February 11–15, 2012
Seattle, WA, USA

Association for
Computing Machinery

Advancing Computing as a Science & Profession

CSCW'12

Proceedings of the ACM 2012 Conference on

Computer Supported Cooperative Work

Sponsored by:
SIGCHI

Supported by:
IBM Research and Google

Volume 2

Association for Computing Machinery

Advancing Computing as a Science & Profession

The Association for Computing Machinery
2 Penn Plaza, Suite 701
New York, New York 10121-0701

ISBN: 978-1-4503-1086-4 (Digital)

ISBN: 978-1-4503-1937-9 (Print Vol. 2)

Additional copies may be ordered prepaid from:

ACM Order Department
PO Box 30777
New York, NY 10087-0777, USA

Phone: 1-800-342-6626 (USA and Canada)
+1-212-626-0500 (Global)
Fax: +1-212-944-1318
E-mail: acmhelp@acm.org
Hours of Operation: 8:30 am – 4:30 pm ET

ACM Order Number: 612121

Printed in the USA

From the Conference Co-Chairs

We welcome you to the ACM 2012 Conference on Computer Supported Cooperative Work!

CSCW 2012 offers the opportunity to hear talks about the latest research results in the field of collaboration and collaborative technologies and to meet researchers and practitioners working on these topics from around the world.

The conference program embraces a variety of perspectives, reflecting how collaboration permeates different aspects of people's work, social, and (increasingly) political lives. This diversity of perspectives is mirrored by geographic diversity among contributors. Following the conference last year in China, CSCW 2012 witnesses an increase in the number of researchers from outside North America contributing to the technical program.

The CSCW 2012 program retains the richly articulated structure of previous conferences in this series. This program of workshops, papers, notes, panels, demonstrations, videos, interactive posters, and forward-looking horizon papers captures both the breadth and depth of the research in this field. At the same time the program offers an opportunity to reflect on the past; a special session discusses the two most-cited papers from CSCW 1992 and CSCW 2002 and the influence of this research on the development of our field.

This is the largest CSCW conference ever. More papers, notes, and interactive posters were submitted and more were accepted. The percentage of accepted papers and notes was also higher, but we believe the conference has retained the exceptionally high quality for which these conferences are known. CSCW 2012 introduces an innovative review process for papers and notes that includes two review phases intended to improve the quality of the contributions. This experiment was successful, and this review process is likely to be adopted in future conferences.

A conference the size of CSCW requires a huge amount of planning. There is a large team behind the scenes carrying out this work: chairs with different responsibilities have been organizing venues, deadlines, reviews, and logistics for more than a year. The success of the CSCW 2012 is due to the tireless efforts of the chairs, the associate chairs and paper reviewers, and the student volunteers: we deeply appreciate their commitment and dedication. It is also dependent on the financial support we received from our generous sponsors, and we all owe them our gratitude.

We hope you enjoy CSCW 2012 and its technical program.

Steven Poltrock
CSCW 2012 Conference Co-chair

Carla Simone
CSCW 2012 Conference Co-chair
University of Milano-Biccoca

From the Program Chairs

Constraint can spur creativity. Approaching the 26th anniversary of the CSCW conference, we were asked to move the submission deadline two months earlier to reduce the reviewing conflict with CHI 2012. In response, we used the additional time to innovate and to increase participation while maintaining or increasing quality, by allowing authors to revise and resubmit their papers and notes. Conference attendees and proceedings readers will ultimately assess the outcome, but overall the feedback from associate chairs, reviewers and authors has been very positive.

Submissions increased 57% from CSCW 2011 to a record 290 papers and 125 notes. We increased the program committee to 67 associate chairs (ACs) to handle them; 21 were women and 20 were from outside North America. They comprised representatives from computer science, social media and social networks, psychology, anthropology, software engineering, management, and design. Fifty were from universities.

Our process most resembled a journal special issue, with a submission deadline, a team of four reviewers, and one revision cycle under a firm time constraint (in this case five weeks). Each submission was assigned to two committee members, designated AC-Coordinator and AC-Reviewer. Each AC assigned one external reviewer. In the first round, each paper or note was blind-reviewed by the AC-Reviewer and the two external reviewers. Reviewers assessed the likelihood that it could be revised within one month to be acceptable. Based on the outcomes, submissions were considered 'conditional accept' (CA, 8.7%), 'revise-resubmit' (RR, 46.5%) or 'reject' (44.8%). In general, papers that received one or more positive assessments were offered the opportunity to revise.

Papers that had no positive assessment in the first round were rejected. We based this decision on an analysis of CSCW 2011 data, which revealed that submissions that did not get an advocate in the initial reviewing had 0% chance of acceptance. Sixty percent of CSCW 2011 submissions had no advocate, compared to 45% of CSCW 2012 submissions. The difference is that the CSCW 2012 submissions had a month in which they could be improved. By immediately rejecting the 45% that had no chance, we streamlined and focused the process, and reduced the number of reviews per submission despite the revision cycle.

The AC Coordinator relied on the reviews in providing written guidance to authors on how to revise RRs. Authors of RR and CA submissions had five weeks to prepare a revision and an explanation of how they had addressed reviewer concerns. Resubmissions of RRs underwent a full second review from the same four-reviewer team; most CAs were checked by just one AC. Reviewing teams were strongly encouraged to resolve decisions prior to the program committee meeting and indeed, only 6% of initial submissions had to be discussed in the meeting.

The program committee split into two subgroups followed by a plenary session to make the final decisions. 127 papers and 37 notes, 39.5% of initial submissions, reached acceptable quality through revision. This is almost twice the number presented in any previous CSCW, in part due to record submissions. ACs and reviewers nominated papers and notes for consideration for Best Paper awards; 4 were selected, with 17 awarded Honorable Mention.

The accepted work represents diverse topics. Relatively new topics for CSCW include crowdsourcing, civic engagement, and social media; more traditional CSCW topics include distributed work, coordination, ethnography, and collaborative software development.

This collaborative effort was an example of computer supported cooperative work. The entire CSCW community provided input throughout the process—many ideas and changes came from outside of the committee. Committee members had to adapt to new ways of working. Our analysis indicates that the work required of reviewers and associate chairs did not exceed that of past years, and authors benefited from two rounds of feedback from committed ACs and reviewers.

Our goal was to maintain a high quality threshold while enabling more papers to reach that threshold. We believe there are many benefits to a review process with more opportunity for constructive interaction between reviewers and authors. Authors benefit by learning more about the CSCW culture, and by producing papers that are better than they could have produced on their own. Reviewers benefit by seeing their work lead to improved papers. The community benefits, because more of its members are successful at producing high quality research each year.

As a community, we must consider new ways to assess conference quality—when a larger volume of high quality work is produced, older metrics no longer hold. Considering the fraction of submitted work that is of low quality to be a measure of conference quality is backwards. We need new measures of process quality and the resulting quality of accepted work. Through continued innovation, CSCW will remain the top venue for leading edge research on collaboration and technology. As with any new process, mistakes were made and much was learned. We look forward to participating as community members in ongoing innovation.

The other technical tracks contribute immeasurably to the program. A record number of interactive posters will be presented. The 14 workshops drew a remarkable number of submissions. With demos, horizon, panels, videos, special sessions, and three plenary keynotes, CSCW 2012 is a great start to the second quarter-century of the CSCW conference.

Jonathan Grudin
Program Co-Chair
Microsoft Research

Gloria Mark
Program Co-Chair
University of California, Irvine

John Riedl
Program Co-Chair
University of Minnesota

CSCW 2012 Table of Contents

CSCW 2012 Table of Contents

CSCW 2012 Table of Contents

CSCW 2012 Table of Contents

CSCW 2012 Table of Contents

CSCW 2012 Table of Contents

CSCW 2012 Table of Contents

CSCW 2012 Table of Contents

CSCW 2012 Table of Contents

CSCW 2012 Table of Contents

CSCW 2012 Table of Contents

CSCW 2012 Conference Organization

Conference Co-chairs	Steve Poltrock Carla Simone *(University of Milano-Bicocca)*
Treasurer	Stephen Hayne *(Colorado State University)*
Papers & Notes Co-chairs	John Riedl *(University of Minnesota)* Gloria Mark *(University of California, Irvine)* Jonathan Grudin *(Microsoft Research)*
Panels Co-chairs	Myriam Lewkowicz *(University of Technology of Troyes)* Michael Twidale *(University of Illinois)*
Videos Co-chairs	Pernille Bjorn *(IT University of Copenhagen)* Matthew Bietz *(University of Washington)*
CSCW Horizon Co-chairs	Gilly Leshed *(Cornell University)* Monica Divitini *(Norwegian University of Science and Technology)*
Workshops Co-chairs	Darren Gergle *(Northwestern University)* M. Antonietta Grasso *(Xerox Research Centre Europe)*
Posters Co-chairs	Cecilia Aragon *(University of Washington)* Hilda Tellioglu *(Vienna University of Technology)*
Demonstrations Co-chairs	Danyel Fisher *(Microsoft Research)* Luigina Ciolfi *(University of Limerick)*
Doctoral Colloquium Co-chairs	Leysia Palen *(University of Colorado)* Dave Randall *(University of Siegen)*
Madness Co-chairs	Sadat Shami *(IBM Research)* Jeff Nichols *(IBM Research)*
Publications Co-chairs	Taemie Kim *(Accenture Technology Labs)* Wendy Ju *(California College of Arts and Stanford University)*
Proceedings Co-chairs	Stacey Scott *(University of Waterloo)* Gina Venolia *(Microsoft Research)*
Publicity Co-chairs	Hideaki Kuzuoka *(University of Tsukuba)* Volker Wulf *(University of Siegen and Fraunhofer FIT)* Bin Hu *(Lanzhou University and Birmingham City University)* Joe McCarthy *(University of Washington, Bothell)*
Industry Liaison Co-chairs	Pamela Hinds *(Stanford University)* John Tang *(Microsoft Research)* Jeremy Birnholtz *(Cornell University)*
A/V Computing Co-chairs	Brian Meyers *(Microsoft)* Steve Abrams *(University of California, Irvine)*
Webmasters and Graphic Design Co-chairs	Victoria Schwanda Sosik *(Cornell University)* Dan Cosley *(Cornell University)*
Social Interaction Co-chairs	Sean Goggins *(Drexel University)* Elizabeth Churchill *(Yahoo!)*

Student Volunteers Co-chairs Norman Makoto Su *(University College Dublin)*
Alex Thayer *(University of Washington)*

Local Arrangements Co-chairs Mark Handel *(Boeing Research & Technology)*
Charlotte Lee *(University of Washington)*

Conference Managers John Lateulere *(IMS-Solutions)*
Joanne Lateulere *(IMS-Solutions)*

Associate Chairs Mark Ackerman *(University of Michigan)*
Daniel Avrahami *(Intel Research)*
Jakob Bardram *(IT University of Copenhagen)*
Jeffrey Bardzell *(Indiana University)*
Shaowen Bardzell *(Indiana University)*
Tora Bikson *(Rand Corporation)*
Jeanette Blomberg *(IBM Research)*
Geoff Bowker *(University of Pittsburgh)*
Barry Brown *(University of California, San Diego)*
Amy Bruckman *(Georgia Institute of Technology)*
Sheelagh Carpendale *(University of Calgary)*
Ed Chi *(Google)*
Luigina Ciolfi *(University of Limerick)*
Noshir Contractor *(Northwestern University)*
Gregorio Convertino *(PARC)*
Dan Cosley *(Cornell University)*
Scott Counts *(Microsoft Research)*
Ed Cutrell *(Microsoft Research)*
Giorgio De Michelis *(University of Milano-Bicocca)*
Alan Dennis *(Indiana University)*
Nicolas Ducheneaut *(PARC)*
Tom Finholt *(University of Michigan)*
Danyel Fisher *(Microsoft Research)*
Andrea Forte *(Drexel University)*
Darren Gergle *(Northwestern University)*
Carl Gutwin *(University of Saskatchewan)*
Tomoo Inoue *(University of Tsukuba)*
Steve Jackson *(University of Michigan)*
Wendy Ju *(California College of the Arts)*
Jofish Kaye *(Nokia)*
John King *(University of Michigan)*
Michael Koch *(Bundeswehr University Munich)*
Bob Kraut *(Carnegie Mellon University)*
Kari Kuutti *(University of Oulo)*
Hideaki Kuzuoka *(University of Tsukuba)*
Cliff Lampe *(Michigan State University)*
Elizabeth Lawley *(Rochester Institute of Technology)*
Charlotte Lee *(University of Washington)*
Catherine C. Marshall *(Microsoft Research)*
Joe McCarthy *(University of Washington, Bothell)*
David McDonald *(University of Washington)*
Hideyuki Nakanishi *(Osaka University)*
Bonnie Nardi *(University of California, Irvine)*
Les Nelson *(PARC)*
Christine Neuwirth *(Carnegie Mellon University)*

Associate Chairs (continued)

Jeff Nichols *(IBM Research)*
Sergio Ochoa *(University of Chile)*
Gary Olson *(University of California, Irvine)*
Judy Olson *(University of California, Irvine)*
Leysia Palen *(University of Colorado)*
Volkmar Pipek *(University of Kaiserslautern)*
Dave Randall *(Manchester Metropolitan University)*
Madhu Reddy *(The Pennsylvania State University)*
mc schraefel *(University of Southampton)*
Frank Shipman *(Texas A&M University)*
Chengzheng Sun *(Nanyang Technical University)*
Stephanie Teasley *(University of Michigan)*
Hilda Tellioglu *(Vienna University of Technology)*
Loren Terveen *(University of Minnesota)*
John Thomas *(IBM Research)*
Michael Twidale *(University of Illinois)*
Doug Vogel *(City University of Hong Kong)*
Dennis Wixon *(Microsoft)*
Volker Wulf *(University of Siegen)*
Naomi Yamashita *(NTT)*
Chen Zhao *(Microsoft Research)*

CSCW 2012 Reviewers

Jose Abdelnour Nocera
Joanna Abraham
Steve Abrams
Lada Adamic
Eytan Adar
Ana Afonso
Agustina Agustina
Ban Al-Ani
Morgan Ames
Margarita Anastassova
Tariq Andersen
Paul André
Judd Antin
Pedro Antunes
Cecilia Aragon
Mark Ashdown
Gabriela Avram
Maribeth Back
Brian Bailey
Aruna Balakrishnan
Elizabeth Bales
Rafael Ballagas
Nelson Baloian
Christoph Bartneck
Maria Cecilia Bastarrica
Scott Bateman
Eric Baumer
Jessica Bayliss
Richard Beckwith
Andrew Begel
Bo Begole
Marek Bell
Steve Benford
Hrvoje Benko
Nicholas Berente
Mark Bergman
Tony Bergstrom
Michael Bernstein
Qingqing Bi
Matthew Bietz
Christian Bird
Jeremy Birnholtz
Konina Biswas
Pernille Bjorn
Mark Blythe
Alexander Boden
Susanne Bødker
Ross Bohner
Alan Borning
Nathan Bos
Claus Bossen
Paolo Bottoni
Erin Bradner
Susan Brennan
Sue Brown
Jed Brubaker
A.J. Brush
Nick Bryan-Kinns
Simon Buckingham Shum
Moira Burke
Georg Buscher
Monika Buscher
Brian Butler
Keith Butler
Ayse Buyuktur
Dara Byrne
Pedro Campos
Matthew Canton
Xiang Cao
Erin Carroll
John Carroll
Julia Cassim
Marcelo Cataldo
Melissa Cefkin
Jilin Chen
Yunan Chen
Zebin Chen
Coye Cheshire
Marshini Chetty
Alvin Chin
Yoram Chisik
Elizabeth Churchill
Luigina Ciolfi
Torkil Clemmensen
Deborah Coleman
Kay Connelly
Eric Cook
Michael Cooke
Lisa Cowan
Lorrie Cranor
Justin Cranshaw
Jeff Cummings
Aaron Curtis
Laura Dabbish
Laurie Damianos
Catalina Danis
Scott Davidoff
Munmun De Choudhury
Anna De Liddo
David De Roure
Cleidson de Souza
David Dearman
Katie Derthick
Sebastian Deterding
Prasun Dewan
Nicholas Diakopoulos
Margaret Dickey-Kurdziolek
Xianghua Ding
Betsy DiSalvo
Alan Dix
Jonathan Donner
Matthew Easterday
Christopher Egert
Hironori Egi
Kate Ehrlich
Margaret Elliott
Nicole Ellison
David England
Ingrid Erickson
Thomas Erickson
JD Eveland
Shelly Farnham
Jesus Favela
Andrew Fiore
Jerry Fjermestad
Kristin Fontichiaro
Jodi Forlizzi
Luis Francisco-Revilla
Christopher Frauenberger
Jeana Frost
Susan Fussell
Jolene Galegher
Alex Games
Monica Garfield
Mike Gartrell
William Gaver
Werner Geyer
Eric Gilbert
Sean Goggins
Jennifer Golbeck
Gene Golovchinsky

Amy Gonzales
Victor Gonzalez
Sam Gosling
Nicholas Graham
Saul Greenberg
Christian Greiffenhagen
Andrea Grimes Parker
Martin Groen
Mark Gross
Tovi Grossman
Ning Gu
Luis Guerrero
Xitong Guo
David Gurzick
Zoltan Gyongyi
Malcolm Hall
Joachim Halse
Christine Halverson
Keith Hampton
Mark Handel
Sean Hannan
Benjamin Hanrahan
Franklin Harper
richard harper
W. Michelle Harris
Chris Harrison
Steve Harrison
Drew Harry
Björn Hartmann
Andrea Hartzler
Kirstie Hawkey
Gillian Hayes
William Hazlewood
Brent Hecht
Libby Hemphill
Valeria Herskovic
Morten Hertzum
Jan Hess
Clint Heyer
Pamela Hinds
Graeme Hirst
Bernie Hogan
Lichan Hong
Gary Hsieh
Hao-Wei Hsieh
David Huffaker
Jina Huh
Susanne Hupfer
Amy Hurst
Claudia-Lavinia Ignat
Michita Imai
Kori Inkpen
Rachael Ip
Lilly Irani
Ellen Isaacs
Petra Isenberg
Brian Jackson
Stephen Jacobs
Sarah Javanmardi
Aditya Johri
M. Cameron Jones
Sasa Junuzovic
Yoram Kalman
Ece Kamar
Anne Marie Kanstrup
Victor Kaptelinin
Karrie Karahalios
Jonas Karlsson
Kostas Karpouzis
Arvind Karunakaran
Andrea Kavanaugh
Michelle Kazmer
Wendy Kellogg
Crowston Kevin
Vijay Khatri
Julie Kientz
Sara Kiesler
Juho Kim
Matthew King
David Kirk
Lorraine Kisselburgh
Aniket Kittur
Cory Knobel
Gwendolyn Kolfschoten
Shin'ichi Konomi
Joseph Konstan
Timothy Koschmann
Gueorgi Kossinets
Adam Kramer
Travis Kriplean
Steinar Kristoffersen
Haewoon Kwak
Peter Lachenmaier
Carl Lagoze
Shyong Lam
Anthony LaMarca
Kristin Lamberty
Brian Landry
Tessa Lau
Christopher Le Dantec
Yoon Suk Lee
Julio Cesar Leite
Thomas Lento
Paul Leonardi
Gilly Leshed
Jim Levin
Sarah Lewis
Brian Lim
Jason Linder
Siân Lindley
Janne Lindqvist
Silvia Lindtner
Heather Lipford
Greg Little
Sophia Liu
Nicholas Lockwood
Danielle Lottridge
Stephan Lukosch
Kurt Luther
Wolfram Luther
Wayne Lutters
Leilah Lyons
Allan MacLean
Anmol Madan
Rui Madeira
Scott Mainwaring
Julie Maitland
Janet Malkovich
Lena Mamykina
Osama Mansour
Wendy March
Adam Marcus
Kai Pan Mark
Paul Marshall
David Martin
Maria Antonia Martínez-Carreras
Paul Marty
Alice Marwick
Tara Matthews
Tom Mattson
David McArthur
David McDonald
Indrani Medhi
Qiaozhu Mei
Helena Mentis
Vera Michalchik
David Millen
Rob Miller
Zara Mirmalek
Jonas Moll

Pascal Molli
Andres Monroy-Hernandez
Troels Mønsted
Alberto Moran
Jonathan Morgan
Daniel Morris
Christian Mueller-Tomfelde
Claudia Müller
Sean Munson
Brad Myers
Mor Naaman
Carman Neustaedter
Mark Newman
Jeffrey Nickerson
Kazushi Nishimoto
Sylvie Noël
Leena Norros
Chris North
Nora O Murchu
Hiroaki Ogata
Corinna Ogonowski
Kenton O'Hara
Masaya Okada
Jacki O'Neill
Michael Oren
Felipe Ortega
Babajide Osatuyi
Florian Ott
Antti Oulasvirta
Tyler Pace
Leysia Palen
Katherine Panciera
Tapan Parikh
Sameer Patil
Sharoda Paul
Thomas Pederson
Samuli Pekkola
Jorge Peña
James Pennebaker
Alex Pentland
Manuel Perez-Quinones
Daniel Perry
Mark Perry
Bruce Phillips
Jeffrey Pierce
Emmanuel Pietriga
Niels Pinkwart
José Pino
Volkmar Pipek
Steven Poltrock
Scott Poole
Sarah Poon
Michael Pope
Vitaliy Popov
Tom Postmes
Wanda Pratt
Reid Priedhorsky
Michael Prilla
Yan Qu
Emilee Rader
Andrew Raij
David Randall
Rebecca Randell
Yolanda Rankin
Rabindra Ratan
Janet Read
Stuart Reeves
Tim Reichling
Yuqing Ren
Paul Resnick
David Ribes
Alexander Richter
Julie Rico
Romain Robbes
Lionel Robert
Toni Robertson
Jennifer Rode
Steven Rohall
Betsy Rolland
John Rooksby
Daniela Rosner
Mary Beth Rosson
Dana Rotman
Mark Rouncefield
Evelyn Rozanski
Karen Ruhleder
Daisuke Sakamoto
Rahul Sami
Aleksandra Sarcevic
Anita Sarma
Steve Sawyer
Karen Schneider
Douglas Schuler
Till Schümmer
Stacey Scott
Taylor Scott
Shilad Sen
Burr Settles
Chirag Shah
N. Sadat Shami
David Shamma
Bin Shao
Patrick Shih
Katie Shilton
Irina Shklovski
David Sirkin
Marc Smith
Timothy Sohn
Diane Sonnenwald
Carsten Sorensen
Patricia Spence
Saurabh Srivastava
Kate Starbird
Charles Steinfield
Igor Steinmacher
Gunnar Stevens
Cristiano Storni
Susan Straus
Simone Stumpf
Fred Stutzman
Bongwon Suh
David Sun
Ja-Young Sung
Elisabeth Sylvan
Leila Takayama
Anthony Tang
Charlotte Tang
John Tang
Alex Taylor
Jaime Teevan
Hilda Tellioglu
Monica Tentori
Alexander Thayer
Jennifer Thom-Santelli
Stella Tian
Marianne Tolar
Catalina Toma
Bill Tomlinson
Michael Toomim
Cristen Torrey
Quan Tran
Manfred Tscheligi
Manas Tungare
Heli Väätäjä
Giuseppe Valetto
Tiffany Veinot
Theresa Velden
Gina Venolia
Janet Vertesi
Iris Vessey

Sarah Vieweg
Jesse Vig
Juergen Vogel
Stephen Voida
Mihaela Vorvoreanu
Ina Wagner
Patrick Wagstrom
Bruce Walker
Jing Wang
Peter Wardrip
Rick Wash
Mark Weal
Anne Weibert
Suzanne Weisband
Taylor Wells
Chunhua Weng
Linda Werner
Torben Wiedenhoefer
Andrea Wiggins
Uffe Wiil
Amanda Williams
Dmitri Williams
Megan Winget
Jill Woelfer
Allison Woodruff
Susan Wyche
Tina Yan
Sarita Yardi
Nick Yee
Jude Yew
Y. Connie Yuan
Masahide Yuasa
Mark Zachry
Massimo Zancanaro
Jun Zhang
Qiping Zhang
Xi Zhang
Shengdong Zhao
Phil Zhou
Xiaomu Zhou
John Zimmerman
Alejandro Zunino

CSCW 2012 Sponsor & Supporters

Sponsor: SIGCHI

Hero: NSF

Champion: Microsoft Research

Benefactors: SMART™

Contributors: Graphisme, animation et nouveaux médias / Graphics, Animation and New Media (GRAND); HUAWEI; NOKIA

Supporters: IBM Research; Google

Finding a New Normal: The Role of Technology in Life Disruptions

Michael Massimi
Department of Computer Science
University of Toronto
mikem@dgp.toronto.edu

Jill P. Dimond
School of Interactive Computing
Georgia Institute of Technology
jpdimond@cc.gatech.edu

Christopher A. Le Dantec
School of Literature, Communication, and Culture
Georgia Institute of Technology
christopher.ledantec@lcc.gatech.edu

ABSTRACT
In recent years, the HCI and CSCW communities have begun to examine the role technology plays in personal, rather than professional settings. Part of this work has begun to address a specific class of life events that are unpredictable, uncontrollable, and destabilizing—what we refer to as *life disruptions*. While each disruption is unique, we find that patterns of social and technical reconfigurations occur in a variety of different contexts. Drawing on three case studies of severe life disruptions—intimate partner violence, homelessness, and death—we remark on the ways that life disruptions prompt a journey towards a "new normal." We enumerate the common lessons learned among our case studies and seek to inform future technology research and design work which may involve life disruptions.

Author Keywords
Disruption, intimate partner violence, homelessness, death, new normal.

ACM Classification Keywords
H5.m. Information interfaces and presentation (*e.g.*, HCI): Miscellaneous.

General Terms
Design, Human Factors.

INTRODUCTION
Following an adverse life event, technology can play a key role in how we react and adapt. Several distinct HCI and CSCW projects have focused on these adverse life events, which we term *life disruptions*. Examples of such disruptions include moving house, divorce, bankruptcy, abuse, and death. While each life disruption is unique, there are patterns in the ways people and technologies are reconfigured following a disruption. In this paper, it is our goal to synthesize three different research projects to identify and characterize these reconfigurations in more detail. In so doing, we provide a resource for HCI researchers and designers working around other life disruptions.

Of the variety of disruptions that might occur, we consider three specific case studies from our research: escaping and recovering from an abusive partner, dealing with episodic homelessness, and coping with the death of a family member. While each of these cases may appear unrelated, they each share the characteristics of being invisible, stigmatizing, and long-lasting disruptions. Escaping a situation of intimate partner violence is often invisible as victims cope with shame; becoming homeless due to job loss is frequently kept private to avoid stigma and discrimination; and while a death in the family will initially be met with sympathy and support, the disruption to individual and domestic normalcy often outlives public forms of mourning and acknowledgement.

In this paper, we reflect on our fieldwork from these three case studies, and share vignettes that vividly depict the lived reality of finding a "new normal." While we recognize that the disruptions themselves—abuse, homelessness, death—cannot be mitigated directly by technological intervention, we find it productive to reach across case studies to illuminate some thematic similarities that these disruptions share. In the discussion, we present three of these themes as ways of thinking through technology's role in life disruptions, and in so doing, contribute to our growing understanding of how people use and relate to technology during times of personal crisis and upheaval. We then conclude with potential directions for technology designers seeking to support individuals and communities in the journey towards a "new normal."

RELATED WORK
Disruptions in HCI and CSCW Work
We often consider the home as a certain kind of place [17] —a "haven in a heartless world" [22]; we assume that families operate on consensus, that family life is fulfilling and restorative, and that routines support cooperative and generative action. These characteristics have led us to appreciate alternate modes of technology use in the home including the repurposing of technologies that might be familiar from the workplace: research has examined technologies for entertainment [46], socialization [7], and family cohesion in the context of the routine and ordinary [39].

Two of the broader themes that tend to run through domestically focused HCI and CSCW research are the role of routine in family settings and the collaborative nature of different forms of domestic work [9,15,33]. Routine-focused research has studied the work needed to set up and maintain home network infrastructure [16] as well as the complex gendered division of domestic work and privacy [39]. Each focuses on different accounts of how domestic routine is

CSCW'12, February 11–15, 2012, Seattle, Washington, USA.

maintained in the face of technological change, acknowledging that the home is a dynamic environment not always denoted by stability or social stasis.

An important part of maintaining these routines is the work done by different members of the home and the negotiation of that work as responsibilities evolve. In examining the social dynamics of the home, researchers have highlighted the collaborative and shared nature of domestic technologies. O'Brien and Rodden, in an ethnographic study of a "set top box" prototype, recommend that technologies for the home should be designed to fit the "cooperative nature of home life" [34]. Similarly, Brush and Inkpen found that the assumption of individual computer accounts—arguably a holdover from workplace privacy protection standards—did not match domestic use, as many of the families in their study shared "pretty much everything" [7].

Beyond the roles of routine and collaboration in the home, we also find work that has focused on the relationship between play [4] and intimacy [20] within the home. Arguably, play and intimacy can be viewed as an important component to the social glue that makes a home and differentiates it from other settings where technology is used, such as the workplace.

This earlier work begins to show how interconnected the home is, both socially and technologically. Family members establish routines of technology use, they divide the work necessary to keep the technology working, and they engage with the technology for reasons of enjoyment, connection, and intimacy. The effects of life disruptions ripple out through these routines, reconfiguring work divisions, and imparting different meaning to the technology mediated experiences shared within the family.

CSCW research concerning divorce provides two examples of how technologies are involved during this life disruption. The first example looks at the role technology can play in helping maintain meaningful contact between children and their divorced (and separated) parents [35,47]. This thread of research directly addresses how families marshal different networked technologies to manage the difficult situations that arise as they attempt to reestablish routine and regular contact after the divorce. In a different example, Dimond *et al.* point to the significant difficulties that arise when family members who were relied upon for technical support are no longer present due to divorce or death [10]. Changes in family membership mean that some family members find themselves having to attend to their technology in new ways as the person they relied on to maintain things like the home network is no longer present. As this more recent work starts to engage with some of the diversity of human experience that plays out in the home, it retains some characteristics of the generative and consensus driven home that pervaded earlier domestic studies. Divorced families are presumed to be actively engaged in easing the burden of separation on their children, and extended families are assumed to be willingly enlisted to help maintain home technologies following separation or divorce.

It is along these lines that we focus our attention: on the serious life disruptions that upend routine and change the social and technological relationships within the family. We recognize that routine, and the effort to reestablish it, plays a crucial role during disruptive life events [31], but that search for routine can often be isolating in unexpected and invisible ways. By examining these conditions—when domestic routines and work are disrupted, when technology use is upset, and when private support networks are stressed to breaking—we gain an analytic perch from which to better understand the range of experience in the home and to consider how technology might be enlisted in reestablishing a new normal.

CASE STUDIES OF LIFE DISRUPTIONS

Building on this previous work, we turn to consider three disruptive life events that occur in private life: intimate partner violence, homelessness, and a death in the family. Each disruption is substantial and grim, however, they collectively represent the extreme realities of domestic life that highlight tensions between public and private. They also expose challenges associated with connecting to and making use of infrastructure —both social and technical. — They highlight the struggles that occur as these disruptions transpire and then pass. Each case study is the result of substantial qualitative fieldwork completed in each of these three settings as well as a technology intervention deployed at one of the research sites.

Case 1: Intimate Partner Violence

Intimate partner, or domestic, violence provides a stark counter example to tranquil visions of domestic life [12]. Intimate partner violence occurs across the world, in many different cultures and is not uncommon even in "developed" countries: in the United States and across Europe, one in four women will be physically or sexually assaulted in her lifetime [44]. Child abuse is often concurrent with partner violence—up to 60% of children are also abused in domestic violence cases [9]. Furthermore, contrary to popular assumptions, in the U.S, partner violence occurs at the same rate in same-sex relationships as it does in opposite-sex relationships [38]. In short, it is a pervasive and often invisible disruption.

The upshot of these statistics is that violence in the home shifts the conversation from how families work together to coordinate their activities, to how affected individuals exercise their need for privacy, separation, and survival. In intimate partner violence research and activism, leaving an abuser is seen as a crucial act for breaking the cycle of partner violence [18]; it requires a reconfiguration of private life and a crossover into publicly provided programs and services. However, with personal technologies, it is unclear that this act severs abuse as completely as we might think.

In the winter of 2010, one of the authors interviewed ten female residents at a domestic violence shelter after volunteering for several months. For data collection, we recorded semi-structured interviews to explore how technology was being used by the women at the shelter. We asked questions such as, "Tell me about how you use your cell phone" and "Tell me what you do on the computer." Interviews were analyzed using thematic analysis; this includes first transcribing the interviews, identifying the different patterns of experiences, and identifying sub-themes within those patterns. The author validated the coding during a "safe technology" workshop at the shelter. Since there are few empirical studies on intimate partner violence and technology, we wanted to understand the landscape of how technology is generally intertwined within these survivors' lives. Survivors of partner violence, after leaving their abuser, have a heightened need to protect their privacy while also coping with new routines and changes in social and resource infrastructure. In this disruption, technology both helps and hinders, as the very same technologies that are used to find jobs, housing, and provide emotional support are also used by abusers to threaten and harass [11].

Harassment and Safety

Text messages were the most frequently reported medium for harassment as seven of the ten participants had received harassing text messages from their abusers. Janelle[1], who fled from her abuser with her four children, explained how her abuser used to threaten her with text messages such as, "*I'm gonna gut you.*" She also experienced harassment from her abuser's family on Facebook: they posted messages on her wall accusing her of stealing the kids. Her abuser posted harassing messages not only on her Facebook wall, but also on her sister's Facebook wall.

In a similar case, another woman at the shelter received a text message from her husband stating that he was tracking her via the GPS on her mobile phone. Despite the technical reality of whether her husband could actually track her location, the mere idea of that possibility prompted the woman to abandon her mobile phone by throwing it out the car window. This may indicate that the perception of privacy when using technologies such as GPS are not always aligned with technical reality. This misalignment has the potential to cause emotional trauma and disconnection as individuals perceive a danger that may not be present and abandon technologies that otherwise provide a life-line to their social support networks. Situations such as these exemplify how privacy needs are enacted [36], indicating a need for designers to consider physical and emotional safety in addition to functional usability.

Tactics to Maintain Social Support

Abusers often exerted control over their partners by isolating them from their social network or other resources; this control often continued even after survivors left. As already pointed out, these threats manifested through mobile phones and social networking sites, but were not limited to direct harassment to the victim. For example, Serena's abuser tried to control who she could communicate with on her cell phone by threatening her family members to get her phone number. As a result, Serena decided to stop calling her family to protect them. For another survivor, Facebook became problematic due to her abuser's harassment. She stopped posting any content, and instead just logged on to view her sister's updates in order to feel connected to her. She said that her "*life on the Internet is over.*" She was also too afraid to apply for jobs online because information she had to release, such as her social security number, could potentially link her to her physical location.

The social isolation experienced by the residents was further compounded when they moved into the shelter. As a result, residents had to work to maintain their social connections. One of the most common strategies the women used was to get a new phone and register it under a pseudonym. As one participant said, "*You can register it under Miss Beyonce Knowles and they don't care.*" In this way, a survivor could replace her phone number if her abuser discovered it. However, this was not always possible if participants could not afford to continually set up new pre-paid accounts or if they relied on government-issued phones such as those provided by SmartLink program sponsored by the federal government of the United States.

Another example of how the women developed creative strategies for maintaining their social support networks comes from Ayana who sometimes talked to her mother-in-law for emotional support (her mother in-law also had an abusive husband). The challenge for Ayana was that her husband sometimes tried to call from his mother's home phone, so Ayana was never sure who was trying to call. To remedy this, Ayana recorded a voicemail stating that she does not answer calls, but will respond to voicemail. Her mother-in-law learned to leave a message, telling her that it was okay to call, and then Ayana would call her back.

Intimate partner violence disrupts social support networks —the friends, family, and institutions upon which we rely. Survivors of partner violence must grapple with prolonged harassment and threats through technology, yet they rely on these same technologies to seek out the support and resources needed to move on—information about counseling, jobs, housing, and childcare. Furthermore, for people escaping an abusive relationship, location information becomes problematic. Due to this, survivors are wary of new technologies as many devices are now embedded with GPS and other tracking mechanisms; these technologies take a certain amount of technical expertise to feel confident that location information is appropriately managed. As seen in the ways that residents of the shelter try to maintain their access to social networking sites or mobile phones, it is not feasible to just quit Facebook, stop using a mobile phone, or otherwise disavow personal technologies. These technologies provide survivors of violence much needed social connections and public resources in times of isolation and change.

Case 2: Homelessness

Starting in 2009, one of the authors began extensive fieldwork and participatory design activities at an emergency homeless shelter for single mothers [27]. The shelter was relatively small, housing up to 8 families at a time for 30 to 90 days. The research conducted at the site began with four months of fieldwork, including ethnographic observation along with semi-structured interviews held twice a week with both shelter staff and residents. Notes from the observations and fieldwork were continuously analyzed and used to further refine the interviews. Following the initial field-

[1] Names throughout the case studies have been changed to protect participants' identities.

work, we worked with the staff and residents to co-design an information and communication system to support the staff and residents.

The deployed system was designed to address three main goals: help the staff more effectively share resources with the residents; enable residents' access to information and expertise when and where they needed it via mobile communication; and provide both staff and residents a means to express their knowledge and expertise together [25]. Each of these goals was formulated in response to the specific ways homelessness disrupted the lives of the women at the shelter. An important point to raise here is that the mothers were homeless for economic reasons such as job loss or sudden medical expense. As such, they identified as working mothers, not as homeless mothers, and viewed their time in the shelter as an unexpected and unwanted disruption to their normal lives.

Given this situation, we focused on the information and social needs of the mothers and on expanding the constraints under which those needs were met. We learned, for example, that the women were coping with information overload and that helping the mothers and the staff impose some order and timing to the information being shared would help the residents make better use of available resources. For the staff, we learned that their contact time with each resident was limited in part because the shelter was only open at night. By providing facilities to encourage mobile communication, the staff could extend their reach, amplifying their support while still managing their case load. Finally, we worked to create a shared message board where both residents and staff could post information, thus providing a way for each to express their knowledge and expertise, and alter the expectations of where to turn for help and knowledge.

"Getting Connected"

Broadly, the challenge of staying connected to different kinds of social and material resources is a primary concern for many homeless individuals [26]. The social support of neighbors and friends becomes strained or broken simultaneously with interruption to the material resources of institutions such as schools and places of employment. As a result, one of the first things the women at the shelter discussed was the need to *"get connected"* to public entities like support groups, childcare facilities, employment services, and entitlement programs to help them reestablish their independence. As we will revisit in the discussion, it is this mix of social and material resources that comprise the durable infrastructure upon which these women depend [23,40].

Within this disruption to social and material access there were some compounding factors with which the single homeless mothers in our shelter had to contend. First, for many of the mothers in our study, a consequence of moving to the shelter was displacement from their social support networks and more isolation as sole providers for their children during a time of extreme instability—an isolation in many ways similar to that of the previous case study. Second, the disruption to material access had an immediate impact on the children at the shelter [37], as they found themselves in new schools or making long bus trips to remain at the school they were enrolled in before moving to the shelter. Both of these interruptions served to displace established routines [31], which, in combination with some of the common risk factors and characteristics of single-mother poor families [28], exacerbated the stress on everyone [3,24].

Two specific examples illustrate how getting cut off from different forms of support affected the women at the shelter. The first, Jacquie, had to contend with the impact of being cut off from friends and family while she tried to find employment and attend to her son (a boy in his early teens). One of the first challenges she faced was finding work that she could balance with her responsibilities as a parent. Initially, Jacquie had found second-shift work—from 2pm to 10pm—but because the shelter would not allow her son to be there alone in the evenings, she had to prolong her stay until she could find first-shift (9am to 5pm) work. Part of the challenge Jacquie faced was gaining employment without being able to enlist the kind of social support she might have otherwise had access to; she could not initially rely on the support of her fellow residents and she was disconnected from her previous life by virtue of having to move to a shelter in a different part of town.

Nancy, another woman at the shelter, was looking after her grandchildren. In some regards, her relationship to her family was reversed. She had been—and continued to be, despite becoming homeless—the stable go-to person for her adult children. She became the guardian of her grandchildren while her own daughter was in a substance abuse program. Nancy became homeless when her unemployment ran out and she was unable to resume work due to severe health problems. As a result, she had to contend with connecting to new forms of institutional support for health and housing while acting as the main support for her family.

Both Jacquie and Nancy became steady users of the system we deployed at the shelter. They actively used the messaging features to stay in contact with the shelter staff, who helped them arrange appointments with employers, receive reminders and supportive messages to secure housing, find childcare, and even manage hair appointments. They also used the shared message board to post messages about resources they found as well as get information on housing programs and job fairs. The routines they developed centered around daily messages sent to their case worker to check on specific programs or follow up with different employment opportunities. They also used the shared message board, passing by it every day and checking to see what new information was there that might be useful. One of the important elements of their interaction with the technology was that it supported different modes of seeking information—either directly from their case worker, or through announcements posted on the shared message board—and it turned information seeking into an active endeavor, where they each took responsibility for seeking what they needed rather than wait for it to come to them.

Case 3: Death of a Family Member

One of the most common disruptive moments in private life is a death in the family. Despite the ubiquity of death, it is a topic that designers and researchers have only recently begun to address as it plays out across various computational platforms. Compared to other life disruptions, death appears frequently; all families will experience multiple deaths as time moves on, and for each member of that family, every loss is unique. Furthermore, a death is irreversible (unlike, for instance, a financial crisis); families must learn to cope rather than struggle to recover what they have lost.

In this case study, we draw on fieldwork conducted by one of the authors with middle-aged parents who had lost a child. Based on three focus groups with 24 bereaved parents, meetings with community support group organizers, and consultations with mental health professionals, we have learned how the death of a child profoundly disrupts the lives of parents. Buckle and Fleming characterize this type of loss thusly: "[t]he fracturing of one's assumptive world results in substantial psychological upheaval, and the reluctant recognition that the world is no longer safe, orderly, and fair leaves bereaved parents feeling fearful and vulnerable" [8]. Over time, parents must learn to live with the death of their child despite their grief and powerlessness, and must adapt their lives to reflect this new reality.

The Journey Following a Loss

In our focus groups and interviews, the time following the death of a child was repeatedly characterized as a "journey" by both the bereaved and professionals alike. This journey, starts with a period of intense emotional turmoil accompanied by the pressing need to organize religious and communal activity. During this time, the bereaved are thrust into a circumstance wherein technology is used to spread the news, receive condolences, and make plans. In an example of this, Charlotte, a bereaved mother, described using email to announce the death of her twins: "*I didn't want to make phone calls, I didn't want to have that conversation. So, I'm writing an email telling people that I just lost my kids, and it felt weird at the time.*"

However, as time progresses, and the flurry of activity fades away, bereaved parents come to value isolation, quiet, and privacy [1]. Focus group participants described "*hiding out at home*" for extended periods following their child's death. Terry, a bereaved mother, decided to shut off her mobile phone and screened calls to her landline in order to control her privacy: "*These people don't understand where you are. They get offended if you don't respond. I know I have to pick up the phone, and I don't want to, but you feel obligated to. Sometimes it just takes everything out of you to return that one call.*" In these cases, technology acts as a double-edged sword. In some ways, it overexposes the grieving parents by making them readily available for phone calls, emails, text messages, and so forth. In response, participants described the need to take actions to shelter themselves from others, and to choose isolation, silence, and disconnection as they reacted to their loss.

As more time passes, the death may usher in social disorder in the personal lives of the bereaved. Grieving family members may be riddled with guilt, anger, or depression. In the case of a child's death, married parents may blame one another for the event, or have different, incompatible styles of grieving; as one participant in our focus groups put it, a child's death "*can make or break a relationship.*" Relationships with surviving children become strained as they must model strength to their children while taking care of themselves [8]. Bereaved parents in our focus groups also remarked on how their child's death was a turning point in their social lives, where they discovered who their "real friends" were by virtue of their continued companionship during this life disruption. The new social arrangements precipitated by a death are rarely considered in the technologies we design, as long-standing patterns of "normal" communication are disrupted by permanent changes in frequency, duration, and emotional timbre.

As the years continue on, bereaved parents slowly come to develop and accept a new definition of their own identities, and what their role is within their social circles.. For example, Rebecca, a bereaved mother whose daughter died 28 years ago, described that even though her child is dead, she is still a part of their family, and Rebecca is still a mother: "*For some of us...we're still sort of parenting in a sense. There is a great need for us to. We're cut short in our parenting—this is still innate in all of us.*" Parents may continue to include their deceased children in domestic routines and events; they may mark the child's birthday or death day, or set an extra place at the dinner table. Continued communication with the deceased is also a common occurrence—beyond simply "speaking" to the deceased, many people will write to them [45]. These writings, traditionally highly private, are moving into the public eye as the bereaved leave public messages on the deceased's Facebook or MySpace profiles [6,14]. The concept of routines as stabilizing forces in technology use and adoption is thus rattled by the inclusion of a dead participant in the routine, and this life disruption can threaten the stability of relationships between living household members. For the bereaved, technology increasingly plays a role in how they cope with their loss over time and rebuild their lives [30].

DISCUSSION

In the case studies above, we presented three different types of life disruption and illustrated how technology is implicated during these disruptions. In reflective discussions between the authors, we noted how the participants in our fieldwork share the search for a "new normal" – a reconfigured lifestyle where previous social and technical infrastructures have been torn down and replaced with tenuous and emerging social groups and resources. In this discussion, we revisit and synthesize the findings from the case studies to identify three thematic lenses that may help technologists think through life disruptions. We begin with thoughts on the shifting landscape of personal relationships as mediated by technology before discussing how social and technical infrastructures are used, broken, and then reformed in light of life disruptions. Cutting across this process, we describe some of the ways that privacy work is performed and in particular how technology and communities work together to achieve this new state of life.

Dynamism of Social Life

Relationships formed in private life are commonly considered to be at-will, desirable, and productive. In Western culture, we often think of families as groups where members contribute to family well-being through the provision of emotional, instrumental, and functional support. Outside the family, we commonly think of fun, enlightening, and nurturing friendships. However, as our case studies have shown, these relationships are not always positive, desirable, or beneficial to an individual's well-being. Personal relationships change over time: good friends can become distant, lovers can become abusive, and our closest confidants may become ill or die.

Our case studies add further nuance to how we conceive of the networks of institutions and personal relationships—what we call the social infrastructure—that families rely upon to create and maintain a sense of stability. First, we must acknowledge that relationships are not permanent; they begin, and they must eventually end. The ending of relationships may occur for reasons outside of one's control (*e.g.*, death), or a person may volitionally end a soured relationship (*e.g.*, intimate partner violence). Many systems pay attention to establishing relationships, but less thought is given to how these relationships represented in the system might gracefully end or change. One study on "unfollowing" behavior in Twitter begins to speak to the dynamics at play [21], but little is known about this behavior in relationship to life disruptions specifically. Harassment through text messaging and Facebook stalking provide two stark examples of technologies that fail to degrade gracefully even when one party attempts to prune their social network or altogether remove themselves from exposure. Similarly, when Facebook began suggesting that users "get in touch" with a dead friend, it sharply demonstrated how a lack of consideration for changing relationships could be problematic [21], and demonstrated the poor tools within the technology for dealing with deceased users and the variety of friends and family who may each have different ideas of appropriate and meaningful ways to mourn and remember.

Relationships are not universally or continually positive; relationships can be roller coasters, with periods of great happiness offset by periods of anger, resentment, or apathy. Bereaved parents sought solace in the home to temporarily escape from friends and family and cope with their grief; alternately, victims of partner violence may be in relationships fraught with mistrust and anger and need to seek refuge in a shelter. This consideration is relevant to systems that aim to design for reciprocity or mutual disclosure [2,19]. While there are certainly healthy relationships, it may be inappropriate for systems to *require* such reciprocity given the range of legitimate reservations someone might have for allowing this sort of technology-mediated intrusion. We must appreciate that human relationships are dynamic, and designers cannot presume that a given relationship in a multi-user system exists as a completely positive and desirable arrangement.

A Shifting Socio-Technical Infrastructure

Disruptions, by their nature, upend the routines, resources, and patterns that we follow during "normal" periods. Our case studies show us that what we take for granted is actually subject to destruction or disturbance. These disturbances are latent foundational parts of our normal lives that provide a unique space for inquiry in domestic HCI. However, by thinking about the vulnerability of the home's social and technical infrastructures, we see how computing plays a part in maintaining, rebuilding, or tearing apart this infrastructure after a disruption comes to pass.

Because relationships are dynamic, so too is the support that comes from them. The people upon whom we rely to install, maintain, and operate personal devices may not always be available. When an individual dies, bereaved family members must make up for a considerable amount of technical resourcing and know-how [10,30]. Furthermore, the ways in which technologies are packaged and consumed sometimes encourage codependence among users; for example, a victim of partner violence may find her mobile phone deactivated by her abusive partner because they signed up for a "family plan."

Further, many relationships need some level of infrastructure stability to maintain continuity. This, in particular, becomes a challenge for the episodically homeless discussed above. The challenge for the homeless mothers was two-fold. First, during the initial experience of homelessness they might stay with friends and family, but soon that becomes burdensome and they are asked to leave. Second, as these individuals find themselves evicted from their homes, they are also often evicted from their neighborhoods as a byproduct of having to move to a shelter or other temporary living arrangement.

In that disruption, we described how Jacquie needed to find work that would not encroach on her responsibilities as a mother, while Nancy needed to enroll in appropriate disability and subsidized housing programs. Even so, both effectively used the system as a way to establish connections to new social and material resources. The creation of these new resources, and the integration of them into daily routines constitutes a kind of infrastructuring [42,43] where the material resources of the deployed system buttressed the formation of routines and social ties with shelter staff. The outcome, then, is that technology aimed at supporting families coping with homelessness acts not only to connect people to needed resources, but also establishes routines around those forms of information [31]. These routines become the basis for creating a new normal and for supporting the mothers as they move toward reestablishing stability in their lives.

For survivors of partner violence, often their abuser isolates them from family and friends who can offer support, as a way to exert power and control. In both cases, their connection to social support is strained or simply not feasible. The breakdown of the infrastructure of the home, also affects the social infrastructure that provides emotional support, childcare, transportation, and information about jobs.

We have shown how social support in the home is subject to disruption. During times of disruption, it is clear that the socio-technical infrastructures present in the home are also vulnerable, and that these breaks in infrastructure serve to make them more visible [41]. Our case studies teach the lesson that a stable home infrastructure is not always available to the technology designer. The technical and material resources of the home are finite and subject to depletion or unavailability. Homelessness presents an obvious example: for affected individuals, access to electrical outlets and the Internet may be a hard-to-find luxury. Similarly, people escaping an abusive partner will find diminished and intermittent access to the technical infrastructure needed to accomplish their goals of safety and independence. In bereavement, this home's technical infrastructure may be dismantled temporarily as the grieving seek peace and quiet, or be subject to degradation over time if the home's technical support specialist has died.

Privacy from Stigma and Harm

Life disruptions of the magnitude described in this paper share a common theme insofar as users find a new need to manage their privacy *vis-à-vis* the event. During these events, information and interaction boundaries shift and "bleed over" between what is usually considered private, such as the home, and what is considered public. Using Altman's privacy and technology framework, Palen and Dourish suggest that what is considered private is reconfigured depending on orientations towards temporality via different social groups, and different contexts [36]. Our case studies illustrate how, specifically, the context of life disruptions may trigger movement and blurring of privacy boundaries, and how technology is implicated in these contexts. Each of these instances demonstrates the heightened need for controlling privacy and the considerable vigilance, action, and the technical know-how needed to defend it. Considering the details of intimate partner violence helps us to paint a vivid picture of Palen and Dourish's observation that privacy is situated and enacted [36].

Moreover, survivors of intimate partner violence must contend with physical and emotional safety as well as safe access to communication technologies. These concerns go beyond the common conceptions of privacy and technology that arise in response to protecting financial information and identity theft. For example, although there are mechanisms to protect the whereabouts of a shelter's location (such as mandating all residents sign a confidentiality agreement), there are no similar mechanisms in which to cope with new ways to "locate" a person through mobile phones and the Internet. Particularly for individuals vested in various social networking sites, the public-ness of their profiles and their connection to their social network often leaves them exposed and accessible to those they are trying to escape.

The larger point here is to draw attention to the complicated privacy work that occurs during a life disruption. The interconnectedness of place, time, interpersonal relationships, and technical possibility beget an intricate privacy-maintenance process where aspect of life previously thought to be safe or stable must be re-evaluated in light of a new set of sensitivities, goals, and standards.

Furthermore, the shifts in boundaries between public and private illustrate a need to scaffold nuanced user agency with respect to privacy management. For example, when a loved one dies, often their Facebook page becomes a sort of public memorial, where people share their memories. Yet, when intimate partner violence survivors escape, often their communication becomes more private. Further, the homeless may have to give up some privacy to receive social services. Homeless people are left with few other choices than to rely upon publicly provided services while simultaneously attempting to "pass" as having a stable private life for their dignity and relationships. In these cases, the magnitude of life disruptions necessitates the intervention of public, legal, or governmental agencies. This kind of involvement may result in a loss of control over personal information.

As we discussed in the beginning of this paper, HCI and CSCW research has only recently come to grapple with some of the important differences between work in the home and that of the workplace. One example of this came from demonstrating that the concept of user identity derived from the workplace does not provide the same utility in the home—for families where everyone "shares everything," the overhead of individual user logins no longer make sense [21]. Based on our fieldwork in diverse contexts, we would argue that the challenge to effectively providing shared computer resources in the home goes beyond dealing with the breakdown in how families use and share login credentials. It is not just that the presumption of *what* is and is not considered private is different, but that the *consequences* of privacy break downs are different as well.

In particular, life disruptions such as those outlined above demonstrate that there are instances where the consequences of privacy mechanisms are unpredictable. In the case study of intimate partner violence, the particulars of the context shape the meaning of the information. Often, tracking the location of family members has been viewed as an instrumental tool in supporting the work of the family [5]; however, using a mobile phone to track the location of a partner can become a threat to personal safety and is difficult to manage, particularly since those family members are reflexively considered trustworthy.

Furthermore, systems concerned with privacy need to understand the home as a place that does, from time to time, interface with the public world. The blurring of these boundaries complicates what is considered domestic HCI. When becoming homeless or escaping partner violence, the construct of the private home as a site of inquiry dissolves. Private life becomes necessarily more public after moving into a shelter and receiving help from different social institutions. It is also especially apparent in the case of dealing with the death of family member. Bereaved parents found that important information needed for a public memorial or for making arrangements following a death was inaccessible because it was private (*e.g.*, data from personal computers or internet accounts such as social networking sites or email).

While the previous examples have highlighted the challenges that arise through domestic disruptions with respect to existing technologies, we would also point to ways that intentionally designed technology interventions impact privacy for disrupted families. Prior to the deployment of the system to the homeless shelter, communication at the shelter was done on an exclusively face-to-face basis. However, once the system had been in use for a couple of months, new habits of communicating between the residents and the staff began to emerge. Importantly, because the system enabled communication to personal devices—residents' mobile phones—the staff stopped feeling that they needed to physically deliver information. This in turn led to a redrawing of social boundaries that empowered residents to communicate with the staff as synchronously or asynchronously as they chose.

While this change might seem small, for the homeless women in the shelter, being able to regain some sense and practice of privacy was important as the rest of their lives were so heavily dictated by external impositions from various care providers (however well-meaning, necessary, and welcomed they may have been). This dynamic also shows how technology can constructively re-introduce social boundaries rather than break them down as is often assumed to be the case in the contemporary breed of social applications.

Designing for a "New Normal"

Life disruptions can result in straining or breaking of existing relationships and access to resources. When this happens, new relationships are often formed which acknowledge the individual's role in moving towards a new normal. A person who loses their home may seek out a homeless shelter, and a person in an abusive relationship may find a domestic abuse shelter. Similarly, bereaved individuals may seek out support groups or other places where they are able to communicate with other people in their situations, and find the resources and information they need. This pattern repeats, and shares commonalities with other life disruptions (*e.g.*, drug addicts entering rehabilitation centers, alcoholics attending Alcoholics Anonymous).

This shift towards a new normal as facilitated by new relationships increasingly involves technology. Technology can play a key role in helping members of these groups communicate more consistently and satisfyingly. In that sense, technology establishes and sustains a new community that eases the transition towards a new lifestyle and new routines following a life disruption. People may also experience periods of "normal disruption", such as episodic homelessness and abuse, and each of our case studies reflect a variance in their levels of permanency. A family that becomes homeless may be able to, one day, move back into their own home. However, for someone whose child has died, there is no way to replace that loss. In this section, we wish to draw attention to the idea of "finding a new normal," and illuminate how families striving towards a new balance in their lives take up technology, and could potentially benefit from new technologies.

Technologies for Socio-Technical Support

Members of the HCI and CSCW communities are uniquely positioned to develop technologies that allow people who are devastated from a severe personal tragedy to find solace or comfort. For example, based on the fieldwork with parents who have lost a child, one of the authors is developing a system that connects bereaved parents together so that they may form mutually-beneficial relationships and move forward together in their losses [29]. Similarly, the system installed in the homeless shelter demonstrates how technology can arm the homeless with an infrastructure that helps them achieve a new form of stability. Technology can provide people with the guidance that they need to ensure their continued safety that allows them to connect to social support—for example, one can imagine the development of a "safe phone" that contains different options for blocking calls and text messages.

New technologies give rise to opportunities for new routines, new traditions, and new ways of making a home (*e.g.*, consider the multitudinous ways in which the television has changed the way that a "typical evening at home" plays out) [32]. There are opportunities to continue to leverage and amplify diverse social resources to aid and support individuals and families recovering from a life disruption.

Designing for Social Interaction During Disruption

One problem that people facing severe life disruption often encounter is the need to explain their situation to interested others. However, explaining what has happened is a difficult prospect for a multitude of reasons, be they related to privacy, dignity, or the sensitivity of the topic. As system researchers and designers, we need to be aware of these concerns as delicate topics come to be expressed through new media and new systems expressly designed for social and familial interaction.

When designing for social interactions through technology, the principles of social translucence [13] such as visibility, awareness, and accountability need to be expanded in the context of life disruptions. For example, visibility about abuse, homelessness, and death, can often be stigmatizing and even dangerous. Similarly, when grieving, the bereaved may feel compelled to hide their feelings in professional or public settings, where their emotions would cause discomfort or unwanted attention. Indeed, many disruptions are events that are emotionally charged and not publically acceptable. There may be criminal or legal issues involved (*e.g.*, in intimate partner violence or with drug addiction).

Often times, people facing homelessness will attempt to pass as a "normal" person in order to gain access to services and resources. In this case, awareness could prevent access to services. We need to realize that the search for a new normal implies a need to develop sensitivities to privacy and infrastructure access that account for the richness and nuance of private life. Technologies that play a role in achieving a new normal must be designed in a way that prevents them from contributing to the stigma surrounding the events of a life disruption.

Importantly, the role of technology in these cases is not to be productive or efficient. It does not necessarily coordinate members in the completion of tasks, or determine the fastest or easiest route towards recovery. Rather, technology supports the members of a community as they establish a new normal in their own ways. Each life disruption is a unique situation, and prescriptive technologies may not offer solutions that work for all. Key to the success of technology in dealing with life disruptions is the open-ended and communicative aspects, and allowing individuals to ask for information, or identify and apply it as they see fit.

Potentially armed with a new appreciation for the pleasant parts of personal life—good friends, a reliable income, a place to call home—people may even find themselves in situations wherein they are more open to new methods for rebuilding and sustaining a new lifestyle. As part of achieving this "fresh start," people may adopt new technologies which make them feel closer to their social networks or help them reconfigure old technologies to reflect their new way of life. Technology also plays a strongly symbolic role in how people achieve this new normal: removing an abusive spouse from your mobile phone plan, changing your Facebook status to single, or creating a web memorial for a deceased loved one are all opportunities to signal—to oneself and to others—that life is continuing on.

CONCLUSION

Across each of the case studies presented here—intimate partner violence, homelessness, and death in the family—we find opportunities for reflecting on interactive systems design that takes in the breadth of experiences that occur during life disruptions. Certainly, the case studies we have presented exist at the extreme ends of personal disruption: they are tragic accounts of some of the most difficult situations in which a family can find itself. Yet, by examining the extremes, we can shed new light on areas of technology use and design, particularly recognizing that as technology becomes an ever more personal, even intimate, accessory, the risk of amplifying negative life events increases.

The three thematic lenses presented in the discussion address a dynamic set of relationships, infrastructures, and privacy concerns. These lenses are intended to inform –and where applicable, extend – existing understandings of technology use during the performance daily living. They suggest ways of beginning to think through other sorts of life disruptions of other varieties. Through such settings we can see both the personal and technical limits, and then from those limits, begin to imagine new or modified systems that would mitigate rather than exacerbate some of the negative consequences.

Clearly, technology cannot "solve" a death in the family, undo the multifarious causes of homelessness, or provide physical and psychological protection against an abusive partner. But it can be used to mitigate the rippling consequences of each of these disruptive life events. By examining these extreme situations, we look to broaden how domestic technologies are considered within HCI and open discussion about a wider range of concerns when conceptualizing technology use in our personal lives. Ultimately, we look to reflect, as designers and as researchers, on the deeply rooted trade-offs that must be reevaluated as our understanding of private life becomes more nuanced and robust.

ACKNOWLEDGMENTS

We'd like to thank the participants and organizations involved in this fieldwork, and Beki Grinter and Lana Yarosh for constructive feedback on earlier drafts of this paper. A portion of the research presented here was supported by the NSF under grant IIS-0915624, and by the Canadian GRAND NCE program.

REFERENCES

1. Aho, A.L., Tarkka, M.-T., Astedt-Kurki, P., and Kaunonen, M. Fathers' Experience of Social Support After the Death of a Child. *Am. J. of Men's Health 3*, 2 (2009), 93-103.
2. Ames, M.G., Go, J., Kaye, J.J., and Spasojevic, M. Making love in the network closet: the benefits and work of family videochat. *Proc. CSCW 2010*, ACM (2010), 145–154.
3. Banyard, V.L. and Graham-Bermann, S.A. Surviving poverty: Stress and coping in the lives of housed and homeless mothers. *Am. J. of Orthopsychiatry 68*, 3 (1998), 479 - 489.
4. Blythe, M.A. *Funology: From Usability to Enjoyment*. Springer Netherlands, 2003.
5. Brown, B., Taylor, A.S., Izadi, S., Sellen, A., Kaye, J., and Eardley, R. Locating Family Values: A Field Trial of the Whereabouts Clock. *Proc. UBICOMP 2007*, Springer-Verlag (2007), 354–371.
6. Brubaker, J.R. and Hayes, G.R. "We will never forget you [online]": an empirical investigation of post-mortem myspace comments. *Proc. CSCW 2011*, ACM (2011), 123–132.
7. Brush, A.J.B. and Inkpen, K.M. Yours, mine and ours? sharing and use of technology in domestic environments. *Proc. UBICOMP 2007*, Springer-Verlag (2007), 109-126.
8. Buckle, J.L. and Fleming, S. *Parenting After the Death of a Child: A Practitioner's Guide*. Routledge, 2010.
9. Crabtree, A. and Rodden, T. Domestic routines and design for the home. *Computer Supported Cooperative Work 13*, 2 (2004), 191–220.
10. Dimond, J., Poole, E., and Yardi, S. The Effects of Death, Divorce, and Life Disruptions on Home Technology Routines. *Proc. GROUP*, ACM (2010).
11. Dimond, J.P., Fiesler, C., and Bruckman, A.S. Domestic violence and information communication technologies. *Interacting with Computers In Press, Corrected Proof.*
12. Edleson, J.L. and Identified, H.F.W. The overlap between child maltreatment and woman abuse. *Violence Against Women 5*, 2 (1999), 134–154.
13. Erickson, T. and Kellogg, W.A. Social translucence: an approach to designing systems that support social processes. *TOCHI 7*, 1 (2000), 59–83.
14. Getty, E., Cobb, J., Gabeler, M., Nelson, C., Weng, E., and Hancock, J. I said your name in an empty room:

grieving and continuing bonds on facebook. *Proc. CHI 2011*, ACM (2011), 997–1000.
15. Grimes, A., Tan, D., and Morris, D. Toward technologies that support family reflections on health. *Proc. GROUP*, ACM (2009), 311-320.
16. Grinter, R.E., Edwards, W.K., Newman, M.W., and Ducheneaut, N. The work to make a home network work. *Proc. ECSCW*, ACM (2005), 469-488.
17. Harrison, S. and Dourish, P. Re-place-ing space: the roles of place and space in collaborative systems. *Proc. CSCW 1996*, (1996), 67–76.
18. Johnson, M.P. and Ferraro, K.J. Research on domestic violence in the 1990s: Making distinctions. *Journal of Marriage and the Family 62*, 4 (2000), 948–963.
19. Judge, T.K., Neustaedter, C., and Kurtz, A.F. The family window: the design and evaluation of a domestic media space. *Proc. CHI*, ACM (2010), 2361-2370.
20. Kaye, J.J., Levitt, M.K., Nevins, J., Golden, J., and Schmidt, V. Communicating intimacy one bit at a time. *Proc. CHI Extended Abstracts*, ACM (2005), 1529-1532.
21. Kwak, H., Chun, H., and Moon, S. Fragile online relationship: A first look at unfollow dynamics in Twitter. *Proc. CHI 2011*, (2011), 1091–1100.
22. Lasch, C. *Haven in a heartless world*. Basic Books New York, 1977.
23. Latour, B. Technology is society made durable. In J. Law, ed., *A sociology of monsters: Essays on power, technology, and domination*. Routledge, 1991, 103–131.
24. Lavee, Y., McCubbin, H.I., and Olson, D.H. The Effect of Stressful Life Events and Transitions on Family Functioning and Well-Being. *Journal of Marriage and Family 49*, 4 (1987), 857–873.
25. Le Dantec, C.A., Farrell, R.G., Christensen, J.E., et al. Publics in practice: ubiquitous computing at a shelter for homeless mothers. *Proc. CHI 2011*, ACM (2011), 1687–1696.
26. Le Dantec, C.A. and Edwards, W.K. Designs on Dignity: Perceptions of Technology among the Homeless. *Proc. CHI*, ACM (2008), 627–636.
27. Le Dantec, C.A., Christensen, J.E., Bailey, M., et al. A Tale of Two Publics: Democratizing Design at the Margins. *Proc. DIS*, ACM (2010), 11-20.
28. Letiecq, B.L., Anderson, E.A., and Koblinsky, S.A. Social Support of Homeless and Housed Mothers: A Comparison of Temporary and Permanent Housing Arrangements. *Family Relations 47*, 4 (1998), 415–421.
29. Massimi, M. and Baecker, R.M. Dealing with death in design: developing systems for the bereaved. *Proc. CHI 2011*, ACM (2011), 1001–1010.
30. Massimi, M. and Baecker, R.M. A death in the family: opportunities for designing technologies for the bereaved. *Proc. CHI*, ACM (2010), 1821-1830.
31. Medved, C.E. The everyday accomplishment of work and family: Exploring practical actions in daily routines. *Communication Studies 55*, 1 (2004), 128–145.
32. Morley, D. *Family television: Cultural power and domestic leisure*. Routledge, 1986.
33. Neustaedter, C., Brush, A.J.B., and Greenberg, S. The calendar is crucial: Coordination and awareness through the family calendar. *TOCHI 16*, 1 (2009), 1-48.
34. O'Brien, J., Rodden, T., Rouncefield, M., and Hughes, J. At home with the technology: an ethnographic study of a set-top-box trial. *TOCHI 6*, 3 (1999), 308.
35. Odom, W., Zimmerman, J., and Forlizzi, J. Designing for dynamic family structures: divorced families and interactive systems. *Proc. DIS*, ACM (2010), 151-160.
36. Palen, L. and Dourish, P. Unpacking "privacy" for a networked world. *Proc. CHI*, ACM (2003), 129-136.
37. Rafferty, Y. and Shinn, M. The impact of homelessness on children. *American Psychologist 46*, 11 (1991), 1170-1179.
38. Ristock, J. and Timbang, N. Relationship violence in Lesbian/Gay/Bisexual/Transgender/Queer [LGBTQ] communities: Moving beyond a gender-based framework. *Violence against women online resources, http://www. vaw. umn. edu*, (2005).
39. Rode, J.A. The roles that make the domestic work. *Proc. CSCW*, ACM (2010), 381-390.
40. Star, S. Power, technologies, and the phenomenology of conventions: On being allergic to onions. In J. Law, ed., *A Sociology of Monsters: Essays on Power, Technology, and Domination*. Routledge, 1991, 26-55.
41. Star, S.L. The ethnography of infrastructure. *American behavioral scientist 43*, 3 (1999), 377.
42. Star, S.L. and Bowker, C. How to infrastructure. In L.A. Lievrouw and S.M. Livingstone, eds., *The Handbook of New Media*. Sage, London, UK, 2002, 151–162.
43. Star, S.L. and Ruhleder, K. Steps toward an ecology of infrastructure: Design and access for large information spaces. *Information Systems Research 7*, 1 (1996), 111–134.
44. Tjaden, P. and Thoennes, N. Extent, nature, and consequences of intimate partner violence: findings from the National Violence Against Women Survey. *Washington (DC): Department of Justice (US) Publication No. NCJ 181867*, (2000).
45. Vale-Taylor, P. "We will remember them": a mixed-method study to explore which post-funeral remembrance activities are most significant and important to bereaved people living with loss, and why those particular activities are chosen. *Palliative Medicine 23*, (2009), 537 -54.
46. Voida, A., Carpendale, S., and Greenberg, S. The individual and the group in console gaming. *Proc. CSCW*, ACM (2010), 371-380.
47. Yarosh, S., Chew, Y.C., and Abowd, G.D. Supporting parent-child communication in divorced families. *International Journal of Human-Computer Studies 67*, 2 (2009), 192 - 203.

An Examination of How Households Share and Coordinate the Completion of Errands

Timothy Sohn[1], Lorikeet L. Lee[2], Stephanie M. Zhang[2], David Dearman[2,3], Khai N. Truong[2]

[1]Google Inc.
1600 Amphitheatre Parkway
Mountain View, CA 94043 USA

[2]Department of Computer Science
University of Toronto
Toronto, ON M5S 3G4 Canada

[3]Nokia Research Center
955 Page Mill Rd.
Palo Alto, CA 94304 USA

ABSTRACT

People often complete tasks and to-dos not only for themselves but also for others in their household. In this work, we examine how household members share and accomplish errands both individually and together. We conducted a three-week diary study with eight households to understand the types of errands that family members and roommates share with each other. We explore their motivations for offering and requesting help to complete their errands and the variety of methods for doing so. Our findings reveal when participants sometimes face challenges completing their errands, and how household members request and receive help. We learned that the cooperative performance of errands is typically dependent on household members' location, availability, and capability. Using these findings, we discuss design opportunities for cooperative errands sharing systems that can assist households.

Author Keywords

cooperative errands, families, roommates, coordination

ACM Classification Keywords

H5.m. Information interfaces and presentation (*e.g.*, HCI): Miscellaneous.

General Terms

Design, Human Factors.

INTRODUCTION

People have a variety of tasks and to-do items that they must accomplish for themselves. Many of these tasks, called errands, require people to make trips outside of their home to complete. Errands often consume a non-trivial amount of time to complete because of the time it takes to travel to and from the locations where the tasks need to be performed, as well as the time and effort that it takes to complete the tasks themselves. As a result, Americans spend on average over 2.5 hours each day at locations outside of their homes [19] to perform a variety of instrumental activities of daily living (*e.g.*, grocery shopping, automobile maintenance).

Those who live with family members or roommates can offer to help other household members complete their errands or ask for help completing their own. For example, a college student who forgot his project report on his desk at home could ask a roommate, who has yet to leave home, to bring the report to class with him. Similarly, a wife may offer to pick up some ice on her way home so that her husband can continue with other preparations for their dinner party at their home later that evening. The availability and assistance of household members can reduce the amount of time needed to perform an errand and allow households to cooperatively perform household tasks.

Although several studies have explored individual task management and family coordination habits [8, 29, 33], few have explored the methods used by households to specifically address errands. What motivates household members to ask for help? What situations influence decisions whether to help with an errand? Understanding how households (*i.e.*, families or roommates) perform errands can provide insights to improve household coordination in cooperatively accomplishing their errands.

In this work, we examine how household members share and accomplish tasks both individually and together. Due to the communal aspect of approaching errands, we refer to errands shared within a household as cooperative errands. We conducted a three-week diary study with eight households to examine the types of errands that family members and roommates share with each other, their motivations for offering and requesting help to complete their errands, and the methods for doing so. Our findings reveal that participants sometimes face challenges in completing errands due to time, location, and circumstances. The urgency of an errand and the resources of other household members are two of the primary factors that influence the sharing of errands amongst a household. Household members were generally willing to help others, but sometimes faced barriers due to not knowing each others' errands or the potential helpers' whereabouts and availability to help with errands. Based on our observations and interviews with participants, we discovered several design opportunities to enhance cooperative errand sharing systems that could improve the communication and coordination of errands within households of both families and roommates. The following sections describe our study methodology, results, and the design opportunities to support cooperative errands.

RELATED WORK

Errands are to-do tasks that require people to make a trip to accomplish. The focus of this work is on how households share and coordinate the completion of errands, which is closely related to task management and reminder systems, and family coordination systems. In a group setting, individuals can share tasks and take advantage of situations where one individual may be better situated to accomplish a task. We first provide a review of previous research that has focused on individual task management, then review previous research that has focused on family coordination of domestic activities.

Task Management & Reminder Systems

Early task management research has examined the artifacts and processes that people use to manage information (such as meetings, contacts, documents) to accomplish their work [20]. These task management systems have focused on tasks typically executed on a desktop workstation to support workplace task management [2, 3, 5, 7, 8].

Although workplace task management is an important domain, many everyday tasks require support away from the desktop [5, 22]. Ludford *et al.* demonstrate that although people pre-plan and create information resources to perform everyday tasks, a location-based reminder system is useful in helping users spatially organize their tasks [22]. Location-based reminder systems provide a contextual method to trigger a reminder at a specified location [14, 17, 18, 22, 23, 27, 29]. These systems allow the user to input a note that is triggered based on her presence at a location. Sohn *et al.* reported that participants in their study used such a system 30% of the time to inform them to make trips and to bring or get items from different locations (*i.e.*, reminders for errands) [29]. These studies have focused primarily only on the user's personal tasks but not those belonging to others, such as those in the user's household.

Family Coordination Systems

Research about how domestic technologies can be built to support family coordination has focused on patterns of interaction within the home [11], and how these interactions relate to everyday artifacts [31, 34] and routines [1, 12, 16]. At the heart of family life is the mutual awareness that household members have of each other's locations and activities throughout each day. This awareness can be gained through location sharing [4, 8] and group calendar systems [25, 10]. Knowing the schedule and whereabouts of other family members can assist in coordinating tasks. However, family calendars can deviate from reported schedules, and in these cases family members often rely on routines that are implicitly communicated and understood amongst family members [12].

In order to address schedule changes and assist in spontaneous family communication, some households coordinate using messaging systems. Taylor *et al.* showed that notes attached to the refrigerator make the fridge's location a significant place for supporting task organization, planning and reminding [32]. Electronic versions of coordination systems can help support family communication and coordination within the home [21, 24] as well as remotely [28]. For example, the TxtBoard system supports family coordination by enabling household members to send text messages to the home that are then shown on an electronic display [26]. Elliot *et al.* leverage user location and context to help people better understand and manage their information and tasks within the home; they demonstrate how to deliver messages at meaningful times and locations based on knowledge of their routines [15].

In this paper, we extend previous research by exploring how errands are communicated and coordinated within households. The key distinction in our work is that we examine the errand sharing practices of families and roommates who cohabitate. Although families have many different kinds of lists that they maintain and create [33], in this work we focus specifically on errands—tasks that require a person to make a trip to accomplish. Further, our work studies also the practices of those who live together as roommates, and not only families.

METHOD

We conducted a three-week diary study to explore the errands that eight different households performed. Diary studies enable us to gather ecologically valid data from participants because they can document an errand when it starts and ends, with minimal disruption to normal activities.

Participants

We recruited eight households (three families, five households shared by roommates) through word-of-mouth and flyers posted in two North American cities. Participation was open to any household with at least three people ages 16 or older who lived together. We used 16 years of age as the lower bound for participation to include families with teenage children who could potentially perform errands on their own. We did not enforce any other restrictions because we wanted to ensure a diverse participant sampling with respect to background and daily experiences given the broad nature of our exploration. The age of our participants ranged from 18-55 with a variety of occupations. In three households (H5, H6, and H7), only individuals who were present in the home during the study and actively contributed to performing errands participated in the study. For example, the H7 household has two children who were younger than 10 years old; they were excluded from the interviews because they did not actively contribute to the performance of errands. Details about the participants can be found in Table 1.

Procedure

We instructed participants to keep a diary of their daily errands (Figure 1) for a period of three weeks. We defined an errand as *a short and quick trip to accomplish a specific purpose, as to buy something, deliver a package, or convey a message*; or *a short trip undertaken to perform a necessary task or commission*. However, we encouraged participants to enter any task into the diary that they perceived as an errand and allow us to determine if it met our definition. Participants were instructed to write down errands as they thought of them, including errands they did not complete, errands they asked others within and outside of their household to help perform, and errands they were asked by others to help perform.

We met with participants weekly to collect the diaries, interview them, and give them new diaries for the next week if needed. Interviews took between 15-60 minutes and followed a semi-structured format, allowing the interviewer to probe further about each diary entry. We asked the participants to explain the intent for each of their errands in greater detail when applicable. If the errand was completed, we asked how it was completed and by whom; alternatively, for errands that were not completed, we probed why they had not been completed. For errands which they were asked by others to help with or ones which they asked others to help perform, we also probed about whom the other the persons were and why they were asked. At the end of the final week, we conducted an exit interview with each household to understand their overall experiences, asking them to reflect on the current practices their household uses to communicate and coordinate errands. Participants discussed several possible design ideas to address many of the barriers faced in the coordination of errands. The weekly and exit interviews were all audio recorded with participant consent for analysis.

We compensated households composed of roommates $50 for the first week, $75 for the second week, and $100 for the final week ($225 total). Households composed of family members were compensated $75 for the first week, $125 for the second week, and $200 for the last week ($400 total). Because we experienced great difficulty recruiting families, they were compensated a higher amount. All households were also entered into a drawing for one of two Microsoft Xbox 360 consoles with Kinect (valued at $299).

Instrument

We designed the diary as a small pocketsize paper journal that participants can carry to make full or partial entries *in situ* [13] as errands were started and completed. Each page of the

Household Code	Participants	Common Errands Performed Top 3 errands during the study	Errands per Week Completed	Uncompleted	Asked others to help	Asked by others to help
H1 - Roommates	A - Female; 18-25; Clinical Research Assistant	Buy/sell, gifting, returning items, transporting	3.7, σ=2.5	1, σ=0.8	1.3, σ=1.2	2, σ=1.6
	B - Female; 26-35; student/teacher	Buy/sell, transporting, gifting	5, σ=5.7	1, σ=0.8	1.3, σ=1.9	4.3, σ=4.8
	C - Female; 26-35; temp	Finance-related, transporting, returning items	3.3, σ=4.7		2.7, σ=3.1	0.7, σ=0.5
H2 – Roommates	A - Male; 18-25; undergraduate student	School-related, planning, transporting	2, σ=1.4	0.3, σ=0.5	0.3, σ=0.5	0.3, σ=0.5
	B - Male; 18-25; undergraduate student	Transporting, finance-related, school-related, planning	1, σ=0.8	0.3, σ=0.5	1, σ=0.8	
	C - Male, 18-25; undergraduate student	Buy/sell, school-related	1, σ=1.4	0.3, σ=0.5		0.3, σ=0.5
H3 – Roommates	A – Male; 18-25; student	Buy/sell, transporting, household chores, school-related	2.7, σ=0.9		0.7, σ=0.9	
	B – Male; 18-25; student	School-related, planning, transporting	0.7, σ=0.9	0.3, σ=0.5	0.3, σ=0.5	0.7, σ=0.9
	C – Male; 18-25; student	School-related, transporting, buy/sell	0.7, σ=0.9	0.7, σ=0.9		0.3, σ=0.5
H4 – Roommates	A –Female; 26-35; Academic Program Assistant at UCSC Extension	Buy/sell, transporting, gifting	8.3, σ=4		0.7, σ=0.9	4.3, σ=3.4
	B - Female; 18-25; Certified Nurse's Aide	Transporting, work-related, maintenance	6.3, σ=3.3			1, σ=1.4
	C - Female; 18-25; student	Buy/sell, returning items, maintenance	6, σ=2.4			0.7, σ=0.9
H5 – Roommates [only roommates who were present in the home during the study participated]	A - Male; 18-25; student	Buy/sell, gifting, school-related	1, σ=0.8			
	B - Female; 18-25; student	Buy/sell, personal, work-related	1.3, σ=1.9			
	C - Male; 26-35; graduate student	Transporting, gifting, buy/sell	2.3, σ=1.7			0.3, σ=0.5
H6 - Family [only siblings who performed errands participated in the study]	A – Female; 18-25; student	Buy/sell, transporting, personal, school-related, assistance	2.7, σ=2.5		1.7, σ=1.7	1.3, σ=1.9
	B – Male; 18-25; unemployed	Buy/sell, work-related, transporting (more)	2, σ=0.8	0.3, σ=0.5	1.3, σ=0.5	1.7, σ=0.5
	C – Female; 18-25; student	Transporting, buy/sell, maintenance	8, σ=3.3		1, σ=0	8.7, σ=3.3
H7 – Family [only family members who are older than 16 years of age participated in the study]	A – Male; 18-25; student	Transporting, buy/sell, maintenance	3, σ=2.2			1.7, σ=1.2
	B – Female; 46-55; stay at home mom	Buy/sell, transporting, returning items	5, σ=0.8	0.3, σ=0.5	0.3, σ=0.5	2.3, σ=0.9
	C – Male; 36-45; press operator	Transporting, assistance, personal (more)	2, σ=0.8	0.3, σ=0.5	0.3, σ=0.5	1, σ=0.8
H8 – Family	A – Female; 55+; social services workers	Transporting, buy/sell, gifting	5, σ=0.8		2, σ=1.4	
	B – Male; 18-25; business systems analyst	Buy/sell, maintenance	0.7, σ=0.5			0.7, σ=0.9
	C – Male; 55+; retired	Gifting, maintenance, transporting, finance-related	1.3, σ=0.9			1.3, σ=1.2

Table 1. Household & errands overview. Table cells are blank if the participant did not report errands matching the specified criteria.

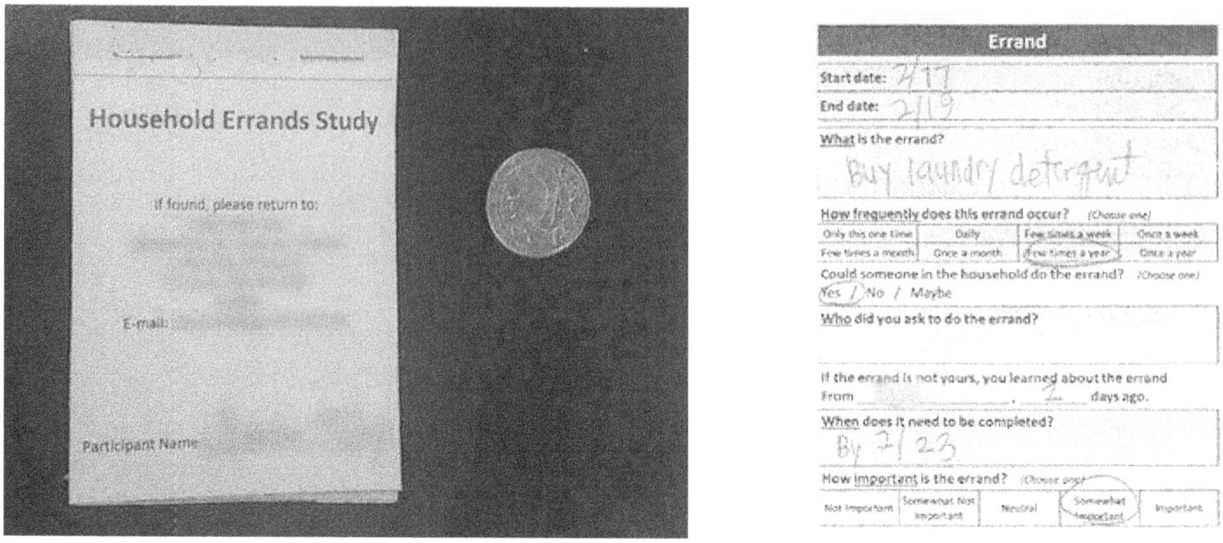

Figure 1. The diary form factor (left). An actual diary page completed about an errand (right).

diary contained a short structured form (Figure 1: right) with the following questions about the errand that the participant needed to perform or was asked to help perform by others:

- A description of the errand
- The date when it started being an active errand
- The date when it ended being an active errand
- The participant's perception of when the errand needed to be completed by
- How frequently that particular errand arises
- Who they might have asked to help with the errand
- If the errand was not their own, who asked them to help and when
- Their perception of the importance of the errand.

A diary study does have some limitations. Self-reported information may not be complete and may also contain inaccuracies. Additionally, participants may forget or choose not to report all qualifying entries. Our specific approach takes these limitations into consideration. To minimize any disturbances, we intentionally designed the diary to ask for very short and specific information to minimize the time burden when completing an entry. Additionally, we performed an interview with each household every week to elicit additional details. A diary study also allows participants to self-filter out sensitive experiences when necessary. At the very least, the number of diary entries gathered using this technique provides a realistic lower bound for the number of times participants experienced the studied effect. We thus chose to use a diary study because we thought it would be the most effective technique to capture data to reveal the nature of individual and cooperative errands.

Analysis

To analyze the errands, one researcher performed an affinity clustering [6] to identify and group similar entries. The affinity clustering was then challenged by the rest of the research team, followed by a round of refinement. The process of challenging and refining the clusters was repeated for 2 additional iterations until a final consensus was reached.

We identified the participants' motivations for cooperatively performing errands and their method for doing so by analyzing transcripts of the weekly interviews using open coding [30]. Three coders participated in the coding activity and discussed the data, forming and grouping codes, until agreement was reached.

RESULTS AND DISCUSSION

In this section, we describe the practices we observed among our participants in completing errands. We first present the errands reported by the participants. We then discuss why participants cooperatively performed errands and how they coordinated such efforts.

Reported Errands

Overall, participants recorded a total of 241 errands, with each household averaging 30 entries over the three weeks of the study. Participants indicated that they were able to complete 226 (93.8%) errands and unable to complete 15 (6.2%) errands. Each participant reported: performing 3.3 errands per week; asking others to help with 0.6 errands per week; being asked to help with 1.4 errands per week; and, not completing 0.2 errands per week.

We used affinity clustering to group the participants' errands into 11 categories (Table 2). The three types of errands most frequently recorded were buy/sell (96 entries), transporting (68 entries), and maintenance (20 entries). Participants most commonly asked for help when performing a transporting (21 entries) and buy/sell (10 entries) errand. These errands typically involve being mobile to move or purchase items. Many of the other categories are not as frequent (*e.g.*, haircuts for personal errands) or are more difficult to ask another household member for help (*e.g.*, work-related).

The majority of errands the participants recorded occur infrequently or do not reoccur; the median frequency of an errand was 3 out of 8 (M=2.9, SD: 2.0) where 1 is only this one time and 8 is daily. Only 3 entries were marked as daily errands and 31 entries were marked as weekly errands. In addition, participants reported their errands as important (median=5, M=4.3, SD=1.0) on a 5-point Likert scale; 1=not important and 5=important. The importance of an errand was generally interpreted based on the urgency of the errand, the number of opportunities to perform the errand, or how impactful the errand would be on their life (*e.g.*, confer with immigration office about Canadian visa).

> H4-C: *If there's no other time to [do the errand] then it'll seem more important.*

Challenges with completing errands individually

The participants faced numerous challenges that hindered their ability to complete errands individually. Our interviews revealed five reasons why errands were often not completed.

Often participants **simply just forget** about an errand. This frequently happened when participants perceived an errand to be **low in priority** and that it did not need to be completed immediately. The longer they delayed in addressing the errand, the less likely it was to be completed or forgotten.

> H3-A: *I had to get a spare key made because I lost mine, but I haven't gotten it yet. I can just call myself and I buzz myself in our main door. I need to talk to my landlord because it is the magnetic key. So I haven't gotten to that yet this week. I just don't feel it's really necessary right now.*

Having a key to get into one's own house is very important, but because this participant had an alternative method for getting into this apartment, he perceived this errand as having low urgency. If he did not have this other method of entry, the urgency of the errand would have likely increased significantly. The urgency of an errand is also affected by its perceived deadline. For participant H2-C, school-related errands were important, but not necessarily urgent because the deadlines could be months away.

> H2-C: *I didn't pick up all my textbooks... cause one of the midterms is in March so I didn't feel like I needed to pick it up right now.*

Participants expressed that the **cost associated with attempting or performing an errand** affects their ability to complete it. For example, participants sometimes delayed completing a task that involves spending a large amount of money for as long as possible. However, simply attempting an errand also involves time and effort, which sometimes participants are not willing to exert.

> H3-B: *I would have to go to IKEA, but it's pretty far. I had planned to go there one day, but found out it was going to take 45 minutes [on bus]...and if we go there and it's closed then we messed up, because we would have spent close to an hour getting there [it would be like] we never went.*

Finally, even when participants have the time and desire to perform an errand, there are **external factors** that may prevent them from completing the task. For example, they may only be free at a time outside of a location's hours of operations or perhaps the weather does not permit them to complete the task.

> H5-B: *I've still yet to go to the bank. This is three weeks now. I was going to go today, but it's closed. It's a holiday. Because I don't have school this week, I have more time.*

Reasons for cooperatively performing errands

Participants described numerous benefits from cooperatively performing errands. Participants gained personally from having help from other household members, but would also cooperatively perform errands due to communal and cultural reasons (*e.g.*, oldest daughter performs most household errands).

Benefits of completing errands cooperatively

Sharing and communicating errands with other household members can help address some of the described challenges that participants faced completing errands individually. Cooperatively addressing errands can take advantage of other household members' time, knowledge, and abilities providing access to additional resources in order to complete errands.

One clear benefit to cooperatively performing errands is that **people can help each other complete important tasks.** The importance of an errand strongly influences a participant's decision to ask others to help with completing that task. The reasons why an errand is important can be multifaceted, strongly influencing how the errand will be prioritized.

> H3-A: *I think it works really well, especially when there are*

Category	Examples	# of Category Entries	# Asked for Help
Buy/Sell	*"Grocery shopping for a party."*	96	10
Transporting	*"Pick up my friend's daughter."*	68	21
Maintenance	*"Get gas for car."*	20	1
Finance-related	*"Go to the bank to close an account."*	12	6
Personal	*"Get a haircut"*	11	2
School-related	*"Get book photocopied."*	8	2
Work-related	*"Job interview."*	8	0
Planning	*"Check out venue for an event."*	6	1
Household Chores	*"Get rid of Christmas tree."*	4	0
Assistance	*"Accompany my wife to the store to take care of the kids while she shops."*	4	1
Gathering Data	*"Take pictures of a house for my mom's insurance business."*	4	1

Table 2. Errand categories.

more than two people, because then you have a backup as well. Anything you have to do, if it is really necessary, then it's going to be done. So I think it's really, really helpful to live with someone who can help you out with your stuff.

Involving the help of others to complete errands helps get such tasks done **more quickly and efficiently** than if participants were to do it personally.

H7-A: *It's about functionality. Whichever way I can do it the fastest, I'll do. It's the same with her and my dad. Whoever can do it fastest within the group, we'll just send him or her.*

H7-B: *The sooner we can do it, the better, so that it's out of our mind. Then we don't have to think about it.*

If they have time and are able to help, participants were generally willing to help each other. For example, participant H4-C stated that her roommate, participant H4-B had *"the most flexible and predictable schedule, so she can run a lot of errands for us."* Household members were able to identify appropriate times to ask for help in performing errands and could rely on the availability of their other household member with more free time.

Often **another person in the household has the knowledge and ability** to help complete one's errands. As described earlier, perhaps their assistance may result in the completion of a task quicker than had the individual tried to complete it herself. A person might simply be located where they are able to help. Their physical ability to perform a task is sometimes the reason a person is asked to help. For example, some participants asked fellow household members to come along on shopping trips to help carry things that they would not be able to carry alone. Another person's assistance can also result in the task being completed better than if one were to attempt to perform it alone. Many times, participants asked for help when they lacked the skills or the expertise to perform the activity.

H7-B: *I don't know how to buy stuff for her music course, like the [strings] for her guitar, they break. I don't know how to buy them, so I call him. I don't know how to call them [sic] and so I don't know where to buy them.*

Communal and cultural expectations for helping others

A large percentage of the errands reported by the participants were not just their own tasks, but reflected activities that benefited the entire house. These **communal factors** made participants feel comfortable asking each other to help with such errands. Participants frequently assisted each other because of their desire to help as common courtesy. This was especially true when the other person was sick or extremely busy.

H3-B *He got sick Thursday night, and he had an assignment due on Friday. Friday morning, he was up at like 8 in the morning and I could tell he was sick. And he asked, "Are you going to school today?" I said "Yeah." And he asked, "Could I get you to submit my assignment on your way?" I said "OK. Just put it on my desk and tell me where to take it."*

H3-A: *I think it's because we're all students. We really understand what the other person needs in terms of if someone asked me to do something, then I know that he really wants that thing to be done...otherwise he would really just do it himself.*

Several households also described **roles and cultural expectations** as a reason why some members of their household helped to perform errands for others. Because of their culture, they assumed particular roles in the family. As a result, many of the errands became their responsibility to complete.

H6-A: *My mom will say "Just do it, just do it."*

H6-C: *He is the eldest son. Even though I'm the oldest [child], my mom will always say "whatever that he says, just do it, no matter how lazy he's being. You're his sister, it's your job."*

In another household, participant H4-A, who is the eldest daughter, would frequently travel home to *"help with a lot of errands for the family."* This included errands such as going to the grocery store, pharmacy, and other miscellaneous household tasks.

Although such expectations differ across different cultures, the notion of roles within a household is one that held true across several different groups of participants in our study. These roles can be defined based on where someone is typically located, as well as their skills and expertise, which we described earlier.

Methods for Cooperatively Completing Errands

In the previous section, we discussed the motivations for why participants cooperatively complete their errands. In this section, we discuss the methods that they use in order to be able to involve each other's help in completing their errands. These methods are not necessarily mutually exclusive and most households employed multiple methods during this study.

Explicitly Coordinate Help

Although they may each do so differently, all households reported some explicit coordination of how members of their household can help each other. Often one person in the house determines what needs to be done and informs those who can help to complete those tasks. In one instance, the coordinator is simply a person through whom information flows. This information can include what needs to be done, by whom, when and where.

H6-A: *We leave notes. It's mostly for my mom. If the note is for my dad, it's so that my mom can read the note and deliver the message to my dad.*

Another strategy used is to negotiate ahead of time how different members of the household can help to complete tasks that happen regularly.

H3-B: *There's a Pakistani supermarket that's far away. So we go there once a month. We do the big grocery shopping there, like chicken and meat and stuff.*

H3-C: *Like in bulk...It's only once a month, so we're like ok, we can come and help carry stuff.*

H3-B: It can be anyone, one of them and me, the two of them… it's whoever is free that week, they can go. The thing is we need chicken and meat and stuff. So whenever that's finished, whenever we have time, we go as soon as possible.

Offer Help Based on Location

Although it did not happen as frequently as we expected, most participants discussed informing other household members when they are able to run errands at specific locations to see if they can help complete other tasks at the same time. Participants also sometimes contacted others in their household from locations where they think they might be able to help perform some errands. Participants offer their assistance because they want to remove the need for others to make an unnecessary trip.

H6-C: Whenever I go out, I tend to call my mom and say, "Do you want anything while I'm here?" I always look out that way. I'm here, I spent $3 to get here on the bus. I might as well make the most of it and see if there's anything someone else needs done so no one else needs to make the trip.

Request Help Based on Presumed Routine

Participants frequently sought help with completing errands by using their knowledge of the other household members' routines. With an assumption of where others might be located and their activities, participants are able to determine who is possibly in position to be able to help them and ask them for assistance.

H3-A: It's just living together and getting to know each other. We're sort of familiar with each other's routines, so we would just know that…OK, so he would be at this guy's place at this time. I don't know how to explain it… it's just instinctual, I don't know.

H3-B: Right, so then the first thing I'd ask is "Hi, where are you?" And he'll say, "Blah, blah, blah." Then I'll ask, "Can you bring back this thing on your way back home?" And he'll say, "Sure."

Participants reported a willingness to help complete errands for others if they are asked in a situation that allowed them to do so.

Figure 2. The "chore *vs.* shame" chart

H6-A: Yeah, I would help if that's something where I'm there. It would be inappropriate [sic] for me to say, "Come do it yourself." Right? So I would do it at that time.

Track Individual Contributions to the Household

Participants were generally aware of how much work different people performed to help complete household tasks. As part of being courteous of others, participants often would attempt to minimize how often they ask for favors from others until they have been able to reciprocate.

H5-C: If I find that I've sort of have been using them more than they've been using me, to put it crudely, then I'm less likely to ask them for a favor until I feel like order has been restored.

One group of roommates leveraged the fact that people within a household will feel compelled to contribute more when they are aware of the amount of work others have performed. They maintained a chart (Figure 2) on which each member of the household can write down the tasks that he or she has recently completed which benefits the group. The purpose of the chart was to make each other more explicitly aware of the amount of work that the different household members have each performed recently.

H5-A: It's called the "chore vs. shame chart." We just hope that it'll put it in everyone's face how much everyone is doing so that they can be like, "Oh crap! So and so has done eight chores and I've only done two" and take more initiative.

In being able to see how much work each person within the household has contributed recently and who was the last person to perform a particular task, work is implicitly assigned to that person without much further explicit coordination.

H5-A: A lot of the time, I'll notice what needs to be done and if I haven't done anything recently or if I feel like it's my turn, then maybe I'll just do it on the spot, or you know plan to in the not-so-distant future. If you weren't that last person to get something, then maybe this time you would get some.

Why Help is Not Always Offered or Requested

Although participants expressed a general willingness to help each other complete their tasks when possible, there are some reasons why help is not always requested or offered for all errands. Each member within a household may have **specific needs that differ from others**, so it may not be easy for participants to ask each other for help. Each participant may want an errand to be done in a particular way, which may make it difficult for others to provide help. These concerns particularly manifested when it came to purchasing food or clothing items. Furthermore, a person might **need to make decisions related to an errand in a contextually dependent manner**. It would be hard for others to make those decisions for a person.

H5-A: I needed [gloves] that were a little bit more agile…It was something where I definitely want to check it out myself, see what the prices are, and try see what the gloves look like on… I can't think of an instance where I would want anyone to buy any clothing item of sorts.

H5-C: You might see fish and go "Oooh!!" And it's just the best selection for what's available that day, so I don't know if other people would be able to make those same decisions that are optimal for me. A lot of the stuff gets to be like that.

Additionally, other people might **lack the knowledge and expertise to complete an errand properly**. As a result, participants perceive that it is easiest for them to perform the task themselves.

H7-B: The two little ones, they have allergies. So some stuff I have to do it myself [sic]. Some grocery stuff [sic], I buy it myself because they don't know if it has to be gluten-free or free of other things. They don't know so it will take them too long to get the same thing. So for example, when I go to buy flours there are special gluten free ones or special products that I personally know because I use it on a regular basis when I'm cooking. For the rest of the family, we use different products, so they can pick up those items, no problem for us, but not for the two little ones.

Roommates, in particular, expressed not wanting to ask too much of their fellow household members. They describe that it is **not their roommate's responsibility to help** them perform tasks that they could otherwise do themselves.

H5-A: You definitely ask more of different people in your life depending on what role they occupy or how much love they get from you, you know? I feel more comfortable asking my sister to do things than some guy in class, or you know the people I live with. I have good relationships with them and I'd like to maintain that.

Often, the **amount of effort that goes into performing an errand** is a factor that the participants also expressed taking into consideration before asking others to help. Participants noted that some tasks were too lightweight to ask others to do; in those instances, those were errands that they could and should do very easily themselves:

H3-A: it's just mailing in a letter, so I didn't really ask.

At the same time, participants were also concerned with asking for help when an errand involved what they perceived as possibly a large amount of inconvenience to others. They feared not being able to return the favor in an adequate manner:

H5-B: If I didn't think it was fair or I couldn't compensate them well enough... like if it's something really big or if it's exceptionally far... it's not their thing to do. I wouldn't make them do something that's out of balance in terms of time, money, distance or effort. I wouldn't ask them, because I don't know if I would be able to reciprocate that.

The **type of errand** and **reimbursement tracking** would sometimes affect whether a household member would ask for help. If the errand was of a personal nature it might be embarrassing or inappropriate to ask for assistance, and the effort involved in maintaining 'who owes who' was more effortful/troublesome than performing the errand:

H4-C: I won't ask to help with an errand if it's a personal item I know I need to reimburse them. If it's a community item and I don't need to reimburse them and its communal then I'd verbalize what I need.

The **dependability of a household member** influenced who a participant was willing to ask for assistance:

H6-B: The reason I won't ask my brother to do anything is because he will say, "Give me five minutes." I'll be sitting there waiting and I'll say, "Five minutes is done," and then he'll go, "Wait five more minutes." We'd be waiting and then time will go by, and my dad will yell at me. We'd all be yelled at, and my brother will still be sitting there. So instead, I'll just do it myself. When I come back, he'll still be sitting there.

If a person is unreliable or sometimes unwilling to help, then participants were less likely to ask that person for help or offer them assistance in the future:

H6-B: If I did something for them and then I want them to do something for me and they don't, and they ask me to help them [again later on], I'll say, "No, I won't help you."

Finally, participants reported that sometimes they preferred to perform their own errands because it is **an excuse for personal time.**

H5-C: I don't know about you guys, but I like the act of going.
H5-A: Uh-huh. Yeah. I definitely use shopping as an excuse to get out that day because I don't have anything else to do other than like homework... it's a way to relax and so I use that as an excuse a lot of the time... to kinda get out of the house too... to take a break from studying, to take a walk, get air.
H5-C: It's kind of social too because there are other people on the street that you can come into eye contact with.

DESIGN OPPORTUNITIES

In the final interview, we asked participants to reflect on the practices used for completing errands within their household and possible opportunities for addressing the challenges that they faced. Participants disclosed how their current methods for sharing errands are problematic, but they also suggested information services that they believe can help in the performance of errands. Three primary themes emerged during the final interview that should be considered in designing tools to support errands: provide the ability to share location information; allow for sharing of a private and communal errands list; and recognize that an errand can have particularities that need to be expressed to the person(s) who will eventually perform the errand. These three themes present opportunities to improve the performance of an errand and errand sharing within a household.

Participants discussed that location and availability are key factors in determining if they would request help to complete an errand and when they would offer to help perform an errand. Although many of the participants disclosed using a variety of communication methods to share their location (*e.g.*, SMS, Facebook Places), few actively used these tools to communicate their location for the purpose of coordinating errands. Instead, participants discussed an opportunity for a collaborative errand service that supports an explicit push model for location sharing and errand availability would support the participants' current behaviors and reduce the overhead of requesting and negotiating availability. In particular, such an explicit push model would help the user maintain her privacy by ensuring that their location and availability are only disclosed when they choose:

> *H5-B:* *I'm not into the idea of having people be able to track my movements during the day, but I do like the idea of if I want to share the information, I can.... I just like the privacy.*

In sharing one's location, participants alluded to a shared errand list that could lower the barrier to help others. Participant H6-B commented that *"if I could see other people's errands and I could do it, then I would do it."* A shared errand list also meets two design requirements discussed by the participants. First, it enables errand sharing to be implicitly initiated by the person who needs help; as participant H3-A explains *"the input should be from the person who wants the thing, instead of the person who might be able to get the thing."* In turn, the ability to share and track the errands of other household members while mobile could foster more opportunistic collaboration. The shared errand list allows users to determine when to push their location to others to offer their help, if it is still needed. When inputting an errand, the user could manually annotate the places she knows where her errand can be performed, or more sophisticated techniques could be used to automatically determine opportunistic places to perform the errand.

> *H5-A:* *Let's say in the next month you know you're going to need a few different things -- sort of long-term errands... so then you put in your database or whatever it is all the items that you need or needed... say you needed it at [large discount department store], and then someone happens to be at [hardware store] and can possibly get it there and then when a person is at such and such a store, they can see it on their phones...a list of things people desire and then they can check in to the group.*

Participants also discussed that *how* an errand is performed and a person's expertise (or ability) to perform the errand strongly influence who they will ask for assistance. For example, participant H7-B discussed her hesitations in asking her family with performing food related errands because they might pick the *"wrong"* item.

> *H7-B:* *My kids are allergic, so I have to go and be sure what to get. I can easily get vegetable and fruits, but not the other stuff, because I have to see if it has colorants, if it has gluten, if it has anything, so...*
>
> *H7-A:* *It's just that I can't remember. And even if she tried to tell me over the phone, I'd see 20 different things and I'll be like, is it this one? Is it this one? So, yeah, it'll be a hell of a lot faster if she did it.*

Thus, participants expressed a desire to have capabilities that would enable them to document how to perform an errand so that others will be able to help when possible.

Finally, the opportunities described could greatly increase collaboration, but the roommate participants in our study still felt that a deterrent from sharing errands was a convenient method to track spent resources and ensure that reciprocity is maintained within the household. Roommates (more so than family members) felt conscious about the time, money and effort spent by other household members on behalf of their personal errands to maintain reciprocity, and ensure that they were not taking advantage of particular relationships:

> *H5-B:* *I guess the biggest problem is how to keep track of how much the items cost because it's a lot of punching in the numbers...I know they have those pixelated bar code things where you can take a picture of it and maybe that can scan the receipt of you want to get super integrated with all those different options...that's really a really personal thing because money can be a very serious issue*

In order to promote awareness of the time, money and effort spent, tools could provide better methods to track and maintain balance between household members.

The design opportunities identified by our participants show areas of exploration to promote further household errand collaboration. Many of these themes can be addressed through mobile applications that help facilitate the sharing of errands and communication among household members. In future work we plan to build and evaluate the usefulness of these tools in promoting errands within households.

CONCLUSION & FUTURE WORK

In this work, we conducted a 3-week diary study with 8 households to examine how family members and roommates share and accomplish tasks both individually and together. We report the types of errands that family members and roommates share with each other, their motivations for offering and requesting help to complete their errands, and the methods for doing so. We uncover that participants would often ask for help based on the location, availability, or capability of other household members.

There are many opportunities to help improve cooperative errands within households of family members and roommates. Based on our observations and interviews with participants we discovered several design opportunities to help facilitate and encourage cooperative errands. Current methods for communicating and sharing errands could be improved by enabling easier sharing of errands, displaying whereabouts of other household members, and communicating the availability of household members to assist with errands. These themes provide the foundation and direction to build mobile tools and evaluate their effectiveness in expressing and communicating errands within households.

REFERENCES

1. Beech, S., Geelhoed, E., Murphy, R., Parker, J., Sellen, A., Shaw, K. Lifestyles of working parents: Implications and opportunities for new technologies, *HP Tech report HPL-2003-88 (R.1)*, 2004.

2. Bellotti, V., Dalal, B., Good, N., Flynn, P., Bobrow, D., Ducheneaut, N. What a to-do: studies of task management toward the design of a personal task list manager. *Proc. CHI 2004*, ACM Press (2004), 735-742.
3. Bellotti, V., Smith, I. Informing the Design of an Information Management System with Interactive Fieldwork. *Proc. DIS 2000*, ACM Press (2000), 227- 237.
4. Bentley, F., Metcalf, C.J. Location and activity sharing in everyday mobile communication. *Ext. Abstracts CHI 2008*, ACM Press (2008), 2453-2462.
5. Bergman, O., Boardman, R., Gwizdka, J., Jones, W. Personal Information Management. *Proc. CHI 2004*, ACM Press (2004), 1598-1599.
6. Beyer, H., Holtzblatt, K. Contextual Design: Defining Customer-Centered Systems. Morgan Kaufmann, 1992.
7. Boardman, R., Sasse, M. Stuff Goes into the Computer and Doesn't Come Out, A cross-tool Study of Personal Information Management. *Proc. CHI 2004*, ACM Press (2004), 583-590.
8. Brown, B.A.T., Taylor, A.S., Izadi, S., Sellen, A., Kaye, J., Eardley, R. Locating Family Values: A Field Trial of the Whereabouts Clock. *Proc. Ubicomp 2007*, Springer-Verlag (2007), 354-371.
9. Brush, A.J.B., Meyers, B.R., Tan, D.S., Czerwinski, M. Understanding memory triggers for task tracking. *Proc. CHI 2007*, ACM Press (2007), 947-950.
10. Brush, A.J.B., Turner, T.C. A survey of personal and household scheduling. *Proc. GROUP 2005*, ACM Press (2005), 330-331.
11. Crabtree, A., Rodden, T. Domestic routines and design for the home. *Computer Supported Cooperative Work 13*, 2 (2004), 191-220.
12. Davidoff, S., Zimmerman, J., Dey, A.K. How routine learners can support family coordination. *Proc. CHI 2010*, ACM Press (2010), 2461-2470.
13. Dearman, D., Kellar, M., Truong, K.N. An examination of daily information needs and sharing opportunities. *Proc. CSCW 2008*, ACM Press (2008), 679-688.
14. Dey, A., Abowd. G. CybreMinder: A context-aware system for supporting reminders. *Proc. HUC 2000*, Springer-Verlag (2000), 172-186.
15. Elliot, K., Neustaedter, C., Greenberg, S. StickySpots: using location to embed technology in the social practices of the home. *Proc. TEI 2007*, ACM Press (2007), 79-86.
16. Fiese, B.H., Tomcho, T.J., Douglas, M., Josephs, K., Poltrock, S., Baker, T. A review of 50 years of research on naturally occurring family routines and rituals: Cause for celebration? *Journal of Family Psychology 16*, 4, (2002), 381-390.
17. Jung, Y., Persson, P., Blom, J. Dede: Design and Evaluation of a Context-Enhanced Mobile Messaging System. *Proc. CHI 2005*, ACM Press (2005), 351-360.
18. Kim, S., Kim, M., Park, S., Jin, Y., Choi, W. Gate Reminder: A Design Case of a Smart Reminder. *Proc. DIS 2004*, ACM Press (2004), 81-90.
19. Klepis, N., Nelson, W., Ott, W., Robinson, J., Tsang, A., Switzer, P., Behar, J., Hern, S., Engelmann, W. The National Human Activity Pattern Survey. *Journal of Exposure Analysis and Environmental Epidemiology, 11*, 3 (2001), 231-252.
20. Lansdale, M. The Psychology of Information Management. *Applied Ergonomics 19*, (1988), 55-66.
21. Lindley, S.E., Harper, R.H.R., Sellen, A. Designing a technological playground: a field study of the emergence of play in household messaging. *Proc. CHI 2010*, ACM Press (2010), 2351-2360.
22. Ludford, P.J., Frankowski, D., Reily, K., Wilms, K., Terveen, L.G. Because I carry my cell phone anyway: functional location-based reminder applications. *Proc. CHI 2006*, ACM Press (2006), 889-898.
23. Marmasse, N., Schmandt, C. Location-Aware Information Delivery with comMotion. *Proc. HUC 2000*, Springer-Verlag (2000), 64-73.
24. Neustaedter, C., Brush, A.J.B. "LINC-ing" the family: the participatory design of an inkable family calendar. *Proc. CHI 2006*, ACM Press (2006), 141-150.
25. Neustaedter, C., Brush, A.J.B., Greenberg, S. The calendar is crucial: Coordination and awareness through the family calendar. *ACM Transactions on Computer-Human Interaction 16*, 2 (2009), 1-48.
26. O'Hara, K., Harper, R.H.R., Unger, A., Wilkes, J. Sharpe, B., Jansen, M. TxtBoard: from text-to-person to text-to-home. *Ext. Abstracts CHI 2005*, ACM Press (2005), 1705-1708.
27. Remember The Milk: Online to do list and task management. http://www.rememberthemilk.com/ Last accessed June 3, 2011.
28. Sellen, A., Harper, R.H.R., Eardley, R., Izadi, S., Regan, T., Taylor, A.S., Wood, K.R. HomeNote: supporting situated messaging in the home. *Proc. CSCW 2006*, ACM Press (2006), 383-392.
29. Sohn, T., Li, K.A., Lee, G., Smith, I.A., Scott, J., Griswold, W.G. Place-Its: A Study of Location-Based Reminders on Mobile Phones. *Proc. Ubicomp 2005*, Springer-Verlag (2005), 232-250.
30. Strauss, A., Corbin, J. *Basics of Qualitative Research: Grounded Theory Procedures and Techniques*. Sage Publications, 1990.
31. Taylor, A.S., Swan, L. Artful systems in the home. *Proc. CHI 2005*, ACM Press (2005), 641-650.
32. Taylor, A.S., Swan, L., Eardley, R., Sellen, A., Hodges, S., Wood, K.R. Augmenting refrigerator magnets: why less is sometimes more. *Proc. NordiCHI 2006*, ACM Press (2006), 115-124.
33. Taylor, A.S., Swan, L. List making in the home. *Proc. CSCW 2004*, ACM Press (2004), 542-545.
34. Tolmie, P., Pycock, J., Diggins, T., Maclean, A., Karsenty, A. Unremarkable computing. *Proc. CHI 2002*, ACM Press (2002), 399-406.

Brothers and Sisters at Play: Exploring Game Play with Siblings

Janet Go, Tico Ballagas, Mirjana Spasojevic

Nokia Research Center

955 Page Mill Rd., Palo Alto, CA 94304

janet@gojanetgo.com | (tico.ballagas, mirjana.spasojevic)@nokia.com

ABSTRACT

To effectively design for families, we must understand familial relationships, which exert a significant influence on children's growth, learning, and play. In particular, siblings can be influential play partners and teachers, providing important scaffolding to each other. We report our observations of eight sibling pairs between ages 6 and 10, playing four popular games of different gaming paradigms. We found that certain patterns of sibling behavior persisted through all game sessions, regardless of the play patterns afforded by the different games, and that parents reports were consistent with our observations. We also observed instances where game design seemed to influence sibling play dynamics. We share our insights into considerations for designing for sibling play, including specialized social dynamics, opportunities for scaffolding, and the particular challenges they present.

Keywords

Games, families, children, siblings, cooperative games

ACM Classification Keywords

H.5.m. Information interfaces and presentation (e.g., HCI): Miscellaneous.

General Terms

Design; Human Factors

INTRODUCTION

Siblings are often a child's earliest and most constant play partners. The sibling relationship constitutes a specialized type of peer relationship, and sibling play differs in many ways from that of peers. However, little research sheds light on the sibling relationship as a context for game design. How do siblings play together? What are the dynamics around how siblings play games?

As part of our research group's effort toward designing technologies for families, we conducted a study of sibling play to inform the design of a collaborative educational game. Our approach was to explore sibling play patterns by using a variety of games as probes. Our goal was to uncover how different design elements might influence play within a typical sibling context, and to identify the unique challenges and opportunities for designing informal learning games that siblings could play *together*. In this work, we share our insights from this experience. We present findings on sibling scaffolding of game play, how important individual dynamics often dwarfed the influence of game design, and some instances where game elements exerted their effect on those dynamics.

Figure 1. Play Sessions: Sisters playing the boardgame Upwords.

BACKGROUND

This work builds on a number of threads within the CSCW and CHI communities, including a growing body of work on designing technologies for families, research on cooperative gaming and group gaming practices, and informal learning with games.

Games and Play in the Home

Many researchers in this community have recently turned their attention to designing for families as a whole [7,16,17], as well as the parent-child relationship [8,33]. Others have expressly studied gaming and play among families or in the home, notably [13,19,31]. Yet none of this work has focused on sibling play or the sibling relationship specifically, despite its ubiquity and importance in family life. Thus, the sibling relationship, which is both significant and formative, is ripe for study as another context for design within families.

Sibling Dynamics and Play

Sibling participants are often inserted as equivalent to peer groups in gaming research. However, there is reason to believe that the sibling relationship is somewhat specialized, and therefore their interactions might be qualitatively different. In general, interactions between siblings have been characterized as polarized, both intensely positive and negative, and are sometimes described as ambivalent rather than one-dimensional [11]. A number of researchers have investigated the negative and positive interactions between siblings, and in particular the influence of gender [1], age, whether siblings are same- or mixed-gender, and the lack of influence of age interval [2]. In addition, Dunn found that negativity and positivity between siblings maintains stability through middle childhood [12].

Older and younger siblings also have the tendency to assume different roles with each other in their interactions. In observations of both structured game play [6] and naturalistic observations [28] in the home, researchers found that older siblings were more likely to take on the dominant role of teacher and manager, while younger siblings were more likely to take on the role of managee or learner. In a lab study of infants and preschool siblings, researchers found younger siblings engaged in more monitoring and imitation of their older siblings, while older siblings initiated more assertive behavior (both nurturing and aggressive). These patterns of behavior were stable at later observations when younger siblings were themselves preschoolers [18]. Researchers have examined factors influencing sibling play roles, and found that they can be influenced by family structures, the gender and temperament of siblings, parental involvement, and cultural factors (See [22] for review).

Siblings and Informal Learning

This work was motivated by the potential for sibling informal learning through games in the home, and thus also extends existing research on social-learning in gameplay [20,24,27], Many educational and developmental researchers argue that learning among siblings is a special case of peer learning that benefits both parties. For example, Gregory characterizes the sibling relationship as a synergistic learning relationship that is reciprocal and bidirectional. In an ethnographic study of language learning in multilingual environments, Gregory described the importance of *shared experience* in the sibling learning arrangement [15].

In another study by Azmitia and Hezzer, older siblings were found to be more effective teachers than familiar peers on an unstructured building task. Children who were taught by their siblings performed better on post-tests, and older siblings provided more explanations, spontaneous guidance, and positive feedback than older peers. Furthermore, younger siblings were more likely to initiate such interactions, prompting for explanations and asking for more control with older siblings [3].

The Study of Group Gaming Practices

Many studies have sought to characterize group gaming practices. Social interactions around games have been described for massively multiplayer online games [10,21], handheld gaming systems [29], and console games [26,32]. However, few have examined how social interactions compare across platforms. Cooperative gaming research distinguishes between competitive, cooperative, and collaborative modes of game play, referring to the goals and incentives designed in the system. Cooperative games model situations where participants have interests to cooperate, but do not force cooperation (e.g. strategies employed in [5]). In collaborative games, players function as a team and share payoffs and outcomes [34].

Some have sought to characterize levels and types of cooperative behavior in group gaming. Seif El-Nasir et al. identified a set of cooperative design patterns and developed Cooperation Performance Metrics (CPMs) for measuring the observed levels of cooperation in screen-based digital games among collocated groups [26]. They used correlations between design patterns and CPMs to recommend different design patterns for promoting cooperation. Taking a more qualitative observational approach, Voida and colleagues investigated group-oriented behaviors around console gaming, identifying different gaming elements that contributed to these behaviors [32].

Other lines of work assert the primacy of social interactions over the designed interaction of the game itself. In another study on Wii console gaming, Voida set al. explicitly emphasized *externally derived* sociability over the internally derived social interactions dictated by rules of the game [31]. Their work draws from Salen & Zimmerman, who distinguish between internally and externally derived social interactions in game play [25].

Although [26,31,32] all included within-family groups and siblings in their study, they did not focus their analysis on siblings specifically. As we have seen, sibling interactions are disparate from peer interaction, and the sibling relationship also has great potential for informal learning. Yet, to our knowledge, in both games research and the literature on designing for families, the sibling relationship has never been given its own attention. In this paper, we attempt to address this gap.

METHOD

With the help of an external recruiter, we recruited 25 participants from diverse economic and cultural backgrounds, including eight sibling pairs and their parents (6 mothers, 3 fathers). Since gender can influence sibling dynamic, we sought to comprise a sample with the full range and balance of older-younger gendered pairings (F-f, F-m, M-f, M-m). In order to minimize variability due to age differences, we chose pairs consisting of younger siblings who were either 6 or 7 years old, and older siblings were either 9 or 10. Thus, all sibling pairs had a three or four year difference in age. We chose this age difference because we believed the corresponding differences in literacy abilities might provide the most opportunity for siblings to learn from each other. Although parents often play an important role at home, we wanted to observe children outside the presence of their parents, in part because we knew from experience that parents often feel the need to manage their children's behavior in front of researchers. However, after play sessions we also interviewed parents about their role in their children's play at home, and include this in our findings.

We chose popular games that represent a variety of archetypal play patterns. Because we wanted to observe whether or how scaffolding could take place, we also chose games that included a literacy component at a level just above the younger sibling's abilities, but within the ability level of the older sibling. We selected a wide variety of gaming paradigms – including a board game, console game, handheld game, and even pencil and paper game – to understand how these paradigms change gameplay. The games included the following:

• *Hangman* is a classic pen and paper decoding game in which one player must guess a word or words that another has chosen by guessing letters. Incorrect guesses are represented by the marking of body parts on the man for each letter, until the man is "hanged." Gameplay ends when a player correctly guesses the word(s) or makes too many incorrect guesses and the man hangs. This game was the most familiar to the children, and all participants had played it before.

• *Upwords* (Fig. 1) is a board game that is similar to the popular (and more adult) Scrabble board game. Players create words by placing letter tiles on a board, building next to or on top of existing words on the board. Players receive points for letters in a word, and the win by attaining the most points. However, none of the participants ended up keeping score in our study (which we discuss later).

• *Scribblenauts* (Fig. 2a) is a handheld game for the Nintendo DS. Like many handheld games, it is meant for single play. A player navigates the character "Max" through different levels and solves puzzles, in part by conjuring objects to use in the world by typing them into the interface. When a puzzle is solved, Max receives a star and points are accrued, unlocking additional levels. Even though this game is designed for single play, it is possible for more than one child to work together. It also represents a common gaming setup among siblings in families who often have a single shared device.

Figure 2. Play sessions: (a) Younger brother looks over his sister's shoulder as she plays Scribblenauts on the Nintendo DSI. (b) Older sister and younger brother play Rock Band.

• *Rock Band* (Fig. 2b) is a popular multi-player console game in which the interface takes the form of popular rock instruments. Each player chooses one instrument to play and scores individual points for hitting correct notes (e.g. on the guitar) or singing at the correct pitch and volume (on a microphone). Players must hit the notes in the proper timing while the notes stream across the screen. To simplify our study, only the guitar and microphone were made available. The singer role relies on a literacy skill element, since the singer follows music lyrics on the screen.

Participants played each game in our lab (Figures 1 and 2) in the order listed above. Each game play session lasted approximately fifteen minutes. If siblings did not know how to play a game, the researcher explained the rules and answered questions as necessary, but otherwise attempted to assume the role of passive observer whenever possible. In cases where siblings engaged in conflict or otherwise monopolized game play, the researcher allowed them to continue without mediation. At the end of a session, if a sibling had not been given a turn to play a game or was otherwise left out of game play, the researcher would ask that they be given an opportunity to play.

Parents were interviewed in a pre-screening phone call about the games their children played and more generally about their playing habits at home. A more extensive semi-structured interview was conducted with parents following play session observations. In this interview, we asked about patterns of play at home and followed up on important observations noted during the study. In most cases this interview was conducted with one parent who would be considered a primary caregiver (5 mothers, 2 fathers). In one case, both parents (mother and father) were interviewed together. Siblings were present during these interviews and sometimes contributed to their responses.

All play sessions and interviews were videotaped and transcribed for both verbal and nonverbal behaviors. Transcripts were then inductively coded for behaviors, beginning with an open coding scheme that was guided by initial research questions. Thus, we were originally oriented toward behaviors related to scaffolding among siblings (in the hopes of understanding possible influencers across the different games), including coding categories such as "helping", "conflict over resources", and "correcting". Codes were subsequently categorized according to emergent themes, forming the basis for the findings presented below.

FINDINGS

We found that sibling dynamics sometimes exerted a primary influence over how sibling pairs played different games together, more than the games themselves: siblings' dominance, competitiveness or cooperativeness, and particular roles were often exhibited across play session for every game played. However, some game elements influenced sibling play in circumscribed ways, sometimes allowing for more or less scaffolding, or mitigating conflict. In the next section, we offer two case studies to illustrate the arc of the play sessions we observed, and to sensitize readers to the findings that follow.

Sibling Dynamics: Case Studies

Tyler and Aaron[1]: Competitive Brothers

The dynamic observed between Tyler (9 years old) and Aaron (7 years old) could best be described as both competitive and antagonistic. Tyler, an extremely dominant older sibling, constantly orders his brother around. He often controls the situation to do what he wants, and rarely accommodates his brother's desires or his participation. Although the younger sibling, Aaron is anything but complacent in asserting his own will. With an ever-present antagonism, every game they play feels like it involves some kind of battle.

Even though they reportedly play Hangman at home together, their session is less about play than Tyler telling Aaron what to do. He impatiently directs Aaron at each guess, issuing curt directives like "Go" and "Hurry!" He provides no feedback other than "Nope. Guess another letter." During one round, Tyler gives him a mere three guesses before pronouncing, "You killed the man. My turn." When it is his turn to guess, Tyler takes an unusual approach. He draws out his own set of blanks to guess and proceeds to spell out the word *of his own choosing*, while having Aaron write down the letters. In the end Aaron refuses to play. He declares, "I give up because you keep on playing," indicating that Tyler has essentially been playing without him. Unfazed, Tyler pronounces that he will play by himself.

During Upwords, Tyler expresses impatience with Aaron when he places letters that do not spell a word: "What does that spell? That ain't a word." He avoids conflict and leaves Aaron's letters in place, but does not bother to correct or help him. The game eventually devolves to a point where instead of taking turns, Tyler and Aaron race to put down letters, sometimes pushing each other out of the way.

When it's time to play Scribblenauts Tyler says, "I call first!" and immediately takes hold of the Nintendo DS. Aaron throws himself on the floor in a tantrum. Finally standing up, Aaron makes a point of not watching Tyler play. At the researcher's suggestion that he help his brother, Aaron starts to look at the game screen, then walks away saying, "I know how to play the game but I can't help him… He knows how to play by himself." After switching turns at the researcher's request, Aaron struggles with the game. In one moment, he seems to look for help, asking his brother a question. But when Tyler approaches to take a look, Aaron taunts him by offering him the DS, then quickly pulling it away. Unable to figure out how to move an object in the game, Aaron quickly loses interest and gives up. Tyler takes the game back.

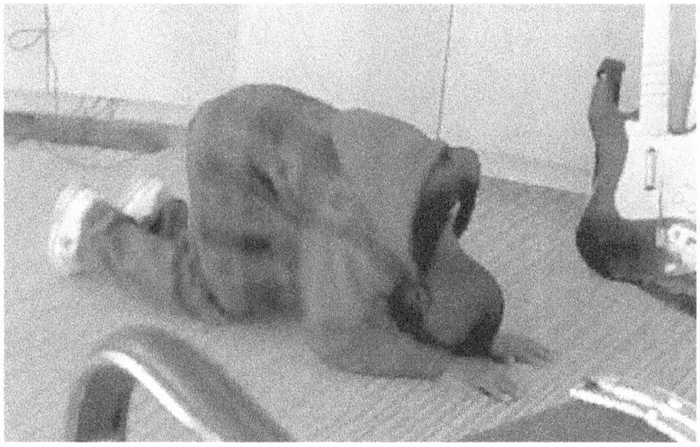

Figure 3. A younger sibling throws himself on the ground in protest to his brother monopolizing play.

In Rock Band, Aaron is excited to sing on the microphone and Tyler is happy to play guitar. Tyler does all the work of picking their characters and choosing a song, while ignoring his brother's requests. Aaron protests with shouts of "No!" and "Oh come on!" at Tyler's choices. As the song starts, Tyler yells commands to his brother: "Don't sing yet. Now. Sing. SING!" He grabs the microphone

[1] *All participant names have been changed.*

away, but Aaron eventually takes it back, asserting, "I want to do it." Although they both initially enjoy playing the game, Aaron eventually asks to play the song that he knows how to sing. He is repeatedly ignored. At the end of one of the songs, Aaron laments, "I lose." He begins to "act out", pushing Tyler's chair and turning up the volume, and eventually asks the researcher if they can play a different game.

In the follow-up interview, the boys' mother shares her insight into their relationship, actually attributing the pattern to her younger son's competitive streak:

They're really competitive. Aaron is more competitive than Tyler. Aaron always wants to win. And then when Aaron wins he rubs it in your face. But then when Aaron loses, he cries and Tyler will laugh at him.

She remarks how this competitiveness often extends to games that are supposed to be cooperative:

Like video games. If it's a two-player game and they're playing together and one's fighting the other one, [but] it's supposed to be ***together*** *fighting something else. They'll not get along...*

She also shed light on a deeper dynamic in their relationship that she believed contributed to their competitiveness:

They may act like they don't like each other but they are inseparable... Aaron really looks up to Tyler.

Talaysia and Jarell: Non-competitive Playmates

For a younger sibling, Jarell seems somehow older and more of an equal to his older sister, compared to some of the other younger siblings we observed. Their relationship can be characterized as a meeting of equals who manage to peacefully coexist, and seem to genuinely enjoy each other's company. Even though Talaysia maintains a degree of control over activities as an older sibling, she never plays the teacher role and rarely shows impatience with her younger brother.

During their Hangman session, Talaysia and Jarrell smile quite a bit, expressing their enjoyment. In hangman, Talaysia allows her brother more guesses by continuing to draw more features on the hangman. They both enjoy teasing and challenging each other, as if it adds fun to their game. At some point when Jarell shares his discouragement at having trouble guessing the final letters of a word, Talaysia gives him progressive hints to help him. During Talaysia's turn to guess, Jarell smiles as much when she guesses correctly as when she gets it wrong. In the end when Talaysia is stuck, he also helps her with a hint.

During Upwords, the two take an unorthodox approach to play, at first making words collaboratively. Each puts down one letter at a time, and they build words together. When Jarell puts down letters that don't make a word, Talaysia starts to benignly question, but doesn't correct him or disallow the move.

During Rock Band, Talaysia wants to sing at first, then after two songs tells Jarell to switch. They both smile often, and neither seems to pay attention to the score.

Their Scribblenauts session is the least oriented around co-play, though devoid of conflict. Jarell calls, "I go first!" and says he wants to play by himself. Talaysia calmly acquiesces and leaves him to play on his own. When Jarell gives up the game because "it's too hard," Talaysia takes over while he watches over her shoulder and calls out suggestions. She ignores most of them, but talks out loud about what she's doing, as if broadcasting for him to hear.

In the parent interview, Talaysia and Jarell's mom reflects that "they do pretty well together" and infrequently fight.

The juxtaposition of Talaysia & Jarell and Tyler & Aaron exemplifies the marked contrast between some sibling pairs, as well as the tendency for some dynamics to exhibit persistence across sessions. Although not every sibling pair expressed behaviors to such extremes, dynamics were often more salient than the effects of the different games they played.

These examples also paint a nuanced picture of the many factors at play in their dynamics, including the disparity of sibling abilities. In the case of Tyler and Aaron, Aaron's lack of ability is a constant source of frustration for both siblings, and sometimes exacerbated their antagonism. In contrast, Talaysia and Jarell experience little if any conflict, but also play more as equals who are able to help each other. In the following sections, we highlight some of the salient issues in the play of siblings, including how levels of games discourage co-play, the nature of persistent sibling dynamics, and the success and failure of sibling scaffolding of play.

Game Levels and an Age Divide

As we have seen, one important aspect of young sibling relationships is that the disparity in their abilities can make it difficult to play the same games. In the age range we chose to study in particular, children experience a number of developmental milestones. Their corresponding cognitive, motor, and education abilities can make for a real difference in game play ability and enjoyment. Games are often designed for different levels of player ability, providing just enough challenge to be fun. However, it is rare for a game to strike the exact balance between challenge and fun for siblings of very disparate abilities. We heard from parents that this separation, by levels of games and siblings' abilities, was a critical factor in determining which games siblings played together at home (and whether they played together at all). As one mother observed:

The things they don't really play well with together are I guess the kinds of things that separate them in level." [Mother of SP8]

Another mother reported the dilemma she felt at the store, looking for games to purchase that all her children could play. She noted a common division in the recommended age requirements of the games popularly found in stores:

And it's unfortunate that there's a break in the games, at like eight [years old] – You can play eight to adult, or three to eight, or four to eight. So eight seems to be the breaking point to me. Where an eight year old can go either way... They start to be able to do logic and problem solving...[The younger daughter] is a lot more linear... [But] Everybody will play Mousetrap. One thing about Mousetrap is it's not one of those games where you really have to strategize or solve. It's a more linear game. [Mother of SP3]

Another result of this "age divide" in games is that games are considered to be predominately "for" specific children. For example, one family explained that the older child had their DS, and the younger had their LeapPad. Console games and some board games were also often considered the domain of the eldest sibling. Additionally, older siblings sometimes saw their younger siblings' games as too infantile, describing them as "for babies".

The fact that children play their own games according to their level is a natural extension of a real difference in children's physical and cognitive abilities, but the consequence is that many children's games aren't actually played together. We consider this gap an especially relevant opportunity for designing for siblings. In order to create games for siblings, designers will need to pay particular attention to how games accommodate players of very different levels of ability.

Sibling Scaffolding

On the other hand, one can also imagine that a difference in abilities can also be advantageous, if more experienced siblings are able to help their less experienced siblings during play, and scaffold them beyond their abilities [23]. In many ways, siblings were extremely adept at scaffolding each other. They were good at choosing levels of play that were appropriate to each other's abilities, and sometimes provided help when the other encountered difficulty.

At times, we witnessed how different aspects of each game enabled scaffolding or hindered it. In Hangman, some older siblings chose words to be easy to guess (e.g., each other's names or words with few letters) and increased the difficulty with their younger siblings performance. As we saw in the example of Talaysia and Jarrell, both siblings provided progressively helpful hints and extra guesses. In Hangman, siblings exercised flexible control over the game, and this allowed them to accommodate each other's abilities.

Although Scribblenauts was a common source of conflict and often resulted in solo play, the multiple-input interface enabled certain kinds of scaffolding. The touch screen, stylus, and buttons, which serve redundant functions, allowed siblings to help by reaching in to spell a word, or moving the character while the other sibling continued to "drive" and maintain control over the device. This worked to a point; sometimes older "helpful" siblings felt compelled to take over the device, resulting in conflict. Similarly, some coaching occurred with one sibling looking over the shoulder of another. However, the small screen size made actions somewhat difficult to see.

Possibly due to rule complexity and lack of system guidance, Upwords seemed to pose the most difficulty for siblings. Younger siblings who were normally capable of spelling sometimes struggled with generating words from the set of letters they had drawn. Older siblings were at a loss to help them, since it required seeing the other's letters. (This sometimes caused the younger sibling to protest their "cheating".) Some siblings applied ineffective (and frustrating) helping strategies; One sister suggested random letters that she knew would make words on the board, rather than starting with the letters that were in her sister's possession. This was a case where enforcing the game rules (i.e. keeping letters hidden from one's opponent) exacerbated the difficulty of the task. Yet helping the other ultimately meant playing for them, and disrupted the point of the game. It is interesting to contrast Upwords with Hangman, in which siblings were able to help each other without playing for them or taking over.

In Rock Band, some younger siblings struggled with the physical coordination necessary to play the guitar, and with reading or knowing the lyrics. Older siblings were usually the one to take the controls, set up characters, and choose songs. They often helped by choosing easier levels for their younger siblings to play. However they did not always want to choose songs that were within their younger sibling's ability, since that affected their own enjoyment. Although many sibling pairs enjoyed playing, once play started, the combination of high engagement and fast parallel play left little opportunity or motivation for helping. In contrast to other games that do not feature fast-paced parallel play, Rock Band leaves little room for in-play scaffolding. Some siblings tried multi-tasking, struggling to help the other sing into the microphone while trying to maintain their role as guitar player (and vice versa).

It is worth noting that when siblings play together, it is often in the presence of parents or other family members, and thus parents often take the role of scaffolding. Some parents reported that sibling game play benefited from their support through a culture of playing together as a family, and at least one family participated in a weekly "game night." Parents stated that during family game play, they were able to scaffold their children's abilities (often through team play), and that children were motivated by the chance to play with parents. However, what siblings were able to play with parents was not the same as what they were able to play by themselves. For instance, an older sibling was able to play a card game with his parents, but would not be able to scaffold that by himself with his younger sibling.

In general, if siblings were willing to help, it could not overly interfere with their enjoyment of the game. Most older siblings who took the time to scaffold their younger siblings showed diminishing motivation as play sessions continued. Even for the most inclined of siblings (such as those who enjoyed playing the role of teacher), helping often seemed to conflict with their own enjoyment of the game. Another aspect of sibling scaffolding was that older siblings were not always in a position to provide correct information to their younger counterparts, sometimes spelling words incorrectly or providing incorrect interpretations of game rules. This does not mean that siblings can never scaffold each other's play. However, it is a reminder that their burden must be balanced against their ability to enjoy the game, and that the help they provide may be imperfect and require its own scaffolding. Another challenge for designers is how to balance system flexibility against the facilitating role it plays in rule enforcement, monitoring correctness, and scoring

Sibling Dominance and Conflict

One common pattern of interaction that we observed was the tendency for one sibling to take a more dominant role during sessions, taking more control of the direction and flow of activities. Reflecting previous findings in the literature, most of the time the dominant sibling was the elder. However, in one interesting case, it was a younger sister who was very assertive of her needs and gave direction for activities, while her older brother usually deferred.

Dominance could be double-edged. It could be used to efficiently direct activities or scaffold to everyone's benefit. (For example, an older sibling assuming the role of "teacher" involves a form of dominance.) However, a dominant sibling might also exclude the other's meaningful participation. In the case of one sister-sister pair, the dominant older sister enacted both sides, alternately playing the patient teacher and the insensitive tyrant. Her mother observed:

I don't know if you noticed but she's [the older sister's] bossy. Yeah she helps her a lot. She'll say, "Wait, Maya. Let me show you, Maya." And Maya wants to try to do something all by herself. [Mother of SP6 (f-F)]

One highly dominant sibling might work to build consensus, while another might assert their will, ignoring that of their partner. (If a younger sibling refused to accept this arrangement it usually ended in conflict.)

Sources of Conflict

One of the largest sources of conflict among siblings was turn-taking. which typically involved a limited resource in a game. Not surprisingly, this usually meant struggles over the Nintendo DS, but also occurred when choosing instruments in Rock Band. One mother commented how turn-taking was such a common source of conflict that she wished for a built-in feature to mediate it:

If you had a game that had a built in timer and would stop and tell them to switch players... It would solve lots of arguments for the game to say "ok time to switch players...." It would sure make my life easier.

One mother reflected on how limited resources led to a basic lack of sharing:

That's the biggest thing, is that we don't have multiples. There's not two computers to play. Two iPods to play. There are two DS's, but there aren't two of the same game. It tends to be that someone's playing something and neither wants to play along too. So there's a lack of sharing... [Mother of SP3]

Another common source of conflict was found in accusations of cheating. Interestingly, this sometimes was simply a consequence of a younger sibling who, not knowing how to spell or perhaps not knowing the rules of the game, tried to play as they could:

That ain't no word. She don't know how to play. She's a cheater. [Older sister, SP6]

This kind of conflict occurred only during Hangman and Upwords, where it is the players rather than the system enforcing the rules.

Parents spoke of strategies for dealing with and avoiding these kinds of conflicts, which they felt were part of their daily lives. Some used pre-emptive strategies such as forced turn-taking. Others motivated siblings to work things out on their own by threatening to take away play privileges if they could not resolve their conflict.

[I say] stop. Play turns. Or get off of it. [Mother of SP8 (m-M)]

Although one can argue that conflicts among siblings are a normal part of family life, these findings raise questions around how a system can avoid or mediate conflict, for example, by enforcing rules or enforcing turn-taking. And while one can surely observe both dominance and conflict among some peer groups, in our observations, it tended to be more intense and pronounced than what is generally reported for peer groups.

Cooperative and Competitive Stances vs. Game Modes

Echoing Voida et al's observations around group-oriented behavior, we found that siblings sometimes assumed competitive or cooperative stances in games that were not aligned with the way the game was intended. Furthermore, different sibling pairs sometimes played the same games in very different ways. In Rock Band, for instance, some siblings focused on their relative scores, appearing to orient to the game competitively. However, others seemed to ignore the score feature entirely and celebrated their performance as a team:

Younger sister: *Ok so let's rock n roll...Ok everyone... Ladies and gentlemen, meet the rock n roll band.*

Older sister: *We about to rock on. [...]*

Younger sister: *Ladies and gentlemen, please welcome...*

Older sister: *The best rock and roll team in the universe!*

Younger sister: *We'll call it the rulers of the world...*

Older sister: *Woohoo!* [SP6]

We have already described other examples of these different orientations. In Upwords, some siblings took turns laying down one letter at a time, building words collaboratively, and in Hangman many siblings helped their "opponent" arrive at the answer with extra hints and leniency. Some siblings were more competition-oriented, paying attention to scores or whether they "won" or "lost". As we saw earlier, Tyler and Aaron reportedly turned a collaborative video game into a competitive conflict. Still other siblings were neither cooperative nor competitive, but rather indifferently engaged in parallel play or playing alone. For most siblings these patterns appeared to be established pattern of mutual preference and habit, perhaps deriving from parent strategies for managing conflict at home. ,The takeaway is that external social dynamics can indeed be more important than the internally derived interactions dictated by the rules of a game, and this is especially true for siblings.

"You always win": Sibling Identities around Knowing and Competency

We found that siblings assigned identities to each other as well as to themselves according to their perceived abilities. For example, one sibling exclaimed, "We're good at this game!" when he guessed a word easily during Hangman. As his sister increased the level of difficulty and he experienced difficulty with a word, he whined, "Aw, I'm a bad guesser." These kinds of attributions were common during play sessions, seemingly stemming from longstanding assumptions of each other's abilities, yet continually negotiated and provoked by events in the game.

One older sister frequently resorted to name calling with her younger sibling:

Older sister: *You gotta fill in the eyes, dummy.*

Younger sister: *I ain't no dummy. That ain't nice to call someone dummy.* [SP6]

It worked both ways, however, as the younger sister was just as critical of the elder's abilities:

Younger sister: *Alice, you don't know how to spell ladder.*

Older sister: *I don't know.*

Younger sister: *Alice, you're 10. And you don't know how to spell!* [SP6]

Such attributions were an indication that these identities are always at play, especially for siblings. In some cases, assumptions about a sibling's ability interfered with game play, such as when a sibling did not trust the other's abilities in Hangman:

Older sister: *Is it 'want'?*

Younger brother: *No*

Older sister [not convinced]: *Michael, is it 'want'?*

Younger brother: *NO. You want me to give you a hint?*

Older sister: *Dude, you spelled the word wrong anyways.*

Younger brother: *No I didn't!* [SP1]

Another thing we did not anticipate in our study was how discouraging it would be for younger siblings to play only games where they were never as able as their older siblings. Many younger siblings became visibly upset over time or lost motivation to continue play. It was a reminder that even if a game can be designed for younger siblings to be scaffolded beyond their abilities, it should be sensitive to the implications of these kinds of attributions. For example, such a game might be designed to highlight a younger sibling's contribution rather than simply calling attention to their deficiency. The way a system attributes achievement and abilities matters, because over time it feeds into identities that are already at play among siblings.

DISCUSSION

Our exploration has suggested a number of directions for designing games for siblings to play together. First, the difference of ability is critical at these ages, and popular leveling of games is a barrier to siblings playing together at all. For siblings to play together, we must find ways to design games that balance their play at different levels, while still providing enough challenge to be fun. One success of Rock Band was that siblings were able to play their role at their own level without drawing too much attention to those differences. Another consideration is how different types of play might be more conducive to accommodating disparate abilities. Informally, we observed and heard from parents that if siblings played together it was more likely to involve creative play. We noticed with Scribblenauts, which involves creative problem solving, that younger siblings were sometimes able to provide an equally valuable contribution (whether or not it was recognized). For instance, a sibling may not have known how to spell a word, but they were able to generate ideas around what objects to create or how to "solve" the puzzle.

We also found that conflict and dominance can be more intense and common for siblings. In anticipation of these dynamics, we can design systems that balance or leverage sibling dominance, and avoid common sources of conflict, such as resource scarcity. For instance, everyone should have their own controller, their own role, and equal view into the system. A system can also play the role as moderator, for example, by enforcing turn-taking. To minimize conflict over cheating (real or imagined), the role of rule enforcement should be offloaded to the system rather than the players.

Another area for consideration is how a system can best support scaffolding of players. In some instances, it was the *openness* and *flexibility* of the system that allowed for siblings to scaffold each other (e.g., being able to show leniency or give hints in Hangman. Sometimes the "rules" of the game made it impossible for scaffolding to occur, as in Upwords where helping required knowing the other player's letters. Thus, to support scaffolding, systems should afford flexibility for players to adjust for each other's abilities or even bend the rules. For example, a game might allow players to take actions back, or to pass resources from one player to the next. ("I need an 'e' to spell this word I know.")

We also learned that the same level of game that a sibling is able to play may not be one they can scaffold. Similarly, a game that can be played together as a family may not be playable by siblings alone. Thus the system needs to anticipate these breakdowns as a function of the group, rather than at the level of individual players. Another implication is that even if siblings are able to scaffold each other, they may not be motivated to do so if it interferes with their enjoyment of a game. We also saw with Rock Band that children are unable to take on a scaffolding role if they are not given space to do so within game play.

Another finding was that siblings tend to exhibit distinct and established identities around *knowing* and competence relative to each other. We observed that any event in game play both reflects on and is influenced by these identities. Older siblings, defending their identity as the more competent one, were reluctant to make or admit mistakes. Younger siblings, discouraged by their inferiority, lost a sense of fun and no longer wanted to play. This seemed like a particularly pronounced phenomenon in our observations of siblings, compared to what might be expected for peers. Researchers who have studied social comparison and identification (and de-identification) among siblings have implicated its role in self-esteem and its influence on behaviors [30]. If games ultimately reinforce ongoing epistemic identities, how can they be designed to support different levels of play without having that understood as levels of deficiency? We saw in Rock Band that players set their characters at different difficulty levels, without invoking comparison. It was also understood by siblings that it was normal to have different abilities based on their different ages. This suggests that it was not so much lower levels of play that communicated deficiency as much as relative scores and failures. One potential direction is to design performance indicators that communicate scores relative to age. Another promising tactic is to have the system adapt with *minimally perceptible* assistance or handicaps, to balance players' skill levels (as exemplified in [4]).

Finally, our findings also suggest that the existing patterns of siblings in relationship can sometimes exert an equal if not greater influence than the designed interaction of the game. Our findings echoed those of Voida et al. on the disconnect between game design and the group dynamics they observed:

In fact, some of the most group-oriented practices we observed occurred in a group that was playing a competitive game. And some of the most individual-oriented practices we observed occurred in a group that was playing a collaborative game. [32]

In our case, we not only observed this discrepancy, we also noted that patterns of competition, dominance, and roles sometimes persisted for siblings across different games. While this might hold true for any group relationship where individuals develop a collective history of relating, take on roles, and ascribe identities to each other, we argue that for siblings this is particularly applicable. This study has implications not only for the design of sibling games, but for the study of group gaming behavior in general. For example, when we evaluate a game for cooperation (as performed in [26]), we often draw on small participant samples that include peers as well as siblings. However, siblings and peers are not equivalent. Further, sibling pairs may exhibit especially strong biases toward competitive or cooperative behavior. There are several possible approaches to balancing for skewed results, including observing baseline behaviors, using self-report questionnaires (such as developed in [14]), or relying on parent reports. We found that parents' description of sibling dynamics exhibited remarkable fidelity to those that we observed. Thus surveys to be used with parents, such as those used in [9], where parents characterize the amount and intensity of children's conflict, might be a promising area for development. In any case, siblings must first be understood as a specialized type of peer group.

CONCLUSION

In this work we have presented considerations for designing for siblings as a user group, as well as implications for game research and evaluation. Many investigations take as an implicit assumption that the *designed* interaction of a system is the major determinant of the group-oriented dynamics around game play. However, as we have seen, there are benefits in examining how externally derived social dynamics influence game play. In future work we intend to compare sibling play to peer play to investigate the extent to which they are different.

ACKNOWLEDGMENTS

We would like to thank the sixteen brothers and sisters and their families who participated in this study. We also thank Glenda Revelle, Lori Takeuchi, Morgan Ames, Daniela Rosner, and Jofish Kaye for their kind feedback, and the rest of the Nokia IDEA team.

REFERENCES

1. Abramovitch, R. and Corter, C. Sibling Interaction in the Home. *Child Development 50*, 4 (1979), 997-1003.
2. Abramovitch, R., Corter, C., and Pepler, D. Sibling and peer interaction: A final follow-up and a comparison. *Child development 57*, 1 (1986), 217.
3. Azmitia, M. and Hesser, J. Why Siblings Are Important Agents of Cognitive Development: A Comparison of

Siblings and Peers. *Child Development 64*, 2 (1993), 430.

4. Bateman, S., Mandryk, R.L., Stach, T., and Gutwin, C. Target assistance for subtly balancing competitive play. *Proc. CHI '11*, ACM Press (2011), 2355.
5. Benford, S., O'Malley, C., Simsarian, K.T., et al. Designing storytelling technologies to encouraging collaboration between young children. *Proc. CHI '00*, ACM Press (2000), 556-563.
6. Brody, G., Stoneman, Z., and MacKinnon, C. Role asymmetries in interactions among school-aged children, their younger siblings, and their friends. *Child Development 53*, 5 (1982), 1364.
7. Brush, A., Inkpen, K.M., and Tee, K. SPARCS: exploring sharing suggestions to enhance family connectedness. *Proc. CSCW '08*, ACM (2008), 629–638.
8. Dalsgaard, T., Skov, M.B., Stougaard, M., and Thomassen, B. Mediated intimacy in families: understanding the relation between children and parents. *Proc. IDC '06*, ACM (2006), 145–152.
9. Deater-Deckard, K. and Dunn, J. Sibling Relationships and Social-emotional Adjustment in Different Family Contexts. *Social Development 11*, 4 (2002), 571-590.
10. Ducheneaut, N., Moore, R.J., and Nickell, E. Virtual "Third Places": A Case Study of Sociability in Massively Multiplayer Games. *Computer Supported Cooperative Work (CSCW) 16*, 1 (2007), 129–166.
11. Dunn, J. Sibling relationships in early childhood. *Child Development 54*, 4 (1983), 787–811.
12. Dunn, J. Brothers and sisters in middle childhood and early adolescence: continuity and change in individual differences. In *Sibling relationships: Their causes and consequences*. Ablex Publishing, 1996, 31-46.
13. Follmer, S., Raffle, H., Go, J., Ballagas, R., and Ishii, H. Video play. *Proc. IDC '10*, ACM Press (2010), 49.
14. Furman, W. and Buhrmester, D. Children's Perceptions of the Qualities of Sibling Relationships. *Child Development 56*, 2 (1985), 448-461.
15. Gregory, E. Sisters and Brothers as Language and Literacy Teachers: Synergy between Siblings Playing and Working Together. *Journal of Early Childhood Literacy 1*, 3 (2001), 301-322.
16. Hutchinson, H., Mackay, W., Westerlund, B., et al. Technology probes: inspiring design for and with families. *Proc. CHI '03*, ACM (2003), 17–24.
17. Kirk, D.S., Izadi, S., Sellen, A., Taylor, S., Banks, R., and Hilliges, O. Opening up the family archive. *Proc. CSCW '10*, ACM (2010), 261–270.
18. Lamb, M.E. The development of sibling relationships in infancy: A short-term longitudinal study. *Child Development 49*, 4 (1978), 1189–1196.
19. Lindley, S.E., Harper, R., and Sellen, A. Designing a technological playground. *Proc. CHI '10*, ACM Press (2010), 2351.
20. McConnell, D. *Implementing computer supported cooperative learning*. Routledge, 2000.
21. Nardi, B. and Harris, J. Strangers and friends: Collaborative play in World of Warcraft. *Proc. CSCW '06*, ACM (2006), 149–158.
22. Oden, S. Sibling and peer influence on play. In D. Fromberg and D. Bergen, eds., *Play from birth to twelve: contexts, perspectives and meanings*. CRC Press, 2006, 297-307.
23. Rogoff, B. *Apprenticeship in Thinking: Cognitive Development in Social Context*. Oxford University Press, USA, New York, 1991.
24. Roschelle, J., Rafanan, K., Estrella, G., Nussbaum, M., and Claro, S. From handheld collaborative tool to effective classroom module: Embedding CSCL in a broader design framework. *Computers & Education 55*, 3 (2010), 1018-1026.
25. Salen, K. and Zimmerman, E. *Rules of play: Game design fundamentals*. MIT Press, 2004.
26. Seif El-Nasr, M., Aghabeigi, B., Milam, D., et al. Understanding and evaluating cooperative games. *Proc. CHI '10*, (2010), 253.
27. Stevens, R., Satwicz, T., and McCarthy, L. In-game, in-room, in-world: Reconnecting video game play to the rest of kids lives. In K. Salen, ed., *The Ecology of Games: Connecting Youth, Games, and Learning. The John D. and Catherine T. MacArthur Foundation Series on Digital Media and Learning*. The MIT Press, 2007, 41-66.
28. Stoneman, Z., Brody, G., MacKinnon, C., and Url, S. Naturalistic Observations of Children's Activities and Roles While Playing with Their Siblings and Friends. *Child Development 55*, 2 (1984), 617-627.
29. Szentgyorgyi, C., Terry, M., and Lank, E. Renegade gaming: practices surrounding social use of the Nintendo DS handheld gaming system. *Proc. CHI '08*, ACM (2008), 1463–1472.
30. Tesser, A. Self-esteem maintenance in family dynamics. *Journal of Personality and Social Psychology 39*, 1 (1980), 77-91.
31. Voida, A. and Greenberg, S. Wii all play: The console game as a computational meeting place. *Proc. CHI '09*, ACM (2009), 1559–1568.
32. Voida, A., Carpendale, S., and Greenberg, S. The individual and the group in console gaming. *Proc. CSCW '10*, ACM (2010), 371–380.
33. Yarosh, S. and Abowd, G.D. Mediated parent-child contact in work-separated families. *Proc. CHI '11*, ACM (2011), 1185–1194.
34. Zagal, J., Rick, J., and Hsi, I. Collaborative games: Lessons learned from board games. *Simulation & Gaming 37*, 1 (2006), 24-40.

I Love You, Let's Share Calendars: Calendar Sharing as Relationship Work

Alexander Thayer[1], Matthew J. Bietz[2], Katie Derthick[1], Charlotte P. Lee[1]
[1]University of Washington
423 Sieg Hall, Seattle, WA 98195
[2]University of California, Irvine
Donald Bren Hall 5042, Irvine, CA 92697-3440
huevos@uw.edu, mbietz@uci.edu, {derthick, cplee}@uw.edu

ABSTRACT
While there has been substantial research into the use of online calendar systems (OCS) within organizations and families with children, no research focuses on adults without children. In our study, we focus on these OCS users' practices of calendar sharing as relationship work, the continually negotiated practice of managing friendships and intimacy. We conducted semi-structured interviews as part of a qualitative user study of Google Calendar users. We report the calendar sharing behaviors and strategies of our participants, who maintain multiple calendars for different purposes and with different users, communicating factual and emotional information through their calendar events. We contribute new knowledge by discussing four strategies derived from our participants' calendar sharing and relationship work activities.

Author Keywords
Calendars; intimacy; groupware; relationship work.

ACM Classification Keywords
H5.3. Information interfaces and presentation (e.g., HCI): Group and organization interfaces.

General Terms
Human Factors; Design.

INTRODUCTION
To date, user studies of online calendar systems (OCS) have focused primarily on the "calendar work" [25, 26] that occurs among members of an organization, or the "life scheduling" [13] that occurs when families with children coordinate their activities using a combination of OCS, paper calendars, and offline digital calendars. These two groups of calendar users have somewhat different scheduling practices and requirements that have been thoroughly explored [cf. 2, 5, 9, 13, 22, 23, 25, 26, 28, 32, 33].

Our user study examines calendar sharing activity in the context of adults who do not have children around whom they must coordinate their activities. These OCS users share calendars with a variety of people in their peer networks (e.g., coworkers, friends, significant others) and use their shared calendars to schedule a variety of events (e.g., professional meetings, vacations with family members, dinners with friends, fertility consultations with doctors). Relationships with members of peer networks are played out, in part, through the sharing of calendars.

As a result of the diversity of people who can view their calendars, as well as the spectrum of event types they enter into their shared calendars, it is not surprising that childless, adult OCS users engage in strategies of calendar use that are similar to those of organizational and familial OCS users [cf. 25, 34]. However, our research finds that calendar use can also be *relationship work*, a set of negotiated practices that foster, maintain, and sometimes damage friendships and feelings of intimacy.

OCS are exceptionally empowering for helping people address the age-old dilemma of staying in touch with others. OCS are powerful partly because they trade in time and intimacy development, which are both extremely valuable relationship work commodities. To use and share calendars for both work and personal lives, as many of our participants do, is to manage what is most important in life. To share calendars is to participate in activities that are much more complex than managing a binary tension between "public" and "private" information, or "personal" and "professional" information.

Taking this perspective as the basis for our work, we enhance the current understanding of OCS sharing behaviors by answering the following research question: *How does calendar sharing among OCS users accomplish relationship work?* For our qualitative user study, we interviewed users of Google Calendar, a freely-available OCS. Our findings contribute new knowledge to the study and design of OCS by describing a set of unique calendar sharing strategies derived from our participants' activities of calendar sharing as relationship work.

In this paper we first explore the HCI and CSCW literature on organizational and familial uses of calendar systems, as well as the psychology and sociology literature on relationship work. We continue with an explanation of our methods and results and conclude with a discussion of the findings that are relevant to OCS researchers and designers.

RELATED LITERATURE

In this section we first discuss the history of OCS studies and the general understanding of the different audiences for these systems. We continue with a discussion of how people generally perform relationship work and enact feelings of intimacy with one another, and close by considering how OCS users express emotions and preserve privacy with and through their shared calendars.

Brief Overview of OCS Studies

The earliest studies of organizational calendar use reflect both a general interest in the potential of OCS and the hazards of implementing such a system within an organization [cf. 18, 19]. OCS are considered communication devices when used among members of an organization [11, 14, 27], an observation that helped designers think about how to meet the challenges associated with transitioning managers, secretaries, and other professionals from paper calendars to OCS. Grudin [15] highlights differences in attitudes toward calendar use among users of different OCS, while [16, 21] examine the differences in meeting scheduling across a ten-year span and the usefulness of group scheduling tools, respectively, during the 1990s when OCS had become more prevalent.

Palen [25, 26] provides the most in-depth investigation of OCS adoption and use within a large organization, determining in part that OCS users perform *calendar work* and *interpersonal boundary management* activities to make coordination happen as smoothly as possible. Calendar work is a set of activities that includes temporal orientation, scheduling, tracking, reminding, note recording and archiving, and retrieval and recall [25]. Organizational OCS users perform these activities while also managing how others perceive them as a function of their calendar information. Calendar owners are aware of the impression that others could get by reviewing their calendars, and they attempt to manage those impressions while protecting the privacy of their information using interpersonal boundary management techniques: restricting and granting calendar access, practicing defensive scheduling techniques, writing cryptic event descriptions, omitting events entirely, and sharing calendars reciprocally with another person [cf. 9, 25, 26]. For example, "Meet with L" might actually be a reference to a tattoo removal appointment that only the calendar owner would understand.

Compared to organizational OCS users, family OCS users engage in relatively different calendaring practices [22]. Family members in charge of their families' calendars perform *life scheduling*, or the process of managing "personal, family, and professional schedules across settings and calendaring tools" [13]. For example, whereas organizational OCS users rely on their calendars for interpersonal coordination, families use OCS along with paper and digital calendars to maintain awareness of scheduled events and plans [cf. 13, 22, 35]. Also, family members do not tend to schedule each other through their calendars: They make plans using other means of communication and then track those plans on their family calendar [9, 13, 22].

The practice of life scheduling highlights another difference between organizational and family calendaring activity: the considerations of privacy and impression management that arise when using shared calendars. Family members are not concerned about the privacy of "personal" information because family calendars are meant to serve as awareness tools [22]. Issues related to calendar access, activity scheduling, and event descriptions are discussed openly among family members rather than negotiated through the calendar [9, 22]. Calendar event descriptions provide important contextual information to family members and are, therefore, quite important to record in accurate detail.

In summary, previous OCS research has focused on organizational and familial calendar users. However, there is another group of calendar users worth studying: childless, adult OCS users. These users rely on their shared calendars to help them schedule their lives and coordinate events with the entirety of their peer network: coworkers, friends, family members, and significant others. The events they schedule range from professional to highly personal, yet a variety of people might have access to those events through their shared calendars. Therefore, these acts of coordination and information sharing necessitate the performance of *relationship work*.

Relationship Work, Intimacy, and Emotional Self-Disclosure

Relationship work is a term used to describe the continually negotiated construction, maintenance, and dissolution of friendships [7], as well as the reciprocal sharing of information to achieve intimacy [6]. Fehr [12] provides a useful model of the process of making friends, a process of relationship work. People typically meet other people because they live or work in close proximity, or because someone else in their social network introduces them. Pairs of people forming a friendship undergo a mutual negotiation process whereby they decide whether they like each other and want to engage in reciprocal self-disclosure; these decisions will solidify budding friendships.

Friends must actively maintain their friendships to preserve their desired level of intimacy with others [29]. This maintenance activity is challenging because people's lives change in predictable and unpredictable ways. Hence, relationship work is a continually negotiated process, which allows friends to be responsive to these changes and which requires significant time and emotional commitment from both parties [36]. Intimate relationships are largely defined by the amount of self-disclosure in which two people engage, as well as the development of similar interests or tastes over time [12] and the responsiveness of each party to requests for communication [20].

When two people discuss personal rather than factual information, they commit to a level of self-disclosure that makes both of them more emotionally vulnerable. These acts of self-disclosure are important in intimate relationships because they promote the development and maintenance of intimacy more effectively than factual disclosures; emotional self-disclosures are recognized as the expression of needs that must be met [20]. It is this type of reciprocal self-disclosure that close friends and significant others engage in more often than acquaintances, casual friends, or even family members [30].

Enacting Intimacy, Emotion, and Privacy through OCS

Following [3], we define the term "emotion" not as an internally-constructed feeling but as an externally-observable product of interpersonal interaction. When people engage in discussion as a method for performing self-disclosing behavior, they are also expressing their emotions to one another. People often express emotion as a way to communicate specific emotional needs and request that those needs be met, but they do so in subtle ways [8].

OCS support this subtlety of expression because users can share their feelings through their event descriptions. These descriptions serve as a distribution channel for the direct expression of emotion, to borrow phrases from [4]. For example, the event description "Salary Review Meeting" has more overt emotional meaning than "meet with Dan." Clearly, OCS users need to be cautious about who can see each event description; given the emotionally sensitive information that shared calendars can convey, privacy of information is quite important. Furthermore, compared to organizational and familial OCS users, the practice of enacting privacy is made more challenging for childless, adult OCS users because they often share the same calendar with various members of their peer networks.

However, as with relationship work, privacy is a continuously enacted social practice [10] rather than a switch than can be turned on or off. As [17] point out, systems designed with interactional principles in mind enable users to manage their privacy concerns by letting them choose which information to share, and which information to keep to themselves. In the context of OCS, this allowance for information privacy occurs in a few ways. For example, users can author event descriptions carefully to avoid sharing sensitive information, or they can maintain multiple calendars to control the information they share with the members of their social networks.

We raise these points about relationship work, intimacy, emotion, and privacy with an eye toward our findings; we will return to these discussions of the enactment of emotion and privacy in the findings section shortly. First, however, we describe the methods we used to design our study.

STUDY METHODS

In this section we describe the specific OCS application we studied, provide an overview of our participants, and explain the methods we used to gather and analyze our data.

OCS Application

We chose to study Google Calendar users because this OCS is freely available and widely adopted. Calendar owners can grant others a variety of levels of access: Users can be allowed to make changes to another person's events or to the list of people who also share the same calendar, view events or event details, or view only free/busy information. Calendar owners can also create and manage multiple calendars, share them in different ways, and view all of their own calendars simultaneously with other people's shared calendars. The most active users of Google Calendar in our study had 15 or more calendars (including other people's calendars) visible at the same time.

Participants

The study took place in the Seattle area from May—August 2009, during which time interviews were conducted with 30 participants (20 women and 10 men). Participants were solicited through e-mail mailing lists associated with our university and snowball sampling was used to gather additional subjects; these sampling methods resulted in a slight imbalance in gender representation among our participants. The criteria for participation included using Google Calendar, sharing a calendar with at least 1 other person, accessing at least 1 other shared calendar, and being older than 18 years of age. Participants were not compensated and were informed of the voluntary nature of the study.

With regard to participant demographics, 18 participants self-identified as Caucasian, 8 self-identified as Asian, and 4 self-identified as multiple ethnicities; 28 participants were US citizens, while 2 were citizens of other countries. The participants ranged in age from 22 to 49 (mean: 31.5, median: 30, SD: 6.66). Thirteen of the participants were undergraduate or graduate university students, 13 participants held jobs in the technology industry, 3 participants were university professors, and 1 participant managed a non-profit organization. Nearly half (14 of 30) participants reported their relationship status as "single, never married," while the rest were either married (14 of 30) or engaged in domestic partnerships (2 of 30). We did not collect demographic data for participants' significant others, friends, and family members with whom participants shared their calendars.

Methods and Data Collection

The research team interviewed each participant once, either in person or over the phone, using a standard semi-structured interview protocol. The questions focused on usage practices with regard to the calendars that participants controlled and shared with others and that were shared with them (e.g., "Have you ever added an event because of who would see it?"). While the protocol ensured all interviews would include a standard set of questions, interviewers were encouraged to ask follow-up questions and probe for greater detail and unexpected insights when possible. All interviews lasted between 16 and 79 minutes (mean: 44, median: 44, SD: 17.37) depending on the number of calendars and intensity of usage. The interviews were recorded and transcribed, and all participant names were replaced with pseudonyms.

We applied a grounded theory approach to analyzing the interviews. In order to develop initial themes describing the data, the research team performed a closed coding pass through the data using a standard codebook developed from the interview protocol. Next, to ensure commonality of interpretation across coders, all team members coded the same 5 interviews using the same codebook and discussed the results. Finally, after writing memos based on the closed codes, the team performed an open coding pass that was focused on locating instances of relationship work and intimacy, and then wrote memos based on those new codes.

In the following sections, we first consider the specific calendar sharing and usage characteristics of our participants. We then discuss how our data diverge from previously reported research on shared calendar use, as well as describe design implications that result from our study.

FINDINGS

We begin this section with an overview of participants' typical Google Calendar usage. Our 30 participants share 88 different calendars (mean: 2.93, median: 2, SD: 2.69); the following list describes the types of people with whom participants share their calendars:

- 73% (22 of 30) share with a significant other,
- 33% (10 of 30) share with a friend,
- 27% (8 of 30) share with a coworker,
- 23% (7 of 30) share with a family member (e.g., mother, father, sister),
- 17% (5 of 30) share with groups of associates (e.g., exercise partners, student group members).

In the sections that follow, we discuss examples drawn from our data that illustrate typical behaviors of our participants. We first examine why the majority of our participants maintain multiple shared calendars. We then examine how some participants rely on emotionally meaningful context when they author and interpret event descriptions. We conclude by describing how participants negotiate shared activities with significant others and with friends, and why certain participants maintain shared calendars with friends who no longer live close enough to see one another on a regular basis.

Distributing Relationship Work across Multiple Calendars

We observed that most participants (20 of 30) partition information across multiple shared calendars; participants shared anywhere from 2 to 13 different calendars. A minority of participants (10 of 30) maintain only one shared calendar; in all cases, these calendars are shared **only** with significant others.

Of the 20 participants who maintain multiple calendars, the typical participant has an unshared calendar containing only tasks or "to-do" information, a calendar shared only with a significant other that lists the entirety of their events in their lives together, and at least one other calendar shared with multiple people that lists a subset of their events. It is these latter calendars that participants share with people outside of their romantic relationships.

For example, Linda and Nathan are a young married couple without children. They each have personal calendars as well as other calendars that they maintain and share. Linda maintains a calendar within which she schedules personal events (e.g., having dinner with a friend) and professional commitments (e.g. taking a professional development class). She shares this calendar only with her husband so they can coordinate their time together. As with other married couples, this calendar is a useful tool for both partners to maintain awareness of their schedules, and a cue to perform specific tasks required of significant others (e.g., making dinner or going to a friend's wedding).

Our participants maintain multiple calendars in order to keep specific people informed about selected areas of their lives rather than opening up their entire lives to scrutiny. Continuing the previous example, Linda is a runner; in addition to the calendar she shares only with her husband, she also maintains a separate calendar that she shares with several running partners. This calendar includes only information about her training regime, which her running partners use to help them train as well, and does not list any of her personal events, such as doctor visits.

Similarly, Harriet maintains a calendar that only her husband can view, as well as work and travel calendars that all of her professional colleagues can read. Through her shared calendar with her husband, she lists every event in her life, even the most sensitive events (e.g., a coffee date with a potential new hire at her office). When updating her work and travel calendars, Harriet avoids including the "personal stuff."

"in terms of what the entire public is seeing, they just see I'm out of the office as opposed to 'get my haircut.'"

Harriet does not include events such as these on her work and travel calendars, which primarily include social events that involve a number of people (e.g., a dinner party with several colleagues) or work-related trips (e.g., a trip to a professional development conference).

Finally, the vast majority of our participants (26 of 30) feel that masking event details and simply saying "busy" is too impersonal, or that setting an event to be described only as "busy" suggests a level of secrecy that could annoy or confuse the people with whom they share their calendar. Linda sums up the general sentiment about how others might perceive "busy" as an event description.

"'Busy,'" I just think, seems suspect. It just seems sort of rude, too."

Events marked as "busy" stand out in calendars with otherwise viewable event details; those "busy" events seem special and exclusive in a way that can harm the perceived level of intimacy between the calendar owner and the people with whom he or she shares that calendar. Fehr [12] cites genuineness as a strong indicator of intimacy within a friendship, and the use of "busy" within a shared calendar clearly damages the perception that feelings of intimacy in a given relationship are genuine.

By maintaining separate calendars, our participants are able to keep specific people informed about certain aspects of their lives rather than opening up their entire lives to scrutiny. As these examples demonstrate, our participants set expectations for their relationships with the people in their peer networks who can view their shared calendars; making only a workout schedule visible, for example, indicates that other types of social engagements beyond those scheduled through the shared calendar are not necessarily desired. In addition, maintaining multiple calendars is a way to avoid making all events visible and describing a subset of those events as "busy."

Negotiating and Maintaining Romantic Relationships and Friendships Using Shared Calendars

In this section we explore a particular facet of calendar sharing as relationship work: the strategies of our participants to maintain or enrich relationships with significant others and with friends. We posit that the use of shared calendars can help people maintain certain levels of intimacy in their romantic relationships and friendships; additionally, the desire to preserve awareness of a friend's activities is sometimes the only reason why friends reciprocally share personal calendars.

Availability, probability of future interaction, frequency of exposure, and responsiveness are four of the most crucial aspects that determine whether two people will become more intimate with one another [12]. Our participants use their shared calendars to negotiate all of these situational hurdles: They use them to determine the availability of others, see how long or how often they can meet with another person (possibly by setting up a recurring meeting), and invite people to a specific event with the expectation that they will receive a reply. They also use the shared calendars of friends and significant others to sustain exposure to their personal lives when spending time together in person is not possible.

When two people commit to a friendship or romantic relationship, they must find time to "hang out" with one another in order to make those relationships last. Being invited to hang out enriches feelings of intimacy because that time is reserved for that relationship alone. However, our participants find it challenging to carve out time for their friends and even their significant others, so they rely on their shared calendars to schedule time together.

Negotiating Shared Activities with Significant Others

Our participants sometimes negotiate shared activities through their significant others' calendars without discussing the details in person first. They use shared calendars in this way in order to accomplish relationship work by scheduling events that are often necessary in the lives of partners engaged in romantic relationships (e.g., fertility planning, meal preparation, and household chores). In so doing, they want to minimize the stress associated with coordinating two busy lives by scheduling events for both partners when necessary.

However, this scheduling technique can cause conflict; Tiffany describes how she argued with her fiancé about scheduling overlapping events.

"We had this argument and...it ended up that I already made plans during this week. And that was the week that he had this...workshop thing that he had to go to. So I got really mad and I'm like, 'You didn't tell me.' He said, 'You didn't look at my calendar.' And I was like, 'I don't look two months ahead.' So we had this argument about it."

To resolve these scheduling conflicts, participants sometimes discuss their plans verbally after noticing the problematic calendar events, and then decide which event will take precedence or whether a specific event can be moved to alleviate the conflict. Other participants who anticipate the potential for conflict use certain event settings (e.g., indicating that an event is "tentative") or special codes within the event descriptions they write (e.g., a question mark to indicate a suggested destination for a meal). They use these settings and codes to indicate that the events they are negotiating through their shared calendars require discussion before they can be considered "scheduled."

For example, Laura uses a special code when planning events with her boyfriend. When she started sharing her personal calendar with him, Laura would enter events and her boyfriend would get upset because he felt obligated to attend every event. After some discussion, Laura developed a new, mutually-agreeable tactic for indicating potential events: She includes a question mark in the description of a calendar event that will require in-person negotiation before any obligations are set. Using this strategy, Laura balances her need for shared time with her boyfriend with his need for a suitable amount of control over his schedule.

We consider this use of shared calendars as a site for the negotiation of shared activities as an example of our participants' stated desire to maintain their feelings of intimacy with the people to whom they feel closest: their significant others. They want to keep their relationships vital, and they look to their calendars as a way to manage the chaos of two different schedules that often provide little in the way of overlapping time.

Negotiating Shared Activities with Friends

Friends who have established emotional bonds with one another also want to keep their relationships vital over time. These bonds are formed by spending time together and by mutually sharing personal information [12]. Our participants cite this desire to spend time with their friends as a primary motivator for sharing and accessing online calendars. They often discuss their interest in coordinating schedules not because of any particular life scheduling necessity (e.g., picking up children from school, working on a project), but because they want to stay close to their friends. Their behavior is driven by their desire to hang out with friends so they can maintain their existing friendships or build stronger feelings of intimacy. The events they schedule with one another often have no agenda: They simply exist to let two friends share a few precious hours together.

For example, our participants tell us that their calendars allow their friends to see what they are up to and whether they are available to see each other soon given their busy schedules. Michael uses his friend's calendar to find time when the two of them can get together for a beer after work.

"This was during one of [our] three-week long attempts to find a date when we could get together for a beer. And toward the end of that process he said that he was just getting online with Google Calendar and he would share it with me and that would be easier."

Friends also rely on their calendars to identify and schedule times to engage in specific activities together. Kevin uses the gaps between events in his friend's calendar to judge when they will be mutually available to play an online game together. For Kevin, these structured times to play games with a friend enable him to stay as close to that friend as he can given his busy schedule.

Having a beer or getting dinner together is a good example of two friends wanting to hang out together in a social situation that grants them unstructured time to simply relax. Therefore, it is a particularly poignant juxtaposition when close friends must resort to an online scheduling tool in order to hang out. Yet our busy participants indicate that relaxation with friends is a special event that must be scheduled, or else it will not happen. They understand that more time spent together leads to stronger feelings of friendship and intimacy.

Staying Connected to Friends' Lives

Shared calendars provide exposure to another person's life even when spending time together face to face is not possible. While shared calendar access can serve as a way to schedule time together or provide talking points for conversations, staying connected to a friend's activities in order to maintain intimacy is sometimes the only reason why our participants reciprocally share personal calendars.

For example, Louise describes shared calendars as diaries that she and her friends use to know what they have been doing lately. She reciprocally shares calendars with one friend specifically because their calendars enable them to keep in touch and up to date on the activities in their lives.

"It's nice to see, like, 'Oh you've been working on your house,' or, 'you've been away in-' he travels, a lot, a lot, a lot, and so I can tell when he's in China or India, or he's in wherever he is."

Louise told us that she goes back and adds certain things that she did just so this friend can see what she has been doing. Similarly, when Julio returned to the US after living in Japan, he and his friend (who remained in Japan) began sharing their personal calendars not to schedule time to chat, but because they wanted their friendship to persist. As with Louise, Julio uses his friend's calendar as a diary of his activities.

"Randomly, out of curiosity...I scroll [through] his events when I want to know if there's something happening that I've missed."

As [12] points out, people understand that the probability of future interaction impacts the level of intimacy that two people feel for one another. Our participants sometimes share calendars with friends who they rarely, if ever, see in person because they consider the intimacy of those friendships worth preserving. In Julio's case, he has no coordinative reason to share calendars. Instead, he reads his friend's calendar to see what he has missed since he moved: a clear example of his desire to maintain a certain level of connection with that friend.

Exploring the Emotional Meaning of Shared Calendars

The event descriptions that OCS users write can serve as expressions of emotion, rather than purely factual communication. The richness of emotion that can be interpreted depends on the social relationships of the participants. Close friends and significant others who have enough shared history with a calendar owner can interpret event descriptions as emotionally meaningful, a level of interpretation that other calendar users who lack the contextual knowledge might not be able to achieve. Some of our participants told us that they interpret event descriptions that appear purely coordinative or factual as emotionally meaningful in order to provide emotional support. We consider this behavior the performance of relationship work to enhance or maintain intimacy.

The shared calendars of close friends and significant others are valuable because they provide the opportunity to read and interpret the emotional states and well-being of the people who matter most in their lives. For example, Harriet told us that she reviews her husband's events to determine whether he will be upset when he comes home that evening.

"now I use [my husband's calendar] somewhat as an awareness thing...just sort of understanding like how stressed out he is going to be or if he needs help with something or whatever."

Others who share the same calendar might not have the depth of contextual knowledge necessary to make the same assessment judging solely by an apparently factual event description (e.g., "Meeting with Paul").

Similarly, Roger describes feeling concerned about his friend after noticing a number of dental appointments on his shared personal calendar.

"my Canadian friend went to the dentist a lot for a while. And I was like 'wow, you've gone to the dentist a lot, what's going on?' and he was telling me about some dental thing that was happening with him."

Roger contacted his friend specifically to see if he was feeling alright, an action that indicates Roger's desire to provide emotional support. It is also worth noting that Roger was geographically removed from his "Canadian" friend, so he used his friend's shared calendar to infer the potential need for support.

Shared calendars are a site for emotional self-disclosure of information partly because event descriptions are a site for expressing emotion, and because calendar events can have the sensitivity of a diary entry [31]. Unlike a diary, however, shared calendars reflect what has happened in the recent past and *what will be happening* in the near future. When viewed as a whole and with the proper contextual knowledge, the set of events in a person's calendar can be a barometer of that person's emotional state and provide friends with cues as to when concern or other types of emotional support may be warranted.

DISCUSSION

In this paper, we have described a number of calendar sharing practices and goals in the context of our participants. Although they perform a combination of calendar work and life scheduling activities reflective of the activities identified by previous research, they also engage in practices that form a set of unique strategies for calendar sharing as relationship work. In this section we describe four strategies of calendar sharing that differentiate our participants' OCS usage from that of organizational and familial OCS users, and consider the broader implications of those strategies with regard to OCS design and use.

Maintaining Multiple Calendars as a Privacy Practice

We observed the majority of our participants *maintaining multiple calendars as a way to control how much knowledge different individuals or groups have of their activities*. By sharing multiple, purpose-built calendars with specific organizing principles and users with access, they can set and manage expectations for their interactions with others and accomplish the relationship work necessary to manage their desired levels of interpersonal intimacy.

This relationship management strategy differs from the calendar work and life scheduling techniques of organizational and familial OCS users, respectively, for a simple reason: Organization and family members are essentially constrained to using only one calendar as the primary shared calendar they update and access. Families with children typically use a "main" or "primary" family calendar supplemented by "secondary calendars" that are not used as the central calendar for coordination [22]. Organizational calendaring usually occurs through one shared calendar to which other members of the organization have access [25]. For these OCS users, issues of event visibility play out through the calendars, necessitating calendar work and interpersonal boundary management techniques to avoid causing interpersonal conflict [25, 26].

We observed that our participants did not actively manage their calendar settings; instead, they might adjust the settings for a specific calendar once and never check those settings again. During our interviews they often had to be shown how to access the settings menu. As a result, even when maintaining multiple calendars as their practice for managing the privacy of their information, several participants still allowed the "wrong" people to see their calendars and events.

Clearly, these participants would appreciate an easier way to control who can see the details of their shared calendars. Although maintaining multiple calendars is the most popular mechanism of control in our study, this strategy can be quite inefficient given that some participants did not want their calendars to be entirely mutually exclusive. What participants really wanted was a provision for different and flexibly controlled views of their events without the overhead of entering items into separate calendars. This could be a productive area for design attention; at a minimum, an alternative to the "busy" event description would be a positive step toward reducing the management issues associated with maintaining multiple calendars.

Ultimately, OCS designers can strike a better balance between the task of managing calendar access and the fact that although users choose not to perform this task regularly, they still need to remain aware of who can access their calendars and events.

Coordinating Life through Shared Calendars

The second strategy is to *use shared calendars to maintain and enhance relationships by maneuvering to spend time together*. Many of our participants in romantic relationships describe their attempts to coordinate their lives **through** their shared calendars. This finding diverges from the familial OCS use reported by [22], who observed that their participants **did not** coordinate through their family calendars. Because familial OCS users need to maintain awareness of family members' plans and locations, they discuss those plans first and use the shared family calendar to broadcast their decisions. By contrast, our participants often use their shared calendars to broadcast their plans and to suggest events to their significant others that require extra discussion before a decision can be made.

These attempts at maneuvering to spend time together stem from the fact that partners in romantic relationships often do things as a couple, creating a requirement for shared time [12]. By contrast, organizational OCS users' requirement for shared time stems from their need to accomplish work tasks collaboratively. Their performance of scheduling as calendar work is an attempt to balance the "constraints and priorities" [25] related to their organizational roles and responsibilities.

We know that our participants maneuver to spend time together in a number of different ways, and using their own systems of nomenclature to do so. However, we believe the most interesting aspect of this strategy is, as several participants described, the use of shared calendars to know when **not** to schedule activities with their significant others. They want to appear available to their partners by leaving gaps in their schedules that align with the gaps in their partners' schedules. This behavior, motivated by the requirement for shared time between significant others, reflects another dimension of the rich emotional behavior that plays out through shared calendars.

As with meeting the emotional needs of others, however, current OCS do not support this behavior effectively enough. In the same way that privacy is not a toggle between binary states, a person's schedule is not simply a distinction between "available" and "busy." When our participants structure their time through their shared calendars, there are times when they are potentially **more or less** available than a simple gap in the schedule might indicate.

Stated differently, not all gaps are created equal: A calendar opening at 6 PM on a Friday is quite different from an opening at 5 AM on a Tuesday. For some couples, a 5 AM jog would be a welcome mutual activity; for others, 5 AM is bedtime. It is up to the partners within the relationship to make ad hoc decisions about availability in order to satisfy their desire to spend time together. While we are not specifically advocating various "shades" of availability within OCS, we do think there is an opportunity here to explore how OCS design could better support this sort of ad hoc maneuvering to spend time together, particularly with regard to OCS users who do not know enough personal details about their colleagues' lives to distinguish which times are more "free" than others.

Sharing Calendars to Prolong Friendships

The third strategy is to *use the calendar to stay in touch with friends*. When friends are unable to spend time together in person, they start or continue sharing calendars as a demonstration of their interest in maintaining their mutual feelings of intimacy. They enact this behavior by browsing friends' calendars to see what they have been up to, and in return they keep the details of their lives documented in their own shared calendars.

This behavior differs sharply from that of organizational OCS users: Although employees at a company sometimes "browse" their colleagues' calendars, they are assumed to have a specifically coordinative reason in mind, such as determining mutual availability for a meeting [24]. They are not skimming other people's calendars to learn more about their personal lives [26]. Similarly, it seems logical that family members would browse the family calendar for primarily coordinative, life scheduling purposes. Families with children use their calendars to see when everyone might be available for a specific outing, for example, or to determine what events each person is committed to over a specific weekend. In short, neither of these groups of OCS users are sharing calendars as a strategy for maintaining mutual feelings of intimacy.

Some of our participants obviously enjoy adding detail to their past events specifically so others could access that information and reminisce about their relationship. OCS can do much more to support the addition of richer, more socially connected information within events. Our participants use their shared calendars to remember what they have done with others, to stimulate new conversations, and to stay connected if only in a small way. Finally, the length of time that OCS preserve past events is of tremendous importance to these participants; they would enjoy being able to travel several months or years back in time so they could see the same events again and again. Given these uses of OCS, we believe the design challenge at hand is to figure out how to support richer conversation and discussion through the interface of the shared calendar.

Meeting Emotional Needs Using Event Descriptions

The fourth and final strategy that emerged from our data is that participants *use the calendars of others to derive or anticipate the need for emotional support or understanding*. Specifically, a few of our participants told us they regard event descriptions, and even the amounts of free and busy time visible in shared calendars, as valuable barometers of emotional needs. This practice of OCS use stems from who has access to shared calendars, and what sorts of information are presented in those calendars.

Familial OCS users need to maintain awareness of their communal activities across all family members. One way they maintain this awareness is by associating "extra information" [22] with their calendars, such as maps, contact information, and additional schedules. This extra information must include clear, actionable details to facilitate the desired level of awareness. Organizational OCS users also attach extra information to their meeting requests, such as project schedules or links to relevant information. For these OCS users, this extra information is purely factual: Maps help family members find the location of an event, for example. It seems unlikely that familial and organizational OCS users would read emotional meaning into this extra information.

A few of our participants chose to extract a different kind of extra information from shared calendar events. These participants rely on their shared history with friends and significant others to understand certain factual information contained in their calendars as emotionally meaningful, and they decide when to act on that information as a way of maintaining intimacy by making contact and providing emotional support. Finally, because this relationship work is occurring through shared calendars, our participants can consider each event in the broader context of all events and determine whether emotional support is necessary.

At this point we recall the distinction between informational and interactional design that [3, 17] make in the context of affective computing systems. In the process of interacting with one another using their shared calendars, our participants decide to request or provide emotional support, which can occur through or outside of the calendar. This activity resembles the affective loop experiences of [17], in which the dialogue with a friend and a system blurs together. The fact that OCS might enable such experiences is a positive yet underexplored attribute of these systems. Given that currently, the onus is on calendar viewers to discern the need for emotional support, a question for future research and development concerns whether, OCS should provide explicit support for the sharing of emotional information with others.

CONCLUSION

Our study has a number of limitations that we hope to address in future studies of the same topic. As an exploratory study, our sampling method resulted in a somewhat homogeneous set of participants with regard to gender, cultural background, and socioeconomic status; we recognize, however, that these characteristics play an important role in technology practices [1] and hope that future studies will include more diverse participants. Future studies could also explore how relationships and calendar sharing activities co-evolve over time, and could include more details about the networks of friends with whom people stay in touch using their calendars.

The strategies outlined here describe how our participants accomplish relationship work using their shared calendars. They perform some activities that are similar to organizational and familial OCS users, but as their motivation for performing those tasks is fundamentally different, their calendaring behavior is also different. In addition to coordinating their own lives and schedules, our participants accomplish a great deal of relationship work with, through, and around shared calendars.

For example, our participants arrange and set reminders for events, invite others to those events, and recall the details of events that have already taken place. They conduct these activities in the service of maintaining or enhancing their relationships and levels of intimacy with members of their peer networks: friends, family members, and significant others, any of whom may have access to one or more of their calendars. The challenge that OCS users such as our participants face, then, is to perform the relationship work required to maintain and enhance their relationships and different levels of intimacy with others who use their calendars, all while avoiding the disclosure of information perceived as negative, insulting, incriminating, and so on.

By studying the calendar sharing practices of adult OCS users, we begin to understand calendaring activities as a type of relationship work. The freely-available OCS we studied supports additional practices beyond calendar work and life scheduling, practices that illuminate the relationship work that occurs when people share calendars. We believe our participants' performance of relationship work using their shared calendars suggests a reframing of OCS as a type of social media. Doing so would open up a larger design space that more accurately reflects the rich and nuanced activities already taking place with, through, and around online calendar systems.

ACKNOWLEDGMENTS

This project was funded by a Google Research Award. Thanks to Karl Frantz, Keith Grochow, Calvin Kaiser, Arsenio Locsin, Natalie Lindner, and Jacob Warren for their work on this study.

REFERENCES

1. Ames, M.G., Go, J., Kaye, J., and Spasojevic, M. Understanding technology choices and values through social class. In *Proc. CSCW 2011*, ACM Press (2011), 55-64.
2. Beech, S., Geelhoed, E., Murphy, R., Parker, J., Sellen, A., and Shaw, K. The lifestyles of working parents. *Tech. rep. HPL-2003-88R1*, HP Labs (2004).
3. Boehner, K., DePaula, R., Dourish, P., and Sengers, P. How emotion is made and measured. *Int. J. Human-Computer Studies 65* (2007), 275–291.
4. Boehner, K., DePaula, R., Dourish, P., and Sengers, P. Affect: From Information to Interaction. In *Proc. CC 2005*, ACM Press (2005), 59-68.
5. Brush, A.B. and Turner, T.C. A survey of personal and household scheduling. In *Proc. ACM SIGGROUP 2005*, ACM Press, (2005), 330-331.
6. Cahill, S.E. Together Alone: Personal Relationships in Public Places. *Contemporary Sociology: A Journal of Reviews 36*, 1 (2007), 32-34.
7. Cahill, S.E. Notably gendered relations: Relationship work in early adolescents' notes. In B. Baron & H.

Kotthoff (Eds.) *Gender in interaction: Perspectives on femininity and masculinity in ethnography and discourse*, (2001), 75–97.

8. Clark, M.S. and Brissette, I. Two Types of Relationship Closeness and Their Influence on People's Emotional Lives. In R.J. Davidson, K.R. Scherer, and H.H. Goldsmith (Eds.) *Handbook of Affective Sciences*, (2003), 824-835.
9. Crabtree, A., Hemmings, T., Rodden, T., and Mariani, J. Informing the development of calendar systems for domestic use. In *Proc. ECSCW 2003*, Kluwer Academic Publishers (2003), 119-138.
10. Dourish, P. and Anderson, K. Collective Information Practice: Exploring Privacy and Security as Social and Cultural Phenomena. *Human-Computer Interaction 21*, 3 (2006), 319-342.
11. Ehrlich, S.F. Social and psychological factors influencing the design of office communications systems. In *Proc. CHI 1987*, ACM Press (1987), 323-329.
12. Fehr, B. *Friendship Processes*. Sage Publications (1986).
13. Grimes, A. and Brush, A. Life scheduling to support multiple social roles. In *Proc. CHI 2008*, ACM Press (2008), 821-824.
14. Grudin, J. Why CSCW Applications Fail: Problems In The Design And Evaluation Of Organizational Interfaces. In *Proc. CSCW 1988*, ACM Press (1988), 85-93.
15. Grudin, J. A case study of calendar use in an organization. *SIGOIS Bull. 17*, 3 (1996), 49-51.
16. Grudin, J. and Palen, L. Why Groupware Succeeds: Discretion or Mandate? In *Proc. ECSCW 1995*, ACM Press (1995), 263-278.
17. Höök, K., Ståhl, A., Sundström, P., and Laaksolahti, J. Interactional Empowerment. In *Proc. CHI 2008*, ACM Press (2008), 647-656.
18. Kelley, J.F. and Chapanis, A. How professional persons keep their calendars: Implications for computerization. *Journal of Occupational Psychology 55* (1982), 241-256.
19. Kincaid, C.M., Dupont, P.D. and Kaye, A.R. Electronic Calendars in the Office: An Assessment of User Needs and Current Technology. *ACM Transactions on Office Information Systems 3*, 1 (1985), 89–102.
20. Laurenceau, J-P, Rivera, L.M., Schaffer, A.R., and Pietromonaco, P.R. Intimacy as an Interpersonal Process: Current Status and Future Directions. In D.J. Mashek and A. Aron (Eds.) *Handbook of Closeness and Intimacy*, (2004), 61-78.
21. Mosier, J.N. and Tammaro, S.G. When Are Group Scheduling Tools Useful? *Computer Supported Cooperative Work: The Journal of Collaborative Computing 6*, 1 (1997), 53–70.
22. Neustaedter, C., Brush, A.J., and Greenberg, S. The calendar is crucial: Coordination and awareness through the family calendar. *ACM Trans. Comput.-Hum. Interact. 16*, 1 (2009), 1-48.
23. Neustaedter, C., Brush, A.J., and Greenberg, S. A Digital Family Calendar in the Home: Lessons from Field Trials of LINC. In *Proc. of Graphics Interface 2007*, ACM Press (2007), 199-220.
24. Palen, L. and Grudin, J. Discretionary adoption of group support software: lessons from calendar applications. In B.E. Munkvold (Ed.) *Implementing Collaboration Technologies in industry: Case Examples and Lessons Learned*, (2003), 159-179.
25. Palen, L. Social, individual and technological issues for groupware calendar systems. In *Proc. CHI 1999*, ACM Press (1999), 17-24.
26. Palen, L. *Calendars on the New Frontier: Challenges of Groupware Technology*. Dissertation, UC Irvine (1998).
27. Payne, S.J. Understanding calendar use. *Human-Computer Interaction 8*, 2 (1993), 83-100.
28. Plaisant, C., Clamage, A., Hutchinson, H.B., Bederson, B.B. and Druin, A. Shared family calendars: promoting symmetry and accessibility. *ACM Transactions on Computer-Human Interaction 13*, 3 (2006), 313-46.
29. Planalp, S. and Rivers, M. Changes in Knowledge of Personal Relationships. In G.J.O. Fletcher and J. Fitness (Eds.) *Knowledge Structures in Close Relationships: A Social Psychological Approach*, (1996), 299-324.
30. Prager, K.J. and Roberts, L.J. Deep Intimate Connection: Self and Intimacy in Couple Relationships. In D.J. Mashek and A. Aron (Eds.) *Handbook of Closeness and Intimacy*, (2004), 43-60.
31. Tomitsch, M., Grechenig, T. and Wascher, P. Personal and private calendar interfaces support private patterns: diaries, relations, emotional expressions. In *Proc. NordiCHI 2006*, ACM Press (2006), 401-404.
32. Tullio, J. and Mynatt, E.D. Use and Implications of a Shared, Forecasting Calendar. In *Proc. INTERACT 2007*, Springer-Berlin (2007), 269-282.
33. Tungare, M., Pérez-Quiñones, M.A. and Sams, A. An Exploratory Study of Calendar Use. arXiv:0809.3447v1.
34. van den Hooff, B. Electronic coordination and collective action: use and effects of electronic calendar and scheduling. *Info & Management 42*, 1 (2004), 103-114.
35. Venkatesh, A. Digital home technologies and transformation of households. *Information Systems Frontiers 10*, 4 (2008), 391-395.
36. Vetere, F., Gibbs, M. R., Kjeldskov, J., Howard, S., Mueller, F., Pedell, S., Mecoles, K., and Bunyan, M. Mediating intimacy: designing technologies to support strong-tie relationships. In *Proc. CHI 2005*, ACM Press (2005), 471-480.

Interacting With Infrastructure: A Case for Breaching Experiments in Home Technology Research

Erika Shehan Poole
College of Information Sciences and Technology
The Pennsylvania State University
321E IST Building
University Park, PA 16802
epoole@ist.psu.edu

ABSTRACT
Why do user experience problems with home computing persist, despite several decades worth of academic study and countless technological innovations to overcome these issues? This paper presents the results of a multi-week trial investigating technical support practices in North American homes using a combination of breaching experiments and custom software. What this study uncovered was not a one-size-fits-all solution to technical problems in residential settings, but instead a rich description of the articulation work required to acquire devices, maintain and configure them over time, and seek help when problems occur. Based on this study, I argue that many of the user experience problems experienced with home computing and electronics are due to issues related to individual agency rather than technical or user interface characteristics of any given technology combination. Additionally, I make a case for the use of breaching experiments to study phenomenon related to technologies infrastructures that are difficult to capture via other traditionally used methods.

Author Keywords
Breaching experiment, computing, home, research methods

ACM Classification Keywords
H5.m. Information interfaces and presentation (e.g., HCI): Miscellaneous.

General Terms
Human Factors

INTRODUCTION
Why do some problems with home computing persist, despite several decades worth of academic study and countless technological innovations to overcome these issues? In this paper, I describe the results of a multi-week trial in which households set up, configured, used, and helped their family and friends with learning more about common home electronics and information technologies that prior studies have shown to be problematic. This study did not lead to a clever solution to the problems of technical advice sharing for homes. Instead, it provided explanations of *why* problems with technical advice sharing and home technical maintenance persist, despite the fact that help-seekers and help-givers both report dissatisfaction with the status quo of home technical support.

This study offers the following contributions to the body of knowledge in CSCW. First, it extends what is known about strategies used by householders to cope with technological difficulties. Prior work suggests that when typical household support patterns are disrupted (e.g., the person who normally takes care of maintenance tasks is unable to do so at a given time), householders must take alternative paths to achieving their goals [7, 10, 20, 29, 30, 37]. However, understanding what people actually chose to do in the moment remains understudied. The majority of studies of household technology support practices rely on retrospective accounts that may be subject to fuzzy memory and recall bias. While there have been a few studies that use interventions to provide richer data, they have either used individuals as a unit of analysis [25] or have focused specifically on installation-related issues [3]. Thus, secondly, I demonstrate how *breaching experiments* [15] can be used to provide richer detail about the coordination problems householders encounter when setting up and maintaining residential computing environments. That is, I provide deeper insight into the articulation work—or work that enables other work—that is required to keep a residential computing environment in working condition [34]. Through using this method, I discuss the impact of acquisition habits, the co-existence of managed (corporate-owned) and unmanaged (householder-owned) equipment, and specific aspects of digital housekeeping practices in maintaining technological order in the home.

RELATED WORK
This section first provides a brief history of computing in American homes and research in understanding and resolving technology troubles associated with home computing. It then turns to methodological challenges in

gaining a more complete understanding of technical support challenges and practices in homes.

Computers and the Internet in American Homes

As home computing rose into popularity from the late 1970s and into the 1990s, computers became more than just technical hobbies or telecommuting tools. Computers became a part the way homes engaged in home finance, leisure, shopping, communication, and educational development [39]. In the mid-1990s, as the popularity of the Internet and World Wide Web grew, researchers began to study the experiences of Americans trying dial-up Internet for the first time. Researchers at US West [14] and Carnegie Mellon University [24] tracked the experiences of families new to the Internet through two studies, tracking families in Minnesota and Pennsylvania, respectively. In both of these early studies, families were eager to be on the Internet, but this excitement was tempered by regular troubles with computers and connectivity, particularly when it came to installation processes or troubleshooting with a technician. (A particular artifact of this early period of home Internet use is that to troubleshoot dial-up connection problems, callers had to hang up the phone in order to try fixes because they typically only had one phone line in the home shared for voice and data).

In the time since these early studies of dial-up Internet practices, the landscape of computer, mobile device, and Internet use in the United States has changed. As of the time of writing, 78% of Americans use the Internet regularly, either through a home broadband connection, connectivity available at a "third place" such as a coffee house or library, or a cellular network mobile device. Of particular note is the increase of broadband adoption in American households; at least 67% of Americans now have broadband access available in their homes [21]. This shift to high-speed Internet connectivity at home also led to changes in how devices are configured and maintained in American homes. Rather than having contention over sharing a single computer, families have, in many cases, shifted to owning *multiple* machines, many of which are portable devices that encourage the adoption of wireless connectivity [40]. As the price of computer hardware decreases, it may also be more affordable to have multiple computers in a home. Thus, more homes are relying on networks within the home in order to provide Internet connectivity simultaneously to computers and other consumer electronics, as well as to share scarce resources such as printers and media.

Resolving Domestic Technology Troubles

A common thread in research on home computing finds families are still faced with vexing problems related to installation and troubleshooting of devices and network connectivity [4, 7, 20, 25, 36]. After nearly two decades of study and commercial product development, why does technical support at home remain an unsolved problem? Why do some technical problems with setup and maintenance of home computing infrastructures continue to exist in spite of many efforts to eradicate them?

Several studies have used ethnographic methods and householder self-reports to understand computing usage and maintenance practices in homes [1, 7, 20, 24, 28]. The majority of these studies depict home computing support as the work of a paid technician or a "lone guru," yet emerging work finds that practices surrounding setup, use, and maintenance of the network can be highly collaborative [29, 30]. Within the home, technical maintenance practices, upon additional scrutiny, may more closely represent a "domestic economy," in which family members specialize in certain aspects of home computing, trading expertise as necessary [32]. For instance, one family member may know quite a bit about spreadsheets or audiovisual equipment, but little about network configurations. Thus, help is not always unidirectional, provided by a single "guru." Similarly, there may collaborations with people who live in a different household, for instance a technician, family member living elsewhere, or a knowledgeable neighbor [19, 20, 37]. Systems that scaffold home support, particularly for easing setup and initial configuration tasks have shown promise [26, 41], yet technology problems beyond installation still abound.

These existing problems may be due to articulation work required to keep home infrastructures afloat. The term *articulation work*, as coined by Strauss, is used to describe "work that enables other work" [16]. In an early article on this topic, Gasser [16], studying computer usage in organizations notes that instead of only trying to find and quickly eliminate problems in computer systems, there is a value in understanding why some problems and human workarounds "persist and evolve" despite technological innovation. Similarly to Gasser's writing, in this paper I provide insight into why "quick fixes" are insufficient for resolving problems seen with networked home computing, and describe the articulation work that occurs within homes to maintain technological order. This articulation work can come in several forms, including changing one's work patterns to accommodate a system, taking on additional tasks, using computing in emergent ways, or avoiding the use of a technology completely.

Methodological Limits of Home Computing Research

Finally, in addition to understanding that there *are* quite a few existing home technology problems that still abound, I would like to also call attention to methodological limits of existing research of home computing practices. Although prior studies identified a broad range of reasons for technology problems in residential settings, they relied on primarily on *retrospective* accounts, particularly those that may have happened long ago. A more limited body of research examines the specific problems householders encounter in-situ. However, this work is limited to understanding the experiences of individuals attempting device installation [3, 25], or in understanding the purpose and functionality of a newly installed research device or device suite [35, 38]. These studies did not examine within-household coordination or divisions of labor within the home, nor did they examine issues extending *beyond* initial installation. In this study, I describe how I have used other methods to capture more in-depth in-situ information about home technology acquisition, usage, maintenance, and troubleshooting patterns.

METHODS: A CASE FOR BREACHING EXPERIMENTS

Studying how people resolve technical difficulties in the home presents two challenges. First, technical problems may happen unexpectedly and infrequently. It can be difficult to study *critical incidents* [13]. The amount of time between critical incidents with respect to home computing setup, maintenance, and troubleshooting are unpredictable; they could be minutes apart or years apart, and thus create challenges for data collection [1]. Secondly, some critical incidents may be so subtle that householders do not recognize them as being an event worthy of noting in studies that rely on them to provide verbal or written recall of incidents. When data is obtained from studies in which people provide retrospective accounts (for instance, of technology difficulties that occurred in the past year), this approach can lead toward shallow accounts of the steps people take to resolve these problems, though they are excellent for understanding the *motivations* for ways they chose to resolve the problem. How then, can we dig deeper into understanding home technology trouble? I turned to using *technology probes* as well as *breaching experiments*, each of which I explain in turn.

Breaching Experiments

Breaching experiments originated with Garfinkel's ethnomethodological approaches to sociology [15]. They are activities that deliberately disrupt the ordinary character of day-to-day life in order to understand social norms and reactions to behavior that does not conform to these norms. Examples of breaching experiments could be demanding to pay more than the stated price of an item in a shop, to intentionally undo a competitor's move in a tabletop board game, or (for the more daring researcher) to drive a car the wrong way down a city street.

I am not the first to discuss the role of breaching in technology research. For example, Crabtree argued for the usefulness of breaching experiments in supporting innovation in design of futuristic ubiquitous computing technologies [8]. In the context of his research, he called for the use of breaching to understand practices surrounding technology in situations where there is an absence of prior practice (as is the case in technological innovations in seen in ubiquitous computing research). More closely to my own work, Tolmie and Crabtree discuss how home technology research deployments of any sort could be considered breaching experiments [35] in their analysis of Gaver's Video Window [18]. Where my work differs from the argument of Tolmie and Crabtree is that they consider deployments of research technology in homes to be *problematic* as these are things typically done by researchers and disrupt the norms of a home's routines.

In contrast, I argue that breaching experiments have a valid and useful place in studies of existing technology infrastructure-related practices in domestic settings. In the context of this study, I did not solely inject a technology for which my research team would be the installer or caretaker. Instead, breaching experiments were used to understand existing infrastructures in the home in ways that are not easily accessible via previously used methods. Specifically, householders were asked to interact with home technological infrastructures in ways that potentially disrupted the social norms of the home, in order to understand the nature of home computing usage and maintenance practices. For example, *all* members of a home enrolled in the study were asked to participate in a series of home technology installation, maintenance, and teaching practices (called "homework assignments"), even if they did not normally do so outside of the confines of the study. By shifting technology-related activities to other members of the home, I could better understand the reasons that households divided technical labor in the ways they did.

Additionally, these homework assignments also provided a mechanism by which participants could discuss technical troubles in terms of recent, specific incidents rather than recalling long past events. The assignments, of which there were up to 11 weekly, included networked hardware setup, media manipulation, teaching others about technology, creating web content, network configuration, sharing websites, and making technology purchasing decisions. They were chosen for several reasons. First, they are representative of the activities that householders may perform with computing infrastructures [6, 7, 9, 12, 20-22, 37, 40]. Secondly, prior research suggests that some of these activities can be difficult. Finally, I also included a subset of intentionally *easy* assignments (e.g., searching for a popular video on YouTube, shopping online, and providing opinions on how to keep kids safe online) in order to prevent undue discouragement or disengagement with the study.

Technology Probes

In combination with the breaching experiments, I also used a technology probe called *Tech Clips*. Within HCI and CSCW, there has been a growing movement to study everyday life using *probes*. Probes, in one form or another, involve the introduction of artifacts into people's lives in order to encourage reflection on existing practices and opportunities for future technologies (c.f. cultural probes [17], technology probes [23], infrastructure probes [11], and

[1] Depending on the time of year, there are a few reliable opportunities to study technical problems in-situ. Research on consumer electronics help requests in online forums [42] showed seasonal peaks in help requests based on events such as the beginning of the academic school year, post-Thanksgiving Black Friday sales, and Christmas gift-giving. A study that tracks consumers who purchase devices or give gifts of computers and electronics around these periods could be another way to approach this type of research.

problem solving probes [25]). I specifically chose to use a *technology probe*, which are software (or hardware) interventions that are intended to be used in long-term field studies. They are technologically robust (e.g., they are not mockups or partially functioning prototypes), and are instrumented to collect usage data. They are also flexible enough so that users may appropriate them in ways that the researchers do not initially anticipate. Technology probes aim to inspire and provoke discussion and ideas about future design possibilities, and much like breaching experiments, they invite reflection on the role of technology everyday life [23]

The design of *Tech Clips* was grounded in previous fieldwork [28-30] suggesting a need for tools that allow families to coordinate and keep track of technology problems they may have in their home. The software was designed to be (1) persistent (e.g., it stayed active on a computer whenever it was powered on); (2) private (available only to a select group of family/friends); (3) supporting of a variety of ways to share information (text, video, and URLs); and (4) allowing for information archival about home technology infrastructures. Householders were explicitly asked to use Tech Clips for some of the homework assignments, but also were encouraged to use it whenever and however they liked.

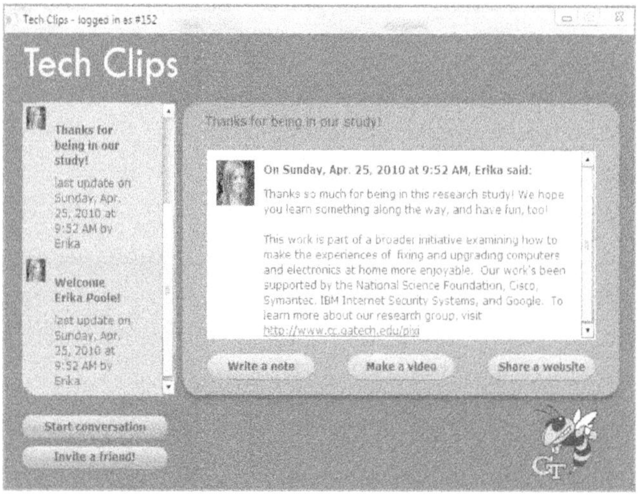

Figure 1. Tech Clips Interface. The left hand panel shows "conversation" threads. The right hand panel shows a thread of conversation. Users may do the following things with the system: write a text or video message, share a URL, browse existing content, or invite a friend to use the program. The software stays active as long as the computer is powered on

Participants

In total, ten homes participated in the study over a three-week period. Two homes piloted the study, and the remaining eight were recruited via a combination of snowball sampling and use of a market research firm. Homes were provided a gratuity of $150-200 for participating in the study, well as a bonus gratuity of up to $150 for completing 75% of the "homework assignments" in the study. Household selection criteria included the presence of two people in the home age 13 or older, a history of giving or receiving technology help over the past 12 months, and having wireless Internet within the home (in order to provide a wider number of homework assignments for families to complete; the pilot study indicated this connectivity was an important thing to have.)[2] During the study, households were also tasked with secondarily recruiting their remote family and friends to try the Tech Clips software; "remote" participants were only asked to install the Tech Clips software and use it in any way they saw fit; they did not have any other specified involvement with the study. These participants received compensation in the form of a $15 Amazon.com gift certificate if they installed the software and completed a short survey at the end of the study. In total, 12 remote participants installed the software.

Study Protocol

The study consisted of three parts: home visits, completion of a set of "homework assignments" without the researcher present, and usage of the Tech Clips software over the entire course of the study. Homes were visited four times during the study; additionally several study participants emailed and called to ask clarifying questions about their participation. Data were collected during these visits using the following techniques.

Pre and post surveys: These questionnaires collected information about demographics, technical background and hobbies, current technical help-seeking and help-giving practices, attitudes and confidence about technology, and attitudes toward helping people. The post survey included questions on Tech Clips usage, and a checklist of possible reasons that for *not* contributing to Tech Clips. This list was derived from Preece et al.'s research on lurkers in online communities, which identified reasons that people may not contribute content to an online resources [31].

Group interviews and home tour: The objective of these activities was to learn about technology acquisition, usage, maintenance, and helping practices. The interviews and home tours were conducted in the style of [5, 7, 20, 33].

Post-study individual interviews: Participants were interviewed individually at the end of the study to discuss topics that might be too sensitive to disclose in a group setting. In addition to a semi-structured interview, participants were shown a customized series of 30 mockups of products (e.g. software, customized hardware) that could be used to give and receive technology help. The mockups were customized for each home and touched on the most common forms of computer assistance outlined in prior research [29], including tools to ask non-urgent questions about technology, tools to gain assistance with hardware

[2] Upon initial interviews, I found that despite the screening criteria used for recruitment, the market research firm accidentally recruited a home that

installation and troubleshooting, and tools to assist with digital housekeeping (e.g. providing reminders to perform these activities). The reason for including these mockups was to deepen the discussion of how recording or data sharing tools besides Tech Clips may be useful for giving and receiving technical help.

Breaching Experiments: Technology Homework
Over the course of the study, each home received weekly "homework," which were activities intended to breach household technology maintenance practices. To encourage participation over the entire study period, a portion of the gratuity for participating in the study hinged upon completing at least 75% of the weekly homework assignments. For each homework assignment, I provided any necessary devices (e.g. hardware, printers, cables), a brief description of the assignment's objective, and a log sheet to document the experience. The log sheet included questions about steps taken to complete the assignment, sources of help used, perceived demands and frustration associated with the assignment, and any other comments that would be considered interesting or relevant.

The homework was intentionally designed to breach household technology installation, usage, and maintenance practices. The assignments the first week served as warm-up to acclimate participants to being in the study; weeks 2 and 3 included more assignments, as well as assignments that are more complicated. Participants were instructed to divide the labor in whatever way they saw fit. For the second week, the participants were instructed to have the *less* technically oriented adult in the home complete the assignments. This choice was made to disrupt the normal family dynamic, and to ensure that the most technologically skilled person in the home did not "take over" all of the assignments. During the third week, participants were instructed to have the *more* technically inclined person in the home complete the week's homework assignments. The assignments during the third week mirrored, but differed slightly, from those during the second week. I had anticipated that by first giving the less technically oriented person an opportunity to try out the assignments, they might be able to turn the tables and help the person who was perceived as the home technical expert. Full reports of householder experiences with study are in [27].

Tech Clips Usage
Householders were instructed to use Tech Clips however they felt best, however, to ensure at least some usage there were homework assignments that had Tech Clips usage integrated into them. Tech Clips automatically logged content created as well as usage data including opening and shutting the software, creating clips, viewing clips, and generating invitations for others to use the software. Full reports of Tech Clips usage can be found in [27].

Table 1: Participant Demographics

	Age/Gender	Describes Self As Technical	Tech Hobbyist	Perceived Responsibility In Home Tech Purchasing	Has Formal Tech Training	Occupation
H1	31-40 (F)	n	n	50%	n	adult education teacher
	31-40 (M)	y	y	50%	n	construction management
H2	23-30 (F)	n	n	50%	n	corporate trainer
	31-40 (M)	y	y	100%	y	database administrator
H3	31-40 (F)	n	n	0%	n	paralegal
	31-40 (M)	y	y	100%	y	real estate agent
	Other occupants: 2 year old son					
H4	51-60 (F)	y	n	50%	n	unemployed
	41-50 (M)	n	y	100%	n	self-employed (audio/visual work)
	Other occupants: 10 year old daughter					
H5	31-40 (F)	n	n	0%	n	stay-at-home parent
	31-40 (M)	y	n	100%	n	engineering management
	Other occupants: 4 year old daughter, 1 year old son					
H6	41-50 (F)	y	y	100%	n	self-employed (freelance writer/editor)
	41-50 (M)	y	n	50%	y	scientist - unemployed
	Other occupants: 11 year old son, 8 year old son					
H7	41-50 (F)	n	n	25%	n	business consultant
	18-22 (F)	y	n	75%	y	k-12 student
	< 18 (F)	y	y	100%	y	k-12 student
H8	23-30 (F)	n	y	75%	n	vocational student
	Other occupants: 1 year old daughter, elderly relative (declined to be in study)					
P1	51-60 (F)	n	n	0%	n	mail carrier
P2	41-50 (F)	n	n	0%	n	stay-at-home parent
	Other occupants: 7 children living at home ranging between age 2-21, husband (His job is another city. Due to frequent travel to worksite he did not participate in the study),					

Data Analysis
I base my findings on 35 transcribed interviews, 191 photographs, and copious field notes written after each home visit. Qualitative data were analyzed using affinity diagramming; these findings were triangulated against survey and software log data collected from each home.

Table 2: Example Technology Homework Assignments

Example Prompt to Participant	Genre
Take 10 photos with the digital camera we provided. Transfer the photos onto your computer. Once the photos are on your computer, share the photos online with someone you know who doesn't live with you. Be sure to share them in a way in which no one else can see the photos.	Digital media manipulation File sharing Security/file permissions
Your wireless access point (the piece of equipment that lets you use wireless internet) will let you do something called "MAC address filtering." 1.Look online or ask someone you know what MAC address filtering is. 2.Once you know what it is, change the settings on your wireless router so that it uses MAC address filtering. Even if it's difficult, remember to try to do this task yourself!	Network configuration
Have you ever wanted to print something from a laptop, but didn't want to be plugged into a printer? This week, your bag includes a printer that you can use to print from any computer in your house (without being plugged in or using a USB stick). Install this printer, and print the collage you created in Task 2 from two different computers in your house. Save your printouts in this binder	Peripheral setup Network configuration

RESULTS

This study aimed to understand broadly how software tools for archiving and sharing information related to technical issues could be useful for households. What the study unexpectedly revealed, however, was not an improvement in home technology information archiving and sharing, but a deeper understanding of *interdependence* involved in the upkeep of home infrastructures. Ultimately, one of the issues that make home computing support so troublesome for householders is a lack of individual agency in making decisions about the entry, usage, and upkeep of home devices. The decisions and actions of other people ripple through and across households in ways that influence technology maintenance practices. In the following sections, I explain how individual agency (or lack thereof) mediates the home technology ecosystem, how the blurring of work and home boundaries with respect to technologies reduces householder agency, and finally how digital housekeeping practices—no matter how well intentioned—may reduce personal agency and control over the home technology ecosystem.

The Home Technology Ecosystem

I present findings that reveal how households acquired computers, maintained technological order at home, modified equipment, and dealt with technology at the presumed end of its life cycle.

Acquisition and Upgrade Habits

Technologies within the home are acquired for a number of reasons; the most common reasons householders purchased new computers were due to planned replacements every so many years, or due to life events that dictated additions of new technologies (e.g. going to college). Who is responsible for decisions about technology purchasing varied among the homes; in some houses, computers were a jointly decided purchase because of their expensiveness. In others, occupants deferred decision making to a single person. For example, in H3 and H10, husbands selected which technologies to purchase without consulting their wives, as the wives were largely uninterested in this sort of decision-making. Intuition might tell us that householders are responsible decision making about the types of technologies that enter their home. However, a counterintuitive pattern emerged in this study: **Householders are not fully in charge of selecting devices that enter their technology ecosystem. Other people can and do implicitly make crucial technological decisions for them.**

For example, technologies entered homes due to gift giving, although gifts may have been unwanted or too advanced for the recipient. In H2, Jessica, who was comfortable using computers and electronics, but had no special interest in them, had received expensive electronics selected by her father. These gifts, while high quality, were often too advanced for the purposes she needed; most recently, she had received a professional-grade digital camera and lens set, which was far beyond her photography abilities. The only way she could make use of the camera was to let a photography guru friend borrow it. Similarly, in H6, a family with two boys under the age of 12, a grandmother (who did not live with the family) would buy the grandchildren computers and other electronics for birthdays and holidays, even though they did not ask for or necessarily want them. Within-home gift giving can also bring technologies that are not used much; Jamar, the husband of the H3 family, bought his wife Deedra a digital music player as a gift, but she refused to use it after trying it a single time and getting confused by the interface.

Acquisition of home technologies can also be opportunistic in nature. In homes where employer-provided laptops were used (e.g. H2, H7, both homes with knowledge workers that traveled as part of their jobs), the users had machines that were standard issue from their workplaces. Householders also, at times, took on cast-off technologies from someone else. Adrian of H8, a single mother and student without a regular income stream, received an old laptop from her father when he upgraded his own, and in H1, Cindy, the female occupant, took in a malfunctioning laptop that her parents thought was beyond repair. She was an adult education teacher, and brought the laptop to her school and had a technically skilled student fix it for her so that it was like new again.

Device Lifespan: Longer than Expected

Once devices enter the home, they may have a longer lifespan than expected. In the H3 and H4 homes, for example, household finances explicitly dictated when purchases occurred; given both home's reliance on irregular income sources (real estate sales and contract work respectively), the homes rarely made electronics purchases.

In other homes, occupants waited until their computer's performance degraded sufficiently enough to convince them it was time to purchase a new machine.

In the H5 and H4 homes, the householders also held a strong regard for *devices that last*. They chose to fix rather than discard items, and took time during the interviews to discuss steps they had taken to keep items in working condition when others would have thrown them away. For example, at the H5 home, the family's laptop fell off a piece of furniture onto the floor, destroying the LCD. With the help of a local relative, Steve, the father of the household refashioned the laptop into a "desktop" machine that (quite literally) was fastened into a computer desk. To enable wireless Internet on the new "desktop" machine, the helpful relative removed the wiring for the laptop's wireless antenna (which had run through the section that was destroyed) and stapled it to the bottom of the desk.

The occupants of H4, Roy and Karen, also took time to discuss the preference for owning long-lasting items extended into other areas of their lives. They showed me antique furniture they owned and loved, and Karen, who was previously married, explained how technology played a role in their engagement. As an engagement gift, Roy gave Karen a 486 computer, because he could not afford to purchase a diamond ring nicer than the one she had from her previous marriage, and "at least this way I'd have something that lasts."

Antiques and Technological Graveyards

Even after usefulness faded, householders kept old computers and electronics in the home. Although these devices may be virus laden, missing pieces, or otherwise malfunctioning, householders kept them within the house, typically in a closet-based "device graveyard." These devices were either held onto because of sentimental value (as an occupant of H3 said, "this was my baby that went all over the country with me"), held extensive digital music libraries, or had important data that one day might be transferred to a working machine. It should be noted that householders did not have any specific plans of when or how they would transfer this data; it was just thought of as something that would happen someday. Finally, in the H6 home, the mother, Jillian, intentionally kept boxes filled with old technologies stored away so that when she had grandchildren, she could show them technological heirlooms.

Blending of Work and Home Computing

In half of the homes, the boundaries of computing at home and computing at work faded. For the occupants of H2 and H7, all used computers issued by their employers in their home, and used them for leisure purposes in addition to work activities. The occupants of the H6 and H4 homes ran home-based businesses from their computers, which presented a wholly different set of challenges. The implications of lax boundaries between work and home computing has been under-investigated in prior literature of home computing environments, while prior literature notes that people use computers for telecommuting, prior work largely ignores how business computers used at home—as well as the presence of small businesses run from the home—impact home technical support practices.

More Support is Available

The benefits of having an employer-owned computer is that it typically also includes access to workplace helpdesk resources, which were viewed as more helpful than calling a public technical support line (e.g. Dell, Comcast, or Microsoft). For instance, Viola, the mother in H7, was a business consultant, and her company had a service where she could call for help. Using a piece of support software installed on the computer, the technician could remotely fix her computer. Similarly, Jessica of H2, who traveled frequently for her job as a corporate continuing education specialist, also relied heavily on calling her workplace helpdesk if she had a computer problem. Both of these employers had contracts with dedicated helpdesk companies, and Viola and Jessica found these services to be extremely satisfactory and helpful. Corporate helpdesks, in contrast to customer-service lines for *all* customers of a brand, have distinct advantages. While their workloads may be just as high, they have more homogenous clientele, and likely have repeated contact with the same clientele over time. Thus, it is more possible to build a personal relationship between the technician and customer, and to know the preferences and habits of the person seeking help. Furthermore, the machines these technicians are servicing are far more likely to have standardized configurations, as well as utilities allowing for remote access by technicians.

What is also important to note is that having access to this high quality workplace helpdesk is a safety net. Jessica and Viola could both ask questions without perceiving that they were putting an undue burden on their helpers; if their preferred helpers were busy or unavailable, then they could call the helpdesk. Furthermore, for the people *within* home who occasionally provided help (e.g. Jessica's fiancé in H2, and Viola's daughters in H7), they experienced situations where they intentionally neglected to help Viola or Jessica, because they knew that if they did not figure it out on their own, the women could choose to call the employer's helpdesk. Given the availability of a reliable, useful professional help source, a tool such as Tech Clips, which facilitated sharing technical information among informal stakeholders did not make sense given their current usage patterns. (The occupants of H7, however, did use Tech Clips in an unanticipated way: they created videos documenting how to make their favorite dinner recipes).

Being Available: Considerations for Home Businesses

In H4 and H6, the occupants relied heavily on freelance contract work to supplement their incomes. This meant they were concerned about having always-working access to email and computers in order to be in contact with existing and potential clients. In particular, for Jillian of H6, Internet connectivity was an important aspect of her business; she used the Internet to communicate with clients and deliver finished products. The need for working connectivity trumped desires for upgrading or making changes to the network; in fact, other occupants of the home were highly reluctant to change settings or install devices in order to prevent disruptions that could have a negative impact on Jillian's business. Thus in the study, any homework assignments (breaching experiments) involving a person other than Jillian changing settings to the home network were especially met with apprehension, and indeed all occupants of H6 opted out of any network-configuration related homework assignments in the study for fear of interrupting Jillian's business continuity.

(Lack of) Control Over Configurations

The availability of workplace technical support was not all positive, though. Spencer, of H2, worked in a technical position for a large firm. Although he was in a technical position at the company, he did not assume responsibility for end-user machine maintenance. Thus, if he had a problem with his employer-owned laptop, the technicians would typically re-image laptops to standard company configurations whenever problems occurred, rather than spending the time pinpointing the actual problem. Spencer found this approach to tech support frustrating, but did not have a better idea of what he could do.

The re-imaging of Spencer's machine was especially problematic during this study. On his employer-issued machine, which he also used at home, Spencer had installed network management software. When the technicians at his office re-imaged the machine several months ago, it erased the network management tool and all of its saved settings. During the course of the study, when he embarked on homework assignments (breaching experiments) asking him to change his network configuration or install new network-enabled devices, he had to find workarounds to not having the software he previously used, and could not remember some of the settings that he had stored within the network management software.

Spencer's work laptop also illustrates another issue with the use of workplace machines in home. Since Spencer could access his workplace network via VPN from home, his employer required the use of restrictive security software. This security suite prevented many types of network-enabled software, including Tech Clips, from properly functioning. When the security suite was enabled, Spencer could not create or watch video content on Tech Clips. However, Spencer, who was very technically enthusiastic, quickly figured out that the security suite was an issue, and found a temporary workaround; he could disable it in order to see videos, though he would have to remember to turn it on and off as needed.

Digital Housekeeping and Ecosystem Instability

Standalone pieces of software for network management can offer a more familiar way of interacting with configuration mechanisms, but digital housekeeping practices within households might result in further sources of difficulty. As previously mentioned, Spencer's example of laptop reimaging offers insight into the limitations of standalone software for network management. Although the IT group at his workplace had removed the software for home network management, Spencer, who was an avid computer hobbyist, was perceptive enough to figure out how to configure his router manually, though he said that it was time consuming to remember passwords and other settings that the utility had stored for him.

More broadly, Spencer's experience speaks to limitations of computer software-based utilities for network management. Across all of the homes in the study, householders performed digital housekeeping[3] that could endanger the longevity of third-party utilities for network management. Even over a period as small as three weeks, they liberally added and removed software (including Tech Clips), for reasons such as "getting back memory" on slow computers. In some cases, they even reformatted their computers (or, in the case of P2, someone else in the house chose to reformat a computer on her behalf, and did not pay attention to what pieces of software were installed). Although software packages that are used to manage network may work well at initial points of installation (c.f. reports of usability trials of the Linksys Easy Link Advisor [12]), will they be available in the long term, given digital housekeeping practices observed? Just because a piece of software is installed does *not* mean that it will be there when there are needs for reconfiguration. In particular, if a third party (another householder, a friend, a workplace IT group) reimages/reformats a machine, he or she may not know or remember to reinstall aftermarket support tools.

Unexpected "Improvements" and "Help"

Participants who were on the receiving end of family provided help, however, were not always positive about these experiences. Most vividly, Nyree of P2, a stay-at-home mother of several children explained how she did not like it that members of her family would upgrade and clean up her computer for her. When her husband and son performed routine digital housekeeping, they would inadvertently remove things such as Internet browser bookmarks or shortcuts that she used to navigate her computer and the Internet—in fact, this occurred during the span of the study. Nyree was *very* cautious of protecting herself from dangers on the web such as viruses; she was concerned of potential security risks of homework assignments (breaching experiments) even as mundane as editing Wikipedia. At the same time, she did not understand the purpose of security-related necessities such as software upgrades. Instead, she wished that systems were not upgraded to the latest-and-greatest versions—she was satisfied with older versions that she knew how to use.

Similarly, Spencer of H2 recounted a somewhat similar experience when he installed the Tech Clips software on his

[3] Householders initiated these housekeeping practices. This housekeeping was *not* requested by the researcher as part of study "homework."

mother's computer during the study. His mother did not understand what the software was for, and every time her computer booted, Tech Clips would start when Windows booted up. She became angry and frustrated with this situation; she found the software popping up upon booting to be annoying, and demanded that Spencer remove it after a couple of days. The perspectives of Spencer's mom and Nyree suggest that forcing things to make one's computing experience better—such as automatically upgrading software or providing new ways to give and receive help—may not work well. Instead, those who would benefit from software systems for the provision of technical help may, in some way or another, be persuaded that these systems will be of use to them. Similarly, it also suggests that people who are *providing* technical help may be well served by both understanding and respecting the needs and preferences of people who do not share the same technical enthusiasm or expertise they do.

DISCUSSION AND CONCLUSION

This paper presented results of a study in which homes interacted with new and existing information technologies in their home, as well as a customized piece of software called Tech Clips, which was intended for facilitating informal technical support interactions. What this study uncovered was not a one-size-fits-all solution to technical advice sharing in residential settings; instead, what emerged from my work was a rich description of how householders acquire devices, maintain and configure them over time, and seek help when problems occur.

Perhaps one of the most striking findings of this study—revealed at multiple points throughout the study, including Tech Clips usage, participation in the homework assignments (breaching experiments), and interviews—is how lack of individual agency is one of the main sources of ongoing technological difficulty in homes. Changes made by one person can ripple out to a number of stakeholders within the home. Similarly, fears of the impact of changes can limit experimentation, playfulness, or enjoyment of engaging with home technology infrastructures. Without addressing this issue, resolving user experience issues with home computing maintenance remains a largely intractable problem.

Crabtree has called for breaching experiments in the design of future ubiquitous computing systems [8]. Similarly, Baumer and Silberman [2] argue for more reflective discussions about system failures when studying user experience. This study touched on both of these issues. Tech Clips, while envisioned as a tool for recording and archiving information that could be used to give and receive home technology help, was not used as intended by the homes in the study, yet the struggles encountered with using Tech Clips revealed information about interdependence and lack of agency in home computing infrastructure maintenance. In closing, I argue that for the study of infrastructures that support home computing, failed systems and breaching experiments should not be swept under the rug, but rather should be considered as an asset and an indispensable part of a researcher's toolbox for understanding existing social norms and practices surrounding technology.

ACKNOWLEDGMENTS

Thank you to Jill Dimond and Lawrence Jarvis for assistance with site visits, and Keith Edwards and Beth Mynatt for providing equipment and material support for the study. An NSF Graduate Research Fellowship supported the author at the time of the study.

REFERENCES

1. Baillie, L. and Benyon, D. Place and Technology in the Home. *Computer Supported Cooperative Work (CSCW)*, 17, 2, 2008, 227-256.
2. Baumer, E. P. S. and Silberman, M. S. When the Implication Is Not to Design (Technology). In *Proc. ACM CHI 2011*, Vancouver, BC, Canada, 2011.
3. Beckmann, C., Consolvo, S. and Lamarca, A. Some Assembly Required: Supporting End-User Sensor Installation in Domestic Ubiquitous Computing Environments. In *Proc. UbiComp 2004*, 2004, 107-124.
4. Bly, S., Schilit, B., Mcdonald, D. W., Rosario, B. and Saint-Hilaire, Y. Broken Expectations in the Digital Home. In *Proc. ACM CHI 2006 Extended Abstracts*, Montreal, Quebec, Canada, 2006, 568-573.
5. Blythe, M. and Monk, A. Notes Towards an Ethnography of Domestic Technology. In *Proc. ACM DIS 2002*, London, England, 2002, 277-281.
6. Brush, A. and Inkpen, K. Yours, Mine and Ours? Sharing and Use of Technology in Domestic Environments. In *Proc. UbiComp 2007*, 2007, 109-126.
7. Chetty, M., Sung, J.-Y. and Grinter, R. E. How Smart Homes Learn: The Evolution of the Networked Home and Household. In *Proc. Ubicomp 2007*, Innsbruck, Austria, 2007, 127-144.
8. Crabtree, A. Design in the Absence of Practice: Breaching Experiments. In *Proc. ACM DIS 2004*, Cambridge, MA, USA, 2004.
9. Crabtree, A. and Rodden, T. Domestic Routines and Design for the Home. *Computer Supported Cooperative Work (CSCW)*, 13, 2, 2004, 191-220.
10. Dimond, J. P., Poole, E. S. and Yardi, S. The Effects of Life Disruptions on Home Technology Routines. In *Proc. ACM GROUP 2010*, Sanibel Island, Florida, USA, 2010, 85-88.
11. Dorner, C., Hess, J. and Pipek, V. Fostering User-Developer Collaboration with Infrastructure Probes. In *Proc. Proceedings of the 2008 international workshop on Cooperative and human aspects of software engineering*, Leipzig, Germany, 2008.
12. Elmore, B., Ivaturi, S. and Hamilton, S. Designing Software for Consumers to Easily Set up a Secure Home Network. In *Proc. Conference on Human Factors in Computing Systems*, San Jose, CA, USA, 2007, 1735-1740.

13. Flanagan, J. C. The Critical Incident Technique. *Psychological Bulletin*, 51, 4, 1954, 327.
14. Franzke, M. and Mcclard, A. Winona Gets Wired: Technical Difficulties in the Home. *Communications of the ACM*, 39, 12, 1996, 64-66.
15. Garfinkel, H. *Studies in Ethnomethodology*. Blackwell, Malden, 1967.
16. Gasser, L. The Integration of Computing and Routine Work. *ACM Trans. Inf. Syst.*, 4, 3, 1986, 205-225.
17. Gaver, B., Dunne, T. and Pacenti, E. Design: Cultural Probes. *interactions*, 6, 1, 1999, 21-29.
18. Gaver, W. The Video Window: My Life with a Ludic System. *Personal Ubiquitous Comput.*, 10, 2-3, 2006, 60-65.
19. Grinter, R. E., Edwards, W. K., Chetty, M., Poole, E. S., Sung, J.-Y., Yang, J., Crabtree, A., Tolmie, P., Rodden, T., Greenhalgh, C. and Benford, S. The Ins and Outs of Home Networking: The Case for Useful and Usable Domestic Networking. *ACM Trans. Comput.-Hum. Interact.*, 16, 2, 2009, 1-28.
20. Grinter, R. E., Edwards, W. K., Newman, M. W. and Ducheneaut, N. The Work to Make a Home Network Work. In *Proc. ECSCW 2005*, Paris, France, 2005, 469-488.
21. Horrigan, J. M. Broadband Adoption and Use in America. *Federal Communications Commission. OBI Working Paper Series No. 1*2010.
22. Horrigan, J. M. and Jones, S. When Technology Fails. *Pew Internet & American Life Project*2008.
23. Hutchinson, H., Mackay, W., Westerlund, B., Bederson, B. B., Druin, A., Plaisant, C., Beaudouin-Lafon, M., Conversy, S., Evans, H., Hansen, H., Roussel, N. and Eiderbäck, B. Technology Probes: Inspiring Design for and with Families. In *Proc. ACM CHI 2003*, Ft. Lauderdale, Florida, USA, 2003, 17-24.
24. Kiesler, S., Zdaniuk, B., Lundmark, V. and Kraut, R. Troubles with the Internet: The Dynamics of Help at Home. *Hum.-Comput. Interact.*, 15, 4, 2000, 323-351.
25. Mcdonald, D. W., Smith, K. A. and Karlova, N. Problem Solving Probes: A Method for Discovering Conceptual Disconnects with Digital Living Technologies. In *Proc. ACM CSCW 2008 Designing for Families Workshop* San Diego, CA, 2008.
26. Newman, M., Elliott, A. and Smith, T. Providing an Integrated User Experience of Networked Media, Devices, and Services through End-User Composition. In *Proc. Pervasive Computing*, 2008, 213-227.
27. Poole, E. S. *Supporting Advice Sharing for Technical Problems in Residential Settings*. PhD Thesis, Georgia Institute of Technology, Atlanta, GA, USA, 2010.
28. Poole, E. S., Chetty, M., Grinter, R. E. and Edwards, W. K. More Than Meets the Eye: Transforming the User Experience of Home Network Management. In *Proc. ACM DIS 2008*, Cape Town, South Africa, 2008, 455-464.
29. Poole, E. S., Chetty, M., Morgan, T., Grinter, R. E. and Edwards, W. K. Computer Help at Home: Methods and Motivations for Informal Technical Support. In *Proc. ACM CHI 2009*, Boston, MA, USA, 2009, 739-748.
30. Poole, E. S., Edwards, W. K. and Jarvis, L. The Home Network as a Socio-Technical System: Understanding the Challenges of Remote Home Network Problem Diagnosis. *Comput. Supported Coop. Work*, 18, 2-3, 2009, 277-299.
31. Preece, J., Nonnecke, B. and Andrews, D. The Top Five Reasons for Lurking: Improving Community Experiences for Everyone. *Computers in Human Behavior*, 20, 2, 2004, 201-223.
32. Rode, J., Toye, E. and Blackwell, A. The Fuzzy Felt Ethnography—Understanding the Programming Patterns of Domestic Appliances. *Personal and Ubiquitous Computing*, 8, 3, 2004, 161-176.
33. Rode, J. A. The Roles That Make the Domestic Work. In *Proc. ACM CSCW 2010*, Savannah, Georgia, USA, 2010, 381-390.
34. Strauss, A. Work and the Division of Labor. *Sociological Quarterly*, 26, 1, 1985, 1-19.
35. Tolmie, P. and Crabtree, A. Deploying Research Technology in the Home. In *Proc. ACM CSCW 2008*, San Diego, CA, USA, 2008.
36. Tolmie, P., Crabtree, A., Egglestone, S., Humble, J., Greenhalgh, C. and Rodden, T. Digital Plumbing: The Mundane Work of Deploying Ubicomp in the Home. *Personal Ubiquitous Comput.*, 14, 3, 2010, 181-196.
37. Tolmie, P., Crabtree, A., Rodden, T., Greenhalgh, C. and Benford, S. Making the Home Network at Home: Digital Housekeeping. In *Proc. ECSCW 2007*, 2007, 331-350.
38. Tullio, J., Dey, A. K., Chalecki, J. and Fogarty, J. How It Works: A Field Study of Non-Technical Users Interacting with an Intelligent System. In *Proc. ACM CHI 2007*, San Jose, California, USA, 2007, 31-40.
39. Venkatesh, A. Computers and Other Interactive Technologies for the Home. *Communications of the ACM*, 39, 12, 1996, 47-54.
40. Woodruff, A., Anderson, K., Mainwaring, S. D. and Aipperspach, R. Portable, but Not Mobile: A Study of Wireless Laptops in the Home. In *Proc. Pervasive Computing*, Toronto, Canada, 2007, 216-233.
41. Yang, J., Edwards, W. K. and Haslem, D. Eden: Supporting Home Network Management through Interactive Visual Tools. In *Proc. Proceedings of the 23nd annual ACM symposium on User interface software and technology*, New York, New York, USA, 2010, 109-118.
42. Yardi, S. and Poole, E. S. Please Help!: Patterns of Personalization in an Online Tech Support Board. In *Proc. Communities & Technologies 2009*, University Park, PA, USA, 2009, 285-294.

Boundary Regulation in Social Media

Fred Stutzman
H. John Heinz III College
Carnegie Mellon University
Pittsburgh, PA
fred@fredstutzman.com

Woodrow Hartzog
Cumberland School of Law
Samford University
Birmingham, AL
whartzog@samford.edu

ABSTRACT
The management of group context in socially mediating technologies is an important challenge for the design community. To better understand how users manage group context, we explored the practice of multiple profile management in social media. In doing so, we observed creative and opportunistic strategies for group context management. We found that multiple profile maintenance is motivated by four factors: privacy, identity, utility, and propriety. Drawing on these motives, we observe a continuum of boundary regulation behaviors: pseudonymity, practical obscurity, and transparent separation. Based on these findings, we encourage designers of group context management systems to more broadly consider motives and practices of group separations in social media. Group context management systems should be privacy-enhancing, but a singular focus on privacy overlooks a range of other group context management practices.

Author Keywords
Privacy, social media, qualitative research

ACM Classification Keywords
H5.m. Information interfaces and presentation (e.g., HCI): Miscellaneous.

INTRODUCTION
In recent years, social media has been adopted by increasingly diverse populations in the United States [21]. Once the domain of the characteristically young, technical elite, social media has achieved mass adoption. As participation in social media diversifies, one particular challenge that arises is the management of group context [19]. As a result of the growth of social media, it is now common for users to interact with a wide range of social groups, such as family members, coworkers, and long-lost contacts [20]. Users are challenged to balance the composition and volume of their disclosures to these wide-ranging groups of differing social composition. To address the challenges of multiple group contexts, users of social media employ a range of strategies, including self-censorship, limitation of group access, or the utilization of technical controls such as privacy settings and access control lists [19, 29].

In the design community, the management of multiple groups in social media is often approached through a lens of privacy, where the intended outcome of a design intervention is an effective private segmentation of social media content by group [2, 5, 11, 13, 17, 28, 33]. Clearly, privacy is a motivation for the management of groups in social media, but as this research evidences, it is not the only motive. By starting with privacy, more functional or mundane needs for group separations may be overlooked in the design of social media group management systems. In this research, we draw on the experiences of individuals that have opportunistically created and employed strategies for group management in social media, identifying a range of motives and methods for the management of groups in social media.

As part of a study exploring the challenges of group management in social media, twenty individuals that maintained multiple profiles on a social media site were interviewed. This baseline criterion was established to recruit individuals that had, at a minimum, actively created segmentation within a social media site that produced differential group audiences. We did not assume motives or outcomes for this criterion. Using a mixture of inductive and deductive analysis, following a grounded approach [30], we explored participant motives for the creation of this explicit group separation. In addition to exploring the methods and motives of the group separations through multiple profile maintenance (MPM), we examined relevant social groups influencing the decision to employ MPM, we explored the outcomes of MPM, and we gauged participant self-evaluation of efficacy and burden of MPM.

Using MPM as an *ex ante* lens through which group separations in social media can be studied, we are unburdened by the assumption of a privacy motive. To this extent, our framing and analysis is guided by theories of boundary regulation, which locate the management of interpersonal disclosure within a framework of optimization [4, 27]. With this frame, we are able to explore how participant group regulation strategies most effectively produce a desired level of disclosure, and how this desired level of disclosure is constructed in relation to the group, the context, and the affordance of the site.

In our analysis, we first identify four motives for group boundary regulation through MPM in social media. These are: privacy, identity, utility, and propriety, which are explicated in depth. We then observe a range of tactics, both explicit and implicit, employed by our interviewees to manage group boundaries in social media. The first tactic is the simple creation of more than one profile on a social media site, to have separate persona within a single site. The second tactic is the use of privacy settings to present a single persona within a single site differently to multiple audiences. The third tactic involves the segmentation of audiences between social media sites, or a systematic limiting of access to certain persona based on contextual setting. We then place these tactics on a continuum of boundary-regulating behaviors that can be addressed in both design and policy.

RELATED WORK

This study examines multiple profile maintenance in the larger context of social media, though a majority of the documented behavior occurred in social network sites. A social network site, as defined by boyd and Ellison [7], has three characteristic features. A social network site allows a user to 1) create a representational profile, 2) articulate their connections in the site, and 3) traverse those connections. As more people adopt social network sites, individuals may find that their list of "friends" covers a broader range of group contexts [e.g., 20, 21], leading to the potentially problematic merging of group contexts. As group contexts merge in social media, individuals must decide how they want to manage disclosure choices with respect to these multiple contexts.

Group Context in Social Network Sites

Researchers have identified a number of strategies individuals use to manage the co-occurrence of multiple social contexts in social network sites. Lampinen et al. [19] identified two meta-strategies for the management of multiple group contexts in a social network site. A user may adopt behavioral strategies, including *division of the platform*, *channel selection*, and *self-censorship*. Alternately, a user may adopt mental strategies, such as the *creation of inclusive identities*, *trusting*, and *being more responsible with content creation* [19, p. 287]. Skeels and Grudin [29], in a situated analysis of social network sites in the workplace, found that tensions exist in the management of multiple social group boundaries. Participants indicated *use of privacy settings*, *content control*, and a desire to *maintain multiple networks* as management strategies [19, pp. 100-101]. These tensions are manifest in a study by DiMicco and Millen [9], in which genres of social network profiles are identified in relation to disclosure in the professional context. Individuals with more business-centric profiles had less personally-engaged profiles than those the authors termed "*Reliving the college days.*"

Information disclosure in social network sites has been extensively studied, with studies often highlighting the disconnect between stated privacy goals and information sharing behavior [1, 3, 8]. Recent work indicates increased awareness of privacy implications of social network site use, as well as increased management of disclosure behaviors [18, 24, 31]. Strategies for management of disclosure include increased use of social network site privacy features, as well as editing of the profile to portray a more acceptable image [18]. These changes in privacy behavior have co-occurred with the growth of popularity of social network sites, a potential reaction to the merging of group contexts in the sites.

According to research by the Pew Internet and American Life Foundation, approximately 57% of adult social network site users have more than one social media profile. Of this group, 17% maintain more than one profile on a single site [20, p. 8]. Reasons for multiple profile management are both functional, with 24% of respondents of the Pew study indicating "*My friends use many different websites so I have more than one profile to stay in touch with them*" and privacy-enhancing, with 19% responding "*Some profiles are professional, others personal*" [20, p. 8]. We do not claim that multiple profile creation (on a single site) is a broad-based trend. Rather, we see this as an emergent phenomenon, whose population is an identifiable group that is likely dealing with the challenges of group context management.

Design Solutions for Group Context Management

The management of group context in socially mediating technologies is an important challenge for the design community [12]. As Farnham and Churchill [12, p. 359] note, a "problematic trend in social media design is the assumption that a single unified user identity is appropriate and sufficient." Technological affordance generally requires that individuals be identified and treated as a unified self, which does not map particularly well onto social practice. One needs only to look to the work of Goffman [15] to understand the essential role selective management of disclosure plays in everyday life: our presentations of self are not the same in all contexts, but are adaptive to circumstance.

In addition to inherent social challenges, the complexities of a unified presentation of self may adversely affect social media business practices. If individuals withdraw and restrict sharing due to the complexities of group context, the end result may be less content shared; as peer-produced content is the engine of social media, designers have clear incentives to address this problem. Indeed, the design community (broadly understood) has responded to this challenge, and put forth a range of potential solutions for the management of group context. We classify these solutions as *recommenders*, *awareness interfaces*, and *alternative structures*.

Recommenders are automated systems that predict group configurations based on graph-theoretic affiliation parameters [e.g., 2, 17, 35; more generally see 32]. These systems automatically predict and configure "friend lists" that foster differential sharing. Awareness interfaces are a class of privacy-enhancing technology that leverage explicit and implicit interaction to make a user aware of an audience [e.g., 10, 11, 22, 26, 33]. These systems play an important role in reducing both the dimensionality and complexity of disclosure rule configuration in a social network site. Finally, alternative structures represent a more general rethinking of the unified model of identity in social network sites [e.g., 5, 13, 16, 28].

The common trait that unifies these solutions is that they are designed for privacy enhancement. Clearly, privacy enhancement is a worthwhile goal, one that has broad benefit. However, privacy may not be the only goal of individuals managing context in social media, and systems of group context management that are designed for privacy may not completely address the needs of users. Consider an individual that wishes to keep family and co-workers separate on a social network site for the simple reason that they do not want to bore family members with posts about work. This situation, one that is not uncommon, is not motivated by privacy in a traditional sense, but out of propriety. As social media expands, and the populations that adopt social media diversify, we must consider the range of motivations for the management of context, realizing that a privacy-centric approach to design may improperly bias solutions.

Group Context Management as Boundary Regulation

To address the challenge of group context in social media, we employ Altman's framework of boundary regulation. This framework, which is increasingly applied in HCI to address the challenges of disclosure management in ubiquitous and mediated social environments, focuses on the "selective control of access to the self" [4, p. 24]. While boundary regulation is, at its essence, a privacy theory, its applicability in HCI is a function of its adaptability. By adapting our desired levels of disclosure to context, Altman argues that privacy, and disclosure regulation is an ongoing, bi-directional, optimizing process. As individuals move through contexts, they perceive stimuli. Based on the individual's goals in the context, boundaries of communication are opened or closed in response to the stimuli. Because regulation is an imprecise state, Altman specifies that individuals continually manage their boundaries with regards to optimizing their privacy or disclosure goals.

Palen and Dourish [25] apply Altman's boundary regulation theory to technologically-mediated social settings, concluding that "privacy management is a dynamic response to circumstance rather than a static enforcement of rules; that it is defined by a set of tensions between competing needs; and that technology can have many impacts, by way of disrupting boundaries, spanning them, establishing new ones, etc." [25, p. 135]. As Nippert-Eng [23] demonstrates, increased socio-technical mediation challenges individuals to define and manage new boundaries; in this we see an extension of the concept of "privacy" beyond disclosure regulation in systems, to active separation or repression of different spheres of life. This socio-technical disclosure management requires ongoing awareness to social context and technological affordance.

Drawing on the theoretical perspective of privacy as boundary management specified by Altman [4], and extended by Palen and Dourish [25], this study explores the use of multiple profiles in social media as a boundary regulation practice. This particular practice was first documented by boyd [6] as the "mirror network" concept, in which the individual maintains two or more discrete identities on a single social media site. boyd describes mirror networks as a structural approach to privacy management, in which individuals create a highly sanitized version of the profile and connect these mirror profiles to each other. The linkage between these profiles creates the impression of authenticity.

Through the lens of Altman, multiple profiles represent an explicit boundary, through which communicative access is granted selectively to specific aspects of an individual's persona. Therefore, multiple profiles serve as locations for observable boundary regulation, which allow an applied analysis of Altman and colleagues' theories of privacy. Between the two (or more) profiles, individuals decide their goals for disclosure, regulate their communicants, and derive the optimizing process with regard to privacy and disclosure goals. With this theoretically specified process in mind, our goal is to explore the motivations and practice of MPM as a boundary regulation strategy. In doing so, we are able to explicate the range of motivations for such a practice, and provide evidence for the design of effective group context management technologies.

THE STUDY

This work was conducted as part of a study exploring the practice of group management in social media. In this study, we interviewed individuals that engaged in the maintenance of multiple profiles in social media, exploring their motives for, and the outcomes of, the use of multiple profile maintenance as an explicit group management strategy.

Methodology

For this study, we interviewed twenty individuals that engage in MPM. We solicited interviews through postings to listserves, blogs and social network sites. Second-stage referrals by participants also resulted in successful recruitment. Individuals were required to meet three criteria for participation in the study. First, we required that participants had, at one point, employed multiple profiles on a social media site. The mechanics of this behavior vary between sites, so we objectively required that participants had maintained more than one identity (i.e., login) on a single site. Notably, some sites, such as Facebook, forbid the practice of MPM; we interviewed subjects that employed MPM on sites where the practice was disallowed, and on sites where the practice is permitted; we did not notice a substantive difference between participants based on MPM permissibility. Second, participants were required to have adopted MPM within the last two years. This criterion was established to increase incidental recall—the participant's recollection of the process regarding the creation and use of multiple profiles. Third, participants were required to be age 24 or older. We believe that the motivations for MPM vary based on stage in the life course, and we explicitly wanted to study the behavior of individuals later in the life course than a college population (studies of social media frequently focus on college populations). We acknowledge that our population size and research methodology does not allow generalization. Still, we purposefully recruited a diverse sample (Table 1) to maximize variation within our data.

Interviews were conducted in-person or via phone, depending on the participant's preference. The researchers jointly conducted all interviews, which lasted between fifty minutes and one hour and twenty minutes (the average was approximately one hour). The interviews were audio recorded; these recordings, in addition to the researchers' field notes and diagrams, comprise the analytic data set. On completion of the interviews, participants were compensated with a ten-dollar gift certificate. We approached the interviews and analysis from both an inductive and deductive standpoint [30]; our interview questions were derived from review of the literature and extant theoretical models of boundary regulation. The interviews were semi-structured, with participants being asked a standard block of questions developed by the researchers. In the interviews, participants were engaged around three core themes: social media self-efficacy, privacy attitudes, and experiences with boundary regulation. The majority of interviews were spent discussing the individual's perception of boundary regulation via MPM; future work may explore audience perceptions of the regulation process. Upon completion of the interviews, the researchers transcribed the recordings, and jointly conducted analysis.

The audio transcription and field notes were imported into Atlas.Ti 6.0, and codes were developed following both an inductive and deductive approach. Our theoretical orientation towards boundary regulation elicited deductive codes for context, separation techniques, and goals of the separation process. Our inductive coding of the transcripts led to the development of codes for audience type, motivation, and thematic types of boundary regulation in social media. In all cases, the codes were refined iteratively between the researchers, and axial coding was employed to identify the major themes of the project, following the grounded theory approach [14].

Identifier	Gender	Age	Profession
F1	F	49	Journalist
F2	F	45	Marketer
F3	F	26	Admissions Counselor
F4	F	32	Lawyer
F5	F	47	Systems Analyst
F6	F	28	Fundraising
F7	F	47	Business Analyst
F8	F	35	Librarian
F9	F	30	Marketing Director
F10	F	29	Office Manager
F11	F	37	University Administrator
F12	F	27	Logistics Expert
M1	M	34	Business Development
M2	M	39	Professor
M3	M	32	Non-profit Director
M4	M	36	Instructional Technologist
M5	M	43	IT Strategist
M6	M	35	Graphic Designer
M7	M	57	Writer
M8	M	29	Entertainer

Table 1. Study participants.

FINDINGS

In the paper, we report our findings in the following order. First, we introduce a typology of boundary regulation via multiple profile maintenance in social media derived from the interviews. We then explicate the typology, describing the interviewees' motivations and tactics for boundary regulation in social media through MPM. We extend this discussion with a reflection on how these findings inform both theory and our evolving understanding of disclosure regulation in social media. We conclude the research with a discussion of how boundary regulation can be supported in the design of group context management systems.

Typology of Boundary Regulation

Figure 1 provides a visual overview of the continuum of practices identified. We observed that individuals crafted a set of strategies, within their technological limits and the limits of the site, to accomplish their disclosure regulation goals through MPM. We place these strategies on a continuum that reflects the state of identification between profiles; this continuum ranges from hidden to public. By regulating boundaries by *site* and *linkage*, and adjusting the type and volume of content shared at each profile, individuals were able to effectively optimize disclosure through MPM. These goals are reflective of a range of motivations and tactics, where the individual bases disclosure goals on knowledge of context, response to stimuli, and goals. Notably, privacy features into some, but not all of the formulations we observed. By considering the range of motives and methods for group boundary regulation, designers of group management technologies may be able to more effectively address the needs of social media users.

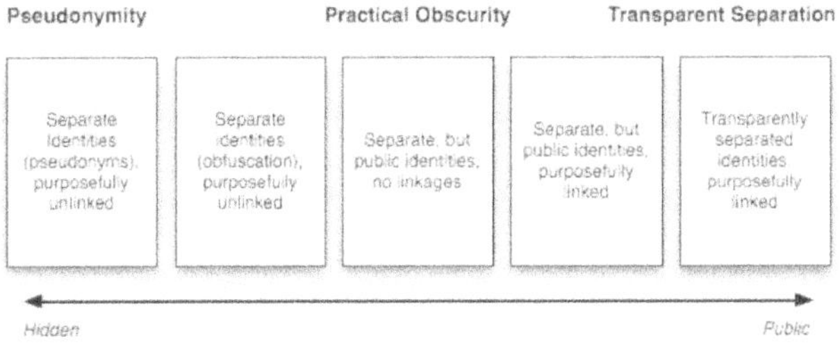

Figure 1. Processes and components of boundary regulation through multiple profiles in social media.

The most concealed profiles were *pseudonymous*. These profiles are fully disassociated from personally identifiable information, they are not linked to the individual's identity or other profiles on social media sites, and they rely exclusively on a pseudonym or obscure name variant for identification purposes. F1, a journalist, employed a pseudonymous account where she could "give a political opinion of something."

On the other end of the continuum, the least concealed profiles were *transparent separations* that made no attempts to obscure either the real identity of the user or any other profiles the user maintained. Often, transparent separations were employed for practical purposes, as the individual had no privacy motives to separate a subset of their profiles. F12, who maintains five Twitter accounts (in addition to other social media accounts), keeps one private, but the other four are transparently separated. She states that the four public accounts are "for everyone, and the only one that is private is my personal one."

The majority of individuals we interviewed employed *practical obscurity*. A profile in a state of practical obscurity is not completely concealed, but it is obscured to the point that the individual felt their "alt" profile could not be located without at least some substantial investment of time or resolve. Practical obscurity can be achieved through a number of means including modification of privacy settings, manipulation of search engines, pseudonymity, and technological separation. F5, a systems analyst, does not use privacy settings on her profile. Instead, she signs her profile with an obscure variant of her name. Only members of her in-group are given access to the name, which is the key referent to the profile; one could not find it by simply searching for her name. It is possible that out-group observers could discover her profile through other means, but F5 feels comfortable her profile is reasonably obscure.

The three states of our typology—pseudonymity, practical obscurity, and transparent separations—are placed on a continuum (Figure 1) as there are not clear-cut determinations between states. Rather, individuals flexibly managed the states of their profiles in response to communication and disclosure goals. To better understand this process that constitutes the typology, we explore the motivations and methods for boundary regulation via MPM.

Motives for Boundary Regulation

We were interested in why individuals engaged in MPM in social media. In our analysis of the creation of multiple profiles on a single social media site, we identified four primary motives. These were: privacy, identity, utility, and propriety (Table 2). In the following section we explore each motive separately. We preface this discussion by noting that these motives are not discrete: they often cross-cut, with many respondents indicating one or more motives in their choice to employ multiple profiles. These motives are not static: an individual's motivations for MPM evolve as time and circumstance change.

Motive One: Privacy

Unsurprisingly, the first motive for MPM was privacy. For the purpose of this paper, the term privacy covers the penumbra of interests effectuated by selective control of access to the self or temporary withdrawal from the public domain as described by Altman [4] and Westin [34]. Because this understanding of privacy implies a continuum of information regulation practices, we identified a number of sub-motivations. The primary sub-motivation was an individuals' desire to selectively control their own disclosures. F5, a systems analyst, identified MPM as a way to safeguard disclosure. In utilizing multiple profiles, F5 is able to socialize online with peers without fear of her behavior negatively affecting her professional life:

"I don't want it to be so divorced from who I am. It's not a total departure from what I think my spirit is or who I am. But it's something that's just a little safe, you know? I want to be able to be real on Facebook without having a lot of repercussions professionally..."

As the quote from F5 illustrates, MPM allows individuals to make disclosures to audiences they trust, without fear of repercussion. In our study, the fear of repercussion was primarily directed towards the individual's professional career. That is, individuals wished to make their disclosures private as to not negatively affect their careers. Other participants linked boundary regulation to physical and emotional safety sub-motives. F1, a journalist who maintains a gender-neutral second profile, was very conscious of the link between privacy and safety. By creating a secondary public persona devoid of gender identifiers, F1 is able to communicate with less fear of repercussions to physical and emotional safety:

"I guess as a woman you kind of want to be gender neutral because it used to be that you had to be careful going online, because if you were a woman you would be the subject of all kinds of either stalking or spamming or, just,

Motive	Outcome
Privacy	Selective withdrawal of access to the self or disclosure
Identity	Management of the self in eyes of multiple audiences
Utility	Optimizing disclosure for appropriate circumstances
Propriety	Normative conformity to prevailing customs and usages

Table 2. Motivations for MPM.

you know, its just not pleasant"

In another segment of the interview, F1 identified the value of an information sparse secondary profile as it does not leak information that can be exploited by malicious others, a discrete privacy-enhancing activity. F1 cites the example of individuals that share information about their real-time physical location:

"I knew some young kids who tweeted 'I'm going to lunch at so and so' and they came back to their apartment and they had been robbed... I assume they have an alarm system or an attack dog or neighbor checking out their house."

Another privacy-related sub-motivation for MPM was the creation of a space for disclosures participants considered confidential. F6, an academic fundraiser, stated that when she first created her personal profile:

"My friend told me when people apply for jobs [potential employers are] searching your MySpace and your Facebook to see what you're like. And I said 'Now, wow, I never thought about that.'"

In F6's case, we observe a withdrawal of information from the public sphere to private, inclusive spheres through MPM. In doing so, the participant is protected, and enabled to share with a known audience. M2, an educator, describes his communication with trusted friends on a private profile:

"More or less those were people to whom I was already presenting myself in other offline or online contexts. It really didn't feel as though I were taking a giant step in terms of self disclosure or awareness of myself as somebody in a social context. "

We found that the privacy benefits of maintaining at least one pseudonymous profile are twofold. Pseudonymity both conceals information and encourages disclosure. Functioning as a shield, pseudonymity protects a user's personally identifiable information such as name, date of birth, address or contact information. As a result of the disassociation with the primary identity, individuals can disclose with less reservation, knowing that the pseudonymous profile is "invisible" to search engine queries on the individual's name, for example. M4, an instructional technologist, describes the use of pseudonymity as a shield:

"I've got [a religious thoughts] page where I'm anonymous. My wife and I blog there. I don't want to be seen as 'Here's some spiritual guidance. Look to us for spiritual guidance.' Which is really not what we're trying to do. We don't want to be perceived as that. So we just don't say anything on that blog about who we are."

Motive Two: Identity Management

The second motive for MPM we identified was identity management, particularly the management of identity in the eyes of others. An example of an identity-based motive for MPM is to proactively create distinct professional and personal identities. F1, a journalist, created a separate professional identity using her real name:

"So that I could use that to be all about business, and to be all about not expressing an opinion on a news story or whatever else I would send out a link to. While I kept my [pseudonymous] profile, because that could be a place where I could have opinions, where I could express personal stuff."

Referring to her pseudonymous profile in the third-person, F1 stated that with a pseudonymous Twitter profile "you can be whatever you want." F2, a marketer, explored the tension between the boundaries in her personal and professional life, identifying context-appropriate spaces for socialization:

"On LinkedIn, I'm a little more professional... I tend to be little more professional with Facebook. I have realized my family is on there, and who I work with. I mean, it's personal, it's business, it's family. When I use Twitter for myself, I'm just me. There's no holds barred. Same with my blog. It's just me."

Notably, F2 employs a strategy of MPM but also considers boundary regulation through a set of by-site separations of context. It is important to note that while all participants employed MPM, MPM was just a part of their overall group boundary regulation strategy. M4, for example, describes how the dynamics of personal and professional identity separation can shift over time. Of Facebook, he states:

"I've had Facebook long before everyone else started using it of course. But I used it first as a professional networking thing, along with other instructional technologists. But then as soon as all my family and friends started getting on there, I started deleting all my professional networking people because it became more of a personal space and less of a professional space."

Consistent with the specification of Altman [4], the separation of identity appears to be an ongoing, optimizing process. Individuals that maintain separate spaces for separate parts of their identity must maintain an awareness of the social dynamics of the space. As the dynamics of the space change, individuals may re-craft or move identities to separate spaces. On the other hand, some individuals create identities in separated spaces that are future-proofed against context merging. Many individuals echoed the statement of F10, an educator and administrator:

"I am consciously aware of how I craft what I write. I don't use swear words... I was trying to keep that in the back of my head when posting."

Motive Three: Utility

The utility and effectiveness of MPM in social media appeared to draw individuals to this boundary regulation strategy. By maintaining division between profiles, participants were able to more effectively promote, collaborate or coordinate their activities in social media. This motive is particularly notable as it is not driven by, or associated with, privacy needs. For example, F2, the marketer, used one of her profiles to promote a restaurant that serves as a meeting place for users of social media. F6, an academic fundraiser, uses one of her MySpace profiles to promote her employer, a school:

"I'm not associated with it... I'm not even a friend because it was set up just for alumni. Since I don't hold a degree it doesn't make sense for me to be a friend."

By having profiles separate from her personal profile, F6 is able to use Myspace and Facebook accounts as part of her job without reflecting on or clouding her personal identity. She also notes that: "Being able to control MySpace really lets me target the audience."

Multiple profiles allow individuals to cater to their audience through segmentation based on the nature and quantity of disclosure. F1 appreciated that one of her profiles allowed her to roam to any topic she chose, posting as often as she liked, whereas her other profile was reserved for specific posts related to journalism. She enjoyed not having to apologize for her off topic posts. She relayed the experience of a woman she was following on Twitter:

"Who I think was sending notes all about gardens and garden sharing. But when all the Iran stuff came up, she just went off on that for probably two weeks. And apologized to her followers about, you know 'I'm sorry. I normally tweet about this, but, right now, I want to tweet about that.'"

F12, a planning expert, uses multiple profiles to segment her volume of information disclosure:

"If somebody on my personal Twitter says 'oh my gosh you are inundating me with too many updates,' I will tell them that they can follow my public profile that I update substantially less."

Notably, F12 also uses the profiles to segment her information consumption by logging in to the different profiles to access different "streams" of information.

F12 was aware that some of her readers might "feel as if they have to read everything" she posts, and that she could shepherd those followers to the profile where she exercised more discretion regarding post frequency and topic:

"If it is an account I use for business [her real name account], I wanted to keep the message on point and I wanted to keep it not full of noise... So it was an effort and understanding that there was a noise level a lot of people didn't like on Twitter, and they won't follow you if you're tweeting 20 times a day about stuff they don't care about."

Finally, a number of interviewees were aware that the content they shared in one domain would not be useful in another. Family members may not care about work business, and vice versa. M1, who works in travel business development, describes boundary regulation for utility:

"There are times where there's a tweet I want to put out, and I have to make the decision – do I want to put it out under [personal name] or [travel tweet account.] And a majority of what I do through [travel] source is [travel] related. But, if you were at a party and all you did was talk about what it was that you sell or whatever, people are going to get tired of hearing from you."

The attention to utility is consistent with theories of boundary regulation. Individuals are motivated to not overwhelm information streams (e.g., Altman's fourth proposition), as there is shared benefit in efficient communication channels. Furthermore, management with an eye towards utility is indicative of an optimizing process, in which communication is effectively managed between two domains, limiting the risk of inadvertent or unwelcome disclosure out of context.

Motive Four: Propriety

Finally, individuals reported regulating boundaries out of a sense of propriety, defined here as a normative conformity to prevailing customs and usages. We commonly observed the propriety motive discussed in relation to the individual's position in a power structure. For example, many individuals would befriend their boss on their professional profile, but not their personal profile out of a sense that it was not customary for employees to have such candid relationships with their superior. F6 describes this power dynamic:

"When I created the pages for the school, she was one of the first fans. She said 'I think this is great.' But there's just a professionalism there that's just we don't need to go there yet. If one of us were to leave the job, then sure. Maybe we would be friends. But I don't want her to see her personal status that says I've had a bad day. That kind of thing."

What is notable about F6's instance is that the boundaries were regulated with both participants mindful to the power dynamics. That is, individuals in power seemed to be aware that the connection to a personal profile represented an incursion into the personal lives of those they supervise. Of course, this was not the case in every instance. Individuals with personal and professional profiles reported several attempts where individuals in the business realm attempted to gain access to a personal profile. The most common reason for rebuffing these requests was a sense of propriety. Regarding disclosure on one of her profiles, F6 stated "now when my boss pops up and Facebook tells me 'we think you should be friends,' I don't say yes because she's my boss."

While the workplace or professional boundaries represent a common location for the management of power dynamics, it was not the only place participants described. Personal relationships, such as the relationships between parents and children, were discussed. F1 describes her experience with the power dynamic between grown children and their parents:

"I have a 71 year old mom. She's on Twitter now. She follows me. So, that is probably more what keeps me in line than anything else. And it probably is the same kind of thing keeping people on Facebook in line from a younger point of view."

Social media enables the connection and re-connection of individuals across large temporal or geographic boundaries. F11, an administrator, describes the challenges of managing a personal contextual sphere, in which some friends are "present" and some friends are from a distant past.

"I know these people from fifth grade, and it seems like people I remember fondly but I was never friends with really, and it seems like it was easier to kind of have them, to keep track of them, for them to see what I was doing, than some of the people that I was actually closer to when I was a kid."

This point is important because it reveals the fluidity of context. Even within a defined space there is rich variation in one's communication and privacy goals. In social media, we are asked to regulate these boundaries of privacy across large groups, often times with little information from the potential communicants. In interpersonal communication, we can draw on cues in a conversation to adjust privacy boundaries. In social media, where hundreds of friends are listeners but not necessarily producers of content, the optimizing function of boundary regulation becomes difficult. MPM represents a blunt segmentation of communication boundaries, one that is optimizing, but lacking in information when compared to an interpersonal context. We envision a number of opportunities for social media sites to provide better tools for the management of context. To explore this opportunity, we turn next to the methods of boundary regulation in social media that we observed.

Methods of Boundary Regulation

Although our criteria for participation in the study was the maintenance of dual profiles on a single social media site, participants employed a wide range of methods to regulate boundaries of group disclosure. In our analysis, we identify two main forms of boundary regulation, broadly classified as *regulation by site* and *regulation by linkage*. Regulation by site refers to the range of technical boundary-setting behaviors that restrict a third party's access to a profile in a social media site. Regulation by linkage covers a range of social and technical practices that restrict linkage between persona. Notably, these methods of regulation are ad hoc, involving an interaction between social practice and technological affordance such as privacy settings.

Regulation by Site

We observed three discrete methods of boundary regulation by site in social media. Due to our participant selection criteria, the primary method of regulation was the creation of multiple profiles on the same service, most commonly Facebook and Twitter. These accounts were most often used for boundary regulation between different disclosure contexts of the individual's life. F9, a marketing director, describes this process:

"My personal Facebook profile, I have friends on there you know, I'm friends with now, that I went to high school with, people I've worked with in past jobs, a lot of relatives, you know, people that I know and interact with in real life. My work profile, it's bare bones."

Another form of boundary regulation observed was the use of a single account with highly segmented privacy controls. For example, an individual may accept friend requests from multiple social groups, but use privacy controls to restrict the disclosure of personal content to one social group. F11 describes the process of using Facebook's privacy list features to separate social groups within a single account:

"I think that with the more kind of customizable privacy stuff that I can generally accept, like I don't get requests from people that I don't know very much. And I've typically accepted requests from people that I don't know very well, but put them in a work-only list where they would not see my status updates or links."

Finally, we observed boundary regulation through "segmenting by site." This class of segmentation involves using different social media sites to engage with explicitly different audiences. F7, a business analyst, describes using multiple social media accounts to afford "segmentation by site:"

"I view them completely separate. Because there are people that I meet on other places on the internet that maybe I just visit once or twice, but I'll tell them I have a Myspace profile and this is it..,if you want to see more about me or something like that. I never give them my Facebook, ever. If it's not somebody that I personally know they don't get on Facebook."

In discussing these strategies, participants commonly focused on ways to keep context separate. For individuals with a "public face," such as marketing directors or sales persons, this was sometimes problematic. Regulation by site allowed powerful management of context and disclosure, but individuals would lose out on the benefit of their rich content creation in various settings. The next set of strategies we discuss, regulation by linkage, describe some of the ways that individuals provided selective pathways between their multiple identities.

Regulation by Linkage

We define a linkage as a connection between identities that cross an established boundary. The first form of linkage we identified is linkage between profiles. M1, who works in business development, has two public Twitter accounts: one for personal reasons, and one for his business. He describes his linkages between the two accounts:

"I decide what's appropriate for [my personal twitter] and what's appropriate for [my business twitter]. And then I stick with it. I may retweet occasionally, between the two, but not often. But I don't try and hide the fact that I'm one or the other... I just think some things are appropriate for the people who follow [my personal twitter] and some things are appropriate for the people who follow [my business twitter]."

In the preceding quote, we see that M1 has first regulated by site, creating two Twitter accounts that allow a separation of the personal and professional context. He regulates access between them through selective linking by "retweeting," which creates a link between the profiles. By creating this link, M1 provides a pathway between the two accounts.

Other participants went to lengths to prevent the discovery of linkages between sites. F9, the marketing manager who maintains a personal and professional Facebook account, makes sure there are no linkages between her two accounts. She complements this behavior with a second obfuscation strategy, using her maiden name on her personal Facebook account to ensure that professional contacts do not locate her personal account. She describes the linkages as follows, with awareness of risks related to linkage.

"I don't really...I do post about work but nothing specific and I try to keep the two very different because even though I only have one coworker on my Facebook, I know how these things can get back."

The first form of linkage, between profiles, is primarily focused on the connections between two digital representations of identity. In theory, two linked identities could be anonymous, providing no information about the person responsible for maintenance. Therefore, the second form of linkages we identified are the connections between the profile and the physical identity. These linkages are how the individual regulates access from the profile to the person. These linkages can be thought of as the chain of *data traces* that would connect a profile to an individual. F8, a librarian, manages her identity linkages by associating a robust set of social media accounts with each persona. F8 describes the process as follows:

"I have two different identities, I have a personal one. Facebook I think it's a little harder to do. I have one presence there but its geared towards my professional stuff, so its not, hardly...there's not much personal information there. But, I do have a separate Flickr account, I pay for pro for both of them. I have separate Twitter accounts, I have separate Myspace pages, I have separate blogs."

In the case of F8, each persona has a separate set of associated content-sharing profiles. This practice reduces the risk of accidental linkage crossing. For example, if each persona connected to the same Flickr account, it would not be difficult to deduce the linkage. However, in F8's case, each persona can publish robust content to a separate associated profile with little risk of linkage to the person.

CONCLUSION

In this research, we have demonstrated there are a variety of motives and strategies for regulating contextual boundaries of disclosure within social media. While group management systems are often designed to be privacy-enhancing, we show that utility, propriety, and identity management are additional salient motivators for boundary regulation. In a socio-technical system, the granting or restriction of boundary access is often concomitant with information exchange. Individuals expressed a desire to regulate boundaries with an explicit goal of regulating information volume and topicality. Participants also indicated a concern for not overwhelming audience information streams as motivation for boundary regulation. With regards to the large amount of information produced in social media sites, this finding is a particularly interesting elaboration of the desire to optimize communication effectiveness.

This study utilized qualitative methodology to develop a better understanding of the motives and methods of boundary regulation via multiple profile maintenance. We found that multiple profile maintenance is motivated by four factors: privacy, identity, utility, and propriety. Drawing on these motives, we observe a continuum of boundary regulation behaviors—pseudonymity, practical obscurity, and transparent separation—that emerge from multiple profile maintenance. Based on these findings, we encourage designers to consider these motives and methods when designing group context management technologies in social media. While these technologies should be privacy-enhancing, a singular focus on privacy misses a range of other potentially useful applications of group boundary regulation.

ACKNOWLEDGMENTS

This work was funded in part by the Kalp and Park fellowships at the University of North Carolina, and NSF Grant CCF-0424422. We thank the anonymous reviewers whose feedback substantially improved this work.

REFERENCES

1. Acquisti, A. and Gross, R. Imagined Communities: Awareness, Information Sharing, and Privacy on the Facebook. *Proc. PET 2006*, Springer (2006), 36-56.
2. Adu-Oppong, F., Gardiner, C. K., Kapadia, A., and Tsang, P. P. Social Circles: Tackling Privacy in Social Networks. *Proc. SOUPS 2008*.
3. Ahern, S., Eckles, D., Good, N. S., King, S., Naaman, M., and Nair, R. Over-exposed?: Privacy Patterns and Considerations in Online and Mobile Photo Sharing. *Proc. CHI 2007*, ACM Press (2007), 357-366.
4. Altman, I. *The Environment and Social Behavior*. Brooks/Cole, Monterey, CA, 1975.
5. Baden, R., Bender, A., Spring, N., Bhattacharjee, B., and Starin, D. Persona: An Online Social Network with

User-Defined Privacy. *ACM SIGCOMM Computer Communication Review 39*, 4 (2009), 135-146.

6. boyd, d. Why Youth (heart) Social Network Sites: The Role of Networked Publics in Teenage Social Life. In Buckingham, D. (Ed.), *The John D. and Catherine T. MacArthur Foundation Series on Digital Media and Learning*. MIT Press, Cambridge, MA, 2007, 119-142.
7. boyd, d. and Ellison, N.B. Social Network Sites: Definition, History, and Scholarship. *JCMC 13*, 1 (2007).
8. Chai, S., Bagchi-Sen, S., Morrell, C., Rao, H. R., and Upadhyaya, S. J. Internet and Online Information Privacy: An Exploratory Study of Preteens and Early Teens. *IEEE Transactions on Professional Communication 52*, 2 (2009), 167-182.
9. DiMicco, J. M. and Millen, D. R. Identity Management: Multiple Presentations of Self in Facebook. *Proc. GROUP 2007*, ACM Press (2007), 383-386.
10. Egelman, S., Oates, A., and Krishnamurthi, S. Oops, I did it Again: Mitigating Repeated Access Control Errors on Facebook. *Proc. CHI 2011,* ACM Press (2011), 2295-2304.
11. Fang, L. and LeFevre, K. Privacy Wizards for Social Networking Sites. *Proc. WWW 2010,* ACM Press (2010), 351-360.
12. Farnham, S. D. and Churchill, E. F. Faceted Identity, Faceted Lives: Social and Technical Issues with Being Yourself Online. *Proc. CHI 2011*, ACM Press (2011), 359-368.
13. Fong, P., Anwar, M., and Zhao, Z. A Privacy Preservation Model for Facebook-Style Social Network Systems. *Proc. ESORICS 2009*, Springer (2009), 303-320.
14. Glaser, B. G. and Strauss, A. L. *The Discovery of Grounded Theory: Strategies for Qualitative Research*. Aldine de Gruyter, Hawthorne, NY, 1967.
15. Goffman, E. *The Presentation of Self in Everyday Life*. Anchor Books, New York, 1959.
16. Guha, S., Tang, K., and Francis, P. NOYB: Privacy in Online Social Networks. *Proc. WOSN 2008*, ACM Press (2008), 49-54.
17. Jones, S. and O'Neill, E. Feasibility of Structural Network Clustering for Group-Based Privacy Control in Social Networks. *Proc. SOUPS 2010*, ACM Press (2010), 9:1-9:13.
18. Lampe, C., Ellison, N.B., and Steinfield, C. Changes in Use and Perception of Facebook, *Proc. CSCW 2008*, ACM Press (2008), 721-730.
19. Lampinen, A., Tamminen, S., and Oulasvirta, A. All My People Right Here, Right Now: Management of Group Co-Presence on a Social Networking Site. *Proc. GROUP 2009*, ACM Press (2009), 281-290.
20. Lenhart, A. *Adults and Social Network Websites*. Pew Internet and American Life Project, Washington DC (2009).
21. Lenhart, A., Purcell, K., Smith, A., and Zickuhr, K. *Social Media and Young Adults*. Pew Internet and American Life Project, Washington, DC (2010).
22. Lipford, H. R., Hull, G., Latulipe, C., Besmer, A., and Watson, J. Visible Flows: Contextual Integrity and the Design of Privacy Mechanisms on Social Network Sites. *Proc. CSE 2009,* ACM Press (2009), 985-989.
23. Nippert-Eng, C. E. *Islands of Privacy*. University Of Chicago Press, Chicago, 2010.
24. Ozenc, F. K. and Farnham, S. D. (2011). Life "Modes" in Social Media. *Proc. CHI 2011*, ACM Press (2011), 561-570.
25. Palen, L. and Dourish, P. Unpacking "Privacy" for a Networked World. *Proc. CHI 2003,* ACM Press (2003), 129-136.
26. Patil, S., Page, X., and Kobsa, A. With a Little Help from My Friends: Can Social Navigation Inform Interpersonal Privacy Preferences? *Proc. CSCW 2011*, ACM Press (2011), 391-394.
27. Petronio, S. *Boundaries of Privacy: Dialectics of Disclosure*. State University of New York Press, Albany, NY, 2002.
28. Shakimov, A., Lim, H., Cáceres, R., Cox, L. P., Li, K., Liu, D., and Varshavsky, A. Vis-à-Vis: Privacy-Preserving Online Social Networking via Virtual Individual Servers. *Proc. COMSNETS 2011*, IEEE Press (2011), 1-10.
29. Skeels, M. M. and Grudin, J. When Social Networks Cross Boundaries: A Case Study of Workplace Use of Facebook and LinkedIn. *Proc. GROUP 2009*, ACM Press (2009), 95-104.
30. Strauss, A. L. and Corbin, J. M. *Basics of Qualitative Research*. Thousand Oaks, CA, Sage, 1990.
31. Stutzman, F. and Kramer-Duffield, J. (2010). Friends Only: Examining a Privacy-Enhancing Behavior in Facebook. *Proc. CHI 2010,* ACM Press (2010), 1553-1562.
32. Terveen, L. and McDonald, D. W. Social matching: A Framework and Research Agenda. *ACM ToCHI 12* (2005), 401-434.
33. Watson, J., Whitney, M., and Lipford, H. R. (2009). Configuring Audience-Oriented Privacy Policies. *Proc. AUSC 2009*, ACM Press (2009), 71-78.
34. Westin, A. F. *Privacy and Freedom*. Athenaeum, New York, 1967
35. Zheleva, E. and Getoor, L. (2009). To Join or Not to Join: The Illusion of Privacy in Social Networks with Mixed Public and Private User Profiles. *Proc. WWW 2009*, ACM Press (2009), 531-540.

A Case Study of Non-Adoption: The Values of Location Tracking in the Family

Asimina Vasalou
HCI Centre
University of Birmingham
Birmingham, B15 2TT UK
a.vasalou@bham.ac.uk

Anne-Marie Oostveen
Oxford Internet Institute
University of Oxford
Oxford, OX1 3JS UK
anne-marie.oostveen@oii.ox.ac.uk

Adam N. Joinson
School of Management
University of Bath
Bath BA2 7AY UK
a.joinson@bath.ac.uk

ABSTRACT
A number of commercial location tracking systems exist which enable parents to monitor where their children are when outdoors. The adoption of these services and whether, through their design, they reflect parental values has not been investigated. This question was pursued with a large-scale survey of 920 parents from the UK. The use of location tracking was not prevalent amongst parents and only a minority had considered using these technologies. Parents favoring location tracking described it in the context of security, peace of mind and the need to reduce uncertainty. Parents who were against location tracking described a general lack of need as they had established reliable mechanisms for security and valued trust in the family as well as children's self-direction. Our findings show that location tracking concurrently *supports* and *threatens* parental values. By focusing on the values it undermines, we are able to suggest new directions for location systems.

Author Keywords
Family, children, parents, GPS, location tracking, control, privacy, security, trust, self-direction, values, adoption.

ACM Classification Keywords
J.4. Social and Behavioral Sciences: Psychology. K4.1 Public Policy Issues: Privacy.

INTRODUCTION
The last decade has seen a rise of commercial location tracking systems (e.g. Nu.M8 digital watch, Guardian Angel, UbiSafe) designed explicitly for families with underage children. Promising to keep children safe, these products provide parents with the facility to track them while outside of the home. Two features are typically shared across different systems: parents have one-directional views of their children's present location and movement history on a map, and they can define a geographical boundary that if trespassed, activates a text notification.

Despite their long-standing presence in the commercial domain, there is growing consensus that 'the commercial success of location awareness applications has been limited' [5]. Tangible evidence to this claim is provided by a recent study: in seeking to recruit users of commercial location tracking systems in the London area, over the course of several months, only a minority of families were identified [2] [3]. The significance of this finding is profound when we compare it to recent statistics on mobile phone use by families with adoption rising from year to year. According to the Childwise Monitor Report, for example, mobile phone adoption among children in the UK has leveled off in 2010 with seven out of ten 5 to 16 year olds owning a mobile phone [6].

The endorsement of children's mobile phone ownership [32] suggests that the non-adoption of location tracking systems is not due to parents' diminished ability to recognize the benefits of technologies in the realm of the family. In seeking to understand why families have not taken up location tracking, recent work that explores the relationship between technology and values is instructive. Sengers et al. argue that designers consciously or unconsciously give prominence to a particular set of values through the socio-technical features they propose [34]. By functioning as guiding principles in people's lives [7] [33], values have been shown to be a motivating force in users' technology adoption decisions [13]. Brown et al. also express this view by positing that commercial location tracking systems may have failed precisely because they have not adequately engaged with the complex dynamics of family values [5].

User research on location tracking systems has primarily focused on understanding the uses and implications of custom-made prototypes amongst select, small cohorts of novice users. In contrast to this research tradition, we turn our attention to commercial location tracking systems to ask why families have not adopted them, focusing in particular on understanding the values this technology supports or threatens. Our work is guided by the belief that in studying users' rejection of these widely-available products we can gain valuable insights on how to redirect their design so that it aligns with the values and needs of the social groups they aim to reach.

This was achieved through a large-scale survey of parents across the United Kingdom. We focused on parents in particular, as they are often the gatekeepers who determine what technologies are introduced in the family [4]. Given the little we know about the adoption of location tracking, adoption was measured using the exploratory framework proposed by Rogers' diffusion of innovations theory [30]. The diffusion of innovations theory formalizes technology adoption with a time trajectory that decomposes the decision to use a given technology into several stages. It begins with users' exposure to the technology's existence (knowledge stage). Once users are aware of the technology, they are influenced by its characteristics, a process that shapes their attitudes towards it (persuasion stage). The persuasion stage is followed by the decision to adopt or reject the technology (decision stage). Finally, people put the technology in use (implementation stage), constantly re-affirming their decision through the outcomes that follow (confirmation stage). To form an initial understanding of the parental values activated by the design of location tracking, we consulted two sources. First, we drew on the values, tensions and anxieties of parenthood as evidenced in the fields of sociology and psychology. Next, we looked at the interplay of these values during the use of location tracking as revealed in previous research.

Our study contributes to the location tracking literature in several ways. It is the first large-scale study to show that families across the UK have not integrated these technologies into their routines with only a small fraction using them. Even though previous research has found that keeping an eye over children through technology is now part and parcel of family life [9], 39% of our panel was not aware that location tracking is available. A minority of parents, 16%, felt that the control location tracking affords would alleviate anxiety over their children's safety. Even so, they had yet to take the leap to implement these technologies. Most importantly, 43% of our respondents felt that location tracking was unnecessary. It did not serve a meaningful purpose in family environments where routines and rules assisted parents to know where their children are. When parents were uncertain about their children's exact location, they trusted their children to keep safe. In line with recent concerns regarding the use of location systems e.g. [22], parents perceived the monitoring facility of location tracking to compromise children's independence and trustworthiness.

BACKGROUND

Parental values

From infanthood, children seek a sense of security established through the reliability of their parents, a psychological process that Winnicott [37] terms 'basic' trust. This interdependency becomes deeply entrenched in familial relations and is constantly affirmed through parents' affection and confirmations of reliability [10]. Personal values shift when becoming a parent from seeking individual achievement to a desire for security [33]. The need for security is framed within, and *modulated* by, the practices of a risk aversive society [11] whose policies have had grave consequences for children's freedom in particular as access to outdoor spaces and its opportunities for play are increasingly replaced by seemingly safer activities [14] [20]. The effect of the 'fear society' on parental perceptions of risk is demonstrable in the results of a recent UK survey, which shows that despite statistical data reporting a low incidence of abductions, a large number of parents maintain that abductions are an imminent threat [19]. Other research has shown that Australian parents discouraged their children to go outdoors by recycling stories of crime incidents that went as far back as 20 years [20].

In moving toward adulthood, children must gradually develop independence both in thought and in action, a rite of passage that takes place under parental direction. Some researchers have warned that without freedom to discover their environment and to make their own mistakes, children may not develop resilience, thus rendering life's risks and dangers a daunting enterprise [14] [20] [22]. Evidence to this, is the finding that children growing up in controlling homes exhibit less self-reliance and confidence [12] [16]. This task is not trivial for parents who must balance the control required in protecting their children, with the openness that allows them to explore their environment in order to develop self-direction. Though self-direction and security are both universal human values [7], they are achieved by antithetical strategies [33].

Trust is often the mechanism through which these tensions are resolved. Indeed, the openness and thus uncertainty required to attain self-direction is a necessary precondition in the process of trust building [22] [27]. Removing uncertainty can bear in different ways on both trustor (parent) and trustee (child). Parents who know more about their children's daily activities report more trust toward them, an effect that holds only when this knowledge is obtained through children's *spontaneous* disclosure [15]. Children whose behavior is regulated through extrinsic forces – such as fear of punishment – are less likely to internalize the values of reliability and honesty as their own in order to go on to become trustworthy people [12] [22].

Location tracking systems for the family

Location tracking systems have been deployed mostly for loose networks of friends with only a few prototypes evaluated in the family context. The Whereabouts Clock was tailored to preserve family privacy. Its aim was to uncover the values evoked by location. Designers positioned the clock within the domestic environment so that it naturally fit into the rhythms of family life and

Figure 1: Examples of existing commercial location tracking systems.

Verizon Chaperone

lok8u num8

UbiSafe

excluded unauthorized parties from accessing it. Each family member was given the choice to set up three coarse-grained location labels ('school', 'work' and 'home') that were displayed on the clock throughout the course of the day. Additionally, users could send custom messages to home members via the clock. In studying the uses of this system, it was found that the clock communicated what families already knew, as such posing few privacy concerns. Location became a token of reassurance, instilling a sense that 'all is well', evoking feelings of connectedness amongst family members and assisting them into smoothly coordinating their everyday routines [5].

Buddy Tracker was a mobile application that allowed family members to search for one another, displaying fine-grained location coordinates on a map. The application sent out a notification to users once they had been tracked. In evaluating Buddy Tracker, it was shown that family members had variable motives for tracking one another including coordination, care and affection, surveillance and curiosity, reassurance and security. Parents, in particular, often sought reassurance and tracked their children in the name of security. They legitimized the intrusion into their children's private spaces, which left their children feeling uncomfortable [21]. A similar set of findings emerged in a study that focused on the uses of commercial location tracking systems (e.g. Follow-us, Google Latitude). This work also revealed that parents rationalized the use of location tracking as a method for trust building, adopted after breaches of trust. The authors of this work argued, that in removing uncertainty, location tracking risked disintegrating the very notion of trust within these families [2].

These studies draw attention to the variable motives of security and the behaviors that establish it. The Whereabouts clock was carefully integrated within users' environment while it gave individual members control and choice when communicating their location. Its use provoked feelings of security, affection, reassurance and ultimately togetherness. By contrast, in making location searches an explicit act that was beyond the control of those who were tracked, Buddy Tracker accentuated surveillance practices in the family. Amongst its positive uses, it also became a tool for alleviating parental anxieties in relation to children's security and at times undermined children's freedom, as well as family trust. Thus, the morality of location tracking is likely to follow from the design sensibilities underpinning different classes of applications. As with the design of Buddy Tracker, commercial location tracking systems (see Fig. 1) feature *control* as the main mechanism to attaining security. Parents can view fine-grained information about their children's location at any given time. Control is asymmetric: parents are the trackers and children take the role of the tracked. Nonetheless, even though there is some evidence that parents have withheld from using commercial location tracking [2] [3], it is unclear whether the moral character of these technologies has influenced parents' decisions. The next section describes a survey study we conducted whose aim was to shed light into this domain.

METHODS

Participants

A panel of 1,130 parents living in the UK whose children were between the ages of 6 and 18 was contacted on our behalf by a market research agency to fill out a survey. A total of 920 (39% male) parents took part in the survey. The average parental age was 43 (SD=8.7) and the average child's age was 11.3 (SD= 4.5). Each household had on average 1.57 children (Median=1). The mean deprivation score for family residence was 22,821 (SD = 16,411), which is comparable with deprivation scores collected in the UK over 2010 (M=21.67; SD=15.51) [35].

Measures

Participants completed the survey online, which was timed to take no longer than 10 minutes. The survey was organized in three parts. In the first section, participants provided demographic information. In the second part, they were asked a question which enabled us to place them in one of several technology adoption stages. The final section measured parental values set in the context of location tracking. The three sets of measures are described by the order in which they were presented.

Controls

Previous work has found that user demographics influence adoption decisions. Younger users are more likely to accept new technologies and similarly, males are quicker to adopt technologies than females [30] [36]. However, in the context of families, mothers' nurturing role often motivates the use of technology so that we might expect a balanced form of participation across gender [29]. To control for these variables, we asked participants to report their age and gender.

The use of domestic technologies in particular can also be driven by concerns that form during specific developmental milestones. For instance, when transitioning from primary to secondary school, children gain more independence. This may in turn fuel new parental fears that encourage the adoption of location tracking. Thus, children's ages were also collected. Since we expected children's ages to have a non-linear relationship with adoption we coded each age point as a categorical variable.

Parents may also have legitimate concerns about their neighborhood safety that in turn bear on adoption decisions. Residential postcodes were collected and used to obtain an objective measure of neighborhood security. For this, we used the index of multiple deprivation (IMD 2007) [23], which is a government-led initiative for measuring deprivation at a small area level. The IMD is a relative measure with higher values indicating higher deprivation. For instance, during the 2010 assessment, the Tendring District (North-East Essex) was the most deprived (M=87.80) and the Three Rivers District (Hertfordshire) was the least deprived (M=0.53) [35]. The IMD combines 37 different indicators measuring income, employment, health and disability, education, skills and training, barriers to housing, living environment and crime. Family postcodes were uploaded to the online GeoConvert tool (http://geoconvert.mimas.ac.uk/) and converted to scores of deprivation.

Dependent variables

After completing the demographic questions, participants were presented with a short introduction about commercial location tracking systems that described their ability to record children's location and transmit it to family members. They were also provided with illustrative examples of three systems available for family use (ChildLocate, IonKids Child Locator and Trackstick). Participants were then directed toward one of four possible paths allowing us to place them at a specific point in the technology-decision process.

- **Knowledge stage**: Participants were asked to report if they had previously heard of location tracking. Those who provided a negative response terminated the survey and were coded as belonging to the knowledge stage.
- **Implementation stage:** Affirmative answers were allowed to progress to a second screen that asked respondents whether they use location tracking with their children. Those who answered affirmatively were categorized in the implementation stage.
- **Persuasion stage:** Participants, who reported not using location tracking, were redirected to a third screen that asked whether they had seriously considered using or decided against using location tracking. Those who had considered using location tracking were coded in the persuasion stage.
- **Decision stage (reject):** Those who had decided not to use location tracking were categorized in the decision (reject) stage.

Independent variables

Except for participants who belonged to the knowledge stage and had thus not formed an opinion about location tracking, the remaining respondents were asked to elaborate on why they would, or would not use, this technology. To avoid biasing responses towards this question with directive items, we measured values through parents' use of language. Language reveals important information about people's psychological states, personality, mental, and social processes [25]. To our present interest, it can show the concerns most salient when raising a family and the associations that parents draw between location tracking and their ongoing needs, values and practices.

Computer-aided content analysis was performed on participants' open-ended responses to convert them to quantitative scores. Using the Wmatrix software [26] (http://ucrel.lancs.ac.uk/wmatrix/), keywords that appeared unusually frequently within the open-ended responses were identified. This was achieved by comparing participants' written responses to a written sample of the British national corpus (BNC). The BNC can be seen as representative of general language use and thus served as a control condition.

Keyword	% of words in the survey	% of words in the BNC	Log-likelihood
Need	1.90	0.05	594.60
Mobile phone	0.33	0.00	203.82
Safety	0.62	0.01	263.64
At all times	0.21	0.00	103.40
Privacy	0.16	0.00	72.00
Knowing	0.21	0.00	72.67

Table 1: Keyword examples from survey responses and the BNC

Keywords retained through this analysis were significant at the .05 level. Table 1 displays a few examples of keywords as they appeared across the two datasets.

This inductive method was followed by thematic analysis. We consulted the texts in which each individual keyword appeared to interpret the issues expressed by participants (see Table 2). This allowed us to identify emergent themes of parental values. For instance, in inspecting the phrase *in case of*, and then subsequently the word *lost*, we found that in both cases participants were describing the security that location tracking would provide during exceptional occasions. These words were coded as describing security concerns and ultimately formed part of the linguistic category *Security*. To ensure that univocal items composed the categories, if a keyword was used in multiple contexts, and thus expressed more than one parental value, it was removed. Our theoretical understanding of parental values (as presented earlier) informed the interpretation of this data. At the same time, our coding scheme remained open to accommodate other sensibilities vital to location tracking that may be unforeseen by our framework. This process yielded 79 words organized across the following six categories:

- **Security** (keyword e.g.: *safe, security, in case of, lost;* Mean category word frequency=4.3%): participants felt that location tracking would keep their children safe and secure when they are not under direct supervision. As one female participant noted 'I can assure their safety when they are away from the house.' They believed these devices would be valuable in exceptional occasions during which children's wellbeing was at stake. In the words of one mother, '...it will also help me track them easily in case of emergencies.' Some participants also perceived the level of outdoor risk to be particularly high noting that modern societies pose unprecedented dangers. This view is encapsulated in one father's response: 'In this day and age you never know what can happen.'
- **Anxiety** (keyword e.g. *peace of mind, worry;* Mean category word frequency=.65%): alongside the need to keep children secure, participants described personal anxieties that would be alleviated if location tracking was put to use. A male participant voiced this worry: '...if anything happened it would give you the peace of mind to know you could track them and find them.'
- **Uncertainty reduction** (keyword e.g. *locate, track, exactly;* Mean category word frequency=1.12%): participants felt that location tracking would allow them to know more about their children's precise whereabouts. Overall, a pressing need to have control over what children are doing at all times transcended many descriptions. As one mother stated, 'I think if my sons are away for a long period of time it would be good to know exactly where they are.'

Safety (37 occurrences)
To know where they are for extra *safety*.
Safety in case of kidnap.
So that I can assure their *safety* when they are away from the house.
... especially while away from home, for *safety* in case of emergency.
We often worry about his *safety*, considering the dangerous people there are.

Table 2: Keyword in context analysis (KWIC) for the word safety

- **Need** (keyword e.g. *do not need, not appropriate;* Mean category word frequency=6.25%): participants expressed a general lack of need for location tracking. Statements such as 'No need for it' echoed in many responses.
- **Awareness and boundaries** (keyword e.g. *mobile phones, don't allow;* Mean category word frequency=2.95%): parents were aware of their children's whereabouts by drawing on numerous practices. Mobile phones, for example, formed part of this repertoire. In line with this, one mother noted, 'My son has a mobile phone and we can contact each other whenever we need.' Many participants had forged rules and agreements over location boundaries with their kids. A female participant described this arrangement: '...I don't let my children roam aimlessly. If they go out somewhere, there are boundaries and times set.' By contrast, those who had younger children felt that their children's movements were sufficiently supervised: 'At the moment my children do not go out unsupervised. We always know where they are, as we are usually with them.'
- **Trust and self-direction** (keyword e.g. *privacy, intrusion, spying, freedom, trust, honesty, responsible;* Mean category word frequency=2.21%): participants viewed location tracking as a threat to their children's freedom and independence. This outlook is reflected in the response of a male participant: 'children need degrees of freedom without feeling like they are been watched.' Furthermore, some participants felt that location tracking was meaningless since they trusted their children. Its surveillance function was thought to undermine trust. A female participant articulated the trust issue by stating: 'I trust my kids not to do or go anywhere they're not supposed to.' A second mother drew the link between trust and the control afforded in location tracking in saying: 'I trust my child and I don't find the need to follow where they are. It is a form of spying.' Issues of trust and self-direction were interwoven as both were achieved through uncertainty: without respect for children's self-direction, trust work

	B	S.E.	Wald	Sig.	Exp(B)	95% CI. For Exp (B)	
						Lower	Upper
Age	.004	.018	.060	.807	1.004	.970	1.040
Area Deprivation	.012	.011	1.030	.310	1.012	.989	1.035
Gender	.600	.321	3.511	.061	1.821	.974	3.411
Security	**-.142**	**.030**	**22.010**	**.000**	**.867**	**.817**	**.921**
Anxiety	**-.192**	**.077**	**6.231**	**.013**	**.825**	**.709**	**.959**
Uncertainty Reduction	**-.313**	**.061**	**26.250**	**.000**	**.731**	**.648**	**.824**
Need	**.374**	**.111**	**11.440**	**.001**	**1.453**	**1.170**	**1.805**
Awareness and Boundaries	**.152**	**.040**	**14.677**	**.000**	**1.164**	**1.077**	**1.258**
Trust and Self-direction	**.303**	**.096**	**9.922**	**.002**	**1.354**	**1.121**	**1.634**
Constant	.218	.845	.066	.797	1.243		

Table 3: Predictor weights (B), significance levels (Sig.) and confidence intervals (95% CI. For Exp(B)).

Note: The coefficients should be interpreted as follows: the persuasion stage was coded as 0, and the decision stage was coded as 1. For gender, females were coded as 1.

was not possible. This is expressed in one father's response: 'Our children know to let us know of their movements all the time. We trust them to be responsible and therefore give them freedom of movement, in return they are honest enough to give us their actual locations.'

RESULTS

Stages of adoption

Over a third of participants, 361 (39%), belonged to the *knowledge stage*. They had never heard of location tracking. A small number of participants, 16 (1.7%), reported using location tracking with their children and were thus classified in the *implementation stage*. The *persuasion stage* group comprised of 148 people (16%) who declared favorable toward using location tracking. The *decision (reject) stage* included 395 (43%) respondents who had decided against the use of location tracking.

Those in the knowledge stage had yet to assign personal meaning to location tracking. We describe the implications of this finding in the discussion section. As expected, only a small segment of users had implemented location tracking in the home (for a full discussion about this user group see [2]). The next stage of our analysis focused on the dominant groups of the technology cycle, parents belonging to the persuasion and decision (reject) stage. Specifically, we investigated how values forge parents' membership across these two stages while controlling for demographics. To verify that the two groups of participants were not qualitatively different, we conducted a multivariate ANOVA with the demographic variables as dependent measures and adoption stage as the independent variable. No significant differences were found.

Predicting stages of adoption

A logistic regression was calculated with two blocks, demographics and parental values, predicting the stage of adoption participants ascribed to. We first explored the data and verified model assumptions. A cross tabulation of the categorical predictors by adoption stage showed that for the variable child's age there were not enough cases in some cells. For instance, only 9 parents with children of the age of 18 belonged to the persuasion stage. This led to the exclusion of child's age from the model. Diagnostic tests suggested that data from 20 participants should be removed because of their undue influence on the model.

The demographics block was non significant (chi-square=3.55, *ns*) explaining less than 1% of variance (Nagelkerke R square=.010). It correctly classified 0% of the cases in the persuasion stage and 100% of the cases in the decision (reject) stage. An examination of the second block which included parental values explained 67% of the variance with the chi-square test showing significance (chi-square=315.987, $p<.001$). 65% of cases were correctly classified in the persuasion stage and 97% in the decision (reject) stage. The log likelihood difference between the two blocks was 316.69 (df=6), which was significant at the .001 level. This indicates that an integrative model of values and demographics fit the data better than the demographics only model.

Table 3 summarizes our findings. All six parental value predictors were significant. The values of Exp (B) were greater than 1 for the following predictors: *need, trust and self-direction, awareness and boundaries*. As these values increase by 1, the odds of deciding against the use of location tracking increase. Conversely, values of Exp (B) were less than 1 for the *security, anxiety, and uncertainty reduction* predictors. The odds of favoring the use of location tracking increase when words from these categories increase. The confidence intervals for each predictor indicate that the values of Exp (B) in the population lie between these two values. From the demographic variables, gender was marginally significant. The odds of being in the persuasion stage increased when the participant was female. This finding should be interpreted with caution however. The confidence interval crossed over zero suggesting that in the population this relationship may be opposite to that observed in our data.

DISCUSSION

This paper reported the results of a large-scale survey that investigated parents' commercial location tracking adoption patterns and the values these technologies activate. The discussion that follows is framed around the contributions of this work, its moral implications and its applications for design.

Families do not use location tracking

It has been previously suggested that location tracking has not had commercial success. Nonetheless, empirical evidence for this claim has not been reported. Drawing from a large sample of parents across the United Kingdom, we showed that location tracking has not reached the home. Only 1.7% parents reported using this technology with their children (*implementation stage*).

Parents have not heard of location tracking

A significant number of parents, over one third of our participants, were not aware these technologies existed (*knowledge stage*). This finding is surprising given that location tracking has been commercially available over the past decade. Although our research cannot directly show why parents were not aware of these services, lack of awareness is suggestive that parents have not *needed* to look for these types of systems [30]. This explanation is viable given that parents in the decision (reject) stage repeatedly noted a general lack of need as a key reason to non-adoption.

Values are the motivating force in the adoption of location tracking

Our findings inform the technology adoption literature by showing that contrary to previous work, demographics (e.g. age and gender) did not predict adoption. Values were the only robust predictors for both persuasion and decision (reject) stages. Before implementing a technology, users will engage in a 'mental exercise of thinking and deciding' [30]. In the domestic context, parents act as technology advocates [4] whose choices ultimately bear on children's wellbeing. Parents acknowledge this responsibility by reflectively evaluating their motives when using technologies with their children [21]. Thus, in the adoption of home technologies, general technology acceptance dispositions may be secondary to the concerns parents have about changing their family practices.

Only a minority of parents is in favor of location tracking

A small group of parents, 16%, were favorable toward location tracking (*persuasion stage*). Location tracking was seen as a tool to reduce uncertainty by providing constant information about children's movements (*uncertainty reduction* category). According to parents, this knowledge would ensure their children were safe and protected. Parents believed that children faced increasing environmental hazards indicating that risk perceptions are a primary driver in the intention to use location tracking (*security* category). Framed within this context, they felt that location tracking would reassure them and give them peace of mind (*anxiety* category).

The decision to track a loved one is often driven by the tracker's desire to relieve personal anxieties. This observation has resulted in concerns over the self-serving nature of tracking [2] [17] [21] [28]. The implication of this practice in our domain is disconcerting as parents' need to calm their short-term worries may cloud concerns over the long-term consequences that tracking poses on children's independence. Indeed, the self-serving nature of location tracking was pronounced in our findings. Parents reported high levels of anxiety. At the same time, adoption was not driven by objective measures of neighborhood safety, i.e., those living in more deprived neighborhoods were not more likely to favor location tracking. As Giddens [11] has argued, 'preoccupation with risk has little to do with life threatening conditions' and in the absence of a direct relationship between neighborhood deprivation and adoption, it seems that positive attitudes toward these technologies are formed on *perceptions* of risk as opposed to tangible and imminent dangers.

More generally, parents' accounts show that location tracking technologies are understood to be 'preventive innovations' that have the ability to reduce the risks facing children. Despite their positive attitudes, however, it is noteworthy that parents had not adopted these systems. The weak relationship between attitudes and behavior (or in the language of the diffusion of innovations theory, the persuasion and implementation stages) has been repeatedly documented in the social sciences. The motivational force of attitudes becomes even weaker in the context of preventive innovations as people ultimately understand the low likelihood of risks becoming dangers [30]. Therefore, not only does location tracking misrepresent the prevailing values of parenthood as we will describe next, but also its preventive function may introduce barriers even to those who are positively predisposed to adoption.

Parents do not need location tracking

Just under half of our participants were positioned against the use of location tracking (*decision stage*). The control provided via location tracking was considered to be a threat to self-direction and trust (*trust and self direction* category). Parents wanted to preserve their children's ability to freely explore their environment without being judged. Similarly, trust was seen as a reliable mechanism for managing uncertainty and particularly vital for personal growth. Keeping children safe was equally important for parents, who established security through various means. After expressing a lack of need for location tracking (*need* category), parents went on to explain that they were generally aware of their children's whereabouts either through adult supervision, by relying on a trusted group of friends, agreeing to rules with their children or using mobile phones to keep in touch (*awareness and boundaries* category).

The reliable routines used by parents to keep their children secure questions the usefulness of location tracking as a purely preventive device. Nonetheless, knowing that one's family is safe is at the very core of parenthood and family life. Indeed, the application of the Whereabouts clock shows that designing to reassure parents that 'all is well' is not a misguided objective. The Whereabouts clock, however, was created with a holistic framework of values in mind. Contrasting the responses of the persuasion stage with those of the decision (reject) stage we find that the current paradigm puts security at center stage, while it undermines trust and self-direction. To address this problem, Boesen et al. propose developing richer privacy settings that will maintain trust and also allow family members to tailor the way they are perceived by others [2]. Follow up work has shown that family members refrain from using privacy settings precisely because they fear how their restrictive actions will be perceived by others [21].

Rogers has argued that technologists must engage people more actively in their current practices, giving them tools to be constructive and allowing them to have choice in their interactions [31]. In a similar vein, Brown et al. have proposed that designers of domestic technologies should be providing families with opportunities to 'do the work of being a family' [5]. Overlaying new controls onto the current paradigm may be a poor application of these sensibilities: firstly, as noted above it is dubious whether privacy settings address the question of choice; secondly, the main emphasis that commercial systems place on security and control certainly does not reflect the mores and practices of family life.

To this end, our data shows that monitoring is not the primary behavior through which families feel safe and connected. Although some of the methods parents applied to keep children secure indeed involved control (e.g. supervision), other practices (e.g., agreements on curfew or activity boundaries) represented negotiations between children and parents where uncertainty was omnipresent. *Trust work* enabled these dynamic arrangements to take place. This balancing act has also been revealed in the uses of a ubiquitous family technology, mobile phones. When children are outdoors, parents tend to initiate communication with a view to reaffirm the agreements that support security [18] [24]. Children respect these contracts, but at the same time they are given the space to use uncertainty to their advantage in the telling of occasional white lies [18]. Systems that feature *spontaneous* location disclosure (e.g. checking-in) might be more reflective of this web of values and behaviors. By weakening the power relationship previously established through one-directional control [2], spontaneous location reports can give choice to children and nurture a sense of responsibility as well as honesty without stifling their freedom and autonomy. For parents, location information can provide peace of mind with the optional nature of sharing restoring or even strengthening their faith in their children.

CONCLUSION

Academic and media discourse has expressed strong concerns about the control location tracking affords arguing that privacy in the family is becoming obsolete, e.g. [1] [22]. In articulating these harms, scholars often overlook people's agency in the partaking of technology. Critical to this debate should be the acknowledgement that our personal beliefs, needs and values are motivating forces in the technologies we choose to use [13]. As Dobson and Fisher [8] rightfully argue in relation to location tracking: 'parents who choose to protect their children through surveillance and location control now may do so in the extreme'. The social determinism encapsulated in this perspective is in line with what our study found: while some parents were ready to relinquish control in the service of self-direction and trust, others sought to reduce uncertainty in the name of security. Therefore, location tracking merely offers a new stage for enacting existing values and concerns, a stage that without doubt may amplify the effects of already harmful practices.

With this perspective in mind, parents willing to use these technologies with their children were a minority. This finding provokes new implications for the current research agenda that tends to study the uses of location tracking by recruiting novice family users, when indeed, the same families would be unlikely to voluntarily introduce these technologies at home. It also suggests that designers of commercial location tracking systems take a critical turn away from the current paradigm. Our findings provided some initial ideas to this end. We hope our work serves as a scaffold for moving forward with fresh prototypes, informed by further research, ethnographic and participatory, that can give us an even deeper understanding of the dynamic interplay of values taking place within this sensitive and multidimensional context.

ACKNOWLEDGEMENT

We gratefully acknowledge Alastair Gill and the anonymous reviewers of our manuscript, whose comments improved our work. This research was funded by the EPSRC through the Privacy Value Networks Project (EP/G002606/1).

REFERENCES

1. Ahmed, M. Google Latitude to allow you to track friends' and families' every move. *The Times*. http://technology.timesonline.co.uk/tol/news/tech_and_web/article5662525.ece (accessed May 29, 2011).
2. Boesen, J., Rode, J. A. and Mancini, C. The domestic panopticon: location tracking in families. In *Proceedings of the International Conference on Ubiquitous Computing*, Springer Berlin/Heidelberg, 2010, 26-29.
3. Boesen J.,,personal communication, August 25 2009.
4. Bonner, J. V. H. Adding critical sensibilities to domestic communication technologies. *International Journal of Human-Computer Studies 67*, 2 (2009), 215-221.
5. Brown, B., Taylor, A., Izadi, S., Sellen, A., Kaye, J. J. and Eardley, R. Locating Family Values: A Field Trial of the Whereabouts Clock. *In Proceedings of the International Conference on Ubiquitous Computing*. Springer-Verlag, (2007), 354-371.
6. Childwise Monitor Trends Report 2010. http://www.childwise.co.uk/trends.htm (accessed May 29, 2011).
7. Davidov, E., Schmidt, P. and Schwartz, S. H. Bringing values back in - The adequacy of the European Social Survey to measure values in 20 countries. *Public Opinion Quarterly 72*, 3 (2008), 420-445.
8. Dobson, J. E. and Fisher, P. F. Geoslavery. *IEEE Technology and Society Magazine 22*, 1 (2003), 47-52.
9. Keeping track of the kids: Parents use Facebook and send 600 texts a year monitoring their children. http://www.dailymail.co.uk/news/article-1392313/Parents-use-Facebook-send-600-texts-year-monitoring-children.html (accessed August 11, 2011).
10. Furman, W. and Buhrmester, D. Childrens Perceptions of the Personal Relationships in Their Social Networks. *Developmental Psychology 21*, 6 (1985), 1016-1024.
11. Giddens, A. *Modernity and self-identity: self and society in the late modern age*. Polity Press, 1991.
12. Grolnick, W. S., Deci, E. L. and Ryan, R. M. Internalization within the family: The self-determination theory perspective. In J. E. Grusec and L. Kuczynski: *Parenting and children's internalization of values: A handbook of contemporary theory*. New York: Wiley, 1997.
13. Isomursu, M., Ervasti, M., Kinnula, M. and Isomursu, P. Understanding human values in adopting new technology-A case study and methodological discussion. *International Journal of Human-Computer Studies 69*, 4 (2011), 183-200.
14. Kernan, M. and Devine, D. Being Confined within? Constructions of the Good Childhood and Outdoor Play in Early Childhood Education and Care Settings in Ireland. *Children & Society 24*, 5 (2010), 371-385.
15. Kerr, M., Stattin, H. and Trost, K. To know you is to trust you: parents' trust is rooted in child disclosure of information. *Journal of Adolescence 22*, 6 (1999), 737-752.
16. Lamborn, S. D., Mounts, N. S., Steinberg, L. and Dornbusch, S. M. Patterns of Competence and Adjustment among Adolescents from Authoritative, Authoritarian, Indulgent, and Neglectful Families. *Child Development 62*, 5 (1991), 1049-1065.
17. Landau, R., Werner, S., Auslander, G. K., Shoval, N. and Heinik, J. Attitudes of Family and Professional Care-Givers towards the Use of GPS for Tracking Patients with Dementia: An Exploratory Study. *British Journal of Social Work 39* (2009), 670–692.
18. Ling, R. and Yttri, B. Control, emancipation and status: The mobile telephone in the teen's parental and peer group control relationships. In: R. Kraut, *Information technology at home*. Oxford Press, Oxford, 2005.
19. Living Streets and Parentline Plus. Is it safe to let our children walk to school? *National charities Living Streets and Parentline Plus*, 2010.
20. Malone, C. The bubble-wrap generation: children growing up in walled gardens. *Environmental Education Research 13*, 4 (2007), 513-527.
21. Mancini, C., Rogers, Y., Thomas, K., Joinson, A., Price, B., Bandara, A., Jedrzejczyk, L. and Nuseibeh, B. In the best families: tracking and relationships. *In Proceedings of the Conference on Human Factors in Computing Systems*, ACM, (2011), 2419-2428.
22. Mayer, R. N. Technology, Familes, and Privacy: Can We Know Too Much About our Loved Ones? *Journal of Consumer Policy 26* (2003), 419-439.
23. Noble, M., mcLennan, D., Wilkinson, K., Whitworth, A. and Barnes, A. *The English Indices of Deprivation 2007 Communities and Local Government*, 2008.
24. Palen, L. and Hughes, A. When home base is not a place: parents' use of mobile telephones. *Personal and Ubiquitous Computing 11*, 5 (2007), 339-348.
25. Pennebaker, J. W., Mehl, M. R. and Niederhoffer, K. G. Psychological Aspects of Natural Language Use: Our Words, Our Selves. *Annual Review of Psychology 54* (2003), 547-577
26. Rayson, P. *Matrix: A statistical method and software tool for linguistic analysis through corpus comparison*. Lancaster University, Lancaster, 2003.

27. Riegelsberger, J., Sasse, M. A. and McCarthy, J. D. The mechanics of trust: A framework for research and design. *International Journal of Human-Computer Studies 62*, 3 (2005), 381-422.

28. Robinson, L., Hutchings, D., Corner, L., Finch, J., Hughes, J., Brittain, K. and Bond, J. Balancing rights and risks: Conflicting perspectives in the management of wandering in dementia. *Health, Risk and Society 9*, 4 (2007), 389–406.

29. Rode, J. A. The roles that make the domestic work. *In Proceedings of the Computer Supported Cooperative Work*, ACM, (2009), 381–390.

30. Rogers, E. *Diffusion of Innovations*. Free Press, New York, 1995.

31. Rogers, Y. Moving on from Weiser's Vision of Calm Computing: Engaging UbiComp Experiences *In Proceedings of the International Conference on Ubiquitous Computing*, Springer Verlag (2006), 404-421.

32. Samkange-Zeeb, F. and Blettner, M. Emerging aspects of mobile phone use. *Emerging Health Threats Journal 2*, 5 (2009).

33. Schwartz. S.H. Basic Human Values: An Overview. *The Hebrew University of Jerusalem,* 2006.

34. Sengers, P., Boehner, K., David, S. and Kaye, J. J. Reflective Design. *In Proceedings of the 4th decennial conference on Critical computing: between sense and sensibility*, ACM, (2005), 49-58.

35. The English Indices of Deprivation 2010. http://www.communities.gov.uk/publications/corporate/statistics/indices2010 (accessed on August 10, 2011)

36. Venkatesh, V., Morris, M. G., Davis, G. B. and Davis, F. D. User acceptance of information technology: toward a unified view. *MIS Quarterly 27*, 3 (2003), 425-478.

37. Winnicott D. *Maturational Processes and the Facilitating Environment*. Hogarth Press, London, 1965.

Going to College and Staying Connected: Communication Between College Freshmen and Their Parents

Madeline E. Smith[1], Duyen T. Nguyen[2], Charles Lai[1], Gilly Leshed[2], Eric P. S. Baumer[1,2]

Department of Information Science[1]
Cornell University
Ithaca, NY 14850

Department Of Communication[2]
Cornell University
Ithaca, NY 14850

{mes369, tn248, ckl22, gl87, ericpsb}@cornell.edu

ABSTRACT
For many first-year college students in their late teen years, communicating with parents provides crucial social support. When going to college involves moving away from home for the first time, students and their parents must rely on technologies to keep communication channels open. We studied the ways in which college freshmen communicate with their parents and the various communication technologies they use. Interviews with nineteen first-year students at a major United States university revealed insights into students' perspectives of their communication and relationships with parents. We found students to use a variety of tools to connect with their parents and identified some considerations they make when choosing tools. Furthermore, the use of these communication tools played a significant role in mediating students' social and emotional closeness with, and independence from, their parents. We conclude by discussing technical and social implications for social support of students and student-parent relationships.

Author Keywords
Communication, domestic, parents, college students, CMC.

ACM Classification Keywords
H5.3. Information interfaces and presentation: Group and Organization Interfaces – CSCW.

General Terms
Human Factors, Design.

INTRODUCTION
Going to college is a major turning point in the lives of many young people. For many high school graduates in the United States, this also involves a residential move away from home, which is in itself a major life event for both students and parents [17]. This move may bring loneliness and reduced social support [21] and the possibility of widening emotional distance from family, especially parents. Reduced connections with parents can have negative impacts on academic performance and social well-being [18, 28]. These negative impacts may be most severe for first-year students who are just beginning to adjust to the college environment and independent life away from home. Thus we feel it is important to study the connection between first-year college students and their parents.

CSCW 2012, February 11–15, 2012, Seattle, Washington.

Shklovski et al. [28] proposed that Internet use for communication with family and friends may help relieve some of the psychological tensions of a residential move. Today's college students combine Internet use and other communication technologies to communicate with family at home. It is therefore interesting to examine how the use of such communication technologies can impact student-parent relationships.

Previous studies have looked at the impact of leaving home for college on the development of student-parent relationships [10,32] and the use of communication technologies among college students [22]. However, little is known about college students', specifically first-year students', use of technology for communication with their parents. Moreover, there has been little work that explored how the use of communication technologies impacts student-parent relationships. Our study hopes to bridge these gaps in the literature and contribute to the understanding of both technical and social aspects of communication technologies used by first-year college students to connect with parents.

In this study we examined the ways in which college freshmen communicate with their parents and the various communication technologies they use, focusing on the following research questions:

1. *How do first-year college students who are away from home for the first time choose among and manage multiple tools for communicating with their parents?*
2. *How do these communication tools contribute to the changes in student-parent relationships during this period?*

We conducted semi-structured interviews with first-year students at a major United States university. Based on qualitative analysis, we identified several themes in students' practices for choosing and using different media to communicate with their parents: convenience, social cues, managing multiple media, the perceived generation gap, and face management. We also found the students we interviewed generally perceived the different technologies including phone, texting, email, instant messaging, video calls and social media to have a positive impact on the relationships with their parents.

This paper contributes in three unique ways: First, we explore the communication practices of first-year college students with their parents, a group that has not been well documented in the CSCW literature. Second, we provide a technical understanding of communication technologies that are currently available and how a sample of users from this population uses them. Third, we investigate the roles technological tools play in these significant and changing familial relationships.

In the remainder of this paper we review related work, describe of our research methods, present our detailed results, and discuss the implications thereof.

RELATED WORK

Student-Parent Relationship & Environment Adjustment

Previous research has examined relationships between parents and college freshmen, and how these relationships can affect students' transition to their new college environments. Flanagan et al. [10] compared the ways that student-parent relationships differed for those students who moved away compared to those who continued to live with their parents, and suggested that the student's process of individuation and redefinition of their relationships with parents might be more problematic for students who still lived at home. Attending college away from home gives the adolescent opportunities to make decisions with less parental support (and monitoring), and may be related to positive perceptions by both the student and parents. Wintre & Yaffe [30] found that good student-parent relationships benefited students' perceived adjustment to the new college environment. Students who feel their parents are responsive to their needs find it easier to adjust socioemotionally during the transition from high-school to college, even when this involves moving away from home [20].

Communication Tool Use Among Students & Parents

A growing body of research investigates teenagers and adolescents' use of various Computer-Mediated Communication (CMC) tools, with some focusing on college students. These studies concentrate primarily on two groups of CMC tools: mobile and Internet technologies.

In the area of mobile technologies, Aoki & Downes [3] looked into the mobile phone use of college students from the behavioral and psychological views, and derived several major themes on the purposes of having cell phones. Notably, some of the participants mentioned their parents while discussing these themes, such as personal safety (e.g., reaching parents in case of emergencies), social interaction, and parental contacts (e.g., keeping in touch with parents). Chen & Katz [6] also found that cell phones for students were a "must" in maintaining contact with family, especially for fulfilling family roles and sharing experiences and emotional support.

Internet technologies have also been very popular among students and well-documented. Students have been found to use more communication media than college faculty and staff [22], including email, social networking sites (SNS), cell phones and voice over IP (VOIP) services. Some of this Internet use is for coping with loneliness, seeking social support, and maintaining family relationships [13]. Even high school seniors still living at home use social networking sites not only for quick and convenient communication with friends, but also to maintain social relationships with family members [2].

There has also been some research exploring parent's perspectives of using communication tools to connect with teenage children. Yardi & Bruckman [33] found that parents struggled with the generation gap between themselves and their teen children in the adoption of and adaptation to new communication technologies. However this study did not focus on parents of children away at college.

Communication Between College Students & Parents

Other research has specifically targeted communication between college students and their parents. In 1995, Johnson et al. [18] found that new students moving away from home felt it necessary to stay in touch with family (especially with parents), and when such family communication was not continued on a regular basis, student-parent relationships can suffer. Sax & Wartman [25] found that over the past two decades college students are increasingly maintaining closer ties with their parents and are communicating with them more frequently. Their findings suggest that these strong student-parent relationships can have positive impacts on students' adjustment to college, identity development and career exploration.

Hofer [15] also documented an increase in frequency of college student-parent communication, finding an average of communicating 13 times per week in 2008. However, more communication wasn't always positive; students who communicated more frequently with their parents also had lower levels of autonomy. High levels of communication with parents often remain consistent over the four years of college, while parents often wish for more contact than students are comfortable providing [16].

Gentzler et al. [12] studied college students' use of four common means of communication with their parents: phone, text messaging, email and SNSs. Students' feeling of loneliness was positively correlated with high frequency of SNS use with parents, while frequency of phone communication was correlated with satisfaction of the parental relationship, high intimacy, support, and instrumental aid.

To sum, previous research has found the importance of maintaining a balanced parent-student relationship for college students, and the overall increase in the use of communication technologies by students and parents to maintain this relationship. Our goal in this exploratory study is to understand qualitatively the point of view of the students and the kinds of interpretations they make of the communication tools they use, their relationships with their parents, and how the two are connected. Our study thus complements previous research that focused on the parents' perspective or on quantifiable measurements of use frequencies and behavior and perceptions measures. We do not focus on measurable frequencies of use, but instead on the idiosyncratic ways in which students choose and use these tools to communicate with their parents, and the understandings they make of the different features and characteristic of these tools in influencing the student-parent relationship.

METHOD

Participants

Nineteen students in a major United States university were recruited for an interview through a university-wide study recruitment system. Students were compensated with extra-credit for a course of their choice with instructor approval or $10 for their participation. All participants were American first-year students who lived on campus and whose parents lived in the United States. We decided to recruit American students only (as opposed to including international students) because we wanted to focus on a more homogeneous group of students for this initial exploratory study. Since this study focuses specifically on students' experiences and perspectives, parents were not interviewed.

Students represented a range of curricula, including engineering, arts, and sciences. We interviewed 16 female and 3 male students, all 18 or 19 years old. Students came to this university from various places across the country, as close as 50 miles from the university and as far as 2,700 miles away (mean 513 miles). No participant had lived away from home for an extended period of time before going to college. At the time of the interviews, 11 participants indicated their parents were married and 8 divorced (these students chose to discuss one or both parents during the interview). Table 1 lists participants' pseudonyms, genders and the technologies they discussed using to communicate with their parents.

Name	Sex	Technologies Used With Parents					
		Phone	Email	Text	VidCall	SNS	IM
Sarah	F	X	X	X	X		
Emily	F	X	X				
Steph	F	X					
Mike	M	X	X	X	X	X	
Megan	F	X	X	X	X		
Jenna	F	X	X	X			
Kayla	F	X					X
Lisa	F	X			X		
Chris	M	X	X	X	X	X	
Julia	F	X	X	X	X	X	
Jamie	F	X		X		X	
Leah	F	X	X	X		X	
Erica	F	X	X		X		
Maria	F	X	X	X			
Erin	F	X	X				
Allie	F	X	X	X		X	X
Matt	M	X	X	X	X		X
Molly	F	X	X	X			
Ariel	F	X	X	X	X		

Table 1. Interview participants (pseudonyms and genders) and the communication technologies they use with their parents.

Procedure

We conducted semi-structured interviews with first-year American college students. Each student was interviewed for up to one hour by one of the researchers in an on-campus interview room during April 2011. Interviews began with general questions about the student, the student's parents, and how they saw their relationships both before and after the student moved to college. The bulk of the interview focused on the various communication tools they used to interact with their parents. The communication tools we focused on were phone calls, texting (SMS), instant messaging (IM), video calling, email, and SNSs. We also asked participants about using blogs, shared tools, shared calendars, and location-based services with their parents, however no student used these tools with their parents, so we do not discuss them in this paper. These tools were chosen due to their prevalence in modern society, and proved to be an exhaustive list; when asked, participants indicated no other communication tools that they used with their parents.

For each tool they reported using with their parents, students were asked to describe both their typical and most recent uses of the tool, their motivations for using this tool, and their understanding and valuing of the roles the tool plays in managing the relationships with their parents. For those tools they did not have experience using with their parents, students speculated why this was and how it might or might not be useful for them. At the end of the interview, participants ranked the technologies they used with their parents in terms of frequency of use, usefulness, favorite, and impact on their relationships. We also asked participants how communication technology might be changed in the future to better support student-parent relationships.

Analysis

All interviews were audio recorded and individually reviewed several times by three of the researchers. Partial transcripts were made when the participant described ideas relevant to the research questions. The three researchers then met and used an open-coding technique to identify the general themes that transpired through the data. This process took place iteratively while developing and organizing the themes described below.

RESULTS

We structure this section in two parts related to the two research questions we posed above. The first part illustrates the ways first-year college students choose and use different communication technologies to communicate with their parents. In the second part we present our findings as to how these technologies contribute to the development of the student-parent relationship in terms of support for the students' adjustment to college and social well-being.

Choosing & Using Communication Tools

With a wide range of communication technologies available, participants described several considerations when choosing which communication tools to use with their parents.

Convenience

The most common consideration students mentioned was the convenience of using the tool. Not surprisingly, tools allowing for easy, immediate, and efficient communication were preferred. For this reason, cell phones were considered very convenient and reported as the most widely used communication tool with parents, both for phone calls (all 19 students) and for texting (13 students). Participants frequently described conveniently talking on the phone with their parents while they were walking around campus:

> *I like to do it walking to or from classes, because that's a time when I know I can't really get anything else done so I'm not losing productivity.* –Chris

Participants considered texting more convenient than calling because of its asynchronicity, which allowed them to respond at their convenience instead of being expected to respond immediately. Similarly, they often chose texting when they did not know their parents' availability and wanted to communicate without interrupting:

> *[I prefer texting] if I have to ask them something in the middle of the day; I don't have to find a time to call them or find a time they're not working to then call.* –Maria

Students also found the asynchronicity of email useful. For example, Allie described using email to share things with her family when she does not need them to get the information and respond right away. In contrast, participants considered IM and video calling to be less convenient and used them less often than phone calls or texting because both parties must be at a computer at the same time. When students did video call with their parents they often first used texting or phone calls to coordinate the video call, consistent with [19]. However, for some parents, the technical barriers of video calling made it inaccessible:

> *I would love for her to just get a high-speed line and a webcam and then we could just talk like that.* –Leah

Although these findings may seem obvious, they should not be taken lightly: given the stressful situation of transitioning to college and the differences in sociotemporal patterns between students and their parents, the convenience of communication technology is especially important to this particular population.

Weighing Social Cues

In choosing which tool to use to communicate with their parents, participants considered the depth of the conversation and the perceived richness of the tool. For in-depth discussions, students prefer phone and video calls that provide richer (audio and visual) social cues:

> *[Phone calling is] more personal than texting or chatting online. You can hear voice, and hear actual emotions like laughing or if she's concerned, stuff like that.* –Mike

Living away from home for the first time, students appreciated these informal, intimate conversations, particularly when they were feeling homesick or stressed. Furthermore, despite the barriers and inconveniences mentioned above, nine students reported talking with their parents over video, describing it as worth the extra effort:

> *If I have the time and it's convenient then I'd rather do Skype. It's more personal and just kind of nicer. It's like a phone call with benefits, pretty much.* –Matt

Students felt their parents were enthusiastic about video calls as well and appreciated the time commitment children made for them. The ability to convey emotions and intimacy and the need to bend one's schedule and to arrange the technical requirements for coordinating a conversation over richer, but more technically-intensive media, were perceived by participants as contributing to enhancing their relationships with their parents.

At the same time, media richness was not always considered positive. Students felt a trade-off between feeling more connected to their parents and sharing more about themselves:

> *When you hear the voice, you'd like to check the tone and how they react to what you're saying... but at the same time you can't hide how you're feeling.* –Steph

In some cases, students found that leaner media could also benefit the student-parent relationship. For example, Emily took her time composing an email to her father after an argument. She felt her thoughts came across clearer and were less likely to be skewed in email than in an emotional phone conversation.

Further, social cues extend beyond the communication channel between students and parents. Some students felt uncomfortable using the phone in their dorm room knowing roommates could easily overhear their conversations. They preferred text-based communication tools in their rooms instead. However, students did not express concern about being overheard when walking and talking on the phone in public.

Taken together, these findings support the view that choice of communication tool is not a simple formula based on message complexity and channel capacity. In other words, it is not simply the "media richness" that dictates when to use which tool and for what purpose [23]. Instead, students considered the entire communication in the larger context of their family relationships and other sociotechnical aspects.

Managing Multiple Media

Despite describing a preference toward one communication tool or another, students frequently used multiple media for communicating with their parents depending on the situation. They described a variety of considerations when deciding which specific tool to use in any individual situation.

First, students considered the specific attributes of the conversation – its purpose, priority, depth, and length. On one end, students reported texting instead of making phone calls when they considered the content something *"not worth calling for"* (Ariel) or not a "*serious conversation*" (Emily). For these messages, texting was considered a faster alternative to calling:

> *Usually when I call they want to have a whole conversation, but texting I can just get a one-word answer.* –Chris

On the other end, some topics called for more focused conversations. For example, Erica described her choice of video calls for a serious discussion about financial aid.

Another factor that students considered was the social norms around the appropriateness of a communication tool to the specific conversation. Many students referred to email as formal and impersonal, and used it exclusively for task-specific purposes:

> *I wouldn't email them to just talk. If we had to send each other forms or something [email] would make it easier.* –Jamie

At the same time, email was occasionally used to share less formal content such as family photos or links to amusing videos. Despite its informality, this kind of content is hard to deliver through voice or short text messages, and is therefore considered socially appropriate for email.

An additional social norm students considered was the expected level of involvement during a conversation:

> *When you video chat you're supposed to like face them and talk to them. ... And I feel rude if I'm doing a bunch of other stuff.* – Kayla

Students also considered the specific affordances provided by each tool. The reviewability of the text-based communication was often appreciated. Jenna described sending a text message as a *"tangible evidence"* of her attempt to communicate when she couldn't reach her parents on the phone, indicating her commitment to persevering the relationships with her parents.

These findings suggest that there is no one-size-fits-all solution for student-parent communication. Instead, students appreciate being able to choose which tool to use in any given circumstances. Students enjoyed having multiple media available and being able to choose the appropriate one for their current purpose.

Overcoming the Generation Gap

While students liked being able to choose which tool to use, their perception of their parents' technological abilities frequently limited their options. Many of the participants described a gap between technology used by themselves and peers in their generation and that used by their parents. Of the 19 participants, 10 reported that their parents were not at all technologically savvy; other parents who work with technology were still considered to be behind the curve by their children.

Participants often felt the generation gap limited their choices of technology to communicate with their parents. Even when parents had the technical ability to use a tool, their level of comfort with the technology may still prevent it from being used:

> *[My mom] went out to the store to get a new web-cam but she just doesn't use it. Maybe she thinks it's too much of a hassle or something.* –Allie (mother is a computer programmer)

Similarly, students who generally preferred texting described using it infrequently with their parents who were less comfortable. When obstacles like this arose, students receded to communications tools that their parents felt comfortable with, particularly the phone, in order to keep the communication channels open.

On the other hand, participants reported influencing their parents to adopt new technologies. While living at home, their parents controlled their access to technology, but as they become more independent, students' exploration of new technologies encourages their parents to expand their own use [see also 24]. Some parents learned to use the tools their children preferred, suggesting a similar effort on the parents' end (from the students' perspective) to maintain communication with their children:

> *I think my parents try to make it convenient for me to talk to them, so there's more opportunity to do that. So as I adopt text messaging or Skype they follow.* –Chris

Some students found creative solutions for using their preferred communication tools. For example, Matt described texting his younger brother who lived at home to ask his mom a question, since she does not use texting. Similarly, his mom interacts with him on Facebook through his sister but does not have an account of her own.

Matt's account exemplifies a trend we observed in communicating with parents while involving other family members in the conversation. Often when students called home the phone was passed around so they could talk to parents, siblings and grandparents in turn. During video calls, everyone at home tended to gather around the computer and talk to the student at once. Other students described email blasts being sent to siblings all over the country at once.

Our findings suggest that students perceive their parents' limited technological proficiency as a major obstacle in the ways they communicate with each other. But at a deeper level, their relationships may be enriched as a result of this perceived generation gap. Having to talk over the phone, even for trivial messages they would otherwise choose to text, forced them to engage in meaningful conversations with their parents. Otherwise, talking with their parents through their siblings or teaching their parents how to use new communication technologies opens up new ways to connect and interact with their family. In other words, overcoming the generation gap required efforts on both ends, which, in turn, strengthened family connections.

Face management

Another aspect in choosing a communication tool revealed in our findings was the tension between awareness and the demand for privacy. Participants thought that an increased level of awareness of their daily activities might benefit their relationship with their parents. At the same time, they were concerned about sharing with their parents specific information such as their exact location or activities such as attending off-campus parties. They wanted the ability to control and filter what information was shared with their parents, especially on social media such as Facebook.

While one-to-one conversations over the phone or other tools allowed students to present only the information they want to share with their parents, broadcasting technologies such as social networking sites frequently treat all of a user's contacts the same way, making it difficult to manage what information is shared with whom [5]. Similar to [9], many of our students preferred to share pictures with their parents via email than by friending them on Facebook.

Of those students who did interact with their parents on social networking sites, many described taking precautions to ensure their parents would not find sensitive information about them online. For example, Mike described how he often untagged pictures of himself and deleted friends' posts on his page so his mom wouldn't see them. He even went as far as to warn his friends to be *"careful"* when interacting with him publicly on Facebook. On the other hand, some didn't worry about this at all. For example, Leah described her mother as *"pretty chill"* and explained that she has nothing to hide from her parents.

Facebook was not the only concern for students; they worried about sharing information with their parents via other media as well. For example, Kayla described her mom checking her status on Google chat and messaging her to go to sleep if she was awake too late. Similarly, many students indicated they would not be comfortable sharing personal blogs with their parents.

After moving to college, students explore new interactions with people their parents may not know and activities that their parents may object to (partying, staying up all night). While this may be an inevitable part of American college life, students still want to present to their parents the identity that they perceive their parents want to see. Our findings suggest that students' choice of tools (e.g., one-to-one over broadcasting) and the ways in which they use them (e.g., filtering information) indicate this tension and point to students' desire to maintain good relationships even as their life is changing.

Impact on Student-Parent Relationships

Our second goal for this study was to explore how communication tools contribute to changing student-parent relationships during the transition to college. As part of the interview, we asked participants if they felt that their relationships with their parents had changed since they moved to college, in what ways that relationship had changed, and how they understand the roles of communication technology in these changes.

Distance Changes Relationships

For some of our participants, moving away from home for the first time helped them become more aware of their parents, less take them for granted, and appreciate the relationships they had with them:

> *After I came [to college] I realized how much I missed my mom.* –Megan

Talking to parents helped these students to relieve some of their frustrations, tensions and anxieties during the stressful transition to college life. They enjoyed personal conversations over the phone or video calls, particularly when they were feeling homesick. Other students and parents struggled at first to adjust to the changing dynamic of their relationship:

> *I think it's changed, But I don't think it's gotten really any better or worse. Clearly we're distant, but I think it's kinda giving us space, which is nice. I think it was hard for [my parents] at first but it's gotten better, so I think it's been good.* –Chris

And some families were still working to figure out how their new relationship should function:

> *Sometimes I wish they could be a little more [laughs] supportive and stuff because some things I'm still confused about and I need their advice* –Julia

These findings indicate that students are sensitive to the changing relationships as they move away from home: they expect empathy and support from their parents, and at the same time they understand that their parents are experiencing difficulties as well in this new situation.

Whether they felt a strong bond with their parents before moving to college or not, seven participants believed that the overall nature of their parent-child relationship had not changed despite the new physical distance and the use of mediated communication:

> *Now a greater proportion of our communication takes place, obviously over the phone, but also over emails, so it's more technological. But I mean as far as the nature of our relationship I don't think [it's changed].* –Sarah

For these students, the available communication technology helped them maintain their relationships with their parents and keep the connection between them alive. As Julia explained, *"If we didn't talk, we wouldn't feel close."*

Preserving existing relationships was particularly important when students went home to visit. Students reported a range of one to six visits home since the start of the school year, over a period of eight months. Erin imagined how these visits would have been different if she had not had access to communication technology:

> *We would have completely lost touch and it would have been all awkward when I went home. As opposed to now when it's like "I spoke to you yesterday, and now I'm here."* –Erin

Many students admitted that they communicated with their parents less frequently than when they lived at home. For example, Erin admitted that she did not put in the expected effort to communicate with her parents:

> *I probably talk to them less [now that I'm at college]. I mean, I only talk to my parents if they call me. If they forget, then I don't talk to them.* –Erin

On the other hand, Lisa would like to talk to her parents more. She felt that the a problem lies with her parents for not learning to use her preferred tools:

> *I don't really think the technology needs to be improved; I just think that my parents should probably learn to use the technology... It'd be great if we talked more often* – Lisa

Erin and Lisa's accounts suggest that the mere effort to maintain frequent communication indicates one's readiness to support the relationship. From the point of view of our participants, both sides of the relationship, the student and the parent, are responsible for bridging gaps in the communication: geographically, temporally, and technologically.

Although they communicated less frequently, none of our participants felt this negatively impacted their relationships with their parents. In fact, eight participants indicated that moving away from home helped to improve their relationships with their parents. Although they were communicating less frequently than when living at home, they now felt closer to their parents. A common explanation for this was that the students were becoming more independent and the relationship with their parents more mature.

Some students, particularly those who had fought with their parents often when living at home, immediately benefited from the mere distance:

> *I know that our relationship has gotten better now that we're not suffocated with each other all day so I guess [technology] creates a good middle point between seeing them all day and not seeing them at all.* –Emily

Emily's account indicates how she perceives the advantages of the geographical distance (not being near each other), the temporal distance (not communicating all day long), and the technological distance (using mediated communication), all helped improve her relationships with her parents by soothing daily, ongoing, face-to-face conflicts.

These findings illustrate the drastic changes that student-parent relationships undergo during the student's transition to college. Students use communication technologies to maintain contact with their parents during this time.

Maintaining "Normal" Relationships

Almost across the board our participants indicated beliefs that more frequent communication would contribute to improved relationships, especially given the new distance. What they considered "frequent communication" with parents, however, varied greatly from one student to another; some talked to their parents multiple times each day (Leah) and others were happy being in contact only every few weeks (Steph).

Some participants compared their communication patterns to those of their friends. For example, Erica second-guessed herself when talking about how close she was to her parents:

> *A lot of my friends are a lot more open with their parents, but I still talk to them a lot...* –Erica

While Kayla found it surprising that her mom doesn't always have time to talk when she calls, but her friends' parents beg them to call more often. She went on to explain that not all students want the same connection with their parents she does:

> *I feel like if college students aren't communicating to their parents it's more so that they just don't want to, it's not like it's hard for them. I think it's fairly easy to communicate with your parents. I think most people just don't really have time, and it's not high on their list of things to do.* – Kayla

During the transition to college, students often compare their own behavior to that of their peers in an effort to determine what is normal and to help themselves fit in. Calling home frequently can contradict the image of becoming mature, independent individuals that students want to project. Finding excuses such as lack of time and playing down their lingering need for emotional and social support from their parents may be ways for students to cope with this tension.

A few students felt that the advances in technology changed the expectations and norms for student-parent communication:

> *Now that there are lines of communication are open, if you don't communicate it's more detrimental to your relationship* – Matt

Similarly, parents expect to be able to contact their children who are away at school and become worried when the communication channel breaks down:

> *One day my phone broke and I was activating a new one, so I didn't have my phone for the day and my dad had BBMed me and it wasn't going through. So then he was like "Where are you, I was getting worried." But then if I didn't have a cell phone he would never have been worried.* –Ariel

These findings demonstrate that communication technologies are seen as inevitable for students to stay in touch with their parents and maintain what they perceive as good relationships even at a distance. However, the reliance on communication tools also creates an expectation of constant contact, which, when the tools cease to function properly, can cause conflict.

To summarize, our findings suggest that, for many of our participants, using communication technologies deepened and strengthened their relationships with their parents. Moving to college also helped students to feel more independent and mature. Communication tools such as the phone, texting, and email allowed them to maintain open communication channels with their far-away parents during this stressful time. Such tools keep students updated about their distant families; relieve stress; provide students with control over the content, mode, and frequency of communication; and overall make the adaptation to college life easier for first-year students. However the expectations about appropriate amounts and frequency of communication need to be constantly reevaluated as students become more independent and parents adjust to their absence at home.

DISCUSSION

Our qualitative interview method allowed us to gather valuable insights into how a sample of first-year college students communicate with their parents from the students' perspectives. The first goal of our study was to better understand how first-year college students make choices between communication tools and their patterns of use when communicating with their parents. The second goal was to investigate the roles these communication tools play in students' changing relationships with their parents.

Our participants described a number of media used to communicate with their parents, including phone calls, video calls, text messaging, email, instant messaging, and social networking sites. Similar to Green's findings about use of cell phones by students and parents to communicate with each other [14], we found that convenience, often correlated with mobility and accessibility, was a prominent factor in choosing which tool to use when contacting their parents. However, our findings highlight a number of additional factors, such as social cues afforded by the tools, the generation gap, and face management, all of which contributed to complex decisions and sets of practices in which each student uniquely engaged.

For example, our findings suggest that parents' willingness and ability to use a communication tool may influence the students' choices, similar to Murnan's finding that students would contact their parents "based on the parents' main mechanism – usually cell phone to parent's cell phone or wired phone, or e-mail to e-mail" [22, p. 269]. On the surface, this may seem as another example of how students' perceptions of their parents' technological incompetence restricts them to a smaller set of tools from which to choose [33]. Yet our participants were sometimes able to bypass this limitation by teaching their parents to use new communication tools such as text messages and Facebook, or by communicating indirectly through other family members. Our results therefore emphasize the importance of communicating through technology not only for staying in touch with parents, but also adding new dimensions to the relationship and signifying willingness to adjust to the other sides' abilities and needs.

A key aspect in this complex sociotechnical arrangement requires consideration of the student's overall relationship with the parent and how communication tools mediate the impacts of physical distance. In 1995, students relied on letters and landline phone calls to stay in touch with their family [18]. Today's students have access to many more and advanced communication technologies. All of our interviewees relied on a constellation of various technologies to stay in touch with their parents, creating what has been described elsewhere as a communicative ecology [11,29]. Students in our study described their relationships with their parents as changing in a variety of ways; some grew closer to their parents emotionally and others felt the nature of their relationships had not changed at all. Furthermore, our findings suggest that students see a direct role that communication technologies play in helping them and their parents actively participate in maintaining these relationships, either enriching, preserving, or toning down the relationships.

Schwartz and Buboltz [26] suggested that while parental support can be highly valuable to students while in college, conflict might also be necessary for students to create their own identities separate from their parents. Although student-parent communication may be on the rise overall [16], our findings illustrate a variety of ways in which students develop independence and confidence in their new adulthood, while staying connected to their parents. They do this by navigating between maintaining parents' awareness of their whereabouts and their growing need for privacy, engaging in faceting their identities [9], and creatively solving technical and socioemotional communication breakdowns.

Overall, our findings suggest that our objects of study, communication tool uses and student-parent relationships, are dialogically related: students' choices and uses of communication tool both shape and are shaped by their relationships with their parents.

IMPLICATIONS

Major life events, including transitioning into college, are significantly intertwined with technology use and are therefore worth considering in the design process of information and communication technologies [7,28]. On the surface, our findings may point to a list of straightforward design recommendations: to create communication tools that are more convenient, mobile, accessible, richer, and easy to use by both students and their parents. However, design implications are not always the most important result of research studies [8]. Instead, we suggest considering the kinds of support students may need as they move out of their parents' home and transition into adulthood. Our exploratory work examines particular circumstances of students moving away to college, and therefore points to future research in other domestic and social relationships as well as to other major life events such as residential move and adjusting to a new job.

Previous findings suggest that strength of relationships with parents before moving to college may help students adjust to college and perform better [20,30]. Our findings suggest that these relationships can change during the first year of college, and that communication tools play an important role in this change. Through the use of communication technologies, many of our participants felt they had grown closer to their parents since moving to college. There may be an opportunity to design technologies that facilitate such familial intimacy [31,34].

However, college is also an important time for children to grow from adolescents to emerging adults. Our findings suggest that one reason these relationships improved was the increased independence provided by living away from home, allowing students room to become independent and mature. "Always on" channels, such as media spaces [4], in which parents and students are constantly connected to each other, provide parents with considerable monitoring and therefore may inhibit students' growth [16]. Instead, we encourage the use of "on-when-in-need" channels supporting open-ended awareness [27]. Such tools could provide students with the comfort of knowing they can instantly connect to their parents when they need the support, while leaving them responsible to independently assess when it is a good time to communicate, using which tool, and what to talk about.

We should also note that parent support is not the only kind available to college students. For example, student peers, especially those who live together, are highly important for satisfaction with the environment and for academic performance [1]. While outside the scope of the current paper, future research may extend our work to examine the roles communication tools play for student services, advising, and peer support for students making the transition into college and growing into adulthood.

Lastly, these results also contain some important implications for theory. CMC is often thought about in a human-computer-human paradigm, where the computer mediates the interaction between two humans. However, our data contain several instances in which another person is also mediating the communication, such as the college student texting a sibling to get in touch with a parent. It may be beneficial to expand CMC theory to account not only for situations where multiple tools form a communicative ecology [11,29], but also for those situations in which another human functions in part as a communication medium within that ecology.

LIMITATIONS AND FUTURE WORK

One key limitation of this study is the relative homogeneity among our participants, such that our findings may not be generalizable to other populations. All of our participants came from a single university, none were international students, most were female, and none were transfer students. This study also took place within a cultural context where it is acceptable for students to leave home and go away to college, but this may not be the case in other cultures. This work should be extended with further studies targeting more diverse students, including more male, community college, vocational school, and international students.

Our method, interviewing first-year students, allowed us to gain deeper insights into the ways students interpret their communication patterns and relationship changes. However, we do not know how close our findings are to actual student-parent communication patterns and relationships. To complement our findings, future studies may benefit from other methods such as diary studies or communication logging and inclusion of parents perspectives to examine these topics.

CONCLUSION

In this paper we explored the ways in which first-year college students communicate with their parents and the various technologies they use. Through qualitative interviews with nineteen first-year students, we gained a valuable understanding of the students' perspectives. We identified a variety of tools used by students to maintain connections with their parents as they transition from adolescents to emerging adults. We also explored students' considerations and preferences when choosing communication tools for this purpose. We discussed the deep impact these communication tools had on students' relationships with their parents and discussed both technical and larger social implications of this work, as well as how these findings may also apply more generally to situations of major domestic and social change. Thus, this paper makes three unique contributions to the CSCW field: 1) exploratory investigation of a new and interesting demographic; 2) technical understanding of communication tool use by a sample from this group; and 3) sociotechnical understanding of impacts on student-parent relationships.

ACKNOWLEDGMENTS

We would like to thank our participants for their time as well as our colleagues for providing valuable feedback throughout the course of this project.

REFERENCES

1. Aitken, N.D. 1982. College student performance, satisfaction and retention: specification and estimation of a structural model. *J. of Higher Edu.*, 53(1), 32-50.
2. Agosto, D. & Abbas, J. 2010. High school seniors' social network and other ICT use preferences and concerns. *Proc. ASIS&T '10*, 1-10.
3. Aoki, K. & Downes, E.J. 2003. An analysis of young people's use of and attitudes toward cell phones. *Telematics and Informatics*, 20(4), 349-364.
4. Bly, S.A., Harrison, S.R., & Irwin, S. 1993. Media spaces: Bringing people together in a video, audio, and computing environment. *CACM*, 36(1), 28-46.

5. boyd, d. & Ellison, N.B. 2008. Social network sites: definition, history, and scholarship. *JCMC*, 13(1), 210-230.
6. Chen, Y.F & Katz, J.E. 2009. Extending family to school life: College students' use of the mobile phone. *Int. J. of Human-Computer Studies*, 67(2), 179-191.
7. Dimond, J., Poole, E. & Yardi, S. 2010. The effects of life disruptions on home technology routines. *Proc. GROUP '10*, 85-88.
8. Dourish, P. 2006. Implications for design. *Proc. CHI '06*, 541-550.
9. Farnham, S.D. & Churchill, E.F. 2011. Faceted identity, faceted lives: Social and technical issues with being yourself online. *Proc. CSCW '11*, 359-368.
10. Flanagan, C., Schulenberg, J. & Fuligni, A. 1993. Residential setting and parent-adolescent relationships during the college years. *J. of Youth and Adolescence*, 22(2), 171-189.
11. Foth, M., & Hearn, G. 2007. Networked individualism of urban residents: Discovering the communicative ecology in inner-city apartment buildings. *Info. Comm. & Society*, 10(5), 749-772.
12. Gentzler, A.L., Oberhauser, A.M., Westerman, D., & Nadorff, D.K. 2011. College Students' Use of Electronic Communication with Parents: Links to Loneliness, Attachment, and Relationship Quality. *Cyberpsychology, Behavior, and Social Networking*, 14(1-2), 71–74.
13. Gordon, C.F., Juang, L.P. & Syed, M. 2007. Internet Use and Well-Being Among College Students: Beyond Frequency of Use. *J. of College Student Dev.*, 48(6), 674-688.
14. Green, K.M. 2007. Understanding college students' and parents' perceptions of cell phone communication in family relationships: A grounded theory approach *Doctoral Dissertation*, U. Minnesota.
15. Hofer, B.K. 2008. The electronic tether: Parental regulation, self-regulation, and the role of technology in college transitions. *J. of the First-year Experience & Students in Transition*, 20(2), 9-24.
16. Hofer, B.K., & Moore, A.S. 2010. *The iConnected parent: Staying close to your kids in college (and beyond) while letting them grow up*. NY: Free Press.
17. Holmes, T.H. & Rahe, R.H. 1967. The social readjustment rating scale. *J. of Psychosomatic Research*, 11, 213-218.
18. Johnson, G.M., Staton, A.Q. & Jorgensen-Earp, C.R. 1995. An ecological perspective on the transition of new university freshmen. *Comm. Edu.*, 44, 336-352.
19. Judge, T.K. & Neustaedter, C. 2010. Sharing conversation and sharing life: video conferencing in the home. *Proc. CHI '10*, 655-658.
20. Larose, S. & Boivin, M. 1998. Attachment to parents, social support expectations, and socioemotional adjustment during the high school-college transition. *J. of Research on Adolescence*, 8(1), 1-27.
21. Magdol, L. 2002. Is moving gendered? The effects of residential mobility on the psychological well-being of men and women. *Sex Roles*, 47(11), 553-560.
22. Murnan, C.A. 2006. Expanding communication mechanisms: they're not just e-mailing anymore. *Proc. SIGUCCS '06*, 267-272.
23. Ngwenyama, O.K., & Lee, A.S. 1997. Communication richness in electronic mail: critical social theory and the contextuality of meaning. *MISQ*, 21(2), 145-167.
24. Palfrey, J. & Gasser, U. 2010. *Born digital: understanding the first generation of digital natives*. NY: Basic Books.
25. Sax, L.J. & Wartman, K.L. 2010. Studying the impact of parental involvement on college student development: a review and agenda for research. *Higher Education: Handbook of Theory and Research*, 219-255.
26. Schwartz, J. P. & Buboltz, W.C. 2004. The relationship between attachment to parents and psychological separation in college students. *J. of College Student Dev.*, 45(5), 566-577.
27. Sengers, P., Boehner, K., Mateas, M., & Gay, G. 2008. The disenchantment of affect. *Personal & Ubiquitous Computing*, 12(5), 347–358.
28. Shklovski, I, Kraut, R, & Cummings, J. 2008. Keeping in touch by technology: maintaining friendships after a residential move. *Proc. CHI '08*, 807-816.
29. Tacchi, J., Slater, D., & Hearn, G. 2003. *Ethnographic action research: a user's handbook*. New Delhi: UNESCO.
30. Wintre, M.G. & Yaffe, M. 2000. First-year students' adjustment to university life as a function of relationships with parents. *J. of Adolescent Research*, 15(1), 9-37.
31. Wong-Villacres, M. & Bardzell, S. 2011. Technology-mediated parent-child intimacy: Designing for Ecuadorian families separated by migration. *CHI Ext. Abst.*, 2215-2220.
32. Wyche, S., Taylor, A., and Kaye, J. 2007. Pottering: a design-oriented investigation. *Proc. CHI '07*, 1895-1898.
33. Yardi, S. & Bruckman, A. 2011. Social and technical challenged in parenting teens' social media use. *Proc. CHI '11*, 3238-3246.
34. Yarosh, S., Chew, Y.C. & Abowd, G.D. 2009. Supporting parent–child communication in divorced families. *Int. J. of Human-Computer Studies*, 67(2), 192-203.

Impression Management Work: How Seniors With Chronic Pain Address Disruptions in Their Interactions

Alison Benjamin[1], Jeremy Birnholtz[2], Ronald Baecker[1], Diane Gromala[3], Andrea Furlan[4]

[1] TAGlab, University of Toronto, Toronto, Canada

[2] Dept. of Communication, Cornell University, Ithaca, NY

[3] SIAT, Simon Fraser University, Surrey, Canada

[4] Toronto Rehabilitation Institute, Toronto, Canada

alison@taglab.ca, jpb277@cornell.edu, ron@taglab.ca, dgromala@sfu.ca
furlan.andrea@torontorehab.on.ca

ABSTRACT
Chronic pain is an illness that affects nearly a third of senior citizens. Uncontrolled chronic pain can manifest constantly and/or intermittently, and can disrupt seniors' ability to plan or to maintain synchronous and scheduled contact with others. Such disruptions can expose seniors to stigma from others who do not understand this illness, social isolation, and a range of challenges to their social autonomy. We present results from an interview study of 27 seniors with chronic pain exploring how they mitigate and manage these disruptions in their lives. Drawing on Goffman's theory of impression management, we found that participants invested significant effort into controlling both the context of interactions and others' expectations, in order to mitigate the potential negative social consequences of disruptions. In performing this work, seniors were selective about what information they revealed to others about their chronic pain and availability. Given such efforts, seniors with chronic pain have unique needs for technologies to support their social interactions.

Author Keywords
Chronic pain, interaction, awareness, impression management, accessibility.

ACM Classification Keywords
H5.m. Information interfaces and presentation (e.g., HCI): Miscellaneous.

INTRODUCTION
Chronic pain is a condition that affects nearly a third of senior citizens [11, 24]. In addition to causing significant discomfort, as a degenerative disease, chronic pain can constrain mobility and can cause unpredictable disruption in the everyday interactions and events that keep seniors active [20, 24] and help them avoid social isolation [30]. Seniors with chronic pain, moreover, have unique needs for communication and social coordination that are often not adequately met by current technologies, and are distinct from many existing technologies designed for seniors (e.g., [21, 25, 26]).

CSCW'12, February 11–15, 2012, Seattle, Washington, USA.

Chronic pain is defined as prolonged or persistent pain that lasts for 3 months or more, or pain that persists after an injury is healed [12]. As an illness, chronic pain is distinct from acute pain, which is more widely understood as a symptom of a treatable injury or disease. Estimated to affect 27-28% of non-hospitalized, non-institutionalized seniors [11, 24], chronic pain's medical consequences include depression, anxiety, sleep disorders, and progressive loss of functionality and mobility [12]. There is often no visible sign of the work people with chronic pain and their caregivers put into its management [28] and they may face barriers accessing health care and social support [9, 19].

Since chronic pain can manifest intermittently, constantly, or both, disruption of routine scheduled events and interactions can be the norm for seniors with the illness, especially during times of intense pain [24, 30]. Moreover, the disruptive nature of chronic pain can constrain availability for interaction [20] and introduce occasions where those with the illness have to take deliberate steps to avoid negative social consequences, including exposure to stigma and misunderstanding [19].

Unlike others who commonly experience disruption in social events – such as on-call medical professionals who may be summoned to an emergency at any moment – sufferers of chronic pain cannot rely on visible or role-based sources of legitimacy in extracting themselves from a social situation. Rather, their pain symptoms are invisible and may not always be perceived as legitimate (e.g., [32]). Seniors with chronic pain may desire interactions and activities with others, but frequent disruptions due to their condition can threaten their ability to remain regularly active. We know little, however, of how seniors with chronic pain are able to do this and how we might better support them in these efforts.

In this paper, we present an interview study of seniors with chronic pain, with an eye toward improving the technologies available to support the social interactions that are critical to their everyday lives, but which are under constant threat of disruption. We argue that living with chronic pain requires vigilance in impression management that has consequences for how seniors interact and live their everyday lives. Decisions about behaviors that deliberately or inadvertently reveal or conceal information related to one's ongoing and current condition play a central role in preventing or mitigating the effects of disruptions caused by chronic pain.

BACKGROUND AND LITERATURE REVIEW

Novel technologies have substantial potential for providing support to individuals with chronic pain. Recent work, for example, has explored the use of immersive virtual reality environments which can have analgesic effects on acute pain [16], and which show promise in treating and managing chronic pain [14].

Another area for potential impact that has not been explored to a great extent is how novel communication technologies might support seniors with chronic pain in their interactions with others, which occur primarily outside of clinical settings (a similarity chronic pain shares with other chronic illnesses (e.g., [1, 7])). These interactions are important because they provide seniors with a critical connection to others, but occur under conditions that are uniquely constrained as compared with others seniors or those living with other chronic conditions.

Aging With Chronic Pain vs. Aging in Place

One point of distinction we wish to make at the outset of our discussion is that the needs of those with chronic pain are unique in many respects, and present challenges that are importantly distinct from prior work on systems for seniors aging in place. That work (e.g., [21, 25]) addresses how aging adults can retain their independence and live in familiar settings as their healthcare needs change. Many seniors do age in place with chronic pain, but our focus is on on the unique needs of those with chronic pain, and the overlap is not complete. We first highlight the overlap and common experience.

In terms of similarities between aging with chronic pain and aging in place, both populations face constraints on mobility and other physical activity, and may face situations where interactions with others are difficult [24, 25]. Another similarity is that both populations often live independently, but have frequent contact with others. In the case of seniors aging in place, a shared understanding of routine activities and rhythms can play a key role in communication with others, such as loved ones, caregivers [3] and senior citizen peers [25]. Daily phone calls and regular visits allow for necessary interaction, social support, and some privacy, and the disruption of these routines can serve as a signal that something may be amiss.

The case of chronic pain is unique in two key respects. First, aging is a life process that carriers with it an expectation of the need for care and attention. Chronic pain, by contrast, is an illness that introduces challenges to quality of life that are above and beyond changes associated with increasing age [12, 17, 24]. Compounding such challenges is the fact that chronic pain often lacks visible symptoms that signal the need for attention, validate a senior's subjective experience, or create expectations of the need for their care - unless the senior chooses to reveal this information and/or ask for help (e.g., [8, 20]).

Second, aging in place lends itself well to routine activities, and disruption of these routines (e.g., failing to make a daily phone call) can be a signal of major problems. The nature of chronic pain, in contrast, is less predictable. Seniors with chronic pain often desire active social lives, but their activities are often disrupted (or prevented from happening in the first place) when episodes of or consistently intense, uncontrollable pain occur.

During these periods of pain, those with chronic pain may be prevented or inhibited from communicating with others in routine or usual ways. For example, pain can temporarily introduce bodily constraints that slow down the speed at which activities or interactions can happen, restrict one's mobility [20], negatively affect one's mood [8, 12], and interrupt ongoing thoughts and physical tasks [10].

Consequences of revealing and concealing pain

These unique properties of chronic pain can mean that there are frequently times in interactions or potential interactions when seniors' behavior deliberately or inadvertently serves to reveal or conceal that they are experiencing pain. The consequences of such behaviors can be nontrivial. Evidence suggests that revealing symptoms of pain can result in possible social isolation and the stigma of negative perceptions by others (e.g., [9, 32]). One reason for this stigma is that chronic pain has only recently been recognized as an illness in and of itself, but this status is not widely recognized, including by many health care practitioners. As such, revealing pain can be met with blame or misunderstanding. At the same time, however, concealing that one is experiencing pain completely can mean the inability to discuss one's experiences with others and that others have unrealistic expectations that cannot always be met.

One key reason underlying this tension between revealing and concealing symptoms of chronic pain is the causes and symptoms of chronic pain are often not visible to others as, for example, a broken limb might be. In some cases, this invisibility – and its accompanying fear of not being believed or taken seriously – has led patients to try to hide their experience of pain or to withdraw from otherwise achievable social interactions if they feel their pain will be called into question [8] or if they fear being blamed or labeled, for example as malingerers [12]. As such, fear of not being taken seriously can lead to attempts to hide pain, sometimes simply by withdrawing from social situations, which can in turn lead to further isolation as contacts may not be aware of what is taking place. In this way, both revealing *and* concealing chronic pain can be perceived to have possible negative consequences.

In addition to possible effects on their general availability and attitude toward social interaction, seniors with chronic pain also experience conditions that can impede their ability to plan and take part in these activities even when they do not deliberately withdraw. These conditions complicate planning and introduce further situations where decisions must be made about revealing or concealing the details of their condition.

These conditions include medical realities such as pain that does not respond to treatment, problems with irregular and unpredictable sleep patterns, and co-morbid conditions such as anxiety and depression; and also difficulties that are non-medical in nature such as lack of social or caregiving support, misunderstanding, and financial strain [12].

In addition, mobility may be restricted, so patients very often experience travel as problematic, for example because of inaccessibility issues, or physical discomfort [20]. As such, they must decide whether or not to request accommodation or make special arrangements when travel is required to participate in a scheduled activity.

These potential threats suggest there can be much at stake when symptoms of chronic pain are revealed or concealed. Of course, it is also important to note that an illness' meaning in a given social world can mediate a person's efforts of what to reveal and conceal [1]. For example, some seniors may hesitate to talk about their chronic pain if they themselves or others have the expectation that suffering because of pain is a "normal" part of aging [9]. Finding medical care can be a problem (e.g., [8, 9]), and patients in such circumstances may have to exert significant effort into making their pain "real" and credible, revealing select aspects of themselves, for example, through attention to appearance or assertiveness strategies [32].

Impression management

So far we have seen that much is at stake in when and how pain is revealed to others. As chronic pain is not acute but rather is constantly and/or intermittently present, the points at which behaviors reveal or conceal symptoms of pain are not one-time happenings, but occur regularly over the course of conducting and planning interactions.

Chronic pain is subjective, and those who live without pain may not understand the degree to which it impacts the ability of people with chronic to maintain a full social, work, or volunteer schedule. Others may think that those with pain will be available on-demand or able to follow-through on plans. Still others may misunderstand or be unaware of the constraints chronic pain, for example, in terms of how it can color interactions of a patient, or in terms of the challenges seniors with chronic pain have to negotiate in order to accomplish interactions.

It therefore seems likely that seniors with chronic pain must make efforts, through behaviors that influence the expectations of others, towards managing and mitigating the ever-present possibility that disruption will be met with misunderstanding, lack of accommodation, and negative attitudes. We know little about how these efforts are currently accomplished, however, and how they could be supported via novel communication technologies.

These efforts may be understood making use of Goffman's [13] work on impression management, which offers a dramaturgical perspective on interaction. This work is underscored by a metaphor of actors operating on social stages, strategically shaping social interactions and others' impressions of themselves. Fundamentally, this is rooted in the notion of face; that is putting forward an image that is likely to be perceived in a positive light and mitigating the effects of possible threats to face [5, 31].

In the case of seniors with chronic pain, we can consider the act of revealing pain or symptoms of pain to be a potential threat to face, given the possible consequences that could cast them in a negative light. As such, theories of impression and face management tactics provide useful insight into how seniors with chronic pain reveal information and shape the context of interactions in ways that forestall or mitigate social disruption. There are two key respects in which this might be considered.

First, Goffman discusses behind-the-scenes tactics through which people shape the context and conditions of interaction in ways that are likely to reflect positively. This type of work is relevant here as it pertains to how seniors with chronic pain can use behind-the-scenes practices in advance of or during interactions to forestall or deal with the effects of disruption caused by pain and/or social factors (e.g., non-accommodative attitudes of others). Examples might include aiming to shape selection of the place, modality, and time of an interaction. Such efforts are invisible from the view of others, but may be critical to accomplishing interactions or maintaining the relationship in a positive light when disruption arises.

Second, steps may be taken to manage the expectations of others to avoid negative impressions or stigma resulting from disappointing them. Such steps may include explicit statements about the feasibility or viability of activities, or additional behind-the-scenes work to shape the context of interactions in ways that are likely to minimize disappointment.

METHOD

From the standpoint of those wishing to understand the experiences of seniors with chronic pain and design technologies to better support their day-to-day social interactions and lives, the present study aims to answer a series of questions.

First, prior work rooted in Goffman (and others) on the use of media in coordinating social interactions shows that people frequently draw on properties of their environment and the media they are using in selectively revealing information about themselves and their situation to others [2, 15]. We are interested in how seniors with chronic pain use known properties of media and of their environment to manage their impressions/social context.

Second, we are interested in how seniors make decisions about revealing and concealing aspects of their chronic pain, the points at which they perceive these choices to occur, and their consequences.

Participants

For the present study, 27 individuals aged 60 or older were recruited from two large cities in North America. People who self-identified as having had chronic pain and who had experienced it for 3 months or more were eligible to participate. The other inclusion criterion was being able to speak and understand English.

Fliers advertising the study were posted in seniors and community centers, university alumni mailing lists, and distributed to chronic pain support groups. In addition, 10 participants were recruited by word of mouth, with help from the fourth author, from a pain clinic. The majority (21) of participants were women. Average age was 72.7 (SD = 8.2, range = 62-96). Average time living with chronic pain was 15.5 years (SD = 14.2, range = .66-47).

Data collection and analysis

Semi-structured interviews were conducted by the first author in-person (18) or over the phone (9). A standardized interview protocol was used that followed several broad topics: background and demographic information; social network structure and media use; interaction challenges; use of mass communication modalities; and the roles of loved ones and caregivers. Participants were encouraged at the outset of the interview to bring up topics not covered by the protocol that they felt they were relevant. Interviews took approximately 1 to 1.5 hours.

After the first 18 participants, the interview protocol was revised to reflect a clearer set of research questions that emerged in these first interviews. The revised protocol included questions on how chronic pain mediates synchronous communication and scheduling practices, and on when seniors decide to talk about their illness. After this revision, the first 18 participants were invited to take part in short follow-up interviews that included the new questions. Twelve participated in follow-ups; 6 did not respond or could not participate for health reasons.

Interviews were audio recorded and fully transcribed. Data was analyzed using grounded theory tools of open coding, constant comparison, and theoretical sampling [29], but this process was guided by our initial research questions. Interview data was read and re-read, then analyzed using open coding. Emerging themes were identified based on coded data and newer data gathered through refined interview protocols and follow-up interviews. These themes were iterated on several times through discussions and exchanges of analytical notes between the authors. While it is not possible to know if we reached true theoretical saturation, towards the end of our sampling it became clear that our data was acceptably dense and varied, and that no new themes were emerging. We thus feel confident making exploratory claims about how chronic pain mediates the communication patterns of our population sample.

RESULTS

Two clear themes are important to mention at the outset of our results. First, it was clear that our participants accorded significant value to their interpersonal relationships and social activities, but that their chronic pain could make it challenging to maintain such engagements while still being sensitive to their own wellbeing and the barriers they might encounter. P22, for example, notes that she would like to take fuller advantage of programs at the art gallery and have a more active social life:

> The art gallery has some wonderful things going on and I would certainly like to be able to go more frequently. But because of the, it's on many floors, because I'm restricted with the walking and pain I don't get to go as frequently as I would like to. I don't get to go out as frequently as I would like to so that I might have a social life. (P22)

Thus, an ongoing concern for our participants was how to accomplish their interactions in the face of possible disruption.

Second, disruption because of pain caused difficulties with scheduled (i.e., planned) and synchronous (i.e., in-the-moment) contact. It could be difficult to keep planned appointments and activities like volunteering, attending classes, or meeting with others. P1 notes the contrast between the fixedness of social plans now and before her chronic pain diagnosis:

> I can say even I'm going to meet [my friend] tomorrow for lunch. I may get up and can hardly walk. So I'm on the phone saying, '...do you mind if we take a rain check' And [my friend with arthritis] could do the same with me. That did not happen before. You could pretty much guarantee, unless a crisis came up, that you were going to meet for lunch... So you can't plan with arthritis. (P1)

Synchronous contact, including unplanned encounters, such as having people drop by without notice, could be difficult during times of intense pain:

> I really don't have any interest in people coming over and talking face-to-face. I can't be bothered because of the pain. It's really hard to concentrate on people gabbing even though it's interesting to them, if my legs are burning and my neck is aching, and that's what my brain is thinking about, it's not that I'm self-pitying, it's just that the pain is there and I can't take it away. It's hard to hold a conversation for very long. (P20)

Thus, our participants desired interaction, but also had to deal with the disruptive effects of chronic pain on synchronous and scheduled contact.

We discuss our results in terms of how impression management tactics were implicated in negotiating these challenges, and group our participants' behaviors into three key themes: setting the stage of interaction, managing the expectations of others, and revealing and concealing pain.

Setting the stage

Participants indicated to us that engaging in regular social activities required a series of tactics that allowed them to avoid or minimize the possible negative effects of disruptions caused by their chronic pain. These tactics were both pre-emptive and reactive, and occurred at all stages of planning and executing social interactions.

The first steps people described involved attempting to set the "stage" – in terms of both the setting and timing – so the probability of disruption was minimized. We use "setting the stage" to refer to the advance or on-the-fly work that participants did to shape or respond to interaction contexts in ways that were consistent with known properties of themselves and interaction media, which we discuss in turn.

Much of this work of setting the stage may not seem like impression management, as it consists of scheduling and generally operating within a set of known constraints. We argue, however, that because much of this work is invisible to others (i.e., behind-the-scenes), the outcome is often an impression. That is, effective stage setting means that others may not even be aware of the chronic pain condition/symptoms, whereas less effective stage setting can mean stigma from both friends and the general public (i.e., strangers on public transit). As such, we present stage setting as a form of impression management behavior that takes place through careful orchestration of events within parameters known to be constrained.

Properties of the self

One key element of stage setting was reliance on self-knowledge in planning interactions. While it is natural to be aware of one's own needs and preferences when scheduling events, what is interesting here is the reliance specifically on knowledge about limitations chronic pain might place on one's energy, cognitive abilities, and physical mobility, and the times at which these are most likely to occur.

First, participants said they are often able to use such awareness to carefully arrange their schedules such that disruptions are unlikely. For example, in the course of planning an outing with friends, one common strategy was consciously scheduling time for respite and self-care before and after the outing:

> I always, if I know I'm going to be doing something that's going to take a lot of time or energy I will take a day before and at least a day after to do very little. And if I'm going out at night which I try not to do but sometimes I want to go to something special, same thing, I'll make sure there's a day after anyhow when I'm doing nothing. (P7)

Another behavior we observed was participants' tendency to plan interactions with others during times when they anticipated that their chronic pain would be less intense. For example, some seniors knew what times of the day were best for them based on how they react to regularly administered medications:

> It's about timing things and at times during the day when I know that my cognitive skills are good that my motor skills are good and that the pain may be less then other times. (P26)

Similarly, those who reported that their chronic pain caused difficulty sleeping through the entire night noted that they avoided making plans during the mornings.

Properties of the Environment

Another way participants relied on self-knowledge to plan interactions and prevent disruption lay in consideration of their ability to access elements of the built environment. This required the combination of self-knowledge with knowledge about elements of the environment that they might have to draw on to have an interaction. For example, P4's chronic hip pain presents in difficulties staying seated, so he says he must pay attention to how and where he sits in social gatherings.

> I look after myself and conversation in a group setting happens... There's a few things I do to protect myself. Like whenever we have a gathering I'm always looking for a chair that's hard because cushiony chairs would disrupt the joint and cause me pain so that's just a piece of logic I work on but I don't mind it. (P4)

For P4, participating in social gatherings was possible if he set the stage in a way that assured his comfort sitting down.

Travel was another attribute of the environment that our participants had to consider in setting the stage. It could be very important to consider when one was traveling, and the type of transportation one used, as both factors could aggravate pain. Some participants indicated, for example, that they found certain modes of transportation difficult or impossible to use due to accessibility barriers or rush hour crowds. As P27 noted:

> I have to depend on Wheel-Trans (a door-to-door accessible public bus service) or taxis which is extremely expensive. And say I want to meet somebody at Harbourfront or the art gallery. I can manage perfectly well along the street or something with a walker, which helps my back. But I can't access [standard] public transit from where I live with the walker if I want to use it [the walker]. You know the escalator or the elevator only goes to one level. I can't go over to St. Clair and Yonge. I can't do that on the streetcar with my walker because the streetcar doesn't accommodate the walker. (P27)

P27's experience highlights how a number of variables - schedules of public transportation, availability of accessible busses, and the physical features of transport stations – had to be taken into account before traveling. Such features would inflect on her self-presentation (her ability to use a walker), autonomy and comfort level during her subsequent outing with a friend. For her, then, setting the stage means ensuring that events take place at events that she is able to access with the transportation options that are easily available to her.

In stage setting, knowledge about oneself and one's ability to travel throughout the environment could also mean forgoing the possibility of contact, as was often the case for P23 in the winter months:

> My social contact [in the winter] is actually quite restricted. It's by virtue of the fact that I don't go out at night, because it's cold and that makes my pain really bad. And I don't like driving at night. (P23)

Known properties of interaction media

Another form of setting the stage entailed consideration of known properties of the media for interaction. Participants tried to anticipate and work around features of interaction media (e.g., phone, computer, face-to-face) that could potentially aggravate pain. One way this played out was in the modality participants used to communicate. For P9, interacting face-to-face was preferred if it occurred in the home as this suited her energy needs:

> People do come and see me normally. It's because I think visitors is a good idea… it saves me the energy of getting to some place else so I have more energy to devote to visiting with people. And I've learned how to throw people out... (P9)

Drawing on the convenience of staying home, P17 often preferred using the phone to speak with others, such as his cousin, who lives in a suburb distant from his own home:

> I get in touch with her [by phone] more often. Not just because of her chronic pain, but cause I suffer from chronic pain and I can't get out there. (P17)

Choosing a modality that required a lower-effort for the person with chronic pain was a very common behavior among our participants. This resulted both in increased comfort, and reduced the likelihood of potentially negative disruptions.

Another way of working with known properties of the environment was participants adapting communications technology to suit their unique needs. Most of our participants reported that form factor, ergonomic, or inaccessibility issues could aggravate pain or fatigue. For example, holding a phone, typing, or staying seated for long periods of time could be difficult:

> [With the phone] it's the positioning. I can't hold it with this arm because of pain in my neck... I still have trouble with full range of motion, my rotator cuff feels like it's burning. I put it on speaker phone. I first ask permission. I'll say that '[my caregiver] is in her room watching TV so I'm just going to put you on speaker phone.' (P17)

Anticipating and working around such problems – finding an appropriate seating position, a preferred position to speak from, etc. – was a way of mitigating factors that could disrupt communication.

What all of these behind-the-scenes behaviors bring into relief is the extent to which seniors with chronic pain must carefully manage interaction contexts in order to accomplish their interactions with others.

Managing the expectations of others

When one is experiencing periods of intense chronic pain, for example times of "breakthrough pain" where pain is uncontrollable, some disruption is often inevitable even after care has been taken in setting the stage. Mitigating the potentially negative and impression-threatening effects of these disruptions was a second clear theme in our findings. In managing the expectations of others, our participants had to be selective about what information was revealed or concealed about their condition. This selectivity played out in the use of both pre-emptive statements that helped prevent their contacts from holding unrealistic expectations, as well as plausible explanations or accounts for their behavior during times of disruption.

One tactic through which the expectations of others could be managed was making pre-emptive statements that sketched feasible boundaries for possible interactions. Such statements influenced others because they aimed to create reasonable expectations in others for an upcoming interaction. Such statements were common in events being planned with contacts who were aware of their chronic pain condition. These statements delineated what was or was not possible, as P7 describes here:

> I do talk about what I need to go with them. They know I walk very slowly, they know I don't walk that far. They know I don't like to go out that much at night. Stuff like that. So they have accommodated me many times. Particularly 2 or 3 of them. (P7)

This example reflects a common strategy of letting others know about one's constraints (e.g., around mobility) in order to seek accommodation.

Another tactic for managing the expectations of others was to warn in advance that social plans could be disrupted in the event of significant pain. As P25 notes:

> Put it this way. All my friends know... if I'm going out somewhere, they know if I call and say, "look, I just can't make it", they understand. So it doesn't become a problem in the sense that the next week they'll say, 'How you feeling now [P25], a bit better? Well let's do it now then.' (P25)

This strategy was used while making plans, and drew on the fact that P25's friends knew and were understanding of his chronic pain.

Importantly, however, the feasibility of these strategies depended on the social and relational context. Some participants did not feel the same level of trust with their contacts. P5, for example, indicated that she sometimes used deceptive excuses, especially if it was suspected that others might not believe her:

> So I usually tell people I'm having a bad few days sometimes you think they don't believe you - but it doesn't matter it's your life. So yeah, some days you just can't face calling anybody or you just say you might even lie, 'I'm busy I just need time out.' (P5)

P5's strategy is interesting because it explicitly communicates boundaries – being busy and needing time out – but this boundary does not draw on and is not explained by the participant's pain status. Rather, it deliberately avoids revealing this information because it is not felt to be believable.

In other cases, participants shaped the expectations of others more implicitly, such as when unavailability for activities was communicated by delaying or avoiding communication with the affected individuals. As P9 describes:

> If it's at all possible I avoid other people. So whereas if I'm having a really bad day and I had nothing particular planned to do – I wasn't going out or anything like that – but I had thought of making some phone calls, the phone calls just don't get made. (P9)

Not answering the phone or delaying contact were common strategies used when social interaction was untenable. It should be noted, however, that such tactics could result in negative consequences for the senior with chronic pain. In the case of P24, who stated she lives with constant pain, putting off engagements with her friends damaged those friendships:

> I'm not as open and as free with cause I always think, well, the pain is there and it's pretty bad. I want to get off, I want to get off the phone… Now there's another thing, you lose friends by because they keep asking to come, you keep saying, 'yes, I will, I will, so I will' and you don't. I will phone and try and make some or send them little notes, which my husband mails them for me. Because you know they send cookies and stuff so I have to write notes to thank them. But otherwise I would be out visiting them all and you know doing things together. It makes it very difficult. (P24)

This quote from P24 illustrates how a tension between signaling boundaries and maintaining contacts could play out in a loss of friends. P24 created expectations that were possibly unrealistic by promising contact later. Such statements had isolating consequences in that they fostered the expectation that she would be able to follow-through.

Revealing and concealing chronic pain

A third theme running through many of the issues discussed so far has been the conditions in which revealing and concealing information related to chronic pain occur.

Pressure to remain silent

An important observation we want to underscore is that our participants often described an impetus to keep silent about the chronic pain that was an ongoing feature of their lives. This means that in many circumstances that spanned both setting the stage and controlling the expectations of others, preserving face and maintaining positive impressions involved concealing their experience of pain. One reason for not revealing this aspect of their life was the expectation on the part of participants that others do not want to hear about chronic pain.

> Your family don't want to hear it. They know you're in pain, and they don't want to hear it... I ran into somebody yesterday and we had a discussion about this. It's perceived as being very negative. Every time you talk to someone and they ask you how you feel. If you really tell them how you do feel, then you're being perceived as being very negative. So you don't do it. (P22)

Another explanation for not showing pain was the idea that chronic pain was a "banal" feature of aging:

> I don't tell [my elderly friends] very much about my problems. Not unless I fall. But I try not to complain. And that's maybe why [my friend who also has chronic pain] irritates me. I mean so many of us at this age have so many aches and pains it just gets rather boring. (P13)

P13 says she would not notify a friend unless an injury occurs that is, as it were, out of the ordinary (e.g., a fall). These quotes may reflect an expectation of others among many of our participants that pain is an obvious or "normal" feature of aging; if this is the case, staying silent may belie the work that goes into sustaining interactions, setting the stage and controlling the expectations of others.

Context matters

Clearly, though, the stakes of revealing chronic pain were different in different arenas. On one hand, a social context might, such as a workplace, not be supportive of revealing illness. For example, at P23's workplace, she felt the need to conceal her pain because she thought her coworkers would perceive her in a negative light:

> [When you work] during the day you can sort of 'muff it' and pretend that you don't have pain, you don't dare tell work colleagues that you have some form of a disability that's pain because that's immediately a downer. (P23)

On the other hand, in supportive contexts, the perceived stakes of revealing pain could be much lower. P2 related that her daughters and granddaughters grew up knowing about her illness; her diabetes and diabetes-related chronic pain was a frequent topic of conversation. For instance, P2 said that and she felt that she could talk about her health in interactions with her granddaughter, who worked as a physician:

> [My granddaughter] tells me from her experience, what I should take, and usually whatever medication she gives me agrees with me… maybe it's psychological, but when this favorite granddaughter of mine talks to me I feel good… as soon as she learned about Neurontin [a drug that can relieve neuropathic pain] she sent me medical samples, she said "Grandma, this is something new you take for your chronic pain." She is always ahead of the time. As soon as she learns something new about chronic pain she calls me right away. (P2)

P2's granddaughter, with whom she had a close and understanding relationship, could be a source of support and information on chronic pain, so this aspect of P2's life was openly discussed.

One benefit of supportive contexts was that when a disruption occurred in a senior's activity or interaction, communicating a need for withdrawal could draw openly on one's chronic pain. This as the case for P3, who plays ping-pong regularly with friends at a local seniors' center, but often must stop during the course of a game:

> Well like every Thursday, I go for lunch and we play ping-pong for at least 2 hours. We're in a group, and instead of playing, as soon as I start feeling the pain, I sit down. I tell them: 'I cannot continue playing, I have this pain.' And then somebody else takes over. So the group knows. (P3)

Likewise P26, who attends a chronic pain support group, noted that withdrawing from its meetings involved a straightforward email:

> I will e-mail the other people in the [chronic pain support] group and I will say, 'I can't make the meeting tonight, I am in too much pain.' (P26)

Both of these quotes illustrate cases where participants disclosed that their chronic pain was causing a disruption in their ability to interact or perform an activity, and where it was possible to disclose this due to the perceived supportiveness of the context.

DISCUSSION

Our study has several implications for understanding and supporting the communication needs of seniors with chronic pain. Our results make it clear that participants value their autonomy and ability to interact regularly with others, but accomplishing these interactions can require substantial effort. This effort stems not just from the disruptive impacts of pain itself, but also on the potentially negative consequences of revealing symptoms of one's pain to others.

The first implication is that fostering a sense of social support and connectedness for those who live with chronic pain is not as simple as increasing opportunities for social interaction. This aligns with research that has established that increased frequency of contact will not necessarily reduce feelings of isolation or increase perceived quality of contact or support [6], as well as studies that identify social barriers, such as stigma and misunderstanding, as uniquely challenging to people with chronic pain (e.g., [9, 12, 32]). Further, while systems intended to support seniors aging in place often aim to support regular and recurring interactions with family and loved ones in new ways [18, 22], chronic pain complicates this scenario somewhat. Pain may cause unanticipated disruption of interactions or potential interactions, a fact that our participants were constantly aware of as they set the stage for their interactions and activities.

Two factors played heavily into participants' efforts in this regard: reducing the likely effects of pain on their interactions, and managing the release of information about their pain. Each of these has implications for how systems might support not only frequency of contact but also the perceived quality, responsiveness, and appropriateness of communications technology.

First, participants put substantial effort into setting the stage for interactions to maximize the probability of success. They were careful to work within their personal limits and constraints imposed by such external factors as transportation schedules or options, and the built environment. As such, one design implication that emerges from these results is to not just help seniors with chronic pain interact, but to *help them set the stage for their interactions* as well. Possible ways to act on this include the development of systems to support seniors that take into account properties of themselves and the environment as they plan interactions. Systems that identify accessible spaces and routes, map transit schedules to one's own calendar, provide mechanisms to support the scheduling of respite time, and possibly even communicate such information to trusted contacts could be useful.

At the same time, seniors were also concerned about how to mitigate the effects of disruption when it did occur. Where disruption for seniors aging in place could be a sign of emergency and a need for immediate attention (e.g., via devices that alert others during a crisis, etc. [21]), disruption for our participants was a sign of temporary withdrawal and a need for an explanation that did not draw negative attention. Thus, a second design implication following from our results would be to *help seniors with chronic pain explain their limitations or disruptions to others.*

This may include systems that selectively reveal details to others, possibly using different explanations for different individuals. Thus, "one status fits all" systems that might indicate seniors' availability for interaction with others (see, e.g., [27]) should allow for different settings for different people or groups of people; and possibly allow for others to "approach" or check availability before starting an interaction (as in [4], for example). As seniors with chronic pain frequently encounter a tension between managing their illness on one hand, and maintaining contact on the other, customizable explanations on the part of the senior with pain, so that this tension might play out more positively, will be important. Systems that support selective revealing would be especially valuable in more ambiguous scenarios, such as where a senior cancels meeting a friend outside the home, but at the same time desires social support, such as having that friend visit them.

Calendar systems could also frame scheduling more flexibly to reflect the possibility of disruption, and give seniors an easy way to opt out of certain activities known to be strenuous. Rather than have event slots appear as "scheduled" or "empty", there could be certain activities that the user knows to be in a "if I feel up to it" category, and the system could send a reminder asking "Do you feel you're up to Activity X?" beforehand, and allow them to easily send a notification to other participants if they are not.

Given the extra work seniors with chronic pain must invest into setting the stage and managing the expectations of others, alongside their own pain and illness management work [8], systems that support seniors foster a sense of participation and contact with others while maintaining necessary personal boundaries could prove very helpful.

Limitations

Our study relied on a limited sample of seniors who self-identified as having chronic pain. This focus enabled us to look at general ways that chronic pain mediated our participants' interactions, and we believe we have presented a range of experiences to that end.

At the same time, it is important to recognize that our participants had diverse health issues that caused them chronic pain, including rheumatoid and osteoarthritis; diabetes; neuropathic pain; post-cancer pain; pain that persisted after injury, and unexplained pain. We acknowledge that these conditions may affect communication in specific ways, and that further studies might be needed to draw out such details. There are at least two implications of this to consider. Firstly, from an impression management perspective, a range of social (and potentially stigmatizing) meanings come with these conditions and may also affect the self-presentation of seniors in specific ways. Secondly, from a design perspective, the range of conditions that are known to lead to chronic pain could motivate illness-specific designs. While it was beyond the scope of the present exploratory study to address such issues, we think that significant value could be gained from a more systematic analysis that uses stratification to target participants with a range of conditions.

Another limitation is that our data were derived solely from interviews with seniors. Their perspectives and accounts of their interaction behaviors provided the basis for our study, but accounts from others are missing. The domestic space is a centre of collaborative work, where multiple stakeholders (people with chronic pain, their loved ones and/or caregivers, health care providers, etc.) are implicated in the management of this illness [1]. Future studies might take this into consideration, and include sampling from broader social networks, or employ ethnographic methods to examine communication patterns in-context.

Future Work

There are many opportunities for future work in supporting seniors with chronic pain. Additional studies with seniors themselves – including possible observation, message log studies, or participatory design endeavors – would deepen our understanding of their day to day lives, concerns, and interaction patterns. Attention to how communication during times of pain is impacted by device accessibility, usability, and form factor, as well as possible cognitive and motor changes that can arise from pain and/or due to aging [23] will be necessary. In addition, field studies of the deployment of novel systems would enable us to understand how specific design choices could help us better support specific scenarios.

CONCLUSION

Chronic pain is a complex illness, but it is clear that where communication is concerned, seniors with chronic pain invest significant work into controlling both the context of interactions and others' expectations so that they may participate in social interactions and minimize disruptions in their lives. Systems that support such efforts could prove to be one component of broader strategies that address the biological, psychological, and social dimensions [12] of chronic pain.

ACKNOWLEDGMENTS

We would like to thank our participants, the O'Neill Long-Term Care Centre, and Dr. Pamela Squire. We are grateful for grant support from NSERC, GRAND NCE, and from Google Research.

REFERENCES

1. Aarhus, R. & Ballegaard, S.A. Negotiating Boundaries: Managing Disease at Home. In *Proc. ACM CHI* (2010), 1223-1232.
2. Aoki, P. and Woodruff, A. Making space for stories: ambiguity in the design of personal communication systems. In *Proc. ACM CHI* (2005), 181-190.
3. Birnholtz, J. & Jones-Rounds, M. Independence and Interaction: Understanding Seniors' Privacy and Awareness Needs for Aging in Place. In *Proc. ACM CHI* (2010), 143-152.

4. Birnholtz, J., Schultz, J., Lepage, M. and Gutwin, C. A Framework for Supporting Joint Interpersonal Attention Management in Distributed Groups. . To appear in *Proc. Interact* (2011),
5. Brown, P. and Levinson, S. *Politeness: Some universals in language usage*. Cambridge U. Press, Cambridge, UK, 1987.
6. Cacioppo, J.T. & Patrick, W. *Loneliness: Human nature and the need for social connection*. Norton, New York, NY, 2008.
7. Chen, Y. Health Information Use in Chronic Care Cycles. In *Proc. ACM CSCW* (2011), 485-488.
8. Clarke, K.A. and Iphofen, R. A phenomenological hermeneutic study into unseen chronic pain. *British Journal of Nursing,* 17, 10 (2008), 658-663.
9. Davis, S. Vancouver Coastal Health Regional Pain Strategy Community Engagement Report, January 2007. http://www.vch.ca/get_involved/community_engagement/reports/2007_reports/
10. Eccleston C. and Crombez G. Pain demands attention: a cognitive-affective model of the interruptive function of pain. *Psychological Bulletin,* 125, (1999), 356–66.
11. Elliott, A.M, Smith, B.H., Penny, K.I., Smith, W.C., Chambers, W.A. The epidemiology of chronic pain in the community. *The Lancet*, 354, 9, (1999): 1248-1252
12. Gatchel, R.J, Bo Peng, Y., Fuchs, P.N., and Turk, D.C. The Biopsychosocial Approach to Chronic Pain: Scientific Advances and Future Directions. *Psychological Bulletin*, 133, 4 (2007), 581–624.
13. Goffman, E. The Presentation of Self in Everyday Life. Harmondsworth, Penguin, 1959.
14. Gromala, D., Song, M., Yim, J.D., Fox, T., Barnes, S., Nazemi, M., Shaw, C., Squire, P. Immersive VR: A Non-pharmacological Analgesic for Chronic Pain? In *Proc. ACM CHI* (2011), 1171-1176.
15. Hancock, J. T., Birnholtz, J., Bazarova, N., Guillory, J., Perlin, J. and Amos, B. Butler lies: awareness, deception and design. In *Proc. ACM CHI* (2009), 517-526.
16. Hoffman, H. G., Richards, T. L., Van Oostrom, T., Coda, B. A., Jensen, M. P., Blough, D. K., Sharar, S.R. The analgesic effects of opioids and immersive virtual reality distraction: evidence from subjective and functional brain imaging assessments. *Anesthesia and Analgesia,* 105, (2007), 1776-1783.
17. Jakobsson, U., Hallberg, I.R., Westergren, A. Overall and health related quality of life among the oldest old in pain. *Quality of Life Research.* 13, (2005), 125-136.
18. Judge, T.K., Neustaedter, C., and Kurtz, A.F. The Family Window: The Design and Evaluation of a Domestic Media Space. In *Proc. ACM CHI* (2010), 2361-2370.
19. International Association for the Study of Pain. Declaration of Montréal. http://www.iasp-pain.org/Content/NavigationMenu/InternationalPainSummit/DeclarationofMontr233al/default.htm
20. Miles, A., Curran, H.V., Pearce, S., Allan, L. Managing constraint: the experience of people with chronic pain. *Social Science & Medicine 61*, (2005), 431-441.
21. Mynatt, E. D., Essa, I. and Rogers, W. A. Increasing the opportunities for aging in place. In *Proc. ACM Conference on Universal Usability* (2000), 65-71.
22. Mynatt, E., Rowan, J., Jacobs, A., Craighill, S. Digital Family Portraits: Supporting Peace of Mind for Extended Family Members, In *Proc. ACM CHI* (2001), 333-340.
23. Newell, A.F. and Gregor, P. Design for older and disabled people – where do we go from here? *Universal Access Information Society*, 2, (2002), 3-7.
24. Ramage-Morin, P.L. *Chronic pain in Canadian Seniors.* Statistics Canada Catalogue no. 82-003-X Health Reports. (2008), 1-17.
25. Riche, Y., & MacKay, W. PeerCare: Supporting Awareness of Rhythms and Routines for Better Aging in Place. In *Proc. ACM CSCW*, (2010), 19, 73-104.
26. Rogers, W. A. and Mynatt, E. D. How can technology contribute to the quality of life of older adults? In M. E. Mitchell, ed. *The technology of humanity: can technology contribute to the quality of life?* Illinois Institute of Technology, Chicago, IL, 2003.
27. Romero, N., Markopoulos, P., van Baren, J., de Ruyter,B., IJsselsteij, W. and Farshchian, B. Connecting the family with awareness systems. *Personal and Ubiquitous Computing*, 11, (2007), 299-312.
28. Star, S.L. & Bowker, G.C. Enacting silence: Residual categories as a challenge for ethics, information systems, and communication. *Ethics and Information Technology*, 9, (2007), 273-280.
29. Strauss, A., & Corbin, J. Basics of Qualitative Research: Techniques and Procedures for Developing Grounded Theory. Los Angeles, California: Sage, 2008.
30. Thomas, S.P. & Johnson, M. A phenomenologic study of chronic Pain. *Western Journal of Nursing Research*, 22, 6, (2000), 683-705.
31. Watts, R. J. *Politeness*. Cambridge U. Press, Cambridge, UK, 2003.
32. Werner, A. & Malterud, K. It is hard work behaving as a credible patient: encounters between women with chronic pain and their doctors. *Social Science & Medicine* (2003), 1409-1419.

Tracking Changes in Collaborative Writing: Edits, Visibility and Group Maintenance

Jeremy Birnholtz
Depts. of Communication & Information Science
Cornell University
Ithaca, NY 14853
jpb277@cornell.edu

Steven Ibara
Dept. of Information Science
Cornell University
Ithaca, NY 14853
ssi9@cornell.edu

ABSTRACT
Systems for collaborative writing have long captured the attention of CSCW researchers, but have only recently come into widespread use. One issue in designing and understanding these systems is awareness of others' actions in a document. On the one hand, making edits and changes visible can improve collaborators' knowledge of who has made edits and what has changed in a document. On the other hand, studies of large scale editing systems such as Wikipedia have suggested that the visibility of certain edits can incite social conflict in groups. In this interview study, we aim to understand how people perceive and consider the potential impacts of their own and others' edits as they write together. Results suggest that edits embody not just changes to a document, but also social messages that have group maintenance implications. Many participants reported that they carefully consider how to make and explain edits so as to minimize social conflict.

ACM Classification Keywords
H.5.3 Group and Organization Interfaces

General Terms
Human Factors; Design

INTRODUCTION
Writing documents with others is a very common activity, and has become more common as teamwork has grown in popularity for work groups [18], research collaborations [39] and student projects in education. It is also possible to write together in new ways using a wide array of popular commercial tools such as Google Docs and the reviewing features of traditional word processors such as Microsoft Word and Apple's Pages, which are widely used [31].

Moreover, collaborative writing has long captured the attention of CSCW researchers. Writing together has been shown to be a complex process involving many discrete activities [32], working and coordination styles [30] and adoption of varied roles in these activities. Early work experimented with the design of tools specifically for the writing process (e.g., [26, 29]), aiming to create taxonomies of processes and roles [32], and also to understand how to design for issues such as version control [25], concurrent access/control [30], change awareness [36] and real-time awareness of others' behavior [12].

Much of this early work involved lab studies of experimental prototype systems, so focused on identifying the utility of specific features in constructing documents together (e.g., [25]). In general, most existing work has focused on understanding and supporting the sub-tasks of the collaborative writing process, such as planning, writing and editing, and providing feedback.

In addition to effective task completion, however, theories of group behavior such as the influential Input Process Output model (e.g., [18]) point to the importance of group maintenance in effective groups functioning. This is further reflected in theories of conflict that distinguish between task and relationship conflict in groups (reviewed in [11]). Group maintenance behavior is targeted toward the maintenance of social relationships with others, as distinct from behavior aimed primarily at efficient or effective task performance. There have been few studies, though, of group maintenance behavior in groups writing together.

Nonetheless, there is reason to believe that group maintenance behaviors may be unique in collaborative writing, particularly when popular collaboration tools are involved. Studies of maintenance [7] and conflicts [24] on the popular Wikipedia site show that visible edits to documents can draw attention to and inflame conflict, often requiring resolution via discussion or moderation. To be fair, Wikipedia clearly differs from small group writing in terms of the number of editors and the coordination mechanisms, but the notion that changes can draw attention in group efforts applies to both scenarios. We know much less about how these processes occur in small groups writing documents together, however, or how we may better support them. Indeed, allowing for some ambiguity around certain changes may sometimes serve a useful social purpose [1, 5].

In the paper that follows, we present data from an interview study of people who write documents with others using commercially available collaborative writing tools. We paid particular attention to how they managed group maintenance alongside task completion. Results suggest that simple edits can carry many messages, and participants took careful steps to ensure that edits were not misinterpreted, and also developed strategies to avoid misinterpretation of others' edits to their work.

BACKGROUND

There are two ways in which we might expect collaborative writing tools to affect group maintenance and performance.

Visibility & Awareness

The first is awareness of others' activities and the visibility of user actions to others. On the one hand, there is clear utility in drawing attention to certain changes via highlighting or other visual cues. Tam and Greenberg [36] discuss the example of a political document in which small, but highly consequential edits went unnoticed by many stakeholders because they were not highlighted as changes, so readers were unaware that changes had been made.

Many systems, including the framework by Tam and Greenberg, have focused on workspace awareness – that is, making users aware of others' actions by making them visible, and by tracking the history of the document [17].

Workspace awareness, however, is only one component. Theories of awareness are rooted in knowing what information people use to interpret what is going on around them, understand these activities, and try to predict likely future states [13]. Awareness has been shown to depend on sensitivity to a range of behaviors and activities [20]. Moreover, when one is building awareness of a situation involving other people, a key element of predicting future states is anticipating others' likely reactions to behavior.

The visibility and presentation of edits in collaborative document editing can affect the likelihood of these behaviors being noticed, and therefore impact others' reactions. The high visibility of edits on Wikipedia – via watch lists and trace histories – for example, can attract attention to a recently changed page [7] and re-ignite conflict among editors who maintain that page [24]. This can be true even if the changes are not substantial, simply by drawing attention to the page.

In this way, the visibility of edits can serve not just to facilitate awareness of changes to a document (along with the details of when these occurred and who is responsible), but also allows edits to act as signals of activity more generally or even be perceived as possible threats to a previously agreed upon way of presenting an issue.

We argue that complete transparency in change awareness may not always be the best option, and that there may be some value in not revealing all details about certain changes to documents, or in considering alternative means for presenting these details to users. Indeed, recent studies have suggested that ambiguity surrounding the details of people's actions or context can serve as a resource in smoothing social relations [1, 5, 19]. Similarly, hiding certain edits in a document could enable minor changes to be made while avoiding unnecessary social conflict.

To design for a balance between transparency and ambiguity, however, we must develop a more systematic understanding of how edits to documents are interpreted by users. While there has been extensive study of edits and conflicts in Wikipedia, there have been fewer field studies of editing in small groups. Kim and Eklundh [23] discuss the importance of *how* changes are made visible, but they do not explore the social *consequences* of these decisions. The first question we ask in this study, therefore, is how people who write together interpret others' edits, and the roles that edits play in both the task and group maintenance components of writing together.

Coordination and Annotation

Beyond understanding how edits are interpreted, we must also understand how people view edits as components of the coordination and revision process. Several studies have examined media usage for commenting and annotating documents, noting that both the substance and interpretation of feedback can be affected by properties of the media being used [25]. In particular, participants using direct text annotation made more detailed comments, and feedback delivered by video has been perceived as less negative than feedback delivered via text [3]. This is an important point from a group maintenance standpoint, as Posner and Baecker note that critiquing work in the writing process can provoke conflict and requires "thick skin" [32].

Another way that visibility of actions can affect group behavior is in self-presentation. One of the ways that people preserve social relationships in the face of potential relationship conflict is by taking actions that are likely to be perceived positively by others [6, 16, 38], or offering explanations that aim to re-cast potentially negative actions in a more positive light [9, 33]. Important here for our purposes is that people are conscious in their actions of how their behavior may be perceived and viewed by others, and of the impact behavior may have on social relationships.

As such, the visibility of behavior can affect people's actions – and the ways in which they explain or present themselves to others [4]. That is, people behave differently when they know others are aware of their behavior [15, 34]. In the context of writing, for example, one might hesitate to change a shared document if it is known that edits will be visible and linked to a particular user. Visibility, as noted above, might draw unwanted attention to edits or spark conflict between collaborators.

Moreover, visible actions in collaborative editing tools reveal only the actions themselves, often leaving the rationale behind them ambiguous. There is evidence, however, that people overinterpret certain cues in impoverished environments, which can lead to exaggerated interpretations or impressions [37], and affect how credit and blame are attributed [2]. This means that people may misinterpret edits to shared documents in ways that result in conflict. For example, they might misinterpret an edit as a sign of a strained relationship with a collaborator.

Large collaborative editing projects such as Wikipedia therefore have "talk" pages that allow people to explain and discuss edits [24], but such tools are not always provided for or used by small groups.

Despite these strong possibilities for effects on how groups are maintained, there has been little discussion of the social effects of change awareness and revision histories. This is the second question we aim to answer in this study. That is, how do people consider the ramifications of their behavior when editing, and what is the effect of edit visibility?

RESEARCH METHOD AND CONTEXT

We conducted an interview study with people who had participated in writing at least one document with others, using a commercially available writing tool with collaborative features. While any tool was acceptable, Microsoft Word and Google Docs were by far the most common. Word documents allow editing by only one user at a time, but the system includes features for tracking and rendering visible (via unique colors for each user) edits to documents, and comments that appear outside the body text. These features are not turned on by default.

Google Docs is web ("cloud")-based and supports multiple concurrent editors in a single document. Real-time awareness of others' changes and cursor locations are provided, but changes are not rendered visible by default in the document. A complete revision history is stored, however, that reveals all edits and who is responsible for them. The system also supports commenting on documents, with comments also appearing outside the body of the text.

Participants

Participants were recruited via a variety of techniques. Initial participants were recruited via: flyers posted on and around our university's campus in the northeastern United States, emails to mailing lists at our and other US universities, speaking with existing contacts, and via advertisements on our university's web-based recruitment system for human participants. Some additional participants were recruited via snowball sampling. All participants were compensated with ten dollars in cash or gift card credit.

Thirty-one people participated in this study between November 2010 and April 2011 (22 female, 9 male). These included eleven undergraduates, eight Ph.D. students, seven students in a pre-professional master's program, three research university faculty, and two university librarians.

Procedure

All interviews were semi-structured and conducted by the second author, either in person or remotely via audio or video conferencing. In-person interviews were conducted in a private office or conference room. Remote interviews were performed from a private space; interviewees were asked to be in a private setting.

The interview protocol was written prior to data collection, but refined through discussion of our own experiences and several pilot interviews (not included in the data set). The protocol was also iteratively refined during the initial interviews, though the set of items was reasonably stable throughout the process. Depending on the participant and context, the order and priority of interview items was sometimes adjusted to fit the flow of the conversation and the applicability of items to the interviewees. Participants were asked about their use of word processing tools, their personal preferences for specific tools and features, and the frequency and nature of their collaborative use of those tools. Interviewees were asked to describe at least one specific example of a collaborative writing project, and at least one example of conflict. Overall, emphasis was placed on change awareness and edit trace history features and related experiences, practices and preferences. Participants were also asked to discuss their interactions with co-authors and editors, and their impressions of specific experiences.

Data Analysis

Interviews lasted between 27 and 87 minutes (M=48.6 minutes). Nearly all were audio recorded and fully transcribed for analysis, with two exceptions: one participant declined to have the interview recorded, and another recording was of poor quality due to unanticipated background noise, so could not be accurately transcribed.

The data analysis process loosely followed a grounded theory approach [14, 21], but was also directed by our initial research questions and ideas. Researchers performed close reading of transcripts, making notes and engaging in constant comparison. Through collaborative discussion and separate memoing, an open coding scheme was developed via annotation of documents, and using a spreadsheet to track categories and relevant data. Throughout the process, the coding scheme was refined, and data were re-coded for the updated categories as necessary. While it is unclear whether we reached true theoretical saturation, there was clear repetition in what our participants told us by the end of the data gathering and analysis. We feel that we have sufficient data to make exploratory claims. Several themes identified in coding are used in presenting our results below. Pseudonyms are used for all participants.

We do not mean to give the impression that our participants' collaborative writing experiences were riddled with conflict. Many had harmonious collaborations as well, but nearly all could recall and describe some conflict episodes. Our focus in analysis was on the management and origin of social conflict when it occurs in writing.

RESULTS

In analyzing our results, we found that participants described a wide range of experiences. Many of these highlighted the importance of being aware of changes to documents via visible edits or change histories, but that they were also conscious of the possible social effects of these edits as they worked together. Awareness information about edits was often interpreted by our participants in ways that go beyond the technical and task-oriented information central to trace and revision history features.

The Many Roles of Edits and Annotations

One key theme in our results was that edits and annotations in documents played several different roles.

Insights about effort and contribution

One role of edits was to serve as a source of insight about collaborators' efforts, both in the aggregate and in understanding the behavior of specific individuals. For example, some users of Google Docs reported that real-time awareness of the amount of text in the document helped them stay aware of group progress. Josie, a graduate student, enjoyed being able to "see the work that's already been done" and "watching [the document] grow" while using Google Docs. This allowed her to monitor the group's progress without having to constantly query collaborators to see if they were doing their part.

Edit histories were also useful in assessing individual effort, in that they allowed for easy determination of who had contributed to a document and how much had been contributed. Some participants, like Carrie, a Ph.D. student, reported that this allowed them to become aware of a disparity or lack of contribution:

> I've worked with people before where there's Track Changes and you get the document back and there's like one thing that has happened. That almost makes you feel like, 'did you read it?'.

Mirah, a professional master's degree student, mentioned that even faculty in her degree program sometimes use the Track Changes feature for evaluation of group work, saying that "sometimes professors want to see the document with these changes so they know everybody has had an equal hand in the creation."

Making the details of changes visible also had the effect that participants could see exactly what had been edited – and thus contributed – by a particular collaborator. Sometimes the detailed nature of the changes affected perceptions of the value of a person's contribution. In reviewing the highlighted changes in a shared Microsoft Word document, for example, one participant saw that a collaborator had made significant edits to a document and was pleased. After a closer look, though, he realized that this person had made primarily grammatical edits to the document, and felt that this indicated a low level of contribution, which was disappointing. This is just one of several ways in which receiving edits on a document or viewing edit information can be alarming or upsetting, and lead to potential conflict as we will discuss further below.

In addition to edits, annotations to documents via commenting also served as indicators of others' activities around the document. Knowledge of these activities could have both positive and negative consequences.

Mirah, for example, said that she saw comments as an indicator that a collaborator had actively engaged with the contents of the document: "if there are comments I know that the person had actively engaged with my material."

Helen, a Ph.D student, referred explicitly to appreciating the amount of time and effort she assumed was behind the extensive editing and commenting performed by her advisor, saying "[it's] a very thoughtful practice that I really appreciate." On the other hand, a lack of comments could be interpreted as signs of disengagement or disinterest, which could have negative implications.

The role of edits in signifying the efforts of others sometimes also went beyond the literal meaning edits and comments in the document. Some participants reported that they could derive insights about what their collaborators were thinking about the work by reading the comments or edits. David, a Ph.D. student, noted that when his colleague gives verbose comments or an extensive set of edits, he "can really get to see what he's thinking, even if [he] can't talk," noting that this wouldn't be the case if he were to simply receive an unannotated revision.

Manipulation, judgment and threat

At the same time, many participants referred repeatedly to being alarmed at the appearance of edits, perceiving certain edits – or certain collaborators – as "overly critical." They said others' edits sometimes forced them to ask themselves "what am I doing wrong?" or referred to their ego being hurt. Participants sometimes used violent verbs (e.g., 'butcher,' 'hack,' 'tear,' and even 'rape') to describe others' edits to their text.

What all of this highlights is that writing can be an act of personal expression that can be hard to detach from the collaborative endeavor of which it is a part. As such, edits to a document can serve as more than mere alterations to content, and be perceived as an attack on one's self or acts of self-expression. This sentiment was common even on projects where responsibility for writing was acknowledged to be shared among all collaborators. This latter point foregrounds a key tension we wish to highlight: many people take their contributions to shared documents seriously, and edits to these sections can have relational effects. This is illustrated by Kaylee, a professional master's student who studied English in college:

> [I was upset] because I cared so much about how my writing comes across, and I'm very careful with the way I write, I was very annoyed, when the person who was charged with putting this book together, didn't give the thing back to me and say, 'This is a little bit too long' ... instead of sending it back to me and saying, 'This is too long,' he just hacked it apart himself. The thing that had my name on it was completely like, 'That's a horrible piece of writing.' I, personally, was mortified – overreacting, sure – but it had my name on it, and it wasn't something I thought was good writing.

Kaylee's experience highlights another key theme that is important for our discussion of edits and group maintenance. It was common for participants to report being upset when edits were perceived as reflecting unilateral decisions by another collaborator, without buy-in or consensus from others. Indeed, Kaylee was upset that editing had been done for her, without her consent or input.

This is about more than just ownership of work, or a challenge to something participants were proud of; there is a distinctly social element. One of Luke's group members made major changes the night of a deadline in a way that offended the rest of the group. He said that "it just didn't seem to us that it was very respectful of the time we had spent working on it for her to come through and just blow all that away," and wished she had discussed it with them.

These examples illustrate several ways in which editing signals had negative social effects, from being bothered by a lack of substantive contribution to being upset by manipulation of one's own work or somebody else's decision about something they felt they had a stake in.

Decisions around Edits: Messages and Relationships

Participants also reported being conscious of the possible negative social effects of editing other people's work. When using tools with edit history features, many described strategies for mitigating the risk of negative social interpretations of their edits.

Visible edits help, but also constrain

The first strategy that most participants described was being careful not to hide edits from collaborators and to use the edit history features available to them. Many felt that this implied that the edit was being presented as a possible revision for collaborators to consider, and not as a unilateral decision to change the document.

In reflecting on their use of these features, many participants discussed being concerned that their edits might be misinterpreted in a negative light. Some, like Kaylee, made direct references to their own experiences:

> I think it's really useful to be able to see what other people have changed about my work, so then I can say, 'OK, I'm OK with this change,' or 'No, I'd like to go back to what I originally wrote.' In the same way, I like other people to see that, so that I feel freer to make more expansive changes, so that they have an easy way to go and reject all of those if they so choose.

As her example illustrates, a key element of this process is consent and respect for others' work. Several participants explicitly described using edit history features as a way of showing respect. Some described it as imperative. Irene, a faculty member at a research university, explained that she typically uses track changes features because "it just shows respect to the co-author. You want to make sure that they're comfortable with the revisions. You just have to use it."

Even though track changes features were a common strategy for softening the potential social impact of edits, many participants reported that there were times when they avoided editing others' text directly or visibly, even with these features enabled. Often this was to avoid potential conflict. For instance, Zeb, an academic librarian, said he was careful to avoid manipulating text he sensed others might feel strongly about:

> Sometimes you [can] tell by the way somebody says something that they're into it. Like that they added a little flourish or something that you think is just awful. I try to be careful about something like that.

Another factor governing whether or not participants would directly edit others' text was expertise in the subject matter. Alice describes a project she was working on that involved some content about therapy, a topic she knew little about:

> I have no background in therapy and I don't understand all the issues that we're talking about there. So if a sentence didn't make sense to me, I wouldn't feel comfortable going and changing that, but I could make a comment.

Many of these responses reflect a common theme that was nicely summed up by Kaylee. In describing what was important to her in considering how her edits might cause awkward or unpleasant situations, Kaylee said, "you just have to try to figure out what value they care about in the actual written product."

Comments allow for explanation

Although refraining from directly editing content was a very common strategy for avoiding potentially relationship-damaging interpretations of their actions, many participants used writing tools as their primary medium for communicating and working with collaborators. That is, they often did not schedule face-to-face or other meetings to discuss the details of specific edits or changes.

Rather, discussions about revisions and negotiation around disagreements were often initiated via a commenting tool:

> Well, he put the note in where he was like, 'Um, I thought, you know... I was thinking that we weren't going to include this.' And so then, yes, [others in the group] would leave a comment and back him up and be like, 'Yes, I really think we should take it out, too.'

Such discussions both facilitated and created the impression of a group consensus and decision process, which served to bolster agreement around edits and reduce conflict.

Participants reported several specific uses for comments, which served as a way of handling the tension between two desires: one to change a document and another to avoid conflicts that could threaten effective group maintenance. In addition to using comments instead of edits, several participants also used comments to explain their edits. Irene, for example, uses comments to explain deletions:

> If I just delete that without telling them, it can be offensive. So, if I delete something, I will leave a reason. If I disagree, I will leave a reason because I want people to treat me the same way I treat them.

Another common strategy was to make general statements about the edits and feedback in an attempt to explain that they were being made without intending to attack others or threaten group dynamics. Ulric, for example, said that he had recently begun to preface his criticism, with a note that he intends no offense and simply wishes to be straightforward and constructive. When asked if he believed if it made a difference, he responded, "Yes... people receive [my straightforward criticism] better." Tessa, a Ph.D. student, did similarly, saying:

> throughout the process [of editing my colleague's masters thesis], ... I hoped that I expressed and I tried to express a couple times that I wouldn't be offended if none of my edits were appropriated.

It is interesting that Tessa used the word "express" in two ways here. The latter use refers to explicit statements, but the first references the way in which she was attempting to present herself via the tone of her communication:

> I don't feel like I moderated my edits [by refraining from making some]. But I do feel like I made extra care to -- in my comments -- to defer to [the primary author] and be strength based, and not be too critical... positing [it] as her choice rather than being, 'this is what you need to do.' And I think maybe some of that deference would have been unnecessary in Google Docs because it's not as glaring. It is transparent because you can go back. But it's not as, maybe, confrontational a format.

Overall, our participants reported many techniques for addressing issues in ways that would not be perceived as overly assertive, disrespectful of another's expertise or effort, unilateral, or otherwise impolite, especially when they knew their edits would be visible.

In contrast, another participant, who used a tool that did not make edits easily visible, said that he sometimes deliberately made changes without telling a collaborator, to avoid a confrontation:

> Like me and one other group member, we're pretty close friends, so we would talk about it. It'd be like "Oh, this person. I can't believe like, their writing is terrible. I don't want to be in a group with them ever again". But, it never got to the point where we confronted the person about it, necessarily. Because I would just go, and change it without her feedback. (Quintin, professional MS student)

Managing Relationships

In discussing these techniques, several participants explicitly noted the need for balance between actions focused on preserving relationships with group members – i.e., group maintenance – and actions aimed at improving the quality of their shared work. Richard, for example, was a student who discussed his attitude toward group projects:

> So, my rule for group work is, generally, you're probably not going to get an A. There's always going to be someone who will want you to do something that will cause you to have a B. But it's much easier to get that B and remain pleasant with the group than it is to fight a long, hard battle with the group over something that, in the long run, will probably not be too effectual.

Mirah noted further that she uses comments and feedback to maintain a positive impression:

> I always want to make sure that whoever I'm editing for knows that I've put time into reading their paper. I want to make sure that I've written comments, that I've given them useful feedback. At the same time, I don't want to hurt them because I'm being too harsh of their work. I'm always walking that line.

Some participants talked about managing social relationships by being conscious of others' impressions of them. David mentioned that he is conscious of when he makes edits, as he believes the timing of the edits in the trace history will inform others' impressions of him as an engaged and thorough collaborator:

> I'm conscious of that when [my colleague] sends me a paper and he says ... I'll take a look at your edits on Monday. He'll be able to see if I did work on it Friday or Saturday or Sunday, or, you know, if I just did an hour's edits before giving it to him on Monday.

Finally, some participants referred explicitly to the impact of their editing behavior on their relationships with collaborators beyond the scope of the current project. For example, Ed, a professor, describes the lasting effect of an incident nearly eight years prior to our interview:

> I had an incident in '03 where I was writing a paper, and the co-author and I didn't really talk very explicitly about how we were going to do the process. So I got the document. I spent like 20 hours one weekend doing a kind of major rewrite of it, because I thought we were sort of collaboratively authoring, and then she just rejected everything that I did as like, "It's my paper," and that led to a not very good collaborative feeling for a long time.

This was emblematic of several participants' feelings about edits perceived as rude or inconsiderate that impacted their relationship with collaborators, and often motivated them to seek other collaborators on future work. This can happen even in the absence of a strong emotional reaction:

> If [a collaborator] changes my idea completely, then I'm like, 'I don't really want to work with them again.' But I'm not really unhappy about it, like "Oh my gosh. I can't believe they did this to me." I'm like maybe next time I shouldn't work with this person. (Vanessa, undergraduate)

Interpretation Strategies

We mentioned at the outset that reduced cues in online environments can affect the interpretation of messages and attribution of credit, blame, and motivation. We have seen that cues about a collaborator's edit actions can be interpreted in negative ways. While our participants described several strategies for mitigating the risk of having their edits perceived in such ways, it also was clear that several participants – especially those with more experience working with others – were able to reduce or avoid negative interpretations of edit actions taken by collaborators.

We found that there were three themes underlying the cases in which participants reported being able to do this.

Presentation style and habits of others

Some participants said they had to develop an understanding that something that might initially seem rude was actually the result of somebody else's routine, habit, or style; or even the way the software presented others' actions. Helen was one of several participants who noted that Track Changes often displays edits in red and that this contributed to a perception of them as harsh and negative in tone. However, she also noted that she's gotten used to this, and does not believe the edits are intended to be harsh:

> especially when somebody has made all their comments red – there is the idea that you've done something wrong. But really, [that's] not [the case]; I think the more that I've done [the more] I've become used to it.

Tessa discussed how her adviser's blunt style of commenting upset her when she first began working with him, but after several terms of working together finds it easier to cope with. She cited knowledge of his habits as one of the reasons that she no longer gets as upset:

> I just got used to [the fact] that that was his communication style. In the same breath he could make all of these sharp criticisms but then also send me an email that same day thanking me or making some other nice comment. So it was clearly separated for me in my mind.

Separating task from social relations

Other times, participants reported learning to assume that others' edits had been made with task-oriented intentions – that is, to improve the joint product. For Tessa, this meant taking her adviser's criticism "a little less personally":

> I think I'm able to have a little bit more of the perspective that he's taking on the role of a article reviewer and trying to help me by spotting out where other people would have criticisms or comments and kind of preempt those by helping me fill in the gaps. I mean I still regret that from the beginning it isn't more of a collaboration because I think that would be [more helpful than just acting as editor]. But I do appreciate that he's looking at it with a critical eye, like, 'how would it be received by reviewers?'

Olivia had similarly positive thoughts about the value of feedback. She described it as an extremely important part of her interactions with collaborators and editors.

> I feel like, I personally have a hard time making drastic changes to someone's paper just because I don't want to hurt their feelings. But as of now, being this far into my degree and studying information, I feel like feedback, receiving good feedback is really important. So now I'm not so concerned about that, because I would also want to receive the best feedback that I could.

Yolanda told us about a new member of her otherwise stable and established lab group, believing that he will adapt to receiving criticism in a more positive way just as she felt she did when she joined the group:

> He's just new to the lab. He's not really that close to us. We try to be friendly. We can't break him in just yet. Whenever we break or rip apart his work, he takes it to heart. We tell him: listen, at the end of the day, the poster is going to have all of our names on it. The manuscript is going to have all of our names on it. Don't take it to heart. We're doing this so that you can be a better writer in life, and that you could just learn from it. Then you could just be part of the team and build on it. I know he's having a hard time adjusting. Anybody would, just to have your work butchered. I was in that position when I was a sophomore and joined the team.

When asked about what she thought was important when writing with others, Helen said the following:

> I think like the easy thing to say would be I don't want to seem like a loser to the person I'm coauthoring with. I want to find the mistakes that I've made before they find them. And be conscientious and upfront in our writing partnership about my own weaknesses and be willing to confront them so that we can be a stronger paper. I think for me one of the worst feelings is when someone feels like they can't critique your work because you're not going to be able to take it well. And so completely like putting the other writer at ease that you're willing to be critical … in a way that sets up everybody to be critical."

Helen's response also illustrates the fact that these issues (a) go both ways, and (b) are relevant not just to a single action or set of edits, but to a series of interactions or even a whole relationship. Indeed, collaboration often involves much more than a single editing pass, and often involves editing by multiple people. Helen discusses the focus on the task-oriented goal as setting the tone of a relationship, rather than a single interaction.

It is worth noting that it is apparent from participants' comments that focusing on edits as constructive criticism – rather than on their potential social meanings –was not their natural tendency when interacting in this way. Doing so required intent and learning.

DISCUSSION

We began with two questions about the social and relational implications of workspace awareness information in collaborative writing. The first was about how people interpret information about others' edits and behavior in shared documents; and the second was about how people take others' possible reactions into account in their own edits and behavior. Generally, we found that participants' reactions to others' actions were affected by social messages perceived in edits, and that many participants do consider how their edits will be interpreted. They try to mitigate the risk of conflict via annotation by ensuring that their edits are not perceived as excessive or unilateral.

Implications for Theory

From a theoretical standpoint, one key implication is that task-focused workspace awareness information – such as visible edits to a shared document – can have relational consequences. Our participants frequently saw edits, particularly when they were perceived as changes being made without the consensus or approval of the group, as a potential threat or personal criticism. This was exacerbated by the fact that edits are shown with little contextual information, so they can be (and were often) misinterpreted as meaning more than the editor intended. As we think about awareness support for collaborative writing, we should therefore focus not just on task (as in [30] and [32]), but also on group maintenance.

Another point is that the conflicts participants described tended to be around relatively large or conceptual changes to documents. Some participants were sensitive to others' making changes to their grammar or spelling, but most were appreciative of these types of edits. Thus, simple change awareness may be suitable for smaller edits, but larger edits may require more attention to relationship management. Size, however, is only one way to assess the magnitude or impact of edits, so this issue merits further study.

Most commercially available systems used by our participants focus primarily on change awareness; that is, highlighting what was changed, when, and who made the change. This approach, in effect, takes "How did things get to be the way they are?" as its motivating question. This can be useful for minor changes and in cases described in [36], but relies on a conceptual model of the writing process that may not always be appropriate.

In contrast to this approach, the processes our participants described as being effective from a group maintenance standpoint had two closely related elements in common. First, they often sought to present changes to shared documents not as definitive revisions, but rather as options for moving forward along with some rationale. What is interesting here from a conceptual standpoint is that the purpose of the group editing features was not to track who changed what and when, but rather to signal attention to the document and frame *possible* changes.

We began the paper with a discussion of how awareness information is used to predict future behavior, and of the potential social value of ambiguity. We argue, in essence, that our participants appropriated the available tools (i.e., commenting) to increase ambiguity around the future state of the document, and then used this ambiguity as a way to propose changes without threatening their collaborators' autonomy. In other words, framing edits as possible future directions or tentative is a way to use ambiguity in being sensitive to others' possible reactions.

Second and relatedly, our participants described actions within shared documents that were shaped not only by awareness of what their collaborators had done in the past, but also anticipating their collaborators' future actions and reactions. This suggests that in thinking conceptually about collaborative writing we aim to ask not just "How did things get the way they are?", but also ask "What are we going to do next?" or "What will happen next?" A consequence of this shift is treating the shared document not just as a collection of past edits, but rather as information about a set of options for moving forward in multiple plausible directions. In the next section we describe some ideas for adopting this conceptual approach.

A second consequence of this shift is allowing for the anticipation of future action. That is, people act in shared documents not just to bring a document closer to its final state, but also because they believe others will react in particular ways or make particular changes. Their actions can also, deliberately or inadvertently, draw the attention of others. We therefore urge viewing the document as a negotiation space, in which all actions – not just explicit comments or feedback – are considered moves in the negotiation process that is the writing of a document together. We might generally frame actions in a document as moves in what Clark [8]describes as "joint action" – in which actions are understood (and assumed to be interpreted) within the larger context of a shared goal, which here is a complete document. As such, the way these moves are presented (as visible or invisible, for example), has significant consequences for the process.

Implications for Design

While much work has examined the functional problems involved in managing multiple versions [40] and resolving conflicts between them [35] – especially in contexts with parallel editing [22, 28], we argue that more consideration of collaboration's social dimensions is necessary. These include people's inevitable reactions to each other's behavior, and the management of relationships between collaborators. This can help avoid the negative social interpretations that our participants reported even in the absence of version conflict or explicit disagreement.

Consider Group Maintenance. Our results demonstrate clearly that participants were conscious not just of their writing tasks, but also of the relational consequences of these task-focused behaviors. They frequently took steps to avoid relational conflict by attempting to create ambiguity around the future state of the document, or by engaging in dialog (via face-to-face conversation or using commenting features) with collaborators. We urge designers to consider not just the task of writing, but also support for group maintenance activities such as conversation, explaining edits and sometimes hiding certain actions. Features in current systems such as chat (in Google Docs) and commenting are steps in this direction.

Additional steps could include hiding certain types of changes (e.g., grammar or spelling fixes) from other collaborators, or even the ability to make specific changes visible to only to selected collaborators. In some ways this is similar to Cohen et al.'s [10] suggestions for selective awareness in adversarial collaborations, but we believe these ideas would be useful in cooperative scenarios too.

This would, of course, necessitate some means for also making those collaborators aware of the possibility. This could be achieved, via options that collaborators could agree to such as "Only make me aware of major changes to this section" or "I agree that John can make changes to this section without notifying me." The fundamental point, however is that we consider ways to allow for some changes to be made without drawing undue attention, while still allowing those who wish to make their edits visible (i.e., for a mentor editing a student's work) to do so.

Present Changes as Possibilities. First, we urge designers to think carefully about ways to visualize changes not as definitive alterations to a document, but rather as potentially ambiguous possibilities for moving forward. This could be as simple as changing a notification such as "John deleted XXX at 12:45 pm on June 3" to "John suggests deleting XXX..." or allowing users to classify certain changes as "suggestions" (or "strong suggestions").

It could also involve more sophisticated changes to writing systems, however. Documents could include multiple plausible versions, allowing for them to be visualized and manipulated with interfaces more akin to the "layers" metaphor in graphics applications (i.e., Adobe Photoshop) than to traditional word processing.

Consider features for new groups. As Leshed et al. [27] note, groups are frequently expected to work together with little knowledge or training about how to do so effectively. We saw that many of our participants developed strategies for interpreting the edits and feedback of others in ways that allowed them to work together more effectively – such as by learning about the habits of others and assuming that feedback was being presented constructively. These are skills that might be taught to new groups of collaborators.

Substantial intelligence has been built into software like Microsoft Word to anticipate common behaviors such as typing the date, misspelling a word or violating basic grammar. Similar features could be built in to help groups work together. Making substantial edits to text written by somebody else, for example, could automatically trigger the appearance of an optional comment box for explanation. Such features could help people anticipate the reactions of their collaborators and work more effectively together.

Limitations and Future Work

One limitation of this study is a limited range of participants. While we spoke primarily with students, many of our participants did have experience writing with others in both academic and professional contexts. Several of the professional master's students described prior work experience (though we did not ask them about this explicitly, so cannot report the exact number), and the librarians and faculty write as part of their current jobs. Undergraduates described writing mostly for course projects, but other participants described writing and editing academic (research) papers, film scripts, short stories, communications to the public, and product evaluations. . It is possible that speaking primarily with students biased our sample somewhat and we do not claim our results generalize, but we do believe their breadth of experience provides exploratory lessons for others interested in collaborative writing. A systematically stratified sample for population and document types would be an excellent starting point for future work.

We also spoke with people who had worked in both voluntary and assigned collaborative groups; and spoke with more women than men. While we did not identify any systematic effects of either of these factors, it is possible that they could affect the prevalence of conflict. Finally, it is possible that people did not accurately recall their experiences, though we have no reason to believe this was the case, and this is common to all interview studies.

In future work we plan to use these results to develop a series of experiments that aim to identify specific sources of social and relational conflict in the group writing process. We also aim to work with system developers to improve and evaluate systems to support collaborative writing.

CONCLUSION

We have presented an interview study of how people write together, with a particular focus on the role of collaboration features in group maintenance. Results suggest that edits and comments often carry social meaning. They may be interpreted as harsh criticism or threats to autonomy, and can have emotional and relational impact. Moreover, participants reported being conscious of this as they work with others, but also noted that aspects of the way these edits are presented and visualized can affect their interpretation. Participants tried to present edits as possible changes, drawing on ambiguity about the future of the document. As such, we conclude by arguing that a conceptual shift may be warranted in how we support collaborative writing. We propose focusing less on answering "How did things get the way they are?" and more on "What is going to happen next?".

ACKNOWLEDGMENTS

We thank Catherine Harley for her assistance with this research, and Google for partial financial support.

REFERENCES

1. Aoki, P. and Woodruff, A. Making space for stories: ambiguity in the design of personal communication systems. In *Proc. ACM CHI* (2005), 181-190.
2. Bazarova, N. and Walther, J. Attribution of blame in distributed work. In P. Lutgen-Sandvik and B. D. Sypher, eds. *The destructive side of organizational communication.* Routledge, New York, 2009.
3. Bietz, M. J. Effects of communication media on the interpretation of critical feedback. In *Proc. ACM CSCW* (2008), 467-476.
4. Birnholtz, J., Guillory, J., Hancock, J., Bazarova, N. "on my way": Deceptive Texting and Interpersonal Awareness Narratives. In *Proc. ACM CSCW* (2010), 1-4.
5. Boehner, K. and Hancock, J. Advancing Ambiguity. In *Proc. ACM CHI* (2006), 103-107.
6. Brown, P. and Levinson, S. *Politeness: Some universals in language usage*. Cambridge Press, New York 1987.

7. Bryant, S., Forte, A. and Bruckman, A. Becoming wikipedian: transformation of participation in a collaborative online community. In *Proc. ACM Group* (2005), 1-10.
8. Clark, H. H. *Using language*. Cambridge Press, New York, 1996.
9. Cody, M. J. and McLaughlin, M. L. Interpersonal accounting. In H. Giles and P. Robinson, ed. *Handbook of language and social psychology*. Wiley and Sons, London, 1990.
10. Cohen, A. L., Cash, D. and Muller, M. Designing to Support Adversarial Collaboration. In *Proc. ACM CSCW* (2000), 31-39.
11. De Dreu, C. K. W. and Weingart, L. R. Task versus relationship conflict, team performance, and team member satisfaction: A meta-analysis. *Journal of Applied Psychology*, 88(2003), 741-749.
12. Dourish, P. and Belotti, V. Awareness and Coordination in Shared Workspaces. In *Proc. ACM CSCW* (1992), 107-114.
13. Endsley, M. R. Toward a Theory of Situation Awareness in Dynamic Systems. *Human Factors*, 37, 1 (1995), 32-64.
14. Glaser, B. G. and Strauss, A. L. *The discovery of grounded theory: strategies for qualitative research*. Aldine de Gruyter, Hawthorne, NY, 1967.
15. Goffman, E. *Behavior in Public Places*. The Free Press, New York, 1963.
16. Goffman, E. *The presentation of self in everyday life*. Anchor Books, New York, 1959.
17. 17. Gutwin, C. and Greenberg, S. A descriptive framework of workspace awareness for real-time groupware. *CSCW*, 11(2002), 411-446.
18. Hackman, R. The design of work teams. In J. Lorsch, ed. *Handbook of organizational behavior*. Prentice-Hall, Englewood Cliffs, NJ, 1987.
19. Hancock, J. T., Birnholtz, J., Bazarova, N., Guillory, J., Perlin, J. and Amos, B. Butler lies: awareness, deception and design. *Proc. ACM CHI*(2009), 517-526.
20. Heath, C. and Luff, P. *Technology in Action*. Cambridge Press, Cambridge, UK, 2000.
21. Huberman, A. M. and Miles, M. B. Data management and analysis methods. In Lincoln and Denzin, ed. *Handbook of Qualitative Research*. Sage, Thousand Oaks, CA, 1994.
22. Ignat, C. L. and Norrie, M. C. Multi-level Editing of Hierarchical Documents. *CSCW*, 17, 5-6 (2008), 423-468.
23. Kim, H. C. and Eklundh, K. S. Reviewing practices in collaborative writing. *CSCW*, 10(2001), 247-259.
24. Kittur, A., Suh, B., Pendleton, B. A. and Chi, E. He says, she says: conflict and coordination in Wikipedia. In *Proc. ACM CHI* (2007), 453-462.
25. Kraut, R., Galegher, J., Fish, R. and Chalfonte, B. Task Requirements and Media Choice in Collaborative Writing. *HCI*, 7(1992), 375-407.
26. Leland, M. D., Fish, R. S. and Kraut, R. E. Quilt: A collaborative tool for cooperative writing. In *Proc. ACM CSCW* (1988), 206-215.
27. Leshed, G., Perez, D., Hancock, J., Cosley, D., Birnholtz, J., McLeod, P. and Gay, G. Visualizing Real-Time Language-Based Feedback on Teamwork Behavior in Computer-Mediated Groups. In *Proc. ACM CHI* (2009), 537-546.
28. Lukosch, S. and Leisen, A. Comparing and Merging Versioned Wiki Pages. In *Proc. WEBIST* (2009), 159-173.
29. Neuwirth, C. M., Chandhok, R., Charney, D., Wojahn, P. and Kim, L. Distributed Collaborative Writing: A comparison of spoken and written modalities for reviewing and revising documents. In *Proc. ACM CHI* (1994), 51-57.
30. Neuwirth, C. M., Kaufer, D. S., Chandhok, R. and Morris, J. H. Computer Support for Distributed Collaborative Writing: A Coordination Science Perspective. In G. M. Olson and T. W. Malone, ed. *Coordination Theory and Collaboration Technology*. Lawrence Erlbaum Assoc, Mahwah, NJ, 2000.
31. Noel, S. and Robert, J.-M. Empirical study on collaborative writing: what do co-authors do, use and like? *CSCW*, 13(2004), 63-89.
32. Posner, I. and Baecker, R. How People Write Together. In *Proc.. HICSS* (1993), 127-138.
33. Scott, M. B. and Lyman, S. M. Accounts. *American Sociological Review*, 33(1968), 46-62.
34. Sudnow, D. Temporal parameters of interpersonal observation. In D. Sudnow, ed. *Studies in Social Interaction*. Free Press, New York, 1972.
35. Sun, C. and Chen, D. Consistency maintenance in real-time collaborative graphics editing systems *ACM TOCHI*, 9, 1 (2002), 1-41.
36. Tam, J. and Greenberg, S. A framework for asynchronous change awareness in collaborative documents and workspaces. *IJHCS*, 64(2006), 583-598.
37. Walther, J. Computer-mediated communication: Impersonal, interpersonal, and hyperpersonal interaction. *Communication Research*, 23(1996), 3-43.
38. Watts, R. J. *Politeness*. Cambridge Press, Cambridge, UK, 2003.
39. Wuchty, S., Jones, B. F. and Uzzi, B. The increasing dominance of teams in production of knowledge. *Science*, 316, 5827 (2007), 1036-1039.
40. Xue, L., Orgun, M. A. and Zhang, K. A Multi-Versioning Scheme for Intention Preservation in Collaborative Editing Systems. *CSCW*, 17, 5-6 (2008), 509-551.

Bon Voyage: Social Travel Planning in the Enterprise

Netta Aizenbud Reshef, Artem Barger, Yael Dubinsky, Ido Guy, Shiri Kremer Davidson
IBM Haifa Research Lab
Haifa, Israel
neta@il.ibm.com, artem.barger@gmail.com, {dubinsky, ido, shiri}@il.ibm.com

ABSTRACT
A proliferation of travel-related web sites enable people to share their travel plans, review hotels, offer advice, and more. In this paper we study social travel planning in the enterprise. While business travelers and leisure travelers have different preferences and needs, employees may benefit from sharing information and travel plans within the enterprise. We present a study collecting the requirements for social travel from employees, detail the design principles of a social travel application in the enterprise, and present Voyage, the outcome. We evaluated Voyage based on qualitative and quantitative data and discuss the results using four perspectives: collaborative activities, social information impact, usage patterns, and sharing behavior. Employees expressed their growing satisfaction from the social information contributed by fellow employees. Moreover, we observed that Voyage shortens the reservation time, thus saving costs for the enterprise.

Author Keywords
Business travel, social activity.

ACM Classification Keywords
H.5.3. Information interfaces and presentation: *Computer-supported cooperative work.*

General Terms
Human Factors; Experimentation; Measurement.

INTRODUCTION
Online social travel sites play a valuable role in helping people plan and book their trips. These sites typically provide the most relevant information about places people can visit, transportation options, and services available. This information is accompanied by social information such as reviews and ratings.

Studies report that 80% of leisure travelers are influenced by of consumer-generated media such as videos, reviews, and blogs [18]. Moreover, the popularity of online social travel sites becomes obvious when looking at the flow of online travel traffic [6]. In online travel sites such as TripAdvisor, Hotels.com, and Yelp, some people share their opinions and experiences about places they visit, hotels they stay in, and services they use. Recently, people have also begun sharing their itinerary details with a select list of friends through services such as TripIt and Dopplr.

Shared social data provides travelers with a variety of benefits, such as feeling actively involved in and satisfied with the trip planning process, more concrete expectations, and greater confidence in the decisions they make [7]. Further, travel-related content contributions have become an important information source for travelers and the majority trust this content [8]. In online hotel bookings, for example, the most important influencing factors are recommendations of friends and online reviews [3]. In addition, travel recommendation systems tend to accelerate the decision-making process [2].

Although social data has proven to be beneficial, findings [8] show that only a small number of travelers engage in content contribution and there is a difficulty in increasing the number of people willing to share information on the web. This is explained, among others, by the lack of a need to post or even the negative effect it might have [14].

People are willing to share more information within the enterprise than on a public site because they are less concerned about the ramifications of sharing personal identifying information [4]. Employees are open to meeting each other on a social networking site for both personal and professional reasons, perhaps because of existing common ground. Likewise, in a study on a social bookmarking service, it was found that in an enterprise there is a willingness to share informational resources for the benefit of the organization [11]. These findings are expected for business travel as well, where employees would be more willing to share their travel plans inside the organization. They would also feel more accountable for the reviews they are providing since their identity is known and they are more likely to trust a recommendation of a fellow worker than of a stranger.

Enterprise (business) travel and leisure travel differ in many aspects [16, 17], including control over the destination, co-travelers, lead time (the time from reservation to trip start), and more. In addition, they have different preferences in services they use in various categories such as planning, reservations, safety and health. Business travelers focus less on the leisure aspect of the trip. For example, one of the most important requirements of a business traveler from a hotel room is the internet connectivity, which might be less important for a leisure traveler. In another example, a business traveler on a tight-schedule might be less interested in leisure activities in the city and more interested in the nearest shop where he can quickly buy presents for his family.

Several studies have found [1, 19] that enterprise travel applications are valuable for the enterprise as a whole. The applications reduce the time spent searching for travel information, reduce the time of discussion with an agent, and also lower travel costs. Providing social capabilities as part of the enterprise travel application is expected to lower travel costs further, as employees are provided with the opportunity to share travel reservations and even travel less, since more business meetings on the same trip may be facilitated due to social awareness. These business meetings can lead to new business opportunities which are one of the goals of the enterprise.

The apparent success of social travel web sites raises the question of whether large enterprises and their employees would also benefit from a social travel application. The expected benefits are both for the employees and for the enterprise. Q1: Would employees feel comfortable sharing their travel plans in the enterprise since they feel less concerned about privacy issues? Q2: How involved would they be in coordinating plans? Q3: Will social information influence them when making a reservation? Q4: How often would they share a taxi ride to save costs? Q5: Would awareness of travel plans from other employees facilitate ad-hoc meetings and reduce travel? Q6: Would it also contribute to the creation of new business opportunities, for example, by learning that a potential customer is going to be at a travel destination?

In this work, we try to answer these questions. We asked employees about the social features they would benefit from when planning a trip using an enterprise travel application. We experiment with Voyage, an enterprise social travel application that is deployed in a big global enterprise. Voyage is based on the Web 2.0 paradigm and is built as a social layer on top of an existing enterprise travel application. We explore potentially valuable social features in an enterprise travel application and its usage patterns.

The contribution of this study is twofold. First, it highlights how including social features as part of enterprise travel can benefit both employees and the organization. Second, based on a thorough analysis of broad data, it reveals patterns for how people use social travel information.

This paper is organized as follows. First we describe a field study aimed at understanding the benefits employees foresee from having a social travel application in the organization. Then we describe the main design principles that guided the implementation of Voyage. We describe the primary features of Voyage and discuss the results of a field study. We conclude with a summary and future work.

SOCIAL TRAVEL NEEDS IN THE ENTERPRISE

To understand the social needs of employees from an enterprise travel application, we collected data from two sources. (1) We conducted qualitative interviews with ten employees, asking which methods and tools they use for travel planning, the issues they encounter, and capabilities they are missing. (2) A user survey was sent to frequent travelers, querying their willingness to share their travel plans and the benefits they envisioned in knowing about others' past reservations and future plans (1431 employees answered this survey). We collected data from employees in Asia, Europe, the Middle East, and North America.

We divide the results into three facets of social capabilities: awareness, sharing, and collaboration.

Awareness

Employees see value in knowing what other employees selected in the past. Of those surveyed, 81% indicated that it is useful to know at which hotel other people from the enterprise usually stay; 83% look for employees they know who stayed at a hotel they are considering; and 69% find it useful to know who recently visited your travel destination.

Many interviewees also indicated that they would like to have a better way to obtain all the relevant information they need to know while preparing for travel. They complained that they need to collect this information from many different sources such as maps for directions, location of offices and the office support items (printers, floor plans, and conference room reservations), weather forecasts, and daily meal allowances.

When circumstances change, employees would want the application to recommend what they should do. One employee who ran into a flight delay scenario suggested: "*If I had known in advance it was delayed, I might have waited elsewhere or taken a train. I would use that time to meet/talk with other employees*".

Sharing

Employees mentioned that they often use external internet web sites to look for hotel reviews and ratings since the travel reservation application used in the enterprise does not contain user reviews. Our survey indicates that employees value reviews and ratings of other employees. Of those surveyed, 75% stated that it can be very useful for them. As one person noted, "*I should be able to see other company traveler's reviews of hotels, and should be able to add reviews concerning specific features of the hotel. For example, how to access their Wi-Fi, specific directions to/from the company office that reflect traffic reality, and comments on really great (or bad) staff*".

From the interviews, we learned that employees are willing to add reviews for the benefit of others and asked to receive an email reminding them to do so.

Employees also appreciate the recommendations of local employees: "*Wouldn't it be nice to know what the locals are saying if you were travelling to Cambridge?*" They are also willing to contribute such data on their home location: "*A place for local people to give local recommendations*".

From the survey it is evident that employees are willing to share their travel plans with different groups of employees in 95% of the cases. Table 1 depicts the willingness of employees to share their travel information with anyone in the enterprise (Anyone), their social network (SN), specific people (Specific), or not at all (No one). As can be seen, there are differences in willingness to share future planned trips versus past trips.

Share \ With	Anyone	SN	Specific	No one
Future plans				
Flight	32%	35%	28%	5%
Hotel	34%	39%	24%	4%
City	29%	37%	28%	6%
Past travels				
Flight	45%	34%	18%	3%
Hotel	48%	37%	13%	3%
City	47%	35%	14%	3%

Table 1: Sharing travel plans

As for sharing resources e.g., car rental, 35% indicated they would share with anyone in the enterprise; 45% would share only with known people; and the other 20% are not willing to share at all. One of the interviewees noted: "*I don't want to sit next to another co-worker on a plane. But I don't mind sharing rides to and from the airport*".

When asked about the importance of controlling the sharing defaults in the system, 16% responded that it is critical for them, 45% indicated it is important for them, 31% said it is slightly important for them, and 8% said they don't care.

Collaboration

Both the interviews and the survey indicate that employees have a need to coordinate their trip plans with others (30% of them indicated so in the survey). Moreover, 35% find it a difficult task. One of the interviewees noted: "*Coordination is the trickiest thing*". Coordination is done using diverse tools, such as email, phone, instant messaging, and face-to-face conversations. All these tools are separate from the travel reservation application that is used in the company. Employees would like better systems for coordination that would ease the task of reserving the same flight and hotel if traveling together, sharing rides, and meeting after hours: "*I should be able to share my specific travel plans with any other employee that I select; that would really help when planning group trips, since then my teammates would see when I'm flying, so we can share ground transport*".

When it comes to coordinating travel plans, 70% of employees stated that it is beneficial to know what flight a colleague is going to take, and 70% want to know who else is attending a meeting/conference/event. On average, 70% of employees find this type of information very useful, while only 2% of employees indicated it is not useful at all. These benefits were raised by employees: "*It's useful to have rough itineraries of when people are arriving*", and "*It's good to take the same flights so we can chat in the terminal*". Employees also see value in coordinating while traveling: "*Would like to know who else is currently traveling to location xyz. Set status message as 'Looking for someone with whom to eat dinner'*".

DESIGN PRINCIPLES

Prior to the development of Voyage, employees used an enterprise travel application (such as Expedia or Orbitz), deployed worldwide that did not include any social features. When designing Voyage, we took the requirements from the previous sections into account so we could provide these social capabilities to the employees. During this process we were confronted with various design decisions, several of which are described below.

Voyage Position

One of the first design decisions we had to make was how Voyage would relate to the existing enterprise travel application. We inspected the following options:

1. Develop Voyage as a separate application, providing social travel features, in such a way that employees can search Voyage for reviews, learn from past travelers, and make decisions. Once settled with their selections, they could use the enterprise travel application to make the actual reservations and purchase.
2. Develop Voyage as a separate application (as in option 1) with integration points to enable exporting/importing a trip itinerary from one application to another and ease the travel reservation process.
3. Tightly integrate Voyage with the enterprise travel application, providing the social features as part of the travel reservation process.

We chose the last option as it seemed optimal for our users, although it was the most complex for implementation. This option did not require the users to learn a new application. The travel reservation process they were familiar with would remain the same, and they would get the benefits from the social features throughout the travel reservation process. The drawback of this approach was that users who were used to the flow of the enterprise travel application might not pay attention to the new social features.

Privacy Controls

Before we introduced social features to the enterprise travel application, each employee would use the application solely for planning her travel, with the travel details visible only to herself. They could have shared travel plans using email or any other means of communication, but could not do so through the travel reservation application itself. Since we were designing a social travel application, we wanted to facilitate the sharing of travel plans through the application. We decided to introduce three levels of privacy to trips: Private, Public, and Confidants.

The 'Private' level allows employees to keep their plans private when confidentiality is required (e.g. when an executive is traveling to a new customer). The 'Public' level enables employees to share their travel plans with anyone in the enterprise.

The 'Confidants' level is meant for employees who do not feel comfortable sharing their travel plans with anyone in the enterprise. It provides a level of sharing that falls somewhere between private and public. We looked at how other social applications share information. Many of them provide a symmetric "friending" mechanism: users can invite others to be their friends. A friend request is sent to the invitee and upon acceptance, the friending relation is formed. In addition, some applications (e.g., Facebook, see http://www.facebook.com) let users arrange friends into different groups and define privacy controls separately for each group. We decided not to follow the Facebook paradigm for the following reasons:

1. We wanted to relieve users from the need to maintain yet another list of friends, this one only for travel.
2. The relation that sharing travel plans imposes in the enterprise context is not symmetric. For example, an employee might want to share his travel plans with a manager, but not vice versa.
3. We believe that there is no fixed group of employees with whom someone wants to share all travel plans, as the purpose of the trip might vary, and the group of people that needs to be aware of it might vary as well.

In keeping with the above, the 'Confidants' level enables users to define the list of people they would like to share their travel plans with on a trip-by-trip basis. To ease this process, the application suggests a list of people with whom to share. This list is based on the user's enterprise social network (calculated by SONAR [9]) and the list of Confidants from past travels. The 'Confidants' relation is asymmetric. The people who are declared as Confidants of a trip can look into its details but not the other way round.

As for reviews entered by employees, we decided that they would be declared public, since we did not see any reason someone would post a review of a hotel, for example, if not for the benefit of all.

Trip Coordination/Conversation

One of the requirements raised by users was the ability to coordinate travel plans. It was clear that we needed to support some place where people could discuss/exchange travel plans. We debated where to best position the conversation place and who should be allowed to participate in it. We decided to attach the conversations to trips. This decision was reinforced by the special asymmetric 'Confidants' relation we defined for trips, which enables only Confidants of this trip to see the travel plans. We used a commenting mechanism to facilitate the conversation. The trip owner and its Confidants are allowed to participate in the conversation by adding comments on a trip and reading comments added to the trip by others. Trip comments inherit the privacy level of the trip itself. If the trip is declared private, only the trip owner can place comments on it and they are visible only to her. This can be used, for example, for personal note taking. If the trip is declared public, its comments are visible to all employees and anyone can add comments. For a 'Confidants' trip, the comments are visible to the trip owner and the trip's confidants, and only they can add comments.

Alerting and Discovery

To encourage ongoing use of the application, and inspire users to add reviews and share their travel plans, it was important to consider mechanisms that notify users of relevant activity in the application. Various notification mechanisms have been shown to contribute significantly to sustaining online interaction in other collaboration applications [12]. We therefore decided to use alerts to notify users of relevant activities in the application. These may include: being added as a confidant to a trip, a new comment added to the user's trip, and more. In addition we use email notifications to encourage users to add reviews of their recent trips for the benefit of others, a few days after the employee returns from a trip.

Serendipity

Support for serendipity was one of our design goals. We perceived it as one of the important aspects of making the travel reservation process more social, especially since meeting with relevant (possibly unfamiliar) people is one of the goals of business travel. Serendipity can raise the awareness of other employees who may not be familiar with each other and helps establish communication. In our opinion, serendipity for business travel is different from serendipity for leisure travel. Leisure travelers care about different types of serendipity, for example, that a festival is taking place during their visit. Business travelers care more about the business context of serendipity.

Hence, we tried to identify places in the application and during the travel reservation process where it would be beneficial to show other people traveling to the same place at the same time. This would facilitate meetings and discussions that were not otherwise planned.

Extensibility

We see Voyage, and its social data, as beneficial to other travel-related applications in the organization. For example, the enterprise expenses reporting system could benefit from the reviews provided. This required enabling capabilities to be exploited programmatically through REST APIs [5]. These capabilities include, for example, the ability to obtain a list of reviews for a travel item, show a list of imminent trips of a user, get useful country information, and more.

Business Considerations

Along with new social features for Voyage, the business aspects that interest the enterprise should also be taken into account, such as enhancing collaboration among employees, promoting new business opportunities and saving costs. These interests are part of the design principles discussed above (coordination, serendipity, sharing) and thus to be also addressed in Voyage.

VOYAGE – TRAVEL MEETS SOCIAL

Voyage extends the enterprise travel application and makes the egocentric travel reservation process more social. The original enterprise travel application supports a travel reservation process similar to common web-based travel reservation applications. It already includes the enterprise policies, such as the list of approved hotels and preferred airlines. The application enables users to search for flights, hotels and car rentals, explore the results, make selections and continue to purchase. Voyage introduces new social features which are divided into the three facets of social capabilities: awareness, sharing, and collaboration. Although similar features are already available in travel applications on the web, we developed these features in the context of the enterprise taking into account their different goals. Table 2 highlights the difference in the context between social travel facets in the enterprise and social travel on the web. A thorough description is provided throughout the following sections.

Context / Facet	Travel in the enterprise	Travel on the web
Awareness	Business awareness	Social awareness
Sharing	Business alignment	Socializing
Collaboration	Business activities	General purpose

Table 2: Enterprise vs. web comparison of social facets

Awareness

Features belonging to this facet enhance awareness to business travel, enabling employees to ask for business tips (who should I meet in the location I am traveling to, what meeting rooms are available), coordinate business meetings, enhance business collaboration and lead to new business opportunities. In addition, the collective knowledge of where people are traveling can be used to negotiate better rates for flights, hotel reservations, and car rentals, thus saving costs for the enterprise. Similar features on travel web sites are mostly meant for social awareness, enabling users to get local tips and coordinate social activities.

Personalized Welcome Page

The original welcome page contained general information such as announcements about changes in the application and enterprise policies, quick links to other features of the application, or links to external travel-related applications that might be useful. With Voyage, we changed this page to be more personalized. This page presents users with their list of upcoming trips, a list of recent trips, and a list of other people's upcoming trips. When collecting the list of other people's trips, Voyage searches for people that the user is likely to know. This list includes confidants of past trips, people from the enterprise social network, and people who shared their trip plans with the user. General details of each trip are shown, including its title, dates, and destinations. Hovering over a trip name opens a popup with a more detailed view of the itinerary. A selection of relevant reviews is also shown. These reviews are related to the user's upcoming trips, such as a review of a hotel with a future reservation. Figure 1 shows a segment of the welcome page, where the user's upcoming trips and the trips of others are shown.

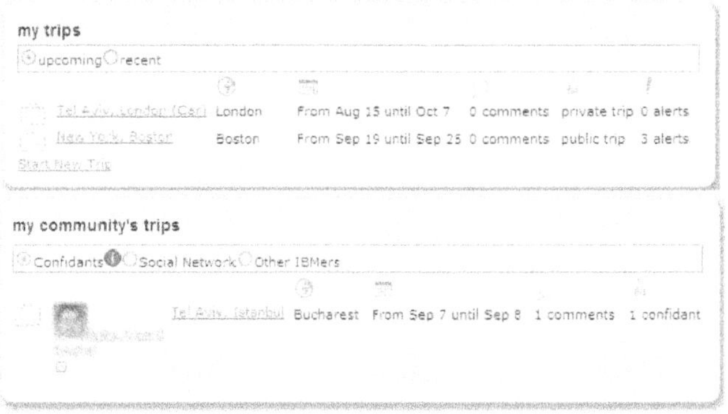

Figure 1: Welcome page

Travel Information in One Place

Voyage introduces the 'places' page where users can find all the travel-related information relevant for a specific city/country in one place. The information is gathered from publicly available sources (such as weather sites and sites providing electrical outlet information) and enterprise-specific sources (such as a meal limit DB or a list of allowed hotels). This frees users from having to search around the Internet and company intranet to collect it. Some of this information is presented in Figure 2(a). Information about other employees who recently traveled to this city or plan to travel there soon is depicted in Figure 2(b).

Learn from Past Travels

During the reservation process, users are presented with different options regarding hotels, flights, and other travel items. To indicate the popularity of the different choices Voyage aggregates information from past reservations of employees and presents statistical measures, such as: the percentage of people renting a car in a specific city, the most frequently reserved hotel, or the flight route usually taken when traveling from one place to another. Statistical measures were also used to help users in an online travel booking service [15]. The statistical measures are mainly shown on result pages. For example, after a user searches for a flight reservation, the search results are augmented with statistical measures of information such as the percentage of employees who flew the same route with the same air carrier in the past. Figure 3 shows one hotel from the outcome of a hotel search within a specific period of time. Along with general hotel details such as name, address, and price, section (a) includes a cue for the percentage of reservations made for this hotel in the past out of all hotel reservations in the city

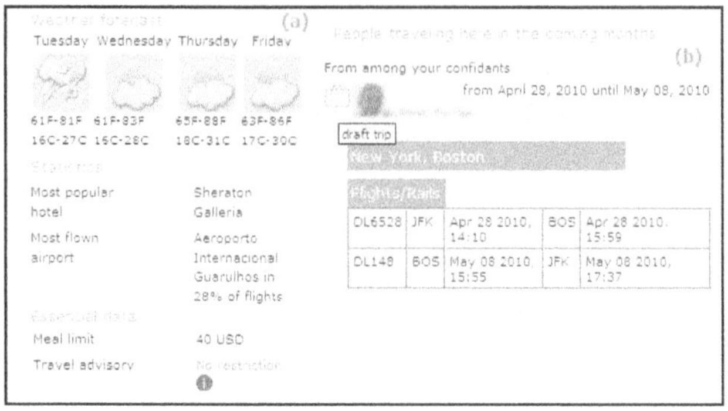

Figure 2. People traveling to a location

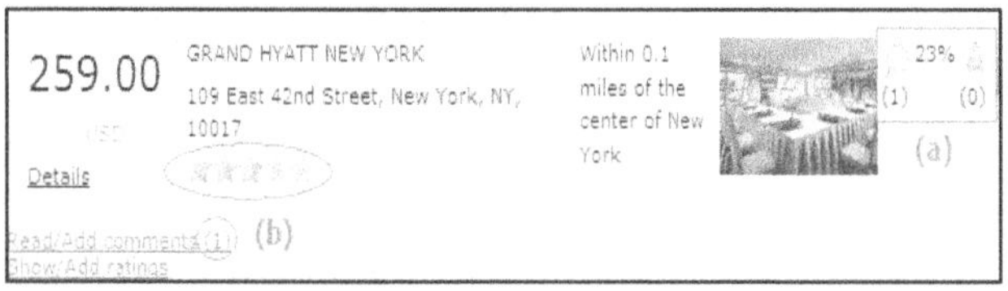

Figure 3. Hotel options augmented with social cues

People Page

Similar to other social applications that contain a 'Home' page showing general information about the user and her latest activity, Voyage includes a 'people' page. The 'people' page shows the latest user activities, such as upcoming trips, recent reviews added by the user and her list of confidants. This page also provides information on other employees. A user can enter the name of another employee and see his recent activity (depending on privacy controls).

Sharing

Features belonging to this facet enable sharing of business travel information with others for better business awareness. Sharing reviews and ratings have impact on both the individual employee and the enterprise as a whole. For the employee, these reviews are business oriented and hence more aligned with the business traveler preferences than those that are found on external sites (e.g. the quality of Internet access services). For the enterprise, aggregating reviews and ratings provided by employees can be used for negotiating for better quality and rates. This aspect is less relevant for travel sites on the web.

Share Feedback

Users can provide reviews and ratings and see information entered by others for any travel-related item in their itinerary such as hotels, flights, airlines, car agencies, airports, and destinations. This capability is provided as part of the search result pages, and the trip itinerary page (e.g., cart). Figure 3(b) shows an example of the reviews and average rating (in a red circle) for a hotel.

Share Travel Plans

Users can share their trips and select the sharing level for each trip. They can set the privacy level of a trip when they are in the last stage of purchasing it. Users can also define a default privacy level to be used for all of their travel plans, without the need to reset it for every trip. Once the trip is purchased, the user can add confidants on the trip details page and change its privacy level. Figure 4 shows one trip itinerary and the people with whom it is shared.

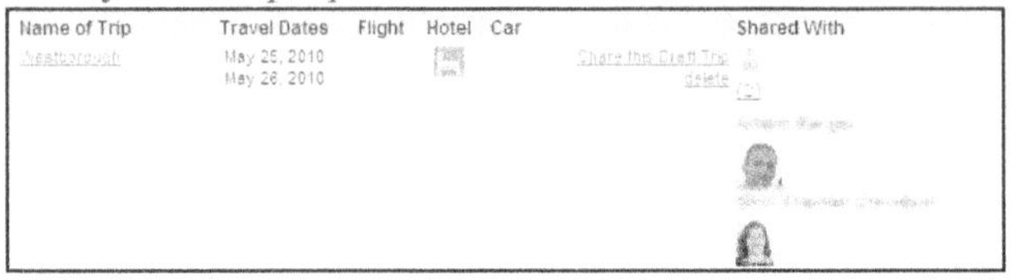

Figure 4. Sharing travel plans

Collaboration

By raising the awareness of other employees' travels and the ability to share travel plans, Voyage encourages communication. In addition, Voyage provides a trip commenting mechanism to facilitate conversation and enable coordination. This feature can save immediate costs (e.g. when used to share transportation) and can facilitate collaboration thus strengthen existing and lead to new business opportunities. On general travel web sites, such a feature is usually used for social coordination.

EVALUATING VOYAGE

In this section, we describe a field study we performed to better understand how enterprise employees are using Voyage, how much they are using the new social features as part of the travel reservation process, what features they value most, and to what extent they are willing to share their travel plans.

Research Setting

We conducted our research in a large distributed organization, collecting data from employees in Asia, Europe, the Middle East, and North America. Voyage has been deployed as a beta version since February, 2010. We used two methods to gather data about Voyage usage to increase the findings' trustworthiness: (1) After Voyage was deployed and employees started to use it for their travel planning, we conducted a survey asking them about the actions they took while planning and the usefulness of the new social features. Of 290 employees who made travel plans through Voyage, 100 answered the survey; (2) We inspected Voyage's logs to determine the actions users took and decisions made throughout the reservation process. Included in the log files are user actions, specific parameters for each action, the user name, and a time and date stamp. The user activity analysis presented here was based on log files covering a 14 month period from February 2010 to March, 2011. During this period, 2500 individuals accessed Voyage, of whom 12% purchased travel components using the tool. Some 700 employees visited Voyage more than once.

The analysis combines qualitative and quantitative results, which involve comparison of triangulated data sources and thick narrative to strengthen each finding.

Result Analysis

We divide the results into four aspects. The first aspect is social actions usage, which reports actions taken by users that involve social activity. The second aspect is the social information impact, which analyses how the social information shown in Voyage impacts decisions taken by employees during the travel reservation process. We list interesting usage patterns as the third aspect. The fourth aspect, the sharing behavior, is of particular interest, since the success of social applications requires a "critical mass" of user participation to provide value, ensure sustainable contribution levels, and encourage vibrant interaction.

Social Actions Usage

Inspecting Voyage's logs, we found that most people used the social feature to see reviews. Indeed, this was found [3] to be the most influential factor for people making travel reservations. The second most used social feature was the addition of confidants to a trip. When we inspected how confidants are added, we saw that most people added confidants from the list Voyage suggested and only a few added confidants manually by typing in names. This finding confirmed our decision to offer users a default list of people from which to select their confidants. Moreover, it confirmed that the list of people suggested was adequate, freeing them, in most situations, from adding confidants manually. As expected, users added confidants to a trip is primarily after trip purchase.

We also noticed that most users examined destination information and read available reviews (via the 'places' page) before making the purchase. This finding is somewhat surprising, since we assumed the 'places' page would become relevant closer to the trip. We estimated that people would want to be updated with the weather, currency exchange rates and latest medical alerts a few days before the trip. This tells us that the 'places' page has the potential to influence users' behavior before they make the reservation, for example by increasing awareness to reviews, ratings, and others' reservations.

Looking at how the 'people' page was used, we were surprised to see that employees mostly viewed other people pages and trip details after they had completed their own trip purchase. This might indicate that 'people' pages did not influence reservation selections still the exposure to others' plans could have been used to enhance communication.

We also examined social actions that involve another person, specifically the following actions: (1) Add a confidant to a trip; (2) Invite someone to use Voyage; (3) View the 'people' page; (4) Explore trip itinerary.

We set out to explore whether the social actions (actions 1-4) imply anything about the nature of the relationships between the people involved. To obtain evidence of these relationships, we used SONAR [10]. SONAR can provide evidence for relationships between two individuals based on different enterprise social media applications. It distinguishes between familiarity evidence items, such as 'they are connected on a social network site' or 'both co-authored a wiki page', and similarity evidence items, such as 'both commented on the same blog post' or 'both used the same tag'. We compared the average number of evidence items for people with whom actions 1 or 2 were performed (overall 309) versus people with whom actions 3 or 4 were performed (overall 174).

When comparing the familiarity relationships, we found that actions 1 and 2 were performed with people who were generally more familiar to the user. On average, there were 3.77 evidence items indicating familiarity for actions 1 and 2, compared to 3.3 for actions 3 and 4. It is indeed natural that users would share travel plans with people they know better, and inform them about a new application they used and liked.

For similarity, we observed the reverse effect. On average, each person with whom actions 1 and 2 were performed had 2.68 evidence items indicating similarity with the user compared to an average of 3.57 evidence items for actions 3 and 4. Both viewing someone else's page and exploring one's itinerary indicate interest in another person's travel plans. These results suggest that employees value the information about other people plans even if these people are not directly known to them. It might also imply that people with similar interests as reflected in enterprise social media activity also share similar travel preferences.

We further investigated the usage of social actions in an enterprise context by referring to the organizational hierarchy and comparing actions of managers to regular employees. Out of the 578 users performing social actions, 151 are managers (26%). Table 3 presents the percentage of actions performed among: two managers (M-M), by a manager to a regular employee (M-E), by an employee to a manager (E-M) and among regular employees (E-E).

Action	M-M	M-E	E-M	E-E
Add confidant to trip	13	12.5	13.5	61
Invite to use Voyage	5.4	3.6	20	70
View 'people' page	8.4	9.6	16.7	65.3

Table 3: Social actions across managers and employees

We observed that a natural social network has evolved, since managers and regular employees add confidants proportionally to their distribution in the sample (25.5% vs. 74.5%). We present two trends that emerge from the data, one for employees and one for managers:

- Employees tend to invite others to join Voyage much more than managers do, and invite managers or employees proportionally to their distribution in the sample (20% vs. 70%). This finding indicates that regular employees play a key role in early diffusion of the tool within the organization.

- Managers seem to watch the travel details of regular employees more often than watching those of other managers. We estimate that in time the trend will become more concrete since managers will use Voyage as a travel management tool to see whether their employees comply with enterprise policies and set examples for others by publishing their own itinerary.

Social Information Impact

In the survey we asked users how useful different pieces of information were for them in making their reservation decisions. From the survey results we learned that users generally find the social information shown on the search result pages to be beneficial (significantly more useful than not useful using One-Way ANOVA $p<0.01$, df=1). This information includes, for each result (e.g., hotel, flight), the percentage of employees who had the same reservation in the past, other people having the same reservation at the time period searched, and any reviews and ratings that are relevant for this reservation. Figure 5 depicts the results for the usefulness of these social features for hotels. It is clear that for all information types the values of usefulness are greater than their counter values.

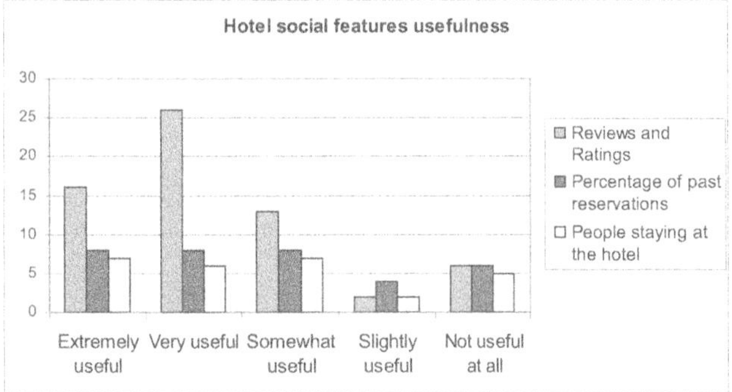

Figure 5. Hotel social features

Looking more deeply into the results, we found that people mostly value reviews and ratings (significantly, using One-Way ANOVA, $p<0.05$, df=1). This aligns with the finding from the previous section of looking into reviews being the most used social action. In addition, for flights and car rentals, people found the information about other people having the same reservation as less useful. This finding is demonstrated in Figure 6. This result for flights aligns well with the observation we got from the interviews that some employees do not feel comfortable sitting next to a colleague during the flight. As for car rental, employees may be less willing to share car rentals with others (20% are not willing to share with anyone).

From the survey we learned that many of the people did not notice the social information (on average 35%). This can result from two reasons: first, the social cues are not prominent enough, and second, the social data is still sparse during the ramp-up period of the system.

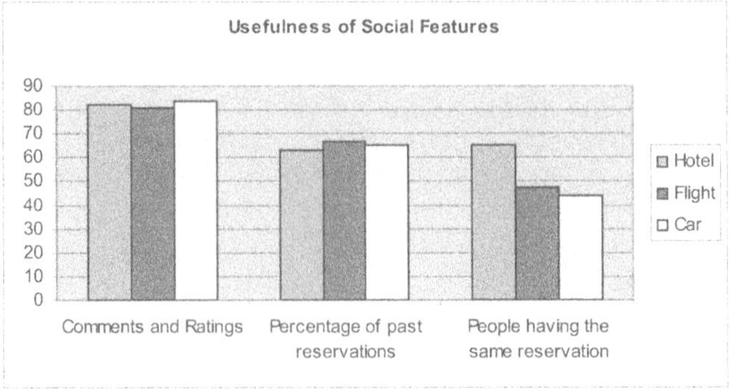

Figure 6. Usefulness of social features

We examined our findings over time, aiming to inspect the evolution of the application's adaptation in the enterprise. Although we cannot say that we crossed the chasm, we found that the number of users is continuously increasing and the user satisfaction is improving. Figure 7 presents the evolution of the survey answers for hotel reviews and ratings; the frequency of extremely useful and very useful answers rises over time. Similar phenomena were observed for other social features as well. This implies that having more social data in the application increases its usefulness.

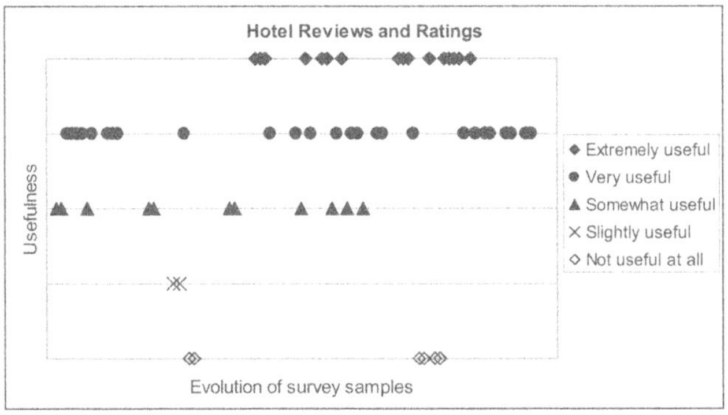

Figure 7. Usefulness over time

Inspecting the reservations made by Voyage users in practice, we found that 76% of the users selected the most popular air carrier in the route they were flying. For hotels, 36% of the reservations were made for the most popular hotel. The difference compared to air carrier can be explained by the wider variety of hotels and also by the fact that the enterprise offers a list of preferred hotels, from which users can choose. Yet, numbers for both hotels and flights are rather high, indicating that many users tend to follow the most popular. As for user input, 37% of the reserved hotels had reviews and ratings. These results indicate that employees found the social information to be useful, and actually used it during the reservation process.

Of the respondents, 78% answered that it was useful for them to see information about other employees traveling to the same destination. Learning about past/future travels of other employees was useful for 40% of them.

As for relieving the users from the need to collect relevant information from many sources, 78% found it useful to see this information in the 'places' page. In addition, 54% agreed that Voyage saved them from having to go to external sites to look for this information.

Usage Patterns

Out of the many possible usage patterns in Voyage, we inspected the existence of the following social patterns. We believe these patterns indicate that Voyage makes the travel reservation process more informative and secure, and enables users to coordinate and communicate. We divided the patterns into categories according to their role in the travel reservation process.

Travel Decisions. In this category we identified patterns that include a travel decision such as which hotel to reserve. We distinguish between social-based travel decisions, where the decision was made based on general social information (the percentage of employees who stayed in a specific hotel in the past), and enterprise-based travel decisions, where the decision was made based on information of a related employee (e.g., a hotel that was reserved by your manager). We believe that these two types of information influence the employee in different ways.

Patterns of social-based travel decisions: 1) before making a reservation, say for a hotel, explore any or all of the general social information about this hotel, such as: the percentage of employees who stayed there in the past, the hotel rating, the reviews on the hotel, etc. 2) On the welcome page, explore relevant reviews for your upcoming trips and decide whether to change any of the reservations.

Patterns of enterprise-based travel decision: look at someone else's itinerary to decide on your reservations or change a reservation you already have.

Travel Coordination. This category includes patterns for coordinating travel plans and communicating before the trip. Patterns in this category: 1) On the 'places' page you see someone else that is traveling there at the same time as you. Enter his trip details page to leave a comment. 2) On the hotel results page you see someone else with a reservation for a hotel. You observe that she is currently on-line. You start a chat with her to discuss travel plans.

Personal Feedback Contribution. This category includes patterns for contributing reviews and ratings for travel-related items. This category could include, for example, the pattern: On the flight results page you see an air carrier you flew with in the past, you add a review to this air carrier.

For all categories of usage patterns, we examined the logs to find user activity sessions that include both a purchase action and social activity in order to identify any of the above patterns. We found that several of the patterns were followed in different ways.

The following is a purchase scenario from the logs, which includes social-based decision making, feedback contribution, and some indication for intended travel coordination: The user started at the welcome page, moved to search for a flight, and made a flight selection. Then the user searched for a hotel and looked at ratings and reviews, decided to add a review for another hotel and made a hotel selection. He then purchased the trip. After that he looked at the trip itinerary and added several confidants. We believe this was done either for awareness or for coordination.

We did not find a strong indication of people using the trip commenting mechanism for trip coordination. The next scenario does indicate that such a trial was made, but the conversation was not established: The user started at the welcome page and checked the definition of confidants and invited several people to join Voyage. Then moved to look at the general section of the page, where enterprise travel information is presented. He then searched for a hotel and made a selection, then moved to search for a flight and made a reservation. Then the user purchased the trip. After purchase completion he looked at the trip itinerary page, added several confidants and added his plans as a comment.

Sharing Behavior

Few employees (1.5%) added reviews and these were mainly for hotels (79%). The ratio of people who read reviews to people who contributed them is still less than the expected 80/20 rule [13]. This could result from Voyage not being the natural place for adding reviews, as people are less likely to add reviews when they are planning their trip, and more likely to do so during or after the trip. Using Voyage REST APIs we plan to integrate the reviewing capability into both a mobile client and the expense-reporting system.

Looking at the privacy settings of travel reservations made in Voyage, we found that employees were less open to sharing than indicated in the survey. While more employees defined their trip as public than declared in the survey (44% vs. 34%), a much higher percentage than expected from the survey defined their trip as private (47% vs. 5%). This behavior was observed both for managers and regular employees. It seems that in theory employees tend to be more open than when they are confronted with the actual travel reservation and must make a real decision. While in theory users want to control who they share their trip with, in practice they tend to opt for the quickest options (private or public), which do not require further input. Nevertheless, employees were willing to expose more about their travel details after they returned from a trip. When queried, 91% of Voyage users who defined their actual travel plans as private expressed this willingness.

SUMMARY AND FUTURE WORK

We studied the topic of social travel planning in the enterprise. We found that social travel planning in this context has unique concepts and characteristics compared to travel on the web. Business considerations are taken into account in all stages of design, development, deployment, and regulations. Although the features are similar to what can be found in travel applications on the web, their meaning and impact are different in the enterprise.

Attempting to answer the questions that we set out to explore, following are the main observations:

Regarding sharing travel plans (Q1): We found out that employees are comfortable sharing their travel plans with others: the second most used social action was sharing travel plans with a confidant. In addition, 44% of employees shared their travel plans with someone. Most of the employees who did not share their upcoming travel plans agreed to share them after returning from the trip.

With respect to trip coordination (Q2, Q4): We did not find a strong indication of people using the trip commenting mechanism for trip coordination; although we found evidence that a trial was made. Possibly, it was not clear enough who is exposed to these comments and how to facilitate a discussion using this mechanism. However, employees indicated that Voyage shortened the travel reservation time, which represents a significant cost savings factors for an enterprise [1, 19].

As for social information impact (Q3): We found that employees see value in different types of social information provided by others, even if these people are not known to them. They used it throughout their travel reservation process and expressed their improved satisfaction from it. Reservation actions tend to follow the popularity indicator, which is calculated and exposed through Voyage.

Regarding business awareness and new opportunities (Q5, Q6): We observed that employees use travel plans of other people with whom they share similar interests to assist in their trip planning. We believe that in the long term, this can lead to new business relationships, which probably would not have been established without Voyage. Such relationships can contribute to better collaboration, contribute to the overall cohesiveness of the enterprise network and help with career development.

We present three directions for future work:

Tooling connectivity and traceability. A tighter integration with common collaboration tools (such as email and instant messaging) is suggested to better facilitate collaboration and track the continued communication that was initiated among employees.

Feature enhancement. More explicit support is required for group travel as part of the evolution of such an application in the enterprise context. For example, this could be used to conduct a large project meeting or to organize a joint trip to a big event. Group recommendation techniques can be applied to identify the optimal location for a meeting, taking into account budget, distance, and even 'green' considerations.

Business value. It is very difficult to show the value of social activities to the enterprise. In this paper we found hints for potential savings from using Voyage. Hence, we suggest developing a quantitative model that could be used to measure the monetary value of adding social features to enterprise travel.

REFERENCES

1. Chircu, A. M. Kauffman, R. J. Keskey, D. Maximizing the Value of Internet-based Corporate Travel Reservation Systems, 2001, *Communications of the ACM,* 44 (11), 57-64.
2. Delgado, J., and Davidson, R. Knowledge Bases and User Profiling in Travel and Hospitality Recommender Systems. *Info. and Comm. Technologies in Tourism 2002*, 1-16.
3. Dickinger, A. and Mazanec, J. Consumers' Preferred Criteria for Hotel Online Booking. *ENTER 2008.*
4. DiMicco, J., Millen, D.R., Geyer, W., Dugan, C., and Brownholtz, B. Caring, Climbing, and Campaigning: Motivations for Social Networking at Work. *CSCW 2008.*
5. Fielding, R.T. Architectural Styles and the Design of Network-based Software Architectures. *University of California, 2000.*
6. Grau, J. US Online travel: Planning and booking. *eMarketer. June 23, 2009*, accessed online at http://www.emarketer.com.
7. Gretzel, U. and Yoo, K.H. Use and Impact of Online Travel Reviews. *Info. and Comm. Technologies in Tourism 2008,* 35-46.
8. Gretzel, U. and Yoo, K.H. Influence of personality on travel-related consumer-generated media creation. *Computers in Human Behavior, 2010.*
9. Guy, I., Jacovi, M., Perer, A., Ronen, I., and Uziel, E. Same Places, Same Things, Same People? Mining User Similarity on Social Media. *CSCW 2010.*
10. Guy, I., Jacovi, M., Shahar, E., Meshulam, N., Soroka, V., and Farrell, S. Harvesting with SONAR: the value of aggregating social network information. *CHI 2008.* 1017-1026.
11. Millen, R.D, Feinberg, J. and Kerr, B. Dogear: Social bookmarking in the enterprise. *CHI 2006*, 111-120.
12. Millen, R.D and Patterson, F.J. Stimulating social engagement in a community network. *CSCW 2002*, 306-313.
13. Ochoa, X. and Duval, E. Quantitative analysis of user-generated content on the web, *Proc WebEvolve 2008*, 19–26.
14. Preece, J. Nonnecke, B., Andrews, A. The top five reasons for lurking: improving community experiences for everyone, *Computers in Human Behavior, 2004.* 20 (2), 201-223
15. Rudström, Å. and Fagerberg, P. Socially Enhanced Travel Booking: a Case Study. *Journal of Information Technology and Tourism,* 6 (3), 2003, 211-221.
16. Swarbrooke, J., and Horner, S. Business Travel and Tourism. *Oxford: Butterworth-Heinemann*, 2010.
17. Tan, E.M.Y., Goa, D.H.L., Theng, Y.L., Foo, S. An Analysis of Services for the Mobile tourist. *Mobile technology, applications and systems 2007*, 490-494.
18. The PhoCusWright consumer travel trends tenth edition. Accessed online (August 1, 2010) at www.phocuswright.com.
19. Voss, A., Schubert, P. User interface integration in corporate travel management: the case of the CWT Connect portal, *Proc. American Conf. on Information Systems 2004.*

A Need-driven Design Approach: Addressing Latent Needs in Collaboration Rooted in Early Childhood

Sheng-Ying Pao
aithpao@media.mit.edu
MIT Media Lab
75 Amherst St
Cambridge, MA 02139

Selene Mota
atenea@media.mit.edu
MIT
77 Massachusetts Ave
Cambridge, MA 02139

Keywon Chung
keywonc@gmail.com
MIT Media Lab
75 Amherst St
Cambridge, MA 02139

Alexander Reben
areben@media.mit.edu
MIT Media Lab
75 Amherst St
Cambridge, MA 02139

ABSTRACT

When the latent needs are un-addressed, collaboration can be easily turned into a non-collaborative activity while the participants are unaware of why. This paper describes a need-driven approach for computer-supported collaborative interaction design, with specific focus on collaboration rooted in early childhood. We conducted a need-identification study, where explicit needs and latent needs in children's collaborative interaction were identified and constructed into a guideline for computer-supported collaboration design. Demonstrating the need-driven approach, a toolkit was designed and the prototype was evaluated based upon the guideline attempting to address the needs identified. The need-driven approach and the design guideline that the toolkit design was based upon may offer new dynamic domains for future computer-supported collaboration design.

Author Keywords

Computer-supported cooperative work, computer-supported collaborative learning, social exclusion, collaboration design guideline, need-driven design approach.

ACM Classification Keywords

H5.2. [Information interfaces and presentation]: Prototyping, User-centered design, Evaluation and Methodology.

General Terms

Design.

INTRODUCTION

Technology provides great opportunities to facilitate the collaboration in many respects between children [1, 8]. The majority of designs encourage collaboration by offering a new variant of approaches to designing shared interfaces [2, 12, 15-16]. However, collaboration does not happen simply because of shared interfaces [5, 8, 13]. What is missing?

In this study, we introduced a need-driven approach to the design of collaborative work rooted in childhood interaction. A qualitative research study to identify people's unmet needs was carried out prior to the design and prototyping. The need-finding strategy offers a different dynamic platform for new design [11]. Explicit needs tend to be obvious to the users, while latent needs may be very non-obvious and very difficult to uncover by the users [9].

In this study we particularly focused on children aged 6-8. Explicit needs as well as latent needs were identified from our need-finding study. Here the latent needs particularly refer to the factors that we discovered which contribute to the break-down of collaboration while participants are unaware of why.

This finding led to a design guideline focusing on children's collaborative interactions. Based on the design guidelines, we developed a toolkit that attempts to enhance children's collaborative experiences. This paper first describes the need-identification study. Based on the need-driven approach, the paper proposes a guideline fo• designs in childhood collaboration. Finally, the paper illustrates the system and the design of the toolkit that attempts to address the explicit as well as the latent needs.

A NEED-IDENTIFICATION STUDY

We conducted a need-identification study to in the process of collaboration. We observed pairs of children of two interacting with each other under the constraint of certain collaborative story-telling and toy playing scenarios in the presence of their parents, each for 20 minutes. In addition, we interviewed their parents. From the observation and interview, explicit needs and latent needs were identified.

Subjects

12 subjects participated in this study. 10 children who participated in this study were pairs of two siblings, including a pair of twins. The rest of the children were friends. They are aged 6-8. Their parents were in their early 30's and were both employed.

Exclusion, Engagement and Attention during Cooperation Activities

The results were categorized into the following domains: (1) unintentional social exclusion, (2) the level of engagement, and (3) the attention from their partners and The interactions from all the subjects showed noticeable patterns in these domains. Children, usually the older one in the pair, unintentionally ignored their partners during the collaboration in both the collaborative story-telling session and the toy playing session. In each pair, the one who responded faster always dominated the pace of the activities. This also occurred in the case in where we had identical twins as participants. For example, we observed that one child among the two usually kept on their own pace and ignored their partner when it should have been the other's turn.

While the dominant person was leading the pace, the engagement level of their partner gradually dropped. They did not usually slow down or to engage their partner. Consequently, the dominant child soon turned the collaboration into an activity performed "alone". The collaboration then broke. The dominant child was not aware that their actions had lowered the engagement level of their partners or had impacted on the collaboration.

Noticeably, the dominant child caught more attention of their parents, while the other child not only got ignored by their partner but obtained less attention from their parents. This further reinforced the dominant child to be more dominant and their partner to be further excluded from the interaction. The collaboration then turned into a non-collaborative activity.

Our study further showed that parents were aware of the changes in engagement level due to such unintentional ignorance. The above observation was further confirmed with the interview results. Parents have reported that they noticed "one child sometimes over-dominated, which seriously obstructed the other child's willingness to collaborate."

Furthermore, parents in our study reported that they found it frustrating to prevent this from happening. When they noticed this, what parents did in response included the following: they purposely initiated interactions with the ignored child between the two; they verbally persuaded the dominant child to collaborate with their partner. However, such interferences by their parents seldom succeeded -- the dominant participant still unintentionally ignored or intentionally rejected their partner than to collaborate.

As oppose to parents' intervention, we observed that only when the dominant participant actively invited their partner to engage, the collaboration continued. This pattern was identified on all the participants in our study.

A NEED-DRIVEN DESIGN GUIDELINE

The Latent Needs in Collaborative Interaction

Explicit needs tend to be obvious to the users. The latent needs here particularly refer to the factors that cause collaboration to break down while the users are unaware of why. When the latent needs are un-addressed, collaboration can be easily turned into a non-collaborative activity and it is non-obvious to the participants.

the third party.

The following latent needs in children's collaborative interaction were identified according to the above results in the observation study and interview:

(1) Participants were not aware of the unintentional ignorance during collaboration. Such unintentional ignorance leads to a break-down of the collaboration.

(2) Following (1), their partner's engagement level is a consequence of their unintentional ignorance and will in turn hurt the collaboration. In addition, the attention on the engagement level needs to be drawn from their partners.

(3) Cooperative signals from the dominating partner, rather than intermediated by a third party (their parents in this case), is crucial to trigger and maintain collaboration. In other words, if the need is unaddressed, it is ineffective to resume a broken collaboration.

The Explicit Needs Specific to Children Collaboration

The explicit needs are rather obvious to the users. The explicit needs in children's interaction identified in this age group included physical contacts, body movements, and self-reflections. Physical contacts dramatically initiated and encouraged the ignored child to participate. Body movements were necessary to draw attention of young children during their collaboration as well as to initiate new collaborative interactions. Self-reflections, such as through role-playing activities, were essential to self-awareness of the engagement and collaborative level, which further reinforces the latent needs.

Design Guideline for Childhood Collaboration

Based on the above findings, we proposed a design guideline for collaboration rooted in childhood interactions.

- A collaboration design should address the latent needs in collaborative interactions so that it (1) allows collaboration to be initiated naturally by the participants, (2) motivate participants to actively engage their partner, and (3) provide ways of self-awareness to reflect and prevent unintentional ignorance.
- Embedded channels to encourage the dominating participant to invite and pay attention to the participant who's fell behind or got ignored is suggested. When collaboration is breaking down, channels that incent the dominating participant to invite their partner and reinitiate the collaboration should be naturally introduced.
- A collaboration design for children satisfies and leverages the explicit needs: involving body movements, physical contacts, and self-reflections.

COLLABORATIVE LEARNING TOOLKIT

We designed a collaborative toolkit that leverages full-body movements, physical contact and self-reflection attempting to address the latent needs in children's collaborative interactions.

System and Prototype

The system consists of the following components (Figure 1-3):

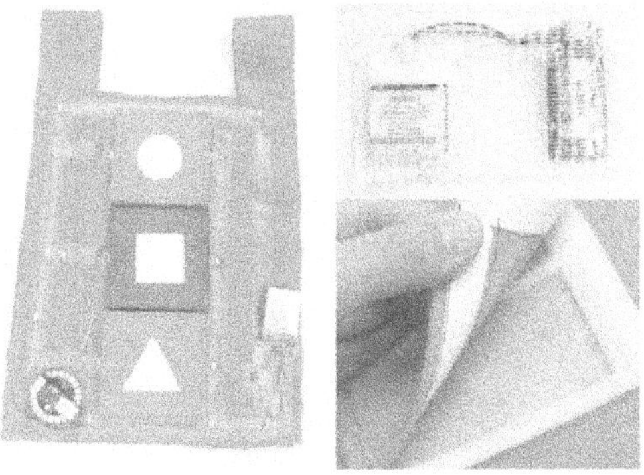

Figure 1. The inner side of the bib (left).Three appliqués shown in the image were attached on the outside of the bib. The top right image shows the wireless accelerometer and the bottom right one is a close-up of the Appliqué.

- Wireless accelerometer sensors were embedded within bibs. The wearable toolkits allow the system to determine the level of collaboration and their body movements using hidden conductive threads, a microcontroller sewn into fabric, as well as wireless communication modules (Figure 1).
- An avatar in the collaboration game where the body parts of the avatar are associated with the body movements of participants, which met the needs of self-reflection of body movements and self-awareness of collaboration (Figures 2 and 3).
- Appliqués attached to the bibs, where their shapes and the positions they attached to the bibs are customizable for physical contacts during the collaboration tasks (Figures 1 and 3).

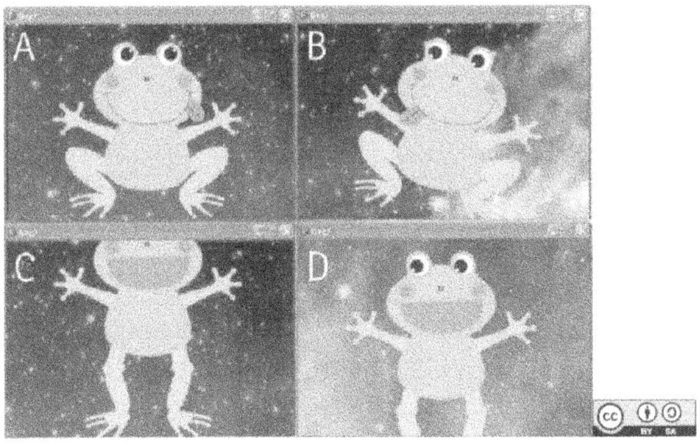

Figure 2. Avatar in the game: (A) initial state; (B) one child lifting his leg can only lift one leg of the frog; (C) only when the partner collaborate to lift the other leg of the frog, the frog can jump to the next scene (D).

From the children's perspective, the goal in the game was the control over the avatar to capture objects through their body movements. The actual goal in the design is to initialize and internalize collaboration through the game. There is only one avatar in the game so each child can only control one body part of the avatar through the wearable toolkit (Figure 3). For example, if one child moves his/her legs, one leg of the avatar will be lifted (Figure 2B). Only when two children collaborate, the avatar can move both legs and jump forward to reach the goals (Figures 2C and 2D.)

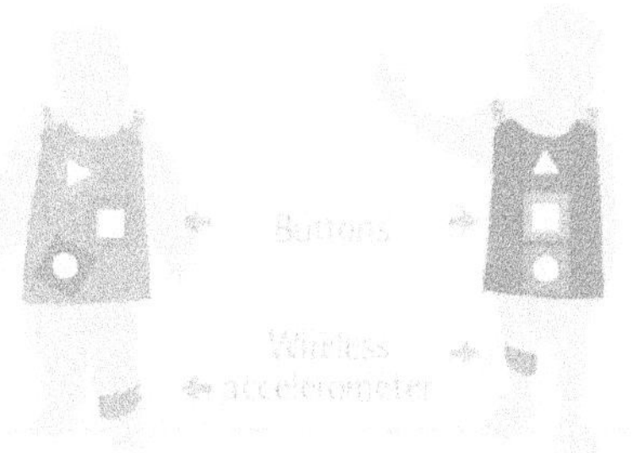

Figure 3. Children wearing bibs interact with each other.

The goal was to move the avatar forward in order to reach and capture objects by hands (Figures 2 and 4). When they collaborated to move the avatar forward, a pair of objects appeared (Figures 4). The shapes of the appliqués attached to the back of the bibs are the same as the objects to be captured by the avatar. They invite and engage their partner by touching the corresponding appliqués on the back of their partner's bib (Figures 3 and 4A). Body movement, physical contacts and self-reflection were leveraged to signal collaboration. The avatar frog for the animation in our game interface was adapted from Open Processing [17] and is licensed under Creative Commons Attribution-Share Alike 3.0 and GNU GPL license.

Figure 4. Touching the appliqués worn by their partner can trigger the avatar to capture the objects and initiate collaboration. (A); collaboration task completed (B).

To detect the children's movement and mapping it to the avatar's legs motion, the system uses two 3-axis wireless accelerometers sensors. The sensors sent the raw data to a PC. The PC processes the data using the MIT Wockets open source software which decodes the accelerometer raw values in real-time [6-7]. The raw values were used to compute the vector of magnitude of the 3-axis accelerometer signal according to the following formula:

$$VM = \sum_{t=0}^{N} VM_t + \sqrt{(Raw_{x,t} - Rm_x)^2 + (Raw_{y,t} - Rm_y)^2 + (Raw_{z,t} - Rm_z)^2}$$

Where VM = Vector of magnitude
Raw = Raw accelerometer sample
Rm = running mean in a 5 seconds window
N = number of raw data samples received in one second

The magnitude of the vector was used as an estimate of the child's level of activity. After all sensor signals coming from both children were processed, the system performs a synchronization step to determine the avatar's action (move one leg or jump with two legs). The synchronization step uses a one second non-overlapping time window to recognize the children's gestures and trigger the action that will move the avatar's legs in the game.

EVALUATION

We tested the current design prototype with three pairs of participants. For safety concerns, we first tested with adult participants. The results showed that the dominant (quick-responding) participants always signaled the partners to collaborate. When they tended to go on their own pace unintentionally, they soon noticed the impact on the collaboration and the attention then was drawn to engage their partner to collaborate. The collaborative and engagement level were made aware through their body movement reflected by the avatar. The partners were also invited and engaged to collaborate through the physical contacts by touching the appliqués. None of the participants turned it into an activity performed alone and none of the participants were ignored by their partner. We also interviewed the observers. No significant delay between the body movements and the avatar was observed.

CONCLUSION

Children who we observed in the need-identification study did not actively exclude others socially, for instance, they never said "you can't play". However, they unintentionally ignored their partner in collaboration activities or went on their own pace without noticing. Collaboration on a shared interface is often turned into a non-collaborative manner while the latent needs are un-addressed and the users are unaware of why.

Social constructionism and collaboration enable children to reach better performance in the long term [3-4, 10, 14, 18]. While difficult to measure the results in relation to collaboration in later life empirically, it is at least possible that this study identified the unmet latent needs in collaboration where the unintentional ignorance of their partner, their engagement level on the collaboration, and the recovering of a broken collaboration are investigated. The need-driven approach and the design guideline that the toolkit design was based upon may offer new dynamic domains for future computer-supported collaboration design.

ACKNOWLEDGMENTS

We thank Prof. Leah Buechley for her valuable feedback. We thank the MIT Media Lab for their resources, and our colleagues in the design for empowerment class for discussion. We also thank Prof. Stephen Intille for the resources regarding the Wockets system, funded by the National Institutes of Health grant #5U01HL091737.

REFERENCES

1. Barfurth, M. A. Understanding the collaborative learning process in a technology rich environment: The case of children's disagreements. In *Proc. CSCL*, L. Erlbaum Associates Inc. (1995), 8-13.
2. Benford, S., Bederson, B. B., Åkesson, K.-P., Bayon, V., Druin, A., Hansson, P., Hourcade, J. P., Ingram, R., Neale, H., O'Malley, C., Simsarian, K. T., Stanton, D., Sundblad, Y. and Tax, G. Designing storytelling technologies to encouraging collaboration between young children. In *Proc. Proceedings of the SIGCHI conference on Human factors in computing systems*, ACM (2000), 556-563.
3. Gardner, H. *Frames of Mind: the theory of multiple intelligences*. Fontana, 1993.
4. Goleman, D. *Emotional intelligence : why it can matter more than IQ*. Bloomsbury, 1996.
5. Harrist, A. W. and Bradley, K. D. "You can't say you can't play": intervening in the process of social exclusion in the kindergarten classroom. *Early Childhood Research Quarterly, 18*, 2 (2003), 185-205.
6. MIT Wcokets software repository. http://code.google.com/p/wockets/
7. MIT Wockets Initiative. http://web.mit.edu/wockets/
8. O'Malley, C. Designing computer systems to support peer learning. *European Journal of Psychology of Education, 7*, 4 (1992), 339-352.
9. Otto, K. N. a. K. L. W. *Product Design : Techniques in Reverse Engineering and New Product Development*. Prentice Hall, Upper Saddle River, NJ, 2001.
10. Paley, V. *You Can't Say You Can't Play*. Harvard University Press, 1993.
11. Patnaik, D. and Becker, R. Needfinding: The Why and How of Uncovering People's Needs. *Design Management Journal (Former Series), 10*, 2 (1999), 37-43.
12. Rogers, Y., Scaife, M., Harris, E., Phelps, T., Price, S., Smith, H., Muller, H., Randell, C., Moss, A., Taylor, I., Stanton, D., O'Malley, C., Corke, G. and Gabrielli, S. Things aren't what they seem to be: innovation through technology inspiration. In *Proc. Proceedings of the 4th conference on Designing interactive systems: processes, practices, methods, and techniques*, ACM (2002), 373-378.
13. Rogoff, B., Turkanis, CG., and Bartlett L., *Learning together: Children and adults in a school community*, 2001.
14. Rogoff, T. *Apprenticeship in Thinking: Cognitive development in social context.* . Oxford University Press, 1990.
15. Stefik, M., Bobrow, D. G., Foster, G., Lanning, S. and Tatar, D. WYSIWIS revised: early experiences with multiuser interfaces. *ACM Trans. Inf. Syst., 5*, 2 (1987), 147-167.
16. Stefik, M., Foster, G., Bobrow, D. G., Kahn, K., Lanning, S. and Suchman, L. Beyond the chalkboard: computer support for collaboration and problem solving in meetings. *Commun. ACM, 30*, 1 (1987), 32-47.
17. Ting, Y. T. Frog Animation. http://www.openprocessing.org/visuals/?visualID=5394
18. Vygotsky, L. S. *Thought and language*. MIT Press, 1962.

To Stay or Leave? The Relationship of Emotional and Informational Support to Commitment in Online Health Support Groups

Yi-Chia Wang
Language Technologies Institute
Carnegie Mellon University
Pittsburgh PA 15213
yichiaw@cs.cmu.edu

Robert Kraut
Human-Computer Interaction Institute
Carnegie Mellon University
Pittsburgh PA 15213
robert.kraut@cs.cmu.edu

John M. Levine
Psychology
University of Pittsburgh
Pittsburgh PA 15260
jml@pitt.edu

ABSTRACT
Today many people with serious diseases use online support groups to seek social support. For these groups to be sustained and effective, member retention and commitment is important. Our study examined how different types and amounts of social support in an online cancer support group are associated with participants' length of membership. We first built machine learning models to automatically identify the extent to which messages contained emotional and informational support. Agreement with human judges was high ($r > 0.76$). We then used these models to measure the support exchanged in 1.5 million messages. Finally, we applied quantitative event history analysis to assess how exposure to emotional and informational support predicted group members' length of subsequent participation. The results demonstrated that the more emotional support members were exposed to, the lower the risk of dropout. In contrast, informational support did not have the same strong effects on commitment. We speculate that emotional support enhanced members' relationships with one another or the group as a whole, whereas informational support satisfied members' short-term information needs.

Author Keywords
Commitment, Online communities, Social support, Natural language analysis, Applied machine learning.

ACM Classification Keywords
H5.3. Information Interfaces and Presentation: Group and Organization Interfaces: Asynchronous interaction, Computer-supported cooperative work, Evaluation/methodology, Web-based interaction.

INTRODUCTION
A large number of American Internet users participate in online health support groups to obtain informational and/or emotional support [8, 9]. A large fraction of these online support groups deal with cancer [11].

Although online support groups are popular, the scientific jury is out regarding their effectiveness in helping participants deal with health problems [20]. It is highly likely that the effectiveness of such groups depends on the communications that members exchange with one another, but surprisingly little systematic research has been devoted to specifying how the quality and quantity of such communications affect groups' outcomes and members' health-related outcomes (see [16, 25, 28] for exceptions).

This paper focuses on member retention and commitment, which are important to individual members and to the maintenance and success of the group as a whole. People who stay in an online support group longer are more likely to receive whatever benefits it provides. Moreover, members are resources in online groups. They share information, provide help, and form social ties with others. Over time, they shift from receiving support to providing it to others [27]. Continued participation, however, cannot be taken for granted. Evidence obtained in a wide variety of online groups indicates that a substantial number of participants drop out before they could plausibly contribute any benefits to the groups or receive many themselves. Thus, in order to understand the effectiveness of online support groups, a critical first step is to understand the factors that influence members' decisions to remain in them.

Maintaining membership in an online (or offline) group is a fundamental component of commitment to that group [2, 4 15]. In their model of group socialization, Levine and Moreland analyzed the antecedents and consequences of individuals' commitment to groups [e.g., 22, 24]. According to their group socialization model, members engage in an evaluation process to determine how well the group can satisfy their needs. In so doing, they consider how rewarding the group has been in the past and predict how rewarding it is likely to be in the future. The outcome of this evaluation process determines members' commitment to the group, which in turn affects the likelihood that they will remain in it and expend effort to achieve collective goals.

The specific rewards that determine commitment vary across groups and are heavily influenced by the functions that groups serve for their members. Since people join health support groups in order to cope with medical problems and the stresses surrounding their illness, the amount and type of social support they receive (as manifested in the communications they receive) are likely to function as important rewards. If so, we would expect receipt of social support to influence members' commitment to groups, as indexed by the length of time they remain in those groups.

Social Support

Of the categories of social support others have identified [10], two have received the most theoretical and empirical attention – emotional support and informational support.

Receiving emotional support. Participants in online support groups can receive emotional support either directly, through messages of caring and concern, or indirectly, through comparisons with others who have had similar experiences [3]. Cancer patients often claim that emotional support is the most helpful type of support they receive [12] and the type of support they actively seek [13]. Research suggests that peer discussion focusing on emotional support enhances cancer patients' psychological adjustment [18, 20].

Receiving informational support. Participants in online support groups also exchange informational support about the course of their disease, treatments, side effects, communication with physicians, and financial problems and other burdens. Research suggests that information available in cancer support groups is an important factor leading to improvements in psychological well-being [19].

Research Question

Our major research question is how exposure to emotional and informational support in online cancer support groups is associated with members' continued participation in these groups. The literature on commitment to groups discussed above suggests that either type of support will increase commitment, because participants are likely to consider them important benefits of participation, even though research in offline groups suggests informational that support may be more valuable, especially for women with breast cancer [19].

RESEARCH SITE AND DATA

The study reported in this paper examines the impact of social support on continued participation in the breast cancer discussion boards[1] operated by Breastcancer.org, "a nonprofit organization dedicated to providing the most reliable, complete, and up-to-date information about breast cancer." This organization also provides a variety of communication platforms, including discussion boards and chat rooms for patients, family members, and caregivers, to exchange support. The discussion board platform is one of the most popular and active online breast cancer support groups on the Internet. It contains more than 90,000 registered members and 66 forums organized by such criteria as disease stage (e.g., Metastatic Breast Cancer), treatment (e.g., Hormonal Therapy), demographic characteristics (e.g., Women 40-60ish), and problems in living (e.g., Breast Reconstruction). In the forums, members ask questions, share their stories, and read posts from others about how to deal with their disease. This discussion board platform is a rich environment for studying the dynamics of online support groups.

We collected all the public posts, users, and their profiles on the discussion board platform from Breastcancer.org from October 2001 to January 2011. During this period there were a total of 90,242 unique users who posted 1,562,459 messages belonging to 68,158 discussion threads. The median length of a discussion thread was 6 messages (mean=23). Figure 1 depicts the distribution of the number of posts per thread. The median lifespan of a thread, from the first thread starting message to the last, was 3 days (mean=33). The distribution of lifespan of threads is shown in Figure 2. Fifty percent of thread-starting messages received a response within 24 hours, but 11% never received any response.

Sixty percent of registered members never logged in after registering. Members posted a median of zero messages and a mean of 24 messages in the forums (Figure 3). Thirteen percent of members filled in a personal profile providing additional information about themselves and their disease (e.g., age, occupation, cancer stage, diagnosis date).

Our goal in this paper was to investigate the association between the amount and type of social support exchanged in the forums and members' continued participation. Our analysis consisted of two parts. First we trained and validated machine learning models to measure the amount of emotional and informational support contained in each of the 1.5 million messages exchanged in the forums. We then used survival analysis [30] to examine how the emotional and informational support that members were exposed to in a particular week predicted their continued participation in the group.

PREDICTING SOCIAL SUPPORT

Most previous research on communication in support groups is based on hand-coding relatively small samples of messages [7, 17, 23, 28, 29]. Even Meier and colleagues' relatively ambitious effort only coded emotional and informational support in about 3,000 online messages [23]. These techniques are impractical for the 1.5 million posts in our data. Previous research has shown that it is possible to

[1] http://community.breastcancer.org/

partially automate some text analysis of conversations in online support groups, but correlations with human judgments were modest [1].

To overcome these methodological challenges, we built machine learning models to automatically identify the extent to which messages exchanged in the breast cancer discussion forums contained emotional or informational support. Machine learning algorithms use statistical procedures analogous to multiple regression to map a set of input features to a set of output categories or numerical values. In our data, the input features include linguistic information from the messages, such as the message length, presence of words from general and domain-specific dictionaries, and higher-level linguistic features such as the presence of questions or advice. The output is a numerical value representing the amount of emotional or informational support the message contained.

Building and validating the machine learning models involved three steps, which we describe in more detail below. First, human judges hand-coded the extent of emotional and informational support in a sample of 1,000 messages. Their judgments represent the "ground truth" or "gold standard" to which to compare the machine learning estimates. Second, we represented the messages as a set of linguistic features as input to the machine learning algorithms. Finally, we constructed the statistical models from part of the handed-coded data, by applying machine learning algorithms, and then evaluated the accuracy of the models on a hold-out sample of data.

Creating the Human-Coded Dataset

In order to construct a hand-coded dataset for training machine learning models, we randomly selected 1,000 messages from the breast cancer data and employed Amazon Mechanical Turk (MTurk) workers to rate each message in terms of the amount of emotional and informational support it contained.

Amazon Mechanical Turk[2] is an online marketplace for crowdsourcing. It allows requesters to post jobs and workers to choose jobs they would like to perform. Jobs are defined and paid in units of so-called Human Intelligence Tasks (HITs). Snow et al. [31] have shown that the combined judgments of a small number (about 5) of naïve annotators on MTurk lead to ratings of texts that are very similar to those of experts for content such as the emotions expressed, the relative timing of events referred to in the text, word similarity, word sense disambiguation, and linguistic entailment or implication. As we show below, MTurk workers' judgments of social support are also similar to those of highly trained, expert coders.

[2] https://www.mturk.com/mturk/welcome

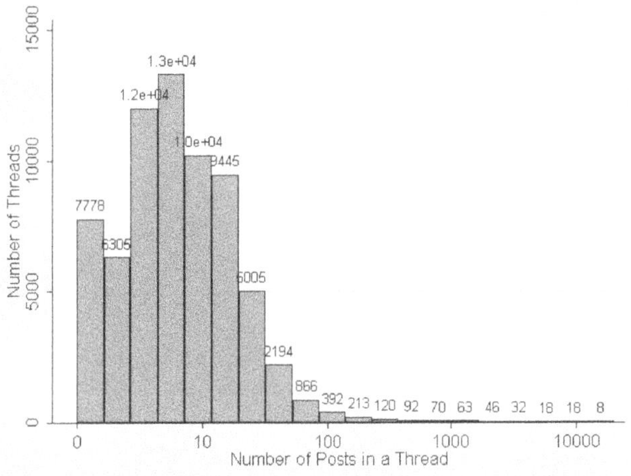

Figure 1. Distribution of Number of Posts per Thread

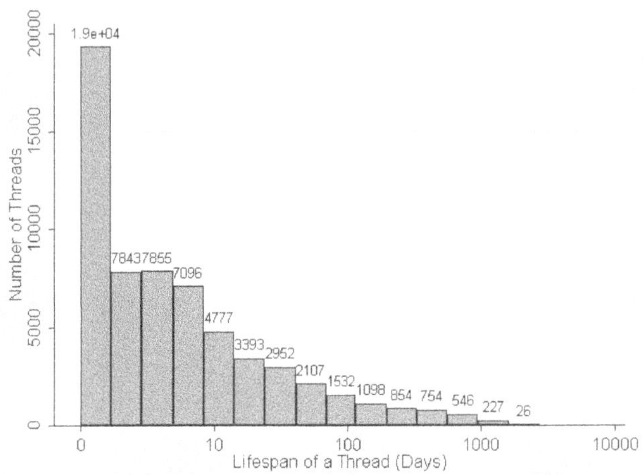

Figure 2. Distribution of Lifespan of Threads

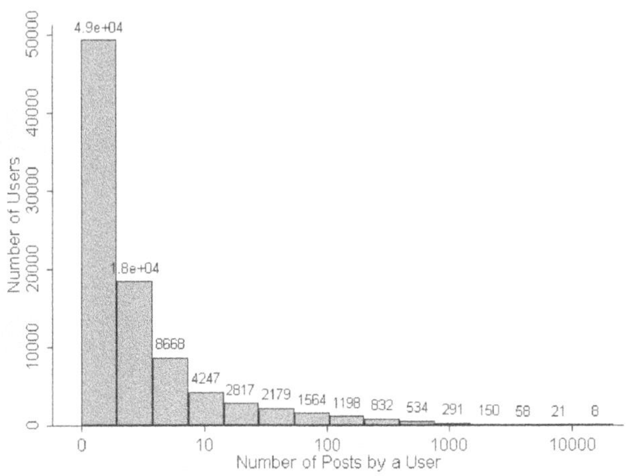

Figure 3. Distribution of Number of Posts per User

Emotional and Informational Support Annotation

The workers were given brief definitions of two kinds of social support, taken from [3]:

- ***Emotional support messages*** *provide understanding, encouragement, affirmation, sympathy, or caring.*
- ***Informational support messages*** *provide advice, referrals or knowledge.*

They were then shown a message and asked: "How much emotional support does this message provide?" and "How much informational support does this message provide?" The workers answered the two questions using a 7-point Likert scale, where 1 meant "none" and 7 meant "a great deal". To encourage workers to take the numeric rating task seriously, we also asked them to highlight words and phrases in the message that provided evidence for their ratings. To further control the annotation quality, we required that all workers have a United States location and have 98% or more of their previous submissions accepted. Ten workers rated each message, with different sets of workers rating each message. Altogether 298 workers participated in the ratings, and a subset of 29 workers completed 80% of all ratings. We paid $0.05 for rating each message.

We aggregated the 10 workers' responses for each message by averaging their ratings. Thus, each message has an average numerical score between 1 and 7 that indicates the amount of emotional and informational support it contains. Following are two examples from our final hand-coded dataset, one providing high emotional support and one providing high informational support. The example messages are lightly disguised using the techniques suggested by Bruckman [6].

- Eg. 1: emotional support=5.7; informational support=1.0

  Julie- you have had such a difficult road, but yet you still manage to do well in school.....I am truly inspired by you. Big cyber hugs and best wishes to you :>

- Eg. 2: emotional support=1.2; informational support=4.5

  Extranodal extension occurs when the tumor extends through the wall of the lymph node. This is noted on pathology reports, but in the main it isn't very significant, and isn't used in assessing cancer stage.

To assess the reliability of workers' ratings, we calculated the intra-class correlation coefficients for the two types of support [21]. Intra-class correlation is appropriate to assess the consistency of quantitative measurements when all objects are not rated by the same judges. The intra-class correlations representing the reliability of the average emotional support rating and the average informational support were high (both = .92).

To assess the validity of their ratings, we also had the workers code 25 messages from the ACOR sample [23] and 25 messages from the Bambina sample [3], which had been previously coded by experts. The correlation of MTurkers' average ratings and the experts' average ratings was moderate for both emotional support (r=.70) and informational support (r=.76).

LIWC Features
Pronoun: i, we, you, she/he, they, impersonal pronoun **Tense:** auxiliary verb, past, present, future **Sentiment:** positive emotion, negative emotion (anxiety, anger, sadness) **Topic:** cognitive mechanism, biological processes, time, religion, death
Linguistic Features
Length: sentence count, word count per sentence **Sentence type:** negation, question **Part-of-speech:** proper nouns, adjectives, cardinal numbers **Sentiment:** strong subjectivity, weak subjectivity **Advice:** advice verb, <please+VERB>, <if+you>, <you+MODAL> **Other:** drug
LDA Topical Features
Pre-diagnosis, Treatment plan, Forum communication, Adjusting to diagnosis, Financial concerns, Lymphedema, Diet, Family and friends, Positive life events, Surgery, Thoughts and feelings, Chemo radiation, Family history, Emotional reaction, Tumor treatment, Spiritual, Emotional support, Routine and schedule, Hairloss and appearance, Post-surgery problems

Table 1. Summary of the Three Kinds of Textual Features

Feature Set

Writers tend to adopt different language strategies when expressing different types of social support in their messages. To capture these strategies, we identified and used three types of textual features in the machine learning models. The first type was a set of generic dictionaries developed by Pennebaker and his colleagues [26] in the Linguistic Inquiry and Word Count program (LIWC), which measures function words (especially various types of pronouns) and topics with psychological relevance (e.g., positive emotion words, negative emotion words, cognition words). Second, we included rule-based structural features of the messages, mainly based on parts of speech, to capture higher-order linguistic concepts such as the presence of questions. Finally, we created specialized, cancer-related dictionaries using Latent Dirichlet Allocation (LDA) topic modeling. We describe each set of features below, summarize the important ones in Table 1, and provide a complete list in the online appendix[3].

LIWC Features: The Linguistic Inquiry and Word Count program (LIWC) is a popular tool which calculates the frequency with which words in a text match each of 68 dictionaries representing linguistic dimensions (e.g., pronouns, tense), psychological constructs (e.g., positive

[3] http://www.cs.cmu.edu/~yichiaw/Data/CSCW2012/CSCW2012-FeatureSet.htm

emotion), and personal concerns (e.g., leisure, death) [26]. Alpers and his colleagues analyzed several hundred posts in an online breast cancer support group using a human rater and LIWC. They demonstrated a moderate correlation between the ratings assigned by the rater and LIWC scores [1]. Motivated by their work, we included LIWC scores in our machine learning models and considered them as the baseline features. LIWC dictionaries were selected based on their relevance to emotional and informational support (Table 1). For example, for emotional support, *we* (e.g., "we," "us," "ours") addresses the feeling of companionship, whereas *positive emotion* (e.g., "love") and *religion* (e.g., "pray") express encouragement. For informational support, *impersonal pronoun* (e.g., "it") and *present tense* are often used to describe objective facts.

Linguistic Features: *Sentence count* and *word count per sentence* are features designed to represent the length and complexity of messages. The *negation* feature is the number of sentences in a message containing negation words or phrases, such as "not", "shouldn't", or "did not." The *question* feature counts the number of question sentences. Since not all questions are asked directly and end with a question mark, we applied heuristic rules to detect question sentences, including sentences starting with a modal verb (e.g., "Does anyone know ...") and indirect questions (e.g., "I am wondering if ..."). Because some parts-of-speech (POS) can signal information or emotion, we counted the number of these specific part-of-speech tags. For instance, professional labels can be signaled as *proper nouns* (e.g., "Dr. Smith"), and emotional states may be signaled by *adjectives* (e.g., "happy" life). We applied the Stanford POS tagger [32] to assign POS tags for words and extracted relevant POS features. Sentiment features describe the subjectivity of a text segment. We counted the number of *strong-subjectivity words* (e.g., "reject", "nervous") and *weak-subjectivity words* (e.g., "idea", "suggest") for every message. These two features were derived from the subjectivity lexicon of OpinionFinder [33]. To identify sentences involving advice or requests, we identified several text patterns or verbs in messages. For instance, the *<you+MODAL>* is a pattern that counts the number of sentences that start with a pronoun *you* and are immediately followed by a modal verb expressing possibilities (e.g., "should", "might", "must"). *<please+VERB>* is a pattern which detects sentences that begin with the word *please* followed by a verb. Furthermore, the *advice verb* feature considers the occurrence of verbs like "make", "suggest", "wish", etc. Finally, the number of *drug* terms in each message was counted. An exhaustive list of medicine names was collected from the Food and Drug Administration website[4].

LDA Topical Features: The features just described are generic, not tailored to the content of cancer support.

[4] http://www.fda.gov/Drugs/

LDA Topic	Sample Vocabulary
Pre-diagnosis	Told, appointment, wait, back
Treatment plan	Clinical, risk, medicine, therapy
Forum communication	Post, read, help, thread
Adjusting to diagnosis	Understand, trying, experience
Financial concerns	Insurance, plan, company, pay
Lymphedema	Arm, pain, swelling, fluid, area
Diet	Eat, weight, food, exercise, body
Family/Friends	Daughter, sister, wife
Positive life events	Love, nice, happy, enjoy, fun
Surgery	breast, surgeon, mastectomy
Thoughts/Feelings	Think, remember, believe
Chemo radiation	Chemo, radiation, treatment
Family history	Mom, children, age, young
Emotional reaction	Better, lucky, scared
Tumor treatment	Biopsy, nodes, positive, report
Spiritual	Love, god, prayer, bless, peace
Emotional support	Hope, hug, glad, sorry, best, luck
Routine/Schedule	Today, night, sleep, work
Hairloss/Appearance	Hair, wig, grow, head
Post-surgery problems	Pain, blood, tamoxifen, symptom

Table 2. Samples of Vocabulary in LDA Topic Dictionaries

Research on analyzing the text in support groups suggests that different topics can signal different types of social support [7]. For example, when messages use surgery-related terms, such as "reconstruction", "skin", "surgeon", they are likely to provide information to others. Latent Dirichlet Allocation (LDA) is a statistical generative model that can be used to discover hidden topics in documents as well as the words associated with each topic [5]. We first trained a LDA model using 30,000 breast cancer messages randomly selected from the entire dataset. The model was set to derive 20 latent topics. For each topic, we chose the 500 words most likely to correspond to that topic and used them to build a topic dictionary. Two experts familiar with cancer manually assigned a label to each topic (Table 2). Examples of topics derived from the LDA analysis include *Emotional Support* (e.g., "hope", "hug", "glad"), *Post Surgery Problems* (e.g., "pain", "blood", "tamoxifen") and *Spiritual* (e.g., "love", "god", "prayer"). Table 2 shows the sample vocabulary for each LDA topic dictionary. Each LDA topical feature calculates the frequency of words in a message matching its corresponding dictionary.

Construction and Performance of ML Models

Our task is a machine learning regression problem. Given the input feature representation of a message, we built two machine learning regressors, one of which outputs a numerical value indicating the amount of emotional support in the message, whereas the other outputs the amount of informational support. We used Weka [34], a machine learning toolkit, to build the regression models. The 1,000 messages coded by MTurk workers were randomly partitioned into training (80%), development (10%), and test (10%) sets. The training set was used to build the models. The development set was used to evaluate the accuracy of different configurations of the models and variations in the features used. Once the models achieved good performance on the development data, we used the test set to evaluate how well the final regressors performed. We evaluated the predictions using the Pearson correlation between the human-coded ratings and predicted amounts of support for the 100 messages in the test sample. Table 3 shows the evaluation results and the twenty most important features of the emotional and informational support models.

Given the adequate validity of these two models (as indicated by the correlations of .76 and .80 for emotion and information, respectively), we then applied them to measure the emotional and informational support contained in the 1.5 million messages in the Breastcancer.org dataset.

Support	Emotion	Information
Correlation	0.76	0.80
Most Important Features (Regression Weight)	*sentence count* (.59) *emotional support* (.45) *we* (.42) *you* (.40) *she/he* (-.37) *spiritual* (.28) *<if+you> (-.26)* *positive life events (-.26)* *adjusting to diagnosis (.24)* *time (-.24)* *word count per sentence (.21)* *strong subjectivity (.20)* *positive emotion (.19)* *present tense (-.19)* *drug (-.19)* *emotional reaction (.18)* *anger (.18)* *financial concerns (-.18)* *treatment plan (-.17)* *religion (.14)*	*sentence count (.89)* *word count per sentence (.41)* *strong subjectivity (-.24)* *<if+you> (.23)* *i (-.22)* *spiritual (-.21)* *we (-.20)* *post surgery problems (.20)* *forum communication (-.17)* *religion (-.16)* *anxiety (-.16)* *<please+VERB> (-.16)* *thoughts and feelings (-.15)* *treatment plan (.15)* *death (-.15)* *anger (-.15)* *impersonal pronoun (-.15)* *diet (.14)* *past tense (.14)*

Table 3. Performance of Social Support Regressors and Top Ranked Features

PREDICTING COMMITMENT TO THE GROUP FROM SUPPORT

We applied survival analysis to test the hypothesis that people who were exposed to more support remain in the forums longer, controlling for the non-support communication they receive. Survival analysis is a statistical technique for investigating influences on time-related outcomes, such as whether an event occurs or when it occurs. In the present research, the event of interest is the time until a member leaves the group (or conversely, the length of time the person continues participating in the group). More specifically, our goal is to understand whether the amounts of emotional or informational support that an individual is exposed to in an online support group can predict that person's length of participation. We use survival analysis because standard regression procedures produce biased estimates. They do not take into account the truncated nature of time-to-event data (i.e., at the time of data collection, some people who will eventually leave the group have not yet left). Because, in many online groups, the probability of leaving is much higher early in members' tenure in the group than later on, we used parametric regression survival analysis to examine influences on length of participation. We assumed a Weibull distribution of survival times, which is generally appropriate for modeling survival.

Data and Methods

The breastcancer.org data does not contain information about which messages people read, but only those they posted. To estimate the amount of support people were exposed to, we assumed that they read all of the messages in the threads to which they posted in the week they posted. This assumption probably underestimates the support individuals received, because they could glean information or compare themselves with others by reading messages without posting. Therefore, our analyses are likely to underestimate the importance of the relationship between social support and people's participation length in the group.

To conduct the analysis, we included only the 30,301 group members who contributed one or more posts, because without overt behavior it is impossible to estimate the amount of support that they viewed. We defined the time intervals as weeks. We considered the timestamp of the first post by each member as her starting date for participating in the breast cancer discussion forums and the date of the last login as the end of participation unless it was within three months before the end of data collection.

Dependent variable

- **Failure:** We consider a user to have left the group if she failed to post within 12 weeks of her last post. According to this definition, a user can drop out from the group and rejoin it multiple times. Because people whose last post was within 12 weeks of end of data collection could still be participating, we treated them as right censored in the analysis. The conclusions we report below are the same if we assume that people leave the group only once.

Control variables

- **HasProfile:** This is a binary measure that describes whether a user had created a profile page (1) or not (0). 31% of the 30,301 subjects had done so.
- **ThreadStarter:** Because people who start conversations may be different from those who participate in conversations started by others, we calculated the percentage of an individual's posts that were thread

starters. This is the number of thread starters a user posted in a week divided by the total post number for that user in that week.

Independent variables

- **PostCountByUser:** This is the number of messages a member posts in the forums in a week.
- **PostCountExposure:** We calculated the total number of posts a user was exposed to by assuming that people read all the messages posted in a thread during weeks when they also posted to the threat. This variable is the count of all posts in the threads in a week in which the user had posted. Since PostCountExposure is inferred from PostCountByUser, they are highly correlated (r=.67). In order to avoid multicollinearity problems, we only included PostCountExposure in the final models.
- **Emotional Support Exposure (EmoSupportExp):** This variable measures the average emotional support per message a user was exposed to in a week. It was calculated by summing all the emotional support in the threads in a week where the user had posted, dividing by the total post number that the user was exposed to in that week.
- **Informational Support Exposure (InfoSupportExp):** This variable measures the average informational support per message a user was exposed to in a week. It was calculated by summing all the informational support in the threads in a week where the user had a post, divided by the total post number that the user was exposed to in that week.

Except for the binary variable HasProfile, all the numerical control and independent variables were standardized, with a mean of zero and standard deviation of one. Table 4 reports the descriptive statistics for the variables entered into the survival regression models before standardization (except PostCountByUser, which, as noted above, was not included in the models).

Who Stays in Groups?

Results of three survival models are shown in Table 5. Effects are reported in terms of the hazard ratio (HR), which is the effect of an explanatory variable on the risk or probability of participants' leaving the group. Because all the explanatory variables except HasProfile have been standardized, the hazard rate here is the predicted change in the probability of dropout from the group for a unit increase in the predictor (i.e., HasProfile changing from zero to one or the continuous variable increasing by a standard deviation when all the other variables are at their mean levels).

	Mean	Median	Std. Dev.	Min	Max
HasProfile	.31	0	.46	0	1
ThreadStarter	.10	0	.27	0	1
PostCntByUser	5.91	2	15.39	1	923
PostCntExp	78.96	25	151.04	0	3790
EmoSupportExp	2.77	2.73	0.65	1	7
InfoSupportExp	2.87	2.91	0.69	1	7

Table 4. Descriptive Statistics for the Variables in the Survival Analysis

Model 1 reports the effects of the control variables and participants' overall exposure to messages. The hazard ratio value for HasProfile means that members' survival in the group is 54% (100% - (100% * 0.46)) higher for those who have entered profile information compared to those who have no profile. Similarly, the hazard ratio for PostCountExposure indicates that survival rates are 39% higher for those who saw a standard deviation more messages than average. Starting a thread in a week has no additional effect.

Model 2 shows that when controlling for characteristics of these members and the total messages they were exposed to, both emotional support and informational support influenced the survival rates, but in different directions. Those who were exposed to messages containing an average of one standard deviation more emotional support (EmoSupportExp) were 16% more likely to *remain* in the group. In contrast, those who were exposed to messages containing an average of one standard deviation more informational support (InfoSupportExp) were 10% more

	Model 1		Model 2		Model 3	
Control/Indep. Variable	**HR**	**Std. Err.**	**HR**	**Std. Err.**	**HR**	**Std. Err.**
HasProfile	0.457***	0.009	0.474***	0.010	0.511***	0.010
ThreadStarter	1.003	0.005	0.875***	0.011	0.853***	0.010
PostCountExposure	0.614***	0.019	0.801***	0.016	0.343***	0.012
EmoSupportExp			0.844***	0.007	0.665***	0.008
InfoSupportExp			1.102***	0.009	1.048***	0.012
PostCountExposure X EmoSupportExp					0.493***	0.011
PostCountExposure X InfoSupportExp					0.953*	0.020

*: $p<0.05$, **: $p<0.01$, ***: $p<0.001$

Table 5. Results of the Survival Analysis

likely to *leave* the group. That is, more emotional support was associated with staying, whereas more informational support was associated with leaving. At 3 months, participants exposed to one standard deviation more emotional support than average were 190% more likely to still be in the group than those exposed to a standard deviation more informational support than average.

Model 3 adds the interaction between the number of messages participants were exposed to and the average amount of emotional and informational support in those messages (PostCountExposure X EmoSupportExp and PostCountExposure X InfoSupportExp). Compared to those exposed to an average number of messages at the average amount of emotional support, members who were exposed to a standard deviation more messages that contained a standard deviation more emotional support than average were 89% more likely to remain on the site[5]. In contrast, members who were exposed to a standard deviation more messages that contained a standard deviation more informational support than average were only 66% more likely to remain on the site[6]. That is, receiving many messages filled with emotional support was much more likely to keep members participating on the site than was receiving many messages filled with informational support. However, when members received few posts, it mattered less when these posts were filled with emotional or informational support. Figure 4 illustrates these results graphically, showing five survival curves. The middle curve shows survival with the number of posts and support exposure at their mean level. The top two curves show survival when the number of posts and average emotional support exposure (or informational support exposure) in the posts were both one standard deviation above the mean, and the two bottom curves show survival when the number of posts was one standard deviation below the mean, and the average emotional support exposure (or informational support exposure) in the posts was one standard deviation above the mean.

DISCUSSION AND CONCLUSIONS

In this paper we built accurate machine learning models to identify the extent to which messages in online breast cancer support groups contained emotional and informational support. We then examined the relationship between types and amounts of social support and commitment. The results demonstrated that the more emotional support members were exposed to, the lower the risk of dropout. In contrast, informational support did not have the same strong effects on commitment.

Although the results for emotional support strongly confirm our hypothesis that social support is associated with increased group commitment, the results for informational

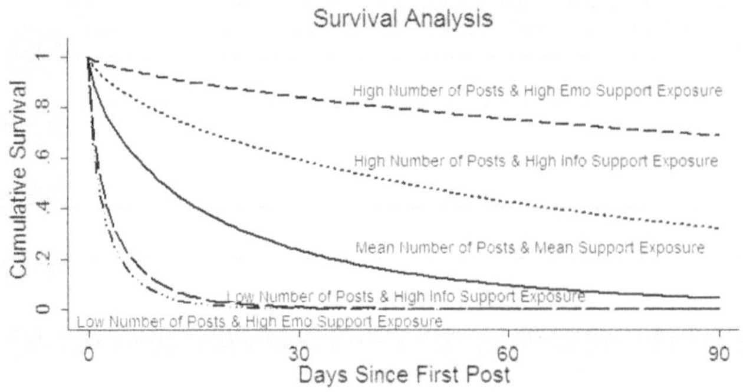

Figure 4. Survival Curves for Members Exposed To Different Levels of Number of Posts and Social Support

support do not. This contrast between the effects of two types of support is interesting, showing how social interaction can have different effects depending upon the content of the communication being exchanged.

How might we explain the unanticipated finding that increased informational support showed a weaker association with commitment than did emotional support? Although our account is necessarily speculative, we would suggest two possible explanations.

First, it may be that many information needs are short term. As a result, people who have information needs and receive informational help from others have these immediate needs met and have little reason to stay in the group, just as one might not continue perusing a dictionary after looking up a definition. On the other hand, the need for emotional support may be longer term and require multiple interactions to be fulfilled.

Second, factual information exchanged in unmoderated health support groups may lack the accuracy, credibility, and usefulness of information from other sources, such as physicians or sites run by the National Cancer Institute or the American Cancer Society. For this reason, people may leave health support groups because they perceive that the information they receive there is not helpful, and the more such information they receive, the more likely they may be to leave.

In contrast, emotional support obtained in a support group is likely to be perceived as more helpful than emotional support obtained elsewhere, because support group providers share many experiences with support group recipients. Moreover, emotional support obtained in a support group may lead recipients to develop relationships with providers or the group as a whole, which in turn increases their feelings of commitment to the group.

Limitations and Directions for Future Work

An important limitation of this study is that, even though we use longitudinal data, our findings are correlational. We examined how the support people were exposed to in one week was associated their subsequent participation in the support groups. The results are consistent with the

[5] 89% = (1-exp(-1.069-0.408-0.708))*100%

[6] 66% = (1-exp(-1.069+0.046-0.049))*100%

assumption that support exposure changes commitment. However, they can also be interpreted in terms of pre-existing differences between those who seek emotional versus informational support. For example, it may be that those seeking emotional support are also seeking long term relationships, while those seeking informational support are not. Only random-assignment experiments will allow us to definitively determine whether exposure to support actually changes commitment. A second limitation is that the reported analysis is based only on the people who had posting experience. It therefore does not shed light on the reason(s) that lurkers continue to participate in these groups. To study the behavior of lurkers, we will need to have detailed records of the activities of all users, such as their browsing and clicking logs. Moreover, because we had no direct measures of reading, we could only estimate exposure during weeks when people posted in the site. This confound led to the high correlation between the two measures and renders the interpretation of the effects of PostCountExposure in Table 5 ambiguous.

We see additional directions for future work. First, although our findings suggest that the effects of social support on commitment vary as a function of the kind of support that one receives, the cause of the difference is still not clear. A natural next step is to conduct surveys or interviews which ask participants in the group why they stay or leave.

Furthermore, although our current analysis was based on a large corpus of data from 66 forums, we only examined one type of disease (breast cancer) in one online health support group. Other online health support groups might produce different commitment levels or patterns given exposure to social support. For example, the positive effect of emotional support on commitment in a prostate cancer support group may be much weaker because men care less about emotional support. Further research studying other online support groups can help us better understand and confirm our findings.

Finally, this research examined only the association between support and commitment to the group. It would therefore be useful to examine the extent to which social support and commitment in online support groups affect participants' health quality of life.

Implications

The impressive performance of our machine learning models for predicting social support implies that it is feasible to utilize computer programs to automatically analyze the conversations in online support groups. In particular, we believe that the proposed feature set can be easily applied to build predictive models for social support for other health support datasets. LIWC and Linguistic features can be directly adopted, since these two types of features are generic in the sense that they are not tailored to any specific data. The only change one might need to make is to recreate LDA topical dictionaries customized to the data of interest, and this step can be done with little effort.

Although we used machine learning models of social support to understand behavior in health support groups, similar models could be the basis for active interventions. For example, it should be possible to assess in real time whether people who tell their disease stories are receiving the emotional support they are seeking or whether those asking a questions are receiving the informational support they are seeking. If not, their posts could be routed to volunteer moderators or to others in the community who have a history of providing the appropriate support.

ACKNOWLEDGMENTS

This research was supported by NSF grant IIS-0968485. We want to thank Dong Nguyen and BreastCancer.org, who helped provide the data for this project.

REFERENCES

1. Alpers, G. W., Winzelberg, A. J., Classen, C., Roberts, H., Dev, P., Koopman, C., et al. (2005). Evaluation of computerized text analysis in an Internet breast cancer support group. *Computers in Human Behavior*, *21*(2), 361-376.
2. Ashforth, B. E., & Saks, A. M. (1996). Socialization tactics: Longitudinal effects on newcomer adjustment. *Academy of Management Journal*, *39*(1), 149-178.
3. Bambina, A. (2007). *Online social support: the interplay of social networks and computer-mediated communication*. NY: Cambria Press.
4. Bauer, T. N., Morrison, E. W., & Callister, R. R. (1998). Organizational socialization: A review and directions for future research. In G. R. Ferris (Ed.), *Research in personnel and human resources management* (Vol. 16, pp. 149-214). Greenwich CT: JAI Press Inc.
5. Blei, David M., Ng, Andrew Y., & Jordan, Michael I. (2003). Latent Dirichlet allocation. *Journal of Machine Learning Research*, *3*(Jan), 993-1022.
6. Bruckman, Amy. (2006). Teaching students to study online communities ethically. *Journal of Information Ethics*, *15*(2), 82-98.
7. Buis, L. R. (2008). Emotional and informational support messages in an online hospice support community. *Computers, Informatics, Nursing*, *26*(6), 358-367.
8. Chou, W. Y. S., Hunt, Y. M., Beckjord, E. B., Moser, R. P., & Hesse, B. W. (2009). Social media use in the United States: Implications for health communication. *Journal of Medical Internet Research*, *11*(4), e48.
9. Chou, W. S., Liu, B., Post, S., & Hesse, B. (2011). Health-related Internet use among cancer survivors: Data from the Health Information National Trends Survey, 2003–2008. *Journal of Cancer Survivorship*, *5*(3), 263-270..
10. Cutrona, C. E., & Suhr, J. A. (1994). Social support communication in the context of marriage: An analysis

of couples' supportive interactions. In B. R. Burleson, T. L. Albrecht & I. G. Sarason (Eds.), *Communication of social support: Messages, interactions, relationships, and community* (pp. 113-135). Thousand Oaks, CA: Sage Publications.

11. Davison, K. P., Pennebaker, J. W., & Dickerson, S. S. (2000). Who talks? The social psychology of illness support groups. *American Psychologist, 55*(2), 205-217.

12. Dunkel-Schetter, C. (1984). Social support and cancer: Findings based on patient interviews and their implications. *Journal of Social Issues*, *40*(4), 77-98.

13. Dunkel-Schetter, C., Feinstein, L. G., Taylor, S. E., & Falke, R. L. (1992). Patterns of coping with cancer. *Health Psychology*, *11*(2), 79-87.

14. Eysenbach, G., Powell, J., Englesakis, M., Rizo, C., & Stern, A. (2004). Health related virtual communities and electronic support groups: Systematic review of the effects of online peer to peer interactions. *British Medical Journal*, *328*(7449), 1166-1171.

15. Fisher, C. D. (1986). Organizational socialization: An integrative review. In G. R. Ferris & K. M. Rowland (Eds.), *Research in personnel and human resources management* (Vol. 4, pp. 101-145). Greenwich, CT: JAI.

16. Han, J. Y., Shaw, B. R., Hawkins, R. P., Pingree, S., Mctavish, F., & Gustafson D. H. (2008). Expressing positive emotions within online support groups by women with breast cancer. *Journal of Health Psychology*, *13*(8), 1002-1007.

17. Hardey, M. (2002). 'The story of my illness': Personal accounts of illness on the Internet. *Health*, *6*(1), 31-46.

18. Helgeson, V. S., Cohen, S., Schulz, R., & Yasko, J. (2000). Group support interventions for women with breast cancer: Who benefits from what? *Health Psychology*, *19*(2), 107-114.

19. Helgeson, V. S. & Cohen, S. (2001). Long-term effects of educational and peer discussion group interventions on adjustment to breast cancer. *Health Psychology*, *20*(5), 387-392.

20. Jacobs C., Ross, R. D., Walker, I. M., & Stockdale, R. E. (1983). Behavior of cancer patients: A randomized study of the effects of education and peer support groups. *American Journal of Clinical Oncology*, *6*(3), 347-353.

21. Koch, Gary G. (1982). Intraclass correlation coefficient. In S. Kotz & N. L. Johnson (Eds), *Encyclopedia of statistical sciences* (pp. 213–217). New York: John Wiley & Sons.

22. Levine, J. M. & Moreland, R. L. (1994). Group socialization: Theory and research. *European Review of Social Psychology*, *5*(1), 305-336.

23. Meier, A., Lyons, E. J., Frydman, G., Forlenza, M., Rimer, B. K. (2007). How cancer survivors provide support on cancer-related Internet mailing lists. *Journal of Medical Internet Research*, *9*(2), e12.

24. Moreland, R. L., & Levine, J. M. (2001). Socialization in organizations and work groups. In M. E. Turner (Ed.), *Groups at work: Theory and research* (pp. 69-112). Mahwah, NJ: Erlbaum.

25. Owen, J. E., Giese-Davis, J., Cordova, M., Kronenwetter, C., Golant, M., & Spiegel, D. (2006). Self-report and linguistic indicators of emotional expression in narratives as predictors of adjustment to cancer. *Journal of Behavioral Medicine*, *29*(4), 335–345.

26. Pennebaker, J.W., Francis, M.E., & Booth, R.J. (2007). *Linguistic inquiry and word count (LIWC2007).* Mahwah. NJ: Erlbaum Publishers.

27. Preece, J., & Shneiderman, B. (2009). The Reader-to-Leader Framework: Motivating technology-mediated social participation. *AIS Transactions on Human-Computer Interaction*, *1*(1), 13-32.

28. Rodgers, S. & Chen, Q. (2005). Internet community group participation: Psychosocial benefits for women with breast cancer. *Journal of Computer Mediated Communication*, *10*(4), np.

29. Shaw, B. R., McTavish, F., Hawkins, R., Gustafson, D. H., & Pingree, S. (2000). Experiences of women with breast cancer: Exchanging social support over the chess computer network. *Journal of health communication*, *5*(2), 135-59.

30. Singer, J. D. & Willett, J. B. (2003). *Applied longitudinal data analysis*. New York: Oxford University Press.

31. Snow, R., O'Connor, B., Jurafsky, D., & Ng, A. Y. (2008). Cheap and fast---but is it good? Evaluating non-expert annotations for natural language tasks. In *Proceedings of the Conference on Empirical Methods in Natural Language Processing* (pp. 254-263). Stroudsburg. PA: Association for Computational Linguistics.

32. Toutanova, K. & Manning, C. D. (2000). Enriching the knowledge sources used in a maximum entropy part-of-speech tagger. In *Proceedings of the Conference on Empirical Methods in Natural Language Processing* (pp. 63-70). Stroudsburg. PA: Association for Computational Linguistics.

33. Wilson, T., Wiebe, J., & Hoffmann, P. (2005). Recognizing contextual polarity in phrase-level sentiment analysis. In *Proceedings of the Conference on Empirical Methods in Natural Language Processing* (pp. 347-354). Stroudsburg. PA: Association for Computational Linguistics.

34. Witten, I. H. & Frank, E. (2005). *Data mining: Practical machine learning tools and techniques* (2nd ed.). San Francisco: Elsevier.

This is Not a One-Horse Race: Understanding Player Types in Multiplayer Pervasive Health Games for Youth

Yan Xu[1], Erika Shehan Poole[2], Andrew D. Miller[1], Elsa Eiriksdottir[3], Dan Kestranek[2], Richard Catrambone[3], Elizabeth D. Mynatt[1]

[1]College of Computing
Georgia Institute of Technology
85 5th Street NW
Atlanta, GA 30332 USA

[2]College of Information Sciences & Technology
The Pennsylvania State University
321E IST Building
University Park, PA 16802 USA

[3]School of Psychology
Georgia Institute of Technology
654 Cherry Street
Atlanta, GA 30332 USA

{andrew.miller, elsa, mynatt, yan.xu}@gatech.edu, rc7@prism.gatech.edu, {djk294, esp13}@psu.edu

ABSTRACT

Technology-based interventions for promoting health behavior-change frequently leverage multiplayer game mechanics such as group-based competitions. However, health interventions successful for groups writ large may not always translate to successful behavior change at the individual level. In this paper, we explore the tension between group and individual success, based on an empirical study on a long-term real-world deployment of a pervasive health game for youth. We report five distinctive player types along the dimensions of motivation, behavior, and influence on others. Based on the findings, we provide design suggestions to help game designers integrate group mechanisms that maximize intervention effectiveness.

Author Keywords

Pervasive Games; Physical Activity; Adolescents; Behavior Change

ACM Classification Keywords

H.5.m. [Information Interfaces and Presentation (e.g., HCI)]: Miscellaneous; K.8.0 [Personal Computing]: Games

General Terms

Human Factors; Design

INTRODUCTION

Many health applications and games leverage cooperation and competition [22], social support [7], and peer pressure [33], with the presumption that social components positively motivate users and foster behavior change. These social components are typically embodied in multiplayer mechanics such as broadcasting progress to a group of friends [7,33] or competing against other groups based on aggregated performance of each member [17,22]. Although group-based mechanics are promising, research studies report conflicting results on their effectiveness. For example, the *Fish'n'Steps* study found that team-based competition did not have a significant effect on step counts compared to a single-user equivalent [22], while the *Step Matron* study showed that participants significantly increased their step counts when sharing the numbers and status updates with a Facebook group [15]. This apparent conflict in the quantitative behavior outcomes calls for qualitative research to gain a deeper understanding of the dynamics of individual participants that may lead to differential effectiveness and enjoyment of multiplayer health games.

In this paper, we describe the diversity of individual participation styles in multiplayer health games, based on our evaluation of a large-scale field trial of a pervasive technology-based health game for youth. Our findings shed light on the concerns and cares of youth participating in health games, and the impact of group-based competition on individual players. Our research identifies and describes the five distinctive player types that emerged during the play of this game: *achievers, active buddies, social experience seekers, team players,* and *freeloaders*. In addition to describing genres of players, we also provide concrete design suggestions for integrating group-based mechanisms more carefully and effectively in health games for youth, as well as populations that are more diverse.

Our findings are timely given the recent increase in commercially available fitness games and group-focused interventions for promoting behavior change; as these programs increase in popularity, there is a need for deeper understanding of real-world gameplay practices and diversity in player styles.

THE AMERICAN HORSEPOWER CHALLENGE (AHPC)

Researching player diversity in multi-user pervasive games is particularly challenging because it is not amenable to lab experiments. To let player diversity in these games emerge, there must be long-term deployments, natural settings, and minimal overt researcher presence.

Thus, the case study we present is the American Horsepower Challenge (AHPC), a multi-user health game created by Humana's Games for Health and sponsored by The Humana Foundation. The AHPC was a multi-month school-based competition to encourage students to increase their daily physical activity levels both inside and outside of school.

What makes the AHPC an ideal candidate for studying individual differences within groups participating in health interventions is its multi-site, long-term, and authentic implementation.

The AHPC Intervention

Youth are an especially important audience for physical activity intervention programs because they often face the challenge of the "*adolescent slump*," which is a significant drop of physical activity occurring at early adolescence [31]. After this slump occurs, many adolescents will transition into sedentary lifestyles as adults. The AHPC aimed to address this slump by incentivizing participation in unstructured physical activity in daily life (e.g. walking rather than riding in a car, or taking the stairs rather than an elevator).

The goal of the game was to win a virtual "race" against other schools participating in the program. Students in the competition wore on-body sensors about their physical activity that fed information into a web-based game. When a student participated in physical activity, he or she earned points for his or her school. To determine each school's rank in the competition, step counts from all students on a school's team were aggregated daily and position on the track was updated accordingly.

It is important to note that the AHPC was *not* intended as an intervention to improve body composition. As such, the program does not use body composition information as an input for the game, nor did the research team collect body composition measurements at any point during the study. Instead, the game focused on increases in physical activity.

Technical Components

The AHPC has three technical components: a wireless pedometer worn on the shoe to collect step data (Figure 1. left), a base station in the school to wirelessly collect step data when students were in range of the device (Figure 1. right), and a password-protected website accessible from school or home (Figures 2, 3).

On the website, each school is represented as a school bus on a racetrack, and the busses' positions on the track represent the schools' rank in the competition. Each player is also represented by a horse avatar, which is customizable using a virtual currency earned by taking steps throughout the day (Figure 2). When using the website, players can check bus positions in the race, purchase items for their avatars, update their individual status messages, or view graphs depicting their recent step history. Players can also view their classmates' horse avatars (see yellow box in Figure 3) and status messages (see yellow box in Figure 2), but they cannot see their classmate's *individual* step counts.

Deployment Sites

Before our research group's involvement with the project, the Humana Foundation recruited eligible schools. The schools, located in a variety of communities across the US, were chosen based on having high participation in the National School Lunch Program, a government-sponsored program offering affordable meals to low-income students. Sixty-one schools participated, with thirty-seven continuing through all three phases of the program. The game was deployed in three "heats" between April 2009 and Feb 2010, each heat lasting 4 to 5 weeks.

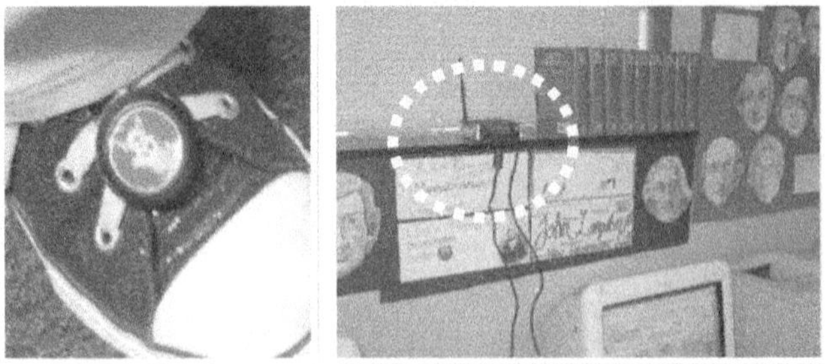

Figure 1. A pedometer clipped to a shoe (left) and the wireless base station (dotted circle) in a classroom (right)

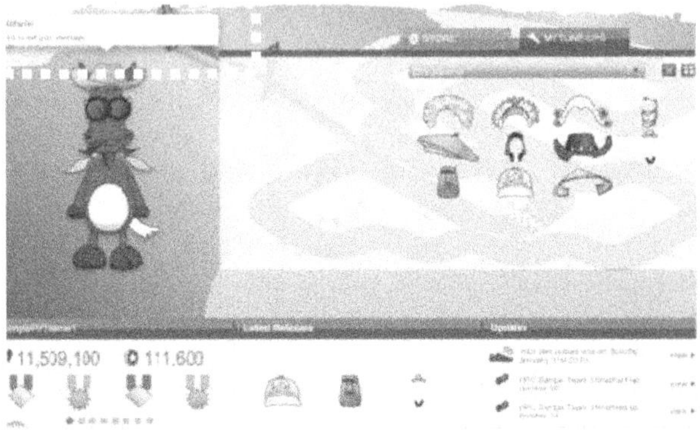

Figure 2. Avatar customization, racetrack in background. Status message bubble appears above the avatar (dotted box at top left)

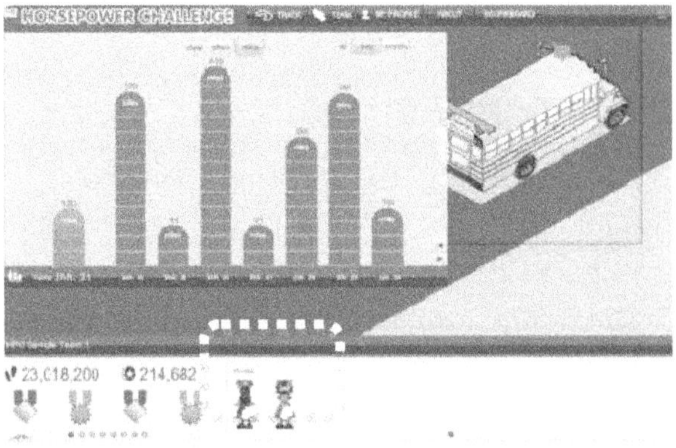

Figure 3. View of aggregate step counts (top left), View of other players (dotted box on bottom)

Participants

In total, 1,743 students participated in at least one of the heats of the AHPC. The majority of the schools had 20 participants each. Within individual schools, there were varieties of mechanisms to select participants, such as first-come-first-served (e.g. students who returned permission slips first) or explicit teacher selection from a pool of student volunteers.

RELATED WORK

The aim of this paper is to describe the diversity of individual player types in group-based health games for youth. Accommodating and coordinating a variety of play styles is critical yet challenging for game design. In this section, we first examine the nature of gameplay in pervasive games, and then we situate the AHPC within the gameplay taxonomy literature.

Defining 'Play' in Pervasive Games

The AHPC is a pervasive game, which extends the traditional boundary of gameplay spatially, temporally, and socially [26]. The core game mechanism of the AHPC is multi-session group-based competition, similar to sports tournaments, a familiar concept to most American schoolchildren. Although the AHPC tracks steps continuously, it does not give real-time feedback, nor does it support real-time communication between remote players. The AHPC is most like *Fish'n'Steps*, [22] which renders the user's steps into the progress of an online character. Because the AHPC is a health intervention, its 'gameplay' is integrated into a user's everyday life [8]. This tight relation between gameplay and real life makes identifying and categorizing styles of play challenging within a traditional pilot deployment, and may require a long-term study that allows players to develop their own ways of integrating a pervasive health game in their environmental and social context [4].

Taxonomies of Play

Game researchers, and more recently psychology and HCI researchers, have categorized play and players based on factors such as motivation [19,28,36], enjoyment [6,20,24], dedication [3], emotional triggers [21], and position in a social network [1]. Indeed, taxonomies of play predate the existence of computer-based games. For example, in 1958 Caillois divided games into four categories based on their structure and rules: *competition*, *chance*, *simulation*, and *vertigo (being physically out of control)* [6]. The advent and popularity of online collaborative games has led to renewed interest in understanding players. For example, Bartle famously analyzed player behaviors in online Multi-User Dungeons (MUDs). Bartle focused on two key dimensions: the degree to which the player emphasizes the virtual world or other players, and the degree to which the player interacts with other objects/players in the game. These two dimensions led to a quadrant of player types: *achievers, explorers, killers,* and *socializers* [2].

In developing our own taxonomy, we employed three dimensions: motivation, behavior and social influence.

Motivation and Behavior

Most game taxonomies address two basic questions: what players seek from the game (motivations and expectations), and how players act during gameplay (behaviors). These questions become heightened in health games, where changes in motivation and behavior are essential. Behavior change theories from health psychology highlight the role of motivation in the behavior change process. For example, in Fisher and Fisher's information-motivation-behavioral skills (IMB) framework, motivation is critical for generating a favorable attitude and affection towards physical activities [14]. When player motivations align with behavior change goals, video games can be an essential tool in increasing healthy behaviors [5]. Accordingly, we derive player types from their motivations—not just for enjoyment, but also for behavior change. We also examine players' behaviors as both outcomes and indicators of the players' motivations. These behaviors might include their interactions with the game, with other players/teachers, and the change of activities for themselves, and so on.

Social Influence

One further recurring theme in the game taxonomy literature is the social aspect of gameplay. For example, Olson et al. surveyed why middle school children play video games, and social motivations include: "*hang out*", "*compete*", "*teach each other*", "*make friends*", and "*lead*" [28]. As pointed out by Lazarro [21], "*it's the people that are addictive not the game.*" Health game designers have incorporated a myriad of multiplayer game mechanics for behavior change [7,15,17,22,33]. For example, one way to motivate physical activity is to mediate social-physical activities in outdoor environments through communication technology [27]. However, social influence may vary depending on the condition and characteristics of the individuals involved, as highlighted by Maitland and Chalmers [23]. In addition to motivation and behavior, we use social influence to generate player types, with the focus on understanding group dynamics.

We also aim to understand the reasons why social influence is sometimes not positive. Although group members oftentimes share a goal and may play cooperatively, rewards for individuals sometimes conflict with those for the group. For example, in World of Warcraft, players might argue when they pick up rare treasures after battling together against a monster [10]. Even when there is no explicit conflict among group members, players still sometimes play in "individual" mode when they are fully engaged with the computer, and sometimes in "group" mode when they construct shared awareness and outcome, and 'sacrifice' for the team [34]. Social reality in a game group is constructed through individuals and their interactions, rather than being pre-defined by the game. Hence, it would be oversimplifying to consider the group as one unit.

METHODS

The main findings of this paper draw upon data from site visits to 15 schools towards the end of the AHPC deployment; for full reporting of survey and step log data, please refer to [12]. At these school visits, we conducted 18 student focus groups with 4-10 participants each, 17 teacher interviews, and 56 individual student interviews. In total, we talked to over 200 participants. We also received tours of facilities and shadowed the teachers during their physical education classes if invited. After each site visit, researchers wrote field notes that included observations about the school.

The profile of the 15 schools we visited was representative of the overall group socioeconomically (71.8% of students receive free or reduced lunch), demographically (male-female ratio=1.03, similar ethnic makeup), and regionally (covering 8 states and a mix of rural/suburban/small town/city schools). We also collected the step count log as a triangulation for the qualitative data.

We derive player types from an inductive, iterative analysis on qualitative data. In prior research, players' reflection on their experience has been used as a key data source for the player taxonomy research [2,28,36]. Due to the emergent nature of multiplayer game experience, we choose an empirical method that focuses on user-reported data over critical analysis, which was most common in the earlier work of play taxonomy in game research [6].

Our data analysis involved four researchers reading and coding each interview focus group transcript, and the field notes. One of the most prominent themes to emerge from this phase of analysis was the variety of play styles students and teachers reported to us, even within the same school, independent of a school's ranking at the game. Our large data set allowed us to verify these observations through cross-school comparison. Based on a player's motivation, behavior, and influence, we extrapolated the player types that were distinctive from each other and happened across multiple schools. We iterated this process until we reached theoretical saturation.

Based on existing literature on player taxonomies and the role of motivation in behavior change, we focused on three dimensions of gameplay experience: motivation (i.e. why did a player care about the game?), behavior (i.e. what kind of things did a player do during the game?), and influence (i.e. what is the social impact that a player brought to the rest of the group?). In the findings section, we describe each type of play by these three dimensions.

FINDINGS

In this section, we describe five types of players found among the AHPC participants. While players naturally varied in their existing athletic skills, social relations, interest in the AHPC system, to form our categories we focus mainly on the differences in their motivation, behaviors, and influence on others in the group. We define the five player types as *achievers*, *active buddies*, *social experience seekers*, *team players*, and *freeloaders*.

Achievers

We define the term *achiever* to be the same as in Bartle's definition of this type on MUDs, meaning players who "give themselves game-related goals, and vigorously set out to achieve them" [2]. In the context of AHPC, achievers are keen on improving their individual step counts and getting confirmation of their improvements from the game system.

Motivations and Behaviors

Achievers were motivated by making individual progress and increasing personal performance. Achievers set step goals for themselves regularly during the AHPC. Some showed us that they wrote numbers down in a notebook to have easier access to their step count trends. They used the AHPC website mainly for checking their steps and the step history.

Although it is logical to assume that highly athletic students would be achievers, we found that it was not the case for the AHPC participants. With respect to athletes, just by doing their existing physical activity routines (e.g. sports practices) they managed to obtain high step counts, so they rarely changed or reflected on their routine. Moreover, as AHPC required almost no athletic skills, it did not reward athleticism in the typical way seen in most sports.

Achievers were oftentimes participants who had previously led sedentary lifestyles and those who were not seen as 'athletes.' Although they were keen on competing with themselves, they typically did not like being compared with others. They tried various physical activities to get more steps, such as walking to school instead of getting a ride, playing more exercise games at home, or walking the dog more. Of note is that these activities were typically low-intensity and non-competitive.

Influence

Achievers exemplify the tension between individual and group performance in the game. For example, in the following dialogue, we asked the student interviewees to give advice to new AHPC participants, and the player emphasized the goal of individual improvement, and remarked on the stress of being picked on during the AHPC:

> *SE_Boy_3: Well, when you're doing the Horsepower Challenge and it's complicated and you're nervous; just set a goal for yourself...*
>
> *Interviewer: Complicated and nervous? – what kind of, exactly, emotion that you're talking about?*
>
> *SE_Boy_3: Nervous that you're going to lose. Like if they change the website and see who has the more points and you have the lowest points. And your team loses, they're going to blame the kid that did the less steps.*
>
> *Interviewer: Did anyone do that to kids in your school?*
>
> *SE_Boy_3: I've heard it before.*
>
> *Interviewer: What kind of things did they say?*
>
> *SE_Boy_3: They'll make fun of other kids. They'll be calling other kids losers and stuff. But the kid is not good at that stuff and he's just trying the thing that the other kids are good at. He's kind of making another goal for himself, because he's trying that thing out but he has never done it.*

This participant wanted to focus on the "*goal for himself,*" but was afraid that it was not good enough for others. Although the boy knew that others could not see his step counts, the stress of being blamed and teased still existed. He hoped to prove himself in front of the rest of the group. Later in the interview, he shared with us his cousin's experience of redeeming himself in another physical activity promotion program with similar group-based competition structure.

Interviewer: What happened to the kid who was teased?

SE_Boy_3: He probably felt bad. Probably eventually he had gotten better at it....And the kid might catch up sometimes.

Interviewer: How do you know?

SE_Boy_3: Well, I had my cousin that used to do this. And he had the lowest points and everybody teased him about it. And at the end of the year he had more points than everybody in the school... He walked from his house to the ____ and back. And his house is like in ___. So he just walks back and forth. Because he told me this and he won. And the school won because of him...

In this example, the boy attributed the success of his cousin's school to his cousin's personal improvement. He considered his cousin a positive example. Overall, the achievers' experience in AHPC had the potential to be inspiring and encouraging to kids who were not typically athletic, as they tried many new and different activities. However, we found that their influence on other members in the group was actually limited. While the achievers might have individually improved more than other types of participant, the group did not always recognize this effort. This was especially true for the students who were overweight and less athletic; they were picked on anyway, irrespective of the fact that others did not have access to their step numbers. The social pressure was stressful and isolating [33]. Here, the current AHPC system design does not seem to support the need of achievers to prove their progress to the group and become positive examples. Instead, a points system based on personalized progress or goals might prove more successful.

In summary, achievers focused on personal improvement. They used the AHPC website mostly for functional purposes of checking the steps. They did not like being compared, although they did want to prove themselves in front of others.

Active Buddies

Active Buddies are players who enjoy the company of a small group of close friends who create and enjoy fun physical activities together.

Motivations and Behaviors

Active Buddies were motivated by social play and physical exertion. During the AHPC, they often paired up with one or two close friends to perform physical activities together. They not only reminded each other to be active, but also joined each other in outdoor games, and even created fun activities that involve physical elements. They sometimes competed against each other to add more tension and more emergent social play was evident, such as "bragging" about who had the highest count. Because the buddies trusted each other, such competitions were playful and fun rather than stressful. The following example illustrates a creative mini-game that two girls invented during the AHPC:

SD_Girl_6: Me and my friend, we would always brag about who had more steps...So at the end of the day, we'd call each other and go on the Internet and see how many steps we got, and whoever got the most had to pay the other $1.00.

Although it is not clear whether this mini-game actually contributed to step count increases, it did add to their enjoyment of AHPC.

The three components of a successful physical game: *sociality*, *engagement*, and *exertion* can reinforce each other [27]. Active buddies enjoy social bonding with physical activities that might seem daunting or boring otherwise:

SB_Girl_7: You're just talking with your friend and you walk more than you wanted to walk and then you get more steps.

Influence

Friends cast a powerful influence through strong social ties, which in the AHPC was beneficial for positively changing the health habits of buddies/peers [32]. The extent of this influence was not limited to participants in the AHPC. For example, a boy mentioned that he turned his sports video game buddies, who were not AHPC participants, into outdoor soccer buddies. However, *couch potato buddies* can have strong influence as well. In the following example, the interviewee intentionally tries to avoid activities with his friend because:

SA_Boy_5: There could be like a football game on TV that he would really wanna watch and you don't really wanna watch it 'cause you don't wanna sit around [but you do anyway]

Although the influence between the buddies was strong, we did not find indications that this influence extended beyond small cliques or existing strong social ties. One of the biggest boundaries we observed is gender. Gender differences were pervasively adopted among adolescents to create clique boundaries. During one of the school visits, the boys and girls in the focus group started a debate about whether everyone worked as a team for the school:

SG_Boy_1: People were doing different things. The guys were playing basketball. Some guys were playing football. Girls doing jump rope and playing volleyball and stuff. And yeah. Like and so we didn't work as a team....

(heated discussion erupts amongst the participants)

SG_Girl_4: Well, I think that like some of the – like all us girls are friend, so we all be with other friends. Some of us got the same friends. So I don't know why he say we don't hang out together because he hang out with boys. We hang out with girls. So and while playing football they wouldn't let nobody else play football so...

While this argument demonstrates the perceived boundary between gender groups, this boundary can also sometimes be enforced from the outside. When talking to the PE teacher at this school, we found that the school divided students by gender into different physical activities during PE class and seminar time. Here it seemed that the externally enforced boundaries between gender-groups were potentially limiting the range of influence between sub-groups.

In summary, active buddies enjoy physical activities as fun, social activities with their close peers and cliques. Nevertheless, between the cliques, there might exist boundaries that constrain spreading their influence. Designing health games that leverage interactions within the boundaries seems to be easier than that across boundaries.

Social Experience Seekers

Bartle defined socializers as players who "use the game's communicative facilities, and apply the role-playing that these engender, as a context in which to converse (and otherwise interact) with their fellow players." In the case of the AHPC, social experience seekers are a subset of the participants who enjoyed entertaining social aspects of the game, rather than physical activity or teambuilding; for this group in the AHPC, dressing up their horse, showing it to others, and talking about it with other players is more engaging than physical activity.

Motivations and Behaviors

These students are motivated by dress-up play, socializing, and showing off new customizations. They decorated their horses and changed their avatar looks frequently. They enjoyed showing their horse to others and chatted about their customizations. The AHPC website allowed a player to view another player's horse as a thumbnail in a list (as shown in the dotted-line frame in Figure 2), and the enlarged image with a username and status message appears when clicked. However, we found that social experience seekers often enjoyed sitting together, looking over each other's shoulder, and talking about their horse customization during class breaks or lunch time. Sometimes they even gave other players their username and password so that they could log onto the account and look at it together.

While dress-up play can be an "escape from the dulling rhythm of salaried work and household labor" [16], it can also be an exploration of self-image in front of others for schoolchildren. It affects their interpersonal behavior and attitude [30]. Some players wanted the dress-up to support them in portraying their self-image:

> *SI_Boy_1: I understand it's called the Horsepower Challenge...but you should be able to like create your own person. You know like get your body shape and stuff like that.*
>
> *SI_Boy_2:Yeah, that'd be more age-appropriate for us.*
>
> *SI_Boy_1: Cause like a horse has a big head, and everybody's head's not big, so—*
>
> *SI_Girl_1: —Most people's heads.*

Although social experience seekers were interested in using the AHPC website, they did not associate it with getting more steps, hence their motivation to improve their fitness was low. The AHPC game made it too easy for them to purchase any costume without striving for more steps, and they could always sell their old costumes with the same amount of points they purchased them with.. Their interest in decorating the horse (and hence their interest in the AHPC) was relatively short-term. Players eventually realized that there were limited dress-up options, which were the same for everyone, and reduced the interest in continuing their conversations about customization.

Influence

The dress-up feature provided opportunities for discussion with friends. In Miller's writing about dress-up play [25], he brought forward the concept of "three selves of fantastic socialization". These three selves involve public dress-up, or costumes worn in a public context; private dress-up, or costumes worn among friends or in the context of family/childhood play; and secret dress-up, which could include both activities that are solitary or intimate. In the context of AHPC, we found that the social experience seekers combined all three representations of self and cared most about interactions with friends. With the current design, they did not connect physical activity behavior with the dress-up play. Therefore, their influence on friends was constrained to fashion tips rather than influence in real-world physical activities.

In summary, social experience seekers are interested in the playful aspects of the AHPC website. Dress-up play, as one example of common interests introduced by games, gives opportunities for players to represent themselves online and offline in a new form, and socialize with their friends around this topic. Social experience seekers do not exhibit much interest in improving their physical activity levels given the current health game design.

Team Players

We use the lay term *team player* to refer to players in the AHPC who were most motivated by group achievement and ranking, and encouraged others to improve the team's performance. Good team players were often defined by other students and the teachers in trait terms; that is, dependable, flexible, or cooperative [9].

Motivations and Behaviors

Team players were motivated by team achievement and a sense of belonging. They were the most enthusiastic about having the opportunity to win for their school, and to contribute to a large cause. They often kept an eye on their schools' rank, tried to improve their own steps with long-term persistence, and reminded others to be more active.

One unexpected behavior of the team players was increased communication with the teacher(s) about their progress. In the AHPC, the team players actively sought attention from the teacher. In the following example, the PE teacher shared her observations about such behavior during the program:

> *SA_Teacher_A: J_ cracks me up. I have seen a change in him as well. He comes to me almost on a daily basis. Oh, I had forgotten. There was a specific story about T__. Shortly after I gave out the pedometers, she came to me, and she said – she*

stopped me. I was out here on the field and she said, "we had to go to the grocery store last night and I talked my mom into walking to the store instead of driving." She said, "Because I had to get steps for my pedometer." ... She goes, "So we walked to the grocery store and got what we needed and walked back." ... It was really neat that she would actually stop me and tell me the story, that she was excited about it. She very much wanted to...feel like she was a part of something, and I think that's something that all these kids have in common is they feel like they belong. They belong to a group.

In above example, the teacher was pleased that the students initiated the conversation about physical activities with her. In this school, most of the participants that the teacher drew from the students who volunteered were not athletes. Instead they were those who the teacher thought might benefit most from the challenge. She also created a ritual in the beginning of every PE class that the whole group checked the rank and step count of their school together on a large display. This ritual helped to create a shared group identity by reiterating the shared group goal. For those participants who had never been involved in a sports team, the AHPC was an opportunity to be a part of one.

Occasionally, leadership in organizing activities might also emerge from team players. During site visits, we found a few cases of one or two students organizing and leading some physical activity for the whole group, with encouragement from teachers. However, as expected the teachers' leadership role was most pervasive and accepted among different schools given their organizing and resource providing abilities in the AHPC deployment.

Influence

Team players have the potential and motivation to influence many people in the team, however, for most this influence is limited to their friends. If they were motivated to attain wider influence, they still typically required assistance from teachers to understand how to do so most effectively. This might be caused by the conventions in middle schools, where the students expect and rely on teachers to make arrangements and organize groups. Indeed, the teachers themselves did play an important role in establishing and promoting group identity, and creating fun group activities for the students. However, we also found that teachers had different availability, dedication, and attitude towards physical activities, which was not always supportive in some cases. Thus, it is important to provide in-game scaffolding mechanics for team players to turn their enthusiasm about group success to day-to-day influence on other members in the group.

In summary, team players care for the group achievement the most. They seek attention and confirmation from their teachers. They use the website for functional purposes of checking school record and rank, and for reinforcing the shared group identity.

Freeloaders

Ang et al. define freeloaders to be those linger on the edge of the social network of a guild in MMORPG games, to "utilize the guild resources" but not contributing to the group growth or providing help to others [1]. Similarly, in the AHPC, freeloaders are those who do not contribute to group achievement but still stay enrolled, often at the cost of the group's performance.

Motivations and Behaviors

Freeloaders were drawn by the buzz generated around the AHPC as a new and interesting program at the beginning of the deployment, but they quickly lost interest and stopped wearing their pedometers regularly. They typically did not quit or ask to be replaced, but hung around to see what personal benefits they could get, for example, free t-shirts and stickers. Although we did not have much chance to talk to them (because they usually did not volunteer to participate in the interview), in focus groups we heard other participants criticizing freeloaders as forces that *"drag the team down"* in multiple schools. The existence of freeloaders is triangulated by step log analysis. We found that a fraction of the participants have exceedingly low average daily steps; 10% of the participants had less than 1,300 average daily steps (0.5 miles[1]), which was one third of the median (1.50 miles). One explanation for this low step count is that these participants failed to wear their pedometers regularly during the challenge.

Influence

In the AHPC, freeloaders' influence is very different from those in online communities who are typically invisible to the rest of the participants. Instead, freeloaders have real social presence at the school. Moreover, unlike the freeloaders in online communities in which the resources they enjoy do not cost extra efforts of the providers, in the AHPC, the less the freeloaders get steps, the more others have to make it up for the group. Unsurprisingly, other students in the group commented negatively about them. However, surprisingly, nobody suggested or reported specifically that they actively tried to change the freeloaders' behavior. The following quote showed what others thought of freeloaders in their team, and how they harmed "*team spirit*":

SE_Boy_1: Can I say something? I disagree about that building the team spirit little thing, because some people just got the little ped thing (referring to the pedometer) just so they can be in something, and they don't want to feel left out because they just wanted to free load and get that shirt and stuff.

This negative comment shows that freeloaders might demotivate other players. The design challenge here is not only to try to motivate freeloaders, but also to minimize their

[1] The step-to-mile conversion rate is 2643:1 (from AHPC website)

negative effect on other players in the group. Although freeloaders' influence is not positive, designers cannot simply ignore or exclude this group—in the end, freeloaders might be a population that behavior change programs intend to reach.

In summary, freeloaders do not care for the game activities or physical activities. They cause frustration among other players because their low participation drags down group performance.

Summary

We presented five types of players that emerged from our evaluation of a group-based competition for promoting physical activity participation in youth. We discussed a tension between *individual* and *group rewards,* and between *behavior change* and *enjoying the online game itself.* Players may be more interested in group achievements (*team players*), interacting with a clique of friends (*social experience seekers* and *active buddies*), or personal improvement (*achievers*). Players may also care more for physical activities (*active buddies, achievers*), online interactions with the game, and offline socialization (*social experience seekers*).

DESIGN IMPLICATIONS

We found a diversity of players in the schools enrolled in this study. Based on our findings, we provide concrete design suggestions about how designers can integrate group-based mechanisms more carefully and effectively in health games for youth.

Group Scale Matters

The AHPC was deployed to groups of approximately twenty participants. Except for the student-teacher interaction, the majority of influence we found is limited to the scope of a small group of friends, at most. There exist boundaries between cliques and gender that constrain the scope of social influence. The effect of peer groups on adolescent's physical activity is paramount. The influence can go both ways as stated by Sallis [32], "If a given adolescent identifies with a peer group that values and participates in physical activity, the group creates a supportive environment for its members. If the main peer group devalues physical activity, this is an effective deterrent." We argue that there may be a benefit to tailoring health interventions to smaller sub-groups within a large competition. We have three main reasons for this suggestion. First, it is easier for players to coordinate and self-organize fun physical activities within smaller groups that have existing social bonds extending beyond the competition. To organize activities for a large group (e.g. all 20 participants in a school) requires shared time, space, and resources that may not be accessible to the students. Second, small groups provide a trusted, safe environment. For example, the achievers had the risk of being teased and isolated because of bullying behavior from other kids in the school. But if grouped with friends they trust, they may become active buddies, who are probably supportive and more likely to enjoy physical activities together. Third, our suggestion is also based on the scale of self-organized social groups observed in online games. For example, the median size of guilds in World of Warcraft is 9 [10]; a survey shows that the cliques among middle school students typically range in size from 3-12 children [13].

When designing for small groups, we note that friends might also *demotivate* each other from being active. For instance, we found that the social experience seeker does not seem to encourage others to be more active even though their interaction with peers makes the online game experience more fun. These social experience seekers sought dress-up play, not physical activity, and focused on decorating the avatars. A simple change in game economics might have helped this group; although outfits cost points, the in-game store had a free returns policy. Creating an in-game cost for the activities social experience seekers like most—such as charging for virtual closet space or for swapping outfits—might increase these players' motivation and that of others in their small group as well.

Online Representations of Self in a Group

Within the AHPC website, the players themselves, other players, and the group were represented independently. Although they simultaneously appear on the same web page (Figure 3), the relations among players and their group cohesion were not represented. We suggest visualizing 'online representations of self in a group' to support the group identity and to create a shared online place. Through this design, the health game creates a *stage* where players can express themselves through the *impression* they give and receive reactions from other players [18]. This stage is clearly wanted by social experience seekers, who are interested in showing off their new looks to friends and classmates. It is also important for team players, who identify themselves with the group strongly. From this representation, team players can view all the members being together, matching with the group identity that team players believe in. This is a first step towards scaffolding team players to think on a higher level of group, and potentially inspire them to try out some social roles in the group (e.g., group leaders).

We also found some players showed interest in portraying an "ideal image" of self by using their online avatars. This tendency was also found in Ducheneaut et al.'s research in which they found that participants with weight issues tended to create idealized avatars [11]. Moreover, Yee et al.'s research showed the "Proteus effect," in which a player's online game avatar changes digital or even offline behaviors [35]; in their study, the researchers found that participants given taller avatars negotiated more aggressively in subsequent offline, face-to-face interactions than those given shorter avatars [35]. It seems promising to leverage players' online avatar creation and customization for health behavior change, especially for social experience seekers who like to talk about their customization with others but lack of interest in being active. However, when players and their avatars are not anonymized in co-located group interactions, it raises concern about privacy and possible bullying issues that may appear in the context of the school setting. In the current design of the AHPC, players have little agency on the physical features of the avatar; they cannot change weight or height, for example. More work is needed to understand how to leverage players' interest in ideal self-image for health behavior change.

Support Play Style Transition

In a long-term deployment such as the AHPC, it would be unreasonable to expect all players to pick a particular style of play and never change. For example, a player may start as an *achiever*, then later her friends join in, and they become *active buddies*. In a health game encouraging players to transition away from less productive player types like *freeloaders* may be critical. Health games that support play style transition must address this dual challenge: allowing players the agency to pick and change their play style while explicitly encouraging less healthy player types to adjust their style of play. This means discerning player types throughout the deployment, encouraging those in less desirable play styles to try a different style of play, and recognizing the period when such transition occurs. Health games need to support players in transitioning to socially engaging and physically active types.

Customizable Privacy

Privacy is an important dimension for any application that shares health information [7], and adolescents might be particularly sensitive to unwanted sharing of their weight or physical activity, especially with peers [33]. Group fitness applications have the potential to leverage positive affirmation, but conversely might contribute to unnecessary taunting, fat-shaming, or body image disorders. As pointed out by O'Dea [29], the most important principle for prevention of child obesity is "*first, do no harm*." Simply making the step counts viewable to all participants without allowing for customizable privacy could create too intense and destructive competition. To prevent this from happening, the AHPC designers made the step counts private; a player can view only other player's horse images and text status, but not individual step information.

However, in some cases, players reported being willing and eager to share their step counts. The important design implication here is to give players control to decide when to share, what information, and with whom. Fixed privacy settings do not allow different player types to share with their ideal level of comfort.

Privacy for Achievers and Freeloaders

For example, achievers might gain many steps but cannot prove it to others easily. Including announcing functions would allow the students to leverage social affirmation but also maintain the control of self-image. Similarly, keeping steps private when not announced protects the well being of freeloaders. We believe this control of self-image is especially important based on our observations at the site visits; during the focus groups we conducted, we observed some instances of bullying and negative remarks toward kids who were overweight, less athletic, or deemed unpopular. When designing multiplayer health applications where social pressure is involved, it is important to minimize the potential for bullying behaviors.

Privacy for Social Experience Seekers and Active Buddies

Another option could be to share step count and in-game activity with a subgroup that a player chooses. For both the active buddies and social experience seekers, the interactions with a small clique of friends provide the main source of enjoyment. Players have tried different ways of sharing game state and activities with their friends, such as betting on step numbers and giving their usernames and passwords to others. These behaviors suggest a desire to share activities within the small cliques.

In summary, we recommend the inclusion of customizable privacy settings that empower players to decide with whom and when to share their physical activity level and progress.

CONCLUSIONS

This long-term, large-scale health game deployment opens a window for researchers to explore the opportunities and challenges associated with group-based health interventions for middle school children. We found that deploying a group-based competition does not automatically lead to cooperative behavior. Instead, it creates a myriad of behaviors based on the players' motivation, existing athletic skills, interest, social relationships, and social status. These players also have different social influences on others in the groups. In summary, we identified five player types in group-based health games for school children, and provide concrete design suggestions for scaffolding health interventions for youth, in ways that maximize player enjoyment while simultaneously providing health benefits.

ACKNOWLEDGEMENTS

We are deeply appreciative to Humana Games for Health and the Humana Foundation for their guidance and support. We would also like to thank the students, teachers, and parents who took our surveys, participated in focus groups and interviews and welcomed us into their schools.

REFERENCES

1. Ang, C.S. and Zaphiris, P. Social Roles of Players in MMORPG Guilds. *Information Communication Society 13*, 4 (2010), 592–614.
2. Bartle, R. Hearts, clubs, diamonds, spades: Players who suit MUDs. *Journal of MUD research*, (1996).
3. Bateman, C. and Boon, R. *21st Century Game Design*. Charles River Media, 2005.
4. Bell, M., Chalmers, M., Barkhuus, L., et al. Interweaving mobile games with everyday life. *Proc. ACM CHI 2006*, 417-426.
5. Berkovsky, S., Coombe, M., Freyne, J., Bhandari, D., and Baghaei, N. Physical activity motivating games: virtual rewards for real activity. *Proc. ACM CHI 2010*,, 243-252.
6. Caillois, R. and Barash, M. *Man, play, and games*. The Free Press of Glencoe, 1961.

7. Consolvo, S., Everitt, K., Smith, I., and Landay, J. Design requirements for technologies that encourage physical activity. *Proc. ACM CHI 2006*, 457-466.

8. Consolvo, S., McDonald, D.W., and Landay, J.A. Theory-driven design strategies for technologies that support behavior change in everyday life. *Proc. ACM CHI 2009*, 405-414.

9. Driskell, J. and Goodwin, G. What makes a good team player? Personality and team effectiveness. *Group Dynamics, 10, 4* (2006), 249-271.

10. Ducheneaut, N. and Yee, N. The life and death of online gaming communities: a look at guilds in world of warcraft. *Proc. ACM CHI 2007*, 839-848.

11. Ducheneaut, N., Wen, M.H., Yee, N., and Wadley, G. Body and mind: a study of avatar personalization in three virtual worlds. *Proc. ACM CHI 2009,*1151–1160.

12. Eiriksdottir, E., Poole, E.S., Miller, A.D., Xu, Y., Kestranek, D., Catrambone, R., and Mynatt, E.D. Assessing health games in secondary schools: an investigation of the american horsepower challenge 2009-2010. *GVU Center Technical Report, Georgia Institute of Technology*, 2010.

13. Espelage, D.L., Holt, M.K., and Henkel, R.R. Examination of Peer–Group contextual effects on aggression during early adolescence. *Child Development, 74*, 1 (2003), 205–220.

14. Fisher, W.A., Fisher, J.D., and Harman, J. The Information-Motivation-Behavioral Skills Model: A General Social Psychological Approach to Understanding and Promoting Health Behavior. *Social psychological foundations of health and illness*, (2003), 82–106.

15. Foster, D. and Linehan, C. Motivating physical activity at work: using persuasive social media for competitive step counting. *Proc. ACM MindTrek,2010* 111-116.

16. Fron, J. and Fullerton, T. Playing dress-up: Costumes, roleplay and imagination. *Philosophyb of Computer Games*, (2007).

17. Gasser, R., Brodbeck, D., Degen, M., Luthiger, J., Wyss, R., and Reichlin, S. Persuasiveness of a mobile lifestyle coaching application using social facilitation. *Persuasive Technology*, (2006), 27–38.

18. Goffman, E. *The presentation of self in everyday life*. Anchor, 1959.

19. Hsu, C.L. and Lu, H.P. Why do people play on-line games? An extended TAM with social influences and flow experience. *Information & Management, 41*, 7 (2004), 853-868.

20. Hunicke, R., LeBlanc, M., and Zubek, R. MDA: A formal approach to game design and game research. *Proceedings of the AAAI-04 Workshop on Challenges in Game AI*, (2004), 1–5.

21. Lazzaro, N. Why we play games: Four keys to more emotion without story. *Talk presented at Game Developers Conference* 2004.

22. Lin, J., Mamykina, L., Lindtner, S., Delajoux, G., and Strub, H. Fish'n'Steps: encouraging physical activity with an interactive computer game. *Proc. ACM UbiComp 2006*, 261-278.

23. Maitland, J. and Chalmers, M. Designing for peer involvement in weight management. *Proc. ACM CHI 2011*, 315–324.

24. Malone, T.W. *What makes things fun to learn? heuristics for designing instructional computer games. Proc. ACM CHI 1980, 162-169.*

25. Miller, K. Dress: Private and secret self-expression. *Clothing and Textiles Research Journal, 15, 4,* (1997), 223-234.

26. Montola, M., Stenros, J., and Waern, A. *Pervasive games: Theory and design*. Morgan Kaufmann, 2009.

27. Mueller, F., Agamanolis, S., Vetere, F., and Gibbs, M.R. A framework for exertion interactions over a distance. *Proc. of ACM Siggraph Game symposium* 2009, 143-150.

28. Olson, C. Children's motivations for video game play in the context of normal development. *Review of General Psychology, 14, 2,* (2010), 180-187.

29. O'Dea, J.A., Prevention of child obesity:'First, do no harm'. *Health Education Research, 20, 2* (2005), 259-265.

30. Rosenberg, M. *Society and the adolescent self-image.* Wesleyan, 1989.

31. Rotwein-Pivnick, R. Getting Kids & Adolescents Excited About Exercise. *IDEA Fitness Journal*, (2006), 1-5.

32. Sallis, J.F. Influences on Physical Activity of Children, Adolescents, and Adults. *PCPFS RESEARCH DIGEST 1*, 7 (1994).

33. Toscos, T., Faber, A., Connelly, K., and Upoma, A.M. Encouraging physical activity in teens: Can technology help reduce barriers to physical activity in adolescent girls? *Proc. of PervasiveHealthcare* 2008, 218-221.

34. Voida, A., Carpendale, S., and Greenberg, S. The individual and the group in console gaming. *Proc. ACM CSCW* 2010, 371-380.

35. Yee, N., Bailenson, J.N., and Ducheneaut, N. The Proteus Effect. *Communication Research 36*, 2 (2009), 285-312.

36. Yee, N. Motivations for play in online games. *CyberPsychology & Behavior*, *9, 6* (2006), 772-775.

Collaborative Help in Chronic Disease Management: Supporting Individualized Problems

Jina Huh
Division of Biomedical and Health Informatics
School of Medicine
University of Washington
jinahuh@uw.edu

Mark S. Ackerman
School of Information and
Department of Computer Science and Engineering
University of Michigan
ackerm@umich.edu

ABSTRACT
Coping with chronic illness disease is a long and lonely journey, because the burden of managing the illness on a daily basis is placed upon the patients themselves. In this paper, we present our findings for how diabetes patient support groups help one another find individualized strategies for managing diabetes. Through field observations of face-to-face diabetes support groups, content analysis of an online diabetes community, and interviews, we found several help interactions that are critical in helping patients in finding individualized solutions. Those are: (1) patients *operationalize* their experiences to easily contextualize and share executable strategies; (2) operationalization has to be done within the larger context of *sharing illness trajectories*; and (3) the support groups develop common understanding towards diabetes management. We further discuss how our findings translate into design implications for supporting chronic illness patients in online community settings.

Author Keywords
Individualized, diabetes, chronic illness, support groups, online health community, collaborative help

ACM Classification Keywords
H5.m. Information interfaces and presentation (e.g., HCI): Miscellaneous.

General Terms
Design

INTRODUCTION
Molly is a 65-year-old female who has been controlling diabetes for the last twenty years. She recently found she is developing liver disease. The new diet plan suggested by her doctor was opposite to what she should eat as a diabetes patient. Molly became frustrated. She scheduled an appointment with a dietitian in two weeks, but until then she wanted to know what other people did in her situation.

Coping with chronic disease is challenging because not only it is a daily problem but also the burden of managing the disease is placed upon the patients themselves. Diabetes, like many chronic diseases, generates *individualized* problems. Molly's example illustrates how chronic illness patients constantly encounter unexpected challenges, uncertainty about the future, and specific problems that do not have easy answers.

Getting professional help from health care providers is costly. Accordingly, hospitals offer support groups to help patients improve and maintain daily health management. But many patients also turn to online; as a recent study showed, 61% percent of Americans search for health information on the Web [1]. Current collaborative help systems such as online message forums and Q&A sites highlight popular, frequently asked questions, and active topics. Getting help to uncommon and individualized problems is still one of the biggest design challenges in collaborative help [14].

Our aim is to address how collaborative help—sharing help among peer-patients—can better support finding individualized solutions. We studied current practices in how patients in support groups help one another solve individualized problems. We found that in order to help solve individualized problems, (1) patients operationalize experiences for easy transfer of knowledge, (2) and the operationalization takes place within the larger context of sharing illness trajectories. Furthermore, (3) operationalization and sharing illness trajectories result in building the community's common understanding towards diabetes management, which helps each member to better generate individualized diabetes management strategies. We end with translating these findings into design implications.

BACKGROUND
We build on prior work that addressed online health community systems, elicitation of experiential knowledge, and information reuse in collaborative help to further discuss what could be done to address better serving patients find individualized solutions. Largely, we build on the discussions around work coordination, information flow, and awareness in CSCW.

The medical community has acknowledged the importance of providing patients with individualized (personalized) health care at the levels of disease, environment, medication, genes, healthcare, and information [9]. Among many aspects of work that facilitate personalized medicine is the information management of personalized medicine—namely through the patient-driven health care model [27]. The use of Health 2.0 technologies, such as online health communities, bookmarks, blogs, and Internet-based applications, serves to personalize medicine and support individualized solutions in health management.

Websites such as Patientslikeme and Curetogether[1] support patients to find similar patients, support one another, and share doctors' opinions. Patientslikeme was shown to be effective in improving psychological experience of living with their conditions and perceived control over their condition [30]. However, integrating health data with conversations, clarifying presentation of health information, and matching of people in similar situations still remains as critical challenges in the field [10].

Allowing patients to share experiential knowledge is a unique opportunity that support groups provide for patients, as noted in the literature [5, 6, 8]. However, transferring such situated experiences from one person to another is often challenging. Accordingly, studies have examined how this tacit knowledge could be elicited. Nonaka and Krogh [15] in their knowledge creation theory discuss "knowledge conversion" as the process by which tacit knowledge becomes explicit knowledge. Knowledge conversion is described as an iterative process of experimenting with words, drawings, models, and language. Ambrosini and Bowman [4] studied how to "operationalize" tacit knowledge in organizational settings through causal maps, interviews, and storytelling. Schatzki et al.'s [23] "practice turn" explained how tightly-knit groups operating in socially stable organizational contexts allow for individuals to acquire tacit knowledge through socialization, similar to the view of Communities of Practice [29].

Even in cases where knowledge is explicitly available for others to adopt, reusing it to make it work for one's settings brings challenges. Issues of information reuse have been extensively discussed in collaborative help literature [2, 12] and this is where patients' sharing experiential knowledge essentially becomes a collaborative help problem.

How patients align with others' experiences for better health management can be seen also as part of the heavily studied theme in CSCW concerning connecting activity, coordination, and information flows. For example, ethnomethodologically-inspired work has viewed this problem from the vantage of awareness and enactment [13], while symbolic interaction work has viewed it from the vantage of articulation work [11] and temporal sequences [24]. Over the last several years, more and more CSCW research has examined coordination and information flows over and within time. For example, Paul et al. [19] examined sensemaking in emergency rooms through information and communication displays. Reddy et al. [22] characterized the medical work in surgical intensive care unit as organized around temporality.

Our work contributes to this CSCW research theme, situating it in health informatics, by examining the interpersonal and interactional work involved in health over time. Our participants, of course, engaged in many of the previously uncovered kinds of interactional work involved in everyday behavior. However, we found several supplemental kinds of work we believe are critical for understanding how people deal with long-term, heavily situated (and therefore individualized) information and health needs. To our knowledge the work which we will describe as *operationalization* and *trajectory alignment work* below, have been previously detailed in the CSCW, HCI, or health informatics literature for diabetes or other chronic conditions.

METHOD

We examined both face-to-face diabetes support groups and an online community for diabetes (dLife.com). We wished to have the findings from the two spaces to inform each other. The two settings largely differed in terms of the role of professionals and demographics. Patients largely led the dLife forum, and health professionals in dLife mainly interacted with patients through the expert Q&A section. In face-to-face support groups (F2F), however, nurses and dietitians led discussions and clarified biomedical concepts. F2F mainly consisted of geriatric patients, whereas dLife had younger members that were recent college graduates, young professionals, and those in their mid-careers. Attitudes towards Internet environment for support also differed. F2F members often distrusted information produced from online communities, whereas dLife members actively utilized information on the Web, such as research articles and patients' forum posts. In both cases, the people we observed had adopted the medicalized view of their condition and were attempting to take control of their diabetes; we follow this viewpoint in this paper. While there are alternative views, these remain controversial. More importantly, there were common activities of members in both settings that helped one another solve individualized problems in diabetes management. We plan to focus our discussions around these common activities.

We conducted field observations of four face-to-face support groups for eleven months and did content analysis of 1,400 threads randomly collected from dLife. At any given session, each face-to-face support group had eight to twenty patients participating. We also conducted 20 semi-structured interviews from both F2F (13) and dLife (7). We

[1] Patientslikeme.com; curetogether.com

studied Type 2 diabetes patients to simplify our analysis. In order to learn peer-help mechanisms among patients, we studied F2F that encourage peer-to-peer discussions among patients over lecture-based support groups. Field notes were taken during the observations; we were not able to audio or video record, because of privacy concerns.

dLife.com was chosen because it has the largest number of members (87,999 as of April 17, 2010) among the diabetes forums and because the conversations in dLife involved practical information sharing rather than giving emotional support like many other communities. We chose to study only the community forum section because our research purpose was to study peer help interactions. We randomly selected threads from the "Type 2 clubhouse" topic for the analysis.

Interviews were recruited through flyers in F2F and messages in the community forum. Interviews were done on the phone, email, or face-to-face depending on the participants' preferences and lasted from thirty minutes to one hour. The interviews were recorded and fully transcribed. We asked the interviewees about what they felt was helpful or not helpful about the support groups, their personal strategies in maintaining diabetes, and their perceptions towards the support group members and support groups in general.

Analysis was done in conjunction with the observations and data collection. The data were analyzed using iterative open coding [25]. We began with descriptive coding for each observation. As our data accumulated, the focus of our analysis continued to evolve. Codes were revised, merged, and broken down as the analysis evolved and more data were collected. We also used findings from the analysis to revise where to focus during field observations. In the end, we aggregated analysis in the form of codes and notes from both F2F and online community studies. These codes were again analyzed using an affinity diagram to find any emerging themes, similarities, and differences for the final report of findings.

Next, we discuss findings about two major help interactions that were taking place in the support groups. One is *operationalization*, a process by which members easily transferred context, directly usable strategies, and ways to modify strategies. Second is *illness trajectory alignment work*, which allowed historical context to be shared as members were helping one another through operationalization. Operationalized experiences and illness trajectories are intertwined in practice. Operationalized experiences provide ways for an individual to understand his or her illness (and thus trajectory), while illness trajectories are part of the context for understanding one's own or others' operationalized experiences. We later discuss how the findings together contribute to design implications.

FINDING 1: OPERATIONALIZING EXPERIENCES

We will first present cases in which operationalizing experiences works well for giving information for contextualizing problems or suggesting solutions. Participants not only objectified tacit knowledge [4], but further operationalized it so that the knowledge could be directly re-used. Operationalization amplifies the material aspect of information and knowledge to become inscribed, transported, and affixed to items [7]. Accordingly, the material characteristics of operationalized strategies makes it easy to share and transfer knowledge.

Operationalizing Context

In collaborative help, (re)contextualization is one of the classic challenges in information reuse [2, 3]. In the support groups we examined, patients carry out operationalizations to contextualize their diabetic conditions and convey various experiences to others. Below, we discuss several forms of operationalized diabetic experiences that are used to connect with others, inspire others, contextualize individualized situations, and understand individual differences from interventions.

Patient Profiles

The most frequently observed indicators for patient profiles include A1C[2], fasting blood sugar (FB)[3], weight, and the dates and times that these indicators were measured. In addition, medication information, date of diagnosis, type of diabetes, age, diet and exercise regimes used, and complications are also important pieces of information for contextualizing one's diabetes.

The patient profiles assumed many forms across dLife and the F2F we observed. In all of the F2F meetings we attended, at the beginning of the sessions patients introduced themselves with patient profile information. This process helped familiarize group members with one another so that they could later ask for help. A typical introduction phase proceeds as follows:

```
Patient #1: John. Diagnosed in 1980. Give 4
shots of insulin a day. Mainly watch diet and
exercise. I passed out 4 times in the last 20
years.
Patient #2: Was diagnosed in January of 2010. I
have heart problems, so I can't take the pills.
I check my sugar 3 times a day, and most of the
time I get sugars below 100.
Patient #3: I've been diabetic for 2 years. The
support group has been helping me in reading
labels and such. I take meds 2 times a day.
Patient #4: Was diagnosed in 2005. I am on
insulin, but other than that I am fine. (July,
2010. FF5)
```

As shown, a typical face-to-face support group consists of patients at diverse stages, ranging from one that has been diagnosed a few months ago to those who have been managing diabetes for more than a decade. They each have

[2] A measurement showing the average plasma glucose concentration over prolonged periods of time.

[3] Blood sugar taken at bed time, before meal, or after 12 hours of fasting.

different complications, regimes for controlling their diabetes, genders, and age. Patients are then able to share experiences about the domains that each is more familiar with. John, patient #1, who mentioned that he had passed out several times, indicated that he has problems with low blood sugar. The nurse who was leading the group asked John about his strategies in getting over low blood sugar. In other groups as well, patients with similar complications, such as an organ transplant, were able to connect through simple introductions, and then members understood with whom to talk when there were specific issues at hand (such as thinking about adopting an insulin pump). In dLife, members used simple textual descriptions and visualizations in their signatures to provide patient profile history, with which members could connect with one another and share strategies from successful cases.

Informal Experiments

Patients also attempted to systematically share their situated experiences through various casual experiment results, such as testing blood sugar changes before and after various diet and exercise regimes. Members also conducted experiments collectively, where they coordinated protocols for the experiments and shared the findings together. Through this collective activity, members were able to collect real life experiences and understand individual differences regarding various interventions for controlling diabetes.

At one F2F meeting (FF1), the group performed a quick five-minute arm exercise together. Blood sugar changes before and after the exercise were significant for some patients and not so much for others. The lesson that the members received was not only to understand how such exercises could change their blood sugar levels, thus motivating patients to exercise even for a short amount of time, but also to help patients understand the individual differences from the interventions.

An interviewee was able to understand from an online forum (diabeticconnect.com) how variations of a pizza slice, such as being whole wheat or having tomato sauce, can affect blood sugar differently. This helped the interviewee to get a sense of how to choose what to eat:

```
I read twenty posts and a lot of people were
saying they have horrible blood sugar readings
even if they had just one piece [of pizza]....
It seems like it affects people in different
ways, but I've got some ideas on how to eat
pizza occasionally. (I, FF2_P12)
```

Collectively sharing small findings from personal experiments with food helps other members make informed decisions, at least in an informal fashion. Conveying context through a standardized form of information makes it easier for patients to interpret and compare shared experiences. A patient shared the value of sharing experiment results of various interventions with other support group members:

```
It's sharing, sharing, sharing, it doesn't
matter what it is but you need to share (I,
FF4_P9)
```

Operationalizing Strategies

Over the course of attempting to control diabetes for many years, patients develop their own individualized coping mechanisms for maintaining control of their diabetes. The members operationalize strategies and daily routines to a form that could easily be adopted, tried out, and tweaked. The forms of operationalization include step-by-step instructions, bullet points of lessons, rules of thumb, blogs, and lists of links, books, and recipes. Such information was especially helpful for newcomers who needed concrete guidelines. At the same time, because not all solutions would work for everyone, the members also help others to learn how to operationalize, deal with exceptions, and find the right individualized solutions. Below, we describe several cases illustrating how members operationalize strategies and share how to generate individualized solutions.

Start Up Solution Kit

A representative set of examples of operationalized strategies is part of the basic knowledge about managing diabetes that is taught at diabetes education classes. It is often useful for newcomers or those who have had diabetes for many years but never knew how to manage it. In dLife, members share what we call a "startup solution kit" for newcomers who ask where to start. The startup solution kit comes with links to blog articles that teach patients about basic diabetes management strategies, simple descriptions of how strategies should be performed, and book recommendations. The solution kit is free of heavy context or verbatim stories, and thus is easy to replicate or post for a variety of situations. The concrete solutions, well-polished through repetitive use, help newcomers who are dealing with extreme ambiguity and do not know where to start.

Collecting Diverse Strategies

As the patients progress with their diabetes treatment, they encounter new problems that are not addressed initially or explicitly by diabetes education materials. By sharing one another's experiential knowledge, patients are able to get solutions for newly encountered problems. For instance, a recently diagnosed patient was unable to check her blood sugar because her blood did not come out well. She had to squeeze her finger in order for the blood to come out. She was not sure whether squeezing was the best thing to do. Instead of answering her question right away, the nurse who led the group asked other group members to share how they checked their blood sugar.

Patients share various strategies of their own, which then lead to a collection of operationalized strategies that the patient herself could try out to see what works better for her. One male patient in F2F said he has been diabetic for so long he developed a callous so he had to get a longer needle to get it working. He then physically demonstrated how he could get the blood monitoring device to work better. Other patients told him to try poking the needle in different areas (other than fingers), to try different fingers, or to run it under hot water. Another patient shared that her doctor had told her to take a baby aspirin before taking her blood sugar. Then the group started talking about a gadget that allowed blood sugar to be checked from the arms.

Solving Unexpected Problems

Problems become more complicated when patients go past the initial learning curve and encounter unexpected problems that are specific to their own situation. In this case, unlike with the startup solution kit or collectively gathering diverse strategies, helpers have to consider the particular individualized situation that the asker is in to provide appropriate solutions.

The following example shows how the operationalization process happens not only in identifying procedural steps of the strategy but also in interpreting the results and applying them to everyday practices. A member, Gary, in dLife encountered unexpected lab results that conflicted with his own readings taken personally at home. Jule assumed there might have been problems resulting from when and how the asker was taking his blood sugar readings at home. Jule suggested a specific blood sugar reading strategy called 'bookend testing,' which would help Gary measure his blood sugar at the right time and to find the glycemic index—how much the food elevates one's blood sugar—of foods that Gary commonly eats:

```
You need to do bookend testing. […] Bookend
testing is as follows. Take the reading before
first bite, then exactly two hours afterwards
(Use an alarm, I like to use the one on my
phone.) You should be around 40 points
difference. So, if you were 103 before lunch,
then you should be around 143 post. If NOT,
then that means you went way higher and are
still coming down from a high. [gives example
from Gary's case](August, 2010. OC. Jule)
```

Here, Jule not only gave step-by-step instructions for how to do bookend testing, but also provided numbers that would help Gary identify whether the results were normal. Operationalization is done in a way that others could not only follow the instructions but also learn how to interpret the results and construct individualized strategies.

Breaking of Operationalization

While the operationalization process makes knowledge exchange efficient, it also unnecessarily simplifies the solution, making it difficult for patients to apply the solution for individualized settings. Operationalization breaks down when the context behind solutions is missing, individual differences are detected, and standards and definitions vary, making it difficult to settle down on a solution. At the same time, the breaking of operationalization works as an opportunity for people to further understand individual differences and learn how to better deal with individualized problems. The conflict, individual differences, and exceptions that challenge existing understandings in the community further facilitates the community's generation of shared understanding about appropriate solutions, which is critical for the long-term understanding of both the community and individuals.

Individualized Problems and Conflicting Philosophies

Each patient has differing personal beliefs and expectations about what constitutes a good strategy. Suggested solutions often go through a negotiation process among the members to arrive at an agreement about what are appropriate solutions for various individualized settings. Through the process of agreement, the community as a whole develops enriched understanding towards the problem where individual differences and exceptional cases are recognized.

As an example, we describe below how sharing personal strategies through operationalized solutions breaks down because of patients' failure to adequately share their personal histories, individual differences, and conflicts in what patients believe are appropriate diabetes management strategies. The members then attempt to come to an agreement about what was an appropriate strategy for checking blood sugar. In the following, the initial asker had been diabetic for 16 years, but still had not found a strategy that would help him choose the right meal plan. David replied with simplified information about a step-by-step procedure that included measuring blood glucose (BG). The asker could follow this procedure in order to find the right food to eat for himself:

```
Take a pre meal BG write it down, write down
how many carbs you eat, eat, take your BG 1
hour after eating, take your BG 2 hour after
eating, take your BG 3 hour after eating. Now
you know how many carbs you ate and you know
how much your BG went up. Adjust one or the
other until you get numbers similar to your
before food BG. (October, 2010. OC. David)
```

While David's suggestion was simple and easy to follow, this post triggered others to discuss how frequent one should check blood sugar. Adam questioned whether checking blood sugar every hour was necessary. Checking blood sugar two hours after the meal is a standard procedure that most diabetes educators suggest, because that is when blood sugar peaks. Adam thought checking blood sugar 2 hours after the meal was sufficient to determine meal adjustments, and checking blood sugar every hour would hurt one's finger tips and waste test strips. This belief indicated his personal preferences towards resources. Others might prefer to waste their test strips than be in danger of going hyper- or hypoglycemic.

In order to explain how he came to the strategy, David provided historical context and personal background. David believed that every time blood sugar spikes, bodies would be damaged. Also, he stated that his body did not do a good job of regulating blood sugar so he had to initially check as frequently as he could until he found a solution that would help him keep his blood sugar levels down. Adam, however, was opposed to David's assumptions about the severe consequences of having acutely high BGs, since his wife who was not diabetic had blood sugar readings of 180 to 200 when she ate high-carbohydrate food.

Bringing in official information put an end to the negotiation about whether taking blood sugar readings at random times is considered important, but the members of the thread continued to discuss what is considered dangerous, citing what their doctors had told them, what they had read, and what they believe to be true. The thread ended with collaboratively coming to understand what is considered severe or normal depends on individual differences such as how high the initial blood glucose was.

Such as this, the key to working around the breakdown of an operationalization is coming to an agreement. The process of agreement helps members to generate shared understandings towards dealing with exceptions and individual differences. During this agreement process, patients' personal understanding of standards and definitions is often discussed. These standards and definitions vary between the patients, creating yet another conflict—a point for negotiation.

Varying Standards and Definitions, Coming to an Agreement

This section will discuss how even standards and definitions are subject to negotiation. For operationalized guidelines and advice that patients will follow, having consistent standards and definitions is important. Inconsistency in standards and definitions, however, was observed both in the information patients gathered from different doctors as well as in varying beliefs among the patients. Below, we will describe two examples that demonstrate how patients are challenged by inconsistency in information given to them. The first is a case where a patient could not get consistent advice from his doctors for what his A1C level should be, and the second is a situation where standards given by lab reports are inconsistent. In both cases, members accept standards that make the most sense to them amongst health professionals or shared interpretations of other members.

FF4_P4 is a geriatrics patient who needs to be extra cautious with hypoglycemia, especially because he uses an insulin pump. He needed to know whether to maintain his current management practice or to try to lower his blood sugar or increase his consumption of carbohydrates so that he would not go too low. Determining this became difficult because the advice given from his doctor, a nurse at one diabetes meeting, and another nurse at another diabetes meeting all suggested different target levels of A1C:

```
I: What is your target A1C that you want to get?
FF4_P4: Well, three months ago I was 5.5, now I'm 5.6. I would like to be around 6. But then that Linda Evans at Domino's says you should be 6.5. And then this new lady at the diabetes meeting, she said to stay in 7~7.2.(I, FF4_P4)
```

The lack of consistency in the standard for FF4_P4 and his A1C level, even among health care providers, made it difficult for him to operationalize what he needed to do to achieve his goal in controlling diabetes because the goal itself was ambiguous. Not only standards—such as what was considered low, high, good, or bad—were difficult to define, but the definitions themselves were often challenged and negotiated. Because there was no unified answer, FF4_P4 just had to pick what made most sense to him.

Varying and conflicting standards were often observed in the support group discussions, and the members handled such conflicts by adopting standards that "made sense" to them. In the following example, a member in dLife found out about a newly changed standard in A1C from his recent lab result. In the ensuing discussion, members negotiated common grounds for what were considered "normal" versus "optimal" numbers, and how interpretations for such terms could change.

```
I got a copy of my labs today, and I noticed that they have new standards on it. It is reflective of the AACE recommendations.
(By the way, this is from Quest Diagnostics Labs...other labs may have different standards, I just thought I would let you know that my lab had changed. Other labs may be different.)
(August, 2010. OC. Fang)
```

When Fang introduced the new lab standard that supposedly differed from the previous standard, another member introduced varying standards that were present across diverse lab testing companies and explained how their standards changed over time. Members then discussed their interpretations for what can be considered 'normal' and 'optimal' numbers for A1C:

```
When I was first diagnosed, the lab said under 6% was normal, and nothing else....You are correct, the change is more reflective of what it should be. (August, 2010. OC. Jule)
There is a vast difference between what is 'normal' and what is 'optimal'. there is a lot of evidence that it's better to be under 5 than under 6. (August, 2010. OC. Nguyen)
```

As seen from the case of conflicting standards referenced above, because members often rely on their own interpretations of standards, definitions, and guidelines, they regularly conflict with the terms and definitions that guide diabetes management practices. This conflict becomes a placeholder for members to understand the individual differences and gage what subjective measurements such as 'normal' or 'optimal' could mean.

In order to discuss personal interpretations and go through negotiation process, members have to reveal their illness histories--historical context of how they maintain diabetes over time. As members reveal their illness trajectories, new kinds of help process also emerge.

FINDING 2: ILLNESS TRAJECTORY ALIGNMENT WORK

Sharing illness trajectories is critical in members' negotiating conflict and individual differences. At the same time, sharing illness trajectories generates interactional work that we call, *Illness trajectory alignment work*. We follow the symbolic interactions in examining "work" as interactional work—one's continuous efforts to act, especially among people within situations that contain socially constructed meanings as well as negotiated senses of order. We use the term "alignment work" not necessarily to denote that patients are trying to have a unified illness trajectory, but to explain how, through the act of comparing and contrasting one anothers' experiences, patients derive personal meanings out of one anothers' illness trajectories. The temporal component in the shared stories allows patients to deal the uncertain future inherent to chronic illness, to understand that the sequence of events could be different depending on the individual, and to be aware of unexpected consequences that might arise at any point.

We will describe illness trajectory alignment work in two ways. First, members attempt to project one's future trajectory through others' trajectories. More experienced patients also share how they deal with a situation in the past that a newly diagnosed patient is currently struggling with, give warnings, and offer reassurances about the likelihood of positive consequences. Through the alignment work of one's future and past trajectories, one can reduce uncertainty about the future, learn shortcuts to problems, and be warned about possible danger to come.

Second, *re-assembling illness trajectories* describes the collective work of the members to build a coherent story about how one might experience a particular problem or intervention over time. Whether the topic is medications, diet regimes, or any number of other subjects, members at different stages share stories about their illness trajectories. These stories are then re-assembled together to construct something the community could use to understand individual differences.

Before we discuss illness trajectory alignment work, we first briefly introduce the Chronic Illness Trajectory Framework (CITF), upon which our analysis builds.

Chronic Illness Trajectory Framework

We use Strauss and Fagerhaugh's [26] Chronic Illness Trajectory Framework (CITF) to borrow terms and analytical tools for understanding how the patients share their stories about managing diabetes over time. In "Social Organization of Medical Work," [26] Strauss defined trajectory as:

> (1) the course of any experienced phenomenon as it evolves over time (an engineering project, a chronic illness, dying ...) and (2) the actions and interactions contributing to this evolution.

In our use of the framework, CITF describes what patients share with peers—the experience of having diabetes over time: how they got diagnosed, what medications are being used, what symptoms and side effects are there, how patients communicate with doctors, what challenges are there in working with the health care providers, and how the patients are dealing with insurance companies. These various stakeholders had to all be considered in order to holistically understand patients' experiences.

The role of the patients today is not limited to attempting to better detect symptoms or to more effectively communicate experiences with the doctors as described in CITF. The patients' work has become diversified and empowered through experiential knowledge gathered from peers, creating a new facet in the illness trajectory framework—the work that is being done among the patients. We next discuss how patients share their illness trajectories as a way to convey their experiences, reduce uncertainty, and help to anticipate possible consequences.

Projecting into the Future and Past

This section will discuss how members share and compare their illness trajectories to help one another project into the future. Not being able to anticipate the timing or severity of things that might happen in the future produces anxiety and stress, and diminishes empowerment for patients [20]. Hearing from experienced patients about how they overcame similar challenges helps to reduce uncertainty about the future. Experienced patients warn less experienced patients about critical events they might encounter and help them become more proactive about problems that might not otherwise have been anticipated.

The following example illustrates a new insulin user attempting to project her future through others' experiences. Sharing past experiences, present struggles, and expectations about the future enables members to encourage one another, find solutions, and reduce uncertainty. The thread began with Tina sharing her excitement about the effectiveness of the insulin, such that she thought she could now eat however she wanted and still enjoy lowered blood sugar levels. However, she was still interested in hearing from experienced patients whether insulin was something she could rely on for a long period:

> I think I just might be in love with insulin!...I feel like I have the freedom to eat the way I want to again without the guilt of high blood sugars. Last night I had spaghetti and garlic bread and 2 hours later a sugar of 99!! […] My only concern is whether or not […] a year of insulin hurt my body in anyway? (Oct, 2010. OC. Tina)

Several patients replied to this, including a patient who also had a positive experience with insulin. Other members expressed concern about Tina's possible weight gain due to the increased use of insulin and the possibility that she might ultimately develop insulin resistance. Members who replied to this thread included several who had experienced gestational diabetes and who enjoyed insulin in the beginning as Tina did—but their recommendations were to start thinking about incorporating appropriate diet change and exercise instead of relying solely on insulin.

As illustrated in Tina's case, patients often cannot anticipate side effects that they might suffer over the years, since little information is given at the time of diagnosis. Accordingly, hospitals arrange support groups to educate patients and to help them become self-sustainable after the acute treatment. Those who choose to engage in support group discussions either F2F or online can get such advice—often from the successful peer patients—and potentially identify negative outcomes that they might have overlooked otherwise.

Re-assembling Illness Trajectories

Our analysis to this point has focused on following the linear trails of each illness trajectory as a form of help, where the transferring of experiential knowledge flowed from directly patient to patient. Now we will further analyze how pieces of illness trajectories from different temporal points on multiple members' trajectories are collected and re-assembled to understand how one might experience medications, diets or exercise regimes differently over time. Rather than attempting to find a solution that perfectly fit each member, awareness of individual differences helps members collectively understand various possibilities so they could adjust their expectations, practices, and decisions accordingly.

The following case illustrates how the community builds an understanding about long-term experiences from a medication. Peter started a thread in dLife after his doctor suggested him to start taking Victoza, a weight loss medication. Victoza was relatively new at the time, thus he wanted to hear about other patients' experiences with the medication so that he could assess whether it would be an appropriate medication for him and also to anticipate what might happen as he continued to use the medication. This thread became helpful not only for Peter, but the community in general.

27 different members replied to the thread, which ended up running for several months and resulted in 41 posts. Some participants had never heard of Victoza, some were thinking of switching to Victoza from other medications, some were about to use it, some had just started using it, and others had been using it for a week to a month. Some of them regularly updated their experiences with the medication. Personal beliefs, past medical history, other medications, and insurance providers varied among the posters of this thread, all factors affecting either the effectiveness of the medication or the consequences of choosing it.

For example, Rick replied to the thread after his third day of using Victoza. In this post, Rick informed readers what they might experience during the first few days of taking Victoza, such as gassiness, and initial fear of injections (Victoza is an injection drug):

```
I just began taking Victoza. Today is only day 3. So far, so good. It has brought my blood sugars down and I am pleased about that. No nausea so far […] I have noticed more "gas". Hopefully this will pass (no pun intended) in a week or two. […] I am very hopeful that Victoza will work for me. (Mar, 2010. OC. Rick)
```

Notice that Rick left it open for what might happen with more protracted use of Victoza. A month later, Rick offered information about how his Victoza experience changed over time. His blood sugar had returned to normal, his dosage had been increased to the normal dose of 1.2 ml, his weight decreased, and new medications were added to his medication plan without side effects. Updating his trajectory over time helped other members anticipate the longer use of Victoza. Hanraty was encouraged by Rick's update:

```
Thanks for your note. I was just given Victoza to try as well- gained 8 lbs and am feeling VERY not happy and reading your note actually gave me a tiny glimmer of hope... (Sep, 2010. OC. Hanraty)
```

Furthermore, the thread allowed eliciting individualized problems around Victoza. Victoza's possible connection with cancer was discussed and which alternative medication—Byetta—could be taken accordingly for those with cancer history. Peter not only had a history of cancer but also had stomach problems in using Byetta. Thus Peter tried controlling his blood sugar levels without the help of Victoza or Byetta for several months, but the risk was too high for him since his blood sugar level was not being controlled. Moreover, contracting pneumonia complicated the situation further. After several months, he was forced to think about how to better manage his use of Victoza—when to take it and where to inject it to minimize the stomach problems:

```
Have a question for those who use it - when do you take yours - morning, afternoon or evening - I know it should be the same time each day but what is the best time - hoping to avoid stomach upset. Any other hints will be appreciated - site of injection (thigh okay?) (Aug, 2010. OC. Peter)
```

Through several months of discussions with other members of the community, Peter was able to develop a fuller understanding of Victoza and how it affected individuals differently. Through re-assembling partial stories from various points in time, members developed a rich picture of what taking the medication was like, and became aware of alternatives that might be pertinent to their own situations. Also, members came to better understand the use of Victoza over time, helping them to adjust their expectations and practices.

Similar activities were observed in F2F, such as their experiences with laser eye surgery, the shingles vaccine and its effects on diabetes, and the progress of the artificial pancreas. This discussion helps them to collectively assemble a more complete picture of what they might anticipate over time and to appreciate individual differences in the experience of various resources, activities, and events.

DISCUSSION

In this section, we discuss how members ultimately involve in constructing common understanding towards diabetes management as they participate in the support groups. We then further examine the relationship between operationalization and illness trajectory alignment work, and how our findings translate into design implications.

Community's Common-Enough Understanding Of Diabetes Management

Knowledge produced by being regular members in a community and all other help processes becomes a foundation for community members' constructing common understanding towards diabetes management. This understanding is common-enough (i.e., not complete) and negotiated [26]. This is similar to Weick's sensemaking [28] in that, during the times of ambiguous and uncertain situations, people collaboratively attempt to share understanding of individuals' perspectives and varied interests. While Weick's analyses largely involve ad-hoc and abrupt situations, the settings we examined involve sensemaking activities happening over years-long period of time. Over time, a community builds a conceptual pool of knowledge containing the community's agreed understanding about appropriate diabetes management strategies. The common understanding then affords members to tailor solutions for themselves or to help others generate solutions for individualized problems. The common understanding becomes a guideline, a reference, and trusted experiential knowledge repository that patients seek out for as ultimate source of help.

The common understanding is not tangible in any way. Similar to what was observed from the workers in a hotline [3] and an emergency room [19], a community's common understanding is embedded in the processes of members' close awareness of one another, continuous negotiation of strategies, elicitation of exceptional cases, and challenges emerging out of operationalization, the breaking of operationalization, and illness trajectory alignment work.

Operationalization and Illness Trajectory Alignment Work

Operationalized information and illness trajectories supplement each other. Operationalized knowledge becomes elements that comprise a more complete story of one's illness trajectory as members share their patient profiles, experiment findings, and current struggles as part of their interaction with the support groups. Still, the missing information between shared operationalized experiences, and the context that surrounds each shared operationalized experience, can only be filled with stories and anecdotes as they become necessary.

Each member's illness trajectory as presented to the support groups is never complete. Only the parts that the members willingly report are visible to the community. One's illness trajectory is in a constant state of progression, thus members need to be kept abreast of one anothers' illness trajectories over time in order to have a "complete" picture.

Design Implications

We now go back to Molly's case introduced in the beginning. How could collaborative help systems support Molly's situation of finding solutions to conflicting diet plans? We discuss three implications.

Facilitate Sharing of Operationalized Experiences

With the advance of Internet technology and increased user participation, sharing operationalized patient profiles in the forms of personal health records (PHR), Microsoft HealthVault, Google Health, or manually reported is actively being explored [16-18]. Personal health information tools integrating above PHR related applications can help find relevant clinical trials for patients' health status, improve patient-doctor communication [16], and monitor one's health in a systematical way (e.g., healthmanager.webmd.com). In the context of support groups, our study found operationalized experiences help members easily [17] share context and strategies. To help further facilitate the process of operationalization, we can imagine a system with a repository of operationalized experiences that includes experimental results of various diet or medication regimes. Molly could then narrow down the pool of patients who have had diabetes for roughly 20 or more years like her and who have had liver disease at the same time. She could then compare diabetes management strategies of those who progressed to the later stages of liver disease more quickly than others versus those who did not. The results may not give her scientifically valid information, but for patients like Molly who are in need of relevant information this could help with the uncertainty of managing chronic illness.

Support Challenging Operationalized Solutions to Elicit Individual Differences

Existing patient networking sites have been critiqued for its disconnection between shared personal health information and narrative discussions [10]. Our findings show that breakdown of operationalization in fact helps members to understand individual differences of a given problem. When a dLife member challenged a strategy for checking blood sugar, the community was able to further understand the need for individualized strategies in checking blood sugars. A repository of operationalized experiences discussed above should not represent each experience as a finished and complete data point. Rather, each data point should be subject to change and the context in which the data point was challenged should be recorded. Examples would include support for conversational threads for each shared data point in the repository. Any data point with long conversational threads could signal that the data point is controversial and is significant.

Facilitate Sharing Individual Trajectories and Help Community's Negotiated Experiences Become Visible

Sharing illness trajectories is critical in not only contextualizing but also generating information about one's future and take preventative measures. The importance of visualizing patient history has been recognized [21]. When Molly narrows the pool of patients diagnosed with liver disease, the ability to see the past history and future plans of those patients would greatly help her reduce uncertainty about the future. Molly could essentially align her future with those who have gone through a similar problem and she could see many cases and exceptions that would help her to anticipate her own future.

In order to support the visibility of the community's common understanding, we could also imagine a system where patients post their problems and the system suggests prior threads that are relevant to their posts. The patient could then link to relevant prior threads in their posts and explain the distinctions between their current problem and prior posts. This feature could not only help the poster learn about prior relevant posts but also help readers to learn about each poster's problem within the larger context of how the community attempts to solve problems.

CONCLUSION

In this paper, we discussed how patient support groups give individualized help and derived design implications. Operationalization facilitates transferring executable experiential knowledge and context. However, operationalization inevitably breaks down due to members' individual and situated differences. Such breakdown in fact works as an opportunity for members to deepen understanding towards exceptions and individual differences, and generates negotiated understandings. The process of operationalization and reflecting upon operationalization breakdowns have to be done within the larger context of sharing illness trajectories. Members also use illness trajectories as resources to help one another anticipate about the uncertain future and understand individual differences. Ultimately, as members continue to participate in the community, they construct common understanding around an ideal way of maintaining diabetes over time.

There are several caveats and remaining questions to be discussed. First, our participants are the group of people who are actively attempting to control their diabetes. A new set of inquiries arises for how we can better support patients who are less proactive about their conditions. Second, our participants come from all around the world, and information they gather from their doctors can conflict. How members can use information they receive from dLife with their health care providers is another question that needs to be answered. Lastly, how our findings relate to online diabetes communities other than dLife and the face-to-face support groups in other parts of the United States is unknown. Devising appropriate environment fit for targeted patient group will become important as we design online communities for varying groups of patients.

ACKNOWLEDGMENTS

This work has been funded in part by NSF 0905460. We thank MISC, the SocialWorlds Group, and the participants and support group leaders for their support.

REFERENCES

1. *The Shared Search for Health Information on the Internet.* Pew Research Center Publications 2009.
2. Ackerman, M.S., *Answer Garden: A Tool for Growing Organizational Memory*, 1993, PhD Thesis, MIT.
3. Ackerman, M.S. and C.A. Halverson, *Organizational memory as Objects, Processes, and Trajectories.* JCSCW, 1999. **13**(2):34.
4. Ambrosini, V. and C. Bowman, *Tacit Knowledge.* Journal of Management Studies, 2002. **38**(6): p. 811-829.
5. Borkman, T., *Experiential knowledge: A new concept for the analysis of self-help groups.* The Social Service Review, 1976.
6. Borkman, T., *Self-help groups at the turning point.* American Journal of Community Psychology, 1990.
7. Bowker, G.C. and S.L. Star, *Sorting things out: classification and its consequences.* 1999, Cambridge, MA: MIT Press.
8. Civan, A., *Understanding and Facilitating Patient Expertise Sharing*, 2009, PhD Thesis, Univ of Washington.
9. Fierz, W., *Challenge of personalized health care.* Med Sci Monit, 2004. **10**(5): p. 111-123.
10. Frost, J.H. and M.P. Massagli, *Social uses of personal health information within PatientsLikeMe.* JMIR, 2008. **10**(3): p. e15.
11. Grinter, R.E., *Supporting articulation work using software configuration management systems.* CSCW, 1996. **5**(4):447.
12. Halverson, C.A. and M.S. Ackerman, *The Bird of an Organizational Resource*, in *Resources, Co-Evolution and Artifacts, CSCW*, M. Ackerman, Halverson, C., Erickson, T., & Kellogg, W., Editor 2007, Springer-Verlag: New York.
13. Heath, C. and P. Luff, *Collaboration and controlCrisis management and multimedia technology in London Underground Line Control Rooms.* CSCW, 1992. **1**(1-2): 69.
14. Huh, J., M.W. Newman, and M.S. Ackerman, *Supporting Collaborative Help for Individualized Use*, CHI, 3141-3150.
15. Nonaka, I. and G. von Krogh, *Perspective--Tacit Knowledge and Knowledge Conversion.* Org Sci, 2009. **20**(3): p. 635-652.
16. Patel, B., et al., *A comparison of web sites used to manage and present home blood pressure readings.* Journal of clinical hypertension, 2010. **12**(6): p. 389-95.
17. Patel, C., et al., *TrialX.* Web Semantics, 2010. **8**: p. 342-347.
18. http://www.patientslikeme.com.
19. Paul, S.A., M.C. Reddy, and C.J. deFlitch, *Information and communication tools as aids to collaborative sensemaking*, in *CHI EA.* 2008, ACM. p. 3105.
20. Piette, J., C. Richardson, and M. Valenstein, *Addressing the needs of patients with multiple chronic illnesses.* American Journal of Managed Care, 2004. **10**(2): p. 152-162.
21. Plaisant, C., et al. *LifeLines: using visualization to enhance navigation and analysis of patient records. AMIA.* 1998. p.76
22. Reddy, M., P. Dourish, and W. Pratt, *Temporality in medical work: Time also matters.* JCSCW, 2006. **15**: p. 29-53.
23. Schatzki, T.R., K. Knorr-Cetina, and E. Von Savigny, *The practice turn in contemporary theory.* 2001: Psychology Press.
24. Star, S.L. and J. Griesemer, *Institutional Ecology, 'Translations' and Boundary Objects.* Social Studies of Science, 1989. **19**(4): p. 387–420.
25. Strauss, A. and J. Corbin, *Grounded theory methodology: An overview.* Handbook of qualitative research, 1994. **273**: p. 285.
26. Strauss, A. and S. Fagerhaugh, *Social organization of medical work*1997: Transaction Pub.
27. Swan, M., *Emerging Patient-Driven Health Care Model.* Int J Environ Res Public Health, 2009. **6**(2): p. **492–525**.
28. Weick, K., *The social psychology of organizing*1979: Addison-Wesley Reading, MA.
29. Wenger, E., *Communities of practice.* 2007:Cambridge Univ.
30. Wicks, P., et al. (2010). Sharing health data for better outcomes on PatientsLikeMe. *JMIR, 12*(2), e19.

Transforming Solitary Exercises into Social Exergames

Taiwoo Park, Chungkuk Yoo, Sungwon Peter Choe, Byunglim Park, Junehwa Song
Department of Computer Science, KAIST
Daejeon, 305-701, Republic of Korea
{twpark, ckyoo, sungwon, blpark, junesong}@nclab.kaist.ac.kr

ABSTRACT
This paper discusses an approach for transforming solitary exercises into social exergames. We frame our discussion by highlighting the relation between the original exercises and game interactions, and by analyzing an example exergame which is successfully transformed from its original solitary exercise. We present a user study of the exergame that evaluates the need for holistic transformation strategies from solitary exercises into social exergames.

Author Keywords
Solitary; Exercise; Social; Interaction; Game Design.

ACM Classification Keywords
H.5.0. Information interfaces and presentation (e.g., HCI).

General Terms
Human Factors; Design.

INTRODUCTION
Sports are an entertaining and engaging means to improve people's athletic abilities and physical condition. Team sports also play an important role in strengthening sociability and solidarity between players. As players act and react to each other, their resulting interactions mesh together. The moment of a clean, perfectly timed pass from a teammate followed by an exquisite shot to a goal, creates an unparalleled feeling of excitement and achievement that is shared among all one's teammates. This kind of extraordinary sensation resulting from synchronized team interaction is an important part of what immerses people in team sports, making it a favored form of physical exercise.

However, it is difficult for many people with their busy and erratic urban lifestyles to engage in such social sports frequently as such activities take place at a strict designated time and place. As a result, many people perform physical training in the form of a solitary exercise that can be done at a more convenient time and place, such as treadmill running at home. It may be difficult for many people to be motivated to perform these monotonous, repetitive, and isolated exercises. Moreover, the results of intrinsic rewards of exercise such as better general health [5] and appearance are not immediately observable. Finally, solitary exercise does not satisfy the need for social interaction, which is important for individual health and sense of well-being [4].

In this paper, we discuss an approach for transforming solitary exercises into social exergames. We frame our discussion by highlighting the relation between the original exercises and game interactions, and by analyzing an example exergame which is successfully transformed from its original solitary exercise. We present a user study of the exergame that evaluates the need for holistic transformation strategies from solitary exercises into social exergames.

We note that a recent work provides a design framework for exergame design [7]. We appreciate that our discussion can be understood as a specialized study framed within the viewpoint of this work. Overall, our work mainly touches on *the moving body* and *the relating body* aspects of *the exertion framework*, through utilizing solitary exercises and providing relationships among players, respectively.

TRANSFORMATION GUIDELINES
While designing exergames based on solitary exercises, designers should keep in mind that the original exercises and game interactions affect each other. Thus, they produce nontrivial problems which are not exposed while being treated independently, thereby requiring the designers to understand the elements from a holistic point of view. That is, exercises expand the design space of games beyond that of traditional games. In detail, designers should integrate a given exercise with a game by utilizing physical actions of the exercise, as well as evaluate whether the game is a suitable fit for the exercise. In this section, we introduce guidelines for the conversion, obtained by analyzing prior studies on traditional games and exergames by Salen and Zimmerman [13], Campbell et al. [3], and Mueller et al. [7]

Exercise-Aware Game Interaction Design
Obtaining Design Primitives from Exercises
As discussed in [13], designing game interaction largely consists of building a meaningful relationship between players and with a game system by defining a set of rules describing the relationship. Specifically, interaction between players is induced by sharing a part of the game system. In the case of social exergames, the shared part of the game system can be derived from a state or outcomes of the original exercise. In this context, it helps designers to create a glossary of a given exercise by thoroughly observing and identifying the states and the outcomes of a target exercise. For example, in the case of running, design primitives from the exercise include the action of taking steps and swinging hands, current speed, elapsed time or duration, distance, and the state of running itself, etc.

Choosing Key Primitives for Interaction

Designers should carefully choose key primitives, depending on the type of experience that they want to focus on delivering: exercising, playing the game, or most likely a mixture of both. The selection should consider the levels of abstraction of the primitives as they can influence aspects of game play and players' experiences. For example, distance is a primitive at a higher level of abstraction than the action of swinging hands while running. These primitives are used as the main inputs in Nike+ iPod [10] and the 100 meters sprint of Wii Olympics [12], respectively. The former preserves the original exercise well; however, it hardly gives players a sense of playing a game while running as indicated by Campbell et al. [3] Conversely, the latter adjusts the original running activity to an easier form, and thus players may feel that they are not running but playing a physical game. We do not aim to discuss what the best form for exergames is, but rather we simply wish to indicate that the key primitives of a game should be chosen depending on the purpose of the game. In Jogging over a Distance [9] and Kukini [3], both also originating from running, these works utilize the players' jogging state and distance, respectively. These games give hints as to ways to create a variety of exergames by choosing different key primitives from the same exercise.

Building Intuitive Interaction

Intuitiveness of interactions should be considered essential in exergame design. In general, the more intuitive an interaction is, the faster players engage in game play. Exergames, in particular, explicitly require interactions which are intuitive enough to perform during exercise. To design an intuitive game interaction based on a certain exercise, *modalities* and *affordances* [6] of the exercise must be identified in advance, i.e., which actions, body parts, and senses are involved in the exercise and to what degree. We refer to actions fundamental to the exercise as primary actions and to other actions as non-primary actions.

Preserving Primary Actions in the Core Mechanics

To make interactions more intuitive, it is often effective to use primary actions that are usually performed throughout the duration of exercise, as the main input for the core mechanics of a game. For example, Table Tennis for Three [8] converted a solitary wall-hitting practice into a social exergame. It preserved and actively employed the primary action of the original exercise into the converted game, namely hitting specific positions using a paddle and a ball.

Utilizing Non-primary Actions

Also, it is possible to utilize additional actions involving non-primary body parts and senses which can be performed concurrently along with the main actions of the exercise. These actions can be useful as additional game inputs to enrich the interactions between players and make the game more dynamic and fun. However, designing non-primary interaction requires careful consideration. The additional interaction should not interfere nor incur any direct physical conflict with the main interaction. Also, the new interaction should be designed not to distract too much attention away from the primary interaction, to guarantee the players' safety and performance of the primary interaction. We present an example later in the Revisiting Design Section.

Motivating Players

In the context of exergames, motivating players becomes more important than in non-exergames, largely because players should exercise as well as play the games. One of the essential components of a game to promote players' motivation is the goal, and the players struggle towards achieving goals [13]. Also, interactions between players, usually conceptualized as competition and cooperation [1], elaborate the struggles, i.e., players actively strive against or assist each other to win the game. In this subsection, we discuss important points on arranging goals and shaping interactions between players in exergames.

Creating and Arranging Micro Goals in Exergames

In general games, it is important to provide micro goals [3], sometimes referred to as short-term goals [13]. Micro goals are used as milestones towards bigger goals and for keeping players engaged in game play. Summarizing discussions in [3, 11, 13], micro goals encourage engagement in three ways; they provide (1) a sense of achievement frequently, (2) an easier way to gauge overall progress, and (3) a path for reaching long-term macro goals. Therefore, in the case of exergame design, it is more important to carefully arrange such micro goals throughout the game play, to keep players involved in strenuous exercise motivated. For example, in Table Tennis for Three players weaken blocks on a screen by hitting them with a ball. The last person to break a weakened block gets the point for the ball, accomplishing this micro goal.

While designing each micro goal, designers should also consider whether the players can achieve the goal given their physical availability. In video games, players learn game objects' characteristics by experience, e.g., the acceleration power of a vehicle or the maximum jumping height of a game character. The players then build strategies to achieve a given goal, taking these characteristics into account. In exergames, some of these characteristics are embodied by the players' physical capabilities, e.g., speeds of vehicles depend on players' running speeds. In that case, the players should adjust their strategies depending on their physical capabilities, as should designers of micro goals. Here we refer to yet another characteristic of exergames which does not exist in non-exergames: 'the outcome of the game is predominantly determined by physical effort.' [7]

Interaction between Players: Competition and Cooperation

Inter-player interactions in exergames resemble those in sports, as indicated in [7, 16]. In general, exciting sports feature highly synchronized interactions between players. Interaction among players can thus be tightly coupled to the point where player's actions are coordinated over very short

[1] In this paper, competition and cooperation refer to explicitly guided ones by game rules.

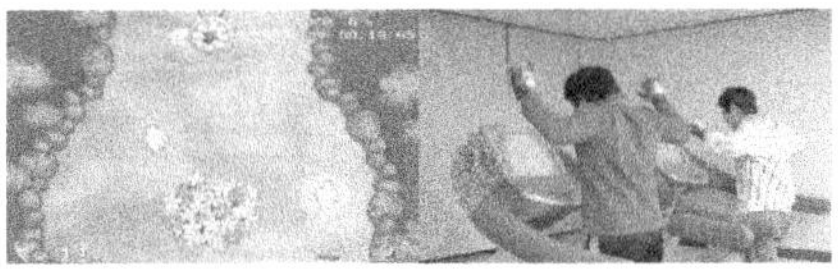

Figure 1. A team playing Swan Boat

time frames resulting in near-simultaneous actions. Actions are time-critical and failure to perform timely actions can result in penalties to the point of losing a game (in competitive cases) or degradation of the quality of the activity to the point where the current iteration cannot continue (in cooperative cases). For example, in Table Tennis for Three, a block must be hit three times before it breaks. Competing players must quickly coordinate their strategy to break the brick, instantaneously adjusting their actions to opponents'.

REVISITING DESIGN: SWAN BOAT

Swan Boat [1] is a social exergame designed for treadmill running (see Figure 1). It enhances the bland experience of running on a treadmill with rich interaction among players, encouraging intensive synchronized movement with their teammates. In the case of treadmill running, we easily observe that the legs are the main body parts used in the exercise and that leg movements are performed repeatedly as the *primary action*. Thus, walking or running actions can be used as the main game input. Also, as the arm and hand movements involve *non-primary body parts* while running, they can be utilized to design additional interactions.

In the game design, the designers adopt a paddle boat-type swan boat and a swan boat race as the game entity and metaphor. The metaphor is used to sketch the outline of the core mechanics: runners compete against each other in teams by cooperatively controlling a team boat. In a two-person team's case, one takes the role of the left paddler and the other, the right. As a result, the difference in speed between team members determines the direction of their boat. For example, if a team wants to steer their boat to port, the member in charge of that direction should run faster than her teammate. Players continuously change their running speed, the *key primitive* of interaction, to fine-tune the speed of their individual steps to adjust to the running pace of their teammates. (The speed of the treadmill is automatically adjusted to the pace of the runners.) This closely harmonized interaction immerses the players in the intense and fun game experience of playing together.

There are a number of *micro goals* designed to enhance the fun of playing Swan Boat by taking advantage of synchronized interaction. Runners promptly change their speed in synchronization with their teammates to steer their boats around *obstacles* and *traps* and rush to acquire *boosters* that temporarily accelerate the speed of their boat.

Simple arm- or hand-gestures are designed for additional fun interactions since they do not incur any conflicts with the main activity of running. Designers added "*punching together*" and "*flapping together*" gestures as additional synchronized interactions. Players in a team flap their arms together to rise back to the surface of the water when their boat is weighed down by a *trap* special item. Team members can also attack nearby opponents by punching together in sync to shove an opponent away with their swan boat's "wing", slowing down the opponent's boat.

Swan Boat supports synchronized interaction with other runners in distant locations over the Internet; players meet other runners of various skill levels and styles in Internet virtual communities to play with. Players can meet up with game partners with whom they meshed well in the past. These partners may forge friendships similar to those found in offline team sports such as soccer.

USER STUDY AND DISCUSSION

We conducted a user study to evaluate the effectiveness of Swan Boat. We compared two conditions: typical treadmill running and team racing in Swan Boat. 4 female and 8 male participants between 20 and 25 years old were recruited via Internet BBS and e-mail. All participants were paired randomly, except two pairs who were previously acquainted. The pairs participated together in each session. Each participant participated in four 20-minute sessions over two weeks. In the first week, participants ran on an interactive treadmill without playing Swan Boat. In the second week, participants ran on the treadmill playing Swan Boat.

Afterwards, participants were interviewed using open-ended questions. To compare energy expenditure in different conditions, we consulted a physical education specialist and decided to use average MET (metabolic equivalent) as a shorthand method for estimating the energy expenditure of the physical activity [2].

Intuitiveness of Game Interaction

The user study confirmed the tightly coupled nature of the design considerations, game play and the original exercise, and highlighted their relationship. Although the game mechanics required synchronization of exercise and close collaboration, most participants played the game well and enjoyed their exercise. All of them (strongly) agreed to the statement 'the game is intuitive to play' and 'the game is compatible with the running activity'. In addition, we carefully observed and interviewed whether *non-primary actions* such as punching together disturbs the primary game play, i.e., the cooperative boat control. Though punching together requires additional attention and gestural inputs, no participants complained about any distraction from the main running activity and when asked about it explicitly, participants simply stated that they did not experience any such difficulty.

Cooperation and Competition Effects

In the interviews, our participants commented on the cooperative effects, particularly on those due to the cooperative boat control game mechanic. Participants noted that they engaged in frequent verbal interaction to coordinate their cooperative play, suggesting that cooperative play increases social interaction: *"During the game play, we continuously discussed each other's running speed"* [P5]. However, some participants reported that they felt inconvenienced during team play: *"I prefer to run at my own pace"* [P20]. Considering the study on the relationship between individual differences in competiveness and the competition experience [14], we can tentatively conjecture that there is a relationship between individual willingness, derived intrinsically or from the relation between co-players, and cooperation and the cooperation experience.

Participants' comments on the competitive nature of the game mainly focused on observations that closely competing with opponents provided strong motivations to keep running hard: "*When the opponents' boat was gaining on us, we ran hard to stay in the lead*" [P4]. This result is consistent with prior works which evaluate competition effects [14]. Competition was reported to make treadmill running much more exciting: *"Passing another boat just before reaching the goal was really thrilling."* [P12].

Interestingly, some participants wondered how the experience would change if a team consisted of more than two players. From on-site discussions with the participants, we could imagine the changes through two example sports, i.e., dragon boat racing and tug of war. That is, as the number of players in a team increases, the sense of belonging to and unity in a group will become still more important, as partially shown in Nike+ iPod [10].

Effects on the Exercise: Balance and Overexertion

Energy expenditure

The estimated energy expenditure while playing Swan Boat was about 54% higher than running on a treadmill; participants' average energy expenditure of Swan Boat playing was 9.47 (MET) and that value for the same time during typical treadmill running was 6.15 (MET). Therefore, we expect that players playing Swan Boat exercise more intensely than conventional treadmill running. The interviews confirmed this assumption as the participants noted that playing Swan Boat encouraged them to run much harder than treadmill running alone. Reasons for running harder while playing Swan Boat include the psychology of competition and not wanting to let down one's teammate.

Inter-player Balance and Overexertion

In incorporating social interaction into an exercise, one must consider how it may affect the original exercise activity itself. Issues not inherent to solitary exercise like differences in physical abilities may threaten fair play between players. Actually, some participants quickly realized their differences in physical ability within a few trials. Also, we observed that excessive motivation can cause overexertion: *"I could not maintain my own pace while trying to catch up with the others' boat. After the race, I realized that I exerted myself too much."* [P4].

Revisiting Game Play Design: Mitigating Imbalance

A potential solution for fine-tuning gameplay balance is to provide a physical ability balancing mechanism between players through the game mechanics. [9, 15] helps mitigate the differences between players' physical abilities by utilizing physical indicators, e.g., individual target heart rates, as criteria for exergame balance. Using such an approach, a player with lower physical ability could compete or collaborate fairly with one with higher ability using handicaps for boat speeds. We can also add game features preventing users from overexerting. For example, a boat can have an attribute called an *overheating gauge*. The gauge fills up gradually when a player runs faster than 7 mph, which is possibly dangerous. The boat slows down automatically when the gauge exceeds its maximum. Now overheating avoidance becomes a part of the game strategy, whereby players control their speed to avoid the penalty.

Field Experiences

We had opportunities to present Swan Boat at a local science festival. During the festival over 100 people tried our game. We observed parents who were unaccustomed to gaming easily interact with our system. The game provided an opportunity for gaming-novice parents to easily play along with their gaming-veteran children.

CONCLUSION

We discussed guidelines for transforming solitary exercises into social exergames, that is, exercise-aware game design, building intuitive interaction, and motivating players. We also analyzed the detailed design of the Swan Boat game to justify our guidelines. We presented a user study of the exergame that evaluates the need for holistic transformation strategies from solitary exercises into social exergames.

ACKNOWLEDGEMENTS

We would like to thank the anonymous reviewers for their helpful comments. This work was supported by the NRF of Korea under grants No. 2011-0018120 and No. 2011-0020519.

REFERENCES

1. Ahn, M., et al. Running or gaming, In *Proc. ACE 2009*, ACM.
2. Ainsworth, B. E., et al. Compendium of physical activities: energy costs of human movement. *Medicine and science in sports and exercise*, 25 (1993), 71–80.
3. Campbell, T., et al. Game design principles in everyday fitness applications. In *Proc. CSCW 2008*, ACM.
4. Cohen, S. Social relationships and health. *American Psychologist*, 59 (2004), 676–684.
5. Fletcher, G. F., et al. Statement on exercise: benefits and recommendations for physical activity programs for all Americans, *Circulation*, 94 (1996), 857–862.
6. Gibson, J.J. *The ecological approach to visual perception.* Lawrence Erlbaum, 1986
7. Mueller, F., et al. Designing Sports: A Framework for Exertion Games. In *Proc. CHI 2011*, ACM.
8. Mueller, F. and Gibbs, M. R. A table tennis game for three players. In *Proc. OZCHI 2006*, ACM.
9. Mueller, F., et al. Jogging over a distance between Europe and Australia. In *Proc. UIST 2010*, ACM.
10. Nike + iPod. http://www.apple.com/ipod/nike
11. Novak, J. *Game Development Essentials*. Delmar, 2007.
12. Wii Olympics. http://www.olympicvideogames.com/
13. Salen, K. and Zimmerman, E. *Rules of Play: Game Design Fundamentals*. MIT Press, 2003.
14. Song, H., et al. Intrinsic motivation in exergames, In *Proc. the annual conference of the int'l communication association*, 2010.
15. Stach, T., et al. Heart rate control of exercise video games. In *Proc. GI 2009*, ACM.
16. Wulf, V., et al. Computer Supported Collaborative Sports, In *Proc. ICEC 2004*, IFIP.

Loosely Formed Patient Care Teams: Communication Challenges and Technology Design

Soyoung Lee[1], Charlotte Tang[3], Sun Young Park[1], Yunan Chen[1,2]

[1]Department of Informatics
[2]Institute of Clinical and Translational Sciences
University of California, Irvine
Irvine, CA, 92697
{soyounl, sunyp1, yunanc}@ics.uci.edu

[3]Department of Computer Science
University of British Columbia
Vancouver BC Canada
V6T 1Z4
scctang@cs.ubc.ca

ABSTRACT

We conducted an observational study to investigate nurses' communication behaviors in an Emergency Department (ED). Our observations reveal unique collaboration practices exercised by ED staff, which we term as "loosely formed team collaboration." Specifically, ED patient care teams are dynamically and quickly assembled upon patient arrival, wherein team members engage in interdependent and complex care activities. The responsible care team then disassembles when a patient leaves the ED. The coordination mechanism required for these work practices challenges nurses' communication processes, often increasing breakdown susceptibility. Our analysis of the ED nurses' communication behaviors and use of communication channels highlights the importance of maintaining team awareness and supporting role-based communication. This points to the need for explicit efforts to coordinate tasks and informative interruptions. These findings call for the design of future communication technologies to meet the needs of loosely formed collaborative environments to provide team-based communication, lightweight feedback, and information transparency.

Author Keywords

Communication Behaviors, Loosely Formed Patient Care Team, Emergency Department, nursing work, collaborative work.

ACM Classification Keywords

H.0 [information systems], K.4.3 [organizational impacts] J3.Life and Medical Sciences: Health, Medical Information Systems.

General Terms

Performance.

INTRODUCTION

Team collaboration in complex workplaces, such as healthcare and transportation domains [9, 13, 15, 23, 24, 31, 37], has been of immense interest to the CSCW community. These settings are characterized as being dynamic and information-rich, such that the success of their collaborative efforts relies upon effective communication among the team members. Previous studies in healthcare [4, 27] have shown that a lack of understanding of effective communication practices can lead to medical errors that threaten patient safety. Yet, effective communication in medical settings is not easily achieved since work collaborations in these settings exhibit distinctly different behaviors from other collaborative settings. In this paper we coin this unique work practice exhibited in medical setting as "loosely formed collaboration".

Collaborative work in many organizational settings is fairly stable [30], with team members generally knowing whom they collaborate with on a daily basis. However medical teams, particularly those in the ED, are often dynamically formed. As such, team members may not know *a priori* who they need to collaborate with when delivering care to individual patients. Furthermore, medical teams may consist of spatially distributed members who may simultaneously belong to multiple medical teams that are dynamically formed to treat different patients. In essence, these collaborative patient care teams are loosely tied together, thus posing considerable challenges to the communication required for time-critical patient care delivery.

Ephemerally formed collaborative teams have been studied previously. For example, trauma resuscitation teams were dynamically formed upon patients' arrival [28]. Without prior knowledge of other team members' roles, the trauma team members had to first explicitly reveal their roles in the collaboration process in order to concertedly perform surgeries under time constraints and stress. Role-based coordination was also common in less critical domains like the film industry where temporary collaborative teams are crucial to their success [5]. Although these studies made efforts to elucidate the importance of roles in dynamically formed team collaborations, they did not detail the communication behaviors and channels used for supporting these collaborative behaviors, nor did they introduce the concept and characteristics of "loosely formed collaboration teams". The current work reported in this paper contributes to a better understanding of the communication behaviors within and between loosely formed collaborative teams.

We present the findings of an observational study conducted in an ED, focusing on nursing communication to understand the communication challenges in loosely formed collaborative teams. We examined ED nurses' work and their use of communication channels *in situ*. The focus on the nurses is justified for studying the communication of loosely formed collaboration since nurses are the ones who "*weave together the many facets of the [healthcare] services and create order in a fast flowing and turbulent work environment*" [1].

This study aims to answer the following questions:

- How does the unique work nature of nursing work influence communication behaviors in the ED?
- What does the use of communication channels reveal about the communication behaviors in the ED?

RELATED WORK

Communication is a fundamental activity for collaborative work. In most office settings, collaboration can be readily achieved through communication among well-structured teams [30] as workplaces often consist of clearly defined work boundaries and explicitly distinguished work teams. In other more dynamic settings such as in the London underground line control room [13], communication could also be quite easily conducted among the collocated Line Controllers, Divisional Information Assistants (DIA) and DIA trainees who coordinated the collaborative work through a variety of cues including eavesdropping of conversations and subsequent responses. Yet, the knowledge gained from studying the collaborative behaviors in these relatively stable work environments may not be applicable to the highly dynamic team collaborations, such as the medical setting.

Comparing with these settings, collaboration in medical field is more complex and dynamic [3, 6, 17, 31]. As such, much research has been conducted to examine important aspects core to work coordination and collaboration in healthcare. These include temporal coordination [2, 24], shift cycles [38], spatiality [3], artifact use [37], redundancy [8, 33], sense-making [23], information sharing [31], and communication breakdowns [24, 35] and workflows [9]. In particular, it has been found that improving coordination-related communication can potentially increase work efficiency in patient care [14]. This is particularly relevant to nursing work as nurses have been found to spend more than 30% of their time on communication-related activities during work [14].

Collaboration in time-critical medical settings is characterized by rapid configuration and reconfiguration of team members [25]. This is due to the increasing specialization of modern medicine [29] that a single patient care team typically requires the involvement of many different professionals [31]. For example, a team treating a chest pain patient usually consists of a cardiologist, a neurologist, a charge nurse, registered nurses, a radiologist, technicians, and a case manager. As patients are continually admitted and discharged, each medical staff is often required to simultaneously participate in multiple patient care teams, each with distinctly different team members [25, 29]. These healthcare teams are often ephemerally and loosely formed within a short period of time, especially in urgent situations such as those formed in emergency departments. Yet members of these healthcare teams may not necessarily be collocated at the time of team formation. Thus it is not uncommon that team members are not immediately aware of other members in the team and their locations.

Given the dynamic nature of medical collaboration, to maintain effective team communication among healthcare providers within and across patient care teams is inherently challenging. Although communication technologies have been widely deployed in medical settings for addressing communication problems found in healthcare, discrepancies have been identified in the intended and the actual use of communication devices in healthcare [32]. Other studies conducted in the highly dynamic and time-critical healthcare settings have reported that role-based information distribution may support coordination-related communication by expediting information gathering and sense-making processes [22], and explicit role-identification facilitated conversations necessary for time-critical coordination [28]. These works have revealed the significance of roles in time-sensitive communication in such collaborative settings, but also called for the need to perform a more comprehensive analysis of the overall communication practice for time-critical teamwork.

Nevertheless, there has been little work done in the specific issue of communication behaviors within and among the dynamic and loosely formed healthcare teams. This paper reports findings from a field study that addresses specific communication problems in the highly dynamic and time-critical healthcare setting of an ED. The goals are to first acquire a better understanding of the communication behaviors exhibited in the loosely formed medical teams, and to provide useful insights to the design of future communication technologies for this type of collaborations.

METHODOLOGY

This study was conducted in an Emergency Department (ED) affiliated with a teaching hospital. The goal of our research was to understand nurses' communication behaviors and the communication channels used in the ED.

Setting

The ED is divided into five areas: triage, ED1, ED2, ED3, and physicians' charting room. In our study, we shadowed ED staff in all five working areas. The ED staff we studied included 3 charge nurses, 15 registered nurses, 2 float nurses, 5 residents and 4 attending physicians, 2 front desk clerks and 1 hospital unit service coordinator (HUSC). The charge nurse of the ED is responsible for managing and expediting patient flow in the entire ED. Float nurses are mainly required to support nursing work in ED1 to help the registered nurses with care for the trauma patients who typically need close monitoring such as acute life support (ALS) procedures.

Since the focus of this paper is on nursing communication, we describe our findings obtained from the entire ED, with the exception of the charting room that is primarily for physicians' use.

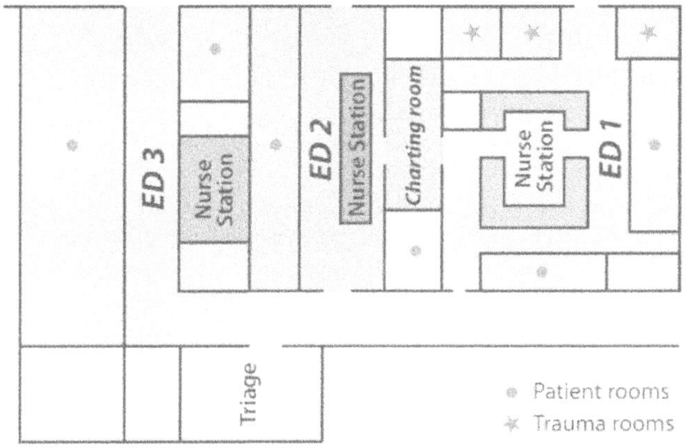

Figure 1. A Floor Map of the ED

Triage is where nurses first conduct a brief assessment on a patient's condition and quickly decide the urgency before handing the patient off to an ED nurse assigned to the patient.

The ED consists of three units depending on the severity of patients' illnesses: ED1, ED2, and ED3. ED1 is a 16-bed unit that is perceived to be the central area in the ED for severely ill and trauma patients. This unit is partitioned into 6 enclosed rooms and a large space with 10 beds separated by curtains. All beds are equipped with a cardiac monitoring machine. ED nurses are assigned with a number of beds at the beginning of each shift. For example, a nurse who is assigned to bed #1 to #4 in ED1 will be responsible for patients admitted to these beds. The nursing station is an open area in the center of ED1 and patients' beds surround the nursing station as shown in Figure 1.

Patients with moderate illness or with psychological problems are assigned to ED2, which has 7 beds assigned to 2 nurses. ED3 is a 9-bed single-room unit for patients with mild illnesses, such as a cold or sore throat. It is located the furthest from ED1and has an enclosed nursing station.

Data collection

Data was collected through field observations, including nurse shadowing, formal and informal interviews. We first observed communication flow in the ED, paying special attentions to nurse communication that mainly took place in the triage, ED1, ED2, and ED3. We also shadowed 20 ED nurses working in all the ED units. The goal was to gain an in-depth contextual understanding of how ED nurses communicate with medical staff both inside and outside the ED, and to identify the communication channels used and the personnel involved in the communication process. When situation permitted, we asked them questions to elucidate the nurses' actions.

In total, 210 hours of observations were conducted over a period of 6 months. Each observation session ranged between 2 and 6 hours. Our observations were distributed across different time periods from early mornings to late evenings on both weekdays and weekends, but not including night shifts. 6 formal interviews were conducted to gather nurses' opinions and perceptions regarding ED communication practices and communication channels. The interviews were recorded and transcribed for analysis.

Data analysis

The data were first analyzed using various diagramming methods including affinity diagram, communication diagram and flow diagram [7]. Communication and flow diagrams helped us understand how and through which communication channels the ED nurses communicated with other staff working both inside and outside the ED. In addition, open coding was used to look for recurring themes emerging from the data regarding nurses' communication behaviors. We specifically coded data for communication channels used in the ED. For example, when mobile phones were used for communication, we identified the process of the phone calls, the sender, the recipient, the content, the objective, and the actions taken. Communication breakdowns were also noted and coded for analysis.

FINDINGS

Through our observation and data analysis we identified critical factors in supporting nursing collaborations at the ED. This section provides a detailed picture of the formation of an ED patient care team, the communication behaviors of the ED nurses, and the important factors contributing to effective patient care in the ED.

Overview of patient care team formation

As described previously, unlike many organizational settings where collaboration occurs in fairly stable teams, patient care teams in the ED are loosely tied together and each ED staff may participate in multiple patient care teams simultaneously. In this section, we describe the formation process of patient care team in the ED and explain why we consider it as "loosely formed team collaboration."

Figure 2 depicts how these patient care teams are loosely formed. Each ED patient care team is made up of a group of core members plus several peripheral members depending on the needs of a patient. An ED patient care team is formed dynamically *in situ* by the assembly of a group of core team members, including an ED nurse, the charge nurse, a resident, and an attending physician upon the arrival of a patient. These core members work together to plan, update, and execute necessary care to the patient until the patient is discharged from the ED. Peripheral members such as a float nurse, a technician, an interpreter, HUSC, and a janitor may join the team as needed. These peripheral team members would leave the team as soon as their designated task is completed. To illustrate, a patient will be assigned to a bed by the charge nurse on his/her arrival and

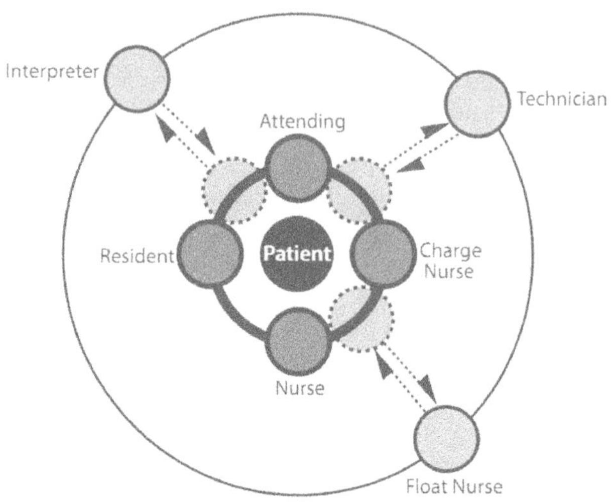

Figure 2. Core and peripheral members of a loosely formed patient care team. Dark and light grey indicate core and peripheral members respectively. The dotted circles show that peripheral members join the care team temporarily.

both the charge nurse and the nurse with the bed assignment become the first core members of the ED patient care team for the patient. ED residents and attending physicians on duty will then be notified of the new patient through the electronic patient board displayed on a desktop computer. An available resident and an attending physician will coordinate the task and subsequently join the patient care team. The core members may call for services of other peripheral staff for ad-hoc collaborations based on the patient's condition. For example, the ED nurse may call a float nurse to temporarily join the care team to help with drawing a blood sample. But the float nurse would typically leave the team as soon as the task is completed so that s/he will be available for work requests from other care teams.

The unpredictable arrival of patients and the variability in severity of their illnesses complicate the formation of ED care teams (Figure 2). Specifically, an ED nurse is often a core member of 4-5 patient care teams simultaneously. Similarly it is not unusual that a resident is accountable for 6-7 patient care teams concurrently and attending physicians are generally involved in an even greater number of care teams. Overall, the charge nurse is a core member to all the patient care teams and is the key coordinator for expediting overall patient flow in the ED.

The underlying team dynamics poses considerable challenges to achieving effective communication. First, the team members are often spatially distributed. Residents and attending physicians usually work in the physicians' charting room and nurses are often found in a patient room or a nursing station. Such spatial separation makes communication between care team members difficult. Thus spatial movement becomes necessary during team collaborations. Moreover, care team members, particularly those of different roles, often work in different shift cycles and temporal horizons [24], adding more challenges to the team formation and reorganization process. This is aggravated by the temporary join-in of peripheral members such as a float nurse and an ED technician. Lastly, the research site being a teaching hospital further complicates the communication process. The involvement of both residents and attending physicians, who have different authorities and responsibilities bound by generally ill-defined work structure [24, 29], in the patient care teams undoubtedly increases the complexity of doctor-nurse and doctor-doctor communications.

ED nursing communication

ED nurses have to constantly communicate with different care team members in order to stay aware of patient care progress within the collaborative work. Consequently, nurses often proactively talk to the charge nurse, residents and attending physicians to obtain updated patient care plan.

Communication channels

Communication technologies in the ED include overhead paging, alpha paging, mobile phones, and stationary phones; face-to-face communication is also common during work. Although other artifacts such as patients' medical records and digital patient boards are also used for communicating important medical information among clinicians, in this paper we only focus on verbal communication behaviors among care team members. The channels through which verbal communication takes place and their typical use by the ED nurses are described in more detail in the following scenario.

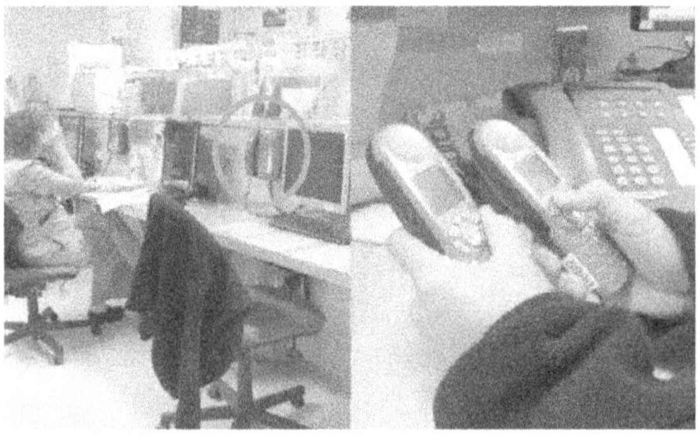

Figure 3. Communication devices at ED – Overhead page and stationary phones (left, in a circle), and mobile phones (right)

Sandy, an ED nurse from ED1, received a call to her ***mobile phone*** *from Sylvia, the charge nurse, and was notified that a patient would be admitted to bed #3. After having examined the patient, Sandy broadcast an* ***overhead paging*** *to the entire ED to request a technician. Soon after,*

David, an ED resident, came to examine this patient. On his way back to the physician's charting room, David briefly stopped by the nursing desk to inform Sandy his initial treatment plan. While Sandy was preparing the orders, she called the radiology department using ***a stationary phone*** *to check the radiology schedule for another patient. When she found out the radiology services were behind schedule, Sandy sent a text message through* ***alpha paging*** *along with her number to Cathy, a resident in another department, to ask her to call back.*

As shown in this scenario, each communication channel has its typical usage: overhead paging for broadcasting impending arrival of ambulance and conveying messages to a particular personnel or a target group; alpha paging for reaching people outside the ED such as an interpreter or a non-ED physician; stationary phones for inquiring about patient situation by other departments and receiving calls in response to alpha paging; mobile phones for reaching ED staff such as technicians, the charge nurse or physicians; and face-to-face interaction for getting immediate response.

Specifically, the mobile phones used in the ED are similar to those available for everyday use (Figure 3: right) except that there is no caller ID feature, nor does it keep a record of incoming calls. Mobile phones are randomly distributed to each ED nurse, physician, and technician at the beginning of a shift and must be returned at the end of their shift. Thus, each person's mobile phone number may vary in different shifts. As such, the charge nurse usually displays a paper list of phone numbers with respective staff's name in the nursing station at the beginning of a shift.

Additionally, a drawback of the overhead paging is that it fails to reach some of the areas in ED3 such as patient rooms in the corner.

Challenges to effective communication

Our study reveals new challenges that are present in the ED that need to be addressed so that nurses can more effectively communicate and collaborate, in addition to those already reported in previous literature [3, 24].

Frequently changing collaborative teams. The need for frequent assembly and subsequent disassembly of patient care teams in the ED poses major threat to effective communication. With the typically high turnover of patients in the emergency medicine setting, each care team member has to frequently adapt to the changing configuration of collaborators for individual care teams that s/he is involved in throughout a shift. Despite the availability of electronic patient boards for identifying the frequently changing collaborators, this information can only be gathered by examining individual patient lists for each ED unit rather than the arrival of patients, which poorly supported the rapid reconfiguration of team members .

Spatial movement for collaboration. Despite the availability of a variety of communication technologies described above, collaboration with spatially distributed and highly mobile personnel in the time-critical ED setting is no trivial task. In a loosely formed patient care team as shown above, the ED nurses communicate with a variety of people, both in and outside of the ED. The people they communicate with are either the core team members or peripheral members in the patient care teams that a nurse simultaneously participates in. Collaborating with many different medical staff who are not always collocated is particularly challenging. To cope with this, some medical staff choose to physically move to their team members' default working area, e.g., the charge nurse spends most of her time in ED1. However, this strategy does not always guarantee one to timely find team members, since medical practices are highly mobile such that ED staff often move around while carrying out their work.

Temporal coordination of collaborative tasks. Coordination of medical work is further complicated by varying shift cycles, temporal horizons, and job nature of collaborators. For instance, the ED nurses and residents have different shift cycles. ED nurses work on 12-hour cycles whereas their bed assignment usually changes every 4 hours. The residents have varying lengths of shift from 8 to 12 hours with different starting times depending on the length of the shift. Thus, the residents may have to work with different nurses for a single patient during a shift, causing troubles in communicating and recognizing team members in loosely formed team collaborations.

Unpredictable interruptions. Since ED work often deals with unexpected and emergent situations, it is almost impossible to foresee and plan for a patient's visit ahead of time. Because of this, interruptions are inevitable in nursing work. Consequently the need to manage these unpredictable interruptions, from both perspectives of being an interrupter and an interruptee, increases the complexity in ED communication. The ED nurses have different strategies to manage interruptions: pausing current task to respond to an interruption, taking notes as a reminder to respond later, or asking a colleague to handle the interruptions.

Coordination across multiple care teams. The communication challenges described above only evolve around a single patient, hence a single patient care team. However, when these challenges are extended to multiple patients and across multiple care teams, the complexity in communication and work coordination become highly intertwined and present amplified challenges to effective communications. Our analysis shows that the available communication technologies in the ED support certain aspects of collaborative work but none of them can address the complexities of communication needs in the loosely formed collaboration dominated in the ED.

Supporting communication in loosely formed patient care teams

Our analysis identified three key factors that are important to ED nurses' communication within the loosely constructed team collaboration process. They are: maintaining awareness within a team, making informative interruption, and supporting role-based calling. Table 1 summarizes our analysis on if and how these three key factors are being supported by the communication channels described earlier.

	Overhead paging	Alpha paging	Stationary phone	Mobile phone	Face-to-Face conversation
Team awareness	++	+	x	x	+
Informative interruption	++	++	x	x	++
Role- based communication	+	+	x	x	x

Table 1. Varied support of communication channels on ED communication needs
(++ : Good Support, + : Partial Support, x : No Support)

Maintaining team awareness

The loosely formed nature of collaboration makes it challenging to maintain awareness of patient care plan and progress among team members. Since each care team is made up of a different configuration of personnel who are often spatially distributed over the ED, it is not easy to maintain a natural awareness of individual teams' operation and the respective patients' status. Our observations also showed that nurses were often required to actively seek information in order to stay aware of the collaborative work. The following scenario shows how a nurse sought to maintain awareness in her care team.

Kate, an ED2 unit nurse, called Tyler, a resident, to update him on a stationary phone call from Internal Medicine that a patient in bed #17 needed a CAT scan. Tyler did not answer so Kate sent him an alpha paging instead. She also needed to update Joan, the charge nurse, to arrange a float nurse and a technician to transport the patient to the Radiology Department downstairs. Joan was passing by ED2 at that moment so Kate stopped her and gave her a verbal update. Joan also told Kate right there that she would look for relevant personnel to take the patient for a CAT scan.

In this scenario, Kate employed several communication channels to try to reach the patient care team members. After failing to reach Tyler at his mobile phone, Kate chose to send an alpha paging so that Tyler would get to the message on his pager later. Kate also grasped the opportunity to have a face-to-face conversation with Joan while she was walking by the unit. In this way, Kate was able to off-load the task of making arrangement for taking a patient for CAT scan to Joan. This scenario shows how spatial distribution, as part of the nature of loosely formed collaborations, is inherently challenging for achieving effective communication. In turn, this challenge aggravates the already loaded nursing work.

Among the communication technologies used in the ED, nurses generally prefer alpha paging to mobile phone since alpha paging will leave records in recipient's pager and it also offers the benefit of *plausible deniability* [20] such that the recipient may postpone responding if s/he is busy at the time when the message arrives. Regardless, face-to-face conversation is often the most preferred channel as it allows direct communication and clarification, as well as getting immediate feedback. Thus, it is not uncommon that nurses make purposeful trips in the ED in order to talk to other team members directly.

On the other hand, overhead paging is frequently used for broadcasting announcements in the ED. It provides rich workplace awareness to all the ED personnel. However, the broadcast nature of the overhead paging may also distract personnel who are not the intended recipient of the message and may be interruptive to other ongoing patient care. The following quote from Brian, an ED nurse, reflects the potential distraction caused by overhead paging.

"...I try to listen to every announcement from overhead paging since I may need to hurry up and help someone."

Informative interruption

Interruptions are inevitable, and sometimes excessive, in ED practices [18]. A simple case is when a new patient is assigned to a bed while the nurse responsible for the assigned bed is busy caring for other patients. In this case, the nurse is notified of, thus interrupted by, the arrival of the new patient. The emergent nature of the ED work makes it ever more important for nurses to constantly re-prioritize their tasks in response to the unpredictability of ED patient care [4]. However, such information, pertinent to interruptions emerged in the course of care, that is needed for task prioritization is not always available. This lack of information appears to be a barrier to effective communication and quality patient care.

Paul, a nurse in ED1, was at bed #5 drawing a blood sample from the patient. His mobile phone vibrated. Not knowing what the call was about, he decided to ignore it, unaware that it was in fact an emergency call to help with a critically ill patient in another room.

This scenario clearly shows the importance of conveying the content of an interruption to nurses so that they can decide whether to respond to the interruption or not. We refer to this need as *informative interruption* in this paper. Informative interruption could have made a difference to the nurse's response to the incoming phone call in the above scenario, which in turn impacted the quality of patient care. Although the lack of caller ID display on mobile phones used in the ED may seem to be the primary cause for this ineffective communication, it is important to note that even if there was a caller ID, the nurse still would not know the content and the urgency of the interruption. Besides, the callee may also be occupied with both hands so that checking caller ID is not possible. Therefore, a caller

ID can offer some improvements but it does not solve the problem.

Instead, informative interruption can be achieved through the use of overhead paging. It however renders itself an interruption to the already highly interrupted ED work practices.

Sandra, a float nurse, heard an overhead paging that a trauma patient would be arriving in 10 minutes. She was taking vital signs of a patient for another nurse, Diana, in ED1. Knowing the imminent arrival of a trauma patient, Sandra quickly documented the measurements and updated Diana before rushing to the trauma room to receive the arriving patient.

Overhead paging, in this case, offers clear benefits in communicating important information to Sandra who can then make informed decisions on how to respond to the unexpected new task. Knowing the content of the interruption allowed her to mentally plan and adjust her workflow accordingly. Nevertheless, while overhead paging offers informative interruption to Sandra, it also creates unnecessary interruption to other ED staff who were not involved in treating the incoming patient.

On the other hand, the informative interruptions can sustain the professional image of nurses in front of patients as patients may not understand that the mobile phone is used for work-related communications, instead of personal matters. To illustrate, Irene, an ED nurse, expressed that,

"...when you are at the bedside with the patient, it [the mobile phone] rings; you pick it up to answer it. Sometimes they may think it's rude. I don't think the patients know it's a work phone. I think they think it's a personal phone. Or it's ringing, ringing, ringing and you are in the middle of doing IV. The patients can go like 'okay it's ringing.' So that is a problem!"

As evident in our study, informative interruption allows nurses to plan their work in response to interruptions, and uphold their professionalism in front of patients. Since unlikely can interruptions be entirely avoided in the ED, it is thus useful to make interruptions as informative as possible without creating an overly disruptive environment and revealing any confidential patient information.

Role-based communication

In medical care, services are often required from a specialty or an expertise rather than a particular individual. In other words, any individual in that specific role will be able to fulfill the requested task or service. Float nurses are a typical example: when an ED nurse needs help with her patient care tasks, any of the available float nurses would be qualified to provide the needed service. Similarly, any available technician can perform an EKG test. This unique practice indicates that the ED communication may rely on specific working roles, instead of individuals. Nevertheless, current communication channels do not provide sufficient support for the role-based work coordination, as indicated in the following case.

Barbara, an ED nurse, needed an EKG at bed #8. She looked at the list of mobile phone numbers and called Kevin, the first technician on the list. Kevin answered that he was with a patient for a CAT scan. Barbara then called Thomas, the second one on the list. He did not answer. Next, she called Carlos who was available.

Apparently mobile phones failed to support desired role-based calling as shown in the scenario. The targeted point-to-point mobile phone calls can be time-consuming when repeated phone calls are needed. Moreover, this has led to an uneven workload distribution since the person at the top of the phone list was always called first, as observed in the study. Thus, to utilize these limited resources more effectively and efficiently, a system should ensure that people in specific roles are aware of and able to promptly coordinate and distribute work requests to a particular role, since a fair distribution of work is essential for sustaining job satisfaction and team morale.

On the other hand, alpha paging and overhead paging can be used to reach recipients based on their roles. Alpha pager numbers are associated with recipients' roles. That is, an alpha page will be broadcast to all the personnel in the specific role as specified by the sender. Needless to say, overhead paging can easily convey messages to the targeted staff working in a particular position.

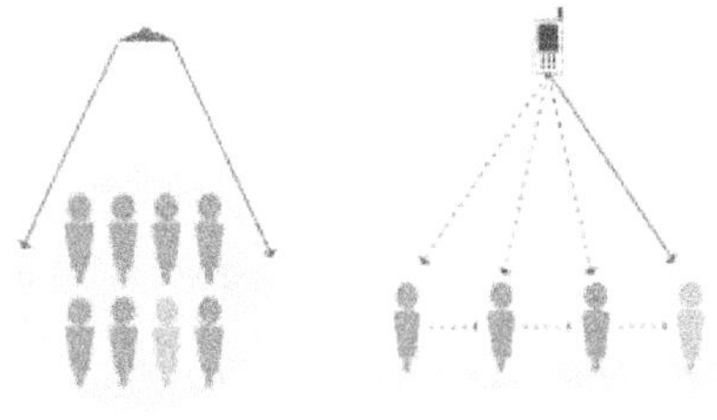

Figure 4. Role-based calling is well-supported by overhead paging (left), and poorly supported by mobile phones (right). Black and orange figurines represent people contacted, but unavailable and people available to work, respectively.

To revisit the above scenario where Barbara was looking for service of a technician, she could have made an overhead paging like *"EKG to bed 8 please."* Kevin and Thomas who were busy at the time would unlikely respond whereas Carlos who was available to take on a work request could then respond by bringing an EKG machine to bed #8 and carrying out the requested task. Nevertheless, without knowing who is available at the time, calling a specific role may cause multiple technicians rushing into the room or none of them reacts due to their unavailability. Therefore, although overhead paging and alpha paging can support role-based calling, they are also inherently limited and even leading to communication breakdowns in team collaboration process.

DISCUSSION

As we described earlier, the loosely formed collaborations challenge the use of traditional communication technologies in the ED. It becomes difficult to maintain team awareness while limiting unnecessary interruptions and miscommunications during work. In this section, we discuss two unique characteristics that we identified as critical issues to consider in order to maintain effective communication in loosely formed team collaborations: *explicit efforts to coordinate tasks* and *information transparency at interruptions*.

Explicit efforts to coordinate tasks

We have already described in the previous sections that the uniqueness of the ED patient care teams being loosely formed is attributed to a number of factors. These factors include ED staff concurrently engaging in multiple patient care teams while working in different shift cycles, their spatial separation as a result of the physical layout of the ED, and most importantly their lack of awareness of their collaborators in each patient care team that they belong to. Therefore, it is imperative for the ED staff to make explicit efforts to communicate patient care information with others for the purpose of coordinating and completing tasks.

To achieve explicit task coordination, role-based calling has been found to be useful such that all the ED staff of the same role will be notified of the same message all at once. In this way the requested task can be more promptly carried out assuming that one of the personnel is available to take on the task. However, role-based calling may decrease the efficiency of resource use when *redundancy of functions* [8] occurs. The problem lies in the lack of a feedback mechanism through which responses can be explicitly delivered to the sender. Thus an explicit feedback mechanism not only helps task coordination but also results in more balanced work distribution.

Information transparency at interruptions

Interruptions have been studied extensively in CSCW and HCI. Many of these studies analyzed interruptions in office settings [12, 21]. Nevertheless, these settings differ from an ED as interruptions in the former are not inherently part of the work practices while it is the case for the latter. In particular, the uniqueness of medical work heightens the complexities in interruption management when ED nurses are with patients. Findings from these previous work, thus, may not be applicable for the time-critical medical settings.

Previous research on interruptions taking place in EDs, reported that interruptions had adverse impacts on patient care work such as substantial threat to trains of thought and job efficiency, as well as contributing to job stress, fatigue, and sleep deprivation [10, 16]. Our work provides a different lens on how to deal with interruptions that interruptions can be utilized to support collaborative patient care work.

We have already presented in the findings section how informative interruptions can help facilitate the collaborative patient care work. By including useful but non-sensitive information with an interruption, people can better determine how and when to respond to interruptions. This can be beneficial not only to the ED personnel but also the patients. As found by Dearden, et al., patients often associate interruptions with potentially disruptive effect on consultation and show negative feelings [11]. Therefore if patients can hear the information and perceive its urgency when interruption occurs, they may believe that the interruption is legitimate and comes from a valid source. Otherwise, they may feel ignored in the middle of a procedure. It is expected that patients will be more receptive to inevitable interruptions even if the interruptions may require the caregivers to deviate their attention and respond immediately.

Since interruptions are inevitable in the emergency setting, it appears worthwhile to design mechanisms to reduce interruptions' potential negative impact while making them better perceived and handled in collaborative work, One way to do this is to increase the level of information transparency when interruptions occur. The degree of transparency is closely related to the amount and the content of information to be revealed to the intended recipient(s) along with an interruption. In essence, if the information within an interruption is appropriately transparent to its recipient, the interruption can facilitate a more informed decision-making or adjustment to a work plan. Our study found that the ED nurses preferred knowing the contents of interruptions so them to decide if they would stop their tasks at hand and respond to the interrupting tasks. This is also why many of them opted for overhead paging, since the message conveyed through overhead paging is transparent to all the ED personnel including its intended recipient. This allows the intended recipient to assess the urgency of the message associated with the interruption and to determine subsequent actions in response. Nevertheless, this transparency afforded by overhead paging may in turn become additional interruptions to the already highly-interrupted ED environment.

DESIGN IMPLICATIONS

Prior studies on communication technologies in medical collaboration presented various design considerations. For example, technologies should be designed to offer communication channels through which an individual can be easily reached by his/her collaborators while the individual can also flexibly adjust his/her availability when needed [26, 32]. On a similar note, the challenges identified in the current study suggest that more robust communication technologies are needed to support the loosely formed collaborative practices in the ED. Specifically, the design of such technologies should encompass the concept of "patient care team" as a unified recipient, rather than only designing for individuals. The goal is to support the intertwined yet complex communicative activities while also allowing individual patient care team members to stay aware of patient situation.

This section presents three design guidelines for supporting loosely formed collaborative practices.

Designing for team-based communication

A loosely formed patient care team allows each team member, including the peripheral members, to join and leave the care team spontaneously as necessitated by changes in patient care tasks or schedule, such as changes in patient reassignment after shift handover or ad hoc collaboration for emergent tasks. Consequently the challenge is to support communication that centers around a patient care team, as opposed to a single recipient or the entire ED staff. Thus the system should allow direct communication with a specific care team to support loosely formed teamwork. In this regard, training for effective teamwork behaviors would be beneficial to the ED staff, which was also reported in [19, 27]. In addition, technology should continually be explored and designed to support these teamwork behaviors.

Another advantage of the team-based design concept is that it supports directed communication to selected members, thus reducing interruptions that may be disruptive to other colleagues. To illustrate, this communication metaphor may be designed in such a way that when a nurse needs to reach the care team responsible for the patient in, e.g., bed #8, s/he can simply press 8 on her mobile phone and leave a verbal message. All the team members involved with patient care for this patient will then receive the information without having to broadcast the message to the entire ED.

Providing lightweight feedback

Our findings echo those identified in prior studies [22, 28] on how role-based communication could help facilitate communication in loosely formed collaborative environments. However, most current technologies that support role-based communication lack the functionality of providing lightweight feedback to the sender [26]. Feedback is important for work coordination so that the sender will know if the work request has been accepted, or the sender may have to look for alternative resources if no feedback is received. On the other hand, feedback is also useful [33] for the recipients working in the same role to coordinate their resources so as to minimize redundancy.

We have shown that it is important to provide lightweight feedback for supporting effective team-based work coordination. However how a feedback mechanism can be designed to be effective and lightweight is challenging. While initiating feedback can be quite easily achieved through, e.g., a simple button press, designing for receiving feedback is more difficult. Factors such as the communication channel used and the timing that feedback is delivered must be considered with prudence, since the arrival of feedback may otherwise present itself as an interruption, thus disruptive, to the recipient's work. Given the heavy workload in the ED, we propose using visual feedback such as pre-defined symbols or color coordination, or audio cues such as designated ringtones to maintain lightweight while less interruptive to support coordination in role-based communications.

Supporting informative interruption

While interruptions are indispensible in medical settings [18], we have already shown that appropriate level of information transparency that is associated with interruptions is crucial for the intended recipient(s) to make informed decisions on work plans, task activities, etc. Therefore when designing communication tools for these settings, it is important to consider how the intended recipient(s) will receive the information and how the content should be delivered so that an optimal degree of transparency is present while still protecting patient confidentiality. In the meantime, the design should also consider that the information communicated would be transparent enough to allow patients to understand the importance and urgency of the information and their caregivers have to promptly attend to other more urgent tasks. For example, communication devices can signal different ring tones based on the urgency of the tasks so both the nurses and patients perceive a sense of information transparency when using them. Nevertheless, the issues of information transparency with respect to how much, to whom and what kinds of information to reveal deserve further investigations.

CONCLUSION

In this paper, we investigated communication behaviors and the use of various communication channels by ED nurses in the context of their collaborative work practices. Our observations reveal a unique collaborative behavior that we term as "loosely formed team collaboration." Our analysis of the ED nurses' communication behaviors and their use of communication channels highlight the importance of maintaining team awareness, making informative interruptions and supporting role-based communication in the ED. Based on these findings, we suggest three guidelines for designing communication technologies for loosely formed collaborative teams: designing for team-based communication, providing lightweight feedback, and supporting information transparency. Beyond ED practices, loosely formed team collaborations are also present in many other work domains, such as firefighter practices [34] and temporary film projects [5]. The knowledge acquired in the current study may also contribute to a better understanding of more general communication and coordination behaviors in CSCW field.

ACKNOWLEDGEMENTS

We sincerely thank the medical staff at UC Irvine Medical Center for their participation. We also wish to acknowledge the inputs from Gloria Mark and Gary Olson to the study.

REFERENCES

1. Allen, D. Re-Reading Nursing and Re-Writing Practice: Towards an Empirically-Based Reformulation of the Nursing Mandate. *In Nursing Inquiry, special Centenary Issue, Wiley-Blackwell* 11, 4 (2004), 271-283.

2. Bardram, J.E. Temporal Coordination - On time and Coordination of Collaborative Activities at a Surgical Department. *Computer Supported Cooperative Work* 9, 2, (2000), 157-187.
3. Bardram, J.E., Bossen, C. Mobility Work: The Spatial Dimension of Collaboration at a Hospital. In *Proc. CSCW 2005*, ACM Press (2005), 131-160.
4. Bardram, J.E., T.R. Hansen. Why the Plan Doesn't Hold: a Study of Situated Planning, Articulation and Coordination Work in a Surgical Ward. In Proc. CSCW 2010, ACM Press (2010), 331-340.
5. Bechky, B. Gaffers, Gofers, and Grips: Role-Based Coordination in Temporary Organizations. *Organization Science* 17, 1 (2006), 3-21.
6. Berg, M. Accumulating and Coordinating: Occasions for Information Technologies in Medical Work. In *Proc. CSCW 1999*, ACM Press (1999), 373-401.
7. Beyer, H., Holtzblatt, K. *Contextual Design: Defining Customer-Centered Systems*. Morgan Kaufmann Publishers, Inc. San Francisco, CA, USA, 1998.
8. Cabitza, F., Sarini, M., Simone, C., Telaro, M. When Once is Not Enough: the Role of Redundancy in a Hospital Ward Setting. In *Proc. GROUP 2005*, ACM Press (2005), 158-167.
9. Chen, Y. Documenting transitional information in EMR. In *Proc. CHI2010*, ACM Press (2010), 1787-1796.
10. Chisholm, C.D., Collison, E.K., Nelson, D.R., Cordell, W.H. Emergency Department Workplace Interruptions: Are Emergency Physicians "Interrupt-Driven" and "Multitasking"? *Academic Emergency Medicine*, 7, (2000), 1239-1243.
11. Dearden A, Smithers M, Thapar A. Interruptions during General Practice Consultations—the Patients' View. *Fam Pract.* 13, (1996), 166–169.
12. González, V. M., Mark, G. Constant, Constant, Multi-tasking Craziness": Managing Multiple Working Spheres. In *Proc. CHI 2004,* ACM Press (2004), 113-120.
13. Heath, C. and Luff, P. Collaboration and Control: Crisis Management and Multimedia Technology in London Underground Line Control Rooms. In *Proc. CSCW 1992*, ACM Press (1992), 69-94.
14. Hendrich, A., Chow, M.P., Skierczynski, B.A., Lu, Z. A 36-hospital time and motion study: how do medical-surgical nurses spend their time? The Permanente Journal 12, 3 (2008), 25-34.
15. Horsky J, Gutnik L, Patel VL. Technology for Emergency Care: Cognitive and Workflow Considerations. In Proc. American Medical Informatics Association Symposium 2006. Washington, DC, 2006. 344-348.
16. Hymel, G., Severyn, F. Typical Shiftwork Interruptions Faced by Supervising EM Faculty in an EM Residency Setting. *Society for Academic Emergency Medicine Midwest Regional Meeting*, Ann Arbor, MI, Sept 1999.
17. Luff, P., Heath, C. Mobility in Collaboration. In Proc. CSCW 1998, ACM Press (1998), 305-314.
18. Melby, L., P.J. Toussaint. Coping with the Unforeseen in Surgical Work. *International Journal of medical informatics.*
19. Morey, J.C., Simon, R., Jay, G.D., et al. Error Reduction and Performance Improvement in the Emergency Department through Teamwork Training: Evaluation Results of the MedTeams Project. *Health Serv Res* 37, (2002), 1553–81.
20. Nardi, B. A. and Bradner, E. Interaction and Outeraction: Instant Messaging in Action. In Proc. CSCW 2000, ACM Press (2000), 79-88.
21. Norman, M. S., Mark, G. Communication chains and multitasking. In *Proc. CHI 2008*, ACM Press (2008), 83-92.
22. Paul, S.A. and Reddy, M.C. Understanding together: Sensemaking in collaborative information seeking. In *Proc. CSCW 2010*, ACM Press (2010), 321-330.
23. Reddy, M.C., Dourish, P., Pratt, W. Coordinating heterogeneous work: Information and representation in medical care. In *Proc. ECSCW 2001*, 239-258.
24. Reddy, M.C. and Dourish, P. A Finger on the Pulse: Temporal Rhythms on Information Seeking in Medical Work. In *Proc. CSCW 2002*, ACM Press (2002), 344-353.
25. Ren, Y., Kiesler, S., Fussell, S. Multiple Group Coordination in Complex and Dynamic Task Environments: Interruptions, Coping Mechanisms, and Technology Recommendations. *Journal of Management Information Systems*, 25, 107-133.
26. Richardson, J.E. and Ash, J.S. The effects of hands-free communication device systems: communication changes in hospital organizations. *J Am Med Inform Assoc* 17, (2011), 91-98.
27. Risser, D.T., Rice, M.M., Salisbury, M.L. The Potential for Improved Teamwork to Reduce Medical Errors in the Emergency Department. *Annals of Emergency Medicine 34*, 3 (1999), 373–383.
28. Sarcevic, A., Palen, L.A., Burd, R.S. Coordinating Time-Critical Work with Role-Tagging. In *Proc. CSCW 2011*, ACM Press (2011), 465-474.
29. Strauss, A.L. *Social Organization of Medical Work.* University of Chicago Press, Chicago, IL, USA, 1985.
30. Suchman, L.A. Office procedures as practical action: Models of work and system design. ACM Transactions on Office Information Systems 1, 4 (1983), 320-328.
31. Tang, C. and Carpendale, S. An Observational Study on Information Flow During Nurses' Shift Change. In Proc. CHI 2007, ACM Press (2007), 219-228.
32. Tang, C. and Carpendale, S. A Mobile Voice Communication System in Medical Setting: Love it or Hate it? In Proc. CHI 2009, ACM Press (2009), 2041-2050.
33. Tjora, A.H. Maintaining Redundancy in the Coordination of Medical Emergencies. In *Proc. CSCW 2004*, Workshop on Social Networks. Sheridan Printing Company. (2004).
34. Toups, Z.O. and Kerne, A. Implicit coordination in firefighting practice: Design implications for teaching fire emergency responders. In Proc. CHI 2007, ACM Press (2007), 707-716.
35. Tucker, A.L. The Impact of Operational Failures on Hospital Nurses and Their Patients. *Journal of Operations Management*, 22, 2, (2004), 151-169.
36. Vastenburg, M., Keyson, D. Ridder, H. Considerable Home Notification Systems: a Field Study of Acceptability of Notifications in the Home. *Personal Ubiquiting Computing* 12, (2008), 555-566.
37. Xiao, Y., Lasome, C., Moss, J., Mackenzie, C.F. and Faraj, S. Cognitive properties of a whiteboard: A case study in a trauma centre. In *Proc. ECSCW 2001*, 259-278.
38. Zerubavel, E. *Patterns of Time in Hospital Life.* University of Chicago Press, Chicago, IL, USA, 1979.

Electronic Medication Management – A Socio-technical Change Process in Clinical Practice

Torbjørg Meum
Telemedicine and e-Health research group.
University of Tromsø.
P.O Box 35, 9038 Tromsø
Torbjorg.meum@uit.no

ABSTRACT
This paper presents a workplace study of the implementation and use of an electronic medication management system (EMMS) at a university hospital in Norway. The strategic plan at the hospital was a fully computerized medication process that included a new application in the electronic patient record (EPR), as well as a fully automated packaging, dispensing, and distributing system using robot technology. A breakdown in the initial phase of the implementation project opened "Pandora's box" and helped visualize the relationship between coordinative practices and artifacts that took place in the new medication management process. Specifically, this paper highlights the redesign of the EMMS as a consequence of the breakdown that led to the development of an electronic chart. Furthermore, the paper characterizes this change process as a transformation in a socio-technical (material) network in which adjustment and innovation are ongoing processes in daily practice.

Author Keywords
Electronic Patient Record, Electronic Medication Management System, Information Infrastructure, Standardization, Change Management

ACM Classification Keywords
H5.m. Standardization, Computer-supported cooperative work

General Terms
Documentation; Performance; Standardization.

INTRODUCTION
Cooperation and collaboration are generally an inherent part of everyday practice in health care, but the technologies that support these practices are still inadequate. Seamless integration and continuity of care processes are prominent objectives of health care policy strategies in which ICT is seen as a means of increasing efficiency and effectiveness [19]. Implementation of an electronic patient record (EPR) has been a priority in Norway and is more or less in use in all hospitals. However, increased specialization, as well as development in medical technology, has involved increased use of specialized decision-support systems that exist side-by-side with EPR. Moreover, paper-based documents are still in use as a supplement, or due to lack of functionality in the EPR, which leads to increased fragmentation. Thus, the national aim of an integrated EPR has not yet been achieved, as it does not support primary activities in clinical practice, such as medication management.

Over the past few years, there has been increased attention on medication management, particularly from research fields in medicine and medical informatics. Medication errors in hospitals are common, and studies have shown that the use of new technology has reduced the incidence of serious errors [24]. Although the use of new technology is a promising strategy to support medication management, such systems have not yet become widely available. Some of the difficulties are the complexity of the medication process. The transition from paper-based to computer-based support of this process is not a straightforward matter, as it involves core activities in clinical practice and encompasses many aspect of patient care. In addition, it involves collaboration between different professions, is distributed across time and space, and is an interplay between multiple tasks and supporting artifacts.

Previous studies of computer-based systems to support medication management have focused mainly on singular technologies, such as computerized physician order entry (CPOE) and barcode verification. In contrast, the focus of this study has been on the whole process of medication management as an integrated part of EPR. This implies a high degree of standardized applications and procedures, as well as integration with an existing portfolio of information systems and practices, the so-called installed base [14]. It is, thus, interesting to explore what such a computerized system does in relation to clinical practice, collaboration, and coordination of work, and it touches on some of the key issues within CSCW. Similar studies have illustrated how the implementation and use of computerized systems is a negotiation between local practice and standardized systems [7], that there are implicated trade-offs and dilemmas [4], and how standards transform work practice through their coordinating roles [29].

The empirical material draws on an ethnographically inspired case study of the implementation and use of an electronic medication management system at a university hospital in Norway. The hospital moved into new facilities in 2008, and a priority in the planning and construction of the new "digital hospital" was to use leading-edge technology to improve patient care and hospital efficiency, including an automated medication management system. Implementation of this highly standardized electronic system was quite ambiguous and revealed a gap between pre-defined plans and challenges in daily practice. Therefore, the system was withdrawn after a short period of use and changes were made, including a redesign and development of a new electronic chart. An interesting question, then, is *what* kind of mechanisms enabled this change process (transformation) and *how* the interplay (interrelation) among technical, social, and material artifacts involved reconfiguration of the system. This paper contributes to an improved understanding of the transformative power of technology in use and characterizes this as an ongoing improvised process of change in relation to socio-technical (material) affordance and constraints.

The structure of the paper is organized as follows: it starts with a brief theoretical description of information infrastructures, standardization, and integration, and characterizes medication management as part of a socio-technical network. This section is followed by a description of the methodological approach, and then a chronological case describing the different phases of implementation, redesign, and use of the electronic medication management system. The next section provides a discussion of some major and subtle changes that emerged after use. Finally, the paper concludes by conceptualizing these changes as situated improvisations in a cooperative infrastructure, as well as the practical and theoretical implications for CSCW system design.

THEORY

From singular tool to network of artifacts

Prior studies of CPOE systems have focused mainly on specific tasks, such as prescription and administration of medication, supported by applications in the EPR or as stand-alone systems [1, 16]. In the CSCW field, the focus has been on single-user and groupware applications, such as workflow systems and decision-support applications [11]. However, in line with the increased use of computers as an embedded part of everyday practice, the scope of cooperative practices has also moved from singular tools to a network of artifacts. As stated by Schmidt and Wagner (2004), *"Contemporary cooperative ensembles depend heavily on a range of highly specialized, standardized coordinative practices involving a concomitant repertoire of equally specialized coordinative artifacts"* [26, p. 351]. In their study of architectural work, Schmidt and Wagner emphasized the complex interrelationship between these classes of artifacts and practices, labeling these clusters as "ordering systems." A similar study in health care highlights the generative power of information technology and emphasizes the mutual shaping of work practice and formal tools that emerge in the interrelation of staff and artifact activities [2]. More recent studies in the field of CSCW have emphasized cooperative practices and artifacts as part of an information infrastructure [3, 9, 14]. What these studies have in common is that they explore different types of "ordering systems" (e.g., medication, laboratories, radiology) and highlight the ongoing work that actors and artifacts undertake to obtain a stable, cooperative arrangement in an interconnected, socio-technical network [1]. A similar study has explored the use of CPOE and also emphasizes the generating effect of communication, as well as transformation of the socio-technical network [1]. A common feature of these studies is that they have focused on different types of ordering devices. When we move the scope of analysis from ordering systems to include the entire medication process, from clinical assessment, to delivery and storage of medication, the complexity of the network also increases. Characterizing medication management as part of an infrastructure arrangement provides a framework for analyzing the dynamic interrelationship between cooperative practice and artifacts. It also blurs the boundaries between the EPR system and supporting artifacts and highlights the interrelation and transformative power of the socio-technical network.

Star and Ruhleder (1996) have defined some key properties that characterize *when* a system becomes an information infrastructure. They emphasize how infrastructure is embedded into other structures, social arrangements, and technologies. Furthermore, they describe infrastructure as a fundamentally relational concept that occurs in relation to organized practices [27].

"An infrastructure occurs when the tension between local and global is resolved. That is, ... when local practices are afforded by large-scale technology, which can be used in a natural, ready-to-hand fashion" (ibid p. 114).

Similar research has also emphasized the interrelated aspect of information infrastructures. These scholars emphasize the dynamic, heterogeneous socio-technical network in which a wide range of activities are supported and shared by a larger community [6]. Moreover, this implies that when we move the focus from a singular system to a socio-technical network, it involves some coordination mechanisms to interconnect the network.

Standardization—the backbone of information infrastructure

Infrastructure arrangement is considered to be the backbone of the management of large-scale information systems [18] and is the invisible glue that binds disciplines together [27]. Standardization and integration are key issues to consider in order to interconnect heterogeneous actors in the network, both human and non-human. Interaction between social and technical subsystems [6] or social and material practices [17] is an ongoing negotiation process to obtain stability. From this point of view, standardization is not just technical artifacts, such as programming language, communications protocols, and exchange format. Scholars within the socio-technical fields have defined standards as any set of agreed-upon rules for the production of (textual or material) objects [4], or as measures established by authority, customs, or general consent to be used as a point of reference [29,p. 24].

Timmermans and Berg (2003) distinguish between four types of standards used in infrastructure arrangements in health care. These standards range from specifications of social and/or technical components (design standards), use of classifications (terminological standards), specifications of results of specific actions (performance standards), and clinical practice guidelines (procedural standards)[29]. Their focus is on procedural standards and how *"proper deployment of procedural standards creates a synergy between staff members' embodied expertise and the tool's coordinating activity, in which expertise and coordination mutually reinforce each other*" [29, p. 78]. From these perspectives, standardization is a negotiation among technical artifacts, work practice, procedures, and so on. Similarly, standards may also be described as coordinative artifacts used as mechanisms of interaction to reduce the complexity of articulating cooperative work [25]. *"Coordinative artifacts concatenate and configure items in certain spatio-graphical ways. They are in the service of imposing order"* [26, p. 47].

Similarly, Carlile (2004) describes the processes of transferring, translating, and transforming as a framework to illustrate the complex movement of knowledge across boundaries [5]. The study illustrates how complexity increases as we move from a syntactic to a pragmatic boundary, and the increased effort required to share and assess domain-specific knowledge as circumstances at a boundary grow more complex. Moreover, another important feature of the socio-technical network that is often ignored is materiality, which involves an artifact's affordance [17].

"*Materiality matters for theories of technology and organizing because the material properties of artifacts are precisely those tangible resources that provide people with the ability to do old things in new ways and to do things they could not do before" (ibid. p. 161).*

From this point of view, the socio-technical dynamic also includes the specific ways in which the features of particular artifacts become entangled in the social practice of people's work, material affordance, and the workaround they develop to address material constraints [17]. Along similar lines, Suchman (2007) introduced the term "situated action," which emphasizes that *"every course of action depends in essential ways on its material and social circumstances"* [28, p. 70]. Related to this, Orlikowski points out the *"recursive intertwining of the social and material as these emerge in ongoing, situated practice*" [20, p. 1438]. She further points out the performativity of the socio-material ensembles and how it may produce intended and unintended outcomes. This illustrates some of the challenges of standardization and implies the need for mechanisms of adjustment to modify an artifact to situated action and to enable people to make dynamically complex systems work in practice. Workarounds and "gateways" are used to compensate for misalignment and/or to link different layers in the infrastructure together [13]. While "gateways" are often standardized, agreed-upon rules to interconnect different layers of the infrastructure [13, 14], workarounds may be ad hoc methods deployed by users of the computer system to fix problems or glitches in their work [23]. On the one hand, workarounds are considered as a prerequisite for maintaining integration and overcoming constraints imposed by a technology. [23]. On the other hand, the use of workarounds may involve additional work and adjustments [10] and may also illustrate the design-use gaps that emerge in the dynamic interaction of the socio-technical network. Of special interest in this case study is the transformative power of standardization, as well as mechanisms involving local adjustments and changes in the interplay between new technology and local diversity.

Change of information infrastructures

Implementation of large-scale information technology is often well grounded in strategic plans and decisions to achieve strategic objectives. In this stream of work, technology is treated as a specific and relatively stable tool to increase efficiency and effectiveness of work practice [12]. However, various studies have shown how implementations of new technology have co-constructed practices [8] and how technologies-in-practice emerge from the ongoing and situated interaction between users and technologies [20]. This illustrates some of the challenges of changing large-scale information systems. First, information infrastructures cannot be built from scratch, but are always developed by extending and improving the old one [13]. Second, representations of infrastructures are multilayered in such a manner that new layers are connected with existing ones, brought together to a larger unit, and become interdependent [13]. Third, it takes time to build an infrastructure, and it is an ongoing, evolving, and dynamic process.

However, applying new technologies to an environment is a major change process. Paramount objectives and needs have to be the driving force, and superior plans have to be adjusted to an iterative implementation process. In a world that is constantly changing, where technology plays a vital role in everyday practices, we need an approach to change management that not only measures "gains and losses" in relation to predefined plans. We need to look at change as a process where new opportunities, as well as challenges, arise in the dynamic interaction in the new socio-technical network.

Orlikowski and Hoffman (1997) have proposed an alternative way of thinking about technological change in organizations. They recognize change management more as an ongoing improvisation than a staged event and have proposed three different types of change: anticipated, emergent, and opportunity-based. In accordance with a socio-technical approach to management of new technology, the emergent and opportunity-based changes are characterized by spontaneous interaction with the new technology over time, and in response to unexpected opportunities [21]. Orlikowski (1996) further suggests a practice-based perspective on organizational transformation, which proposes changes as "enacted through situated practices of organizational actors as they improvise, innovate, and adjust their work routines over time" [22, p. 63]. This perspective on change highlights micro-level changes and the power of transformation that is grounded in the socio-technical dynamics. This view on change management is not an argument against the planned change model, but a complement to traditional theories by emphasizing innovation and a proactive approach to change [22]. Thus, it is specifically interesting to explore changes in large-scale information infrastructures, particularly considering the challenges of changing such systems (i.e., installed base) [13]. A key issue in balancing strategic plans with the co-evolving, improvised change model outlined above is to study the interrelation between social and technical (material) agency across development, implementation, and use of technology.

METHODOLOGY

The study applies the interpretive approach to case study research and aims at producing an understanding of the context of EMMS and the mutual influence between the system and its context over time [30]. The study is further guided by methodological principles outlined by Klein and Myers (1999) in terms of preparing the research questions, data collection, and analysis. First, selection of the case was motivated by the author's involvement in an ongoing, longitudinal research project on the implementation and use of EPR in Norway, with special attention to the documentation of nursing. Second, the empirical setting was selected because it was the first hospital in Norway that implemented EMMS as an integrated part of EPR and was, therefore, a continuation of existing research activities.

Research setting

The empirical setting investigated is a neurological department at a large university hospital in Norway. The hospital has approximately 6,000 employees and deals with 60,000 admissions each year. The hospital moved into a new building in 2008 and is one of Europe's most modern university hospitals. The use of new technology was a key issue during planning and construction of the new hospital, where the main objective was to use technology to promote organizational development and support work processes. The hospital has undertaken major efforts to standardize the hospital infrastructure for computer technology, such as EPR, EMMS, IP telephony, and automated transportation (robot technology). This study focuses on the implementation and use of EMMS and the electronic medical chart in the neurological department and traces the process as illustrated in Figure 1.

Fall 2008	"Big Bang" implementation of EMMS at all bed units
Fall 2008	Withdrawal of the system after ten days' use
Spring 2009	Stepwise implementation of automatic local storage of medication
Winter 2010	Pilot implementation of the medication module and Panorama clinical chart at one bed unit
Fall 2010	Step-by-step implementation of the medication module and Panorama clinical chart at the other department (ongoing process)

Figure 1. Timeline of the implementation of EMMS at the hospital

The electronic medication management system included a new medication module in the EPR, a logistics management information system at the pharmacy, and an automated packaging, dispensing, and distributing system. The EPR vendor played a key role in this process, as it is a leading provider of EPR systems in Norway and this project was an important strategy to expand its EPR portfolio. A medication module was developed first, followed eventually by an electronic chart (Panorama Clinical Chart) that was piloted in the neurological department.

The 29-bed neurological department provides care and treatment to patients with acute and chronic neurological diseases. The organization of work in the department is further divided into four-bed units, and a group of three or four nurses is responsible for each bed-unit during the day. The bed units are characterized by modern design, and the patient rooms are located in small units in close proximity to the nursing workstation to enhance the contact between patients and staff. Moreover, facilities such as local medication storage and a locking system for pneumatic dispatch are located between units for shared use. In this way, the bed units are designed to support collaboration, and they are provided with modern technology to increase efficiency in daily practice.

Data collection and analysis

The design and implementation of the EMMS has been a long process that started in 2005 and is still ongoing (see Figure 1). One of the key tasks in interpretive research is seeking meaning in the social and historical context [15]. To obtain a contextual understanding of the implementation process, data collection was conducted, which included a combination of archival documents, participant observation, and semi-structured interviews. First, various documents, such as strategy documents, minutes of meetings, evaluations, and e-mails were collected. Second, observations of design meetings between the vendor and the local project group (two meetings), user training (three sessions), and the use of the system in clinical practice (64 h) were conducted between February 2010 and April 2011. Participant observations focused on following actors and artifacts in the medication management process. This process included participation in morning meetings between physicians and nurses, medication administration by nurses, and related activities and material/technical artifacts used in work practice. Finally, various interviews were conducted to gain additional insight into the process. These included semi-structured interviews (one head nurse and one nurse), informal telephone interviews (one representative from the vendor and a project member from the hospital), and in situ interviews during the observation sessions. Data from the interviews were collected mainly to supplement and complement data from the observation studies. During the observations and in situ interviews, notes were taken and then transcribed, and semi-structured interviews were taped and then transcribed consecutively.

Analysis of data was based on the hermeneutic circle, which is a fundamental principle for interpretive research: *"The process of interpretation moves from a precursory understanding of the parts to the whole and from a global understanding of the whole context back to an improved understanding of each part"* [15, p. 71]. Using a hermeneutics approach, data collection and analysis were conducted in an iterative process. After each observation session, the field researcher took analytical notes that guided further data collection and literature searching. This process constituted emerging issues that provided a new understanding about the case [30]. Finally, data and the case were discussed with fellow researchers for purposes of critical thinking and reflection of the interpretation process [15]. This group of colleagues has extensive experience with research in the implementation and use of information systems in health care.

FINDINGS

Strategic decisions to streamline medication management at the new hospital

ICT has had a major impact during the planning and construction of the new hospital in terms of increasing efficiency and effectiveness, as well as ensuring seamlessness and continuity in the clinical care process. Standardization has been an important strategy for achieving the objectives of a functional hospital, and it includes the standardization of work processes, equipment, procedures, treatment lines, and documentation. Medication management has been a priority in this context and is a work process that involves cooperation among different professions, work practices, and technologies. In this study, we mainly use the concept EMMS to describe this process, as it covers the entire hospital medication cycle, including prescribing by doctors, review and dispensing of medication orders by pharmacists, and administration of medication by nurses. Traditionally, manual work processes and a paper-based medication sheet supported medication management at hospitals. First and foremost, the physician had to prescribe medication on the medication sheet. Second, the nurse needed to maintain a well-organized and available medication storage system to facilitate day-to-day medication administration. Maintenance of the medication storage system required daily review to ensure access of the most commonly used medications in the ward, as well as emergency preparedness. Ordering and delivery of medication from the pharmacy were performed by manual procedures. Paper requisitions were sent by internal mail to the pharmacy, which delivered drugs back to the ward via a porter. The last step in the medication process was the administration of the right medication to the right patient at the right time. For example, in the paper-based system, the nurse had to check the medication sheet to get an overview of the prescribed medication and specify the time that each medication was given to the patient. As illustrated, medication management involves a number of work processes that require collaboration and integration among various different actors. In the new information infrastructure at the hospital, a main objective was to standardize this process further by using new technology. Implementation of a medication module was a continuation of the EPR strategy at the hospital. For several years, the use of EPR has been a key player in the hospital's information infrastructure, and to computerize medication management was a strategy to complement the EPR portfolio. The strategy involved major change processes, as well as pioneering work. First, a new medication module was designed and configured to ensure the prescription and administration of medication. The work on the medication module was carried out as collaboration between the vendor of the EPR system and the hospital. Second, communication and coordination between the wards and the pharmacy were computerized. A fully automated packaging, dispensing, and distributing system (pill pick) were introduced by using robot technology and bar coding of unit doses, as illustrated in Figure 2.

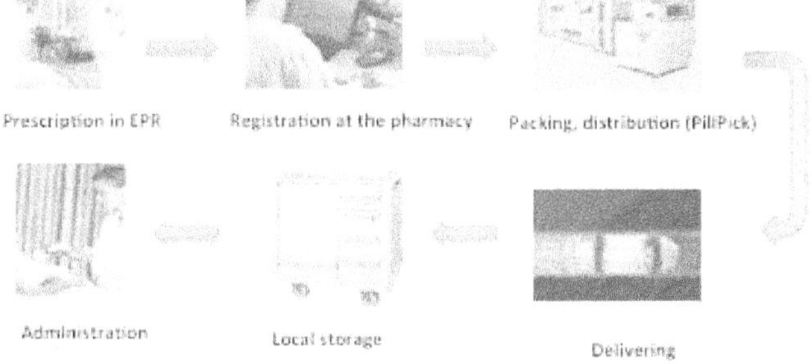

Figure 2. EMMS workflow

As briefly outlined above, the strategic plan to support the medication management workflow was highly ambitious.

All applications were thoroughly tested prior to implementation. Tests were conducted in both the test environment and the production environment. There were also integration tests between systems. After extensive testing, the system was put to use in 2008 in all units of the hospital. The EMMS and paper-based medication sheets were used synchronously to finally carry out an in situ test of the EMMS as an integrated part of daily work practices. The first step in the new work practice was the prescription of drugs that was supported by the new medication module in the EPR. The main objective of the prescription interface was to enable the prescription of drugs, as well as to provide an overview of current medications prescribed for the individual patient, the route of administration (how the medication should be given), and frequency (how often the medication is to be given). In addition, it provided decision support, such as access to Pharmacopoeia, which is the national consolidated catalogue of pharmaceutical compounds marketed in Norway, as well as access to a drug interaction database. When the selected drug was enabled in the user interface, it appeared in the overview in the prescription interface in the medication module. Meanwhile, the prescription was transferred to the pharmacy computer system and then transferred to the distribution system for packaging in unit doses. This process was controlled by robot technology that distributed medication and delivered it back to the ward in unit doses via a pneumatic tube system. Medications were then stored in a dispensing trolley until further administration. The dispensing trolley was designed to support the administration process, and there was one in place in each unit. Further medication management was carried out at the bedside; i.e., a trolley with a laptop was brought around to the patients where the drug was given. First, the nurse picked up the prepared medication from the pill dispenser. The next step was to enable the patient and the time field in the administration interface in the EPR system, where all drugs prescribed to the patient in the specified period were listed. The drug list was organized in tabular form and sorted by ascending date/time. Exceeded administration times were highlighted in red. By using the barcode scanner on the unit dose package and on the patient's wristband, the drug was recorded as delivered and removed from the list. The main purpose of using a barcode scanner was to support efficiency and accuracy of the medication process.

Moreover, the local electronic storage system was designed to support monitoring of daily supplies of medication. To gain access to the medication store, the nurse needed to use an identification card that served as a key to the storage system and have access to an application designed to support the overview of medication supplies, the location of medication, and so on. By scanning the medications that were removed from the local storage system, information was sent to the pharmacy so that they might send new supplies when needed.

This complex workflow system was implemented at all units in the hospital at once. However, experiences during the first ten days revealed various discrepancies, which led to termination of the pilot. Consequently, the new technology was taken out of daily operation and the hospital returned to the old paper-based procedures. The main reason for this termination was the discrepancy in the distribution of medication; the automatic packing machine failed to distribute the prescribed medication at the right time. This breakdown initiated re-establishment of two new projects: new strategies for automatic drug supplies and redesign of the medication management in the EPR system. The strategy was changed from a "Big Bang" to a more stepwise implementation in order to reduce the complexity of the information infrastructure, as well as the scope of users.

Re-establishment of computerized distribution and storage of medication

The breakdown of the automated medication chain was caused by various factors, not just the distribution system. It was, rather, that the process in general that did not work because of the complexity and heterogeneity of the actors involved. First, patient-specific drug administration involved frequent interruption of the nurses' work, as drugs delivered from the tube system frequently had to be picked up from the locking chamber. Second, the process required a more standardized schedule for prescribing medication, which is a challenge in daily practice. Third, employees at the pharmacy were assigned several new tasks, resulting in an increased workload. Along with the technological elements, it was a challenge to achieve seamless integration among the various actors in the new computerized process, which resulted in some delays and incorrect distribution of drugs.

Despite some of the above-mentioned challenges and the breakdown of automated medication management, efforts were immediately initiated to develop a new restrained strategy with a step-by-step implementation. Instead of patient-specific delivery of medication, the new strategy was initially aimed at computerized communication between the pharmacy and the local storage system. Thus, the "pill pick" system was used to facilitate the traceability of drug supplies. Most drugs were prepared in unit doses by the "pill pick" system and, as mentioned earlier, barcode scanning was put into use to record drugs that were retrieved from the local storage system. Simultaneously, another project initiated the re-design of the medication management in the EPR, as well as the use of barcode readers to support drug administration.

Redesign of the EMMS workflow

As mention above, a modification of the new strategy was not to include integration between the medication module in the EPR and the distribution system. After using the medication module in the EPR during the first project period, the experience showed that the application was a useful support in the medication management process. However, access to more clinical information in the application was requested in order to replace paper-based procedures. Information recorded in the medical chart is closely interlocked with the medication management process. For example, clinical information, such as blood pressure and fluid balance, are important pieces of information to have when prescribing cardiac medication. Although the electronic medication module was available across time and space, the staff still had to use the paper-based medical chart to gather clinical information as a support in the prescription process. Accordingly, key users at the hospital demanded additional functionality in order to support the work process. Demands from hospital management involved both challenges and opportunities for the vendor. On the one hand, functionality demands resulted in the development of a new user interface for graphical and numeric representation of clinical information. On the other hand, it gave the vendor an opportunity to expand its EPR portfolio. However, the vendor responded to the challenge and started working on the design and development of an entirely new interface for recording and visualizing clinical information.

The new user interface, called Panorama Clinical Chart, is an interdisciplinary and graphical user interface that provides the ability to integrate and visualize other information from EPR (e.g., medication, lab results) in one interface. In addition, it provides support for recording and displaying clinical parameters, such as blood pressure (BP), heart rate, temperature, and fluid balance.

The medical chart was designed and constructed in a step-by-step manner, and key users from the hospital participated in the project team. They provided input to the design process, and they verified and tested the new application. As learned from the initial project, the implementation was also carried out as a step-by-step process. Implementation of the new EPR modules (both medication modules and Panorama) was first conducted in a pilot ward in February 2010. Since then, several wards at the hospital have gradually adopted the system in a process that is ongoing.

Use of the computerized medication process in clinical practice

Panorama Clinical Chart has become a key player in the medication management process in the department. For example, it is used as a main source of information-seeking during the daily pre-rounds, which is a multidisciplinary meeting between physicians and nurses. During these meetings, they share clinical information and plan care and treatment. Usually, the physician navigates in the clinical chart to obtain an overview of medication, measurements, and so on. When it is decided to prescribe a new drug, it is easy to navigate to the prescription interface in the EPR.

While doctors mainly use the graphical interface in Panorama to seek information to support the decision-making process, the nurses are responsible for recording clinical information in the clinical chart. As such, clinical information such as BP and heart rate are available to all clinicians involved in the care team. In addition, the system provides an overview of medications and provides a more accurate accounting of when medications are actually given. It is also easy to scroll back and forth on the timeline to get an overview of the last hours or the last week. Thus, Panorama Clinical Chart provides an overview of clinical information and replaces the paper-based medical chart. Moreover, it is easy to navigate between the different interfaces and the clinical chart, thus, it supports the various steps involved in medication management. However, there have been local adjustments to the medication process and supportive artifacts.

Adjustments to local practice

At the start of the pilot, the dispensing trolley, laptop, and barcode scanner were used as a support in the bedside medication administration. The main objective with this bedside procedure was to ensure the five "rights" of medication administration: right patient, drug, dose, route, and time. However, it soon became apparent that this work process was cumbersome in daily practice. First, the size of the trolley was a challenge, and it was hard to move it in and out of patient rooms. Because all doors in the hospital are built in accordance with fire safety regulations, the doorstep is not easy to change. Second, many of the patients are not confined to bed, and it was cumbersome to move around with the trolley when a patient was in the bathroom, living room, and so on. Consequently, part of the medication process was changed, and the trolley was instead placed at the workstation in each unit, where part of the administration of medications currently takes place. Parts of the process are the same, but instead of using the barcode reader, the medication is taken out of the unit dose package and dispensed into a medication cup for each patient. Thus, nurses do not use the barcode on the unit doses in the administration process to verify the "five rights." Instead, they use manual procedures to verify medications and manual input in the administration interface to confirm that the medication is given to the patient.

Other adjustments also include the use of supportive artifacts, such as paper-based lists. For example, monitoring of fluid balance is a regular intervention in nursing, and a paper-based list is kept at the bedside for recording during the day. Nurses on night duty are responsible for summarizing the total amount of liquid given in a day, which was a straightforward task in the paper-based chart. However, this feature in Panorama Clinical Chart involves both benefits and disadvantages. On the one hand, fluid intake is automatically summarized, and medication fluids recorded in the medication plan are transferred to the fluid list in the clinical chart. On the other hand, they have to "fix and trick" to get an exact fluid balance. For example, intravenous infusions are summarized in the fluid balance at start-up time. When 1000 ml saline is recorded as being started at 10 p.m., the total amount is summarized in the fluid balance. At midnight, the nurse has to subtract the residual amount in the intravenous bag as fluid loss in order to obtain an exact fluid balance. Although the fluid balance is accurate, it is not true that the reminder of intravenous fluid is a loss.

Despite some of the challenges described above, the users are quite satisfied with the new computerized system. In light of experiences from the pilot department, hospital management has decided to implement the system in all departments during the next year. In the meantime, it is an ongoing process to optimize medication management, as well as further development of Panorama Clinical Chart.

DISCUSSION

The dynamic interaction in the new practice of medication management may be characterized as an ongoing cycle of design, use, and modification, in which coordinative practices and artifacts induced changes. Some key issues that will be further elaborated on are how the breakdown in the initial project involved innovation, and how adjustments and improvisation in everyday practice were a response to socio-material constraints and affordance.

The dynamics interrelation in the cooperative infrastructure

Several studies have illustrated the trade-offs and dilemmas of changing large-scale information infrastructures [3, 9, 14]. The power of the so-called installed base makes it difficult to change and control, due to its complexity and interconnectivity [14]. This includes not only hardware and software, but also the information itself that is embedded in the structures and processes of cooperative practices. However, the main aim of the implementation of new technology is to change and improve existing practices. As illustrated in this case, the implementation of EMMS involved a complex change process, although the changes were not in accordance with pre-defined plans. The new infrastructure arrangement of the medication process was a complex assemblage of hardware components, software applications, and standardized procedures that had to be aligned to support daily practice. Coordination mechanisms, such as standardization and integration, are essential to interconnect heterogeneous actors in the network [13, 25]. Just consider the whole range of different actors involved in the automated packaging, dispensing, and distributing system. This highly standardized process requires integration at multiple levels. For example, it involved changes in the work practice at the pharmacy, new procedures for local storage of drugs, fixed schedules for prescribing medications, and a new standardized practice for administration of medication. Thus, standardization was a negotiation among technical artifacts and procedures, as well as the skills and knowledge embedded in clinical practice. Moreover, use of standards transform the practice that they become part of and are a dynamic process of change [29]. The complexity of this infrastructure implies that it cannot be changed instantly, but co-evolves slowly over time [14]. As illustrated in this case, misalignment of the new infrastructure caused a breakdown, which in turn resulted in delays and a redesign of the whole system. As stated by a member of the project team, *"The technical system worked in a way; it was more the overall solution that was immature."* Although the technical system was tested in advance, the challenges and problems were only visualized when the new technology was implemented as part of coordinative practice. This illustrates the interdependent relationship between the components that constitute the new infrastructure arrangement. When one of them is changed, the others often needs to change as well [13]. Star and Ruhleder (1996) emphasize the relational aspect of infrastructures and also highlight that *"it becomes infrastructure in relation to organized practice"* (ibid. p. 113). Accordingly, the new medication management process was more complicated than anticipated and required adjustments to local practice in order to be "ready at hand."

Redesign as improvisation

One of the key dimensions of working infrastructures is the normally invisible quality that becomes visible upon breakdown [27]. The breakdown of the initial plan helped visualize the coordinative practice of the medication process, in which new emerging needs and opportunities led to the development of the Panorama Clinical Chart. This graphical user interface was not part of the pre-defined plan and was not a demand in the requirement specification. However, it was an emerging need that occurred in order to integrate the new medication module into the local work infrastructure, and it demonstrates the interrelation between the medication process and clinical information. In accordance with the improvisational model of change management described by Orlikowski and Hoffman (1997), this case illustrates how the breakdown in the project also uncovered new emergent needs and opportunities [21]. For example, one of the advantages of the new system was distributed access to information, as well as distributed coordination of work across time and space. Accordingly, the physician is able to prescribe medication to patients from all areas of the hospital as long as he/she has access to the computer system. Still, the decision process to prescribe medications is based on clinical assessments and clinical information, such as BP, fluid balance, and so on. To achieve seamless integration between clinical information and prescription of medications, there was an emergent need to integrate the medical chart into this process. However, this new requirement was a surprise to the vendor and was not part of the requirement specification. Yet, in order to complete the implementation of the new medication module, they chose to respond to user requirements and needs and developed the Panorama Clinical Chart. Despite some of the challenges, the process has been quite successful for both the users and the vendor.

The Panorama Clinical Chart has become an integrated part of the EMMS and is about to be implemented by all departments at the hospital. Moreover, it has become an important application in the vendor's EPR portfolio and has received high priority for further progress.

A socio-material reconfiguration

Changes and adjustments have also been realized in daily practice, and the new standardized procedure has been integrated into local practice. This means paying attention to how the new standardized practice is aligned with the coordinative practice, as well as paying attention to a new technology's material constraint and affordance. In this socio-material configuration, both the social and the material are considered as emerging, evolving, and intertwined [17, 22]. Improvised procedural changes emerged to accommodate their evolving use of technology [22]. Just consider how the use of the barcode reader was adapted to local practice. The use of a barcode reader was regarded as an improvement to ensure the "five rights" in the administration of medications. Barcode verification was not a replacement of the nurse's manual verification (medication, dose, and patient's identity), but an additional layer of safety. Hence, administration of medication was automatically documented in the interface in the medication module and provided some alerts if medication, dose, and patient's identity did not correspond. As illustrated in the case, the new verification process included various artifacts, such as a computer, barcode reader, dispensing trolley, and the organization of the work practice. The gradual reconfiguration of the new work practice evolved as a consequence of local adjustment. Both the material constraints mentioned in the case, as well as the organizing of the work practice, shaped workarounds to compensate for misalignments in the new infrastructure. Workarounds, such as bypassing barcode validation, were constituted through the relationship of materiality. Accordingly, the challenges faced included not only the difficulties of bringing the technical equipment to the patients, but also how it corresponded with the local work practice. Consequently, the material constraints caused interruptions in the new medication process, and the gradual improvisation of workarounds was a way to establish smooth coordination and get the work done in daily practice. This is what Leonardi and Barley (2008) calls a cascading pattern, and it demonstrates how work was tied to the technologies' materiality and the nature of affordance and constraints that the materiality provided [17].

Similarly, there have been other changes and workarounds. Clinical information, such as the fluid list, is recorded and stored in the Panorama Clinical Chart and provides an overview of fluid balance that is available across time and space to all members of the care team. However, they have to "fix and trick" to get the fluid balance accurate. Representation of fluid balance is not just a passive feature; the specific way in which the fluid list is filled in creates a brief history [2]. Input such as oral and intravenous fluid is set against fluid that "goes out," such as urine and wound fluid. This input and output provides valuable information that is "lost" in the new electronic chart. As a result, they still use a paper-based list to record fluid balance as a support in daily practice. Moreover, the paper-based list has some supportive features compared with the computer system. For example, it is easy to carry around and easy for all workers in the department to update. In comparison, the computer system is less mobile and requires a login procedure each time they use the system. This example illustrates the interplay between materiality and agency in cooperative practice and how the new practice emerges as a negotiation among coordinative artifacts. Some of the key constraints and affordances are difficult to anticipate in advance; they are more easily identified in daily practice. A key issue in this context is how new technology provides people with the ability to do old things in new ways and to do things they could not do before. This means paying attention to the material constraints and affordances of the new computerized systems and how workarounds arise and evolve to address material constraints [17]. Furthermore, medication management is based on clinical assessments of the patient's trajectory. Particularly when the patient suffers from severe organ failure, fluid balance is an important parameter of clinical assessment. This illustrates how the medication process is entangled with clinical information and how medication management is continually assessed and performed in relation to the interpretation of clinical information. The examples discussed above illustrate the dynamic interplay between materiality and agency across implementation and use of EMMS, and demonstrate some of the challenges to the further development of the Panorama Clinical Chart.

CONCLUSION AND IMPLICATIONS

This study illustrates the mutual interrelation between social and technical (material) artifacts in cooperative practice and how changes emerge in a dynamic interaction in the socio-technical network. The complexity of this network illustrates the difficulties of making pre-defined changes in cooperative practice, such as medication management. However, it is necessary to explore and unfold this complexity, because it is in the relation between cooperative practices and coordinating artifacts that changes are visualized. As illustrated, these changes were improvised in relation to social, technical, and material artifacts in an ongoing process. These findings have both theoretical and practical implications. First, they provide increased insight into how to manage and change information infrastructures. Second, the case illustrates how medication management is entangled with clinical information, and it suggests that further development of EMMS also includes an electronic medical chart. Finally, the case illustrates the transformative power activated by the dynamics in the socio-technical network and suggests that this feature is used as a resource in the further design and development of EMMS.

REFERENCES

1. Ash, J.S., Berg, M., Coiera E. Some unintended consequences of information technology in health care: The nature of patient care information system-related errors. *JAMIA*. 11, 2 (2004), 104-112.

2. Berg, M. Accumulating and coordinating: Occasions for information technologies in medical work.*Computer Supported Cooperative Work*.8, 4 (1999), 373-401.

3. Bossen, C., Markussen, R. Infrastructuring and Ordering Devices in Health Care: Medication Plans and Practices on a Hospital Ward. *Computer Supported Cooperative Work* . 19,6 (2010), 615-637.

4. Bowker, G., Star, S. *Sorting things out: classification and its consequences,* The MIT Press. Cambrigde, USA, 2000.

5. Carlile, P.R. Transferring, translating, and transforming: An integrative framework for managing knowledge across boundaries. *Organization Science*.15, 5 (2004), 555-568.

6. Ciborra, C. *From control to drift: the dynamics of corporate information infrastructures,* Oxford University Press, New York, USA. 2001.

7. Ellingsen, G., Monteiro, E. A patchwork planet: Integration and cooperation in hospitals. *Computer Supported Cooperative Work,* 12, 1 (2003), 71-95.

8. Ellingsen, G., Monteiro, E., Munkvold, G. Standardisation of work: co-constructed practice. *The Information Society*.23, 5 (2007), 309 - 326.

9. Ellingsen, G., Røed, K. The role of integration in health-based information infrastructures. *Computer Supported Cooperative Work,* 19, 6 (2010), 557-584.

10. Gasser, L. The integration of computing and routine work. *ACM Tranaction on Information System*.4, 3 (1986), 205-225.

11. Grudin, J. Groupware and social dynamics: eight challenges for developers. *Communications of the ACM*.37, 1 (1994), 205-225.

12. Hammer, M. Reengineering work: don't automate, obliterate,*Harvard business review*.68, 4(1990), 104-112.

13. Hanseth, O. The Economics of Standards. In: Ciborra C, From control to drift: the dynamic of corporate information infrastructures, Oxford University Press, New York, 2001. p. 56 - 70.

14. Hanseth, O., Lundberg, N. Designing Work Oriented Infrastructures. *Computer Supported Cooperative Work,* 10, 3 - 4 (2001), 347 - 372.

15. Klein, H., Myers, M.D. A set of principles for conducting and evaluating interpretive field studies in information system, *MIS Quarterly* 23,1(1999),67 -94.

16. Koppel, R., Wetterneck, T., Telles, J.L., Karsh, B.T. Workarounds to barcode medication administration systems: their occurrences, causes, and threats to patient safety. *JAMIA*.15, 4 (2008), 408-23.

17. Leonardi, P.M., Barley, S.R. Materiality and change: Challenges to building better theory about technology and organizing. *Information and Organization*.18, 3 (2008), 159-176.

18. Monteiro, E. Actor-Network Theory and Information Infrastructure. In: Ciborra C. From control to drift: the dynamic of corporate information infrastructures, Oxford University Press, New York, 2001. p. 71 - 83.

19. Norwegian Ministry of Social Affairs and Health, Interaction 2.0. National strategy for electronic cooperation in health sector 2008 - 2013. http:www.helsedirektoratet.no/samspill/

20. Orlikowski, W. Sociomaterial practices: Exploring technology at work. *Organization Studies*.28, 9 (2007), 1435-1448.

21. Orlikowski, W., Hoffman, D. An Imporvisational Model for Change Managment: The Case of Groupware Technologies. *MIT Sloan Management Review*.38, 2 (1997), 11 - 21.

22. Orlikowski, W.J. Improvising organizational transformation over time: A situated change perspective. *Information systems research*.7, (1996), 63-92.

23. Pollock, N. When is a work-around? Conflict and negotiation in computer systems development. *Science, Technology & Human Values*.30, 4 (2005), 496 - 514.

24. Poon, E.G., Keohane, C.A., Yoon, C.S., Ditmore, M., Bane, A., et al. Effect of bar-code technology on the safety of medication administration. *The New England Journal of Medicine*.362, 18 (2010), 1698 - 1707.

25. Schmidt, K., Bannon, L. Taking CSCW seriously. *Computer Supported Cooperative Work,*1,1 (1992), 7-40.

26. Schmidt, K., Wagner, I. Ordering systems: Coordinative practices and artifacts in architectural design and planning. *Computer Supported Cooperative Work* .13, 5 (2004), 349-408.

27. Star, S., Ruhleder, K. Steps toward an ecology of infrastructure: Design and access for large information spaces. *Information System Research*.7,1 (2000),111-134.

28. Suchman, L.A. *Human- Machine Reconfigurations,* Cambridge University press, New York, USA, 2007.

29. Timmermans, S., Berg, M. *The gold standard: The challenge of evidence-based medicine and standardization in health care,* Temple Univ Pr. Philadelphia, USA, 2003.

30. Walsham, G. Interpretive case studies in IS research: nature and method. *Eur JInf Systs* 4, (1995), 74 - 81.

Fragmentation and Choreography: Caring for a Patient and a Chart during Childbirth

Kathleen H. Pine
University of California, Irvine
226G Social Ecology I, Irvine, CA
khpine@uci.edu

ABSTRACT
CSCW has long been concerned with how work is coordinated. A rich body of literature examines the mechanisms underlying cooperative work and the articulation of discrete tasks into meaningful sequences of action. However, there is less treatment of how workers balance multiple streams of work at once. In hospitals, the introduction of Health Information Technologies coupled with increased requirements for documentation means that workers must simultaneously care for and integrate two work trajectories: that related to the patient and that related to the medical record. Using data from an ethnographic study of labor & delivery nurses in a mid-size hospital, I describe the situated, embodied, and effortful work of coordinating multiple streams of action into a single coherent performance of work, a process I refer to as choreography, and present a number of choreography practices. I then describe implications of this perspective for CSCW.

Author Keywords
Coordination; HIT; Documentation; Choreography.

ACM Classification Keywords
H5.3 Computer Supported Cooperative Work: Miscellaneous.

General Terms
Documentation; Design; Human Factors

INTRODUCTION
The field of CSCW has long been concerned with coordination of work. This paper expands on previous conceptualizations of coordination by describing a new type of coordination work, which I refer to as choreography. Choreography is the embodied work of balancing and maintaining multiple simultaneous streams of work and bringing them together into a single coherent stream of actions. I ground this theoretical proposition in ethnographic data focusing on how obstetrical nurses balance documentation work with patient care during childbirth.

This case provides an especially rich and timely context in which to examine choreography work. Documentation has long been a central feature of medical work [7,35]. Recently, documentation has been changing as an influx of Health Information Technologies (HITs) coupled with increasing regulation, legal pressure, and public demand for transparency and accountability of hospitals and medical providers has led to a profusion of documentation requirements [37]. The intensification of documentation requirements coupled with technological changes in the work system makes it increasingly difficult to balance and integrate documentation work with patient care.

This work contributes to CSCW and extends the literature on work coordination by describing choreography work. Work in general requires bringing multiple disparate tasks into a coherent sequence of actions. I analyze how nurses, through a variety of effortful embodied, social, and cognitive practices, choreograph the practice of documentation to manage competing work trajectories and goals. The rest of the paper is structured as follows; first, I ground my research in past CSCW studies on coordination. I then describe methods. In the finding section, I discuss the logics underlying the current documentation work system and describe how nurses engage in choreography practices both to produce a viable medical record and to integrate this documentation work with the work of caring for a patient during childbirth. I conclude by drawing out implications for CSCW research on supporting choreography of multiple work trajectories simultaneously.

BACKGROUND

Coordination in CSCW

Coordination is a central topic in CSCW research and a rich body of literature has contributed to our understanding of workplace coordination [see 14, 28, 29, 31 among many others]. Although coordination has been defined in multiple ways, three general postulates underlie research on workplace coordination: 1) people work collaboratively; 2) work is interdependent; and 3) this interdependent work is in the service of some particular goal or piece of work [25]. Schmidt [30] proposes a distinction between cooperative work and articulation work. The term cooperative work describes the technical (causal, temporal, and logical) connections between interdependent tasks. In contrast, articulation work as described by Strauss et al. [31] is the second-order work of coordinating and integrating tasks and clusters of tasks together in a meaningful way that will accomplish the intended goal. A number of mechanisms, or organizational arrangements that facilitate a collaborative performance [25], have been identified. These include routines [16, 17]; boundary objects [29]; and co-location [1], among others.

An important concept for the present research drawn from medical sociology [30] is that of "trajectories." Strauss uses the term trajectory to describe the physiological unfolding of a disease process along with the entire organization of work done over the course of a disease process and the impact on the people doing this work. Over the course of a single trajectory countless routines, artifacts, and rules are articulated in order to provide a course of treatment for a single patient. Therefore, the notion of trajectories provides a useful way for talking about the entirety of the coordination efforts and mechanisms that come into play in service of a collective piece of work.

Situated and Agentic Coordination

A pivotal development in research on coordination is the emergence of a perspective that focuses on the situated, emergent, and effortful nature of coordination [see for example16, 20, 28, 33]. Suchman [33] makes the point that action is necessarily situated and improvisatory; people often have a plan in mind of how to act but the plan is constantly re-adjusted based on the specifics of the situation at hand and the embodied skills and knowledge available to a person in a situation. In the medical world, articulation work involves maintaining control of a disease trajectory by both coordinating work along expected paths associated with a condition and also re-articulating as problems and interferences arise [30]. Another important contribution in understanding coordination is Feldman's [16] work on the performative aspect of coordinating. Focusing on routines as a coordination mechanism, Feldman demonstrates how people performing routines change courses of action through processes of ongoing reflection. The thoughts, feelings, and actions of people are resources that shape the performance of coordinated work on an ongoing basis.

Coordination and Multi-tasking

A rich body of work describes the mechanisms through which work is coordinated and the emergent, situated, and agentic nature of coordination work. However, much research up to this point has focused on how work is coordinated to pursue a single work trajectory; for instance, the complex articulation work required to collectively perform activities such as auditing an accounting invoice [32], driving a train [15], or caring for a patient with lupus [30]. A more recent body of literature examines the problem of work fragmentation, defined as "a break in continuous work activity" [22] and the ways in which information workers multi-task to accomplish multiple streams of action [19]. These studies, however, focus on characterizing the nature and frequency of interruptions and describing how people use information technologies to maintain continuity in multiple tasks. The present study draws on Suchman's [33] work on situated action and Feldman's [16] work on the role of agency in coordination. In contrast to previous studies on multi-tasking described above, the present study focuses on *choreography*, or the embodied, social, and cognitive practices of carrying out a situated and improvisatory performance that involves multiple trajectories of work.

METHODS

I used ethnographic methods consisting of observation and interviews with informants. A qualitative methodology is appropriate since the objective was to examine in intricate detail what people were actually doing and thinking, processes not readily apparent through other methods [11]. The Labor & Delivery (L&D) unit of H1 has 14 beds and approximately 55 nurses who work 12 hour shifts from 7AM to 7PM. About 1,000 deliveries per year occur in H1. H1 is well-equipped to handle both very high risk pregnancies and sick and premature infants, so the unit sees an exceptionally large number of high-risk cases.

I conducted observations in the L&D unit of H1 for 16 months for periods of time ranging from four to fourteen hours during all times of the day as well as at night. Observations took place once or twice per week, intersected by three four-week periods away from the field in order to reflect and analyze data. I also conducted observations of unit and hospital-wide staff meetings, daily rounds, Practice Council, grand rounds, computer documentation training sessions, and various other education and training activities. Field notes were recorded using pen and paper and typed after leaving the field in the manner described by Emerson, Fretz, & Shaw [13].

My informants include bedside nurses, charge nurses, nurse managers, and several other interdisciplinary personnel. I focused on the practices of nurses in relation to the larger context of the obstetrical team. I also conducted a focus group interview with twelve L&D nurses and nine formal semi-structured interviews with L&D bedside nurses, as well as interviews with nurse managers and others who work in or collaborate with L&D (see table 1 for a description of data collected).

I analyzed data using a set of steps outlined in grounded theory [11]. In grounded theory, data collection, data analysis, and theorizing occur continuously, and each activity overlaps and informs the others. One of the hallmarks of this approach is that as soon as researchers begin to tentatively form categories in the data, a process of constant comparison begins and all new pieces of information are held up against those that already populate the category; in this way, the researcher is pushed to challenge and refine their description of the phenomenon. Additionally, I used data analysis to guide future data collection as analysis pointed me towards categories and properties that required further development and explication [11]. Essentially, I used a process of reading through my interviews line by line performing open coding, then organized these codes into categories and went through my data again, coding according to the categories I had developed. During this process, I wrote extensive memos about key themes I saw emerging from the data, which I later refined through the process of writing. During data analysis, I presented my findings to participants, including the nurse manager and bedside nurses, in a series of informal conversations to contest findings and clarify pre-conceptions [21].

Observations. Observations were conducted in the labor & delivery unit of H1. Individual nurses were shadowed as they went about their work. The researcher observed all aspects of care, from triage through delivery (in a delivery room for vaginal births and in an operating room for surgical births).
Informal conversations. The researcher engaged in countless informal conversations with participants in H1 during fieldwork. These included conversations with nurses, nurse managers, residents, unit secretaries, scrub techs, anesthesiologists, quality analysts, nurse informatics workers, and others.
Interviews. Individual semi-structured interviews and focus groups of labor & delivery nurses were conducted with participants both from H1 and from a number of surrounding hospitals (conducted as part of preliminary field work). H1: L&D RN's (9) nurse managers (2) perinatal educator (1) medical students (4) resident (1) blood bank personnel (1) perinatal coordinators (2) focus group of L&D nurses and nurse managers (12 participants) Preliminary interviews conducted with participants outside H1: L&D RN's (6) physicians (3) nurse managers (3) nursing directors (3) certified nurse-midwives (2) public health official (1) focus group with L&D nurses and nurse managers (10 participants).

Table 1: sources of data

FINDINGS

I will first provide an overview of the two work trajectories the nurses manage, the patient work and the documentation work. I then describe several choreography practices that nurses engage to integrate these two streams of work into a single coherent flow of actions.

Caring for a Patient

L&D nursing presents a unique situation where patients are (for the most part) healthy people doing something that is, while potentially risky, very personal and meaningful. Additionally, L&D nursing work is unique in some other important ways: 1) while patients across the hospital are enrolled in various kinds of work related to their care [30], L&D patients are required, by the nature of the task, to take on a much more significant role as "workers" than in most units. Consequently, duties placed on L&D nurses as manager and coach are also greater than those of other types of nurses. 2) L&D seems to generally have higher requirements for documentation than other units, at H1 and otherwise. Explanations given by hospital workers for this center on the fact that obstetrics is a highly litigious specialty where malpractice verdicts frequently favor families and the unique patient situation, described next. 3) L&D nurses are in the unusual situation of having a "two patient problem;" they must care for two patients but one (the baby) is only visualizable, and thus nurse- and doctor-able, through the use of an assemblage of technologies. All nurses must balance documentation with patient care; this is a commonality of hospital work. However, the qualities outlined above may exacerbate the tension between documentation work and patient work in L&D, particularly during the intense pushing phase and the birth itself.

Each patient is assigned a primary nurse. Nurses conduct continuous close observation of mother and baby, looking for potential signs of distress. This nurse is also responsible for performing various procedures, assisting physicians, and administering medications, among other tasks. The primary nurse is a "hub" who serves as the main source of communication between the patient and the team; nurses coordinate the actions of residents, anesthesiologists, assistant nurses, pediatricians, scrub techs, and so on to ensure that the necessary people and equipment are in the right place at the right time as a labor progresses. An important part of L&D nursing and an ethos of nursing care in general is to maintain physical presence and connection with patients [10]. As one nurse described it, she strives to "...be the eyes that my patient sees and the voice that my patient hears." This becomes particularly important as a labor progresses and a patient starts pushing. The primary nurse engages in intensive coaching, encouragement, and physical support as she "pushes with" a patient.

Typically, two to three nurses come to the room to assist the primary nurse during a vaginal birth. Support nurses help in a variety of ways. During a vaginal birth, there is a lot of talking and cheerleading during pushing ('c'mon, c'mon, almost there, little more!'). The primary nurse heads up this effort, with other nurses forming a supportive chorus. Nurses also physically hold and support the patient. During a contraction, a nurse on either side will hold one of the patient's feet in her hands and wrap her other arm around the patient's bent leg, forming a human structure the woman braces herself against as she pushes. Nurses outside the room, including the charge nurse, also coordinate with nurses in the room to assist with work in a variety of ways.

Caring for a Medical Record

Accountability and Health Information Technologies

"We will make sure that every doctor's office and hospital in this country is using cutting edge technology and electronic medical records so that we can cut red tape, prevent medical mistakes, and help save billions of dollars each year." -President Barack Obama, 12/6/2008

The practice of documentation in hospitals is enmeshed in the social and political landscape of medicine. In the past 20 years concern has grown that hospitals are sacrificing quality in the name of cost containment, leading to the emergence of an accountability imperative in the medical field [37]. Patient-consumers and third-party buyers of healthcare along with regulatory agencies are now demanding an unprecedented degree of transparency and accountability [35]. The accountability endeavor is in large part contingent on what has been called the "next major change" in medical record keeping practices [26], the shift away from paper-based records and toward computerized records [35]. Implementing HITs for documentation has been advanced as a key to improving health care. HITs are expected to increase efficiency and safety of care as well as provide a multitude of other benefits [2]. Despite skepticism from the medical community and studies showing mixed results from HIT implementation [3], adoption of HITs, particularly Electronic Medical Record (EMR) programs, has escalated and is expected to increase as the government is now offering major incentives to hospitals for purchasing EMR systems [18]. With this in mind, I will now describe the documentation work that takes place in the L&D unit of H1.

Documentation in H1

The documentation work system in H1's L&D is highly fragmented. Multiple computer- and paper-based artifacts are used by the nurses, and these artifacts exist in multiple sites in the physical and information workspace. This infrastructure has accrued in layers over a period of decades. Nurses must "care" and tend to the medical record and the assemblage of documentation technologies just as they must care for and tend to patients.

The most important part of the documentation work system for the L&D nurses is a computer flowsheet program (quantitative sentinel or "QS") that nurses use to chart throughout a birth. A key feature of QS and the reason it is so important is that it is linked with the electronic fetal monitor (QS thus ties back in with the "two-patient problem" described above). Nurses watch the pattern created by the fetal heart rate (called the "strip") and contractions over time and make notations at regular intervals as well as noting any aberrations; this gives the team information about how the baby is coping with the labor process and whether intervention is needed. The strip is also used as a marker of time. Nurses click on the strip to open the flowsheet and chart on what is happening at any specific moment, often on a minute-by-minute basis. The flowsheet thus provides a "blow-by-blow" account of what is happening during a birth.

H1 uses two additional computer programs for documentation, a new electronic medical record implemented in 2010 ("Quest") and the older linked program Quest is intended to replace ("TDS"), implemented in 1990. QS and Quest cannot be interfaced due to cost and technical issues. Therefore, nurses must log in and navigate between two separate computer programs to complete documentation in each; for a variety of reasons, nurses must often move between workstations and locations to access each of the programs. Although many functions were migrated to Quest from TDS, a few tasks continue to be performed using TDS (see table 2). Finally, the unit continues to maintain a paper chart for each patient. The paper chart contains a multitude of forms that must be completed for each patient. One form of particular importance during a birth is the L&D Record, a tri-fold sheet filled out gradually over the course of the labor and typically set out on a wheeled table in the hallway outside the patient's room during the birth.

Clearly, the documentation work system is quite complex. One of the most frequent complaints from nurses is that they chart the same piece of information over and over. For example, if a patient is given pitocin (a drug used at some point in almost all births that stimulates uterine contractions), the nurse must complete documentation in the pyxis (medication room computer system), type a series of notes in the QS flowsheet on pitocin administration, complete documentation in another section of QS that tracks fluid given from each IV bag, complete a series of documentation tasks in Quest related to carrying out medication orders, and note on the L&D record and the QS delivery summary that labor was augmented with pitocin.

Documentation is time-sensitive and limited by the cognitive capabilities of humans to remember information-some pieces of information will be lost if they are not recorded somewhere (even if somewhere is a paper towel, a random piece of paper, or on one's scrubs) at the time they occur. Additionally, if nurses do not keep up with charting, there is a feeling of being "buried" under it- nurses do not want to let too many documentation tasks accrue or they will have difficulty remembering what needs to be charted where and when. Nurses have different tolerances for letting documentation work pile up without feeling overwhelmed, but documentation in general is not a kind of work that can be "put down" for any length of time; the medical record must be attended to just as the patient must be attended to. The larger legal, political, and organizational context surrounding medical work has placed increasing emphasis on completeness and rigor of documentation. The fragmentation of charting tasks means that documentation requires elaborate situated coordination in order to keep up and produce a healthy medical record. Each component of the chart serves a purpose with regard to accountability, which I will describe next.

Accountability logics

Different pieces of the medical record serve different accountability functions (see table 2 for a brief overview of the function and logic associated with key documentation artifacts). The computerized flowsheet is a key piece of evidence in legal cases. Providers refer to this as cover-your-ass ("CYA") charting. The flowsheet also serves professional interests, as it demonstrates work done by the nurses and serves as a source of legitimation. When a bad outcome, an error, or a near-miss occurs, these pieces of the chart are reviewed during debriefs, rounds, and practice council meetings.

Form	Function	Logic
Labor & Delivery Record (Paper)	Summary of key information from a delivery. Quality analyst extracts data for statistics reported to various regulatory/QI agencies.	Regulatory accountability
Flowsheet (QS)	Ongoing record of patient data, aberrations, actions taken. Linked with fetal monitor.	Legal & Professional accountability
Delivery summary (QS)	Summary of key information from a delivery. Physicians use for statistics.	Inter-organizational accountability
Patient Outcome Plan (TDS)	Plan for addressing psycho-social problems identified by the nurse, required by CMS.	Regulatory Accountability
Orders, worklist (Quest)	Notes on completed orders, nurses charge patients for supplies, medications, and procedures.	Fiscal & Regulatory accountability

Table 2: Function and logic associated with some of the documentation forms used in L&D

Other pieces of the chart satisfy accountability requirements from regulatory agencies, accreditation organizations, and consumer advocacy organizations who make the results publicly available. For example, the quality analyst uses the L&D Record to extract statistics for a database of information reported to the state public health department. The new EMR system, Quest, is designed to adhere to best practices for patient safety including extensive documentation intended to prevent medication errors. Quest is also the primary site for fiscal accountability, where nurses enter charges for equipment, medications, and procedures.

Choreographing Patient and Chart

I now turn my attention to the integration of the two fragmented trajectories of work, caring for the patient and caring for the medical record. I begin with an ethnographic vignette to illustrate a typical scene during a birth; using this vignette along with additional examples, I then describe a set of *choreography practices* that nurses engage in to integrate the trajectories into one coherent flow of actions.

> 2:15 PM
>
> The nurse is adjusting the monitor machine, turning a knob that makes the blood pressure cuff contract- she wants to keep an eye on the pressures. Then she moves her hands up and fiddles with the computer monitor- the computer screen went off for some reason, so she gets it back on. On the screen, the line of the tocometer, which measures contractions, is going up- the patient is having a contraction. "Here we go!" The nurse calls, and moves quickly back to the bed, taking the patient's left foot in her right hand. "ready? push!" Her other hand is pressing down on the fetal monitor so the baby's heart rate won't be lost during the contraction. A second nurse, who had been prepping a label for a sample, puts down her work and moves to the patient's other side, mirroring the first nurse's pose. The resident sits on the end of the bed, feeling for the baby's head in the birth canal as the patient pushes. Meanwhile, the nurse is counting slowly to ten while the patient pushes, her face tight with strain. Through the contraction, the nurse continuously coaches, holds the leg, and works the monitor with her left hand to keep the baby's heart rate visible on the screen. The second nurse leans over the watch the perineum as the patient pushes and gives further direction as the first nurse counts- "that's it, strong strong strong- push in your bottom. No, don't make noise! Save it for pushing. Good!" As the contraction fades, the first nurse releases her grip. She looks at the resident: stop the pit? Resident: yeah, please.
>
> 2:16 PM
>
> The nurse talks out loud to herself- 'oxygen going, pit stopped, patient repositioned...' as she pivots to the IV pump, quickly navigating a series of screens to stop one medication and change the volume on another. She then takes two quick steps to the computer, clicks on the strip and opens the flowsheet, clicking rapidly through several screens to get to a screen for general comments where she quickly types 'pit stopped, bolus started, O2 given, pt. repositioned...' The patient has her eyes closed on the bed, head turned to the side, husband standing next to her looking a little lost. 'Keep breathing...' the nurse says, her eyes on the screen. Meanwhile, in the hallway, a paper form sits open on a table. Another nurse stops by to see what's happening. On her way out she stops at the table, picks up a pen, checks a box, then moves on.
>
> 2:18 PM
>
> The first nurse, at the computer in the room, clicks on the fetal monitor strip to enlarge it just as another contraction starts to build. She turns away from the computer, back to the bed and gets in position for another push...

Choreography Practices

Research on coordination typically considers how workers collectively execute a single work trajectory. However, L&D nurses are managing two work trajectories- a patient trajectory and a documentation trajectory. Each trajectory involves divergent work routines and skillful care. Nurses engage in *choreography practices* to connect the two trajectories together into one coherent workflow, including:

Moving

Choreography requires more then mentally balancing tasks; the choreography work of L&D nurses is very physical, and physically demanding. Nurses change the position of their body, hands, and eyes as they engage with and transition between different tasks. Movements are both small (moving hands, glancing) and large (pivoting, stepping, power walking) as nurses travel between the patient and the different sites of work- the computer, the IV pump, the table in the hallway, the medication room down the hall.

Synching

Nurses must synch charting work with the events that are unfolding with the birth and with the other providers. The nurse in the vignette engages in a common synching strategy by pushing with the patient during contractions and charting on the computer (as well as completing a multitude of other tasks) in the few minutes between contractions. It is almost as if the nurse is present during a contraction and then disappears between contractions, as she has space to attend to documentation tasks. If a nurse attempts too much in the space between contractions, she will lose track of the patient. If she does not smoothly transition away from the patient when there is a rest, she will lose track of the chart. Nurses find, maintain, and adjust a rhythm during each birth.

Juggling

Juggling involves choreography to handle multiple tasks at once, keeping an eye on different tasks simultaneously. A nurse's eyes and hands are divided between multiple sites of work. Between contractions, nurses do the supportive work of caring for a patient- coaching ("keep breathing"), encouraging ('you're doing great'), answering questions (yes the epidural is working, but you feel pressure as the baby comes down)- while standing at the computer clicking through boxes and typing notes on whatever just happened ('pit stopped...'). The nurse's focus on the computer screen and keyboard is punctuated by glances at the patient, but the nurse types about one thing and talks about another at the same time or in close rapid succession.

Prepping

Nurses prep constantly. On an ongoing basis, nurses attempt to anticipate their own future documentation and patient care tasks and the tasks of others and ready things so they can be completed with fewer steps later on, smoothing out their path so they can flow more easily through and between tasks seconds, minutes, or hours in the future. For example, if a nurse knows she will need to chart on a patient's vital signs, she opens the computer flowsheet to the first screen of a series of screens involved in charting vital signs, then goes to check the patient's vitals so she can enter the vitals a few minutes later without logging in.

Collaborating

Choreographing documentation involves skillful teamwork. Multiple nurses coordinate their actions to care for the chart. At some point during a birth, the physical work of delivering a baby becomes so intense that the primary nurse has to stop tending to documentation all together. Helping a patient to push involves holding legs back and up, manipulating the fetal monitor and watching the strip on the screen, and coaching the patient while she pushes. When this work becomes too consuming and the nurse can no longer make it back to the computer between contractions, another nurse moves to the computer and picks up the charting, recording the "blow by blow" on the computer flowsheet. In many cases, a third nurse tends to the L&D Record and the rest of the paper chart, looking around the curtain to watch the action and fill out the record while doing other small tasks like preparing containers and labels for specimens, getting ID bracelets ready, and manning the phone. This collaborative choreography occurs wordlessly- monitoring the chart, in its different locations, is something all of the nurses keep an eye on.

Triaging

Nurses engage in a cognitive process in order to maintain and integrate dual trajectories. This process involves constant attention- or at least partial attention- to the tasks at hand and ongoing, moment to moment decisions about what needs to be done next:

"You really have to be able to know how to multi-task and know how to prioritize what you're going to be doing at every minute, basically..." -RN, L&D

During intensive phases of birth, nurses may have many tasks related to both documentation and the patient. At any given time, they have to assess all of the things that need to be done and make decisions about what needs their attention most, how they will fit in the urgent but slightly less pressing tasks, and what can be left for later. Nurses also engage in cognitive work to keep information straight- the nurse in the vignette talks out loud to herself, repeating the things that need to be charted as she walks to the computer.

DISCUSSION

Choreography

"In dance, choreography is also known as dance composition. Dance compositions are created by applying one or both of these fundamental choreographic techniques:

Improvisation, in which a choreographer provides dancers with a score (i.e., generalized directives) that serves as guidelines for improvised movement and form...

Planned choreography, in which a choreographer dictates motion and form in detail, leaving little or no opportunity for the dancer to exercise personal interpretation."
-Wikipedia.com entry for "choreography"

Nurses work individually and collectively to choreograph the actions of two competing trajectories into one coherent flow of actions through a variety of practices, described above. I do not use the term "choreography" in the sense of a highly choreographed ballet that is planned and rehearsed before a performance. Instead, I initially borrowed the term from William Whyte [36], who studied the life of city streets. Using time-lapse video, Whyte showed how people walking across a crowded plaza choreograph their movements. The ease with which people are able to move purposefully across a busy place without ever colliding is surprising and, he argues, requires a high degree of skill; the success of a plaza's design is reflected in the degree to which it supports its occupants in the service of this choreography. Similarly, nurses have directives about what needs to be done, along with a set and props on which to carry out their work. Choreography is emergent as the nurses perform and transition between tasks, creating a single flow of actions. This is consistent with a situated action perspective: "..the organization of situated action is an emergent property of moment-by-moment interactions between actors, and between actors and the environments of their actions…the emergent properties of action mean that it is not predetermined, but neither is it random" [33:179].

However, Whyte's notion of choreography does not adequately describe the coordination work of L&D nurses. Dancers in a ballet and commuters walking through a plaza have a distinct advantage over L&D nurses. Each group has a single overarching goal: perform a ballet, get to the other side without bumping into anyone. The notion of choreography in the hospital is further complicated as it becomes clear that nurses are actually engaging in two simultaneous performances: caring for a patient dyad in order to produce a healthy mom and a healthy baby and documenting their actions in order to produce a viable account that will stand up to all of the rigors it may be subjected to. Here's how one nurse described charting:

"It's just constantly writing what you've been doing so that if you ever have to go back… if you're writing every single thing down, they'll be able to say, 'Okay, you were doing this at 10:31 in the morning and then this happened at 10:33…'and...If you didn't write it down, then you didn't do it. That's what they always say. Even if you really did do it (laughs)." –RN, L&D

So nurses do work and then document that they did work. In the view of the organization, one of these kinds of work does not exist without the other. When considering the embodied practice of the nurses, however, these tasks are quite different. Taken separately, each could occupy almost all of the time and attention of one worker (recent reports in the media of a newly emerging role for medical "scribes" who follow physicians and complete documentation attest to this), yet nurses must find a way to accomplish both. An apt metaphor can be drawn from the book *Harry Potter and the Prisoner of Azkaban*, in which over-achiever Hermione secures a magical device called a time-turner so she can literally be in two different classes at once[1]. During intense phases of work, L&D nurses are essentially attempting to do something similar, but without magical aid. Instead, they regularly engage in a series of choreography practices to bring the patient work and the documentation work together. These practices are highly physical, and often physically demanding. Choreographing patient and chart involves movement, tempo, and rhythm and necessitates ongoing collaboration and attention, resulting in a single improvisational performance.

Skillful Choreography

Benner, Tanner, and Chesla [4] describe how nurses go from novice to expert. Much of clinical expertise, they argue, is more embodied, engaged and practical than it is typically depicted in rational technical models of decision making. Similarly, skill in choreography requires an artfulness that develops over time. Part of becoming an expert nurse is becoming familiar with the artifacts-learning to properly complete a multitude of forms and quickly navigate the computer systems involved in documentation. This set of skills becomes especially apparent when a nurse is away from the hospital for a period and then comes back to practice. One nurse re-orienting in L&D after three years working as a research nurse told me:

'My skills just aren't there right now. It's not the medical stuff, it's all of this [indicates the computer], the computer and the documentation.' –RN, L&D

Expertise extends beyond how to simply complete different tasks, however; nurses also learn to transition gracefully between tasks and perform a cohesive dance given multiple competing directives. This becomes apparent as we examine another dimension of skillful nurse choreography. Just as one of the rules of Hermione's time-turner was that no one could find out she was in two places at once, nurses attempt to choreograph their work in a way that keeps charting invisible to patients:

"I try not to make my patient feel that that's my primary task. That should be, kind of, behind the scenes. And it's…it's an art. And I'm still learning how to do it best." -RN, L&D

To better understand this, I turn to a discussion of the intersections between care, documentation, and the professional identity of nurses.

Caring, Documentation, and Identity

Nurses have a unique professional identity. They are highly trained, clinically skilled individuals who value caring for patients through intimate observation and connection [9]. It takes years of professional experience to develop nursing expertise [4]. None of the nurses I shadowed mentioned wanting to work with technology and computers as a reason they went into nursing. All cited a desire to take care of patients. Some were drawn to the idea of a collaborative work environment or particularly chose H1 because it is a teaching hospital where they can continually improve their clinical skills and contribute to training young providers.

---

[1] Thanks to Martha Feldman for suggesting this metaphor. It is worth noting that at the end of the book, Hermione cedes the time turner, saying "I can't stand another year like this one. That Time-Turner, it was driving me mad. I've handed it in."

Some are drawn to the challenge of taking care of very high-risk patients and the adrenaline rush of dealing with emerging crises. Many of the L&D nurses I spoke to mentioned that they derive a sense of honor from participating in an important moment in a family's life. Nurses derive satisfaction and identity from activities such as caring, doing skillful medical work, teaching, learning, dealing with crises, and witnessing important life events.

Most of the nurse participants in my study expressed frustration at the amount of work fragmentation they experience due to documentation. It is clear that although the nurses balance documentation and patient care, they ground their identity in only one of those tasks. Feldman [16] conducted her research on the crucial role of agency in the ongoing iteration of routines in the student housing unit of a university. She uses an example of a situation in which building directors alter a routine for moving out of the dorms because they feel the current routine does not allow them to perform their core duty as educators. Similarly, L&D nurses at H1 draw on their nursing identity as they attempt to choreograph a performance that foregrounds patient care and backgrounds documentation and computer work. For instance, by stepping in (and physically stepping up to the computer) to take over documentation in the moments before birth, nurses collaborate to create pockets of time and space in the stream of actions- like an eddy in a river- for the primary nurse to maintain a continuous presence at the bedside as birth becomes more intense.

Sometimes the nurses are unable to successfully produce a performance that satisfies all of the directives they are tasked with. Busy nurses engage in a near constant process of triaging, deciding what to do next and what to put off. Generally, nurses prefer to prioritize the patient whenever possible. However, nurses sometimes feel that if they privilege patient care over charting there will be sanctions:

'Some nurses are always writing, trying to keep up with the documentation. I always choose my patient over the chart, but my charting isn't very good. I **should** do better documentation. So far I haven't gotten in trouble for it, but someday I might.' -RN, L&D

The nurse above expresses a truth that documentation is an important part of her job, and something she feels by all rights she should be doing better. However, she also feels that if she were to document more, she would be compromising the patient. As political and technological changes lead to increasing fragmentation of documentation tasks, it becomes increasingly difficult to maintain this balance. Nurses find it more of a struggle to work in a way that they feel is meaningful, energizing, and aligned with their identity as nurses. This tension plays out in nurses' satisfaction with their jobs. A few experienced nurses at my field site mentioned that they sometimes felt so frustrated with the computers and documentation that they were considering retiring. These complaints escalated when Quest was implemented. This is a real concern as it is widely acknowledged that there is a shortage of nurses in the U.S. Finding ways to support choreography to keep documentation "behind the scenes" is not just a matter of producing more efficient work, but effectively drawing on nurses as highly skilled professionals with a unique professional and personal commitment to giving care.

The Logic of a Fragmented Work System

There are different layers of fragmentation in the work of L&D nurses. One is the fragmentation between the two major tasks, patients and documentation. Fragmentation exists within each of these work trajectories as well. Turning to the documentation work system, we can see that documentation work is fragmented into multiple artifacts and environments. Nurses complain that they engage in double, triple, and quadruple charting, documenting the same information in multiple places. Fragmentation is, to some extent, inherent in the nature of documentation- even when there was just a single paper chart in H1, the chart was organized into different sections. Berg and Bowker [7] describe how the medical record is multiple and, taken in its entirety, consists of a large corpus of artifacts including notes on scraps of paper and official documents. What is interesting about H1 is how many different systems are involved in documentation- almost all participants agree the work system is a mess.

However, there is a logic underlying the fragmentation of H1's work system. As described above, the different charting tasks represent different documentation requirements. Layers of infrastructure accrue as new systems are added but old systems are not completely removed. This is logical in the moment as there are functions that may be performed in the old but not the new system. Over time, however, the result is ever-increasing fragmentation. This environment constitutes the set and stage nurses use to carry out their performance, thus inevitably shapes the aesthetics of the performance.

Returning to a situated action perspective, we can see that in the situated practices used by nurses to choreograph multiple work trajectories, fragmentation places physical constraints on action. Accountability requirements constitute a social circumstance that both shape the environment in which the L&D nurses conduct their work (expressed in the fragmentation of the documentation work system) and directives placed on the nurses (to produce a complete chart that stands up to a variety of assessments). Nurses also draw on physical and social resources, particularly the focus that nurses place on caring for patients, to guide the performance and the manner in which they balance work trajectories on an ongoing basis. This research extends current literature on situated action and coordination by examining the physical, social, and cognitive practices that workers use to create an ongoing, situated performance that balances multiple simultaneous work trajectories and the qualities of person and environment that shape the resultant choreography. Future research could examine the choreography practices, as well as the requirements and resources that constrain and enable choreography performances, in other situations where workers must balance multiple work trajectories.

Implications for CSCW

Broad Implications for CSCW Research

This paper provides a starting point for a choreography perspective of action, applicable both in medical contexts and other work contexts. All systems of work, even those that are seemingly mundane, require people to bring disparate heterogeneous tasks together into coherent sequences of action. Choreography takes seriously the actions that connect tasks together in addition to examining the routines and actions involved in completing work. When conducting research on workplace coordination, CSCW researchers should look for choreography practices, such as synching, juggling, and moving, described above. Additionally, this research points to a number of crucial questions that CSCW researchers should confront in a wide variety of studies on work practice and coordination, including: what are the work trajectories, and what are the loci and implements involved in carrying out these different trajectories? How is the infrastructure impacting the choreography? Is the choreography excessively complicated and difficult, in a way that intrudes on successful completion of work trajectories? What are the aesthetics of the choreography, and how do inherent resources of workers, such as ethics and identity, shape the choreography? Do workers find it difficult or easy to choreograph work in way that is satisfying and pleasing?

Implications for Design and Implementation of HIT

The current research also has several practical implications for design of HIT systems. Past CSCW research calls for HIT designers to consider how medical work involves physical movement in space [5] and temporal rhythms of different members of the medical team [27]. Similarly, documentation work systems should be designed with an eye to the multiple performances that medical workers must choreograph and the quality and aesthetics of the performance that providers would like to achieve. Artifacts could be designed to directly facilitate choreography practice. For example, Chen et Al. [10] found that providers using workstations-on-wheels engage in small adjustments of computer screens throughout an encounter with a patient, moving the screen to strike a balance between the need to document and maintain social contact with a patient. The mobility of the computer enables the provider to juggle the computer and the patient more effectively since she can continuously adjust the computer based on the configuration of computer and patient tasks the provider is balancing at any given time. Designers need to pay attention not just to the tasks that providers engage in, but also how providers transition between tasks.

Although there is a general perception in HI that "backcharting," or charting things after the fact, is bad practice, strategic use of backcharting is an important skill that nurses develop over time. Knowing when and how to backchart can help nurses maintain attention on the patient. Designers should seek to find ways to make it easier for nurses to put down documentation work and return to charting later, thus enabling nurses to more effectively background documentation work as they deem necessary.

Finally, managers and other stakeholders should work to decrease fragmentation of documentation tasks. Task fragmentation is to some extent a natural and inevitable part of work [6]. However, fragmentation in the documentation work stream could be reduced by removing programs from the system and making different parts of the chart multi-task to serve more functions. Finding ways to mitigate fragmentation must take into account the specific context of the work system, including the sedimentary layers of documentation infrastructure and the unique requirements present in each setting.

CONCLUSION

This paper draws on past research on the situated and agentic nature of coordination to describe how nurses choreograph the work of caring for a patient with the work of documenting information during childbirth. Choreography involves physical, social, and cognitive practices in an ongoing and situated performance that is constrained by accountability requirements underlying a fragmented documentation work system and shaped by the inherent resources nurses bring to their practice, including expertise developed over time and a professional identity that places primacy on patient care.

ACKNOWLEDGMENTS

I sincerely thank the providers and women as well as the Agency for Healthcare Research and Quality, the Johnson Chair, The Center for Organizational Research, and the UCI Graduate Division for supporting this work.

REFERENCES

1. Allen, T. (1977). Managing the flow of technology. Cambridge, MA: MIT Press.
2. Armijo, D., McDonnell, C., & Werner, K. (October 2009). Electronic Health Record Usability: Evaluation and Use Case Framework. Rockville, MD: Agency for Healthcare Research and Quality.
3. Ash, J. S., Berg, M., & Coiera, E. (2004). Some unintended consequences of information technology in health care. JAMIA, 11(2), 104-112.
4. Benner, P., Tanner, C., & Chesla, C. (2009). Expertise in Nursing Practice. New York: Springer.
5. Bardram, J. E., & Bossen, C. (2005). Mobility work: the spatial dimension of collaboration at a hospital. Computer Supported Cooperative Work, 14(2), 131-160.

6. Berg, M. (1996). Practices of reading and writing: the constitutive role of the patient record in medical work. Sociology of Health & Illness, 18(4), 499-524.
7. Berg, M., & Bowker, G. (1997). The multiple bodies of the medical record: toward a sociology of an artifact. The Sociological Quarterly, 38(3), 513-537.
8. Bowker, G.C., & Star, S.L. (1999). Sorting Things Out. Cambridge: The MIT Press.
9. Chambliss, D.F. (1996). Beyond Caring. Chicago: The University of Chicago Press.
10. Chen, Y., Ngo, V., Harrison, S., & Duong, V. (2011). Unpacking exam-room computing: negotiating computer-use in patient-physician interactions. CHI'11, 3343-3352.
11. Corbin, J., & Strauss, A. (2008). Basics of Qualitative Research: Techniques and Procedures for Developing Grounded Theory. Los Angeles: Sage.
12. Dickerson, K., & Manheimer, E. (1998). The Cochrane Collaboration: evaluation of health care and services using systematic reviews of the results of randomized controlled trials. Clin Obst & Gyn, 41(2), 315-331.
13. Emerson, R.M., Fretz, R.I., & Shaw, L.L. (1995). Writing Ethnographic Fieldnotes. Chicago: The University of Chicago Press.
14. Dourish, Paul: Where the Action Is: The Foundation of Embodied Interaction, MIT Press, Cambridge, Mass., 2001.
15. Heath, C., Hindmarsh, J., & Luff, P. (1999). Interaction in isolation: the dislocated world of the London Underground train driver. Sociology, 33(3), 555-575.
16. Feldman, M. (2000). Organizational routines as a source of continuous change. Organization Science, 11(6), 611-629.
17. Feldman, M., & Pentland, B. (2003). Reconceptualizing organizational routines as a source of flexibility and change. Administrative Science Quarterly, 48(1), 94-118.
18. Ford, E.W., Menachemi, N. P., Thad, M. (2006). Predicting the adoption of electronic health records by physicians: when will health care be paperless? JAMIA, 13(1), 106-112.
19. Gonzalez, V. and Mark, G. (2004). "Constant, Constant, Multi-tasking Craziness": Managing Multiple Working Spheres. Proceedings of ACM CHI'04, 113-120.
20. Kellogg, K.C., Orlikowski, W.J., & Yates, J. (2006). Life in the trading zone: structuring coordination across boundaries in postbureaucratic organizations. Organization Science, 17, 22-44.
21. Klein, H., & Myers, M. (1999). A set of principles for conducting and evaluating interpretive field studies in information systems. MIS Quarterly, 23(1), 67–93.
22. Mark, G., Gonzalez, V.M., Harris, J. (2005). No task left behind?: examining the nature of fragmented work. Proceedings of the SIGCHI Human factors'05.
23. McQuaid, L. et Al. (2010). Socio-technical considerations in epilepsy electronic patient record implementation. Int J Med Informatics, 79(5), 349-360.
24. Mentis, H. M., Reddy, M., & Rosson, M. B. (2010). Invisible emotion: information and interaction in an emergency room. CSCW'10, 311-320.
25. Okhuysen, G.A., & Bechky, B.A. (2009). Coordination in organizations: an integrative perspective. The Academy of Management Annals, 3(1), 463-502.
26. Ornstein, S.M., Oates, R.B., & Fox, G.N. (1992). The computer-based medical record: current status. J Family Prac, 36(3), 556-565.
27. Reddy, M. 2002. A Finger on the pulse. temporal rhythms and information seeking in medical work. CSCW'08, 344-353.
28. Schmidt, K. (2011). Cooperative work and coordinative practices. New York, New York; Springer.
29. Star, S.L., & Griesemer, J.R. (1989). Institutional ecology, "translations" and boundary objects. Social Studies of Science, 19, 387–420.
30. Strauss, A., Fagerhaugh, S., Suczek, B., & Wiener, C. (1997). The Social Organization of Medical Work. Chicago: The University of Chicago Press.
31. Strauss, A. (1988). The articulation of project work: an organizational process. Sociological Quarterly, 29(2), 163-178.
32. Suchman, L. A. (1983). Office procedure as practical action: models of work and system design. ACM Transactions on Office Information Systems, 1(4), 320-328.
33. Suchman, L.A. (1987). Plans and Situated Actions. Cambridge: Cambridge University Press.
34. Tang, C.M. & Carpendale, S.T. Evaluating the deployment of a mobile technology in a hospital ward. CSCW'08, 205-214.
35. Timmermans, S., & Berg, M. (2003). The Gold Standard: The Challenge of Evidence Based Medicine and Standardization in Health Care. Philadelphia: Temple University Press.
36. Whyte, W. H. (1980). The Social Life of Small Urban Spaces. New York: Project for Public Spaces Inc.
37. Wiener, C. L. (2000). The Elusive Quest: Accountability in Hospitals. New York: Walter de Gruyter.

The Work of Play: Supporting a Pervasive Health Behavior Change Intervention for US Middle School Students

Andrew D. Miller[1], Erika Shehan Poole[2], Yan Xu[1], Elsa Eiriksdottir[3], Daniel Kestranek[2], Richard Catrambone[3], Elizabeth D. Mynatt[1]

[1]College of Computing
Georgia Institute of Technology
85 5th Street NW
Atlanta, GA 30332 USA

[2]College of Information Sciences & Technology
The Pennsylvania State University
321E IST Building
University Park, PA 16802 USA

[3]School of Psychology
Georgia Institute of Technology
654 Cherry Street
Atlanta, GA 30332 USA

{andrew.miller, elsa, mynatt, yan.xu}@gatech.edu, rc7@prism.gatech.edu, {djk294, esp13}@psu.edu

ABSTRACT

Technology-based health behavior change interventions involving passive on-body sensing and feedback interfaces show promise for increasing participation in physical activity. However, the majority of prior studies are small-scale interventions that heavily rely on research teams for programmatic support. In larger-scale deployments, participants may have to take over setup and maintenance tasks. In this paper, we examine the "hidden work" involved with the large-scale deployment of a behavior change application in American schools. We offer insight into the coordination required to maintain such deployments, and identify unique challenges that arise when schoolchildren are the target of a behavior change intervention. Our findings highlight the behind-the-scenes coordination and management work required of adult facilitators in order to support pervasive health interventions for children in school environments. We offer advice to researchers and project managers attempting integration of technology-based health behavior change applications for children.

Author Keywords

Health Informatics, Pedometers, Longitudinal study, Wellness, Articulation work, Children

ACM Classification Keywords

H5.m. Information interfaces and presentation (e.g., HCI): Miscellaneous.

INTRODUCTION

With rising concerns about obesity and sedentary lifestyles, particularly in childhood, the CHI and CSCW communities have correspondingly been interested in understanding how pervasive and ubiquitous computing technologies such as passive on-body sensing can support health behavior change. In pilot deployments, researchers often provide logistical and support functions, such as setup and troubleshooting. As these technologies move beyond the pilot stage and into large-scale deployments, there is a need for a deeper understanding of the coordination work needed to support such deployments, and the structural and environmental challenges that emerge in the context of real adoption [1]. Moreover, little research has addressed the challenges involved in deployments with children. Child-focused interventions differ from those described in the literature because children lack the autonomy in their daily decision making usually assumed in adult-focused interventions (such as [2,6]); hence one must also consider the role of adults who support the deployment.

In this paper, we describe the experience of teachers who took local responsibility for a school-based health intervention for early adolescents called the American Horsepower Challenge (AHPC). Developed by Humana Games for Health and sponsored by the Humana Foundation[1], the AHPC used real-world fitness data to create a multi-week walking competition among schools. The AHPC was deployed in 61 schools on three different occasions, involving the participation of over 1,700 students. In each participating school, a team of approximately 20 students wore wireless pedometers. A base station within the school automatically collected step data. Individual and school standings were displayed on a password-protected website that could be accessed either in the classroom or at home.

At first glance, the AHPC appears to be a relatively simple deployment in a well-ordered environment. In promotional materials, the game was described as a "turnkey solution" requiring "minimum support" from schools [5]. The relative simplicity of the intervention design (commercial pedometers seamlessly connecting to base stations and a web interface) seemed robust enough to sustain a large-scale longitudinal deployment. Furthermore, as a student-focused health intervention without a required curricular component or mandated

[1] The philanthropic arm of Humana, Inc., a health benefits company.

activities, the AHPC looked like it would place minimal burdens on teachers. However, our study reveals a more complicated picture of the system in use. To make the system work, the role of the *teacher* is crucial. As pervasive health systems move out of the lab and into everyday use, it is essential to understand the support networks required to manage novel technological deployments.

RELATED WORK

Pervasive health interventions have been an object of study within HCI for several years. As opposed to "exertion interfaces" [7] that often enable real-time collaboration in a pre-defined setting, pervasive health interventions facilitate asynchronous interaction "in the wild," and offer computational support for individual health goals, augmented by tracking and visualization technologies [2,3,6]. There are two main types of systems in this area: personal informatics systems that focus on the needs of individuals [2], and group deployments aimed at small groups of friends [3,6]. These systems typically focus on healthy individuals, as distinct from other systems designed for those living with chronic conditions.

Pilot deployments of collaborative and pervasive technologies often involve significant researcher-provided support. For example, in Fish'n'Steps, an influential pedometer-based fitness competition, researchers employed Wizard-of-Oz techniques for data capture and goal management, and installed and maintained the central kiosk. Additionally, participants were selected from office workers in the same company, to whom the researchers had easy access [6]. In contrast to this pilot approach, Bardram and others have called for studies of pervasive health systems to move "out of the lab" and examine long-term deployments in real-life healthcare settings [4].

In all deployments, someone must perform what Strauss termed *articulation work*, or work that enables other work [10]. By its nature, articulation work is "invisible within rational models of work or work planning" and is generally "undertaken in support of a high level end goal" [8]. Without researchers to perform articulation work, participants must negotiate this invisible work themselves. Additionally, research suggests articulation work is cumulative, meaning that the longer a deployment, the more articulation work is likely to pile up over time [8]. In a distributed, minimally supported, long-term deployment like the AHPC, articulation work is likely to emerge but difficult to account for preemptively.

METHODS

After a small-scale pilot in the Louisville metro area, Humana conducted a large-scale field trial with 61 schools across the United States in 2009 and 2010, and ran three "heats" over two school years: one in Spring 2009, one in Fall 2009, and one in Spring 2010. The top performing schools in Spring 2009 and Spring 2010 received grants for fitness programs. Our independent research team studied the AHPC's impact and effectiveness during this period.

Participant Demographics

Schools were selected by The Humana Foundation based on high participation in the National School Lunch Program, a federally assisted meal program in the US; 73.5% of students in AHPC schools received free or reduced lunch. The schools were situated in a range of environments, from large cities to rural areas [11]. Thirty-seven schools continued in the AHPC across all three heats of the game; 1,377 students started in the first heat and 1,743 students participated in at least one of the heats. Most students were in 6th grade (age 11-12) when they began the challenge, and in 7th grade (age 13-14) when the challenge ended. Students joined or left the program for various reasons, including student transience (students sometimes became too busy for the program or moved schools) and teacher preference (teachers often lost daily access to students when they started 7th grade, and some teachers recruited new students).

Data Collection and Analysis

During the field trial, members of our research team visited 15 schools participating in the AHPC, speaking with over 200 students and teachers. The profile of the 15 schools we visited was representative of the overall group socioeconomically (71.8% of students receive free or reduced lunch), demographically (male-female ratio=1.03, similar ethnic makeup), and regionally (covering 8 states and a mix of rural/suburban/small town/city schools). At each school we conducted a student-only focus group, teacher interviews and individual student interviews, and wrote field notes with observations of interest. We also gathered pedometer log data from each child, and surveyed participating students, teachers and parents. The bulk of our findings in this paper are from qualitative analysis of the interview and focus group data. During analysis, four researchers qualitatively coded and analyzed transcripts and field notes in a multi-step process aimed at identifying themes and stakeholder relationships. A more complete discussion of the AHPC evaluation can be found in [12].

Program Administration and Support

Our research team did not recruit schools, set up equipment, or provide technical support. Representatives from Humana contacted schools and enrolled them in the program, and were available to assist schools and teachers with setup and troubleshooting tasks. The AHPC project managers operated remotely, and each managed a region comprised of multiple schools. Teachers contacted them when they needed assistance. Each school selected a teacher or teachers responsible for the AHPC.

FINDINGS

The AHPC was, at first glance, technologically simple. Students wore wireless pedometers on their shoes all day during each period of gameplay. Their steps were automatically wirelessly uploaded via a base station at school, and students could access the game website from a web browser. In practice, however, the interaction between various participant groups proved much more complex, and the teacher emerged as an important stakeholder not to be overlooked in the design of school-based health interventions.

The AHPC Teacher as System User

Before conducting our on-site visits, we assumed that the students participating in the AHPC were the primary users of the system. They are, after all, the people whose behavior and attitudes the system sought to change. What was less obvious was the interconnectedness of several other stakeholders in the network: administrators, other teachers, friends, siblings, parents, and, most prominently, the teacher or teachers in charge of the AHPC at each school. Teachers responsible for administering the AHPC performed much of the articulation work required for the AHPC to function. For example, they selected students, worked with administrators for gym resources, contacted project managers at Humana to coordinate technology, set up the base stations with the help of the school's IT personnel, distributed pedometers, monitored students' progress using the website and organized physical activities for the participating students.

Therefore, the AHPC relied heavily on the teachers' ability to coordinate stakeholders. As the students' closest advocate within the school environment, teachers took on tasks the students could not do themselves, such as setting up technology and securing support from administrators. In Strauss's terms, they "meshed" the actors and activities without performing the step-gathering "task" at the center of the Challenge [10]. Although the teachers could to some extent observe and control the core interactions with the game—uploading steps, accessing the website, troubleshooting technology—the business of getting steps was largely left out of their control. Teachers' ability to coordinate and support students was thus their primary goal because they could not always accompany students as they acquired steps. Although teacher-supervised exercise took place, students also walked and played between classes and after school, and these are times outside a teacher's direct influence.

In the AHPC, teachers played a vital coordination role by encouraging students to be physically active and engaging with the program more generally. But they also helped mitigate two other larger challenges: limited computing and gym resources in the schools, and technology troubleshooting and repair. If the deployment environment was Oz, the teachers were definitely Wizards.

Resource Availability

A prominent feature of participating AHPC schools was the low socio-economic status of students and insufficient funding of school districts. When the AHPC was deployed in these schools, we observed two primary challenges with respect to school resources: computer infrastructure and availability of facilities and playgrounds for physical activity.

In the surveys, teachers cited limited computing resources as one of the primary de-motivating factors in the AHPC and we saw evidence of this in our site visits. The processor-intensive Flash-based AHPC website placed a strain on lab computers, and the limited availability of computer lab time in many schools created additional barriers. The AHPC also requires some involvement from school district IT personnel, who were often unable to resolve technical difficulties with the base stations or website as quickly as the teachers desired. Additionally, many of the schools we went to lacked adequate gym resources, including funding for equipment and facilities as well as regular access to PE teachers. For example, the teacher survey indicated that the average student-to-teacher ratio for PE classes was 247:1. Resource constraints became apparent in our site visits as well; one school we visited lacked an indoor gym, so students could not exercise when it rained.

These structural factors of the environment had a significant impact on the technical deployment. As CSCW systems engage with ever "messier" environments, accounting for the presence or lack of resources will become essential.

Troubleshooting and Repair

Troubleshooting and repair involved the greatest number of stakeholders and proved the most challenging administrative tasks for teachers. The scenario played out similarly at many schools we visited. If a student checked the website and saw no new progress recorded, he or she might mention it to the AHPC teacher, who would then attempt to troubleshoot the problem by contacting the project manager. The project manager might then send a replacement device. However, even this proved complicated. In one school we visited, no AHPC students in the school were able to register their steps at the beginning of the Fall 2009 heat. In this case, the teacher had to negotiate with the school district's IT department, the Humana project manager, and even a representative from the pedometer and base station provider in order to solve the issue. One AHPC teacher reported that:

> *We kept going back with the technology people... And for the first two weeks it didn't work at all. And I think for this year that's what lost the kids because they were coming up to me and they're like, 'I logged on and it's saying I have zero steps.' By the time we got it working...it was too late.*

More than a technical glitch, this delay lowered student motivation and contributed to a steep drop in step-counts for the following heat. Had the teacher not been vigilant about coordinating support, the school might have dropped out of the program entirely. Teachers performed vital articulation work during these times, and the normally "invisible" technical infrastructure of the AHPC became painfully visible during these breakdowns [9].

Overall, it surprised us just how critical and complicated this troubleshooting process appeared to be. The apparent simplicity of pedometer/base station and connectivity belied the complexity of school firewalls, longitudinal hardware deployments, and the difficulty of troubleshooting in an environment without dedicated technical expertise. Additionally, as the deployment progressed and the technology experienced the stress of a long deployment, step upload failure became more common. Failures of this sort will be a challenge for any real-world deployment and one that future researchers in this area will likely encounter.

DISCUSSION: SUPPORTING SUPPORTERS

Despite expectations of a "turnkey" solution, the AHPC is far from automatic. We found that the program requires constant upkeep, both to support the technology across a long deployment, and to manage the students' experience of the game. While an analysis of all supporters is beyond the scope of this note, our analysis of the role of the teacher serves as a key example. Teachers took on additional work by helping students remember to wear their pedometer and by monitoring their progress in the game. They also had the additional responsibility of ensuring that students uploaded steps as well as dealing with lost pedometers and countering flagging motivation. As the central users of the AHPC, teachers deserved more support from the system, both in helping them see students' progress and more effectively delegating troubleshooting.

We must stress that this finding, which seems sensible and even obvious in hindsight, was not apparent to us or to the design team in advance. The extent of articulation work performed by teachers was truly hidden until our fieldwork exposed it. Therefore, in addition to conducting pilot trials to test hardware or software interfaces, researchers working towards large-scale or long-term deployments of this kind might want to conduct pilot trials that test the support networks. These pilot trials could be done by providing the technology with as little hand-holding as possible and studying the emergent practices that evolve to meet gaps in the design.

CONCLUSIONS

Pervasive health applications enter environments and lives already filled with existing practices, values and relationships. Even interventions that seem simple on the surface, like the AHPC, require nontrivial management and support as well as situated invention to make these interventions successful in the localized context.

ACKNOWLEDGMENTS

Thanks to our hundreds of participants, Humana Games for Health and the Humana Foundation for collectively making this research possible.

REFERENCES

1. Carter, S., Mankoff, J., Klemmer, S., and Matthews, T. Exiting the Cleanroom: On Ecological Validity and Ubiquitous Computing. *Human-Computer Interaction 23*, 1 (2008), 47-99.
2. Consolvo, S., McDonald, D., and Toscos, T. Activity Sensing In The Wild: A Field Trial Of Ubifit Garden. *Proc. CHI 2008*, ACM Press (2008), 1797-1806.
3. Consolvo, S., McDonald, D.W., and Landay, J.A. Theory-Driven Design Strategies For Technologies That Support Behavior Change In Everyday Life. *Proc. CHI 2009*, (2009), 405-504.
4. Hansen, T.R., Bardram, J.E., and Soegaard, M. Moving Out of the Lab: Deploying Pervasive Technologies in a Hospital. *IEEE Pervasive Computing 5*, 3 (2006), 24-31.
5. Humana Games For Health and Exergame Fitness. The Horsepower Challenge Overview. 2009. http://www.exergamefitness.com/horsepower-challenge-overview-humana-games.htm.
6. Lin, J.J., Mamykina, L., Lindtner, S., Delajoux, G., and Strub, H.B. Fish'n'Steps: Encouraging Physical Activity With An Interactive Computer Game. *Proc. Ubicomp 2006*, Springer (2006), 261–278.
7. Mueller, F., Gibbs, M.R., and Vetere, F. Towards Understanding How To Design For Social Play In Exertion Games. *Personal and Ubiquitous Computing 14*, 5 (2010), 417-424.
8. Sawyer, S. and Tapia, A. Always Articulating: Theorizing on Mobile and Wireless Technologies. *The Information Society 22*, 5 (2006), 311-323.
9. Star, S.L. and Ruhleder, K. Steps Toward an Ecology of Infrastructure: Design and Access for Large Information Spaces. *Information Systems Research 7*, 1 (1996), 111-134.
10. Strauss, A. Work and the Division of Labor. *Sociological Quarterly 26*, 1 (1985), 1–19.
11. US Department of Education. National Center for Education Statistics. 2010.
12. Xu, Y., Eiriksdottir, E., Miller, A. D., Poole, E. S., Kestranek, D., Catrambone, R., & Mynatt, E. D. (2011). *Assessment of Health Games in Secondary Schools: An Investigation of the American Horsepower Challenge*. GVU Technical Report.

Sustaining the Development of Cyberinfrastructure: An Organization Adapting to Change

Matthew J. Bietz
Department of Informatics
University of California, Irvine
Bren Hall 5042, Irvine, CA 92697, USA
mbietz@uci.edu

Toni Ferro, Charlotte P. Lee
Human Centered Design & Engineering
University of Washington
423 Sieg Hall, Seattle, WA 98195, USA
{tdferro, cplee}@uw.edu

ABSTRACT
Cyberinfrastructures are virtual organizations comprised of people and large-scale scientific computational infrastructures. Cyberinfrastructures endeavor to support "cutting-edge" science and must continually evolve and be under development in order to maintain their relevance and usefulness. This qualitative study of a cyberinfrastructure development project to support the new science of metagenomics investigates how sustaining cyberinfrastructure entails continually realigning the relationships among people, technologies, and organizations.

Author Keywords
Cyberinfrastructure, e-Science, Sustainability, Synergizing, Infrastructure, Organizations.

ACM Classification Keywords
H.5.3. Group and Organization Interfaces.

General Terms
Design; Management.

INTRODUCTION
Cyberinfrastructures (CIs) are virtual organizations comprised of people and large-scale scientific computational and networking infrastructures. In order to answer pressing scientific questions in areas like human disease and global warming, scientists are engaging in large-scale distributed and interdisciplinary collaboration around very large data sets from a wide variety of sources. New infrastructures are needed to meet the communication and computation demands of contemporary collaborative science.

There is an emphasis on sharing tools and data in order to enable new forms of collaborative scientific production while making the most efficient use of available resources. However, as the scale of science grows to include larger aggregated data sets and to depend on greater levels of computational power, the question arises of how to ensure that the infrastructures that support this digital scientific knowledge base will be preserved and maintained over time. Long-term sustainability of systems and resources has become a key concern for large-scale scientific computing (a.k.a. cyberinfrastructure, e-Science, scientific Grids, etc.).

Building on the work of Star and Ruhleder [27,29], we adopt a relational view of infrastructure. Infrastructure is less a thing in and of itself than a set of relationships among people and technologies. When we refer to CI, we are referring to arrangements of technologies, individuals and organizations [15]. This research explores and reframes the sustainability of cyberinfrastructure as an ongoing process of relational maintenance.

Our research site is the Community Cyberinfrastructure for Advanced Microbial Ecology Research and Analysis (CAMERA). This project is developing advanced computational resources to support and promote the emerging community of scientists working in the new field of metagenomics. In this paper, we investigate how the developers of CAMERA understand, manage, and respond to change, and we use these findings to understand relational maintenance as a set of strategies necessary for accomplishing infrastructure.

LITERATURE REVIEW

Cyberinfrastructure
Trends toward big science and big data [2,10] are increasingly pushing scientists to collaborate across traditional organizational, geographical, temporal and disciplinary boundaries. The development of large-scale cyberinfrastructures is part of this trend. A US National Science Foundation (NSF) Blue Ribbon Panel defined cyberinfrastructure as follows: "Cyberinfrastructure refers to infrastructure based upon distributed computer, information and communication technology. If infrastructure is required for an industrial economy, then we could say that cyberinfrastructure is required for a knowledge economy" [3]. Spurred on in part by the findings of this panel, there have been significant investments made by the NSF and other agencies in developing cyberinfrastructure.

Cyberinfrastructure is more than software and hardware. It also encompasses the human infrastructure of CI, which in

CSCW'12, February 11–15, 2012, Seattle, Washington, USA.

large projects is "a vast series of overlapping traditional organizations, consortiums, loosely organized groups, and networks" [15]. In this paper our concern is with understanding the processes through which infrastructural relationships are created and sustained [13,28]. We draw heavily on the work of Star et al. [27,28,29] that understands infrastructures to be fundamentally relational. Infrastructures are embedded inside other structures and technologies, function beyond the scope of a single event or site, and are closely linked to communities of practice [29]. Our goal is to recognize, understand, and ultimately better support the collaborative work of infrastructuring.

Cyberinfrastructure and Organizational Sustainability

Cyberinfrastructure is becoming increasingly important for the conduct of science, but many early CI projects were developed as short-term endeavors without much consideration of what would happen to the infrastructural resources when the projects concluded. As more science depends on cyberinfrastructure and early CI development projects are coming to an end, the sustainability of CI has become a pressing issue [24].

Sustainability can be a difficult concept to pin down, however. To sustain cyberinfrastructure means to make it last or endure for long (or even indefinite) time periods. But this leaves open questions about what exactly should be preserved and how to choose among potentially competing infrastructure priorities like sustainability, innovation, growth, and robustness. Our goal here is to inform this conversation by studying and theorizing the work of maintaining cyberinfrastructure. The discussion of CI sustainability has tended to focus in two areas: sustainable institutional resources and preservation of scientific products.

In terms of the issues of sustainable institutional resources, researchers have discussed how to continue to fund cyberinfrastructure given the challenges of long-term planning and resource allocation. Organizations like the National Science Foundation that have funded much of the early development of cyberinfrastructure are poorly placed to provide long-term, ongoing support. Concerns in this area have focused on issues like the reusability of code and components to ensure efficient development and deployment of technological resources [26]. Another set of concerns revolves around incorporating cyberinfrastructures into existing institutional structures like university libraries or IT departments as a way to transition from short-term development projects to a more sustainable funding model [19].

The second factor driving the push for sustainability is a concern that we may be losing valuable (and sometimes irreplaceable) knowledge if scientific outputs are not adequately preserved [13]. In this era of "big data" research, datasets are seen as knowledge products in and of themselves, and it is important to ensure long-term storage and curation of the data [18]. Similarly, as models and algorithms are becoming an increasingly central part of the scientific method, there is a push to save research-related software as well [30]. The preservation of scientific artifacts would ideally allow future scientists to judge the validity and accuracy of scientific conclusions. Just as important, however, is that data and codes must be preserved for potential reuse by future scientists [16].

This paper advances our understanding of a third aspect of sustainability, specifically, how to maintain the persistent human and technological arrangements that comprise cyberinfrastructure. Ribes and Finholt discuss the dilemma of building a sustainable infrastructure in the world of software development, which is known for rapidly advancing hardware, development platforms, and programming languages [23]. They see cyberinfrastructure as a sustainable, human-technical collective and articulate a set of tensions which infrastructure developers face when thinking about long-term sustainability. For example, the "development vs. maintenance" tension arises from the necessity of doing ongoing upkeep work even though developing new tools and resources tends to be more valued and rewarded. These tensions describe the pressures that drive infrastructure development. This framework has much in common with the approach taken here, especially in its recognition that developing cyberinfrastructure "requires creative attention to issues of sustainable technology, persistent human arrangements, and institutional resources" (p. 379). This paper builds on this observation that sustainability is needed, and investigates the work of a CI development team to demonstrate how sustainability can be achieved.

Developing Cyberinfrastructure Through Synergizing, Leveraging, and Aligning

Recognizing the challenges and necessity of sustaining cyberinfrastructure, CSCW research has turned to investigating how sustainability is accomplished. In order to investigate organizational sustainability and organizational change in CI, Bietz, et al. [6] introduce the concept of *synergizing*. Synergizing recognizes that infrastructure is necessarily woven into existing structure, social arrangements and technologies" [29]. Synergizing is "the work that developers of infrastructure do to build and maintain productive relationships among people, organizations, and technologies." Synergizing specifically draws on the concept of synergy, the increased effectiveness resulting from combined action or cooperation [22]. This systems-level, relational view of infrastructure work provides the framing for our discussion of cyberinfrastructure sustainability.

Synergizing encompasses two specific kinds of work activities: leveraging and aligning. Leveraging is the work a development team does when it uses its existing relationships (between people, organizations, or technologies) to build or strengthen other productive relationships. For example, a development team may leverage connections within its own university to gain access to cutting edge technology or other resources. In addition, leveraging an existing network can result in less alignment work (because an existing relationship indicates that some level of alignment work has been done previously).

Aligning is the work that developers do to make relationships among people, organizations and technologies productive and functional within a specific CI. An example of alignment work is developing an application programming interface (API) that allows two component technologies to communicate with each other. However, alignment work is not limited to creating connections between technologies and includes the work required for individuals and organizations to be able to collaborate. Alignment work can include the work of developing data sharing policies that are amenable to all participants, or ensuring that technological security arrangements are in line with those policies. Alignment work is "the work necessary to create enough compatibility between entities so that the relationship can be productive."

Synergizing is distinct from articulation work [11,25] because it ensures that a common field of work exists, whereas articulation ensures that work goes well and that complexity is controlled within an existing field of work. Synergizing creates the situation in which articulation work can be enacted. However, both synergizing and articulation work are fundamentally concerned with the work done to make other work possible.

Relationships among human and technological components (like the components themselves) change over time, and must be maintained and tended if they are to continue to exist. Synergizing affords a consideration of cyberinfrastructure sustainability that concentrates on how these relational structures are managed over time.

SITE AND METHODS

The Community Cyberinfrastructure for Advanced Microbial Ecology Research and Analysis (CAMERA) is a cyberinfrastructure development project intended to provide resources for high-volume data storage and analysis in metagenomics. Metagenomics is a "new science" aimed at understanding the genomic characteristics of microbial populations [21]. New laboratory technologies, in combination with advanced computational capabilities, allow scientists to change the level of analysis from the single organism (as in traditional genomics) to entire populations of microorganisms. For example, the Human Microbiome Project [32] is focused on characterizing the bacteria and other microbes that live in the human body in order to understand how these microorganisms contribute to human health and disease.

Metagenomics depends on access to large databases of genomic data and significant computational and networking power [5]. Microbiologists in our study report a shift away from traditional hands on research in the field or laboratory so that now more than 90% of their research is conducted "*in silico*." Genetic sequencers produce vast amounts of data about each biological sample, which scientists analyze with a variety of statistical techniques, many of which require comparing the new sample to large databases of reference genomes. While other genetic and genomic databases exist, scientists were concerned that none were capable of supporting the specific data and analysis demands of this new science. In response to this concern, the Gordon and Betty Moore Foundation (http://www.gbmf.org) commissioned the development of CAMERA. The foundation funded the California Institute for Telecommunications and Information Technology (Calit2) at the University of California San Diego (UCSD) and the J. Craig Venter Institute (JCVI) to build a new cyberinfrastructure for metagenomics. The project began in 2006 and was funded at $24.5 million over seven years.

Data Collection and Analysis

The CAMERA cyberinfrastructure development project was the site for the current research. We engaged in two extended periods of investigation with the CAMERA project team. In both periods, our investigation included a mix of interviews with project participants and observation of everyday activities and meetings. We will refer to these two periods as "Round 1" and "Round 2."

Round 1 began in the late summer of 2007, but most observations took place between January and May of 2008. During that 4-month period, the lead author attended weekly project meetings, ad hoc meetings, and spent at least one day per week working from an assigned desk in the development team area. We interviewed as many members of the development team as we could, some of them multiple times.

Round 2 of our investigation took place from May through September 2010. Again, the lead author attended various project meetings, observed daily work (although there was no assigned desk in Round 2), and interviewed as many members of the development team as would participate.

These two time periods were chosen to be approximately two years apart and to fit with both the researchers' and participants' schedules, but there were no other theoretical motivations for choosing these specific dates. Our goal was to develop two snapshots in the life of the project that could serve as a basis for comparison and help us understand how projects may change over time. It should also be noted that this time period is relatively short in the life of infrastructures. Ribes and Finholt [23] borrow the concept of the "long now" to discuss issues of the long-term in infrastructure development. Our three-year study period gives us some perspective on change, but would be better described as the short- to medium-term. This time period does not allow us to comprehensively catalog all of the potential aspects of long-term change.

Even so, investigation at this scale covers substantial organizational change and yields important characteristics of the work of cyberinfrastructure sustainability. In late

2008, the CAMERA development team underwent a significant reorganization which also included a major staff shakeup. When we conducted Round 2 of our investigation, one of the earlier PIs was no longer on the project, and of the development team professional staff, only three individuals were still working on the project. Coupled with the rapid pace of change in the developing science of metagenomics, we saw a number of interesting changes between the two rounds of investigation.

While our primary investigations involve those individuals and organizations who are directly involved in the work of development, we take a broad view of the site and include a wide swath of stakeholders including funders, the "users" of the system, project collaborators and competitors, and members of broader scientific communities who hold a stake in the development of this and similar cyberinfrastructures.

During the two-year period when we were not on site with the CAMERA team, our focus shifted to developing a broader understanding of the landscape of cyberinfrastructure for metagenomics research. We interviewed microbiologists, bioinformaticists, computer scientists, and representatives of funding agencies. We interviewed both users and developers of several major genomics and metagenomics databases. We attended conferences and workshops devoted to metagenomics research, database development, and the development of standards for genomic data and metadata. Over a period of five months, one of the authors attended weekly laboratory meetings at an academic molecular biology laboratory engaged in metagenomics research.

In all, we conducted 43 semi-structured interviews with 33 CAMERA team members, other stakeholders, and scientists in the metagenomics field. Interviews lasted from 20 to 102 minutes (median: 52 minutes). We attended 30 regularly scheduled CAMERA meetings, numerous ad-hoc meetings, and observed the ongoing work of the CAMERA development team, resulting in over 100 hours of observation. Transcripts of interviews and field notes were analyzed using grounded theory techniques and Atlas.ti qualitative data analysis software [4,7,12]. All participants are identified by pseudonyms. Data were open coded as they were generated. Coding continued as new data came in, both building on and extending the existing code list. Descriptive and analytic memos were written during ongoing analysis of the data. Coding and memoing were iterative: after writing memos, we would return to the texts to further enhance and refine the coding scheme. Through this process, we developed the set of themes that we discuss in this paper.

FINDINGS

Like others who have studied sustainability, we observed that a state of ongoing change is the norm for cyberinfrastructure. Sustainability cannot be a matter of maintaining the status quo. Only by responding to new organizational arrangements, technologies and scientific needs can an infrastructure remain useful. In this section, we use the analytical lens of synergizing to explore in detail how cyberinfrastructure responds and adapts to ongoing change. Cyberinfrastructure development is a process of creating and maintaining relationships among people, organizations and technologies. Documenting synergistic activity is difficult because the complexity of the systems requires an analytic complexity that cannot be captured by a focus on a single analytical unit. The findings below take only elements of cyberinfrastructure—human infra-structure, technology, and science—and trace how those elements interact and co-evolve with other infrastructural elements in order to illustrate the work of how organizational stability is accomplished.

Human Infrastructure: Changing and Stabilizing

Understanding sustainability through the lens of synergizing requires a consideration of how infrastructures adapt. The notion of human infrastructure underlines the importance of recognizing the multitude of collaborative forms (organizations, networks, teams, etc.) necessary for accomplishing infrastructural work. Therefore in order to understand how the sustainability of cyberinfrastructure is managed, we explore how those entities interact.

When we returned to the CAMERA project for Round 2 of our study, the most obvious change was that the project had undergone a significant shift in the human infrastructure. This began as a change in the organizational alignments of the project. CAMERA was originally a partnership of Calit2 and the J. Craig Venter Institute (JCVI). Calit2 is a research institute of the University of California, and the CAMERA team was located entirely on the UC San Diego campus. JCVI is an independent genomic sciences institute with most of its staff in Maryland, USA. During Round 1 of our study, JCVI had decided to leave the CAMERA project, and interactions with individuals at that institution were becoming less frequent. JCVI had provided a good deal of biological and technological expertise, and there was a concern that their leaving could represent a loss of capability. CAMERA's leadership felt that the project needed to quickly partner with another organization to deliver on the promises made to the funders and the scientific community. As our Round 1 engagement was wrapping up, the project leaders had decided to partner with the Center for Research on Biological Systems (CRBS) in order to benefit from their experience with other similar projects. CRBS is another research unit at UCSD with significant experience developing cyberinfrastructures, including the Neuroscience Information Framework, the National Biomedical Computation Resource, and the Biomedical Informatics Research Network. While CRBS and Calit2 are independent units, they have become closer collaborators, especially since they began working together on CAMERA. In Round 2, even though Calit2 was still involved, CRBS was clearly the lead organization for the development work, with key project leadership positions occupied by CRBS-affiliated staff.

This change in organizational arrangements had also resulted in significant staff turnover. Of the Round 2 staff, only two of three members of the Executive Committee, one of six members of the Leadership Team, and three of twenty-five professional staff had been on the project during Round 1. Many of the staff working on CAMERA in Round 2 had previously worked with CRBS on other cyberinfrastructure projects.

The synergizing lens, which focuses attention on the work of building and maintaining infrastructural relationships, helps us understand how this transition was managed. The decision to collaborate with CRBS was seen as a way to sustain infrastructural capabilities after it became clear that JCVI was going to leave the project. However, the alignment work necessary to make the new relationship with CRBS productive would take time. A CRBS staff member on the Round 2 CAMERA team explained how CRBS took over support of JCVI-developed applications:

> *"We had a phased transition plan... where our teams worked together with their teams, and that was to gain an understanding of the system.... And then after a certain period of time we took over the primary support for the components for the entire system.... So, it wasn't an abrupt cutoff." (Johann, CRBS staff, Round 2)*

Switching partnerships from JCVI to CRBS was not an instantaneous change, but was managed in phases so as to minimize disruption to the infrastructure. This transition in the human infrastructure involved first bringing in the new organization (CRBS) and personnel and working to make those new relationships productive before JCVI transitioned out of the project. We also found that while only a few of the professional staff were still on the project, those staff had assumed larger responsibilities in the project, and they played important roles in providing historical information to the new team members.

The transition was easier than it might have been because CRBS and the new participants were already embedded in many of the same structures as Calit2 and the Round 1 CAMERA staff. CRBS was also based at UCSD, had been involved in cyberinfrastructure development for years, and had worked closely with scientists in biology and related fields. This simplified the alignment work in a number of areas. For example, mechanisms for moving money between Calit2 and CRBS were already in place because they were both part of the UCSD financial systems, and CRBS was already familiar with the UCSD computer networks and other technological resources on campus. Synergizing highlights that being embedded in multiple, overlapping networks and systems is an important resource for cyberinfrastructure development, as existing infrastructural relationships are *leveraged* to create new relationships.

To understand how CAMERA was sustained through this organizational change, it is also important to recognize that the human infrastructure of cyberinfrastructure is larger than the development team. Even as these changes were going on within the project staff, other stakeholder groups remained relatively constant. CAMERA's 10-person scientific advisory board played a significant role in setting the project's vision and priorities, and between Rounds 1 and 2, only two people left and one new person joined this board. In both rounds, we saw that not only did the project funding come from the same source, the same program officer was involved. And even though the development team was almost completely different, they were still working with many of the same scientists and the same laboratories in Round 2.

CAMERA's ability to serve the metagenomics community was preserved, even as organizational arrangements and development staff shifted. We see this stability resulting from a variety of factors, including a phased transition, leveraging other infrastructural relationships, and drawing on the stability of the project's other stakeholders. Maintaining this stability of the whole even as various aspects change is an important part of cyberinfrastructure sustainability.

Changing Technologies: Causes and Consequences

The relational embeddedness of cyberinfrastructure implies a degree of dependency or contingency among infrastructural components. Changes in one area lead to changes and adaptations in others. For example, changes in human infrastructure, precipitated changes in technology, which in turn precipitated still other changes in human infrastructure and technology.

We found that certain changes in the technological infrastructure of CAMERA were a direct result of the reorganization of the human infrastructure. During Round 2 of our study, the CAMERA team released version 2 of the CAMERA resource, the first major release since CRBS had joined the project. One participant discussed the tight coupling between the human infrastructure and the new technologies:

> *"I mean with the changeover to CRBS it's not - I wouldn't say it's just a management change. With the change to CRBS completely changed the site itself." (Martin, Professional Staff, Round 2)*

After CRBS joined the project, CAMERA adopted a set of technologies that included portal technology for the web site, a different database platform, and various project management and development tools. While some of these technologies provided new or improved functionality, many replaced existing similar technologies. However, the new team was already familiar with the new technologies, and they were used widely in the CRBS organization. By adopting these technologies, CAMERA could benefit by leveraging a number of other relationships: the team would gain access to a wider pool of expertise from other CRBS

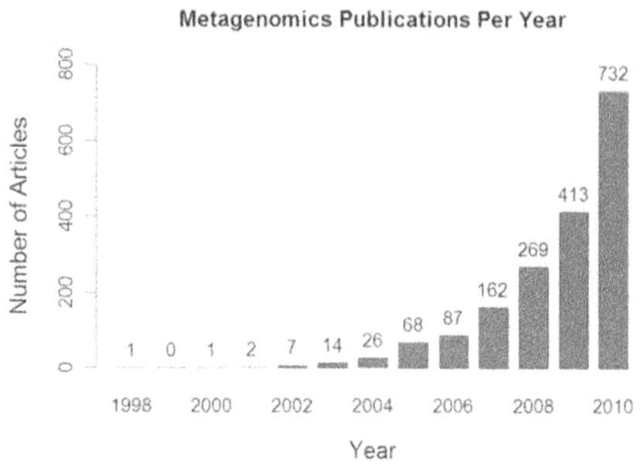

Figure 1: Number of publications per year returned from a PubMed search for "metagenom*" (April 30, 2011).

projects, they could shift some of the burden of system administration outside of CAMERA and onto the CRBS infrastructure, and they could participate in CRBS license agreements for commercial technologies.

However, adopting the new technologies also required making adjustments elsewhere in the system. Pieces of the JCVI code had to be rewritten to interface with new database software. New instructions had to be written to help users manage their accounts on the system. These changes fed back into the human infrastructure, with roles in the projects shifting slightly to accommodate the new technology. This spreading out of actions and responses through infrastructural relationships can be a path to innovation in infrastructure, and in fact, this coupling of infrastructural components is often part of the reason for initiating changes (e.g. making a technology change may draw in a new stakeholder community that needs the new capabilities). In order to realize this innovation and sustain the infrastructure, the CAMERA developers had to engage in an ongoing process of adjusting and tweaking relationships between components to keep them in alignment.

Changing Science

In order to sustain the CAMERA cyberinfrastructure, developers had to adapt to changes in the science and communities they were serving. In the previous sections we discussed the work that developers do to keep the human and technological structures in alignment within the CAMERA cyberinfrastructure. However, in order for the CI to maintain its value to the community of users, it is necessary to maintain relationships that may be outside of CAMERA's control. This work involves similar synergizing processes, but with an emphasis on managing relationships with other systems and infrastructures.

To some extent, the need to adapt to external changes is driven by the development of the scientific domain. During the period in which we were studying CAMERA, we observed a number of changes in the scientific context. 2008-2010 was a period of significant growth for this scientific community, as can be seen in the number of published metagenomics papers per year (see Figure 1). When we started working on this project, metagenomics was still on the fringes of microbiology, and some of our scientists reported that it was difficult to convince journal reviewers that metagenomic studies were valid. By 2010, metagenomics was on a much more established footing.

The growth of the metagenomics community and the development of metagenomics science created another set of sustainability-related pressures on the CAMERA cyberinfrastructure. At the same time that some scientific controversies were closed, others opened. Research questions and methods in the community shifted. In order to stay current and continue to provide useful services, the CI had to adjust to what was going on around it.

For example, in Round 1, the developers were dealing with what contextual metadata—data about the environment from which the metagenomic samples were collected—should be stored in the CAMERA database. One of the key differences between metagenomics data and data from genomic studies is the importance of metadata. While this is a simplification, traditional genomics research has focused on the genomes (hereditary information encoded in DNA and RNA) of individual organisms or species. Metagenomics, on the other hand, uses genetic material to understand the relationships between populations of microorganisms and their environments. For example, metagenomic studies have investigated how populations of organisms are affected by acid mine drainage [1], and whether particular communities of organisms in the gut are related to obesity [31]. In order to understand these phenomena, it is necessary not only to store the genetic sequence information, but also to store information about the environment, e.g. the pH of the mine runoff, or the weight of the study participants. This metadata is also crucial for data aggregation and recombination. Several scientists in our study expressed a hope that soon it would be possible, using a database like CAMERA, to combine datasets in new ways to answer new research questions. For example, even though the two studies mentioned above are looking at very different 'environments,' the data from both may be useful to discover whether all microorganisms that live in acidic environments share certain characteristics. This kind of aggregation across studies requires that all studies in the database share a consistent set of standardized metadata. However, because the metadata are closely tied to particular research questions and disciplinary approaches, deciding which metadata are included in the database can become a contentious negotiation [5].

In Round 1, CAMERA was struggling to decide which metadata fields should be in their database. One participant stated,

> *"Another challenge is the – there are really no standards associated with the metadata* per se....

There's no sort of well-defined, organized checklist... that a scientist in the field would use as part of the data collection process. So – and that's ongoing and the challenge is to sort of work with the community and other practitioners to generate those standards." (Philip, Executive Committee, Round 1)

At this time, there was basically no agreement in the community about what metadata should be stored. However, by Round 2, this question was no longer a pressing concern. The Genomics Standards Consortium (GSC, http://www.gensc.org), a group of stakeholders from across the genomics and metagenomics communities published a standard metadata checklist in mid-2008 [8]. While there were still ongoing metadata negotiations, these discussions now took place under GSC auspices. The publication of the standard checklist allowed CAMERA to treat the controversy as closed (at least until the next version was published). The CAMERA development team quickly adopted the GSC checklist: "In the data query application, we follow the standard very strictly" (Alvin, Professional Staff, Round 2). The publication of the standard created a pressure on CAMERA to adapt, but the standard also signaled a level of agreement within the scientific community and allowed CAMERA to shift its attentions elsewhere.

At the same time that some issues were becoming less salient, others were becoming more problematic for the developers. One of these revolved around how CAMERA would support analysis of metagenomic data. In Round 1, the developers were focusing primarily on analyses that would be widely useful to metagenomics researchers. Users could choose from a predefined set of analyses to run against either datasets already in the CAMERA system or datasets that they had uploaded. There were plans to bring community-created analyses into the CAMERA system. The developers believed that software created by end users would be more useful to other community members.

"Software coming in from the community is absolutely, absolutely a priority for me. That is something we are working on quite hard.... The software being developed externally is by biologists with a little bit of skill in computer science that know exactly what they're doing scientifically and by definition there's a much higher probability that what they're doing is of interest to the scientific community." (Morgan, Leadership Team, Round 1)

Even though these scientists may not have significant skill or experience in computer science or software engineering, they are developing software specifically to fill a scientific need that they have experienced. Working with members of the scientific community, the CAMERA team would identify the software that could be useful more broadly. They would then bring this software into the CAMERA systems so that other scientists could use it to run their own analyses.

When we came back for Round 2 of investigation, we discovered that incorporating user-generated analysis software was a much larger part of the project. However, the model for doing so was significantly different and was a response to new pressures from the scientific community. Metagenomic datasets were getting larger and stretching the capacity of in-lab computing resources. The breadth of metagenomics approaches and research questions was also increasing, so that it was less likely that a small number of pre-selected analyses would serve the entire community. The focus shifted from providing a few basic analysis tools to being a more open analysis platform for metagenomics research.

This change in approach involved incorporating a new technology. Whereas before each analysis used its own custom script and operated independently of other analyses, now analyses were conducted using a "scientific workflow" system called Kepler [17]. Kepler allows scientists to create graphical flowchart-like versions of their analyses. These workflows can also be loaded and run on the CAMERA systems, allowing scientists to relatively easily run their own analyses on high-performance computers. Like the community software concept that we saw in Round 1, the workflows create a framework for bringing scientist-generated software into CAMERA. However, in Round 2 the emphasis is on allowing scientists to run their own individual analyses using the CAMERA data and computational resources without necessarily sharing their scripts or having to interact with the CAMERA developers. If scientists do want to make their workflows public, it is simply a matter of changing the sharing settings in their CAMERA account.

The workflow system was a way to respond to the changing needs of the scientific community the cyberinfrastructure was serving. The community was becoming more diverse in terms of its analysis requirements, and the workflows allow scientists to conduct analyses on the CAMERA system that are specifically tailored to their needs. In this case, the work needed to sustain the CI so that it would remain valuable to the labs included leveraging an existing technology (Kepler) which had been available for some time and had a robust open-source academic development community. As a way to help the alignment work of integrating Kepler into the CAMERA systems, the CAMERA team partnered with researchers and developers from the San Diego Supercomputing Center who had been involved in the Kepler project from its beginning. Bioinformaticists on the CAMERA development team created sample Kepler workflows to provide basic functionality and guiding examples for the scientists who would now be asked to create their analyses scripts as workflows. Training sessions were planned and curricula were developed to train graduate students to create and use workflows. This is an example of the ongoing leveraging and aligning work that is necessary to sustain cyberinfrastructure. Without these types of gradual sustaining changes, the CI will become less and less valuable to the community over time.

DISCUSSION

Given that cyberinfrastructures like CAMERA are in a state of ongoing change, sustainability can be seen as matter of tending to a set of infrastructural relationships to maintain productive alignments. Only by responding to new organizational arrangements, technologies and scientific needs can an infrastructure remain relevant.

However, it is also clear that changes in the cyberinfrastructure take time. If change is too rapid, or affects too much of the relational structure of the CI, it is more likely to have negative consequences. In CAMERA, we saw changes and their consequences happening over time scales of two or more years. We also see change happening at different rates in different systems. Even while the middleware has changed significantly in this time period, the computing hardware has remained quite stable. We expect that as the infrastructure matures, the overall pace of change may slow down or speed up, but we do not expect change to stop.

In the rest of this discussion, we address some of the implications of our findings for how we think about and design for sustainability of cyberinfrastructure.

Coupling Human and Technological Infrastructure

The value of infrastructures lies in their ability to connect other systems and infrastructures. The current research reveals that in the richly embedded and interconnected sets of relationships among the human and technological components that comprise cyberinfrastructures, changes in one component lead to shifts in other connected components.

A change in one component of the infrastructure cannot be understood without understanding the way that the component is connected to others. We observed, for example, a very close coupling between technological changes and changes in human infrastructure. In CAMERA, a change in organizational participation (JCVI leaving the project, CRBS joining the project) also involved a set of changes for individuals (some staff leaving the project, others joining) and technologies (switching to different middleware applications). The perturbations in the technological components then enable other changes, for example, developing new collaborations with the Kepler open source project, or shifting more of the responsibility for application development to the scientist users. These responses propagate through the networks and webs of relationships that make up the infrastructure, as each component adjusts (or is adjusted) to changes going on around it.

The *synergizing* concept reminds us that even though these complex systems have emergent properties and far-reaching effects, they are not beyond the reach of design. In the rest of this discussion, we will consider what the example of CAMERA reveals about what it means to design for sustainable cyberinfrastructure.

Ongoing Maintenance Work

Sustainability of a cyberinfrastructure over time is a process of ongoing maintenance of infrastructural relationships among people, organizations, and technologies. This maintenance work is taking place against a constant backdrop of change. A change in one component produces a spreading set of responses as other components and systems adjust and adapt to each other. These adaptations spread through the cyberinfrastructure at different rates, with some components adapting quickly (e.g., a bug fix in a script may be complete in a few minutes) while others take years (e.g. getting community buy-in for a new data standard). Making these adaptations is the work required to sustain cyberinfrastructure.

It is important to realize that this work operates not only on the components themselves but also on the relationships between them. The kind of adaptation varies depending on the circumstances. Some relationships remain relatively stable (e.g. the relationships between the CAMERA project and the stakeholders on its advisory board), with only minor changes to keep the relationships productive. In other cases, it may make more sense to end a relationship than to try to keep it active. Frequently, new relationships are cultivated, perhaps to expand the scope of the cyberinfrastructure, or replace another relationship that is no longer active. This work takes place against an always-changing backdrop of evolving stakeholder needs, developing science, new technologies, unpredictable funding, and shifting organizational attachments. A cyberinfrastructure that does not keep pace with these changes will quickly become obsolete.

This perspective helps to reframe the tension between innovation and upkeep. While we agree with Ribes and Finholt [23] that creating something perceived as new is often seen as more valuable than maintenance, the synergizing lens reveals that the day-to-day work of maintaining the CAMERA cyberinfrastructure is not fundamentally different than the work of developing new capabilities. In fact, maintenance work could be better described as continual redevelopment work.

Designing for Flexibility

Sustaining cyberinfrastructure requires continual adaptation. Ribes and Finholt find that there is a tension in infrastructure development between maintaining flexibility in the face of pressure to have concrete and detailed plans [23]. We see this tension as a design opportunity and believe there are opportunities to make flexibility and responsiveness a design consideration for the development of cyberinfrastructure. For example, an active and evolving research area is to consider how to flexibly connect heterogeneous data sources using semantic web technologies [9].

When designing infrastructures, it is important to consider both flexibility and stability. As components become more embedded within infrastructures, the networks of relationships tend to reinforce each other and become stronger and more productive [6]. Too much flexibility in a cyberinfrastructure could lead to more instances of breakdown and a loss of robustness.

Flexibility need not be uniform across the entire infrastructure. Some components and relationships can be more flexible while others are more rigid. Similarly, flexibility can be adjusted over time. We saw the CAMERA developers using this to their advantage. For example, when CRBS joined the project, most of the technological components were kept unchanged while the human and organizational components were in flux. It was not until two years later, when the human infrastructure was more established, that the team released the new version of the software. The timing of changes was carefully managed in order to maintain the balance between flexibility and stability.

Although it is somewhat counterintuitive, we believe that standardization can be an important part of designing for flexibility. In CAMERA, we saw the adoption of genomic data and metadata standards, and the use of the Kepler workflow system to standardize the representation of data analysis scripts. In both of these cases, adopting the standard freed up resources that could be used to address other areas where flexibility was more important. The key design decisions involve which aspects to standardize and which need to remain flexible. A good standard can lead to greater efficiencies, but standardization that happens before stakeholders have reached agreement can stifle necessary innovation [14].

CONCLUSION: CI SUSTAINABILITY

In this paper we have explored how one cyberinfrastructure project, CAMERA, reacted to and managed change in pursuit of sustainability. By conducting investigations at two time periods we were able to highlight aspects of change that might not be as salient in shorter time periods. We recognize that the three-year time period covered in the study is still short compared to other work that has focused on longer time spans (e.g. [23]). Certain sustainability issues are beyond the scope of this study, like how to ensure long-term funding on decade-long scales or what to do when it is decided that an infrastructure has outlived its usefulness. However, we argue that with CAMERA, we were able to see many of the same kinds of changes that cyberinfrastructures will face in the longer term: refactoring of organizational and human resources, changing demands from user communities, and the introduction of new technologies. We hope that these findings can inform not only the work of developing cyberinfrastructure, but also policy and planning discussions.

Viewing sustainability through the lens of synergizing highlights that the work involved in maintaining a productive CI involves managing the infrastructural relationships among organizations, individuals and technologies. The human and technological infrastructures are tightly coupled, and changes in one area often require adjustments in others. As CAMERA faced fluctuations in its human infrastructure, technologies, and scientific user community, the developers actively moderated the pace of change to prevent major disruptions, and paid careful attention to the balance of flexibility and stability within the cyberinfrastructure.

This case provides a better understanding of the work necessary to sustain cyberinfrastructure. Preserving the components of the CI is not enough. Myers and McGrath [20] argue that when faced with the question of what should be sustained, "sustaining capabilities and architecting to enable change are often the better choice, particularly when one considers the costs and consequences of maintaining a specific software product." In other words, CI sustainability is less about maintaining any particular technology than it is about being prepared to accommodate technological, scientific and organizational change. The capabilities of cyberinfrastructure are a product of a relational development process that we call synergizing. Preserving the artifacts and technological elements of cyberinfrastructures is important, but much of the value of the cyberinfrastructure is lost if these are taken out of their relational context. The usefulness of cyberinfrastructure arises out of the rich interconnectedness of the human and technological infrastructures. Sustaining a cyberinfrastructure requires maintaining these relationships.

ACKNOWLEDGMENTS

This research was supported in part by NSF awards IIS-0712994 and OCI-0838601. Thanks to our participants and to our anonymous reviewers for their feedback.

REFERENCES

1. Allen, E. E., & Banfield, J. F. Community genomics in microbial ecology and evolution. *Nature Reviews Microbiology*, 3, 6 (2005), 489-498.
2. Aranova, E., Baker, K. S., & Oreskes, N. Big Science and Big Data in biology: From the International Geophysical Year through the International Biological Program to the Long Term Ecological Research (LTER) Network, 1957-Present. *Historical Studies in the Natural Sciences*, 40, 2 (2010), 183-224.
3. Atkins, D. E., Droegemeier, K. K., Feldman, S. I., et al. Revolutionizing science and engineering through cyberinfrastructure: Report of the National Science Foundation blue-ribbon advisory panel on cyberinfrastructure. National Science Foundation, Washington, D.C., 2003.
4. Atlas.ti v. 6. (2011). [computer software]. Berlin: ATLAS.ti Scientific Software Development GmbH.
5. Bietz, M. J., & Lee, C. P. Collaboration in metagenomics: Sequence databases and the organization

of scientific work. In *Proc. ECSCW 2009*, Springer-Verlag (2009), 243-262.

6. Bietz, M. J., Lee, C. P., & Baumer, E. P. S. Synergizing in cyberinfrastructure development. *Computer Supported Cooperative Work*, 19, 3-4 (2010), 245-281.
7. Corbin, J., & Strauss, A. *Basics of Qualitative Research: Techniques and Procedures for Developing Grounded Theory* (3rd ed.). Sage, Thousand Oaks, CA, 2008.
8. Field, D., Garrity, G., Gray, T., et al. The minimum information about a genome sequence (MIGS) specification. *Nature Biotechnology*, 26, 5 (2008), 541-547.
9. Futrelle, J., Gaynor, J., Plutchak, J., et al. Semantic middleware for e-science knowledge spaces. In *Proc. MGC 2009*, ACM Press (2009).
10. Galison, P. *Big Science: The Growth of Large-Scale Research*. Stanford University Press, Stanford, CA, 1992.
11. Gerson, E. M. Reach, bracket, and the limits of rationalized coordination: Some challenges for CSCW. In *Resources, Co-Evolution and Artifacts: Theory in CSCW*. M. S. Ackerman & C. A. Halverson & T. Erickson & W. A. Kellogg, Eds. Springer, London, 2008, 193-220.
12. Glaser, B. G., & Strauss, A. L. *The Discovery of Grounded Theory: Strategies for Qualitative Research*. Aldine de Gruyter, New York, 1967.
13. Karasti, H., & Baker, K. S. Infrastructuring for the long-term: Ecological information management. In *Proc. HICSS 2004*, IEEE Computer Society (2004), 10020c.
14. King, J. L., & Frost, R. L. Managing distance over time: The evolution of technologies of dis/ambiguation. In *Distributed Work*. P. J. Hinds & S. Kiesler, Eds. MIT Press, Cambridge, MA, 2002, 3-26.
15. Lee, C. P., Dourish, P., & Mark, G. The human infrastructure of cyberinfrastructure. In *Proc. CSCW 2006*, ACM Press (2006), 483 - 492.
16. Lee, J. W., Zhang, J., Zimmerman, A. S., et al. DataNet: An emerging cyberinfrastructure for sharing, reusing and preserving digital data for scientific discovery and learning. *AIChE Journal*, 55, 11 (2009), 2757-2764.
17. Ludäscher, B., Altintas, I., Berkley, C., et al. Scientific workflow management and the Kepler system. *Concurrency and Computation: Practice and Experience*, 18, 10 (2006), 1039-1065.
18. Lynch, C. Big data: How do your data grow? *Nature*, 455, 7209 (2008), 28-29.
19. Mackie, C. J. Cyberinfrastructure, institutions and sustainability. *First Monday*, 12, 6 (2007).
20. Myers, J. D., & McGrath, R. E. *Sustaining capabilities not codes by architecting for innovation. In Cyberinfrastructure Software Sustainability and Reusability: Report from an NSF-funded workshop*. C. A. Stewart & G. T. Almes & B. C. Wheeler, Eds. Indiana University, Bloomington, IN, 2010, 100-102.
21. National Research Council (U.S.) Committee on Metagenomics: Challenges and Functional Applications. *New science of metagenomics: Revealing the secrets of our microbial planet*. National Academies Press, Washington, D. C., 2007.
22. The Oxford English Dictionary. (1989). *OED Online* (2nd ed.). Oxford, UK: Oxford University Press.
23. Ribes, D., & Finholt, T. A. The Long Now of Technology Infrastructure: Articulating Tensions in Development. *Journal of the Association for Information Systems*, 10 (2009), 375-398.
24. Ribes, D., & Lee, C. Sociotechnical Studies of Cyberinfrastructure and e-Research: Current Themes and Future Trajectories. *Computer Supported Cooperative Work (CSCW)*, 19, 3 (2010), 231-244.
25. Schmidt, K., & Simone, C. Coordination mechanisms: Towards a conceptual foundation of CSCW systems design. *Computer Supported Cooperative Work (CSCW)*, 5, 2 (1996), 155-200.
26. Schopf, J. M. Sustainability and the Office of CyberInfrastructure. In *Proc. Eighth IEEE International Symposium on Network Computing and Applications, 2009*., IEEE Computer Society (2009), 1-3.
27. Star, S. L. The ethnography of infrastructure. *American Behavioral Scientist*, 43, 3 (1999), 377-391.
28. Star, S. L., & Bowker, G. C. How to infrastructure. In *The Handbook of New Media*. L. A. Lievrouw & S. Livingstone, Eds. SAGE Publications, London, 2002, 151-162.
29. Star, S. L., & Ruhleder, K. Steps toward an ecology of infrastructure: Design and access for large information spaces. *Information Systems Research*, 7, 1 (1996), 111-134.
30. Stewart, C. A., Almes, G. T., & Wheeler, B. C. *Cyberinfrastructure Software Sustainability and Reusability: Report from an NSF-funded workshop*. Indiana University, Bloomington, IN, 2010.
31. Turnbaugh, P. J., Backhed, F., Fulton, L., et al. Diet-induced obesity is linked to marked but reversible alterations in the mouse distal gut microbiome. *Cell Host Microbe*, 3, 4 (2008), 213-223.
32. Turnbaugh, P. J., Ley, R. E., Hamady, M., et al. The Human Microbiome Project. *Nature*, 449, 7164 (2007), 804-810.

Cooperative Documentation: The Patient Problem List as a Nexus in Electronic Health Records

Xiaomu Zhou[1], Kai Zheng[2,3], Mark S. Ackerman[3,4], David Hanauer[5]
[1]School of Communication and Information, Rutgers University; [2]School of Public Health, [3]School of Information, [4]Department of EECS, [5]Medical School, University of Michigan

ABSTRACT
The patient Problem List (PL) is a mandated documentation component of electronic health records supporting the longitudinal summarization of patient information in addition to facilitating the coordination of care by multidisciplinary medical teams. In this paper, we report an ethnographic study that examined the institutionalization of the PL. Specifically, we explored: (1) how different groups (primary care providers, inpatient hospitalists, specialists, and emergency doctors) perceived the purposes of the PL differently; (2) how these deviated perceptions might affect their use of the PL; and (3) how the technical design of the PL facilitated or hindered the clinical practices of these groups. We found significant ambiguity regarding the definition, benefits, and use of the PL across different groups. We also found that certain groups (e.g. primary care providers) had developed effective cooperative strategies regarding the use of the PL; however, suboptimal usage was common among other user types, which could have a profound impact on quality of care and safety. Based on these findings, we provide suggestions to improve the design of the PL, particularly in strengthening its support for longitudinal and cooperative clinical practices.

Author Keywords
Patient problem list, electronic medical records, EMR, EHR, patient-centered medical records, documentation, coordination, CSCW.

ACM Classification Keywords
H.0 [information systems]; K.4.3 [organizational impacts]: Computer-supported cooperative work.

General Terms
Human Factors; Design; Documentation.

INTRODUCTION
The Problem List (PL), as the name suggests, is a place where essential descriptors about a patient's illness are recorded. In practice, the PL not only serves as an index and summary of the patent's presented symptoms and differential (tentative) or final diagnoses (i.e., "problems"), but also provides clinicians a quick access to other types of critical patient information such as allergies and medication prescriptions and treatments. Given its direct relevance to quality of care and patient safety, a comprehensive and timely documentation of the PL is mandated by the Joint Commission, [1] and therefore constitutes an essential function electronic health records (EHR) system [4].

An appropriately structured and documented PL is instrumental in facilitating the coordination of care and enhancing clinicians' ability to understand patient cases more effectively and efficiently—by eliminating the need to peruse every document in a large collection of historical patient records. It also plays a key role in proactively arranging long-term care plans both for the benefit of patients and for the cost containment goals of healthcare providers [3, 5]. Nonetheless, while the PL is mandated by the Joint Commission, how it should be implemented is largely a decision by individual healthcare institutions. Therefore, its designed objectives, actual usage, and quality of implementation can vary greatly from setting to setting. Existing research has shown that in many healthcare institutions, the implementation of the PL is very problematic which is partially responsible for its suboptimal usage and consequently underachieved value [5].

The PL's documentation summarizes a patient's information after an ambulatory visit or hospitalization to provide a comprehensive overview of this patient for future care. Therefore, it does not directly support the current episode of care. Furthermore, the "documenters" of the PL are, sometimes, not going to be the *direct* beneficiaries of the information in the future. This unique nature introduces many interesting dynamics into how different clinicians may perceive differently their anticipated responsibilities and rewards in this cooperative documentation activity, in which reciprocal benefits, tacit negotiation, and other types of incentives may all play critical roles.

To better understand this cooperative nature that has profound implications on the design and use of the PL, we conducted an ethnographically based study at a large teaching hospital in a Midwestern state in the U.S. Our

CSCW'12, February 11–15, 2012, Seattle, Washington, USA.

[1] Formerly JCAHO, i.e. Joint Commission on Accreditation of Healthcare Organization. It is an independent and non-profit organization that accredits and certifies more than 19,000 health care organizations and programs in the United States.

investigation involved observations of and interviews with different types of clinicians (e.g., specialists, general medicine hospitalists, primary care physicians, and nurse practitioners), and was focused on how the PL functions supports, as well as hinders, their group practices. The central objective of our research was to further examine the issues involved in information sharing – to examine the critically important differences between local settings and the needs for standardized processes, particularly in providing for the long term while dealing with short-term needs and incentives.

In the next section, we describe the PL in more detail and present a review of the extant research literature related to its design, implementation, and use, and similar research issues documented in CSCW. Then, we describe our empirical study setting and the data collection processes. In the following sections, we present our research findings and discuss how these findings further our understanding of the necessity of acknowledging local practices [17] in relation to standardization, and how the findings from the healthcare context may inform CSCW research in general. We conclude the paper with several design implications that may contribute to improving the PL function in EHRs.

BACKGROUND AND LITERATURE REVIEW

The PL, either on paper forms or in electronic systems, is often presented in a "table of contents" format serving as an index to most essential patient data. The entries on the "table of contents" provide not only pointers to the referenced information, but also high-level summaries of a cogently selected set of patient data to help clinicians quickly build an accurate and comprehensive understanding of the patient's illnesses, conditions, and treatments. Because of this nature, the PL represents a patient-centered, problem-oriented medical records approach (which requires careful thinking and synthesis) as opposed to a "laundry list" approach documenting data according to discrete clinical processes. Previous research has shown that these two different document practices could lead to distinct outcomes [14], and that identifying an optimal balance between describing the patient vs. medical processes that occur to the patient is vitally important [18].

First introduced by Weed in 1969 [16], the concept of the PL has been widely adopted in healthcare and is now mandated by the Joint Commission as a key component of patient records. However, there has been a lack of general consensus in the medical community with regard to what should be included on the PL in order to effectively and comprehensively present a patient case. Some emphasize "significant diagnoses and treatments" [2], while others argue for the inclusion of additional relevant information elements such as patients' psychosocial histories [10]. Due to a lack of agreement, the institutionalization of the PL has been very problematic, which has resulted in varied practices, inaccuracy (and thus distrust) of the data recorded, and consequently lack of user acceptance and suboptimal use [5].

Researchers and practitioners have strived to address these issues in order to unleash the true power of the PL. Such efforts include studies on automated construction of the PL by extracting medical concepts from narrative patient records, development of more pertinent taxonomies and vocabularies to help formalize the PL in structured and codified formats [3], and incorporation of the PL in the clinicians' sign-out process to improve efficiency and patient safety [15].

However, significant gaps remain in understanding clinicians' perception of *how* the PL should be designed and used to better support their cooperative work. For example, what are the medical and social implications that may result when the PL is missing certain information? How should the PL be constructed and presented more effectively to help clinicians make sense of patient cases? For chronically ill patients whose medical records may accumulate to an unmanageable amount over time, can the PL serve the function of helping clinicians quickly identify most critical areas in the data? Such gaps have severely constrained our ability to design more useful and usable PL functions in EHRs to help clinicians manage complex data [18]. While the study described in this paper attempted to answer these questions based on an investigation conducted in one hospital, we believe the research findings may be generalizable to other settings.

The use of the PL in a health care setting is an ideal case to further examine information sharing in a collaborative setting. Information sharing has been a consistent theme within CSCW. For example, Grudin noted that when an information object is shared across multiple parties, there are always tensions between different parties due to the unevenly distributed workload and benefits [7]. Further, Ackerman and Halverson, in their study of a hotline [1], found that when the same information object is maintained by multiple parties, there can be tensions between information provenance, i.e. who creates it, and information governance, i.e., who manages it. This is especially true when an information object is shared across communities whose expertise and practice are inherently different, and is even more complex when such information is politically or psychosocially sensitive in medical settings [18].

Long-term use of information has become more a prevalent interest in recent years. Medical care is an especially good place to examine this problem, not only because of the need but also because of the relative complexity of the work. Patients often present 'one-off' problems, and care is contingent and situated. On the other hand, medical care is not ad-hoc; it consists of sequences of standardized routines [11]. Furthermore, this work is done within a complex landscape involving a large number of clinicians from distinct specialties and backgrounds cooperating over a long period of time to provide high quality care services to patients. As such, the PL both documents those routines and the problems as well as attempts to provide an overall view of the patient.

This study was informed, then, by the research findings from both medical informatics and organizational studies in CSCW. We believed that a close examination of the PL problem would not only benefit medical practice, but could also lead to a better understanding of information sharing and reuse—specifically in trying to balance localized versus standardized practice and in ameliorating tensions between long-term and short-term needs.

STUDY SETTING

Our observation field site was an internal medicine unit at a large teaching hospital. An in-house developed electronic health records system, eCare, has been implemented in this hospital for over a decade. It allows clinicians to document various kinds of clinical notes, such as Emergency Department (ER) notes, (inpatient) admission notes, progress notes, nursing notes, discharge notes, and (outpatient) clinic visit notes. In an inpatient setting, discharger planners and social workers also document patients' discharge and long-term care plan and any social issues that may be discovered and affect patient illness management. In addition, eCare also serves as interface to pull lab/radiology results and medication information from the clinical data repository (CDR) so that clinicians largely can do their information work within eCare.

The research reported in this paper is part of our larger study which aims to explore any issues related to medical information reuse from a long-term perspective. This objective led us to search for a research site that could provide rich data related to patients with chronic illness trajectories. We selected an internal medicine unit that hosts four internal medicine doctor teams and one nursing team. The unit receives a diverse range of patients. Many patients have a long history of chronic illness accompanied by various psychosocial issues in their daily lives.

Among the four doctor teams, one general medicine team granted us the opportunity to shadow their work almost without any restriction. The nursing manager also provided us access to all aspects of the nurses' work. Therefore, our field observation focused on this general medicine team (3 attending doctors and 21 residents working on a monthly rotation) and nursing team (56 nurses).

DATA COLLECTION

The data collected and reported in this paper consist of field-based observations augmented by the examination of patients' medical records and clinicians' working documents, including both paper and electronic due to the transition to a more computerized environment. In addition, we also conducted semi-structured formal interviews with the clinicians from several units of the hospital system, such as specialists, primary care doctors, and nurse practitioners in order to get a much broader understanding of the issues.

The first author performed the field observations, semi-structured interviews, and all other data collection. She shadowed clinicians' day-to-day work, including doctors' morning rounds, diagnostic interviews, constructing notes, nursing shift-change, etc. She often engaged the clinicians to conduct informal interviews with them during quiet periods. Her fieldwork was typically from three to five hours per each session. In total, she spent over 750 hours through 18 months.

Our semi-structured interviews about the issues of PL use included 13 physicians (including inpatient general medicine, ER and specialized services, and outpatient primary care) and 2 nurse practitioners, who were all required to contributed to the PL. We also included an IT project manager who was responsible for improving the PL design and for implementing a structured PL, and who had a broad perspective about PL use across the hospital.

We employed the grounded theory [6] approach to begin our data analysis. This approach allowed us to identify emerging themes from broad observational activities and to gradually evolve into more focused data collection. For instance, the issues with PL use appeared repeatedly during our observations of work activities in the general medicine team, such as the attending doctor pushing residents multiple times to document certain information on the PL. This theme gradually emerged as an interesting research topic that led us to focus on the PL when we interviewed the clinicians, and we extended our interviewees to include a spectrum of caregivers who are all required to use the PL in their patient care. Therefore, the grounded theory method served not only as an approach for analyzing the data but also a guide for data collection. In this paper, field notes, interview transcripts, and examination of the PL function within eCare were used to corroborate one another during the data analysis process.

PROBLEM LIST IN MEDICAL PRACTICE

To comply with the Joint Commission regulations, the institution we studied requires that a Problem List (PL) be maintained for any patient who has had more than three encounters in the health system (including hospitalizations and clinic visits), and that the PL must be shared among clinicians. It is the responsibility for every clinician who treats the patient to document any "major" problems based on the categories defined.

The PL in this health system is a large table divided into six sections: Diagnoses, Procedures, Medications, Allergies, Health Maintenance/Chronic Care, and Patient Education / Counseling. For simple patients, the PL can be viewed on a couple of screen pages; but for complex patients with a long past medical history, the PL will require many pages. The first four categories are mandatory. The Health Maintenance section became primarily an automated process, pulling relevant data entries from CDR and populating them on the PL, which includes whether the patient gets services such as mammography, cholesterol screening, Pap smears, immunizations, etc. Patient Education/Counseling is not required, and is almost never used. All of the other categories require clinicians to manually enter the data. For instance, Diagnoses should contain the "significant" medical diagnoses or other problems for a patient through her or his entire lifetime for which knowledge of the items could impact future medical decision making; Procedures records a patient's surgical history and other "significant" medical procedures; Medications should list a patient's current and past medications; Allergies should contain a list of all allergies and intolerances to not only medications but foods and environmental exposures as well.

The PL was initially begun with free-text entry for all sections. Gradually, Allergies and Medications required structured input in order to build a foundation upon which inpatient computerized provider order entry (CPOE) and outpatient electronic prescribing (E-prescribing) could be implemented. Currently, the hospital system is preparing for a transition from free text to coded diagnoses as well. In this study, we will focus on the Diagnoses section.

In the rest of this section, we attempt provide a rich account of the use of the PL from different stakeholders. We report 1) how the PL provides an overview of a patient's medical record, 2) how primary care, specialists, inpatient doctors, and ER doctors perceive and use the PL differently, 3) how the PL can be over- or under-documented, depending on the type of clinician, 4) how it has become the primary care clinicians' responsibility to maintain and clean up duplicate entries on the PL, and 5) the upcoming transition to coded diagnoses from the current free text.

Mixed Perceptions and Uses of the Problem List

Our findings reveal that clinicians have mixed perceptions of what the PL is about, which further manifested in how they use the PL in their practice. It is interesting to note, for all primary care clinicians (including pediatricians) we interviewed, when asked what was their last time they used a PL, they all said something like "five minutes ago" or "I use it for every single patient I see," whereas the specialists answered the same question, "a long time ago" or "honestly I don't use it very much." In this section, we introduce how several groups of clinicians use the PL, focusing on how their perceptions are dramatically different and how these perceptions and uses may affect the continuity of care.

Primary care clinicians—heavy users

In a clinic environment, primary care clinicians almost always look at the PL just before meeting a patient (unless the patient is new and has no data in the system yet). The PL allows for a quick review of the patient's overall medical issues and helps prompt the clinicians to consider further evaluations or tests for the patient.

For primary care physicians, support staff such as nurses or medical assistants (MAs) print out a paper PL when the patients are being prepared for the physician. The physicians often update the paper PL *during* the clinical encounter and return it to the support staff for adding or updating the entries in the electronic PL. One of our interviews was with a physician who sees patients three days a week and 20 patients a day. She largely relies on her assistants to maintain her patients' electronic PL via handwritten notes, and admitted that she usually would not go back to check whether the new problems were appropriately interpreted and documented. Further, sometimes the paper PLs were just left behind and thus the official electronic PL was never updated.

Some physicians update the PL electronically by themselves due to concerns that their assistants may not understand what they wrote or to allow for more contemplation before adding the diagnoses to the records. Their use of the PL is often streamlined into their practices while they are seeing patients. One nurse practitioner reported,

```
[For] "any patient I take my laptop into the room and the problem summary list is the first thing I look at, with the patient, I have them looking at the screen actually. So, they can see the diagnoses they can see the medications and they are the ones who will say no, no that's not right I am not on that medicine anymore.... Then the patient knows what's in the system and can help me update it."
```

This nurse practitioner reported that usually after a patient's visit she would dictate the clinic visit notes and sometimes forget to update the PL. In one of the most recent peer audits (which is an institutionalized activity for nurse practitioners), among ten of her patients' records, her peer found out two cases where the diagnoses weren't updated on the PL. Since then, she has double-checked to ensure that everything is entered.

For primary care services, clinicians reported that updating a single patient's PL required an average of 1–3 minutes for an existing patient, and about 5 minutes or longer for a patient who is new to the system. However, considering that they need to see up to 20 to 30 patients per day, updating the PL within their routine workflow indeed adds significant documentation time.

Regardless, primary care clinicians recognize that the PL is essential for them because they can save a lot of time for a patient's next visit and avoid reading through the clinical notes. For them, the PL will be beneficial to whomever will see the patient subsequently, including themselves. Updating the PL, while time consuming, is a process they "pay forward" in order to maintain the continuity of care.

Specialists' view of the problem list

In contrast with the primary care clinicians, the specialists in the hospital systems seem to find that the PL requires too much "additional work," is "redundant," or is "doing the same thing two times." While we only interviewed two specialists in this study, primary care clinicians also commented on the lack of input to the PL from specialists.

It is interesting that one of the specialists (a developmental behavioral pediatrician) labeled herself as "the other end of the spectrum" of PL users. She created a template to remind her of work activities. During the interview, she recalled a recent case in which she did not enter a diagnosis of ADHD in the PL because "I haven't been careful to do that."

Another specialist (a pediatric cardiologist) commented that the PL has no direct role in the workflow of his unit. As specialists, the information they want to capture is of a very precise nature. They spend a lot of time creating precise clinical notes, and thus heavily rely on the notes when they see the patients. Their method of documentation is through dictation with subsequent refinement of their notes. In this context, documenting in the PL is perceived as an extra effort with no direct benefit for their practice. Doctors in this division never look at PL for diagnostic information.

This specialist also pointed out that what is considered as a "significant" problem is very local to each service. For instance, in their work the most significant birth defect should always be listed first with subsequent complications labeled with lower priorities. The new "problems" in their field may include a series of anatomic diagnosis of a patient's heart (e.g. certain abnormal vessels of the heart), whereas a primary care physician may only need to know that the patient has a "heart problem."

One specialist commented that unless there was a way to automatically populate the PL directly from their detailed notes, it was just not compelling for them to take extra time out of their workflow to summarize a patient's medical problems during the visit in a note and then manually key the significant problems into the patient's PL, because all they need is the detailed clinical note from the patient's last visit. However, summarized information about a patient's recent visit to a specialist and the subsequent diagnosis is critical for the patient's primary care clinicians to know.

It should be noted that not all specialists or special units have the same practice or attitude towards the PL. One primary care physician observed that certain special units (e.g. pulmonary) are "doing better" than the others.

Inpatient doctors—using the PL as hospitalization summary
Our observations, based on one general internal medicine team using informal and formal interviews, showed mixed use of the PL among inpatient doctors.

When admitting a patient who needs to be hospitalized, some of the doctors like to start gathering information from the PL to get a brief overview about the patient's prior conditions, whereas others may read the admission or discharge note from the patient's *last* hospitalization, since these notes contain more detailed information. Updating a patient's PL only takes place as the patient is being discharged from the hospital. It is the doctor who took direct care of the patient, i.e. usually the resident in a teaching hospital with the attending doctor's supervision, who is responsible for documenting in the PL for the major issues arising from the hospitalization.

For an internal medicine team, which normally consists of one attending doctor, one or two residents, and two interns (i.e. first year residents), they admit about eight patients every four days. Summarizing and documenting new diagnoses should not be a huge burden for them; however, some admit that they neglect to do this. Regardless, issues arise in considering which specific diagnoses should be included or excluded (which we will discuss in detail later) in order to make the PL useful, but not overwhelming, to other inpatient, primary care, and ER doctors.

Emergency Department doctors' use of the PL
About 80% of the patient admissions for hospitalization come through the ER in this health system. In order to make an informed decision about a patient, ER doctors need to see a quick overview of their past medical history due to the time pressures. The first priority of their work is to address the patient's acute situation and then move them to an inpatient unit or send them home.

For ER doctors, obtaining the most critical information about a patient's medical history in a highly time-sensitive fashion is a concern. A well-maintained, concise PL is ideal for this purpose. However, due to the inconsistent use across the hospital system and different interpretations of what a PL should contain (which we will discuss in detail next), certain critical information is often not documented. This information can be either medical or psychosocial. (For instance, some patients may have serious behavioral issues and they come to ER only to receive a controlled substance). On the other hand, a patient's single diagnosis can be recorded multiple times if they have had multiple prior encounters, which results in a PL that is many pages long. This situation often frustrates ER doctors who then have to sift though many non-essential items.

During our observations, one general medicine attending doctor was very upset when he made a special warning in a patient's admission note not to prescribe narcotic to a patient because she was abusing it with no diagnosis found (after multiple hospitalizations), but ER doctors missed the warning, prescribed large doses of the drug, and admitted the patient for further treatment. One ER doctor responded why they often missed a warning and did not read the note,

"If you have millions notes (in eCare), I don't know where to start."

Indeed, an ER doctor may only have a few seconds to glance at the information about a patient's critical problems (either medical or psychosocial) in their decision making process. How to construct a PL that fits into ER doctors' needs is still an open question. During our interviews, acknowledging that the PL may be constructed at different levels, some argued that a PL should only include the most important elements for a patient such that if they came into an emergency room unconscious, the ER doctors could still make informed decisions without causing harm.

Different Interpretation of 'Problem' on the PL
What is considered an appropriate "problem" that should be on a patient's PL and should it be presented? Surprisingly, there is no common agreement among clinicians, which partially explains why certain critical information is

missing while other entries are repeatedly documented. However, for some physicians, the redundancy in certain contexts has great utility [13]. In this section, we focus on how clinicians interpret the notion of a 'problem.'

As described earlier, a patient's PL has four sections that clinicians must manually update. Among these four, Medication, Allergies, and Procedures are clearly defined. However, clinicians have very different opinions about what should be put in the Diagnoses section, which is presented at the top of the PL page.

For some clinicians, only significant medical diagnoses that may affect how *later* doctors may treat the patient should be documented in the Diagnoses section. For instance, a patient's diabetes should always be on the PL. However, inpatient doctors tend to list every single diagnosis that the patient received during the hospitalization, such as 'dehydration,' 'respiratory distress,' 'diarrhea,' and 'vomiting.' Some of these diagnoses, such as dehydration may be secondary to a more important primary diagnosis, or may have resolved quickly; these may not be critical for subsequent caregivers to know.

This situation became worse after the eCare implemented a function last year that automatically extracts items from the diagnoses section from a patient's inpatient discharge note and subsequently updates the PL. The feature was a remedy for the lack of contribution to PL from inpatient doctors (only about 30%). However, it created many duplicate PL entries, because it simply included each visit-level diagnosis rather than a general summarized overview about a patient's medical history. In fact, the new feature requires the doctors who discharge the patient to synthesize and refine the PL rather than just leave it as it is after the automatic extraction.

In addition to the issue with duplicate diagnoses, many clinicians may also interpret the PL differently depending on what other information is on the PL. As the name Problem List suggests, any observed problematic situations (e.g. symptoms, patients' complaints, diagnoses) relevant to a patient hospitalization or clinic visit could be documented as a means to inform other care providers. The IT manager we interviewed, who was in charge of the improvement of PL design and use, also commented on this extended use. For instance, symptoms such as 'throat pain' and 'headache' in the PL may not be related to a clear diagnosis or may be simply a manifestation of an encompassing diagnosis such as 'strep throat.' One primary care physician pointed out that having symptoms documented provided one more dimension of the information to understand a patient's illness situation.

However, this extended use of the PL can go too far, as one primary care physician said,

"We use that for anything that we think is important because no one else is going to look at any other part. We will use it even for a reminder to ourselves you know, (such as) 'parents have chosen not to vaccinate this child' or 'remember to do serology at the nine-month visit'."

In this situation, a group of physicians used it as a place to put comments about the patient that they wanted someone else in the group to know about. Surprisingly, the use of PL as a sort of quick work list is not uncommon. For these clinicians, "these are the *key* things that we need to know whether it's a problem or not."

The lack of the consensus of what should be documented in the PL results in a messy PL that is not universally accepted by all clinicians. However, inflexible rules may not be the best way to solve the problem, as one physician said,

"I don't think that we want to restrict clinicians from entering a problem. It is always good when people enter problems. We want it as complete as possible, and the key is how to display and summarize it…if your rules are 'we don't want you entering this problem because we don't want the list cluttered', I think that's a problem. I think the better way is consider how we can make a scattered list manageable. Because if you basically say 'don't enter a problem', you are losing information."

Information Provenance vs. Governance

As described above, the PL should be a shared responsibility so that each clinician has a different role for updating the list—primary care clinicians focus on the general situation, inpatient doctors contribute the hospitalization summary, and specialists add detailed diagnoses. The PL should help coordinate care activities and maintain the continuity of patient care.

In preparation to transition from the free-text based PL into a structured format entry list, the administration has asked all clinicians to take some effort to clean up their patients' PLs by removing redundant or minor diagnoses, or other elements that will not transition well to a structured format such as comments. This task eventually was delegated to primary care clinicians, whom the patients see most often. As a result, many primary care clinicians are frustrated because a lot of this work is perceived to be clerical, even though they acknowledge that those without enough medical background could not do the work.

However, deleting or altering "problems" someone else created (as part of maintenance) raises important issues about data provenance and governance. One may not fully understand another person's intention and may remove or edit important information. This further escalates clinicians' distrust about the PL. One primary care nurse practitioner reported that she had been actively deleting duplicate entries in the PL. For instance, if she saw multiple entries of 'asthma' or 'hypertension,' she would delete the duplicates then add 'multiple' before the diagnosis. However, another clinician had a strong reservation about this practice:

"Was it (multiple) three times or 30 times? Was it just all in the last month or was it within the last five years? I think it helps to know frequency and intervals because if you had no problems and then all of a sudden you're having the same problem five times in the last month, then something is very wrong; if you had it every other year for the last ten years maybe it's not a big deal, but the context of timing matters."

In this context, a certain level of redundancy conveys much more meaning than a single mention of diagnosis.

While some primary care clinicians were actively cleaning up the 'mess' on the PL, others were hesitant because they were "afraid to get rid of somebody else's entry." In addition to the additional meanings resulting from duplicate diagnoses provided by different care providers, the use of the PL as a reminder or work list further complicates the situation. For instance, whereas one physician may enter "depression secondary to physical abuse" as a reminder about the patient's problematic situation, another physician may think such an entry is inappropriate because the Diagnosis section of a PL should only include pure medical diagnoses. If the second physician deletes the entry, the first physician will lose the valuable reminder. As described in last section, these data entries, although not clearly defined medical diagnoses, depict a richer picture about a patient, which are all important for physicians to know in order to provide appropriate care.

The conflicts between information provenance and governance created distrust about the veracity of data in the PL. One primary care physician stated that she would only print out the PL for *her own* patients when the patients need to visit other health organizations and request a copy of their PLs because she had carefully gone through their PLs manually and made sure every data element was correct.

Psychosocial Context of the Problem List

In eCare, the design for documenting a patient's major social history is a separate page accessible via a tab on the primary page, requiring an extra click. Due to this separate click, poor interface design, and perceived lack of overall utility, the page is rarely used. Documenting psychosocial history as a reminder to other care providers usually occurs either in the hospital admission notes or clinic visit notes. In addition, physicians also key in entries as a diagnosis in the PL when a patient's psychosocial issues become critical and worthy of warning to other care providers whom the patients may see.

For instance, along with some medical diagnoses, "domestic violence" also appeared on a patient's PL. The nurse practitioner who documented it wanted other care providers to know about the patient situation right at the front page of the PL. In the context of pediatric practice, entries such as "Parents divorced" or "Child adopted from another country" are not medical diagnoses, but they are very important for pediatricians to know.

The use of the PL for psychosocial problems has raised concerns among some clinicians. One primary care physician worried that information like "depression" and "anxiety" on the PL would affect the patient's ability to receive disability insurance later, because the insurers may request the patient's entire medical records, and since the PL is an overview of the patient, the company is likely to look at it first. This physician expressed,

"I don't feel comfortable putting this in the problem list; I don't think we should do that. The opposite argument is this is really important information that we need to know about that patient and we need to have it in some place where other people who are taking care of this patient can easily find it."

In the inpatient setting, the internal medicine unit deals with a large number of the patients who have chronic medical conditions with a psychosocial issue. If their frequent hospital visits are driven more by their psychosocial issues related to managing their illness rather than the illness itself, the attending doctors often push the residents to document critical and problematic psychosocial issues in the PL. In an extreme case, one attending doctor put his warning message in all capital letters at the very top of the PL, saying:

"DO NOT EVER PRESCRIBE CONTROLLED SUBSTANCES FOR THIS PATIENT. HE IS A DRUG DEALER AND FORGES PRESCRIPTIONS."

This is a way to warn ER doctors not to give certain controlled substances to patients who are drug seeking. This active and alarming description ensures that no one who reads the patient's PL will miss it. However, some residents still hesitate to enter this. One resident said while the person indeed exhibited some pain-medicine-seeking behavior that should not be encouraged, a similar warning might prevent someone in actual pain from receiving appropriate care. The subjective interpretation about a patient's psychosocial behavior has presented a unique account about the complex use of the PL. As one physician put it, "we haven't come up with an answer to that question yet."

Looking Forward: Structured Problem List

The hospital is in the process of implementing a transition to a structured Diagnoses section on the PL, preparing for the transfer of eCare data to a newly purchased commercial EHR that will be in practice next year. The new system requires structured data entry for many components.

In anticipation of the new system, some clinicians are optimistic because it has the potential to automatically populate data from clinical notes to the PL; others have a lot of concerns. The structured PL will be substantially different from how the PL is used right now. For instance, a large portion of psychosocial problems will not get transferred into the new system. Clinicians are concerned that they would lose valuable information that would affect their understanding of the patients.

DISCUSSION

Our findings provide a detailed account of clinicians' perceptions about the value of the PL and consequently how they may use the PL function in an EHR system differently. We found that while the use of the PL does support patient care among certain clinician groups, the practices are highly variable due to the lack of a common agreement on the intended purposes of the PL, which is caused by, and perhaps also a cause of, the technical design of the PL function in the EHR system used in the site.

We believe that these findings can be readily applied to better understand the tensions originating in the use of shared information objects in cooperative clinical work, in addition to informing better designs of the PL in clinical settings. This study also speaks to collaborative issues in information sharing, balancing local differences and standardization, and information reuse from a long-term perspective.

First, the use of the PL among the primary care clinicians has been well institutionalized and well integrated into their workflow. These primary care clinicians highly appreciate the value of well-constructed summary data in the PL, in supporting their patient care activities across multiple episodes. This is indeed a reflection of the nature of the longitudinal, holistic patient care services that primary care clinicians are primed to render. The reason that specialists and inpatient hospitalists are poor contributors to the PL is multifold, such as the PL not being adapted to their workflow nor specific enough. Most importantly, the lack of systematic contribution to the PL by other types of clinicians (specialists and inpatient hospitalists) echoes a classic CSCW story: people are reluctant to contribute unless they see direct rewards for them in return [7].

Second, there are situations where the PL has been "over-documented," i.e., populated with redundant data entries. This issue may be a result of the lack of a consensus what to include (and what not to) in the PL in the institution. Some clinicians adhere to the "general PL" concept, such as primary care clinicians who see that the PL documentation should be patient-centric, a snapshot of a patient, only presenting significant issues. Other clinicians, however, such as inpatient doctors, adopt the episodic approach and thereby choose to record all issues presented during the hospitalization, which can be repeating from last hospitalization or temporary symptoms quickly solved. This deviated understanding of the purposes of the PL has resulted in conflicts frustrations and suboptimal utilization. Increasingly, EHR systems are required to have a dual PL design that is intended to support both needs (and beyond, unique needs by ER doctors).

Relatedly, because eCare is shared among all patient care services in the hospital system, our field investigation uncovered interesting behaviors regarding how clinicians maintain and manage information created by other people, particularly other types of clinicians. For instance, primary care clinicians attempt and sometime are obligated to remove duplicate entries created by other care providers (inpatient doctors) further discouraging their already limited contributions. This also creates tensions between the people who generate the data (provenance) and those who manage the data (governance) [1]. The politics of information in this context not only involves the debates on data ownership but also interpretations of what is considered to be appropriate as integral parts of the PL.

Third, in both health informatics and CSCW, researchers have paid close attention to the complex use of patients' psychosocial information to facilitate patient care [10, 17, 18]. The deficiencies identified have led to arguments whether a separate set of codes for accurate and comprehensive description of patients' psychosocial information should be developed [10]. In our study, the hesitation from certain clinicians about documenting sensitive information in the PL (the judgmental comments such as "patient needy for pain medications") is reasonable, which reflects their concerns about anticipated future use of the information (e.g., seen by other clinicians, insurance company, or patients themselves through personal health records or patient portals in the future). That is, when one decides what information should be entered in a shared information object, the nuance of expressing the information is subject to anticipated downstream use [9]. If there is no clear anticipated downstream use, or there may be uncertainties with regard to how the information will be used later, clinicians are inclined not to document the information into patient records. These findings hence suggest that the PL should be considerably designed to accommodate such sensitive psychosocial information, or it will be lost. This may be an indication that there is a tension in everyday practice between short-term, specialized use and long-term use. Earlier CSCW studies have suggested to allow more flexibility in providing "informal" information and establishing communication channels to handle work-in-progress or sensitive data ([e.g. 8, 17, 18]).

Fourth, in the context of the PL, the key challenge is how to connect the dots (critical yet fragmented information from multiple episodes) into a bird's-eye view of patient cases (understanding the patient's illnesses and conditions as a meaningful whole). To have clinicians construct and maintain the PL in a manner that is primed for long-term use would require substantial effort, and this effort fails much of the time. The tensions that occur between localized practice and standardized procedures, and between acute (short-term) and chronic (long-term) issues, warrant further study. In this study, however, it is apparent that they make one unified PL difficult.

In addition, while significant progress has been made on structuring the PL, which provides the promise of automated populating the PL using existing patient records data [12], automation will not be able to deliver desirable results if no consensus has been achieved on how the PL should be constructed, as illustrated in this study. On the contrary, automation could exacerbate the situation if there is not a mindful strategy of what to include in the PL and what not to, as well as the nuances in how to properly present certain information such as patients' psychosocial data. After all, a task cannot be effectively automated if human experts do not know how to handle it properly.

Automated approaches that are capable of meeting this objective will still require significant future research.

Finally, our study not only describes the complexity of long-term information use in healthcare. It also speaks to the issues in designing a computerized system to accommodate the differences of local settings (e.g. primary care, ER, specialized care, and inpatient care) in order to better support the cooperation in future work (e.g. collaboratively documenting the patient's critical information to be used as a whole in the future). As our results show, even within the same local setting, information requirements and practices can deviate to a great extent. For instance, general medicine in inpatient care may have more patients with complicated psychosocial issues and therefore have a greater need for mechanisms to communicate psychosocial information to future care teams. Our study hence provides insights about the issues and tensions in creating information for 'work in the future', i.e. how multiple groups (with distinct expertise) can collaborate in an attempt to maintain the continuity of the work over time. We believe a better understanding of cooperation in light of work in the future is critically important in both healthcare and non-healthcare settings.

DESIGN IMPLICATIONS

Based on our findings we can suggest several design elements, including user interface modifications, to enhance the functionality, usability, and usefulness of the PL across clinical domains, ranging from general practitioners to specialists. Many of the elements we suggest would depend on significant amounts metadata to enrich the diagnoses, some of which might still have to be developed..

First, diagnoses should be coded and should provide a hierarchy so that generalists can pick higher-level codes (e.g., 'heart disease') whereas specialists could select more granular codes (e.g., 'double outlet right ventricle,' a subset of 'heart disease'). The PL itself could then include a 'slider' to adjust the level of granularity as needed, based on the clinical hierarchies, for the clinician reviewing the list. Additionally, having coded data could allow grouping by categories including 'organ system' (e.g., 'heart') or even 'disease process' (e.g., 'diabetes').

Second, diagnoses should support labels such as

- *acute* or *chronic*, so that episodic diagnoses can be distinguished from long-standing diagnoses. This is to acknowledge the differences in disease processes that may affect patients for just a short period of time versus many years.
- *active* or *resolved*, dates, relative dates, or ages at disease onset or resolution should be selectable if known. This is to record the times at which different disease processes occurred which helps clinicians determine whether they may or may not still be affecting the patient.
- *major* or *minor*, or potentially a continuum, to allow for the ranking of diagnoses in terms of perceived importance for a patient. Such labels should be modifiable over time so that if a major issue is corrected, or a minor issue flares, the PL can accurately reflect that.
- *department*, from which the diagnoses was entered in or to which it pertains. This would allow for specialists to quickly filter out the diagnoses that may not primarily be of interest to them.
- *clinician,* who entered the diagnosis or who saw the patient in which the diagnosis was made. This would allow a clinician to view everyone who may have taken care of the patient for a specific diagnosis which may be important when interdisciplinary teams are involved.

Third, diagnoses should support the ability to view the *number* of times a diagnosis was entered, especially for acute issues. This contrasts with some policies that either discourage the entry of such diagnoses or require that they be entered only once, to avoid clutter. This could be done by simply appending a number in parentheses next to the diagnosis (e.g., 'acute otitis media (10)', ear infection ten times in the past). This can provide valuable information for diagnoses in which the frequency of an event can provoke further work-up or investigation (e.g., ear tubes for too many ear infections, or a tonsillectomy for too many strep throat infections). Furthermore, the list should be expandable so that each individual episode with time stamps can be viewed individually. Even in cases where a repeated diagnosis probably has no clinical significance, such as the case with 'seasonal allergies', it may still be worthwhile to show all of the care episodes in which the diagnoses was addressed. Multiple instances for such diagnoses might suggest either a misdiagnosis or help identify a patient that is not being treated adequately.

Fourth, diagnoses should be linked to the original care episode in which each diagnosis was made, so that clicking on the diagnosis would bring up a display of the detailed note, such as an admission note by an inpatient doctor, or an outpatient clinic note by a primary care doctor.

Fifth, one should enable embedded displays of ancillary data associated with a subset of common diagnoses. For example, if a diagnosis of obesity were added, one should be able to click a link to view all weights for a patient in tabular or graphic form trended over time. Similarly, blood pressures could be displayed for patients with a diagnosis of hypertension (high blood pressure), or kidney failure so that the trends are evident immediately. Lab data could also be incorporated. This represents a hybrid model between a PL and what is often viewable on dashboards, but it would enhance the value of the PL for many clinicians.

Sixth, one should allow specific diagnoses to be flagged for internal viewing only. This is important at institutions where the PL is accessible by patients through a portal, or even by insurance companies. While the merit of such a practice is debatable, some clinicians may be reluctant to add certain diagnoses to the PL if they know that the patient will view them. This is especially true in adolescent medicine in which sensitive information (e.g., sexually transmitted infection) is supposed to be kept confidential from parents. Additionally, concerns about affecting a patient's eligibility for insurance might also drive this decision.

Last, in a rigid, structured approach, we suggest having an area where free text notes can be added. Previously, clinicians often added notes that were important for themselves or other clinicians to view on subsequent visits. These included reminders about tests that needed to be done, or even details about the patient that were important to always remember (e.g., 'tremendous fear of white coats—take off before seeing patient' or other types of psychosocial issues). With the move from paper to electronic documentation, and from free text to structured data entry, the ability to add such small notations is diminishing even though the need still exists.

In summary, we believe that while maintaining an accurate and complete problem list may require extra work by some clinicians, if such a list were constructed properly, it would become a more central source of patient-centered information for all clinicians, and thus greater incentives would exist to maintain up-to-date documentation. Our findings provide rich insights for redesigning the PL in a much more general context.

CONCLUSION

The patient Problem List (PL) is a mandated documentation component of electronic health records supporting the longitudinal summarization of patient information, in addition to facilitating the coordination of care by multidisciplinary teams. We conducted an ethnographic investigation that examined the institutionalization of the PL, investigating the use of the PL among primary care clinicians, inpatient internal medicine doctors, specialists, and emergency doctors. We found significant ambiguity regarding the definition, benefits, and use of the PL from different clinician groups. Additionally, we found that some clinician groups (e.g. primary care) had developed effective cooperative practices regarding the use of the PL; however, suboptimal usage was common in other groups which could impact quality of care and safety. We studied various issues related to information sharing, integrity, and long-term reuse in the context of clinician use of electronic health records (EHR). We described in-depth issues and tensions involved in designing a computerized system that can enable multiple user groups to collaboratively document information to support 'work in the future.' Based on the findings, we provided several design suggestions to improve the PL, particularly regarding the longitudinal cooperative clinical practices that the function should support.

ACKNOWLEDGMENTS

This work was supported in part by a Univ. of Michigan Rackham Barbour Scholarship, NSF (0325347), and the National Institutes of Health (UL1RR024986). We thank the clinicians at the study site for their incredible support.

REFERENCES

1. Ackerman, M.S. and Halverson, C. Organizational Memory as Objects, Processes, and Trajectories, *Journal of CSCW*, 13, 2(2004), 155–189.
2. Benson, D.S. et al. Quality ambulatory care: The role of the diagnostic and medication summary lists. *Qual. Rev. Bull.* 14, 6 (1988) 192–197.
3. Campbell, J.R. and Payne, T.H. A comparison of four schemes for codification of problem lists. *Proc Annu Symp Comput Appl Med Care.* (1994), 201–205.
4. The Joint Commission on Accreditation of Healthcare Organizations, *Comprehensive Accreditation Manual for Hospitals*. Oakbrook Terrace, IL, 1996.
5. Galanter, W.L. et al. Computerized physician order entry of medications and clinical decision support can improve problem list documentation compliance. *Int J Med Inform.* 79, 5(2010), 332–338.
6. Glaser, B. and Strauss, A. *Discovery of Grounded Theory.* Aldine Publishing, 1967.
7. Grudin, J. Groupware and social dynamics: *Communications of the ACM.* 37,1 (1994), 92–105.
8. Hardstone, G. et al. Supporting informality. In *Proc. CSCW'04*, ACM Press (2004), 142–151.
9. Hertzum, M. Six roles of documents in professionals' work. *ECSCW '99*, 41–60.
10. Katzenberg, B., Pickard, F. and McDermott, J. Computer Support for Clinical Practice: Embedding and Evolving Protocols of Care. *CSCW '96*, 364-369.
11. Kuperman, G, and Bates, D.W. Standardized coding of the medical problem list. *J Am Med Inform Assoc.* 1, 5 (1994), 414–415.
12. Meystre, S.M., and Haug, P.J. Randomized controlled trial of an automated problem list with improved sensitivity. *Int J Med Inform.* 77,9(2008), 602–612.
13. Munkvold, G., et.al Formalizing work: reallocating redundancy. *Proc. of CSCW '06*, 59–68.
14. Østerlund, C. Mapping Medical Work: Information practices across multiple medical settings. *Journal for Information Studies*, 3(2004), 35–44.
15. Sarkar, U. et al. Synopsis: integrating physician sign-out with the electronic medical record. *J. Hosp. Med.* 2, 5 (2007), 336–342.
16. Weed, L.L. *Medical Records, Medical Education, and Patient Care.* Yearbook Medical Publishers, 1969.
17. Zhou, X., Ackerman, M.S., and Zheng, K. I just don't know why it's gone: Maintaining informal information use in inpatient care. *Proc. of ACM SIGCHI '09*, 2061–2070.
18. Zhou, X., Ackerman, M.S., and Zheng, K. Doctors and Psychosocial Information: Records and reuse in Inpatient Care. *Proc. of ACM SIGCHI '10*, 1767–1776.

Medical Secretaries' Care of Records: The Cooperative Work of a Non-clinical Group

Claus Bossen[1], Lotte Groth Jensen[2], Flemming Witt[2]

[1]Information Studies, Aarhus University
Helsingforsgade 14, 8200 Aarhus N, Denmark
imvcb@hum.au.dk

[2]Health Technology Assessment, Aarhus University
Oluf Palmes Alle 15, 8200 Aarhus N, Denmark
{Lotte.Groth; Flemming.Witt}@stab.rm.dk

ABSTRACT
We describe the cooperative work of medical secretaries at two hospital departments, during the implementation of an electronic health record system. Medical secretaries' core task is to take care of patient records by ensuring that information is complete, up to date, and correctly coded. Medical secretaries also do information gatekeeping and articulation work. The EHR implementation stressed their importance to the departments' work arrangements, coupled their work more tightly to that of other staff, and led to task drift among professions. While medical secretaries have been relatively invisible to health informatics and CSCW, this case study identifies their importance, and suggests that they and other non-clinical groups should be considered, when developing health care IT. We propose the term 'boundary-object trimming', to conceptualize their contributions to hospitals' cooperative work arrangements.

Author Keywords
Electronic health records, health care, medical secretaries, invisible work, non-clinical groups.

ACM Classification Keywords
H.5.3 Group and Organization Interfaces – Computer supported cooperative work.

General Terms
Human Factors; Theory

INTRODUCTION
In this paper, we describe the work of medical secretaries, and their role in the cooperative work arrangements of hospitals. Medical secretaries are part of any larger medical practice or hospital, and schedule patients, transcribe physicians' notes, and ensure the completeness of records. The medical secretaries' importance became evident during the study of the implementation of a comprehensive electronic health record system (EHR) at a Danish regional hospital. Among other things, implementing the EHR slowed medical secretaries' writing-up of physicians' notes, with repercussions for physicians and nurses in particular, in terms of their proceeding with their work. Consequently, the implementation plan changed radically: The first scheduled upgrade consisted almost entirely of upgrades that mitigated the challenges the EHR presented to the medical secretaries.

The implementation of the EHR was part of ongoing efforts in Denmark, where, since the mid-1990s, national IT strategies have set high goals for the development and implementation of cross-professional, structured records that enhance clinical work, planning, and research. Substantial capital and high expectations have also been, and continue to be invested in EHRs and health information systems in the USA [9] and in European countries, such as the UK [15], Austria [16], and Norway [18]. Greenhalgh et al. present a comprehensive overview of EHR studies [23].

CSCW has contributed to the efforts to develop IT systems for health care, with studies of emergency departments, surgical wards, inpatient wards, and laboratories [5; 10], analyses of temporal and spatial aspects of cooperative work and awareness [4; 27], discussions of the role of representation and categorization in developing EHRs, and the challenges involved in their implementation [3; 12; 31].

Most studies focus on the cooperative work of physicians and nurses, while non-clinical staff, such as pharmacists and hospital porters, receive less attention. We argue that medical secretaries have a central role in hospital work arrangements. Along with other non-clinical groups, they are likely to become increasingly relevant to the design and implementation of health care IT, in the shift from stand-alone systems to integrated infrastructures. We suggest the term 'boundary-object trimming', to conceptualize their contributions to health care.

BACKGROUND
The focus on physicians and nurses in EHR-study design and implementation is understandable, considering the important and emblematic roles of these professions in health care. When browsing the ACM library portal and two medical informatics journals (*Int J Med Inform*; *J Am Med Inform Assn*), we found only one study that focused on medical secretaries: It describes the central role of the unit secretary in the information-seeking activities of a multidisciplinary team at an emergency department [40]. Medical secretaries are also mentioned in passing in other research on collaborative information-seeking [34; 37; 38].

We also found one study on patient transfers, which mentions an unspecified group of non-clinical staff [1].

Along with other non-clinical hospital staff, medical secretaries seem to be mostly invisible, a fate they share with secretaries and assistants more generally. Erickson et al. (2008) found that 'There appear to be no studies that *explicitly* focus on the work of administrative assistants in the HCI or CSCW literature.' [19: 610]. Erickson et al. describe the skills and knowledge required for administrative assistant work, and suggest the term 'articulation workers' for administrative assistants. One reason for the invisibility of secretaries and administrative assistants may be that their work, like that of technicians, is typically regarded as routine, unskilled, or not 'knowledge work' [7; 21]. Yet, as several studies in CSCW reveal, the work of telephone operators and copy machine technicians, for example, requires knowledge and skill, and is important to their organizations [11; 32; 33]. Since making work visible is pertinent to CSCW [42; 45], the apparent invisibility of clerical work is something of an enigma.

Occupations, Cooperative Work, and Tasks

Medical secretaries are part of hospitals' organizational orders, which may be understood as the result of the actors' ongoing interactions and technologies, which facilitate and stabilize complex, cooperative work arrangements [39; 43].

Strauss's interactional approach to action aims to make visible the efforts involved in the actions and interactions between actors [43]. Cooperative action and work emerge as accomplishments arising from actors' alignment of their actions with those of co-actors, task articulation, and the coordination of work trajectories with the requirements of other co-actors' work and recursive interdependencies. The effort of alignment and articulation may be minimized by routinizing interaction, and working out standard operating procedures (SOP), which may stipulate courses of action and interaction. As cooperation becomes more complex and broader in scope, actors may work out *arrangements*: temporarily stabilized agreements that may include division of work and work roles, including, for example, descriptions of responsibilities, required skills, and accountability [43]. SOPs and arrangements are often formalized and inscribed on paper or in computers. As *coordination mechanisms*, they facilitate cooperative action, enable communication, and provide updated information on work status. Multiple coordination mechanisms may be organized into *ordering systems*: complexes of interrelated practices and artefacts. These enable cooperative, coordinated interactions of greater complexity and scope than otherwise possible [39].

The multiple actors or groups of actors involved in a cooperative effort often do not share the same work objects. The analytic advantage of keeping this in mind is evident in the case of pregnant women, who, during foetal surgery, become two work objects: To surgeons, the unborn child is the primary work object, while the mother is secondary, a practical and juridical barrier to be addressed; on the other hand, nurses regard the mother as their primary work object, and concern themselves with her survival and well-being [14]. Similarly, cooperating groups of actors may be unfamiliar with the perspectives, aims, and scope of other actors' work. Hence, the coordination mechanisms become *boundary objects* that facilitate and stabilize cooperation between different social worlds, whose actors relate differently to, but cooperate through these [41].

From this perspective, hospitals emerge as temporarily stabilized orderings of actors and technologies, in which roles, groups, divisions of work, and so forth, are established through cooperative work arrangements, enabled and stabilized by coordination mechanisms and ordering systems. Professions such as medicine and nursing, and occupations such as medical laboratory technician, hospital porter, and medical secretary, align their tasks and actions, and cooperate through SOPs and arrangements inscribed on whiteboards, paper, and in IT systems such as EHRs. As boundary objects, these enable cooperation across the various social worlds of professions and departments.

Sustaining work arrangements requires ongoing effort, and they are under constant pressure for renegotiation. Since coordination mechanisms are constitutive of the complex arrangements, changes in technologies are likely to entail changes in work arrangements, including work roles, task distribution, and responsibilities. The outcome of the changes emerges from the interactional processes following the changes in technology, and may lead to the expanded or reduced role of a profession or group, with regard to responsibility, tasks, remuneration, and so on, depending, amongst other things, on the acumen and power of the various groups, including management [2; 6; 13].

RESEARCH SETTING, CONTEXT, AND METHODS

We conducted qualitative and quantitative studies at the endocrinology and emergency departments at Regional Hospital in Central Region, one of five regions in Denmark.

Regional Hospital has a staff of about 2000, including 300 physicians, 970 nurses, 130 medical secretaries, and 80 physiotherapists. It is one of the most effective nationally, has 360 beds, and 30,000 admissions annually, of which 85% are acute cases. Yearly, the outpatient clinics receive 110,000 patients. The endocrinology department has 167 beds, and about 12,500 admissions yearly, of which 90% are acute cases. It has a staff of 65 physicians, 169 nurses, 8 physiotherapists, and 30 medical secretaries. It consists of eight wards: stroke services, dialysis, cardiology, rheumatology, gastroenterology, diabetes, outpatient cardiac care, respiratory medicine. Its outpatient clinic receives about 15,000 patients yearly. The emergency department treats 32,000 acute cases annually, and employs 40 nurses, 12 health-care workers, and 5 medical secretaries.

Context: Implementation of a Comprehensive EHR

The study of the medical secretaries was conducted in the context of the implementation of a 'comprehensive' EHR.

The EHR comprises modules for booking, test requisitions and results, administration of medication, patient administration, and clinical documentation. The Booking, Requisition/Results, and Medication modules had already been implemented at Regional Hospital some years earlier. A previous patient administrative system (PAS) called the GREEN SYSTEM was to be replaced by a new module, which we will henceforth call 'PAS'. The module for documenting clinical work, CLINICAL PROCESS, was entirely new, and replaced all paper-based records kept by physicians, nurses, physiotherapists, midwives, and so on. It was the first time the Central Region implemented an EHR that included such a broad and integrated range of functionalities. The EHR did not integrate the picture archiving and communication systems or the microbiology system. Thus, the region described it as 'comprehensive', and not 'complete'.

Of special interest to this study is the PAS, since one of the core tasks of medical secretaries is patient administration. In the PAS, patient data (name, social security number, address, relatives, etc.) are registered along with admissions to, and discharges from departments at Regional Hospital, as are transfers to other hospitals. Of interest is also CLINICAL PROCESS, in which clinicians were to document treatment and care in a structured manner, using a wide range of menus and fields shaped by staff at Regional Hospital. Where appropriate, codes for documenting treatment and care are linked to the menus and text fields. For example, the new EHR automatically reports codes for Diagnosis Related Groups (DRG) – used for reimbursing the hospital for its activities – to the National Board of Health. Registration and reporting of DRG codes was, and to some extent remains a core task of medical secretaries.

The EHR was implemented in three phases in the spring of 2010. The first and major phase involved the endocrinology and emergency departments, discussed here.

Data Collection and Analysis

This paper builds on data generated during a larger study conducted in the first half of 2010. It was commissioned by the region, and aimed to evaluate the clinical applicability of the EHR and changes in work practices at the endocrinology and emergency departments at Regional Hospital. Because the region urgently needed to decide whether or not to implement the EHR at other hospitals, the study was conducted during the shakedown phase, just before and after implementation. It may take up to a year before an organization stabilizes, since further changes evolve, as work practices and arrangements are recursively aligned. However, evaluation studies during the shakedown phase are important, and may provide valuable insights [26].

The larger study was devised as a mixed-methods case study [47], and focused on four professions (physicians, nurses, physiotherapists, and medical secretaries). It combined qualitative interviews, ethnographic observation, and a quantitative survey. Observations of the four professional groups were mainly conducted before implementation, to learn about their work practices and organization (in all, 64 hrs; 42 hrs before, 22 hrs after implementation). Also included was observation of expert-user meetings (10), and implementation management meetings (14), following implementation. Observation notes were written up as extended text immediately afterwards. This data also informed interview guides and the design of the survey. All interviews were conducted after implementation, to obtain the staff's evaluation of the EHR: 13 individual interviews were conducted before the survey, and were also used to inform its design; 7 group interviews were conducted after the survey, and also used to validate survey results.

The project was approved by the hospital directors and department heads, and presented at staff meetings, noting that participation was voluntary. Permission to observe and interview was obtained verbally, as research advanced. All interviews were transcribed and analysed by two of the authors. The quantitative survey was conducted six weeks after implementation (n=225, 58% response rate), and analysed for significant patterns. Nurses, therapists, physicians, and medical secretaries were generally satisfied with the EHR, though there was room, and at some points a need for improvements. The latter two groups were most critical. Not all data from the survey (40+ questions) is relevant to this paper, and is only included where medical secretaries deviated from the general trend.

The analysis of the medical secretaries' responses draws on data generated by the larger study, as well as the data specifically concerning medical secretaries. This includes three individual interviews (lasting between 54 and 67 min.) and one group interview (lasting 80 min.; 4 participants), eleven hours of observation, and the survey data (n=6 medical secretaries, response rate 87%). The latter sample is very small, and would be unreliable on its own. However, the medical secretaries' relatively critical stance in the survey is supported by the interviews and observations of the expert-user and implementation management meetings, where they were very vocal. When possible, their concerns led to immediate software upgrades, as well as to a radical rescheduling of the first planned upgrade, three months after implementation. The generated data have been read and reanalysed, in order to understand the work of medical secretaries, their cooperation with other professions, use of various artefacts, and the changes the EHRs involved.

MEDICAL SECRETARIES' WORK PRECEDING THE EHR

To become a medical secretary in Denmark, one must have a high school degree, followed by a certified, two-year vocational education that includes courses in medical terminology, office software, transcribing and information technology. In this section, we describe their work at Regional Hospital, prior to the implementation of the EHR.

Maintaining Accurate Records

Ruth arrives at her office in the Gastroenterology Department at 7.00, and starts her computer. From a letter tray on her desk, she takes printed discharge summaries for patients discharged the previous day. She transcribed the summaries yesterday, but could not enter them into the record until the nurse had finalized her notes, and left the record on Ruth's desk. The discharge summary is filed under the appropriate tabs, first in the record, but also in the file for physicians' ongoing notes, of which the summary is also part. She writes the discharge date on a table on the front page of the record, and places the record on one of two shelves. One shelf is for records with summaries dictated by junior physicians, which must be checked by a senior physician before an internal messenger takes them to the record archive. Another shelf is for records with summaries dictated by senior physicians, which the messenger may take directly to the archive. Ruth then turns to her computer, finds the data file for a given patient by entering her or his social security number, enters the discharge date, and closes the patient's admission record.

Medical secretaries participate in the cooperative work surrounding patients. Although they are only infrequently in contact with patients, they contribute to the maintenance of patient records, and do so in a way that is aligned with departmental work arrangements. In the case of discharged patients, the medical secretaries 'tidy' the records before they go into the archives. 'Tidying' includes a number of tasks: Medical secretaries ensure that all transcribed physicians' notes and examination results are in the record folder. They enter the physicians' final diagnoses into the GREEN SYSTEM as DRG codes, based on the discharge summaries. The system accumulates codes, and, on a monthly basis, reports them to the National Board of Health, which uses them to reimburse the hospital, thus, entering the codes in the GREEN SYSTEM is one of the medical secretaries' crucial tasks, as far as the hospital administration is concerned. Tidying records also includes entering the status of a discharged patient in a table at the front of the paper-based record, and in the GREEN SYSTEM. Furthermore, records are sorted into two stacks, to facilitate a quality-control procedure between junior and senior physicians: Discharge summaries written by the former are read and evaluated by the latter. All records are kept in Ruth's office for a week following discharge, in case test results arrive, and have to be added to the record. Ruth and her colleagues are also in charge of communication between her department and the archive, and of requesting and returning records on behalf of nurses and physicians.

Ruth accomplishes her work by using several ordering systems. One comprises paper-based records, and consists of folders, drawers, binders, and trolleys sized for A4 paper. Another consists of digital systems, such as the GREEN SYSTEM, the database in which patients' personal data, and admissions and diagnosis codes are registered. Whereas paper-based records are primarily used by clinicians when treating and caring for patients, the GREEN SYSTEM is mainly used by medical secretaries, to track patient admissions, discharges, and bookings, and store transcribed physicians' notes. However, nurses may also use it, when the medical secretaries are busy.

Locating Patient Records

Continuing to go through the records, Ruth stops at one particular record. She enters the GREEN SYSTEM, and writes a message to the records archive, headed 'Write on the bag': 'Hey archive girls! I'm sending this record to the outpatient clinic'.

'The bag' is a record's folder in the archives, whose staff Ruth addresses jocularly as 'archive girls'. Her message is intended to remind the archive staff to write the record's destined location on the folder. It is quicker, and less work to send the record directly to the other department, instead of via the archive, which does, however, need to know the record's location, should someone else need it. Locating patient records is often a challenge. Patients move between departments, and may have multiple admissions, and the location of the record is not always noted on 'the bag'. According to Ruth, there are generally two ways to locate a record whose location is unknown: look it up in the GREEN SYSTEM to see whether the patient has admissions or bookings at other departments, or contact the department to which the patient was last admitted.

Transcribing Physicians' Notes

Having taken care of the records of discharged patients, Ruth returns to her computer, and enters the SPEECH DICTATE SYSTEM, to see whether there are physicians' notes that have not yet been transcribed. There are three sets. She listens to the first seconds of the first note, for the patient's social security number, and enters the number in the GREEN SYSTEM, to find the patient's file in the system. In the patient's file, she clicks on a link to start the digital NOTE EDITOR, and begins writing. She puts on headphones, and starts and stops the SPEECH DICTATE SYSTEM by pressing a pedal. Having finished the first dictation, she clicks on a button in the NOTE EDITOR, which sends the written text to the GREEN SYSTEM, from which Ruth prints it. She picks up the notes from the printer in the nurses' office, and puts it into the patient's record, in a letter tray on a shelf in the nurses' office.

One of the medical secretaries' core tasks is writing out physicians' notes. This is achieved by switching between three digital systems. The SPEECH DICTATE SYSTEM stores sound files of physicians' dictation, using recorders kept in the nurses' office, where the patient records are kept, and rounds planned and finalized. The sound files are stored centrally in a common database, though sorted according to priority and by department. Hence, medical secretaries can take care of their own department's dictation, and also help colleagues at other departments if they fall behind, and they have spare time. Hence, transcribing is shared among medical secretaries at different departments. On the recorder, physicians must enter numerical codes, to identify the kind of note they have made. In order of priority, these are: '11' for new or acute patients, '12' for ward round dictation, '22' for outpatients, and '14' for discharge summaries. The codes show up in the SPEECH DICTATE SYSTEM, and allow medical secretaries to prioritize transcribing, though they also consider the work pressure on their own ward.

Transcribing is a Skilled Activity

In her office at the at the haematology department, Karen repeatedly listens to the same sound bite. The physician states a treatment, but Karen can only distinguish the last part: '... [incomprehensible] manoeuvre...'. She phones a colleague at another ward, who is better acquainted with the terminology of this medical specialty, and plays the sound bite into the receiver. However, the colleague cannot make out the term either, so Karen transcribes the rest of the note, prints it, marks the problematic term in red, and sends it by internal mail to the physician who dictated the note.

Situations such as this abound, when medical secretaries transcribe. They have to check terms in medical dictionaries, or consult colleagues with more expertise in a particular medical area. Accuracy is crucial, since slight differences may completely alter a diagnosis. For example, as one physician explained: 'encephalitis' is an inflammation of the brain, whereas '(hepatic) encephalopathy' is caused by liver dysfunction, and the two diagnoses entail entirely different treatment. Hearing the difference between terms may be difficult, and requires a trained ear. As is typing in general [22], transcribing notes is a skilled activity: Secretaries switch between digital systems, and simultaneously listen, type, and use the pedal, while differentiating between similar, sometimes unintelligible medical terms.

Booking

At about 9.00, Ruth starts to book patients for enteroscopy. She goes through the small stack of requisitions on her desk, checks that each enteroscopy requisition is registered in the GREEN SYSTEM, searches for a time slot in the BOOKING MODULE, and books the examination. Then she puts the requisitions into binders on one of the shelves in her office.

Because Ruth is working on a ward that also has an outpatient clinic, one of her tasks is to book examinations. After booking an examination, she prints a patient notification letter, and sends it, together with informational folders about the examination, and dietary and fasting requirements, by ordinary post. Later, patients may phone to inquire about examinations, rescheduling, or cancellations.

Information Gatekeepers

During her transcribing of physicians' notes, Karen is interrupted several times by phone calls. In one instance, a relative wants to hear more about what occurred when a now-discharged patient was on the ward. Karen puts the relative on hold, phones the nurses' office, and is fortunate to be answered by a nurse who cared for that patient. She connects the relative and the nurse, and terminates the call at her end. In another instance, the local suicide prevention centre would like to see the summary for a newly discharged patient. Luckily, the record is still on a shelf in her office, and she can take the summary from the record, and fax it to the suicide prevention centre.

Medical secretaries handle numerous inquiries by clinicians and other staff at the department, other departments, relatives, and other entities, external to the hospital. They are contacted about matters that concern the location of patient records, non-clinical data (addresses, DRG codes, etc.), bookings, or more generally, connecting people with questions to people with answers. Thus, being information gatekeepers is one of their central tasks [40].

Miscellaneous Tasks

Medical secretaries also take care of a range of other tasks, such as ordering and returning office equipment, or special mattresses for patients with bedsores, and guiding relatives and taxi-drivers bringing flowers to the patients' rooms.

The Cooperative Work of Medical Secretaries

Medical secretaries may be said to handle the non-clinical aspects of patient treatment trajectories and patient records. They record and coordinate admissions, bookings, and discharges, register and report DRG codes to the National Board of Health, request and retrieve records from the archives, locate records, or pass them along to other staff. They transcribe physicians' notes, act as intermediaries between relatives, patients, and staff, and carry out various other tasks. Their work is not mere routine, but requires skill and applied knowledge. They are information gatekeepers, as well as articulation workers [19; 40].

Since the 1980s, medical secretaries' work has been undergoing computerization, to which the GREEN SYSTEM, SPEECH DICTATE SYSTEM, and NOTE EDITOR testify. Though not integrated with the patient records, these systems are parts of the department's ordering system. The secretaries' primary work arrangement is that of the department and its physicians and nurses, with whom they align and coordinate their work. But they are also part of a cooperative arrangement of other medical secretaries, whom they help with transcribing and the handling of records.

While patient records form an ordering system shared by medical secretaries, nurses, and physicians, their stance on it is different. The primary work object of physicians and nurses is the patient: The patient record, its information channels and formal aspects, merely document and record patient care. To medical secretaries, the records and the information channels themselves are the primary work objects, whose completeness, integrity, and formal aspects they take care of. Whereas clinicians are patient caretakers, medical secretaries are record caretakers.

THE NEW WORK OF MEDICAL SECRETARIES

The most apparent and immediate change for the medical secretaries was the replacement of the GREEN SYSTEM with the new PAS that was integrated into the EHR. The GREEN SYSTEM had been used at most hospitals in Denmark, including Regional Hospital, since the late 1980s. Thus, medical secretaries were very proficient in its use, and could manoeuvre about in it with optimal speed. Therefore, the implementation group and the secretaries themselves anticipated that deploying the EHR would cause frustration, since it was expected that it would take some time for the medical secretaries to recover their previous proficiency.

The implementation strategy was based on minimal instruction in the new system prior to implementation, with extensive local support during the first 14 days of use. Nevertheless, the medical secretaries received more training than any other group, because their learning curve was expected to be steeper. As it turned out, that prediction was correct, and, along with the physicians, the secretaries were the most critical group in the survey. Their difficulties had repercussions for the other groups, and included shifts in tasks and responsibilities, some being abolished, new ones emerging, and others shifting between occupations.

Transcribing Becomes More Cumbersome

One immediate effect of the new EHR was that transcribing notes took longer. Statistics from NOTE EDITOR reveal that during the first 12 weeks following implementation, the transcription ratio (min. of writing/min. physician dictation) rose from an average of 6, preceding the implementation of the EHR, to 9 during the first week of use, then settled near an average of 7, during weeks 5 to 12 after implementation (Table 1). The total number of untranscribed notes grew steadily to 813 during the first 12 weeks following implementation, compared to about 50 to 60 unwritten notes previously. Since the statistics from NOTE EDITOR also show that neither the number nor the length of notes grew (Table 2), the increase in untranscribed notes must be attributed to the rise in the transcription ratio caused by the PAS module. Hospital management initially asked the medical secretaries to work overtime, but later had to hire outside help.

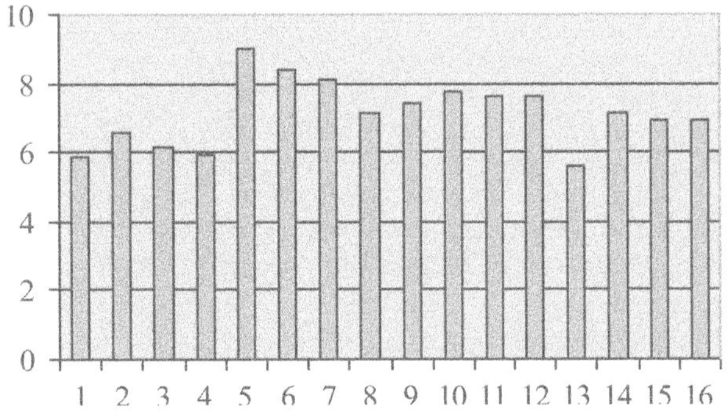

Table 1. Transcription ratio (min. of transcribing/min. of dictation). Weeks 1–4 before implementation, weeks 5–16 after

During our interviews, and in the reports to the hospital's implementation group, the medical secretaries identified a combination of HCI issues and slow functionality as the causes of their predicament. For example, when writing discharge summaries, they first had to enter the current date and the physician's name in fields at the very bottom of the screen, and then write the actual note in a field at the very top of the screen. This meant scrolling up and down when writing each summary. They also complained of too many mouse-clicks, and a lack of keyboard short cuts.

The new PAS also made some tasks more rigid. Previously, medical secretaries just wrote the name of a physician or a diagnosis code in a discharge summary, but they now had to upload these through a browser from a database. However, both the diagnosis and the physician identification browsers were frustratingly slow: 'I start the browser, then I go to the shelves for records while I wait', Karen stated.

The untranscribed notes were a major problem for physicians and nurses, since the notes are the primary means of communication about patients among staff and across shifts. Without notes, they lacked access to previous diagnoses, plans, and prescriptions, unless they could contact the physician responsible for these. Proceeding with treatment and care became difficult, a serious situation with critically ill patients. As the problem of untranscribed notes was not resolved, despite investing more resources and hours in transcribing, the implementation group and the system supplier renegotiated the next upgrade of the EHR, scheduled for a few months later, and designed functionality that addressed medical secretaries' highest priorities, a move that stresses the importance of their work to the department.

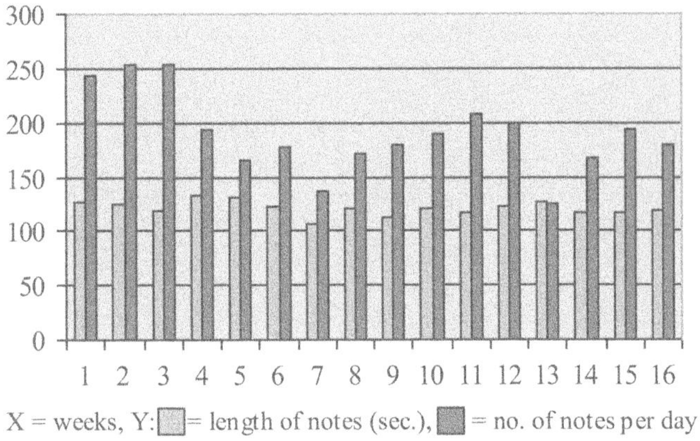

Table 2. Average number and length of notes

Tighter Coupling to Other Professions

The new EHR combined the GREEN SYSTEM and the paper-based physicians' and nurses' records into one integrated system. Medical secretaries, nurses, and physicians now shared the same artefact, and could respond immediately to updates. This also meant that their work practices became more tightly coordinated and interdependent. For example, previously, medical secretaries discharged patients via the GREEN SYSTEM, after having written up the physician's discharge summary, while nurses finalized their documentation in parallel to, and independently of that. The new, cross-professional record integrated nurses' and physicians' notes in CLINICAL PROCESS. Physicians often dictated their discharge summary before the nurses had completed their documentation of a patient's care, and while the secretaries could write the summary, they could not send it until the nurses had finished their documentation, and the patient was registered in the PAS as discharged. Hence, they had to check patient records occasionally, to see whether this had occurred, which entailed a bit more work for them.

This tighter coupling also affected physicians' notes more generally. When dictating, physicians at the department usually followed a recommended structure for going through diagnosis, treatment, prescriptions, and so on. In the EHR, the elements of this structure appear as separate fields, in order to structure data on patients, diagnoses, treatment, and so forth. For example, a note of a physician's round must have the following structure: Record for <patient name>, <patient social security number>, by <physician name>, Objective observations, Conclusion (e.g. diagnosis), Plan, and Prescriptions. If physicians follow this structure, transcribing is no more complicated than previously, since they can 'jump' down the screen in the same order as that in the dictated notes. If physicians do not follow the template, transcribing takes significantly longer, since medical secretaries have to scroll up and down to enter the information in the correct fields. Physicians may not follow the template, either out of habit or because they think it leads to notes of lesser quality: For patients with multiple diagnoses, the template requires that these be listed separately from the prescriptions (diagnoses in one field, prescriptions in another), which means that the reasoning behind prescriptions is listed separately, and must be inferred, instead of being explicated in the case narrative.

Medical secretaries' and nurses' tasks also became more tightly coupled. For example, nurses are responsible for initiating the plans to which care, examinations, and treatment are linked, and which are basic elements of the EHR. Since nurses are often busy, they do not always register activities in the EHR in real time. To nurses, this makes little difference, since they seldom document in real time. However, for the medical secretaries this means that they cannot register the actual time of admission when transcribing admission notes. They have to either use the start time indicated in the EHR, which may be three hours late, or correct the time of admission in the EHR. The former is incorrect; the latter requires more effort and time.

Organizing Records

> …as a medical secretary, you've been taught that your work must be in order. Times must be exact. It is really important. When a patient dies, you register the exact time that it happens. Now it happens that nurses do not have time to register a death until sometime during the night. Then we register a death at 23.00, even though the patient died at 19.00. It is not right. It is frustrating, when you have been taught to register when things happen. (Head medical secretary)

The implementation of the EHR imposed changes that affected the work ethic of the medical secretaries, as described in the statement above. They regarded the maintenance of orderly and accurate records as one of their core tasks. Not registering data at the correct time was one challenge to this ethic, while finishing records following discharge was another. As mentioned, the EHR makes use of plans that health care staff activate on admission, and when commencing new treatment or care activities. These plans must be closed once completed, but, particularly when patients are discharged, this is not always done. Medical secretaries tried to close them, and tidy the records as part of the process of writing the discharge summary, as they had done previously with the paper-based records. However, this was not always possible, because some plans were ongoing, and might be part of a patient's visits to the outpatient clinic, for example. Only physicians and nurses have the clinical insight to judge whether or not plans should be closed, and therefore the medical secretaries could not tidy the records as accurately as they wished.

Task Drift among Professions

The problems related to initiating and closing plans are linked to task drift, that is, tasks originally performed by one group being executed by another group. Usually, the trend is for routine tasks to move down the hierarchy. With the EHR, PAS functionality is no longer a separate system like the GREEN SYSTEM, but integrated with other functionalities. Hence, these functionalities are more easily accessible to others, as well as to secretaries. For example, nurses can now access the functionality for discharging patients, which poses the question of whether nurses should register discharges, which would make sense if real-time registration is pursued, or whether the secretaries should continue to do this, which might mean that they are not be registered until the next morning, when they write the discharge summary. Similar examples of task drift are physicians themselves writing (short) notes or registering diagnosis codes in the EHR, and nurses printing labels.

Discarding Old Tasks and Acquiring New Ones

> A funny incident occurred the other day. We have medical secretaries who work at home. This raised the question: Who is going to tidy, take transcriptions from the printer, and put them into record binders? And I said: 'But there is nothing coming out of the printer'. (Head medical secretary)

An important effect of the EHR, almost overlooked in the interviews, is that medical secretaries no longer have to print and distribute notes into the (paper-based) records anymore: Transcriptions go directly into the EHR. Similarly, they do not have to spend as much time locating records as previously, though this still requires some of their attention, since paper records are still relevant for some patients. Another obsolete task is the registration of certain services by therapists and nurses, for which they previously had to register the codes, in order for the hospital to be reimbursed by the National Board of Health. Before, physiotherapists would document their work with patients in their own records, and leave a note in the nurses' office. The medical secretary would pick it up, and register the service codes in the GREEN SYSTEM. Now, the therapists' records are part of the EHR, and the codes are automatically reported.

As already mentioned, nurses did some of the same administrative tasks as medical secretaries, and still do. Nurses now transfer patients between departments at the hospital, or to other hospitals, and discharge them from the hospital. However, this creates more work for the secretaries: Nurses sometimes transfer patients incorrectly, and since only the receiving department can correct the error, medical secretaries have to wait for that to happen. Therefore, they maintain lists of incorrectly transferred or discharged patients, so that they can complete the administrative work on a patient, when the error has been corrected (e.g. send a discharge summary to the general practitioner). Tidying has become more complicated, since the work arrangement surrounding it is more complex, and tasks and responsibilities drift between professions.

Whether medical secretaries now have fewer or more tasks, and less or more work is difficult to assess, since the gains of not having to print, distribute print-outs, locate records, and request records and return them to the archives are currently overshadowed by the extra work needed for transcribing. As the only group surveyed, they did not think that EHR had reduced their work load.

The New Cooperative Work Arrangement

The problem of physicians' untranscribed notes made clear the importance of the medical secretaries' work to all at the two departments and to management, as evidenced by the revision of the first scheduled upgrade of the EHR.

The EHR involved a systemic integration of medical secretaries' work with that of physicians and nurses. The previous division of work had been partly effected and supported by the media used for patient administration. In the integrated, comprehensive EHR, the GREEN SYSTEM was replaced by the PAS, and physicians' and nurses' records were replaced by CLINICAL PROCESS, which was accessible to all groups. This more tightly coupled tasks, which became more dependent on one another, with regard to accuracy and timeliness. Also, some tasks, such as registering discharges, entering diagnosis codes, and assuming responsibility for initiating the closing of plans in the EHR, tended to drift among groups of staff. While a major benefit of the EHR for the medical secretaries was that they no longer had to print and distribute physicians' notes, or request, return, and locate patient records, they also acquired new tasks, such as keeping records of patient files that were not yet in order. The tighter coupling, task drift, and new tasks meant that they could no longer tidy records as thoroughly as before, which challenged their work ethic.

The formal distinctions among occupations and professions remain, but the new work arrangements that had to be established created possibilities for desirable and undesirable expansion and reduction of roles. For example, some physicians regarded the option of writing notes themselves as a yet another effort on the part of management to delegate more tasks to them. Nurses did not reject the tasks of admitting and discharging patients in the PAS, because it integrates with the writing of care summaries. Medical secretaries, however, were more anxious during this process, since some of their tasks were now automated (e.g. DRG coding) or partly assumed by other groups (e.g. note writing, admission, and discharge), and the extent of their new tasks was not entirely clear. The results remain to be seen, as the outcomes of implementing new technology are not givens [2; 6]. At the time of our study, shortly after implementation, a new arrangement had not yet stabilized.

DISCUSSION

Computerization of medical secretaries' work has been ongoing since the late 1980s, though unnoticed by CSCW, CHI, and medical informatics. Yet, as efforts to develop health care IT move from stand-alone systems to integrated infrastructures such as EHRs, medical secretaries' work may receive more attention. Moreover, as the information infrastructures in health care incorporate more groups, other non-clinical staff may also become increasingly relevant.

The invisibility of medical secretaries to CSCW and related fields may have several explanations: Until recently, private and public efforts to digitize health care have focused on physicians and nurses, and research may have reflected that focus; medical secretaries may appear to work alone in their offices, cut off from the hum of other staff activity by headphones (Figure 1); or, they may have been perceived as holdovers from the field of Office Automation, which faded in the mid-1980s, when the field of CSCW emerged [24].

Medical secretaries are unlikely to become obsolete. The skills of registering, transcribing medical terms, and information gatekeeping are unlikely to be fully replaceable by IT. Moreover, the emergence of infrastructures such as EHRs is part of an increasing demand for accountability to other parties, such as management and health care authorities [36]. This will demand continued effort, to ensure the accuracy, completeness, and integrity of data. Since clinicians are costly, on call, and prefer clinical tasks to administrative ones, medical secretaries' care of records should continue to be in demand. The roles of clerical staff as intermediaries, information gatekeepers, and articulation workers should not be underestimated [17]. As studies have revealed, clerical work is rarely mere routine, but requires knowledge and skill. If this is disregarded, the development of IT may lose central functionalities. Archive staff may execute tasks important to hospitals' work arrangements: As medical secretaries do not merely 'transcribe notes'; archive staff may not just 'archive records'.

There seem to be at least two ways to increase the visibility of medical secretaries and other non-clinical staff: one is to conduct studies with and of archive staff, pharmacists, porters, and so on, to describe their work, which may prove relevant to the development of health care IT; another is to pursue a research strategy of 'following the object', rather than following the actors [25; 28]. With patient records, this might have led researchers into the offices of the medical secretaries, and down to the cellar, to the records archives. It might also have led from the ward to hospital management, and to the National Board of Health: What kind of work relevant to the design of EHRs might be performed there?

Boundary-object Trimming

The primary work object of the medical secretaries is the EHR, to which they attend in its formal aspects. They are not concerned with the actual diagnoses and care plans, but with whether diagnoses have been entered, care and treatment properly coded, and with the completeness of information: Has all dictation been transcribed and entered into the EHR? Are all examination and test results recorded? Have appropriate plans been initiated and terminated?

Until now, we have informally called this work 'tidying', and contrasted medical secretaries' care of records with clinicians' care of patients. In the interactional approach's efforts to make visible the interaction and work [42; 45], we propose defining this as *boundary-object trimming*. Originated by Star and Griesemer [41], the concept of the boundary object has been widely used, and several studies have contributed to a nuanced understanding of it. Fujimura emphasizes the need to augment the robustness rather than the plasticity of boundary objects, when these have to travel between diverse social worlds, and suggested the term 'standardized package' [20]. Lee argues that not all objects that travel between social worlds are boundary objects: Non-standardized, temporary objects may be used to negotiate boundaries between groups [29; See also 35]. Finally, boundary objects should not be considered static. Lutters and Ackerman describe boundary objects that are in flux, as the work of which they are part changes. They are 'punctuated crystallizations' of information, interpreted in the context of their production [30]. Subrahmanian et al. describe how changes in organization threaten to make boundary objects useless, as their information becomes irrelevant, and interpretations in different social worlds diverge [44]. The two last-mentioned studies indicate the importance of the ongoing maintenance of boundary objects. To a large extent, this is what medical secretaries do, when they 'tidy' medical records. In the paper record, they wrote notes and inserted these, along with examination and test results, into the record folders. They added codes, ensured the completeness of the record before sending it to the archives or another department, and kept track of its location. Though somewhat differently executed, much of this tidying work continues with the EHR: Secretaries write notes, add codes, and try to ensure the completeness of the record by closing initiated plans. They maintain the records, so that they may function effectively as boundary objects.

Strauss called actors' reflexive monitoring of their own and other actors' actions, and the projection of future ones, the 'gyroscopic source' for coordinating different courses of action for common goals [43, p37]. Boundary objects have a similar stabilizing effect on the interactional courses of cooperative work, as long as they are useful and appropriate to that work: Their structural forms and informational content must be maintained and updated, which may be accomplished during use, but may also be delegated to a group of staff. In the same way, 'articulation work' may be an integral part of action, but may also be the main task of some (e.g. secretaries and project managers). We suggest calling this 'trimming', in the aeronautical sense of levelling an airplane to ensure smooth flight, or in the nautical sense of distributing the load and adjusting the sails of a ship, to reach optimal speed and stay on course. 'Trimming' stresses the dynamic and directional aspects of the work, in contrast to 'upkeep' or 'maintenance', which suggest a more static extension of a given state. The concept of boundary-object trimming may be a third way of making visible the efforts of medical secretaries and other non-clinical groups.

CONCLUSION

We have described the cooperative work of medical secretaries, and their central role in the work arrangement at a hospital, based on a mixed-methods case study of the implementation of a comprehensive EHR. We propose the term 'boundary-object trimming' to characterize a central feature of their work; they and other non-clinical groups have been relatively invisible to CSCW and medical informatics, but may require more attention, as health care IT moves from stand-alone systems to integrated health care infrastructures, and hence incorporates more groups of health care professionals.

Figure 1. Medical secretary doing cooperative work

ACKNOWLEDGEMENTS

Our sincere thanks to the staff at Regional Hospital.

REFERENCES

1. Abraham, J. and Reddy, M.C. Moving patients around. In *Proc. CSCW'08*, ACM (2008), 225-228.
2. Aydin, C.E. and Rice, R.E. Bringing Social Worlds Together. *Journ. Health and Social Behavior,* 33(2) (1996), 168-185.
3. Balka, E. and Wagner, I. Making things work. In *Proc. CSCW'06,* ACM (2008), 229-238.
4. Bardram, J. and Bossen, C. Mobility Work. *Journ. of CSCW, 14*, Springer (2005), 131-160.
5. Bardram, J., Hansen, T.R., Søgaard, M. AwareMedia. In *Proc. of CSCW'06*, ACM (2006), 109-118.
6. Barley, S.R. The Alignment of Technology and Structure through Roles and Networks. *Adm. Science Quarterly* 35(1) (1990), 61-103.

7. Barley, S.R. Technicians in the Workplace. *Adm. Science Quarterly* 41(3) (1996), 404-441.
8. Berg, M. Accumulating and Coordinating. *Journ. of CSCW.* 8(4) (1999), 373-401.
9. Berner, E.S., Detmer , D.E., and Simborg, D. Will the Wave Finally Break? *Journ. of the American Medical Informatics Association,* 12(1) (2005), 3-7.
10. Bjørn, P. and Rødje, K. Triage Drift. *Journ. of CSCW,* 1(4) (2008), 395-419.
11. Blomberg, J., Suchman, L., and Trigg. R. Reflections on a Work-Oriented Design Project. In Bowker, G. C., Star, S. L., Turner, W., and Gasser, S. (eds): *Social Science, Technical Systems, and Cooperative Work.* Mahwah, Lawrence Earlbaum (1997), 189-215.
12. Bossen, C. Accounting and co-constructing. *Journ. of CSCW,* 20(6) (2011), 473-495.
13. Bowers, J. The Work to Make a Network Work. *Proc. of CSCW'94,* (1994), 287-98.
14. Casper, M. Working On and Around Human Fetuses. In Berg, M. and Mol, A. *Differences in Medicine.* Durham and London, Duke University Press (1998), 28-52.
15. Comptroller and Auditor General. *The National Programme for IT in the NHS.* Department of Health, London, The Stationery Office (2011)
16. Dorda, W., Duftschmid, G., Gerhold, L., Gall, W., and Gamball, J. Austria's Path Towards Nationwide Electronic Health Records. *Methods of Inf. in Medicine,* 47, 2 (2008), 117-123.
17. Ehrlich, K. and Cash, D. The Invisible World of Intermediaries. *Journ. of CSCW,* 8(1) (1999), 147-167.
18. Ellingsen, G. and Røed, K. The Role of Integration in Health-Based Information Infrastructures. *Journ. of CSCW,* 19(6) (2010), 557-584.
19. Erickson, T., Danis, C.M. , Kellogg, W.A., and Helander, M.E. Assistance: the work practices of human administrative assistants and their implications for IT & organization. *Proc. of CSCW'08*, ACM (2008), 609-618.
20. Fujimura, J. Crafting Science: Standardized Packages, Boundary Objects, and 'Translation'. In Pickering, A. (ed) *Science as Culture and Practice.* Chicago & London, University of Chicago Press (1992), 168-211.
21. Glenn, E. and. Feldberg, R.L. Degraded and Deskilled. *Social Problems*, 24(1) (1997), 52-64.
22. Goodman, S.E. and Perby, M-L. Computerization and the skill in women's work. In Olerup, A., Schneider, L. and Monod, E (eds) *Women, Work and Computerization.* Amsterdam, North-Holland (1985), 23-42.
23. Greenhalgh, T., Potts, H.W., Geoff, W., Bark, P. and Swinglehurst, D. Tensions and Paradoxes in Electronic Patient Record Research. *Milbank Quarterly,* 87(4) (2009), 729-788.
24. Grudin, J. Computer-Supported Cooperative Work: History and Focus. *Computer,* 27(5) (1994), 19-26.
25. Harper, R.P. *Inside the IMF*. Aca. Press, Orlando (1997)
26. Häkkinen L., Hilmola O. ERP evaluation during the shakedown phase: lessons from an after-sales division. *Information Systems Journal,* 18 (2008), 73-100.
27. Heath, C., Svensson, M.S., Hindmarsh, J., Luff, P. and Lehn, D.v. Configuring Awareness. *Journ. of CSCW,* 11 (2002), 317-347.
28. Latour, B. *Science in Action.* Harvard UP (1987)
29. Lee, C. P. Boundary Negotiating Artifacts. *Journ. of CSSW,* 16 (2007), 307-339.
30. Lutters, W.G. and Ackerman, M.S. Beyond Boundary Objects. *Journ. of CSCW,* 19(3) (2007), 341–372.
31. Martin, D., Hartswood, M., Slack, R. and Voss, A. Achieving Dependability in the Configuration, Integration and Testing of Healthcare Technologies. *Journ. of CSCW,* 15(5-6) (2006), 467-499.
32. Muller, M. J. Invisible Work of Telephone Operators. *Journ. of CSCW,* 8(1-2), Springer (1999), 31-61.
33. Orr, J. E. *Talking about Machines. An Ethnography of a Modern Job*. Ithaca, Cornell University Press (1996).
34. Paul, S. A. and Reddy, M.C. Understanding together. *Proc. of CSCW'10,* ACM (2010), 321-330.
35. Pennington, D. The Dynamics of Material Artifacts in Collaborative Research Teams. *Journ. of CSCW,* 19(3) (2010), 175-199.
36. Power, M. *The Audit Society.* Oxford, OUP (1997).
37. Reddy, M., Dourish, P. and Pratt, W. Coordinating Heterogeneous Work. *Proc. of ECSCW'01*, Klüver (2001), 239-58.
38. Reddy, M. and Spence, P.R. Collaborative information seeking. *Inf. Process Management,* 44 (2008), 242-255.
39. Schmidt, K. and Wagner, I. Ordering Systems. *Journ. of CSCW,* 13(5-6) (2004), 349-408.
40. Spence, P. R. and Reddy, M.C. The 'active' gatekeeper in collaborative information seeking activities. *Proc. of GROUP '07,* ACM (2007).: 277-280.
41. Star, S. L. and Griesemer, J.R. Institutional Ecology, 'Translations' and Boundary Objects. *Social Studies of Science* **19**(3) (1989), 387-420.
42. Star, S.L. and Strauss, A. Layers of Silence, Arenas of Voice. *Journ. of CSCW,* 8 (1999), 9-30.
43. Strauss, A. *The Continual Permutations of Action*. New York, Aldine de Gruyter (1993).
44. Subrahmanian, E., Monarch, I. Monarch, I., Suresh, K., Granger, H., Milliken, R. and Westerberg, A. Boundary Objects and Prototypes at the Interfaces of Engineering Design. *Journ. of CSCW,* 12(3) (2003), 185-203.
45. Suchman, L. Making Work Visible. *Communications of the ACM,* 38(9), (1995), 56-63.
46. Webster, J. *Shaping Women's Work. Gender, Employment and Information Technology.* London & New York, Longman (1996).
47. Yin R.K. *Case study research. Design and Methods.* Newbury Park USA: Sage, (1991).

Social Scientists and Cyberinfrastructure: Insights from a Document Perspective

Steve Sawyer
School of Information Studies
Syracuse University
Syracuse NY 13244-4100 USA
+1-315-443-6147
ssawyer@syr.edu

Elizabeth Kaziunas
School of Information Studies
Syracuse University
Syracuse NY 13244-4100 USA
+1-315-443-2911
eskaziun@syr.edu

Carsten Østerlund
School of Information Studies
Syracuse University
Syracuse NY 13244-4100 USA
+1-315-443-8773
costerlu@syr.edu

ABSTRACT
Contemporary cyberinfrastructure (CI) efforts are most often directed to meeting the needs of physical and natural scientists. We wonder: might the CI needs of social scientists be different? To provide insight into this question we report on a pilot study of social scientist's distributed and collaborative work practices. To frame this study we drew from the literatures of science studies and e-science and followed a mixed-methodological research design. Findings suggest focusing on documenting practices provides novel insights into the distributed work practices and the CI uses of social scientists.

Author Keywords
Cyberinfrastructure, social scientists, work practices, documents.

ACM Classification Keywords
H.4 [**Information Systems Applications**] K.4.3. [**Computers and Society**]: Organizational Impacts – *computer-supported collaborative work* J.4 [**Computer Applications**]: Social and Behavioral Sciences – *sociology*.

INTRODUCTION
We report on a pilot study of social scientist's distributed collaborative practice as a means of gaining insight into the needs of these scholars relative to cyberinfrastructure (CI). We observe that much of the current uses of CI are oriented towards supporting natural and physical scientists. And, the emphasis of these CI have been to supporting increased access to large data sets, providing greater computing resources and broadening the uses of a range of scarce or unique instruments and sensors [2]. We further note that CI provides a means for more scientists to work together across time and space while pursuing larger scientific problems. We wonder: do the same needs and motivations hold true for social scientists? [e.g. 15][14]

We continue with a too-brief introduction to CI and its roles in the social sciences. We then review literature from several intellectual communities regarding the work practices of social scientists. In the third section we outline and highlight insights from our pilot study, situating our findings within the current CI discourse. In the final section we offer tentative next steps.

Cyberinfrastructure and Social Science
Cyberinfrastructure encompasses a range of digital resources such as computational capacity; access to data sources; tools to support access, use and analysis of this data; and the needed networking infrastructure to support access and use. Seen this way, CI is: "the sharing of computational resources, distributed access to massive datasets, and the development of tools for collaboration and communication" [5]. Often CI is advanced as a neutral technological platform imbued with the potential to extend research practices beyond any one laboratory and to transform scientific practice [1] [7] [15].

Contemporary evaluations of social scientists' uses of CI often echo the excitement of these ICT-enabled platforms as a n ew frontier for social science research [29] [14]. However, these studies also highlight a number of socio-technical issues that impede the widespread adoption of CI in the social sciences. Others find that many social scientists often resist sharing data and collaborating – key assumptions in the design of CI – as there are disincentives in their intellectual communities for doing so [3][19][28].

While CI proponents argue such obstacles can be overcome with better design, more usability testing and training, others are less sanguine. Some argue CI are far from being generic research platforms as they emphasize computational and quantitative approaches to doing science [5] [10] [24]. One implication of this emphasis is that simply extending CI principles for social scientists might fail to lead to the kinds of advances these infrastructures are seen as enabling. In response, we and other social science-oriented CI advocates call for an empirically-driven view of CI usage.

Social Scientists
For this paper social science are those intellectual communities whose central phenomenon of interest is the

human condition. This definition encompasses sociology, economics, anthropology, political science, linguistics, geography and others (and community inclusion is socially negotiated) [26]. One characteristic which helps define the social sciences is that knowledge is built from facts or evidence in support of theories (that are partial explanations of the world) and not typically represented as laws.

While a rich body of literature details the working lives of scientists in the laboratory (e.g., [16] [17] [33]), and more recently the virtual collaboration of scientists in e-science collaboratories [9] [21], much less has been written on the work practices of social scientists; distributed or otherwise. In fact, with the exception of Ellis' work on the information seeking behavior of social scientists, "...studies investigating academic social scientists have been in steady decline since the mid-1970s" [20]. And, there exists little research focused on the design and evaluation of collaboratories for pursuing social science [15] [25] [31].

This lack of empirical insight into social scientists' work practices, combined with the practical problems being routinely encountered in CI-oriented initiatives, leads to: 1) odd extrapolations being made from studies of current CI to the needs of social science [25] [31]; and 2) nascent social science CI efforts falling short of becoming the kind of transformative research envisioned. To help achieve transformative uses of CI by social scientists, we are wise to better understand their distributed collaborative practices.

STUDYING DISTRIBUTED SOCIAL SCIENCE PRACTICE

To help advance our understanding, we conducted a pilot or "micro" study of distributed collaboration among four social scientists. These scholars collaborated across three different time zones and never met face-to-face during the 13 months we studied them across 2009-2010. To do this study we employed a document-centric methodology that involved mapping their uses of physical and digital documents, personal and shared repositories, and shared online interactions. We used software to track uses of desktop and online repositories; gathered participant-generated images of physical documents and desktops; collected documents; conducted interview and behavioral inquiries; and did participant observation.

Following this intensive micro-study, we did follow-up interviews with a convenience sample of another seven social scientists involved in distributed collaborative projects in order to explore in more detail our initial findings. Here we present our observations from this data relative to the five elements of social scientist's work practices that are drawn from the literature.

SOCIAL SCIENTISTS' WORK PRACTICES

To advance our understanding of social scientists' distributed collaborative work practices, we build on the current literature. In particular we build from Bealieu and Wouters [5] [36] who theorize social science research practices as characterized by five inter-connected elements:

1. Epistemic diversity
2. Lack of consensus
3. Low technology (ICT) research environment
4. Historically grounded solitary research practices
5. Specificity of writing and reading as features of knowledge creation

Relative to the specificity of writing and reading we focus on documents. Our premise is that documents are at the center of most scientists' work. This centrality can be seen in a range of practices: from reading and writing research to doing email with colleagues. And, document-centered interactions are increasingly (but not exclusively) reliant on digital forms. We define documents broadly as material, geographic, temporal and socially constructed communication. This can include traditional, paper-based, material forms such as memos, reports. This can also include publications, online documents, web pages, and text-based communications such as email.

Documents provide a tangible entree for observing both the dynamic nature of coordination work in virtual collaborations and the uses of digital infrastructure. This approach takes into consideration: 1) the nature and uses of social ties in virtual organization 2) the web-like arrangements of documents and material and digital artifacts (i.e. computers, sheets of paper, whiteboards, software) along with the rules and norms that govern them, and 3) the everyday work practices that produce and reproduce socio-technical structures [13][23].

Negotiating Epistemic Diversity

Articulated by Karin Knorr-Cetina, "epistemic culture" is an analytic framework highlighting the unique ways researchers "maintain and adapt a particular culture that distinguishes them from other researchers" [36]. The four scholars were trained in and pursue their craft in different intellectual areas: information systems, organizational studies, information science, and social networks. Examining documents from the study highlights that this negotiation continued throughout the collaboration. Short-but-frequent email exchanges, messy document drafts, and the sharing of numerous whiteboard sketches suggest a constant state of negotiation and boundary-spanning.

Documents of Consensus and Uncertainty

Social science is often characterized by a lack of consensus among participants and a high-level of task uncertainty [35]. Collins [8] argues the basic pattern of intellectual life among the social sciences is disagreement. One consequence is that in "...many hard areas research takes place, and can be reported, within a known framework of assumptions; in soft areas, the context has often to be separately elaborated" [35]. Our findings support Collin's [8] and Whitley's [35] claims that social scientists often disagree as to what counts as empirical knowledge and how best to frame their research efforts, given their constant attention to negotiating meanings, goals and issues.

Technology (ICT) Use

For technology we focus on ICT use, noting use is common and there are shared patterns. But, ICT uses are distinctly individualized. The most common ICT are commodified (e.g. laptops and computers, word processing, statistical and network visualization software). This does not differentiate social scientists from others. While CI often is seen as helping physical and natural scientists share sophisticated technological equipment such as earthquake sensor networks, radio telescopes, and computational resources, this is less common in the social sciences and nothing like this was seen in our single group of scholars.

It may be the lessened need for shared instrumentation via CI means is because the analysis of social science data is more individualized (i.e. done by a researcher at their office or home instead of the laboratory) [18] [8] [29]. We observe two aspects of this in our pilot study: (a) the pervasive and enduring uses of email and (2) the importance of pre-existing and personalized infrastructure in structuring work practices.

The Enduring Power of Email

Despite the many ICT-based tools available, and as expected, the scientists in our pilot study used email as the primary way of sharing information and communicating. This seems to be a "lowest common denominator" as email was a routine part of everyone's day-to-day work practices. Documents arrived into each other's email inbox: a push-in reminder of workflow, tasks to-be-done and deadlines. Scholars typically 'cc'd' collaborators on any email involving the project to keep everyone in the communication loop. Emails amongst collaborators also tended take the form of numerous short threads. Many of these were "negotiating" emails such as: Where do I fit in? What are my responsibilities? How can I help? These emails served to inform and provide feedback about a specific issue rather than engage a wider project discussion.

Shifts in Work Practice/Work Structures

The scholars in our pilot study explored various ICT to better support collaboration on project tasks. For example, at the study's outset the researchers used a university-provided document management system (Sharepoint). Use made clear this was a static repository of the group's materials rather than an active place for collaboration. This led them to explore (and adopt) "Dropbox" (see http://www.dropbox.com) as a more useful means to share and store documents because its design allowed for more indications of use and interactivity through desktop notifications of changes to the shared document repository (a form of social transluscence to support distributed collaboration [e.g., 16].

Independent Research Practices

We know social scientists are trained to be critical and independent scholars [35]. So, co-authorship is more common in the natural and physical sciences than in the social sciences [6] [19]. The research practices of study participants reflect this individuality. The four worked individually and stored project documents (physically and digitally) in highly personalized ways, following their own provenance, storage and retrieval systems. Shared digital resources were secondary. This made it easier to make ICT changes (like the Sharepoint-to-Dropbox swap) as these were not critical to any one scholar's personalized work practices. This suggests collaborative practices are layered on, or are secondary too, individual efforts.

Evidence suggested to us that the social scientists' digital infrastructure evolves organically over time and is largely premised on providing ways to link individual work patterns. In doing this social scientists are entrepreneurial, drawing on commodified technologies and organizational ICT infrastructures at hand and layering these onto their existing work practices through exploration and debate.

Documents in the Reading and Writing Practices

In the natural and physical sciences, collaborative work is more common, research teams are typically larger, and publications tend to emphasize succinctness and precision of language. Ambiguity is reduced via formalized and standardized reporting procedures such as lab notes and short articles [35]. In contrast, the literature and writing practices in the social sciences are typically "... diverse, unsettled and open to interpretation" [4]. The scholars in our pilot study reflect this. They typically chose to write alone and followed personalized work practices regarding the uses of digital and material documents. Their writing was often directed towards publishing venues which differed from their collaborators. This led each to emphasize different points and to develop these in rhetorically different styles.

What became clear from the pilot study is that explicitly focusing on document and documenting practices made it easier to discern social scientists' distributed and collaborative work practices. Moreover, we found that by focusing on documenting practices, we were able to learn about ICT uses, communication patterns, and these scholar's approaches to pursuing shared scientific efforts. In returning to the literature, we find that contemporary CI studies that mention documents typically do s o only in passing [19][25][28]. This may be due to the perceptions of the roles documents play in the physical and natural sciences, or it may be a r eflection of the importance of documents for social scientist's work practices.

NEXT STEPS

Initial findings, albeit from a small pilot study, suggest that a document-centric approach is useful for studying distributed collaborative work. These findings also suggest CI needs for social scientists may be different than that which is currently provided or envisioned [27][19][16]. A larger-scale empirical effort is both needed and next.

ACKNOWLEDGMENTS

We thank the participants in our pilot study for their willingness to allow us to study their work practices. We acknowledge financial support of Syracuse University's Faculty Assistantship Program.

REFERENCES

[1] American Council of Learned Societies. 2006. *Our cultural commonwealth*. New York: ACLS. DOI=http: //www.acls. org/cyberinfrastructure/acis.ci.report.pdf.

[2] Atkins, D. 2003. Report of the National Science Foundation Blue–Ribbon Advisory Panel on Cyberinfrastructure. The National Science Foundation, Arlington VA. DOI= http://www.nsf.gov/od/oci/reports/toc.jsp.

[3] Barjak, F., Lane, J., Kertcher, Z., Poschen, M., and Robinson, S. 2009. Case studies of e-infrastructure adoption. *Soc. Sci. Comput. Rev*. 27, 583-600.

[4] Bazerman, C. 1981. What written knowledge does: three examples of academic discourse. *Phi. Soc. Sci.* 11, 335-359.

[5] Beaulieu, A. and Wouters, P. 2009. E-research as intervention. In *E-research: Transformations in Scholarly Practices* N.W. Jankowski, Ed. Routledge, New York, NY

[6] Beecher, T. and Trowler, P. 2001. *Academic Tribes and Territories: Intellectual Inquiry and the Culture of Disciplines* (2nd Ed.). Open U. Press, Milton Keynes, UK.

[7] Berman, F. and Brady, H. 2005. *Final Report: NSF SBE-CISE Workshop on Cyberinfrastructure and the Social Sciences*. DOI=http://www.sdsc.edu/sbe /reports/SBE-CISE-FINAL.pdf

[8] Collins, R. 1994. Why the social sciences won't become high-consensus, rapid discovery science. *Soc. Forum*. 9, 2, 155-177.

[9] Cummings, J. and Kiesler, S. 2003. Collaborative research across disciplinary and organizational boundaries. In *Sci. Collaboration on the Internet*, G. Olson, A. Zimmerman, and N.Bos, Eds. The MIT Press, Cambridge, MA.

[10] Dutton, W.H. 2007. Reconfiguring access to information and expertise in the social sciences: the social shaping and implications of cyberinfrastructure. In *Proc. 3rd Intrn'l. Conf. on e-Social Science.* (Ann Arbor, Michigan, October 7-9).

[11] Dutton, W.H. and Meyer, E.T. 2008. E-social science as an experience technology: distance from, and attitudes toward, e-research. In *Proc. 4th Intrn'l Conf. on e-Social Science* (Manchester, UK, June18-19).

[12] Erickson, T. and Kellogg, W. 2000. Social translucence: An approach to designing systems that support social processes. *Transactions on Computer-Human Interaction*, 7(1), 59-83.

[13] Fleck, J. 1994. Learning by trying: the implementation of configurational technology. *Res. Policy*. 23, 1, 637-652.

[14] Fry, J. 2006. Coordination and control of research practices across scientific fields: implications for a differentiated e-science. In *New Infrastructures for Knowledge Production: Understanding e-Science*, C. Hine, Ed. Info. Sci. Pub., Hershey, PA.

[15] Fry, J. and Schroeder, R. 2009. Towards a sociology of e-research. In *E-Research: Transformations in Scholarly Practices,* N.W. Jankowski, Ed. Rutledge, New York, NY.

[16] Hine, C. 2006. Computerization movements and scientific disciplines: the reflexive potential of new technologies. In *New Infrastructures for Knowledge Production: Understanding e-Science,* C. Hine, Ed. Info. Sci. Pub., Hershey, PA.

[17] Knorr-Cetina, K. 1999. *Epistemic Cultures: How the Sciences Make Knowledge*. Harvard Press, Cambridge, MA.

[18] Latour, B. and Woolgar, S. 1986. *Laboratory Life: The Social Construction of Scientific Facts*. Sage, Beverly Hills, CA.

[19] Lin, Y.-W., Procter, R., Halfpenny, P., Voss, A., and Baird, K. 2007. An action-oriented ethnography of interdisciplinary social scientific work. *Proc. Of the 3rd e-Social Science Conf.* (Ann Arbor, MI, October 7-9).

[20] Meho, L. and Tibbo, H. 2003. Modeling the information-seeking behavior of social scientists: Ellis' study revisited. *J. Am. Soc. Inf. Sci. Tec*. 54, 6, 570-587.

[21] Merz, M. 2006. Embedding digital infrastructure in epistemic culture. In *New Infrastructures for Knowledge Production: Understanding e-Science*, C. Hine, Ed. Info. Sci. Pub., Hershey, PA.

[22] Olson, J., Hofer, E., Bos, N., Zimmerman, A., Olson, G., Cooney, D. and Faniel, I. 2003. A theory of remote scientific collaboration. In *Scientific Collaboration on the Internet*, G. Olson, A. Zimmerman, and N.Bos, Eds. The MIT Press, MA.

[23] Østerlund, C. 2008. Documents in place: demarcating places for collaboration in healthcare settings. *CSCW*. 17, 195-225.

[24] Pieri, E. 2009. Sociology of expectation and the e-social science agenda. *Info., Comm. & Society*. 12, 7, 1103-1118.

[25] Ponti, M. 2010. *Actors in Collaboration: Socio-technical Influence on Practice-Research Collaboration*. Doctoral Thesis. University of Gothenburg. DOI=http://bada.hb.se/ bitstream/2320/5458/2/Avhandlingen.pdf.

[26] Rosenberg, A. 2008. *Philosophy of Social Science, 3rd Edition,* Westview Press, Boulder, CO.

[27] Sawyer, S. and Tapia, A. 2007. From findings to theories: institutionalizing social informatics. *Info. Soc.* 23 4, 263-275.

[28] Schroeder, R., and Fry, J. 2007. Social science approaches to e-Science: Framing an agenda. *JCMC*. 12, 2, 229-248.

[29] Schroeder, R. and Spencer, D. 2009. Social scientists and the domestication of e-research tools. In *Proc. 5th International Conf. on e-Social Science* (Cologne, Germany, June 24-26).

[30] Smith, D. 1990. *Texts, Facts, and Femininity: Exploring the Relations of Ruling*. Rutledge, London, UK.

[31] Sonnenwald, D.H., Lassi, M., Olson, N., Ponti, M., and Axelsson, A-S. 2009. Exploring new ways of working using virtual research environments in library and information science. *Libr. Hi. Tech.* 27, 2, 191-204.

[32] Star, S.L. and Ruhleder, K. 1996. Steps toward an ecology infrastructure: design and access for large information spaces. *Inform. Syst. Res.* 7, 1, 111-134.

[33] Traweek, S. 1988. *Beamtimes and Lifetimes: The World of High Energy Physicists*. Harvard University Press, MA.

[34] Wessels, B. and Craglia, M. 2007. Situated innovation of e-social science: integrating infrastructure, collaboration, and knowledge in developing e-social science. *JCMC* 12, 358-7.

[35] Whitley, R. 2000. *The Intellectual and Social Organization of the Sciences* (2nd Ed.). Oxford U. Press, Oxford, UK.

[36] Wouters, P. and Beaulieu, A. 2006. Imagining e-science beyond computation. In C. Hine (Ed.), *New Infrastructures for Knowledge Production: Understanding E-Science.* Information Science Publishing, Hershey, PA.

Organizing without Formal Organization: Group Identification, Goal Setting and Social Modeling in Directing Online Production

Haiyi Zhu, Robert Kraut, Aniket Kittur
Carnegie Mellon University
5000 Forbes Avenue, Pittsburgh, PA15213
{haiyiz, robert.kraut, nkittur}@cs.cmu.edu

ABSTRACT

A challenge for many online production communities is to direct their members to accomplish tasks that are important to the group, even when these tasks may not match individual members' interests. Here we investigate how combining group identification and direction setting can motivate volunteers in online communities to accomplish tasks important to the success of the group as a whole. We hypothesize that group identity, the perception of belonging to a group, triggers in-group favoritism; and direction setting (including explicit direction from group goals and implicit direction from role models) focuses people's group-oriented motivation towards the group's important tasks. We tested our hypotheses in the context of Wikipedia's Collaborations of the Week (COTW), a group goal setting mechanism and a social event within Wikiprojects. Results demonstrate that 1) publicizing important group goals via COTW can have a strong motivating influence on editors who have voluntarily identified themselves as group members compared to those who have not self-identified; 2) the effects of goals spill over to non-goal related tasks; and 3) editors exposed to group role models in COTW are more likely to perform similarly to the models on group-relevant citizenship behaviors. Finally, we discuss design and managerial implications based on our findings.

Author Keywords

Online Production Communities, Group Identification, Governance Mechanisms, Directing Behaviors, Group Goals.

ACM Classification Keywords

H.5.3 [Information Interfaces and Presentation]: Group and Organization Interfaces – Collaborative computing, Computer-supported cooperative work, Web-based interaction; K.4.3 [Computers and Society]: Organizational Impacts – Computer supported collaborative work.

INTRODUCTION

Online production communities are becoming increasingly important in creating innovative products in the networked world. These organizations have successfully aggregated the efforts of millions of volunteers to produce complex artifacts such as GNU/Linux and Wikipedia. Currently most large online projects primarily rely on a paradigm of self-direction in which contributors work primarily on the tasks they are interested in. This paradigm provides a number of benefits. Contributors are motivated to work on the tasks in which they are intrinsically interested in and are likely to choose tasks in which they already have some expertise [4]. However, this approach breaks down when there are conflicts between the interests of the contributors and the interests of the project as a whole. Many people may want to work on the same popular areas (e.g., an article on "Barack Obama" in Wikipedia) while ignoring less popular areas that require work. Contributors may not want to perform maintenance and other unattractive tasks, even though these tasks are important to the continued functioning and health of the project.

Many techniques used in conventional employment organizations are not effective in managing online volunteers due to the fundamental characteristics of online communities, including lack of employment contracts, weak external incentives, weak interpersonal bonds, impoverished communication, large size, and high turnover [20]. For example, if a project tries to exert too much managerial control, volunteers can simply leave, with fewer economic or social consequences than if they had quit a job or left a real-life social group.

Instead, communities must turn to other means of motivating volunteers to accomplish tasks that are important for the welfare of the group. One technique is by leveraging group identification—the perception of belonging to a group. If volunteers feel that their identities are tied to the identity of the group, their goals may be more likely to reflect those that are important to the group [1,15,19,32]. However, group identification by itself does not specify *which* particular tasks to work on.

In contrast, direction setting—for example by specifying goals—can be an effective mechanism for accomplishing specific tasks [3,21,22]. However, direction setting by itself may not be enough. For example, Cosley and his colleagues found that task recommendations based only on the community's needs are less likely to interest members than those that consider personal needs [9]. These challenges may become even more pronounced for tasks that are considered unpleasant or unrewarding.

We hypothesize that group identification and direction setting can complement each other in managing volunteers' efforts. Group identification can align the individual volunteer's goals with the group's goals, while direction setting can channel their effort toward specific group goals. Thus people who identify themselves as group members may voluntarily follow directions based on group needs and perform tasks valued by the group because they believe that investing effort in these tasks is important for the group and thus validates their own identity.

This paper describes a mechanism to motivate and manage volunteers when standard managerial mechanisms deployed in conventional organizations are not available. This mechanism combines group identification and direction setting. Particularly, two sources of direction setting are investigated – explicit direction based on publicized group goals and implicit direction based on role modeling. We test the effectiveness of the mechanism in the context of WikiProjects, subgroups within Wikipedia. After presenting the main findings we also discuss design implications for governance in online communities.

TRADITIONAL MANAGEMENT MECHANISMS

Markets

The market mechanism relies on individuals to make independent decisions about the tasks they want to undertake and how they will do them. In contrast to simple self-direction, market mechanisms use external incentives, such as price, to regulate participants' behaviors. Amazon's Mechanical Turk, a popular crowd sourcing website, uses price to encourage subscribers to undertake tasks that employers care most about. If Wikipedia applied a monetary market mechanism, it would pay editors more for editing important but unpopular articles or for engaging in important but tedious tasks such as maintenance work. However, volunteer peer production systems rarely have the resources to provide external incentives to get important work done. External incentives may undermine people's intrinsic motivation to contribute if they become focused on the extrinsic rewards [11]. Finally, they may be inconsistent with the ideology that drives some volunteer communities.

Bureaucratic Control

Three primary controlling strategies evolved in the history of modern organizations [2]. First was "simple control", which represents direct and personal supervision by factory owners. The second was "technological control", in which simple control was reinforced by physical technology such as the assembly line in traditional manufacturing. The most familiar is bureaucratic control, which derives control from hierarchical social relations between supervisor and supervisee and sets of systemic rules that reward compliance and punish noncompliance [2]. A supervisor can legitimately assign employees tasks and rewards and punish them based on their amount and quality of work.

Bureaucratic control legitimizes the roles of managers, so that employees see themselves as having an obligation to adhere to the decisions made by their managers. External incentives, including monetary rewards such as raises and bonuses, and social ones including promotions and better assignments, supplement this legitimacy and are also important in causing employees to follow the direction of their managers.

Bureaucratic control has become the primary control strategy in conventional modern organizations. Some degree of bureaucratic control exists in online production communities, as well. For many years, Linus Torvalds had significant control in the community developing the Linux operating system. Although by definition managers cannot use wages as incentives to get volunteers to comply with their directives, they can motivate contributors through promotion from rank-and-file positions to more important ones, such as committer status in open source software development projects [29] or administrator status in Wikipedia [6].

However, the effectiveness of bureaucratic control is limited by other characteristics of online production communities. As with market mechanisms, online production communities cannot afford external incentives. Furthermore, tight managerial control of volunteers, including regular supervision and communication with them, is associated with higher turnover rates in offline volunteer organizations. According to Hager and Brudney, bureaucratic control may cause their "volunteer experiences to feel too much like the grind of their daily work rather than an enjoyable avocation," [14, p. 9] and thereby drive them away. In addition, impoverished communication and weak interpersonal bonds in online communities weaken the managers' ability to exert bureaucratic control [10].

INCORPORATING GROUP IDENTITY AND DIRECTION SETTING

Group identity

Tajfel and his colleagues conducted a series of laboratory studies in the early 1970s showing that the mere perception of belonging to a group – that is, social categorization per se – is sufficient to trigger intergroup discrimination favoring the in-group [32, 33, 34]. For example, when assigned to groups on the basis of trivial criteria, participants tend to award more rewards to in-group members than outgroup members. Tajfel and his colleagues introduced the concept of social identity and developed classic social identity theory. Social identity is "the individual's knowledge that he belongs to certain social groups together with some emotional and value significance to him of the group membership" [32]. Social identity rests on intergroup social comparisons, in which members attempt to establish or confirm ingroup-favoring evaluative distinctiveness between ingroup and outgroup. Social identity is motivated by an underlying need for self-esteem [34]. That is, to the extent people have incorporated the group's identity into their personal identities, positive evaluation of the group results in enhanced self-esteem.

The relationship of social identity and in-group favoritism plays out in work environments. In offline organizations, social identity leads individuals to perform behaviors beneficial to the groups of which they are part (see [1] for a review). The outcomes associated with social identity involve cooperation, effort, participation, organizationally beneficial decision making, intrinsic motivation, task performance, information sharing, and coordinated action. Recently work has extended the analysis to online volunteer communities as well. Kittur and his colleagues [19] examined the effects of group identification in Wikipedia, finding that joining a WikiProject (a subgroup in Wikipedia) was associated with increased production work, coordination work and citizenship behaviors.

Direction setting: Goal setting & social modeling

The in-group favoritism that results from group identification alone is often too diffuse to effectively direct volunteers toward specific actions. Volunteers, who identify with a group and want to benefit it, have wide latitude in selecting behaviors that benefit the group. Therefore, we hypothesize that direction setting could complement group identification by focusing people's group-oriented motivation towards important and necessary tasks for the group.

Previous researchers interested in increasing contribution in online communities have often focused on getting volunteers to provide more of what they already contribute. For example, Beenen et al. examined the effects of goal setting in MovieLens [3]. They assigned performance goals (e.g., number of movies to rate), while allowing volunteers to self-select specific targets (e.g., which movies to rate). Cosley and his colleagues designed task recommendation systems in Wikipedia and MovieLens. However, these systems focused on matching individuals with tasks they are already interested in [8,9]. Below we discuss how two direction setting mechanisms—explicit goal setting and implicit social modeling—can motivate self-identified group members to work on tasks important for the group's interests, rather than their own interests.

Goal setting

A goal is the object or aim of an action, usually within a specified time limit [22]. Goal setting can be an effective technique to direct human attention and efforts toward goal-relevant activities and away from goal-irrelevant activities [22, 23]. For example, students with specific learning goals attend to and learn goal-relevant passages better than goal-irrelevant passages [30]; similarly, when people receive feedback, they only improve their performance on dimensions for which they have goals even when receiving feedback on multiple dimensions [21]. In addition to the directive function, goals can motivate high task performance. Goals have an energizing function – high goals lead to greater effort than low goals. Goals also affect persistence – they extend directed effort over time. Finally, goals also affect action indirectly by leading to strategy development and action plans for attaining ones' goal [22].

Group goals, which highlight important tasks for the group as a whole, can direct people's attention and efforts towards these tasks and improve their performance on these tasks. The effects are strongest when people perceive goals as desirable and important for them and thus are committed to the goal [22]. As we discussed previously, people who identify with the group align their own interest with the group's interest; therefore they are more likely to invest their efforts to achieve group goal than people who do not identify with the group because they believe the goals are important to the group and thus important for themselves.

> **Hypothesis 1** (Direct effects of goal setting).
> **H1a.** Highlighting tasks important to the group through goal setting directs people' efforts towards these tasks and improves performance on these tasks. **H1b.** The effect is stronger for people who identify with the group than those who do not identify with the group.

If we assume volunteers' total efforts are fixed, group goals would only redistribute their efforts. However, there are reasons to expect that volunteers' total efforts will be increased by group goal setting. Specifically, group goals might lead to motivational spillover, in which people increase their efforts on behalf of the group beyond that demanded by the original goals. Because of expectancy effects, success and failure on one task may change motivations for subsequent tasks [18, 23, 28]. Accomplishing group goals can lead to rewards such as recognition and reputation, activating people to continue working after the initial task is accomplished. Furthermore, publicizing group goals may activate people's awareness of the group, which then leads to more group relevant activities and contributions.

> **Hypothesis 2** (Spillover effects of goal setting).
> Group goals increases people's general contributions to group-related tasks.

Social modeling

There are often a set of prototypical members in groups who best embody the features that are valued by the group [15, 35]. In volunteer associations and online production groups, the prototypical members are often a small set of core members who perform large amounts of work, engage in coordination activities, and have significantly more knowledge of the group and the community than peripheral members [26, 27]. The prototypical group members serve as models, providing cues for what behavior is valued, and make salient the situational needs for certain actions.

According to social identity and self-categorization theories, individuals who identify themselves as group members tend to spontaneously change their behaviors to be more similar to these prototypical members [15, 35]. In contrast, prototypical members should have less of an effect on those who does not consider themselves as group members [15, 35].

However, for social modeling to occur, the prototypical members should be visible, so that group members can perceive them as role models and to imitate their behaviors.

Hypothesis 3. (Effects of social modeling)
H3a Exposure to prototypical group members should lead people to perform more group-valued behaviors that prototypical members engage in. **H3b** The effect is stronger for people who identify with the group than those who do not identify with the group.

STUDY PLATFORM

Wikiprojects – groups in Wikipedia

We chose Wikiprojects, subgroups in Wikipedia, as the domain in which to investigate the effects of group identification and direction setting. Wikiprojects are collections of editors interested in specific topics such as military history, psychology, or even copyediting. As of March 2008, Wikipedia contained more than 2000 Wikiprojects.

Each Wikiproject has dedicated pages (known as project pages) on which editors can coordinate and organize the writing and the editing of project-related articles. Wikiprojects have a loose membership structure; any editor can participate in project activities and contribute to articles within projects as they see fit. Editors often express their identification with a project by adding their name to a member list or tagging their personal user pages with the project template. Some projects have explicit coordinators, who are responsible for coordinating maintenance tasks and keeping the project functioning.

Wikiprojects employ a variety of techniques to direct members' attention to project valued-tasks [19]. These techniques include: 1) *Open task lists or article alerts*. Many Wikiprojects list from dozens to hundreds of open tasks in their project pages. These lists identify articles that need to be expanded, assessed, copy-edited or reviewed and discussions that need more participation. 2) *Important article lists*. Some Wikiprojects list their most valued articles in their project pages, encouraging people to improve these. 3) *Contests*. Some Wikiprojects set goals and then reward people who contribute the most to them over a defined time period. 4) *Collaborations of the week (COTW)*. Projects set one or two articles need to improve during a defined time period (usually one week to one month).

Collaborations of the Week (COTW)

In this paper, we investigated a specific mechanism, collaborations of the week, which designate one or two articles to improve in a defined period. Collaborations of the Week (COTW) are a widely-applied mechanism in Wikiprojects. As of March 2008, 189 Wikiprojects had conducted COTWs for at least part of their history.

COTWs usually have two phases - selection and collaboration. In the selection phase the project chooses one or two articles on which members will collaborate. In some projects, the article is chosen through voting. Other projects rely on the judgment of coordinators for article selection. In other cases, the choice is made by an automated program. During the collaboration phase, the project tags the chosen article(s) with a special template in its talk page (as shown in Figure 1). This template is visible to all editors who read the article talk page, not just those who are members of the Wikiproject. In addition, the project typically announces the targets of the collaboration on its project pages (as shown in Figure 2). Some projects also send special reminders to project members (those editors with names on member list) on their personal talk pages.

Figure 1. An example template identifying an article as a collaboration of the week.

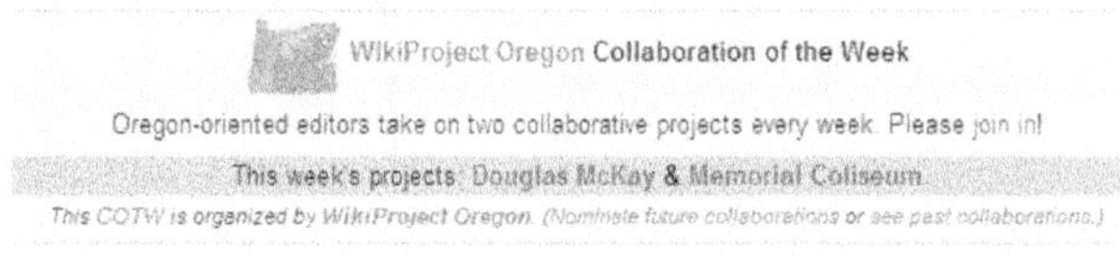

Figure 2. A collaboration of the week announcement in a project page

We chose to examine the Collaborations of the Week as group goal setting mechanism for a number of reasons:

- COTWs are a project goal setting mechanism that highlights tasks crucial for the Wikiproject. For example, some projects explicitly claim that the goal of collaborations is to "fill the gap" of the Wikiproject [38]; collaboration targets are typically articles rated as high importance but having low quality [40]. Furthermore, COTWs have many properties of effective goals, according to the goal setting theory [22]. Compared with a diffuse open task list, for example, COTWs set specific, concrete and time-limited requirements for editors. The limited number of articles and defined time period focus editors' attention on these articles, potentially leading to both production and social benefits.
- COTWs are also social events. COTWs focus volunteers towards specific targets during a defined period, providing opportunities for volunteers to discuss plans and progress with each other, and potentially to influence each other. According to a small survey we conducted with COTW participants, COTWs are "a chance to get to meet your collaborators and their interests". COTW participants are "virtually surrounded by peers who are into the topic and you all have the common goal of sharing knowledge together".

- COTWs are salient. Notices for COTWs are prominent on project pages, thereby attracting people who care about the project, and on the talk pages of the articles which are targets of the collaboration, thereby attracting editors interested in the specific article. Also, the effects of COTWs are amenable to analysis. Firstly, COTWs are widely-used so we can obtain sufficient data for analysis. Secondly they have clear-cut start times and end times. We can compare editors' behavior on the same articles when they are the subjects of collaborations and at other times.

METHOD

Data Collection

In the following analysis, we used a complete download provided by the MediaWiki Foundation from Wikipedia's inception to March 2008 (approximately 182 million revisions). To handle this data volume, we used the Yahoo! M45 computing cluster running Hadoop and Pig. Among the 189 projects that ever used COTW for goal setting, we chose projects with at least five collaborations that had explicit time periods and complete collaboration histories. We also excluded redirected projects and two collaboration-oriented projects which do not have their own topics. The remaining 26 projects carried out a total of 618 collaborations, which lasted 17.7 days on average.

The 26 projects were large and important ones in Wikipedia. They include eight of the ten largest projects in Wikipedia. On average, each project encompassed 26,553 articles (median = 4,632) and 471 members (median = 255.5). Overall, these 26 projects contained 68.5% of all articles associated with any project in Wikipedia.

ANALYSIS AND RESULTS

1. Direct Effects of Goal Setting (H1)

1.1 Analysis Strategy

H1 predicts that, although any editor can participate in the Collaborations of the Week, people who identify themselves as group members in particular will be especially likely to work more on goal-related articles.

We included in our sample editors who had edited the collaborated target articles either during the collaboration period (week or month) or the pre- and post-collaboration period (week or month). We assume that all of these editors were aware of the event, at least from the advertisement notice on the article talk page.

To test the direct effects of group goals, we examined whether these editors' contributions increased during the goal period (the period when the articles are selected as collaboration targets) compared to the non-goal period (the pre- and post-collaboration period). For the effects of group identification, we further investigated whether the contribution increase during the goal period was larger for editors who self-identified as group members than for those who did not.

1.2 Dependent Variable

Goal-relevant Contribution: We measured editors' contributions towards goal-related articles through their revision count on that article. Revisions are a measure of editors' effort, indicating the number of changes they make to articles during a period of time. Each revision comprises a set of editing actions, for example adding, changing, deleting or reverting text, references or illustrations, or communicating with other editors. In this analysis, the dependent measure was the number of revisions the editor made to the COTW articles or their associated discussion pages.

1.3 Independent Variables

Goal period: Collaborations of the Week are explicit group goals that designate one or two articles as targets of work during a defined time period. When editors revise and add to these articles during that period, we consider that they are following the group's goals. However, editing other articles or editing the COTW articles at other periods did not fulfill the group goals in this context. To assess the effectiveness of these goals, we compared contributions towards the same target articles in different time periods – pre-collaboration, during collaboration and post-collaboration. In the analysis, pre-, during and post-collaboration periods were of the same length. For example, if the collaboration lasted one week, pre-collaboration is the week before the start of collaboration; while post-collaboration includes the week after the end of the collaboration. In particular, the dummy variable "Goal period" in our analysis was defined as 0 during the pre-collaboration and post-collaboration periods, and 1 during the collaboration period.

Group identification: Originally, we operationalized people who identified with the group as those who edited the project member lists. However, we found edits to the project members list page were not always a good indicator of group identification, as members often added the names of others to the page (e.g., if the page was copied or repurposed from another source). Therefore, we determined self-identified group members to be all editors who have edited any project page, under the assumption that editors who are involved in the organization of project activities are more likely to consider themselves group members. We used a dummy variable to indicate group identification: 0 indicates the editor has not identified as a group member, while 1 indicates the editor has identified as a group member.

1.4 Control Variables.

Goal length: the number of weeks the collaboration lasts.

Project articles: the total number of articles in the scope of the project during the given period.

Project members: the total number of project members during the given period.

1.5 Statistical Model

We conducted an editor-level analysis, with revision count of contributors to the article as the dependent variable. Because revision counts are count data with a non-normal distribution truncated at zero, we used a negative binomial regression model. Because the analysis compared the contributions from the same editor in different time periods and one of the explanatory variables is constant for an individual, we used random effects methods to deal with the panel data set [16].

1.6 Analysis Results

Figure 3 shows the average number of revisions per editor on collaboration targets in different time periods. We found that people in general contributed more during collaboration periods, but the effect is dramatically larger for those who identified with the group: editors who identified with the group contribute approximately three times more during the collaboration period than they did before the collaboration period, and four times more than editors who did not identify with the group.

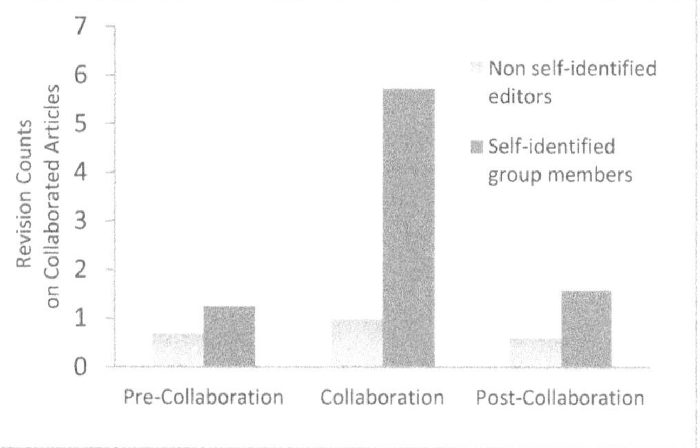

Figure 3. Average revision counts on collaboration target articles in different time periods from different types of editors.

Predictors	IRR.	Std. Err.	P>|z|
Group identification (1-self-identified; 0-not identified)	1.424	.301	<.001
Goal period (1- collaboration period; 0 – pre & post collaboration)	2.066	.036	<.001
Goal period * Group identification	2.975	.102	<.001
Goal length	.996	.001	0.002
Project members	1.000	2.16e-5	<.001
Project articles	1.000	1.07e-7	.105
Log likelihood	-42894.534		

Table 1. Negative binomial regression model predicting goal relevant contributions (revision counts on collaboration target articles). IRR: the ratio change of the dependent variable by increasing an independent variable by a unit.

The negative binomial regression model with random effects methods predicting revision counts on COTW articles tests the significance of these results we ran. The results of the analysis are shown in Table 1, with the effects reported as Incidence Rate Ratios (IRR), which can be interpreted as the ratio change of the dependent variable when increasing an independent variable by one unit. The model assumes that contributions from non-self-identified editors during non-collaboration periods are the baseline level. During collaboration periods, non-self-identified editors increased their contributions 107%, while self-identified editors increased 515% compared to non-collaboration period. The main effect ($P_{Goal\_period} < 0.001$) and interaction effect ($P_{Goal\_period*Group\_identification} < 0.001$) are both highly significant. These results support H1, suggesting that COTWs have a strong motivating effect on contribution, and the effect is especially strong for editors who identify with the project.

The results also suggest that the number of weeks a COTW lasts has a slight negative effect on contributions. Although statistically significant, the size of this effect is quite small, suggesting care must be taken in making too much of it. Factors such as the total number of project articles and project members do not have significant effects. Together, these results suggest that the group goal settings coupled with projects is robust and applies across variations in the length of goal period, and project characteristics.

2. Spillover Effects of Goal Setting (H2)

2.1 Analysis Strategy

The previous analysis demonstrated that group goals set via Collaborations of the Week energized editors, especially self-identified project members. We now examine whether accomplishing these COTW-set group goals influence these project members' editing contributions beyond the targets of the group goal.

We examined the 26 projects in different time periods. We investigated whether the projects received more contributions on goal-irrelevant articles when group goals were posted compared to the period when there were no group goal goals at all.

2.2 Dependent Variable

Non-related contributions: the average number of revisions done by each self-identified project member on all articles in the scope of a given project (including associated discussion pages) in a given month, *excluding the revisions on COTW target articles.*

2.3 Independent Variable

Goal period: a dummy variable indicating whether the project posted COTW goals in a given month. Even though all of the projects in the sample used COTWs at some time in their histories, they used them in only 46% of the months in the dataset.

2.4 Control Variables

Project articles: number of articles in the project.

Project members: total number of project members signed up before the end of the given month.

Project coordination activity: number of revisions made to the project pages in the given month. Since these project pages are where editors organize and discuss project activities, this variable reflects the overall activity of the group during the time period. We used this variable to control for other project activities which might influence contribution towards the project.

Project age: number of months the project has been in existence, starting month one (the month when the project was created). We used this variable to control for the maturity of the project which might influence how much effort people will devote towards the project.

2.5 Statistical Model

For reasons similar to those for the previous analysis, we also applied a negative binomial regression model with random effects to fit the data.

2.6 Analysis Results

The results reveal that the presence of a Collaboration of the Week substantially increased the average number of edits done by project members (IRR = 2.14, P<0.001). The effect is substantial: the presence of COTW goals induced project members to approximately double their contributions on non-target articles. To put this in context, during the month the project posted COTW goals, self-identified group members on average made 9 edits to the collaboration target articles and 60 more edits to other articles in the scope of the project compared to non-COTW month. Thus it appears that employing shared group goal mechanisms such as COTWs can have large benefits to contributions to the project that go beyond the articles identified as collaboration targets.

	IRR	SE	P value
Setting goals	2.140	.097	<0.001
Project Activities	1.000	3.61e-05	<0.001
Project Members	1.000	9.13e-05	0.002
Project Articles	1.000	4.26e-07	<0.001
Project Age	1.043	0.002	<0.001
Log likelihood	-3121.773		

Table2. Negative binomial regression model with random effects predicting goal-irrelevant group-related contributions

3. Effects of Social Modeling (H3)

3.1 Analysis Strategy

Group goal presents explicit direction setting while social modeling is more implicit. When editors work together to accomplish group goals, they can be exposed to prototypical project members, who may serve as role models, and whose behavior provides implicit direction to others (especially self-identified group members).

According to prior research, social modeling may be a useful way to influence a particularly important kind of contribution: citizenship behavior [31]. Citizenship behavior has been defined by Organ [25] as the types of "extra-role" behaviors that are not explicitly recognized by the formal reward system, but are vital to the continued functioning of the organization. For example, the central and most valued work in Wikipedia is creating good quality articles. Adding content to articles is not sufficient. Established editor brag about the number of articles they have brought to "featured article" status. In contrast, maintenance tasks, such as copy-editing, formatting citations, welcoming newcomers, reverting vandalisms, and assessing articles, are actually important to wikipedia as a whole, but less explicitly value or rewarded. Wikipedians wrote of them as "tedious, often unrewarding, and usually unappreciated" tasks [39]. Many of the non-writing wikiwork identified by Kriplean et al [17], such as teaching rewarding welcoming others, finding sockpuppets, reverting vandalism, assessing articles and creating templates, comprise citizenship behavior in Wikipedia. In the analyses below, we treat reverting vandalism and article assessment as representative citizenship behaviors.

We define prototypical members as those who were the heaviest contributors in project pages and at the same time participated in collaborations of the week in a given period. We selected regular editors as non-prototypical members who also participated in COTWs at least once. To measure the influence of role models, we calculated the correlation between their citizenship behaviors with the citizenship behaviors of regular editors, considering 1) whether the regular editors identified themselves as project members or not, and 2) whether the regular editors participated in COTWs in the given period or not. According to hypothesis 3, the correlation between prototypical members' behaviors and the behaviors of the regular editors will be higher when the regular editors participated in COTWs than during other periods. Furthermore, people who self-identified as group members and participated in COTWs should have the highest correlation with prototypical members.

3.2 Dependent variables: citizenship behaviors

Anti-vandalism correlation: Vandalism is defined as "any addition, removal, or change of content made in a deliberate attempt to compromise the integrity of Wikipedia" [36]. Anti-vandalism is the behavior of reverting the vandalized version to a previous state. Following previous research [19], we quantified anti-vandalism as edits annotated with common vandalism-fighting comments, such as "Reverting vandalism" or variants such as "rvv". We measured this variable in two steps. First, we calculated the (log transformed) number of revisions with anti-vandalism comments on articles within the project done by each editor in the given month. We then used this data to calculate the correlation of regular members with prototypical members. To compute this correlation, we matched regular members with prototypical members whom they would meet if they participated in COTWs in that month (multiple editors can match the same prototypical member in a given month).

Assessment correlation: Each article within the scope of a Wikiproject can have a quality rating and an importance rating in its Wikiproject template. Assessing an article involves adding or changing the rating of an article. Assessing articles is an important task for Wikiproject in order to recognize excellent contribution and identify important topics in need of further work; there have been over 2.1 million assessments made over the history of Wikipedia, with most being driven by individual projects. Similar to the anti-vandalism correlation, we measured this variable by 1) calculating the (log transformed) number of revisions done by the editor which change the rating of any article within the project, and 2) calculating the correlation of regular members with prototypical members.

3.3 Analysis Results

The results are shown numerically in Table 3, and graphically in Figure 4 and Figure 5. For assessments, the results are consistent with the Hypothesis 3. Compared to editors who did not participate in collaborations of the week, editors who were exposed to prototypical members through the Collaborations of the Week performed more similarly to prototypical members in terms of helping assess articles. Editors who self-identified as group members and participated in the Collaborations of the Week acted most similar to prototypical members (r=0.36), compared to self-identified members in other months (r=0.24) or to non-self-identified editors, either in the month participating collaborations (r=0.08) or other months (r= 0.07).

For anti-vandalism, editors who participated in collaborations also behaved more similarly to prototypical members (average r=0.11) compared to editors who did not participate (average r=0.06). Surprisingly, however, the difference between participants and non-participants has higher among editors who did not identify as group members (non-self-identified editors: r=0.13 versus r=0.05) compared to those who did (self-identified members: r=0.09 versus r=0.06). Thus we have mixed results about the interaction effects of group identification and social modeling in the case of vandalism reversion. One possible explanation for the latter findings is that, reverting vandalism, although an important citizenship behavior, is not an activity that is strongly identified with any particular Wikiproject. This suggests that social modeling may not be effective for behaviors that are not specific to the group. Additional research is needed to further understand the mechanism of social modeling in these settings: why are models more likely to influence other community members on some citizenship behaviors but not others?

Correlation with prototypical group members	Regular editors			
	Editors who self-identified as group members		Editors who did not identify as group members	
	The month when participated in COTWs	The month when not participate in COTWs	The month when participated in COTWs	The month when not participate in COTWs
Assessment	0.3631	0.2378	0.0759	0.0697
Anti-vandalism	0.0852	0.0599	0.1292	0.0525

Table 3. The correlations of the behaviors of regular editors with the behaviors of prototypical project members.

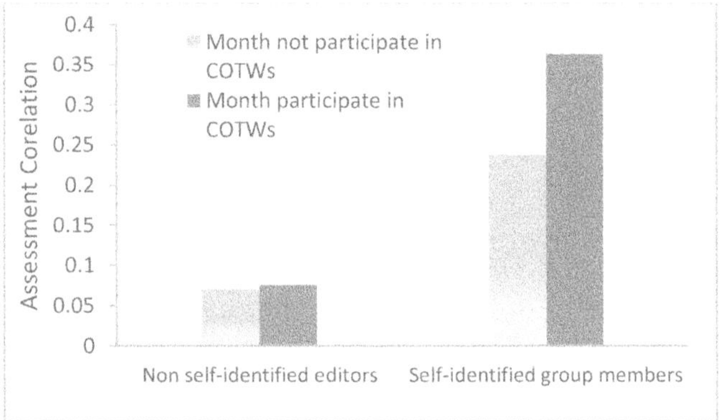

Figure 4. The correlation of regular editors' assessment with the prototypical project members' assessment

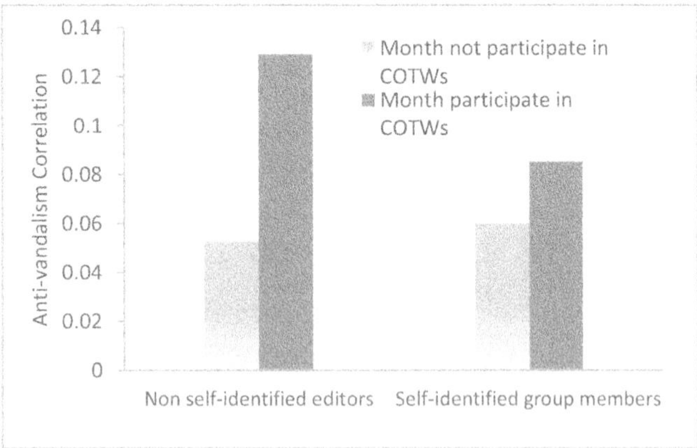

Figure 5. The correlation of regular editors' anti-vandalism with the prototypical project members' anti-vandalism

DISCUSSION

Lessons from Collaborations of the Week

Despite the success of Collaborations of the Week in Wikipedia, many Wikipedia projects that successfully used them ultimately abandoned them. In our data, only 13 of the 26 projects that started to use Collaborations of the Week continued to use them throughout the period of our research (as of March 2008). According to interviews with project leaders [37] the explanation is not related to their effectiveness but instead to the bureaucratic cost of running them. Like any recurrent event, they need an organizer responsible for managing the collaboration process, such as monitoring the nomination progress and maintaining the announcement. In addition, groups and organizers need appropriate strategies to choose collaboration targets. These problems suggest opportunities for computer support for coordinating the collaboration process, such as helping to choose collaboration targets and announcing and running the collaboration process.

Critics might suggest that computer supported coordinated goal setting is not as optimal as goals selected by group organizers or voted by members. However, goal-setting theory suggests that all these types of goal selection can be equally effective as long as group members become committed to the group goal [24] and furthermore some projects have already implemented an automated topic selection program which chooses targets from a collectively maintained list [40].

Although Collaborations of the Week are occasions for social interaction and modeling, their design could enhance these attributions. For example, some Wikiprojects has instituted temporally synchronous editing sessions for project members to get together to work on common tasks, with the explicit purpose of increasing social interaction.

Managerial implication

Although these results were obtained in the context of projects within Wikipedia, we believe that the basic idea of combining group identification and direction setting, as an unobtrusive management method, may generalize to other kinds of online communities and offline organizations. For example, these ideas may work well in organizations emphasizing creative work, such as art design or scientific research, where strong managerial control may harm creativity. Deadlines for major releases in many open source software projects serve similar functions.

There may be limits to the applicability of group goal setting, which simply highlight tasks important for the group. If these tasks involve high coordination costs, the benefits of adding more effort may be offset by the difficulties of coordinating that effort; or, as Brooks aptly states, "Adding manpower to a late software project makes it later" [5]. However, in the cases when group goal setting can be used, our results suggest it is remarkably powerful and leads to benefits not only to the targeted goals but also to other group-relevant tasks.

Compared to group goal setting, which focuses attention on a specific set of tasks, social models may be especially effective in drawing in peripheral members and training them in a wide range of subtle behaviors. Therefore, we recommend practitioners pay close attention to encouraging the desired behaviors from core members and then providing social opportunities (such as communication channels and collaboration tasks) for core members to interact with and potentially influence the others.

CONCLUSION

This paper investigated how combining group identification with direction, either explicit direction through group goals or implicit direction through social modeling, can motivate volunteers in online communities to accomplish tasks important to the success of the group. We tested our hypotheses in the context of subgroups within Wikipedia (Wikiprojects), examining a common group activity (Collaborations of the Week). Our results demonstrate that 1) highlighting important group goals can have a strong motivating influence on editors who have self-identified as group members compared to comparable others who have not self-identified; 2) the positive effects spill over to non-goal related tasks; and 3) editors exposed to prototypical group members are more likely to behave similarly to those members on group-relevant citizenship behaviors than editors not exposed to prototypical members.

ACKNOWLEDGEMENT

We thank the members of the Social Computing Group at Carnegie Mellon University for helpful feedback. We also thank Yarun Luon and Raechel Lee for editing help. This research was supported by NSF grants OCI-09-43148, IIS-0968484, IIS-1111124 and a grant from Carnegie Mellon's Center for the Future of the Work.

REFERENCES

1. Ashforth, B.E., Harrison,S.H., and Corley, K.G (2008) Identification in Organizations: An Examination of Four Fundamental Questions. Journal of Management.
2. Barker, J. (1993). Tightening the iron cage: Concertive control in self-managing teams. *Administrative Science Quarterly, 38*(3), 408-437.
3. Beenen, G., Ling, K., Wang, X., Chang, K., Frankowski, D., Resnick, P., and Kraut, R. E. (2004). Using social psychology to motivate contributions to online communities. In *CSCW 2004*
4. Benkler, Y. (2002). Coase's Penguin, or Linux and the Nature of the Firm. *Yale Law Journal*, Vol. 112.
5. Brooks, F.P. (1975). The mythical man month. Addison-Wesley Longman Publishing Co., Inc. Boston, MA, USA
6. Burke, M., & Kraut, R. E. (2008). Mopping up: Modeling Wikipedia Promotion Processes. In *CSCW 2008*.
7. Cheney, G., & Tompkins, P. (1987). Coming to terms with organizational identification and commitment. *Communication Studies, 38*(1), 1-15.
8. Cosley, D., Frankowski, D., Terveen, L., and Riedl, J., 2007. SuggestBot: using intelligent task routing to help people find work in wikipedia. In Proceedings of the 12th

international conference on Intelligent user interfaces (IUI '07).

9. Cosley, D., Frankowski, D., Terveen, L., and Riedl, J., 2006. Using intelligent task routing and contribution review to help communities build artifacts of lasting value. In Proceedings of the SIGCHI conference on Human Factors in computing systems (CHI '06)
10. Daft, R., & Lengel, R. (1984). Information richness: A new approach to managerial behavior and organizational design. *Research in Organizational Behavior, 6*, 191-233.
11. Deci, E. L., Koestner, R., & Ryan, R. M. (1999). A meta-analytic review of experiments examining the effects of extrinsic rewards on intrinsic motivation. *Psychological Bulletin, 125*(6), 627-668.
12. Feather N.T.; Rauter K.A., (2004) Organizational citizenship behaviours in relation to job status, job insecurity, organizational commitment and identification, job satisfaction and work values. *Journal of Occupational and Organizational Psychology*, 77(1), 81-94.
13. Forte, A., & Bruckman, A. (2008). Scaling Consensus: Increasing Decentralization in Wikipedia Governance. *Hawaii International Conference on System Sciences, Proceedings of the 41st Annual*, 157-157.
14. Hager, M., & Brudney, J. (2004). Volunteer management practices and retention of volunteers. *The Urban Institute*
15. Hogg, M. A., & Terry, D. J. (2000). Social identity and self-categorization processes in organizational contexts. *The Academy of Management Review, 25*(1), 121-14.
16. Kennedy, P. (2001). A guide to econometrics (4th ed.). Cambridge, MA: MIT Press.
17. Kriplean, T., Beschastnikh, I., and McDonald, D.W.(2008). Articulations of wikiwork: uncovering valued work in wikipedia through barnstars. In Proceedings of the 2008 ACM conference on Computer supported cooperative work (CSCW '08).
18. Kernis, M., Zuckerman, M., Cohen, A., & Spadafora, S. (1982). Persistence following failure: The interactive role of self-awareness and the attributional basis for negative expectancies. *Journal of Personality and Social Psychology, 43*(6), 1184-1191.
19. Kittur, A., Pendleton, B., & Kraut, R. (2009). Herding the cats: The influence of groups in coordinating peer production In *WikiSym 2009.*
20. Kraut, R. E. & Resnick, P. (Under contract). *Evidence-based social design: Mining the social sciences to build online communities.* Cambridge, MA: MIT Press.
21. Locke, E. A., & Bryan, J. (1969). The directing function of goals in task performance. Organizational Behavior and Human Performance, 4, 35–42.
22. Locke, E. A., & Latham, G. P. (1990). *A theory of goal setting and task performance.* Englewood Cliffes, NJ: Prentice-Hall.
23. Locke, E. A., & Latham, G. P. (2002) Building a Practically Useful Theory of Goal Setting and Task Motivation American Psychologist, Vol. 57, No. 9, 705–717
24. O'Leary-Kelly, A., Martocchio, J., & Frink, D. (1994). A review of the influence of group goals on group performance. Academy of Management Journal, 37(5), 1285-1301
25. Organ, D. W., & Ryan, K. (1995). A meta-analytic review of attitudinal and dispositional predictors of organizational citizenship behavior. *Personnel Psychology, 48*(4), 775-802.
26. Pearce, J.P., (1993) Volunteers: the organizational behavior of unpaid workers, Published by Routledge, 11 New Fetter Lane, London
27. Preece, J. and B. Shneiderman (2009) "The Reader-to-Leader Framework: Motivating Technology-Mediated Social Participation," AIS Transactions on Human-Computer Interaction, (1) 1, pp. 13-32
28. Quintela, Y., & Donovan, J. (2008). A model of motivational spillover. In K. H. Kiefer (Ed.), *Applied Psychology Research Trends*. New York: Nova Science, 141-160.
29. Roberts, J. A., Hann, I.-H., & Slaughter, S. A. (2006). Understanding the Motivations, Participation, and Performance of Open Source Software Developers: A Longitudinal Study of the Apache Projects. *Management Science, 52*(7), 984-999.
30. Rothkopf, E., & Billington, M. (1979). Goal-guided learning from text: Inferring a descriptive processing model from inspection times and eye movements. Journal of Educational Psychology, 71, 310 –327.
31. Smith, C. A., Organ, D. W., Near, J. P. (1983) Organizational citizenship behavior: Its nature and antecedents. Journal of Applied Psychology, Vol 68(4), Nov 1983
32. Tajfel, H. 1972. Social categorization (English translation of "La cat6gorisation sociale"). In S. Moscovici (Ed.), Introduction a la psychologie sociale, vol. 1: 272-302. Paris: Larousse.
33. Tajfel, H., Billig, M. G., Bundy, R. P., Flament,C., 1971 Social categorization and intergroup behaviour, European Journal of Social Psychology, Volume 1, Issue 2.
34. Tajfel, H., & Turner, J. C. 1979. An integrative theory of intergroup conflict. In W. G. Austin & S. Worchel (Eds.), The social psychology of intergroup relations: 33-47. Monterey, CA: Brooks-Cole.
35. Turner, J. C. 1985. Social categorization and the self-concept: A social cognitive theory of group behavior. In E. J. Lawler (Ed.), Advances in group processes: Theory and research, vol. 2: 77-122. Greenwich, CT: JAI Press.
36. Vandalism. http://en.wikipedia.org/wiki/Wikipedia:Vandalism
37. Wikipedia:Wikipedia Signpost/Archives/WikiProject report. http://en.wikipedia.org/wiki/Wikipedia:Wikipedia_Signpost/Archives/WikiProject_report
38. Wikipedia:WikiProject_Anime_and_manga/Collaboration_of_the_Week http://en.wikipedia.org/wiki/Wikipedia:WikiProject_Anime_and_manga/Collaboration_of_the_Week
39. Wikipedia:WikiProject_Council/Guide http://en.wikipedia.org/wiki/Wikipedia:Wikiproject_Council/Guide
40. Wikipedia:WikiProject_Video_games/Collaboration_of_the_week http://en.wikipedia.org/wiki/Wikipedia:WikiProject_Video_games/Collaboration_of_the_week

All-for-One and One-for-All? A Multi-Level Analysis of Communication Networks and Individual Performance in Geographically Distributed Software Development

Kate Ehrlich
IBM Research
Cambridge, MA, USA
katee@us.ibm.com

Marcelo Cataldo
Carnegie Mellon University
Pittsburgh, PA, USA
mcataldo@cs.cmu.edu

ABSTRACT
It is well established that distributed software projects benefit from informal communication. However, it is less clear how patterns of informal communication impact the performance of the individual developers. In a study of communication networks in a large commercial software project, we found that individuals performed better when they were central within a team's communication network but their performance worsened if they were central within the communication for the whole project. On the other hand, individuals embedded in a dense communication cluster at the team and at the project level perform better than those who were not embedded. The effects for both network positions were maintained even after controlling for formal role, individual differences in communication, workload and other factors that drive communication. We discuss the implications of the results for intra- and inter-team communication and for the inclusion of network structure into the design of collaborative and awareness tools.

Author Keywords
Communication, Coordination, Centrality, Closure, Software Development, Social Network Analysis.

ACM Classification Keywords
H5.3. Group and Organization Interfaces: Asynchronous Communication, Computer-supported Cooperative Work.

General Terms
Human Factors, Management, Measurement.

INTRODUCTION
Research on geographically distributed product development teams has established the importance of informal communication for coordination within and across teams (e.g. [12, 26]), for building shared knowledge (e.g. [16]) and for locating and leveraging expertise (e.g. [22]). However, the effect of communication on individual performance is less well understood. While individuals can benefit from increased communication [13], too much communication can interfere with completing tasks (e.g. [11, 19, 28, 34]). Recent research suggests that there are more varied communication requirements at the individual level compared with the team or project level [15]. This paper brings some focus to individual performance in distributed software projects by using social network analysis to examine the effect of position within a communication network on individual performance.

CSCW researchers are turning to social network analysis as a method of understanding the effect of communication on distributed software development (e.g. [11, 13]) especially in the context of open source development (e.g. [5, 17]). However, this research has generally looked at performance outcomes at the team or project level (e.g. [45, 46]). Few studies have looked at the role of communication and individual-level performance in software development. One exception is a recent study by Cataldo and Herbsleb [12] who found project-level communication tended to follow a core-periphery pattern where developers who were part of the core also contributed more to the development effort of the project. The absence of research on individual performance is especially noteworthy in the context of collaborative and awareness tools which are designed for individual use. By examining individual performance we can better pinpoint what enhancements to bring to these tools.

A different approach to communication patterns comes from investigations into the effect of network position on performance. A body of research has demonstrated that an individual's position within a communication network affects how well they share information and knowledge with others (e.g. [36]). Especially important are positions of centrality [24] and positions within highly dense clusters, typically referred to as closure [9]. Individuals who are central in a communication network generally benefit from exchanging more important and varied information [1]. Individuals embedded within a cluster of people benefit from sharing information with others who they trust and with whom they have shared knowledge (e.g. [14, 30, 32]).

Communication demands are further complicated when there is a need to coordinate work across rather than within teams since there is less certainty and higher cost associated with cross-boundary interactions [10, 18]. For instance, Hinds and McGrath [28] report that a higher level of communication is detrimental to cross-site communication. Recent research has refined this finding to suggest that amount of communication is related to the kind of outcome under study as well as to cross-boundary effects [11].

In this paper, we studied the effect of structural position in an evolving communication network on individual performance in a commercial software development project. In the next section we describe related research on centrality and closure, followed by a description of the research setting, and the empirical methods we used to collect and analyze the data and the results. We conclude by drawing the implications of our findings for research on distributed software teams and especially for development of collaborative tools.

NETWORK POSITION AND PERFORMANCE IN TEAMS AND PROJECTS

Centrality and Performance

Research on positional effects in social networks has largely focused on centrality, which is associated with positive outcomes for the individual [8, 24]. For instance, individuals who are central within a friendship or advice network are more powerful and influential because they gain from being connected to more people (e.g. [29, 40]). Individuals who are central in a communication network benefit because they are in a position to distribute or transfer information more efficiently (e.g. [36]), or gain influence through visibility as a communication partner (e.g. [1]). However, being centrally located in a communication network requires additional effort that may detract from an individual's performance [9, 11, 34]. Furthermore, the benefits of communication centrality may depend on the ability of the individual to absorb and act upon the information they receive [29]. There is therefore some uncertainty whether centrality within a software team's communication network will help or hinder the ability of an individual to complete their assigned coding tasks on time.

RQ1: Does centrality in team-level communication network help or hinder individual performance?

Closure and Performance

Individual-level cohesion or closure in social networks refers to relationships that are embedded in a dense web of third-party ties, resulting in strong relationships conducive to cooperative behaviors and trust [14, 30]. Recent work on innovations that builds on Simmelian ties theory [31] argued that triadic communication, in which two people who communicate directly with each other also communicate with a common third person, provides the necessary mechanism to make sense of new information [41].

A clustered set of relationships creates the willingness to devote time to assist others and in turn increases the likelihood of successful knowledge sharing and transfer [36]. Team members who might struggle to make sense of new knowledge and effectively integrate it into the relevant context because of differences in perspectives, lack of common understandings [4] and lack of familiarity working together [6] benefit from being positioned within closed clusters.

Although this line of research has not yet been extended to software development, there is evidence to suggest that clusters of developers tend to form organically in open source projects, especially around technical issues [5]. Recent research also points to the importance of team-level clustering for producing higher quality code [11]. The principle of modularity along with the practice of splitting work into separate teams is a tacit endorsement of the need to keep work, and hence communication to a small, manageable group of people. [2]. Based on these principles and the previous research, it is plausible that individuals who are positioned within more clusters, i.e. have a higher level of closure should have a higher level of shared information resulting in completion of more code. However, closure is also associated with "group-think" and an unwillingness to consider alternate approaches and solutions [7], which could inhibit development of new features or reinforce poor development practices.

RQ2: Does closure in team-level communication network help or hinder individual performance?

Project-level Communication Networks

The work of a large-scale product development project is generally distributed across separate teams. Moreover, the use of modular designs to limit the number of dependencies among those teams tends to be the norm [2]. Most of the coordination effort occurs within each team and is handled through informal communication amongst the developers involved. Responsibility for cross-team coordination usually falls to a few people who may undertake a larger burden of communication [12]. While cross-team communication is a vital part of coordination there is a greater cost to the individual associated with sharing information across boundaries (e.g. [10, 20]).

Network positions of centrality and closure can be considered with respect to the position of the individual within a team or the position of the individual within the set of teams comprising the overall project. Individuals who are highly central at the project level will have more cross-team communication. On the one hand, cross-team communication can improve project coordination and reduce the number of bugs [13, 39]). On the other hand, maintaining communication with a more diverse and distributed set of people is more costly which makes it harder for the individual to maintain a high level of performance.

RQ3: Does centrality in project-level communication network help or hinder individual performance?

Similarly, individuals who have high levels of closure will be exposed to a more diverse set of expectations. Since conflict and disagreement is common in distributed workgroups [27], the increased trust and willingness to share information that is associated with closure could be beneficial. However, individuals with higher levels of closure might also get involved in resolving conflict, which interferes with their own development tasks.

RQ4: Does closure in project-level communication network help or hinder individual performance?

RESEARCH SETTING

We studied the software project that developed the IBM® Rational® Jazz™ (RTC) collaboration platform[1]. RTC is a software development environment that integrates development, collaboration and project management features in the same platform [25]. IBM made available the data from the software repositories that the project generated during the development of the first version of the product. Although development activities started as early as May 2006, we focused our analysis on the 13 months prior to the release of the product's first version, which was the period of time between July 2007 and August of 2008. The reason to focus on this particular period of time is two-fold. First, in July of 2007 the project underwent a significant change in process opening up the development process to the Jazz community. Second, prior to July 2007, the amount of development activities, referred to in this study as work items, was a small fraction (498 out of 12,886 work items) of the overall development effort. We focused on development activity corresponding to release 0.6. A total of 161 developers, worked on the project during the period analyzed. There were 26 functional teams distributed in 21 different sites across the U.S., Canada and Europe. Project members belonged to one or more of these teams, and, each team had its own leader.

The project organized its development effort using iterations, which are short-lived (e.g. 6 to 8 weeks) units of development activities. The tasks to be performed for each iteration and by each development team, were planned at the beginning of each iteration. However, the amount of development work varied across teams, and, within teams across iterations, based on the technical responsibilities of the teams and the properties of the product features being developed at different points in time. Release 0.6 of the product, which consisted of 14 iterations, was the focus of our analysis. The nature of the project is such that there are also teams who are part of the development effort for only a short period of time, who are very small or who are called upon to contribute a small amount of code. Where most of the teams had well beyond 100 work items per iteration there were a few teams who had fewer than 20 work items in multiple iterations. In order to focus on the main continuous development, we used 20 work items as a cutoff to determine which teams to include in our analysis. This resulted in data for 16 out of the 26 teams. Those 16 teams were distributed across 15 development sites. The 10 excluded teams were very small in size (1 to 3 members) and represented a very small fraction of the overall amount of development activity (7.2%) and communication (0.9% among the project members. We discuss the analytical implications of this decision at the end of the results section.

Description of the Measures

In order to examine our hypotheses, we collected a number of measures from various data sources including the project's software repositories. We collected information about each project member's location from personnel records. The rest of the section is organized as follows. First, we describe our outcome measure, Individual Performance. Second, we describe how we captured the communication measures and the network measures that constitute our independent variables. We conclude with a description of the control factors that we included in our analyses. Table 1 reports the descriptive statistics of all our measures.

Measuring Individual Performance

Assessing individual-level performance is a challenging endeavor in software development. Past research has proposed different approaches to measure individual-level software development performance such as subjective measures of performance (e.g. [35]), units of source code per some unit of time (e.g. [21]), time to complete a development task (e.g. [23]) and number of tasks and commits completed (e.g. [12]). This study considers individual-level performance as the amount of contribution to the development effort as captured by the number of defects fixed. In the development project, there were three different types of tasks: defects, enhancements and tasks. Defects represent development activities associated with fixing a bug in the system. Enhancements referred to development tasks that involved adding new functionality to the system under development or extending existing functionality. Finally, tasks involved a wide range of activities such as design of certain features of the system, documentation, and support for the RTC online community. Defects represented the largest category and were a relatively homogeneous group in terms of the development work associated with the task. Therefore, we opted to use the number of defects a project member resolved in an iteration as our outcome measure. A defect was considered completed or "resolved" when its resolution state in the software repository was set to *fixed* and its status was set to "*resolved*", "*closed*" or "*verified*".

Construction of the Communication Networks

The RTC development environment offers a number of features for contextualized communication for work items. Our study focused on the comments on a work item, allowing us to identify the work item, the individuals that made the comment(s) as well as the content of the comment. Unlike traditional threaded discussions tools (e.g. chat/IRC) where linking the content of a conversation to a task is not trivial, the work item comments are directly

[1] IBM, the IBM logo, ibm.com, and Rational are trademarks or registered trademarks of International Business Machines Corporation in the United States, other countries, or both.

associated with development tasks. In separate conversations, four developers from the project, confirmed that the comment field was used as the primary mode of communication for technical issues, in part to satisfy a goal of making the development process transparent to everyone and, by the need to create a traceable record of decisions.

Since multiple work items could refer to the same issue and later be resolved as duplicates, we considered a work item and all its duplicates as a single work item. In this way, the comments made in the different work item reports were all combined under a single report. Once all the work items associated with a particular iteration and with a particular team were identified, we constructed an iteration-team-level network using the following procedure. First, we considered only those comments made in the work item reports that were within the time frame of the iteration. Second, the first comment in the work item linked the person that made the comment with the owner of the task at the time the comment as made. If the owner and the commenter were the same person, the link was ignored. Third, and for the subsequent comments in the work item report, a link in the communication network between two project members was made if the comments were sequential in time and they were associated with the task at hand. These comments also resulted in a link between the commenter and the owner of the work item at the time it was made. We identified comments in the work item report that were requesting status rather than providing information or contributing to the resolution of the work item. We removed these comments from our analysis.

Finally, it is important to point out that we considered the sequence of the communication. An examination of a random sample of work items revealed that interaction tended to follow sequences of questions or requests for information followed by answers. Identifying the directionality of the flow of information is important to understand how communication patterns evolved during the development effort. This approach is consistent with, other methods used to extract communication patterns from software repositories (e.g. [5, 42, 45]). Our approach is conservative relative to other approaches because it only establishes a communication link between pairs of individuals that made the communication explicit. Other approaches (e.g. [45]) tend to assume communication among individuals when they are subscribed to the notifications generated by the tools, which could result in biased structural patterns of communication.

We illustrate how the construction of the communication networks was done using an example from one of the work items. Figure 1 shows the comments associated with work item id 4276, which was about hiding "check-in" actions when auto-save is enabled. For simplicity sake, we consider that all the comments were made during a single iteration. Developer A (Dev A) is the owner of the task. Developer B (Dev B) made the first two comments, which provide suggestions on how to address the issue, generating a link from Developer B to developer A in the communication network. Developer C (Dev C) expresses his/her opinion regarding Developer's B suggestion generating a link between developer C and B as well as a link between Developer C and Developer A (the owner of the task). Then, Developer D (Dev D) made a comment related to Developer C's suggestion which generated a link between Developer D and Developer C. Developer A (the owner) then follows up with a response to D's comment so a link from Developer A to Developer D is created in the communication network. The process continues in this manner until all the comments associated with the work items that fall between the start and end time of an iteration are processed. Using this method we constructed communication networks for each team for each iteration.

Dev B:	We could disable it. But again, I still have a problem tying the enablement of the action to the global setting. What happens if the setting is set but the check-in failed?
Dev B:	Would it make more sense to show a dialog when the preference is on explaining auto check-in and possibly allowing the user to toggle it directly from there? I'm not sure that removing or changing the visibility of an action based on a global preference is prudent.
Dev C:	... would leave the action visible and enabled, and let the user know that there are no changes to check in for the selected resource(s). I think that hiding the action when auto-check-in is on is too much of an implicit mode.
Dev D:	This is only an implicit mode if the user sometimes works with auto-checkin on and sometimes works with it off. In most cases I've seen, users always work one way or the other but rarely switch between the two. This is similar to the "pin editor" action in Eclipse.
Dev A:	Auto check-in can fail (e.g. server behaves crazily for 15 minutes). Then user must rearm it by manually checking-in (e.g. after user reads an email saying server has been patched live). In that scenario it is nice to still have this action.
Dev D:	> Auto check-in can fail (e.g. server behaves > crazily for 15 minutes). Then user must > rearm it by manually checking-in(e.g. after > user reads an email saying server has been > patched live). In that scenario it is nice to > still have this action. Good point. However, the action is still available from the Pending Changes view. That should be enough to cover this use-case.

Figure 1: Sample Communication in a Work Item

We constructed project-level communication networks by aggregating the information from the team level networks and re-computing the network metrics such that position in the project-level was separate from the position in the team-level. The aggregation process consisted in performing the union of all team-level networks, resulting in a project-level network per iteration. In other words, we used two types of communication networks. One communication network captured the interactions among members of each organization team within an iteration and the second type of network captured the communication patterns across all teams within each iteration. Finally, the aggregation process results in a communication network with weighted edges that represent the number of interactions by one developer directed at another developer.

Computing the Independent Measures

The communication networks have two properties: directionality of the interaction and the weight or amount of interactions between a pair of developers. We computed the *In-flow and Out-flow Centrality* measures based on Barrat and colleagues' [3] normalized weighted centrality measure. *Closure* was calculated as the normalized number of triads considering the weights on the edges as proposed by Barrat and colleagues [3]. It is worth pointing out that such a measure is equivalent to the normalized Simmelian ties [31] for each individual when considering the networks as binary. These independent measures for Centrality and Closure were used to examine our 4 research questions.

Additional Control Factors

Past research work suggests a wide range of factors that impact individual-level performance in the context of knowledge-intensive tasks and software development in particular (e.g. [6, 26, 46]). We organized our control variables into five groups:

Controls for role-related factors: Within each team, each individual was assigned a role of team lead, developer or admin. The assignment of roles was done by the project's higher management. To the extent that these assigned roles may describe job requirements or expectations, the role could impact an individual's communication. Therefore, we computed several binary variables that captured the various roles that an individual could have within each team for each iteration. *Team Lead Role* is set to 1 if the individual had the team lead role in the team for a particular iteration otherwise was set to 0. *Developer Role* is set to 1 if the individual had the contributor or part-time contributor role in the team for a particular iteration otherwise was set to 0. In addition, there were a number of administrative-related roles that involved collecting information for different purposes such as maintaining the project's dashboard. Then, *Admin Role* is set to 1 if the individual had any of the administrative roles in a team in a particular iteration. Finally, there were a few additional roles that involved activities such as building and integrating the system. *Other Role* is set to 1 if the individual had any other roles in a team in a particular iteration. It is important to point out that a project member could have multiple roles across iterations within a team.

Controls for communication-related factors: Individuals communicate with colleagues based on both specific needs and for general purposes. *Coordination Needs* captures the extent to which an individual needs to communicate with other members of the project given the set of task dependencies that the individual has in a particular team and iteration. We used the approach proposed by Cataldo and colleagues [12, 13] to compute a coordination requirement matrix for each team in each iteration. Then, for each individual we computed the density of their ego network which was our measure of *Coordination Needs*.

Individuals may also have a general tendency to share information with other project members on tasks that might not be directly related to their responsibilities for their team and iteration. We computed *Commenting Propensity* as the number of work items where an individual made a comment in the work item report but the individual did not directly work on that work item (e.g. did not own the task, or did not make any of the changes to the system associated with the task). Members in the same team may have more opportunities to interact face-to-face, for instance, through periodic meeting than members that belong to different teams. Thus, we computed *Commenting Propensity Other Team,* which is similar to the previous measure but only considering those tasks that were performed by project members that belong to other teams but were in the same location as the focal individual. These last two measures allow us to control for the overall propensity to comment on other tasks within and outside the team as well as the differences that might exist in such propensity when the coworkers as collocated or not.

Finally, we controlled for the density of communication in which an individual is involved. We assess *Communication Density* as the density of the neighborhood of the ego network of each individual not considering ego. In other words, this measure is the local clustering measure proposed by Watts [43]. This measure was computed for the team-level network and the project-level network.

Controls for task-related factors: We also measured *Overall Workload* as the number of tasks that the individual worked on including the resolved defects. This control is important since position in the communication network is independent of the amount of work a person is assigned.

Controls for unobserved effects: Finally, we included a few additional controls for unobserved, team- and location-specific factors. These dummy variables effectively control for any factors, which we could not explicitly measure such as the cultural or organization aspects of the teams as well as of the development locations involved in the project. These were recorded as Dummy A through D for the teams and dummy Location A through D for the sites. Table 1 shows the descriptive measures for all dependent, independent and control factors for our dataset consisting of 3978 <iteration, team, individual> data points.

Description of the Model

Our data is a repeated-measures longitudinal dataset. As is typical in these situations, variations of the outcome may be the result of the idiosyncratic aspect of each project as well as time (e.g., variation may be due to the current development state of a project). Traditional regression models are not able to properly account for those variations. Therefore, we utilized a multi-level modeling approach, which allows variation at several levels within the model (for a more complete overview of multi-level modeling of longitudinal data see [38]). In our data we have a stream of data for each individual that worked in one or more teams over one or more iterations. Then, in our multi-level model, we introduced the individual id, team id and iteration id as random effects factors. In this way, we account for the fact that individuals, teams and iterations may be different across a wide range of factors. Since our dependent variable is a count variable, we used a multi-level negative binomial model to examine our research questions.

	Mean	S.D.	Min	Max
Individual Performance	2.02	6.85	0	92
Team Lead Role	0.07	0.26	0	1
Developer Role	0.28	0.45	0	1
Admin Role	0.02	0.13	0	1
Other Roles	0.05	0.23	0	1
Coordination Needs	0.17	0.11	0	0.52
Comm. Propensity	2.52	5.09	0	88
Comm. Propensity (loc)	9.77	12.8	0	90
Comm. density (team)	0.39	0.37	0	1
Comm. density (project)	0.39	0.18	0	1
Overall Workload	6.75	15.3	1	175
In-flow Centrality (team)	0.15	0.25	0	1
Out-flow Centrality (team)	0.17	0.23	0	1
Closure (team)	0.04	0.09	0	0.66
In-flow Centrality (project)	0.32	0.25	0	1
Out-flow Central. (project)	0.30	0.24	0	1
Closure (project)	0.08	0.07	0	0.34

Table 1: Descriptive Statistics

RESULTS

We examined our hypotheses by creating several negative binomial models, which included the different control variables as well as our independent measures. In order to assess the fit of each model, we report the log-likelihood of each model as well as the percentage of deviance explained by the model. Deviance is defined as -2 times the log likelihood of the model. The percentage of the deviance explained is a ratio of the deviance of the null model (containing only the intercept) and the deviance of the final model. We report the regression coefficients associated with each factor in our models in Table 2. Model 1 is the null model used to determine the baseline log-likelihood to compare the subsequent models against. Model II is our baseline model with only the control factors.

Team-level Interaction and Individual Performance

Model III in Table 2 examined the impact of different structural positions in the team-level communication network on individual performance (RQ1 and RQ2). The results show statistically significant effects for our independent variables. Higher levels of *in-flow centrality* and *closure* within the team-level network are associated with improvements in individual-level performance. On the other hand, higher levels of *out-flow centrality* within the team-level network are associated with lower individual-level performance. Given that these factors are relevant in terms of individual performance, it is useful to take a closer look at their relative impact. One approach is to compute the incidence rate ratios (IRRs) associated with each measure. The IRRs indicate the rate at which the dependent variable, in our case the number of tasks resolved in an iteration, change for one unit change in one independent variable keeping the rest of the measures constant. The IRRs are calculated as the $exp(\beta)$ where β is the regression coefficient. Using the regression coefficients reported in Table 2 - Model III, the IRRs for in-flow centrality, out-flow centrality and closure are 2.82, 0.91 and 21.11, respectively. These IRRs show that *Closure*, in particular, has a very strong effect on individual performance. In sum, we found that centrality impacts performance (RQ1) in two distinct ways depending on the direction of the communication. While in-flow of communication helps individuals perform better, out-flow of communication hinders performance, We also found that closure at the team-level network has a major positive impact on performance (RQ2) providing support for the theoretical argument that clustered interactions and relationships are key enablers to share and assimilate the information relevant to resolve challenging innovative tasks [41].

Project-level Interaction and Individual Performance

The second step in our analysis involved examining the impact of position within the communication network for the overall project (RQ3 and RQ4). Model IV in Table 2 reports the regression coefficients for the project-level independent measures as well as the team-level ones. The results show higher levels of *in-flow centrality* in the project-level communication network are associated with lower levels of individual performance (RQ3) while higher levels of *closure* are associated with better individual-level performance (RQ4). Unfortunately, our results do not provide evidence of a relationship between *out-flow centrality* and individual performance. These results suggest that inter-team communication imposes a cost on highly central individuals which adversely affects their performance, but the cost for those embedded in a closed, albeit diverse, cluster is not sufficient to interfere with task completion. It is also worth pointing out that the impact of in-flow centrality and closure at the team level remained statistically significant in Model IV suggesting a complementary positive impact of individual performance to closure at the project level. We also examined the relative impact of all six independent variables using the incident rate ratios in Model IV. The results showed the following IRRs: *in-flow centrality* (team) = 1.73, *out-flow centrality* (team) = 0.55, *closure* (team) = 10.46, *in-flow centrality* (project) = 0.88, *out-flow centrality* (project) = 1.01, and *closure* (project) = 1.95. The IRRs of out-flow

	Model I	Model II	Model III	Model IV
Controls				
Team Dummy A		0.344**	0.217**	0.312**
Team Dummy B		-0.264**	-0.158**	0.091
Team Dummy C		-0.088	-0.023**	-0.111*
Team Dummy D		0.105*	0.015**	-0.113
Location Dummy A		-1.059**	-0.914**	-0.764**
Location Dummy B		1.128**	0.807**	0.769**
Location Dummy C		-0.901**	-0.595**	-0.456**
Location Dummy D		0.896**	0.818**	0.590**
Team Lead Role		0.130**	0.202*	0.174*
Developer Role		4.091**	3.668**	3.671**
Admin Role		-0.751**	-0.454**	-0.396**
Other Roles		0.380**	0.430**	0.422**
Coordination Needs		0.484**	0.218*	0.214
Commenting Propensity		-0.044**	-0.041**	-0.041**
Commenting Propensity (collocated)		-0.028**	-0.027**	-0.021**
Communication Density (team-level)		-0.186*	-0.091*	0.141+
Communication Density (project-level)		0.239*	0.624**	0.273*
Overall Workload		0.038**	0.027**	0.027**
Independent Variables				
In-flow Centrality (team-level)			1.037**	0.551**
Out-flow Centrality (team-level)			-0.104**	-0.601*
Closure (team-level)			3.050**	2.348**
In-flow Centrality (project-level)				-0.117**
Out-flow Centrality (project-level)				0.008
Closure (project-level)				0.671**
Log-Likelihood	-17395	-3899.8	-3525.5	-3519.2
Deviance Explained	-	77.58%	79.73%	79.77%

(+ $p < 0.10$, * $p < 0.05$, ** $p < 0.01$)

Table 2: The Impact of Centrality and Closure on Individual-level Performance

centrality at the team level and in-flow centrality at the project level are below 1 indicating that increases in those independent variables lead to a decrease in the outcome. The magnitude of those IRRs, suggest that closure at both levels, team and project, as well as in-flow centrality at the team level are the main factors that contribute to improvements in individual performance. In sum, our analyses showed that only one dimension of centrality in the project-level networks matters to performance (RQ3), in-flow centrality, and in fact its impact is detrimental to performance. Finally, we found that closure in the project-level network also helps individual performance (RQ4) providing a complementary impact to the effect of closure in the team-level network.

Additional Analyses

We performed a collection of additional analyses for two reasons. First, we made methodological decisions that deserve further discussion. We also performed a second analysis considering the entire dataset. As discussed in the Research Setting section, we removed the data from 10 teams because the amount of work performed by these teams as teams as well as the amount of communication that contributed by them was minimal and they represented outliers that could lead to over-fitting in the models. We ran the regression Model IV with our independent measures on the entire dataset. The results were consistent with those reported in Table 2. Furthermore, the deviance explained for the models was lower than the one associated with Model IV in Table 2.

Second, we also re-ran our analyses considering the communication networks as binary to further explore the relationship between the role of the amount of interaction as well as the role of just the existence of interaction. We constructed *in-flow* and *out-flow centrality* measures using traditional social network normalized measures of in- and out-degree. Closure was measured using Krackhardt's measure [31]. Interestingly, the results were consistent with those reported in Table 2. Furthermore, the deviance explained for the models was slightly higher than the one associated with Model IV in Table 2. These results suggest that the existence of a communication linkage between two individuals seems to be a more significant driver of performance than the actual amount of information exchanged.

DISCUSSION

Informal communication is essential for software development especially in large, geographically distributed teams. But communication is not evenly distributed across all members of a team or the project. Some individuals participate in more of the discussion than others (e.g. [12]). Current research is not clear on which patterns of communication are helpful or detrimental (e.g. [34]) to individual performance. We began to address those gaps in the literature by examining actual communication that occurred in the context of specific work items and the associated development. Specifically, we examined two distinct structural positions, centrality and closure, within a team and across teams, over 14 development iterations. Each structural position has been associated with higher individual performance [1, 36] but also with negative consequences [7, 29]).

Individuals who are central in the communication network, participate in discussions with a larger number of people. In the context of within-team communication, we found that centrally located individuals fixed bugs at a higher rate than did individuals who were less central. These results suggest that participating in communication with a wider range of people is beneficial to getting work done. Whatever cost may be associated with the communication is more than balanced by the benefit of the information exchanged. Moreover, since we controlled for the propensity of each individual to communicate with project members as well as the task dependencies individuals had, we can further conclude that it is the number of people with whom one communicates that matters, not the total amount of communication. The benefits of being central, however, are not sustained, when communication extends to the overall project. In that case, individuals who are at the center of the network fix bugs at a lower rate than those individuals who are less central suggesting that the cost of cross-team communication outweighs the benefits.

Individuals may also be embedded in closed communication clusters made up of people who not only communicate with each other but also communicate with additional people in common. Over time, participants in these closed communication clusters evolve a high degree of shared knowledge (e.g. [36]), which can be helpful for coordination. We found that individuals embedded in many triadic communication patterns (Simmelian ties) fixed defects at a higher rate than individuals with less clustered communication patterns. The benefits of closure were found when the cluster was made up of people across as well as within teams. This result suggests that this form of close, shared communication is always beneficial.

Since our communication networks captured patterns of inter- and intra- team interaction we also examined the dominance of one over the other by comparing the size of the effect. We found that intra-team communication was stronger for both centrality and closure. This result is consistent with the tendency for large software projects to segment the work into nearly independent teams [2]. It does, however, reinforce the importance of cross-team communication, which is often achieved by people in an informal liaison role [12]. Furthermore, it emphasizes the importance, if not the dominance, of inter-team communication based on closed clusters. Finally, it is worth pointing out that our findings were obtained while accounting for a comprehensive number of control variables, which underscores the robustness of our findings.

Limitations

We address several limitations of the study. First, our analysis is based on a single project and a single product release created by such a project. Although ideally considering multiple projects from multiple organizations would improve the external validity of our results, we do not have any reason to believe that this particular project is significantly different than other large-scale geographically distributed projects. Costa and colleagues [15] showed that the Jazz project, the basis of the current study, exhibits coordination needs patterns similar to those from 4 other projects belonging to 2 distinct companies.

Second, our study focused solely on CMC-based communication. Although it is common to rely on one form of communication in network studies (e.g. [12, 28]), there is always some risk of a communication bias. To counter the possibility that direct communication amongst collocated team members contributed to the results, we included a control variable, which considered the propensity of individuals to use CMC-based communication with collocated project members. Our results thus are robust with respect to other communication. Finally, although our analyses considered only one measure of individual performance, namely completed bug fixes, we are following the tradition established in other studies (e.g. [12, 37]).

Implications for Future Research on Communication in Large-scale Product Development Projects

Our results also carry implications for issues of trade-offs between communication and other work. Since both communication and development activities such as fixing defects involve effort, it is often argued in the literature that there is a tradeoff between communication and other work [34]. In the context of a work group, our results suggest that there need not be such a trade-off. In fact, there seems to be tangible benefits for individuals who communicate with more people or with the same people because those individuals fix bugs at a higher rate than others. In terms of communication across teams, however, there may be a tradeoff between the number of communication partners and individual-level performance suggesting that the increased effort associated with communication across team boundaries (e.g. [10, 20]) may be higher than the benefits that can be realized. However, such a tradeoff may be beneficial for the team or the overall project [9]. Moreover, such tradeoff may be contingent on the outcome being considered [11]. Then, future research should examine the role of such tradeoffs across different levels of analysis (e.g. individual-, team- and project-level) as well as across various types of outcomes such as productivity, quality or success.

Our results on the differentiating impact of centrality at the team and at the project-level points to the need for further research on how teams can manage their cross-team communication. One suggestion is to promote the use of liaisons who seem able to handle both the level of communication and the level of work [12]. It is not clear, however, whether these people are able to handle the communication and work demands at the same time. Those differences could be due to distinctive individual characteristics or particular aspects of the management of the project that allows individuals to manage that duality of communication load and traditional task load. Further research is needed to shed light on these issues.

Past research on geographically distributed workgroups has shown the important role that managers and leaders play in facilitating and enabling the flow of information across the various sites (e.g. [44]). The present results showing strong benefits of closure which in turn relates to shared knowledge, trust and redundancy, suggests that project leaders and executives could do well to find ways to reinforce existing groupings of people. However, further research is needed to better understand how to integrate such activities within the context of traditional activities that leaders carry out as well as avoiding detrimental effects such as turning highly clustered groups into non-overlapping cliques which could lead to unnecessary conflict [27].

Implications for the Design of Collaborative Tools

The results of this study carry valuable implications for the extension and enhancement of existing communication, coordination and awareness tools, especially those focused on large-scale product development. First, tools designed to identify relevant task dependencies are currently limited by the size of teams and projects [15]. Current approaches to manage scalability focus primarily on techniques that synthesize information in order to identify and rank the most relevant individuals to interact with given a particular set of coordination requirements. Our results suggest an alternative approach. Tools might recommend communication partners based on a combination of task dependencies and historical interaction patterns based on patterns of closure.

A second group of tools that would benefit from our results are those that support awareness of expertise. Our results point to the benefit of adding awareness of "*who knows who*" in addition to the traditional notion of "*who knows what*". Individuals are not always aware that two people who they communicate with often also communicate with each other. In fact, product development researchers have documented cases where individuals, for instance A and B, would interact through a third party C [12, 39]. Although numerous reasons could lead to such behavior, it is clear that tools could facilitate this type of communication pattern, For instance, if individuals are able to be more productive in cross-team communication when embedded in clustered interaction patterns as our results suggested, then it should be helpful to identify people known in common. Inline with social networking tools that make recommendations for friendship based on common "friends", we could envision a similar technique that leverages the historical data of interaction patterns to make recommendations for communication that follow patterns that would improve individual level productivity.

REFERENCES

1. M. Ahuja, *et al.*, "Individual centrality and performance in virtual R&D groups: An empirical study," *Management Science,* 49, 21-38, 2003.
2. C. Y. Baldwin and K. B. Clark, *Design rules.* Cambridge, Mass.: MIT Press, 2000.
3. A. Barrat, *et al.*, "The architecture of complex weighted networks," *Proceedings of the National Academy of Sciences of the United States of America,* 101, p. 3747, 2004.
4. B. Bechky, "Sharing meaning across occupational communities: The transformation of understanding on a production floor," *Organization Science,* 14, pp. 312-330, 2003.
5. C. Bird, *et al.*, "Latent social structure in open source projects," 2008, pp. 24-35.
6. W. F. Boh, *et al.*, "Learning from Experience in Software Development: A Multilevel Analysis," *Management Science,* 53, pp. 1315-1331, 2007.
7. S. Borgatti, "The Network Paradigm in Organizational Research: A Review and Typology," *Journal of Management,* 29, pp. 991-1013, 2003.
8. S. Borgatti, "Centrality and network flow," *Social Networks,* 27, pp. 55-71, 2005.
9. R. Burt, *Brokerage and closure: An introduction to social capital*: Oxford University Press, USA, 2005.
10. P. Carlile, "Transferring, translating, and transforming: An integrative framework for managing knowledge across boundaries," *Org. Sci.,* 15, pp. 555-568, 2004.
11. M. Cataldo and K. Ehrlich, "The Impact of the Structure of Communication Patterns in Global Software Development: An Empirical Analysis of a Project Using Agile Methods," Institute for Software Research, Carnegie Mellon University2011.
12. M. Cataldo and J. D. Herbsleb, "Communication networks in geographically distributed software development," presented at the Proceedings of the 2008 ACM conference on Computer supported cooperative work, San Diego, CA, USA, 2008.
13. M. Cataldo, *et al.*, "Identification of coordination requirements: implications for the Design of collaboration and awareness tools," presented at the Proceedings of the 2006 20th anniversary conference on Computer supported cooperative work, Banff, Alberta, Canada, 2006.
14. J. Coleman, "Social capital in the creation of human capital," *A. journal of sociology,* 94, pp. 95-120, 1988.

15. J. M. Costa, *et al.*, "The Scale and Evolution of Coordination Needs in Large-Scale Distributed Projects: Implications for the Future Generation of Collaborative Tools," presented at the International Conference on Computer-Human Interaction, Vancouver, Canada, 2011.
16. C. Cramton, "The mutual knowledge problem and its consequences for dispersed collaboration," *Organization Science,* 12, pp. 346-371, 2001.
17. K. Crowston and J. Howison, "The social structure of free and open source software development," *First Monday,* 10, p. 1-100, 2005.
18. J. Cummings and R. Cross, "Structural properties of work groups and their consequences for performance," *Social Networks,* 25, pp. 197-210, 2003.
19. J. N. Cummings, "Work Groups, Structural Diversity, and Knowledge Sharing in a Global Organization," *Management Science,* 50, pp. 352-364, 2004.
20. J. N. Cummings, *et al.*, "Crossing Spatial and Temporal Boundaries in Globally Distributed Projects: A Relational Model of Coordination Delay," *Information Systems Research,* 20, pp. 420-439, 2009.
21. B. Curtis, *Human factors in software development.* Los Angeles: IEEE Computer Society Press, 1981.
22. K. Ehrlich and K. Chang, "Leveraging expertise in global software teams: Going outside boundaries," presented at the Proceedings of the IEEE international conference on Global Software Engineering, 2006.
23. J. A. Espinosa, *et al.*, "Familiarity, Complexity, and Team Performance in Geographically Distributed Software Development," *Org. Sci.,* 18, pp. 613-630, 2007.
24. L. C. Freeman, "Centrality in social networks conceptual clarification," *Social Networks,* 1, pp. 215-239, 1979.
25. R. Frost, "Jazz and the eclipse way of collaboration," *IEEE Software,* pp. 114-117, 2007.
26. J. D. Herbsleb and A. Mockus, "An Empirical Study of Speed and Communication in Globally Distributed Software Development," *IEEE Trans. Softw. Eng.,* 29, pp. 481-494, 2003.
27. P. Hinds and D. Bailey, "Out of sight, out of sync: Understanding conflict in distributed teams," *Organization Science,* 14, pp. 615-632, 2003.
28. P. Hinds and C. McGrath, "Structures that work: social structure, work structure and coordination ease in geographically distributed teams," 2006, pp. 343-352.
29. H. Ibarra, "Network centrality, power, and innovation involvement: Determinants of technical and administrative roles," *The Academy of Management Journal,* 36, pp. 471-501, 1993.
30. D. Krackhardt, "The strength of strong ties: The importance of philos in organizations," *Networks and organizations: Structure, form, and action,* 216, p. 239, 1992.
31. D. Krackhardt, "Simmelian ties: Super strong and sticky," *Power and influence in organizations,* pp. 21-38, 1998.
32. D. Obstfeld, "Social networks, the tertius iungens orientation, and involvement in innovation," *Adm. Science Quarterly,* 50, pp. 100-130, 2005.
33. G. M. Olson and J. S. Olson, "Distance Matters," *Human-Computer Interaction,* 15, pp. 139 - 178, 2000.
34. L. A. Perlow, "The time famine: Toward a sociology of work time," *Adm. Sci. Quarterly,* 44, pp. 57-81, 1999.
35. R. H. Rasch and H. L. Tosi, "Factors affecting software developers' performance: an integrated approach," *MIS Quarterly,* pp. 395-413, 1992.
36. R. Reagans and B. McEvily, "Network structure and knowledge transfer: The effects of cohesion and range," *Adm. Sci. Quarterly,* 48, pp. 240-267, 2003.
37. J. A. Roberts, *et al.*, "Understanding the Motivations, Participation, and Performance of Open Source Software Developers: A Longitudinal Study of the Apache Projects," *Mgmt. Sci.,* 52, pp. 984-999, 2006.
38. J. Singer and J. Willett, *Applied longitudinal data analysis: Modeling change and event occurrence*: Oxford University Press, USA, 2003.
39. M. E. Sosa, *et al.*, "The Misalignment of Product Architecture and Organizational Structure in Complex Product Development," *Management Science,* 50, pp. 1674-1689, 2004.
40. R. Sparrowe, *et al.*, "Social networks and the performance of individuals and groups," *Academy of Management Journal,* 44, pp. 316-325, 2001.
41. M. Tortoriello and D. Krackhardt, "Activating cross-boundary knowledge: the role of Simmelian ties in the generation of innovations," *The Academy of Management Journal (AMJ),* 53, pp. 167-181, 2010.
42. P. Wagstrom, *et al.*, "Communication, Team Performance and the Individual: Bridging Technical Dependencies," In Proc. of the Academy of Mgmt. Annual Meeting, Montreal, Canada, 2010.
43. D. J. Watts, *Small worlds : the dynamics of networks between order and randomness*. Princeton, N.J.: Princeton University Press, 1999.
44. S. P. Weisband, "Leadership at a distance: research in technologically-supported work," 2007.
45. T. Wolf, *et al.*, "Predicting build failures using social network analysis on developer communication," 2009, pp. 1-11.
46. T. Zimmermann and N. Nagappan, "Predicting defects with program dependencies," In Proce. of the 3rd International Symposium on Empirical Software Engineering and Measurement, 2009.

The Personality of Popular Facebook Users

Daniele Quercia[§], Renaud Lambiotte[‡], David Stillwell[*], Michal Kosinski[†], Jon Crowcroft[§]
[§]The Computer Laboratory, University of Cambridge
[‡]Institute for Mathematical Sciences, Imperial College
[*]School of Psychology, University of Nottingham
[†]The Psychometrics Centre, University of Cambridge
daniele.quercia@cl.cam.ac.uk, r.lambiotte@imperial.ac.uk, david@mypersonality.org, mk583@cam.ac.uk, jon.crowcroft@cl.cam.ac.uk

ABSTRACT
We study the relationship between Facebook popularity (number of contacts) and personality traits on a large number of subjects. We test to which extent two prevalent viewpoints hold. That is, popular users (those with many social contacts) are the ones whose personality traits *either* predict many offline (real world) friends *or* predict propensity to maintain superficial relationships. We find that the predictor for number of friends in the real world (Extraversion) is also a predictor for number of Facebook contacts. We then test whether people who have many social contacts on Facebook are the ones who are able to adapt themselves to new forms of communication, present themselves in likable ways, and have propensity to maintain superficial relationships. We show that there is no statistical evidence to support such a conjecture.

General Terms
Measurement, Theory, Verification

ACM Classification Keywords
J.4 Computer Applications: Social and Behavioral Sciences.

INTRODUCTION
There is no definite answer to the question of whether digital representations of ourselves on Facebook can capture much about human social relations. This question is important yet difficult to measure. Literary intellectuals and scientists alike have recently debated that question and have formed two camps. Members of the first argue that Facebook simply supplements traditional forms of communications (e.g., text messages, face-to-face contacts) and additionally helps to maintain weak and loose ties [8, 36]. This implies that people are doing online what they have been already doing offline, with the only difference that coordination and communication costs online are lower [48].

Members of the second camp argue, instead, that social-networking sites create and promote radically new forms of communication. Jaron Lanier, for example, thinks that communication on Facebook is inherently "self-reduced" [34]. On signing up, users are asked to fill in a questionnaire in which they should specify, for instance, what they looking for; that is, whether they are looking for 'friendship', 'dating', 'relationship', or 'networking'. Those are the available conditions in Facebook world, and no other condition is available. In the same vein, a large body of academic work is coming round the idea that design decisions have profound implications on people's social capital and well-being [6, 16, 26]. For example, Burke *et al.* found that directed communication among Facebook users is associated with greater feelings of bonding social capital and lower loneliness [7]. Surprisingly, they also found that users who passively consume greater levels of content report reduced bridging and bonding social capital and increased loneliness. These findings might consequently suggest that designing a social media site that emphasizes content consumption over peer interactions would accommodate specific user needs. Worryingly, design decisions are often taken by a very small number of technologists and impact what gets broadcasted between half a billion Facebook social contacts.

There is a corollary to the two camps' arguments: users who will become popular on Facebook are the ones who are able (have the "right" personality) to *either* attract many friends offline *or* "reduce" themselves in order to make their Facebook profiles appear more likable. This corollary reflects two extreme viewpoints but, in reality, this dichotomy might not be strict: offline and online friendship creation might well be both affected by similar factors such as being skilled at social interaction (e.g., self-presentation) or being motivated by social status. To verify the extent to which this is true, we study popularity (defined as number of social contacts) on Facebook. As we shall see in Section "Related Work", one widely-used measure of sociometric popularity in the literature is number of friends, but this measure has been predominantly studied at a small scale. We analyze data from a Facebook application (named myPersonality) that offers its users a set of genuine personality tests and researchers access to high quality and representative samples that are comparable or better than traditional samples used in psychology research (Section "MyPersonality"). We test two competing ideas that explain creation of Facebook contacts by comparing two personality traits related to offline friend creation - Extraversion and Neuroticism - and one trait related to "reducing" oneself online - self-monitoring. In so doing, we make the following contributions:

CSCW 2012, February 11–15, 2012, Seattle, Washington, USA.

- We study the relationship between number of contacts and personality traits that are typically associated with offline popularity, i.e., with high number of real-world friends (Section "Traditional Explanation"). We build a simple linear regression model that predicts number of contacts based on the 'big five' standard personality traits. Similar to what holds for offline friends, we find that also number of Facebook contacts is positively associated with Extraversion and negatively with Neuroticism. Our analysis shows that Extraversion is a predictor (albeit weak) for number of social contacts. Interestingly, despite weak individual-to-individual correlations, we find that a linear relationship between number of contacts and Extraversion is borne out extremely cleanly at population level.
- We also study the relationship between number of social contacts and a personality trait called "Self-monitoring" that predicts the ability of individuals to present themselves in likable ways and maintain superficial relationships (Section "Alternative Explanation"). We find that the relationship between number of contacts and self-monitoring is statistically negligible, if one controls for Extraversion. More specifically, based on partial correlations, one concludes that, if Extraversion is controlled for, self-monitoring does *not* explain number of contacts; by contrast, if self-monitoring is controlled for, Extraversion does explain number of contacts.
- We finally discuss theoretical implications of our findings on personality research and practical implications for viral marketing and social media security (Section "Implications").

RELATED WORK

Social-networking sites such as Facebook not only support the maintenance of existing social ties and the formation of new ones (as Ellison *et al.* has found in the US [16] and Lewis and West in the UK [36]) but they also impact how profile owners are socially judged in the real world. Researchers have studied the factors that might influence the perception (including popularity) of a profile. The most obvious factor is the profile itself. In 2007, Kleck *et al.* found that even just the number of social contacts shown on one's Facebook profile triggers positive social judgments in terms of popularity, pleasantness, heterosexual appeal, and confidence [32]. A year later, Tong *et al.* conducted a study among 153 US undergraduates and found that the relationship between Facebook friend count and positive social judgment is not linear (the bigger one's count, the more positive he/she is judged to be) but quadratic: beyond a certain number (typically 300), friend count may reach a point of incredulity or foolishness [52]. By contrast, in 2010, Utz conducted a similar experiment among 124 users of the largest Dutch social-networking site and found no evidence of any linear or quadratic relationship: positive social judgment (e.g., perceived extroversion) was only weakly related to friend count. One important difference between Tong *et al.*'s study and Utz's is that the subjects in the first study had almost twice as many social contacts as the subjects in the second.

How a profile is perceived depends not only on the profile itself but also on who views the profile. Gogolinski recently created two fictitious Facebook pages that differed from amount and type of information they displayed [18]. She showed the two profiles to 134 US undergraduates and found that the way the profiles are perceived changed depending on the viewer's personality: lower self-monitors preferred the less detailed and more cautious profile, while higher self-monitors preferred the more detailed and generous profile. The problem is that the subjects in this study were largely women enrolled in undergraduate courses. It is not clear whether men and, more generally, individuals of different generations would hold the same view. More recently, for 167 Facebook users, Golbeck *et al.* successfully predicted these users' five personality traits (which we will describe in Section "The Big Five") out of their personal information and posts [19]. In Section "Discussion", we will spell out how our work extends Golbeck *et al.* 's.

This brief literature review has offered contrasting results that are telling examples of how hard it is to generalize any finding upon a very limited and biased sample of users, largely few hundreds of undergraduates of WEIRD (White, Educated, Industrialized, Rich, and Democratic) countries [25]. Also, personality research of social-networking users has long suffered from a severe measurement problem: personality information is hard to measure, especially at scale, over time, and at the same time as unobtrusively observing user behavior.

It thus seems that a new way of measuring personality information of social-networking users is needed. Ideally, this new way should use well-establish tests to record personality scores of *unbiased* and *large* samples of users whose behavioral measures are recorded *directly* as the users are on the social-networking site.

MYPERSONALITY

myPersonality is a Facebook application that users install to take a variety of genuine personality and ability tests (Figure 1). Users can also opt in and give their consent to share their personality scores and profile information, and around 40% of its 5.5 million users choose to do so. The problem with any web-based survey (including myPersonality) could be that users might respond in a careless, dishonest, or mischievous way, and that might compromise data validity [5, 46]. So it is worth emphasizing the measures that myPersonality undertakes to assure the highest quality of its databases:

1. *The right incentives for participants are in place.* As opposed to what often takes place in traditional research, subjects are not paid nor receive college credits. myPersonality users are solely motivated by the prospect of receiving reliable feedback and test results that accurately describe their personalities. Respondents can leave as many questions unanswered as they like (while researchers can easily discard tests with unanswered questions).
2. *Unreliable results are removed.* Numerous validity tests

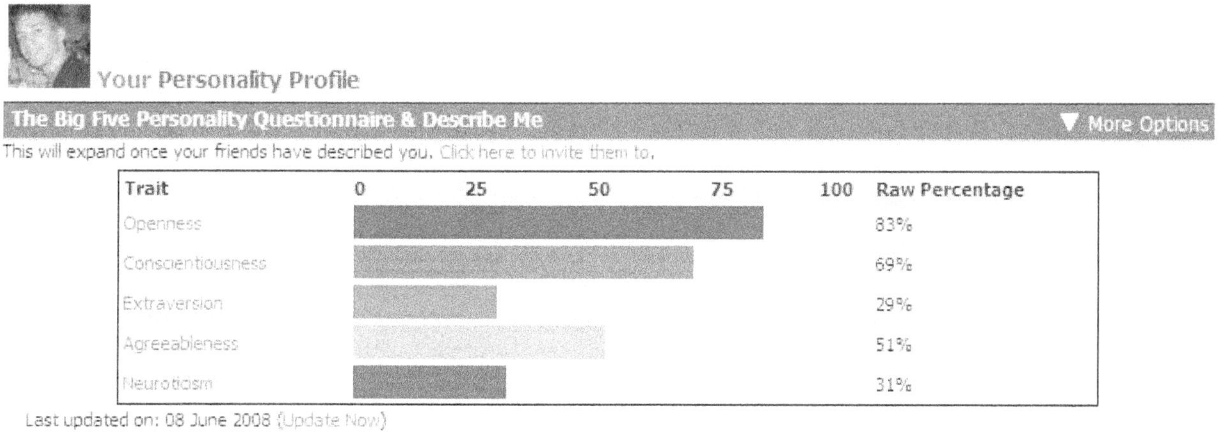

Figure 1. Part of the myPersonality user interface.

are applied to remove the protocols that may be a product of inattentive, language incompetent, or randomly responding individuals. Consequently, the quality of the responses in our sample is at least as high as in traditional pen-and-paper studies. This is demonstrated by the scales' reliabilities which are on average higher in myPersonality samples than reported in test manuals[1]. Additionally, the discriminant validity of myPersonality sample (average $r = .16$) is better than one obtained using traditional samples (average $r = .20$ [29]).

After ensuring the right incentives are in place and removing unreliable results, myPersonality is able to obtain test results that are more reliable than those in pen-and-paper studies. Also, compared to pen-and-paper studies published in the highly-regarded Journal of Personality and Social Psychology (JPSP) in 2002 [22], myPersonality users are far less biased than those studies' subjects for gender, age, and geography. However, our dataset has its own limitations and we will later discuss those that are specific to our study (Section "Discussion").

TRADITIONAL EXPLANATION

Having this data at hand, we are able to study the relationship between personality and Facebook popularity. Previous research suggests that personality influences both offline and online activities [23]. So it is reasonable to test whether personality traits that predict popularity offline would also predict popularity online.

The Big Five

The five-factor model of personality, or the big five, consists of a comprehensive and reliable set of personality concepts [10, 20]. The idea is that an individual can be associated with five scores that correspond to five main personality traits. Table 1 lists the big five personality traits along with descriptive terms that are typically associated with them. Personality traits predict a number of real-world behaviors. They, for example, are strong predictors of how marriages turn out: if one of the partner is high in Neuroticism, then divorce is more likely. "People high in Extraversion really do talk a lot ... When asked to think about or view something stressful and unpleasant, people high in Neuroticism really do become more upset than people low in Neuroticism. When people high in Agreeableness listen to stories, they really do pay more attention to the mental states of the characters than those low in Agreeableness" [41].

Personality Trait	High scorers	Low scorers
Openness	Imaginative	Conventional
Conscientiousness	Organized	Spontaneous
Extraversion	Outgoing	Solitary
Agreeableness	Trusting	Competitive
Neuroticism	Prone to stress and worry	Emotionally stable

Table 1. The big five personality dimensions.

Research has consistently shown that people's scores are stable over time (they do not depend on quirks and accidents of mood) and correlate well with how others close to them (e.g., friends) see them [41].

Since the 1980s, the relationship between popularity and the big five personality traits has been widely studied. Individuals who are more outgoing and social (Extraverted) tend to report greater numbers of people in their social network [51]: they are more inclined to approach others and are more likely to receive/give social support as compared to more introverted individuals [4].

Next, we will consider the (big) five personality trait and their relationships with popularity and, more generally, with social support.

The trait of *Extraversion* is associated with descriptive terms such as sociability, activity, and excitement seeking. Individuals higher in Extraversion tend to report larger social networks, greater contact with network members, lower

[1] http://www.mypersonality.org/wiki/

Personality Trait	r
Openness	0.013
Conscientiousness	0.018
Extraversion	**0.2**
Agreeableness	0.039
Neuroticism	**-0.068**
Sex	0.012
Age	**-0.154**

Table 2. (Pearson) correlation coefficients between the logarithm of the number of social contacts and each of the big five personality traits, Sex and Age, as measured in the large dataset ($172,952$ users).

number of conflicts, and greater social status [2, 3, 24, 47, 51]

The trait of *Neuroticism* is associated with descriptive terms such as emotional liability and impulsiveness. Individuals high in Neuroticism are prone to more negative mood states (e.g., anxiety, depression), tend to withdraw from other during times of stress [35, 39, 43], and generally report less satisfaction with the support received by their social networks [30, 31].

The trait of *Agreeableness* is associated with descriptive terms such as trusting, altruistic and tender-minded. Research has shown that individuals who are high in *Agreeableness* are motivated to maintain positive relationships with others [28]. However, less is known about the relationship between *Agreeableness* and structural social support (e.g., network size, contact with network members).

The trait of *Conscientiousness* is associated with descriptive terms such as ambitious, resourceful and persistent. It is not clear the relationship between Conscientiousness and number of friends or, more generally, social support: although social support is available to those high in Conscientiousness, given their competence and resourcefulness, they may simply not require as much support from others [12, 38].

The trait of *Openness* is associated with descriptive terms such as imaginative, spontaneous, and adventurous. Openness has been found to be positively associated with network size ($r = 0.23$) [50]. More generally, studies about the relationship between Openness and social support have been inconsistent.

To recap, the trait of Extraversion has been found to be associated with number of real-world friends and with structural measures of social support, including network size and contact with network members. Instead, Neuroticism has been associated with negative social interactions. Finally, the findings for the traits of Agreeableness, Conscientiousness and Openness are inconsistent.

Results

We take a sample of $172,952$ Facebook users who live in the United States[2] and have taken the big five personality test, whose number of social contacts is between 30 and 1000 and whose age is comprised between 18 and 54. This group is composed of $103,482$ women (60%) and $69,470$ men (40%) with a median age of 23. Figure 2 plots their age and degree distributions. Our analysis unfolds in three steps:

[2]In Section "Discussion", we detail why we have chosen users from a single country.

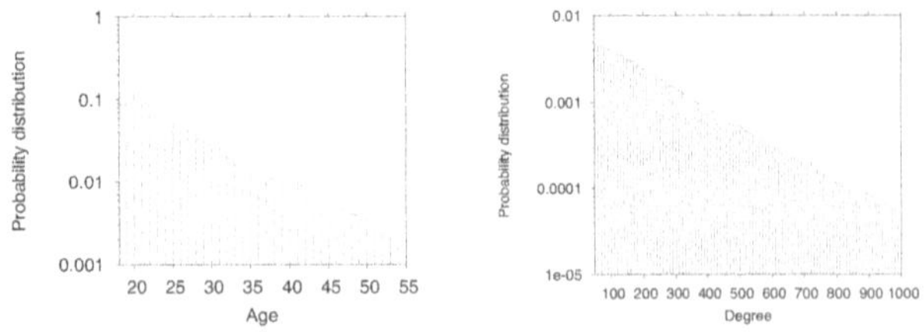

Figure 2. Probability distributions of age ($left$) and number of friends ($right$).

Variables	β	t-test	β	t-test
Openness	-0.031	-12.6	-	-
Conscientiousness	0.004	1.5	-	-
Extraversion	0.174	**79.7**	0.171	79.8
Agreeableness	0.013	5.1	-	-
Neuroticism	0.005	2	0	0
Sex	0.005	1.4	-	-
Age	-0.015	**-64.5**	-0.014	-64.7

Table 3. Prediction model for number of friends. ($left$) A linear regression model between $\log(k)$ and the big five personality scores, plus Sex and Age. ($right$) A linear regression model between $\log(k)$ and Extraversion, Neuroticism and Age. The table reports t test statistics rather than p-value because, in this case, t test statistics reflect statistical significance of variables better than p-value. In fact, in the linear regression on the left side: Openness, Extraversion, Agreeableness and Age have all p-value$< 10^{-4}$. Openness and Agreeableness are not significant for the prediction.

1. *Determine relevant predictors for number of Facebook contacts.* We study the relationship between personality traits and the logarithm $\log(k)$ of the number of social contacts. We are interested in the logarithm rather than the number of social contacts simply because of the large variability of number of contacts (right graph in Figure 2). The five traits are all normally distributed, suggesting the lack of selection bias among our subjects. We study the Pearson product-moment correlation between $\log(k)$ and each of the (big) five personality traits, plus two additional attributes, namely sex and age. Pearson's correlation $r \in [-1, 1]$ is a measure of the linear relationship between two random variables. Table 2 summarizes the results. Weak correlations are found with Extraversion (0.2), as expected, and with Age (-0.154). The latter indicates that older individuals tend to have significantly fewer Facebook contacts than younger ones. Among the remaining personality traits, Neuroticism (-0.068) has a very weak negative correlation with $\log(k)$. These correlations and corresponding magnitudes are consistent with previous research about both offline and online popularity.

2. *Determine the statistical significance of the predictors.* Since Pearson correlation coefficients are low, it might be

worth checking the statistical significance of each predictor. To this end, we build a regression model that predicts $\log(k)$ based on the previous variables. That is, we model the logarithm of number of friends as a linear combination of the big five personality scores, plus Sex and Age:

$$\log(k_i) = \alpha + \sum_{l=1}^{5} \beta_l R_{l;i} + \beta_S S_i + \beta_A A_i + \epsilon_i$$

In the previous equation, k_i is user i's number of contacts, R_i is a vector that contains user i' big five personality scores, S_i is i's Sex (0 if female or 1 if male), A_i i's Age and ϵ_i is the error term. The extent to which the regression predicts $\log(k_i)$ is reflected in a measure called R^2 - the higher R^2, the better the fit of the model. In this case, $R^2 = 0.064$, which is small. However, to understand the statistically significance of each predictor, one examines the predictor's t statistic - the higher in absolute value, the more significant the predictor. From Table 3, we learn that Extraversion and Age have the highest t statistics. This implies that, to model the logarithm of number of Facebook contacts, Extraversion and Age are sufficient. This hypothesis is verified by checking that the addition of any other variable in the regression (e.g., Neuroticism, Openness) does not improve results (R^2 remains roughly the same).

3. *Determine the nature of the linear relationships of predictors.* We now know that Extraversion is the personality trait that correlates with the logarithm of Facebook contacts. However, since R^2 (the model's predictive power) is small, it is not clear yet to which extent the relationship between the logarithm and Extraversion is linear. To find this out, we segment our users in 40 bins depending on their number of social contacts (depending on $log(k)$) and we measure the *average* personality score for each of the (big) five traits in each bin. Interestingly, despite high individual-to-individual variability reflected in our R^2, the linear relationship between $\log(k)$ and Extraversion is borne out extremely cleanly by the aggregate data (Figure 3). Also, people at the extremes of the Extraversion scale greatly differ for number of contacts: extreme extroverts are expected to have two times as many contacts as extreme introverts.

ALTERNATIVE EXPLANATION

So far we have assumed that the meaning of friendship on Facebook is comparable to that in the real-world, but friendship on Facebook does not always have traditional connotations. Research suggests that an individual can maintain 10-20 close relationships [44] and 150 social relationships [15]. An average Facebook user has 130 friends[3], which is close to the "default" size of the social group for humans [15]. However, Facebook friendships do not simply mirror offline relationships. While some Facebook friendships may represent real life strong ties, others might be more superficial links between acquaintances. Indeed, Jaron Lanier writes [34]:

> "The most effective young Facebook users - the ones who will probably be winners if Facebook turns out to be a model of the future they will inhabit as adults - are the ones who create successful online fictions about themselves.
>
> They must manage offhand remarks and track candid snapshots as carefully as politician. Insincerity is rewarded, while sincerity creates lifelong taints. Certainly, some version of this principle existed in the lives of teenagers before the web came along, but not with such unyielding, clinical precision."

[3]http://www.facebook.com/press/info.php?statistics

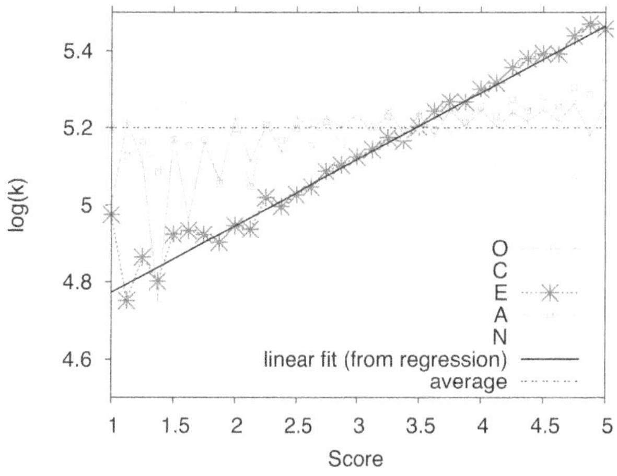

Figure 3. Average $\log(k)$ as a function of score for the 5 big personality traits. The dashed line indicates $\langle log(k) \rangle$ across the whole population. The solid line indicates the linear fit obtained from a linear regression of $\log(k)$ with Extraversion alone.

In Section "Related Work", we have seen that one's profile impacts one's ability to attract social contacts. Hence it is reasonable to posit that users who are able to adapt to new forms of 'self-presentation' are likely to become popular. To test whether this is true, we need a personality trait associated with the way people present themselves.

Self-monitoring

In 1974, Mark Snyder realized that personality research had failed to consider that some people's personalities are more 'fluid' than others'. Hence, he conducted in-depth interviews and found that some people are more prone to pick up on social cues and adjust how they act and how they are perceived by others. He called such individuals 'high self-monitors' [49]. High self-monitors tended to agree with statements like "I can make impromptu speeches even on topics about which I have almost no information". By contrast, low self-monitors tended to agree with statements such as "I find it hard to imitate the behavior of other people" and "I have trouble changing behavior to suit different people and different situations".

Snyder also found that high self-monitors had distinct attributes. They had unusual ability to pick up social cues and modulate their emotional expression; to quickly learn what behaviors were appropriate in various situations; and to easily manage the perceptions of others.

Although high self-monitors modulate their behavior to fit the situation, they do not actively manipulate others to get people to like them but are actually just as genuine and principled as low self-monitors. They just pick on social cues in an unconscious effort to establish a genuine connection with others. For example, it has been shown that high self-monitors mirror their peers' body languages without even realizing they are doing so [9].

The end result is that a high self-monitor modifies his/her behavior (and self-presentation) to fit the situation and the people in it, while a low-self monitor does not try to alter behavior very much across situations. Successful politicians, for example, tend to be high self-monitors [40].

High self-monitors modify their behavior not only offline but also online. In 2008, Lin studied the personal pages created by users of web portals [37]. He found that high self-monitors would display limited and generic information on their pages to represent themselves in likable ways, while low self-monitors would display more personal and in-depth information to accurately portray themselves. More recently, it has been shown that the same holds for Facebook [18]: high self-monitors tend to have less detailed and more cautious pages, while low self-monitors prefer more detailed pages.

Results

We take a sample of $2,165$ users who live in the United States and have taken not only the big five personality test but also the self-monitoring test. Those users have a number of social contacts between 30 and 1000, with the same age interval as in the large dataset studied in the previous section. Compared to the large dataset, the correlations with the big five traits are similar (Table 4) and the regression with all variables has $R^2 = 0.041$. The only new result is that there is a weak correlation between $log(k)$ and self-monitoring ($r = 0.089$). It follows that self-monitoring could help to predict $log(k)$. To see the extent to which it does so, we build a linear regression with Extraversion alone. We find that the addition of self-monitoring to the regression does only marginally improve the regression's predictions (R^2 goes from 0.037 to 0.038). That is simply because there is a strong interaction effect between self-monitoring and Extraversion ($r = 0.312$ between the two): if a regression model has Extraversion, then it would not improve its prediction by adding self-monitoring, as the two variables are strongly related. We conclude that self-monitoring does not contribute in explaining the number of Facebook contacts. This argument is also supported by the low value of self-monitoring for the *t* statistic (Table 4).

Also, the lack of direct dependence of $log(k)$ on self-monitoring (SM) and its dependence on Extraversion (E) are also confirmed by partial correlations. By construction, partial correlations measure the degree of association

Variables	r	β	t-test
Openness	0.038	-0.013	- 0.5
Conscientiousness	0.052	0.02	0.9
Extraversion	0.191	0.155	7.5
Agreeableness	0.04	0.01	0.4
Neuroticism	-0.069	0.005	0.3
Age	-0.045	- 0.006	-2.9
Self-monitoring	0.089	-0.014	1.3

Table 4. **($left$) Correlation coefficients between $\log(k)$ and each of the big five personality traits, Age and self-monitoring, as measured in the small dataset ($2,165$ users). ($right$) A linear regression model between $\log(k)$ and the same variables.**

between two random variables by controlling for the effect of a third variable. We compute two correlations and obtain $r(\log(k), E|SM) = 0.16$ (with $p < 10^{-5}$), and $r(\log(k), SM|E) = 0.03$ (with $p = 0.17$). The comparison of these two correlations clearly confirms our interpretation that self-monitoring is mainly correlated to $log(k)$ due to its association to Extraversion. Finally, there is no correlation between self-monitoring and any of the four personality traits other than Extraversion.

DISCUSSION

We will now discuss the limitations of our dataset and our study, the novelty of our big five study, and the theoretical and practical implications.

Limitations of personality data. All users of myPersonality choose to participate motivated primarily by the prospect of taking and receiving feedback from a high quality personality questionnaire used in actual scientific research. Although this encourages them to respond to the questions accurately and honestly, it means that the sample is a convenience sample of self-selected users interested in their personality, and so the results may not represent the Facebook population as a whole. For example, the number of contacts for the average myPersonality user is 194 whereas Facebook reports an average of 130[4]. This is most likely because number of Facebook contacts is confounded by Facebook activity, and active Facebook users are more likely to use applications. In future, Facebook activity should be controlled for, although this information is not available automatically from Facebook's API. Nevertheless, there are reasons to be confident in our conclusions. First, the demographic and geographic distribution of myPersonality users is closer to that of the general population than that reported in social psychology studies which typically rely on undergraduates [22]. Second, our results concentrate on the relationships between personality and number of Facebook contacts, so any sampling bias would have to affect this relationship, and it is unclear why application users would have a different association between personality and number of contacts than the general Facebook population.

[4] http://www.facebook.com/press/info.php?statistics

Limitation of our study. The only variable under study has been number of contacts, and that is because it is the only unbiased network metric readily-available from our application. Ideally, we would have included other variables of interest, but those variables either have not been captured because of technical limitations imposed by Facebook (e.g., frequency of interaction among users) or are biased if taken at face value (e.g., since we do not have information about non-myPersonality users, one's network clustering coefficient could be computed, but only upon a biased network that contains myPersonality users and excludes non-myPersonality ones). We are currently exploring techniques that would allow us to reduce such biases or, at least, quantify them.

Novelty of the Big Five Study. In section "Traditional Explanation", we have analyzed the results for the Big Five test, and Golbeck *et al.* have already done so [19]. We build upon their work in that we use the same (data analysis) methodology and extend previous experimental results as follows:

- The results in Golbeck *et al.*'s work are about 167 participants, 82.6% (138) of whom are from the United States and the remaining subjects come from India (8), Australia (7), Italy (7), and others (7). Our results are about 172,952 subjects in United States. We chose subjects from a single country for two main reasons. First, our test is the commonly-used US version of the Big Five test. Second, the Big Five factors were found to function differently across samples from different countries: although the same traits may exist in different cultures, there is a large bias at the metric and scalar levels of analysis across cultures [42]. Therefore, mean-level cross-cultural comparisons should be done only after ensuring measurement equivalence. To interpret our results correctly, we have users from the United States - the country from which we had the most representative sample.

- In our study, all the five personality traits have statistically significant (albeit weak) correlations. Furthermore, age is an additional factor that shows a statistically significant correlation and its magnitude reflects a weak yet important correlation as it is comparable to that with Extraversion. Also, the correlation is negative (i.e., younger people tend to have more social contacts on Facebook). By contrast, the opposite holds in Twitter: we have studied the personality of Twitter users and have found a positive correlation between number of followers/following and age [45]. These contrasting results reflect the different user demographics in the two platforms and reflects the importance of controlling for age.

- In line with previous work, our individual-to-individual correlations are all weak. Yet, at population-level, we report, for the first time, a clear linear relationship between number of contacts and Extraversion (Figure 3).

Theoretical Implications. It is important to study the nature of Facebook relations, not least because they do not stay confined online but do impact access to real-world opportunities. They have been shown, for example, to: (1) *Increase social capital:* A large number of weak social ties on Facebook becomes a source of social capital [16]; (2) *Trigger positive social judgments in the real world:* Just the number of social contacts on one's Facebook profile triggers positive social judgments in terms of popularity, pleasantness, heterosexual appeal, and confidence [32].

By studying the self-monitoring trait and the big five personality traits, we have tried to understand the nature of Facebook relationships and have asked whether they are either superficial (typical of high self-monitoring individuals) or "real" (individuals who are high in Extraversion and low in Neuroticism typically have a large number of offline friends). As our Introduction has exemplified, the dichotomy real *vs.* superficial has been widely debated, but we have now partially quantified it. Extraversion is not only weakly correlated with number of online social contacts (as it is with number of offline friends), but its relationship with number of contacts is also strongly linear (Figure 3). By contract, self-monitoring, which correlates with superficial relationships in the real world, does not have any explanatory power for number of contacts.

Practical Implications. Past research has shown that, from textual content accessible (e.g., blog posts, Facebook pages dedicated to brands), one could infer personality scores [19, 21, 33, 54]. We have shown that, from those scores, one is then able to partially predict the number of social contacts on Facebook based on the three variables Extraversion, Age, and Neuroticism. If we then build a simple Naive Bayesian model with those three variables, we find that we are able to predict whether Facebook users are likely to be social hubs or poorly-connected. More specifically, if we define all user with number of social contacts in the range $[500, 1000]$ to be social hubs and perform a 10-fold cross-validation on the big dataset (that of Section "Traditional Explanation"), we obtain that 83.68% of the social hubs are correctly classified by the model. The ability to identify social hubs may benefit a variety of individuals such as:

Social Media Marketers. Those individuals are interested in identifying social hubs and poorly-connected users in order to:

- Launch marketing campaigns that, to be successful, either target few social hubs [14] or many poorly-connected individuals who are passionate about certain brands and have spare time at hand [13].
- Measure brand awareness. Marketing agencies often measure, for a given brand, the quality of a community around it and they do so based on the presence of social hubs in that community [1].

Phishing Attackers. Those individuals are interested in avoiding social hubs and finding poorly-connected users who tend to be more gullible and less technological-savvy than typical Internet users [27].

Those examples not only point to the use of public data for questionable (marketing) reasons but also inform two research areas other than personality research. First, they inform the privacy literature in that our results might raise awareness among online users about the privacy-sensitive predictions that are possible from publicly-available data. This is similar to Crandall *et al.*'s very recent work, which showed that, from publicly available geo-referenced Flickr pictures, one is able to infer several coincidences (eg, two people taking picture at the same place at the same time) that in turn reveal people's personal social contacts [11]. More importantly, in addition to raise awareness around privacy issues, our findings might well inform the design of new privacy protection mechanisms. Having the necessary means to identify the social-networking users who are likely to be targeted by viral campaigns or phishing attacks, one could design feedback mechanisms for those targets. That is important not only for underage targets (e.g., for designing child protection mechanisms) but for targets of any demographic. That is largely because, although feedback on "who views what" has been shown to be a central element for helping people manage their privacy, social-networking sites currently provide very little of it [53].

The second area is social network modeling. Our research suggests that people are not alike in that they have different tendencies of attracting attention/creating links and, consequently, adding hidden properties such as personality traits could be crucial for modeling online social networks in realistic ways.

CONCLUSION

Creators of social-networking sites make specific design choices and those choices may impact the way people communicate on those sites. Facebook, for example, allows its users to 'poke' social contacts or to exchange personal trivia. However, based on that, one cannot conclude that Facebook is surely "reconfiguring" our ways of communicating with each other or that "the most effective young Facebook users ... are the ones who create successful online fictions about themselves" [34]. Those are seemingly reasonable speculations for which, unfortunately, we found little evidence. Popular Facebook users tend to have the same personality as popular people in the real world, suggesting that the nature of online interactions does not significantly differ from that of real world interactions. So, if design choices were made by Facebook creators, then those choices had little impact on which personality traits determine popularity. We could speculate that it is more likely that Facebook users simply devise their own patterns and structures within status/comment free-form fields outside the narrow creators' original straitjackets. If that is the case, to explain interactions on social-networking sites, the words of William Gibson might have been more apt: "The street finds its own uses for things" [17].

Acknowledgments. We thank EPSRC for its financial support. This work was in part funded by RCUK through the Horizon Digital Economy Research grant (EP/G065802/1). We also thank Paul Expert for his assistance in the statistical analysis. We finally thank the three anonymous reviewers.

REFERENCES

1. R. Algesheimer, U. Dholakia, and A. Herrmann. The Social Influence of Brand Community: Evidence from European Car Clubs. *Journal of Marketing*, 69, July 2005.
2. C. Anderson, O. John, D.Keltner, and A. Kring. Who attains social status? Effects of personality and physical attractiveness in social groups. *Journal of Personality and Social Psychology*, 81, July 2001.
3. D. S. Berry, J. K. Willingham, and C. A. Thayer. Affect and personality as predictors of conflict and closeness in young adults' friendships. *Journal of Research in Personality*, 34, March 2000.
4. N. Bowling, T. Beehr, and W. Swader. Giving and receiving social support at work: the roles of personality and reciprocity. *Journal of Vocational Behaviour*, 67, December 2005.
5. T. Buchanan and J. Smith. Using the Internet for psychological research: Personality testing on the World Wide Web. *British Journal of Psychology*, 90, March 2002.
6. M. Burke, R. Kraut, and C. Marlow. Social Capital on Facebook: Differentiating Uses and Users. In *Proceedings of the* 29th *ACM Conference on Human Factors in Computing Systems (CHI)*, May 2011.
7. M. Burke, C. Marlow, and T. Lento. Social Network Activity and Social Well-Being. In *Proceedings of the* 28th *ACM Conference on Human Factors in Computing Systems (CHI)*, April 2010.
8. J. T. Cacioppo and W. Patrick. *Loneliness: Human Nature and the Need for Social Connection*. W. W. Norton & Company, 2008.
9. C. M. Cheng and T. Chartrand. Self-Monitoring Without Awareness: Using Mimicry as a Nonconscious Affiliation Strategy . *Journal of Personality and Social Psychology*, December 2003.
10. P. Costa and R. Mccrae. *The Revised NEO Personality Inventory (NEO-PI-R)*. SAGE Publications, 2005.
11. D. Crandall, L. Backstrom, D. Cosley, S. Suri, D. Huttenlocher, and J. Kleinberg. Inferring social ties from geographic coincidences. *Proceedings of the National Academy of Sciences*, 107, December 2010.
12. C. Dehle and J. Landers. You can't always get what you want, but can you get what you need? Personality traits and social support in marriage. *Journal of Social and Clinical Psychology*, 24, November 2005.
13. P. S. Dodds, R. Muhamad, and D. J. Watts. An Experimental Study of Search in Global Social Networks. *Science*, 301:827–829, August 2003.

14. W. Duan, Z. Chen, Z. Liu, and W. Jin. Efficient target strategies for contagion in scale-free networks. *Physical Review E*, 72:026133, August 2005.

15. R. Dunbar. Coevolution of neocortical size, group size and language in humans. *Behavioral and Brain Sciences*, 16, 1993.

16. N. Ellison, C. Steinfield, and C. Lampe. The benefits of Facebook "friends": Exploring the relationship between college students' use of online social networks and social capital. *Journal of Computer-Mediated Communication*, 12, July 2007.

17. W. Gibson. *Burning Chrome*. Ace Books, 1987.

18. T. B. Gogolinski. Effects Of Self-Monitoring and Public Self-Consciousness on Perceptions of Facebook Profiles. *Colonial Academic Alliance Undergraduate Research Journal*, 1, 2010.

19. J. Golbeck, C. Robles, and K. Turner. Predicting personality with social media. In *Proceedings of the 29th ACM Conference on Human Factors in Computing Systems (CHI)*, May 2011.

20. L. Goldberg, J. Johnson, H. Eber, R. Hogan, M. Ashton, R. Cloninger, and H. Gough. The international personality item pool and the future of public-domain personality measures. *Journal of Research in Personality*, 40, February 2006.

21. S. Gosling and S. Vazire. Personality impressions based on facebook profiles. In *Proceedings of the International Conference on Weblogs and Social Media (ICWSM)*, March 2007.

22. S. Gosling, S. Vazire, S. Srivastava, and O. John. Should we trust web-based studies? A comparative analysis of six preconceptions about Internet questionnaires. *American Psychologist*, 59, February 2004.

23. E. Hargittai. Whose space? Differences among users and non-users of social network sites. *Journal of Computer-Mediated Communication*, 13, 2008.

24. S. Henderson. Neurosis and the social environment. *New York: Academic Press*, 1981.

25. J. Henrich, S. Heine, and A. Norenzayan. The weirdest people in the world? *Behavioral and Brain Sciences*, 33, June 2010.

26. B. Hogan. The Presentation of Self in the Age of Social Media: Distinguishing Performances and Exhibitions Online. *Bulletin of Science Technology Society*, December 2010.

27. T. Jagatic, N. Johnson, A. Nathaniel, M. Jakobsson, and F. Menczer. Social phishing. *Communications of the ACM*, 50, October 2007.

28. L. Jensen-Campbell and W. Graziano. Agreeableness as a moderator of interpersonal conflict. *Journal of Personality*, 71, January 2004.

29. O. P. John and S. Srivastava. The Big Five trait taxonomy: History, measurement, and theoretical perspectives. In *Handbook of Personality: Theory and Research*. Guilford Press, 1999.

30. G. D. Jong, E. V. Sonderen, and P. Emmelkamp. A comprehensive model of stress: the roles of experience stress and Neuroticism in explaining the stress- distress relationship. *Psychotherapy and Psychosomatics*, 68, 1999.

31. B. R. Karney and T. N. Bradbury. The longitudinal course of marital quality and stability: a review of theory, methods and research. *Psychological Bulletin*, 118, July 1995.

32. C. A. Kleck, C. A. Reese, D. Z. Behnken, and S. S. Sundar. The company you keep and the image you project: Putting your best face forward in online social networks. In *Proceedings of the International Communication Association*, May 2007.

33. A. Kramer, D. Adam, and K. Rodden. Word usage and posting behaviors: modeling blogs with unobtrusive data collection methods. In *Proceeding of the 26th Annual Conference on Human Factors in Computing Systems (CHI)*, April 2008.

34. J. Lanier. *You Are Not a Gadget: A Manifesto*. Knopf, 2010.

35. D. Lee-Baggley, M. Preece, and A. DeLongis. Coping with interpersonal stress: role of Big Five traits. *Journal of Personality*, 73, July 2005.

36. J. Lewis and A. West. 'Friending': London-based undergraduates' experience of Facebook. *New media and Society*, 11, September 2009.

37. C. S. Lin. Exploring the Personality Trait of Self-Monitoring on Technology Usage of Web Portals. *CyberPsychology and Behavior*, 11, April 2008.

38. L. Lu and M. Argyle. Receiving and giving support: effects on relationships and well-being. *Psychology Quarterly*, 5, April 1992.

39. R. McCrae and P. Costa. Personality, coping, and coping effectiveness in an adult sample. *Journal of Personality*, 54, 1986.

40. A. Mehra, M. Kilduff, and D. Brass. The Social Networks of High and Low Self-monitors: Implications for Workplace Performance. *Administrative Science Quarterly*, 11, March 2000.

41. D. Nettle. *Personality: What Makes You the Way You Are*. Oxford University Press, 2007.

42. C. D. Nyea, B. W. Robertsa, G. Saucierb, and X. Zhouc. Testing the measurement equivalence of personality adjective items across cultures. *Journal of Research in Personality*, July 2008.

43. T. B. O'Brien and A. DeLongis. The interactional context of problem-, emotion-, and relationship-focused coping: the role of the Big Five personality factors. *Journal of Personality*, 64, December 1996.

44. M. Parks. *Personal networks and personal relationships*. Routledge, 2006.

45. D. Quercia, M. Kosinski, D. Stillwell, and J. Crowcroft. Our Twitter Profiles, Our Selves: Predicting Personality with Twitter. In *Proceedings of the 3rd IEEE Conference on Social Computing (SocialCom)*, October 2011.

46. U. Reips. *The Web Experiment Method: Advantages, disadvantages, and solutions*. CA Academic Press, 2000.

47. D. Russell, B. Booth, D. Reed, and P. Laughlin. Personality, social networks, and perceived social support among alcoholics: a structural equation analysis. *Journal of Personality*, 65, September 1997.

48. C. Shirky. *Here Comes Everybody*. Allen Lane, 2008.

49. M. Snyder. Self-monitoring of expressive behavior. *Journal of Personality and Social Psychology,*, 30, 1974.

50. R. Swickert. Personality and social support processes. *The Cambridge Handbook of Personality Psychology*, 2009.

51. R. Swickert, C. Rosentreter, J. Hittner, and J. Mushrush. Extraversion, social support processes, and stress. *Personality and Individual Differences*, 32, April 2002.

52. S. T. Tong, B. V. D. Heide, L. Langwell, and J. B. Walther. Too Much of a Good Thing? The Relationship Between Number of Friends and Interpersonal Impressions on Facebook. *Journal of Computer-Mediated Communication*, April 2008.

53. J. Y. Tsai, P. Kelley, P. Drielsma, L. F. Cranor, J. Hong, and N. Sadeh. Who's viewed you?: the impact of feedback in a mobile location-sharing application. In *Proceedings of the 27th International Conference on Human factors in Computing Systems (CHI)*, 2009.

54. S. Vazire and S. Gosling. e-Perceptions: Personality Impressions Based on Personal Websites. *Journal of Personality and Social Psychology*, 87, July 2004.

Tracking "Gross Community Happiness" from Tweets

Daniele Quercia[§] Jonathan Ellis[‡] Licia Capra[‡] Jon Crowcroft[§]
[§]The Computer Laboratory, University of Cambridge, UK
[‡]Department of Computer Science, University College London, UK
dq209@cl.cam.ac.uk, j.ellis@cs.ucl.ac.uk, l.capra@cs.ucl.ac.uk, jac22@cl.cam.ac.uk

ABSTRACT
Policy makers are calling for new socio-economic measures that reflect subjective well-being, to complement traditional measures of material welfare as the Gross Domestic Product (GDP). Self-reporting has been found to be reasonably accurate in measuring one's well-being and conveniently tallies with sentiment expressed on social media (e.g., those satisfied with life use more positive than negative words in their Facebook status updates). Social media content can thus be used to track well-being of individuals. A question left unexplored is whether such content can be used to track well-being of entire physical communities as well. To this end, we consider Twitter users based in a variety of London census communities, and study the relationship between sentiment expressed in tweets and community socio-economic well-being. We find that the two are highly correlated: the higher the normalized sentiment score of a community's tweets, the higher the community's socio-economic well-being. This suggests that monitoring tweets is an effective way of tracking community well-being too.

General Terms
Measurement, Theory, Verification

ACM Classification Keywords
H.5.m Information Interfaces and Presentation: Miscellaneous

INTRODUCTION
Policy makers have recently suggested that measuring community well-being will help governments do a better job at directing public policy towards promoting quality of life (happiness) rather than material welfare (GDP). The French president Nicolas Sarkozy recently announced he intended to include well-being in France's measurement of economic progress [13]. The UK prime minister David Cameron is initiating a series of policies, under the rubric "Big Society", that seek to make society stronger by getting more people running their own affairs locally all together. To assess how different "Big Society" policies will impact the well-being of communities, the UK Office of National Statistics will shortly be asked to produce measures of "general well-being" [13].

Measuring the well-being of single individuals can be easily accomplished by administering questionnaires such as the Satisfaction With Life (SWL) test, whose score effectively reflects the extent to which a person feels that his/her life is worthwhile [3]. Self-reporting has been shown to be reasonably accurate, and recent studies have further highlighted that it tallies with, for example, sentiment expressed in Facebook status updates [9].

To go beyond single individuals and measure the well-being of communities, one could administer SWL tests to community residents. But that would be costly and is thus done on limited population samples and at a frequency of years. Recent research findings suggest that the costing problem may be ameliorated by monitoring implicit data generated by community members. For example, in a 2010 Science article, Eagle *et al.* monitored the diversity of the communication networks formed by community residents, and showed that socio-economic well-being of communities strongly correlates with network diversity (with a striking correlation of $r = .74$). In particular, they built communication networks from phone records across the entire United Kingdom, cross-referenced it with socio-economic census data, and showed that members of well-off communities have diverse networks, while members of economically and socially disadvantaged communities have insular social relations [5].

Another way of tracking community well-being is to extract community residents' emotional state from text they produce on social media websites such as blogs, Twitter, or Facebook. As a result, "sentiment analysis", that is, extracting emotional state from text, is receiving a lot of attention from the research community [8]. Since self-reported content on social media is ready available, researchers can monitor sentiment without having to go through the time-consuming process of asking people explicit questions. Kramer, for example, has built a sentiment metric out of Facebook status updates (he used a standardized difference between percent of words that are positive and those that are negative), found that the metric correlates with self-reported satisfaction with life (it correlates with SWL scores with a statistically significant coefficient of about $r = .17$), and aggregated the metric at national US level. In so doing, he observed that the temporal graph of the aggregate US metric

CSCW 2012, February 11–15, 2012, Seattle, Washington, USA.

(named "Gross National Happiness") showed peaks occurring on national and cultural holidays [9].

Although Kramer's study suggests that one might be able to gauge a whole nation's well-being and overall emotional health from the sentiment expressed on social media, it is not clear whether the correspondence between sentiment of self-reported text and well-being would hold at *community level*, that is, whether sentiment expressed by community residents on social media reflects community socio-economic well-being. We test the hypothesized correspondence between sentiment and community well-being by making the following contributions:

- For a variety of London communities, we crawl tweets produced by their residents and obtain census data of their socio-economic well-being (Section "Dataset"). More precisely, we crawl Twitter accounts whose user-specified locations report London neighborhoods. We geo-reference those accounts by converting their locations into longitude-latitude pairs. We also obtain the 2007 UK government's Index of Multiple Deprivation (IMD), which is a composite measure of relative prosperities of 32,482 communities, 78 of which are in London [11].

- We analyze the sentiment of tweets using two algorithms (Section "Sentiment Analysis"). The first is the word count technique proposed by Kramer and is based on computing the standardized difference between percent of words that are positive and those that are negative. The second is the Maximum Entropy classifier, which is a state-of-the-art method for classifying sentiment of single tweets [6]. We implement both classifiers and show that their results correlate and are accurate.

- We study the relationship between sentiment and socio-economic well-being (Section "Results"). We find that the higher the normalized sentiment score of a community's tweets, the higher the community's socio-economic well-being. The correlation coefficients are statistically significant and are as high as $r = .350$ for sentiment based on word count, and $r = .365$ for sentiment computed with Maximum Entropy. These results suggest that monitoring the sentiment of tweets may well be an accurate and cost-effective way of tracking the well-being of communities.

DATASET

Twitter Profiles. To control for any variability in the use of language across geographic areas, we have preferentially chosen Twitter profiles from London and did so as follows. We chose three popular London-based seed profiles of news outlets: the free subway newspaper Metro, the center-left newspaper The Independent, and the tabloid The Sun. These news outlets cover the entire UK political spectrum and have high penetration rates in the city. Each Twitter user who follows these seed profiles was crawled. This resulted in 250K profiles, 157K of which specified geographic locations (mostly city names) and 1,323 specified London neighborhoods (e.g., Hackney, Mayfair). For those 1,323 profiles, we converted user-specified home locations into longitude-latitude pairs using the Yahoo! PlaceMaker API[1]. To filter out profiles that are likely to be spam accounts or are not of real people, we crawled the PeerIndex realness score for each profile. This score is generated upon information such as whether the profile has been self-certified on the PeerIndex site and or has been linked to Facebook or LinkedIn. "PeerIndex realness score is a metric that indicates the likelihood that the profile is of a real person, rather than a spambot or twitter feed. A score above 50 means this account is of a real person, a score below 50 means it is less likely to be a real person"[2]. We filter out profiles that scored below 50 and are left with 573 profiles.

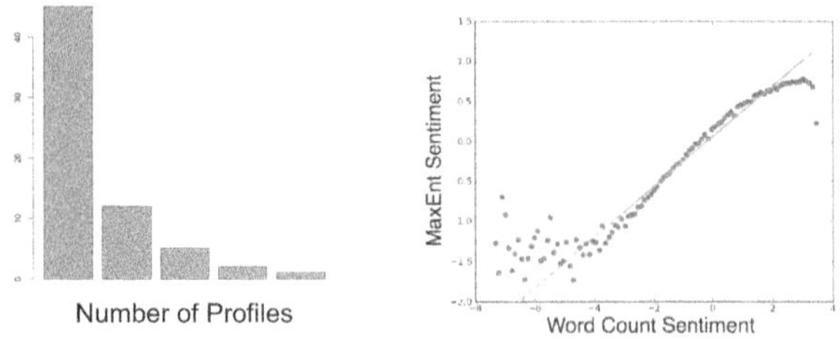

(a) Number of Profiles per Community

(b) Sentiment Scores: Word Count vs. Maximum Entropy

Figure 1. (a) Frequency distribution of the number of Twitter profiles in each community. (b) Maximum Entropy Sentiment vs. Word Count Sentiment: the two sentiment scores are highly correlated at aggregate level.

Socio-demographic Data. From the UK Office for National Statistics, we obtain the Index of Multiple Deprivation (IMD) score of each of the 78 census areas in London. We consider a census area to be a community. We choose such a definition of community because it has been widely used in studies of social deprivation (including the related article by Eagle *et al.* [5]) and because using IMD scores with any other definition of community would lead to results that are not ecologically valid. IMD is a composite score based on income, employment, education, health, crime, housing, and the environmental quality of each community [11]. The higher a community's IMD score, the more socially deprived the community (e.g., Tottenham, Hackney); whilst the lower the score, the less deprived the community (e.g., Mayfair, Belgravia). Of these 78 census areas, 51 contained at least one of the Twitter profiles we crawled; Figure 1(a) shows the frequency distribution of the number of profiles per community.

SENTIMENT ANALYSIS

After collecting tweets between the dates of 27 September and 10 December 2010, we measure the sentiment expressed by a profile's tweets and then compute, for each census region, an aggregate community-sentiment measure of all the profiles in the region. So, for starters, we need to measure the sentiment of a profile, and we do so using two classifications: Word Count and Maximum Entropy.

[1]http://developer.yahoo.com/geo/placemaker/
[2]http://www.peerindex.net/help/scores

Word Count. We use a dictionary called "Linguistic Inquiry Word Count". LIWC is a standard dictionary of 2,300 English words that capture 80% of the words used in everyday conversations and reflect people's emotional and cognitive perceptions. After removing stop-words from tweets, we count, for each profile, the number of words that are positive and those that are negative (words matching the two categories of 'positive emotions' and 'negative emotions' as defined in LIWC) and aggregate both counts to produce the "Word Count Sentiment" score, which is similar to the score proposed by Kramer [9]:

$$Sentiment_i^{WC} = \frac{p_i - \mu_p}{\sigma_p} - \frac{n_i - \mu_n}{\sigma_n} \quad (1)$$

where p_i (n_i) is the fraction of positive (negative) words for user i; μ_p (μ_n) is the fraction of positive (negative) words, averaged across all users; and σ_p (σ_n) is the corresponding standard deviation. The normalization using means and standard deviations accounts for the unbalanced distribution of positive and negative words of the English language [9].

Maximum Entropy. A limitation of the Word Count technique is that the vocabulary it uses does not contain all English words that are positive or negative. We thus need a classifier that can learn new positive/negative words. To this end, we resort to a machine learning technique called Maximum Entropy (MaxEnt for short). The technique has been proven to be effective in a number of natural language processing applications, including sentiment classification of tweets [1, 6]. To train MaxEnt, we used a dataset provided by a group of students from Stanford University that consists of 232,442 "smiley" tweets (containing the :-) emotion) and 151,955 "frowny" tweets (containing the :-(emotion). We consider "smiley" and "frowny" faces to reflect the ground-truth sentiment of the corresponding tweets, similarly to previous work by Go *et al.* [6]. After being trained on the ground-truth, MaxEnt is then able to classify future tweets. We do so for the tweets in our London dataset, and compute a profile's "Maximum Entropy Sentiment" using, again, formula (1).

Effectiveness of classifiers. Having the two classifiers at hand, we now need to measure how well they perform. Upon 10-fold cross validation, we find that the two classifiers show very similar *accuracy* upon tweets they are able to classify (precision is around 66%) but different *recall* in that Word Count leaves more tweets unclassified than what MaxEnt does (recall is 38% for Word Count and 68% for MaxEnt). However, these results are for single tweets. At profile level, the two classifiers perform similarly. We plot one classifier's profile sentiment scores versus the other's in Figure 1(b) and clearly observe that the two quantities are strongly correlated (Pearson correlation coefficient of $r = .73$): each profile, on average, is considered to be positive/negative to a very similar extent by both classifiers. Given these results at profile level, one concludes that the two classifiers perform similarly, all the more so at community level.

However, critics might rightly say that words not reflecting positive moods such as greetings during Christmas might well wrongly skew our sentiment classifications. This bias holds but is alleviated in three ways. First, we study profiles in the single area of London and, as a result, we control for any variability in the use of words across geographic areas. Second, our sentiment analysis is a comparative one - time-specific or area-specific words (e.g., greetings) do introduce biases but do so across all profiles and, as such, have little impact on a comparative analysis. Third, any bias left (e.g., one could argue that deprived areas always use less greetings) is of little concern because our classification is not of single tweets but of entire profiles in which the importance of individual greetings is largely diluted.

Gross Community Happiness. Upon the sentiment classifications of profiles, we finally compute "Gross Community Happiness" (*GCH*) as the mean sentiment score of the profiles in a community: $GCH_C = Mean\{Sentiment_i\}_{\forall i \in C}$, where $Sentiment_i$ is the sentiment score (computed with either word count or maximum entropy) of each profile i in community C. We choose the metric of *GNH* to ease the interpretation of our results: the mechanics behind *GNH* are easy to understand, as opposed to machine learning approaches that often act as black boxes, and *GNH* also makes our correlation results comparable with previous work. Furthermore, as for *GNH*'s input sentiment classifications, we have just shown that classifying (not tweets but) *profiles* does not require sophisticated techniques - Word Count does a reasonable job.

RESULTS

We now use the previously computed sentiment scores across different communities to make two assessments. First, we aim to gain an insight into the geographic distribution of sentiment across London neighborhoods. We do so by overlaying "Gross Community Happiness" (*GCH*) scores onto a city map using the Google Maps Javascript API (Figure 2). The map loosely indicates that the North West is the happiest quadrant of the city, whilst South East London is fairly awash with blue, indicating unhappy sentiment. Indeed, conventional wisdom among Londoners holds that "Generally London has a North West/South East gradient of posh to rough areas. It's not so much 'West end' vs. 'East end' as 'North West' vs. 'South East'. Many of the really dodgy parts of London are in the South East"[3]. These anecdotes are quantitatively supported by the gradient of IMD scores between North West London and South East London [11].

Second, we compute the Pearson correlation coefficient between IMD and "Gross Community Happiness" scores. In so doing, we learn that the two quantities are correlated to a significant extent: $r = .350$ if *GCH* is computed with word count ($p < 0.05$), and $r = .365$ if *GCH* is computed with MaxEnt ($p < 0.01$). These correlations are statistically significant. However, for areas with less than 9 profiles, correlation coefficients do vary but their variations are not easy to interpret as they are not statistically significant. For the 33 areas with more than 9 profiles, correlation coefficients become stable (around .35) and statistically significant, and the corresponding IMD distribution is still nor-

[3] What's the worst part of London? http://tinyurl.com/3ldhu8q

Figure 2. Mapping "Gross Community Happiness" in Greater London (best seen in color).

mally distributed. More generally, there is no correlation between one area's number of Twitter profiles and its IMD. Correlation coefficients are rather high considering that, at individual level, sentiment expressed on social media correlates with self-reported life satisfaction with a coefficient of about $r = .17$ [9]. These results ultimately suggest that users in more deprived London communities tweet, on average, more negatively than those in less-deprived communities.

DISCUSSION

Our analysis has demonstrated that the relation between sentiment and well-being does not only hold for individuals but scales to the level of communities too, so much so that we have created an aggregate metric out of community residents' tweets and have successfully validated it: the metric correlates with census socio-economic well-being of communities. This result suggests that it is possible to effectively track the emotional health of local communities from their residents' tweets in an unobtrusive way, as tweets are publicly available and easily crawled.

The significance of these results extends beyond merely tracking emotional health of local areas: they provide evidence that users' offline communities have a noticeable effect on their online interactions. To appreciate the importance of this insight, consider that past research has suggested two relations relevant to this study. The first is between where people live and their subjective well-being: income inequality, unemployment rates, urbanization, safety and deprivation of an area have all been shown to relate to people's subjective well-being across different countries and time periods [4]. The second relation is between subjective well-being and what people write on social media: sentiment expressed in user-generated content gets more positive as people are increasingly satisfied with their lives [9]. From these two relations, a third one might transitively follow but has never been tested: the relation between where people live and social media content they generate. We have now tested this third relation and found that, indeed, tweets from residents of socially deprived communities contain more negative emotions than those from residents of well-off communities. Interestingly, this link between offline and online worlds counsels cautions against claims that social-networking sites like Twitter "dehumanize" community life [7, 10]; on the contrary, they seem to reflect important aspects of physical communities. Our recent findings further support this view. We have studied the Twitter network and have recently found that one's sentiment strongly correlates with the average sentiment of one's Twitter friends and followers. This suggests, once again, that dynamics observed in the physical world such as homophily are reflected in digital interactions.

This study has three limitations that call for further investigation in the future. The first is demographic bias: 63% of Twitter users are less than 35 years old and 68% have a total household income of at least $60, 000 in the United States. The results we presented thus disproportionately represents the happiness of some citizens over others. This is one of reasons why we have chosen London: it had been the top Twitter-using city in the world until the beginning of 2010 [2], and as the service penetration rate increases, demographic bias is bound to decrease. The second limitation is that our results do not speak to causality. Though the causal direction is difficult to be determined from observational data, one could repeatedly crawl Twitter over multiple time intervals and use a cross-lag analysis to potentially observe causal relationships. The third limitation is that we have tracked sentiment but have not studied *what* actually makes communities happy. To that end, we are currently extracting the *subject matter* of tweets using topic models [12] and will then compare topics across communities. For example, given two communities, one talking about yoga and organic food, and the other talking about gangs and junk food, what can be said about their levels of social deprivation? The hope is that topical analysis will answer this kind of questions and, in so doing, assist policy makers in making informed choices regarding, for example, urban planning.

REFERENCES

1. L. Barbosa and J. Feng. Robust sentiment detection on Twitter from biased and noisy data. In *Proc. of the* 23rd *COLING*, August 2010.
2. M. Butcher. London is the capital of Twitter, says founder. TechCrunch Europe, August 2009.
3. E. Diener, M. Diener, and C. Diener. Factors predicting the subjective well-being of nations. *Journal of Personality and Social Psychology*, 69(5):851–864, 1995.
4. P. Dolan, T. Peasgood, and M. White. Do we really know what makes us happy? *Journal of Economic Psychology*, 29(1):94–122, 2008.
5. N. Eagle, M. Macy, and R. Claxton. Network diversity and economic development. *Science*, 328(5981):1029–1031, 2010.
6. A. Go, R. Bhayani, and L. Huang. Twitter Sentiment Classification using Distant Supervision. In *Stanford Tech Report*, December 2009.
7. C. Irvine. Twitter CEO dismisses claims that social networking 'dehumanises'. The Telegraph, August 2009.
8. F. Kivran-Swaine and M. Naaman. Network properties and social sharing of emotions in social awareness streams. In *Proc. of the ACM CSCW*, March 2011.
9. A. Kramer. An unobtrusive behavioral model of "Gross National Happiness". In *Proc. of the* 28th *ACM CHI*, April 2010.
10. J. Lanier. *You Are Not a Gadget: A Manifesto*. Knopf, January 2010.
11. M. Noble *et al.* The English Indices of Deprivation 2007. The Department of Communities and Local Government, March 2008.
12. D. Ramage, S. Dumais, and D. Liebling. Characterizing Microblogs with Topic Models. In *Proc. of the AAAI ICWSM*, 2010.
13. A. Stratton. Happiness index to gauge Britain's national mood. The Guardian, November 2010.

What Makes Users Rate (Share, Tag, Edit...)? Predicting Patterns of Participation in Online Communities

Paul T. Fuglestad, Patrick C. Dwyer, Jennifer Filson Moses, John S. Kim, Clelia Anna Mannino, Loren Terveen, and Mark Snyder
The University of Minnesota
Minneapolis, Minnesota USA
{fugl0025, dwyer092, fils0007, kimx1073, manni114, msnyder}@umn.edu, terveen@cs.umn.edu

ABSTRACT
Administrators of online communities face the crucial issue of understanding and developing their user communities. Will new users become committed members? What types of roles are particular individuals most likely to take on? We report on a study that investigates these questions. We administered a survey (based on standard psychological instruments) to nearly 4000 new users of the MovieLens film recommendation community from October 2009 to March 2010 and logged their usage history on MovieLens. We found that general volunteer motivations, pro-social behavioral history, and community-specific motivations predicted both the amount of use and specific types of activities users engaged in after joining the community. These findings have implications for the design and management of online communities.

Author Keywords
Online communities, volunteers, motivation, participation, surveys

ACM Classification Keywords
H5.3 [Group and Organization Interfaces]: Collaborative Computing, computer-supported cooperative work, web-based interaction

General Terms
Human Factors, Design, Experimentation.

INTRODUCTION
Online communities derive great value from the contributions of their users. For example, Wikipedia editors have created the largest encyclopedia in history. Yahoo! Answers users have provided over one billion answers. And contributors to open source software projects have produced operating system, web browser, and web server software that rivals software produced by the largest software companies in the world.

Nevertheless, online communities have significant problems of contribution. Many communities fail [4]. Only a small percentage of users contribute content, and only a small proportion of these contribute significant amounts of content [24,35]. Even successful communities like Wikipedia face problems such as a large backlog of pending tasks [38], low retention of new editors [25], and highly unequal participation by men and women [8, 14].

Thus, it would be useful for website maintainers to be able to quickly identify whether a new user is likely to become an active participant. If the signs are not promising, perhaps an immediate "rescue" attempt could be made, e.g., getting an experienced user to welcome the newcomer and suggest ways for the newcomer to get started. Further, online communities typically offer multiple ways for users to participate, and users often specialize in particular tasks and roles [6, 18, 37]; thus, being able to quickly identify roles that suit a new user and guide the user appropriately also may aid retention.

The present investigation frames the problem of attracting and maintaining user participation in online communities as analogous to the "problem of inaction" identified for participation in offline communities [31]. Volunteerism, for example, is a form of community participation that is widely valued throughout society. When it comes to actually volunteering one's time, however, people's actions fall short of their attitudes and beliefs, with barely 1 in 3 people serving as volunteers in their communities on a regular basis [11].

We believe that participation in many types of online communities can be conceptualized as a form of volunteerism. While one may not immediately view online participation as volunteerism, the defining characteristic of numerous online communities, such as Wikipedia, arXiv.org, Slashdot, open source software projects, or MovieLens (a movie recommendation community) is that people volunteer their time and effort to accomplish valued tasks together. These activities are neither required nor socially mandated. Rather, users choose to perform these activities for the benefit of the community, just like people who serve as volunteers in offline communities [39]. And by participating, they may discover additional ways of involvement beyond those that drew them to the site in the first place.

Of course there may be other types of online participation where a volunteerism model is less appropriate, such as consumers shopping on sites driven by financial incentives (Ebay, Amazon). As such, our research is specifically aimed at online communities that benefit from the unpaid, discretionary behaviors of community members.

In this research, guided by relevant theory and research on participation in volunteer communities [22, 33] we investigate the utility of several different types of information for predicting future behavior of new members of an online community:

- The general motivations they have for engaging in volunteer activities (e.g., to understand and learn about the world),
- Their relevant pro-social behavioral history (e.g., past volunteer behaviors), and
- Specific reasons they have for joining this community (e.g., to get movie recommendations or to have fun).

Our goal is to determine whether people's motivations for volunteering, history of pro-social behavior and motivations for joining MovieLens predict overall participation in an online community and whether different motivations predict different types of behavior.

RESEARCH SITE: MOVIELENS

We conducted our study on MovieLens (www.movielens.org), an online community started in 1997 as one of the first Web recommender systems. In MovieLens, a user rates movies, and the system compares the user's ratings to those of all other users in the system in order to identify and recommend other movies the user is likely to enjoy. Getting movie recommendations was the original – and remains an essential – purpose of the site.

However, over the past five-plus years, MovieLens has been transformed into an online community with new and extensive opportunities for interaction and participation. Users so inclined can suggest new movies to be added to the database and edit the details (e.g., actors, directors, release date) of movies already in the database. They can tag movies to aid navigation through the movie database (and rate the tags others have assigned to movies). They can create personal profiles to represent themselves to other users, choose to make their ratings visible to other users, and interact on a Q&A-style discussion forum.

MovieLens is an active medium-sized online community. It has over 165,000 registered users, and about 30 new members join every day. Users collectively enter about 2500 new ratings and apply 150 new tags daily. Still, like most online communities, MovieLens has problems of contribution. For example, less than 2% of registered users have been active in the past year, the Q&A forum is little used, and it is a challenge to keep the database updated with timely and accurate information about new movies. Therefore, a better understanding of what motivates users to participate could be quite helpful in devising new techniques to elicit and direct user participation.

Next, we discuss the related research and theory that serves as a foundation for this work.

RELATED WORK

There is a substantial body of prior work that aims to apply psychological theory to online communities. Most closely related are studies that analyze people's motivations for participating in online communities or that invent new techniques to elicit participation. For example, Ridings and Gefen [26] found that, across several different types of online communities, the desire to exchange information with other members was the most frequently cited reason for joining. However, the second most cited reason varied depending on community type. While the desire to obtain and receive social/emotional support was the second most important reason for joining communities oriented around health/wellness and professional/occupational issues, the desire simply to make new friends was the second most important reason for joining communities oriented around personal interests/hobbies, pets, or recreation.

Further research has focused on assessing the motives of members of specific kinds of online communities. Lakhani and Wolf [13] surveyed open source software developers, identifying motivations such as intellectual stimulation, desire to improve programming skills, and adherence to the principles of open source software. Nov [19] found that fun and adherence to the principles of open source were leading motivations for Wikipedia editors, and that the fun motivation was moderately positively correlated with higher self-reported participation. Oreg and Nov [23] surveyed Wikipedia editors and open source contributors, finding differences in motivations between the two domains and uncovering relationships between psychological dispositions and motivations. And among members of a professional legal association, contributions to the association's online message board were significantly predicted by members' perceptions that doing so would enhance their professional reputations [36].

Lampe et al. [15] studied members of the Everything2 online encyclopedia and creative writing community using surveys and behavioral log analysis. They identified a range of theory-derived motives and found that different motives were associated with different behavioral patterns. Similarly, Butler et al. [5] found that specific benefits derived from participation were linked to specific self-reported patterns of participation among Internet listserv owners and other members. Finally, Ling et al. [16], Cosley et al. [7], and Vassileva [34] reported on theory-based interaction techniques and intervention studies designed to elicit user participation in online communities.

The present research builds on and extends prior work in the following ways. Unlike nearly all the analytical work, we combine the use of survey data and behavioral log data. It is quite useful to be able to analyze actual behavioral data, since the relation between self-reported behavior and actual behavior is not as strong as one might expect [3]. In this way our work is similar to that of Lampe et al. The current work also complements Lampe's work in several important ways. We study a different community with different properties. MovieLens is interesting to study because of the wide range of behaviors it provides. This work evaluates the roles of different psychological motivations and prior behaviors in predicting MovieLens behaviors. And it focuses solely on new members of an online community, which is useful since their expectations and attitudes have not yet been influenced by participation in the community, and the earliest stage of membership is the point of maximum leverage for potential interventions. Finally, while the current work does not create or test design interventions, the results suggest promising directions for intervention.

We next outline the theoretical approach guiding our investigation.

A FUNCTIONAL APPROACH TO COMMUNITY PARTICIPATION

This research takes a functional approach, a theoretical perspective on motivation that has guided much research on volunteerism and community involvement [6, 20]. The functional approach has shown that people may have distinct motivations to participate in the same behavioral domain [32]. In other words, different people can perform the *same behavior* to satisfy *different psychological needs*. Guided by previous theory and research on motivations for volunteering [6, 20, 33], we consider three general classes of motivations that we hypothesized might influence user participation in online communities: general volunteer motivations, pro-social behavioral history, and community-specific motivations.

General Volunteer Motivations

Research on volunteerism has identified several key motives for volunteer behavior [6, 22]. For example, people might volunteer to express or act on important values, to learn more about the world, or to grow and develop psychologically. By identifying people's underlying motivations and corresponding behavioral patterns, one can encourage volunteerism by matching individual volunteers to the activities for which they are best suited and that they are most interested in performing. A growing body of empirical research has supported this theoretical framework and extended it to a wide variety of volunteer endeavors, e.g., recreation volunteerism [30], and types of volunteers, e.g., senior volunteers [21]. There also has been some application to participation in online communities [19].

We build on and deepen the application of this approach to online community participation. We investigate whether, for example, people who volunteer for relatively more self-oriented reasons engage in more activities that benefit them directly, and whether people who volunteer for relatively more other-oriented reasons engage in more actions that benefit the community as a whole. If such relations do exist, and if user motivations can be assessed, online community maintainers gain a powerful tool for directing users to activities that they are likely to find appealing.

Pro-Social Behavioral History

We also consider people's history of engaging in pro-social behaviors, including their history of volunteerism, level of community involvement, and engagement in everyday altruistic behaviors (e.g., giving up their seat on a bus). These behaviors are plausible predictors of online community participation since they all are activities that people freely choose (or don't choose) to perform for the benefit of others [33, 39]. Therefore, in MovieLens, it is reasonable to conjecture that people with a history of engaging in pro-social behaviors may be more likely to engage in community-benefiting activities like adding new movies into the database and editing details about a movie. Additionally, according to Omoto and Snyder [22], individuals feel compelled to act on behalf of a group if they feel a sense of connection to and identification with the group. Previous research on participation in online communities [2] has also found members' level of commitment to a specific online community to be an important predictor of participation in that community. Therefore, among new users of MovieLens, we hypothesize that people who are generally more inclined towards feeling a sense of community connectedness also should be more likely to participate in MovieLens.

Community-specific Motivations

Finally, any group or community, online or offline, will have specific attractions for potential members: people may join a book club for the intellectual stimulation, an adult hockey league for the fun of physical activity, and a sports website to get the latest scores and news and to chat with fellow fans. We therefore also examine reasons for joining MovieLens that are specific to the site's domain (movies) and the site itself, such as getting accurate movie recommendations and expressing one's opinion about movies. While these reasons are community-specific, there may be cross-community generalizations. For example, whatever the online community, one motive to join always will be to use the essential function of the site (such as getting movie recommendations), while other common classes of motives – communicating with fellow enthusiasts, expressing one's opinions, having fun – transcend utility.

STUDY AND METHODS

The goals of our study were to determine whether people's motivations for volunteering, history of pro-social behavior and motivations for joining MovieLens predict overall participation in MovieLens and whether different motivations predict different types of behavior.

To make these determinations, we had to first identify users' motivations. We did this by developing a survey to administer to new MovieLens users.

Survey

In October of 2009, we modified MovieLens to administer a survey to new MovieLens users immediately after completing the signup process (which includes rating 15 movies) and before they continued on to the normal MovieLens site. The survey contained measures (based on standard instruments where available) for each of the three classes of motivation. Users who agreed to take the survey were entered into a raffle for the chance to win Amazon.com gift certificates. 3,904 users provided usable data, although most users did not provide data for all measures. Response rates for the different measures were dependent on survey order. 3,890 users completed the community specific measure (presented first), 2,307 completed the volunteer motivations measure (initially presented toward the end of the survey and later presented just after the community specific measure), and 1,651 completed the pro-social behavioral history measures (presented toward the end of the survey). Participants who completed the survey were given a tracking number so that we could link their survey data with their actual behavior on MovieLens. We next describe the measures included on the survey.

General Volunteer Motivations: The VFI

We measured general psychological motives for volunteer participation using an abridged 18-item version of the Volunteer Functions Inventory (VFI) [6]. The VFI assesses six volunteer motives on a 7-point scale (from *1 = not at all important* to *7 = extremely important*). The motives are defined as follows:

- *Protective* – volunteering to reduce negative feelings, such as guilt, or to address personal problems ($M = 3.03$, $SD = 1.64$);
- *Values* – volunteering to express or act on important values, such as humanitarianism and helping those less fortunate ($M = 4.61$, $SD = 1.81$);
- *Career* – volunteering to gain career-related experiences and benefits ($M = 3.31$, $SD = 1.71$);
- *Social* – volunteering in order to strengthen one's social relationships ($M = 3.13$, $SD = 1.66$);
- *Understanding* – volunteering to learn more about other people and the world ($M = 4.03$, $SD = 1.72$); and
- *Enhancement* – volunteering to grow and develop psychologically ($M = 3.82$, $SD = 1.70$).

Consistent with suggestions [20] that much of the variability in motivations for volunteering is captured in a two category classification system in which motivations are grouped into those that focus on *others* who are the beneficiaries of volunteerism (e.g., values and understanding motivations) and those that focus on the *self* and the benefits that accrue to the self from volunteering (e.g., career advancement, esteem enhancement), we combined these six motives to get at relatively more *self-oriented* volunteer motivation (a combination of the Enhancement, Social, Career, and Protective motives) and relatively more *other-oriented* volunteer motivation (a combination of the Values and Understanding motives). Exploratory factor analysis (using maximum likelihood extraction with promax rotation) confirmed these interpretable other and self-oriented volunteer motives. The motives, though distinct, were highly correlated ($r = .78$, $p < .001$).

- *Other-oriented* – volunteering to learn about or benefit others ($\alpha = .92$, $M = 4.33$, $SD = 1.67$); and
- *Self-oriented* – volunteering to gain benefits for the self (e.g., friends, skills, or mood enhancement) ($\alpha = .94$, $M = 3.31$, $SD = 1.47$).

Pro-Social Behavioral History

We assessed three distinct aspects of prior pro-social behavior:

Volunteer History. Participants were asked to list all past volunteer positions held, along with the average number of hours per week served in each position. Our measure of volunteer history was the sum across all past positions of the average hours served per week ($M = 2.39$, $SD = 6.72$).

Altruistic Behavior. This measure was an abbreviated version of one created by Rushton, Chrisjohn, and Fekken [29]. It simply asked the user how frequently he/she engages in five helpful everyday behaviors (e.g., giving up one's seat on a bus). We created a composite score by averaging the user's responses over those five behaviors ($\alpha = .86$, $M = 2.83$, $SD = 1.21$).

Community Involvement. We developed a unique measure to capture community involvement. We simply asked participants to list all the communities (subjectively defined) to which they belonged (e.g., church, New Yorker, hunting, Labour Party, vegetarian, American, etc.). We then operationalized community involvement as the number of communities listed ($M = 1.96$, $SD = 2.81$). This is a reasonable operationalization, since studies have found that the number of communities people report is associated with how closely they identify with their communities as well as their volunteer history [17].

Altruistic behavior was not related to volunteer history or community involvement (*r's* $< .03$); volunteer history and community involvement were positively correlated ($r = .19$, $p < .001$).

Community-specific Motivations

We used an 11-item scale that asked participants to rate the extent to which various reasons for joining MovieLens were important to them (from *1 = not at all important* to *7 = extremely important*). Although the items could be viewed as assessing a single dimension ($\alpha = .88$, $M = 4.07$, $SD = 1.17$), exploratory factor analysis (using maximum likelihood extraction with promax rotation) showed that the items captured three distinct reasons for joining

MovieLens. These reasons were (a) getting movie recommendations (e.g., "I want to receive accurate movie recommendations," α = .69, *M* = 5.85, *SD* = 1.17), (b) having fun (e.g., "I like to rate movies," α = .87, *M* = 3.92, *SD* = 1.82), and (c) connecting with other users and expressing oneself (e.g., "I like to share my opinions with other people," α = .91, *M* = 3.24, *SD* = 1.55). We refer to these as *utilitarian, fun*, and *social/expressive* reasons. Utilitarian reasons were modestly related to fun (r = .31, $p < .001$) and social/expressive reasons (r = .26, $p < .001$); fun and social/expressive reasons were highly correlated (r = .64, $p < .001$). Utilitarian reasons for joining were more common (*M* = 5.85) than fun (*M* = 3.92) and social/expressive (*M* = 3.24) reasons ($F(2,3886) = 4759, p < .001$).

MovieLens Behavioral Indicators

We analyzed the behavior of users for their first three months of MovieLens membership. We consider this sufficient time to understand the range of actions MovieLens provides. We studied the following specific behaviors: (1) logging into MovieLens (*M* = 3.5 , *SD* = 9.0), (2) rating movies (*M* = 70.3 , *SD* = 210.6), (3) editing movie descriptions (1% of users edited a movie), (4) applying tags to movies (*M* = 1.9 , *SD* = 23.5), (5) voting on the quality of previously applied tags (*M* = 2.2 , *SD* = 20.0), (6) sharing ratings with others (76% of users share ratings), (7) adding other users as "buddies" (3% of users had a buddy), (8) editing one's user profile (3% of users edited their profile), (9) visiting the Q&A forum (*M* = 2.8 , *SD* = 27.2), and (10) visiting the volunteer center (3% of users visited the volunteer center).

For clarity of analysis and ease of presentation, we group these behaviors into three clusters:

Basic. These behaviors are either required (logging in) or essential to the purpose of the community. Rating movies is the one truly essential behavior because you cannot join MovieLens and get recommendations without rating at least 15 movies. Logging into MovieLens and rating movies were highly positively correlated (r = .59, $p < .001$).

Discretionary. These behaviors are not required and are not necessary to use the site, but are still closely related to the community purpose, which for MovieLens is learning and thinking about movies. We therefore put editing movies, applying tags to movies, and voting on tags in this cluster. Editing a movie was positively related to tagging movies (r = .23, $p < .001$) and voting on tags (r = .16, $p < .001$); tagging movies and voting on tags were highly positively correlated (r = .49, $p < .001$).

Social/Community. The final cluster consists of behaviors that are less closely related to the core purpose of the site, but are more social and community oriented (rather than oriented on individual benefits). We include sharing one's ratings, adding buddies, editing one's user profile, using the Q&A forum, and going to the volunteer center in this cluster. Sharing ratings was positively correlated with having a buddy (r = .06, $p < .001$), editing one's profile (r = .08, $p < .001$), visiting the forums (r = .08, $p < .001$), and visiting the volunteer center (r = .06, $p < .001$). Having a buddy was positively correlated with editing one's profile (r = .17, $p < .001$), visiting the forums (r = .21, $p < .001$), and visiting the volunteer center (r = .13, $p < .001$). Editing one's profile was positively correlated with visiting the forums (r = .24, $p < .001$) and the volunteer center (r = .31, $p < .001$). Visiting the forums was positively related to visiting the volunteer center (r = .28, $p < .001$).

We make no large claims for this categorization. Its purpose is simply to help us organize and present our results, and we analyze each behavior individually. We think it has some generality (e.g., to sites whose primary purpose is obtaining information and that also have a social component), but exploring its scope is beyond the concerns of this paper.

ANALYSIS AND SUMMARY OF RESULTS

We did two classes of analyses to assess how the various motivations are associated with and predict user behavior. We first computed correlations to provide an overview of the bivariate relations between predictors and behavioral outcomes of interest (see Table 1). We then did a set of regressions to investigate these relationships more deeply (see Table 2). Table 2 groups the results of three separate sets of regressions, one for Community-specific Motivations, one for General Volunteer Motivations, and one for Pro-Social Behavioral History. Continuous criterion variables (e.g., counts of logins, ratings, and tags) were log transformed to correct for outliers and skewness. Ordinary least squares regression was used when the criterion variable was continuous and logistic regression was used when the criterion variable was dichotomous. In Table 2, overall model R^2 values are reported for each regression analysis. Standardized beta weights are reported for continuous variables, whereas odds ratios are reported for dichotomous variables. An odds ratio greater than 1 indicates that the behavior becomes more likely as the predictor increases, and an odds ratio less than 1 indicates that the behavior becomes less likely as the predictor increases.

	Basic Behaviors		Discretionary Behaviors			Social/Other-Oriented Behaviors				
	Logins	Ratings	Movie Edits	Tags	Tag Votes	Shares Ratings	Has a Buddy	Profile Edits	Forum Visits	Volunteer Visits
Community-specific Motivations										
Utilitarian	.11***	.12***	.02	.06***	.05**	.08***	.01	.03^	.09***	.02

Fun	.08***	.14***	.001	.07***	.08***	.19***	.04*	.07***	.11***	.04*
Social/Expressive	.05**	.04*	.02	.04*	.05*	.30***	.07***	.08***	.07***	.04*
General Volunteer Motivations										
Other-oriented	-.005	.01	-.01	.01	-.01	.09***	-.03	.03	.01	.002
Self-oriented	-.06**	-.06**	.004	-.02	-.04	.09***	-.03	-.005	-.04*	-.01
Pro-Social Behavioral History										
Volunteer History	.02	.04	.07**	.02	.03	.03	-.02	-.02	.02	.01
Altruistic Behavior	-.08**	-.11***	-.02	-.07**	-.05*	.03	-.01	.00	-.09***	-.05*
Community Involvement	.06*	.05*	-.01	.05	.04	.06*	.04	.06*	.07**	.01

Table 1: Correlations between different classes of motivation and clusters of behaviors. Logins, Ratings, Forum Visits, Tags, and Tag Votes are log transformed. Shares Ratings, Has a Buddy, Profile Edits, Volunteer Visits, and Movie Edits are dichotomous. Key to significance: ^ p < .10, * p < .05, ** p < .01, *** p < .001.

General notes. The reader might notice that the effect sizes in Tables 1 and 2 are fairly low even when the p-values indicate a significant relationship between a motivational factor and a behavior. However, as Rosnow and Rosenthal [28] have argued, a small effect can have a powerful impact on outcomes over time, especially in the aggregate. Further, since the behaviors we are predicting are (somewhat or very) rare, small effect sizes are to be expected. Additionally, the large number of analyses conducted arguably increases the likelihood of type I error. As such, the significance levels for the correlation table should be interpreted with caution. Furthermore, to preserve a true family-wise type I error rate of .05 for statistical significance and .10 for marginal significance, a Holm's procedure was employed for each family of regression analyses [1]. That is, each family of predictors was treated separately and a Holm's correction was made within the community specific motivations analyses, the VFI analyses, and the pro-social history analyses.

	Basic Behaviors		Discretionary Behaviors			Social/Other-Oriented Behaviors				
	Logins	Ratings	Movie Edits	Tags	Tag Votes	Shares Ratings	Has a Buddy	Profile Edits	Forum Visits	Volunteer Visits
Community-specific Motivations										
(*n*=3869)	R^2=.01	R^2=.03	R^2=.01	R^2=.01	R^2=.01	R^2=.14	R^2=.02	R^2=.03	R^2=.02	R^2=.01
Utilitarian	.10***	.09***	1.28	.05^	.03	1.01	.95	1.03	.06**	1.05
Fun	.05	.19***	.85	.06^	.08**	.98	.98	1.13	.08**	1.08
Social/Expressive	-.01	-.10***	1.25	-.01	-.009	1.71***	1.30*	1.22	.003	1.08
General Volunteer Motivations										
(*n*=2295)	R^2=.01	R^2=.01	R^2=.01	R^2=.002	R^2=.003	R^2=.01	R^2=.004	R^2=.01	R^2=.01	R^2=.003
Other-oriented	.11*	.14***	.80	.06	.05	1.09	.97	1.24	.12**	1.12
Self-oriented	-.15***	-.16***	1.26	-.07	-.08	1.07	.91	.82	-.14***	.85
Pro-Social Behavioral History										
(*n*=1643)	R^2=.01	R^2=.02	R^2=.03	R^2=.01	R^2=.01	R^2=.01	R^2=.01	R^2=.01	R^2=.01	R^2=.01
Volunteer History	.02	.03	1.05^	.01	.03	1.01	.97	.97	.01	1.01
Altruistic Behavior	-.08*	-.11***	.85	-.07*	-.05	1.07	.98	1.01	-.09**	.80^
Community Involvement	.06	.05	.91	.04	.03	1.05	1.09	1.11	.07^	1.02

Table 2. Using multiple regressions to evaluate how different classes of motivation predict MovieLens behaviors. Coefficients are standardized beta weights for continuous dependent variables and odds ratios for dichotomous variables.
Key to significance: ^ p < .10, * p < .05, ** p < .01, *** p < .001, using a Holm's correction for multiple tests.

General Volunteer Motives

Tables 1 and 2 show that the self- and other-oriented motives from the Volunteer Functions Inventory were related to specific MovieLens behaviors. As a reminder, the other-oriented motive is defined as volunteering to learn about or benefit others while the self-oriented motive is defined as volunteering to gain benefits for the self (e.g., friends, skills, or mood enhancement). Table 1 shows that the other-oriented motive was modestly positively correlated with sharing ratings (r = .09, p <.001). The self-oriented motive was modestly positively correlated with sharing ratings (r = .09, p <.001), but was negatively correlated with logins (r = -.06, p <.01), ratings (r = -.06, p<.01), and forum visits (r = -.04, p <.01). The regressions reported in Table 2 provide a better understanding of the unique predictive power of self- versus other-oriented volunteer motives by considering the motives together and controlling for inflated type 1 error. Other-oriented motivation positively predicted the basic MovieLens behaviors of logging in (β = .11, p <.05) and rating movies (β = .14, p <.01), as well as participating in the Q&A forum (β = .12, p <.01). Conversely, self-oriented volunteer motivation negatively predicted those same behaviors (β's = -.15, -.16, -14, p's < .001).

Pro-Social Behavioral History

Our measures of pro-social behavioral history were volunteer history, altruistic behavior, and community involvement. Table 1 shows that volunteer history was modestly positively correlated with movie edits (r = .09, p <.01). Altruistic behavior was negatively correlated with logins (r = -.08, p <.01), ratings (r = -.11, p <.001), tag applications (r = -.07, p <.01) and votes (r = -.05, p <.05), forum visits (r = -.09, p <.001), and visits to the volunteer center (r = -.05, p <.05). Community involvement was positively associated with logins (r = .06, p <.05), ratings (r = .05, p <.05), sharing ratings (r = .06, p <.05), profile edits (r = .06, p <.05), and visits to the Q&A forum (r = .07, p <.01). As with the general volunteer motivations, the regressions in Table 2 provide a clearer picture of the unique associations of pro-social history variables with MovieLens behaviors. Volunteer history positively predicted editing movies (OR = 1.05, p <.10). Community involvement positively predicted Q&A forum visits (β = .07, p <.10). Conversely, altruistic behaviors negatively predicted logins (β = -.08, p <.05), ratings (β = -.11, p <.001), tag applications (β = -.07, p <.05), forum visits (β = -.09, p <.01), and visits to the volunteer center (OR = .80, p <.10).

Community-specific Motivations

As discussed above, a factor analysis revealed three community-specific motivations to join MovieLens: (a) *utilitarian* (e.g., getting accurate movie recommendations) (b) *fun*, and (c) *social/expressive* (i.e., connecting with other users and expressing one's opinions). Table 1 revealed all three community-specific motivations were positively associated with most MovieLens behaviors, with a few exceptions. Movie edits was not associated with any community-specific motivation, and the utilitarian motive was not associated with having a buddy nor volunteer center visits. The Table 2 regressions, which consider these predictors together and control for inflated Type 1 error, show that these community-specific factors differentially predict MovieLens behaviors. Utilitarian reasons positively predicted logins (β = .10, p <.001), ratings (β = .09, p<.001), tag applications (β = .05, p <.10), and forum visits (β = .06, p <.05). Fun-related reasons positively predicted ratings (β = .19, p <.001), tag applications (β = .06, p <.10) and votes (β = .08, p <.01), and forum visits (β = .08, p <.01). Finally, social/expressive reasons negatively predicted ratings (β = -.10, p <.001), but positively predicted having a buddy (OR = 1.30, p <.05) and sharing ratings (OR = 1.71, p <.001).

DISCUSSION AND IMPLICATIONS

Our findings shed light on our guiding questions: Can we predict who will participate in an online community? What activities are specific individuals most likely to engage in? We now summarize and interpret our findings and draw out some implications for design.

Predicting Participation

Both general and community-specific motives predicted the most basic form of participation, simply logging in. Specifically, the two general VFI motives, a personal history of altruistic behavior, and the community-specific motive of receiving accurate recommendations each predicted logging into the site. Interestingly, other-oriented volunteer motivation predicted more logins, whereas self- oriented volunteer motivation and altruistic behavior negatively predicted logins.

Predicting Specific Patterns of Participation

Consistent with functional theorizing, we found that different motivations, and different histories of pro-social behavior, led to different patterns of behavior. We interpret the findings, first considering only positive predictions and organizing the discussion around the three classes of predictors:

- General motivations for engaging in volunteer activities (e.g., to understand and learn about the world),
- Pro-social behavioral history (e.g., past volunteer behaviors), and
- Specific motivations for joining the community (e.g., to get movie recommendations or to have fun).

General Volunteer Motives. People's volunteer motivations were related to general participation in MovieLens. Specifically, the other-oriented motivation predicted more basic engagement in MovieLens through returning to the site and rating movies as well as connecting with other users via the Q&A forums. The Q&A forums allow users to ask/answer questions for other users about the site or movies. It is possible then that some people use MovieLens and the Q&A forums to help satisfy an other-oriented motivation to volunteer. That is, users may come to MovieLens and use the forums partially to connect with and help others. This finding is consistent with functionalist theory and research that finds that people prefer and are more likely to engage in behaviors if those behaviors match their specific volunteer motivations [12].

Pro-Social Behavioral History. Users' pro-social behavioral histories also were related to specific patterns of behavior in MovieLens. People with more volunteer experience were more likely to edit movies. Editing movies is a task similar to editing a Wikipedia page and requires more effort and thought than other behaviors on MovieLens. Indeed, this behavior is non-compulsory and other-oriented. The main objective is improving the MovieLens experience for all users. This is similar to traditional offline volunteering where people engage in effortful, non-compulsory behaviors for the benefit of others. Thus, past volunteerism may be a useful predictor of who will go "above and beyond" in online communities similar to MovieLens.

Likewise, people with higher community involvement were more likely to invest effort in MovieLens, notably the discretionary and other-oriented behavior of visiting the Q&A forums. These findings suggest that people who see themselves with higher general community involvement may be more likely to form a sense of community towards MovieLens and engage in behaviors that go beyond just rating movies. This complements findings that show a psychological sense of community to be an important predictor of volunteer behavior [22]. That is, it seems reasonable that those who are more oriented towards communities in general might be more likely to engage with MovieLens as a community and as a result be more likely to engage in discretionary behavior in that community. In future research, it will be important to determine which users develop a sense of community regarding MovieLens and if this sense of community predicts behavioral engagement.

Community-Specific Motives. Different community-specific reasons for joining MovieLens predicted different patterns of behavior. Utilitarian and fun reasons for joining predicted engaging in the basic behavior of rating movies, whereas social/expressive reasons predicted connecting and sharing with others. Interestingly, people with a greater desire to connect with other users and to express themselves were less likely to engage in the most basic behavior of rating movies. However, these users appeared able to find other behaviors, such as finding a buddy and sharing their ratings with others, which did match their reasons for joining. Although we did not measure users' satisfaction with their experience, prior research on volunteerism suggests that people whose experiences fulfill their motivations are more satisfied and more likely to continue participation in the long term [6]. In future research, it will be important to assess the motivations and experiences of established users as a way to understand and affect rates of attrition and continued participation.

One Site Does Not Fit All

We also found that certain motives actually led to less participation in MovieLens. We will now consider this in some detail.

Our results suggest that MovieLens may not be a place to satisfy certain types of motives. For example, users high in self-oriented motivation to volunteer were less likely to login to MovieLens, rate movies, or visit the Q&A forums. It is possible these users did not perceive MovieLens or using the Q&A forums as ways to satisfy their more self-directed motivation to volunteer. Indeed it may be that these users are choosing other activities to fulfill this motivation; for example, the self-oriented motive of career-building is prominent for open source software participation [13].

We also found that different aspects of pro-social behavioral history predicted different kinds of activities. While volunteer history and community involvement generally led to increased participation, greater self-reported altruistic behavior led to lower levels of several behaviors we tracked. It may seem contradictory that different measures of prior pro-social behavior would differentially predict MovieLens behaviors. However, careful consideration of how volunteerism and everyday altruistic behaviors differ helps explain these findings. While both volunteering and altruistic behavior benefit others, volunteering and altruistic behavior are distinct and were not correlated in our study.

Altruistic behaviors (as measured by our instrument) explicitly require face-to-face interaction, but may not require great effort (e.g., giving up a seat on a bus). Volunteering, on the other hand, may not require social interaction, but often requires a substantial commitment of both time and effort [26]. Indeed, research on informal helping and volunteerism finds that although these are similar forms of pro-social behavior, they are not identical. For example, helpfulness is an important predictor of person-focused pro-social behavior but not task-oriented pro-social behavior [9]. Consistent with this finding, our research suggests that those who are generally more helpful in their day-to-day interactions are not more likely to engage in volunteer-like behavior in sites like MovieLens. It may be that volunteering in MovieLens is more task-oriented and that the kind of active helpfulness captured by our altruistic behavior measure requires a social contract that only actual interaction can provide. At best, MovieLens provides limited ways for users to help each other.

Implication: Personalized Community Interface. Many new users of MovieLens and other similar sites do not connect with the community, participate little, and eventually drop out. Most online communities are complex and users may find that the opportunities these communities afford do not suit their motivations. Our findings suggest that we can identify the features of a site most likely to appeal to individual users. Community designers can tailor the interface to highlight for a user features most likely to appeal to the user, thus increasing retention and participation. Moreover, communities may want to actively seek new members with prior behavioral histories that correlate with increased participation in activities that benefit the entire community.

Implication: New Features to Attract New Users. We have seen that MovieLens does not satisfy a number of possible motivations. Several types of new features have the potential to attract and retain users with these motivations. For example, enhanced opportunities to help other users directly, e.g., by directly recommending movies for them to view, and enhanced social interaction (say, Facebook-style social networking) might satisfy the community-specific social motive or attract users who engage in altruistic behaviors offline.

Implication: Recommender System. Given our finding that other-oriented volunteer motives and community-specific social motives predict MovieLens behaviors, connecting users to each other may help increase engagement with MovieLens. As a part of the basic MovieLens experience of rating movies, users provide a great deal of information about their preferences. Using this information, the MovieLens system could recommend similar users to connect with as buddies. Such recommendation systems have been shown to be effective at increasing engagement in socially oriented sites [10].

Implication: An Efficient Survey. The survey we administered to new MovieLens users was not terribly long: it typically took about 12 minutes to complete. Nonetheless, we still think the survey must be streamlined significantly before it could be deployed permanently in a site like MovieLens. Given our findings, the most promising route would be to ask just about Community Involvement, Volunteer History, Utilitarian and Social/Expressive motives for joining MovieLens, and the general volunteer motives. Such a survey could be completed in less than 5 minutes.

SUMMARY

We identified three classes of motivations that we thought might impact the amount and type of participation in the online community of MovieLens. We developed and administered a survey to new MovieLens users to assess these motivations. We then analyzed behavioral data to determine the power of the motives for predicting behavior. We found a number of interesting relationships, discussed their meaning, and drew several implications for design that we believe can be generalized across a range of online communities.

ACKNOWLEDGMENTS

We are grateful to the MovieLens users who took our survey and to Rich Davies and Michael Ludwig for invaluable programming support. This work was supported in part by NSF Grant IIS-0808692.

REFERENCES

1. Aickin, M., and Gensler H. Adjusting for multiple testing when reporting research results: The Bonferroni vs. Holm methods. *American Journal of Public Health 86,* 5 (1992), 628-629.
2. Bateman, P. J., Gray, P. H., and Butler, B. S. The impact of community commitment on participation in online communities. *Information Systems Research: isre.1090.0265,* (2010).
3. Baumeister, R. F., Vohs, K. D., and Funder, D. C. Psychology as the science of self-reports and finger movements: Or, whatever happened to actual behavior? *Perspectives on Psychological Science 2,* 4 (2007), 396-403.
4. Butler, B. S. Membership size, communication activity, and sustainability: A resource-based model of online social structures. *Information Systems Research 12,* 4 (2001), 346-362.
5. Butler, B. S., Sproull, L., Kiesler, S., and Kraut, R. E. Community effort in online groups: Who does the work and why? *Leadership at a Distance.* S. Weisband and L. Atwater, Eds., Lawrence Erlbaum Associates, Mahwah, NJ (2007).
6. Clary, E. G., Snyder, M., Ridge, R. D., Copeland, J., Stukas, A. A., Haugen, J., and Miene, P. Understanding and assessing the motivations of volunteers: A functional approach. *Journal of Personality and Social Psychology 74,* 6 (1998), 1516-1530.
7. Cosley, D., Frankowski, D., Terveen, L., and Riedl, J. Using intelligent task routing and contribution review to help communities build artifacts of lasting value. In *Proceedings of CHI 2006.*
8. Define Gender Gap? Look up Wikipedia's Contributor List. http://www.nytimes.com/2011/01/31/business/media/31link.html
9. Finkelstein, M. A., and Brannick, M. T. Applying theories of institutional helping to informal volunteering: Motives, role identity, and prosocial personality. *Social Behavior and Personality 35,* (2007), 101-114.

10. Freyne, J., Jacovi, M., Guy, I., and Geyer, W. Increasing engagement through early recommender intervention. *In Proceedings of Recommender Systems 2009.*
11. Houle, B. J., Sagarin, B. J., and Kaplan, M. F. A functional approach to volunteerism: Do volunteer motives predict task preference? *Basic and Applied Social Psychology 27*, (2009), 337-344.
12. Independent Sector *Giving and volunteering in the United States*. Washington D.C. (2001).
13. Lakhani, K., and Wolf, R. Why hackers do what they do: Understanding motivation and effort in free/open source software projects. *Perspectives in Free and Open Source Software*, MIT Technical Report. J. Feller, B. Fitzgerald, S. Hissam, and K. Lakhani, Eds. MIT Press, Cambridge and London (2005).
14. Lam, S. K., Uduwage, A., Dong, Z., Sen, S., Musicant, D. R., Terveen, L., and Riedl, J. WP: Clubhouse? An exploration of Wikipedia's gender imbalance. In *Proceedings of Wikisym 2011.*
15. Lampe, C., Wash, R., Velasquez, A., and Ozkaya, E. Motivations to participate in online communities. In *Proceedings of CHI 2010.*
16. Ling, K., Beenen, G., Ludford, P., Wang, X., Chang, K., Li, X., Cosley, D., Frankowski, D., Terveen, L., Rashid, A. M., Resnick, P., and Kraut, R. Using social psychology to motivate contributions to online communities. *Journal of Computer-Mediated Communication, 10,* 4 (2005), 10.
17. Mannino, C., and Snyder, M. Unpublished raw data, (2010).
18. Masli, M., Priedhorsky, R., and Terveen, L. Task specialization in social production communities: The case of geographic volunteer work. In *Proceedings of ICWSM 2011.*
19. Nov, O. What motivates Wikipedians? *Communications of the ACM 50*, 11 (2005), 60-64.
20. Omoto, A. M., and Snyder, M. Sustained helping without obligation: Motivation, longevity of service, and perceived attitude change among AIDS volunteers. *Journal of Personality and Social Psychology 68*, 4 (1995), 671-686.
21. Omoto, A., Snyder, M., and Martino, S. Volunteerism and the life course: Investigating age-related agendas for action. *Basic and Applied Social Psychology 22*, 3 (2000), 181-197.
22. Omoto, A. M., and Snyder, M. Considerations of community: The context and process of volunteerism. *American Behavioral Scientist 45*, 5 (2002), 846-867.
23. Oreg, S., and Nov, O. Exploring motivations for contributing to open source initiatives: The roles of contribution context and personal values. *Computers in Human Behavior 24*, 5 (2008), 2055-2073.
24. Ortega, F., Gonzalez-Barahona, J. M., and Robles, G. On the inequality of contributions to Wikipedia. In *Proceedings of HICSS 2008.*
25. Panciera, K., Halfaker, A., and Terveen, L. Wikipedians are born, not made: A study of power editors on Wikipedia. In *Proceedings of Group 2009.*
26. Penner, L. Dispositional and organizational influences on sustained volunteerism: An interactionist perspective.
27. Ridings, C. M., and Gefen, D. Virtual community attraction: Why people hang out online. *Journal of Computer-Mediated Communication 10*, 1(2004).
28. Rosnow, R. L., and Rosenthal, R. Statistical procedures and the justification of knowledge in psychological science. *American Psychologist 44*, 10, (1989), 1276-1284.
29. Rushton, J. P., Chrisjohn, R. D. and Fekken, G. C. The altruistic personality and the self-report altruism scale. *Personality and Individual Differences 2*, (1981), 293-302.
30. Silverberg, K. E. Understanding American parks and recreation volunteers utilizing a functionalist perspective. *Volunteering as Leisure/Leisure as Volunteering: An International Assessment.* S. Arai and J. Benoit, Eds. CAB International, Willingsford, Oxfordshire, UK, (2004), 87-101.
31. Snyder, M. Basic research and practical problems: The promise of a "functional" personality and social psychology. *Personality and Social Psychology Bulletin 19*, 3 (1993), 251-264.
32. Snyder, M., and Cantor, N. Understanding personality and social behavior: A functionalist strategy. *The Handbook of Social Psychology.* D. T. Gilbert, S. T. Fiske, and G. Lindzey, Eds. McGraw Hill, New York (1998), 635-679.
33. Snyder, M., and Omoto, A. M. Volunteerism: Social issues perspectives and social policy implications. *Social Issues and Policy Review 2,* 1 (2008), 1-36.
34. Vassileva, J. Motivating participation in peer to peer communities. *Engineering Societies in the Agents World III, Lecture Notes in Computer Science 2577.* P. Pett., R. Tolksdorf, and F. Zambonelli, Eds. Springer, Berlin / Heidelberg (2003), 141-155.
35. Voss, J. Measuring Wikipedia. In *Proc. of the 10th International Conference of the International Society for Scientometrics and Infometrics 2005.*
36. Wasko, M. L., and Faraj, S. Why should I share? Examining social capital and knowledge contribution in electronic networks of practice. *MIS Quarterly 29,* 1 (2005), 35-57.
37. Welser, H., Gleave, E., Fischer, D. and Smith, M. Visualizing the structure of social roles in online discussion groups. *Journal of Social Structure 8*, 2 (2007), 1-32.
38. Wikipedia. For example, 1487 articles were tagged as "needing expansion" in September 2010 alone. See http://en.wikipedia.org/wiki/Category: Articles_ to_be_expanded_from_September_2010.
39. Wilson, J. Volunteering. *Annual Review of Sociology 26,* (2000) 215-240.

Recommending Routes in the Context of Bicycling: Algorithms, Evaluation, and the Value of Personalization

Reid Priedhorsky,* David Pitchford,† Shilad Sen,‡ Loren Terveen†

*IBM Watson Research Center
Cambridge, MA, USA
reid@reidster.net

‡Macalester College
St. Paul, MN, USA
ssen@macalester.edu

†University of Minnesota
Minneapolis, MN, USA
{pitch006,terve002}@umn.edu

ABSTRACT
Users have come to rely on automated route finding services for driving, public transit, walking, and bicycling. Current state of the art route finding algorithms typically rely on objective factors like time and distance; they do not consider subjective preferences that also influence route quality. This paper addresses that need. We introduce a new framework for evaluating edge rating prediction techniques in transportation networks and use it to explore ten families of prediction algorithms in Cyclopath, a geographic wiki that provides route finding services for bicyclists. Overall, we find that personalized algorithms predict more accurately than non-personalized ones, and we identify two algorithms with low error and excellent coverage, one of which is simple enough to be implemented in thin clients like web browsers. These results suggest that routing systems can generate better routes by collecting and analyzing users' subjective preferences.

Author Keywords
geographic recommenders, geowikis, recommender systems, route finding

ACM Classification Keywords
H.5.3 Group and Organization Interfaces: Collaborative computing, computer supported cooperative work

General Terms
Algorithms, Human Factors

INTRODUCTION
Modern websites frequently personalize users' online experiences. For example, Amazon and Netflix depend on recommender systems to help users find books and movies, Google can display a personalized selection of news stories [8], and social networking sites use personalized algorithms to help users make new connections [7]. This paper explores whether and how personalization can improve route finding, doing so in the context of Cyclopath, a route finding service for bicyclists in the Minneapolis/St. Paul metro area of Minnesota.

Rather than returning a route that is optimal according to some objective metric like time or distance, a personalized route finding system returns a route which is optimized to meet the personal preferences of the user who requested it. For example, one person might prefer slightly longer routes (in time or distance) if they are scenic, while another might prefer the opposite tradeoff – i.e., the quality of a route can be influenced by users' *subjective preferences*. This notion is supported by prior work in the automobile and wheelchair domains [4, 15, 21]. In addition, during the design of Cyclopath, users reported a desire for personalization [24, 25].

All but the most prolific users express preferences for only a tiny fraction of the transportation network. Because route finding algorithms such as A* require information about the entire network, systems that personalize routes must *infer* a user's preferences for the bulk of the edges in the network. This paper explores algorithms for making these inferences by studying the following questions:

1. Which preference prediction algorithms have both good accuracy and good coverage?
2. Do *personalized* route finding algorithms that account for subjective user preferences yield better routes than objective algorithms that do not?

Three key characteristics of route finding domains provide a novel challenge for personalization: (a) the structure of the rating datasets are different (items dramatically outnumber users rather than the other way around, and ratings are much sparser); (b) items have structured relationships and the output is a sequence of items (a route); and (c) 100% coverage is essential (no location pairs can be unrouteable due to lack of rating data).

This paper seeks to close this gap. We introduce a three-stage framework for evaluating personalization in the context of route finding and evaluate 10 families of algorithms using this framework.

We first survey related work and evidence suggesting the need for personalized routing. We then describe our evaluation framework, present the results of the algorithms we tested under that framework, and close with a summary and directions for future work.

RELATED WORK
Recommender systems
These systems use algorithms that detect patterns in users' past preferences to predict their future preferences. *Collaborative filtering* approaches include user-based [27] and item-

based [30] algorithms, with later refinements such as dimensionality reduction using singular value decomposition [11] and *ensemble recommenders* which combine the output of multiple algorithms [5]. While collaborative filtering leverages patterns among users' preferences for items, some recommender systems also use *content-based* algorithms [2] that leverage patterns in the attributes of items.

More recently, researchers have begun to explore geographically aware recommender systems. Some systems recommend items near a user's current or future location, such as restaurants [23, 34] or tourist destinations [1, 28]. Others assume that a user's location contains preference information. For example, Li et al. found that similarity of users' location histories predicts social tie strength [19]. Zheng et al.'s GeoLife2 social networking system does both, drawing on location to infer user similarity and recommending social activities between potential friends who are near each other [35]. Our work resembles these types of systems in that it predicts user satisfaction for edges in the transportation network, but we go beyond prior work to explore how these individual predictions affect their assembly into a complete route.

Finally, researchers have also studied recommending collections of items. Ziegler et al. showed that user satisfaction with a set of recommended items was enhanced when diversity of items within the set was considered, rather than simply minimizing the total prediction error [36]. Felfernig et al. explored recommending product configurations, where different components required or conflicted with other components [10]. Our work builds upon these ideas by addressing recommendation of large collection of items (the sequence of edges which forms a route) and the new types of structure relevant to route finding applications.

Route finding

Modern route finding systems are supported by a large scholarly literature. For example, geographers have explored the effects of transportation on human beings: the meaning of mobility and distance, economic and political influences, and where people choose to live and travel within their communities [29]. Computer scientists have studied the technical aspects of route finding, exploring issues like algorithm performance and scalability [9], uncertain costs [16], and multimodal routing (e.g., trips by both car and bus) [6].

Researchers have also begun to explore *personalized* routing. Bederson et al. motivate personalization by pointing out the need for "subjective human experience" in route finding, proposing a system for recording such experiences [4]. Personalized algorithms that accommodate these differences in routing preferences have been shown to outperform traditional routing algorithms. The OurWay system created by Holone et al. asked nine users in wheelchairs to rate route segments in order to receive personalized route recommendations, and these outperformed traditional algorithms [15]. McGinty and Smith used case-based reasoning to find a route by drawing on data from other users with similar route preferences [21].

Our work improves upon these personalized routing ideas in two ways: we draw upon a much larger dataset from a mature production route finding system, and we apply established techniques from the machine learning and recommender systems communities.

Route finding for cyclists

There are numerous websites that address various aspects of bicycle route finding. Gmaps Pedometer,[1] Bikely,[2] and others let users manually define and share routes. Wayfaring[3] enables collaborative editing of routes and places of interest. Open Cycle Map[4] is a cyclist-focused rendering of Open Street Map data. A few offer automatic route finding, such as YTV Journey Planner for Cycling[5] and Fietsrouteplanner,[6] and others offer automatic route finding based on Open Street Map user-contributed data, such as the Cambridge Cycling Campaign's "journey planner" for cyclists.[7] Biketastic[8] is a research system which uses a mobile phone application to share information about rides, collected using both built-in sensors (pavement roughness, noise level) and user contributions (photos, videos, and text descriptions) [26]. Finally, Google recently introduced bicycle route finding in Google Maps for many American cities [18]. This was a key advance for cyclists across the country, most of whom previously had no online bicycling map or automated route finding at all.

A variety of metrics for computing the bikeability of streets exist, but they are generally impractical because they require an unrealistically large number of attributes for each street; for example, Sorton's bicycle stress level [33] requires 6 to 14, and an analysis at Macalester College [20] identified 16. Cyclopath currently uses a metric developed by the Chicagoland Bicycle Federation [3], which requires 4 attributes; of these, we have moderately complete data for only 3 (speed limit, daily traffic volume, and shoulder width) and we must estimate the last one (lane width).

Many of these systems let users express preferences each time a route search is initiated. However, none support rich user profiles that capture preferences about specific streets and trails. We take advantage of such preference data in Cyclopath to explore personalized route finding algorithms, developing a systematic framework for evaluating route finding algorithms and using that framework to draw empirical conclusions about specific algorithms.

ROUTING AND PERSONALIZATION

Route finding in Cyclopath, at a high level, works as follows.[9] The streets and trails traveled by cyclists form a graph, where street intersections are nodes and the city blocks between them are edges; we call this graph the *transportation network*. Figure 1 shows a small portion of this network as it is displayed in the web application, along with the underlying graph representation.

[1] http://gmap-pedometer.com
[2] http://www.bikely.com
[3] http://wayfaring.com
[4] http://opencyclemap.org
[5] http://kevytliikenne.ytv.fi/?lang=en
[6] http://fietsersbond.nl/fietsrouteplanner/
[7] http://www.camcycle.org.uk/map/route/
[8] http://biketastic.com
[9] Technical details are available by consulting the Cyclopath source code: http://cyclopath.org/wiki/Tech:Source_Code.

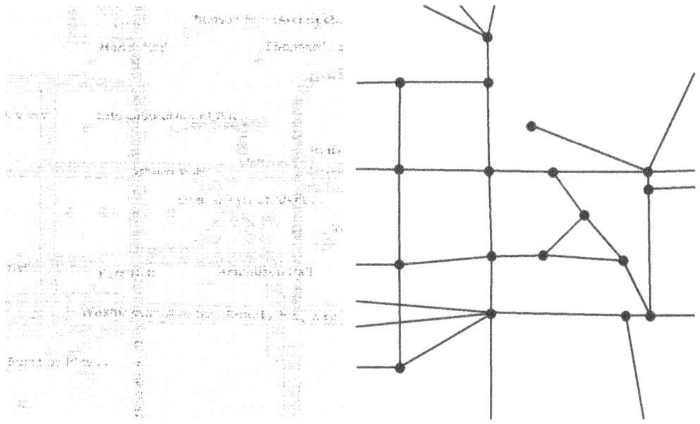

Figure 1. A portion of the Cyclopath web map covering the University of Minnesota campus (left) and its representation as a graph (right).

Cyclopath users can rate the subjective *bikeability* of the graph on an edge-by-edge basis, on a five-level scale from "impassable" through "excellent". We provide user interface support to make it easy to enter many ratings at once. For the purposes of analysis, we treat bikeability as a number ranging from 0 (impassable) to 4 (excellent).

When searching for a route, a user can also express preferences for that particular search, making both a tradeoff between higher bikeability and shorter distance as well as specifying bikeability penalties and bonuses for tags that edges might have (e.g., *bumpy* or *caution with merging*).

These notions are brought together as follows. Cyclopath uses A* search [14] to compute the minimum-cost route through the transportation network. In addition to small costs for traversing notes, the weight of an edge is a function of that edge's bikeability score and the route search preferences. The challenge is thus to accurately estimate bikeability for each edge that A* might evaluate during its search (as all but the most prolific raters have actually rated only a tiny fraction of the edges in the graph).

Evidence for personalization

Several informal analyses of the Cyclopath ratings database suggest that personalized route finding would be useful. As of April 2011, Cyclopath had 68,274 ratings by 481 users on 35,608 edges, with a mean rating of 2.78 and standard deviation of 1.13; in MovieLens, a movie recommendation site operated by our research group, these statistics are 3.51 and 1.06, respectively (as of April 2010). Also, of the 110,671 instances when two users rated the same edge, they gave the same rating 53% of the time, disagreed by one star 34% of the time, and disagreed by two or more stars 13% of the time. In other words, nearly half the time, users disagree on the appropriate rating for an edge, and about one eighth of the time, this disagreement is at least two stars (the difference between "fair" and "excellent" or "poor" and "good").

Another way to quantify disagreement is: to what degree would different users' ratings actually lead to different decisions by the graph search algorithm? We explore this by examining the preference order of edges rather than actual rating values; the intuition is that even if two users give different ratings, but graph search would make the same choices regardless, the two users' ratings are effectively the same.

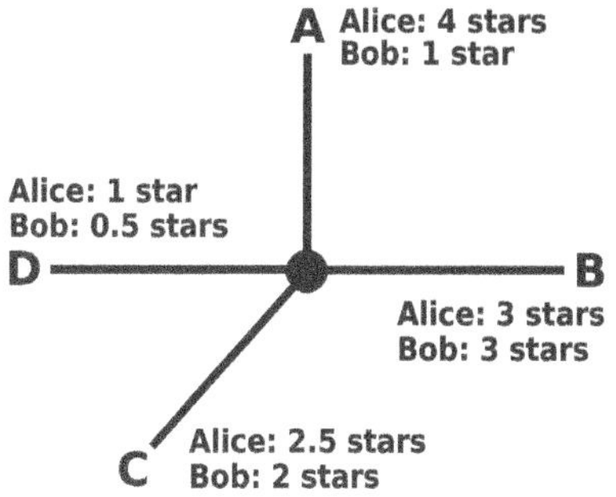

Figure 2. A hypothetical node in the transportation network. Bikeability ratings by two users are shown.

Figure 2 shows a hypothetical graph node with four adjacent edges, A through D, and bikeability ratings from two users, Alice and Bob. The predicted preference order of the four edges is ABCD according to Alice but BCAD according to Bob. For example, Edge B has the same rating (3 stars) from both users, but only for Alice is it the most preferred edge adjacent to this node.

This is relevant because graph search algorithms such as A* wander through a graph, choosing at each node the best edge to wander next. For example, if a graph search algorithm arrived at this node via Edge C, it would next choose Edge A if using Alice's bikeability ratings, but Edge B using Bob's ratings (assuming that other considerations such as edge length are the same).

Results of this analysis over Cyclopath ratings[10] are as follows. Given adjacent edges A and B and users U and W who have each rated both edges, in 87.3% of the 81,903 observations, U and W agree: either all four ratings were the same (84.7% of observations) or both users prefer A to B (2.6%). On the other hand, 12.7% of the time, they disagree; either U prefers A to B and W rates them equally (12.0%) or U prefers A to B but W prefers B to A (0.7%). At first glance, this result is cause for skepticism – users give a different preference order only one eighth of the time. However, the average computed route contains 76 edges, and the graph search to produce this average route evaluates thousands of edge pairs; together these results imply that each set of 23 edge pairs is 95% likely to contain a disagreement ($0.873^{23} = 0.044$). Thus, even this fairly low level of disagreement will result in graph searches that encounter many points of disagreement where the computed paths could diverge.

These three informal analyses suggest that route personalization is valuable. The remainder of this paper is a systematic evaluation of this hypothesis.

Challenges for personalization

As noted earlier, there are three core challenges in applying personalization techniques to route finding systems. First, the structure of the user/item rating matrix is less favorable. As noted in Table 1, when considering all edges (not just those that are rated), as is needed to address the first challenge, the Cyclopath dataset is 10-42 times more lopsided than active MovieLens or the Netflix Prize dataset [13], and in the opposite direction; for example, MovieLens has 7.6 users per

[10] This analysis uses ratings data as of April 2010.

Dataset		Users	Items	Aspect	Ratings	Sparsity
MovieLens		102,757	13,608	7.6 u/i	17,488,416	0.013
Netflix Prize		480,189	17,770	27 u/i	100,480,507	0.012
Cyclopath	rated edges	481	35,608	74 i/u	68,274	0.0040
	all edges		154,242	321 i/u		0.00092

Table 1. Descriptive statistics for MovieLens, Netflix Prize, and Cyclopath ratings datasets. We include only Cyclopath users who have made at least one rating, in order to permit comparison with other systems; for the same reason, we present the number of rated edges as well as the total number of edges in Cyclopath. The latter is of greater interest in our analysis due to the 100% coverage requirement.

item, but Cyclopath has 321 items per user. Furthermore, the Cyclopath dataset is 13 times sparser.

Second, both items and the output of the system have significant constraints. Items (edges) have highly structured relationships defined by the topology of the transportation network, and rather than outputting one or a few individual items, recommenders for route finding must produce a structured sequence of items – a route.

Finally, universal coverage is required. In contrast to systems that recommend products (e.g., 17% of movies in MovieLens are unrecommendable), graph search algorithms need edge weights for every edge in the graph in order to produce a path for arbitrary starting and ending points.[11]

EVALUATION FRAMEWORK

We propose the following basic structure for the design and evaluation of personalized routing systems. *Prediction algorithms* predict bikeability ratings for individual edges, which are then used by a graph search algorithm to compute the complete route. Our framework tests performance at three stages – individual edge rating predictions, node-level graph search decisions, and the final route – enabling analysis at each stage to see if differences between algorithms remain meaningful.

Stage 1: Predicting edge ratings

The goal of this stage is to assess the accuracy of edge rating predictions when compared against actual user ratings; it corresponds to the "predict" task in traditional recommender systems [31]. Here, items are the edges in the transportation network: given an edge and a user, predict the user's rating of that edge. The procedure is straightforward: (a) define and implement different prediction algorithms, (b) evaluate them using standard k-fold cross-validation, and (c) report coverage and error for each algorithm, using standard metrics like mean absolute error (MAE) and root mean squared error (RMSE).

Stage 2: Comparing node-level decisions

This stage considers whether edge weights created by different prediction algorithms would lead to different decisions by a graph search algorithm. Similarly to the discussion of user ratings above, the intuition is that even if Algorithm A has better accuracy than Algorithm B, but graph search would make the same decisions regardless, there is no effective difference between the two. It corresponds to the "recommend" task in traditional recommender systems [31], where a system tries to choose the best available item (e.g., "find me the movie I would most like"); the key difference is that in recommending routes, this decision is made thousands of times per high-level operation (find a route), rather than a few times (find a movie to watch).

We introduce a metric called *best edge agreement* (BEA) for this analysis: given two algorithms and a set of nodes, the BEA is the fraction of nodes where the two algorithms select (from the edges adjacent to the node) the same edge as best. This metric is hard to operationalize, however, because it requires both algorithms to predict *all* edges adjacent to a particular node in order to assess their BEA at that node; as we show below, many algorithms have poor coverage, so this requirement is often not met. Thus, we take a pairwise approach, introducing a variant metric, *pairwise best edge agreement* (PBEA): given two algorithms and a set of pairs of edges such that both edges (a) are adjacent to the same node and (b) have predictions from both algorithms, the PBEA is the percentage of pairs where both algorithms select the same edge as best.

PBEA can be used to estimate BEA. For example, suppose that Algorithm X's predictions for four edges adjacent to a node give preference order ABCD; in particular, Edge A has a higher predicted rating than B, C, and D. The probability that Algorithm Y chooses the same best edge (A) is the probability that its own rating prediction for Edge A is also higher than for the other three edges, i.e., Y must agree with X on the predicted preference order of three edge pairs: AB, AC, and AD. Assuming that edge predictions are independent,[12] the probability of the algorithms agreeing three times is the probability that they agree once raised to the third power: we estimate BEA on this four-edge node as PBEA cubed. Cyclopath nodes have on average 3.2 edges (excluding dead ends – nodes with degree 1 – which don't affect graph search decisions), so we estimate BEA $\approx$ PBEA$^{2.2}$ for this context.

Stage 3: Comparing paths

This stage evaluates how much *paths* produced with different prediction algorithms differ. The motivation is similar to

[11]To be pedantic, this is not strictly true. One need not predict *all* edge weights; rather, one must predict edge weights for all "important" edges – those which have a realistic chance of being considered for routes (not just included in the result). However, 100% coverage is achievable with good performance, as we elaborate below, and it is a simple way to meet this stricter criterion.

[12]This assumption is probably untrue – i.e., ratings of adjacent edges are probably correlated – so it's likely that this technique underestimates BEA. However, if we assume that the ratings of adjacent edges are positively (and not negatively) correlated, this underestimation is bounded, as the true BEA must then lie between PBEA and the estimated BEA.

Stage 2: even if different algorithms produce different low-level graph search decisions, if the resulting paths are the same or essentially the same, the algorithms are effectively equivalent. However, it differs from Stage 2 in two important ways. First, it requires a corpus of route searches to recompute. Second, only algorithms with 100% coverage can be tested, because now rating predictor and graph search algorithms are combined. As our results below show, often an ensemble predictor is needed, because there is a tradeoff between accuracy and coverage.

We next turn to our application of this framework, using data from Cyclopath to test several bikeability prediction algorithms and explore the value of personalized route finding.

ALGORITHMS TESTED

We tried 10 families of algorithms, which we divide into four classes: objective algorithms which do not consider user ratings, algorithms which average user ratings in simple ways, collaborative filtering algorithms, and machine learning algorithms.

"Objective" algorithms

These two algorithms, which make use of only edge attributes rather than ratings (i.e., objective rather than subjective data), represent the general approach of current state-of-the-art route finding.

We first consider *Objective-CBF*, a bikeability metric developed by the Chicagoland Bicycle Federation which takes into account speed limit, daily traffic volume, lane width, and shoulder width [3]. While simpler than other metrics created by the bicycling community, it is the only one we could find whose input attributes had sufficient coverage in Cyclopath, which is based on the best available data (and data availability for our area is typical for American cities). Our implementation has minor modifications to make it usable in Cyclopath, motivated by data availability, the first author's expertise as a bicyclist, and feedback from Cyclopath users (again, the technical details are available by consulting the Cyclopath source code).

We created *Objective-Simple* to achieve 100% coverage. This ad-hoc metric predicts a base rating depending solely on the edges' type (e.g., major road, local road, bike path) and then applies a few of the same adjustments as in *Objective-CBF*.

Simple averaging algorithms

We next turn to algorithms that average ratings in a simple ways. First, we tested two very simple baseline methods. *Global-Mean* predicts the mean of all ratings in the system, while *User-Mean* predicts the mean rating by the user for whom the prediction is being made.

Second, we tried a family of algorithms which predict the mean of other users' ratings on a particular edge; for example, if an edge is rated 2 stars by User A and 3 by User B, the prediction for other users would be 2.5 stars. We varied the threshold of ratings required for prediction, only considering a prediction valid if there are more than n ratings on an edge. We tried $n = 1, 2, 3, 5, 10$, and we refer to these algorithms as *Edge-Global-Mean.n*.

Finally, we tried algorithms which group edges into clusters and then predict using average edge ratings within each cluster. We took advantage of existing structure in the data, creating clusters based on the 9 edge types as well as the presence or absence of a bike lane. For example, major roads with a bike lane were one cluster, major roads without a bike lane were another, bike paths were a third (as bike lanes on bike paths do not make sense), and so on.

This yielded two algorithms. *Type-Global-Mean* predicts the mean of all users' ratings on edges of the same type, while *Type-User-Mean* predicts the mean of the searching user's ratings on edges of the same type.

Collaborative filtering

Collaborative filtering (CF) is one of the most powerful recommendation techniques in other contexts [5]. We expected CF to give accurate ratings but have problems with coverage, given our extremely sparse dataset. We implemented collaborative filtering according to [31] and [32], with several variations: user-based vs. item-based, different distance metrics (Pearson correlation, Euclidean distance, cosine similarity), and adjusting or not adjusting ratings by the user average. We used a similarity threshold of just one co-rating in an effort for more coverage (except for the Pearson distance metric, which is not defined for one co-rating).

Machine-learning algorithms

Finally, we tried machine learning techniques similar to linear regression. The regressions take as input a training set of $\langle r(u,e), f_1(u,e), f_2(u,e), \ldots \rangle$ examples, where $r(u,e)$ is a rating by user u for edge e, and each $f_i(u,e)$ is a numeric or categorical feature giving information about the user or edge associated with a rating (e.g., speed limit). They then analyze the relationships between features and ratings and generate predictions for unknown ratings based on these relationships. Machine learning regression algorithms are well-suited to our task because they are fast and regularized to avoid over-fitting. We used the Vowpal Wabbit conjugate gradient descent software [17] because it efficiently handles large datasets with many features.

We tried two algorithms based on these ideas. First, *ML-User* creates a separate regression model for each user. We included seven features in total: mean rating by all users on that edge, mean rating by the user in question on all edges, and 5 edge attributes (speed limit, lane width, log-transformed average daily traffic, tags, and lane count).

Because this algorithm builds an independent model for each user, it cannot analyze rating patterns across different users. We addressed this with *ML-Global*, which builds one shared regression model for all users, with 6 additional features (for 13 total) to support personalization in the shared model. First, we added user ID as an indicator variable. Second, we added a user profile vector that captured how users felt about the five edge attributes; a value in the profile was either the Pearson correlation between the attribute and the user's ratings (for numeric attributes) or the fraction of of the user's rated blocks with that feature (for categorical features). Finally, as personalized algorithms must capture how a specific user (or type of user) feels about a specific edge, we added in-

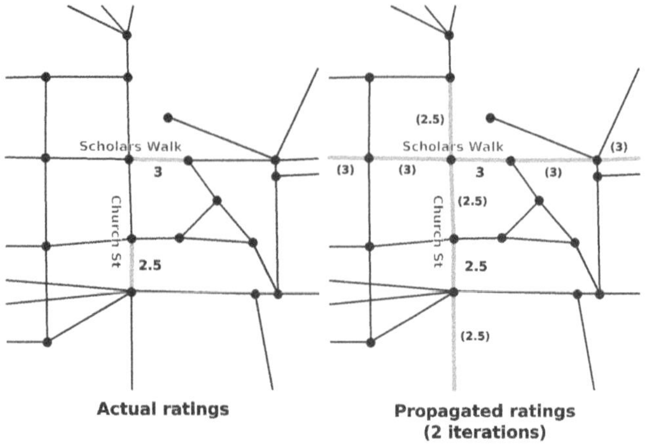

Figure 3. Ratings propagation. This illustration shows our (largely failed) technique to address the sparsity of ratings.

teractions between the edge attributes and both user ID and the profile vector. (Vowpal Wabbit optimizes interactions directly, eliminating the need to add them as separate features.)

For both of these algorithms, we normalized all feature and rating values to the interval [0,1], as recommended by the Vowpal Wabbit documentation.

STAGE 1: PREDICTING RATINGS

We begin by analyzing the coverage and accuracy of these rating prediction algorithms, to find which are promising in the context of route finding.

Method

We implemented the algorithms in Python and evaluated their accuracy with 10-fold cross-validation, using Cyclopath ratings as of April 2011. This dataset contains 68,274 ratings by 481 users on 35,608 of 154,242 edges.[13]

We report accuracy using MAE and RMSE. Coverage is computed statistically: we took a random sample of 5,000 user,edge pairs and tried to predict each, counting how many times we succeeded. We use the full dataset for this estimate, i.e., without cross-validation, which is not needed because we are not using prediction values.

We report coverage for users who have made at least one rating. Cyclopath also computes routes for users who have made no ratings, but we report as we do for two reasons. First, it allows for comparison with other recommender systems. Second, it is impossible to compute coverage including users who have rated no edges, because this set contains an unknown and unbounded number of anonymous users. However, some algorithms can make predictions for a user without any ratings from that user: in these cases, coverage for both classes of users is equal. We point out such algorithms in our discussion below. In particular, when we claim an algorithm has *universal coverage*, that means it can predict a rating for any user,edge pair even if that user made no ratings.

[13] We removed 1,400 ratings on expressways made before the system was complete, when rating was the only way to prevent certain expressways from being offered in routes, as working around this missing feature was unrepresentative of typical rating behavior.

We were concerned about the sparsity of our dataset (recall that only 0.092% of user,edge pairs actually had a rating, 13 times sparser than MovieLens or Netflix), and we tried to address this by inferring some ratings. Our approach is similar to Good et al., who inferred rating profiles based on movie attributes such as genre and keywords [12]. The intuition is that unrated edges "near" rated edges are likely to have similar ratings (i.e., edges show *spatial autocorrelation*). Figure 3 gives an example; two ratings are shown, one on Scholars Walk and one on Church St. We can reasonably infer that topologically adjacent edges of the same street have the same rating, as do edges adjacent to those, and so on. The example shows two iterations of this propagation – we have inferred 7 ratings, increasing the number of rated edges from 2 to 9.

We did this for 8 iterations, creating 58,066 inferred ratings for a total of 126,340; 49,277 edges then had at least one rating, up from 35,608. This reduced sparsity from 0.00092 to 0.0017, still 7 times more sparse than MovieLens or Netflix and much less improvement than we expected. We speculate that this is for two reasons. First, some ratings were near the "end" of a street, so it was not possible to propagate for the full 8 iterations. Second, rated edges are not uniformly distributed. For example, if a user has rated 20 edges, they are frequently in an adjacent sequence already (e.g., Hennepin Ave. between 20th and 40th St.), so propagation only expands the first and last ratings in the sequence – yielding closer to 20 inferred ratings than 400. Unsurprisingly in light of this, the technique turned out to be not very helpful: coverage was improved only modestly, and accuracy was damaged (perhaps due to the obvious risk that inferred ratings are necessarily guesses), for all algorithms except the *ML-* pair. Details are given below as algorithm results are summarized.

Results

Table 2 lists our full results, divided into sections according to algorithm class. Below, we discuss key results and interpretations for each algorithm.

Objective algorithms. *Objective-CBF* has coverage of 88% and MAE of 0.709, while *Objective-Simple* has universal coverage (its motivation) and MAE 0.770. While both of these algorithms have excellent coverage, their accuracy is uncompetitive compared with other algorithms.

Simple averaging algorithms. *Global-Mean* has universal coverage and MAE of 0.882, while *User-Mean* has 99.8% coverage (the gap from universal arising from a few users having rated only edges which were later deleted from the system) and MAE of 0.802.

Accuracy of *Edge-Global-Mean.n* is surprisingly good; even copying a single other user's rating (*Edge-Global-Mean.1*) is slightly more accurate (MAE of 0.684) than a moderately sophisticated objective algorithm (*Objective-CBF* with MAE 0.709). *Edge-Global-Mean.2* and higher are competitive with the more complex algorithms below, with MAE from 0.633 to 0.440. However, coverage is poor. *Edge-Global-Mean.1* can be stretched to 31% using ratings propagation with essentially no penalty in accuracy (MAE declines by 0.004), but other algorithms are superior in both coverage and accuracy, and a higher threshold quickly leads to very

Algorithm	Without propagation MAE	RMSE	Cov.	With propagation MAE	RMSE	Cov.
Objective algorithms						
Objective-Simple	0.770	1.035	1.000 ⋆		no effect	
Objective-CBF	0.709	1.031	0.882 ⋆		no effect	
Simple averaging algorithms						
Global-Mean	0.882	1.122	1.000 ⋆	0.903	1.123	1.000 ⋆
User-Mean	0.802	1.015	0.998	0.818	1.021	0.998
Edge-Global-Mean.1	0.684	0.975	0.212 ⋆	0.688	0.963	0.307 ⋆
Edge-Global-Mean.2	0.633	0.871	0.078 ⋆	0.650	0.879	0.153 ⋆
Edge-Global-Mean.3	0.601	0.830	0.041 ⋆	0.627	0.846	0.096 ⋆
Edge-Global-Mean.5	0.556	0.778	0.015 ⋆	0.604	0.821	0.043 ⋆
Edge-Global-Mean.10	0.440	0.653	0.005 ⋆	0.563	0.776	0.014 ⋆
Type-Global-Mean	0.674	0.887	1.000 ⋆	0.704	0.908	1.000 ⋆
Type-User-Mean	0.482	0.698	0.609	0.520	0.736	0.637
Collaborative filtering						
CF-User.pearson	0.614	0.895	0.029	0.636	0.907	0.059
CF-User.euclid,unadj	0.553	0.845	0.076	0.502	0.777	0.116
CF-User.euclid,adj	0.621	0.911	0.075	0.624	0.911	0.119
CF-User.cosine,unadj	0.675	0.961	0.080	0.677	0.947	0.140
CF-User.cosine,adj	0.610	0.885	0.049	0.623	0.886	0.087
CF-Item.pearson	0.410	0.637	0.007	0.461	0.664	0.021
CF-Item.euclid,unadj	0.582	0.797	0.082	0.614	0.807	0.145
CF-Item.euclid,adj	0.582	0.797	0.082	0.614	0.807	0.145
CF-Item.cosine,unadj	0.638	0.862	0.072	0.674	0.881	0.130
CF-Item.cosine,adj	0.566	0.785	0.067	0.590	0.790	0.118
Machine learning algorithms						
ML-User	0.558	0.799	0.650	0.514	0.723	0.664
ML-Global	0.495	0.719	1.000 ⋆	0.477	0.677	1.000 ⋆

Table 2. Results of predicting edge ratings. Coverage includes only users who have made at least one rating. Algorithms which can make predictions for a user without any ratings from that user are marked with ⋆. For these algorithms, coverage for the (unbounded) set of no-rating users is equal to what is listed; for the others, coverage is undefined for no-rating users.

poor coverage (*Edge-Global-Mean.2* has just 15% coverage even with ratings propagation). Furthermore, *Edge-Global-Mean.1* is vulnerable to trivial attacks – for most of the edges in the system, one user can destroy the ability of the system to predict ratings for that edge by entering a bogus rating (which then becomes the predicted rating for everyone).

Finally, both *Type-* algorithms performed very well. *Type-User-Mean* has excellent accuracy (MAE 0.482) and reasonable coverage (61%), while *Type-Global-Mean* achieves universal coverage and has reasonable accuracy (MAE 0.674). Additionally, they have several further advantages. They are amenable to an easy cold start process – simply rate one edge in each cluster – and users might not even need to rate any actual items at all (e.g., "what rating do you typically give to bike paths?"). They are difficult to attack because users' ratings do not influence other users in *Type-User-Mean* and have weak influence in *Type-Global-Mean*. Finally, the models built by these algorithms are very simple and can be easily communicated to lightweight client software like web applications; in Cyclopath, this would be useful as ratings could be predicted even for newly created edges that have not yet been saved, without a round-trip to the server.

Collaborative filtering. Our hypotheses for CF algorithms we tried were confirmed, more dramatically than we expected – these algorithms are not useful in this context. One variant (*CF-Item.pearson* without ratings propagation) is the most accurate of anything we tried (MAE of 0.410), but coverage is extremely poor, just 0.7%. Other CF variants have better, though still poor, coverage (at most 15%), but other algorithms have much better coverage and better accuracy.

Machine Learning algorithms. These algorithms also both performed very well. *ML-User* had coverage of 65% and MAE 0.558, improving to 66% and 0.514 under ratings propagation. However, *ML-Global* was superior on both dimensions, with universal coverage and MAE of 0.495; this algorithm too improved under ratings propagation, though modestly, decreasing MAE by 0.02. (Because this improvement was small, our further analyses consider the non-propagated variant for simplicity.)

Summary. Figure 4 summarizes the performance of the algorithms we tried. Three of the four groups (objective, simple averaging, and machine learning) produced algorithms with sufficient coverage and accuracy to be of plausible use. For further evaluation, we analyze the best algorithm from each:

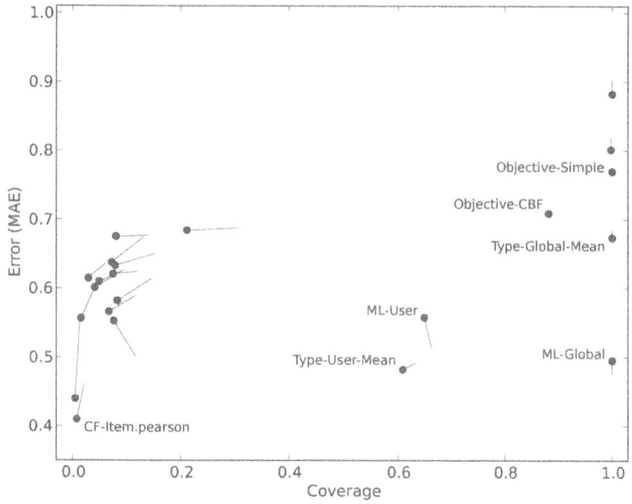

Figure 4. Scatter plot of prediction algorithm coverage vs. error. Algorithms lower and more to the right are better. Dots are results without ratings propagation, while the flags show the effect of propagation. Key algorithms are labeled.

	Objective-CBF	*Type-User-Mean*	*ML-Global*
Objective-CBF		0.75	0.44
Type-User-Mean	0.75		0.48
ML-Global	0.44	0.48	

Table 3. Pairwise edge order agreement (PBEA) between "plausible" rating prediction algorithms.

Objective-CBF, *Type-User-Mean*, and *ML-Global*. We next explore the question of whether these accuracy differences are meaningful at Stage 2.

STAGE 2: COMPARING NODE-LEVEL DECISIONS

Prediction accuracy is irrelevant if different algorithms do not lead to different graph search decisions. This section describes our evaluation of the agreement of the three plausible algorithms in this context, using the metrics and ideas explained above.

Stage 1 produced a set of user,edge,value predictions for each fold in the 10-fold cross-validation. For every pair of algorithms in each fold, we counted the number of pairs of adjacent edges where the two algorithms gave the same predicted rating ordering and the number where the orderings were different. This yielded the pairwise best edge agreement (PBEA) for the two algorithms.

Our results are summarized in Table 3. PBEA is at most 75% (an estimated BEA of 53%, suggesting that graph search would make the same low-level decisions at least 53% of the time), itself a large difference. Further, *ML-Global* has an even larger difference with both other algorithms (PBEA at most 48%), despite its modest MAE difference with *Type-User-Mean* (0.495 vs. 0.482). We speculate that this is due in part to the granularity of the predictions made by the different algorithms. For example, *Type-User-Mean* can make only 16 distinct predictions for any given user, because it returns the mean rating of one of 16 clusters; on the other hand, *ML-Global* yields continuously varying predictions in the appropriate range. The result is that *Type-User-Mean* frequently makes exactly the same prediction for a given pair of edges, while *ML-Global* rarely does, lowering the likelihood that the two algorithms will agree. In other words, the differences evident in Stage 1 do not collapse, and in fact other factors may dominate the agreement level.

This relatively low agreement between the algorithms at the node level suggests that optimal routes from different algorithms may diverge at many nodes. We next explore the degree to which this is true.

STAGE 3: COMPARING PATHS

In this stage, we examine whether differences in the desirability of edges when examining nodes in isolation translate into meaningful differences between entire routes.

Our methodology allows us to report differences between predictors in this stage, but not their quality directly, for two reasons. First, our ratings data is extremely sparse – the tiny number of edge ratings a user is likely to have made on a given route may not reflect that route's overall quality. Second, based on our experience working with cyclists, we believe that users evaluate routes holistically rather than as a collection of edges.

However, we believe that our findings in this stage do allow us to form plausible hypotheses about quality. Stage 1 let us establish low-level quality differences: for any given edge, certain predictors yield better predictions than others. Stage 3 (via Stage 2) then lets us test whether a better predictor yields different routes. Thus, it seems plausible that if a predictor is *better* at Stage 1 and *different* at all stages, it is better overall.

In this stage, we continue discussion of the three "plausible" prediction algorithms: *Objective-CBF*, *Type-User-Mean*, and *ML-Global*. However, recall that in order to be used in graph search, an algorithm must have 100% coverage. *Objective-CBF* and *Type-User-Mean* do not have this property and thus must be augmented. Accordingly, we tested the following three prediction algorithms:

- *Type-Ensemble*, an ensemble predictor [5] which first attempts *Type-User-Mean*, and if that does not yield a prediction, *Type-Global-Mean*. Recall that *Type-User-Mean* has 61% coverage; i.e., on average, 61% of prediction attempts will use *Type-User-Mean* and the remainder *Type-Global-Mean*.
- *Objective-Ensemble* is similarly a fall-through ensemble predictor which attempts *Objective-CBF* (88% coverage) and then *Objective-Simple*.
- *ML-Global* in isolation.

We randomly selected 5,000 of the 57,116 route searches made by Cyclopath users since the site went live in May 2008. For each of these, we recomputed the search (i.e., we reissued the same source, destination, and route preferences as the user who originally issued the search) using ratings

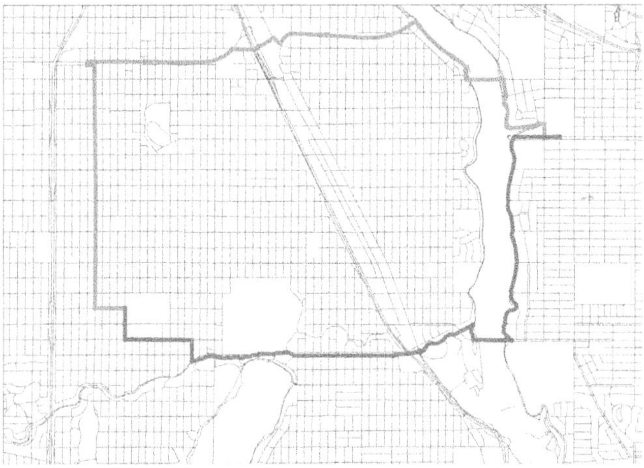

Figure 5. An example route search from Steele Flats (bottom left) to St. Thomas University (top right). The *Objective-Ensemble* predictor yielded the red upper route, while *Type-Ensemble* yielded the (almost completely different) blue lower route.

	Objective-Ensemble	*Type-Ensemble*	*ML-Global*
Objective-Ensemble		0.62	0.38
Type-Ensemble	0.62		0.44
ML-Global	0.38	0.44	

Table 4. Mean fraction of edges shared between route searches using each pair of ensemble prediction algorithms.

predicted by each of the three algorithms. We then compared the routes produced by each pair of predictors on each route. For example, Figure 5 shows an example route search which yielded two very different routes using different predictors.

Our results are summarized in Table 4. For each pair, we report the mean fraction of edges shared by the two predictors over the set of routes; for example, if predictor A produces a route of 12 edges and predictor B a route of 10 edges, and 5 edges are found in both routes, then the fraction of edges shared is $(5 \times 2)/(10 + 12) \approx 0.45$. (We also computed the mean fraction of distance shared, but it differed by no more than 2% from the mean fraction of edges shared, so we omit it for brevity.)

Different prediction algorithms do indeed produce different routes. While *Objective-Ensemble* and *Type-Ensemble* agree most often, they only share 62% of edges. This agreement indicates that attribute-based methods, such as *Objective-CBF*, do capture typical user preferences to some degree. Overlap between *ML-Global* and the other algorithms are quite low (38-44%). The low agreement with *Type-Ensemble* (44%) is particularly surprising, as both algorithms are personalized and draw upon edge ratings. This divergence suggests that the two algorithms achieve their Stage 1 accuracy through independent signals of user preference.

CONCLUSIONS

These results represent a step forward in two distinct ways. First, we have shown that personalized route finding algorithms that use edge ratings can be valuable in a production system. This is of additional interest because in many contexts, particularly open-content ones, qualitative data such as subjective ratings are easier to obtain than the quantitative data needed for objective rating predictors.

Second, our new framework and our algorithm evaluations are an advance for personalization research. Specifically, we identified two edge rating prediction algorithms that work excellently, one of which (*Type-Ensemble*) leverages a tiny model and whose algorithm to make predictions given the model is trivially simple. This makes it easy to pass the model to a thin client such as a browser and make predictions for edges of which the server has no knowledge.

There is much future work. First, the meaning for users of the differences identified in Stage 3 should be explored with a user study. Second, a deeper understanding of the relationship between Stages 2 and 3 would be useful; such an understanding may make it possible to eliminate Stage 3 and its more complex prerequisites. Third, other algorithms to predict edge ratings should be tested using our analysis framework. Fourth, rating predictions based on sensing could be fruitful: for example, cyclists could carry accelerometers to measure bumpiness, power sensors to measure effort, and/or physiological sensors to measure emotional stress.

Furthermore, route finding presents a number of additional complications. For example, we suspect that the subjective cost of a path is a nonlinear function of the (also subjective) weights of its edges. We already exclude some routes if one or more edge ratings fail to meet a minimum threshold. Another possibility is that each additional unit of poorly-rated edge distance has exponential additional cost; this notion is similar to the finding of Ziegler et al. that the desirability of a set of books differed from the average desirability of the individual books in the set [36]. Alternately, we might want to compute the path with with the smallest distance on poorly-rated edges or the highest worst rating ("least misery" [22]).

Finally, users have asked us numerous times for loop routes; e.g., "I am at Point A and I want a one-hour loop that I would enjoy". In general, we believe that there is much richness in route finding, particularly bicycle and other human-powered route finding, which we have not yet explored. Future research should do so, and new graph search algorithms may be required.

ACKNOWLEDGEMENTS

We thank the Cyclopath team at GroupLens Research and the Cyclopath user community. Ryan Kerwin did the analysis work in "Evidence for Personalization". This work was supported in part by the National Science Foundation, grants IIS 05-34692, IIS-0808692, IIS-0936043, and IIS-0964697.

REFERENCES

1. Liliana Ardissono et al. Intrigue: Personalized recommendation of tourist attractions for desktop and hand held devices. *Applied Artificial Intelligence*, 17(8):687–714, 2003.

2. Marko Balbanovic and Yoav Shoham. Combining content-based and collaborative recommendation. *CACM*, 40:66–72, 1997.
3. Ed Barsotti and Gin Kilgore. The road network is the bicycle network: Bicycle suitability measures for roadways and sidepaths. In *Proc. Transport Chicago*, 2001. http://bikelib.org/roads/roadnet.htm.
4. Benjamin B. Bederson et al. Enhancing in-car navigation systems with personal experience. In *Proc. Transportation Research Board*, pages 1–11, 2008.
5. Robert M. Bell and Yehuda Koren. Lessons from the Netflix Prize challenge. *SIGKDD Explorations*, 9(2):75–79, 2007.
6. Joel Booth et al. A data model for trip planning in multimodal transportation systems. In *Proc. Extending Database Technology*, pages 994–1005, 2009.
7. Jilin Chen et al. Make new friends, but keep the old: Recommending people on social networking sites. In *Proc. CHI*, pages 201–210, 2009.
8. Abhinandan S. Das et al. Google News personalization: Scalable online collaborative filtering. In *Proc. WWW*, pages 271–280, 2007.
9. Daniel Delling et al. Engineering route planning algorithms. In *Algorithmics of Large and Complex Networks*, pages 117–139. Springer-Verlag, 2009.
10. Alexander Felfernig et al. Personalized user interfaces for product configuration. In *Proc. IUI*, 2010.
11. Simon Funk. Netflix update: Try this at home, 2006. http://sifter.org/simon/journal/20061211.html.
12. Nathan Good et al. Combining collaborative filtering with personal agents for better recommendations. In *Proc. AAAI*, 1999.
13. Ilya Grigorik. Dissecting the Netflix dataset, Oct 2006. http: //www.igvita.com/2006/10/29/dissecting-the-netflix-dataset/.
14. Peter E. Hart et al. A formal basis for the heuristic determination of minimum cost paths. *TOSSC*, 4(2):100–107, 1968.
15. Harald Holone et al. Aspects of personal navigation with collaborative user feedback. In *Proc. NordiCHI*, pages 182–191, 2008.
16. William H.K. Lam and G. Xu. A traffic flow simulator for network reliability assessment. *Advanced Transportation*, 33(2):159–182, 1999.
17. John Langford et al. Sparse online learning via truncated gradient. *Machine Learning Research*, 10:777–801, 2009.
18. John Leen. It's time to bike, 2010. http: //google-latlong.blogspot.com/2010/03/its-time-to-bike.html.
19. Quannan Li et al. Mining user similarity based on location history. In *Proc. ACMGIS*, pages 1–10, 2008.
20. Macalester College. Collecting bikeways data in Minnesota, 2006. http://www.macalester.edu/geography/civic/BikewaysProject_Geog364_Spring2006.pdf.
21. Lorraine McGinty and Barry Smyth. Shared experiences in personalized route planning. In *Proc. FLAIRS*, pages 111–115, 2002.
22. Mark O'Connor et al. Polylens: A recommender system for groups of users. In *Proc. ECSCW*, pages 199–218, 2001.
23. Moon-Hee Park et al. Location-based recommendation system using Bayesian user's preference model in mobile devices. In *Proc. Ubiquitous Intelligence and Computing*, pages 1130–1139, 2007.
24. Reid Priedhorsky et al. How a personalized geowiki can help bicyclists share information more effectively. In *Proc. WikiSym*, pages 93–98, 2007.
25. Reid Priedhorsky and Loren Terveen. The computational geowiki: What, why, and how. In *Proc. CSCW*, 2008.
26. Sasank Reddy et al. Biketastic: Sensing and mapping for better biking. In *Proc. CHI*, pages 1817–1820, 2010.
27. Paul Resnick et al. GroupLens: An open architecture for collaborative filtering of netnews. In *Proc. CSCW*, 1994.
28. Francesco Ricci. Travel recommender systems. *IEEE Intelligent Systems*, 17(6):55–57, 2002.
29. Jean-Paul Rodrigue et al. *The Geography of Transport Systems*. Routledge, 2006.
30. Badrul Sarwar. Item-based collaborative filtering reccomendation algorithms. In *Proc. WWW*, pages 285–295, 2001.
31. J. Ben Schafer et al. Collaborative filtering recommender systems. In *The Adaptive Web*, chapter 9, pages 291–324. Springer-Verlag, 2007.
32. Toby Segaran. *Programming Collective Intelligence*. O'Reilly, 2007.
33. Alex Sorton and Thomas Walsh. Urban and suburban bicycle compatibility street evaluation using bicycle stress level. In *Proc. Transportation Research Board*, 1994.
34. Fan Yang and Zhi-Mei Wang. A mobile location-based information recommendation system based on GPS and WEB2.0 services. *WSEAS Transactions on Computers*, 8(4):725–734, 2009.
35. Yu Zheng et al. GeoLife 2.0: A location-based social networking service. In *Proc. Mobile Data Management*, pages 357–358, 2009. Demo.
36. Cai-Nicolas Ziegler et al. Improving recommendation lists through topic diversification. In *Proc. WWW*, pages 22–32, 2005.

Searching for the Goldilocks Zone: Trade-Offs in Managing Online Volunteer Groups

Loxley Sijia Wang*, Jilin Chen, Yuqing Ren*, John Riedl****

*Carlson School of Management
University of Minnesota
321 19th Ave. S., Minneapolis, MN 55455
{wang1290, chingren}@umn.edu

**Dept. of Computer Science and Engineering
University of Minnesota
200 Union St. SE., Minneapolis, MN 55455
{jilin, riedl}@cs.umn.edu

ABSTRACT

Dedicated and productive members who actively contribute to community efforts are crucial to the success of online volunteer groups such as Wikipedia. What predicts member productivity? Do productive members stay longer? How does involvement in multiple projects affect member contribution to the community? In this paper, we analyze data from 648 WikiProjects to address these questions. Our results reveal two critical trade-offs in managing online volunteer groups. First, factors that increase member productivity, measured by the number of edits on Wikipedia articles, also increase likelihood of withdrawal from contributing, perhaps due to feelings of "mission accomplished" or "burnout". Second, individual membership in multiple projects has mixed effects. It decreases the amount of work editors contribute to both the individual projects and Wikipedia as a whole. It increases withdrawal for each individual project yet reduces withdrawal from Wikipedia. We discuss how our findings expand existing theories to fit the online context and inform the design of new tools to improve online volunteer work.

Author Keywords

Online volunteer groups; Wikipedia; trade-off; productivity; withdrawal.

ACM Classification Keywords

H.5.3: Group and Organization Interfaces; K.4.3: Organizational Impacts

General Terms

Design; Human Factors; Management; Theory.

INTRODUCTION

The past decade has observed tremendous growth in the number of online volunteer groups that self-organize on the Internet to accomplish tasks that used to be performed in traditional organizations. One successful example is Wikipedia, the free online encyclopedia. In just ten years, millions of volunteer editors have collaboratively created more than three million articles in English – and nearly twenty million across all languages. Despite its success, Wikipedia and similar online collaboration efforts face challenges in recruiting and retaining active contributors.

Active contributors are crucial to the success of online volunteer efforts. Without a steady rate of participation and a critical mass of contributors, online groups may suffer sustainability issues [10]. Contributors may leave for many different reasons. Some may leave due to outside influences in their lives, such as school, work and family. Others may leave due to conflict within the community [26]. Still others, who work on many articles or participate in multiple projects, may leave due to burnout.

Much of the existing research on Wikipedia and other online volunteer efforts has focused on understanding what motivates members to contribute and how they coordinate and resolve conflict (e.g., [14, 24, 26]). Our research, instead, focuses on the opposite problem: understanding why members stop contributing to a group and the implications of their withdrawal behaviors. Are newcomers or old-timers more likely to withdraw? Are active or inactive contributors more likely to withdraw? For what reasons? What about the impact of social connections between editors? In addition to retaining members, another crucial goal for online volunteer groups is to complete work. In the context of Wikipedia, continued edits to articles are important and have been used repeatedly to measure group activity and individual productivity [25, 39]. By comparing factors that affect individual productivity and withdrawal, we hope to explore a critical trade-off between the two: Can the goals of increasing productivity and reducing withdrawal be pursued simultaneously, or does one need to be sacrificed for the other?

The second key trade-off we investigate is between subgroups within a community and the larger community as a whole. Many online groups have a subgroup structure that allows members to participate in more intimate settings (e.g., sub-forums in web discussions and guilds in online games). In Wikipedia, these subgroups are known as WikiProjects, where members organize to work on Wikipedia articles related to specific topics. The relationship between the subgroups and the community is subtle. Some members of online groups may need to decide whether to focus their efforts on a specific subgroup or to split their efforts among multiple subgroups [17].

In this paper, we examine the two trade-offs in the context of Wikipedia and WikiProjects. We analyze data from 648

WikiProjects to explore the effects of member tenure, tenure dissimilarity, past performance, and involvement in multiple projects on members' productivity and withdrawal behaviors at the project level. We then examine the effects of these factors on member productivity and withdrawal at the Wikipedia level. Our results provide evidence for both trade-offs and highlight the challenges in balancing multiple desirable outcomes of community health within a large online volunteer effort like Wikipedia.

The rest of our paper is organized as follows: (1) We review organization science and volunteerism literature on member productivity and withdrawal and propose how they may generalize to online groups. (2) We describe our research setting of Wikipedia and WikiProjects as well as how we assembled the data set. (3) We present our main results and discuss their implications for the management of online collaboration efforts.

THEORIES AND HYPOTHESES

We focus on studying productivity and withdrawal, two common ways to measure participation in online volunteer groups. In traditional organizations, productivity can be measured as the quantity of work output, such as the number of papers and reports produced in a research lab. In Wikipedia, number of edits is a common measure of productivity [23, 24, 25, 39]. In traditional organizations, withdrawal includes behaviors such as "psychological withdrawal, lateness, absenteeism, and turnover" [7]. In Wikipedia, the primary evidence of withdrawal is for a formerly active editor to cease contributing.

Research on productivity and withdrawal behaviors in traditional groups and organizations sheds light on studying similar behaviors in online groups [15]. At the same time, insights from offline groups may not be readily applicable to online groups for three reasons: 1) online groups have low entry and exit barriers. In traditional organizations, employees need to follow established procedures to enter or exit the organization or its subunits. In contrast, members of most online groups can enter and exit at their will. 2) Online volunteer groups have little leverage to mandate active participation. Members are motivated by different incentives [36]. There is a wider variation in member participation [25], and factors that predict productivity in traditional organizations, such as tenure, may not predict productivity in online groups. 3) Compared to traditional organizations, online volunteer groups like Wikipedia often don't have formal training and socialization programs, both of which could help new members learn the ropes and form relationships with other members to increase productivity and reduce withdrawal.

Furthermore, the voluntary nature of online groups like Wikipedia poses additional challenges in encouraging productivity and discouraging withdrawal. Similar to members of offline volunteer organizations, online volunteers also may suffer from burnout and subsequently withdraw from these groups [42]. Because withdrawal may happen suddenly without a formal process, project work may be left unattended until new volunteers take over [36].

Trade-Offs Between Productivity and Withdrawal

While Wikipedia strives to encourage productivity and reduce withdrawal, it is unclear whether the two goals can be accomplished equally well. Ideally, online volunteer groups should achieve both goals simultaneously. In reality, there may be tension between the two. For instance, research has shown that members working in larger groups tend to contribute less than members working alone or in smaller groups. There is a greater penchant for "free-riding" [1] in larger groups. Free-riding occurs when members retain their membership in a group and receive benefits or credit without providing the same amount of work as others. When free-riding behaviors are frequent, the group may have a seemingly large membership but does not actually benefit from these extra members.

The tension between productivity and withdrawal may also arise from overburdening the core set of active contributors. It is common for a core group of productive members to be the driving force behind a successful online collaboration effort [25]. Studies on Wikipedia have shown how important that core group is in helping to maintain the overall productivity of the free online encyclopedia, compared to the bulk of community members [23, 34]. Although these core members are highly committed and dedicated to the effort, shouldering a heavy workload may erode their energy and enthusiasm and increase their likelihood of withdrawal. An alternative explanation for why active members leave may be that they feel they have accomplished their mission by contributing all that they know, and that further contribution would require much more research and effort [40].

In summary, both productivity and withdrawal are important outcome measures to study, along with potential trade-offs between the two. A successful online collaboration effort requires both a "critical mass" of participants [28] and a reasonable level of contribution. Both the amount of activity within an online volunteer group and its size have a strong impact on the ultimate sustainability of the group [10].

Factors That Affect Productivity and Withdrawal

In this section, we identify a set of factors that have been linked to individual productivity and withdrawal in the organization science literature. We first summarize the insights from the existing literature and then speculate how they may generalize to online volunteer groups.

Tenure. Tenure has been conceptualized and measured as the amount of time that an individual has been part of a group or organization. Organization science literature posits a curvilinear, inverted-U relationship between tenure and employee productivity [38]. When a newcomer first joins an organization, productivity is expected to increase over time as the person acquires skills, accumulates experience, and becomes familiar with organizational routines and policies. After a number of years of effort, participants are more prone to a burnout effect. The idea of job burnout is based on the potential buildup of stress and exhaustion that may cause workers to decrease productivity [13]. Research suggests that certain people may be especially prone to burnout over time [4], and burnout especially affects members with longer tenure who have felt frustration on the job [13]. Some of the nonlinear effects may be due to the aggregation of a plateau effect [22]. In essence, most workers improve at first but then reach a plateau, while others may start strong and begin to decline later.

Tenure has also been shown to be a strong predictor of withdrawal behavior across different professions [2]. Longer tenure allows for more experience, which would help increase productivity while reducing withdrawal [3]. In addition, newcomers have been consistently shown to be more likely to leave an organization than those with longer tenure [19]. We expect a similar effect of tenure in the context of Wikipedia collaboration, because newcomers who lack the experience of doing the work and interacting with other editors may feel frustrated or perceive a lack of fit with individual work groups [39]. In addition, research has shown that when newcomers' edits are reverted by old-timers, the newcomers are more likely to leave Wikipedia permanently [20]. We thus expect tenure to increase productivity and decrease withdrawal.

Tenure dissimilarity. Another strong predictor of productivity and withdrawal is interpersonal similarity. Studies of traditional organizations have shown that members in the minority component of a group are discouraged from making substantial contributions due to assumptions that they may be weak performers and because they may have more trouble aligning their interests with the rest of the group [35]. These arguments hold true for demographic attributes such as age and tenure [41]. A newbie in a group that consists of mostly experienced members may feel uncomfortable or inadequately prepared to contribute. Similarly, an experienced member in a group with mostly newbies may have different goals and ideas that are hard to communicate to the rest of the group. Hence, we expect tenure dissimilarity to be negatively associated with productivity.

Tenure dissimilarity may also affect withdrawal [41]. The homophily literature suggests that people tend to interact with others who are similar to them on attributes like age, race, ethnicity, etc. Ties between people will dissolve if there is too much dissimilarity [31], while groups that are more homogeneous, in terms of age and tenure, have fewer members leaving than heterogeneous groups [33]. We expect that members whose tenure differs more from the rest of the group are more likely to withdraw.

Past productivity. In traditional organizations, past performance has been shown to be a reliable predictor of future performance. We therefore expect a strong association between an individual's past and future productivity.

The effects of past productivity on withdrawal are more complicated. In traditional organizations, poor performers are generally more likely to leave than good performers, which implies that withdrawal may not be detrimental for the organization [29]. Although some past research suggests that high performers can find alternate opportunities and therefore be enticed to leave the organization, more recent studies usually show that poor performers are more prone to voluntary turnover. In addition, these members more often consider other factors, such as job satisfaction, in evaluating whether to remain in the organization [37].

We expect the effects of past productivity on withdrawal to be even more complicated in online volunteer groups. There are reasons to expect poor performers to voluntarily leave the project due to lack of contribution. However, there are also reasons to expect good performers to voluntarily leave, either because they have contributed what they know and accomplished their mission or because they are burnt out from maintaining a high level of contribution.

Concurrent projects. Being involved in multiple groups within a community affects member productivity and withdrawal. Similar to traditional organizations that compete for limited resources [5], online groups that are created on the same platform or have similar functions also compete for scarce resources like members' time and effort. Online volunteer groups need dedicated members, who put in the most time and effort, in order to survive as a group [10]. However, from a resource-based view, the amount of time spent on one activity is time that cannot be spent on another [6]. Those who are involved in multiple subgroups need to decide how to allocate their time to each group, making them physically unable to spend as much time on any one group. We thus expect members who are involved in multiple projects in Wikipedia to do less work for each project. Being involved in multiple projects increases the demand for members' time and effort and, thus, may increase the likelihood of withdrawing from the projects.

An alternative view on the effects of multiple subgroups or projects is job or social embeddedness theory [32]. Members who are affiliated with multiple projects are more socially embedded within Wikipedia, which should reduce their likelihood of withdrawing from Wikipedia as a whole, and may reduce their likelihood of withdrawing from the individual projects as well.

Communication and social integration. Social identity has been shown to be positively correlated with performance measures [35]. Members who strongly identify with a group are willing to exert greater effort and make more contributions to the group than those who do not identify with the group. This leads to greater social integration of members into the group. As members become more active within a group, they are more likely to be productive and display better performance [33]. Interpersonal relationships or psychological contracts are especially important to increase participation and reduce withdrawal intentions in not-for-profit volunteer organizations [18]. Communication with others is an important way for members of online volunteer groups to be socially integrated and feel like an essential part of the group [21].

Communication may occur internally within subgroups or externally across subgroups within a large community. Internal and external communication may have different effects on individual behavior. Social integration and frequent communication with members of one's group is likely to focus members' attention on the group goals and needs, and thus increase their contributions to the group and reduce their likelihood of withdrawal from the group [33].

In contrast, when members have many ties or frequent communication with those outside of a group, they are more likely to be pulled away from the focal group [30]. External connections have been shown to affect performance and withdrawal differently in traditional organizations. On one hand, an individual's connections with external groups have been shown to improve performance due to access to novel and relevant information [16]. On the other hand, social networks research has shown that employees or community members who are on the outskirts of groups and have strong external connections are more likely to leave [30]. Increased communication and socialization outside of a project is therefore likely to increase both individual productivity and withdrawal.

Trade-Offs Between the Community and its Subgroups

Online groups often consist of subgroups, such as projects within Wikipedia. Membership in multiple subgroups, on one hand, creates tension around how an individual allocates time and effort to different subgroups; on the other hand, this strengthens connections between an individual and the larger entity by enriching the web of connections tying the member to the community. It is important to understand more precisely how this trade-off works and how individual commitment and contribution to subgroups might transfer to the community as a whole.

Two mechanisms may be at work in determining how an individual's involvement in multiple subgroups affects the individual's involvement with the larger community. The first mechanism is the competition argument. As mentioned earlier, members participating in multiple subgroups must dole out their time and effort to each subgroup [6]. Because members have limited time to spend on volunteer work overall, splitting their efforts is likely to cause decreased productivity and increased withdrawal for individual subgroups [17]. Reduced productivity and increased withdrawal for individual projects does not necessarily mean reduced productivity and increased withdrawal for the community. Reduced levels of contribution to multiple projects, when aggregated, may exceed the average level of contribution to a single project. Similarly, for members who are involved in multiple projects, leaving one project doesn't conclude the person's affiliation with Wikipedia.

The second mechanism is job or social embeddedness. Job embeddedness theory suggests that more investment in a job increases the quitting cost, which is negatively correlated with the likelihood of leaving the organization [32]. Someone who is highly embedded (or involved) in an organization would be less likely to withdraw. In the context of Wikipedia, involvement in multiple projects increases the extent to which individual editors are socially embedded within Wikipedia, which makes them less likely to leave the Wikipedia community as a whole.

Furthermore, affiliation with multiple projects can lead to effective knowledge transfer across the projects, and thus increase the amount of work done within each project [16]. In these instances, members increase their ability to draw from outside sources and gain new knowledge that is useful to their productivity within the group. Furthermore, in the online context, member participation is socially driven by perception of and interactions with other members [11, 18]. The social embeddedness perspective implies that involvement in multiple projects may increase member contribution to Wikipedia as a whole.

To explore these trade-offs, our research questions are:

R1: How do individual tenure, past productivity, project involvement, and communication affect productivity and withdrawal at the project level?

R2: How do individual tenure, past productivity, project involvement, and communication affect productivity and withdrawal at the Wikipedia level?

R3: Are there any trade-offs between productivity and withdrawal? Are there any trade-offs between these outcomes at the project level and the Wikipedia level?

WIKIPEDIA AND WIKIPROJECTS

In this section, we describe our research setting – Wikipedia and the WikiProjects subgroups. Wikipedia is a free online encyclopedia that anyone can edit. An edit is simply a revision, large or small, to any article, talk, or user page. If users perform edits, they may also choose whether or not to register for a user account. Those who have accounts may then interact with other registered users, or editors, to coordinate work and discuss articles. Each article page has an associated talk page enabling editors to collaborate while working on the article.

A WikiProject is defined as "a group of pages in the 'Wikipedia' article namespace which are devoted to the management of a specific topic or family of topics within Wikipedia; and, simultaneously, a group of editors who use those pages to collaborate on encyclopedic work"[1]. Since 2002, more than 20,000 Wikipedia editors have joined more than a thousand projects. WikiProjects provide a way to organize editors with the goal of improving a specific subset of articles in Wikipedia. Members may choose to join or leave a project by adding or removing their names on the project's member list. The main page of a WikiProject typically includes a brief description of the project and its scope, a list of project members, guidelines, and tasks that require member contribution.

In this study, we focus on editors who have contributed to Wikipedia as a part of one or more WikiProjects. We chose

[1] http://en.wikipedia.org/wiki/Wikipedia:WikiProject_Philosophy

to study WikiProjects because they have clearly defined goals and boundaries, which make it easy to assess individual productivity and withdrawal at the project level.

DATA AND VARIABLES

The dataset we use in this study is extracted from the January 2008 dump of the English Wikipedia, which includes the full text of all pages and their complete edit histories from the creation of Wikipedia to the end of 2007. To gather information about projects and their members, we traversed the main directory page of WikiProjects and included all projects that are topical (thus excluding projects such as WikiProject Citation Cleanup). We also excluded projects that never grew to have at least three members (the minimum size of a group), projects that do not have a member list to track membership, and projects whose scopes could not be estimated using categories. Our final data set has 648 WikiProjects and 14,464 individual editors who are or have been members of these projects.

We determined each WikiProject's membership and scope following the approach in Chen et al. [12]. We used historical edits of a project's member list to identify members of each WikiProject. We considered an editor to have joined a project when her username appeared on the member list and to have left when her username was removed or contribution stopped. To determine the scope of a WikiProject, we first found the Wikipedia category that matched the title (like category *Computer science* for WikiProject *Computer science*). We then traversed all subcategories of the matched category down to the 4th level and considered all articles in those categories to be within the scope of the WikiProject (see Chen et al. [12] for more detail).

We constructed a longitudinal dataset to temporally separate the independent and dependent variables. Each observation records the characteristics and activities of an individual editor as a member of a project for each quarter in that project's lifespan. Within each project, each quarter is a 90-day period in a project's lifespan, with the first quarter beginning immediately after its creation date. Within each quarter, every editor who was a member of the project in that quarter was measured once for that project. The level of the analysis is therefore *project individual quarter*, with quarters nested within individuals and individuals nested within projects. For any given WikiProject, the first quarter is the first 90-day period following its date of creation. If the project had 10 members in this quarter, the dataset would have 10 observations for the project during this quarter, with each observation measuring the activity of one editor within the project. In total we had 85,105 project individual quarters in the WikiProject dataset.

Dependent Variables

Project-Level Productivity: We measured an editor's project-level productivity as the number of edits performed by the editor on articles *within the scope of the WikiProject* during the current quarter.

Project-Level Withdrawal: We measured an editor's project-level withdrawal as a binary variable, i.e. either 1 or 0. The variable is 1 if and only if the editor was an active member of the project in the current quarter, but removed her username from the project member list or stopped contributing within the scope of the project by the end of the next quarter.[2] We considered a member to be active if the person had at least one edit during that quarter to any of the following: an article within the project scope, the talk page of such an article, any project organization page, or the user pages or user talk pages of another project member.

Wikipedia-Level Productivity: We measured an editor's Wikipedia-level productivity as the number of edits performed by the editor on *any and all Wikipedia articles* during the current quarter.

Wikipedia-Level Withdrawal: We measured an editor's Wikipedia-level withdrawal as a binary variable, i.e. either 1 or 0. The variable is 1 if and only if the editor had performed at least one edit in Wikipedia during the current quarter but made no edits in Wikipedia in the subsequent quarter.

Independent Variables

Tenure: We measured an editor's tenure by how long the editor had been a member of Wikipedia, that is, the number of days elapsed from a member's first edit in Wikipedia to the end of a quarter [12].

Tenure Dissimilarity: We measured an editor's tenure dissimilarity from the rest of the project members using Euclidian Distance as follows [41]:

$$\sqrt{\sum_{j=1}^{n}\frac{(S_i - S_j)^2}{n}}$$

where S_i is tenure for the editor in question, S_j is the tenure of the j-th member in the project, and n is the total number of members currently in the project.

Past Productivity: We measured an editor's past productivity as the total number of edits performed by the editor on articles within the scope of the WikiProject before the current quarter.

Concurrent Projects: We measured an editor's concurrent projects by the total number of projects of which the editor is currently listed as a member. A higher number means that the editor is involved in more projects at the same time.

In-Project Communication: We measured an editor's in-project communication by the number of edits that other members of the project have made to the editor's user page and user talk page. We only counted edits by others on the editor's pages, not the editor's own edits, for two reasons. First, it is easier to track one user page than two. Second, strong ties tend to be reciprocal, so the amount of inbound

[2] 11% of editors returned one or more times after withdrawing, with a majority returning after one inactive period. Excluding these editors from the analysis did not significantly affect our results. In the analysis below we consider only the last and final instance of withdrawal for each editor.

	Descriptive Statistics							Correlations											
	Mean	Std Dev	1%ile	25%ile	50%ile	75%ile	99%ile	1	2	3	4	5	6	7	8	9	10	11	12
1. Project-Level Productivity	34.63	162.3	0	0	0	5	6810												
2. Project-Level Withdrawal	0.213	0.409	0	0	0	0	1	.02											
3. Wikipedia-Level Productivity	200.5	656.7	0	0	2	91	18226	.52	.05										
4. Wikipedia-level withdrawal	0.262	0.440	0	0	0	1	1	-.01	.50	-.02									
5. Quarter	5.292	2.864	1	3	5	7	14	-.07	.04	-.10	.14								
6. Project scope	20681	58493	10	871	4618	15605	1054242	.07	.03	.01	.01	.02							
7. Project size	58.83	49.95	1	22	44	82	275	-.07	-.01	-.10	.07	.41	.01						
8. Tenure	527.7	341.8	0	271.4	473.3	713.7	2447.9	.00	.06	.04	.08	.24	.01	.03					
9. Tenure dissimilarity	405.3	166.8	3.14	300.5	372.1	469.4	1781.1	.00	.06	.01	.08	.21	.05	.00	.48				
10. Past productivity	239.3	832.2	0	3	20	132	34529	.43	.07	.24	.03	.07	.08	-.02	.14	.05			
11. Concurrent projects	3.253	4.154	1	1	2	4	50	.02	.06	.12	.06	.00	.05	-.07	.16	.08	.07		
12. In-project communication	0.964	5.800	0	0	0	0	275	.34	.02	.19	-.01	-.06	-.02	-.02	-.02	-.02	.21	.03	
13. Out-project communication	14.44	36.83	0	0	1	9	300	.28	.08	.50	-.01	-.11	.01	-.10	.05	.00	.17	.22	.30

Table 1. Descriptive Statistics and Correlations of Variables

Variables	Project-Level Productivity	Project-Level Withdrawal	Wikipedia-Level Productivity	Wikipedia-Level Withdrawal
Intercept	2.151**	- 2.981**	5.343**	-5.495**
Quarter	- 0.191**	0.473**	- 0.567**	1.236**
Project Scope	0.464**	- 0.111	0.127**	- 0.446**
Project Size	- 0.216**	0.104*	0.254**	-0.122
Tenure	- 0.165**	- 0.129**	0.024+	-0.073**
Tenure Dissimilarity	0.085**	0.108**	0.029*	0.079**
Past Productivity	0.596**	0.362**	0.113**	0.133**
Concurrent Projects	- 0.287**	- 0.061**	- 0.116**	0.034**
In-Project Communication	0.611**	- 0.042**	0.290**	- 0.047**
Out-Project Communication	1.006**	0.350**	2.390**	0.188**
BIC	317209	56144	347630	53816
Deviance	35867**	2361**	57519**	1185**
N	N = 85105	N = 65393	N = 85105	N = 65393

Table 2. Predicting Member Productivity and Withdrawal Behaviors

We use the following notation in tables to represent p-values: ** p < .01, * p < .05, + p < .1

communication to an editor should be a good measure of how socially integrated the editor is within Wikipedia.

Out-Project Communication: We measured an editor's out-project communication by the number of edits that non-members of the project have made to the editor's user page and user talk page.

Control Variables

Quarter Index: The index of time within the project was measured in quarters (90-day periods), starting with quarter 0 from the moment the project is created until the last full quarter before the end of 2007.

Project Scope: Measured as the number of articles falling under the project scope. Project scope was determined using the same approach as Chen et al. [12].

Project Size: Measured as the number of project members during the current quarter.

RESULTS

Descriptive statistics and correlations of the variables in the dataset are displayed in Table 1. Most of the variables are highly skewed to the right so we performed base-2 logarithmic transformations for normality considerations. Because our data is nested by nature, we analyzed the data using Hierarchical Linear Models (HLM) [8], with member productivity and withdrawal as the dependent variables and project and individual characteristics as the independent variables. HLM is an advanced form of linear regression that allows us to examine the effects of independent variables on dependent variables while taking into account potential correlations across observations that are nested within a high-level entity (e.g., individuals nested within projects). Our dataset is cross-nested between projects and individuals, meaning an editor can belong to multiple projects. Thus, we ran the analysis using the lmer function in R.

Our main results are displayed in Table 2. The first two columns show how project and individual characteristics relate to individual productivity and withdrawal at the project level, and the second two columns show the relationships at the Wikipedia level. We standardized all independent variables for ease of comparing coefficients across variables. We estimated our HLM models using maximum likelihood estimation, random intercepts, and unstructured covariance structure. For each dependent variable, we ran two models: the base model with the intercept and quarter as predictors, and the complete model with two project level variables and six member level variables. Due to the large size of our data set, we examined Bayesian Information Criterion (BIC) across the models. BIC punishes models with a large sample size and a large number of parameters [9]. We included BIC and deviance between the complete model and the base model in Table 2. In all analyses, the deviance is greater than 10, meaning the complete model fits the data better than the base model.

The first two columns of Table 2, respectively, predict member productivity, measured as the number of edits performed by an individual member within a project in the current quarter, and member withdrawal, measured as either removing one's username from a project or stopping contribution to the project in the next quarter. Our analysis revealed a negative relationship between tenure and both productivity and withdrawal ($p < 0.01$). Compared to newcomers, old-timers contributed fewer edits and were less likely to withdraw. Our analysis also revealed a positive relationship of both tenure dissimilarity and past productivity with productivity and withdrawal in the current quarter ($p < 0.01$). Members with tenure different from the group contributed more edits than those with similar tenure and were more likely to withdraw from the project. Members who had made more edits in the past continued contributing more but were also more likely to withdraw from the project.

Our analysis revealed a negative relationship of the number of concurrent projects with productivity and withdrawal ($p < 0.01$). Members who took on more projects contributed fewer edits than those with fewer projects. Contrary to our predictions, members involved in multiple projects were less likely to withdraw from any individual project. We also found a positive effect of communication both within and outside of the focal project ($p < 0.01$). Members who engaged in communication, either with other project members or editors outside of the project, contributed more edits than those who engaged in less communication. Communication within and outside of the focal project had opposite relationships with withdrawal from the project, with more internal communication being associated with less withdrawal and more external communication with more withdrawal. These relationships are consistent with our predictions.

The last two columns of Table 2 show how project and member characteristics relate to productivity and withdrawal at the Wikipedia level, i.e. the total number of edits within Wikipedia during the quarter and whether an editor stopped contributing to Wikipedia after the next quarter. Most of the effects on productivity at the Wikipedia level are similar to those at the project level, with tenure being the only exception. While editors with longer tenure contributed fewer edits to individual projects, they contributed more edits to Wikipedia as a whole ($p < 0.1$). Contrary to our predictions, members who belong to multiple projects contributed less work, both to an individual project and to Wikipedia as a whole. The standard coefficient for project-level productivity is greater than the one for Wikipedia-level productivity, implying greater negative impact on the former.

The results on withdrawal at the Wikipedia level versus the project level are similar as well, with three exceptions. First, while project scope had no significant effect on project-level withdrawal, larger scope was associated with reduced withdrawal from Wikipedia as a whole. Second, members of projects with more total editors were more likely to withdraw from the project but not significantly more likely to withdraw from Wikipedia. Third, while belonging to multiple projects was associated with a lower likelihood of withdrawing from any single project, it was associated with a higher likelihood of withdrawing from Wikipedia as a whole ($p < 0.01$).

DISCUSSION

We set out to understand two critical trade-offs in online volunteer groups like Wikipedia: the trade-off between productivity and withdrawal and the trade-off between subgroups within a community and the community as a whole. Our quantitative analysis of WikiProjects provides evidence for both types of trade-offs. Table 3 summarizes some of the critical trade-offs revealed in our analysis.

For the ease of illustrating the trade-off, we summarize our results as the impact on *productivity* and *retention*, where retention is the opposite of withdrawal. A trade-off exists when a factor increases one outcome while decreasing the other or increases the same outcome at one level while decreasing it at another level. The left-hand side of Table 3

	Tradeoffs between productivity and retention			Tradeoffs between projects and Wikipedia as a whole		
Project Characteristics	No tradeoffs			Mixed tradeoffs		
	(+) project scope	→	(+) productivity (+) retention	(+) project scope	→	No effects on project retention (+) Wikipedia retention
	(–) project size			(+) project size	→	(–) project productivity (+) Wikipedia productivity
Member Attributes	Major tradeoffs			No tradeoffs		
	(–) tenure	→	(+) productivity (–) retention	(+) tenure	→	(–) project productivity (+) Wikipedia productivity
	(+) past productivity					
Member Connections	Mixed tradeoffs			Mixed tradeoffs		
	(+) concurrent projects	→	(–) productivity (+) retention	(+) concurrent projects	→	(–) project productivity (–) Wikipedia productivity (+) project retention (–) Wikipedia retention
	(–) out-project communication					
	(+) in-project communication	→	(+) productivity (+) retention			

Table 3. Summary of Main Findings

refers to trade-offs between productivity and withdrawal, while the right hand side refers to trade-offs between projects and Wikipedia as a whole. For instance, the second row in the left column shows some major trade-offs between productivity and withdrawal when tenure and past productivity are the independent predictors. The display of (–) tenure → (+) productivity and (–) retention means that shorter tenure is associated with higher productivity and lower retention.

In the rest of the section, we discuss these trade-offs, speculate on their underlying processes, and highlight implications for managing online collaboration.

Trade-off between Productivity and Retention

Our first main finding is a critical trade-off between how many edits an individual editor contributes to a project and her likelihood of staying with the project. A typical factor with such opposite effects is an editor's past edits, which is associated with increased productivity but a reduced retention rate. Contrary to traditional organizations where poor performers are more likely to leave an organization [29], we find that good performers are more likely to leave or stop contributing in online volunteer groups. One possible reason is the "mission accomplished" effect, as illustrated in the following quote:

"Having done all I can on the Andorra rugby and womens sevens pages (aside from keep them up to date), I am going to see if I can help with the Shannara project."

Another possible reason is the burnout effect, as illustrated in the following quotes from conversations between active editors who have experienced "wikiburnout" or "wikistress":

"I am suffering from wikiburnout and chronic Wikistress. [...] I probably won't be able to log in as frequently and contribute as much as I would like."

"On another point; I noticed your wikistress level is high, and your contributions may be dropping. [...] I'd like to add something else; avoid burnout. You are a very active contributor. It is easy for highly active contributors to get caught up in burnout."

Stress management seems to be a major issue among active contributors. For dealing with stress, the meta-wiki of Wikimedia (the mother organization of Wikipedia) lists 154 tips contributed by editors[3]. The meta-wiki also suggests that stressed people leave Wikipedia for a short while so they can recover[4].

Many active Wikipedia editors created "wikistress meters" on their user pages to indicate their stress levels to fellow editors[5]. The use of these stress meters may help alleviate the burnout effect of productive editors by increasing awareness of stress levels among editors. However, the effectiveness of such a solution remains limited due to the effort and skills required to create and update the meters. In addition, some research has shown that focusing on the negative aspect of stress may lead to unintended effects such as depression [27].

A design opportunity lies in improving the ease of use and functionality of stress awareness tools like stress meters. For instance, software agents can be developed to automatically estimate stress levels from an editor's recent activity and comparison with historical patterns. Stress information can be customized or hidden from the focal editor to avoid negative impact. Instead, it can be made available to other editors and project leaders who can use the information to proactively manage the stress of project members and avoid overburdening already-active members. Tools like these can be promising for alleviating the stress of productive editors, thus helping to maintain high productivity while improving member retention.

Trade-off between WikiProjects and Wikipedia

Our second main finding is a critical trade-off between members' continued contributions to individual projects versus Wikipedia as a whole. Membership in multiple projects reduces one's likelihood of leaving an individual project but increases the likelihood of leaving Wikipedia. In contrast, membership in multiple projects reduces the amount of work editors contribute at both levels. The negative effects of multiple project membership on productivity have wide implications because about 45% of the editors in our data were involved in more than one project, with 10% being involved in five or more projects. Our results suggest the detrimental effect is not limited to individual projects. Instead, it may have spilled over to affect other types of work an editor does for Wikipedia.

Anecdotal evidence we found on talk page conversations further highlights the challenge for active editors to take on and juggle too many projects and the risk for project leaders to over-draft from the same pool of active editors.

"Goodnes[sic]; I should have abolished this article last month but got too many projects on my plate and forgot."

"I'm working on too many projects atm. I'm going to be moving slowly here."

"Ditto. PS. Considered joining us in this fine wikiproject? :)" "Thanks. I can definitely occasionally lend a hand here and there, but I already am involved in too many projects for the limited time budget I am on."

The real trade-off lies between withdrawal behaviors at the project level and those at the Wikipedia level. Being involved in multiple projects showed decreased likelihood of leaving a specific individual project, possibly because multiple projects give members more opportunities to remain involved. At the same time, being involved in too many projects may increase their stress level, which could eventually cause them to abandon the site altogether. The challenge is how to leverage the benefits of multiple project membership while minimizing its negative impact. Resolving this challenge requires both change to Wikipedia's policies and guidelines and the development of software tools to improve awareness of editors' activity and commitment across projects. Tools can be developed to share information across projects, such as how many projects an editor has joined, how many edits an editor has made for each of these projects in recent

[3]http://meta.wikimedia.org/wiki/Wikistress
[4]http://meta.wikimedia.org/wiki/Wikibreak
[5]http://en.wikipedia.org/wiki/Template:Wstress3d

months, etc. Wikistress meters may also be an indication of instances in which editors have been overtaxed by too many projects. We expect such information to provide insights into an editor's workload that may help coordination efforts to avoid competition among projects for member attention. Tools can also be developed to use a combination of signs such as involvement in a large number of projects and sudden or significant drops in recent editing behaviors to generate alerts for editors or project leaders.

Does old wisdom on individual productivity and withdrawal apply to online volunteer groups?

At a high level, many of the insights from social and organizational theories still apply to the online context. Both individual productivity and withdrawal are affected by factors such as group characteristics, individual attributes like tenure and past performance, and social connections within and across projects. We were able to replicate many relationships between variables in traditional organizations, such as the negative relation between tenure and withdrawal, the positive relation between internal and external communication and productivity, and the positive relation between external communication and withdrawal. However, there are subtle differences between our findings and what we expected from reviewing old theories.

One example is the negative relationship between tenure and productivity and the positive relationship between past productivity and withdrawal. Following the organization science literature, we expected old-timers to be more productive and members with low levels of productivity to be more likely to withdraw. Yet we found the opposite of these effects. The discrepancy can be attributed to the informal and voluntary nature of online groups compared to formalization and bureaucracy in traditional organizations. Members of online groups don't have fixed roles (except those who become administrators) and self-select to take on certain tasks and responsibilities. The goal of many members may be to find or share information and contribute to a good cause, rather than sticking around and climbing corporate ladders. Therefore, members who have contributed much of their knowledge may either feel a sense of "mission accomplished" or become burnt out and leave or stop contributing.

Another discrepancy between our findings and the organizational literature is the effects of the number of concurrent projects on productivity and withdrawal. The variable itself is somewhat unique to the online context. Although employees of traditional organizations may work on multiple projects, they are limited in how many they can join, either by their billable hours or managerial oversight. The voluntary nature of online collaboration allows members to join as many projects as they wish, up to or even beyond what their time and effort allow. With greater control and less individual autonomy in choosing projects to join, we expect some differences in the effects of multiple project membership on individual behaviors. For instance, being involved in multiple projects does not necessarily increase one's likelihood of withdrawal. Instead, individuals may develop social networks with different units within the organization, reducing their likelihood of withdrawing from these units though they may not have strong bonds with the organization itself.

Comparison with the organization science literature reveals a limitation in our measure of productivity. It does not consider the type of work or quality of work. This may help explain the interesting dilemma we found with old-timers – they stay longer with a project but do not contribute as much as newcomers. Because our measure of productivity only considers the quantity of contribution, it is possible that, with more experience, old-timers shift their focus to administrative work or more challenging tasks, which is not reflected in a simple edit count. Examining type and quality of work would be fruitful for future research.

Overall, our study confirmed the applicability of social science theories to at least one online group, while also highlighting the importance of reconsidering and modifying the assumptions and propositions to fit the online context.

ACKNOWLEDGMENTS

Thanks to the Wikimedia Foundation for providing the data. Thanks to Robert Kraut, members of GroupLens Research Lab at the Department of Computer Science and Engineering, and the OB Research Group at the Carlson School of Management for their feedback and support. This work is supported by National Science Foundation Grant IIS-0808692, IIS 0729344 and IIS 0534939.

REFERENCES

1. Albanese, R. and Van Fleet, D.D. Rational Behavior in Groups: The Free-Riding Tendency. *Academy of Management Review, 10*, 2 (1985), 244-255.
2. Arnold, H.J. and Feldman, D.C. A Multivariate Analysis of the Determinants of Job Turnover. *Journal of Applied Psychology, 67*, 3 (1982), 350-360.
3. Arthur, J.B. Effects of Human Resource Systems on Manufacturing Performance and Turnover. *Academy of Management Journal, 37*, 3 (1994), 670-687.
4. Bakker, A.B., Van Der Zee, K.I., Lewig, K.A., and Dollard, M.F. The Relationship Between the Big Five Personality Factors and Burnout: A Study Among Volunteer Counselors. *The Journal of Social Psychology, 146*, 1 (2007), 31-50.
5. Barron, D.N., West, E., and Hannan, M.T. A Time to Grow and a Time to Die: Growth and Mortality of Credit Unions in New York City, 1914-1990. *American Journal of Sociology, 100*, 2 (1994), 381-421.
6. Becker, G.S. A theory of the Allocation of Time. *The Economic Journal, 75*, 299 (1965), 493-517.
7. Beehr, T.A. and Gupta, N. A Note on the Structure of Employee Withdrawal. *Organizational Behavior and Human Performance, 21*, 1 (1978), 73-79.
8. Bryk, A.S. and Raudenbush, S.W. Hierarchical Linear Models for Social and Behavioural Research: Applications and Data Analysis Methods. Newbury Park, CA: Sage Publications (1992).

9. Burnham, K.P. and Anderson, D.R. Multimodel Inference: Understanding AIC and BIC in Model Selection. *Sociological Methods Research, 33* (2004), 261-304.
10. Butler, B.S. Membership Size, Communication Activity, and Sustainability: A Resource-Based Model of Online Social Structures. *Information Systems Research, 12*, 4 (2001), 346-362.
11. Butler, B.S., Sproull, L., Kiesler, S., and Kraut, R.E. Community Effort in Online Groups: Who Does the Work and Why? In S. Weisband & L. Atwater (Eds.), *Leadership at a Distance*. Lawrence Erlbuam Associates (2007).
12. Chen, J., Ren, Y., and Riedl, J. The effects of diversity on group productivity and member withdrawal in online volunteer groups. In *Proc. CHI 2010*, ACM Press (2010).
13. Cordes, C.L. and Dougherty, T.W. A Review and An Integration of Research on Job Burnout. *Academy of Management Review, 18*, 4 (1993), 621-656.
14. Cosley, D., Frankowski, D., Terveen, L., and Riedl, J. Using intelligent task routing and contribution review to help communities build artifacts of lasting value. In *Proc. CHI 2006*, ACM Press (2006).
15. Cotton, J.L. and Tuttle, J.M. Employee Turnover: A Meta-Analysis and Review with Implications for Research. *Academy of Management Review, 11*, 1 (1986), 55-70.
16. Cross, R. and Cummings, J.N. Tie and Network Correlates of Individual Performance in Knowledge-Intensive Work. *Academy of Management Journal, 47*, 6 (2004), 928-937.
17. Daniel, S.L. and Diamant, E.I. Network Effects in OSS Development: The Impact of Users and Developers on Project Performance. *ICIS 2008 Proceedings*.
18. Farmer, S.M. and Fedor, D.B. Volunteer Participation and Withdrawal: A Psychological Contract Perspective on the Role of Expectations and Organizational Support. *Nonprofit Management and Leadership, 9* (1999), 349-368.
19. Griffeth, R.W., Hom, P.W., and Gaertner, S. A Meta-Analysis of Antecedents and Correlates of Employee Turnover: Update, Moderator Tests, and Research Implications for the Next Millennium. *Journal of Management, 26*, 3 (2000), 463-488.
20. Halfaker, A., Kittur, A., Riedl, J. Don't Bite the Newbies: How Reverts Affect the Quantity and Quality of Wikipedia Work. In *WikiSym 2011*.
21. Haythornthwaite, C. Crowds and Communities: Light and Heavyweight Models of Peer Production. In *Proc. HICSS 2009*, IEEE (2009).
22. Hofmann, DA., Jacobs, R., and Gerras, S.J. Mapping individual performance over time. *Journal of Applied Psychology, 77*, 2 (1992), 185-195.
23. Kittur, A. and Kraut, R.E. Harnessing the Wisdom of Crowds in Wikipedia: Quality Through Coordination. In *Proc. CSCW 2008*, ACM Press (2008).
24. Kittur, A., and Kraut, R.E. Beyond Wikipedia: coordination and conflict in online production groups. In *Proc. CSCW 2010*, ACM Press (2010).
25. Kittur, A., Chi, E., Pendleton, B.A., Suh, B., and Mytkowicz, T. Power of the Few vs. Wisdom of the Crowd: Wikipedia and the Rise of the Bourgeoisie. *Alt.CHI at CHI 2007*.
26. Kittur, A., Suh, B., Pendleton, B.A., and Chi, E.H. He says, she says: conflict and coordination in Wikipedia. In *Proc. CHI 2007*, ACM Press (2007).
27. Lyubomirsky, S. and Nolen-Hoeksema, S. Effects of Self-Focused Rumination on Negative Thinking and Interpersonal Problem Solving. *Journal of Personality and Social Psychology, 69*, 1 (1995), 176-190.
28. Markus, M.L. Toward a "Critical Mass" Theory of Interactive Media. *Communication Research, 14*, 5 (1987), 491-511.
29. McEvoy, G.M. and Cascio, W.F. Do Good or Poor Performers Leave? A Meta-Analysis of the Relationship between Performance and Turnover. *Academy of Management Journal, 30*, 4 (1987), 744-762.
30. McPherson, J.M., Popielarz, P.A., and Drobnic, S. Social Networks and Organizational Dynamics. *American Psychological Review, 57*, 2 (1992), 153-170.
31. McPherson, M., Smith-Lovin, L., and Cook, J.M. Birds of a Feather: Homophily in Social Networks. *Annual Review of Sociology, 27* (2001), 415-444.
32. Mitchell, T.R., Holtom, B.C., Lee, T.W., Sablynski, C.J., and Erez, M. 2001. Why People Stay: Using Job Embeddedness to Predict Voluntary Turnover. *Academy of Management Journal, 44*, 6 (2001), 1102-1121.
33. O'Reilly, C.A., III, Caldwell, D.F., and Barnett, W.P. Work Group Demography, Social Integration, and Turnover. *Administrative Science Quarterly, 34*, 1 (1989), 21-37.
34. Priedhorsky, R., Chen, J., Lam, S.K., Panciera, K., Terveen, L., and Riedl, J. Creating, Destroying, and Restoring Value in Wikipedia. In *Proc. GROUP 2007*, ACM Press (2007).
35. Randel, A.E. and Jaussi, K.S. Functional Background Identity, Diversity, and Individual Performance in Cross-Functional Teams. *Academy of Management Journal, 46*, 6 (2003), 763-774.
36. Robles, G., Gonzalez-Barahona J.M., Michlmayr, M. Evolution of Volunteer Participation in Libre Software Projects: Evidence from Debian. In *Proc. First International Conference on Open Source Systems 2005*.
37. Spencer, D.G. and Steers, R.M. Performance as a Moderator of the Job Satisfaction-Turnover Relationship. *Journal of Applied Psychology, 66* (1981), 511-514.
38. Sturman, M.C. Searching for the Inverted U-Shaped Relationship Between Time and Performance: Meta-Analyses of the Experience/Performance, Tenure/ Performance, and Age/Performance Relationships. *Journal of Management, 9*, 5 (2003), 609-640.
39. Suh, B., Convertino, G., Chi., E.H., and Pirolli, P. The Singularity is Not Near: Slowing Growth of Wikipedia. In *Proc. WikiSym2009*, ACM Press (2009).
40. Taylor, L.C. Thousands of Editors Leaving Wikipedia. Thestar.com, Nov. 23 (2009).
http://www.thestar.com/news/sciencetech/technology/article/729552--thousands-of-editors-leaving-wikipedia.
41. Wagner, W.G., Pfeffer, J., and O'Reilly, C.A., III. Organizational Demography and Turnover in Top-Management Group. *Administrative Science Quarterly, 29*, 1 (1984), 74-92.
42. Wilson, J. Volunteering. *Annual Review of Sociology, 26* (2000), 215-240.

Asking Questions of Targeted Strangers on Social Networks

Jeffrey Nichols
IBM Research – Almaden
650 Harry Rd, San Jose, CA 95110
jwnichols@us.ibm.com

Jeon-Hyung Kang
USC Information Sciences Institute
4676 Admiralty Way, Marina del Rey, CA 90292
jeonhyuk@usc.edu

ABSTRACT
When people have questions, they often turn to their social network for answers. If the answer is obscure or time sensitive however, no members of their social networks may know the answer. For example, it may be difficult to find a friend who has experience with a particular feature or model of digital camera or who knows the current wait time for security at the local airport. In this paper, we explore the feasibility of answering questions by asking strangers. In this approach, strangers with potentially useful information are identified by mining the public status updates posted on Twitter, questions are sent to these strangers, and responses are collected. We explore feasibility in two ways: will users respond to questions sent by strangers and, if they do respond, how long must we wait for a response? Our results from asking 1159 questions across two domains suggest that 42% of users will respond to questions from strangers. 44% of these responses arrived within 30 minutes.

ACM Classification Keywords
H5.m. Information interfaces and presentation (e.g., HCI): Miscellaneous.

General Terms
Experimentation, Human Factors

Author Keywords
Social Q&A, Twitter, qCrowd

INTRODUCTION
Unlike many other social networking sites, much of the content posted by users to Twitter is publicly accessible. This creates a unique opportunity for a Q&A system; users who may be able to answer questions can be identified from the content of their previous tweets and questions can be sent to those users directly using features such as the @reply. This approach is different from typical Q&A on social networks because it targets answerers who are strangers rather than friends. This approach is also different from other existing Q&A systems, which rely on a potential question answerer to find the question on a web site (e.g.,

Figure 1. An example question/answer regarding the airport security wait time at SeaTac Airport.

Answers.com and StackOverflow) or on users to submit expertise profiles to help automatically identify potential answerers (e.g., Aardvark [1] and IM-an-Expert [7]).

We believe there are advantages of this "targeting strangers with questions" approach, at least for certain classes of questions. One particularly interesting class is *questions about an event that are best answered soon after the event.* The real-time nature of Twitter allows a question asker to identify strangers experiencing relevant events based on keywords in status updates and send relevant questions immediately. E.g., asking about the current wait time at an airport security checkpoint (see Figure 1). Another class is *questions for which there may be a diversity of opinion.* A Twitter-based Q&A system could target knowledgeable users across a range of different biases as detected from their social media posts (e.g., camera users that prefer Nikon or Canon, or political party affiliations [6]) and extract answers across that range.

We foresee at least two different implementations of this approach. A semi-automated dashboard implementation would allow users to enter a question, search for people that might be knowledgeable in that area, and send questions to a subset of those people. An automatic approach could also be useful in some situations. For example, a retailer's CRM system might identify complaints about service and send questions to learn more about the problem before engaging a human representative to provide a solution.

There are at least two challenges to building a Q&A system based on this approach. First, we must be able to identify strangers who can answer our questions based only on the content of their tweets. We have found that this varies based on domain and is easier for heavily trafficked locations, such as airports, and popular technology products, such as high-end digital cameras. We expect growth in social networks and improvements in text analytics to make this more reliable for less popular topics in the future. Of course, we would not expect to be able to find strangers for topics that are not routinely discussed on social networks, such as personal health issues [4]. Second, strangers must be willing to respond when receiving a question. Here we focus on the second challenge and examine the following questions:

- Will users respond to unsolicited questions sent by strangers?
- How will providing an incentive for answering affect their response rate?
- If users respond, what is the duration between question and response?

To answer these questions, we conducted a series of experiments in which we watched a live stream of status updates from Twitter, manually sent questions to relevant users, and collected response rates and times. We asked questions in two different domains, airport security tracking and digital camera reviews, and in the airport domain we also tried questions with and without the incentive statement seen in Figure 1. Our overall finding from asking 1159 questions is that users responded to 42% of initial questions, and that 44% of all responses arrived within 30 minutes of sending the question. We also found that removing the incentive statement did not affect response rate, but seemed to result in a greater number of questions being marked as spam by recipients.

RELATED WORK

Numerous web services provide forums for posting questions and providing answers, including Yahoo! Answers, Answers.com, StackOverflow and Quora. All of these sites rely on experts to visit the site and provide answers to questions for which they are knowledgeable. There are also a myriad of question answering services that use Twitter, including TweetQA[1] and AskOnTwitter[2]. The Twitter-based services primarily offer two capabilities: aggregating questions asked by users on Twitter and tracking responses to those questions. We have not found a service that helps users direct questions to appropriate strangers, especially to strangers who have not previously opted-in to the service.

Several studies have been conducted of Q&A in a variety of settings. Zhang et al. [8] conducted a study of the Java Developers Forum and found the average response time to a question to be nearly 9 hours. Hsieh and Counts [2] found the average response time on Microsoft's Live QnA site to be 2 hours and 52 minutes, and that 20% of questions posted were never answered. Mamykina et al. [3] found that StackOverflow provides answers to software development questions in a median time of 11 minutes. Morris et al. [4] conducted a survey of Q&A within social networks and found that questions were answered in a comparable amount of time to other sites, such as those previously mentioned, but that users tended to trust the opinions of people they knew compared to those of strangers.

Paul et al. [5] conducted a study of question asking on Twitter. They found the response rate for questions in their corpus was only 18.7%, but the median response time was 10 minutes for questions that were answered. They also found that 67% of responses came within 30 minutes and 95% came within 10 hours. Later in the paper, we will discuss our results in the context of these numbers.

EXPERIMENTAL SETUP

Our goal for the design of the feasibility study was to maximize the chance that users would respond to our questions, because we expected the response rate might be very low even in favorable conditions. We also hoped to establish an upper bound on how well such a system might perform, which could be used in the future to judge the performance of automated systems. We built a simple dashboard application to help us choose which status updates to respond to and which questions to ask. We were conservative in choosing which users were sent questions.

We chose two question domains to which we believed strangers might be willing to respond: airport security wait time tracking and digital camera product reviews. We chose these two domains because:

- The desired information is not personal in nature (In the airport case we asked questions of people who had already reported their location publicly);
- There is enough traffic on these topics that it is easy to find relevant status updates;
- The initial question is easy to answer. Reporting a wait time can be two words (e.g., 10 minutes), and our initial camera question had a yes/no answer (the question was, "Do you have <camera model>?").

Airport Security Wait Time Tracking (TSA Tracker)

In this domain, we watch for users who report that they are at a US airport via a real-time stream from the Twitter streaming API. Once we have identified a relevant user, we send them one of two questions:

> **Q1:** If you went through security at <airport code>, can you reply with your wait time? Info will be used to help other travelers
>
> **Q2:** If you went through security at <airport code>, can you reply with your wait time?

The only difference between the two questions is the final sentence of Q1, which attempts to motivate users to respond because they will be helping others. We anticipated that users might view the profile of the Twitter account from which the message originated, so we used separate accounts

[1] http://www.tweetqa.com/
[2] http://www.askontwitter.com/

for each question: Q1 was asked by @tsatracker, whereas Q2 was asked by @tsatracking. Note that we use accounts with institutional sounding names. We plan to experiment with using accounts with personal names in the future.

For each response, we posted the wait time on a web site that we created to store the data: http://tsatracker.org/. We also sent back a thank you message with a link to the site.

Digital Camera Q&A

In this domain, we watch for users who mention specific model numbers for any of 8 different digital cameras (e.g., Nikon D7000, Canon 7D, etc.), again via a real-time stream. Once we have identified a user, we send a question asking whether the user owns whichever camera they mentioned. All questions were sent by @productqa.

A key difference between this domain and the previous is that we ask multiple questions. If the user responded that they did own the camera, we followed-up with a camera-related question such as, "How is the image quality?" We asked up to 3 follow-up questions based on their replies.

RESULTS

For our experiment, we have 3 conditions: 2 in the airport domain (Q1 vs. Q2) and 1 in the digital camera domain. Table 1 shows a summary of the results for the first question asked in each condition. Figure 2 shows a histogram of response times for each of the 3 conditions, coupled with line graphs showing the percentage of total responses received over time. Note that the response times follow a power law distribution.

To examine whether the response rate in any of the conditions differed, we performed 3 pairwise two-tailed Fisher's exact tests and found no significant difference between the groups. To test differences in response time, we performed a Kruskal-Wallis test that showed a marginal difference between the conditions ($H=5.7$, $df=2$, $p < 0.06$). This likely reflects the shorter tail in the distribution of response times in the Airport Q2 condition, which occurred because Twitter suspended the @tsatracking account within an hour or two after its last question. This prevented late responses and altered its response time distribution. No significant difference was found when comparing just the set of response times until the Q2 account was suspended across all 3 conditions. We were unable to collect any quantitative data that would allow a comparison to our

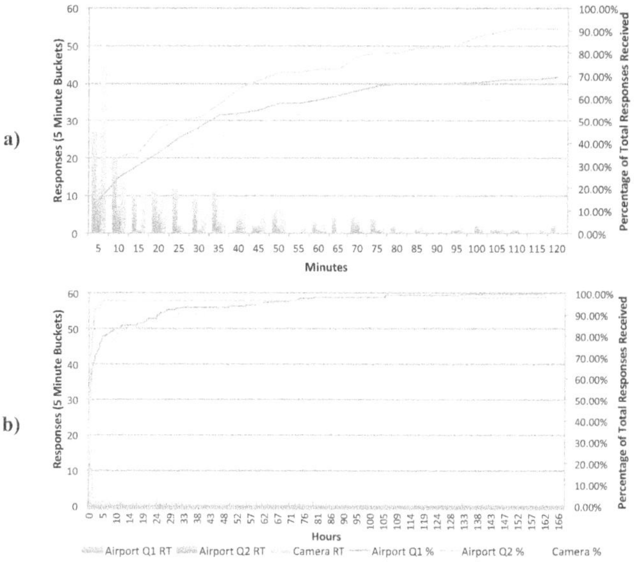

Figure 2. Total responses in 5 minute buckets and percentage of total responses received for each condition. a) The first two hours of data, b) All responses received within a week. Note that the percentage of total responses for Airport Q2 grows more quickly because that account was suspended, which artificially capped responses.

other conditions where many more questions were asked. A Twitter representative told us the account exceeded a threshold for tweets marked as spam or user blocks.

Table 2 shows a summary of the results for the follow-up questions asked in the camera condition. A pairwise two-tailed Fisher's exact test found significant differences in response rate between the first question and the first follow-up ($p < 0.0001$) and the first and second follow-up questions ($p < 0.0001$), but no significant difference between the second and third follow-ups. A significant difference in response time behavior was found between all four questions ($H=50.12$, $df=3$, $p < 0.0001$, Kruskal-Wallis) and just the three follow-ups ($H=25.46$, $df=2$, $p < 0.0001$, Kruskal-Wallis). This suggests that conversations were more likely to continue with users that responded quickly.

DISCUSSION

The first thing to note is that our results are different than those found by Paul et al. [5]. This is expected, because our questions have different properties from the questions they studied. In particular, each question in Paul et al.'s set were

Table 1. Summary of experimental results for the first question in each condition. *The Airport Q2 account was suspended after asking 150 questions, which distorts some of these numbers.

	Asked	Responses	Response Rate	Median Response Time (minutes)	% Responses Within 30 minutes	95% Responses Received In (hours)
Airport Q1	424	189	45%	25.5	47%	55.4
Airport Q2*	150	56	38%	33	52%	4.1
Cameras	585	245	42%	47	42%	47.0

Table 2. Summary of results for follow-up questions in the Camera condition

	Asked	Responses	Response Rate	Median Response Time (minutes)	% Responses Within 30 minutes	95% Responses Received In (hours)
1st follow-	245	151	62%	18.5	58%	17.5
2nd follow-	61	55	90%	2	84%	11.2
3rd follow-	24	23	96%	6	78%	2.0

sent by one user to all of that user's followers, as compared to our questions, each of which was seen by only one user. This difference in the number of potential answerers may explain the shorter response rate found by Paul et al. Our questions were also targeted at specific users who were likely to be able to answer the question and required a relatively basic response, whereas Paul et al.'s questions were more varied and may have required a more thoughtful response or expertise not possessed by anyone who saw the question. This difference may account for our much larger response rate (42% compared to 18.7% for Paul et al.).

Including the motivational sentence clearly had an effect on behavior, as not including the sentence resulted in suspension of the question asking account. Unfortunately, Twitter would not provide specific numbers on blocks or spam flags so it is not possible to compare these values across each of the 3 accounts used in our experiments. It does seem that the @tsatracking account exceeded some threshold for suspension whereas both of our other accounts, which together sent many times more questions, did not. We found it surprising that including the motivational sentence did not have a significant effect on response rate or time. Overall, these results suggest that the incentive sentence may not affect people who would be willing to respond to the question but does have an affect on those who are not willing to respond. Without the motivational sentence, users who would not be willing to respond may be more likely to mark the question as spam or block the user.

Despite being suspended, our question asking approach complies with Twitter's Terms of Service. With respect to unsolicited @replies, the Terms explicitly disallow sending large numbers of duplicate @replies or using @replies to spam a link or service. Our question tweets are all customized to the particular user they are sent to, so they are not duplicates. We also explicitly do not include a link in our initial question, which both complies with the terms and avoids the misperception that the question could be a phishing attack.

The responses that we received in all conditions were almost uniformly positive. The most negative comment that we received came from one user (in the non-incentive airport condition), who remarked that our question was "creepy," but also provided a wait time. We also received a lot of positive feedback, primarily in the airport conditions where we built a web site to display the data for everyone. Comments especially came from people who said they were frequent travelers and looked forward to making use of the tool in the future. The @tsatracker account, from which we asked many of our questions, also picked up 16 followers over the course of our experiment.

Our goal in this work was to determine the feasibility of building a Q&A system using our approach of asking targeted strangers, and we believe our results demonstrate that this approach can be feasible, at least in our two domains. Whether the approach can translate to other domains depends on the ease of finding strangers with potential to answer the question and the nature of the question being asked. Obviously, questions about personal information or other sensitive topics are likely to be ignored or blocked, and it will be difficult to find strangers to answer questions on topics that are not frequently discussed on Twitter. Although certainly not conclusive, our results suggest that asking questions of targeted strangers can be a viable approach if these other challenges are overcome.

CONCLUSION

In this paper, we have explored the feasibility of a system that obtains answers by sending unsolicited questions to people based on their public status updates on social networks. We found that 42% of people will respond to these questions, at least in the "best case" scenarios that we explored. Going forward, we plan to build technology that provides a dashboard to assist users in applying this approach in custom domains and an automated system that can be used to assist in customer support and crowd data collection scenarios.

REFERENCES

1. Horowitz, D. and Kamvar, S.D. (2010). "The anatomy of a large-scale social search engine," in *Proceedings of WWW*, 431–440.
2. Hsieh, G. and Counts, S. (2009). "A market-based real-time question and answer service." In *Proceedings of CHI'09*. 769-778
3. Mamykina, L., Manoim, B., Mittal, M., Hripcsak, G., and Hartmann, B. (2011). "Design lessons from the fastest q&a site in the west," In *Proceedings of CHI '11*. 2857-2866
4. Morris, M.R., Teevan, J., and Panovich, K. (2010). "What do people ask their social networks, and why?: a survey study of status message q&a behavior," In *Proceedings of CHI '10*. 1739-1748.
5. Paul, S.A., Hong, L., and Chi, E.H. (2011). "Is Twitter a Good Place for Asking Questions? A Characterization Study," In *Proceedings of ICWSM'11 Posters*.
6. Pennacchiotti, M., and Popescu, A. (2011) "A Machine Learning Approach to Twitter User Classification," in *Proceedings of ICWSM'11*. 281-288
7. White, R.W., Richardson, M., and Liu, Y. (2011). "Effects of community size and contact rate in synchronous social q&a," In *Proceedings of CHI '11*. 2837-2846
8. Zhang, J., Ackerman, M., Adamic, L. and Nam, K. (2007). "QuME: A Mechanism to Support Expertise Finding in Online Help-Seeking Communities," In *Proceedings of UIST'07*. 111-11

Collaboratively Crowdsourcing Workflows with Turkomatic

Anand Kulkarni[1], Matthew Can[2], Björn Hartmann[3]
Department of IEOR[1], Computer Science Division[3]
University of California, Berkeley
anandk@berkeley.edu, bjoern@cs.berkeley.edu
Computer Science Department[2]
Stanford University
mattcan@cs.stanford.edu

ABSTRACT

Preparing complex jobs for crowdsourcing marketplaces requires careful attention to workflow design, the process of decomposing jobs into multiple tasks, which are solved by multiple workers. Can the crowd help design such workflows? This paper presents Turkomatic, a tool that recruits crowd workers to aid requesters in planning and solving complex jobs. While workers decompose and solve tasks, requesters can view the status of worker-designed workflows in real time; intervene to change tasks and solutions; and request new solutions to subtasks from the crowd. These features lower the threshold for crowd employers to request complex work. During two evaluations, we found that allowing the crowd to plan without requester supervision is partially successful, but that requester intervention during workflow planning and execution improves quality substantially. We argue that Turkomatic's collaborative approach can be more successful than the conventional workflow design process and discuss implications for the design of collaborative crowd planning systems.

Author Keywords

Crowdsourcing, task decomposition, workflows.

ACM Classification Keywords

H5.3. Information interfaces and presentation (e.g., HCI): Group and Organization Interfaces.

General Terms

Algorithms, Design, Human Factors

INTRODUCTION

Crowdsourcing marketplaces are increasingly used to solve computational problems that require human intelligence, such as audio transcription and data verification [11,16]. Many problems on markets like Amazon Mechanical Turk are solved as a series of *microtasks*: narrowly focused, brief tasks designed to be completed in a few minutes, such as labeling an image or checking the accuracy of data through web search. For quality assurance and to accomplish complex work, multiple microtasks are frequently chained together into *workflows*. Such workflows may decompose larger tasks into smaller subtasks, and later recompose subtask solutions into an overall work product. For example, a text editing workflow may ask one group of workers to *find* problems, another set to *fix* the identified problems, and a third to *verify* these edits [6]. A fundamental challenge in the use of crowdsourcing markets is the *workflow design problem*: how can employers divide a complex task into a set of microtasks that can be accurately solved by a pool of crowd workers?

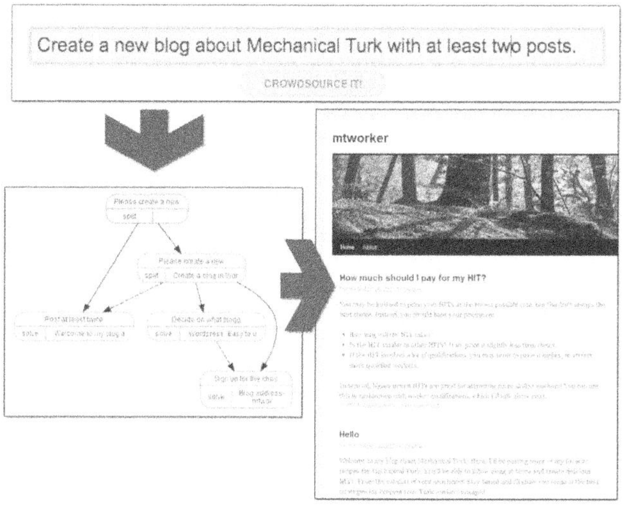

Figure 1: Turkomatic harnesses crowds to design and execute workflows in collaboration with requesters. A request (top) is subdivided into steps by the crowd. Turkomatic shows a task graph as work is progressing (left). Multiple workers execute steps of the created workflow until a global solution is produced – in this case, a new blog (right). Requesters can modify workflows in real-time.

Effective workflow design remains a major challenge today, involving both substantial planning, software development, and testing. Absent formal design methodologies, requesters commonly rely on an iterative process to construct good workflows. Requesters guess at a viable workflow, implement all of its steps as software that interfaces with a crowd platform, test it live with workers, identify points of failure, then iterate and modify the workflow. The cost and complexity of this process limits participation in crowdsourcing marketplaces to experts willing to invest substantial time. These barriers to participation also limit the kinds of work that are crowdsourced today.

We propose that the responsibility for workflow design can be shared between the crowd and the requester. Turkomatic (Figure 1) is a novel crowdsourcing tool that allows the crowd to collaboratively design and execute workflows in conjunction with a requester. Turkomatic accepts a requester's specification of a broad objective, then asks workers on Amazon's Mechanical Turk to determine how to structure workflows to achieve the objective. The requester is able to monitor and edit the resulting workflows as they are produced.

Turkomatic uses a novel meta-workflow to induce the crowd to design and execute workflows. The system executes a continuous *price-divide-solve* loop that asks workers to recursively divide complex steps into simpler ones until they are at an appropriately simple level, then to solve them. Other workers are asked to verify the solutions and combine the results into a coherent answer to the original request. The use of pre-structured task templates and the participation of the crowd enables requesters to produce workflows without implementing software or designing intermediate tasks themselves. Compared to existing toolkits for programmatic workflow design, *e.g.*, TurKit [14] and Jabberwocky [4], these features lower the threshold for employer participation in crowdsourcing.

The price-divide-solve loop produces directed, acyclic *task graphs*: nodes represent subtasks and links describe task dependencies. The task graph is constructed during divide steps, and completed during solve steps. Turkomatic's graphical user interface allows the requester to visualize, monitor and interact with task graphs in real-time. Requesters can delete or modify plans made by workers, request the crowd to re-plan components of workflows, or seed the system with partial plans to evaluate their effectiveness. Real-time visualization of workflow structures and partial solutions enable requesters to debug many of the common failure modes that arise in multi-step workflows. These include cases where workers misunderstand tasks, give inadequate solutions, or where the requester's original language is unclear.

Following a review of related work, we introduce the algorithmic foundations of the *price-divide-solve* loop and discuss how Turkomatic operates from both the requester and worker perspectives. A first experiment explores how workers succeed and fail to plan tasks without expert supervision. A second experiment demonstrates how workers and requesters can successfully interact through Turkomatic on a variety of planning and execution tasks. We close by reporting on usage of Turkomatic outside the lab. Our findings lead to a number of design implications for collaborations on crowdsourcing platforms.

RELATED WORK

Early work in human computation emphasized its utility as a tool for efficiently processing large datasets in applications like tagging and classification that were outside the reach of autonomous algorithms [5]. Artificial intelligence researchers emphasized the utility of crowds for supporting active learning problems [17,19]. Most paid microtask work today remains batch data processing [11]. Quinn and Bederson's taxonomy of human computation does not include any creative or integrative tasks [16].

More recent research has attempted to expand the types of tasks that can be solved via distributed human computation. VizWiz is capable of handling open-ended, natural-language requests from users [7]. Soylent provides crowd-powered text editing services in a word processor [6]. Its "find-fix-verify" design pattern divides work in a manner that maintains consistency and accuracy. Legion enables multiple crowd workers to control existing user interfaces in real-time [13].

New toolkits seek to support such complex applications. TurKit aids requesters in deploying iterative tasks on Mechanical Turk; its crash-and-rerun architecture saves intermediate results to avoid redundant crowd assignments [14]. Jabberwocky can target workers in both paid and volunteer workforces [4]. In these toolkits, it is assumed that task designers (not workers) will determine how tasks are broken down in all cases.

While most crowdsourcing tasks are designed manually based on prior experience and intuition, formal techniques can also play a useful. By optimizing task parameters programmatically [10], modeling the market [8], or introducing auction mechanisms [18], response quality and response rate can be improved. Task templates can also be automatically created for data gathering tasks based on an underlying database schema [9].

Both text-based and visual workflow languages have been devised in prior work; Stohr presents a survey of such systems [20]. Some workflow languages have recently been extended to connect to crowdsourcing marketplaces. Crowdsourcing companies such as Crowdflower use the domain-specific workflow language Ruote [1] to implement complex tasks. Ruote is only accessible to expert programmers. RunMyProcess is a commercial service to author and execute business processes in the cloud [2]. It uses Business Process Modeling Notation [21], a standard diagramming convention, as the basis for a visual workflow design tool. Olsen used RunMyProcess to post tasks and receive answers from Mechanical Turk [15].

Most recently, CrowdForge introduced a map-reduce paradigm to divide complex work into smaller steps for crowdsourcing platforms [12]. We also employ a divide-and-conquer strategy, but introduce a recursive algorithm. In addition, Turkomatic adds workflow visualization and editing capabilities not present in CrowdForge.

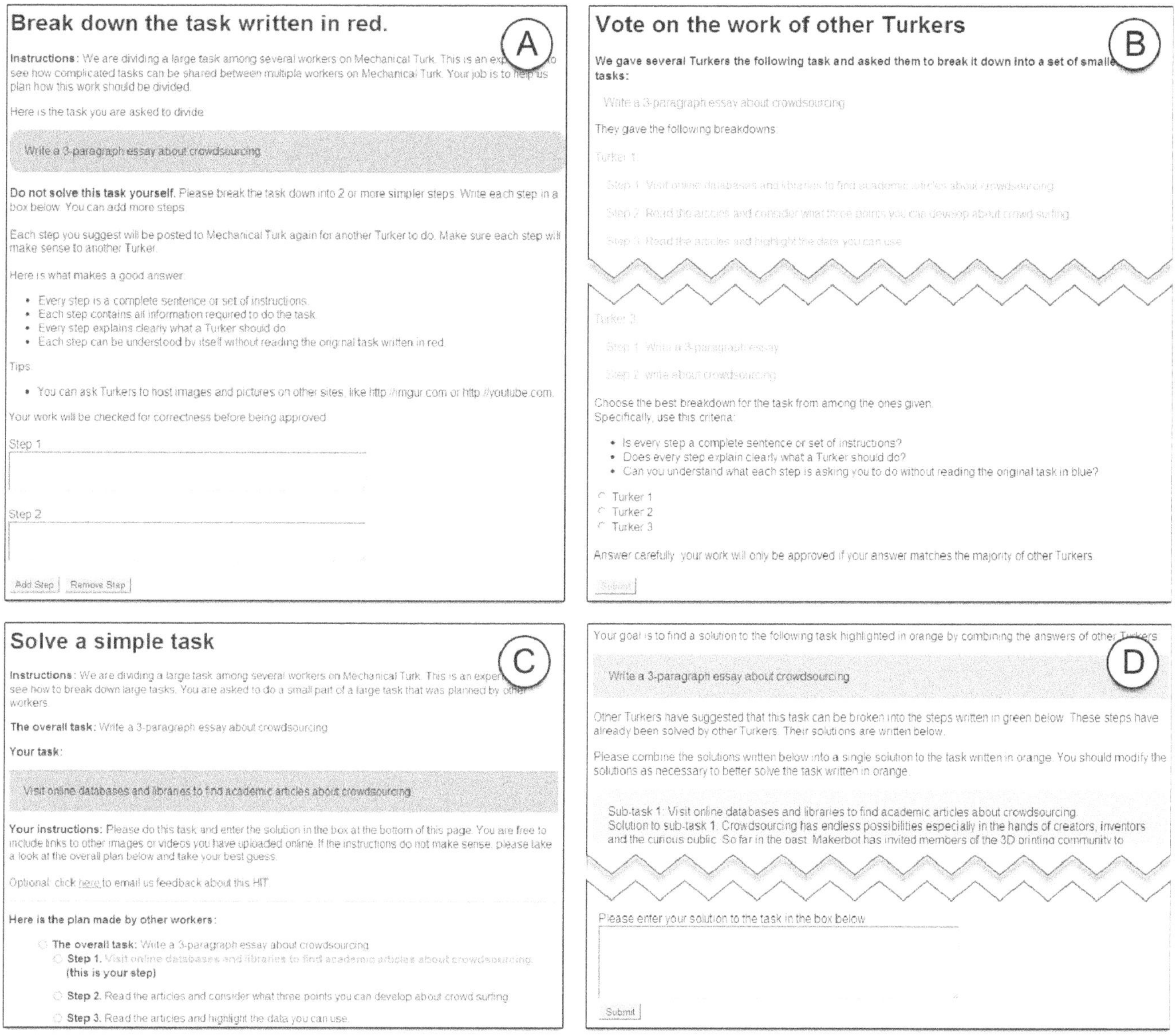

Figure 2: The worker interface: HITs corresponding to (A) subdivision, (B) verification, (C) solution and (D) merging.

THE TURKOMATIC SYSTEM

Turkomatic consists of two major components. First, a *meta-workflow* uses the crowd to assist in the design of the workflow, and to execute it. Our novel *price-divide-solve* algorithm (PDS) uses a divide-and-conquer strategy to let workers decide how to split up tasks. Second, an *editable workflow visualization* enables requesters to observe and manage work being executed by the crowd. We discuss the algorithm and the associated worker interfaces first, then describe Turkomatic's requester interfaces.

Algorithmic Model: Price-Divide-Solve, Then Merge

PDS is a general-purpose algorithm for inducing the crowd to generate workflows for tasks specified by the requester. The algorithm guides workers through the process of converting large, complex tasks into microtasks appropriate for crowd markets. Once all the microtasks for a given component of the workflow are solved, a *merge* stage asks workers to recombine work back into a coherent single solution to the original task. Both stages rely on *verification* functions that determine when work needs to be checked or repeated. For each step in the algorithm, task templates are automatically instantiated with task context and posted to a crowd marketplace (see Figure 2). Turkomatic posts Human Intelligence Tasks (HITs) on Amazon Mechanical Turk, through the algorithm is independent of this particular platform.

Price-Divide-Solve

The *price-divide-solve* phase splits work into fairly priced sub-tasks. An initial pricing HIT presents the overall task goal and asks whether or not this task can be solved for a fixed price (in our implementation, twenty cents). If a worker indicates the task can be solved directly at the stated price, a new HIT will be posted, asking another worker to do so

```
PDS(Task t, Price p, Redundancy r):
  if crowdIsFairPrice(t,p):
    return solve(t,r)
  else:
    subtasks = divide(t,r)
    for s in subtasks:
      subsolutions += PDS(s,p,r)
    return merge(t,subsolutions,r)

divide(Task t, Redundancy r):
    for j in [1,r]:
      divisions += crowdSubdivide(j)
   return crowdChooseBest(divisions)

solve(Task t, Redundancy r):
    for j in [1,r]:
      solutions += crowdSolve(t)
   return crowdChooseBest(solutions)

merge(Task t, Subsolutions s, Redundancy r):
    for j in [1,r]:
      merges += crowdMerge(t,s)
   return crowdChooseBest(merges)
```

Figure 3: Pseudocode for the PDS algorithm. Calls to crowd

(Figure 2C). If the task is judged too complex, the next worker is asked to divide the task into two or more subtasks that are easier to solve than the original task (Figure 2A). To capture information dependencies, workers indicate whether the subtasks can be worked on in parallel or whether they must be completed sequentially.

The set of subtasks is then posted to Mechanical Turk. This process is recursive: subtasks generated by the subdivide step may themselves be broken down by another step. Figure 3 shows pseudo-code for the entire PDS algorithm.

Merge Phase

The *merge* step combines subtask solutions elements produced during *divide* steps. Once all the subtasks produced in a given subdivide step have been solved, the solutions are listed together in a *merge* HIT (Figure 2D). The HIT instructs a worker to combine the subtask solutions in a way that solves the overall goal at the given level of the task hierarchy. The merge process continues until the requester's original task is solved.

Verification

Turkomatic validates the quality of work produced by subdivide, solve, and merge functions by asking the crowd to vote on the best of several redundant answers. For each of these functions, Turkomatic requests r answers from the crowd, where r is an initial redundancy parameter specified by the requester (see Figure 3). For simplicity, r is kept uniform across all types of HITs, though this parameter could be optimized for each HIT independently. In *verification* HITs (Figure 2B), a worker is presented with a task and its candidate decompositions or solutions; the worker is asked to vote on the answer that best accomplishes the task. Using workers to select from redundant answers for quality control is a common strategy in many crowdsourcing applications [6,14].

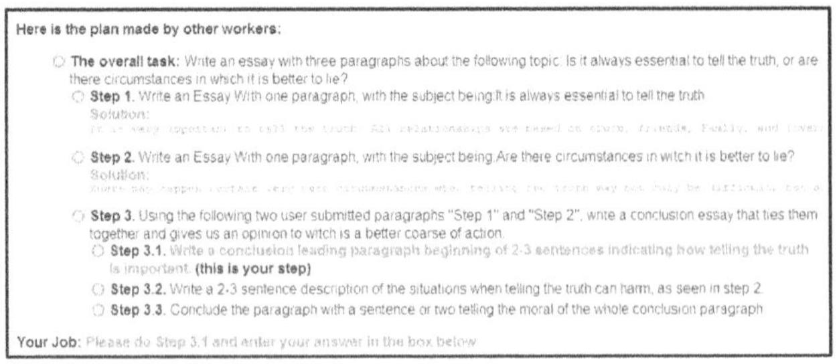

Figure 4: Turkomatic shows task context to workers.

Task Design Strategies

Designing general-purpose HITs that fit a wide variety of tasks while still conveying specific requirements of the decomposition and merge phases to a worker is challenging. In our experience, two design techniques proved especially useful and necessary: 1) including larger task context in subtasks, and 2) visually separating task language from context language.

Show Context of Tasks in a Workflow

Providing workers with a birds-eye view of the overall decomposition is critical. Workers can easily become confused if their role in the larger process is not made explicit. In addition, workers may need to refer to information contained in prior answers to adequately solve their sub-task. To communicate the larger goal, and the work completed towards this goal, Turkomatic shows an indented list view of the decomposition generated by other workers (Figure 4), highlighting the current subtask. This view shows all available information. However, presenting complete task status can also lead to confusion if the task is already extensively subdivided. We reserve further study of the optimal amount of context information that should be presented to future work.

Visually Separate Task Language from Context Language

The HITs for subdivide and merge steps contain complex information and require careful attention of the worker. Workers can have difficulty identifying which task in a complex plan they were being asked to carry out. We used background colors to emphasize and separate the primary task instructions from explanatory and context information. Type treatment, e.g., bold, red text, was used as an effective second level of emphasis. In pilot testing, these attributes were more effective than indentation or whitespace.

Requester Interfaces

This section reviews interaction with Turkomatic from the requester's perspective.

Requesting Work

Requesters post new Turkomatic jobs through a natural-language web interface (Figure 1). Inspired by web search, it offers a single text box where the requesters specify what they want to accomplish.

Expert requesters can also author decompositions that serve as a starting point for the PDS algorithm. Such decompositions may be preferred if the requester believes

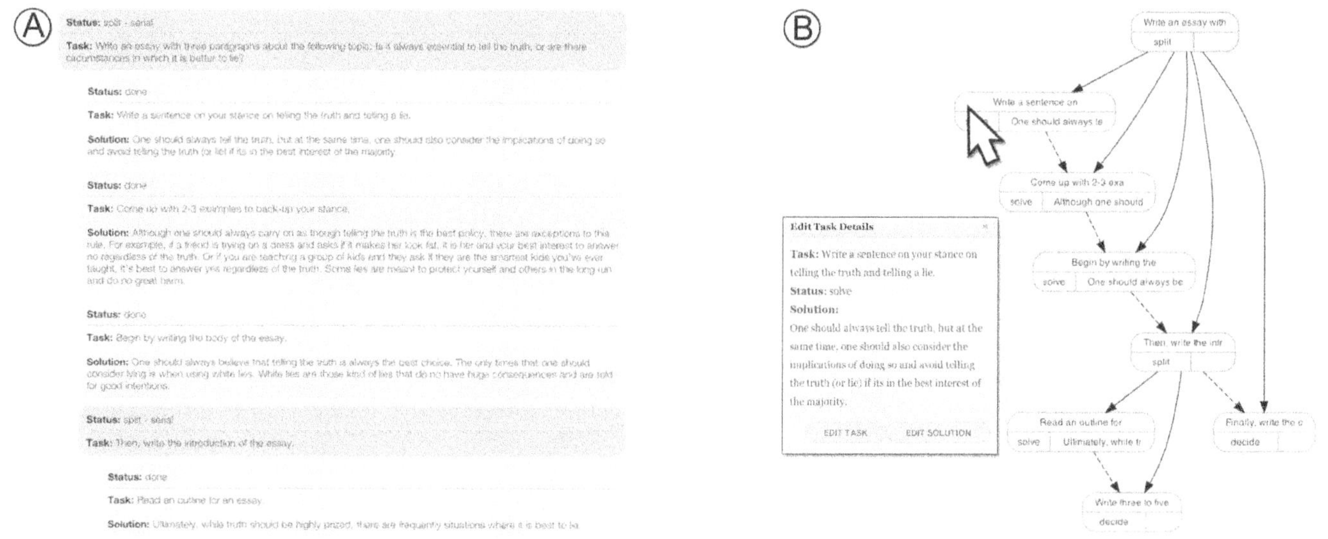

Figure 5: The requester interface: To see content, requesters use an indented list view (A). To see the dependency structure of the workflow, requesters use a graph view (B). A complete task description is shown in a floating panel. In both views, steps are color-coded to indicate their status: waiting (orange), in progress (red/cyan), completed (green).

that crowds will not be able to properly decompose a given task, *e.g.*, because the decomposition requires significant domain expertise. A decomposition specifies a tree structure where the leaves of the tree are the tasks that have to either be solved or further sub-divided. Turkomatic provides an indented list interface for authoring decompositions (Figure 6). Once a new task prompt or task tree is loaded, the PDS algorithm recruits crowd workers to price, subdivide, and solve the leaf tasks, and eventually merge solutions to accomplish the root task.

Visualizing Ongoing Work

To enable requesters to gain insight into partially completed work, Turkomatic provides a workflow visualization that shows the current state of an ongoing job as either an indented list (Figure 5A) or a decomposition graph (Figure 5B). The list view allocates most screen space to task content (*i.e.*, written descriptions and solutions). The graph shows hierarchy, as well as parallel and serial decompositions. Both visualizations inform requesters how much of the work has been accomplished, what strategies have been taken, and whether subtask solutions or decompositions are of sufficient quality.

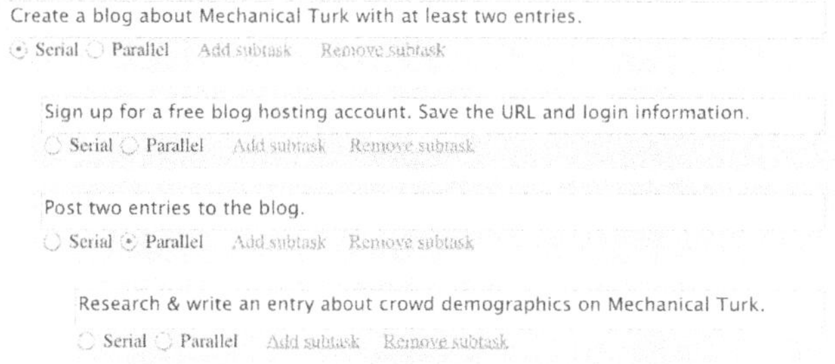

Figure 6: Requesters can author partial workflows before starting the PDS algorithm.

Turkomatic uses GraphViz [3] to render decomposition graphs. Nodes in the graph represent the component tasks of a job. Solid directed edges show the relationship between tasks and sub-tasks (*i.e.*, when there is a subdivision). Dashed directed edges indicate the order of tasks in a serial split, where one sibling must complete before another sibling can be posted.

Each node contains a summary of the task prompt, the solution to the prompt (if available), and a status indicator. A task can either be a) waiting on a decision whether to split or solve (orange in Figure 5B); b) in-progress and waiting for subtasks to complete (cyan); or c) solved (green). The tree visualization is interactive: brushing over nodes displays complete instructions and solutions in a floating panel, as the text often cannot fit in the node. This visualization remains legible for tasks with tens of nodes. For complex graphs, additional interaction techniques such as collapsible branches may become necessary.

Editing Workflows

Ongoing work can be unsatisfactory for multiple reasons: a crowd-authored decomposition may be flawed, or a solution to a subtask may be of low quality. Requesters can edit existing workflows in real-time to address such challenges (Figure 7). Requesters edit the task description, decomposition, or solution for any node. Once an edit is completed, Turkomatic computes which tasks will have to be performed again by additional workers.

When a task *description* is changed (Figure 8A), any subtasks created for this task by the crowd may also no longer be valid. Turkomatic therefore invalidates the entire sub-tree below the edited task and reissues the task (Figure 8B). If the task already had a solution, all upstream solutions of parents that used this stale information have to be reissued

Figure 7: Requesters select a node to edit a workflow (A), and enter new content (B). Turkomatic computes which subtasks have to be re-issued due to the edit and restarts the PDS algorithm (C).

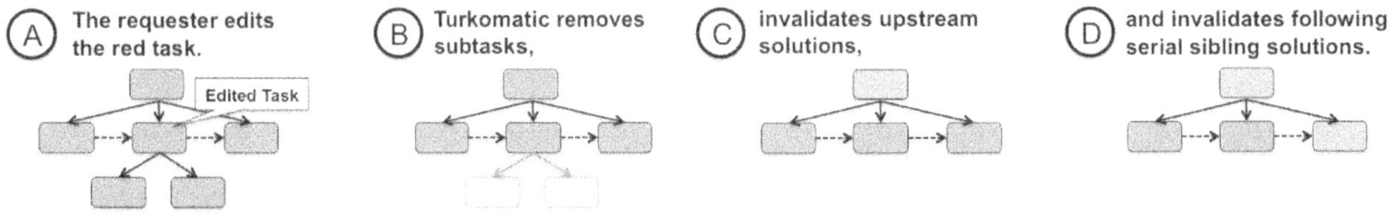

Figure 8: When requesters edit subtasks, children, parent solutions, and sibling solutions may have to be recomputed.

to the crowd as well (Figure 8C). Finally, subsequent siblings in serial decompositions also have to be reissued (Figure 8D). When a requester edits a task *solution* or *decomposition* directly, the entire sub-tree of that task is discarded. Tasks in this sub-tree that are currently being answered will also be discarded. As with task instructions, serial siblings and solutions of parents are also invalidated.

HOW WELL CAN CROWDS PLAN AND EXECUTE?

To explore how effectively crowds can be used to support the execution of complex work, we performed two evaluations. First, we examined how crowds performed in producing and solving workflows without expert intervention. Second, we looked at how expert intervention can improve the crowd's performance. Additionally, we informally observed use of the Turkomatic platform outside the lab. We discuss each of these evaluations in turn.

Unsupervised Crowd Planning

Can the crowd be guided algorithmically to plan and solve problems without any input from requesters? Undirected crowd planning seems *a priori* unlikely to produce usable workflows: design problems often require extensive communication and coordination between client (requester) and designer (worker). In addition, correct interpretation of a prompt may rely on specific domain knowledge. If that knowledge is not shared between requester and worker, instructions are likely to be misinterpreted. To provide a baseline of success and failure patterns, we ran the PDS algorithm with no monitoring by the requester.

Procedure

Via Turkomatic, we requested that the crowd plan workflows for and compute answers to several types of objectives, including essay writing, natural language queries, itinerary planning, Java programming, and multimedia content generation. We ran more than twenty distinct kinds of queries in total. If the crowd had not completed planning and solving a task within 5 days, we posted it a second time. In each of these experiments, we paid $0.05 for *price* and *verify* HITs; and $0.20 for *divide*, *solve* and *merge* HITs. Workers were given 20 minutes to complete each HIT; payments were automatically approved after 24 hours. For five of these tasks, we also systematically modified the redundancy parameter. Requests given to the crowd were phrased as follows:

- **Essay writing**: "Write a 3-paragraph essay about crowdsourcing."
- **Natural language query**: "Create a list of the names of the Department Chairs of the top 20 computer science college programs in the US."
- **Itinerary planning**: "Plan a complete road trip from San Francisco, California, to New York City. Completely include the locations of all necessary hotels, restaurants, and sights along the way."
- **Java programming**: "Please write a short piece of Java code to reverse a string. The algorithm should take as input a string and output its reverse. Make sure it compiles."

For each of these queries, we posed the objective to the crowd through Turkomatic with redundancy levels of one (no redundancy), two, and three.

Results and Observations

We observed both successes and systematic failures. Table 1 shows some task outcomes. The results can be grouped into a small number of classes, described below.

Task Description	Outcome	Subtasks	Sample Data & Observations
Three-paragraph essay: Is it always essential to tell the truth, or are there circumstances in which it is better to lie?	Success with complex planning	7	Top level breakdown was to write one paragraph arguing for one position, another paragraph arguing for the other position, and a conclusion paragraph reconciling the two.
Three paragraph essay: Do we learn more from finding out that we have made mistakes or from our successful failure?	Failure: Starvation	17	Sample response: "I've been through a lot in my life and one thing I've learned is never, ever, ever, even think about smoking or doing drugs. I spent years quitting from smoking and I've learned that lesson."
Write Java code to reverse a string	Success: Snap judgment	1	
Plan a road trip from San Francisco to New York City	Derailment	55	Cyclic behavior: workers recomputed a list of landmarks at least 3 times.
List department chairs of top 20 Computer Science programs in the US	Derailment	5	Loss of context: Solution was a list of IKEA chairs.

Table 1: Experimental results for several unsupervised tasks. Outcome indicates type of success (snap judgment, complex planning) or type of failure (derailment, starvation).

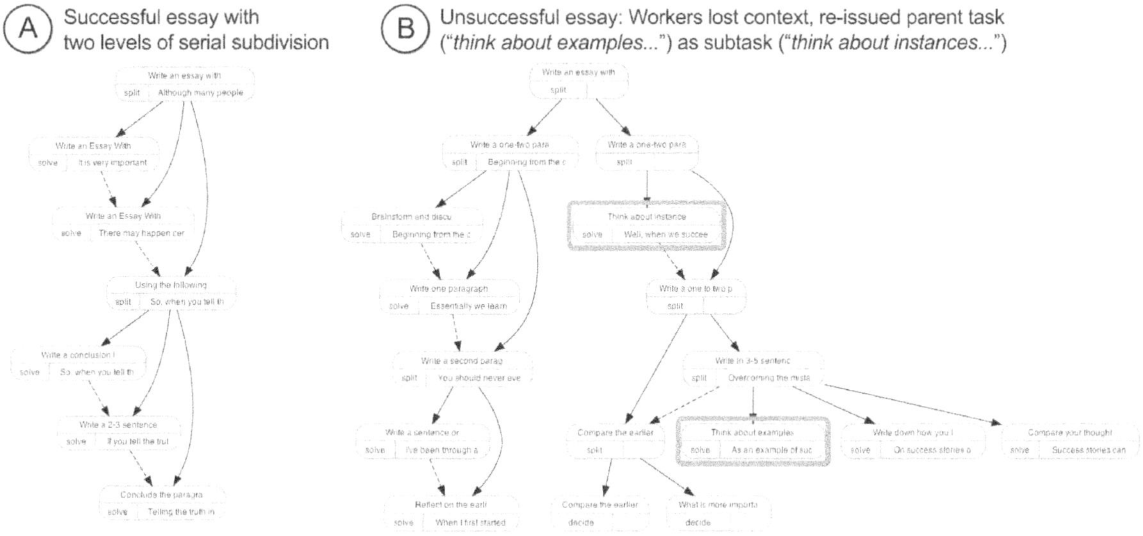

Figure 9: (A) Successful essay decomposition. (B) Derailment due to task cycling Highlighted nodes mark repeated tasks.

Snap Judgments

On a subset of the work, the crowd provided reasonable, correct solutions. One class of successes were *snap judgments*: cases where there was no decomposition of the input task, but where a worker marked the first task as solvable, and a subsequent worker provided a correct, coherent and complete answer. In these outcomes, a correct result is produced without additional decomposition or planning. This success is unsurprising, as no collaboration is involved when no workflow is required: the same worker both determines how to solve a task and solves it.

Successful Planning

In some cases, groups of workers broke down tasks in line with requester intentions, and this was sustained over multiple iterations. For two writing tasks taken from sample SAT essay questions, Turkomatic produced coherent essays with reasonable arguments (Figure 9A – here the task tree has two levels of serial subdivision; each division split the original task into three subtasks).

This outcome occurred infrequently, which is not surprising: it required a shared cognitive model of how work should be decomposed to be maintained by multiple workers in the execution process. We found that the active participation of one or more highly eager workers early in the process made a substantial difference in downstream quality. The strongest workers provided instructions that were self-contained and encapsulated all necessary information independently in each subtask. Downstream workers tended to pattern their contributions after models established by earlier workers.

Challenges:
Task Derailment, Emergent Complexity and Cycling

In the majority of cases, the unsupervised crowd produced unsuitable workflows or unsuccessful results. The most frequent type of failure was *derailment*, a phenomenon that occurred when the PDS algorithm failed to terminate and continued to produce steps indefinitely. An example of this phenomenon is shown in Figure 9B. Derailment occurred for multiple reasons. First, workers were confused about appropriate task granularity. For instance, to write a paragraph as part of an essay-writing task, one worker determined the first subtask for another worker should be to "acquire a writing utensil or a computer" – losing track of the original objective in an effort to subdivide as small as possible. Second, workers authored subdivisions that could be executed by a single worker, but not split across separate workers (e.g. "think about what to write for the next paragraph" followed by "write it down"). Finally, workers who had lost the context of the overall workflow generated decompositions that restated previous tasks as subtasks, leading to cyclic behavior (Figure 9B, red highlight).

Task Starvation

Some workflows failed to complete due to *starvation* – after a while, no new workers attempted the available tasks, and the time limit for the experiment expired without the execution of work continuing further. Task starvation has been observed in other projects [6,7] and has been counteracted in those contexts through listing optimization or chaining sets of tasks to retain workers. In the context of the PDS algorithm, starvation occurred most often when a worker marked a task as solvable when, judging by its complexity, it should have been subdivided.

Standard Quality Assurance Techniques are Insufficient

Surprisingly, adding redundancy by asking more workers to contribute and vote on subdivisions at each step failed to yield more successful decompositions. This is in contrast to other forms of collaborative content creation such as Wikipedia, where increasing the numbers of workers tends to improve the quality of content. One explanation is that Turkomatic's model for redundancy does not allow workers to iterate towards correct answers, but simply increases the parallelism in each step. Workers tended to vote for decompositions that were more detailed and produced more subtasks, introducing more potential failure points.

Interestingly, eager workers sometimes arrived in already derailed workflows and made efforts to correct the state of the system. In several cases workers accepted Turkomatic HITs, but were not satisfied with the workflow provided by previous members of the crowd: these workers chose to email the authors directly to suggest improvements to the task. This suggests that making the Turkomatic requester interface available to motivated workers to allow the crowd to self-police and improve its own work.

COLLABORATIVE PLANNING AND EXECUTION

The results of the previous section suggest that the crowd can sometimes produce acceptable results in planning and executing solutions to general requests, but more frequently faces challenges. At least two different strategies to address these challenges are plausible. The first strategy is to *recruit more expert workers*: it may be that the pool of workers available on Mechanical Turk is not sufficiently qualified to participate in planning tasks. The second strategy is to *allow requesters to monitor and selectively intervene* in the workflow design and execution process. In this section, we describe informal experiments for both approaches: first, with an expert crowd of workers recruited at UC Berkeley; and second, with a Mechanical Turk crowd, augmented through active requester participation using Turkomatic's monitoring interface.

Task instructions	Condition	Outcome
Create a list of the names of the Department Chairs of the top 20 computer science college programs in the US (each school has 1 Department Chair)	Expert workers	Completed without intervention
	Requester monitoring	Task completed after 3 interventions
Write a 3-paragraph essay about crowdsourcing	Expert workers	Completed without intervention
	Requester monitoring	Task completed after 4 interventions
Please create a new blog about Mechanical Turk, with a post and a comment on that post.	Expert workers	Completed with 1 intervention
	Requester monitoring	Task completed with requester termination

Table 2: Results from the second set of Turkomatic Experiments.

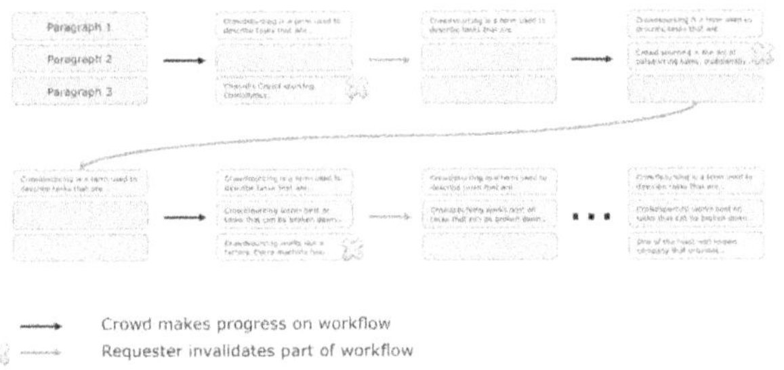

Figure 10: Requesters can intervene repeatedly to increase the quality of the work. Here, different paragraphs of a three-paragraph essay are independently written by different workers. Some work is not acceptable to the requester, so she reissues subtasks.

We re-ran Turkomatic with the essay-writing, blog creation, and natural-language query tasks discussed earlier, in two conditions. In the first condition, we used a pool of five expert workers drawn from a graduate computer science course who had reported experience using Mechanical Turk both as workers and requesters. The experts were males with ages ranging from 21 to 33. These experts were broadly aware that Turkomatic was a system for crowdsourcing complex work, but were not given additional instructions beyond those provided in the HITs. In the second condition, we continued to use Mechanical Turk to recruit workers, but used the requester interface to monitor and edit tasks. To avoid snap judgments, we seeded initial decompositions into the workflow. HITs were priced identically to the unsupervised experiments.

Outcome

Table 2 summarizes the results we obtained, counting the number of interventions required for planning and execution of the tested tasks. Both conditions avoided starvation and derailment and resulted in usable solutions. When expert workers carried out decomposition and solution of the subtasks, solutions were reached rapidly.

When requesters intervened using the workflow editor, the resulting workflows were executed correctly in all cases (*i.e.*, they reached a correct solution without derailment or starvation). Figure 10 shows an example of how an essay-writing workflow evolved during the experiment as requesters intervened to invalidate and re-request specific components of workflows. Requesters did not edit any solutions provided by workers to reach this outcome; only rejection of inconsistent work was required.

Discussion: Why Does Collaborative Workflow Creation Succeed?

When requesters used workflow editing tools to guide the crowd's efforts, tasks completed successfully. Intervention enabled requesters to provide feedback and to iterate on unsuccessful tasks. If a workflow is executed without input from the requester (unsupervised), workers must design plans or create content with only a limited understanding of the requester's intent or preferences. This is in striking contrast to the traditional model of design where designer and clients to converge on a solution through repeated iteration. For complex work, it seems especially important for the requester to provide feedback. Manual intervention and editing of a crowd-generated workflow is an effective (if indirect) way to do so.

For example, requester instructions in our tasks were sometimes inadequate in expressing what a requester actually wanted. In an essay-writing task, when crowd workers submitted solutions to individual paragraphs that were clearly copied from Wikipedia, we used Turkomatic's editing interface to modify the task instructions (asking not to copy text from another source) and reissue the task. Improving task instructions in response to the crowd's initial failed attempts can be seen as an application of iterative design to crowd programming. Such iterations allowed tasks to succeed.

USER EXPERIENCES WITH TURKOMATIC

The authors have been using Turkomatic as a platform since its creation to test a variety of tasks. We have also shared Turkomatic with a number of end users within academia and the computer science community who requested solutions to various tasks. Two use case patterns have emerged: first, Web search and data processing, such as finding real estate listings, email addresses, or cross-checking multiple web documents; second, one-time experimentation to see if particular new classes of tasks can be solved by workers on a crowd platform. Results from some of these tasks are illustrated in Figure 11. Some users indicated that the extra monetary cost involved in using Turkomatic over regular crowdsourcing tasks was made up for by its simple, fast interface.

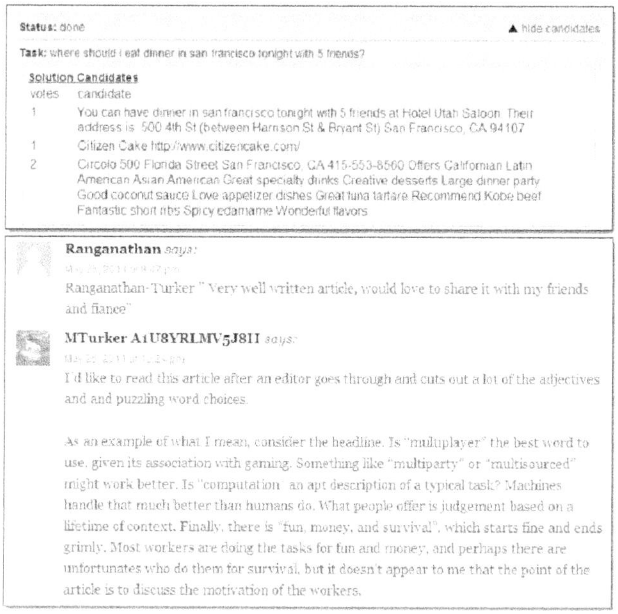

Figure 11: Results from two example tasks submitted by Turkomatic users. Above: asking for restaurant recommendations. Below: requesting blog comments.

These outcomes illustrate two additional benefits of Turkomatic: It has value in quickly evaluating the ability of crowds to solve particular kinds of work, and it can reduce the complexity of accessing crowd platforms for casual use. These additional benefits stem from the fact that Turkomatic's initial interface requires only a goal stated in natural language. We hypothesize that crowdsourcing marketplaces can grow substantially if the process of sending work to crowds is simplified.

DISCUSSION

We close with several observations that arise from our work with the Turkomatic system on collaboratively designing workflows with the crowd.

Instructional Writing is Difficult for Workers

Composing good instructions is not trivial and takes time and effort. This requirement stands in tension with the goal of workers to maximize the number of tasks they complete per unit of time. While we observed that some workers were able to write excellent instructions, few other tasks on Mechanical Turk require such careful attention, and workers may thus be disincentivized from delivering nuanced work.

Reputation Effects Arise from Worker Planning

Turkomatic assigns responsibility for wording tasks to the workers. Interestingly, this means that poor choices by Turkers may negatively affect the requester's reputation. We noticed that workers on Turker Nation, a discussion forum, posted messages about tasks created by Turkomatic, complaining about poor wording or excessive scope. Workers were not aware that these tasks were in fact created by other workers and assigned their dissatisfaction to the requester.

Excessive Structure Limits the Effectiveness of Leaders

We noticed that expert workers provided more detailed instructions in their subdivisions and attempted to communicate corrections to requesters through external channels of communication. The PDS algorithm does not yet offer workers the ability to contribute at different levels commensurate with skill and interest. This phenomenon suggests that more effective platforms for collaboration with the crowd should permit workers to edit workflows much as requesters do in the current systems.

Scaling Requires Context-Free Workflows

Batch processes send many different problem instances through the same workflow (*e.g.,* filtering a database of business addresses through an address verification workflow). This implies that such workflows must be designed in a *context free* manner – the instructions have to be written independently of any particular problem instance. Turkomatic currently does not offer a guarantee that crowd-planned workflows are context free. One promising idea for future work is to first ask the crowd to produce a concrete workflow; and afterwards generalize it to fit multiple problem instances.

CONCLUSION

This paper introduced Turkomatic, a system that harnesses crowds to design and execute workflows for complex tasks. Turkomatic is based on a price-divide-solve algorithm that guides workers through the steps of decomposing and solving tasks; and on generic task templates that are instantiated with particular task contexts. Our experience with Turkomatic suggests that unsupervised workers face planning challenges. However, experiments also showed that planning succeeds for an interesting range of tasks when more knowledgeable workers are recruited and when requesters can review and edit crowd work in real-time.

However, the one-size-fits-all model of Turkomatic trades off simplicity of use for runtime supervision: workflows can be generated without exhaustive planning, but require requester monitoring at runtime to guarantee quality of results. In future work, we plan to investigate to what extent this supervisory function can again be assigned to crowd workers, and how the pricing structure of Turkomatic can be optimized. Effective workflow design is among the most common problems facing crowdsourcing researchers today. Why not collaborate with workers in solving it?

ACKNOWLEDGMENTS

This work was supported by gifts from Intel and Google.

REFERENCES

1. Ruote. http://ruote.rubyforge.org/.
2. RunMyProcess. http://www.runmyprocess.com/.
3. Graphviz. http://www.graphviz.org/.
4. Ahmad, S., Battle, A., Malkani, Z., and Kamvar, S. The Jabberwocky programming environment for structured social computing. *Proceedings of UIST 2011*, (2011), 53-64.
5. Ahn, L. von. Games with a Purpose. *IEEE Computer 39*, (2006), 92–94.
6. Bernstein, M.S., Little, G., Miller, R.C., et al. Soylent: a word processor with a crowd inside. *Proceedings of UIST 2010*, ACM (2010), 313–322.
7. Bigham, J.P., Jayant, C., Ji, H., et al. VizWiz: nearly real-time answers to visual questions. *Proceedings of UIST 2010*, ACM (2010), 333–342.
8. Faridani, S., Hartmann, B., and Ipeirotis, P.G. What's the Right Price? Pricing Tasks for Finishing on Time. *Proceedings of HCOMP11: The 3rd Workshop on Human Computation.*
9. Franklin, M.J., Kossmann, D., Kraska, T., Ramesh, S., and Xin, R. CrowdDB: answering queries with crowdsourcing. *Proceedings of SIGMOD 2011*, (2011), 61-72.
10. Huang, E., Zhang, H., Parkes, D.C., Gajos, K.Z., and Chen, Y. Toward automatic task design: a progress report. *Proceedings of the ACM SIGKDD Workshop on Human Computation*, ACM (2010), 77–85.
11. Ipeirotis, P.G. Analyzing the Amazon Mechanical Turk marketplace. *XRDS: Crossroads, The ACM Magazine for Students 17*, (2010), 16–21.
12. Kittur, A., Smus, B., Khamkar, S., and Kraut, R.E. CrowdForge: Crowdsourcing Complex Work. *Proceedings of UIST 2011*, ACM (2011), 43-52.
13. Lasecki, W.S., Murray, K.I., White, S., Miller, R.C., and Bigham, J.P. Real-time crowd control of existing interfaces. *Proceedings of UIST 2011*, (2011), 23.
14. Little, G., Chilton, L.B., Goldman, M., and Miller, R.C. TurKit: human computation algorithms on mechanical turk. *Proceedings of UIST 2010*, ACM (2010), 57–66.
15. Olsen, T. Incorporating crowdsourcing into business processes. *Adjunct Proceedings of CSCW 2011*, (2011).
16. Quinn, A.J. and Bederson, B.B. Human computation: a survey and taxonomy of a growing field. *Proceedings of CHI 2011*, ACM (2011), 1403–1412.
17. Sheng, V.S., Provost, F., and Ipeirotis, P.G. Get another label? Improving data quality and data mining using multiple, noisy labelers. *Proceeding of the 14th ACM SIGKDD international conference on Knowledge discovery and data mining*, ACM (2008), 614–622.
18. Singer, Y. and Mittal, M. Pricing Tasks in Online Labor Markets. *Proceedings of HCOMP11: The 3rd Workshop on Human Computation*, (2011).
19. Sorokin, A. and Forsyth, D. Utility Data Annotation with Amazon Mechanical Turk. *Proceedings of CVPR 2008*, (2008).
20. Stohr, E.A. and Zhao, J.L. Workflow Automation: Overview and Research Issues. *Information Systems Frontiers 3*, (2001), 281–296.
21. White, S. *BPMN modeling and reference guide*. Future Strategies Inc., Lighthouse Point Fla., 2008.

Shepherding the Crowd Yields Better Work

Steven P. Dow[1], Anand Kulkarni[2], Scott R. Klemmer[3], Björn Hartmann[4]

HCI Institute
School of Computer Science
Carnegie Mellon University
spdow@cs.cmu.edu

Industrial Engineering & Operations Research[2]
Computer Science Division[4]
University of California, Berkeley
anandk@berkeley.edu, bjoern@cs.berkeley.edu

Stanford HCI Group[3]
Computer Science Department
Stanford University
srk@stanford.edu

ABSTRACT

Micro-task platforms provide massively parallel, on-demand labor. However, it can be difficult to reliably achieve high-quality work because online workers may behave irresponsibly, misunderstand the task, or lack necessary skills. This paper investigates whether timely, task-specific feedback helps crowd workers learn, persevere, and produce better results. We investigate this question through *Shepherd*, a feedback system for crowdsourced work. In a between-subjects study with three conditions, crowd workers wrote consumer reviews for six products they own. Participants in the *None* condition received no immediate feedback, consistent with most current crowdsourcing practices. Participants in the *Self*-assessment condition judged their own work. Participants in the *External* assessment condition received expert feedback. Self-assessment alone yielded better overall work than the None condition and helped workers improve over time. External assessment also yielded these benefits. Participants who received external assessment also revised their work more. We conclude by discussing interaction and infrastructure approaches for integrating real-time assessment into online work.

Author Keywords

Crowdsourcing, human computation, feedback system.

General Terms

Experimentation, Design.

ACM Classification Keywords

H5.3. Information interfaces and presentation (e.g., HCI): Group and Organization Interfaces.

INTRODUCTION

Modern crowdsourcing systems enable distributed human problem solving on an unprecedented scale [17,35,36]. On micro-task platforms like Mechanical Turk, people perform short tasks for small amounts of money. This rapid, decontextualized, anonymous work provides few motivational incentives and little time for reflection [16,19,30]. Consequently, workers often expend minimal effort to complete tasks, yielding low-quality results.

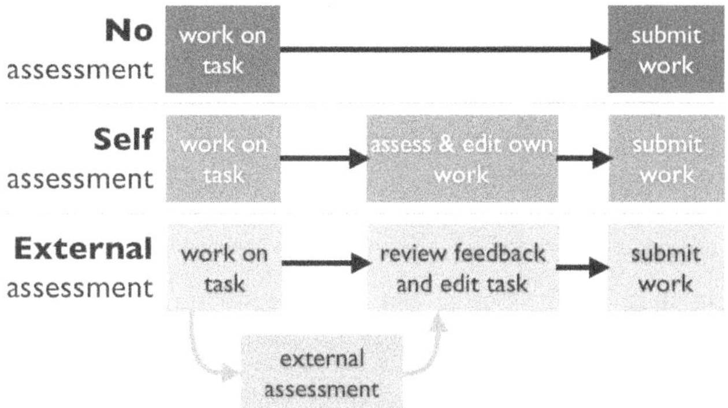

Figure 1: (A) Micro-task workers today receive no feedback. This paper investigates two interventions. (B) Workers reflect and edit their own work and (C) Workers review and edit after reading an external assessment.

How can we increase work quality in micro-task platforms? Increasing payment can improve individual performance, but paying more actually reduces quality after a certain point because it incentivizes speed [12]. Requesters can also increase quality by aggregating answers from multiple workers [2,16,23], filtering spammers by inserting test problems with known solutions [19,37], or using intelligent redundancy to simultaneously filter and aggregate [18]. Moreover, providing context about the rationale for a task can be a powerful motivator [5].

This paper explores the value of providing real-time assessment to help motivate and teach online workers to produce high-quality results. In many micro-task platforms, requesters and workers remain largely anonymous to each other, and little direct interaction occurs between them. We hypothesize that *task-specific feedback will help workers in micro-task markets perform better, learn over time, and persevere longer*. Concrete expert feedback can help people understand and strive toward key metrics in a task domain [28,29,31]. Assessments also provide motivation by making workers cognizant that other people are judging their work [1]. However, external feedback requires the time of someone with sufficient domain knowledge. Alternatively, a well-structured self-assessment may be able to provide guidance without the additional overhead [34]. Self-assessments can help workers see how their work aligns with key performance criteria and may be less discouraging than external assessments [7].

To examine the effects of different kinds of assessment in crowds, we introduce the *Shepherd* system, which provides targeted, real-time assessment as workers complete a series of tasks. In a between-subjects experiment, 105 participants wrote consumer reviews for products they own. This paper compares three scenarios (Figure 1): micro-task work with *No* assessment (the current status quo), work with instant *Self*-assessment, and work with real-time *External* assessment. Participants in both the *External* and *Self*-conditions were encouraged to make edits to their earlier work.

Both external and self-assessment led to significantly more highly-rated work than no feedback at all. There was no overall performance difference between external and self-assessment. External and self-assessment both led participants to produce better work across a series of tasks, indicating a learning effect. Participants in the External condition produced significantly more changes to their work than the other conditions, leading to more overall writing output.

In short, both external and self-assessment helped participants produce better work. External assessments lead workers to submit more work for the same payment, however this incurs the cost of an assessor's time. These results suggest that crowds can be shepherded through the use of concrete rubrics. The following sections elaborate the study's rationale and hypotheses.

Feedback supports community and transfer of expertise

In many communities, senior members help novices learn and stay motivated, often through implicit feedback [21]. Enabling social interaction among peers provides a learning opportunity [1]. (However, biased information can nullify these benefits or have a negative impact [15].) Traditional work environments foster employee development through formal performance reviews and feedback, and informally through apprenticeship, collocated awareness, and observation [21]. Likewise, online communities often provide infrastructure for moderators to review others' content and to encourage the growth of newer members [6,20]. Members choose where to devote resources, and through transparency and reputation systems, the community defines standards and quality control mechanisms [33]. Peer interaction also has motivational benefits [6,14]. LiveOps, a distributed online call center, enabled chat interaction between at-home agents to recreate a "water cooler" setting and to foster cohesion among their workforce [26]. Online freelancing platforms (e.g., oDesk) typically enable requesters and workers to send each other e-mail.

In contrast with traditional labor, peer-production, and freelance systems, micro-task platforms such as Amazon Mechanical Turk typically offer few formal or informal methods for worker-requester communication. In general, these systems provide no way for crowd workers to see what their peers produce, instructions are often the sole means for requesters to communicate to workers during the task, and there is no in-task channel for workers to communicate with requesters. At best, novice workers can only observe expert behavior from a few curated examples provided by the requester. Feedback from external reviewers can complement other quality-improvement efforts such as worker qualifications and clearer instructions. However, real-time communication is difficult to achieve on high-throughput micro-task platforms, where workers perform tasks at a small granularity, on the order of a few seconds to a few minutes.

Self-assessment rubrics capture domain knowledge

Self-assessment activities can help students reflect, learn skills, become more autonomous, and more clearly draw connections between learning goals and evaluation criteria [7,27,31]. Well-designed rubrics can help students align their own work with concrete grading criteria, leading them to better grasp a domain's key principles [7,31]. These benefits diminish when self-assessment rubrics are overly complex or use special domain language difficult for novices to understand [4]. Without clear criteria, learner's performance and their self-assessment often exhibits little correlation, unless the learner believes he/she will be later assessed by an authority [4]. In general, high performers tend to underrate and low-performers tend to overrate – and self-assessment can be used to make learners more aware of gaps between their standards and those of external assessors [25]. Peer assessment can also be valuable, especially when a concrete rubric effectively captures domain knowledge [10,32]. Social forces, such as friendships, can alter peer assessments, but in general, students still learn [24].

Hypotheses: shepherding leads to better work, learning, and perseverance.

This paper hypothesizes that shepherding workers through task-specific rubrics will produce better results, help workers learn, and lead to greater perseverance than current micro-task crowdsourcing practices. Further, we hypothesize that expert rubrics will be more impactful when delivered through an external assessor, rather than assessed by the workers themselves.

Hypothesis 1: *Assessment (both through worker self-assessment and by an external expert) will help crowd workers produce better quality work.*

Hypothesis 2: *Assessment will help crowd workers learn and improve their work over time.*

Hypothesis 3: *Assessment will motivate crowd workers to produce more output.*

Hypothesis 4: *The effect sizes for H1, H2, and H3 will be larger for external assessment than self-assessment.*

To measure work quality, a blind-to-condition expert rated the work results. To examine learning effects, we monitor each worker's progression in terms of expert rating over their set of assignments. To measure perseverance, we look at the percent of modified assignments, the change in number of characters between the original and modified assignments, and the overall amount of text produced.

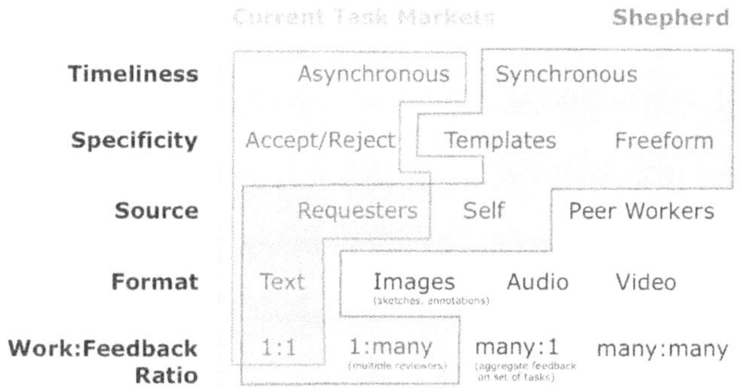

Figure 2: A design space for crowd feedback. Orange: current task markets deliver accept-reject feedback days later. Blue: *Shepherd* explores synchronous feedback with detailed rubrics.

DESIGN SPACE FOR CROWD FEEDBACK

To effectively design feedback mechanisms for micro-task platforms—and to support our goal of improving learning, engagement, and work quality—we generated a possible design space for crowd feedback and analyzed it along several key dimensions (Figure 2).

Timeliness: When should feedback be shown?

In micro-task labor, many workers perform tasks for a short time (seconds to minutes), and then move to other tasks by other employers [12,19]. This implies two timing options: synchronously deliver feedback when workers are still engaged in a set of tasks, or asynchronously deliver feedback after workers have completed the tasks.

Synchronous feedback may have more impact on future task performance since it arrives at a teachable moment, while people are still thinking about the task domain [11]. However, synchronous feedback places a burden on the feedback providers, because they have to review work quickly. Asynchronous feedback gives feedback *providers* more time to review and comment on work. However, *workers* may have forgotten about the task or feel unmotivated to review the feedback or revise their work.

Most current micro-task platforms provide support for asynchronous feedback, often days later (Figure 2, orange). Requesters can provide feedback at payment time, but at that point, workers may care more about getting paid than improving submitted work. More importantly, unless requesters have more jobs available, workers cannot act on requesters' advice. In our *Shepherd* system, we explore the efficacy of synchronous feedback (Figure 2, blue).

Specificity: How detailed should feedback be?

Currently, workers on most micro-task platforms receive a single bit of feedback—acceptance or rejection of their work. (In a few cases, micro-task workers receive feedback on training questions with known answers – but importantly not on actual work [37].) While additional freeform communication is possible, it is rarely used unless workers file complaints. It is feasible a micro-task platform could enable external reviewers to provide detailed and personalized feedback on each micro task. However, this requires external reviewers to spend time authoring open-ended feedback.

Assessment rubrics provide an alternative to freeform feedback. Rubrics codify domain knowledge into pre-authored statements providing an effective and efficient form of feedback [7,31]. However, rubric authors may struggle to completely encapsulate domain knowledge. Moreover, assessors may want to make comments that are not embodied in the rubric. *Shepherd* employs a pre-authored feedback rubric and provides a place for open-ended comments.

Source: Who should provide feedback?

Crowdsourcing requesters post tasks with specific quality objectives in mind; they are a natural choice for assuming the feedback role. However, experts often underestimate the difficulty novices face in solving tasks [13] or use language or concepts that are beyond the grasp of novices [8]. Moreover, as feedback volume increases or feedback becomes more specific, requesters may find it more difficult to complete work assessments in real-time (synchronously).

Alternatively, workers may benefit from assessing their own work [7,10]. By viewing assessment rubrics such as scoring templates, workers become aware of desirable work characteristics and can learn by aligning these characteristics with their own work [31].

As a third approach, workers can be paid to provide feedback to their peers. In theory, peer feedback increases the scalability as more crowd workers can be recruited to handle the volume of feedback needs. Our preliminary trials indicate that workers do perform tasks simultaneously and overlap (Figure 3). Systems like VizWiz demonstrate the feasibility of recruiting workers for tasks in nearly real-time [3]. Such a peer feedback system could have two tiers; more experienced workers could be promoted into the feedback role. This introduces the challenge of identifying and promoting knowledgeable and responsible workers. This paper leaves the possibility of peer feedback for future work. *Shepherd* supports self-assessment and rich synchronous feedback from a singe external reviewer.

SHEPHERD: SYSTEM DESIGN

To study the effects of different feedback mechanisms, we created *Shepherd* to visualize work progress and provide real-time work assessments. The *Shepherd* system manages workflows for tasks posted to Amazon Mechanical Turk. Task hosting and data collection occurs on our Web server. We developed *Shepherd* as a web application in PHP with a MySQL database and XMPP for instant notifications.

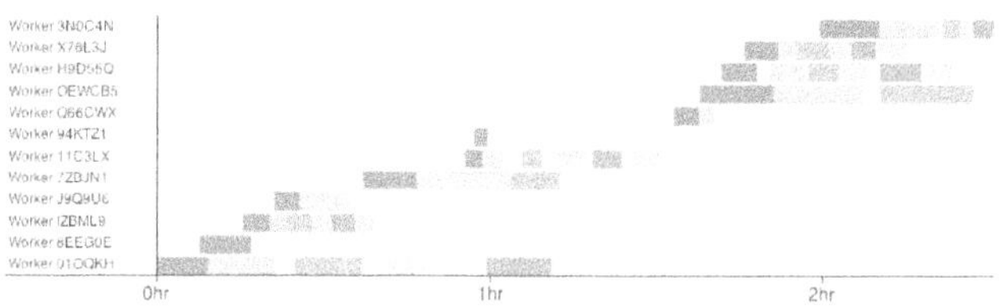

Figure 3: Shepherd's Gantt chart view.

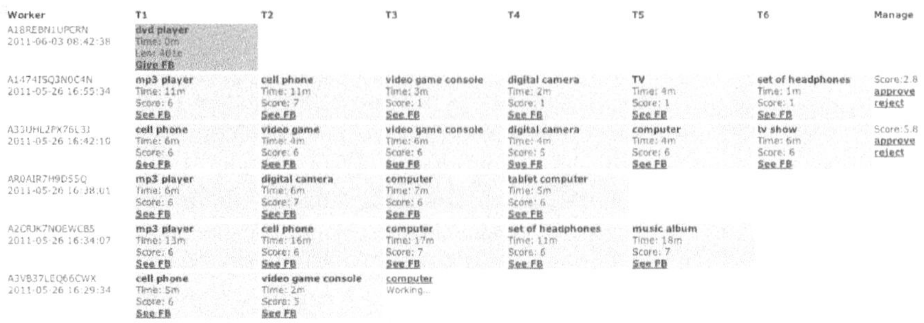

Figure 4: The dashboard interface displays completed tasks (green), in-process tasks (yellow), and tasks that need feedback (red). Requesters are notified via instant messaging.

Figure 6: As a study task, participants write reviews for six products they own.

Shepherd's requester interface provides two different real-time views of workers and results. A Gantt chart view shows when workers accept a task, the length of time workers spend on each task, and how many tasks a worker completes within a batch (Figure 3). A dashboard view (Figure 4) displays tasks in each column and workers in each row. Each box represents one worker's single piece of work (e.g., a mobile phone review) and includes status details. The color corresponds to different task states: in progress (yellow), work needs feedback (red), or feedback applied (green). Requesters can monitor incoming work and click on any task to provide feedback using an assessment rubric (Figure 5). The rubric prompts the requester select from a set of feedback statements, to rate the consumer review on a scale from 1 to 9, and to enter freeform comments.

Shepherd supports three feedback modes for the worker: *No* assessment, *Self*-assessment, and *External* assessment. With no assessment, the work environment resembles any other task on micro-task platforms. For self-assessment, a rubric appears after each assignment. For external assessment, an

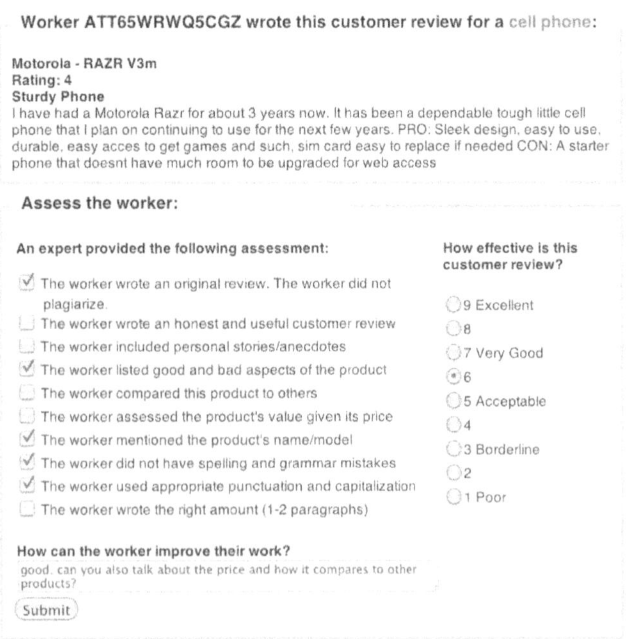

Figure 5: An assessment for the External condition. The Self condition uses the same rubric, but statements are phrased in first person (e.g., "I compared this product to others").

expert assesses one task while that worker completes a subsequent task. The system automatically notifies assessors via instant messages when new product reviews arrive (Figure 7). The assessor follows the instant message link to immediately judge the work. By default, *Shepherd* delivers any new assessments to the worker before he or she begins a subsequent task.

METHOD

A between-subjects study manipulated the writing process for a set of consumer reviews (Figure 6). This task fulfills key criteria: ① The task domain has precedence and relevance to the crowdsourcing community. ② Tasks solutions are open-ended, so expert feedback has the potential to improve results. ③ Performance can be measured.

Study Design

Participants write consumer reviews for six products they own. In the *External a*ssessment condition, an expert reads and judges each consumer review using a grading rubric (Figure 5). The expert performs the assessment while the participant completes the next consumer review. Before the subsequent task, the participant reads the expert assessment and optionally edits his/her consumer review. In the *Self-a*ssessment condition, participants reflect on their own work directly after each consumer review using a grading rubric. The rubric mirrors the external feedback condition's expert grading rubric, but frames each in first person (e.g., "I included personal stories/anecdotes in my review"). Self-assessment participants have the opportunity to edit their reviews. In the *None* condition, participants advance directly from one review to the next; they do not get an opportunity to modify their reviews.

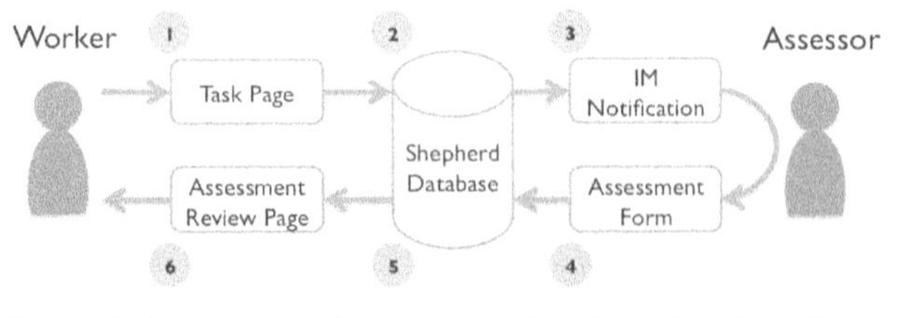

Figure 7: A worker writes a product review (1); when Shepherd receives the completed review (2), the assessor is immediately notified via instant messaging (3). The assessor provides feedback (4), which is again stored in the database (5). The form is shown to the original worker between tasks (6).

Participants

We recruited participants on Amazon Mechanical Turk over seven days in May 2011; 207 workers wrote reviews. Workers were assigned to conditions in round-robin fashion. Their average age was 25; 55% were from the United States, 35% from India, and 10% from other countries.

Procedure

The online experiment includes four main steps. First, participants select six out of twenty possible product categories they wish to review (Appendix A). Second, participants receive instructions on writing effective reviews. Instructions include the basic points of the assessment rubric and examples of high- and low-quality reviews. Third, participants write six reviews – one per chosen category. Fourth, participants fill out a short questionnaire and provide basic demographics. In accordance with current market rates on Mechanical Turk, participants earned $1.50 for their work. Regardless of quality, workers were paid if they completed all six reviews. Moreover, the instructions did not say their payment would be adjusted based on quality.

A member of the research team served as the external assessor in the experiment. To avoid bias, the researcher assessed every review in all three conditions in real-time without knowledge of the assigned condition. The assessor checked for plagiarized consumer reviews through an automated web search on the submitted text. The expert assessment took approximately 60 hours over seven days. Participants who self assessed or got an external assessment could revise their reviews. The assessor only judged the original, unedited version in real-time; the revised versions were judged independently after the experiment.

Dependent Measures

Task Performance

During the experiment, the expert assessor judged consumer reviews as they arrived. Each review received an *expert rating* between 1 (poor) and 9 (excellent). Each review was also scored on a checklist comprising ten features of effective consumer reviews (Figure 5). The number of checked features provides an *expert criteria count*.

After the experiment, all consumer reviews were re-posted to Mechanical Turk for a crowd assessment. Up to five workers judged each review using the same assessment rubric as expert assessors, but without freeform feedback (Figure 5). This yielded two additional performance measures: *crowd rating* and *crowd criteria count*. 615 crowd judges participated and received $0.02 per assessed review. To filter for erratic workers, assessments completed in less than 20 seconds were excluded, resulting in 408 crowd judges and 2229 valid assessments.

Learning

An individual's change in performance over a set of consumer reviews provides an indication of whether participants learned. The amount of learning for a condition was calculated by regressing expert ratings on condition, review order, and worker. Constant scores have a *slope coefficient* of 0; increasing scores have a positive coefficient; decreasing scores have a negative coefficient. This study did not measure long-term learning effects.

Perseverance

Participants could edit their consumer reviews after they self assessed or reviewed external assessment. The amount of revision provides a measure of a participant's willingness to persevere and improve their work. We measured the *ratio of revised reviews* to the total number of reviews. We also examined the length of reviews before and after edits using *overall character length* and *Levenshtein string edit distance* (number of character edits needed to transform the original into the revised review) [22]. As another measure of perseverance, we recorded the *length of time per review*.

To judge the value of revisions, a single independent assessor judged the original and revised versions of reviews, in randomized order and blind to condition. This provides *expert ratings and expert criteria counts for both original and revised reviews*. The expert assessor—a copy editor hired through odesk.com—earned a flat rate of $80 for 380 assessments and used the same rubric form (Figure 5). Likewise, the crowd assessments provide *crowd ratings and crowd criteria counts for both original and revised reviews*.

RESULTS

207 participants wrote product reviews in our experiment: 67 in the None condition, 67 in Self, and 77 in External (Table 1). 71 additional participants signed up but never submitted reviews. We excluded participants from our analysis for three reasons: First, 25 participants plagiarized reviews. The number of plagiarizing participants is not significantly different across conditions (X^2=1.60, df=2, p=0.44). Second, 52 participants were not assessed by the external assessor in time, due to work breaks. Third, 25 participants dropped out early, before experimental manipu-

Condition	None	Self	External	Totals
Participants entered	67	67	73	**207**
Plagiarizers	*-6*	*-8*	*-11*	*-25*
Missed assessments	*-12*	*-27*	*-13*	*-52*
Early dropouts	*0*	*-12*	*-13*	*-25*
Participants analyzed	49	20	36	**105**
Reviews analyzed	240	101	197	**538**

Table 1: Summary statistics

Category: **Game Console**
Title: **Nintendo Wii gets old, fast.**
Rating: **2 / 5**

At first, the Nintendo Wii was great fun, but the appeal quickly faded into boredom. The controls are gimmicky and tiresome. Compared to the other consoles out there, PS3 and XBOX 360, the Nintendo Wii just doesn't have the staying power. I had quite a bit of fun the first month or so of owning the Wii, but lost interest not too long after. I came to realize most of the games were the same concept over and over and over. Very boring. If you're buying this for kids, it may be a good plan, as it is very simple. For adults, I would recommend getting a more complex and versatile system with a better variety of games. I eventually sold my Nintendo Wii with all the games for a measly $75. Don't waste your money like I did.

Figure 8: One participant's consumer review.

lations could affect their work (before two reviews in Self, and three reviews in External). The number of dropouts in Self and External is not significantly different (X^2=1.09, *df*=1, *p*=0.30). The analyzed data set comprises 538 consumer reviews from 105 participants. Figure 8 shows an example review. The average review length was 570 characters (SD=223.1). Most participants were positive towards products, assigning an average rating of 4.29 (SD=0.90) on a scale of 1 to 5.

Both external and self assessment led to better work

Self-assessment participants start assessing themselves after review one; External participants see the first assessment after review two. To gauge whether assessment has an effect, we consider reviews 2-6 in the Self-condition, 3-6 in the External condition, and 1-6 in the None condition.

A single expert judged all reviews on a 9-point scale (1=poor and 9=excellent). Figure 9 (left) shows the distribution of expert ratings. An analysis of variances was performed with condition (External, Self, and None) as a factor, participant (worker ID) as a random effect and expert overall rating as the dependent variable. The External condition (μ=6.01, SD=1.38) and the Self condition (μ=6.35, SD=1.63) outperformed the None condition (μ=5.69, SD=1.19) ($F(2,102)=3.02$, $p<0.05$). Pair-wise comparisons with Welch two-sample t-tests indicate a significant difference between *None* and *External* ($t(222)=2.48$, $p<0.05$) and between *None* and *Self* ($t(110)=3.35$, $p<0.05$). There was no significant difference between *External* and *Self* assessment ($t(150)=1.40$, $p=0.18$). Participants produced higher-rated reviews when they self-assessed and when they received external feedback (Figure 10, left).

For the criteria count, the expert selected up to ten assessment criteria for each review (an excellent review satisfied all criteria; a poor review satisfied none). Figure 9 (right) shows the distribution of criteria counts. A one-way repeated-measures ANOVA was conducted with condition (External, Self, and None) as a factor, participant (worker ID) as a random effect and criteria count as the dependent variable. The ANOVA did not show a significant difference in the criteria count across conditions ($F(2,102)=1.78$, $p=0.17$, Figure 10, right).

To examine the crowd assessments, an analysis of variances was performed with condition (External, Self, and None) as a factor, judge (crowd ID) as a random effect, and crowd rating as a dependent variable. Crowd ratings were not significantly different across conditions ($F(2,405)=0.93$,

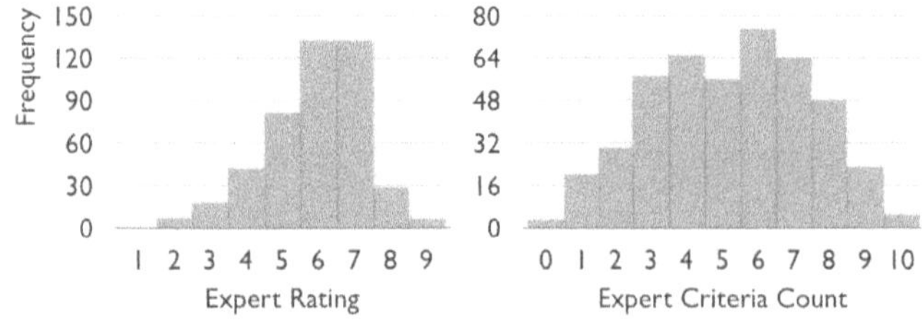

Figure 9: Distributions of expert ratings and expert choice of checkboxes (criteria counts) across all reviews.

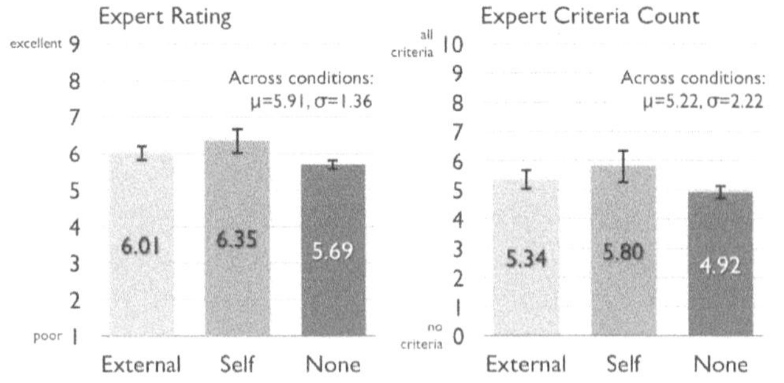

Figure 10: External and Self assessment led to higher overall expert ratings.

$p=0.40$). A second analysis of variances was performed with condition (External, Self, and None) as a factor, judge (crowd ID) as a random effect, and crowd criteria count as a dependent variable. Crowd criteria counts were not different across conditions ($F(2,405)=1.43$, $p=0.24$).

In summary, the independent expert assessor rated the reviews in the Self and External conditions higher than the None condition. Self-assessment had the highest scores, but not significantly higher than External assessment. The expert selection of satisfied criteria also favored Self and External assessment, although there were no significant differences across conditions. The crowd ratings and criteria counts did not yield useful data for distinguishing conditions; the discussion section further describes the tradeoffs of using the crowd to generate assessments.

Self assessment helped people learn

An expert rated each review; this analysis considers how those ratings changed over time. A multilevel linear regression was carried out, regressing expert rating on condition (External, Self, and None) and review order (0-5) as fixed effects, and participant (worker ID) as a random effect. We analyze interactions between condition and review order, since we are interested in differential effects of assessment conditions on learning. In the Self-condition, review ratings improved over time (Figure 11). The estimated coefficient with the Markov Chain Monte Carlo method was 0.25 (95% HPD credible interval = [0.09, 0.44]). This effect is significant ($p=0.001$). Review ratings in the External feedback condition also improved, but the effect was borderline significant (coefficient: 0.10, 95% HPD credible interval = [-0.03, 0.23], $p=0.08$). For the None condition, reviews did not improve, and order was not significant (coefficient: -0.03, 95% HPD credible interval = [-0.13, 0.06], $p=0.38$).

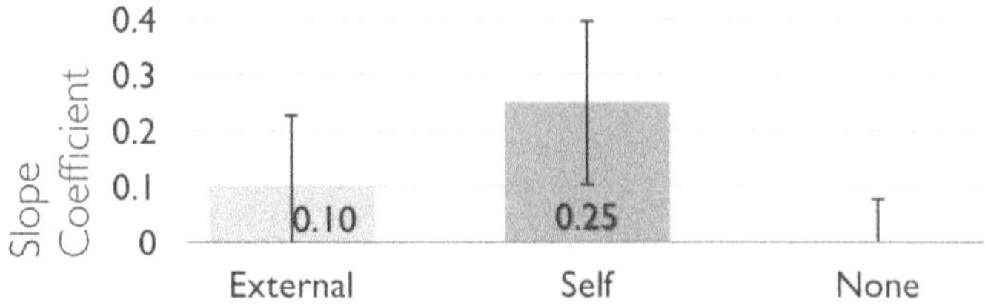

Figure 11: Participants' review ratings in the External and Self condition increased over time; Participants without feedback did not improve. Error bars indicate 95% HPD credible interval.

As a musician, the 3rd generation iPod Touch has helped me immensely in my music studies and in learning to play guitar. The app store is huge, and most of the apps are free or only $1. I was skeptical at first about buying this product because of its size (I like to carry my mp3 in my pocket). This is simply not a problem, even with a rubber case on it. My iPod is a music player, web browser, video player, metronome, synthesizer, video game system, graphing calculator, notebook, and much more. I base the iPod's value on the fact that I saved $100 by getting a graphing calculator app for only $1. I can't believe I kept my iPod Nano for so long when I could've had an iPod Touch. The only problem is the Facebook app, which is often very slow and unresponsive, even with updates. This is no a problem with the iPod, though. I strongly recommend this product for anyone, even my grandma has one!

Figure 12: An External assessment participant responded to feedback by adding text (in red and underlined). The original review received a rating of 5 and a criteria count of 4; it did not fully mention the product name, assess the product's value, and list good and bad aspects of the product. The revised review received a rating of 7 and a criteria count of 7.

In summary, self-assessors improved throughout the series of tasks; external assessment led to only marginal increases. The fact that the expert assessor could see the review order on the Shepherd dashboard presents a potential confound. However, the expert *was* blind to condition, so exposure to ordering cannot explain the observed differential effects.

External assessment encouraged more work revisions

Participants in the External and Self assessment conditions could edit their reviews in the feedback stage. In total, participants edited 184 reviews. 56.5% of External assessment participants changed their review, while only 24.8% of Self-assessment participants changed their review. External assessment led to a significantly larger ratio of revised reviews than Self-assessment (χ^2=47.24, $p<0.05$). Table 2 summarizes the work effort differences between conditions.

Participants who changed their reviews added an average of 119.8 characters (SD=157.8). In the External assessment condition, this was typically in response to expert feedback (Figure 12). An ANOVA was performed with condition (External and Self) as a factor, participant (worker id) as a random effect and review length change as the dependent variable. External assessment (μ=137.1, SD=175.8) led to (weakly significantly) longer revisions than Self-assessment (μ=84.0, SD=104.4) ($F(1,81)=3.26$, $p=0.07$).

Levenshtein string edit distance counts the number of characters that change between original and revised reviews. Participants' average string edit distance was 141.42 characters (SD=145.97). An ANOVA was performed with condition (External and Self) as a factor, participant (worker ID) as a random effect and string edit distance as the dependent variable. External assessment (μ=165.4, SD=158.6) led to significantly greater string edit distances than Self-assessment edits (μ=91.8, SD=98.8)($F(1,81)=8.20$, $p<0.05$).

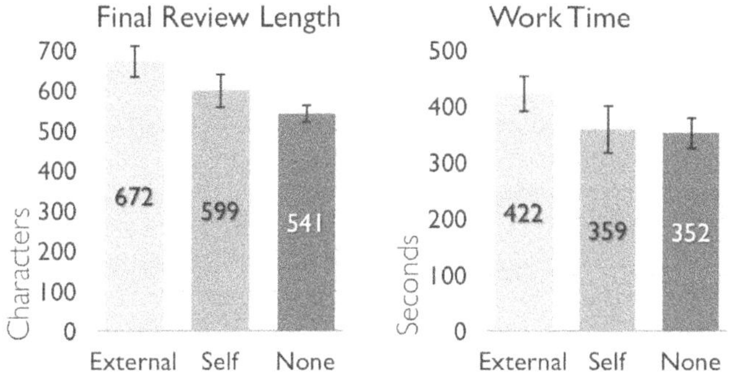

Figure 13: External feedback resulted in longer consumer reviews and more time spent.

Condition	None	Self	External
Num of revised reviews	N/A	60	124
Length change (characters)	N/A	84.0 (104.4)	137.1 (175.8)
Edit distance (operations)	N/A	91.8 (98.8)	165.4 (158.6)
Length before revision	541 (191.8)	577 (210.8)	600 (257.7)
Length after revision	N/A	599 (225.8)	672 (300.0)
Seconds to write original	352 (229.5)	359 (224.6)	422 (236.4)

Table 2: Differences in work effort across conditions: External assessment led to more changes, longer reviews, and more participation time for the same payment. Lengths are reported in characters (with standard deviation in parentheses).

For review length, an analysis of variances was performed with condition (External and Self) as a factor, participant (worker id) as a random effect and overall length as the dependent variable. Condition did not significantly affect the length of the original, non-revised reviews ($F(2,102)=1.06$, $p=0.35$). When we also consider revised reviews, the same ANOVA shows a significant difference between conditions ($F(2,102)=4.10$, $p<0.05$) (Figure 13). Post-hoc pair-wise Welch two-sample t-tests show that the difference between None and External is significant ($t(321)=5.28$, $p<0.001$), while None-Self ($t(164)=2.261$, $p=0.025$) and Self-External ($t(256)=2.339$, $p=0.020$) differences are weakly significant with respect to the Bonferroni corrected significance level of 0.017.

For the amount of time spent writing the original reviews, an ANOVA was performed with condition (External and Self) as a factor, participant (worker ID) as a random effect and time to write each review as the dependent variable. Condition did not significantly affect the amount of time spent on the original reviews ($F(2,102)=1.43$, $p=0.24$).

Revisions resulted in better overall consumer reviews

An expert and the crowd rated the quality of all original and revised reviews. A paired-samples t-test found that expert ratings were significantly higher for revised reviews (μ=5.87, SD=1.36) than for original reviews (μ=5.58, SD=1.34) ($t(188)=2.09$, $p<0.05$). A second paired-samples t-test found that expert criteria counts were higher for revised reviews (μ=6.12, SD=1.34) than for original reviews (μ=5.89, SD=1.23), but the difference is only weakly significant ($t(188)=1.68$, $p=0.095$) (Figure 14).

To examine the crowd assessments, an ANOVA was performed with version (Original and Revised) as a factor, judge (crowd ID) as a random effect and crowd rating as the dependent variable. Crowd ratings were (weakly signif-

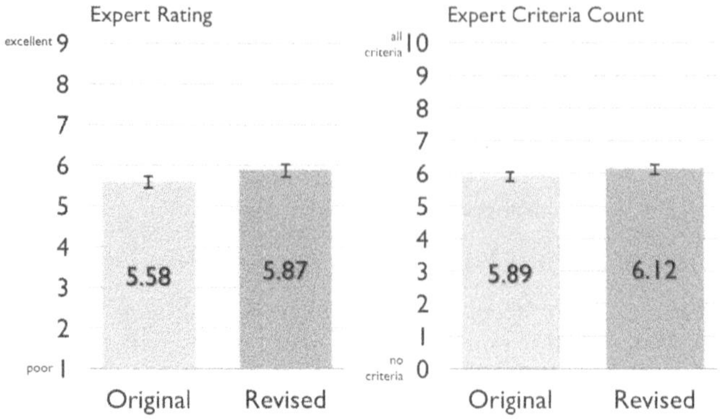

Figure 14: Mean expert ratings and criteria counts for original and revised reviews. Error bars indicate 95% CI.

icantly) higher for revised reviews (μ=6.37; SD=1.76) than for original reviews (μ=6.07; SD=1.90) ($F(1,291)=3.19$, $p=0.08$). Another ANOVA was performed with version (Original and Revised) as a factor, judge (crowd ID) as a random effect and crowd criteria count as the dependent variable. Crowd criteria counts for revised (μ=6.02; SD=2.06) and original reviews (μ=5.74; SD=2.01) were not significantly different ($F(1,291)=0.97$, $p=0.32$). The results suggest that revised consumer reviews receive better expert assessments than the original reviews. Crowd assessments favor revised reviews, but not significantly.

To examine whether revision quality improved differentially across conditions, an analysis of variances was performed with condition (External and Self) and version (Original and Revised) as factors and expert rating as the dependent variable. The ANOVA revealed a main effect for assessment condition ($F(1, 374)=4.55$, $p<0.05$), and a weak main effect for version ($F(1,374)=2.76$, $p=0.099$). There was no interaction effect between condition and version.

DISCUSSION

Both external and self-assessment led to better writing results and helped participants improve over time. These performance advantages were calculated on the original, non-revised versions of work. About 34% of participants in External and Self conditions also revised reviews. Revisions scored better than original reviews. External assessments also led participants to do more work per payment unit than self-assessments alone (although, this did not lead to differentially better quality on the revised versions).

The study confirmed some of our hypotheses about assessment: that feedback leads to better work, helps workers learn over time, and motivates more production. However, our hypothesis that external assessment produces larger effect sizes than self-assessment is not fully supported. While self-assessment did not lead to as many work revisions, it was just as effective as external assessment in increasing work quality in micro-task platforms. From a system evaluation perspective, we provide evidence that *Shepherd* improves crowdsourcing results. This section analyzes the effects of our interventions and discusses implications for future crowdsourcing systems.

Why did external and self-assessment help crowd participants improve their work?

In many contexts, assessment helps people improve performance and learn. However, it was not a foregone conclusion that assessment could improve micro-task work, given that workers perform tasks remotely and anonymously. Workers may not see—or comprehend—expert assessments; or they may not carry out self-assessments carefully. Future work assessments may include verification methods (e.g., [19]) to ensure that workers absorb the feedback.

Many workers dropped out before completing all reviews (and getting paid). We observed higher attrition rates in the Self (78%) and External (61%) than in the None condition (47%). Poor performing workers may have dropped out upon realizing they would be assessed and would need to put in extra effort. The fact that Self and External assessment led to higher quality work may be due to a combination of driving poor performers to drop out and actually helping the remaining workers learn the task. Future work should disentangle these two effects experimentally.

For workers who attempted to write consumer reviews in good faith, the assessment rubric served as an expert checklist [9]. Notably, there were no performance differences between workers who self-assessed and those who got external feedback. The concrete rubric enabled participants to understand key success criteria without external involvement. Including self-assessment in micro-task workflows provides a practical and scalable way to improve results.

Why did external assessment encourage more work?

Participants in the External assessment condition revised more of their consumer reviews, resulting in more text written and more time on task. There are several possible reasons for this increase in production over self-assessment. The fact that someone else is paying close attention may motivate workers to take more responsibility for their work. The power status of an external "expert" assessor may have led workers to make obligatory changes to their work out of fear of payment forfeiture. Finally, workers received open-ended comments from external experts, but self-assessors did not. Comments included suggestions for improvement that were more concrete than the general grading criteria.

Can we trust self-assessed ratings?

Self-assessing participants produced better work than those who receive no assessment. Can self-assessment scores inform filtering algorithms or guide the promotion of workers into leadership roles? In our study, self-assessors rated themselves 1.8 points higher (μ=7.9; SD=1.01) than experts' ratings of the same work (μ=6.1; SD=1.49). Criteria counts were also much higher (by 3.2 points) for self-assessors. The significance of the respective paired t-tests ($t(86)=9.96$, $p<0.05$ and $t(86)=13.02$, $p<0.05$) suggests that self-assessors systematically over-rate the quality of their own contributions. There is a moderate positive correlation between self-ratings and expert ratings (Spearman's rho=0.20, $p=0.057$). While self-ratings do not serve as an accurate measure of performance, concrete assessment criteria help people reflect and make appropriate adjustments to current and subsequent work. Future work should investigate whether the difference in self-assessed and expert-assessed scores—the amount of score inflation—can help identify undesirable workers.

Can peer workers be effective shepherds?

If crowd workers can effectively assess each other, they could realize the benefits of external assessment at a much larger scale, without requester intervention. There are two key challenges for real-time peer assessment: scheduling and variance. Timely feedback is important for engaging workers before they complete a set of assignments. Participants spent an average of 6 minutes and 8 seconds per product review (SD=232.9) (Figure 15). Crowd workers hired after the experiment took an average of 58 seconds (SD=55.3) to assess a review (Figure 16). Therefore, real-time feedback by crowd workers is plausible if assessors can be recruited within this five-minute difference.

Bigham *et al.*'s success with real-time crowds [3] suggests that short recruitment times are achievable. In addition, we already observed simultaneous work occurring during our experiment: Figure 15 shows a Gantt chart of a subset of workers reviewing products. A fraction of these simultaneous workers could perform assessor roles. With deeper analysis of the arrival time data, we hope to develop algorithms for recruiting assessors within a desired time frame.

The high variance of peer assessment is also problematic. Our expert and the oDesk editor had moderate agreement on their ratings (Cohen's Kappa=0.41 using squared weights, Spearman's rho=0.39). The expert and crowd workers had lower agreement (treating the crowd as a single aggregate rater for comparison: Cohen's Kappa=0.20 using squared weights; Spearman's rho=0.28). Even when collected redundantly and averaged, crowd ratings can vary widely from an expert's opinion. To improve consistency among the crowd assessors, our filtering heuristic eliminates workers who completed the assessments too quickly, although more sophisticated techniques to infer worker quality exist [16,18]. Such techniques often rely on comparing answers to ground-truth values, but such "gold standards" may not exist for inherently creative tasks. An alternative approach would be to recruit only *experienced* workers who have been previously rated favorably by others. Future work should explore approaches for identifying expert workers suitable for the assessment role.

What tradeoffs do crowdsourcing platforms present for controlled experiments?

This study recruited participants through Amazon Mechanical Turk and paid $1.50 per task for an average of 27 minutes and 46 seconds of participation. This yields an effective hourly rate of $3.26; which is consistent with current crowd market rates [17] and much less than paying a freelance writer (currently $10-$15 per hour on oDesk.) From a crowdsourcing business perspective, a corpus of 881 consumer reviews (total non-plagiarized data) cost about $220 to generate. Despite the low costs, using crowd participants created two main challenges: many workers dropped out early and many submitted plagiarized work.

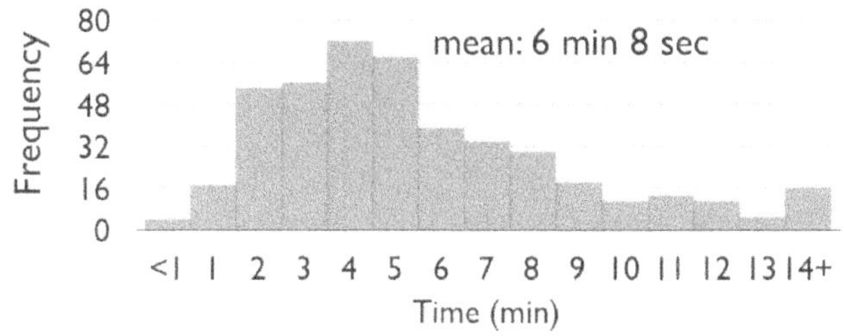

Figure 15: Distribution of time to complete reviews.

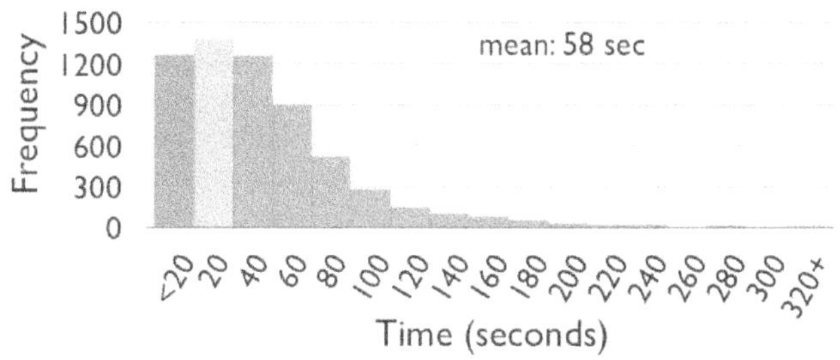

Figure 16: Distribution of time to assess reviews. Workers in red were excluded from our analysis; workers in orange are suspect as well.

CONCLUSIONS AND FUTURE WORK

This paper found that online workers produce better results when they self-assessed or received external feedback. External assessment led to more work output than self-assessment, but not necessarily better overall work. The results suggest a practical implication for requesters on crowd platforms: enumerate concrete criteria for the work output and then ask workers to self reflect on their prior work along those criteria. For task domains with more complex success criteria, a real-time expert assessor may also prove effective. Alternatively, the two approaches can be combined. Prompting for frequent self-assessment and providing intermittent expert feedback may deliver the benefits of both approaches at acceptable extra cost.

One direction for future work is to study whether crowd workers can effectively assess other workers. It may be prudent to recruit promising assessors based on prior task performance and domain knowledge by interspersing short test questions. In a related question, how does the quality of feedback affect work production and results? Follow-up studies may explicitly manipulate how good and bad feedback propagates within a peer assessment system. Further studies are needed to understand whether feedback provides advantages in different task scenarios and how feedback compares to other incentives for improving performance, such as adjusting worker pay based on quality measures.

ACKNOWLEDGEMENTS

We thank Truc Nguyen and Brie Bunge for early prototypes and CMU's Social Computing Lab for feedback. Funding support provided by the Hasso Plattner Design Thinking Research Program, Intel, and Google.

REFERENCES

1. Annett, J. Feedback and human behaviour: the effects of knowledge of results, incentives, and reinforcement on learning and performance. Penguin Books, 1969.
2. Bernstein, M.S., Little, G., Miller, R.C., Hartmann, B., Ackerman, M.S., Karger, D.R., Crowell, D., and Panovich, K. Soylent: a word processor with a crowd inside. *Proc of ACM Symposium on User Interface Software and Technology* (2010), 313–322.
3. Bigham, J.P., Jayant, C., Ji, H., Little, G., Miller, A., Miller, R.C., Miller, R., Tatarowicz, A., White, B., White, S., and Yeh, T. VizWiz: nearly real-time answers to visual questions. *Proc of ACM Symp. on User Interface Software and Technology* (2010), 333–342.
4. Boud, D. Sustainable Assessment: Rethinking assessment for the learning society. *Studies in Continuing Education* 22, 2 (2000), 151.
5. Chandler, D. and Kapelner, A. Breaking monotony with meaning: Motivation in crowdsourcing markets. *University of Chicago mimeo,* (2010).
6. Cheshire, C. and Antin, J. The Social Psychological Effects of Feedback on the Production of Internet Information Pools. *Journal of Computer-Mediated Communication* 13, 3 (2008), 705-727.
7. David, B. Enhancing Learning Through Self-Assessment. Routledge, 1995.
8. Ericsson, K.A., Charness, N., Feltovich, P.J., and Hoffman, R.R. The Cambridge Handbook of Expertise and Expert Performance. Cambr. Univer. Press, 2006.
9. Gawande, A. The Checklist Manifesto: How to Get Things Right. Metropolitan Books, 2009.
10. Hanrahan, S.J. and Isaacs, G. Assessing Self- and Peer-assessment: The students' views. *Higher Education Research & Development* 20, 1 (2001), 53.
11. Havighurst, R.J. Human Development and Education. Longmans, Green and Co, 1955.
12. Heer, J. and Bostock, M. Crowdsourcing graphical perception: using mechanical turk to assess visualization design. *Proc of ACM conf on Human factors in computing systems* (2010), 203-212.
13. Hinds, P. The Curse of Expertise: The Effects of Expertise and Debiasing Methods on Predictions of Novice Performance. *Journal of Experimental Applied Psychology* 5, (1999), 205-221.
14. Horton, J.J. Employer Expectations, Peer Effects and Productivity: Evidence from a Series of Field Experiments. *SSRN eLibrary*, (2010).
15. Hullman, J., Adar, E., and Shah, P. The impact of social information on visual judgments. *Proc of conf on Human factors in computing systems,* ACM (2011), 1461–1470.
16. Ipeirotis, P.G., Provost, F., and Wang, J. Quality management on Amazon Mechanical Turk. *Proc of ACM SIGKDD Workshop on Human Computation*, (2010), 64–67.
17. Ipeirotis, P.G. Analyzing the Amazon Mechanical Turk marketplace. *XRDS: Crossroads, The ACM Magazine for Students* 17, 2010, 16–21.
18. Karger, D., Oh, S., and Shah, D. Budget-optimal Crowdsourcing using Low-rank Matrix Approximations. *Proc. of the Allerton Conf. on Communication, Control, and Computing*, (2011).
19. Kittur, A., Chi, E.H., and Suh, B. Crowdsourcing user studies with Mechanical Turk. *Proc of SIGCHI conference on Human factors in computing systems, ACM* (2008), 453-456.
20. Lampe, C. and Resnick, P. Slash(dot) and burn: distributed moderation in a large online conversation space. *Proc. of the SIGCHI conference on Human factors in computing systems*, ACM (2004), 543–550.
21. Lave, J. and Wenger, E. Situated Learning: Legitimate Peripheral Participation. Camb. University Press, 1991.
22. Levenshtein, V.I. Binary codes capable of correcting deletions, insertions, and reversals. *Soviet Physics Doklady* 10, 8, 707-710.
23. Little, G., Chilton, L.B., Goldman, M., and Miller, R.C. Exploring iterative and parallel human computation processes. *Proc. of the ACM SIGKDD Workshop on Human Computation, ACM* (2010), 68–76.
24. Masten, A.S., Morison, P., and Pellegrini, D.S. A revised class play method of peer assessment. *Developmental Psychology* 21, 3 (1985), 523-533.
25. Mattheos, N., Nattestad, A., Falk-Nilsson, E., and Attstrom, R. The interactive examination: assessing students' self-assessment ability. *Medical Education* 38, 4 (2004), 378-389.
26. Musico, C. There's No Place Like Home. *destinationCRM.com*, 2008.
27. Orsmond, P., Merry, S., and Reiling, K. A Study in Self-assessment: tutor and students' perceptions of performance criteria. *Assessment & Evaluation in Higher Education* 22, 4 (1997), 357.
28. Sadler, D.R. Formative assessment and the design of instructional systems. *Instructional Science* 18, 2 (1989), 119-144.
29. Shute, V.J. Focus on Formative Feedback. *Review of Educational Research* 78, 1 (2008), 153 -189.
30. Silberman, M.S., Ross, J., Irani, L., and Tomlinson, B. Sellers' problems in human computation markets. *Proc ACM SIGKDD Workshop on Human Computation,* (2010), 18–21.
31. Taras, M. Using Assessment for Learning and Learning from Assessment. *Assessment & Evaluation in Higher Education* 27, 6 (2002), 501.
32. Taras, M. To Feedback or Not to Feedback in Student Self-assessment. *Assessment & Evaluation in Higher Education* 28, 5 (2003), 549.
33. Viégas, F., Wattenberg, M., and Mckeon, M. The Hidden Order of Wikipedia. *In Online Communities and Social Computing.* 2007, 445-454.
34. Zimmerman, B.J. Becoming a self-regulated learner: Which are the key subprocesses? *Contemporary Educational Psychology* 11, 4 (1986), 307-313.
35. http://en.wikipedia.org/.
36. http://www.thejohnnycashproject.com/.
37. Crowdflower. Crowdflower.com/.

APPENDIX A:

Twenty product categories for writing reviews

MP3 player	Refrigerator	Digital camera	TV
Mobile phone	Microwave	Computer	Headphones
DVD player	Vacuum	Printer	TV show
Video game	GPS device	Tablet	Music album
Game console	Camcorder	Washer/dryer	Set of speakers

Community-based Web Security: Complementary Roles of the Serious and Casual Contributors

Pern Hui Chia
Q2S NTNU*
Trondheim, Norway
chia@q2s.ntnu.no

John Chuang
UC Berkeley
Berkeley, CA
chuang@ischool.berkeley.edu

ABSTRACT
Does crowdsourcing work for web security? While the herculean task of evaluating hundreds of millions of websites can certainly benefit from the wisdom of crowds, skeptics question the coverage and reliability of inputs from ordinary users for assessing web security. We analyze the contribution patterns of serious and casual users in Web of Trust (WOT), a community-based system for website reputation and security. We find that the serious contributors are responsible for reporting and attending to a large percentage of bad sites, while a large fraction of attention on the goodness of sites come from the casual contributors. This complementarity enables WOT to provide warnings about malicious sites while differentiating the good sites from the unknowns. This in turn helps steer users away from the numerous bad sites created daily. We also find that serious contributors are more reliable in evaluating bad sites, but no better than casual contributors in evaluating good sites. We discuss design implications for WOT and for community-based systems more generally.

Author Keywords
Web Security, Wisdom of Crowds, Web of Trust (WOT)

ACM Classification Keywords
K.4.3 Computers and Society: Organizational Impacts

General Terms
Measurement; Security.

INTRODUCTION
Despite the efforts of a multi-billion dollar computer security industry, web security remains a largely unsolved problem. Large numbers of malicious sites continue to serve as platforms for phishing, malware, and other security exploits. Provos et al. [20] found over 3 million URLs (hosted on more than 180,000 sites) that initiated drive-by downloads – automatic installation and execution of malware on the machines of unsuspecting visitors. Zhuge et al. [26] found that 1.5% of Chinese websites, sampled using popular keywords on Baidu and Google search engines, were malicious. Meanwhile, the Anti-Phishing Working Group recorded more than 67,000 phishing attacks worldwide in the second half of 2010 [2].

Detection, blacklisting, and takedown of malicious sites have been traditionally handled by security vendors such as antivirus and brand protection companies. Detection and blacklisting of suspicious sites are typically done with automated sensing and classification using heuristics and machine learning. Given that the takedown of a malicious site can be cumbersome and protracted in time, tools have been created to warn the users about suspicious sites on the web.

However, many of the automated risk signaling tools, including McAfee's SiteAdvisor [15] and Norton's Safe Web [17], fall short in identifying 'bad' sites that try to trick or harm users in a variety of subtle ways. Problems of increasing concern that are not adequately handled by security vendors include the misuse of personal information, scams and fraudulent sites such as illegal online pharmacies. The automated tools also do not evaluate content appropriateness. While it is a personal judgment whether adult content is appropriate, the fact that adult sites regularly rank among the top 50 most visited sites and are often associated with malware, script-based attacks and aggressive marketing strategies [25], do indicate a serious problem. Furthermore, verifying the goodness of sites is not a straightforward task. Online certification issuers, such as BBBOnline and TRUSTe, strive to distinguish the 'good' sites from the 'bad' ones, but conflicts of interest can sometimes arise. When certifiers adopt lax requirements in certifying sites in the 'gray' category, the problem of adverse selection may result in the certified sites having lower trustworthiness than those that forego certification [9].

The limitations of automated tools and the potential risks of centralized judgment have prompted the alternative approach of leveraging community input for web security. Encouraged by the success of peer-production systems such as Wikipedia, yelp, and reCAPTCHA, the crowdsourcing of website security evaluation holds the promise of scalability. Yet, there remain concerns on the ability of community members in providing timely and reliable evaluation of a large number of websites. In addition to the typical problem of malicious or misinformed contributors present in a peer-production system, there are additional challenges in the context of web security. First, one would expect a certain level of security expertise, and therefore a higher contribution barrier, to evaluate the security of a website. Determining if a website en-

*Centre for Quantifiable Quality of Service in Communication Systems (Q2S), Centre of Excellence, appointed by the Research Council of Norway, is funded by the Research Council, Norwegian University of Science and Technology (NTNU) and UNINETT.

CSCW'12, February 11–15, 2012, Seattle, Washington, USA.

gages in a variety of security exploits is different from bookmarking a page using reddit or reviewing a book on Amazon. Second, attackers play a game of cat-and-mouse by creating large numbers of malicious websites every day, typically with short lifespans. The challenges of coverage and timeliness are therefore different from the case of Wikipedia, where the number and content of articles are relatively static.

Despite these concerns, several community-based systems for web security such as Web of Trust (WOT) [22] and PhishTank [19] have achieved significant impact. PhishTank collects user reporting and voting on suspected phishing sites. Its assessments are used by popular vendors including Yahoo!, McAfee, Mozilla and Opera. On the other hand, WOT collates individual user ratings into aggregate ratings on four aspects of web security, namely trustworthiness, vendor reliability, privacy, and child safety. Facebook has recently incorporated the assessments by WOT to protect its users from potentially harmful URLs [10]. A recent study by Chia and Knapskog [5] found that WOT was more comprehensive than three automated counterparts namely SiteAdvisor, Safe Web, and Safe Browsing Diagnostic Page in identifying bad domains among the frequently visited sites.

There is certainly value in leveraging on community inputs for web security. Beyond comparing the overall reliability of community-based systems against the automated counterparts, in this paper, we set out to study how different types of contributors (casual and serious) play their parts in advancing WOT in the challenging domain of web security. Understanding the roles of different contributors can lead us to a clearer picture of the underlying success factors and potential pitfalls. Specifically, in this work: (I) We ask how do the casual contributors add value to WOT given the steep contribution barrier of assessing web security? (II) We study how different types of contributors may choose to focus on different types of websites (popular/unknown, malicious/benign) or different trustworthiness aspects of websites (e.g., phishing, spam, inappropriate content). (III) We also seek to characterize the contribution patterns of casual and serious contributors, and to examine if there is a room to better coordinate the limited human resources. (IV) We also determine if different types of contributors realize different levels of reliability in their assessments. We hope that these questions can yield insights applicable to other contexts beyond web security.

In the following, we first describe the related works before detailing on how WOT works in practice and our methodology. We then present our analysis results focusing on the coverage, coordination, and reliability of inputs by the serious and casual contributors. Finally, we discuss the design implications to WOT and community-based systems more generally.

RELATED WORK

Collective Wisdom in General

A large number of prior works on collective wisdom have focused on the participation patterns in Wikipedia (e.g., [3, 12, 18, 23]), its potential pitfalls and risks (e.g., [8]) as well as its success factors and how to improve it (e.g., [6, 7, 11, 13]). Our work is related to that of Kittur et al. [12] and Welser et al. [23] in the way that we are interested in the roles played by different types of contributors for collective intelligence. While Kittur et al. [12] has observed a shift of workload from the elite class contributors to the less active ones over time, Ortega et al. [18] concluded that the contribution pattern in Wikipedia has remained highly skewed even in the stable phase. We note that however contribution should measure more than just the count of article edits and submissions. Indeed, even though the role by the less active contributors might appear overshadowed by the few serious contributors, prior research (e.g., [3]) has pointed out that even the readers (lurkers) can and do contribute to a collaborative system like Wikipedia. In this work, rather than focusing only on the count of comments and ratings, we measure the roles of different types of contributors judging from the coverage, coordination and reliability of their assessments.

Wilkinson [24] describes two macroscopic characteristics in peer production systems and shows how the two regularities arise from simple dynamic rules. First, he demonstrates that the probability a person stops contributing is inversely proportional to the number of contributions he has made, which in turn leads to a power law contribution distribution in all four systems (Wikipedia, Bugzilla, Digg and Essembly) he investigated. He found also a lognormal distribution of per topic activity – a small number of very popular topics accumulate the vast majority of contributions due to a multiplicative popularity reinforcement mechanism. We do not evaluate if the contribution patterns in WOT follows a specific distribution in this paper, but we observe that both the distributions of per person contributions and per site inputs do have a heavy tail. The skewed attention distribution among sites evaluated by the casual contributors is interesting as it suggests the possibility of better coordinating the security crowds for a higher level of efficiency.

Mamykina et al. [14] argued that the success of Stack Overflow attributes not only to the careful design considerations, but also to the high visibility and interactive involvement of the design team in the community. The authors further highlighted that this model of continued community leadership presents challenges to port the success of Stack Overflow easily over to other domain specific systems. This argument has only made it more appealing to better understand the roles played by different contributors as we aim for in this paper.

Collective Wisdom for Web Security

Denning et al. [8] highlighted six areas of potential risks in Wikipedia, namely accuracy, motives of contributor, uncertain expertise, volatility of content, sources of information and coverage. The first five areas relate to the correctness of information, suggesting a heavier focus on content reliability. All six areas are valid concerns facing the community-based web security. We note that however coverage is just as important given that it is the strategy of attackers to create numerous new bad sites to thin the resources of the defenders.

Moore and Clayton [16] evaluated the effectiveness of PhishTank – a community-based system for reporting and voting against suspected phishing sites. They found that the participation ratio in PhishTank was highly skewed (following a power-law distribution), making it particularly susceptible to manipulation. Compared to a commercial phishing report, they found that PhishTank was slightly less comprehensive and slower in reaching a decision. 3% of the sites reported as suspicious (out of a total of 176,654) were found to be invalid phishes. A large percentage of the incorrect submissions came from the less active contributors. However, considering the eventual assessment outcomes (when the initial reporting is validated or corrected by the subsequent voting mechanism), they have found only 39 false positives and 3 false negatives in total.

The study by Chia and Knapskog [5] was the among the first that evaluated WOT comparing it with the assessment outcomes of SiteAdvisor, Safe Web and Safe Browsing Diagnostic Page. They found that the participation ratio in WOT was also highly skewed. However, WOT was in fact more comprehensive than the three automated systems in identifying bad domains (amongst the top million most visited sites as published by Alexa [1]). The study also concluded that user concerns on web security are not limited to malware and phishing. Scams, illegal pharmacies and misuse of personal information are regular issues raised by WOT's community while they are not evaluated by the automated services. In a similar study, Ayyavu and Jensen [4] rejected the unfair generalization on the low reliability of community-based rating systems as they found that, among frequently visited sites that have been co-evaluated by WOT and SiteAdvisor, the disagreement in assessments was actually less than 10%.

Building on the above studies, our work here looks beyond the overall reliability of crowdsourcing for web security. Acknowledging the potentials of such systems, we examine the roles being played from different types of contributors to better understand the underlying success factors and potential pitfalls. We center our analysis around the coverage, coordination and reliability of user assessments in line with the typical concerns of collaborative systems and web security.

WEB OF TRUST (WOT)

WOT is a reputation system that collates community inputs into aggregate ratings for different websites. It takes the form of an open source browser add-on and a website (mywot.com) with a number of community features including a personal page per registered user, discussion forums, a wiki as well as messaging and polling tools. The add-on has been downloaded for more than 23 million times by August 2011.

User Ratings and Comments

Individual user ratings and the aggregate ratings for different sites in WOT are structured around four aspects: trustworthiness, vendor reliability, privacy and child safety. The ratings range from very poor (0-19%), poor (20-39%), unsatisfactory (40-59%) to good (60-79%) and excellent (80-100%).

WOT weighs the input ratings differently based on the reliability of individual contributors. The reliability of a contributor, decoupled from his activity level or contribution count, is computed with Bayesian inference based on his past contributions. Individual user ratings are kept private to the contributors. The rating aggregation formula is also not publicly available. WOT argues that the hidden formula and individual inputs, plus the Bayesian inference rule, help to mitigate gaming behaviors. We learned from the developers that they have built in automated mechanisms to monitor for suspicious contribution behaviors. They have also factored in the freshness of user ratings by setting the weight of individual ratings to decay over time (until the rater re-visits the site).

Positive category	Negative category	Other
Entertaining	Useless	Other
Useful, informative	Annoying ads or popups	
Child friendly	Ethical issues	
Good customer experience	Hateful, violent/illegal content	
Good site	Bad customer experience	
	Browser exploit	
	Spyware or adware	
	Adult content	
	Phishing or other scams	
	Malicious content, viruses	
	Spam	

Table 1. Comment categories of positive or negative nature in WOT.

Other than numerical ratings, users can also evaluate a site by textual comments. To give a comment, they must first register themselves on mywot.com. There are more than 2 millions registered users to date. Unregistered users (i.e., anyone who has downloaded the add-on) can only rate a site through the add-on, which assigns a unique pseudonym to the user. When submitting a comment, the user selects one out of 17 comment categories that best describes their concern. As shown in Table 1, excluding the category 'Other', 5 of the comment categories are positive in nature, while the remaining 11 are negative. Comments do not count towards the aggregate ratings, but they provide a way of reasoning as to how a user has rated a particular site. Unlike the individual ratings, comments are publicly accessible on the *scorecard* of each evaluated site. The scorecard of a particular site refers to a uniquely reserved page on mywot.com that shows the aggregate ratings and user comments given to the site along with other details such as its traffic ranking, server location, description and links for further information.

Mass Rating Tool

WOT ranks the community members starting from rookie, bronze, silver, gold to the platinum level. The ranking is done based on the activity score which is computed from the total ratings and comments contributed, different from the reliability score that is kept private and designed to incentivize the users to contribute responsibly. Platinum members are given the privilege to use the *mass rating tool* which allows them to evaluate (at maximum) 100 sites at the same time with the same rating and comment. It is a handy tool for those who have access to some blacklists (e.g., on spamming, phishing and malicious sites) to submit the bulk evaluations conveniently.

Trusted sources

Besides user ratings and comments, WOT does factor in inputs given by trusted third parties. For example, it receives blacklists of phishes, spamming sites and illegal online pharmacies from PhishTank, SpamCop.net and LegitScript.com respectively. Inputs from the trusted third parties play an important role in improving the coverage and timeliness of WOT in responding to new bad sites created by the attackers daily. We do not have access to the inputs from these trusted sources (nor the ratings from individual contributors). We will focus only analyzing the user comments in this paper.

Risk Signaling and Warning

WOT signals the reputation of different URLs through the browser add-on using colored rings (red for 'bad', yellow for 'caution', green for 'good', gray for 'unknown'). By default, the reputation of a site is computed based on the trustworthiness (tr) rating which covers whether a site can be trusted and is safe to use (without malicious content). A site is considered bad if tr<40, caution if 40≤tr<60, good if tr≥60, and unknown if tr is not available or if a minimal confidence level has not been obtained. A special case is when WOT finds a *credible warning* in either aspect of vendor reliability or privacy and thus treating the site as bad. By credible warning, we refer to the case when a particular aspect is given an aggregate rating below 40% with a confidence level above 8%. The confidence level is computed based on both the number of ratings and the reliability scores of the contributors. In the presence of a credible warning, besides displaying a red ring next to the URL, WOT prompts a large warning dialog to the user if he clicks on the link. The child safety rating is ignored by default. The settings for risk signaling and warning can however be configured to suit the needs of different users.

Evaluation Statistics

According to its statistics page, WOT has evaluated more than 32 million sites by August 2011. The community may however have quite some catch-up to do considering that there are more than 205 million domain names now (as estimated in [2] and [21]), giving WOT an overall coverage of 15.6%. As found in [5], the coverage of WOT among Alexa's top million most visited sites was 51.2%, but still lower than SiteAdvisor (87.9%) and Safe Web (68.1%). Among the 32 million sites evaluated by WOT, 3.4 millions (10.6%) are regarded as bad with a low trustworthiness rating. While no one can be sure about the total bad sites on the web (given that many of them are undetected), researchers found that 1.5% of the frequently visited Chinese sites were malicious [26], and 1.3% of Google search queries received more than one malicious URL in the result page [20]. Putting the above figures together, WOT does appear to have a better coverage for bad sites than the good ones in its current state. Indeed, WOT was found to be more comprehensive than SiteAdvisor, Safe Web and Safe Browsing Diagnostics Tool in identifying bad domains among the frequently visited sites [5].

METHODOLOGY AND DATA COLLECTION

For this study, we have obtained two valuable datasets from the WOT developers (hereafter referred to as DS-Comment and DS-Activity). DS-Comment consists of 600,000 comments randomly selected from more than 12 millions in total in WOT in early 2011. The comments evaluate a total of 504,874 sites and were submitted by 20,657 unique contributors. Each comment in the dataset is accompanied by details including the user ID, date of writing, evaluated domain as well as a comment category as specified by the contributor. We made use of the positive or negative nature of a comment category (as classified in Table 1) to determine the positive or negative sentiment of the contributor's assessment. We thus refer to a negative (positive) comment as one that has been given a negative (positive) comment category in this article. On the other hand, DS-Activity describes the total ratings and comments that each of the 20,657 contributors has given considering the entire database of WOT. The dataset thus indicates the activity level of the contributors in WOT in entirety; we made use of it to distinguish between different types of contributors (casual or serious). Put together, these two datasets allow us to evaluate the coverage (attention) provided by different types of contributors, various characteristics of sites they attend to, and the potential coordination among themselves.

To evaluate the reliability of inputs given by different contributor types, we then randomly selected 5,000 domains from the 504,874 evaluated in DS-Comment and queried for their aggregate ratings from WOT. Note that the aggregate ratings of WOT have factored in the reliability scores of different contributors and additional inputs (if any) from trusted third parties. For each of the 5,000 sites, we queried also the assessments by SiteAdvisor (SA) and Safe Web (SW) – two services provided by McAfee and Norton respectively. SA evaluates a site based on proprietary and automated tests on aspects such as downloads, browser exploits, email, phishing and annoyance factors (e.g., pop-ups). It also receives inputs from TrustedSource.org (also owned by McAfee) which evaluates aspects including site behavior, traffic and linking patterns, and site registration and hosting. Similarly, SW run automated tests to determine if a site imposes threats such as drive-by download, phishing, spyware, Trojan, worm, virus, suspicious browser change, joke program and identity theft. Both SA and SW do collect user comments (and ratings in the case of SW) but these inputs do not count towards the eventual assessment. We parsed the reports and obtained the assessment outcomes which constitute our third dataset, DS-Reliability. The querying process took place in April 2011. We repeated the queries in mid May and found no significant changes in the assessment outcomes by all three services.

Limitations

We list here several limitations to our study. First, given that we do not have access to the ratings given by individual contributors (which are kept private in WOT), we will be projecting the attention and concern of different contributor types judging from their comment contribution. This should not be problematic as we find a strong correlation (r=0.89 with $p<.001$) between the total ratings and total comments one has contributed from DS-Activity.

Secondly, for our analysis on coverage and attention, we will assume that the contributors have specified a category that fits their comment correctly. The same assumption is used as we will leverage on the nature of a comment category (positive or negative) to evaluate the reliability of different contributor groups in assessing bad and good sites. We note that this assumption is reasonable given that there is no motivation for a user to cheat or game the system by choosing a false category as comments do not affect the aggregate outcome.

Another limitation relates to the fact that we will measure the coverage and reliability of different contributor groups based on the sites evaluated in DS-Comment. The ratio of comments given a category of negative nature is much higher than the positive ones in DS-Comment, in line with the statistics on mywot.com. While this gives us an accurate representation of the state of contribution distribution in WOT, it may be misleading to take, for example, the loss of coverage in the absence of the casual contributors to be minimal (2.16% as we will show in the next section). The impact will be larger if we consider sites relevant to the daily browsing patterns of ordinary users. For example, among the top million most visited sites, WOT rated 45.9% of them as good [5] – a stark difference to the small proportion of positive comments (5%) in DS-Comment. This suggests a more important role played by the casual contributors than it may appear.

We note that also DS-Comment contains comments that may have been later removed by the contributors (e.g., when a negative comment is disputed by other users as a false positive). We pay attention to this when evaluating the reliability of different contributor groups given that the test sample is smaller.

ANALYSIS / RESULTS

We will first describe the macroscopic contribution patterns in WOT and how we categorize the contributors based on their activity level. Then, we delve into the characteristics of the two extreme types of contributors (serious or casual) and measure their roles in covering sites of different natures as well as evaluating them reliably. We study also how the different contributors may have (mis-)coordinated themselves.

Characterizing Different Types of Contributors

Figure 1 plots the contribution distributions of ratings and comments using DS-Activity. Both of them do not fit a power-law distribution (different from in [5] where the comment contribution was found to be following a power-law distribution). We did not test if they fit some other types of heavy tailed distributions (e.g., log-normal, Weibull) but it is visually intuitive that the distributions are skewed. This is not entirely unexpected; a skewed contribution distribution of a community-based system can be characterized by the 'participation momentum' [24] – the more contributions one has made, the lower it is the likelihood of him quit contributing. An interesting observation (not shown in figure) is that not all the highly active contributors actually arrived from the beginning. WOT has managed to attract new highly active members as the community evolves.

While more ratings have been given than comments (per person) on average, the difference is not statistically significant. There is a strong correlation (r=0.89 with p<.001) between the number of ratings and number of comments contributed per person. This indicates the feasibility to study the different characteristics of the contributors based on the comments given instead of ratings that are not publicly available.

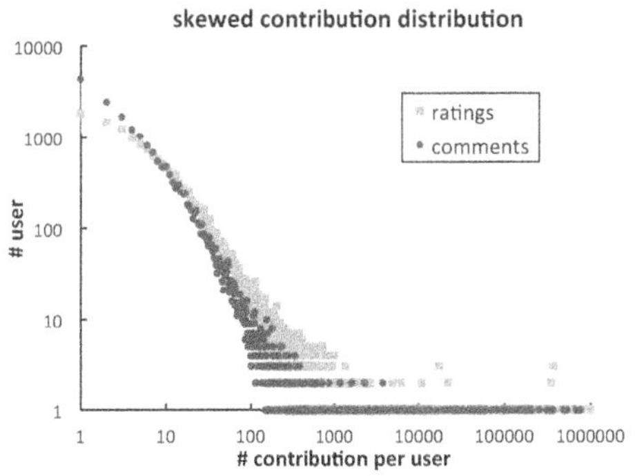

Figure 1. Distribution of comment and rating contribution.

Contr. group	Total comments (from DS-Activity)	Statistics from DS-Comment: # comments contributed	# sites evaluated	# unique users
u0	1 – 9	15,493	12,932	13,924
u1	10 – 99	18,727	17,306	5,850
u2	100 – 999	8,569	8,197	703
u3	1000 – 9999	16,956	16,641	106
u4	10000 – 99999	80,607	73,965	44
u5	100000 or more	459,648	407,778	30
	All groups	600,000	504,874	20,657

Table 2. Grouping based on total comments one has given in WOT.

We categorize the contributors according to the number of comments one has given, with *u0* denoting the group of *casual* contributors who have provided less than 10 comments, and *u5* denoting the group of *serious* contributors who have given at least 100,000 comments. In other words, each contributor group corresponds to a different contribution level measured in terms of the base 10 magnitude order of the total comments contributed. Table 2 details on the categorization rules, total comments, total unique sites covered and the size of each contributor group. 67.41% of the contributors belong to the casual type while more than 76.61% of the comments comes from the few serious contributors. As demonstrated in [14, 23], there may be ways to refine the contributor categorization using various structural attributes (e.g., the temporal patterns of comment submission, the nature of sites evaluated). However, we note that an activity-based categorization scheme does serve the research questions we pursue in this paper. In addition to comparing the characteristics of the casual (u0) and serious (u5) contributors, we include also the results of comparing the combinations of u0+u1 (less active members) and u4+u5 (highly active members) whenever suitable. We expect the combination of u4 and u5 to represent those who have the privilege of using the mass rating tool.

Coverage: Complementary Attention and Concern

We first analyze the attention and concern by different contributor groups judging from the comments they have given.

Attention Divide on Goodness and Badness of Sites

Figure 2 (right) depicts the percentage breakdown of comments given by different contributor groups in each comment category. Notice that the first 5 categories are positive in nature, followed by 11 others that are negative, as classified in Table 1. We made use of the positive or negative nature of a comment category to determine the contributor's attention

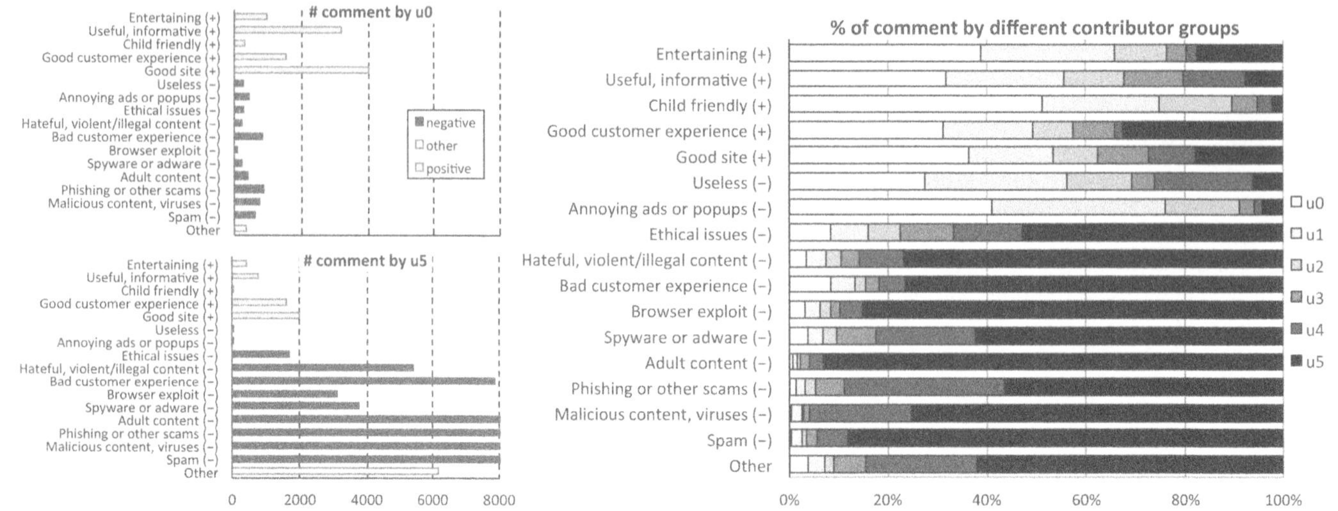

Figure 2. (Left) Total comments given by u0 and u5 in each comment category with the horizontal bars truncated at value=8000. (Right) Percentage breakdown of comments given by different contributor groups. + and – denote the positive and negative nature of a comment category respectively.

on the goodness or badness of a site. An interesting finding is that a large percentage of attention or concern on the goodness of sites (i.e., whether they are entertaining, useful, child friendly, offers good customer experience, or good) actually comes from the less active contributors (especially u0). Conversely, other than the 'Useless' and 'Annoying ads or pop-ups' categories, a large percentage of comments among the negative categories actually come from the highly active contributors (especially u5). These include the attention on the technical security of sites (e.g., whether a site contains malware, spyware, browser exploits, or whether a site is related to spamming, phishing or scams) as well as the attention on adult and other potentially inappropriate content. While this may be largely due to the fact that the serious contributors have been rating and commenting a large number of sites based on some blacklists they maintain or reference to, the distinctive divide on the attention for the goodness and badness of sites does highlight the role of the casual contributors.

The finding is consistent when we look at the ratio of positive versus negative comments that have been given by the casual and serious contributors respectively. As shown in Figure 2 (left), the casual contributors (u0) are indeed more inclined to comment about the good aspects of a site, different from the serious contributors (u5) who have produced much more negative comments versus the positive ones. Next, we quantify the roles of serious and casual contributors in covering for sites of specific nature in Table 3. Specifically, we measure the loss of coverage should a particular contributor is absent in the community. Most notable is that, without the inputs from the highly active contributors (u4 and u5), 92.77% of the 473,273 potentially bad sites would have gone undetected. Meanwhile, the loss of coverage for potentially bad sites should u0 and u1 are absent is 2.55%.

While it may appear that the casual contributors provide little value to web security, we argue the reverse is true as they enable a system like WOT to signal against sites that are good from those that have not been evaluated. Indeed, without the less active contributors (u0 and u1), 50.1% of potentially good domains (i.e., those that have received at least a positive comment in the our dataset) would have been given an 'unknown' status. This is important, as attackers tend to leverage on a large volume of bad sites to thin the defenders' resources. Given an adequate coverage of good sites, users who are conservative on web security can regard sites with an unknown status as potentially questionable.

Attention Divide for Popular Sites and The Long Tail

Among sites that have been attended to by more than one contributors, we find that 4.91% of these sites were in fact first discovered (first commented) by a member of either u0 or u1. This is close to the 4.69% loss of coverage on all kinds of sites (as shown in Table 3) should we ignore the inputs from u0 and u1 contributors. The corresponding figures considering the u0 contributors only are 1.98% and 2.16%.

Note that however the above figures are computed based on the total number of sites covered in DS-Comment, which contains a disproportionately large share of bad sites (93%) typically found in the long tail of the web popularity. The value of the casual contributors will be larger should we consider only sites that are more relevant for daily browsing. Not surprisingly, we find that only 3.4% of the sites evaluated by the u5's comments appear on Alexa's list of top million most visited sites. On the other hand, 51.9% of the sites attended to by u0 are among the top million most visited sites. The corresponding figure is 29.6% for u1 and 4.3% for u4 respectively. Considering only those that appear on Alexa's list, the mean traffic ranking of sites attended to by u0 is lower than that of attended to by u5 ($p<.01$). The mean traffic ranking comparing u0+u1 to u4+u5 is also significantly lower ($p<.01$).

While serious contributors identify most of the bad sites in the long tail of web popularity, we note that the coverage for the more popular sites by the casual contributors is equally important. Following our earlier argument, coverage for known sites would allow the users to be correctly cautious about un-

	Comment category	# comments	# unique sites	Loss of coverage (%)			
				without u0	without u0 & u1	without u4 & u5	without u5
	All	600,000	504,874	2.16	4.69	89.60	75.53
	Positive only	29,018	24,697	31.04	50.10	27.01	17.79
	Negative only	561,006	473,273	0.80	2.55	92.77	78.61
positive	Entertaining	2,496	2,219	36.64	62.33	21.54	19.51
	Useful, informative	9,985	8,841	29.51	51.85	21.66	7.86
	Child friendly	607	577	49.39	73.31	5.37	2.25
	Good customer experience	4,948	4,595	29.36	46.49	36.28	34.86
	Good site	10,982	9,999	33.69	50.06	28.58	18.43
negative	Useless	950	929	26.37	55.33	26.91	6.46
	Annoying ads or popups	1,040	905	37.46	72.71	5.75	4.64
	Ethical issues	3,149	3,038	7.83	14.91	67.08	53.32
	Hateful, violent or illegal content	7,044	6,927	2.86	6.63	86.73	77.83
	Bad customer experience	10,300	10,117	7.44	12.32	82.67	77.38
	Browser exploit	3,660	3,609	3.02	5.99	89.86	85.23
	Spyware or adware	6,052	5,902	3.49	6.25	82.68	62.15
	Adult content	53,879	52,856	0.60	1.19	95.99	93.74
	Phishing or other scams	65,259	58,011	1.29	3.13	88.01	54.67
	Malicious content, viruses	171,175	139,711	0.47	1.84	95.19	72.82
	Spam	238,498	210,529	0.26	2.13	93.89	87.12
	Other	9,976	9,861	3.31	6.45	85.16	62.29

Table 3. Total comments and unique sites evaluated per comment category, and the loss of coverage in the absence of casual or serious contributors.

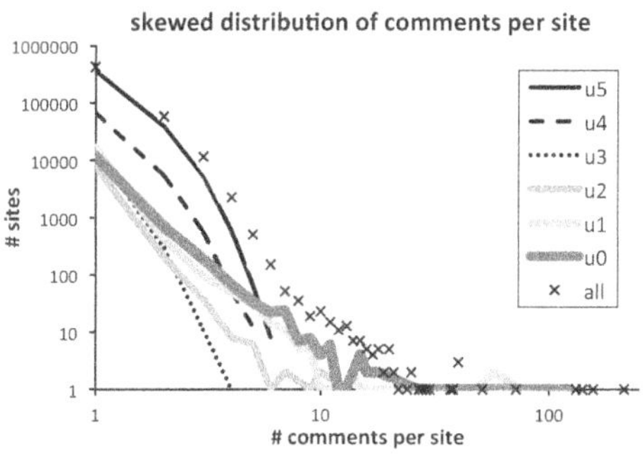

Figure 3. Distribution of comments per site considering all contributors (× markers) and each contributor group separately (black/color lines).

rated or unknown websites. Evaluations for the more frequently visited sites are also of a higher relevance and can thus be of a higher value. There is however a potential pitfall. Sites from well-known vendors should not be unnecessarily occupying the attention of the contributors. We look into the issue of efficiency and redundancy in the next section.

Coordination: Redundancy versus Efficiency

Figure 3 plots the distribution of comments per site considering all contributors together (depicted by the × markers), and considering the individual contributor groups separately (depicted by the black and color lines). An interesting observation is the heavy tail of the overall distribution of comments. This is largely due to the highly redundant coverage given by the less active contributors (u0 and u1). Notice that both the u0 and u1 lines exhibit also a long tail. In particular, a number of sites have received tens of comments from u0 alone. The redundancy is much larger in practice given that our dataset represents only a 5% sample of all available comments.

While a certain degree of redundancy is needed to ensure a reliable assessment outcome (the law of large number), excessive redundancy indicates inefficiency. It may be reasonable to expect controversial sites to receive more attention than the others. We examine the cases where u0 contributors have given more than one comments to a site, and measure the controversy of a site as $1 - |n_i - p_i|/(n_i + p_i)$ with n_i and p_i denoting the number of negative and positive comments given to site i respectively. However, we find only a low correlation (r=0.08, p<.01) between the number of comments of a site and its level of controversy. Indeed, the top most commented sites by u0 (and their controversy level) include WOT's own website, mywot.com (0.17) and other well-known sites such as google.com (0.38), facebook.com (0.95), youtube.com (0.66) and mail.google.com (0.10). This suggests the potential to coordinate the casual contributors for a higher efficiency.

The distributions of comments given by u4 and u5 seem to follow a different trend. A large number of sites evaluated by the serious contributors (u5) have actually received only one or two comments (in DS-Comment). While it may appear that there is an implicit coordination, we find that the three most common issues (spam, phishing and malicious sites) are actually attended to by 27 out of the 30 serious contributors. 15 of them have used the blacklists on malwaredomains.com for malicious sites, while 14 have referred to joewein.net for spamming activities. While further investigation is necessary, there may be also some room to better coordinate the volunteering efforts by the serious contributors.

Reliability and Verifiability

Thus far, we have studied various characteristics of the comments given by different contributor groups but we have yet to consider the reliability of their inputs. We would expect some of the comments (and ratings) to be invalid due to errors or potentially gaming behaviors. To evaluate the validity of the individual inputs, we first work out the *true risk status* of different sites using the dataset DS-Reliability, which contains the assessment outcomes by WOT, SiteAdvisor (SA) and Safe Web (SW) on 5,000 sites randomly selected from DS-Comment. This is however not a straight forward task; the assessment outcomes of different services are known to

Contr. group	Among sites identified as bad: by WOT # c (–)	# c (+)	by WOT & SA # c (–)	# c (+)	Among sites identified as good: by WOT # c (–)	# c (+)	by WOT & SA # c (–)	# c (+)
u0	30	34	1	1	15	50	15	48
u1	99	7	34	-	11	28	11	28
u2	32	4	7	-	8	27	7	27
u3	107	3	20	-	3	18	3	15
u4	698	1	326	1	1	20	1	16
u5	3,826	4	1,232	-	9	41	7	38

Table 4. Error rate of different contributor groups in assessing bad and good sites comparing the number of positive (+) and negative (–) comments to (i) the sole assessments by WOT, and (ii) the common assessment outcomes (bad/good) of WOT and SiteAdvisor (SA). Texts in red denote the counts of false-negative or false-positive cases accordingly.

Contr. group	% comments with web link	mean comment length (# char)
u0	3.10	91
u1	8.07	118
u2	10.07	76
u3	26.56	99
u4	64.29	108
u5	49.38	138

Table 5. Percentage of comments containing a web link, and average comment length (in terms of the number of characters) excluding comments containing non-Latin characters.

be disagreeing with each other [5]. We map the assessment outcomes of SA (Green, Yellow, Red, Gray) and SW (Safe or VerisignTrusted, Caution, Warning, Untested) to the default risk signals of WOT (Green: good, Yellow: caution, Red: bad, Gray: unknown). We find that, among the 302 good sites identified by WOT, a majority of them receive the same verdict from SA and SW respectively. However, out of the 4544 sites identified as bad by WOT, 1230 are co-identified as bad by SA while only 47 sites are warned by SW. The large discrepancy between SW and WOT can be attributed to the extremely low coverage of SW (29%) on the 5000 sites in our test sample. This leads us to ignore the assessments from SW in the subsequent analysis. On the other hand, SA (with a coverage of 78%) has come short in evaluating sites with an IP address and those hosted on shared domain or free hosting services. Another factor contributing to the discrepancy between SA and WOT is the larger evaluation scope of WOT. For example, SA does not evaluate the vendor reliability aspect as WOT does. For these reasons, to study the reliability of different contributor groups, we approximate the true risk status of sites based on (i) the aggregate assessment outcomes by WOT alone, (ii) the common outcomes of WOT and SA.

Reliability in Evaluating Good and Bad Sites

Table 4 shows the number of positive and negative comments given by different contributor groups that match the assessments by WOT alone, and that match the common verdicts by WOT and SA. Note that we have excluded comments with the 'Adult content', 'Child friendly', 'Hateful, violent or illegal content', 'Ethical issues' and 'Entertaining' categories given that both SA and the default risk signaling strategy of WOT do not evaluate content appropriateness or fun level.

There are several interesting findings here. First, notice that among sites that have been co-identified as bad by WOT and SA, there are only two positive comments wrongly made for these sites (see Table 4, 5th column). A similar trend can be observed for sites that have been identified as bad by WOT (a superset of the previous case); the ratio of positive comments (error rate) is small except for the case of u0 (see Table 4, column 2-3). Here, the casual contributors (u0) could be misinformed about the badness of the sites or attempting to game the aggregate outcomes. Either way, the large error rate suggests the limitation of the casual contributors as a whole in assessing bad sites reliably. On the other hand, the reliability of serious contributors in assessing bad sites is applaudable. In fact, u5 has found many more bad sites than SA.

Next, we look at the reliability of different contributor groups in assessing the good sites. Notice that there is a higher error rate (the ratio of negative to positive comments) in general. Indeed, labeling a site as good involves a higher level of subjectivity. Different from the objective assessment on whether a site is malicious, is a phishing site and so on, there is also a lack of well-defined terminologies in general to measure the good properties of a site. Interestingly, the error rate does not differ much across different contributor groups. To be exact, the difference in the ratios of positive to negative comments given by u0 and u5 is not statistically significant considering sites evaluated as good by WOT (Table 4, column 6-7) (Fisher's exact test, p=0.64), as well as sites co-evaluated as good by both WOT and SA (column 8-9) (p=0.34). The casual contributors are thus not inferior to the serious contributors when it comes to evaluating a good site correctly. We look into the error cases by u5 and find that 4 out of 9 false positive comments have actually been removed from the scorecards of the related sites.

Verifiability: Reference and Comment Length

Table 5 shows the percentage of comments that come with at least a URL link. While it is not always the case, URLs in the user comments often lead to some specific resources (e.g., further discussion) or references (e.g., to some online blacklists) where the contributors have become aware of the evaluated sites. We use the presence of a URL as an estimator of the verifiability of a comment. Notice that only 3% of the comments given by the casual contributors (u0) contain a URL. At the same time, only 49% of the comments given by u5 potentially contain a reference URL, typically pointing to a blacklist provided by, for example, joewein.net, cert.at, uribl.com, atma.es, malwareurl.com, spamtrackers.eu and malwaredomains.com. Also given in Table 5 is the mean length of comments provided by different contributor groups, excluding comments containing some non-Latin characters. The mean comment length increases going from casual to serious contributors; however, the increment is not statistically significant. These findings do signal the need of actions from WOT to improve the verifiability of user inputs. We outline some potential pitfalls and suggestions in the following.

DISCUSSION

Complementary Roles in Web Security

An important lesson learnt from our study is the complementary roles of casual and serious contributors for community-based web security. Contrary to the skepticisms that security is out of reach for ordinary users given that it is a highly specialized domain requiring expert knowledge, our work shows that the casual contributors can be helpful in differentiating the good and known sites from those that have yet to be evaluated. Availability of such a 'whitelist' is valuable considering the large number of bad and gray sites created daily. In addition, while serious contributors may be sharp in evaluating the badness of a site (given the access to some reliable blacklists and expert knowledge on malicious activities on the web), their judgment on good sites (subjective) is not significantly better than the less active contributors.

Applicability to Other Contexts

The complementary roles we find in this paper are probably unique to web security where conventional approaches are being overloaded with a large number of new sites, and where there is a need for subjective judgment (where personal experience matters) and objective evaluation (where expert knowledge is required) on different aspects of sites. While the exact complementarily may not apply to other collaborative systems directly, the finding that different members play different roles and exhibit different potentials should be capitalized by community-based systems across different domains. Leveraging on the different roles and natures of tasks, we outline several design implications relevant to WOT and community-based systems more generally in the following.

Design Implications

Context based Reliability

The ability to gauge and make use of the reliability of a contributor is an important building block to many community-based systems. WOT currently weighs the user inputs differently based on the reliability of individual contributors when computing the aggregate outcomes. This provides an incentive for the community members to contribute responsibly. Nevertheless, the actual formula used is hidden (arguably to mitigate potential gaming behaviors). Our findings that different contributor types attend to sites of different natures and realize different levels of reliability in evaluating bad and good sites, raise several important issues in designing the reliability weighting mechanism. First, should the weighting be computed at per contributor or per contributor-and-site-category level? We argue that the latter would be more appropriate. Specific to WOT, a serious contributor who has been consistently giving reliable evaluations on potentially malicious sites should not be automatically given a heavy weight when, for example, evaluating the goodness or content appropriateness of a site. Another issue lies with the subjective evaluation aspects that WOT and many other reputation systems actually deal with. Does the reliability weighting punish those who may have a different expectation and opinion than the majority on a subjective aspect? This is a tricky matter which further highlights the need to acknowledge the differences across multiple evaluation aspects: subjective or objective, requiring expert knowledge or not, and so on.

Verifiability of Objective and Subjective Evaluation

A way to increase the reliability of a community-based system is probably by improving the verifiability of user contributions. WOT details on the use of inputs from third party sources (if any) on the scorecard of each evaluated site, but the community inputs seem to be lacking in verifiability currently. WOT requires the users of the mass rating tool (the highly active members) to include a comment describing the reasons of their ratings and to be always contactable on mywot.com. However, our analysis shows that only 49% of the comments provided by the serious contributors do potentially contain a reference URL. The percentage is much lower among the comments given by the casual contributors. These suggest a lack of verifiability that could affect user confidence in the long run. We suggest putting in place a referencing system for objective evaluation (e.g., on whether a site is malicious) and a more structured process when eliciting subjective evaluation. For example, requiring the mass rating tool users to always include the supporting reference will help especially in the cases of false positives. This will also restrict the tool from being wrongly used on aspects that are subjective and objectionable in nature. On the other hand, casual contributors who we find to be more likely to attend to subjective aspects such as the goodness of a site, should be guided to detail on their personal experience in a more structured manner. This can include indicating if they are affiliated with the site, how frequently they visit it, how does it matches a list of keywords, and so forth. The use of a referencing system and a structured way of eliciting subjective inputs are not new. However, different from the Wikipedia and many other systems that deal with either objective or subjective contributions solely, WOT exemplifies the case where both methods will be needed at the same time to cater for a mix of objective and subjective evaluations.

Role based Coordination and Socialization

Reliability issues aside, under-provisioning is perhaps the most challenging problem in community-based systems. Our study yields interesting insights on how we can better coordinate and socialize the contributors depending on the roles they play in the community. Currently, WOT does allow the site owners to reach out to the community members and call for their assessments. We note that it could be interesting to automatically distribute these requests to selected highly active members with the necessary skill sets and experience, similar to SuggestBot presented in [7]. WOT can also consider introducing a more explicit community structure (e.g., establishing sub-communities that would specialize on certain objective aspects e.g., privacy and malicious contents) such that a core team of contributors could help to set directions and guide the new contributors (as proposed for Wikipedia in [13]). On the other hand, the heavy tailed attention distribution among the less active contributors (as shown in Figure 3) hints on the possibility of coordinating the ordinary members to increase productivity. While there may be a privacy issue, WOT could innovate on an *opt-in* feature that would automatically suggest to the casual contributors to rate the unevaluated sites that they have been visiting. Generally, these should be done with care as certain socialization tactics may adversely turn away the contributors [6]. All in all, coordination and socialization efforts should be done with a good understanding on the different roles and potentials of different contributors.

CONCLUSIONS

We have found the interesting complementary roles of serious and casual contributors in Web of Trust (WOT). Serious contributors play an important role in reporting most of the malicious sites while casual contributors provide a large percentage of attention to the goodness of sites. Although the casual contributors do not evaluate malicious sites extensively and reliably, their evaluations on the good sites are valuable as they enable WOT to differentiate the good and known sites from those that have yet to be evaluated accordingly. This helps to steer users away from the numerous bad sites created daily. In addition, while serious contributors give reliable evaluations on bad sites, their evaluations on good websites are not significantly more reliable than the casual contributors. While the complementarity we find in this paper may be specific to web security, the finding that different community members contribute in different roles and exhibit different potentials in different tasks should be better capitalized by community-based systems across different domains.

ACKNOWLEDGMENTS

This research was supported in part by the National Science Foundation under award CCF-0424422 (TRUST). We are grateful to the anonymous reviewers for their constructive comments. We thank also the WOT developers for providing us two valuable datasets.

REFERENCES

1. Alexa Top Million Sites. http://www.alexa.com/topsites.
2. Anti-Phishing Working Group. Global Phishing Survey: Trends and Domain Name Use in 2H2010. http://www.antiphishing.org/reports/APWG_GlobalPhishingSurvey_2H2010.pdf.
3. Antin, J., and Cheshire, C. Readers are not free-riders: reading as a form of participation on Wikipedia. In *Proc. CSCW*, ACM (2010), 127–130.
4. Ayyavu, P., and Jensen, C. Integrating user feedback with heuristic security and privacy management systems. In *Proc. CHI*, ACM (2011), 2305–2314.
5. Chia, P. H., and Knapskog, S. J. Re-evaluating the wisdom of crowds in assessing web security. In *Proc. Financial Cryptography and Data Security (FC)*, Springer (2011).
6. Choi, B., Alexander, K., Kraut, R. E., and Levine, J. M. Socialization tactics in Wikipedia and their effects. In *Proc. CSCW*, ACM (2010), 107–116.
7. Cosley, D., Frankowski, D., Terveen, L., and Riedl, J. Suggestbot: using intelligent task routing to help people find work in wikipedia. In *Proc. IUI*, ACM (2007), 32–41.
8. Denning, P., Horning, J., Parnas, D., and Weinstein, L. Wikipedia risks. *Communications of the ACM 48*, 12 (2005), 152.
9. Edelman, B. Adverse selection in online "trust" certifications and search results. *Electronic Commerce Research and Applications* (2010).
10. Facebook partners with WOT to protect its users. http://www.arcticstartup.com/2011/05/12/facebook-partners-with-wot-to-protect-its-700-million-users.
11. Geiger, R. S., and Ribes, D. The work of sustaining order in Wikipedia: the banning of a vandal. In *Proc. CSCW*, ACM (2010), 117–126.
12. Kittur, A., Chi, E., Pendleton, B. A., Suh, B., and Mytkowicz, T. Power of the few vs. wisdom of the crowd: Wikipedia and the rise of the bourgeoisie. *Algorithmica 1*, 2 (2007), 1–9.
13. Kittur, A., and Kraut, R. E. Harnessing the wisdom of crowds in Wikipedia: quality through coordination. In *Proc. CSCW*, ACM (2008), 37–46.
14. Mamykina, L., Manoim, B., Mittal, M., Hripcsak, G., and Hartmann, B. Design lessons from the fastest Q&A site in the west. In *Proc. CHI*, ACM (2011), 2857–2866.
15. McAfee SiteAdvisor. http://www.siteadvisor.com.
16. Moore, T., and Clayton, R. Evaluating the wisdom of crowds in assessing phishing websites. In *Proc. Financial Cryptography and Data Security (FC)*, Springer (2008).
17. Norton Safe Web. http://safeweb.norton.com.
18. Ortega, F., Gonzalez-Barahona, J. M., and Robles, G. On the Inequality of Contributions to Wikipedia. In *Proc. HICSS*, IEEE Computer Society (2008).
19. PhishTank. http://www.phishtank.com.
20. Provos, N., Mavrommatis, P., Rajab, M. A., and Monrose, F. All your iframes point to us. In *Proc. Security*, USENIX (2008), 1–15.
21. Verisign Domain Name Report. http://www.verisigninc.com/en_US/why-verisign/research-trends/domain-name-industry-brief/index.xhtml.
22. Web of Trust. http://www.mywot.com.
23. Welser, H. T., Cosley, D., Kossinets, G., Lin, A., Dokshin, F., Gay, G., and Smith, M. Finding social roles in wikipedia. In *Proc. of the 2011 iConference*, ACM (2011), 122–129.
24. Wilkinson, D. M. Strong regularities in online peer production. In *Proc. of the 9th ACM Conference on Electronic commerce (EC)*, ACM (2008), 302–309.
25. Wondracek, G., Holz, T., Platzer, C., Kirda, E., and Kruegel, C. Is the Internet for Porn? An Insight into the Online Adult Industry. In *Proc. of the 9th Workshop on the Economics of Information Security (WEIS)* (2010).
26. Zhuge, J., Holz, T., Song, C., Guo, J., Han, X., and Zou, W. Studying Malicious Websites and the Underground Economy on the Chinese Web. In *Proc. of the 7th Workshop on the Economics of Information Security (WEIS)* (2008).

CrowdWeaver: Visually Managing Complex Crowd Work

Aniket Kittur, Susheel Khamkar, Paul André, Robert E. Kraut
Carnegie Mellon University
5000 Forbes Avenue, Pittsburgh, PA, 15213
{nkittur, pandre, kraut}@cs.cmu.edu, susheelkhamkar2@gmail.com

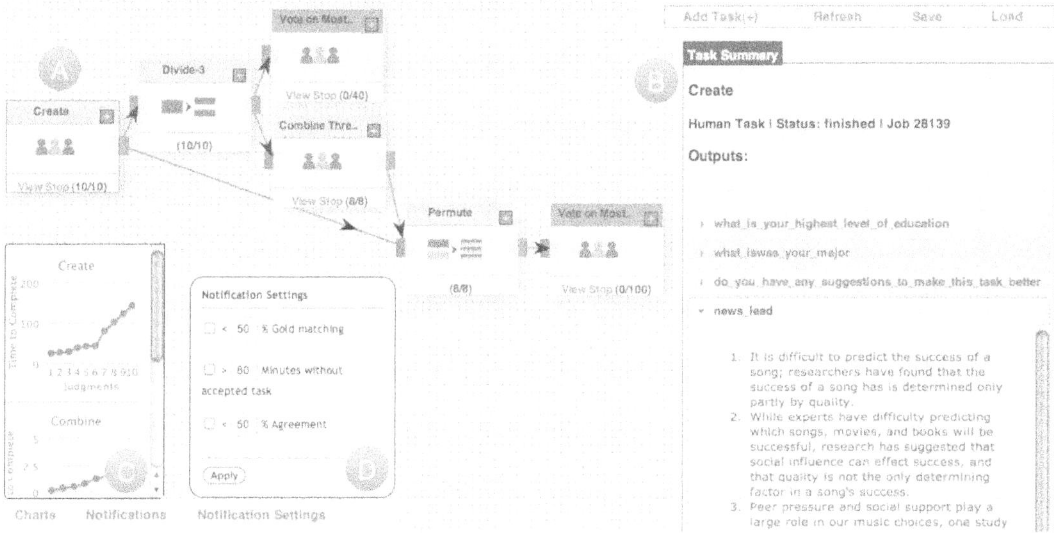

Figure 1. The CrowdWeaver workflow management interface. (A) The workflow consisting of human tasks (), e.g., "create (news leads)", and machine tasks (e.g., divide, permute). (B) The Task Summary pane details the selected task, with the "news lead" field expanded showing worker outputs. (C) Graphs to track 'crowd factors' such as arrival of workers to a task. (D) Settings to alert the requester if crowd factors such as uptake, quality or time to complete become cause for concern, allowing the requester to edit task design or instructions in real-time to optimize time and quality of results.

ABSTRACT
Though toolkits exist to create complex crowdsourced workflows, there is limited support for management of those workflows. Managing crowd workers and tasks requires significant iteration and experimentation on task instructions, rewards, and flows. We present CrowdWeaver, a system to visually manage complex crowd work. The system supports the creation and reuse of crowdsourcing and computational tasks into integrated task flows, manages the flow of data between tasks, and allows tracking and notification of task progress, with support for real-time modification. We describe the system and demonstrate its utility through case studies and user feedback.

Author Keywords
Crowdsourcing, workflow, visualization, coordination.

ACM Classification Keywords
H5.m. Information interfaces and presentation (e.g., HCI).

General Terms
Design

INTRODUCTION
Crowdsourcing has become a powerful mechanism for online production, but is currently mostly used for simple, independent tasks. Recently, a number of toolkits have been created to programmatically support more complex tasks and workflows [4,5,6]. However, though a requester of work now has advanced tools and algorithms to *create* workflows, there remains limited support for *management* of those workflows. Managing workflows can be as or even more challenging than their creation: requesters must experiment and iterate with different tasks, instructions, rewards, and flows to optimize the process. For example, in interviews we conducted with employees of CrowdFlower (a commercial crowdsourcing platform), they noted that when working with a crowd "*a major issue is stringing tasks together.*" To achieve successful output requires a "*significant cost in time, [and involves experimentation with] what's the right [task] that gets to the most effective results most quickly and cheaply.*"

This discussion points to the unique challenges posed by managing crowdsourced workflows. In other forms of computational task flow management (e.g., visual programming languages [2], online mashups [7]) experimentation and execution is essentially free, instantaneous, and deterministic. In contrast, each run of a crowdsourced workflow requires an investment of time and money, and may give different results each time. This suggests that crowd-based computational task flow systems should not only manage tasks but also address crowd-specific factors such as: *latency*, the delay between requesting and commencing work; *price*, understanding what price is appropriate, and how varying prices may affect work [1]; the varying *quality* of worker and output; and the varying *time* to completion of a unit of work.

To address these challenges we present CrowdWeaver, a system to visually manage complex crowdsourcing tasks, with no need for programming knowledge. Our contributions include:

- A visual interface for task and workflow creation and monitoring that serves as an external mental model of a task flow;
- The management and reuse of templates, including both human and machine tasks;
- Tracking and notification of crowd factors (e.g., latency, price, time and quality);
- Support for real-time experimentation.

In the remainder of this paper we provide a brief overview of the architecture of the system, illustrate its features through an example task flow, and discuss feedback from task designers using the system.

THE CROWDWEAVER SYSTEM

CrowdWeaver is built on top of CrowdFlower, a commercial crowdsourcing platform that provides certain advantages over platforms such as Mechanical Turk, including the ability to post tasks on multiple markets (including MTurk), a rich API, and a robust template editor. The CrowdWeaver system consists of a MySQL database that stores information about the tasks, data, and connections between tasks; a JQuery-based web visual interface with which users view, create and manage tasks; and a Ruby controller that powers the interface, manages the database, and synchronizes with CrowdFlower.

Scenario

Imagine a task designer is trying to generate a news lead for a newspaper article as part of a larger task crowdsourcing the writing of the article. She wants to determine whether voting to select the best lead or merging leads together is a better task design. In one method, she has workers each generate a news lead, splits them into groups of three (to simplify the voting), and has workers vote on the best. In another method, she takes the same generated leads, splits them into groups of three, and has workers generate a new lead that merges the best aspects of the three they are given. Finally, she compares each combination of original and merged news lead and has workers vote on which is better.

Throughout the process, she wishes to monitor the workflow and be alerted if there are problems such as poor uptake or lack of agreement between workers. If so, she may step in and review the work to understand where the problem lies, and modify the task design or instructions. (This task is similar to that used in Kittur et al. [4].)

Figure 1-A presents this task flow as created and managed by CrowdWeaver, with the top path corresponding to the voting method and the bottom path the merging method, including permutation with the original leads and voting. The interface integrates both crowdsourced and machine tasks, and reflects all key data collection and manipulation steps, including the flow of data between tasks. Monitoring is achieved through real-time update of the number of completed assignments, and details of the task including outputs are shown in the Task Summary pane (Figure 1-B). Since manually keeping track of every detail could be overwhelming, notifications can be triggered (Figure 1-C) when crowd factors such as latency or worker agreement generate cause for concern. We discuss CrowdWeaver's core functionality and design in more detail below.

Task and Workflow Creation

Visual Representation

A key challenge is choosing how to visually represent a task, data fields, inputs, and worker outputs. For example, a simple image labeling task could include multiple data fields (e.g., each label, demographics), thousands of input images, and tens of thousands of worker outputs. Complex flows may involve many such tasks, each with potentially thousands of interconnected inputs and outputs. With workflows such as these, approaches which visually represent each input and output (e.g., [5]) can quickly get overwhelming. Instead, we chose a higher-level representation, visually depicting each task and the data flow between them, with details about inputs and outputs available on demand in a dynamic pane (Figure 1-B).

Another important consideration was to enable the interface to act as a user's external mental representation of the workflow. To support this, users can alter the spatial arrangement of tasks to match their mental model of the workflow, with spatial positions saved across sessions, enabling the construction of a persistent task landscape.

Creating and Reusing Templates

One of the most significant costs in time, effort, and money for crowdsourcing complex tasks is in experimenting and iterating with the instructions and materials. Even small changes in instructions can lead to dramatic differences in output quality [3]. To help with this costly process of iteration, CrowdWeaver saves each human task created and allows the user to create and modify (via the CrowdFlower editor) new instances of it for future tasks. Properties such as instructions and HTML, answer fields, pricing, market choice, and worker qualifications are inherited from the original template, while new input streams can be selected. A basic set of common human tasks are included as starter templates, including generate, vote, and merge tasks.

In addition to crowdsourced tasks completed by humans, CrowdWeaver supports tasks performed by machines, such as data manipulation, which use the same data structure

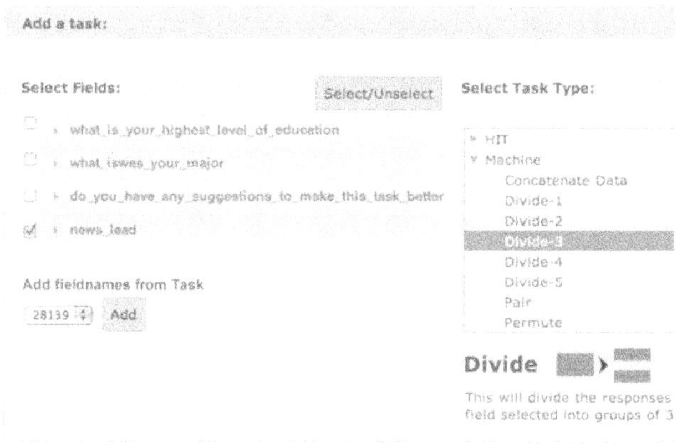

Figure 2. The Add Task screen, with the "news_lead" data field from the previous task selected as input, and a machine "divide" task chosen.

(data fields, inputs and outputs). A basic set of machine tasks are included, such as divide, concatenate, pair, and permute; users can add new machine tasks by adding a wrapper function within the controller code, and a class to implement the new machine task.

Data Flow Between Tasks

CrowdWeaver uses a dataflow paradigm [2] supporting the visualization and flow of data between tasks. For example, in our scenario, the designer wishes to determine whether voting on news leads or merging them together is a better workflow. To create the voting flow (top path in Figure 1), the designer passes the news leads generated by workers in the original task to new *divide* and *vote* steps. She wants to group the data into sets of three, so she selects the "news lead" data field and the *divide* task. For convenience, descriptive text and images of machine tasks are shown in a preview when selected (see Figure 2). The designer creates the *vote* task in a similar way, passing through data from *divide* and repurposing the generic *vote* template.

The system also supports branching and combining multiple data flows. As illustrated in the scenario, the designer creates the alternate branch in which workers merge the best aspects of three news leads and vote on the merged version (bottom path in Figure 1). These results are compared to the originally generated leads by combining the original and alternate data flow branches (specifically, by adding additional fields from the original task; see bottom left of Figure 2).

Tracking and Notification of Task Progress

As identified in the Introduction, crowd work poses challenges in terms of latency, price, time, and quality. Rather than wait for a task to complete (or never attract enough workers) to determine if there is a problem, CrowdWeaver offers a task progress system to easily view and be alerted of common signifiers of task problems.

Monitoring

As data comes in, summary statuses are viewable at a glance. The bottom of each task shows the number of outputs collected, and graphs updated in real-time (Figure 1-C) help monitor crowd factors. To drill down into the data, one can expand the Task Summary pane (Figure 1-B). This makes it easy to trace data across tasks and to compare different task versions as all data is immediately available from the main interface.

Notifications

Figure 1-D shows the current notifications available in CrowdWeaver. In terms of latency, if a task does not attract new workers for a period of time, it may be that the instructions are unclear or unattractive, or the task is incorrectly priced [1]. Identifying this early could save hours or days waiting for workers. Similarly, quality can either be compared against a gold standard (as CrowdFlower currently does) or inferred from the percentage of workers whose answers agree with each other. In cases where a problem occurs in a task, the requester can stop a poorly functioning flow and create a new branch to fix the problem while preserving their existing work.

SYSTEM USAGE

We have experimented with creating and managing a variety of tasks using CrowdWeaver, including product research, article generation, and science journalism. Furthermore, functionality from crowdsourcing frameworks such as CrowdForge [4] including partitioning, map, and reduce tasks can be replicated in CrowdWeaver. For example, Figure 3 shows a flow involving two *create* tasks (generating eReader models and features to evaluate them); a *permute* task creating all combinations of models and features; a *find information* task gathering evidence about each combination; and a *divide* task splitting the data into groups relevant to each model (in this example, two).

Interviews and Usage

To gather initial feedback about the usefulness of CrowdWeaver for complex workflow management, and reaction to and usage of the tool in a workflow creation task, we conducted two interviews and recruited two participants for a formative study.

In interviews with two CrowdFlower employees who create workflows for corporate clients, the general approach of CrowdWeaver for dealing with time-consuming workflow creation and management was appreciated ("*awesome concept!*"). The employees were particularly enthusiastic about the potential to "*string jobs together, visualize all running jobs, and [see] stats on a given workflow.*"

To gather feedback about the usefulness of CrowdWeaver, we recruited two participants (graduate students) familiar with designing tasks for MTurk but with no prior exposure to CrowdWeaver. Participants were assigned the example problem described earlier: given a set of news leads, decide whether a vote or a merge task resulted in better outcomes. They were asked to draw a flow indicating how they would complete the task using MTurk and their current tools. They were also given a 10 minute tutorial on CrowdWeaver's

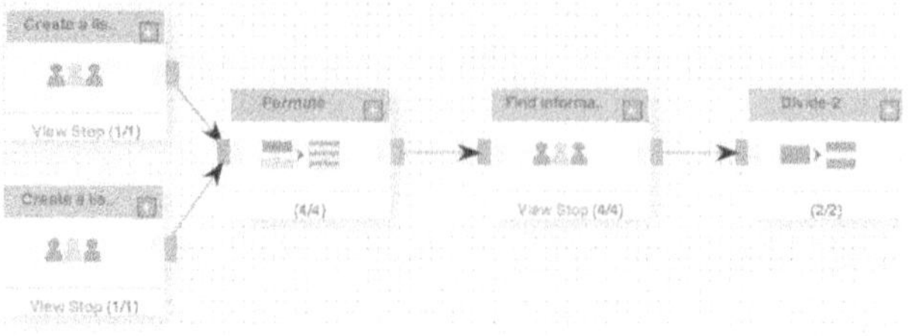

Figure 3. Task flow for researching an eReader.

functions, then asked to create the flows in CrowdWeaver, and finally to fill out a questionnaire.

In the drawing task, both sketched flows very similar to Figure 1, although their projected data manipulation steps were done either through scripting (e.g., Python) or by hand (copy-paste). Both participants were able to generate the entire working flow, including splitting and merging tasks with multiple connections. Participants rated the usefulness of CrowdWeaver very highly, with answers between 6 and 7 on a 7-point Likert scale for "viewing and managing tasks visually was helpful", "connecting tasks to each other was helpful", "I enjoyed using CrowdWeaver", and "I would like to use software like CrowdWeaver in the future". One participant noted that it "*fit [his] intuition about workflows nicely*", and that "*the visual component helps me model what I'm doing with workers and data*", suggesting that it did support his mental model of the task flow.

DISCUSSION AND FUTURE WORK

One of our design goals was to visualize task flows such that they provided useful externalized mental representations. To do so we chose to represent tasks at the level of the subtask rather than visualizing each individual workers' output. However, an important lesson we learned is that even this level of representation may be too low level for many users, suggesting an opportunity for future research to better visually represent multiple levels of detail (i.e., task, data fields, inputs/outputs). A related challenge is that both participants found it difficult to adapt to the CrowdFlower nomenclature, editing interface, and task structure, giving CrowdWeaver relatively low scores on ease of use (mean = 4.5 on a 7-point Likert scale) and suggesting that making a visual task management system such as CrowdWeaver easier to use for those less experienced with existing crowdsourcing paradigms may be a valuable area for future research.

We further investigated these issues with employees of CrowdFlower who were responsible for managing the design of tasks for corporate clients but not actually programming the tasks themselves. We found that for these users, the level of abstraction presented in CrowdWeaver was lower-level than they desired. While our system enables the user to stay "close to the data", these employees thought about flows in higher-level steps such as "generate", "vote", etc., without the intermediate linking data manipulation tasks.

This suggests that instead of the visualization of individual workers' outputs or even of subtasks, a fruitful area of research may be how to enable the aggregation and visualization of subtasks as meaningful patterns of work (e.g., combining divide, vote, match and filter into a single useful pattern for interacting with the crowd). Such an approach could be instantiated as a "simple" interface for CrowdWeaver in which users create and manage entire subflows, with data manipulation steps (such as splitting the data into threes) surfaced as user-configurable parameters. Supporting interaction at both the pattern level and the task level could be helpful for more advanced users who need greater customization, and enable sharing and customization of useful patterns.

CONCLUSION

We present CrowdWeaver, a system for visually creating and managing crowd workflows. CrowdWeaver functions as a "mental model" for the task designer, integrates human and machine tasks, supports template reuse, manages dataflow, and does not require programming knowledge. In particular we address unique factors of crowd work, allowing monitoring and alerting based on task progress in terms of: latency, price, time to completion and quality.

CrowdWeaver can benefit task designers through easier iteration and experimentation for complex flows, leading to time and cost savings. We describe how the system can be used for a variety of tasks, gather feedback from participants using CrowdWeaver, and discuss future opportunities for research on the visual management of crowdsourcing flows, notably in the level of representation, and aggregating subtasks into reusable patterns of work.

ACKNOWLEDGMENTS

This research was supported by NSF grants OCI-09-43148, IIS-0968484, IIS-1111124 and a grant from Carnegie Mellon's Center for the Future of Work.

REFERENCES

1. Faridani, S., Hartmann, B., & Ipeirotis, P. G. What's the Right Price? Pricing Tasks for Finishing on Time. *Proc. HCOMP 2011.*
2. Johnston, W.M., Hanna, J.R., & Millar, R.J. Advances in dataflow programming languages. *ACM Computing Surveys (CSUR) 36*, 1 (2004), 1–34.
3. Kittur, A., Chi, E., & Suh, B. Crowdsourcing user studies with Mechanical Turk. *Proc. CHI 2008.*
4. Kittur, A., Smus, B., Khamkar, S. & Kraut, R. E. CrowdForge: Crowdsourcing complex work. *Proc. UIST 2011.*
5. Kulkarni, A., Can, M., & Hartmann, B. Collaboratively Crowdsourcing Workflows with Turkomatic. *Proc. CSCW 2012.*
6. Little, G., Chilton, L.B., Goldman, M., & Miller, R.C. Turkit: Human computation algorithms on Mechanical Turk. *Proc. UIST 2010*, 57–66.
7. Yu, J., Benatallah, B., Casati, F., & Daniel, F. Understanding mashup development. *IEEE Internet Computing*, (2008), 44–52.

Phrases That Signal Workplace Hierarchy

Eric Gilbert
School of Interactive Computing & GVU Center
Georgia Institute of Technology
gilbert@cc.gatech.edu

ABSTRACT
Hierarchy fundamentally shapes how we act at work. In this paper, we explore the relationship between the words people write in workplace email and the rank of the email's recipient. Using the Enron corpus as a dataset, we perform a close study of the words and phrases people send to those above them in the corporate hierarchy versus those at the same level or lower. We find that certain words and phrases are strong predictors. For example, "thought you would" strongly suggests that the recipient outranks the sender, while "let's discuss" implies the opposite. We also find that the phrases people write to their bosses do not demonstrate cognitive processes as often as the ones they write to others. We conclude this paper by interpreting our results and announcing the release of the predictive phrases as a public dataset, perhaps enabling a new class of status-aware applications.

Author Keywords
computer-mediated communication (CMC), email, natural language processing (NLP), text, status, power

ACM Classification Keywords
H5.3. Group and Organization Interfaces; Asynchronous interaction

INTRODUCTION

Email 1:
Please take a look at these spreadsheets and calc the gas usage by plant and by pipe in CA. Mike is telling us that most of these palnts [sic] will be shutting down in the next few weeks due to credit exposure. Let's discuss the impact on sendouts. Thanks.

Email 2:
Thank you! The itemization was absolutely no problem, and please let me know when I can do things like that to make your job go more smoothly. I know the market got chaotic late yesterday . . . So I thought I'd ask in the future, is it you I should come to, or real-time? Thanks again for your help.

Which email message comes from someone's boss and which goes to someone's boss? In the first message, we see softened calls to action in "please take a look" and expectations of future work in "let's discuss." In the second, we see confidence exuded in "absolutely no problem," offers of help in "please let me" and hedging in "so I thought." As you may have already guessed, the first message comes from the boss. This paper is about email phrases like these and what they reveal about corporate hierarchies.

Despite years of new social media platforms and experiences, email is still central to how we communicate, especially at work. Nielsen recently reported that Americans use email for a third of all their online communication [20]. Email is the most frequent mode of communication on mobile devices [20]. In a 2008 study, 37% of respondents said they check their work email "constantly," up from 22% in 2002 [17]. With smartphones now everywhere, we can only imagine this figure has gone up.

At the same time, email is not only a place where we chat and exchange information: it is a performance [10]. At work, we have a place within the hierarchy. We have bosses and perhaps people who work for us. The people around us expect that we act like someone who occupies the role. Bosses ask for things; employees provide them. And yet the boss versus employee dichotomy is a false one: we can occupy either role depending on who's around. At work, email is the performance of power and hierarchy captured in text.

In this paper, we search for signs of hierarchy in the phrases people use in email. We closely study the particular words and phrases people send to those above them in the corporate hierarchy versus those at the same level or lower. We adopt the Enron email corpus as our dataset, coupling it with a dataset of Enron employee job titles. By applying penalized logistic regression, we tease apart the relative power of certain words and phrases to signal hierarchy within workplace email. We find that certain phrases are strong predictors, such as the hedge "thought you would" (an upward phrase) and the aforementioned "let's discuss" (a lateral or downward one). Other intuitively good predictors of hierarchy, like "glad to" or "can be reached," carry little weight. Surprisingly, and perhaps disturbingly, we also find that upward phrases do not show evidence of active thinking as often as downward or lateral ones.

After presenting and reflecting on the most powerful phrases for signaling hierarchy, we announce the release of all 7,222 phrases (and associated β weights) as a public dataset. We hope to do for power and hierarchy what LIWC [23] has done for so many other categories. We also think the phrases dataset may lay the groundwork for status-aware CMC applications. For instance, an email client might analyze the content of your messages and notify you differently based on the inferred rank of the person sending the message.

CSCW'12, February 11–15, 2012, Seattle, Washington, USA.

RELATED WORK

Next, we review related work on power and hierarchy in the workplace. We also discuss analytic efforts similar to ours: work aimed at extracting socially relevant information from text. Finally, we conclude this section with research sparked by the Enron email corpus.

Power and Hierarchy

We focus on two bodies of research most relevant to this work: hierarchy and power in CSCW and linguistics research. From its earliest days, CSCW has been concerned with the relative power of individuals collaborating over networked systems (e.g., [3, 30]). For example, [3] reports on the role of power and status in an early CSCW system called *The Coordinator*. In recent years, we've seen power and hierarchy in the emerging social computing literature [2, 28]. For example, researchers have looked at Wikipedia through the lens of power, where people exercise it informally by marking territory with templates [28] and formally through the Wikipedia bureaucracy [2].

Social structures like power also leak into the words we use. (See [31] for an overview from a linguistic perspective.) For example, managers often employ directives (as might be expected), but also wrap those directives in hedging phrases to make them more palatable to those under them (e.g., "when you have time" as a euphemism for "now"). For years, researchers accepted the common wisdom that men use directives more when talking to subordinates, but recent work has shown that women use just as many when put in similar contexts [32]. Bosses will often inject humor to soften the blow of their words and to build loyalty [12]. They also use collective talk (e.g., "let's all give it a try") to build support for themselves as leaders [33]. We look for evidence of this theory later in the paper when we examine the structure of the most predictive phrases.

Processing Text for Social Information

Social scientists have been interested in the interpersonal dimensions of text for decades. Much of this work, including the well-known LIWC [23], descends from Harvard's General Inquirer [27], a dictionary for measuring social science concepts in unstructured text. In recent years, researchers have applied more refined and targeted dictionary techniques (e.g., [6, 9, 11]). For example, in [6] the authors demonstrate that a dictionary-based method can compute happiness over a wide variety of modern text corpora, like blogs.

Over the last decade or so, roughly corresponding to the rise of the social internet, the natural language processing community has also moved into this space. Whereas the methods above employ dictionaries vetted by experts, machine learning research applies algorithms to learn its social concepts directly from data. Most notably, techniques for inferring sentiment have exploded. (See [22] for a review.) Meta projects like SentiWordNet have fused the dictionary and machine learning approaches, generating reusable dictionaries by overlaying many experiments that predict the same dependent variable (i.e., sentiment) [7]. Our work follows in this tradition: we aim to learn from existing data and produce a reusable dictionary of power and hierarchy.

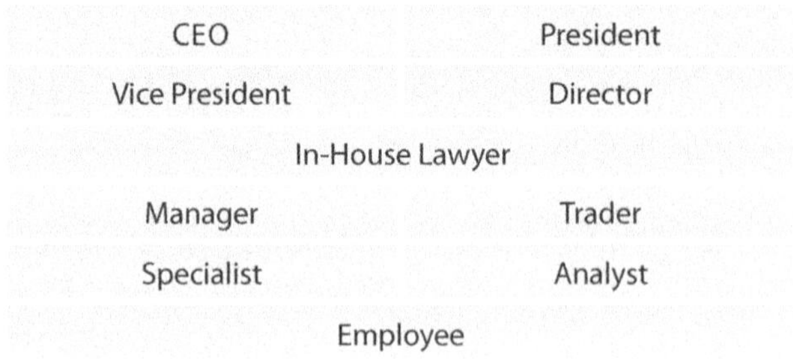

Figure 1. A visual depiction of the hierarchy of Enron job titles. We use the job titles of senders and recipients to determine whether an email goes up or down the hierarchy.

The Enron Corpus

The purchase of the Enron corpus after the company's collapse [15] sparked many new email studies. ([25] presents the corpus's basic descriptive statistics.) Using the corpus, researchers have inferred important nodes in social networks [26], improved spam filtering [18] and developed new NLP techniques for name resolution [4].

We are not the first to search the corpus for signs of power and hierarchy. Relevant to the present work, [5] and [24] show how social network features (computed across the network inferred from all messages) can signal power relationships. In [19], the researchers show that a small set of unigrams (single words) have predictive information for inferring power relationships. [19] inspired this work. We build on it by closely studying the power of words and phrases, aiming for insight into why and how people construct hierarchy through CMC. We think this approach (i.e., features rather than black box accuracy) is more relevant to the CSCW community.

METHOD

To search for hierarchy in text, we turn to two datasets: the Enron email corpus [15] and an Enron job titles dataset. The Enron email corpus is the only large email dataset available to researchers. It contains 517,431 email messages sent by 151 people over the span of nearly four years [25]. The job title dataset, formed from trial documents by researchers at Johns Hopkins and USC[1], contains titles for 132 Enron employees. For example, it maps *Jeffrey Skilling* to *CEO* and *Michelle Lokay* to *Employee, Administrative Assistant.*

Pairing this dataset with an account of the ranks of each job title within Enron's corporate culture [21], we were able to fit each employee into a rank within the company. Figure 1 presents the relative ranks of job titles. CEOs and Presidents have the highest rank; Vice Presidents and Directors report to CEOs[2]; In-House Lawyers follow next; Managers and Traders form the next two levels; Specialists and Analysts sit at the hierarchy's second lowest level, above Employees. By combining all three sources of data, we can say that an email

[1] `http://www.isi.edu/~adibi/Enron/Enron.htm`

[2] We made custom rules for Sally Beck, Rod Hayslett, Rick Buy and Jeff Dasovich, all of whom held special positions within Enron. Dasovich was an appointed liaison between Enron and government investigators; we discarded his email entirely.

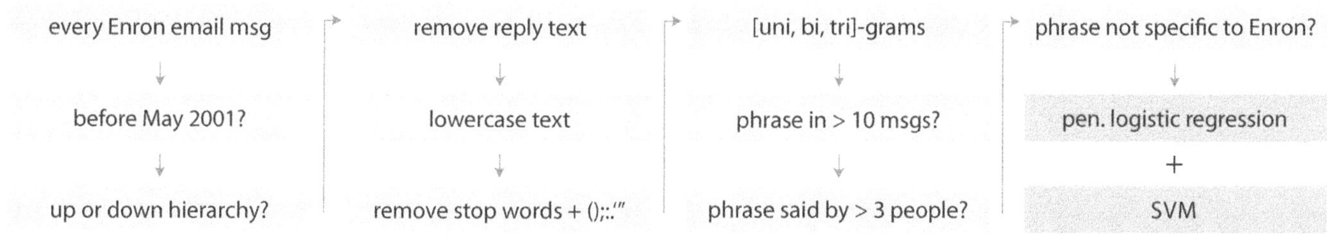

Figure 2. A map of the steps taken in this paper to prepare text for modeling. All phrases go to the penalized logistic regression model and the SVM. We cover these steps in detail in the main body of the paper, but include this figure for overview and reference.

from Michelle Lokay to Jeffrey Skilling went six levels up the corporate hierarchy.

The unit of analysis in this paper is an individual email message combined with status information. We will treat an email as doing one of three things: traveling up the hierarchy (e.g., Manager to VP), staying at the same level (e.g., Employee to Employee) or going down the hierarchy (e.g., CEO to Trader). Furthermore, the models presented here will try to predict whether an email message simply goes up the corporate hierarchy or not. In other words, we will treat email messages which stay at the same level or go down the hierarchy as the same. This simplification means that we can apply traditional statistical techniques but still induce an ordering of employees. In other words, we can reproduce the corporate hierarchy without making our models unnecessarily complex.

The Enron Confound

This entire paper hinges on the idea that our models reproduce a power relationship between two people in a company. And yet the models build on data from a profoundly dishonest company which ultimately fell apart. At the same time, the Enron email corpus is without parallel in the research community. Nowhere else can you find such a rich, complex and naturally occurring email dataset.

Therefore, we have taken steps to guard against this problem. It seems reasonable that up until a certain point—-the point when everything started to fall apart—-Enron behaved like a normal company internally. Even if certain people knew of or suspected malfeasance, it seems likely that they behaved towards their coworkers the way other people behave toward their coworkers. The trick is finding the point after which all of that may have changed. For example, perhaps as word got out regarding how executives had steered the company into the ground, lower level employees started looking for parachutes and challenging the authority of their bosses.

After reviewing a history of Enron [13], we decided to discard all data after May 1, 2001. The SEC did not launch its investigation until many months later in October (the first by any agency). Enron executives did not begin to sell their stock until later—something we only learned after Enron's fall. By contrast, in February 2001 Fortune magazine named Enron the "most innovative company in America" and Enron executives gave well-received presentations proclaiming the company's bright future. With the private selling of Enron stock by executives, we think May 1 was a sea change moment: executives admitted (to themselves) that Enron would probably collapse. Before, on the other hand, it seems likely that Enron employees behaved toward one another the way people do in countless other companies.

Preparing the Email Text

We include in our corpus only those email messages which clearly go up the Enron hierarchy or clearly do not. In other words, we label an email message as *upward* only when every recipient outranks the sender. Conversely, we label an email message as *not-upward* only when every recipient does not outrank the sender. (We make use of both *To:* and *Cc:* headers.) At first it seemed attractive to allow mixtures of ranks (e.g., an email from a Trader to both a VP and a Specialist) because it results in a bigger dataset. But it is possible that the sender speaks differently to each person, perhaps even addressing each one individually. This would confuse any model and cloud the results. While we approach classifying messages conservatively, the upside is that we have greater confidence in the phrase findings. After filtering this way and removing duplicate messages (the Enron corpus has many duplicates), our corpus has 2,044 email messages.

From each message, we discard any text that looks like a quoted reply or a forwarded message by searching for conventional textual markers (e.g., *Original Message*, *— Forwarded by* and lines beginning with >). Next, we convert all text to lowercase and remove the punctuation characters *();:.'"*, while letting the punctuation characters *?!,* remain. We allowed these particular characters to stay because we hypothesized they may signal hierarchy, whereas we thought others—like the period—would not. Keeping punctuation marks can sometimes degrade model performance. For example, keeping all punctuation marks would partition predictive power between "however" and "; however." Therefore, we use punctuation sparingly. From here we adopt a trigram "bag of words" model, a common approach in computational linguistics. That is, we use single words (unigrams), two-word phrases (bigrams) and three-word phrases (trigrams) as the inputs to our models.

However, we cannot include every possible unigram, bigram and trigram. This is not because there would be too many, but because many phrases subtract information or even endanger the validity of the results. Following convention, we discard all phrases consisting solely of "stop words" like "at," "it" and "here." We also look for phrases too obscure to matter in other domains or in other companies: we discard any phrase which does not appear in at least ten email messages, ensuring that we build models only around common English phrases.

More subtly, a phrase could occur at least ten times, but only matter to energy companies like Enron. We could not devise a way to handle this case automatically with code, so two independent raters familiar with Enron looked over every phrase and marked any that appeared specific to Enron's business. Both raters followed the company during its demise, read a history of the scandal and had reviewed trial documents. (We explored using the Google 1T corpus [1] to mark Enron-specific phrases, but it measures web text—not email text—and produced poor results.) Because our dataset is so large and so asymmetric (both in terms of proportions and weights assigned to mistakes), traditional metrics of agreement like Cohen's κ are inappropriate. Instead, we again take a conservative approach: any phrase marked by either rater as Enron-specific was deleted from the list of possible phrases. This process removed proper names like "Frank" and "Stacey," as well as phrases like "gas markets."

Since our models will predict relationships, we also have to guard against phrases that uniquely identify a single relationship. For example, a particular trader and assistant might use the phrase "transfer the memo" uniquely across the corpus. Any model would interpret "transfer the memo" as an important phrase, even though it only serves to identify the trader and assistant. To guard against this, we discard any phrase not written by at least three different people. After these steps, our models have 7,222 different phrases available to them. Figure 2 presents an overview of the entire process.

Statistical Methods

In this paper, we employ two techniques to predict the dependent variable *upward*. Each one has a different objective. Our statistical technique, penalized logistic regression [8], allows us to determine the relative importance of each phrase for predicting hierarchy. Implemented in the R package `glmnet`[3], penalized logistic regression predicts a binary response variable while guarding against the collinearity of phrases, something traditional logistic regression does not do. This is important in our context since English phrases exhibit highly correlated behavior: the word *cone* will appear after the phrase *ice cream* much more often than the word *house*. This implementation of penalized logistic regression handles correlated predictors by shifting most of a coefficient's mass into the most predictive feature, often leaving others out of the model all together. The implementation also handles sparsity well, an important feature in natural language processing where a message only contains a small percentage of the possible phrases.

In the penalized logistic regression model, we include fixed effects for the sender of each message. We instantiate this by including dummy variables in the model representing each sender. This means that any predictive power assigned to the phrases comes after controlling for who said it. The fixed effects also guard against "catchphrases," phrases often associated with one person more than anyone else. In the Results section, we use a model comprised only of sender variables as a substitute for the null model to make a stronger claim about the predictive utility of email phrases. We cover this in more detail later.

[3]`http://cran.r-project.org/web/packages/glmnet`

Model	Dev. (Acc. %)	df	χ^2	p
Null	2,722.66	0		
Senders-only	1,628.60	98	1,094.10	$< 10^{-15}$
Phrases + senders	224.21	974	1,404.39	$< 10^{-15}$
SVM	(70.7%)	7,222	43.35	$< 10^{-10}$

Table 1. A summary of our different model fits for the progression of models in the Results section. *Null* refers to an intercept-only model. *Dev.* refers to deviance, a measure of the goodness of fit similar to the better-known R^2.

The penalized logistic regression model allows close inspection of the relative power of the phrases. Yet, it is not the strongest purely predictive model. It cannot, for instance, support higher-order interaction terms without considerably more data than we have available to us. (Here, a higher-order interaction might look something like a *thanks* phrase co-occurring with a *best regards* without *see attached*.) To explore how much information phrases have in purely predictive terms, we also employ a Support Vector Machine (SVM) model, validating it using three-fold cross-validation. We use the well-known `SVMlight` implementation[4]. The NLP literature documents many instances where SVMs outperform other machine learning techniques on text [14].

RESULTS

Instead of comparing our phrases model against a null model (i.e., an intercept-only model), we use as our baseline a model that only knows a message's sender. Whereas the null model has deviance 2,722.66, the sender-only penalized logistic regression model has deviance 1,628.6. (The deviance is related to a model's log-likelihood. It is an analog of the R^2 statistic for linear models.) The difference in deviances approximately follows an χ^2 distribution. Simply knowing the sender of an email message provides considerable explanatory power: $\chi^2(98, N{=}2{,}044) = 2{,}722.66 - 1{,}628.6 = 1{,}094.1, p < 10^{-15}$.

Adding phrases to the penalized logistic regression model, we find that the model undergoes another dramatic reduction in deviance. The model containing both the phrases and the senders has deviance 224.21. Comparing this to the sender-only model above, the phrases model has significantly more explanatory power: $\chi^2(974 - 98, N{=}2{,}044) = 1{,}628.6 - 224.21 = 1{,}404.39, p < 10^{-15}$. The phrases add considerable predictive information after controlling for the identity of the sender (i.e., after controlling for fixed effects). The `glmnet` implementation of penalized logistic regression only activates those variables which have an effect on the dependent variable. As with most computational linguistics work, most phrases do not affect *upward*: only 974 of the 7,222 possible phrases have coefficients significantly different from zero (at the 0.001 level). Table 1 presents a summary.

Table 2 presents the 100 phrases with the most positive β weights. Table 3, on the other hand, shows the 100 phrases

[4]`http://svmlight.joachims.org`

↑ phrases	β	↑ phrases	β
the ability to	6.76	attach	6.72
I took	6.57	that we might	6.54
are available	6.52	the calendar	6.06
kitchen	5.72	can you get	5.72
thought you would	5.65	driving	5.61
, I'll be	5.51	thoughts on	5.51
looks fine	5.50	shit	5.45
voicemail	5.43	we can talk	5.41
tremendous	5.27	it does	5.21
will you	5.17	involving	5.15
left a	5.07	the report	5.04
I put	4.90	please change	4.88
you ever	4.80	issues I	4.76
I'll give	4.69	is really	4.65
okay ,	4.60	your review	4.56
to send it	4.48	europe	4.45
communications	4.38	weekend .	4.35
a message	4.35	have our	4.33
one I	4.28	interviews	4.28
can I get	4.28	you mean	4.26
worksheet	4.15	haven't been	4.10
liked	4.07	me . 1	4.07
I gave you	3.95	tiger	3.94
credit will	3.88	change in	3.88
you make	3.86	item	3.84
together and	3.82	a decision	3.82
have presented	3.78	a discussion	3.74
think about	3.71	sounds good	3.65
lot to	3.64	units	3.62
bills	3.61	you are the	3.61
october	3.57	proceed	3.56
keeping	3.55	agreement for	3.50
anything we	3.49	you have an	3.47
don't know what	3.47	february	3.44
the email	3.43	do we want	3.40
in the process	3.34	me or	3.32
head	3.29	, yes ,	3.24
be a great	3.21	case of	3.18
be my	3.17	remedy	3.16
administration	3.15	invite you	3.13
worked on	3.12	conflict	3.11
is doing	3.11	by our	3.11
compensation	3.10	asked if	3.08
candidate	3.08	that night	3.07
this afternoon	3.05	listed	3.04
thanks a	3.03	excellent	3.00
you may	3.00	were pulling	2.99
here's	2.99	factor	2.96
change my	2.95	final draft	2.95
looked at	2.95	wed	2.93

Table 2. The 100 most powerful phrases for predicting that an email message goes up the corporate hierarchy. The table flows left to right, then top to bottom. All phrases are significant at the 0.001 level.

↔↓ phrases	β	↔↓ phrases	β
have you been	-8.46	to manage the	-6.66
you gave	-6.64	let's discuss	-5.72
we are in	-5.44	publicly	-5.24
title	-5.05	promotion	-5.02
need in	-4.80	good one	-4.62
opened	-4.57	determine the	-4.47
initiatives	-4.38	is difficult	-4.36
. I would	-4.34	man	-4.26
we will probably	-4.12	number we	-4.11
any comments	-4.06	contact you	-4.05
you said	-3.99	the problem is	-3.97
I left	-3.88	you did	-3.78
can you help	-3.68	cool	-3.54
send this	-3.47	your attention	-3.44
whether we	-3.44	to think	-3.44
the trade	-3.40	addition to the	-3.30
and I thought	-3.28	great thanks	-3.24
should include	-3.19	selected	-3.16
please send	-3.14	ext	-3.13
existing	-3.06	and let me	-3.05
mondays	-3.02	security	-3.01
presentation on	-2.95	got the	-2.94
let's talk	-2.94	get your	-2.88
the items	-2.78	this week and	-2.77
i hope you	-2.77	team that	-2.75
did it	-2.75	a deal	-2.71
test	-2.69	yours .	-2.68
be sure	-2.65	briefing	-2.60
fri	-2.53	notes	-2.51
forgot to	-2.50	funny	-2.48
confirmations	-2.45	sessions	-2.43
pay the	-2.39	your group	-2.37
implement	-2.35	resolve	-2.34
would need to	-2.34	will be making	-2.33
enter into	-2.32	numbers and	-2.28
and i discussed	-2.28	are you	-2.27
should look	-2.27	calendar	-2.27
helping	-2.26	email	-2.24
doing a	-2.21	to suggest	-2.19
use the	-2.19	the confusion	-2.19
and I am	-2.17	fyi I	-2.16
months to	-2.15	in charge	-2.15
look for	-2.13	meeting will	-2.10
fyi ,	-2.09	that we should	-2.06
know this	-2.05	sent this	-2.04
confirming	-2.03	give me	-2.03
included on	-2.00	prior to the	-1.99
problem with	-1.90	, I thought	-1.89
location	-1.89	supposed to be	-1.88
you take a	-1.85	. I just	-1.83

Table 3. The 100 most powerful phrases for predicting that an email message *does not* go up the corporate hierarchy. (Table flows same as Table 1; all phrases significant at the 0.001 level.)

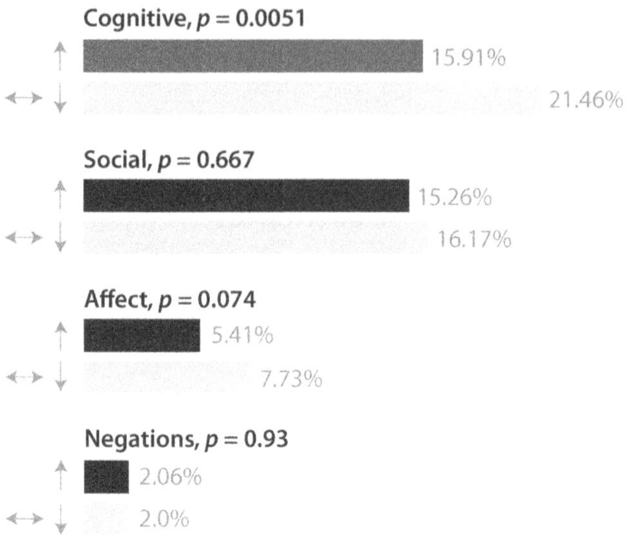

Figure 3. Testing the predictive phrases for structure. We use the LIWC program to test phrases for membership in seven categories. Four are shown here. After a Bonferroni correction, we find that the phrases you say to your boss do not demonstrate cognitive processes as often as the phrases you say to others.

with the most negative β weights. (We have deleted the senders from these lists to showcase the more generalizable set of phrases. 23 senders appeared in the top 100 positive predictors; 12 senders appeared in the top 100 negative predictors.) Tables 2 and 3 affect a message's likelihood of having gone *upward* most strongly—when they appear. It is important to note that a phrase's β corresponds not only to its discriminative power, but also to its obscurity. Recall that we limited the set of possible phrases to only those that appeared in at least ten messages. We should expect that more obscure phrases (i.e., longer phrases) will have higher β coefficients since they occur fewer times and therefore may more easily skew toward one side or the other.

Do the phrases in Tables 2 and 3 cluster together in some meaningful way? To explore this question, we used the LIWC program [23] to compute categories to which the predictive features belong. After reviewing the LIWC categories, we picked seven we hypothesized might relate to workplace hierarchy: *Cognitive Processes, Social, Affect, Negations, Certainty, Money* and *Assent*. Due to these seven simultaneous tests, we allow for a Bonferroni correction, letting $\alpha = 0.05/7 = 0.0071$. Figure 3 presents proportions of membership in four of the LIWC categories along with p-values associated with the corresponding χ^2 test. We find that *Cognitive Processes* yields the only non-random result: 21.46% of the *not-upward* phrases belong to this category while only 15.91% of the *upward* phrases do, $\chi^2(1, N{=}974) = 7.83$, $p = 0.0051$. The three categories not shown in Figure 3—*Certainty, Money* and *Assent*—have random results, $p = 0.88$, $p = 0.34$ and $p = 0.73$, respectively.

Figure 4 provides a deeper view into the structure around the predictive phrases. It shows Word Tree visualizations [34] of searches for "thank" and "talk" in the two halves of the corpus. For example, Figure 4 shows that the phrase "thank you for your" appears many times in the corpus across multiple email messages. We think this is an intriguing, deeper look into the text behind our statistical techniques. The visualizations come from the online site Many Eyes [29].

Support Vector Machine Approach

The penalized logistic regression model allows us to inspect which phrases have the most impact on the dependent variable *upward* while controlling for senders' identities. However, as noted earlier, this approach does not allow us to get the most predictive information out the phrases. We now turn to an SVM to see how well the phrases can predict hierarchy when we give up introspection and let phrases interact in high-dimensional (and opaque) ways.

The SVM here does not have access to the identity of the sender; it only has access to the phrases. The reason behind this is that an SVM would project lots of predictive information onto the identities (i.e., it would know the *upward* baselines for each person). The SVM performs with 70.7% accuracy under three-fold cross-validation, a non-random improvement over the baseline of 60.5%, $\chi^2(1, N{=}1{,}900) = 43.35$, $p < 10^{-10}$. The 60.5% baseline corresponds to picking the most likely class, *not-upward*, every single time. We employ *three-fold* cross-validation—instead of a more standard technique like ten-fold cross-validation—because it allows us to collapse all relationships in the test set onto a single prediction. By way of an example, suppose in the test set the same relationship occurs three times. Our SVM makes an independent prediction for each one, and they are often different. In a post-hoc step, we unify all predictions about the same relationship by voting.

DISCUSSION

We find that certain words and phrases signal hierarchy while others do not. Tables 2 and 3 provide an intriguing look into how we express power and hierarchy through email at work. As is perhaps to be expected, "attach," a top predictor of *upward* ($\beta = 6.72$), suggests that the majority of documents flow up through organizations. "thought you would," also a top *upward* predictor ($\beta = 5.65$), has the ring of hedging and politeness. Some words unexpectedly signal one way or the other. For instance, "weekend" surprisingly suggests an *upward* email—perhaps used to signal how hard the employee works. "sounds good," on the other hand, unsurprisingly predicts a *upward* relationship.

> Hi Carol, my home number is [redacted] — **weekends** [$\beta = 4.35$] would work fine so give me a call any time. (↑76)

> Louise, thanks for your reply to my email. The fixes implemented over the **weekend** appear to have worked extremely well. I am sure that the changes your team made also contributed to the record 147 external and 263 total trades that I executed today. Thanks for all your help. (↑111)

> Hey, sorry I haven't read my e-mail in the past day and a half. Too busy selling, but that **sounds good** [$\beta = 3.65$] Fletch. (↑778)

(In the quotes above and below, the number corresponds to a message's place in either the *upward* or *not-upward* dataset.) Many of the most predictive *not-upward* phrases relate to checking on a subordinate's current status, exemplified by "have you been" and "I hope you." "I hope you" subtly communicates expectations from a boss to a subordinate, whereas "have you been" is more direct.

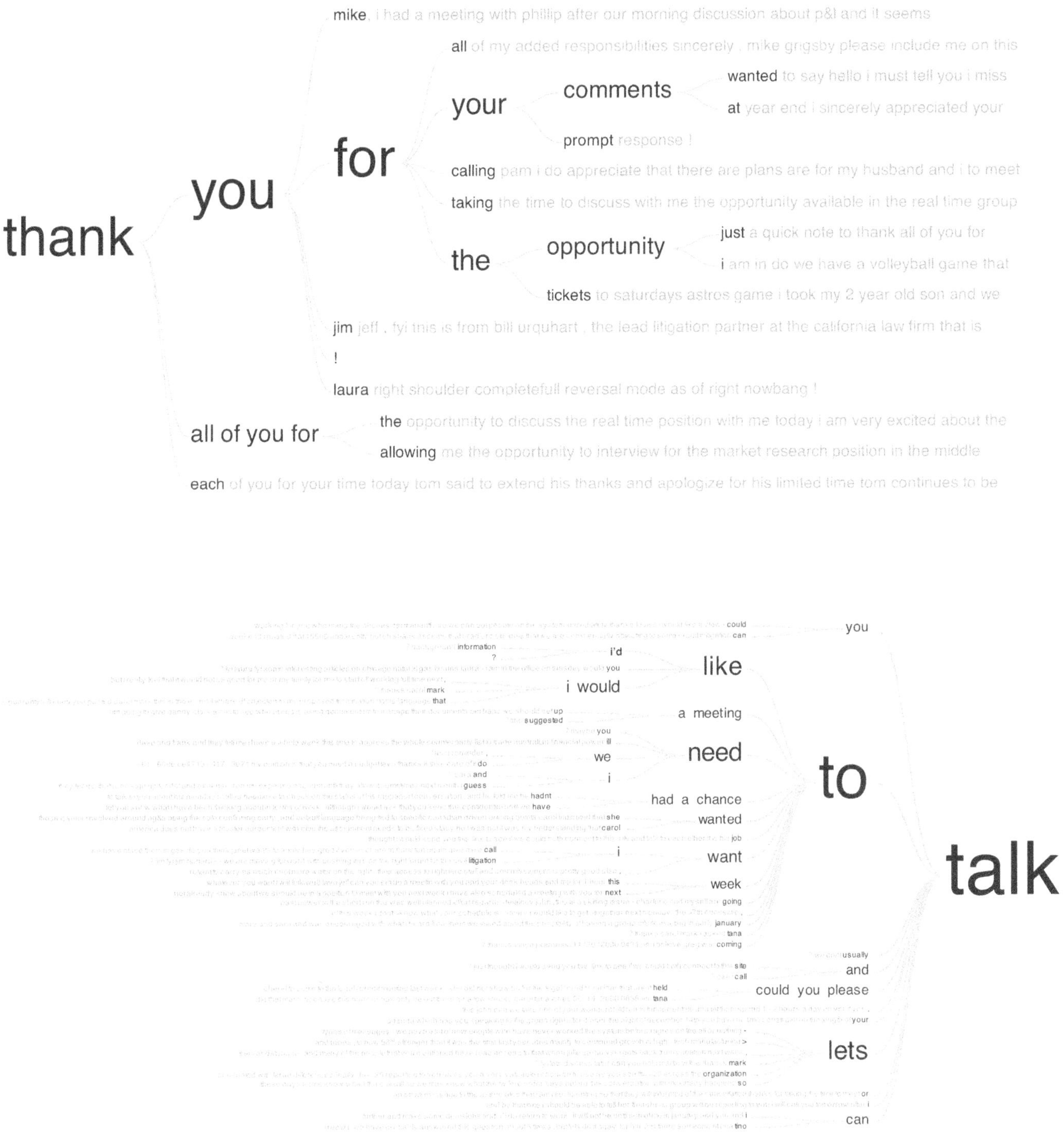

Figure 4. Word Tree visualizations of searches in the two halves of our dataset. At top, a visualization depicting a search for "thank" in only the *upward* part of our corpus. The visualization shows phrases that branch off from "thank" across every message in this part of the corpus. A larger font-size means that the word occurs more often in the corpus. "thank" appeared in the *upward* part of the corpus 16 times and is present in the most powerful predictors listed in Table 2. At bottom, a Word Tree visualization of a search for "talk" in the *not-upward* part of our corpus. Here, we show all phrases that terminate in "talk," with "need to talk" and "like to talk" the most likely trigrams. "talk" appeared in the *not-upward* part of the corpus 64 times. The visualizations come from the site Many Eyes.

Did Tim already send you these documents for your review? If he did, **have you been** [β = -8.46] working with the Houston group on them or do you want to tell me about any problems? (↔↓412)

How **have you been**? I have not had much of your mail lately, but am guessing this one is yours. Have a great weekend! (↔↓1,080)

What **have you been** smoking? (↔↓716)

Dan, **I hope you** [β = -2.77] haven't wasted much time on this one so far. Let me know where this stands. C (↔↓65)

Aaron, I sent you a file a few days ago. **I hope you** could open it. Vince (↔↓1,188)

A limitation in our text-cleaning algorithms highlighted an unexpected finding. Many messages are tagged at the end with a short version of the message's date, outside the traditional *Date:* email header. Coming right after the message's signoff (e.g., "Best regards, Jim"), the models had access to these words. Wednesday's ("wed," β = 2.94) saw more messages going *upward*, while Fridays ("fri," β = -2.53) saw more messages going the other way. This is a finding we would like to see examined in more detail in the future.

A few of the words and phrases in Tables 2 and 3 raised concern. For example, consider "October" (β = 3.57). In reviewing where it appears in the corpus, it often occurs in the context of travel:

Jeff, Christ, Mark and myself are planning to visit Tom Piazze in **October**. I talked to Christy about Wharton and she will be calling Tom to set it up. (↑661)

Despite our efforts to control for it, some of the phrases may reflect Enron culture more than corporate culture. At the same time, perhaps "October" signals an uptick in travel associated with the new fiscal year and the money that comes with it. Future work may need to address these tricky issues.

Figure 3 reveals a surprising and somewhat concerning finding: people demonstrate active thinking more often to those below them than they do to their bosses. (Depending on your perspective, however, this isn't surprising at all—perhaps only surprising that NLP can detect it.) Now, that means that LIWC sees less evidence in the text of actively working things out in email, as measured by its internal word-stem list named *Cognitive Processes*. It seems reasonable to think that people only go to their bosses when they have an answer, not when they want to work out the answer. In pouring over our data, we also noticed a seemingly disproportionate number of misspellings in the *not-upward* emails. The example that opens this paper contains one. We suggest that future researchers explore misspellings as a feature: they may indicate someone has little incentive to proofread.

While we find reliable signals of hierarchy in certain phrases, the SVM did not perform particularly well. We see two possible explanations for it. First, a good amount of predictive information lies elsewhere: in the interaction timing patterns, social network data, etc. Or, we constrained the data so tightly that the SVM has a hard time not over-training. This seems more likely to us, because when we expand the dataset to go past May 2001 (yielding 11K messages total), the SVM's accuracy goes to 91%. In our focus on the phrases, we probably hamstrung the SVM.

not-[↑↔↓] phrases

have been working	opportunity to	agreement	comments
in the meantime	we discussed	remember	customers
I am forwarding	can't believe	available	suggested
can be reached	the meeting	decision	everyone
would like to	interested in	exceeds	private
in the office	your new	money	annual
take a look	can talk	suite	wait

Table 4. A small sample of phrases with no power to signal hierarchy (i.e., β = 0). While many seem like intuitively good predictors, the predictive power lies in phrases like those in Tables 2 and 3.

Phrases Dataset

We have released the predictive phrases that form the basis of the penalized logistic regression model[5]. We extracted the phrases in Tables 2, 3 and 4 from it. It contains every phrase available to the penalized logistic regression model plus the identities of the senders in the corpus. Each line in the file corresponds to a phrase and its β weight, sorted from smallest to largest. Most of the phrases have zero β weights; we include them so that researchers can also see which words and phrases *do not* signal hierarchy. Table 4 presents a sample of these β = 0 phrases.

Theoretical Implications

Even today, most CMC generates text [16]. Methods that can transform raw CMC text into meaningful inferences about social life are valuable to researchers. Compared to things like positive and negative sentiment, we know very little about how people express power and hierarchy through CMC. We hope that this work open lines of research in the CSCW community unavailable before. For example, imagine a study investigating who in a organization disproportionately attracts *upward* language. Do they move up the ladder faster?

By releasing the model's predictive phrases, we hope to do for power and hierarchy what LIWC [23] has done for other categories: reveal hidden social processes by analyzing the text we write to one another. While CSCW research has often incorporated power and status in its studies, we have not had a way to scalably operationalize that concept. That's the reason we performed such a close study of the words and phrases behind hierarchy: we wanted to build a portable dictionary capable of operationalizing hierarchy across organizations.

We studied a formal corporate hierarchy in this paper, marked by clear reporting lines. You might imagine that by applying the phrases in this paper to a corpus of workplace email you could discover informal power and reporting structures. Sometimes power exists in unlikely, undocumented places within companies. The phrases dataset may highlight them.

Design Implications

We also believe this work may enable a new class of status-aware applications. For example, imagine a mobile email client that can guess when somebody above you in the hierarchy just sent you a message. You might set the client to

[5] http://comp.social.gatech.edu/hier.phrases.txt

interrupt you at any time after 5 p.m. if the message comes from above you in the hierarchy (i.e., you might want to seem always available to them). Otherwise, however, you might set the client to hold notifications until after business hours. These notions of power and hierarchy are so crucial within workplace applications, yet no current tools know about them without considerable manual effort: you would have to input the org chart. Furthermore, organizations change all the time, and a software provider would want to build a product that scales to many companies without rebuilding the application for every client. We believe this textual work could form the basis of such a product.

However, more work may need to be done. As our SVM results showed, there is probably predictive information outside the text. Perhaps future work building on these purely textual results could improve the accuracy. Predictive features like response time, social network descriptors and amount of text come to mind. We focused on text because it is so universal and an application would have access to it (within your email archives). An application might not have access to the entire corporate network structure, on the other hand.

CONCLUSION

We believe this work addresses a fundamental force in the workplace: hierarchy. In this paper, we have revealed phrases which signal power and hierarchy in workplace email. These phrases shine a light on the ways CMC captures embedded and often undiscussed aspects of social life. We hope other researchers will be able to address new theoretical questions using the results in this paper, perhaps by making use of the phrases made available as a public dataset. Our results may also lay the groundwork for new status-aware applications, such as email clients that can differentially notify you of new messages based on the rank of the sender.

ACKNOWLEDGEMENTS

We would like to thank the comp.social lab at Georgia Tech for reviewing early drafts of this work. Aaron Bobick contributed valuable feedback on our analytic approach. Google helped support this work.

REFERENCES

1. T. Brants and A. Franz. Web 1T 5-gram Version 1. *Linguistic Data Consortium, Philadelphia*, 2006.
2. M. Burke and R. Kraut. Mopping up: Modeling wikipedia promotion decisions. In *Proc. CSCW*, pages 27–36, 2008.
3. R. Carasik and C. Grantham. A case study of cscw in a dispersed organization. In *Proc. CHI*, pages 61–66, 1988.
4. C. Diehl, L. Getoor, and G. Namata. Name reference resolution in organizational email archives. In *SIAM International Conference on Data Mining*, pages 20–22, 2006.
5. C. Diehl, G. Namata, and L. Getoor. Relationship identification for social network discovery. In *Proc. NCAI*, volume 22, page 546, 2007.
6. P. Dodds and C. Danforth. Measuring the happiness of large-scale written expression: Songs, blogs, and presidents. *Journal of Happiness Studies*, pages 1–16, 2009.
7. A. Esuli and F. Sebastiani. Sentiwordnet: A publicly available lexical resource for opinion mining.
8. J. Friedman, T. Hastie, and R. Tibshirani. Regularization paths for generalized linear models via coordinate descent. *Journal of Statistical Software*, 33(1):1, 2010.
9. E. Gilbert and K. Karahalios. Widespread Worry and the Stock Market. In *Proc. ICWSM*, 2010.
10. E. Goffman. *The Presentation of Self in Everyday Life*. 1959.
11. J. Hancock, C. Landrigan, and C. Silver. Expressing emotion in text-based communication. In *Proc. CHI*, pages 929–932, 2007.
12. J. Holmes and S. Schnurr. Politeness, humor and gender in the workplace: negotiating norms and identifying contestation. *Journal of Politeness Research. Language, Behaviour, Culture*, 1(1):121–149, 2005.
13. Z. Jelveh and K. Russell. Interactive timeline: The rise and fall of enron. *The New York Times*, 2006.
14. T. Joachims. Text categorization with support vector machines: Learning with many relevant features. *Machine Learning: ECML-98*, pages 137–142, 1998.
15. B. Klimt and Y. Yang. Introducing the Enron corpus. In *First conference on email and anti-spam (CEAS)*, 2004.
16. A. S. Lee Rainie, Kristen Purcell. The Social Side of the Internet. Technical report, Pew Internet & American Life Project, 2011.
17. M. Madden and S. Jones. Networked Workers. Technical report, Pew Internet & American Life Project, 2008.
18. V. Metsis, I. Androutsopoulos, and G. Paliouras. Spam filtering with naive bayes. In *Proc. CEAS*, pages 125–134, 2006.
19. G. Namata, L. Getoor, and C. Diehl. Inferring formal titles in organizational email archives. In *Proc. of the ICML Workshop on Statistical Network Analysis*. Citeseer, 2006.
20. Nielsen. What Americans Do Online: Social Media And Games Dominate Activity. Technical report, 2010.
21. S. Palus, P. Bródka, and P. Kazienko. How to analyze company using social network? *Knowledge Management, Information Systems, E-Learning, and Sustainability Research*, pages 159–164, 2010.
22. B. Pang and L. Lee. Opinion mining and sentiment analysis. *Foundations and Trends in Information Retrieval*, 2(1-2):1–135, 2008.
23. J. W. Pennebaker and M. E. Francis. *Linguistic Inquiry and Word Count*. Lawrence Erlbaum, August 1999.
24. R. Rowe, G. Creamer, S. Hershkop, and S. Stolfo. Automated social hierarchy detection through email network analysis. In *Proc. WebKDD*, pages 109–117, 2007.
25. J. Shetty and J. Adibi. The Enron email dataset: database schema and brief statistical report. Technical report, University of Southern California, 2004.

26. J. Shetty and J. Adibi. Discovering important nodes through graph entropy: the case of enron email database. In *Proceedings of the 3rd international workshop on Link discovery*, pages 74–81, 2005.
27. P. Stone, R. Bales, J. Namenwirth, and D. Ogilvie. The General Inquirer: a computer system for content analysis and retrieval based on the sentence as a unit of information. *Behavioral Science*, 7(4):484–498, 1962.
28. J. Thom-Santelli, D. Cosley, and G. Gay. What's mine is mine: territoriality in collaborative authoring. In *Proc. CHI*, pages 1481–1484, 2009.
29. F. Viegas, M. Wattenberg, F. Van Ham, J. Kriss, and M. McKeon. Many Eyes: a site for visualization at internet scale. In *InfoVis*, pages 1121–1128. Published by the IEEE Computer Society, 2007.
30. S. Viller. The group facilitator: a cscw perspective. In *Proceedings of the second conference on European Conference on Computer-Supported Cooperative Work*, pages 81–95, 1991.
31. B. Vine. *Getting things done at work: The discourse of power in workplace interaction.* John Benjamins Publishing Company, 2004.
32. B. Vine. Directives at work: Exploring the contextual complexity of workplace directives. *Journal of Pragmatics*, 41(7):1395–1405, 2009.
33. B. Vine, J. Holmes, M. Marra, D. Pfeifer, and B. Jackson. Exploring co-leadership talk through interactional sociolinguistics. *Leadership*, 4(3):339, 2008.
34. M. Wattenberg and F. Viégas. The Word Tree, an interactive visual concordance. In *InfoVis*, pages 1221–1228, 2008.

Predicting Tie Strength in a New Medium

Eric Gilbert
School of Interactive Computing & GVU Center
Georgia Institute of Technology
gilbert@cc.gatech.edu

ABSTRACT
We have friends we consider very close and acquaintances we barely know. The social sciences use the term *tie strength* to denote this differential closeness with the people in our lives. In this paper, we explore how well a tie strength model developed for one social medium adapts to another. Specifically, we present a Twitter application called We Meddle which puts a Facebook tie strength model at the core of its design. We Meddle estimated tie strengths for more than 200,000 online relationships from people in 52 countries. We focus on the mapping of Facebook relational features to relational features in Twitter. By examining We Meddle's mistakes, we find that the Facebook tie strength model largely generalizes to Twitter. This is early evidence that important relational properties may manifest similarly across different social media, a finding that would allow new social media sites to build around relational findings from old ones.

Author Keywords
tie strength, social media, social networks, computer-mediated communication (CMC), collapsed contexts, streams

ACM Classification Keywords
H5.3. Group and Organization Interfaces; Asynchronous interaction; Web-based interaction.

INTRODUCTION
While different on the surface, many social media share some fundamental similarities. They let people build relationships, primarily using language. We type messages to one another. Those messages happen at certain moments in time. Whether we articulate them publicly or not, we form our own micro social networks embedded within macro ones.

These building blocks suggest that we should be able to ask questions about relationships which transcend a particular medium. For example, we have colleagues with whom we correspond intensely, but not deeply; we have childhood friends we consider close, even when we fall out of touch. Do we leave clues in social media signaling our closeness with these people? How often we talk? Our places in a broader social network? The words and phrases we use?

The academic literature refers to this differential closeness by the name *tie strength*. We rely on our strong ties for emotional support, but our weak ties keep us in touch with current information [11]. People with many weak ties to other work groups often command higher salaries [2]. When our strong ties find happiness, we sometimes find it too [5]. In a 2009 paper, [7] reported a way to reconstruct tie strength using the data we leave behind in social media. Although it builds its model from Facebook data, [7] speculates that the model may adapt to relationships in other social media too.

Here, we explore that idea. We present *We Meddle*, a Twitter application built around [7]'s Facebook model. Simultaneously an experiment and a real-world system, We Meddle's central feature is that it infers tie strength between you and everyone you follow on Twitter. It generates exportable Twitter lists based on tie strength. The lists allow you to filter your Twitter stream to just a subset of people instead of everyone you follow, similar in spirit to "circles" in the recently released Google+ [9]. At the time of this writing, 2,114 people from 52 countries have used our site. After analyzing more than 200,000 We Meddle tie strength predictions, we arrive at early evidence that tie strength manifests similarly in Twitter and Facebook. To the best of our knowledge, this is the first paper to study in-depth how an aspect of relationships manifests *across* social media. Our method—a hybrid between building something people use voluntarily and studying social life online—has limitations, however. We also examine those limitations in this paper, hopefully directing future work toward ways of achieving greater precision.

We begin by reviewing work on tie strength, socially-rendered social media and the collapsed context problem. Next, we describe how we mapped [7]'s model from Facebook to Twitter. We then introduce We Meddle, which uses the model to generate Twitter lists. Adopting both quantitative and qualitative methods, we examine the model's generalizability and how people used We Meddle. The paper concludes by contextualizing our results within theory and design.

LITERATURE REVIEW
Tie strength refers to a general sense of closeness with another person. When that feeling is strong, we call it a *strong tie;* when it is weak, we call it a *weak tie.* Tie strength is also one of the most influential concepts in sociology. In the years since "The Strength of Weak Ties" introduced tie strength [11], the paper has attracted over 15,000 citations [10] from fields as diverse as Organizational Studies, Finance and Computer Science. Here, we focus on the most seminal and relevant papers from this literature.

We usually trust our strong ties, and their social circles tightly overlap with our own. Often, they also share our values, tastes and interests (i.e., homophily) [11, 20], yet this effect diminishes for people who live in cities [19]. Happiness even *flows* along strong ties in a network [5]. Weak ties, on the other hand, are our acquaintances. Most notably, they provide access to new information, information not flowing through our dense networks of strong ties. For instance, scientific discoveries seem to flow more efficiently through weak ties than through strong ones [12]. In a re-creation of a classic Milgram experiment [21], Lin et al. [18] asked participants to deliver a booklet to some unknown person in a distant place. They found that people who used more weak ties in their paths had greater success reaching the destination. People with weak ties outside their organizations often command higher salaries [2] and obtain better deals for their firms [29].

There are many reasons to care about tie strength, but historically simple heuristics have substituted for it. Communication reciprocity [6], one mutual friend [26], communication recency [18] and interaction frequency [8, 11] have all stood in for tie strength at one time or another. New research claims that we severely skew analyses when we use coarse heuristics like these [3], and leading scholars have called for more refined metrics [33]. Our data support these claims: we estimate that a heuristic like "call it a strong tie if they message each other at least N times" performs at 61% accuracy (at best) on a *strong vs. weak* classification task, with a baseline of 52%. Richer computational models, like the one presented in [7], perform with nearly 90% accuracy on the same task. In this paper, we reappropriate the model presented in [7], a computational technique for predicting tie strength from 74 Facebook interaction variables. Whereas other computational tie strength models have appeared between then and now [16, 34, 32], we chose to use [7]'s model because it builds in two things: simplicity as a path to generalizability and a large set of predictors. We put both properties to work when we map it from Facebook to Twitter.

With the present work, we ask if tie strength has a recognizable signature in social media, perhaps irrespective of a medium's implementation details. This idea, that some CMC phenomena persist across communities and media, has recently emerged in the literature [17]. We believe this is the first work to study a relational one.

Socially-rendered Social Media

Can social media interfaces reflect the social relationships they foster? Primarily, social media interfaces rely on *time* to organize themselves. Twitter, email, IM, IRC and many others all use time as their central design concept. We may call it "social media," but it's not a stretch to instead call it "temporal media."

In the short body of literature on socially-rendered social media, two research projects have laid the groundwork. SNARF [4, 22] and ContactMap [31] each explore using interaction histories to reconfigure interfaces. As these two projects represent the extent of the literature on socially-rendered interfaces, we will discuss them in some detail. (Currently, the Facebook News Feed prioritizes information by some metric. However, its details are proprietary.)

SNARF, the "Social Network and Relationship Finder," is a social sorting prototype designed to solve the email overload problem. SNARF uses features from past email exchanges to visually depict which people are most important to its users. The features include things like "emails sent to each person from the user" and "replies to each person from the user." In total, SNARF extracts 11 features. You can then select any of them as the key upon which the system sorts your email. ContactMap, on the other hand, explores an approach more like our own. Its authors developed hypotheses about things likely to be "important" and perform logistic regressions to predict it from six features.

Our work draws inspiration from these systems and builds on them in main two ways. First and foremost, it works on the open internet. We have as a primary goal testing theory. By putting our work on the open web, we lift sampling frame problems, encounter unexpected contexts and collect enough data to test theory. Second, We Meddle is the first application we know of to put a *relational* model at the heart of its design, as opposed to something defined in a single medium. With a model calibrated against a large relational dataset, we may be able to improve on the relatively low satisfaction scores users gave automatic importance in ContactMap [31].

The system we present in this paper groups Twitter accounts together, something a handful of commercial systems also do. Features like TweetDeck's groups [28] and Facebook's Friend Lists provide ways to group your friends. We have little information on their usage. However, the blog TechCrunch quoted Mark Zuckerberg [27], the founder of Facebook, as saying "Guess what? Nobody wants to make Lists," probably referring to how much time it takes to create a Friend List. Users put friends in lists one by one. The system we present here focuses on subtracting mispredictions, rather than adding each friend individually.

The Collapsed Context Problem

We Meddle attacks the *collapsed context problem.* We often think about it with this analogy: imagine living your whole life at your own wedding. Everyone you know from various parts of your life is there: grandmothers, in-laws, coworkers, cousins, childhood friends, etc. Writing a status update on a social media site is like forgetting you left the microphone on. Everyone hears everything. Consuming content (e.g., reading Twitter or the Newsfeed) is very much like standing in the receiving line. Everyone you know passes by in random order. danah boyd has termed this the *collapsing of context* [1], concentrating mainly on how it affects self-presentation. Do you want to share your latest party pictures with everybody, including the people you didn't invite? But it has other consequences too. In social streams, people from every part of life collapse into one channel, in temporal order, with nothing distinguishing one from any other.

If you want to monopolize your followers' streams, write about what you're eating, seeing or doing every ten minutes. Because of collapsed context, your messages will crowd out others and get more attention. In the real world, and even with varied media [13], we can enforce boundaries: turn on the TV to hear about the movie star; use the phone to talk to your best friend. Today's social streams make this harder.

Facebook predictors	Twitter predictors	β
Days since last comm.	Days since last comm.	-0.587
Days since first comm.	Days since first comm.	0.581
Intimacy x Structural	Intimacy x Structural	0.308
Wall words exchanged	@-reply words exchanged	0.230
Mean *ts* of mutual friends	Mean *ts* of mutual friends	0.198
Educational difference	Follower difference	-0.123
Structural x Structural	Structural x Structural	0.150
Reciprocal x Reciprocal	Links x Links	-0.146
Initiated wall posts	Initiated @-replies	0.112
Inbox thread depth	Direct message headers	-0.105
Number of friends	Following count	-0.105
Soc. Distance x Structural	Soc. Distance x Structural	0.100
Number of applications	no analog	
Wall intimacy words	@-reply intimacy words	0.085

Table 1. The top predictors as measured by standardized betas for the *How strong?* model in [7] and their Twitter analogs. *Follower difference* (gray) substitutes for the original social distance predictor, *Education difference*. It captures a difference in fame on Twitter.

METHOD OVERVIEW & RESEARCH QUESTIONS

To explore the adaptability of predicting tie strength, we built a website called *We Meddle*, open to anyone on the internet who uses Twitter. Users sign in and have the tie strength model applied to their own Twitter accounts. We Meddle is a hybrid, simultaneously an experiment and a system we hoped people would find useful. Via We Meddle, this paper addresses the following research questions.

R1: Does the computational tie strength model in [7], trained on Facebook data, adapt to another social medium?

R2: Can feedback from users improve the model? If so, how does it change?

MAPPING FACEBOOK TO TWITTER

When a user first signs into We Meddle, an agent gathers relational histories from the Twitter API to compute tie strengths. However, first we had to map [7]'s model from Facebook to Twitter. Table 1 presents the mapping: we directly reappropriated the coefficients from [7] for use on Twitter. (The coefficients here differ in absolute terms from [7] because this model only uses the top predictors (not all 74). They are proportionally the same and move in the same directions.) This was one of [7]'s goals: identify predictors that draw on the breadth of Facebook, but have analogs in other media.

In building We Meddle's model, we tried to find the most natural analogs to [7]'s predictors, changing it as little as possible to study how well it adapts. All of We Meddle's predictors are also internally normalized as z-scores and logged—the approach taken by [7].

Predictors

We now visit each We Meddle predictor in turn, discussing what it measures and how it compares to the predictors from [7]'s original Facebook model. Below, + denotes a replication of [7]; ++ refers to a minor deviation from [7], usually an analogy between the two sites; +++ denotes a significant departure from [7]'s original Facebook model.

+ ***Days since last communication*** measures the number of days between the last time two people interacted, accounting for both @-replies and direct messages.

++ ***Days since first communication*** measures the same concept in the same way as the predictor above, but from the first known time two people interacted. In addition, it has access to the order in which a user followed someone, a feature [7] wanted but could not obtain. For example, if I followed you 3rd in my list of 200 followees, but have never communicated with you, this predictor chooses $3 \div 200$.

+ ***Intimacy x Structural*** measures the interaction between [7]'s *Intimacy* and *Structural* dimensions. LIWC intimacy words proxy for the *Intimacy* dimension and *Median strength of mutual friends* proxies for *Structural*.

++ ***@-reply words exchanged*** measures the raw number of words exchanged by the dyad in the form of @-replies. On Twitter, the @-reply is the natural analog of Facebook's wall post: a semi-public, directed message.

+ ***Mean tie strength of mutual friends*** measures the mean tie strength of mutual friends in the ego network. We follow the same iterative regression approach as [7].

+++ ***Follower difference*** measures the difference in follower counts between a We Meddle user and someone they follow. The original Facebook *Educational difference* predictor has no convenient Twitter analog. Instead of omitting it entirely, leaving our model without a representative from [7]'s *Social Distance* dimension, we substitute *Follower difference*. On Twitter, a big difference in follower counts (i.e., orders of magnitude since predictors are logged) is a fame differential. Rather than copy its coefficient directly from *Educational difference*, *Follower difference* derives its coefficient from the average of the four social distance predictors in [7]. This is the only predictor to change its coefficient substantially from the original model.

+ ***Structural x Structural*** measures the multiplicative effect of structure, where *Structural* is again proxied by *Median strength of mutual friends*.

+ ***Links x Links*** measures the multiplicative effect of link-sharing via @-replies. While [7] named its predictor *Reciprocal Services x Reciprocal Services*, [7] also used link-sharing as the underlying proxy variable.

++ ***Initiated @-replies*** measures the number of @-replies initiated by our user. This contrasts with *@-reply words exchanged*, which measures aggregate traffic. By contrast, this predictor is directional, measuring how often our user initiated contact.

++ ***Direct message headers*** measures the number of times a user corresponded with someone via direct messages. (No content was examined.) Direct messages are the Twitter-equivalent of the Facebook inbox: an internal messaging technology very much like email.

Figure 1. The We Meddle web interface, grouping a user's Twitter contacts via a computational model of tie strength. (This image has been modified to preserve privacy. Normally, different profile pictures appear in each spot.) On first log-in, We Meddle computes tie strengths for everyone the user follows. The "Inner Circle" and the "Outer Circle" correspond to strong ties and weak ties, respectively. We Meddle also computes lists corresponding to social communities in the underlying social network, labeled as "Birds of a Feather" and "Flock Together" here. Users can store these lists inside Twitter and use them in their client.

++ ***Following count*** measures how many people a user follows. [7] used *Number of friends* to discount the tie strength of any one friend as the number of friends grew. Since We Meddle computes tie strength over those you follow, this predictor is the natural analog.

+ ***Social Distance x Structural*** measures the interaction effect between the *Social Distance* dimension and *Structural*. As before, *Social Distance* is proxied by *Follower difference* and *Structural* is proxied by *Median strength of mutual friends*.

++ ***@-reply intimacy words*** measures the number of LIWC intimacy words among @-reply words.

Model Limitations

This is not a perfect mapping. In some cases, we took advantage of data not available to [7]; in others, we had to settle for imprecise analogs, such as fame difference substituting for education difference. Surely, we lose some precision. We aimed for the most natural analogs available, one of [7]'s goals. We hope that later work can resolve some of our inconsistencies. As this is the first in-depth study of how relational features manifest across media, we suggest that the mapping presented here provides first-order insight on an topic we know very little about today.

WE MEDDLE

We Meddle is a web application which uses this model to infer tie strengths between a Twitter user and the people they follow. We Meddle calculates tie strengths in the background, the first time a user logs in. It then generates lists of Twitter accounts, including lists of strong ties and weak ties. We chose to create lists simply because the opportunity presented itself. We moved into the space shortly after Twitter announced the Lists infrastructure, while it was new and there were few competitors. Figure 1 shows the interface (modified to preserve privacy)."Inner Circle" and "Outer Circle" are synonymous with strong and weak ties. We call someone a strong tie when they score one-half standard deviation above the mean, and vice versa for weak ties. This serves to reduce clutter in the interface, making We Meddle usable for users who follow many, many people.

A user can drop someone from a list by clicking on that person's profile picture. When she clicks, the profile picture goes to 25% opacity, holding its place to remind the user that she dropped the account. When she's happy with the list, she can create it, storing the list in Twitter. Storing it in Twitter means that she can access it from any Twitter client, using the list in ways the particular client affords. For instance, the Seesmic client [25] lets you view each list in its own column, meaning that you can slice the conventional Twitter stream into multiple views. A We Meddle user can go to Seesmic and see their Inner Circle flowing in a separate column beside the main stream, using the split view to make sure she does not miss any strong-tie tweets. A short demo video on the site shows users how this could look.

We Meddle takes its inspiration from real life social relationships. In real life, we do not pay everyone equal attention. Returning to the wedding analogy from earlier, imagine yourself standing in the receiving line while everyone in your life comes to talk to you, one by one, in random order. They can talk as long and as often as they want, effectively blocking the people you truly care about. Anyone who already finished can cut back into line anywhere they like. We permit something very similar from our stream clients. We Meddle tries to improve this by making guesses about a user's relationships with everyone they follow, and then lets users slice their stream by those guesses.

Users cannot add people to the lists We Meddle generates. Adding accounts to the We Meddle lists could change their meaning. If a user adds people, can we be sure that Inner Circle still corresponds strong ties? Perhaps the user started from We Meddle's suggestions but branched off to create a list with a different meaning. Limiting users to deletions is an important decision. It allows us to argue that the Inner Circle and Outer Circle retain their meanings. When a user removes an account from the Inner or Outer Circle, we learn where the model makes mistakes. These clicks are crucial data: during the natural process of using We Meddle, users leave a trail from which we study tie strength. (Note that the way ties are classified does not imply that everyone appears as either a strong tie or a weak tie. These two lists do not add up to everyone.)

Communities

When people discuss their social networks, they usually do so in two ways: tie strength and communities [14]. While this paper is about tie strength, We Meddle tries to support this practice. We Meddle uses a community detection algorithm to decompose a user's following network into as many as four social communities. These communities often correspond to groups we can easily name when we see them, like "College Friends," "Former Colleagues" and "Researchers." Users can store these lists in Twitter, too. We Meddle uses a freely available community detection algorithm, called the Markov Cluster Algorithm [30], to generate them. The algorithm does random walks of a network, noting that nodes within a community have more paths between one another than nodes in different communities. The algorithm then works to optimize modularity [23]. While not central to this paper, we built the communities feature to give users another reason to visit We Meddle.

Architecture

The We Meddle tie strength engine is written in Perl, appropriating the output of an R statistical model. When a user first signs in to We Meddle, the system builds a database of tie strengths for each account the user follows. The sign-in forks off hundreds and sometimes thousands of API requests against Twitter.

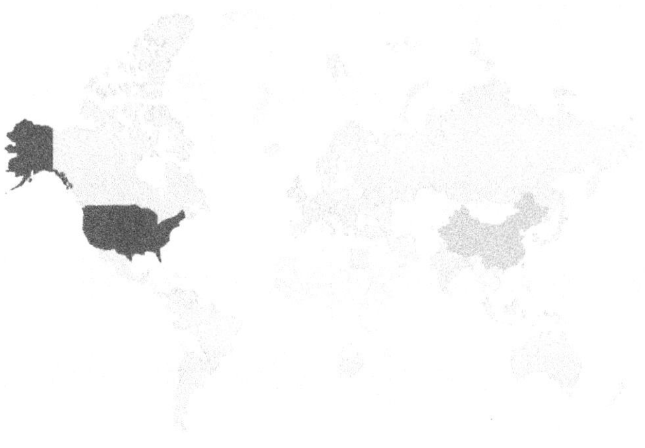

Figure 2. A heatmap of We Meddle's 2,114 users spread over their 52 countries. Most users come from the United States, but China also has a strong presence, accounting for about 10% of We Meddle's users.

As the API requests come back, they first filter through the non-structural parts of the tie strength model. When they all come back, the Perl-based model percolates the non-structural tie strengths through the user's network. People often formulate this as an eigenvector centrality problem, but in practice a simple percolation loop with a few iterations seems to always converge (and consumes far fewer resources). Near the end of the tie strength computation, the engine projects all tie strengths onto a [0, 1] interval by mapping the mean to [7]'s mean and capping at the ends of the interval. The web interfaces seen by We Meddle users are written in PHP and Javascript, making use of the jQuery [15] toolkit for animations and asynchronous communication.

Deployment

In January 2010, we made We Meddle open to any Twitter user on the web. We Meddle was available at `http://wemeddle.com`. After announcing it on a few mailing lists and through our Twitter accounts, the site spread by word of mouth. We considered doing a lab study: recruit Twitter users from around campus to tell us whether We Meddle's guesses match how they feel about their networks. But, we decided on an open web deployment for two reasons. First, releasing We Meddle on the web means people can choose to use it. Voluntary usage is good in our view. Second, by lifting the college campus sampling frame, we have more confidence in the results that come from the present study. We Meddle has seen users from all over the world—something we never could have replicated in the lab. Figure 2 illustrates We Meddle's user distribution by country. At the time of this writing, 2,114 people from 52 countries have used We Meddle.

At the same time, We Meddle largely spread by word of mouth, starting with our personal networks. This is called snowball sampling, and some research traditions see it as problematic. This does introduce complications. Yet, this is primarily how social applications spread on the web. Putting it online also means it reached much further than we ever could come in the lab. Since We Meddle spread relatively wide, less than 5% of its users were our Twitter followers or their followers (i.e., 2 hops away). We argue that this reduces snowball sample validity threats.

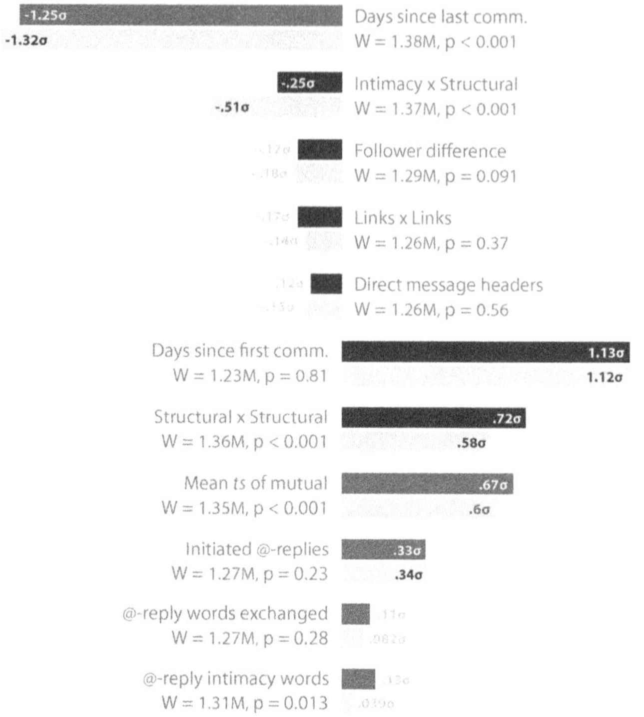

Figure 3. An analysis of We Meddle's *strong tie* mistakes in terms of the model's input predictors. Each pair of bars compares two groups, correct predictions (black) and mistakes (gray). At the end of each bar is the within-user, standardized median for the predictor. *W* refers to the Wilcoxon statistic. Note the recency effect indicated by *Days since last communication* and many strong effects by network-based predictors: *Intimacy x Structural, Mean strength of mutual friends,* and *Structural x Structural.* These highlight differences between Twitter and Facebook.

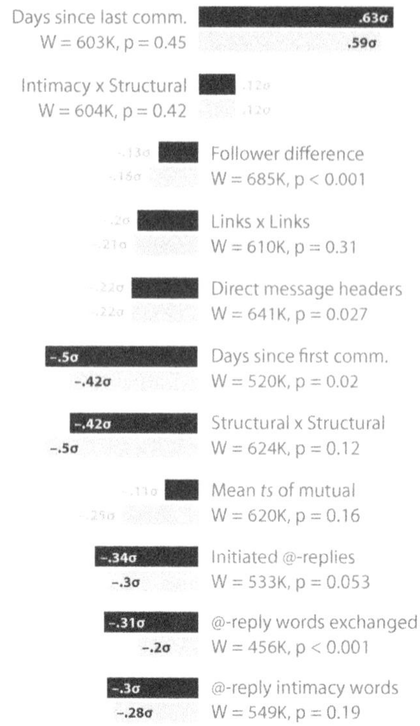

Figure 4. An analysis of We Meddle's *weak tie* mistakes in terms of the model's input predictors. Colors and statistics have the same meaning as in the figure to the left. We see very different reasons for weak tie mistakes than we do for strong tie mistakes. The network-based predictors vanish. Instead, we see strong effects by *Follower difference* and *@-reply words exchanged,* perhaps signaling the ease with which you can message a higher-status user on Twitter.

We Meddle's Limitations

We Meddle allows users to perform a first-pass sort of the people they follow on Twitter. One limitation is that the interface does not give users the ability to create lists with finely tuned meanings, such as the intersection of social circles. For example, perhaps someone would like a research circle only composed of people they feel close to (i.e. strong ties). While We Meddle takes a step toward enabling better consumption of social streams, we hope that future work can improve on some of these design limitations. This seems especially relevant and timely given the rise of Google+.

GENERALIZATION

When a user drops someone from the Inner Circle or Outer Circle, we can infer that the model made a mistake. Whether the model generalizes hinges on the question "How many mistakes did We Meddle make?" We argue that the tie strength model generalizes when we see a comparable error rate to the one seen in [7]. In other words, it generalizes to Twitter if it gets about 87–88% of its predictions right. We Meddle received 1,105 corrections from 236 different users. Most We Meddle users made no corrections. We could view this as a huge success: the majority of users experienced complete and utter success with We Meddle. Of course, this is a blindly optimistic interpretation. Some of them probably thought We Meddle got everything right. (Some qualitative data support this.) However, other people probably did not realize they could correct We Meddle (qualitative data also support this), or felt it wasn't worth the effort to make the clicks. Because We Meddle straddles the boundary between an experiment and a system people want to use, we have to correct for issues like these.

First, we consider only data from the 236 We Meddle users who made at least one correction and at least one list, putting aside users who did not. This method leaves out anyone who felt We Meddle's predictions closely matched reality and did not make corrections. (Several hundred people made lists without a correction.) But, we know these 236 users understood the process by which they could correct We Meddle and subsequently made a list. We cannot guarantee that these users corrected *all* of We Meddle's mistakes, but remember that they ultimately created a list for their own use within a Twitter client. They had every incentive we could provide—short of forcing them—to make the tie strength lists they wanted. We Meddle observed 27,529 relationships from these 236 users. Of these, users had a chance to correct accounts that We Meddle marked as a strong tie or a weak tie, a total of 14,075. So, users corrected 1,105 out of 14,075 relationships, or 7.85%.

However, as explained in the previous section, users had no way to tell We Meddle that it had forgotten someone: they could only drop people from lists. Since We Meddle is as likely to underestimate tie strength as it is to overestimate it (see Figure 4 in [7]), we double this percentage, obtaining an upper bound of 15.7%. While slightly higher, it closely resembles [7]'s error rate of 12–13%, especially considering that 15.7% is an upper bound. ([7]'s error rate was based on the difference between model predictions and participant-provided scores; We Meddle's user corrections are a direct analog.) Primarily from this number, but with support from qualitative data presented next, we find evidence that [7]'s tie strength model largely generalizes to a new social medium.

Mistakes in Terms of Predictors

Next, we analyze how We Meddle's mistakes express themselves in terms of the model's input predictors. This can tell us in what subtle ways the Twitter tie strength model differs from the Facebook model, and where we should look to improve it. Figures 3 and 4 summarize the results. For example, Figure 3 shows that true strong ties have a lower *Days since last communication* predictor than mistakes, Wilcoxon $W = 1.38\text{M}$, $p < 0.001$. (Use of Wilcoxon tests reflects the non-normality in the data.) We within-user standardize every predictor. That is, we compare numbers standardized against all relationships corresponding to a user. As the same model generated both the correct predictions and the mistakes, differences stem from differences between correct predictions and mistakes, not artifacts of the model.

What jumps out most is the contrast between strong and weak tie mistakes, particularly the role of the network in strong tie mistakes. Three network predictors have large effects: *Intimacy x Structural* (0.263 standard deviations), *Structural x Structural* (0.134 standard deviations) and *Mean strength of mutual friends* (0.073 standard deviations). Interestingly, something outside the model itself suggests why. The strong tie mistakes disproportionately belong to big clusters, evidenced by their membership in the lists generated by community detection on the underlying social network, $\chi^2 = 37.43$, $p < 0.001$. Recall that the model blends tie strength recursively through the network: it is a function of the tie strengths of mutual friends. Due to the summary statistics over the cluster, this means that many relationships benefit from a single strong tie in a big cluster. These network predictors make a strong case for a more refined view of the network in the tie strength model, something we discuss in more detail later.

Weak tie mistakes, on the other hand, express themselves most definitively in *@-reply words exchanged,* with correct predictions lower than mistakes. Perhaps this stems from how easily you can message someone you do not know on Twitter. Whereas on Facebook someone must confirm my friend request before we can exchange messages, on Twitter I can send messages to President Obama if I like.

HOW USERS EXPERIENCED WE MEDDLE

The quantitative data address the generalizability question, but they do not tell us how users felt toward We Meddle. To understand it, we conducted interviews with our users. We picked We Meddle users at random from the logs and @-mentioned them on Twitter. After they replied, we conducted eight semi-structured interviews in whatever medium they preferred (e.g., phone, IM or email). (This is a typical response rate and sample size for follow-up interviews.) The participants ranged widely in backgrounds and in how they used Twitter, from young coders to small business owners

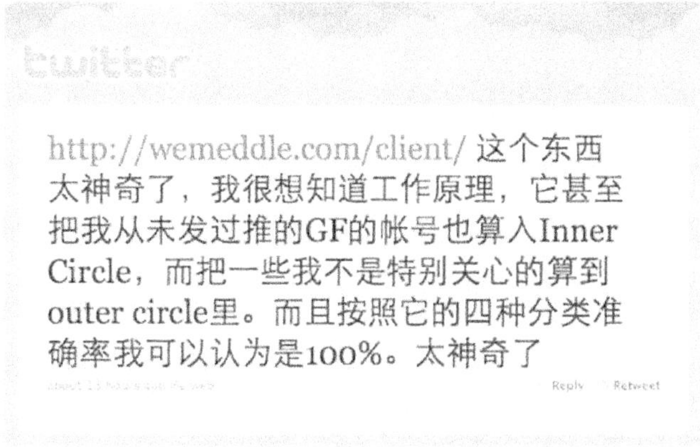

Figure 5. A comment on We Meddle via Twitter. The user writes, "This thing is miraculous. I really want to know how it works. It even classifies my GF's account into Inner Circle, but I never send tweets to her account, and it also classifies accounts I don't care about into outer circle. The four categories are very accurate, almost 100%."

who primarily used Twitter for promotional reasons. We Meddle also received many hundreds of comments via Twitter, and we present a selection of them at the end of this section. The point of the interviews was to elicit feedback from people who did not say anything on the web, hopefully removing the inherent self-selection bias that comes from speaking up publicly. The interviews took about 30 minutes. Email interviews consisted of questions similar to IM and phone interviews, but we often had follow-up conversations to clarify points. Typically, participants logged into We Meddle to look at the lists while we talked.

When asked about the composition of the tie strength lists, participants reflected on the lists' accuracy and the tie strength concept in their lives.

> [Did the lists reflect your real social life?] Um, I was pretty amazed to tell you the truth. Really amazed cause, um, the one I had an extreme [sic] hard time with trying to figure out was the Outer list. And this was probably the same with most people cause they're not people you communicate with much. So, I only remember one person I actually recognized on the Outer list. But the other three [Inner Circle, two communities] were pretty close to right on.

> It's actually kind of fun to look at the Inner Circle and say, "Wow, look at that person. I haven't talked with him in a long time, but they totally fit there." Yeah, there's some of those in here.

> It's kind of astounding and scary how good it is. [The people it chose for your Inner Circle, did they fit?] I would say the Inner Circle is about 70% accurate, maybe 80%. And it does actually a fairly—well, it's such an interesting question, right? So, it includes my wife, which is *good.* And people like [name] who runs [my online community], which is *good.* And my baby blogs, but doesn't tweet. But mostly what it is, is the Inner Circle is a sort of a blend of my immediate personal universe and probably my two most important social universes.

The last statement captures the way scholars often talk about tie strength: it skims off people from different social circles. In some cases, users expressed surprise when We Meddle correctly identified certain people in their lives.

> A few of the . . . well I remember a few of the people in the Inner Circle are actually relatives, and that was pretty cool. I didn't expect that.

> It's interesting that it actually placed my girlfriend four rows down versus at the very top, where I would expect her to be. [But she's in the list?] She's in the list, yeah absolutely, most of the lists actually. I hope she doesn't see the four rows down part. [participant laughs]

However, we did hear about problems. For instance, two users discussed relational contexts which fell outside We Meddle's built-in assumptions.

> Some people on Twitter just say stupid things. Or, they might say something that's inaccurate. So there's a few people I see who are not in my Inner Circle, you know, my group ... people I actually hang out with. But we have had disagreements on Twitter. We argued.

> The Inner Circle is actually not super accurate. Yeah, the Inner Circle is basically all the people I used to work with ... But I talk with them, sort of irregularly, now that I'm not at [company] anymore. [How close were you when you worked there?] Yeah, I was close to them while I was there, so it's fun to see them here from an old job. Maybe there should be a category for them: like people you used to be close to, but you know, aren't anymore.

Relationships can be intensely *negative*. (In fact, we received a handful of mildly annoyed emails from We Meddle users wondering why their ex-partner appeared in the Inner Circle.) The tie strength model does not understand these relationships. The former colleague story shows how a *biographical break* can influence someone's viewpoint. This participant felt close to his co-workers one month, and then did not the next. [7] saw similar problems, and future work could do better by trying to resolve them. However, a perhaps strange way to see these problems is as a sign of generalization: the model makes the same kind of mistakes as [7].

Reactions via Twitter

We Meddle received hundreds of unprompted comments via Twitter. In addition to Figure 5, we include a selection of these tweets here.

> wemeddle.com is a very cool idea for making twitter lists. It was good enough to re-create lists I made myself! Worth checking out.

> Fascinating clustering of those you follow by strong and weak ties.

> Oh geez, this application is a great filter for your Twitter contacts. [translated from Romanian]

> trying we meddle. [... six minutes later ...] didn't like we meddle.

> Liking what the folks at We Meddle are doing with the @TwitterAPI!

> Easiest Twitter list maker from @wemeddle.

> @[previous tweet] Just did and guess what, you are in my inner circle.

> If you are too lazy to take the time to make lists, we now have a new choice. We Meddle automatically analyzes your friends to generate several lists, which you can then make. [translated from Japanese]

> We Meddle is really good. It automatically divides my friends into groups, so that occasional tweets from my important friends won't be buried in an ocean of other tweets. [translated from Chinese]

These tweets speak to the value users found in We Meddle. Each tweet originally included a link to direct people to the site, which we edited out in the interest of brevity. We see this willingness on the part of our users to spread the site as evidence of its value to them. We Meddle did not have any prompt anywhere asking users to share the site with others.

DISCUSSION

From our data, we arrive at early evidence that [7]'s predictive tie strength model largely generalizes to a new social medium. The error structure, based on the intersection of quantitative and qualitative data, resembles what we see in [7].

If the model aligned precisely with social dynamics in Twitter, Figures 3 and 4 would show no effects for any predictors. However, the error analysis reveals wrinkles in the tie strength model. Remember, though, that these mistakes represent at most 15.7% of the data; their effect on an updated model would be subtle. Some predictors from Figures 3 and 4 probably reflect Twitter itself. For instance, the part played by *Days since last communication* in strong tie mistakes suggests that Twitter is more recency-driven than Facebook: tie strength seems to decay faster there. *@-reply words exchanged* in strong tie mistakes may suggest that people need to use more evocative language to maintain relationships in Twitter's lean medium. The role of *@-reply words exchanged* in weak tie mistakes probably reflects non-reciprocal ties in Twitter. [7]'s model learned a social structure in which a handshake precedes any communication. In Facebook, we have to accept friend requests; Twitter usually has no barrier.

Figure 6. A way to update the network component of the tie strength model. 1) A user's ego network, including links between mutual friends. 2) We want to estimate the tie strength of the link in gold. Instead of weighting the two mutual tie strengths equally, we weight them by low-fi tie strengths on the cross-cutting links, 0.09 and 0.74 in this example. We think it could reduce noise associated with big clusters; however, the extra crawl costs time.

We also find that intensely negative relationships often confound the model. [7] indicts "asymmetric friendships," friendships with big power differentials. How can we account for these relationships? This remains an unanswered and attractive target for future research. We tentatively propose a direction: measure politeness. We could measure it textually (e.g., hedges, deference, formal greetings, etc.) or via inter-message response time. For example, we know that in corporate contexts, upper-level management often lets messages sit for long periods of time before responding [24]. Similar temporal dynamics may happen in everyday social media. Politeness may signify asymmetry; lack of politeness coupled with *Intensity* may signify negative relationships.

A New View of the Network

The network predictors truly stand out in Figure 3. In [7]'s model, every mutual friend contributes equally to the network part of the tie strength model. But, why should my wife's sister contribute to my best friend's tie strength, if they only felt obligated to become friends in the first place? Instead, we propose a new, weighted network model, one where each mutual tie has its own tie strength. Practically speaking, this is easier said than done. Not only would we have to estimate every ego-centric tie (as We Meddle does), but also every cross-cutting tie between alters. In other words, not only would the model have to estimate tie strength for you and all our mutual friends, but also *between* you and all our mutual friends. To operate in web-response time, this is probably intractable; plus, from the outside we simply cannot see everything every dyad does.

Instead, consider low-fi tie strengths on the ties between alters. Draw a few roughly orthogonal tie strength predictors: we could pick *Days since last communication* and *@-reply intimacy words*. The model could use tie strengths made only from these two predictors to weight contributions to the tie strength of interest. Figure 6 illustrates the idea. This would of course require deeper knowledge of the communication record (e.g., being inside Twitter) or extra crawls at prediction time. But, as we see in Figures 3 and 4, it's the easiest way to bring down the error rate. With it, perhaps 90-95% prediction accuracy is within reach.

Theoretical Implications

This paper looks at *one* new medium. We see this as a substantial step for the study of social media and CMC: we believe this is the first work to quantitatively study how an important property of relationships manifests in two social media. However, many others remain. It is an open question how or even if tie strength can be reconstructed in all of them. Does it work in email? Does it work in IM? Perhaps it will need modifications. What modifications? Future work may find traction with the approach presented here: offer [7]'s model in the new medium; let your users tune it via feedback.

Our findings suggest that some important properties of online relationships resist sites' implementation details. This is important not only because we have so many social media, but because they change so often. Facebook has changed, perhaps substantially, since [7]'s study in 2008. Among many changes, Facebook has added comments directly on statuses, photos and videos. In 2008, everything happened threadlessly on the Wall. Maybe practices have changed in response. But, how much? [7]'s model worked for We Meddle, built a year and a half later. We see this as a deep question for future study: Do some fundamental properties of online relationships manifest the same way, regardless of design?

We have a vast literature on how tie strength modulates all kinds of social phenomena, from financial trading to the spread of values to the cohesion of groups. Consequently, we see opportunity to study other things by predicting tie strength. For example, what mix of ties keeps users on sites the longest? Mostly strong? A core of strong, but otherwise mostly weak? Do certain mixes of ties promote prosocial behavior online? Answers would have profound consequences for how we see online communities and how owners operate them. Or, instead of asking questions *about* social media, we might ask questions that simply use social media as a setting. For example, we could re-ask Fowler & Christakis's question [5]: Does tie strength modulate happiness in online networks?

Design Implications

In this paper, we take a step toward showing that computing tie strength helps users deal with the consumption side of the collapsed context problem. However, if we controlled all of Twitter, we would not have picked the consumption side of the collapsed context problem. We would have picked the production side: imagine sending messages only to strong tie colleagues (e.g., the intersection of the Inner Circle and a community list) without having to work at generating those lists yourself. We hope that our We Meddle case study encourages designers to experiment with tie strength. Whereas [7] briefly sketches many ways tie strength could inform design, here we conclude by drawing a longer scenario showcasing tie strength.

Imagine a woman interacting with her friends and family via a social network site. She posts photos, talks about her job, her family life and how night classes are coming along. And she uses it to keep up with everybody's busy lives. Now let's imagine that when she next logs in, she's been on vacation for two weeks with limited internet access. She wants to catch up. What should the system show her? All 5,000 things that happened?

In addition to topics she cares about, we might want to show her what happened to the most important people. Maybe her best friend changed jobs, or her sister took some great photos of her vacation. Maybe she missed a few strong tie birthdays and can sneak in belated congratulations. Perhaps a weak tie posted an inspiring web video that got everybody talking. We think understanding tie strength is the first step to building systems that can do these things.

LIMITATIONS

We used an imperfect mapping to build We Meddle, a system that could not support deep fine-tuning of social circles. We see this as a first step in an area we know very little about today. At the same time, we hope future work can improve upon the precision and design flexibility of what we present here. Systems that flexibly understand social life stand a chance to improve a wide range of social media.

CONCLUSIONS

In this paper, we find early evidence that [7]'s predictive tie strength model generalizes to a new social medium, one in which it did not train. This was a critical step: a model that works only in Facebook has little value outside that site. Perhaps most importantly, our findings suggest that a core property of online relationships may manifest similarly across social media. We see this as an important new step for social media and CMC theory.

Via We Meddle, we also show how computing tie strength can help users cope with the collapsed context problem. We find this encouraging and hope to see practitioners exploring new interfaces which incorporate tie strength. Perhaps we do not have to think linearly and temporally: we could bubble old but important messages to the top of a linear interface using tie strength. By intersecting tie strength and community detection, perhaps we might make a dent in social media's privacy problem.

We believe this is the first work to study in-depth how something fundamental about online relationships manifests *across* social media. But, we also think this work raises as many questions as it answers. Does tie strength continue to manifest this way in other social media, like email and IM? Do other core aspects of relationships manifest in their own ways across media?

ACKNOWLEDGEMENTS

We would like to thank the Social Spaces group at Illinois, as well as the comp.social lab at Georgia Tech. Amy Bruckman, Sarita Yardi and Ethan Zuckerman contributed valuable feedback on We Meddle's design. Google helped support this work. We also thank our users for giving We Meddle a try, and for chatting with us when we asked.

REFERENCES

1. d. boyd. Faceted id/entity: Managing representation in a digital world. Master's thesis, MIT, 2002.
2. R. S. Burt. Structural holes and good ideas. *American Journal of Sociology*, 110(2):349–399, 2004.
3. M. De Choudhury, W. Mason, J. Hofman, and D. Watts. Inferring relevant social networks from interpersonal communication. In *Proc. WWW*, pages 301–310, 2010.
4. D. Fisher, B. Hogan, A. J. Brush, M. Smith, and A. Jacobs. Using social sorting to enhance email management. In *Human-Computer Interaction Consortium (HCIC'06), Fraser, Colorodo*, 2006.
5. J. H. Fowler and N. A. Christakis. Dynamic spread of happiness in a large social network: longitudinal analysis over 20 years in the framingham heart study. *BMJ*, 337:a2338+, 2008.
6. N. E. Friedkin. A test of structural features of granovetter's strength of weak ties theory. *Social Networks*, 2:411–422, 1980.
7. E. Gilbert and K. Karahalios. Predicting tie strength with social media. In *Proc. CHI*, pages 211–220, 2009.
8. E. Gilbert, K. Karahalios, and C. Sandvig. The network in the garden: an empirical analysis of social media in rural life. In *Proc. CHI*, pages 1603–1612, 2008.
9. Google Plus. http://plus.google.com.
10. Google Scholar. http://scholar.google.com/scholar?q=strength+weak+ties.
11. M. Granovetter. The strength of weak ties. *The American Journal of Sociology*, 78(6):1360–1380, 1973.
12. M. Granovetter. The strength of weak ties: A network theory revisited. *Sociological Theory*, 1:201–233, 1983.
13. C. Haythornthwaite and B. Wellman. Work, friendship, and media use for information exchange in a networked organization. *J. Am. Soc. Inf. Sci.*, 49(12):1101–1114, October 1998.
14. B. J. Hogan. *Networking in Everyday Life*. PhD thesis, University of Toronto, 2009.
15. jQuery. http://jquery.com.
16. I. Kahanda and J. Neville. Using transactional information to predict link strength in online social networks. In *Proc. ICWSM*, 2009.
17. A. Kittur and R. Kraut. Beyond wikipedia: coordination and conflict in online production groups. In *Proc. CSCW*, pages 215–224, 2010.
18. N. Lin, P. Dayton, and P. Greenwald. Analyzing the instrumental use of relations in the context of social structure. *Sociological Methods & Research*, 7(2):149, 1978.
19. P. V. Marsden. Core discussion networks of americans. *American Sociological Review*, 52(1):122–131, 1987.
20. M. Mcpherson, L. S. Lovin, and J. M. Cook. Birds of a feather: Homophily in social networks. *Annual Review of Sociology*, 27:415–444, 2001.
21. S. Milgram. The small world problem. *Psychology today*, 2(1):60–67, 1967.
22. C. Neustaedter, A. Brush, M. Smith, and D. Fisher. The social network and relationship finder: Social sorting for email triage. In *Proc. CEAS*, 2005.
23. M. E. J. Newman. Modularity and community structure in networks. *Proceedings of the National Academy of Sciences*, 103(23):8577–8582, 2006.
24. D. Owens, M. Neale, and R. Sutton. Technologies of status management: status dynamics in e-mail communications. *Research on Managing Groups and Teams*, 3:205–230, 2000.
25. Seesmic. http://seesmic.com/app.
26. X. Shi, L. A. Adamic, and M. J. Strauss. Networks of strong ties. *Physica A: Statistical Mechanics and its Applications*, 378(1):33–47, May 2007.
27. TechCrunch. http://tcrn.ch/cuzaqp.
28. TweetDeck. http://www.tweetdeck.com.
29. B. Uzzi. Embeddedness in the making of financial capital: How social relations and networks benefit firms seeking financing. *American Sociological Review*, 64(4):481–505, 1999.
30. S. van Dongen. *Graph Clustering by Flow Simulation*. PhD thesis, University of Utrecht, 2000.
31. S. Whittaker, Q. Jones, B. Nardi, M. Creech, L. Terveen, E. Isaacs, and J. Hainsworth. Contactmap: Organizing communication in a social desktop. *ACM TOCHI*, 11(4):445–471, 2004.
32. A. Wu, J. M. DiMicco, and D. R. Millen. Detecting professional versus personal closeness using an enterprise social network site. In *Proc. CHI*, pages 1955–1964, 2010.
33. S. Wuchty. What is a social tie? *Proceedings of the National Academy of Sciences*, 106(36):15099–15100, September 2009.
34. R. Xiang, J. Neville, and M. Rogati. Modeling relationship strength in online social networks. In *Proc. WWW*, pages 981–990, 2010.

Tie Strength in Question & Answer on Social Network Sites

Katrina Panovich, Robert C. Miller, David R. Karger
MIT CSAIL
{kp, rcm, karger}@mit.edu

ABSTRACT

Asking friends, colleagues, or other trusted people to help answer a question or find information is a familiar and tried-and-true concept. Widespread use of online social networks has made social information seeking easier, and has provided researchers with opportunities to better observe this process. In this paper, we relate question answering to tie strength, a metric drawn from sociology describing how close a friendship is.

We present a study evaluating the role of tie strength in question answers. We used previous research on tie strength in social media to generate tie strength information between participants and their answering friends, and asked them for feedback about the value of answers across several dimensions. While sociological studies have indicated that weak ties are able to provide better information, our findings are significant in that weak ties do *not* have this effect, and stronger ties (close friends) provide a subtle increase in information that contributes more to participants' overall knowledge, and is less likely to have been seen before.

Author Keywords

Social search, Social networks, Q&A, Social Network Q&A.

ACM Classification Keywords

H5.3. Information interfaces and presentation (e.g., HCI): Hypertext/Hypermedia: Collaborative computing.

General Terms

Human Factors, Design

INTRODUCTION

We all have information needs—How's the weather? Who's the actor in this movie? Where can I find the best latte in Seattle?—and we have long found a variety of ways to satisfy these needs. Some questions are easily satisfied by a trip to the library, some by a phone call to a knowledgeable friend, and many are now best handled by using the internet. The internet has become a fully integrated utility in many people's lives, and *the* place to find an answer to many questions. Besides the obvious, and most common [9], option of using a search engine, one might post to a Q&A (question and answer) site, where community members help find answers. Some people use the internet to contact specific friends, using IM or email. One option that's gaining traction is using a social network site, such as Facebook, MySpace, LinkedIn, or Twitter [22]. In this case, people ask *all* of their friends or followers at once—they have no need to direct questions at specific people, or even to specific lists of people, they just simply broadcast their question.

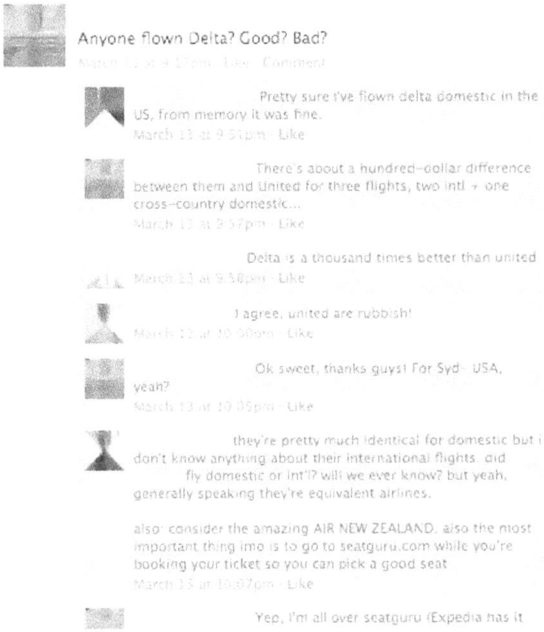

Figure 1. Question from study with some of the answers.

Using social networks for information seeking long predates current research. In this work, we are particularly interested in Granovetter's "The Strength of Weak Ties" [11]. This influential paper defined tie strength as the strength of a friendship—close friends are strong ties, and acquaintances are weak ties. He observed job finding practices, and saw that the job opportunities his participants found were largely through word-of-mouth communication with weak ties—this very useful information came from acquaintances who traveled in different circles and so had access to different information, not from strong ties or close friends.

Do our friends *offline* travel in the same circles *online* as us? Do they frequent the same places and sources of information online? In the broadcast question-asking mechanism concerning us here, one's entire network of friends has the ability to answer questions, and so both *who* answers questions (strong ties? weak ties?) and *how* they answer them (does one type of tie tend to provide more useful information, as in Granovetter's work?) are important to understanding the practices of social network-based information seeking.

We build off of tie strength work by Gilbert and Karahalios [10], who constructed a model of tie strength on Facebook using profile characteristics. We employ their techniques in our paper.

In this paper, we argue that tie strength *does not* have the same effect in question answering as would be predicted. In fact, there seems to be a subtle increase in answer quality from strong ties, rather than weak ties.

Some previous work, discussed in more detail below, has looked at who answers questions. For instance, popular question answering service Aardvark [15] found friends-of-friends to be more effective than strangers in answering questions. Morris et al [21] found that, in a small study, many participants' questions were answered by friends they rated as close. Granovetter's work suggests that perhaps the most useful answers would *not* come from close friends, but from acquaintances instead. Work by Morris et al [22] saw that closeness of a friendship was a motivator to answer questions, though many also responded to friends who weren't yet close, in an effort to improve the friendship, suggesting that friends of all strengths would respond to questions.

We have these research questions: we ask *if tie strength has the same 'strength of weak ties' effect in SNS Q&A*, and *how the relation between tie strength and answer quality plays out*. We found that it does *not* have the same effect, and strong ties may actually contribute slightly more to the overall knowledge gained by participants, and share less information the participant already knew. To do this, we conducted a lab study attempting to correlate tie strength with various measures of answer quality. In this paper, we first discuss related work, then our methodology for the study, followed by our results and a discussion, and potential design implications.

RELATED WORK

This research is beholden to several different areas of research: online question and answer tools, social search, social networking systems, and tie strength, a sociological principle spawned from interest in information exchange.

Online Q&A Tools

Electronic bulletin boards, newsgroups, and question-answering sites enable users to post questions targeted either at a particular community or to the world at large. We refer to sites where users post questions to be answered by people not known personally as *Q&A sites*. Question asking and answering behavior on Q&A sites has been well studied (e.g., Harper et al. [14]; Hsieh and Counts [16]; Liu et al. [19]; Mamykina et al. [20]). For example, Harper et al. [14] identified two categories of questions posted to Q&A sites: conversational questions, which are intended to spark discussion, and informational questions, which solicit specific facts. They found informational questions have higher archival value.

Other question asking opportunities include third-party applications that Facebook users can install designed specifically for Q&A purposes (*e.g.*, "My Questions" [slide.com]). Facebook also has a feature called Facebook Questions [7]. We did not collect data on use of this application and we are unaware of any research focusing on its use. We focus on the use of status messages for question asking, which does not require the installation of additional applications and thus has a lower barrier to entry, as well as for its unique role in repurposing social network tools.

Some researchers have explored the factors affecting answer quality on Q&A sites. Raban and Harper [25] point out that a mixture of both intrinsic factors (*e.g.*, perceived ownership of information, gratitude) and extrinsic factors (*e.g.*, reputation systems, monetary payments) motivate Q&A site users to answer questions. These questions come from complete strangers or near-strangers using the same system, as opposed to friends or followers online. Ackerman and Palen [1] and Beenan et al. [2] confirmed that intrinsic motivations, such as visibility of expertise and the feeling of making a unique contribution, influence participation in such systems. Results regarding extrinsic motivators have been more mixed; Hsieh and Counts [16] found market-based incentives did not increase answer speed or high-quality answers, but did decrease the number of low-quality responses, but Harper et al. [14] found fee-based sites produced higher quality answers than free sites. In this work, we look at answers from social networks, rather than Q&A sites — there are no extrinsic motivators besides social ones. Harper et al [13] also looked at questions on Q&A sites to determine the difference between informational and conversational questions — objective and subjective questions — and included "non-questions". These "non-questions" are of particular interest as many status message questions are not in typical question form. We incorporate their precedent and include information seeking sentences like these (often prefaced with "I wonder...") in the same group as general questions. These sentences are information seeking, and can be reframed in the form of a question, so can be considered questions.

Question-and-answer systems (Q&A systems) are of commercial interest as well. One commercial system of note is Aardvark [15], a site which routes questions through an instant messaging bot to an appropriate user in one's extended network, comprised of friends-of-friends and strangers. Aardvark prioritizes friends-of-friends for responses, and in fact, this appears to be a good way to increase the quality of the response. When asked for feedback about the answer the user received, 76% of the answers from within the user's extended network were rated 'good', and only 68% of answers from outside the user's network were rated 'good.' We hypothesize that extended network effects here mirror the effects of weak ties or acquaintances providing novel information.

Social Search

Broadcasting a question to one's social network, as in status message questioning, is one way to find information online; other common methods include using a search engine or emailing a question to a particular person. The term *social search* refers broadly to the process of finding information online with the assistance of social resources, such as by asking friends, reference librarians, or unknown persons online for assistance. Some researchers have built special tools to integrate social information with search engine use, such as HeyStaks [27].

Some researchers have proposed formal models to describe the interplay of online information seeking with the use of social resources. For example, Pirolli [24] developed a model of social information foraging, and Evans and Chi [5] described the various stages in the search process when users engaged with other people.

To compare social search with more traditional search, Evans *et al.* [6] conducted a study in which eight participants completed two search tasks. For one task, participants used only non-social, online resources (*e.g.,* search engines); while in the other they used only social resources (*e.g.,* calls or emails to friends, and social network or Q&A sites). Evans *et al.* found that in the social condition targeting questions to specific friends versus asking a social network had similar outcomes in terms of task performance; questions posed to the social network received more answers, but those targeted to individuals received in-depth answers.

Social Network Site Q&A

Our work draws directly from previous work on social network question answering (SNS Q&A). Morris et al [22] provide a survey of this behavior, including the types and topics of questions asked. The most popular type was recommendation, and the most popular topic was technology; our study capitalizes on these trends and uses them as the basis for questions in our study. They also addressed motivation for asking, the biggest factor of which was trust of friends, and motivations for answering. The most popular motivation was altruism ("being friendly"), though over 35% of participants cited the nature of the relationship, connecting socially, and creating social capital. Morris et al [21] also looked at searching, vs. asking questions, and saw similar motivations in trust, as well as the additional benefit of personalization from friends. Participants in their study also stated that they knew the friends who answered their question quite well. This serves as an interesting counterpoint to Granovetter's and others' work (discussed below).

Social Network Sites

While we position our work in the space of social search and question asking, and specifically SNS Q&A, the fact that it happens on social networks is non-trivial. Social network sites enable users to specify other users that they are connected to. Examples of popular social networking services include Facebook, Twitter, and MySpace. A December 2008 survey by the Pew Internet Project [18] found 35% of adult internet users in the U.S. have a profile on a social network, as do 65% of U.S. teens. We focus on work conducted on Facebook, as opposed to sites like Twitter, where "social network" has a different meaning.

The popularity of these social network sites (SNSs) is a big part of the reason this research is interesting: there are many users and their use is only increasing. Addressing unmet information needs in such a well-used medium means that more people are able to participate, as opposed to installing a tool or signing up for another service. This low barrier to entry is similar to simply searching on a search engine.

Researchers have explored many aspects of how social networking services are used. Lampe et al. looked at how university students' perceptions and use of Facebook changed over time [17]. In particular, Lampe et al found that the number of participants who used Facebook "to get useful information" increased from 2006 to 2008, pointing toward potential social information seeking behaviors, though it's unknown if this "useful information" consisted primarily of social awareness information or if it also included content gleaned from practices such as question asking.

Others have looked more specifically at expertise finding on social networks. Bernstein et al [3] generated a body of informational tags for users from their friends using a social game, and then were able to leverage that information for a system suggesting who might be able to answer a question.

Tie Strength

In our introduction, we discussed Granovetter's work looking at tie strength. His seminal paper "The Strength of Weak Ties" [11,12] discussed the value of weak ties (acquaintances). The primary idea behind tie strength is that, amongst our network of friends (online or offline), we have friends with whom we are close (*strong ties*) and friends who are less close, acquaintances or *weak ties*. Granovetter identified this after observing friendships in an offline social network, and pointed toward the idea that one's weak ties might be an effective information source because they traveled in separate social circles, and so could better transmit new information. Constant et al. [4] looked specifically at the role of weak ties in seeking technical advice, rather than job finding, in an enterprise setting. They found that, in cases where strong ties lacked the knowledge to answer questions, weak ties were able to provide good answers, given motivation. Recent work by Gilbert and Karahalios [10] looked at Granovetter's denotation of strong and weak ties within real-life offline social networks and found a series of features (number of mutual friends, number of words exchanged, and so on) that can effectively predict tie strength between friends in an online social network. Granovetter highlighted the role of tie strength in information exchange between people, and as such, models of tie strength online can help us to understand the exchange of information through questions and answers online. We build upon their algorithm in our work looking at what kinds of friends provide valuable answers to questions on SNS.

METHODOLOGY

In this study, we analyzed responses to status message questions - questions that were asked through the status message feature of the popular SNS Facebook. Note that this is distinct from questions asked in directed messages to friends, public or not, or using systems built specifically for question asking, such as Facebook Questions [7].

In an effort to assess how tie strength between friends affected answer quality, we collected information to determine tie strength and asked for feedback about responses participants received to questions they had asked. In this section, we detail the process of generating a tie strength value for participants, the feedback we requested from participants, and general information about our participants.

Participants

We had 19 participants complete the study. Participants were recruited through mailing lists to engineering students at a northeastern university; recipients were also invited to forward the information to friends. Most participants were from the university. Of these participants, 31.58% were female. While this is not proportionate to the Facebook population, it is a better percentage than some previous work in the field [22]. The mean age was 25.8 (median 25). Participants were largely seasoned users of Facebook, with a mean length of time with profiles on the site being 5.26 years (median 6), and with an average number of friends at 607.42 (median 505). This is far above the average of 130 friends of the general Facebook population [8], but is largely explained by the length of time participants have been members of the site, and could be considered a way to forecast use of Facebook as more and more participants reach this duration of time as members. Our findings should be interpreted in light of the generalizability of this population. As with many such studies, future work is needed to fully understand the generalizability of these findings.

Generating Tie Strength

Our process for generating tie strength is drawn directly from Gilbert and Karahalios [10]. In their method, they predicted tie strength using features and content from Facebook. They listed their top 15 predictive variables and their corresponding beta coefficients; we have used a subset of those for our model.

Our Predictive Variables	β
Days since last communication	-0.76
Days since first communication	0.755
Words exchanged	0.299
Mean tie strength of mutual friends	0.257
Positive emotion words	0.135
Intimacy words	0.111

Table 1. Our predictive variables and their associated beta coefficients. Beta values are drawn directly from Gilbert and Karahalios

We list our variables in Table 1. We used the same beta coefficients as Gilbert and Karahalios for all variables. The variables we omitted were Intimacy × Structural, Educational difference, Structural × Structural, Reciprocal Serv. × Reciprocal Serv., Participant-initiated wall posts, Inbox thread depth, Social Distance × Structural, and Participant's number of apps.

The variables not used were omitted because of the increased difficulty in obtaining the information. For instance, educational difference: at the time of the study, the Facebook API call for education did not return meaningful information. Asking each participant about each of their friends would not have been feasible, and so we omitted it from our study.

Since we used a simplified version of Gilbert's model, we attempted to calibrate our results by asking participants a question in the survey portion about how much they valued information from each of the answerers in general. The correlation was statistically significant. Several months after the initial study, we asked participants to rate the tie strength of a selection of their friends as well. The correlation was strong.

The data required for generating tie strength was gained primarily from Facebook's Download Your Data feature [29]. This allowed us to capture all of the communication between the participant and her friends. Participants were asked to download their data before the study and before asking a question for our study, so that participation in the study would not affect generated tie strengths.

We parsed this information to get our necessary numbers: the days since first and last communication, quantity of words exchanged, intimacy words, and positive emotion words. Communication between each friend was parsed with LIWC to label words as positive emotion or intimacy words. LIWC, Linguistic Inquiry Word Count, is a tool for text analysis developed by social psychologists [23]; Gilbert and Karahalios used this tool to generate the same data in their study. We also gathered the mutual friends

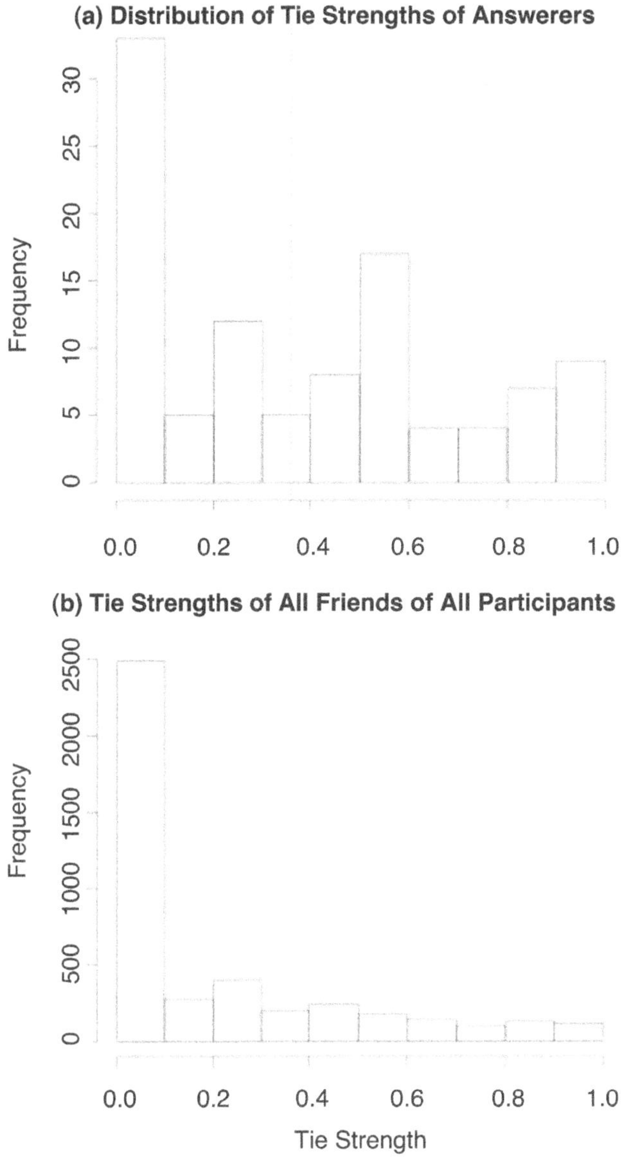

Figure 2. Distribution of tie strengths of (a) answers of questions during the study and of (b) all friends of all participants. The dotted line in (a) represents the median: 0.36, indicating that more weak ties answered questions than strong ties. The median in (b) was 0.01, a very weak tie.

between each participant and their friends to generate the mean tie strength of mutual friends.

We chose to calculate tie strength from a trained model instead of asking about it outright because of potential biases that would be introduced. Participants would be more likely to rate the closeness of a friend highly when presented with an example that they had just helped them; using this model to generate tie strength was an effort to remove this bias.

We saw confirmation of this effect in our study. Several participants had friends that answered their question multiple times. Two of our questions (detailed below) were about the friend in general, such as how much they valued input from this friend, and some participants increased the score for those friends on subsequent times we asked.

After several months had elapsed, potentially negating this bias, we asked participants to rate the strength of their friendship with some of their friends, as detailed in the Followup Surveys section. We found a strong correlation between our generated tie strength and their responses.

The distribution of generated tie strength between answerers of questions and our study participants is shown in Figure 2(a). The distribution of all of tie strengths for all of the friends of our participants is in Figure 2(b). As in Gilbert and Karahalios, the range is normalized to between 0 and 1 for each participant, where 0 is the weakest tie strength of a friend, and 1 is the strongest.

Answer Quality Survey

To determine the quality of responses from friends, 24 hours before the study, we asked each participant to ask a recommendation question about technology, such as "Can anyone recommend some places to get good information on cameras?" Participants were asked to use the question to address an existing information need.

While this is more specific in scope than the entire spectrum of questions typically asked on Facebook, previous work by Morris et al. points to recommendations being the most popular form of questions asked, and technology being the most popular topic.

Each participant asked a question, and in some cases, we reviewed other questions the participant may have asked if the participant wished to do so. An example question, drawn (with permission) from a participant in our study, is in Figure 1.

Questions included the following examples (somewhat altered to preserve anonymity):

- recommendations please: what are your must-have smartphone apps?
- does anyone have a good camera to recommend? Size-wise, I'm looking for something between a giant DSLR and a tiny point-and-shoot
- anyone got a website they use to track relevant new academic papers?
- Anyone flown Delta? Good? Bad?

Our 19 participants received a total of 104 responses, with a median response rate of 3 answers (not counting any clarification or comments by the participant) (average 5.47 responses, minimum 1 answer, maximum 19). All of the questions covered in our study were answered.

We asked participants nine questions about each answer they received. Questions were either about the *person* answering the question or about the *specific answer*. The questions and the distribution of answers are in Figure 3. Each participant was asked to give a response on a 7-point scale, with 1 being the least and 7 being the most. The questions we asked, along with clarification given, are as follows:

- How on topic is this answer? (where 1 is not at all related, 7 is 100% only about what was asked)
- What value do you place on answers from this person in general? (1-7)
- How knowledgeable or trustworthy is this person about this topic? (1 is not at all, 7 is expert level)
- How supportive is this answer? (1 is not at all, 7 is completely) *with example provided, see below*
- How interesting is this answer? (1-7)
- How much does this answer contribute to your overall knowledge? (1-7)
- How much does this answer provide information you haven't seen before, that's novel? (1-7)
- How much does this answer verify information you already knew? (1-7)
- How much do you trust this answer? (1 is not at all, 7 is don't need to verify anywhere, complete trust)

Three of the questions (how much the answer contributes to overall knowledge, how much is novel information, how much you already knew) address knowledge gained from the answer. We asked this general question in three specific ways in an effort to tease out any subtleties. Two of the questions (value placed on answers from this friend, how trustworthy/knowledgeable about the topic the friend is) asked about the friend in general. This was an effort to understand if answer quality was simply related to qualities (not necessarily tie strength related) of the answerer.

We conducted the data collection and survey portion of the study in the lab for several reasons. The main reason was that we conducted unstructured interviews with participants after the survey.

Participants could also qualify answers and give general impressions. We also had participants come into the lab in an effort to mitigate privacy concerns about sharing their downloaded Facebook data. Participants seemed more comfortable sharing their data when they were able to observe the investigator generating the tie strength metrics without actually reading messages.

We also conducted the study face-to-face in an effort to help participants calibrate answers; when asking about how supportive an answer was, for instance, we gave this example of an unsupportive answer: "Don't buy a new camera! What a waste of money!"

Previous work often simply discusses evaluating answer quality by having independent coders rate answers. The questions we asked participants were based largely on interviews with participants from a pilot study and others who self-identified as question-askers. Our nine questions are an attempt to unpack what constitutes answer quality in social questions.

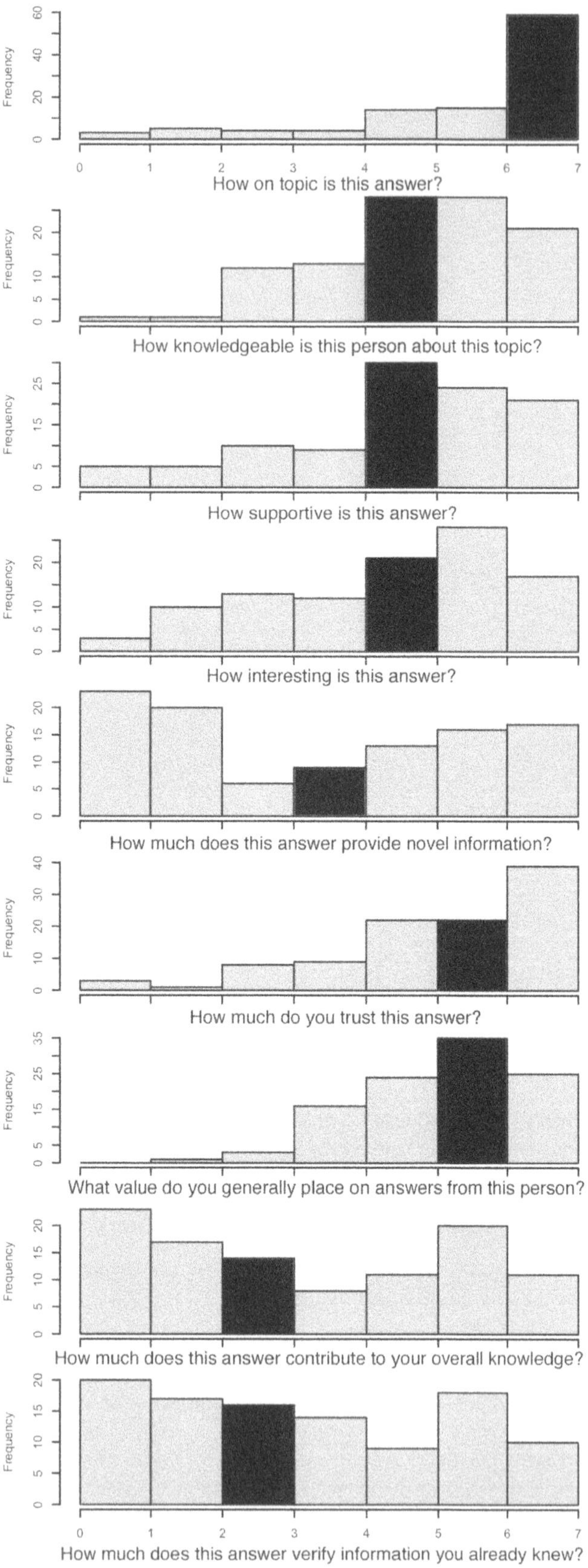

Figure 3. Questions asked of participants and their distributions. Medians are highlighted.

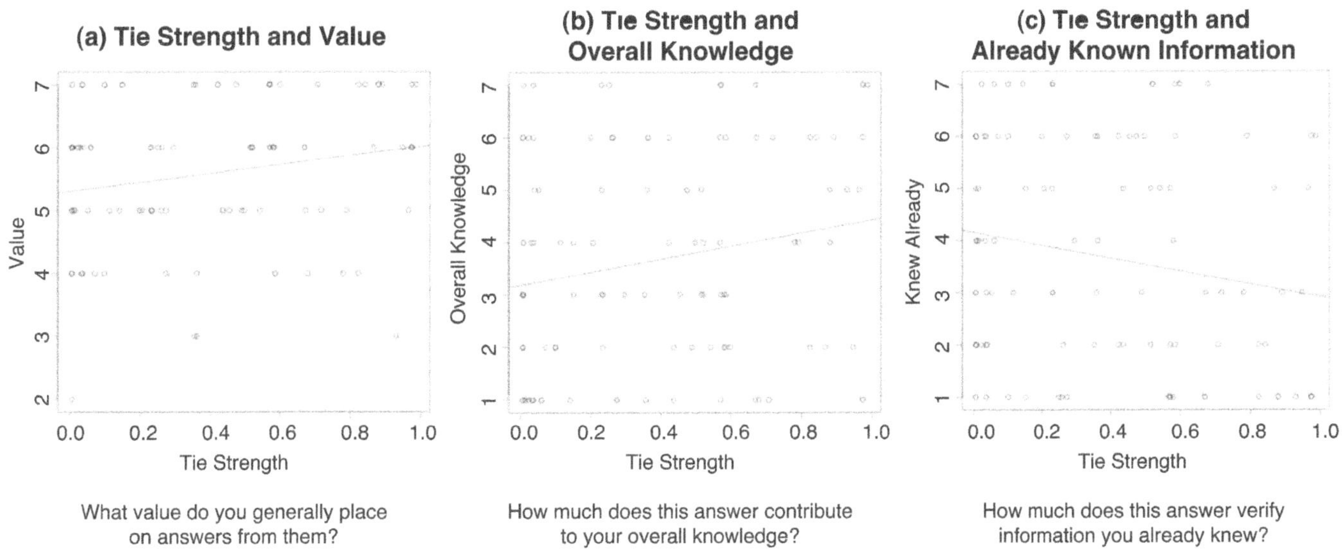

Figure 4. Tie strength and (a) value of answers in general, (b) overall knowledge gained from each answer, and (c) information already known by the participant.

We chose not to use an independent rater because of the inherently social nature of the site. For instance, friends could exchange an inside joke that was on topic, even if it didn't appear so to outside raters.

We asked how interesting the answer was to capture answers that may be good in a non-traditional sense. Someone answering with a pun, for instance, may not be very helpful, but it may be interesting. We also asked if participants would trust the answer, in the sense that they wouldn't feel the need to verify it at all. A trusted answer, for instance, would be an answer a participant would repeat to another friend, if she asked a similar question.

For questions that were directly about the answer, rather than the answerer, we followed up with participants several months later, in attempt to reduce bias or memory of the answers, and asked them to rate their answers without being able to see who provided them. More details are below.

Followup Surveys

Several months after the initial study, we contacted our participants for two more surveys. In the first, participants were asked to rate the strength of their friendship with some of their friends. We specifically asked participants to "adjust [a] slider to represent how strong your relationship is with [each] person", for a set of friends comprised of the friends that answered their question, the friends we found to be the highest and lowest tie strength with our generated metric, and random friends, totaling 15 friends. We received participation on this portion from all but one participant. We measured the correlation between the tie strengths we generated and the tie strengths our participants provided and found a Pearson's coefficient of 0.50, indicating a strong correlation.

We also asked participants to re-rate the answers that they had received to their questions. We used the same questions as above, focusing only on questions that are about the answer, rather than the person who provided it. After they had responded to those questions, we asked them to rate how much each answer had contributed to any decision they made for their question, and how they made that decision. We also asked if participants remembered who provided the answers.

Fifteen of 19 participants completed this survey. These 15 participants had a total of 101 answers, of which participants remembered the author 56% of the time. We discuss the differences in rating in the following section.

RESULTS

In this section, we discuss the results from our survey and tie strength metrics, as well as our followup work. To do this we calculated a correlational analysis between tie strength and each of our survey questions, as well as between other variables, when noted below.

Our analysis did not control for the number of answers a participant had received. Our analysis also does not include any analyses of likelihood of getting a response or of getting a high quality response. This information was impossible to obtain, given the data available. Further discussion of this appears in the Limitations section.

Surprisingly, the bulk of our results were not statistically significant. We initially found no significant correlation between tie strength and how on topic an answer was, how knowledgeable a friend was about the topic, how supportive the friend was perceived to be, how interesting an answer was, how novel the information was, or how much the answer was trusted. However, the correlations between the value placed on a friend's feedback, the overall knowledge gained from an answer, and whether or not the answer verified already known information were statistically significant. We discuss these results in more detail below. In some cases our followup survey or the tie strength numbers provided by our participants conflicted with our initial findings; these are noted when this is the case.

	On topic	What value for friend in general	How knowledgeable	How supportive	How interesting	How much added to overall knowl.	How much already known	How novel	How trusted was response
How on topic was this answer?		not sig	0.51***	0.60***	0.32***	0.32***	0.16*	0.21**	0.48***
What value do you generally place on answers from this friend?	not sig		0.32***	not sig	0.20**	0.17**	not sig	0.11*	not sig
How knowledgeable/trustworthy is this friend about this topic?	0.35***	0.44***		0.43***	0.32***	0.30***	not sig	0.17**	0.31***

Table 2. Correlations with beta coefficients between survey variables and how on topic a question was, what value participants generally placed on answers from that friend, and how knowledgeable/trustworthy on this topic they are.

*** $p < 0.05$, ** $p < 0.01$, *** $p < 0.001$**

We also discuss a subset of significant correlations between survey questions. We focus on the things that were predicted by qualities about the answerer, the friends of the participant – the value placed on answers from that friend, and the perceived knowledge and trustworthiness of the friend on the topic of the question. These qualities of the answerer can help us understand factors that *do* predict answer quality, if tie strength does not.

How on topic is this answer?

While initial ratings and generated tie strengths showed no statistically significant correlation, the tie strengths from participants *did* correlate negatively with the ratings from our followup survey ($R^2 = 0.049$, $\beta = -0.040$, $p < 0.05$). This effect size is minimal.

What value do you generally place on answers from this person?

The value placed on answers is correlated positively with tie strength ($R^2 = 0.065$, $\beta = 0.071$, $p < 0.05$). R^2 indicates that about 4% of value is predicted by tie strength; the low p value indicates that it is a statistically significant fit. β indicates that, as ties become stronger, value increases, though not greatly. Figure 4(a) shows a plot of tie strength and value, with the line of best fit. When correlated with participants' ratings of tie strength, we saw a similar correlation with a slightly larger effect size ($R^2 = 0.020$ $\beta = 0.114$, $p < 0.001$).

We also compare the value placed on answers with other measures of the answers. Those results are in Table 2. Value is correlated significantly with how knowledgeable the friend is, how interesting the answer is, how much the answer contributes to the participant's overall knowledge, and how novel the answer was.

How much does this answer contribute to your overall knowledge?

The overall knowledge gained by answers is correlated positively with tie strength ($R^2 = 0.036$, $\beta = 0.031$, $p < 0.05$). About 4% of knowledge gained is predicted by tie strength; Figure 4(b) shows a plot of tie strength and knowledge gained, with the line of best fit.

How much does this answer verify information you already knew?

How much answers verify known information is correlated negatively with tie strength ($R^2 = 0.062$, $\beta = -0.038$, $p < 0.01$). R^2 indicates that about 6% of how much of the answer is known is predicted by tie strength; the p value indicates that the fit is nearly statistically significant. β indicates that, as ties become stronger, answers are less likely to have already been known. Figure 4(c) shows a plot of tie strength and how much the answer was known, with the line of best fit.

How knowledgeable/trustworthy is this person about this topic?

Specific numbers are in Table 2. Knowledge on the topic is correlated significantly with how on topic the answer is, the value placed on answers by that friend in general, how supportive the answer is, how interesting it is, how much it contributed to overall knowledge, how novel the answer was, and how much the participant trusted the response. It was not, however, correlated with tie strength.

How much do you trust this answer?

How much participants trust specific answers is correlated positively with tie strength, only when participants *do not remember* who provided the answer in the followup survey ($R^2 = 0.092$, $\beta = 0.058$, $p < 0.05$). There was no initial correlation. In a followup survey, which took place months later, we asked this question again. Fifteen of 19 participants completed this portion, and a combined total of 44 of 101 answerers were forgotten.

How much did this answer contribute to your decision?

We asked participants how much each answer contributed to their ultimate decision regarding their question. Fifteen of 19 participants completed this portion, and there was no statistically significant correlation between tie strength and the decision.

DISCUSSION

In this section, we discuss the meaning behind our results and possible explanations for them.

Our research question asks *if tie strength has the same 'strength of weak ties' effect in SNS Q&A, and how the relation between tie strength and answer quality plays out.* In our introduction and related work we detailed some of the places where tie strength and the transmission of information have been studied. While job finding may be different from question asking, at its crux, it is still about solving an information need. In these cases, research pointed toward *the strength of weak ties*, where weak ties provided better information than strong ties.

Surprisingly, our data show no correlation in this direction. Participants in our study even rated answers from strong ties as having a slightly stronger contribution to their overall knowledge. Weaker ties were more likely to answer with information that the participant had already seen, and participants valued answers from closer friends more in general. Both strong and weak ties provided decision making information, though no correlation between the two was found.

We asked participants how much they valued answers from each of their friends in general, and saw a statistically significant positive correlation with tie strength. Though the beta is low, we see this as evidence that our implementation of Gilbert and Karahalios's model is valid. Several months later, we surveyed participants and found that their reported tie strengths were strongly correlated with our initial values.

There are several potential explanations for why our contrary findings may be the case. We saw that strong ties were slightly more likely to contribute more to a participant's overall knowledge, and that weak ties were more likely to share information the participant already knew. One potential, though unlikely, explanation is that information diets, even between close friends, are varied and diverse. As such, question askers might gain benefits like personalization without losing breadth in information known by their close friends.

The ability for friends to personalize information when answering questions alone may also help explain our findings. Strong ties' increased knowledge of the participant may have enabled them to direct their answer, despite their overlapping knowledge bases. Even when participants could not remember who provided an answer, they rated answers from strong ties more trustworthy than those from weak ties. Future work is needed to unpack these interactions and to verify these results.

Perhaps topical knowledge matters more. There was no statistically significant correlation between how knowledgeable/trustworthy a friend was and tie strength, but the correlation between how much the answer contributed to participants' overall knowledge and how trustworthy/knowledgeable the answer *was* significant, and predicted 66% of the overall knowledge gained.

Many participants confirmed this and said that the answers they liked best were answers that seemed reliable, and came from a reliable source. One participant said, "*I look for answers where people didn't just recommend a product but gave reasons from their experience or pointed to reviews online. So I guess I want citations.*"

Others echoed this remark: "*I guess a lot of evaluating is my estimation of the source reliability (the person).*" One of our questions asked how much participants trusted their friend about the particular topic – this had no statistically significant correlation with tie strength, though it seems to be a big factor in determining answer quality for many participants.

Another said, "*[It's] just kind of a personal experience with products that I'm looking for. For example, I know* [friend with tie strength 0.006] *does a lot of camera work, and* [tie strength 0.718] *is a professional photographer, so I value their answers more.*" In this case, the best answers were from friends with wildly different tie strengths.

One interesting anomaly in our study is that very few things seem to be correlated with how much the answer verified information that was already known. Part of the reason we asked several questions about knowledge was to allow for survey questions that may have been perceived as confusing or unclear.

IMPLICATIONS FOR DESIGN

Perhaps most significantly, designers should consider drawing on close friends more strongly within the question-asking process. Systems such as Aardvark [15] bypass all friends, including close friends, for friends-of-friends and strangers. While some questions may be better suited for strangers, due to an embarrassing nature, or extremely localized knowledge, other questions may do better when routed to close friends. For instance, a participant may want to ask *any* close friend for advice about something, but selecting a specific friend is unimportant. Were one to have access to a social network at a higher level, it would make a great amount of sense to route questions that were posted to strong friends first.

LIMITATIONS

This paper suffers from several limitations. One is that work on Facebook must acknowledge unknowns about the Newsfeed algorithm. This algorithm, at time of writing, selectively displays posts to participants, instead of displaying all recent posts. This means that we cannot make any claims as to who saw posts or make any useful statements about percentages of answers from strong or weak ties; it also means that the weak ties that answered questions in our study may have been a poor subsection of the population. We are also unable to predict the likelihood of getting a high quality response to a question for this reason.

Our participants may likewise not be a generalizable population, though it is possible that the length of time our participants have been on the site can help us predict what longer term use looks like.

We also did not completely replicate the tie strength model proposed by Gilbert and Karahalios. While we argue that the parts of the model we used were the most significant parts, there may be subtleties we are missing.

CONCLUSION

In this paper, we presented a study relating tie strength to answer quality for questions asked as status messages on social network sites. We found that there was no statistically significant correlation between tie strength and these values, contrary to previous literature on tie strength.

In our study, 19 participants asked technology recommendation questions of their social network. We compared participant-rated answers to a tie strength metric drawn from Gilbert and Karahalios [10]. We saw that, instead of weaker ties providing better answers, there was minimal correlation at best, and in fact, for some measures of answer quality, stronger ties actually provided better answers.

We also saw that friends who were rated as more knowledgeable and trustworthy about the given topic provided answers that were better (more interesting, supportive, contributed more to overall knowledge).

Social network system Q&A lies at the intersection of several different areas. We hope that our effort to better understand some of the social mechanisms in play can also translate to other areas. It is important to understand this process – it has been happening for a long time, and will continue into the future for a long time as well.

ACKNOWLEDGEMENTS

We thank Greg Vargas, Karrie Karahalios, Mark Ackerman, and our participants, as well as grants from Xerox, the NSF and Google. We also thank the reviewers for their incredibly helpful comments in the revision process.

WORKS CITED

1. Ackerman, M. and Palen, L. The Zephyr help instance: Promoting ongoing activity in a CSCW system. CHI 1996.
2. Beenan, G., Ling, K., Wang, X., Chang, K., Frankowski, D., Resnick, P. and Kraut, R.E. Using social psychology to motivate contributions to online communities. CSCW 2004.
3. Bernstein, M., Tan, D., Smith, G., Czerwinski, M. and Horvitz, E. Collabio: A game for annotating people within social networks. UIST 2009.
4. Constant, D. and Sproull, L. and Kiesler, S. The kindness of strangers: The usefulness of electronic weak ties for technical advice. Organization Science, 1996.
5. Evans, B. and Chi, E. Towards a model of understanding social search. CSCW 2008.
6. Evans, B., Kairam, S., and Pirolli, P. Do Your Friends Make You Smarter?: An Analysis of Social Strategies in Online Information Seeking. IP&M, 2010.
7. Facebook, Inc. Facebook Questions. http://www.facebook.com/questions (accessed June 2, 2011).
8. Facebook, Inc. Statistics. http://www.facebook.com/press/info.php?statistics (accessed June 2, 2011).
9. Fallows, D. Search Engine Use. Pew Internet and American Life Project. August 6, 2008.
10. Gilbert, E. and Karahalios, K. Predicting tie strength with social media. CHI 2009.
11. Granovetter, M. The Strength of Weak Ties. American Journal of Sociology, May 1973.
12. Granovetter, M. Threshold Models of Collective Behavior. American Journal of Sociology, November 1978.
13. Harper, F.M., Moy, D. and Konstan, J.A. Facts or friends? Distinguishing informational and conversational questions in social Q&A sites. CHI 2009.
14. Harper, F.M., Raban, D., Rafaeli, S. and Konstan, J.A. Predictors of answer quality in online Q&A sites. CHI 2008.
15. Horowitz, D., and Kamvar, S. The Anatomy of a Large-Scale Social Search Engine. WWW 2010.
16. Hsieh, G. and Counts, S. mimir: A market-based real-time question and answer service. CHI 2009.
17. Lampe, C., Ellison, N. and Steinfield, C. Changes in use and perception of Facebook. CSCW 2008.
18. Lenhart, A. "Adults and social network websites." Pew Internet and American Life Project, January 2009.
19. Liu, Y., Bian, J., and Agichtein, E. Predicting information seeker satisfaction in community question answering. SIGIR 2008.
20. Mamykina, L. and Manoim, B. and Mittal, M. and Hripcsak, G. and Hartmann, B. Design Lessons from the Fastest Q&A Site in the West. CHI 2011.
21. Morris, M. R., Teevan, J., Panovich, K. A Comparison of Information Seeking Using Search Engines and Social Networks. ICWSM 2010.
22. Morris, M.R., Teevan, J., and Panovich, K. What Do People Ask Their Social Networks, and Why? A Survey Study of Status Message Q&A Behavior. CHI 2010.
23. Pennebaker, J.W., Chung, C.K., Ireland, M., Gonzales, A., & Booth, R.J. The development and psychometric properties of LIWC2007. Austin, TX: LIWC.net, 2007.
24. Pirolli, P. An elementary social information foraging model. CHI 2009.
25. Raban, D. and Harper, F. Motivations for answering questions online. In New Media and Innovative Technologies. 2008.
26. Slide, Inc. Slide.com. http://www.slide.com/ (accessed June 2, 2011).
27. Smyth, B., Briggs, P., Coyle, M. and O'Mahoney, M. Google shared: A case study in social search. UMAP 2009.
28. Torrey, C., Churchill, E. and McDonald, D. Learning how: The search for craft knowledge on the Internet. CHI 2009.
29. Zuckerberg, M. Giving You More Control. Oct. 6, 2010. http://www.facebook.com/blog.php?post=434691727130 (accessed June 2, 2011).

Removing Gamification from an Enterprise SNS

Jennifer Thom, David R. Millen, Joan DiMicco
IBM T J Watson Research
1 Rogers Street
Cambridge, MA 02142
{jthomsa, david_r_millen,joan.dimicco}@us.ibm.com

ABSTRACT
Gamification, the use of game mechanics in non-gaming applications, has been applied to various systems to encourage desired user behaviors. In this paper, we examine patterns of user activity in an enterprise social network service after the removal of a points-based incentive system. Our results reveal that the removal of the incentive scheme did reduce overall participation via contribution within the SNS. We also describe the strategies by point leaders and observe that users geographically distant from headquarters tended to comment on profiles outside of their home country. Finally, we describe the implications of the removal of extrinsic rewards, such as points and badges, on social software systems, particularly those deployed within an enterprise.

Author Keywords
Gamification, organizational social networking

ACM Classification Keywords
H5.3. Group and Organization Interfaces: Computer-supported cooperative work

General Terms
Human Factors

INTRODUCTION
Designers of social software systems have employed aspects of gamification – the integration of game-inspired elements – to incent repeat usage, increase contributions, and establish user reputations. These incentives can come in the form of points, badges and leveling that can help the player advance in status. In the workplace, game-like systems have been employed to collect information about employees [6] and incent contribution within enterprise social software [5]. Ultimately, gamification aims to create a sense of playfulness in non-game environments so that participation becomes enjoyable and desirable.

Game mechanics draw heavily from theories of social psychology that predict how users can be motivated to participate in collective systems for individual benefit [1]. For instance, badges and points can be categorized as extrinsic rewards for participation (e.g. posting a comment, checking into a location). There is, however, evidence that extrinsic rewards can undermine intrinsic motivation to complete a task, particularly if the task is interesting and beneficial to the user [2]. This suggests if members of a community find participation in a social site enjoyable, the addition of specific reward structures (e.g. levels, badges) may actually decrease already existing intrinsic motivation to contribute.

In this paper, we focus on the implications of the wholesale removal of such features from an enterprise social networking service and answer the following main research question:

How does the removal of gamification features affect user activity within an enterprise social networking service?

Our data suggests that the removal of such features does negatively impact continued participation in the SNS, and that the removal of the extrinsic rewards also decreased the activity by geographically distant users, despite factors that might increase their motivation to maintain activity. We make a secondary observation that there were geographic differences in how users employed commenting strategies within the system, where those outside of the United States tended to reach out to those outside their home locations.

METHOD
The current study focuses on a points-based system on an enterprise SNS deployed within a large IT enterprise headquartered in the northeastern United States with a globally distributed workforce of approximately 400K employees. The goal of the incentive scheme was to encourage content contribution, so points were awarded for the addition of lists, photos and comments. Each user received 5 points for each contributed photo or list, while comments on a profile page, photo and list received 15 points.

Log analysis had revealed that comments helped to draw visitors back to the SNS, so this particular scheme rewarded commenting behavior [5]. The incentive design also

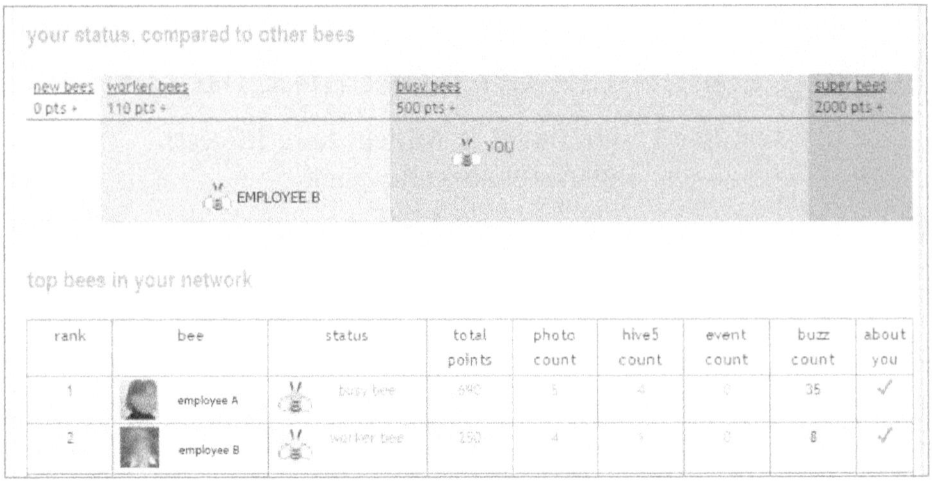

Figure 1. Member status display (top), leaderboard showing point totals and count of content contributions (bottom).

included a leveling component, with 4 tiers of status depending on accumulated points (Figure 1) and the appropriate badges displayed on user profile pages. Those who received the most points were spotlighted on a leader board, accessible from the user's login page (Figure 1).

To measure the impact of the points deployment on the social system, an experiment was run for six months in which half of the site was able to earn points and the other half of the site was unaware of the existence of the points system. In an analysis of the first three weeks of the experiment, the incentive scheme dramatically increased the overall levels of content contributed upon introduction, followed by a decayed impact [5]. Over the entire six months, usage analysis revealed that as new users joined the site, those who could earn points added more content over time, both short and long-term, yet the proportion of new users who contributed content was the same between the points-earning and non-points-earning users [3]. After the six-month deployment, the points deployment became available to all members of the SNS.

The current study focuses on a specific event that has heretofore not been reported in prior research – the complete removal of the points system from the site 10 months after their introduction as an experimental feature. Points removal entailed the deleting of all interface features related to the incentive, such as the profile badges, leaderboards and display of point totals to users. Site administrators announced the removal of the points system via the user forums found on the employee intranet. The data in the current study consists of four weeks of usage logs from two weeks before and after points were removed from the site. We limited the users of the study to those that had used the system at least once during that time period.

RESULTS

Our analysis focuses on 3486 members of the site that had contributed at least one item of content during the four-

	Points Deployed Total (#/user)	**Points Removed** Total (#/user)
Photos	4502 (2.6)	2926 (1.7)
Lists	1277 (1.0)	780 (.64)
Profile comment	8983 (5.5)	4056 (2.5)
Photo comment	2598 (2.9)	1348 (1.5)
List comment	1770 (2.5)	873 (1.2)

Table 1. Contribution of content type during points deployment (2 weeks) and after points removal (2 weeks).

week analysis period. Table 1 presents the total number of contributions by each of the content types before and after the removal of the points system for these members.

Because the distribution of contributions is non-normal, we conducted all analysis on log-transformed data; however, we report all results as non-transformed for readability. A repeated measures GLM (points deployed/no points) reveals that the removal of the points significantly decreased contributions of photos (df=1,1717, F=38.24, $p<0.001$) and lists (df=1, 1211, F=39.07, $p<0.001$). The analysis also reveals a main effect of the removal of points over all types of comments (df=1,710 F=49.50, $p<0.001$; df=1,885, F=308.78, $p<0.001$; df=1,1627, F=603.95, $p<0.001$ for lists, photos and profiles respectively).

We conducted a qualitative analysis of the comments left by the point leaders reveals that types of comments contributed by the most active users during this time period differed in content and formality. One type of comment observed was extremely concise and greeting-oriented, placed on a profile page.

"HI"

"Hiee..."

"howz work goin on..?"

"Nice.."

Another type of comment left by the points leaders were placed on the associated and generally focused on the target content of interest.

"Love the pics. Have some ideas on articles for you, but might want to give you the lowdown first. Up for a chat sometime?"

"Connect back to me and then you can see some great pictures I know you'll enjoy!"

After the removal of the points systems, we observed that the prevalence of terse greeting-oriented comments subsided. One possible explanation can be linked to the design of the site. In this case, adding comments to a profile page takes one click from the homepage, while adding comments to a content type (e.g. photo or list) takes at least two clicks.

Finally, we investigate in more detail whether the points-based incentive system had a differential effect on globally distributed employees. Based on prior research that suggested that motivations for SNS usage differ between employees who are geographically central and those who are geographically distant from headquarters [9,10], we analyzed points activity of the 1815 members from the United States and the 287 members from India, the two most active geographies in the study sample (Table 2). Repeated measures GLM (points/no points) and country (India/USA) as a between subjects variable reveals a main effect of the removal of points over all types of comments for both countries (df=1,478 F=15.822, $p<0.001$; df=1,596, F=27.62, $p<0.001$; df=1,733, F=51.93, $p<0.001$ for lists, photos and profiles respectively).

The analysis also revealed a main effect of country for profile comments (df=1,733, F=444.88, $p<0.001$), with users from India contributing more profile comments than those from the United States. While the total (raw) numbers for India is generally below those of the US, the contribution levels are quite similar when normalized by number of active contributors for that content type. The noteworthy exception is the number of profile comments contributed by employees from India. The total number of profile comments is larger than those from US employees in total (3543 vs 3502) and considerably higher per active contributor (20.7 in India versus 4.1 in the US).

	USA	India
	Total (#/user)	Total (#/user)
Photos	4090 (4.1)	550 (5.6)
Lists	1159 (1.7)	104 (1.5)
Profile comment	3502 (4.1)	3543 (20.7)
Photo comment	2430 (1.3)	189 (5.6)
List comment	1584 (3.6)	102 (2.6)

Table 2. Contribution of content type by country over all four weeks.

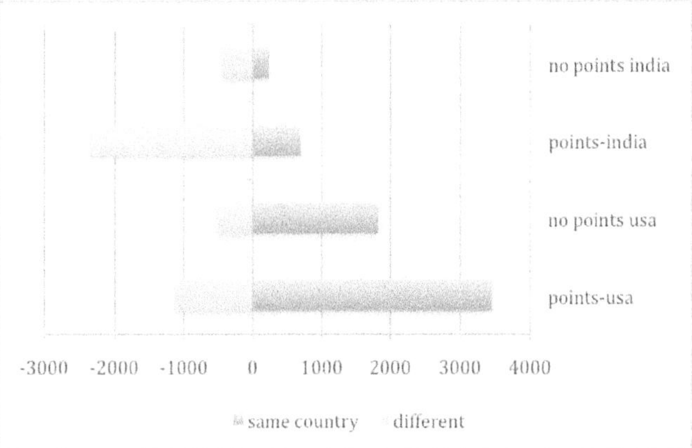

Figure 2. Comments within and between countries before and after the removal of points.

To further characterize differences in commenting patterns, we recoded comments to indicate whether or not users in each geography left comments on member content or profiles in different countries and same country. Figure 2 describes the directionality of comments between and within countries, normalized by posts/total number of members inside and outside the country (e.g. for users from India, the number of members inside and outside India).

These results suggest that users in the United States tended to comment on content contributed by users in the same country, while users in India tended to comment on content created by those outside the country. Closer investigation of the points leaders from India reveals that their organizational affiliation is from the Services division, which is one that provides operational and technical support for internal and external clients. This finding is consistent with prior research detailing the proportion of friend connections between and within countries for India and the US [9] and lends additional support to previous observations regarding differing motivations for SNS usage across factors such as geographical distance and organizational function within an enterprise.

DISCUSSION

The main contribution of this study is the observation of the impact of the removal of a gamification feature within a social networking system. The removal of the points system made a significant negative impact on the user activity of the site, and our analysis suggests that contribution of content significantly decreased after the deactivation of the points system. This suggests that such extrinsic rewards did influence a segment of the user population to participate more intensely while the point system was in place.

We also observed that the removal of the gamification feature decreased activity by users in the two most active geographies, the United States and India. However, compared to users in the United States, users in India commented more often on profiles outside of their home country. This is consistent with research that suggests that geographically distant members of an enterprise, far from headquarters, have been observed to use social software systems as a way to learn about its organizational culture and build one's reputation [7]. Again, however, there was a negative effect of the removal of the extrinsic rewards system, suggesting that intrinsic motivation to participate may not be consistent across individuals.

We suggest two main implications for the design of gamification systems that result from our findings. First, the complete discontinuation of a game-like capability should not be taken lightly, as they do seem to motivate participation within a social system even for a short period of time. If the particular game functionality seems stale and in need of a redesign, one approach would be to have an immediate transition to another game-like system to incent new players or those who do participate primarily for extrinsic rewards. In the case of this particular system, the designers implemented a new feature to encourage viewership of a more diverse set of content [4].

Second, we observed differences in the way users reacted to the incentive system and that there were different strategies adopted by the points leaders. However, other members of the SNS may perceive unsolicited profile comments as disruptive. One possible intervention would be a clearer delineation of the rules of engagement and fair play. This could be stated in policy by the site administrators or through moderation within the system. Another approach would be an incentive that increased common ground, as a way to encourage collaboration or shared identity as way to possibly reduce disruptive gaming from participants who follow a different set of game values.

While we did not specifically study the cultural consequences of this specific form of gamification, we propose that game-like incentives can embody certain values, such as competitiveness, which may not be consistent with the culture of the organization [8]. In this case, employees may not feel comfortable participating in a system, which encourages such behavior. On the other hand, members of organizational cultures that value public competition may be extremely motivated by features, such as leaderboards. Further, local culture may play a role in the design of such systems. For instance, a point-based currency on a Chinese online community reproduced norms of social exchange and sharing within that culture, such as guanxi and renping [11]. As a result, gamification features in such cultures would require incentives that included ideals of reciprocity, social obligation and face-saving.

LIMITATIONS

This study was conducted within a single global organization and so was necessarily influenced by the culture of that organization. Our results should be interpreted in that light. Future work in other organizations and settings is needed to better determine the generalizability of our findings. Given the high levels of interest in gamification and enterprise social computing, we think that this research will serve as a useful foundation for future work in this area.

ACKNOWLEDGMENTS

The authors thank Rosta Farzan, Beth Brownholtz, Casey Dugan and Werner Geyer.

REFERENCES

1. Beenen, G., Ling, K., Wang, X., Chang, K., Frankowski, D., Resnick, P., and Kraut, R. Using social psychology to motivate contributions to online communities. *Proc.CSCW2004*, ACM (2004), 212-221.
2. Deci, E.L., Koestner, R., and Ryan, R.M. A meta-analytic review of experiments examining the effects of extrinsic rewards on intrinsic motivation. *Psychological Bulletin, 125*, 6 (1999), 627.
3. Farzan, R., DiMicco, J.M., Millen, D.R., Brownholtz, B., Geyer, W., and Dugan, C. When the experiment is over: Deploying an incentive system to all the users. *Proc.AISB*, ACM (2008).
4. Farzan, R., DiMicco, J.M., and Brownholtz, B. Spreading the honey: a system for maintaining an online community. *Proc.GROUP2009*, ACM (2009), 31–40.
5. Farzan, R., DiMicco, J.M., Millen, D.R., Dugan, C., Geyer, W., and Brownholtz, E.A. Results from deploying a participation incentive mechanism within the enterprise. *Proc.CHI2008,* ACM (2008), 563-572.
6. Guy, I., Perer, A., Daniel, T., Greenshpan, O., and Turbahn, I. Guess Who?: Enriching the social graph through a crowdsourcing game. *Proc.CHI2011*, ACM (2011), 1373–1382.
7. Morrison, E.W. Information Seeking Within Organizations. *Human Communication Research, 28*, 2 (2002), 229-242.
8. Schein, E.H. *Organizational Culture and Leadership*. Jossey-Bass, San Francisco, 1992.
9. Thom-Santelli, J., Millen, D.R., and DiMicco, J.M. Characterizing global participation in an enterprise SNS. *Proc.ICIC2010*, ACM (2010), 251–254.
10. Thom-Santelli, J., Millen, D.R., and Gergle, D. Organizational acculturation and social networking. *Proc.CSCW2011*, ACM (2011), 313–316.
11. Yang, J., Ackerman, M.S., and Adamic, L.A. Virtual gifts and guanxi: supporting social exchange in a chinese online community. *Proc.CSCW2011*, ACM (2011), 45–54.

Setting the Stage for Interaction: A Tablet Application to Augment Group Discussion in a Seminar Class

Drew Harry
MIT Media Lab
Cambridge, MA 02139
dharry@media.mit.edu

Eric Gordon
Emerson College
Boston, MA 02116
eric_gordon@emerson.edu

Chris Schmandt
MIT Media Lab
Cambridge, MA 02139
geek@media.mit.edu

ABSTRACT
We present a tablet-based system to collaboratively track discussion topics and ideas in a seminar-style discussion classroom. Each student uses his or her own tablet to share text ideas in a synchronized, visual environment. The system is designed to promote diverse participation and increase engagement. Our findings are based on observations of twelve class sessions and interviews with participating students. Instead of simply introducing an additional text-based communication channel into the classroom, we find that the system creates a new "stage" (in the Goffman sense) on which students could perform in ways that the main spoken stage could not support. This stage coexists with spoken communication, and augments how students attend to the material and each other. We conclude that spoken participation alone poses barriers for some participants and the addition of a non-oral, text-based stage can help establish equitable and engaging discussions in the class.

Author Keywords
Computer mediated communication, backchannel, tablet, small group discussion, education

ACM Classification Keywords
H.5.3 Information Interfaces and Presentation: Group and Organization Interfaces

[Synchronous Interaction]

General Terms
Design; Theory; Experimentation

INTRODUCTION
The physically co-located small group discussion is often viewed as the gold standard for effective collaboration and communication. It can provide a space for participants to voice their opinions and can readily lead to deliberation and collective problem solving [4]. Not surprisingly, it is often the case that designers seek to virtually reproduce the characteristics and norms of the small group discussion in technologically mediated communication media. Hollan and Stornetta [12] provide a valuable counterpoint to this approach arguing against viewing experiences mediated by the "physically proximate" reality as necessarily superior to those mediated by technology. We have adopted the following challenge: instead of assuming that the small group discussion is good enough and the only appropriate design consideration is its preservation and replication, we seek to appropriately apply the unique properties of a technological system to the established affordances of a small group discussion. We would not deny that face-to-face interaction offers many substantial benefits when compared to interactions mediated by, for instance, a video conferencing system; nevertheless, we argue that there is room to improve the physically proximate small group discussion by intervening in the assumed normal frameworks of turn-taking and attention.

In this paper, we describe the design and enacted use of a tablet-based system for a discussion-based graduate seminar. Although this is not a common educational venue for intervention (lecture classes are a more traditional venue, e.g. [13] or [1]), it is one in which we identified a number of potential problems with pure face-to-face discussions that a tablet-based system might effectively address. We had two major goals for this work: first, create a class discussion context that encouraged more diverse participation in class; and second, to help students feel engaged and connected to the learning environment.

To meet these goals, we sought to expand notions of legitimate participation beyond speaking, using the affordances of a text-based communication system. Our system creates an alternate communication space within the learning environment. Typically, in group communication contexts, spoken participation is viewed as the primary or dominant interaction medium, one that is often the target of modification as in, for example, *Second Messenger*[6] or *Meeting Mediator*[16]. Like the *Cognoter*[23] system, our system placed emphasis on the combinatory possibilities of text-based and verbal participation in a co-located group communication environment. Unlike *Cognoter*, however, we focus on enhancing the performative space of group interaction. Consequently, our goal was not to create alternate communication channels; instead, it was to expand the space of performance. As part of this conceptual shift, we argue for moving from the metaphor of a "front", spoken channel and a "back" channel to the metaphor of a "main" performance stage and "side" performance stage.

CSCW'12, February 11–15, 2012, Seattle, Washington, USA.

This study seeks to understand how having simultaneously accessible stages in the context of a group discussion affects the methods and outcomes of participant engagement. We start by describing how our system, called *Tin Can*, is related to existing systems that similarly augment face-to-face communication. We introduce the idea of *stages* and contrast it to previous models of *channels*. We then describe in detail the critical design elements of the *Tin Can* application and the class context in which it was implemented. Then, we present the results of the study, based on class observations, process traces, and interviews. In our discussion, we return to the concept of stages and describe how this formulation of participation can be productive for thinking through how people can interact with additional stages introduced into the dominant context of face-to-face communication. Finally, we discuss some specific insights about the the tablet as a platform and describe the extent to which the design met our initial goals and how our results compare to those from past findings in the literature.

RELATED WORK

There is a rich field of research on the topic of augmenting co-present group communication with socio-technical systems. One significant area of investigation concerns how systems can "level the playing field" of face-to-face communication through reflecting information about a group's behavior back on itself. Karahalios and Bergstrom [14] refer to this as a "social mirror"; a real-time visualization of social dynamics that is shared by the whole group and can cause changes in group dynamics. They suggest that "social mirrors become another channel for interaction (or a back channel) and, in the process, become a signal that influences interaction." Their exemplar social mirrors measure behavior in an audio channel and visualize different aspects of it on on shared Displays. This strategy is shared by *Second Messenger*[6] and *Meeting Mediator*[16]. In these systems, presenting real-time participation visualizations tended to close the gap between over-participating group members and under-participating members, although in most cases this effect was primarily from over-participating members decreasing their participation. This work demonstrates how visualizing main stage spoken participation in different ways can impact relative participation rates by encouraging individuals to censor or otherwise alter the nature of their communication to correspond with perceived group norms and group behavior.

Another strain of this work is less interested in altering the verbal channel of group communication, and more focused on creating separate, productive backchannels. There are a variety of contexts where people have added communication channels. Yardi describes how a chat-based backchannel operates over a semester in a class [26], McCarthy et al. describe a similar approach at a conference [18]. This early work focuses on characterizing the kinds of use that occur in backchannels using existing systems like chat, but do not engage specifically with design issues in backchannels. Harry et al. [11] propose a new design for projecting question-oriented backchannels in panel presentations. Yankelovich et al. [25] discuss verbal backchannels during verbal meetings, and the "social translucence" research stream (*Rendezvous* [15] is most closely related to this work) explores the design of systems to represent engagement in different kinds of mediated social situations.

Tin Can is designed specifically for use in a class, and is thus influenced by the systems designed for this specific context. Like much of the backchannel work described above these systems are typically concerned with creating new channels for communication in, for example, a large lecture hall. Bergstrom's lecture class system [1] supports question-asking and commenting and Kam et al's [13] *Livenotes* supports taking shared notes on lecture presentation slides. The *ActiveClass* project [21] creates a channel between students and instructors for asking anonymous questions during a lecture from PDAs. Each of these systems seeks to increase participation in very large group settings by establishing separate channels for participation. Work in this space is typically not focused on directly influencing spoken participation because the expectation is that there is none; the lecturer is (except for question-asking) the only legitimate participant.

In *Tin Can*, we take a different approach. We seek to expand the stage of participation by diversifying the sites of performance. In other words, we are not interested in creating better oral or better text-based channels; instead, through their correspondence, we seek to create a rich environment for participation composed of multiple, simultaneous stages. Perhaps the earliest research to explore this sort of approach is Tatar et al.'s [23] work on *Cognoter*. They pointed to some interesting problems with creating stages, namely the limits of the "parcel-post" model of communication—where a message is sent and subsequently received and interpreted. Although this model works well for written correspondence, they found that within *Cognoter*, because the written contributions were designed to be interspersed with verbal dialogue, it was difficult for users to understand them "within the time frame of the actual communication" unless the verbal conversation paused while written contributions were processed. In other words, in actual practice, users resorted to channel switching in order to accommodate the written or the verbal modes. Another example is the *Thoughtswap*[5] project which takes a much more structured approach by interspersing periods of engagement with the system with freeform discussion. In *Tin Can*, we employed a similar model of written communication to *Cognoter* and *Thoughtswap*, but we found that we were able to successfully create simultaneous stages for participation instead of stages one at a time. We will discuss the reasons for this disparity at more length in the conclusions. Work in this space on how alternate communication channels are selected and used owes a clear debt to Ochsman and Chapanis's [20] early work on mediated collaboration.

SETTING THE STAGE

Platforms for discussion and commenting that are outside official discourse channels have widely been referred to as "backchannels." Backchannels, traditionally defined, create a space where audience members to some "front channel" can share information with each other, typically about the content of the front channel. Audience members can alternate their attention between the two channels but are only legitimate participants in the backchannel. Presenters, on the other hand, often have a very hard time staying aware of backchannel content if they are aware of it at all, which gives it its outsider flavor that can lead to snarky and disrespectful content [3]. In this configuration, the front/back channel distinction is a useful one because in a very practical sense the backchannel is usually somewhat covert or hidden and participants in the backchannel rarely have the ability or opportunity to communicate on the front channel.

Although this front/back channel metaphor works in situations where audience members have no access to the front channel, it is less effective in situations where the backchannel is intended to influence the front channel. As discussed in the related work, much recent work is focused on bridging these front and back spaces and we argue that a new metaphor is useful for understanding how these parallel communication spaces interact. We turn to Erving Goffman[9] for his description of *stages* to illuminate this new sort of situation. He uses the example of a waiter behaving politely with a problematic customer and then walking into the kitchen and complaining to the cook about the customer's difficult behavior. Each interaction is performative and represents the waiters' competence at performing his role appropriately for different audiences in a different setting. In the waiter example, these audiences are disjointed, and the door into the kitchen represents a gateway between the "front" performance space with customers and the "back" performance space among restaurant staff. The notion of stages shifts our attention from spaces where a small number of people can broadcast information to many recipients (like a lecture hall or conference) and instead focuses on negotiated sites of performance like the restaurant dining room and kitchen, where people can perform different aspects of their identity for different audiences.

A stages metaphor also more actively recognizes the way that audiences to a performance are themselves constantly performing in small ways, while a channel metaphor limits the audience to simply receiving a broadcast. For example, in a class, students learn what it looks like to be attentive to a teacher's performances and what it sounds and looks like to be engaged. In a large lecture hall, the nature of the individual performance is not that precise. If there is an open laptop policy, students might be checking their email or Facebook, or engaging in an official backchannel. They are able to, as Goffman says, "get away with going away," because the act of *going away* is an expected part of the front stage performance. But in a seminar environment, attentiveness and participation are more scrutinized because of the size and nature of the group. This suggests that integrating new communication technology into groups of smaller size might be more challenging because *going away* is more difficult to politely incorporate into the front stage performance.

The traditional response to this has been an acceptance of the quality and sufficiency of the front stage in small groups and to eschew the addition of other communication channels because they might be distracting. A seminar class already adheres to the gold standard of face-to-face communication. It is often assumed that the pressures of the performance are

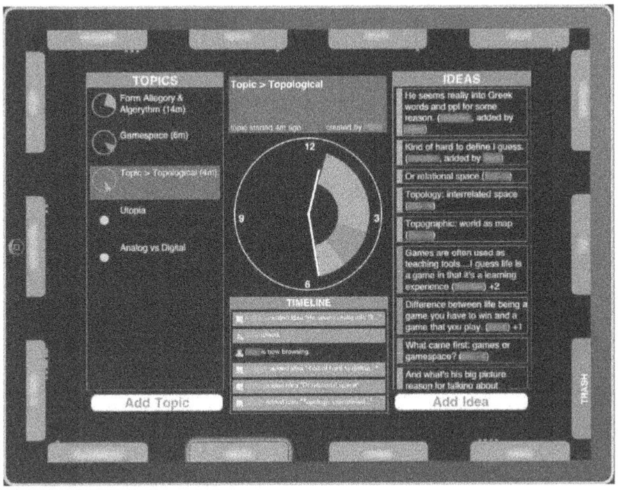

Figure 1. A screenshot of the *Tin Can* interface running on a tablet.

exactly what we want them to be—students talk and the professor evaluates. But there are two faulty assumptions here. The first is that engagement in a co-present discussion can be manifested only in established methods of performance, e.g. speech. And the second is that all students are equally capable of convincing performances. Social psychology research suggests that introverts rely more heavily on written communication to express themselves [22] [24]. But when there is only one legitimate kind of performance in a class, when there is only one way to perform on the front stage, the structure of the learning environment may not be as equitable as it could be, and it may not even be as productive as possible, even for extroverts.

Consequently, when designing for the seminar, we sought to intervene in the established norms of the front stage by adding a well-crafted additional stage. The goal was to create a context for the legitimate performance of the back stage without having to *go away* from the front stage. As such, we move away from the front/back distinction, preferring the notion of a main stage with a side stage. We sought to design a system where performers could be on both stages at once, where performances were simultaneous, not alternating. Furthermore, the front and back stage as Goffman uses it implies different audiences for front and back performances. Moving to main and side stages reinforces the shared audience of the two stages, which has a big influence on how people perform on each stage and makes it easier to integrate those performances in a meaningful way. We use the terms main stage (face-to-face, spoken conversation) and side stage (text input) to explain the context of performance created as a result of using *Tin Can*.

SYSTEM DESIGN

Tin Can is a tablet-based application to support class discussions. It provides a synchronous environment shared by the students and teacher. Each user has his or her own device and are physically co-located. Students arranged their tablet in different ways. Some kept them on their laps, some on the table in front of them. All users (including the professor and

Figure 2. The classroom environment. The student at the head of the table is presenting and controlling the projector. The professor is to the presenter's right.

researcher) had the same capabilities in the system. The system serves as a visualization of the current state of the group discussion. It focuses on three main parts of a class's process: topics, time, and ideas. Figure 1 shows the interface in action.[1]

Topics

The topics pane in the UI collects past, current, and potential future discussion topics. These topics can be added using the "Add Topic" button at the bottom of the pane. The current topic is highlighted in a topic-specific color. All topics have a short text description. Past and current topics show a kind of clock pie chart, illustrating the start and end times of a discussion topic (or the current time in the case of ongoing topics). The total duration in minutes of past and current topics is also shown as part of the topic text. Topics can be tapped to bring up an interface for changing their state: starting future topics, stopping current topics, and restarting past topics.

Time

The clock in the center of the screen serves as a reminder both of the current time as well as a concise visual representation of the history of discussion topics covered in the class. The time spent on each topic is swept out radially on the clock such that large blocks of color represent topics that occupied a longer period of the class. When an hour of time has passed, the central area in the clock is cleared and the colored record of the previous hour appears at the edge of the clock. Up to four hours can be easily represented in this way. The clock is non-interactive.

Ideas

The ideas pane contains a time-sorted list of ideas. An idea is simply a text contribution. Although we had presumptions about what would be posted here (as indicated by the terminology we used in the interface). Ideas evolved to include statements, questions, recording main stage discussion themes, and a simple Twitter-like reply syntax. When entering an idea, the author of the idea could do one of two things: "add idea" or "add idea to group." The former option would store the idea in the user's "personal" idea drawer. The latter option would immediately put the idea at the top of the group idea timeline, as well as adding it to their personal drawer. Users can tap and hold to "like" an idea. The idea will flash and get a "+X" notation in its text, where X is the number of likes that the idea has received. Ideas in the group timeline have their author's name displayed in parentheses after the text of the idea. Ideas are colored based to match the color of the current topic.

[1]A video of the interface and the classroom context is available at `http://www.youtube.com/watch?v=ztVllLuCcTM`

Users

Each user logged in to the system is displayed on a tab around the edge of the screen. The arrangement is essentially random. Tapping a user extends that user's idea drawer. This drawer contains all ideas created by the user, whether shared or not. These ideas are differentiated in the list by "(shared)" being appended to ideas that have been shared. Any unshared idea in the idea drawer can be dragged from the drawer to the group idea area, even if the user didn't originally author the idea. Ideas dragged by other people are attributed differently in the main timeline. For example, an idea created by Alice and shared by Bob would say "(Alice, shared by Bob)". By design, personal folders are not private. They are semi-public spaces meant to give users some choice in how their contributions are read by the group.

Archive

All ideas and topics are recorded on the server. At the end of each class session, the server emails everyone who attended the class with a list of their personal ideas and a link to a shared Web page that had a list of all student ideas sorted by topic and by user.

RESEARCH CONTEXT AND METHODS

We deployed the *Tin Can* system in two sections of a graduate seminar on media and social theory taught by one of the authors at a liberal arts college. One section met in the morning, the other in the afternoon, twice a week. Class assignments were reading-based. Each discussion class was usually lead by a student or pair of students. While what it meant to lead class changed somewhat over the course of the study, the pre-study norm was to prepare a slideshow and accompanying media (images and video were quite common) and present it to the class. The morning session had eight regular students and the afternoon session had eleven regular students. In total, thirteen students were male, six were female. There were five non-native English speakers in both classes.

Our study lasted for six weeks and utilized mixed methods, including classroom observations, capture of text inputs, and semi-structured interviews.

Throughout the deployment, user interactions were captured. This did not, notably, include live recording of class audio, only text-based interactions with the *Tin Can* system itself. We made the decision not to record audio because we felt that this would make students self-conscious and would be too disruptive to main stage interactions. In lieu of audio recordings, for most class sessions, a researcher other than the professor was present to observe the class. We employed a form of direct observation known as continuous monitoring, where the researcher documented everything he saw throughout the study period, including the description of the environment and participant actions, as well as inferences about their meaning [19]. The researcher's observations were not prescribed before the study, because of the exploratory nature of this first deployment. We did not know what to expect, so the observations were designed to be generative and not conclusive. We documented patterns of student attentiveness to peers and professor; interactions with tablets (i.e. position of tablets on the table or in laps); and correlations between speaking and writing. The students were aware that their use of *Tin Can* was being studied and they were aware of the presence of the researcher. Because the students were invested in the use of *Tin Can*, the presence of the researcher was not disruptive, but instead added to the excitement they had about testing a new system. The field notes were recorded by hand and subsequently transcribed and shared with the teaching researcher.

All text inputs into *Tin Can* were recorded over 22 hours of usage across twelve class sessions. Each class was about two hours long, but classes often had a non-discussion logistical content from the professor at the beginning of sessions. The average *Tin Can* session was 105 minutes long. After the deployment, the inputs were categorized into types, including topics and ideas, shared and non-shared.

Finally, at the conclusion of the discussion-based component of the class, the researchers conducted semi-structured individual interviews with fifteen of the nineteen students (79%). Interviews were conducted by the non-teaching researcher to alleviate student concerns about sharing judgements about the teaching researcher, although there were no sections of any of the interviews that students did not want to be shared with the teaching researcher. All interviews were recorded and transcribed and entered into *Dedoose*, a qualitative analysis tool. Because we view this work as generative, we iteratively coded the transcribed interviews, letting themes (and codes) arise organically as we reviewed the interview data, observational data, and process traces from the class. This strategy closely resembles Glaser and Strauss' [8] grounded theory approach. All names mentioned in interviews or shown in screenshots have been obscured or changed to pseudonyms to protect the identities of those participating in the research.

PROCESS TRACES

Over the course of the deployment of *Tin Can*, 839 ideas and 119 topics were created. The majority of ideas created were shared: 72% of ideas were shared on creation. Another 5% were private ideas that were turned into public ideas by being dragged by another user from a users' personal idea drawer to the public idea area. The balance, 23% of ideas, were never shared. The distribution of these different idea types on a per participant basis can be found in figure 3.

Over the course of the study, 119 topics were created in total. Of these, 79 were actually discussed and the remainder were raised as potential topics but never actually used. The average class had 6.5 started topics, with a standard deviation of 2.3. Topic duration had a much wider variation: the average topic lasted 851 seconds with a deviation of 673 seconds. This is skewed largely because of very short topics.

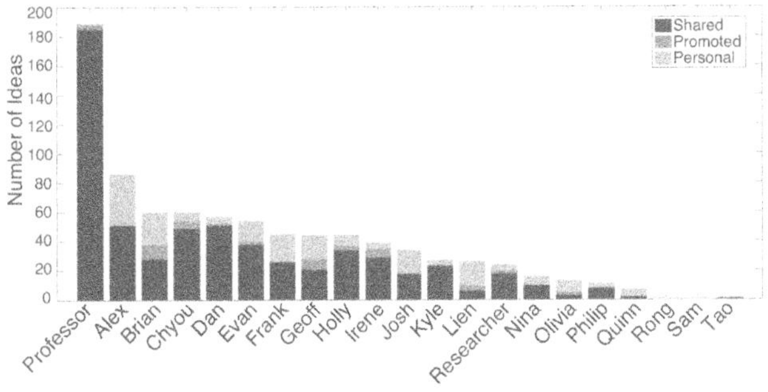

Figure 3. Distribution of ideas per participant per idea type: personal, promoted, and shared.

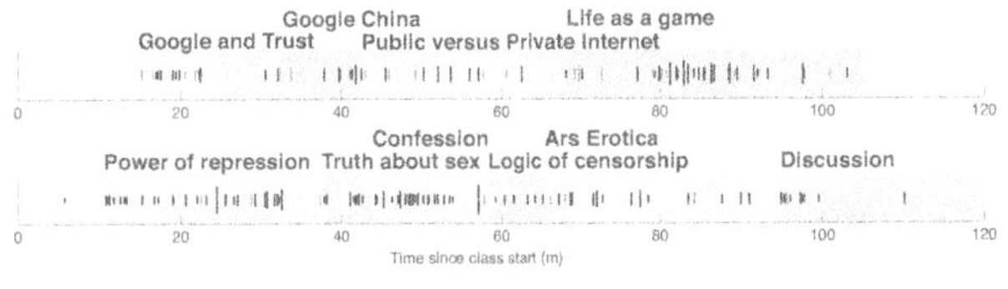

Figure 4. Timeline of topics and ideas posted in two example class sessions. Ideas posted by students are in black, ideas from the professor are in red. The height of the line indicates the length (in characters) of the idea. Topic names are shown above their corresponding section of the class.

A deep analysis of temporal patterns within the data is beyond the scope of this paper, but to provide a rough sense of what topic and idea posting activity looked like we have provided two example timelines in figure 4. The most striking thing about the data from this perspective is that the temporal distribution is very uneven. In Kleinberg's terms, we see a bursty structure [17] in idea posting. This is a common structure in communication systems and it is no surprise that it appeared in our study results.

DISCUSSION

Much of the existing literature on backchannels focuses on situations in which the audience has one stage to perform on and the presenter has a separate one. [26] [18] *Tin Can*'s symmetry, where anyone can use either stage at any time, is the focus of our analysis. In this section, we use the stages metaphor introduced earlier to describe how students managed their attention to stages. Then, we discuss how students made decisions about when and how to perform on the available stages.

Attention

Attention, for our purposes, is best understood not as an innate characteristic of someone's behavior, but as a value-laden socially situated performative behavior. "We are always to a certain extent in a state of distraction," according to sociologist Emile Durkheim. [7] Every situation is composed of stimuli that disrupts some fictional conception of undivided attention. Likewise, every situation requires some aspect of performance, as individuals are required to communicate their attentiveness in response to specific social contexts. In a lecture, attentiveness is typically demonstrated by looking at the presenter and potentially taking notes. In a small group discussion, attentiveness might be expanded to include looking through class reading material or looking at other people.

Traditional approaches to managing attention in education tend to take as their starting point the desire to maximize audience attention on the presenter through the physical architecture of lecture spaces, presentation media, and rhetorical strategies. Gordon and Bogen [10] argue that attention and distraction are best understood as being "hand-in-hand. The very same new technologies and landscapes that cultivate a state of distraction are themselves directed simultaneously toward the cultivation of attention." Educators tend to look to technology (broadly construed) to help manage overwhelming sensory inputs while simultaneously blaming the lack of attention of students on that same technology.

Of course, it is not simply a definitional matter to decide what constitutes attention in a class using *Tin Can*. To understand how students and professor understood attention in this context we can look to how they talked about attention and distraction. Students predominantly viewed participation as obligatory. Speaking to his motivation to use *Tin Can*, one student said "to be part of the class I had to use it." Students were never admonished for interacting with tablets, and didn't report feeling like they needed to minimize their performance on the side stage to avoid negative perceptions of themselves by the professor or others, except to the extent that students felt like over-participation on either stage might crowd out other students. A student who was particularly active on the side stage worried that "I take so much space that people that are shy...have more problems ... standing up when they have personal ideas [to share]."

To the extent that students were concerned with attention, the most common problem was not being viewed as inattentive, but struggling to track performances on both stages simultaneously. Although students were not concerned with annoying the professor, they were worried about offending their peers who were presenting that day: "It is a little tough to keep your attention on both [stages], and sometimes you get a running conversation on *Tin Can*, which can be interesting but it is maybe a little unfair to the presenter." Although this perspective represents a pull towards enacting traditional models of attention, it wasn't enough to significantly diminish involvement (either as a performer or an audience member) on the side stage. Student presenters often used *Tin Can* as a way to gauge interest in future discussion topics and to decide on whom to call.

In resolving the conflict between compelling simultaneous performances, students could fall back on the persistence of performances on the side stage. In making a choice to attend to the main stage, they could, in Josh's words, "have a comfort that you're not going to miss anything because you can always go back and see other people's posts whenever." Still, there seemed to be a difference between browsing posts later and being part of the live conversation. This came up most frequently when students expressed frustration with text entry on the tablet and missing the right moment to post something: "I didn't get it out as fast as I'd hoped and it was already passed and it wasn't worth typing it anymore."

Deciding between stages was really only a problem when both stages were compelling. If only the main stage was compelling, students could freely attend to that. The reverse was also common, and students frequently reported attending to the side stage as an escape from an un-engaging main stage, as in this quote from Quinn:

> "I can remember a particular ... presentation that he was doing a lot of PowerPoint, I think he was completely oblivious to the *Tin Can* conversation and [the *Tin Can* conversation] ended up going in a very good direction ... as a result, I do not remember anything he said, because ... the conversation on *Tin Can* was a little more engaging"

Moments like this highlight the extent to which our characterization of stages as "main" and "side" is itself a product of attention. The presence of a system like *Tin Can* does not automatically create a side stage, nor does the ability for spoken communication guarantee that such communication will create a main stage. The addition of a mediated communication platform simply creates the *possibility* of a new stage. Whether or not it becomes a viable stage, and whether the mediated stage is a main stage or a side stage is all the result of people's attention to the system. Furthermore, the designation "main" or "side" is not fixed. The situation Quinn describes is a moment where the main stage ceased, for a little while, to command people's attention and *Tin Can* took on some main stage properties. Although such moments were rare, they point out how stages are not created by technology or decree: they are designated and sustain by the collective attention of people using them.

The professor's high level of activity on *Tin Can* throughout the class can be seen as playing a role in setting the main/side distinctions. His activity was a way of giving students permission to take the side stage seriously, both because it was clear that he was going to notice contributions from students, but also because he was frequently entering ideas himself and not looking at the current speaker. This underlines the extent to which this was an ideal context for testing a system like *Tin Can*. Had we deployed in a class where the professor was neutral or hostile to people attending to *Tin Can*, traditional class expectations of attention would more likely have been practiced by students, reinforcing those norms and making a side stage much less viable.

There was a moment towards the end of our study when the professor brought in a colleague over video chat to discuss his work and answer questions from the class. The remote presenter had a very limited view of the room from the professor's laptop video camera and could see only a few students. Although the *Tin Can* system was available for this section of the class, it went almost entirely unused. This may simply be because the activity on the main stage was engrossing, but the total lack of side stage performance was still well outside of the bounds of normal disuse during a particularly engaging presentation in class. This suggests to us that the students were concerned with enacting the traditional model of attention for this outsider to the class. He could have viewed intense tablet use (something that was normal and viewed as attentive during normal class sessions) as inattentive or disrespectful and so his presence (even though his view of the classroom was quite limited) triggered a reversion to the more restrictive expectations of attention in a traditional class context.

Performance

The presence of an additional participation stage complicates the experience of being a member of the class. When should you submit an idea on the tablet rather than say it out loud? When is the right time to say something? Should you share an idea or make it a personal idea? The enacted (and self-reported) answers to these questions can provide some insight into the experience of using the system as well as deepen our understanding of the stages metaphor. In many cases, students viewed the side stage as complementing the main stage and valued its presence in situations where a range of problems with the main stage impeded their participation. In this way, *Tin Can* acted as a kind of escape valve: when the main stage was working for people, they used it; when they felt like they could not use it or did not want to use it, they turned to the side stage and valued its complementary affordances.

Performance on the main stage was widely viewed as more challenging and having higher stakes than side stage performance. Among the students who were reluctant oral participants in class, this was particularly acute. Geoff, a very rare oral participant in class before *Tin Can*, was particularly frank on this point: "I don't really talk a lot in class because I'm scared of sounding stupid." Geoff was a more frequent side stage participant. Although he would still rarely speak up directly in class, he was often called on by others in class to speak about ideas he had posted on *Tin Can*; he would happily speak in those instances. This change in behavior on his part was frequently brought up by other students as being a major benefit of using *Tin Can* because they valued the opportunity to hear and see what he was thinking. Irene, a more talkative student, characterized Geoff as a member of a "good chunk of people who I think are thinkers and they would just think and write down what they were thinking" as opposed to speaking on the main stage. This feeling was common among people who were comfortable on the main stage, who acknowledged that "not everyone feels comfortable speaking in class, so I think [*Tin Can*] definitely allowed for certain ideas to be shared that probably would have been either suppressed or just ignored or forgotten."

Students' comfort with the different properties of the main stage and side stage influenced which stage they chose for a performance. Students for whom English was a native language were more comfortable in spoken conversation, and when faced with complex ideas preferred to express them orally, turning to *Tin Can* to express simpler ideas because typing complex ideas was slow. Students who did not speak English natively had the reverse logic, preferring to type complicated ideas so they could, according to Rong, "organize my language a lot before I actually talk because I want my thoughts to be systematical and clear, I want people to get it." In both groups, though, students viewed the revisability of written contributions as a potential benefit: "[*Tin Can*] gave me the advantage of thinking it through in a writing sense a little bit before I vocalized the idea."

A lack of confidence about one's performances was not the only reason to choose the side stage over the main stage. Students had a clear sense of etiquette surrounding when they could participate on the main stage and in what ways. Because only one person could be talking at once and conversations were fundamentally linear, students often felt like speaking up themselves would be changing the flow of the conversation in an inappropriate way. Instead, students would prefer to write their comments on the side stage instead of "interrupting" on the main stage. This was intertwined with ideas of timeliness. Performances seen as being closely related to the current main stage conversation were more appropriate than performances that might drag the conversation in a significantly different direction. Although similar, these concerns are not precisely the same. The worry about interruption was primarily a desire to not unduly influence the path of the conversation because that was perceived by some students as the role of the professor or presenter, not the role of the individual student. In contrast, ideas that were seen as "not quite as relevant [and not] really [fitting] into the conversation" were not really valid performances on the main stage at all because not only would they move the conversation significantly, they did not necessarily have anything to do with the existing main stage conversation.

Both of these worries, though, led to the same thing: increased use of the side stage. Because turn-taking was not a concern on the side stage, it easily supported ideas going in different directions simultaneously. To the extent that those directions were interesting to other people, they could serve as the basis for future ideas. If they were not, it was not seen as problematic to have put them there in the first place. When an idea did not seem to lead to any future ideas, students "didn't think anything of it. Not all ideas are great."

Sharing and Promotion

Key to our argument about stages is moving from a model where we view people as "tuning in" to a single channel to one where we recognize that computer-mediated communication systems offer new simultaneous stages on which we can perform and be observed. It is critical, then, that we describe how performances shifted between stages, influencing what students said and how they said it. One common pattern was the positive reception to ideas on the side stage encouraging those ideas to be performed on the main stage. This same process happened even within *Tin Can*, when personal ideas were dragged by someone (usually the professor; 57% of ideas promoted from personal to shared were promoted by the professor) to the public idea timeline. Students also viewed "likes" and replies as good indicators of interest in their ideas. Geoff, the quiet student discussed earlier, captured the impact of these promotions nicely: "At first I started just putting them in my box [i.e. making them personal ideas] without even sharing with the class. Then I saw that [the professor] started dragging them out and putting them in discussions so afterwards I was more open to sharing my ideas within the class discussion."

Activity on the side stage was sometimes explicitly moved onto the main stage. In most cases, the professor or student presenter called on someone based on something they had said on *Tin Can* and asked them to re-perform the idea on the main stage. The professor might say, for instance "Olivia, you had a nice point here on *Tin Can*, do you want to expand on it?" and Olivia could elect to take a speaking turn (and nearly always did). The other common strategy was for a speaker (particularly a student presenter) to use an idea recorded on the side stage as a starting point for a comment of their own or to introduce a topic known to be of interest to students based on side stage activity. Promotion moves by the professor were valued over those by other students, but both were appreciated and clearly remembered by students.

In the stages framing, we can understand note-taking as moving performances from the main (verbal) stage to the side (text) stage. For example, these were ideas entered into *Tin Can*: "Play is no longer having fun, it is work", "Question of self-efficacy in public sector" or "Consumption leads to feeling good about yourself." When posted by students, ideas of this form were frequently attempts to move the discussion, but when they were posted by the professor they were seen as records of the main stage. Students characterized the professor's role in this process as "the note taker person so if ... the presenter said something [the professor] would summarize what they just said." This was seen as a valuable contribution by the students that showed interest in reviewing the archives after class: "I liked the way [the professor] used it. Because that also meant that I didn't need to take notes ... because he posted it in *Tin Can* and I could get access to that later."

As is evident from figure 3, the professor was a significant outlier in terms of his performance on *Tin Can* and his participation clearly had a big impact on how students understood and used the tool. Beyond his role as a note-taker, students also viewed his performances as oriented towards trying to guide the main stage conversation in particular ways. Students characterized this use pattern as, variously, "guiding", "influencing", or "driving." He was particularly interested in "[initiating] conversation", primarily by posting thought-provoking questions like "Why do we feel responsible for a corp's feelings?" or "What is the role of god in modernism?" Most students avoided starting or stopping topics (or proposing them at all), arguing that it was the professor's job to do that, although some students took more active roles in administrating topics when they were in the presentation role. In total, 53% of topic-related state changes were done by the professor.

On the main stage, the professor was also a frequent promoter of side stage activity. Sam characterized the professor's role in a particularly evocative way:

> "I feel like [the professor] would be a speaker for people who couldn't speak, you know. The fact that he was really into *Tin Can*, so he would read something that [a student] had written and be like oh, I want to quote this or talk about it and [act] as a spokesman for people who aren't really comfortable speaking"

This underlines the professor's role as a bidirectional bridge between the stages. By taking notes on main stage performances, he reenforced *Tin Can*'s note-taking role. By speaking out about side stage performances and drawing people into the discussion based on written ideas, he legitimated their side stage performances. It is very hard to imagine *Tin Can* being as well integrated into the class as it was without the extensive involvement of the professor. This does not, in our minds, diminish the contributions of this work. Although we cannot speak to how a skeptical teacher might react to the system, having a fertile classroom situation gives us an opportunity to make important insights into the potential for this design space that we might not have otherwise been able to access.

Hardware

While one could easily imagine *Tin Can* working on a laptop, its deployment on tablets substantially affected use and outcomes in a variety of ways. First, there is a simple visual benefit to using tablets. Unlike laptops, which can create strong visual boundaries between people, tablets lie flat (or nearly flat) on the table or in people's laps. When organized around a rectangular seminar table, tablets do not disrupt sight lines between people. In general, laptops give people something to hide behind while tablets more strongly signal availability.

Accordingly, tablets offer less privacy than laptops. Participants can easily see when other participants are using the system, and typing is easily distinguishable from browsing other people's ideas. Surprisingly, we frequently saw students looking at other students' tablets while they interacted with them, even though everyone's view of the space was the same. Students seemed to be interested in knowing how other people were using the system.

Because of the way the tablet program was administrated at the school, students did not have any particular ownership over a specific tablet. This inhibited any sense of ownership; students talked about the tablets as being essentially disposable, e.g. "sometimes the [tablet] would run out of battery and kick you off and you'd have to get a new one." The benefit of this lack of ownership was that it limited the tablets' non-*Tin Can* uses. Unlike a laptop, on which the Web and communication tools were a click away, the tablets were not personalized. Even using Web tools was tedious, because they had to log in to each one which was both slow and obvious to people around them.

The biggest challenge with tablets is data entry. The most frequent complaint about the system was how slow and difficult they found accurate text entry to be. Students complained about slow typing speed making it hard to post timely ideas ("I didn't get [an idea] out as fast as I'd hoped and it was already passed and it wasn't worth typing it anymore") and distracting them from the main stage ("it takes time to type on the [tablet] and so probably it takes you away from the presentation sometimes"). We also saw a number of ideas correcting typos and autocorrect mistakes in previous ideas. These problems mitigate the system's utility as a conversational stage and seemed to depress overall use.

CONCLUSIONS

In deploying *Tin Can*, we had two major goals: increase the diversity of participation and increase engagement. We feel that we were successful in each of these goals.

When judging participation, we consider activity on each stage. In terms of the main stage, we saw some evidence that people who might not have spoken up in class were prompted to speak by *Tin Can*. Most often, this came from the promotion processes described earlier. This moderately increased the diversity of participation on the main stage. Side stage participation was viewed by both students and teacher as a legitimate way to be a class participant, and we saw much broader participation in *Tin Can* than we saw on the main stage. The distribution of side stage participation was relatively flat, setting aside the professor, especially when compared to the steep power law reported in a chat backchannel[26]. Based on our discussion of how and when students chose to participate, it is clear that the distinct affordances of the main stage and side stage meant that each captured kinds of participation that would not have been effective on the other. It is not the case that adding *Tin Can* detracted from the main stage and that there is a simple conservation of participation across all formats; we saw a more subtle case in which having a communication outlet with different properties drew out contributions that otherwise would not have happened at all.

This system was consciously designed for students who were less likely to participate verbally in class. We were surprised at the extent to which attitudes about the system aligned along active oral participant / reluctant oral participant lines. Active oral participants tended to be indifferent about how *Tin Can* affected their personal participation in class. However, they acknowledged its effect on less active participants. Members of this group almost always commented on the increased diversity of involvement that *Tin Can* promoted, with observations like: "it tends to be a certain group of people who would talk and a certain group of people who were thinking but not talking. So I would like to see what they were up to." Philip, an active oral participant with essentially zero *Tin Can* participation noted of reluctant oral participants "maybe [reluctant participants] would have something to say but maybe there's like some sort of reluctance to actually to speak the thing aloud. So it gave another sort of channel to express ideas." Knowing that reluctant participants had a place to participate made active participants feel less guilty about their own participation on the main stage.

Reluctant oral participants broadly relished the opportunity to participate in new ways with which they were more comfortable. Students described the system as "more efficient", it "gave more people a chance to say things that they wouldn't say", and it helped students "feel more connected to the other students." Olivia poignantly described the system as "something that was on my side, so to speak. You know what I mean? ... Like it was a resource."

This dynamic between reluctant and active main stage participants suggests a new view on the findings of DiMicco et al. [6]. They found that although visualizing participation decreased participation among over-participators, it did not boost participation of under-participators. In contrast, we found that although *Tin Can* did not decrease oral participation among active oral participants, it *did* boost oral participation among reluctant participants by letting them try out potential comments in a less intimidating medium and gather support for those ideas before speaking about them to a wider audience. Furthermore, if we include non-spoken participation, reluctant participants increased their participation substantially. This suggests that a lack of participation is not simply an issue of under-participators not finding conversational space to jump in, but can represent low conversational confidence that needs to be specifically addressed to boost participation.

We can also compare this boost in participation to Bergstrom and Karahalios' [2] finding that under-participators on the verbal stage were also under-participators in voting. Our findings suggest that if participation rates are strongly correlated, perhaps the votes do not represent a different stage. This would fit with Tatar et al's [23] findings with *Cognoter*; although *Cognoter* had more communication opportunities than *Conversation Votes*, participation in *Cognoter* nonetheless frequently stalled audio conversation while discussants processed the contribution. Simply providing another communication venue does not necessarily create a stage.

Our findings are also surprising in light of Tatar et al.'s analysis[23] of the "parcel-post" style of communication. Although it would be fair to describe ideas in *Tin Can* as parcel-post, we did not observe any of the breaks in main stage participation resulting from submitted ideas that were observed in *Cognoter*'s use. Students frequently talked about waiting to read ideas when there was down-time on the main stage, something Tatar et al. view as a central problem with the parcel-post model in a face-to-face environment. We suspect that the main difference is group size. At small group sizes (like Bergstrom's table-based work and the *Cognoter* studies) it is quite difficult to maintain separate stages because participation on the side stage is so conspicuous and attracts immediate attention. In Goffman's terms, it is a venue where it is difficult to "get away with going away". At larger group sizes like those we observe in this work, it is difficult to constantly participate on the side stage (either as a reader or a writer), so immediate awareness or consideration of all side stage contributions is simply not feasible. In fact, this lack of obvious immediate attention on each contribution could be a big part of why reluctant participants were more comfortable making side stage contributions.

Based on our study, we conclude that the introduction of a tablet-based system into a seminar classroom can have positive effects on the engagement of students and diversity of their participation without sacraficing the primary mode of interaction: spoken conversation. Unmediated face-to-face group discussions can be high pressure situations. Participating in face-to-face discussions requires participants to perform "live" (performances cannot easily be composed in advance); they also typically come with predetermined notions of etiquette to which one must adhere in order to preserve the integrity of the performance. We wanted to design for this context in order to take advantage of the rich texture of participant attention and performative attributes the seminar setting presents. Our study demonstrated that *Tin Can* gave a voice to students who otherwise were not confident enough to perform on the main stage or who needed to "test out" ideas before sharing them on the main stage. It also demonstrated a need for a new model of thinking about how computer mediated communication systems can work in face-to-face discussion settings. *Stages* are not tied to particular technologies, nor are they predictive of specific behaviors. They are a way of conceiving of modes of communication within situations that are flexible and that emerge from participant performance.

ACKNOWLEDGEMENTS

Many thanks to Wanda Orlikowski, Jon Chambers, and Katrina Panovich for reviewing drafts of this work. Thanks, as well, to the provocative and thoughtful anonymous reviewers who strengthened this work substantially.

REFERENCES

1. T. Bergstrom and A. Harris. Encouraging Initiative in the Classroom with Anonymous Feedback. In *Proceedings of INTERACT*, 2011.
2. T. Bergstrom and K. Karahalios. Vote and Be Heard: Adding Back-Channel Signals to Social Mirrors. In *Proceedings of INTERACT*. INTERACT, 2009.
3. d. boyd. Spectacle at Web2.0 Expo... From My Perspective, Nov. 2009.
4. S. Burkhalter and J. Gastil. A Conceptual Definition and Theoretical Model of Public Deliberation in Small Face—to—Face Groups. *Communication Theory*, 2002.
5. M. Dickey-Kurdziolek, M. Schaefer, D. Tatar, and I. Renga. Lessons from thoughtswap-ing. In *Proceedings of CSCW*, 2010.
6. J. M. DiMicco, K. J. Hollenbach, A. Pandolfo, and W. Bender. The Impact of Increased Awareness While Face-to-Face. *Human-Computer Interaction*, 22, 2007.
7. E. Durkheim. *Sociology and Philosophy*. Free Press, Nov. 1974.
8. B. G. Glaser and A. L. Strauss. *The Discovery of Grounded Theory*. Aldine Transaction, 1967.
9. E. Goffman. *The Presentation of Self in Everyday Life*. Anchor, 1959.
10. E. Gordon and D. Bogen. Designing Choreographies for the "New Economy of Attention". *Digital Humanities Quarterly*, 3(2), Apr. 2009.
11. D. Harry, J. Green, and J. Donath. backchan.nl: Integrating Backchannels in Physical Space. In *Proceedings of CHI*. ACM Press, 2009.
12. J. Hollan and S. Stornetta. Beyond being there. *Proceedings of CHI*, 1992.
13. M. Kam, J. Wang, A. Iles, E. Tse, and J. Chiu. Livenotes. In *Proceedings of CHI*, 2005.
14. K. Karahalios and T. Bergstrom. Social Mirrors as Social Signals: Transforming Audio into Graphics. *IEEE Computer Graphics and Applications*, 29(5), Sept. 2009.
15. W. A. Kellogg, T. Erickson, T. V. Wolf, S. Levy, J. Christensen, J. Sussman, and W. E. Bennett. leveraging digital backchannels to enhance user experience in electronically mediated communication. In *Proceedings of CSCW*. ACM, 2006.
16. T. Kim, A. Chang, L. Holland, and A. S. Pentland. Meeting Mediator: Enhancing Group Collaboration using Sociometric Feedback. In *Proceedings of CSCW*. ACM Press, 2008.
17. J. Kleinberg. Bursty and hierarchical structure in streams. *Data Mining and Knowledge Discovery*, 7(4), 2003.
18. J. F. McCarthy, d. boyd, E. F. Churchill, W. G. Griswold, E. Lawley, and M. Zaner. Digital backchannels in shared physical spaces: attention, intention and contention. In *Proceedings of CSCW*. ACM, 2004.
19. B. M. Montgomery and S. Duck. *Studying interpersonal interaction*. Guilford Press, 1991.
20. R. B. Ochsman and A. Chapanis. The effects of 10 communication modes on the behavior of teams during co-operative problem-solving. *International Journal of Man-Machine Studies*, 1974.
21. M. Ratto, R. Shapiro, and T. Truong. The activeclass project: Experiments in encouraging classroom participation. *Proceedings of CSCL*, 2003.
22. C. Ross, E. S. Orr, M. Sisic, J. M. Arseneault, M. G. Simmering, and R. R. Orr. Personality and motivations associated with Facebook use. *Computers in Human Behavior*, 25(2), Mar. 2009.
23. D. Tatar, G. Foster, and D. Bobrow. Design for conversation: lessons from Cognoter. *International Journal of Man-Machine Studies*, 34(2), Feb. 1991.
24. K. Wilson, S. Fornasier, and K. M. White. Psychological Predictors of Young Adults' Use of Social Networking Sites. *Cyberpsychology, Behavior, and Social Networking*, 13(2), Apr. 2010.
25. N. Yankelovich, J. McGinn, M. Wessler, J. Kaplan, J. Provino, and H. Fox. Private Communications in Public Meetings. In *Proceedings of CHI*. ACM Press, 2005.
26. S. Yardi. The role of the backchannel in collaborative learning environments. In *Proceedings of ICLS*, 2006.

Social Visualization and Negotiation: Effects of Feedback Configuration and Status

Michael Nowak[1], Juho Kim[2], Nam Wook Kim[3], Clifford Nass[1]

[1]Department of Communication
Stanford University
Stanford, CA, USA
{mnowak, nass}@stanford.edu

[2]CSAIL
MIT
Cambridge, MA, USA
juhokim@mit.edu

[3]Samsung Techwin
Republic of Korea
namwkim85@gmail.com

ABSTRACT
We describe a social visualization system that monitors the vocal arousal levels of the participants in a simulated two-party employment negotiation. In a 3x2 factorial experiment (N = 84), we manipulate two variables of interest for social visualization systems: the *feedback configuration* of the system's display (participants receive self feedback vs. partner feedback vs. no feedback) and the *status* of the interactants (high vs. low). Receiving feedback about one's own arousal level has negative consequences for performance in and feelings about the negotiation. Receiving feedback about one's partner's arousal level interacts with status: high-status individuals benefit from the visualization, while low-status individuals do not.

Author Keywords
CSCW, social visualization, negotiation, arousal, feedback systems.

ACM Classification Keywords
H.5.3 Group and Organization Interfaces: Computer-supported cooperative work

General Terms
Human Factors; Experimentation; Theory; Design.

INTRODUCTION
A great deal of human communication relies on the exchange of information through non-linguistic channels [19]. For example, posture can convey engagement [25], physical distance can convey intimacy [12], and unstated group dynamics can shape the course of interactions [26]. For both individuals and groups, these hidden social behaviors often surface involuntarily, leading many to view them as authentic ways to convey information [22].

In recent years, a number of studies have looked at the effects of *social visualizations*, which are systems that monitor such implicitly exchanged social information and make it explicit in real-time interactions. Many of these have focused on representing aspects of group dynamics, particularly balance in participation [3, 9, 10, 16, 17], while other efforts have focused on representing attributes of individuals, most commonly arousal [8, 14, 29].

In general, social visualizations have been designed with the intent of supporting or enhancing communication, but their actual effects on interactions have been mixed. Many studies have reported both positive and negative results: DiMicco et al.'s shared display reduced the over-participation of dominant individuals but may have stunted within-group trust [9]; Leshed et al.'s GroupMeter caused more agreement but less discussion of ideas [17]; Wang et al.'s arousal-based animated chat client was seen as engaging, but some participants were reluctant to share their arousal data with their partners [29].

In addition, some studies have reported social visualization effects that were moderated by individuals' characteristics: Kim et al. found that groups with a dominant member reacted differently from those with no dominant member [16], and both DiMicco et al. [10] and Bergstrom and Karahalios [3] reported that over-participators and under-participators responded to visualizations differently.

Against this complex empirical backdrop, it is difficult to infer much about social visualizations in general. This is due, at least in part, to the fact that most studies have taken what Nass and Mason [21] call a *holistic approach*, which considers the effects of a complex intervention as a whole rather than the effects of an intervention's component dimensions. This approach has allows for clear tests when the intervention and situation of interest are well defined. But the approach is of limited utility for making inferences that extend beyond the specific context under study.

To build a more general body of knowledge, a better alternative is to adopt a *variable-centered approach* [21], in which the goal is to understand the effects not of interventions per se, but of dimensions that span technologies and situations. Some researchers have indeed isolated and manipulated such dimensions within their studies; for example, Leshed et al. [17] and DiMicco et al. [10] varied aspects of the feedback display, and Kim et al. [16] manipulated the collocation of participants. However, the literature as a whole has put little emphasis on developing theories around the fundamental dimensions underlying social visualizations. A principal focus of the present work is to adopt precisely such a variable-centered approach, with the goal of contributing to a broader and more basic understanding of social visualization systems.

Feedback Configuration

The primary variable of interest in this study is *feedback configuration*. This refers to how the visualization is configured with respect to the constellation of interactants – that is, whose behavior is displayed and to whom the display is shown. This represents one of the fundamental design decisions of any social visualization: the experience of using a social visualization is certain to be radically different if, e.g., one sees feedback about oneself versus about one's partner, or if the system shows the visualization to all people in the interaction versus only to some.

Yet no study to date has addressed this as a variable of theoretical concern. This is somewhat surprising given that prior work has been quite divergent in its treatment of this issue. For example, in Iwasaki et al. [14], interactants only saw their partners' behaviors and were unable to tell how they themselves were perceived; in Janssen, et al. [15], only one person per dyad was monitored, while the other person received feedback about the monitored individual; while in a number of studies [8, 9, 10, 16, 17], all interactants saw representations of each other's actions (a configuration that Erickson has set forth as one of six "claims" for how social visualizations should be designed [11]).

Despite these diverse approaches, we are only aware of one report in which the social-visualization configuration was explicitly manipulated. Wang et al. [29] describe two pilot studies in which a chat client visualized participants' arousal levels. In one study, two partners were shown feedback about each other. In a second study, only one partner was monitored, while the other saw that person's feedback. Unfortunately, this manipulation was confounded by a change in situation (from a conversation between peers to a teacher/student tutorial), and the number of participants (four dyads total) was too small to make broader inferences.

For the present study, we focus on three configurations of a social visualization in a dyadic interaction: feedback about oneself, feedback about one's partner, and no feedback. In all three conditions, both interactants were given the same type of feedback; that is, both interactants saw feedback about themselves, saw feedback about each other, or saw no feedback at all. We kept the configuration symmetric within dyads so as to avoid conferring different status levels on the interactants through differential access to the visualization – a particularly important consideration given that we also manipulated status in the experiment (discussed below).

It is relatively simple to imagine how having feedback about either oneself or one's partner might improve one's experience in an interaction. In both cases, individuals have more information about the emotional content of the interaction, which can aid in managing self-presentation (in the self-feedback case) or in establishing rapport (in the partner-feedback case).

However, it is also possible that either self-feedback or partner-feedback could have negative effects, for at least two possible reasons. First, objective self-awareness theory [7] states that increased self-focus often leads to a state of discomfort as people try but fail to conform to ideal standards. In the self-feedback case, self-awareness may be heightened as people see explicit representations of social signals that they normally convey unconsciously. Prior work suggests that self-awareness might also be increased in the partner-feedback case as well, as stimuli that increase the salience of an audience have been known to activate self-awareness impulses [30].

Second, either self- or partner-feedback may hurt interactions if they increase participants' cognitive loads. While prior social visualization studies [10, 17] have failed to find evidence for this, it is possible that certain feedback configurations make greater cognitive demands than others.

The above considerations led us to pose the following research questions:

RQ1: Does receiving feedback about oneself or one's partner help or hurt one's experience in an interaction, as compared to receiving no feedback?

RQ2: Can either self-awareness or cognitive load explain any observed negative effects of feedback configuration?

It is important to note that even participants in the no-feedback condition knew that a system was monitoring their behaviors. Studies have often compared interactions in which social visualizations were present versus absent. Unfortunately, this approach confounds the presence of the visualization itself with the fact that individuals' behaviors are being monitored. Because the mere presence of an audience can affect behavior [e.g., 31]—a finding that has been extended to human-computer interaction via media-equation theory [24]—it is impossible to know whether differences should be attributed to the representation of one's behaviors in a social setting or to the fact that one is being monitored by a system. Because our concern here is not with being monitored per se but with who sees representations of monitored behaviors, participants were monitored even in the "control" condition, thereby ensuring that the only differences across levels of *feedback configuration* were who had access to the feedback.

Status

The second variable of interest is the *status* of the individuals within the interaction. Status differences play a critical role in many situations in which social visualizations are likely to be deployed. For example, workplace monitoring systems are generally not designed to be egalitarian: lower-level workers are more likely to be monitored by their bosses than the other way around. It therefore seems likely that one's status could influence the effects of social visualizations. Unfortunately, this topic has been absent from prior social-visualization research.

In this study, we assigned one participant in each dyad to a high-status role and the other to a low-status role. We were not interested in the main effects of status, because that is not a computer-mediation question. Instead, we were interested in possible interactions between status and feedback configuration:

RQ3: Are the effects of self- or partner-feedback moderated by one's status in the interaction?

As a methodological point, we emphasize that we manipulated rather than measured individuals' status levels in the interaction. Previous work on individual-level differences in social visualizations has measured variables via self-report [16] or observer coding [10]. This leads to tenuous inferences because measured variables are likely to correlate with unobserved factors (e.g., dominance may correlate positively with extraversion or negatively with agreeableness). By randomly assigning individuals to high- and low-status roles, we can ensure that any differences are attributable to differences in this variable alone.

Negotiation and Arousal

We situate the present study within the context of a mock employment negotiation scenario. This scenario has a number of properties that make it a useful context for social-visualization research. Employment negotiation is an instance of what McGrath [18] has called "mixed-motive tasks," in which interactants must resolve differing preferences to come to an agreement. This represents a largely unexplored domain for social-visualization research, which has primarily focused either on unstructured conversations [3, 29] or on what McGrath terms "creative," [16, 17] "intellective," [10, 16] or "decision-making" [17] tasks. In addition, as negotiation is a vital activity in a number of contexts, any effects of social visualizations on negotiation outcomes should be of broad interest even outside the CSCW and HCI communities.

Social cues play an important role in predicting negotiation outcomes, making explicit feedback about these cues a potentially useful intervention. In particular, Curhan and Pentland [6] demonstrated that arousal (or "emphasis") is negatively correlated with negotiation outcomes: people who speak with higher arousal tend to perform worse in negotiations. No other social signal in their study was significantly predictive of negotiation outcomes for both high- and low-status actors, suggesting that arousal plays a particularly salient role in the negotiation context.

Negotiation scenarios involve both objective outcomes, which indicate the amount of economic value gained or lost, and subjective outcomes, which describe one's perceptions about the nature of the interaction [5]. In the present scenario, objective performance is determined by allocating points in accordance with each individual's performance in the negotiation. Subjective experience is evaluated using multiple metrics: individuals' own overall perceived experience quality, the degree to which they felt their dyads were competitive or cooperative, and their perceptions of their partners.

METHODS AND SYSTEM DESCRIPTION

Eighty-four participants (48 female; mean age 21.5) were recruited via campus mailing lists and course announcements. Participants came to an on-campus lab and were told that they would be participating in a simulated employment negotiation between a middle manager and a vice president (roles randomly assigned within dyad). The study lasted approximately 1.5 hours. Participants were offered either course credit or $30 in exchange for participating. As an incentive for thoughtful participation, one pair was randomly selected to receive a cash prize, distributed in accordance with their performance in the negotiation. All experimental sessions were conducted using same-gender pairs in order to avoid known issues of gender differences in negotiation outcomes [27].

Computer Monitoring of Arousal

Before the start of the negotiation, participants were shown a web page that explained that previous research had shown that people who spoke in an excited fashion in negotiations tended to have worse outcomes than people who spoke in a calm manner [6]. All participants were told that their voices would be monitored during the negotiation by a computer that was designed to detect differences in excitement as manifested through vocal cues.

Participants in the self-feedback condition were also told:

> As you talk, you will see feedback about the excitement level of your voice. Meanwhile, your partner will similarly see feedback about the excitement level of his/her own voice.

Similarly, participants in the partner-feedback condition were told:

> As you talk, you will see feedback about the excitement level of your partner's voice. Meanwhile, your partner will similarly see feedback about the excitement level of your voice.

Participants in both the self-feedback and partner-feedback conditions were shown a screenshot of the VoiceScan application (Figure 1). Participants in the no-feedback condition were not told about the VoiceScan visualization nor shown a screenshot.

Negotiation Scenario

Next, participants were given 15 minutes to review the instructions outlining the negotiation scenario. In the scenario, which has been used in various negotiation studies and classroom settings [6, 23], the middle manager has requested a transfer to a new branch of a multinational corporation overseen by the vice president. The two must come to an agreement on an employment package consisting of eight issues, such as salary, health insurance, and vacation days. Each issue has five possible outcomes, with corresponding positive or negative point values. Participants were told that the vice president had the final say on whether or not to approve the transfer; however, it was emphasized that it was in both participants' best interests to come to an agreement if they could find one such that both earned any number of points above zero.

The eight issues in the scenario reflect three different issue types [23]. *Distributive* issues are ones in which the two participants' values are diametrically opposed: every point that the vice president earns is a point that the middle manager loses, and vice versa. *Compatible* issues are ones in which the parties' values are perfectly aligned: every point that the vice president earns is a point that the middle manager also earns. *Integrative* issues are ones in which the parties have opposite but unequal incentives: one issue is worth more to the vice president while another is worth more to the middle manager. Integrative issues require cooperation and synthesis for both parties to receive high scores. Thus, it was possible for both parties to score relatively low or both to score relatively high, regardless of who "won" the negotiation. If both parties earned high scores, it indicated that they were communicating effectively and balancing competition with cooperation.

Calibration Phase

After reviewing the negotiation instructions, each participant went through a "calibration phase" to establish baseline calm and excited states so that the system could accurately analyze his or her voice. During this phase, the participant made two calls using provided PSTN telephones to an Asterisk telephony server [28], which bridged each call to a voicemail repository. During the first call, the participant was instructed to speak as calmly and steadily as possible; during the second call, he or she was told to speak as excitedly and dynamically as possible. For each call, a short passage was provided for the participant to read aloud. To make the task of performing calm and excited states easier for the participants, a descriptive passage with long, florid sentences was chosen for the calm call, while an action-filled passage with short, choppy sentences was chosen for the excited call.

For each call, a Java module connected to Asterisk via the Asterisk Gateway Interface extracted the first 30 seconds of the call and saved the recording as a .wav file on the server. This .wav file was then processed by Praat [4], a speech-analysis software package, which extracted the pitch median and interquartile range from the 30-second recording. Thus, after the two calls in the calibration phase were complete, the system had four readings for each participant: his or her pitch median and range in a calm state, and his or her pitch median and range in an excited state. These values were then associated with the participant's unique ID and stored in a MySQL database.

Live Phase

After both participants completed the calibration phase, they were instructed to begin the negotiation itself. The vice president dialed a new phone number that again activated the Asterisk telephony server, though this call was bridged to the middle manager's phone. Thus, the two participants were able to talk directly over standard landlines while the system monitored their speech signals in real time.

Speech signals from each participant were processed through different channels by the telephony server. During the negotiation, the Java module extracted speech signals for each participant at seven-second intervals and saved them as .wav files on the server. The pitch median and pitch range of each seven-second chunk of speech was then extracted by Praat. Arousal scores were calculated for each feature as follows:

$$A_{median} = (M_{live} - M_{calm}) / (M_{exc} - M_{calm})$$

$$A_{range} = (R_{live} - R_{calm}) / (R_{exc} - R_{calm})$$

where A_{median} is the score for pitch median, A_{range} is the score for pitch range, M represents the pitch median, R represents the pitch range, *live* denotes values in the live negotiation, *calm* denotes calm calibration values, and *exc* denotes excited calibration values. To protect against outliers, the maximum *live* value for each feature was limited to 25% above the corresponding excited calibration value and the minimum was limited to 25% below the calm calibration value. Scores for each feature were summed to compute a composite arousal score, which was scaled to fall between a minimum of 0 and a maximum of 4.

The validity of this approach was demonstrated during a pilot phase in which participants were shown a real-time feedback graph with data generated via the parameters above. All pilot participants reported being able to manipulate the graph easily by alternating between calmer and more excited speaking states.

During the negotiation (mean length = 13.6 minutes), participants were shown a webpage with a series of form fields for each issue. For each issue, participants checked a radio button next to the agreed-upon level; at the conclusion of the negotiation, they entered their selections via a form submission button. Next to the form fields, participants in the self-feedback and partner-feedback conditions were also shown a Flash visualization labeled "VoiceScan" that

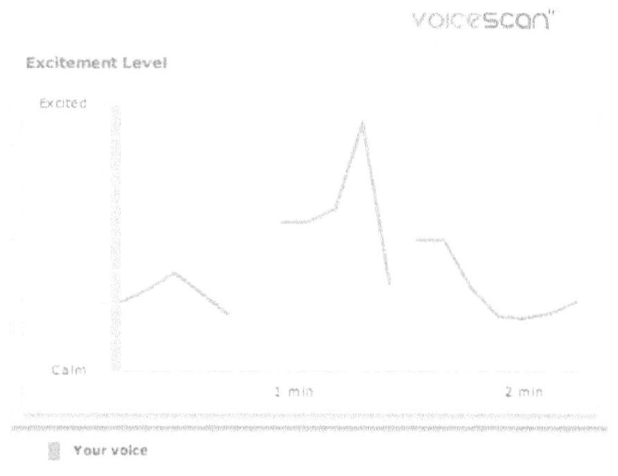

Figure 1: VoiceScan screenshot, self-feedback condition

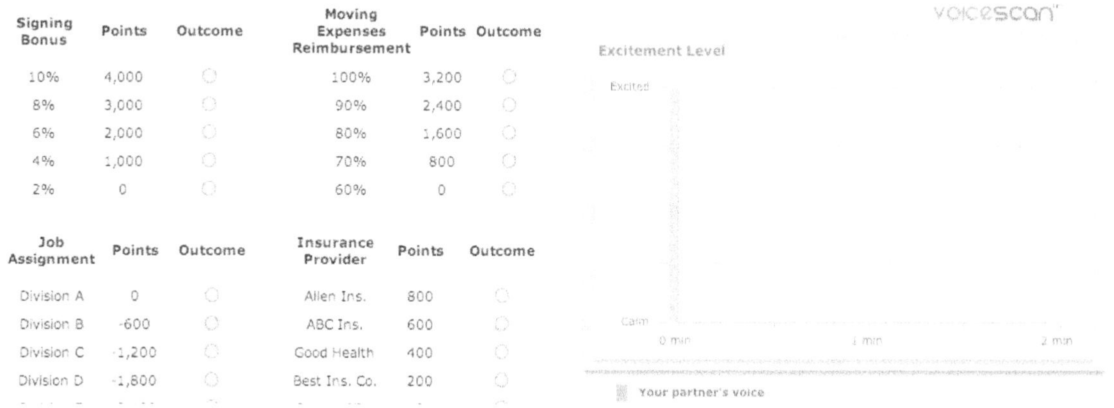

Figure 2: Negotiation interface (partial view); partner-feedback / middle-manager perspective.

displayed an animated line chart showing time on the x-axis and arousal on the y-axis. The graph was captioned "your voice" in the self-feedback condition and "your partner's voice" in the partner-feedback condition (Figure 2). In the no-feedback condition, no graph was shown.

Post-Questionnaire and Debrief

After completing the negotiation, participants filled out a post-questionnaire and were then debriefed, compensated, and dismissed.

Measures

Negotiation points. Because the scenario involves both integrative and distributive issues, negotiation points can be considered in two ways. The total points created by the dyad indicate the total amount of "value creation," or how well the counterparts worked together. The points earned by each individual within a dyad reflect "value claiming" – that is, how effective the individual was at winning points for him- or herself [6].

Subjective Value Inventory. This 16-item scale measures the subjective value that each participant felt that he or she gained from the interaction [5]. The concept of *subjective value* includes the fairness of the process, the perceived quality of the working relationship, and the impact of the negotiation on one's self-image. Subjective value is a critical component of the negotiation process, particularly in cases, such as employment, in which the two counterparts have to work together after the negotiation. The scale was very reliable (Cronbach's $\alpha = 0.93$).

Cooperativeness. This scale was comprised of three items, each measured on 10-point Likert scales: *How well did you and the other person work together?* ("Not well at all" (=1) to "Very well" (=10)), *How much did the other person cooperate with you?* ("Not at all" (=1) to "A lot" (=10)), and *How much did you cooperate with the other person?* ("Not at all" (=1) to "A lot" (=10)). The scale was very reliable ($\alpha = 0.81$).

Competitiveness. Two questions, both measured on 10-point Likert scales, gauged the competitiveness of the parties in the interaction: *How competitive was the other person?* and *How competitive were you?* ("Not at all competitive" (=1) and "Extremely competitive" (=10)). Because these questions were uncorrelated ($\rho = 0.11$), we include each as a single item in our analysis.

Perspective taking. Two statements gauged the degree of perspective-taking in the interaction: *I worked hard to think about things from my partner's perspective* and *My partner worked hard to think about things from my perspective*. Each statement was accompanied by a 7-point Likert scale with labels ranging from "Strongly disagree" (=1) to "Strongly agree" (=7). Because these questions were not highly correlated ($\rho = 0.57$), we include each as a single item in our analysis.

Partner friendliness. Participants rated how well *friendly*, *likable*, and *easy to talk to* described their partners, using 10-point Likert scales ("Describes very poorly" (=1) and "Describes very well" (=10)). The scale was very reliable ($\alpha = 0.88$).

Self-consciousness. Participants rated how well *self-conscious* described themselves, using a 10-point Likert scale ("Describes very poorly" (=1) and "Describes very well" (=10)).

Task Load Index. Five questions from the NASA Task Load Index [13] measured cognitive load. One item from the standard index measuring physical demand was omitted because it was irrelevant to this task. The scale was only somewhat reliable ($\alpha = 0.66$), but we include it here because it has been extensively validated.

RESULTS

Three dyads were removed from the data set prior to analysis;[1] thus, all analyses were conducted on a data set of

[1] In one case, this was due to a technical problem with the system calibration; in another, experimental protocols were not followed properly by the researcher; in the third, the two participants realized that they knew each other partway through the phone call and mentioned in the debrief that this affected their negotiation.

78 total participants. For *feedback configuration*, there were 24 participants in the self-feedback condition, 28 in the partner-feedback condition, and 26 in the no-feedback condition. *Status* was a within-dyad variable, so both levels of status were equally represented within each level of *feedback configuration*.

The focus of this study is on how receiving no feedback differs from receiving feedback either about oneself or about one's partner. This would normally call for analyses using Dunnett's t, which is commonly used when multiple treatments are compared to a single control. However, because we are also interested in potential interactions between *feedback configuration* and *status*, Dunnett's t is not appropriate. Instead, we simply compare the no-feedback condition to the self-feedback and partner-feedback conditions in turn, and apply a conservative Bonferroni correction: we use a critical α value of 0.025 (two-tailed) instead of the standard 0.05. All post-hoc tests on interaction effects were performed using Tukey's HSD.

As the main effect of *status* was not of theoretical interest in this study, we do not included detailed statistics in the results below. We did include this factor in our models; there were no significant main effects of *status* for any outcome measures.

Analyses were conducted by fitting multilevel models [2] using *feedback configuration* and *status* as fixed effects and *dyad* as a random effect. We also included *gender* as a random effect to reduce the variance associated with gender differences in negotiation outcomes [27]. Because the calculation of degrees of freedom for t statistics in such models is known to be problematic, p-values were generated via Markov-Chain Monte Carlo sampling [1].

Negotiation points. For self feedback vs. no feedback, there was a marginally significant main effect of *feedback configuration*, $t = 2.27$, $p < 0.03$, resulting from a marginally significant interaction between *feedback configuration* and *status*, $t = 2.05$, $p < 0.05$. In the no-feedback condition, middle managers scored higher than vice presidents, $p < 0.02$; in the self-feedback condition, there was no difference, $p > 0.9$.

For partner feedback vs. no feedback, there was no significant effect of *feedback configuration*, $t = 0.82$, $p > 0.4$. There was a significant crossover interaction between *feedback configuration* and *status*, $t = 3.94$, $p < 0.001$. In the no-feedback condition, middle managers scored more points than vice presidents, $p < 0.02$; in the partner-feedback condition, vice presidents scored more points than middle managers, $p < 0.06$ (Figure 4).

Subjective value. For self feedback vs. no feedback, there was a significant main effect of *feedback configuration*, $t = 3.14$, $p < 0.01$. Participants in the self-feedback condition felt less subjective value than those in the no-feedback condition. There was no significant interaction between *feedback configuration* and *status*, $t = 1.39$, $p > 0.1$.

For partner feedback vs. no feedback, there was no significant main effect of *feedback configuration*, $t = 0.40$, $p > 0.6$. There was a significant interaction between *feedback configuration* and *status*, $t = 2.67$, $p < 0.02$. Vice presidents felt greater subjective value in the partner-feedback condition than in the no-feedback condition, $p < 0.10$, but for middle managers there was no difference between conditions, $p > 0.4$ (Figure 5).

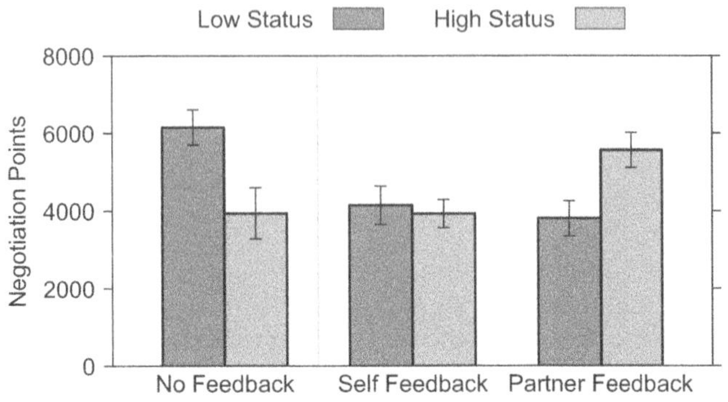

Figure 4: Negotiation points. Means = {6,158, 3,942, 4,150, 3,933, 3,806, 5,563}; SEs = {458, 658, 494, 361, 450, 455}

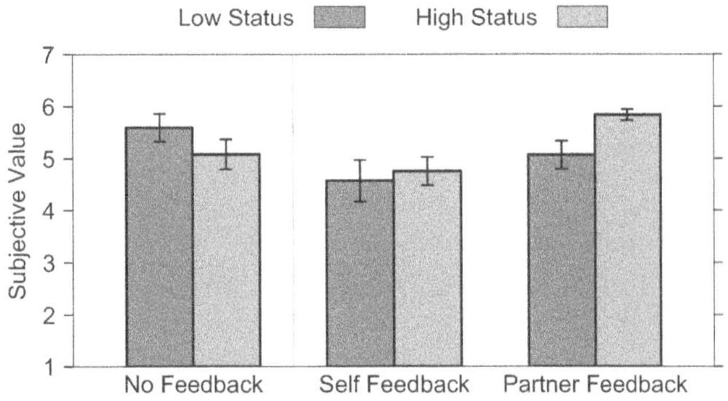

Figure 5: Subjective value. Means = {5.59, 5.08, 4.57, 4.76, 5.07, 5.84}; SEs = {0.27, 0.29, 0.40, 0.27, 0.27, 0.11}

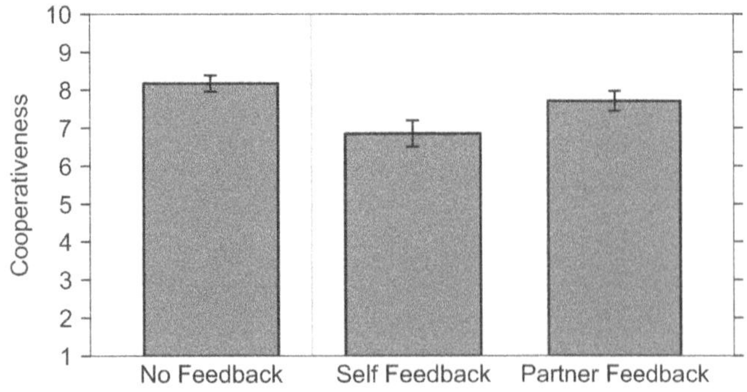

Figure 6: Cooperativeness. Means = {8.17, 6.85, 7.70}; SEs = {0.21, 0.35, 0.26}

Cooperativeness. For self feedback vs. no feedback, there was a significant main effect of *feedback configuration*, $t = 3.43$, $p < 0.02$. Participants in the self-feedback condition felt that their interactions were less cooperative than those in the no-feedback condition. There was no significant interaction between *feedback configuration* and *status*, $t = 0.92$, $p > 0.3$.

For partner feedback vs. no feedback, there was no significant main effect of *feedback configuration*, $t = 1.22$, $p > 0.2$, and no significant interaction between *feedback configuration* and *status*, $t = 1.50$, $p > 0.1$ (Figure 6).

Partner competitiveness. For self feedback vs. no feedback, there was a significant main effect of *feedback configuration*, $t = 2.34$, $p < 0.025$. Participants in the self-feedback condition felt that their partners were more competitive than those in the no-feedback condition. There was no significant interaction between *feedback configuration* and *status*, $t = 1.56$, $p > 0.1$.

For partner feedback vs. no feedback, there was no significant main effect of *feedback configuration*, $t = 0.06$, $p > 0.9$, and no significant interaction between *feedback configuration* and *status*, $t = 0.98$, $p > 0.3$ (Figure 7).

Self competitiveness. For self feedback vs. no feedback, there was no significant main effect of *feedback configuration*, $t = 1.49$, $p > 0.1$, and no significant interaction between *feedback configuration* and *status*, $t = 0.77$, $p > 0.4$.

For partner feedback vs. no feedback, there was no significant main effect of *feedback configuration*, $t = 1.11$, $p > 0.2$. There was a significant interaction between *feedback configuration* and *status*, $t = 2.37$, $p < 0.025$. Vice presidents felt more competitive in the partner-feedback condition than in the no-feedback condition, $p < 0.09$; there was no difference for middle managers, $p > 0.9$ (Figure 8).

Partner perspective taking. For self feedback vs. no feedback, there was a significant main effect of *feedback configuration*, $t = 2.53$, $p < 0.02$. Participants in the self-feedback condition felt that their partners did not try as hard to think about things from their perspectives as did those in the no-feedback condition. There was no significant interaction between *feedback configuration* and *status*, $t = 0.18$, $p > 0.8$.

For partner feedback vs. no feedback, there was no significant main effect of *feedback configuration*, $t = 0.50$, $p > 0.6$, and no significant interaction between *feedback configuration* and *status*, $t = 1.09$, $p > 0.2$ (Figure 9).

Self perspective taking. For self feedback vs. no feedback, there was no significant main effect of *feedback configuration*, $t = 0.34$, $p > 0.7$, and no significant interaction between *feedback configuration* and *status*, $t = 1.43$, $p > 0.1$.

For partner feedback vs. no feedback, there was no significant main effect of *feedback configuration*, $t = 0.83$, $p > 0.4$, and no significant interaction between *feedback configuration* and *status*, $t = 0.34$, $p > 0.7$.

Partner friendliness. For self feedback vs. no feedback, there was a significant main effect of *feedback configuration*, $t = 2.53$, $p < 0.02$. Participants in the self-feedback condition felt that their partners were less friendly than those in the no-feedback condition. There was no significant interaction between *feedback configuration* and *status*, $t = 0.45$, $p > 0.6$.

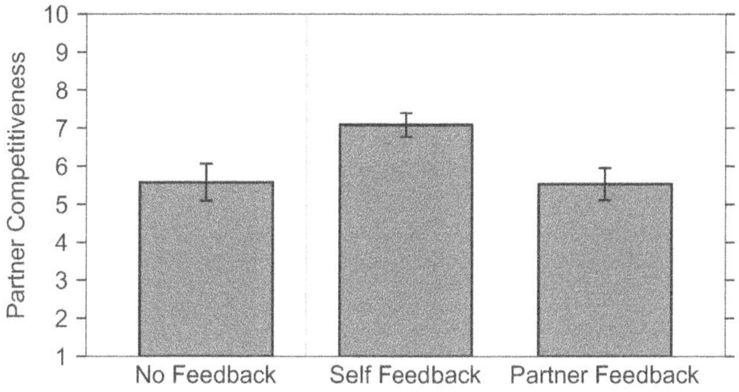

Figure 7: Partner competitiveness. Means = {5.58, 7.08, 5.54}; SEs = {0.48, 0.31, 0.42}

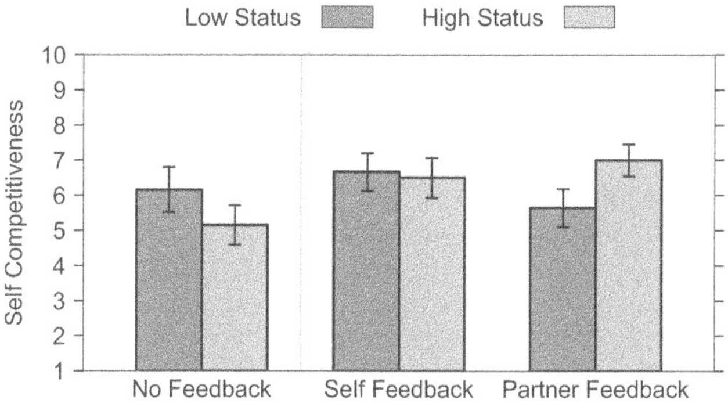

Figure 8: Self competitiveness. Means = {6.15, 5.15, 6.67, 6.50, 5.64, 7.00}; SEs = {0.64, 0.56, 0.54, 0.57, 0.54, 0.46}

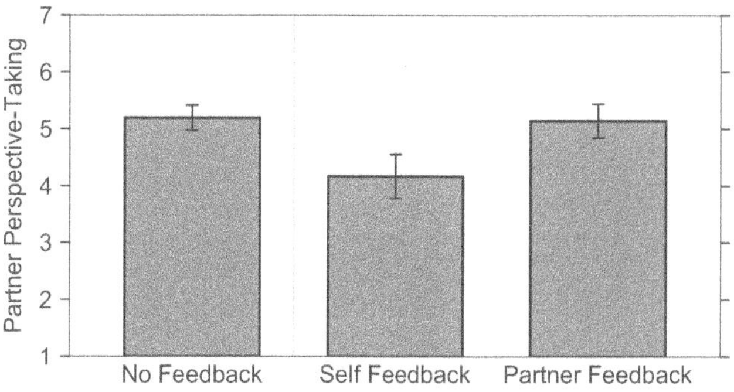

Figure 9: Partner perspective taking. Means = {5.19, 4.17, 5.14}; SEs = {0.22, 0.39, 0.30}

For partner feedback vs. no feedback, there was no significant main effect of *feedback configuration*, $t = 0.70$, $p > 0.4$, and no significant interaction between *feedback configuration* and *status*, $t = 1.40$, $p > 0.1$ (Figure 10).

Self-consciousness. For self feedback vs. no feedback, there was no significant main effect of *feedback configuration*, $t = 0.16$, $p > 0.8$. There was a significant crossover interaction between *feedback configuration* and *status*, $t = 3.78$, $p < 0.001$. Middle managers were more self-conscious in the self-feedback condition than in the no-feedback condition, $p < 0.06$; vice presidents were less self-conscious, $p < 0.03$.

For partner feedback vs. no feedback, there was no significant main effect of *feedback configuration*, $t = 0.66$, $p > 0.5$. There was a significant interaction between *feedback configuration* and *status*, $t = 2.69$, $p < 0.01$. In the no-feedback condition, vice presidents were more self-conscious than middle managers, $p < 0.01$; in the partner-feedback condition, there was no difference, $p > 0.9$ (Figure 11).

Task load. For self feedback vs. no feedback, there was no significant main effect of *feedback configuration*, $t = 0.68$, $p > 0.5$, and no significant interaction between *feedback configuration* and *status*, $t = 1.45$, $p > 0.1$.

For partner feedback vs. no feedback, there was no significant main effect of *feedback configuration*, $t = 0.07$, $p > 0.9$, and no significant interaction between *feedback configuration* and *status*, $t = 0.80$, $p > 0.4$.

DISCUSSION

Self Feedback

With respect to RQ1, we find that receiving feedback about one's own arousal level had negative effects on many aspects of the negotiations. When participants received feedback about themselves, they felt subjectively worse about the negotiations, found their interactions to be less cooperative, and found their partners to be more competitive, less friendly, and less willing to see things from their perspectives.

For RQ3, we find evidence that *status* may have moderated the effects of *feedback configuration* for objective performance: low-status individuals claimed less value when self-feedback was present, while high-status individuals claimed the same amount of value (though this effect was only marginally significant). Interestingly, however, we find no interactions in terms of people's subjective perceptions of the negotiation: self-feedback hurt low- and high-status people alike.

Addressing RQ2, we find no evidence that these negative effects were caused by additional cognitive load. Meanwhile, we find mixed support for the possibility that the negative effects are due to heightened self-awareness. Low-status individuals indeed reported feeling more self-conscious when self-feedback was shown than when no feedback was shown; however, the opposite trend was true for high-status individuals.

One possible explanation for these results is that heightened self-awareness did indeed interfere with the interactions for all participants, but the single *self-consciousness* item was too simplistic a measure to provide a reliable indicator of this. It is possible that participants construed "self-consciousness" in its colloquial sense as referring to anxiety about the self, rather than as referring to a broader notion of awareness the self. In this case, all individuals may have felt heightened self-awareness in the presence of self-feedback, but this may have only implicated related anxiety for low-status individuals.

If self-awareness but not anxiety is responsible for the negative effects of self-feedback, it is possible that rapport was stunted simply because people focused more on how they were being perceived and less on the social cues that their partners were giving off. Additional work should examine the role of objective self-awareness in explaining social-visualization effects in more depth.

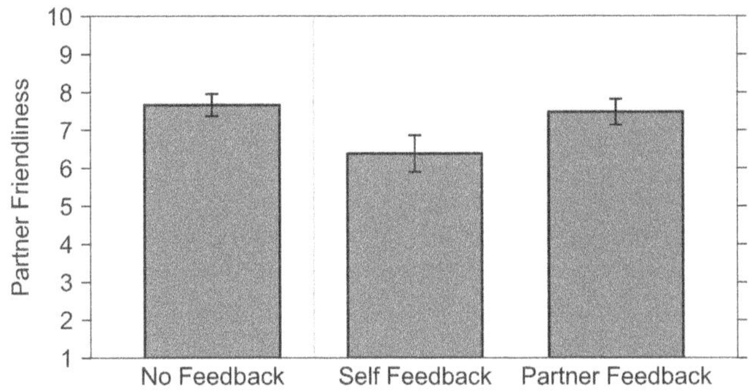

Figure 10: Partner friendliness. Means = {7.67, 6.38, 7.48}; SEs = {0.29, 0.48, 0.34}

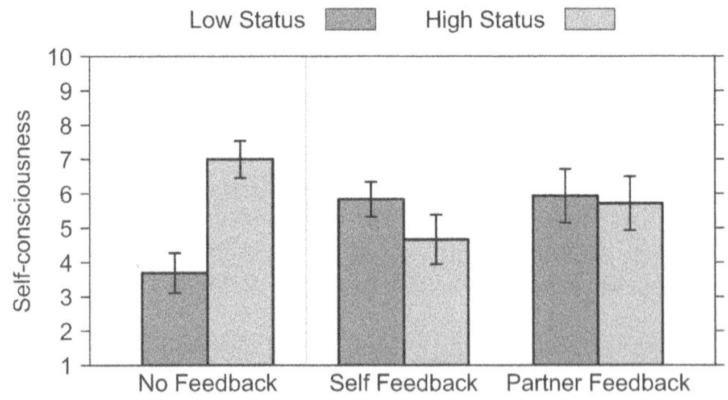

Figure 11: Self-consciousness. Means = {3.69, 7.00, 5.83, 4.67, 5.93, 5.71}; SEs = {0.58, 0.54, 0.51, 0.72, 0.78, 0.78}

Partner feedback

In contrast to the effects of self-feedback, the effects of receiving feedback about one's partner's arousal level were strongly influenced by one's status in the interaction. The higher-status vice presidents clearly benefitted from receiving feedback about their partners, as it caused them to score more points and feel greater subjective value. Interestingly, it also caused them to feel more competitive. Conversely, the effects of partner-feedback on lower-status middle managers were less apparent. Middle managers did claim less value in the partner-feedback condition than in the no-feedback condition, but there was no discernible difference in their subjective experiences. Thus, we find evidence that partner-feedback affects people's interactions (RQ1) but that the effects differ significantly depending on one's status (RQ3).

With respect to RQ2, we once again find no evidence that cognitive load had any bearing on the observed effects. Taken together with the results for self-feedback, as well as similar null results reported in previous work [10, 17], this suggests that people are actually quite capable of incorporating peripheral social visualizations without overloading their cognitive resources.

As with self-feedback, we find mixed support for the notion that heightened self-awareness, as measured by the *self-consciousness* item, can explain the observed results. We do note that in the partner-feedback case, lower-status individuals both created less value and were more self-conscious than in the no-feedback case; however, as per the discussion above, we treat these results as suggestive rather than conclusive.

One interpretation for the positive effect of partner-feedback on high-status individuals is that this subject population—primarily consisting of undergraduate students with little work experience—had inherent difficulty adopting the more powerful role of the vice president. However, receiving feedback about one's partner's voice may have been empowering for the vice president role in a way that it was not for the middle manager role, because in real life monitoring another individual is almost exclusively the purview of higher-status individuals. In other words, monitoring other people may actually be more helpful to high-status individuals (who are presumably in a position to act on that information) than to low-status individuals (who are presumably not in such a position). Particularly given these real-world issues, status is an important topic for future work on social visualizations to explore.

CONCLUSION

This work has several limitations. The present experiment examines the visualization of only one type of social behavior (vocal arousal), in one interactional context (negotiation), between same-gender pairs, in a single setting. It is possible that other social cues may be more appropriate for feedback in negotiations, or that people may benefit from receiving feedback about their own arousal levels in a different situation. It also seems reasonable to conjecture that feedback about one's social cues may be more effectively provided as part of a long-term training regimen rather than in a single laboratory session. All of these would be fruitful areas for future work.

In addition, as with much work in social science, this study makes use of certain contrivances that, while useful for research purposes, should be taken into account when making general inferences based on the findings. Notably, the experiment involves a simulated negotiation and restricts dyads to same-gender pairs. Real-world negotiations are certain to have higher stakes for the parties involved and to often take place between opposite-gender dyads. Examining the issues raised here in more naturalistic scenarios would be a useful extension of this work.

While we are aware of the limitations of the present work, we hope that it provides at least the beginnings of a foundation, grounded in dimensions rather than holistic interventions [21], on which others interested in psychological effects of social visualization systems can build. At a minimum, we hope that this work encourages others to manipulate those specific aspects of system, role, and situation that are likely to help construct a larger theory of social visualization systems.

ACKNOWLEDGMENTS

We thank Nokia Research Center for their generous support of this work.

REFERENCES

1. Baayen, R.H., Davidson, D.J., and Bates, D.M. Mixed-effects modeling with crossed random effects for subjects and items. *Journal of Memory and Language 59* (2008), 390-412.
2. Bates, D.M. and Maechler, M. lme4: Linear mixed-effects models using S4 classes. http://cran.r-project.org/web/packages/lme4/index.html.
3. Bergstrom, T. and Karahalios, K. Seeing more: Visualizing audio cues. *Proc. INTERACT 2007*, Springer (2007), 29-42.
4. Boersma, P. and Weenink, D. Praat: Doing phonetics by computer. http://www.praat.org.
5. Curhan, J.R., Elfenbein, H.A., and Xu, H. What do people value when they negotiate? Mapping the domain of subjective value in negotiation. *Journal of Personality and Social Psychology 91*, 3 (2006), 493-512.
6. Curhan, J.R. and Pentland, A. Thin slices of negotiation: Predicting outcomes from conversational dynamics within the first 5 minutes. *Journal of Applied Psychology 92* (2007), 802-811.
7. Duval, S. and Wicklund, R. *A Theory of Objective Self-Awareness*, Academic Press, New York, 1972.
8. DiMicco, J.M., Lakshmipathy, V., and Fiore, A.T. Conductive Chat: Instant messaging with a skin

conductivity channel. *Proc. CSCW 2002*, ACM Press (2002).

9. DiMicco, J.M., Pandolfo, A., and Bender, W. Influencing group participation with a shared display. *Proc. CSCW 2004*, ACM Press (2004), 614-623.
10. DiMicco, J.M., Hollenbach, K.J., Pandolfo, A., and Bender, W. The impact of increased awareness while face-to-face. *Human-Computer Interaction 27* (2007), 47–96.
11. Erickson, T. Designing visualizations of social activity: six claims. *Ext. Abstracts CHI 2003*, ACM Press (2003), 846-847.
12. Hall, E.T. *The Hidden Dimension*, Anchor Books, New York, 1966.
13. Hart S.G. and Staveland, L.E. Development of a NASA-TLX (Task Load Index): Results of empirical and theoretical research. In Hancock, P.S. and Meshkati N. (eds.), *Human Mental Workload*. North-Holland, Amsterdam, 1988.
14. Iwasaki, K., Miyaki, T., and Rekimoto, J. AffectPhone: A handset device to present user's emotional state with warmth/coolness. In Kim, J. and Karjalainen, P. (eds.), *Bio-Inspired Human-Machine Interfaces and Healthcare Applications*. INSTICC Press, Valencia, Spain (2010), 83-88.
15. Janssen, J.H., Bailenson, J.N., Ijsselstein, W.A., and Westerink, J.H.D.M. Intimate heartbeats: Opportunities for affective communication technology. *IEEE Transactions on Affective Computing 1*, 2 (2010), 72-80.
16. Kim, T., Chang, A., Holland, L., and Pentland, A. Meeting Mediator: Enhancing group collaboration using sociometric feedback. *Proc. CSCW 2008*, ACM Press (2008), 457-466.
17. Leshed, G., Perez, D., Hancock, J.H., Cosley, D., Birnholtz, J., Lee, S., McLeod, P.L., and Gay, G. Visualizing real-time language-based feedback on teamwork behavior in computer-mediated groups. *Proc. CHI 2009*, ACM Press (2009), 537-546.
18. McGrath, J.E.. *Groups: Interaction and Performance*. Englewood Cliffs, NJ: Prentice-Hall, 1984.
19. Mehrabian, A. *Nonverbal Communication*, Aldine-Atherton, Chicago, 1972.
20. Murray, I.R. and Arnott, J.L. Toward the simulation of emotion in synthetic speech: A review of the literature on human vocal emotion. *The Journal of the Acoustical Society of America 93*, 2 (1993), 1097-1108.
21. Nass, C. and Mason, L. On the study of technology and task: A variable-based approach. In J. Fulk and C. Steinfeld (eds.), *Organizations and communication technology*. Sage, Newbury Park, CA, 1990.
22. Pentland, A. *Honest Signals: How They Shape Our World*, The MIT Press, Cambridge, 2008.
23. Pinkley, R.L., Neale, M.A., and Bennett, R.J. The impact of alternatives to settlement in dyadic negotiation. *Organizational Behavior and Human Decision Processes, 57*, (1994), 97-116.
24. Rickenberg, R. and Reeves, B. The effects of animated characters on anxiety, task performance, and evaluations of user interfaces. *Proc. CHI 2000*, ACM Press (2000), 49-56.
25. Scheflen, A.E. The significance of posture in communication systems. *Psychiatry 27* (1964), 316-331.
26. Shaw, M. *Group Dynamics: The Psychology of Small Group Behavior*. McGraw-Hill, New York, 1976.
27. Stuhlmacher, A.F. and Walters, A.E. Gender differences in negotiation outcome: A meta-analysis. *Personnel Psychology 52* (1999), 653-677.
28. Van Meggelen, J., Madsen, L., and Smith, J. Asterisk. http://www.asterisk.org.
29. Wang, H., Prendinger, H., and Igarashi, T. Communicating emotions in online chat using physiological sensors and animated text. *Ext. Abstracts CHI 2004*, ACM Press (2004), 1171-1174.
30. Wicklund, R.A. Objective self-awareness. In Berkowitz, L. (ed.) *Advances in Experimental Social Psychology 8*, Academic Press, New York, 1975.
31. Zajonc, R.B. Social facilitation, *Science 149* (1965), 269-274.

Taking as an Act of Sharing

Helena M. Mentis, Siân E. Lindley, Stuart Taylor, Paul Dunphy*, Tim Regan, Richard Harper
Microsoft Research Cambridge, Cambridge, UK
*Culture Lab, School of Computing Science, Newcastle University, Newcastle upon Tyne, UK
{hementis; sianl; stuart; timregan; r.harper}@microsoft.com, *p.m.dunphy@ncl.ac.uk

ABSTRACT
We present findings from the deployment of a mobile application, *Take and Give*, which allows users to place image files in a virtual folder or 'Pocket' on a mobile phone. This content can be viewed by a set of 'Buddies', who can, if they wish, attempt to take ownership of a file for themselves, following which they can keep it, delete it, or place it in the Pocket of someone else. There is only one version of each file, creating a twist on traditional sharing technologies. We report findings from a three week trial of the application in an office space, and describe how Take and Give provided a means of self-presentation and supported a sense of awareness, mutual attentiveness and connectedness. Our findings suggest that the taking of unique content can be an engaging form of sharing and can facilitate awareness and connectedness between people.

Author Keywords
Ownership, connection, awareness, self-expression, work.

ACM Classification Keywords
H5.m. Information interfaces and presentation (e.g., HCI): Miscellaneous.

General Terms
Human Factors; Design.

INTRODUCTION
Traditional communication technologies tend to be built on the metaphor of giving in order to share content. Letters, emails and text messages are all examples in which content is pushed from one person to another. More recently, blogs, micro-blogs and social networking sites allow people to post content online to be consumed more broadly. We might think of such behaviour as being closer to pulling; 'friends' and 'followers' can access content at their convenience. In this paper we present a system that permits users to *take* unique content from one another. Further, and unlike systems such as Facebook, Twitter and many file-sharing sites, where content is copied or duplicated, in this instance taking is based on the metaphor of material things: it means a passing of ownership. To be specific, we explore content taking rather than content giving, through a system where there is only ever one copy of each file. Our interest is to investigate the affordances of an alternative mechanism for sharing – one that is based on a very robust pulling of content – with a view to addressing new opportunities around shared collections of content.

The system we present is *Take and Give*, a mobile phone application that was designed to provoke reflection on the way people perceive and manage the taking of digital content and the social outcomes of such behaviour. In Take and Give, the mobile phone is converted into a personal web server, known here as a 'Pocket'. Images placed in this Pocket can be viewed freely by other Take and Give users who, if they wish, can attempt to take them. Successful instances of taking content result in a transfer of ownership: the prior owner loses their copy whilst the person doing the taking gains a version for themselves. To allow people to retain possession of their files, the system was also designed to support monitoring of taking-related behaviours in real time. So content-owners are made aware, firstly, whenever their Pocket is being viewed, and secondly, if the viewer is attempting to take a file from them. If they are sufficiently attentive, the content holder can prevent their content from being taken in the moment. Users can also give files to each other by placing them in each other's Pockets. Thus, the system design supports the transfer of ownership of unique content amongst those within a network, in terms of pull and push, but emphasises the pull mechanism by alerting of such acts.

During a deployment of the application, emerging patterns of use suggested that by twisting the dynamics of content transfer in this way, Take and Give provided a means of self-presentation and supported a sense of awareness, mutual attentiveness and connectedness. Our findings suggest that, somewhat surprisingly, taking can be as engaging as giving in forging connections between people.

BACKGROUND
There is a wealth of research within, and beyond, CSCW on supporting connections between people. In terms of the literature on communication, much of the focus has been on the giving of content in some corporal form [3], and the systems of obligation by exchange that emerge around this. For instance, research into texting practices amongst contemporary teenagers demonstrates how the sending, or gifting [20], of a text message is bound up with the expectation that a message will be sent back in return. Some such mes-

sages are of sufficient value that they are kept, an inviolate proof of a connection between two people, sender and receiver. Harper [8] has argued that the values inherent in the design of content sharing technologies support diverse and complex social bonds, which create a weave, almost a texture, of communicative obligation.

Acts such as these are rooted in deep sets of norms related to reciprocity, performativity and solidarity – norms that require both give and take behaviour. Research that has demonstrated the importance of taking in this context includes a study of *Glancephone* [9], a mobile phone application that allows users to determine each other's availability by taking a 'glance' at the intended recipient before making a phone call. In practice, the system was appropriated as a means for provoking glances at oneself; users quickly realised that if someone glanced at them, this meant that they wished to be glanced at themselves. This was especially sought after when users were doing something that they wanted to share; in other words, they wished for their friends and colleagues to look at them during key moments. Here, returning a glance demonstrated attentiveness and underpinned connectedness.

We might think of this use of Glancephone as a clever means of broadcasting; one wishes to share what one is doing and so elicits glances from others. This is somewhat reminiscent of other social pull environments, such as social networks and micro-blogs, where 'friends' and 'followers' can view content that is shared, and act upon it though 'liking' and posting comments. These acts perform a similar purpose to the returning of a glance; they can be seen as a demonstration of attentiveness. Unlike Glancephone, however, the form of these broadcasts means that they are understood to become a resource for further action by others. In Twitter, for example, the act of re-tweeting means that content is copied and proliferated throughout the network. Studies of Twitter users highlight how the notion of ownership in this online environment is nuanced: re-use is accepted, so long as authorship is attributed, and users feel that they have the right to store or archive tweets posted by others in addition to their own [15]. In other words, it is deemed as acceptable for content broadcast in this way to be re-used or kept for oneself.

Other types of broadcasting include publically displaying one's possessions. In an investigation of iTunes music sharing in an office-space, participants were found to put a lot of thought into crafting an identity through their music collections, which were shared with others on the same network [22]. Ownership of content, and decisions relating to which content others could use, were a means of portraying identity to co-workers. Furthermore, participants gained an awareness of their co-workers' personalities by perusing the music libraries that they had shared.

Another study that illustrates the links between ownership and identity is *Urbanhermes* [14], which allows for the exchange, adoption, and removal of digital images displayed on a handbag. If a user sees an image on another bag that they like, they can download it to their own bag. Much like in the fashion world, images accrue intrinsic value if a particularly high-status or popular individual originally owned it, or has copied it. Those high in status are more selective regarding the types of images they display. In this system, copying an image does not require permission from the holder, and users saw the adoption of images from their bags as a compliment rather than 'stealing' or 'copying'.

This can be contrasted with systems in which there is only one version of the item that is taken. Systems designed along this principle are most commonly gaming applications. For instance, *Treasure* allows for players to steal coins from one another in an outdoor mobile game [1]. Unsurprisingly, having one's coins stolen was found to lead to changes in game play over time to prevent such occurrences from happening. In examples such as this, the coins are valued due to their role in their game, but their value is also linked to a sense of possession. Through the act of taking, issues of ownership become more pronounced.

As a final and related example, systems where there is only one version of an object (such as a Wikipedia page or other shared document) illustrate how feelings of ownership can have a strong negative effect on interaction. For instance, Wikipedia editors signal ownership over a page through territorial markings, such as the *Maintained* designation [17, 21]. These markings represent the boundaries between social actors and ultimately shape interactions in the space, such as controlling which contributions will be accepted. It has been shown that a Wikipedia editor's feeling of ownership will have a strong effect on whether another's edit will be rejected, independent of factors such as quality [7].

So, issues of ownership are bound up with identity and play a role in the types of content that people share, broadcast, and make available, as well as how the act of taking is perceived. However, it is much more common to design systems that support sharing through giving or copying, than through the taking of content that is unique within a shared pool. In this paper, we explore how self-presentation and connectedness are underpinned through use of a system, designed as a research probe, which enables the taking of unique content. We view our approach as part of a turn towards inventing new acts of communication, as an attempt to foster greater creativity for human expression [11]. In the section that follows, we describe the system we devised.

SYSTEM DESCRIPTION

The design of Take and Give as a research probe encompassed a number of features including enabling users to add images to their Pocket; look at content in the Pockets of others; remove that content and place it in their own Pocket; be aware of their own content being viewed; and allow them to stop content being removed, should they wish to do so. With Take and Give, users need to attend to their phone in order to see what is happening with their content, to know that it is being seen or taken in the here and now, and

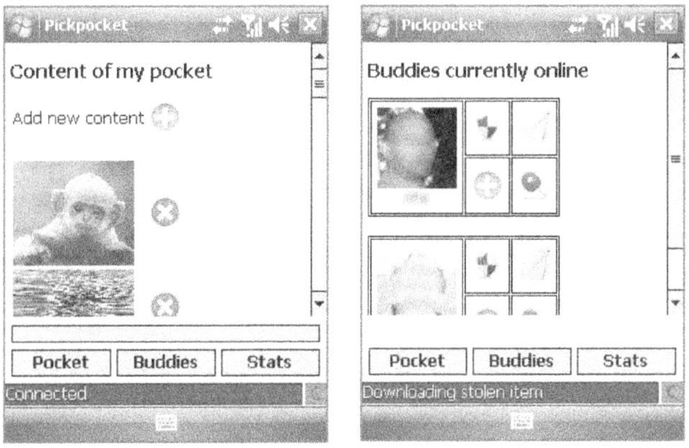

Figure 1. (i) Pocket; (ii) Buddies with snoop, message, add and ping (for debugging) buttons.

Figure 2. (i) View of a Buddy's Pocket; (ii) Stop Thief button displayed during an attempt to take content.

for them to be able to manage this process accordingly, stopping the removal of content in some instances, allowing it in others. Vigilance was important since there exists only one copy of each file across the network of users; these were understood to move about, in the same way that a material object might move from one person to another. Users could also 'give' in the traditional sense through the system, either by placing content in one another's Pockets, or by sending text messages.

The Take and Give client application was developed around two separate, but interconnected components: A GUI based application and a custom web server. The application hosts an embedded web browser through which the user interacts with the system. The web server, which runs continually in the background, provides the necessary functionality to serve files to other users and allow files to be uploaded.

The Web Server

The system was designed to support quick access and loading over a network, to facilitate real-time responsiveness. Central to this was support for point-to-point data communication between mobile devices, so as to enable the transfer of content files. Thus, we employed a web server running on each mobile device.

We chose to develop the Take and Give client software to run on Windows Mobile 6.5 devices as these provided a number of key features including multi-tasking, which was required to ensure the local web server was always active. Each of these clients then connected to a gateway server that was developed and deployed on a Windows Server PC with Internet access. This gateway server was required since the network address of each of the clients is allocated by the mobile phone operator and as such, is private and inaccessible to other devices. Routing network traffic through the gateway thus allowed each of the clients access to all other clients.

The User Interface

The Take and Give application comprises three main sections: *Pocket*, *Buddies* and *Stats*. Tapping on the *Pocket* button from the start screen allows a user to view, add and delete content to/from their Pocket (Figure 1(i)). The *Buddies* button allows a user to display a list of Buddies in a network (i.e. the other Take and Give users) who are currently online (Figure 1(ii)). A table of number of views and attempts to take content (both successful and prevented) can be accessed by clicking on the *Stats* button.

From the Buddies list, firstly, one can view the Pockets of others. Tapping on the *Snoop* button beside a Buddy's profile picture brings up a list of thumbnails representing the images stored in a Buddy's Pocket (Figure 2(i)). However, this cannot be done in secret: the act of looking also triggers an alert on the Buddy's phone, which vibrates once and displays a message detailing who is doing the viewing. Once viewing the content of a Buddy's Pocket, tapping on a thumbnail initiates an attempt to take the associated image. This action also triggers an alert on the Buddy's phone, which vibrates twice and displays a warning message, during which time the user has the opportunity to tap a *Stop Thief* button (Figure 2(ii)). If the button is tapped within these three seconds, the attempt to remove the content is stopped and the user trying to undertake this is notified with a message in the status bar. Otherwise, the file is deleted from the Buddy's phone and a copy is added to the Pocket of the user doing the taking.

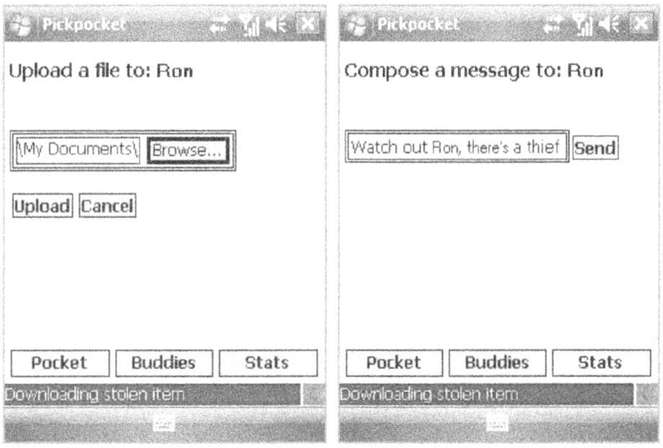

Figure 3. (i) Uploading a file to another user; (ii) Sending a message to another user.

A second way in which one can interact with one's Buddies is through adding content to their Pockets. This can be done by tapping the *Add* button displayed next to a Buddy's profile picture and subsequently selecting an image file to be uploaded (Figure 3(i)). The file is added to the Buddy's Pocket, but without explicit notification. This design decision was taken because we wanted to highlight the taking action of the system as opposed to acts of giving.

Finally, one can interact with one's Buddies by sending them short messages, by tapping on the *Message* button next to a Buddy's profile picture (Figure 3(ii)). This is similar to, but independent of, regular SMS messaging.

Users were provided with a number of options for adding new content to their Pockets, including syncing content when the phone was connected to their PC and grabbing images using the phone's built-in camera. In addition, since the phone was running a web server with image upload capability, users were able to quickly and easily add content to their own Pocket using any web browser.

THE FIELD TRIAL

Having developed Take and Give in accordance with our aims of enabling users to take, as well as give, expressive content, we deployed the application amongst a group of colleagues in an industry research lab, an environment that we could observe closely in order to elicit a rich description of how ownership and taking of content is perceived and experienced. This approach clearly has limitations in that our closeness to the participants could instil bias; however, considering the paucity of work in this area, we wanted to first gain a better understanding of the space to identify salient issues for future research.

Participants

The participants included the two engineers who had developed Take and Give and six of their colleagues, who were recruited due to their availability and diversity in terms of demographics (age, gender, disciplinary background). Participants also differed in terms of their relationship to the overall group. Two were previous interns who were now located off-site. The first of these was one of the engineers who had developed the application and who was located at his university, 230 miles away, during the deployment; the other was studying at a local university and occasionally came on-site for meetings. Of the six co-workers located on-site, one was a visiting researcher who was new to the group, one was a post-doc researcher who had been in her post for two months at the time of deployment, and the others had been working together for at least three years. Further details are provided in Table 1.

Participant Alias	*Gender*	*Group Tenure*	*On- or Off-site*
Ron	M	6 yrs.	On
Steven	M	5 yrs.	On
Titus	M	6 yrs.	On
Simone	**F**	3 yrs.	On
Heidi	**F**	**2 mo.**	On
Adam	M	**2 wks.**	On
Peter	M	6 mo.	**Off**
Tony	M	1 yr.	**Off**

Table 1. Participant details. Notable differences are in bold.

Procedure

Take and Give was deployed for three weeks. Participants were given the dedicated phones running the application and were instructed on the possibilities for use offered by the application – putting images in one's Pocket, viewing another's images, taking another's images, stopping others from taking their images, giving images to another, and sending messages. They were told that they could use the application as much or as little as they liked and in whatever manner they chose. Since this was an exploratory study it was explained to the users that we were simply interested in how the application would be used.

Data Collection and Analysis

Data collection entailed a combination of self-reporting diaries, discussion groups, interviews, and logged transaction data. All interactions with the system, including views, takes and messages, were logged. This data was collated, parsed into a database, and analysed using tSQL. Participants maintained diaries of key events during the deployment and took part in two group discussions, one at the end of the first week and another towards the end of the three weeks. Discussions were focused on unpacking participants' evolving use of Take and Give, their feelings towards it, and their interpretations of any events that they had recorded in the diaries, such as funny moments or their observations of changing strategies. Both off-site participants took part in the first discussion (with one of the remote participants dialling in), but neither were able to attend the second. They were interviewed individually instead – the remote participant by telephone, the local participant face-to-face. Discussions and interviews were audio recorded and transcribed. Quotes that are presented in this paper illustrate the participant and the data source, where 'D1' represents the first group discussion, 'D2' the second group discussion, and 'I' represents individual interviews with off-site participants. As an additional point, we also include observations made by co-workers who did not participate in the study, which were noted in the diaries. The on-site participants represented half of their workgroup, and so their use of the system was visible to and impactful upon others.

In our analysis, we utilized a grounded theory inspired method [19]. We began by inspecting the transcripts, diaries and visualisations of the log files for themes related to use and outcomes of use. Early on in the deployment most participants related stories of how Take and Give had an impact on their sense of connectedness to others in the group. We then continued to search for evidence relating to how this sense of connectedness was supported. In what follows, we report themes that emerged through cross referencing the three sources of data, and then discuss the mechanisms and consequences of *taking* expressive content.

FINDINGS

The results shown in Figure 4, derived from the logs, reveal that viewing the Pockets of others and attempting to take content were much more frequent than other actions permitted by the system. They were surpassed only by clicking on the Buddies screen, which was a necessary precursor to many of the system's functions. To a much lesser degree did people give content to others (282 instances over the three weeks) or message their Buddies (112 instances). However, viewing one's own Pocket was a reasonably frequent activity (844 instances), and there is some evidence that this was bound up with the curation of one's Pocket through deletion (207 instances). Over 250 pictures were also uploaded to the pool during the course of the study.

A final point in Figure 4 worth highlighting is that, despite the focus on viewing and taking, participants paid little attention to how these behaviours were rated in Stats. It is clear in Figure 4 that Stats was the least viewed screen in the Take and Give application. More so, views of the Stats page dropped from 26 views in the first week to 7 views in the last week of the study. Use of the system was not motivated by the accumulation of 'gaming points'.

However, the logs indicate that Take and Give was used fairly consistently over the three weeks, although principally during working hours. Long term breaks in usage were found during the second and third weekends and outside office hours during the week. The only participants to show a more general drop-off in use of the system were the off-site participants (we say more about this later) and Ron, a manager (all participant names are pseudonyms). He stopped engaging with the application within the first few days of the trial. This led to an eventual disinterest in Ron's Pocket; after the first week of the study, other participants rarely bothered to view it (log).

The analysis that follows is divided into four sections, which explore how Take and Give was used and how this was influenced by, and fed into, the social environment in which it was situated. The first explores the importance of image choice when populating one's Pocket with content, and how this related to self-expression and being an active Take and Give user. The second relates to motivations for taking content within the system. The third discusses how taking was mediated by an understanding of social boundaries. In the fourth section we unpack the sense of awareness and connectedness that taking engendered.

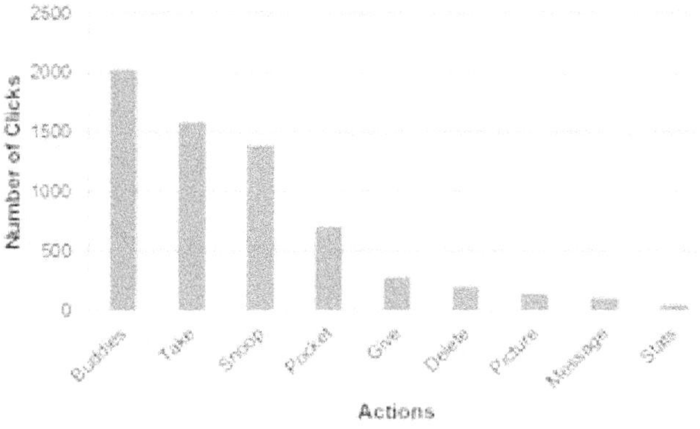

Figure 4. Actions taken over the course of the trial.

Self-Expression and Attracting Attention

Perhaps the most immediately apparent way in which Take and Give could be used was in providing a novel mechanism for self-presentation through the tailoring of one's Pocket. At the beginning of the deployment, an initial pool of images was made available by one of the engineers who had developed the application. However, participants quickly curated the content of their Pockets, using this as a way of demonstrating their participation, expressing themselves, and seeking to attract the attention of others.

For example, some participants uploaded images that related to their interests (e.g., Titus uploaded content linked to tea-drinking and Harry Potter), some captured images using the camera-phone to reflect things that happened during the trial (e.g. Simone took photos of a snapped key and a new pair of shoes), and some sought out images that represented interests shared with others (e.g. Steven added a picture of a punk band that he and Titus both liked). Additionally, some participants became associated with certain images simply because they were known to like them (e.g., Heidi's picture of Wonder Woman). As the trial progressed, the notion of curating a collection of images, which worked together as a whole, became more pronounced. Some participants became focused on having images that were "weird ... but interesting" (Simone, D2), or "stuff you thought about" (Titus, D2). This was taken to its extreme at the end of the third week by Titus, who created a set of images that spelt out 'STEAL-THIS!' (Figure 5) (log).

Having interesting content in a Pocket put participants at risk of being targeted for takes. However, far from being an annoyance, this was an important part of how Take and Give was used. As shown in Figure 4, taking was a very frequent activity in use of the system. If one's Pocket was empty, or devoid of noteworthy content, this was manifest in the lack of attempted takes that one attracted (and eventually, a lack of views, as happened in Ron's case). Being part of the interaction supported by the system was predicated on having content that others would want to take.

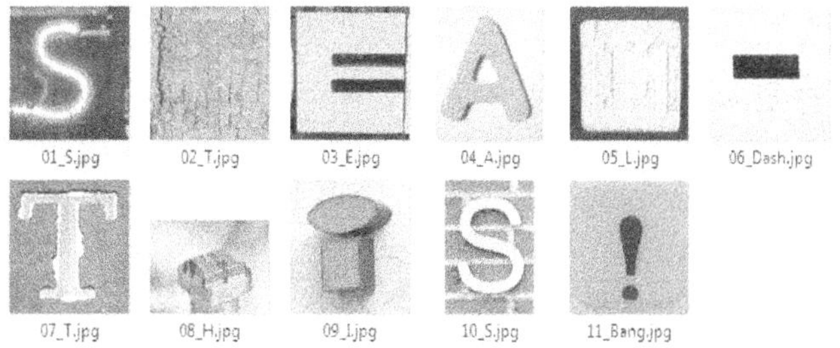

Figure 5. Curating a collection of images

Related to this, some participants adopted clear strategies in order to attract the attention of others. Titus describes an instance in which he placed an image in Steven's Pocket, which related to an on-going project they were involved in, in order to "tantalize him" into visiting his own newly curated collection of images. In other cases, images that were known to be valued by others were placed in Pockets. For example, Heidi noted in her diary early in the study, "Uploading stuff now to see if people take it. See what entices them. I know I can always take it back later." One of the more subversive ways of attracting attention involved the uploading of pictures of Titus to the image pool. This initially began when Tony placed a photo of Titus in Simone's Pocket. The discovery of this led Titus to make repeated attempts to take the image, in order to delete it. This incident led to other participants downloading multiple images of him from the web and adding them to their own Pockets, in a behaviour that was certain to make them a target:

"I guess it attracts people's attention as well ... it's almost kind of like I put that stuff in my Pocket thinking, right, Titus is going to come and get this stuff and it's almost kind of a honeypot ... you're attracting the hit" (Peter, I2).

However, the creation of enticing Pockets did not mean that participants were willing to easily let go of their content. That content was sought after meant that it had some value, and the act of acquiring a collection of highly-valued objects served as an expression of one's aptitude at, firstly, curating interesting content and, secondly, guarding against others taking it from you. Because users invested so much time in curating their Pockets, the motivation to protect and retain what was viewed as theirs quickly led to a fierce sense of connection through competition. Images tended to be defended against other's attempts to take them, and when such attempts were successful, they often triggered counter-attempts to take the file in question back (log).

Thus, the development of norms surrounding the taking of content meant that participants did not only actively engage in taking from each other, but also almost immediately realized the importance of curating an interesting Pocket to entice others to try to take content from them. To be an active Take and Give user, it was necessary to be perceived as someone worth taking from.

Motivations for Taking Content

The other side of this practice is the taking itself. We have identified three motivations for the taking of expressive content: wanting something to be in one's own Pocket or out of the loop, opportunity for challenge, and to elicit a satisfying reaction from another participant.

We have already described how taking could be an attempt to curate the shared pool, as in the example of Titus's attempting to retrieve and delete pictures of himself. Participants also attempted to take and hold on to images as a means of self-expression. For example, early in the study an image of a cat with a watermelon on its head was taken from Steven by Heidi because she loves cats and thought the image was hilarious. She wanted the photo in *her* Pocket to represent her likes and her sense of humour (D1).

Motivations for taking that were less bound up with self-expression include the challenge associated with the act itself. During the study, strategies for taking quickly evolved. Some participants would spend hours "sitting in someone's Pocket" (Heidi, D2) after having an initial look, enabling them to make an unexpected take. Other strategies included the launching of "sustained attacks" (Steven, D2), in which repeated attempts to take were delivered until the target gave in, and, more elaborately, distracting another participant, for example by phoning their office phone whilst simultaneously taking an item from their Pocket (Steven, D1). Participants often shared amongst themselves stories of cunning strategies like this one.

Counter-strategies to protect one's content also developed, including always having one's phone close to hand or on one's lap. Stealing from those participants who were considered to be particularly "on the ball" (Adam, D2) or "taking this quite seriously" was considered a "victory" (Tony, I2), and an act that required a different approach:

"[W]hen I try to steal stuff from Heidi or Simone, my assumption is that they have their phones right there so you have to get in as quickly as possible and so there isn't time to scroll through. It is all a question of trying to get as quickly as possible. You just hit whatever is first" (Adam, D2).

Consequently, an attempt to take an image is a compliment of sorts to the target. It is saying, firstly, 'I want something that you have because it is neat' and secondly, 'I think you are a worthy adversary'.

The third motivation for taking content was in order to elicit a reaction or see "the effect" (Titus, D2). Looking into someone's Pocket was often done when they were in view. This not only made it more difficult to take an image, thus increasing challenge, but could also trigger telling exchanges of looks, with participants glancing at each other to indicate that they were attending to their phone and were ready to defend themselves. Furthermore, successful taking in this context meant that the bemoaning of loss of an image could be witnessed first-hand. Use of Take and Give often became an undercurrent in meetings or at lunchtimes, with participants hurriedly retrieving their phones when they noticed another participant carrying theirs, or reacting out loud when images were taken from them.

For those who were unable to see first-hand the effect of their takes, the importance of eliciting a reaction was still important, but realized in a different way. When Peter (I2) talked about making the "ultimate steal", he envisaged completely ransacking someone's Pocket and leaving a "calling card" to show that he had been there. When describing an example in which he had accomplished this with Steven's Pocket, he went on to say, "Even though I wasn't there I knew exactly what his reaction would be and it was kind of more, it spoke to me a bit more" (I2). In this case, the existing strong social relationship was an important factor in taking files, enabling Peter to imagine and take pleasure in what the reaction might be.

Thus, motivations for the taking of content were bound up with self-presentation and social interaction. Take and Give was a means of self-presentation, both through the curation of images and through displays of strategy and skill. Further, use of the application was bound up with provoking reactions from and issuing challenges to others. In the next section, we describe how this was done in a way that was mindful of the boundaries of other Take and Give users.

Understanding and Pushing Boundaries

It is important to note that while taking was an act that was normally considered mischievous, it could also be potentially annoying, demanding and disruptive. Views of content could interrupt one's colleagues when they would prefer not to be distracted, and takes could entail the removal of a target's favourite image. Consequently, use of the application needed to be undertaken in a way that was sensitive to the boundaries of other participants, and strategies were gradually adapted accordingly. As the deployment progressed and participants crossed more of these "boundaries" (Heidi, D2), they were able to test out and discover new aspects of one another's character. They reported being sometimes surprised by the competitiveness that was displayed, this being a characteristic not typically associated with the workplace, or participants, in question.

One example of a strategy that emerged more slowly was the sustained attack. Whilst participants were prepared to be somewhat sneaky at the beginning of the deployment, sustained attacks were only adopted once they had a better sense of each other's tolerance for this kind of behaviour, and their willingness to take it in good humour. For example, Steven commented that he was prepared to target Heidi for a particularly intense sustained attack only towards the end of the trial (D2), an act that was indicative of the developed knowledge of one another's boundaries.

However, there were some boundaries that were rarely crossed. Even for participants who were somewhat inept at, or disinterested in, participating, it was rare for Pockets to be completely emptied. Instead, participants generally tended to show a degree of restraint when easy opportunities arose, taking only one or two images. This is partly bound up with the lack of challenge this presents, as already discussed, but it also reflects a sense of fairness and of not wishing to push others out of participating (as already noted, it was important to have content in one's Pocket to participate). Participants who were particularly inattentive, such as Ron, also found themselves the recipient of gifted images, as a way of trying to sustain their participation in the trial. As previously mentioned though, Ron did not really want to participate. He later expressed a sense of unease at peering into his employees' Pockets; as a manager, use of the application seemed too personal to him. In this case, using the application involved crossing a boundary that was not surmounted; Ron's lack of participation is clearly illustrated in Figure 6.

Titus also described himself as being somewhat disturbed at the introduction of pictures of himself into the image pool, saying, "It is very distressing if you look in someone's Pocket and they have a photo of you" (D2). However, the amusement that he expressed on top of this dismay meant that others felt this was a boundary that could be pushed, and joined in.

Evidence of the importance of understanding boundaries can also be seen in the different ways in which Take and Give was used by on- and off-site participants. Tony (who was off-site) reported that it felt a bit "bizarre" (I2) to take an image from people that he did not know well, such as Adam and Heidi who were new to the workgroup. Further, Peter (also off-site) observed that "you need to figure out where someone's level is" as an integral part of using the application, and that face-to-face "feedback" (I2) is an important component of this. This was one reason why Peter did not feel comfortable taking from many participants; Figure 6 clearly shows how his strongest connection was with Steven, who he knew best out of the group. Both Peter and Tony, the two off-site participants, are plotted away from the core on-site group. Social relationships mediate the impact of co-presence, and we suggest that this is because boundaries are better understood.

Effect of Taking on Awareness and Connection

The above section indicates how Take and Give affected social relationships within the group more generally. The application presented an opportunity for participants to attend to one another, watching or listening for moments when others appeared distracted, for example, or observing their reactions to views, takes and the occasional gift.

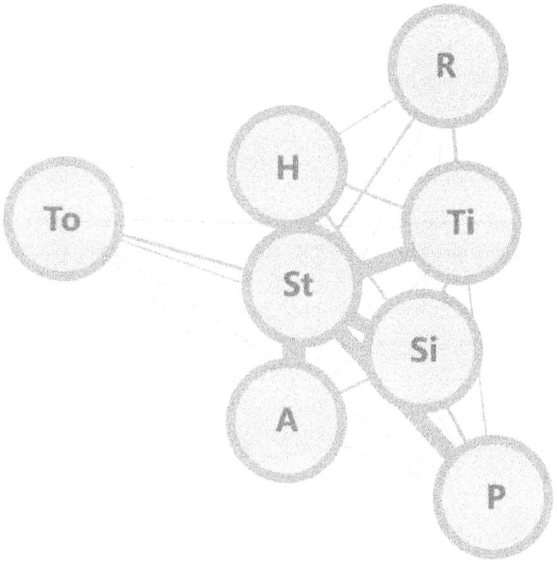

Figure 6. Force-directed graph of participants based on successful takes; line strength represents the amount of taking across any one pair of participants.

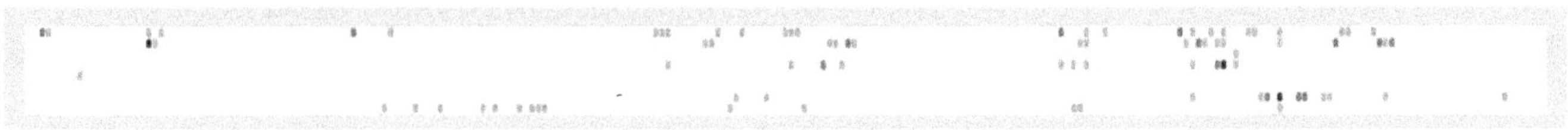

Figure 7. Views per minute over a typical trial day. Each row is a single participant's data for a typical day of the trial (Day 4). The total number of views of a Pocket in each one minute span is rendered – darker means more views.

We have outlined so far that the process of curating a Pocket could support self-expression and also led participants to learn how to entice each other into their own Pockets. We have also seen that participants learnt about one another's competitive streaks, strategies and boundaries. More generally, participation in the trial led to a sense of awareness within the group. One behaviour that emerged was the counter-view: participants often responded to someone viewing their Pocket by returning the view. This gave the impression of the recipient being "attentive to my poking" (Steven, D2), and provided a potent sense of presence through the application. Views and counter-views also extended outwards across the group, in what was described as "social cascading" (Steven, D2). Figure 7 shows this cascade in action: each row draws from a single participant's data for a typical day of the trial (in this case day 4). The total number of views in each one minute span is rendered (light grey for one view, darker grey for two, and black for three or more). The figure demonstrates how views are often clustered together, occurring in bursts. These cascades, in which multiple participants looked at each other's Pockets in quick succession, were noted for providing a sense of the group's connection and attentiveness.

In addition to this, images that were highly valued often led to the formation of transient sub-groups of participants. For example, an image of a lava-lamp was particularly sought after by four participants, Adam, Heidi, Steven, and Titus, and once acquired by Heidi it was enjoyable for her to hold on to it whilst the others attempted to take it from her. Yet when this image was mentioned at the second group discussion, Simone reported not knowing of the image in question, nor was she aware of the intense activity that had centred on it. Thus, certain images could bind some participants together, but these sub-groups could be invisible to the wider group.

In other cases, sub-groups formed around joint action, in a way that was obvious to other participants. In one example, three participants simultaneously targeted the off-site Tony during their lunch break, bombarding him with takes. Tony later described how he felt that the three must have been together; "It couldn't have been otherwise", and Peter also recognized when he was the victim of an organised assault, explicitly sending a message: "your feeble collaboration will come to no good" (log).

Sub-groups tended to be fleeting however, and participation in the deployment engendered a sense of awareness and connection amongst the group as a whole, and particularly amongst the on-site participants. This sense of companionship was also apparent to other members of the workplace. The behaviours witnessed were described by those not involved as "quite funny to watch" (Outside Member 1), and were noted to have generally brought a sense of camaraderie to the workplace. However, they was also described as "excluding" (Outside Member 1) and (somewhat jokingly) as being "unbearably cliquey" (Outside Member 2).

It is worth additionally noting that this sense of connection did not fully extend to the off-site participants. The application was used more frequently, and this use was sustained better, within the on-site group than with off-site participants. Those that were on-site felt that the two remote users were "dropping off" (Heidi, D2) in their usage by the third week, and off-site Peter (I2) also expressed that he felt the application was best suited to "collocated tomfoolery".

These findings suggest that an application that facilitates the taking of unique content within a group of people can provide a mechanism for awareness and connectedness. However, this is strongest between those that already know one another well and that can interact face-to-face outside of using the application. We suggest that this is related to boundaries, and the need to be able to push these gently.

DISCUSSION

This deployment of Take and Give, and the twist on traditional content sharing practices that it entails, provides an illustration of how the taking of unique content can serve to facilitate awareness and underpin social connection. The ways in which this is achieved are numerous and diverse, and echo prior research in related spaces. Use of Take and Give became a means of self-presentation [cf. 6] through image curation. Like the music collections belonging to iTunes users [22], Pockets were curated with a view to the way they would be perceived and, in a pattern of behaviour that resonates with Glancephone users [9], this was bound up with eliciting reactions from, and attending to, others. Relatedly, the movement of images across participants, and the knowledge of who preferred what, meant that some images came to be more valuable than others, similar to those in the Urbanhermes system [14]. In this case though, having a highly-valued image was likely to provoke action, rather than admiration. Further, the system provided a mechanism for views and counter-views, which could cascade throughout the group and underpin a sense of presence much as Glancephone [9] users glanced at others because they wanted to provoke a glance at themselves. Given these features, it is perhaps not surprising that the application was felt to create a sense of awareness and connectedness amongst the participants.

In the discussion that follows, we focus on two aspects of the system design. Firstly, we consider the consequences of our design decision to support the taking of ownership of unique content, rather than copying of content and discuss the implications of this for future design endeavors. Secondly, we consider Take and Give's playful qualities and how this affected the use of the system in the workplace.

Taking Ownership of Unique Content

The fact that there was only one version of each file within the image pool underpinned a sense of ownership, which was reminiscent of gaming and triggered the development of strategies to hold on to content [cf. 1]. This can be clearly contrasted with systems such as Twitter, where ownership of expressive content is more nuanced and it is perceived as acceptable to copy, proliferate, and keep content that originates elsewhere [15]. Notably, a (sometimes fierce) sense of ownership developed around Take and Give content, despite the fact that images placed in Pockets were, in a manner of speaking, 'broadcast'; they were placed there to be viewed by others, and this placement was done with full knowledge that they could consequently be taken.

This wish to hold on to content was bound up with an implicit value system that developed through use of the application. Images were known to be valuable because others would attempt to acquire them and so, through interactions via the system, users could learn how their own content was perceived by others. Further, there being only one version of each image made it very clear which images were most wanted, and by whom. The fact that taking was bound up with ownership of a unique image strengthened the association between certain individuals and certain images; ownership was bound up with self-presentation in a way that may be less exaggerated when multiple people own the same item. This provided an additional incentive to curate and protect one's Pocket. Finally, the development of strategies around taking and keeping content was also a way in which participants presented themselves through the system. Attempts to take content were an outlet for behaviour that was mischievous, sneaky or competitive, allowing participants to express different sides of themselves, and to extol the skill of others.

This suggests that systems with only one version of each file may underpin a stronger sense of ownership of content and, if that content can be taken, a value system that is bound up with knowledge of individual preference. For instance, we might consider a shared digital book repository for an office space that allowed each group member to 'own' a selection of the books, thus indicating their current interests or knowledge area. As well, this would provide a mechanism to spark conversation when someone else wishes to take ownership of another's book. A system like this could be in line with Digital Rights Management, while allowing co-workers to share content.

However, there are a number of further design decisions that could be added to an application for taking of unique content that we did not explore. Much as Twitter users feel their content can be reused as long as authorship is attributed [15], and fashionistas are enticed by lineage [14], we posit that a history of ownership could enhance an environment for taking, and would be particularly compelling when there is only 'one' version of each item. Such ideas resonate with other attempts to show the 'wear' of digital objects [10]. In addition, further ways for explicitly marking boundaries, such as Wikipedia page maintainers do [21], may be important when designing for online spaces that feature unique content and underpin a keen sense of ownership. Exploring these additions is a rich area of further work.

Playful Taking in the Workplace

A further topic for discussion is the playful aspect of the taking act and situating this within the workplace. While not a game as such (see Kaprow [13] for the distinction between play and games), the pattern of use that emerged resonates with classical sociological and anthropological descriptions of play. Huizinga [12] and Caillois [4] have described play as being separate from 'ordinary' life, proceeding freely with its own boundaries of time and space, and engaging a restricted circle of people. Huizinga has underscored this separation from reality as fundamental to the role of play as a 'safe' domain, in which learning can be undertaken without fear of negative social consequence.

The playful quality of the taking act became a useful connection mechanism for on-site colleagues who did not necessarily know each other well at the beginning of the field trial. Nardi [16] argues that flirting, joking and everyday chitchat can serve as a resource for further work-related communication by creating a sense of affinity and trust, and it was clear that Take and Give occasioned conversation and provided opportunities for co-workers to get to know each other. Further, we see how these points of connection need not always be respectful. Participants interrupted one another's work by launching sustained attacks, adopted cunning strategies to distract targets before taking images, and provocatively uploaded photos of each other to the image pool. In the same way that a deployment of Loki [5], an agent that propagated gossip and lies amongst co-workers, was found to act as a resource for communication, our findings show that playful taking can be an act that bonds at work.

However, it is crucial to acknowledge that the ways in which participants appropriated Take and Give were not malicious or disrespectful. Fieldwork by Roy [18] demonstrates how delicate the balance for joviality at work can be - if a co-worker is somehow offended then the result can be an end to all frivolity. In this deployment too, it was clear that participants took care not to cross one another's boundaries. They avoided overzealous or callous thievery at moments of vulnerability, choosing not to empty each other's pockets when the opportunity arose. Participants were careful about pushing each other's boundaries, with off-site participants being especially reluctant to test the limits of others. Through the act of not taking, participants were able to express a degree of consideration for one another.

Thus, the sense of playfulness engendered by Take and Give was essential to allowing participants to test one another's boundaries in a 'safe' space within the workplace, and through doing so discover aspects of one another's character that might not otherwise emerge.

CONCLUSION

In this paper we have described how Take and Give, an application that promotes the taking of unique content from others, served as a mechanism for awareness and connection. Firstly, we have highlighted how ownership of unique content, and the strategies that were used to obtain and keep them, were bound up with self-presentation underpinning a value system in which it was understood who wanted what images. Secondly, we have described how use of the system was influenced by the context in which it was deployed, the workplace. We have suggested that Take and Give provided a safe environment in which users could test one another's boundaries, and conversely, demonstrate restraint when a target was vulnerable. We conclude that systems built on the premise of taking unique content provide an interesting metaphor for interaction, which can be as engaging as giving in sharing content.

ACKNOWLEDGMENTS

We would like to thank Alex Soojung-Kim Pang for his input on initial drafts of this paper, and the Microsoft Cambridge Socio-Digital Systems group for tolerating our use of the Take and Give system.

REFERENCES

1. Barkhuus, L., Chalmers, M., Tennent, P., Hall, M., Sherwood, S. & Brown, B. Picking pockets on the lawn: The development of tactics and strategies in a mobile game. In *Proc. UbiComp 2005*, 358-374.
2. Beggan, J.K. On the social nature of non-social perception: The mere ownership effect. *Journal of Personality & Social Psychology 62*, 2 (1992), 229-237.
3. Berg, S. Taylor, A. & Harper R. Mobile phones for the next generation: Device designs for teenagers. In *Proc. CHI 2003*, 433-440.
4. Caillois, R. *Man, Play and Games*. University of Illinois Press, Urbana and Chicago, 1958.
5. Foucault, B., Mentis, H.M., Sengers, P. & Welles, D. Provoking sociability. In *Proc. CHI 2007*, 1557-1560.
6. Goffman, E. *The Presentation of Self in Everyday Life*. Penguin Books, London, 1959.
7. Halfaker, A., Kittur, A., Kraut, R. & Riedl, J. A jury of your peers: Quality, experience and ownership in Wikipedia. In *Proc. WikiSym 2009*,155-164.
8. Harper, R.H.R. *Texture: Human Expression in the Age of Communications Overload*. The MIT Press, London, 2010.
9. Harper, R. & Taylor. S. Glancephone: An exploration of human expression. In *Proc. MobileHCI 2009*, 1-10.
10. Hill, W.C., Hollan, J.D., Wroblewski, D., McCandless, T. Edit wear and read wear. In *Proc. CHI 1992*, 3-9.
11. Hollan, J. & Stornetta, S. Beyond being there. *Proc. CHI 1992*, 119-125.
12. Huizinga, J. *Homo Ludens: A Study of the Play Element in Culture*. The Beacon Press, Boston, 1950.
13. Kaprow, A. *Essays on the blurring of art and life*. University of California Press, Berkeley, 2003.
14. Liu, C.M. *Urbanhermes: Fashion signalling and the social mobility of images*. Master's Thesis (2006). Downloaded November 15, 2011: http://smg.media.mit.edu/ projects/urbanhermes/thesisfinal.pdf.
15. Marshall, C.C. & Shipman, F.M. Social media ownership: using Twitter as a window onto current attitudes and beliefs. In *Proc. CHI 2011*, 1081-1090.
16. Nardi, B. Beyond bandwidth: Dimensions of connection in interpersonal communication. *Computer-Supported Cooperative Work 14*, 2 (2005), 91-130.
17. Pierce, J.L., Kostova, T. & Dirks, K.T. Toward a theory of psychological ownership in organizations. *Academy of Management Review 26*, (2001), 298-310.
18. Roy, D.F. Banana Time: Job satisfaction and informal interaction. *Human Organization 18*, (1959), 158-168.
19. Strauss, A.L. *Qualitative Analysis for Social Scientists*. Cambridge University Press, Cambridge, 1987.
20. Taylor, A. & Harper, R. The gift of the gab: A design oriented sociology of young people's use of mobiles. *Computer-Supported Cooperative Work 12*, 3 (2003) 267-296.
21. Thom-Santelli, J., Cosley, D. & Gay, G. What's mine is mine: Territoriality in collaborative authoring. In *Proc. CHI 2009*, 1481-1484.
22. Voida, A., Grinter, R.E., Ducheneaut, N., Edwards, W.K. & Newman, M.W. Listening in: Practices surrounding iTunes music sharing. In *Proc. CHI 2005*, 191-2000.
23. Wang, Q.Y., Battocchi, A., Graziola, I., Pianesi, F., Tomasini, D., Zancanaro, M. & Nass, C. The role of psychological ownership and ownership markers in collaborative working environment. In *Proc. ICMI 2006*, 225-232.

Video Threads: Asynchronous Video Sharing for Temporally Distributed Teams

Jeremy T. Barksdale[†‡], Kori Inkpen[†], Mary Czerwinski[†], Aaron Hoff[†], Paul Johns[†], Asta Roseway[†], Gina Venolia[†]

[†]Microsoft Research
One Microsoft Way
Redmond, WA 98052
{kori, marycz, aaronho, pauljoh, astar, ginav}@microsoft.com

[‡]Department of Computer Science
Virginia Tech
Blacksburg, VA 24060 USA
barksdale@vt.edu

ABSTRACT
Work teams are often geographically distributed, and in some cases, experience large time-zone differences with no overlap in working hours. We explored the use of asynchronous video in temporally distributed teams. We developed VideoThreads, which provides a novel thread-based visualization of video messages. Based on a deployment to four teams, we offer design recommendations and insights about the benefits of asynchronous video sharing.

Author Keywords
Computer-mediated-communication, video, asynchronous, CSCW, time-shifted collaboration, office and workspace.

ACM Classification Keywords
H5.3. Group and Organization Interfaces (CSCW).

General Terms
Design; Human Factors; Management

INTRODUCTION
Workgroups are often geographically distributed and can span large time-zones. Temporal and geographic dispersion can complicate group-based communication as various cues and signals available in face-to-face interaction are absent.

When there is some overlap in normal working hours, teams can schedule synchronous communication. However, not all teams have this luxury. A number of text-based asynchronous communication tools exist to help distributed teams work together more effectively. Such media, however, do not necessarily facilitate nuanced communication.

The goal of our research is to explore whether asynchronous video conversations could be beneficial to temporally distributed teams, and how they might be used. The contributions of this work are three-fold: we introduce a thread-based visualization tool to manage asynchronous video conversations, we contribute an understanding of how temporally distributed teams use asynchronous video, and we provide design recommendations for asynchronous video messaging tools.

TEMPORALLY DISTRIBUTED TEAMS

Distributed Team Communication
Distributed team communication has been studied extensively [1, 11, 13]. Grinter et al., found that team members could mitigate some coordination challenges by using their personal networks nurtured by face-to-face time [5]. They also found that cross-site work has interdependencies that introduce delays [6, 7]. In comparing video to face-to-face communication, Issacs and Tang found that participants used video to express understanding or agreement, enhance verbal descriptions, and express attitudes through posture and facial expression [8]. Similar research found that video was beneficial for non-native speakers and that groups who used both audio and video in a social dilemma game did as well as face-to-face [14].

Temporally distributed teams that experience a time-zone difference of eight hours or greater likely have very different work-life boundary experiences than teams that are two or three time-zones apart [12]. Common means of communicating within highly temporally distributed teams are email, voicemail, and shared repositories. However, none of these media provide teams with the ability to capture visual cues or other information that assists in communicating effectively.

Asynchronous Video Communication Tools

Commercially available asynchronous video communication tools, such as Techsmith's Camtasia Studio and Jive Systems, allow users to send or broadcast individual videos and screencasts to a number of recipients. However, there is limited support to visualize the flow of conversations, and some are complex to use. Our tool specifically focuses on providing lightweight interaction and conversation visualization.

AIR (Accelerated Instant Replay) Conferencing and PAVE (PAL Virtual Environment) are related non-commercial tools. AIR Conferencing allows distributed attendees to catch-up on missed content during a meeting using various modalities – audio, video, shared workspace, and text [9]. PAVE was designed to support asynchronous collaboration among distributed researchers by allowing users to asynchronously replay captured media (audio, text, and drawing) used in a virtual meeting room [1]. Given the cost of using video (in file size) at the time PAVE was developed, it was not included in the tool. Our work revisits this scenario, but with the use of video and screen recording threads, to provide richer interactions.

Thread Metaphor

Frustration from incoherent conversations can contribute to communication challenges in highly temporally distributed teams. Conversational coherence is the semantic meaning gained by the sequence of temporal and topical exchanges among people where the relationship between previous and successive turns is clear and easy to follow and where individual messages contribute to an overall topic [4]. A threaded visualization can help improve coherence and reduce the cognitive load that might otherwise be required to follow along in a conversation.

VIDEOTHREADS

VideoThreads enables team members to capture video, record their screen, and send, receive, and reply to a message. When screen recording, team members can share parts of their screen while simultaneously narrating. Notifications and related metadata of new messages are sent via email with a link to open the message. VideoThreads inherently facilitates many-to-many distributed conversations since many people can receive updates for, and contribute to, a conversation.

The VideoThreads user interface (Fig. 1) is comprised of three windows: the conversation window, the message window, and the screen recording frame. The conversation window displays a hierarchical visual representation showing the flow of one conversation and a list of all conversations along with the properties of each conversation (i.e., the number of messages in the conversation, the date and time of the last update, the people involved in the conversation, and the number of unread messages). A camera icon is shown in the top left corner if the message contains a screen recording. The message window enables users to record a message, preview a recording, or play a received message. The screen recording frame is used to select the area of the screen that will be recorded.

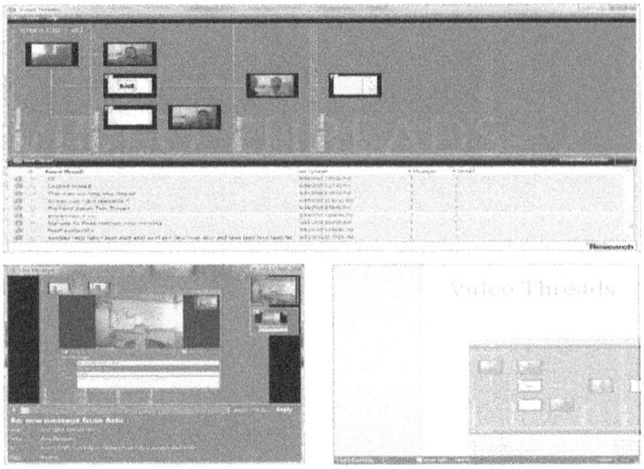

Figure 1: VideoThreads conversation window (top), message window (bottom left), screen recording frame (bottom right).

VideoThreads uses a central server that is a repository for videos and the related message, user, and conversation metadata. Videos are stored in the server file system while event log data and metadata are stored in a SQL Server database accessible to client components via a secure asp.net web service layer. The client component is built using Windows Presentation Foundation (WPF) and Microsoft's Expression Encoder library (for video recording and processing). Messages in a thread are rendered according to a hierarchical layout algorithm and their creation date.

TRIAL DEPLOYMENT

We deployed VideoThreads to four teams (totaling 29 participants) over a two week period. Team A (5 members) and D (8 members) were each distributed between Redmond, WA and Shanghai. Team B (8 members) was distributed between Redmond and Zurich. Team C (8 members) was distributed between Redmond and India. Each team had at least one highly temporally distributed member and at least one month of collaboration experience to reduce variability inherent in newly formed teams. Participants used their own computers and received a gratuity for their participation. No guidelines were provided to participants on how or when to use VideoThreads. They decided which communication medium best suited their needs. To better determine when participants would use video instead of email, we prevented users from sending a message without either a video or screen capture in VideoThreads. We surveyed participants on their current communication practices, then deployed VideoThreads, and finally surveyed the participants again to measure any perceived changes. Microsoft Outlook, which allows message threading, was the email tool used for comparison and was the primary email client used by our participants.

Results and Insights

Participants did not collaborate on software development tasks using VideoThreads as expected. Instead, they used the tool for congratulating and becoming familiar with one another. There were 18-56 messages per team (with an average of 38 messages), 11-28 threads created (with an average of 20 threads per team), and the tool was used between 3-9 days (with an average of 7 days). Most threads had 1 or 2 messages; however, others had 3-7 messages. This is consistent with the distribution of email thread lengths reported in [10]. Usage was lower than hoped given the challenge of motivating participants to incorporate the tool into their workflow, although this result is consistent with previous literature on tool adoption [2].

Regarding thread visualization, 55% of participants reported that following the flow of a conversation in email was easy, whereas, 69% reported that following the flow of a conversation in VideoThreads was easy. Additionally, 16% of participants reported moderate or extreme difficulty with following the flow of conversation in email, whereas no moderate or extreme difficulty was reported for VideoThreads. Almost half of our participants, 14/29 (48%), were satisfied with message threading in VideoThreads and no participants were dissatisfied. Fully experiencing the message threading feature requires multiple exchanges on a specific topic. Some participants did not engage in this level of conversation. We believe that one primary reason the remaining participants rated message threading as "neither satisfied nor dissatisfied" is because they did not engage in enough conversation on a topic to evaluate the message threading feature.

In comparison to email, results showed that 15/29 (52%) participants found VideoThreads either more useful or much more useful than email. Other participants seemed to find VideoThreads less useful because they could not edit videos as easily as they could edit email, re-recording videos decreased productivity, it was difficult to quickly seek to a specific point in the video, they could not search the audio or video content, video required more write/read time than email, and most of their close team members were in the same geographical area. For VideoThreads', 20/29 (69%) participants indicated they were satisfied or very satisfied with the visualization component while only 1/29 (3%) indicated that they dissatisfied (Fig 2).

The following four benefits surfaced from a thematic analysis of our qualitative survey data.

Emotional and Personal Feel. One of the key benefits of VideoThreads was that it enabled users to see the personality or emotion of other team members through video. For example, a participant from one team that initiated a thread to congratulate one another for completing a milestone remarked "*it was quite satisfying to see people reacting positively to [the completed milestone], and I could actually see them.*"

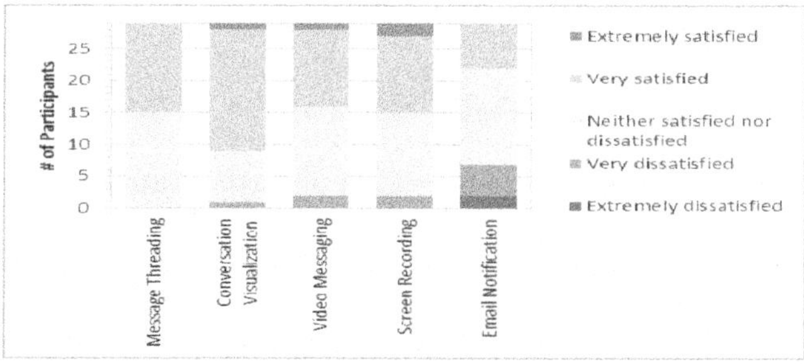

Figure 2: Responses for VideoThreads Features Satisfaction

Participants also reported that they felt more connected with other team members when sharing video asynchronously and that they appreciated the social niceties of video that are less prevalent in email. As one participant explained "*...I grabbed my laptop and just walked around and showed him what the office looked like today, who was doing what, and got everyone to wave and say hi to the camera to try and make him feel more connected.*"

Benefits from being able to see each other on video have been reported in other research [3,8,11]; however, it is important to remember that people on temporally distributed teams rarely see each other, and asynchronous use of video is rare. Some of our participants had never seen some of their teammates and appreciated being able to connect a person's image with their name. One participant commented, "*I haven't met him at all, so it's good to put [a] name to a face and see him actually amusing himself. That always helps.*" Another participant commented that there were elements in the background of his video which he chose to keep visible so that it would communicate some of his personal interests to other members of the team.

Communication Efficiency. Efficiency was seen as both a benefit and a disadvantage of VideoThreads. For example, "*Sending these kinds of announcements verbally... often actually using screen capture, seemed much more efficient to me cause it took less time for me to put together a quick narrated video message of what I was trying to illustrate.*"

However, others missed the efficiencies of email such as the ability to quickly search through and scan across a lot of emails and edit discreet sections of a message. One participant commented that "*with email you can kind of sit, formulate it a little, and type it out, whereas with video [you have to] record and re-record to make sure ... you didn't lose your train of thought midstream.*" Others commented on the overhead associated with video, in particular since it isn't a part of everyday work culture: "*Video at this point takes more work. Email - you just start typing. Video, you have to fire up the application, make sure the camera is on, take a look, and sometimes record and [you're] like 'did that sound right?'* "

Value of Video as a Medium. Several participants found value in using video because it helped them explain complicated things such as demoing use of an application, reproducing a bug, or showing a drawing by pointing the webcam at the whiteboard. As one participant explained: "*I set up a screen capture window [to show] how we should do work item tracking. And so I just pulled up a report that showed what we were making use of. It was easy to show people... and use my mouse to illustrate what pieces of it I was trying to draw attention to.*"

One downside of video was that some people were uncomfortable being seen on video and felt it was too invasive at times. Some also noted the shyness associated with team members who speak English as a second language. As one participant expressed: "*I didn't think this would happen, but trying to take a video capture of myself and sending it to people felt a little unnerving. It's not as simple and straight forward as a voice call or an email.*"

Visualizing Conversations. Conversation visualization was one feature that participants specifically liked in VideoThreads over approaches commonly used in email, "*... the conversation history comes through nicer than in email, so it's easier to see date progression and things like that.*" However, albeit messages were easy to follow within VideoThreads, the overall conversation was sometimes difficult to follow since it was spread across various media, "*you couldn't shift from an existing email thread to add video to that context and say 'well I'd like to add video or screen capture.' And it was hard to do the reverse too.*"

DESIGN RECOMMENDATIONS

From our results we provide three design recommendations.

Integrate with existing communication tools. Not surprisingly, most of our participants wanted VideoThreads integrated into their email tool. They wanted to be able to leverage the address book and email notifications. Also, enhanced thread visualization would allow participants to see all messages related to a conversation, regardless of the media (i.e., email, IM, and phone messages) within the thread visualization. Providing access anytime and anywhere was also important to participants. They wanted more ubiquitous access to the tool—outside the firewall and on mobile devices. Users wanted to be able to quickly scan messages from home or other non-work locations.

Enable Searchability / Editability. The users in our study wanted ways to search videos to find particular content or quickly browse a conversation. Additionally, users wanted more video editing related features to enable them to more creatively compose their video messages and screen shots in personal ways.

Provide Social Aids. Some users found value in the screen capturing and recording feature because it helped them communicate complex ideas more clearly. Some enjoyed the more creative features that allowed them to add virtual artifacts via camera effects to their video message. These features can allow users that are shy and uncomfortable with video a means to communicate more confidently. Translation, transcription, and annotation could assist those users whose primary language is not English communicate more confidently.

CONCLUSIONS

Asynchronous video sharing has its place among temporally distributed work teams when well integrated with existing tools. However, the cost of using video is still high relative to text. Our findings indicate that video can provide opportunities to help teammates gain exposure to each other's personalities and ease complex demonstrations. Team members found fun and interesting ways of incorporating video into their routine to enhance group communication.

REFERENCES

1. Adams, L., Toomey, L., and Churchill, E. Distributed research teams: Meeting asynchronously in virtual space. *HICSS-32*, (1999).
2. Bradner, E., Kellogg, W., and Erickson, T. The adoption and use of 'Babble': A field study of chat in the workplace. *ECSCW'99*, Springer (1999), 139-158.
3. Fish, R.S., Kraut, R.E., and Chalfonte, B.L. The VideoWindow system in informal communication. *Proc. CSCW*, ACM (1990), 11.
4. Goodwin, C. and Heritage, J. Conversation analysis. *Annual review of anthropology 19*, (1990), 283-307.
5. Grinter, R.E., Herbsleb, J.D., and Perry, D.E. The geography of coordination: dealing with distance in R&D work. *Proc. GROUP*, ACM (1999), 315.
6. Herbsleb, J.D., Mockus, A., Finholt, T.A., and Grinter, R.E. Distance, dependencies, and delay in a global collaboration. *Proc. CSCW*, ACM (2000), 328.
7. Herbsleb, J.D., Mockus, A., Finholt, T.A., and Grinter, R.E. An empirical study of global software development: distance and speed. *Proc. ICSE*, IEEE Computer Society (2001), 81-90.
8. Isaacs, E.A. and Tang, J.C. What video can and cannot do for collaboration: a case study. *Multimedia Systems 2*, 2 (1994), 63-73.
9. Junuzovic, S., Inkpen, K., Hegde, R., Zhang, Z., Tang, J., and Brooks, C. What did i miss? In-Meeting Review using Multimodal Accelerated Instant Replay (AIR) Conferencing. *Proc. CHI*, ACM (2011), 513-522.
10. Kerr, B. Thread arcs: An email thread visualization. (2003).
11. van der Kleij, R., Maarten Schraagen, J., Werkhoven, P., and De Dreu, C.K.W. How Conversations Change Over Time in Face-to-Face and Video-Mediated Communication. *Small Group Research 40*, 4 (2009), 355.
12. O'Leary, M.B. and Cummings, J.N. The spatial, temporal, and configurational characteristics of geographic dispersion in teams. *MIS Quarterly 31*, 3 (2007), 433-452.
13. Olson, G.M. and Olson, J.S. Distance matters. *HCI 15*, 2 (2000), 139-178.
14. Veinott, E.S., Olson, J., Olson, G.M., and Fu, X. Video helps remote work: Speakers who need to negotiate common ground benefit from seeing each other. *Proc. CHI*, ACM (1999), 309.

Patterns of Team Processes and Breakdowns in Information Analysis Tasks

Marcela Borge, Craig H. Ganoe, Shin-I Shih*, & John M. Carroll
College of Information Sciences and Technology & Department of Psychology*
The Pennsylvania State University, University Park, PA, USA
{mborge, szs215}@psu.edu,{cganoe, jcarroll}@ist.psu.edu

ABSTRACT
In this paper we present findings from a laboratory study of teams of three, collaborating to complete a complex information sharing, synthesis, decision-making task. We use interaction analysis, communication analysis, and task analysis methods to identify the primary activities teams engaged in as they solved a complex information dependant decision-making task. These activities serve as the foundation to present findings related to common team problems and patterns of interaction associated with team performance. We found differences between high and low performing teams related to verbal equity and how they shared and synthesized information.

Author Keywords
Information Analysis, Shared Authority, Cognitive Specialization, Team Performance, Information Synthesis, Communication Analysis, Verbal Equity, Information Artifacts

ACM Classification Keywords
H.5.3- Group and Organization Interfaces

General Terms
Human Factors; Experimentation; Performance

INTRODUCTION
Teams often lack the ability to use their interactions as a resource for effective problem solving [2, 3, 13, 14, 16, 17, 27]. In formal learning environments, poor collaborative interactions can lead to lower team learning and task performance outcomes when compared to teams with more effective interactions [2, 3]. The same is true in emergency/crisis work contexts, but with far higher stakes and the potential for catastrophic outcomes [17]. In business contexts differences in processes can be determinants of economic success or an organizations ability to learn [26, 11]. West (2007) argues that successful teams are those that have a greater level of diversity in terms of backgrounds, expertise, and knowledge, and can use those diverse members as resources when engaging in joint team knowledge-building activities. Team knowledge building activity is the act of creating new knowledge that did not exist anywhere in the team prior to collaboration [23]. One person sharing expert knowledge with their team would be an example of information transfer. An example of knowledge building would be the team using that information to draw new conclusions or extend what was previously known.

CSCW'12, February 11–15, 2012, Seattle, Washington, USA.

Our aim is to understand the patterns of activities teams engage in when completing a complex, dynamic task, where the task fluctuates and changes over time, in order to understand how those patterns are associated with performance. Our research questions are as follows: 1) what are the primary activities teams engage in during complex, dynamic collaborative activity (i.e., task analysis and related breakdowns), and 2) what differences exist in the patterns of interaction between high and low performing teams.

Prior research has identified issues of verbal equity and the use of visual representations to mediate understanding as important factors in the learning processes and success of teams [12, 19, 24, 25]. For this reason we chose to comprehensively analyze communication, interaction, development of information artifacts, i.e., visual representations, and compare patterns across teams. By comparing differences between high and low performing teams we aim to identify critical processes associated with performance. Thus we developed a complex scenario to serve as the basis for a lab study where we can control for amount of distributed task knowledge and expertise and meticulously track activity.

We previously developed similar types of scenarios as a means to observe team behavior and inform the design of collaborative tools. We have validated these scenarios with actual fieldwork, and demonstrated that this development process produces tools that improve average performance of collaborative teams [4, 7, 8, 9, 22].

Study design
We used a collaborative information analysis scenario as a means to study information dependent decision-making activity. The scenario needed to fulfill certain requirements

in order serve as a representative information dependent decision making task: maximize generalizability, provide diverse but equitable roles, and present a complex information rich, non-linear problem that requires team members to share specialized information in order to make decisions. We decided to develop a complex crime-solving task and utilized a military information analysis scenario as means of informing the structure of an information synthesis task [26].

In order to maximize ecological validity, the scenario is designed to emulate the characteristics and processes of a real police task force team. For example, having investigators that are familiar with the neighborhood and general context of the environment where a crime occurs is crucial to ensuring for an effective investigative team [1, 5]. Consequently the scenario uses local landmarks and crimes that would be more familiar to our participant pool. This is done to provide participants with some inherent expertise, similar to the type of knowledge that real experts might have.

The scenario is divided into three parts and is similar to a proactive investigation tactic employed by police departments when dealing with burglaries, where the ultimate goal to predict and prevent the next crime [5]. Participants must use a mix of inductive and deductive reasoning much in the same way real police officers or information analysts would [1, 20] in order to accurately solve each part of the scenario. Participants must use shared information as a means to accomplish different objectives in each part of the scenario: (part one) narrow down a list of 26 Persons of Interest (POIs) to a list of the eight most likely suspects; (part two) identify thieves for each of four thefts, instigators or accomplices, motives, and whether there were connections among the four thefts; and (part three) predict the thief, time and place of the next crime.

In total, the scenario contains 222 unique pieces of information divided evenly between three information analyst roles: Interview Analyst, Web Analyst, and Records Analyst. Each team member is provided a General Mission Statement and a set of Role Documents. Each set of Role Documents contains unique information that other specialist roles lack. For example, Records Analyst has information on bank transactions, receipts, and class schedules, Web Analyst has information gathered from Facebook, Twitter, Ebay, and other online resources, and Interview Analyst has information gathered from questioning POIs and people they know, and tailing POIs in order to determine regular routines or contacts.

The General Mission Statement is the same for all roles: it contains crime descriptions, explains reliability of the information, and provides "rules" associated with alibis and opportunity to commit the crime. Participants play the same role throughout the scenario, and in order to do well on the task, they need to share their specialized information as a means to draw accurate conclusions.

Pilot tests were conducted to ensure that our participants understood the scenario and had sufficient knowledge of local landmarks and related events. Furthermore, in every trial, we found that participants relied on their knowledge of places and events to make claims. For example, they would make statements like: "Well they could walk from the IST Building to the White Building in 5 minutes; I have done that before."

METHODS

Video data from ten microanalyzed teams, five consistently high performing and five consistently low performing, is the primary data source for the findings presented in this paper. This data is used to unpack the types of cognitive activities and process problems experienced by our teams and whether patterns exist between particular processes and performance. Such statements support that participants used their own knowledge and experience with local landmarks to inform decisions.

Participants

Participants were recruited from a large northeastern United States university. Twenty-two teams took part in the study. Each team was comprised of three participants, for a total of sixty-six participants. The majority of the participants were recruited from undergraduate information sciences and psychology courses. Fifty-three percent of the students were male.

Protocols

Upon arrival, each participant was randomly assigned one of the three roles, which they took on as part of the scenario. In each part of the scenario, the three participants were provided with information particular to their role and were told that only by integrating information and resources would they be able to provide accurate recommendations and successfully complete each task.

The video recorder was set-up to capture the entirety of the lab portion of the study, from the experimenter instructions to behaviors of all team members as they completed each part of the scenario.

Participants had a set amount of time in which to complete each decision-making task: 50 minutes for part one, 45 minutes for part two, and 30 minutes for part three. At the end of each task, participants needed to come to a joint decision and write down a team recommendation or answer for that part of the scenario.

Assessing task performance

Task performance was scored based on accuracy of solutions in each part of the task: total points received/total possible points. There were eight points possible in part 1, 16 in part two, and three points in part three.

Selection of microanalysis teams

Ten teams were selected for microanalysis and their sessions were transcribed and coded. Teams were selected based upon consistent performance across the three parts of the scenario: consistently high performing teams and consistently low performing teams. Though selection was based on consistency of performance, for the purpose of conciseness these teams are referred to as high and low performing teams in the paper.

In order to identify objective cut offs that could be used as a means of designating performance categories, quartile rank scores were identified for each part of the scenario. Teams were categorized as high, medium, or low teams based on these cut offs. For example, cut offs for part one were 50% accuracy (50th percentile), and 63% accuracy (75th percentile). Teams in the 75th percentile and above were designated with an "H" (high), teams below the 50th percentile received an "L" (low) designation, and teams between the 50th and 75th percentile were designated as mid "M" performers. Teams with the most "H" designations were selected as high performing teams and teams with the most "L" designations as low performing teams. In cases where more than one team had the same frequency of "H" or "L" designations across the three parts of the scenario, average percent accuracy across all three parts was used as a secondary filter.

Transcription of video
Each of the ten selected teams' videos was transcribed following a similar format. Each new speaker utterance and or behavior was numbered, denoting a new "turn". A "turn" ended when a different speaker introduced a new utterance. These turns were then split up into dialogue acts: separate sentences. Compound sentences were split into separate acts as well. The participants were referred to by the role they played and were given pseudo-names in the transcript. Parentheses were used to label nonverbal gestures and events (i.e., leaving the group, making faces, using hands, etc). Brackets were used for codes, time stamps, and notes relevant to the analyses, but not found in the video itself. These transcripts were utilized along with video when analyzing the artifacts and detecting common task errors.

Identifying primary activities
The identification of primary activities was the result extensive qualitative analysis headed by the first and third author and informed by members of our lab. Students were trained to observe and take notes on teams while the experiment was running. The first author developed content logs and notes of behaviors for each of the microanalyzed teams (for description of content logs see [15]). These notes and logs were used to develop conceptual models of the activities the teams engaged in. These conceptual models were then compared to student observations from all of the teams. The third author in collaboration with students then went through the videos again, with transcripts, to identify common team problems. Group discussions between the authors and students were used as a means to verify observations, organize the primary tasks and related activities. This process often included sharing notes, conceptual models, and discussing video segments. This method is similar to methods of interaction analysis [15]. Through this process we identified the primary activities teams engaged in, subactivities, problems encountered by teams in each category, and the relationship between dialogue coding patterns and primary activities.

Coding dialogue patterns
A method of analyzing communication was used that built on previous work [8], but modified to better meet the needs of the current research. Inter-rater reliability for the new coding schema was Kappa= .67, indicating substantial inter-rater reliability [18].

In the coding schema, dialogue is divided into four classes (in bold below) and then broken down into acts. These acts can be compared to other variables such as performance in order to distinguish patterns between successful and unsuccessful teams.

Information Transfer- How new information (existing prior to collaboration) is added
(AI): Add Info- Add new information w/o prompting
(Q): Question- Prompt someone for new information
(R): Reply- Provide new information in response to a prompt
Check Understanding- How previously added info is checked, confirmed, or repaired
(CH): Check- verifying information
(CL): Clarify- clarifying or restating information
(AC): Acknowledge- signaling receipt or understanding of information
Management of Processes- How work is orchestrated
(MN) Management- discussions centered on interactions, how to do the work, and what has been done
(CM) Command for action, order, or instruction that does not take others into account
(RQ) Request for action- posed as a question or indirect prompt (not a question)
Interpretation- How task information is interpreted
(J): Judge- Individual preference, opinion, or claim, with or without deliberation
(RA): Rational that supports a judge (J) or alternative (AT) act.
(AT): Proposing alternative to a (J) OR (RA) act.
(CO): Confirmation- Requesting agreement on a proposed decision
(AG): Agreement- Indicating agreement for prior judgment or decision

Once dialogue was coded, the raw scores for each team were normalized. This was accomplished by calculating the percentage of specific dialogue acts to total dialogue acts. In this way comparisons could be made across teams and we could control for amount of talk. Dialogue act coding was used as a means of looking for patterns of interaction as they occurred in different primary activities within the scenario.

Measuring verbal equity
Verbal equity scores were based on amount of variance of speech turns. Each team's members were designated as high, medium, and low verbal contributors based on

number of speech turns. For example, when calculating scores for overall talk, "percent of total talk" was calculated for individuals by dividing their total number of speech turns by the total number of speech turns for the entire team. The standard deviation of variance was calculated for percentage of total talk across all teams: Mean amount of talk was .33 (33% of talk), SD = .07, (7% of talk). This standard deviation was used as a means to score and categorize teams into three categories of verbal equity.

Verbal equity scores distinguish between patterns of communication: score of 3, or equitable verbal participation, score of 2, or shared authority, and score of 1, or dominance of one team member. The method of calculating scores is detailed below:

h = # of turns of high speaker
m = # of turns of mid speaker
l = # of turns of low speaker
t = Total # of turns
SD= standard deviation of talk

Score of 3: $(h/t)-(l/t)<2SD$
Score of 2: $(h/t)-(l/t)>2SD$
$(h/t)-(m/t)<1SD$
Score of 1: $(h/t)-(m/t)>2SD$ or
$(h/t)-(l/t)>2SD$ and $(h/t)-(m/t)>1SD$

Each team received three verbal equity scores, one for each part of the task. Average verbal equity scores were calculated for each team and used as a means to compare to outcome measures.

Collection and coding of information artifacts

Multiple sources of data were used to assess and code information artifacts: information provided by participants, information from video and transcripts, and also measures of team accuracy at solving the task.

Shared information artifacts are visual representation utilized by the entire team. They were scored for epistemic fidelity [10] and type of use. Epistemic fidelity (accuracy and completeness) was measured by matching the information needed to solve each phase with the information contained in the artifact.

Type of use refers to the primary function that an information artifact served. After videos were fully transcribed, they were coded to highlight any time shared information artifacts were created or in use. This allowed for the identification of when artifacts led to the creation of other artifacts, when artifacts were referred to or used, and when artifacts were used in conjunction with other artifacts. This information was used as a means to differentiate between note-taking or knowledge-building activities. Note-taking activities describe instances when teams use the information artifact to write down what the team is saying, but no evidence exists of the team pulling information from the artifact to lead to a new conclusion. Knowledge building activities, on the other hand, refer to instances when a team will pull information from an artifact to guide discussion in new directions, ask novel questions, or create new artifacts.

RESULTS

Primary team activities

Six primary activities emerged from the microanalysis: 1) reading/searching intelligence reports, 2) sharing information, 3) synthesizing information, 4) interpreting information, 5) making final decisions, 6) and receiving new information. These activities were not carried out in a linear fashion and patterns of flow from one to the other varied by team and by the strategy they chose as a means of sharing information. For example, teams that chose to proceed through the task by sharing information from one POI to the next were more likely to cycle through the primary activities than those who shared information based on crime location, or with no clear strategy. Thus far, no relationship has been identified between the order of activity flow (i.e., how teams move from one activity to the next) and their performance, but more work remains to be done.

During *reading/searching the intelligence report* participants worked independently as they learned about the task, their role, and their unique role information. The documents our participants received contained information similar to the types of real-world documents that specialists might read prior to engaging in a real-world information synthesis scenario: a brief containing the general problem, situation as it stands, their role in the team, and, in keeping with the scenario, a summary of all of the information their specialized team had gathered to date. During this activity participants familiarized themselves with the intelligence: reading, searching, interpreting, highlighting information, and writing on the documents. Individuals also used information from the intelligence report to create individual information artifacts: notes or visual representations. At this point in the task, team members did not speak to each other.

During this time, the primary cognitive activity was individual knowledge building: developing knowledge individuals lacked prior to the start of the scenario. Individuals were instructed to use the given information to generate preliminary judgments about potential suspects. Individuals read over the information, highlighting information and creating notes of their interpretations. The primary tools used in this category were pens, markers, and separate pieces of paper: pens to underline information, markers to highlight, and paper to keep separate notes. Maps, sticky notes, and calendars were generally not utilized at this point in the activity.

Most individuals spent more time searching and interpreting crime related information (POI information in the role specific documents) than they did searching and highlighting mission goals and objectives, and understanding the problem. After reading through the information and forming an understanding their role, individuals wrote down their initial interpretations of the information and prepared to introduce themselves and their role to team members.

Once participants finished reading the documents and writing notes they moved on to the next primary activity: *sharing information*. This activity includes all actions where participants discuss preexisting knowledge: knowledge already gathered and represented in the intelligence documents. There were five categories of actions that occurred as part of information sharing activity: 1) sharing information relevant to the crimes, 2) sharing information about the crime-solving task, 3) filtering information, 4) checking/clarifying information, 5) and prompting for more information.

Sharing information relevant to the crimes refers to the sharing of role specific document information, i.e., information about POIs that one role has, but another may lack. This type of information comes directly from the Role Documents and contains no inferences. One example could be, "I have that Tay was in his statistics class on the 5th."

Sharing information about the task refers to instances when participants refer to information contained in the Mission Statement and General Instructions, i.e., information about the crime-solving scenario context. This would include sharing of any of the task rules, goals, or background information contained in the documents participants received. For example, "Well it says here that even if they are listed as attending a class, they can still sneak out for 10-15 minutes depending on what type of class it was."

Information can be shared with a group in one of two ways: though *push* acts and *pull* acts [8]. A push act refers to instances where a team member shares information from intelligence documents without being asked to do so. We code this as an *add information* act (AI). Information can also be shared in response to someone prompting for it; this is referred to as a pull act, or a *reply* act (R) in our coding schema. Prompting for more information refers to instances when participants would ask questions to illicit more information transfer, such as, "Do you have any more information about Dante?"

Participants also checked and clarified transferred information. These types of behaviors include questions and answers that are not aspects of creating new knowledge, but rather clarity and full understanding of previously shared existing knowledge. For example, "Wait, what building did you say Isabel was in", would be an example of a *check* behavior in this category. A clarify behavior that could follow would be, "She was in the White building." Clarify behaviors in a sense are repeated information.

The primary collaborative breakdowns that occurred during *sharing of information* were lack of shared understanding due to imprecise sharing and ignorance of team members' questions and opinions. These breakdowns had negative consequences either with overall team performance or for a particular interpretation or decision act. They were primarily present in teams where one person dominated most of the verbal contributions.

Lack of shared understanding can lead to synthesis problems as false conclusions result from misinterpretations. Even superficial examples where teams do not realize they are talking about different POIs (Cristian vs. Kristin) or different Starbucks café locations could have a large impact on decision-making. This is due to the fact that such information serves as the foundation for synthesis from which a team draws final conclusions.

There were several incidents related to problems with dominance where one team member repeatedly asked for a piece of critical information, but was ignored by a dominant member. Thus key pieces of information were not shared that could have helped the team to connect opportunity or motive to a suspect.

There is no real team knowledge building that occurs within this category. *Individuals* may build new knowledge, but since the information already existed in some form within the team, team members are simply transferring knowledge between members. This shared knowledge is then synthesized to some extent by the team. This is the next main activity that teams engaged in.

During *information synthesis*, teams figured out how to combine the separate bits of shared information to create a collective whole. They figured out how to create a shared understanding of the problem, or a shared representation of the problem. Sub-activities within this category include, 1) discussing strategies for sharing information, 2) summarizing information, 3) creating personal notes, 4) creating information artifacts, and 5) referring to information artifacts.

One aspect of the synthesis category is related to verbalization of strategies for information sharing. These are the rules that teams set up for how they would contribute information, e.g., organizing information sharing according to POIs' first names and going in alphabetical order, turn taking, etc. Many teams came up with an agreed upon order to share information and then synthesized information in a personal or shared artifact. However, relationships between strategy use and effectiveness have yet to be examined in the dataset.

Summarizing information was another sub-activity in this category. Summarizing was more frequent when teams did not create detailed externalized shared representations as information artifacts. Thus teams would provide a summary of all of the information the team had already discussed: this included transferred information and inferences made from transferred information. For example, "Okay so Tay and Isabel where both at work as were Edgar and Frank. And we decided that Tay and Isabel could not have committed the crime, but we're unsure of Edgar and Frank." Summarizing information was also used as a means of checking the accuracy and completeness of information artifacts or as a means of determining the team's current knowledge state.

Many individual team members kept personal notes of the information that other team members presented. However, personal notes even when containing synthesized information, were associated with collaborative process problems. There were instances where individuals wrote down correct solutions, or critical bits of information in their notes, but still failed to share them with the group. Below is an example of this type of problem as it occurred in one team. One team member had critical information written down in his personal notes, but failed to share it with the team. The team identified this breakdown during the reflection period following part two of the scenario:

Turn	Role	Utterance
1.	Record	Yeah. Nicky hit York's car. Nowhere does it say George needed his car repaired. I don't have anything on that do you have that?
2.	Interview	No, I have nothing.
3.	Record	Do you have anything for George?
4.	Web	Um, let me look through it again. Um, no, but I told you George looks like a shady character. Oh, yeah (looking at notes), right here- Oh s***! This is all my fault. I did say something about George having really aggressive- It says, "I can't believe Upton f*** up and vandalized my car, I saw him." I think this would have been really helpful.
5.	Record	Oh, well. That's good to know. Aw, well.
6.	Web	Sorry guys.

In this example, the team was comparing the solutions they provided for part two with the correct solutions that the experimenter provided them to reflect on before beginning part three. They were having difficulty understanding how George could have been a thief since they recalled no real mention of him or any motives for committing the crime (turns 1, 2, and 3). In turn 4, the Web Analyst remembers saying that George was suspicious at some point, but realizes he failed to provide his team with a rationale as to why. He had made a note about George, but hadn't shared this information with the team. The information stated that one of the victims of the laptop theft had vandalized his car. That information, he claimed, would have been helpful to solving the crime.

Unlike personal notes, shared information artifacts, by definition were utilized by the entire team. Information artifacts are visual representations developed as a means to synthesize shared information. Both high and low performing teams engaged in elaborate discussions centered on how to orchestrate the creation and development of a shared artifact: what type of representations to create, how to highlight, organize, and filter information, and who should write on the artifact. Not all teams engaged in these types of discussions and preliminary data does not indicate that these discussions lead to higher task accuracy.

One of the most important activities teams engaged in when orchestrating the creation of a shared information artifact was deciding how to filter information. Filtering of information was something that many teams struggled with and that led to problems with synthesizing and interpreting information. Teams used variables related to the scenario, i.e., crime locations, POI relationships, events, etc., as a means to select and organize information depicted on the shared artifact

Once teams created information artifacts they engaged in other subtasks of information artifact related behaviors: they followed rules, ignored rules, added information, created new related information artifacts, and created new unrelated artifacts. Following or ignoring rules refers to whether the information artifact had systematicity, i.e. whether they followed uniform rules of correspondence [10]. For example, if eliminated suspects were to be written in green ink, was this rule applied uniformly. Lack of systematicity was a common occurrence in both high and low performing teams. When symbols and rules were not uniformly followed it made searching for and retrieving information from the artifacts more difficult. This was particularly true of overly complex artifacts such as one created by a consistently low performing team that had so many symbols and rules that teammates had problems keeping track of them and as a result added and interpreted information incorrectly.

Though *interpreting information* was often tied with synthesis, it could technically occur after any of the primary activities: reading intelligence reports, sharing information, or, synthesizing information. Interpretation begins once a judgment has been made. A judgment act is a hypothesis, opinion, or claim, made with or without deliberation. Judgments can be made about crime information, the preexisting information the team has shared about suspects, locations, relationships, etc. Judgments can also be made about how to do the task, i.e., what counts as evidence or alibis, what types of representations are best, etc.

Once a judgment is made teams can respond to them in one of four ways: they can ignore them, reject them, accept them, or they can discuss them. Similar categorizing of utterances has been used when evaluating team interactions in educational settings [2]. Ignoring a judgment means that a judgment is simply disregarded and no evidence exists in transcript that any team member paid attention to. Rejecting a judgment means that teammates refuse to accept the judgment without providing any rationale. For example, they could reply to a judgment by saying, "that's ridiculous", or "you're wrong" and moving on. Accepting a judgment means that a teammate agrees with it without adding any comments, (i.e., "Yeah, you're right", "Yeah, [repeats judgment]), denotes judgment on shared artifact, adds related information, or connects shared information.

Discussing a judgment means that the judgment is not accepted outright, but rather is examined or considered. Examples of discussion type utterances include, "Why do you think he is suspicious", "Just because he has class doesn't mean he has an alibi, he could have snuck out", or "yeah, but you don't have any evidence to support that".

Collaborative process problems related to interpretation included, decisions based on partial information, and faulty hypotheses-guided information gathering. Partial information refers to instances when teams made decisions without having all of the facts relevant to the crime. Faulty hypotheses-guided information gathering occurred when information gathering and, thereby, judgments were biased by pre-mature hypotheses. For example, in part one, some groups hypothesized that all the thefts were connected (a false assumption) and were associated with two competing teams. Therefore, they judged that everyone on the victim's team innocent (another false assumption). Similar events occurred in other groups. This pattern of interpretation was associated with over rationalization: high frequency of rationale acts. Not surprisingly consistently low performing teams had higher frequencies of rational dialogue acts than consistently high performing teams. Groups with patterns of faulty hypotheses-guided information gathering also had problems with synthesis activities: information artifacts were not properly filtered, or information from artifacts was not synthesized to develop new artifacts or knowledge.

After teammates respond to judgments they *make final decisions*: the fifth activity teams engaged in. Final decisions were made with and without confirmation acts. Confirmation acts were speech acts where team members attempted to establish certainty about a judgment. Examples of confirmation speech acts include such questions as, "So, we are eliminating Tay, right?", and "So, yes to Isabel?"

Errors related to making final decisions primarily centered on poor time management. Most of the lower performing groups made hasty final decisions because they ran out of time. These decisions also tended to be made by the dominant member, often written down without any discussion at all. Our highest performing team had one member who took responsibility of time management. This person kept the team focused and encouraged them to share all relevant information rather than spend too much time on one person. In contrast low performing teams spent a great deal of time on a few suspects and therefore did not have time to discuss them all.

Finally, as the team progresses through the crime-solving scenario they *receive new information*. This information could be related to previous information or it could stand-alone. For example, part two of the scenario requires the team to combine new information with previous information from part one. New information can also be unrelated to previous information: to solve part three, the team did not need to look at information from parts one or two, though they were not told this.

Differences in patterns of interaction

Once we had identified the different activities inherent of the task we used these activities to compare the interactions of our consistently high performing groups to those of our consistently low performing teams. This was done by looking at patterns of verbal equity and use of specific dialogue acts.

Verbal equity was assessed for a team's overall talk (as determined by turns of speech) as well as for each of the primary activities (as determined by dialogue acts). As detailed in the methods section, an equity score of 1 denotes domination: one person dominates the group. A score of 2 signifies a shared authority pattern, where two people share most of the talk and one person is significantly lower. A score of 3 indicates a pattern where all three members contribute equally to the talking space and no significant differences exist in frequency of talk between any two members for a specific activity.

There was a significant difference between the verbal equity patterns of overall talk for high performing teams and those of low performing teams, $t(8) = -3.01$, $p < .05$. High performing teams had a mean equity score of 2.7, SD = .58. Whereas low performing teams had a mean equity score of 1.6, SD = .55. However, verbal equity fluctuated depending on the type of activity that teams engaged in, as defined by our dialogue acts and the primary activities. For example, one of the highest performing teams (team 13) had overall equity scores of 3, but when examined closely this overall equity pattern was actually the result of shared dominance in different activities and not equity throughout the differing activities. Shared dominance describes a pattern where or one person dominates one type of dialogue class, i.e., synthesizing information, and another person dominated a distinct class, i.e., interpretation.

Verbal equity was assessed for dialogue acts related to *sharing information, information synthesis, and interpreting information*. The average score across all ten

	Team	18L	21L	17L	1L	8L	15H	7H	14H	13H	2H
	Ave. Performance	25%	28%	29%	36%	39%	50%	54%	57%	57%	60%
Verbal Equity Score	Info. Transfer	3	1	1	3	1	3	3	3	3	3
	Synthesis	2	1	1	1	1	1	1	3	1	1
	Interpretation	1	1	1	1	1	3	3	1	1	1

Table 1. Table of verbal equity scores of the ten microanalysis teams for three of the primary activities. High performing teams (H) are on the right and low teams (L) are on the left.

teams for *sharing information* behaviors was 2.4 with a standard deviation of 0.84. The average verbal equity for *information synthesis* and *interpreting information* were lower. The average verbal equity score was 1.3 (SD = 0.64) for synthesis and 1.4 (SD = 0.84). As Table 1 illustrates, both high and low teams were more likely to have one person dominate synthesis and interpretation activities than they were to have one person dominate information-sharing activities. However there were noticeable differences between high and low teams with regards to how information was shared and synthesized, and how authority shifted depending on the primary activity.

Consistently high performing teams had significantly higher proportions of *push* acts to total information transfer (IT) acts than did our low teams, $t(8)=-2.506$, $p < .05$. Consistently high performing teams also had significantly lower proportions of *check* and *clarify* acts to total IT acts as compared to consistently low performing teams, $t(8)= 2.99$, $p < .017$.

When it came to synthesizing information, consistently high and low performing teams used visual representations to support different functions. Consistently high performing teams used them to record and guide externalized knowledge-building behaviors: they built on prior information, correlated data from multiple artifacts, and used it to come up with new forms of externalized information. In contrast, lower performing teams used artifacts primarily for note-taking purposes: to synthesize verbalized information or to write down solutions. In fact the proportion of artifacts used as knowledge-building tools to total artifacts for consistently low teams was 22.2%. Whereas, the proportion of artifacts used as knowledge-building tools to total artifacts for consistently high teams was 88.9%. The information contained in the artifacts of consistently low performing teams was often disjointed and artifacts were rarely used in conjunction with other artifacts. This led to misinterpretation of data based on incomplete information. Consistently low performing teams externalized shared information, but rarely externalized knowledge-building activity.

There were also differences between the amount of variables high and low performing teams used to organize and narrow down represented data. For example, when creating lists, low performing teams recorded all information that fell under one variable, e.g., date of crime. Low performing teams would then list any shared information related to that date, i.e., where all the POIs were at the time. In contrast, high performing teams used multiple variables to reduce the amount of depicted information from the amount of shared information. For example, they would use the same list with the crime date heading, but only list information related to people who were at or near the scene of the crime at the time of the crime. This facilitated data reduction.

Another difference between consistently high and consistently low performing teams had to do with authority shifts between primary activities. The biggest difference between the high and low performing teams was not in terms of the equity scores related to the primary activities, but rather how dominance varied by person between synthesis and interpretation activities. When an individual dominated the synthesis related activities in a high performing team, a different person dominated the interpretation of information, or decision-making activities. For example if a high performing team had a member contribute 50% of the dialogue acts for synthesis, a different member would dominate around 50% of the interpretation acts. In contrast, a low performing team would have the same person dominate both activities. The difference in shifting authorities is depicted in Figure 1. In this figure the first team, with a verbal equity score of 1, has the same member dominate regardless of activity. The second team, a consistently high performing team with a verbal equity score of 2, has one member dominate synthesis and a different member dominate interpretation. This "cognitive specialization" or shared authority was present in the two highest performing teams out the 22 teams we ran; this pattern was not present in any of the low performing teams.

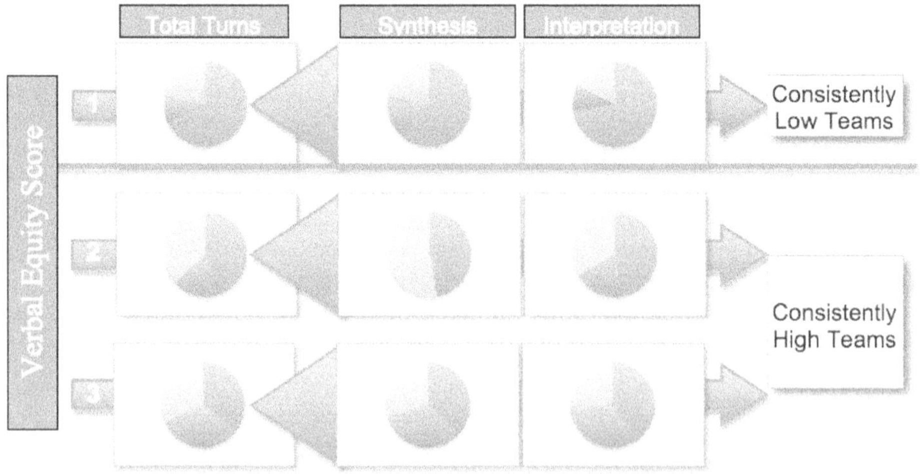

Figure 1. Depiction of most common verbal equity (VE) patterns for the three members of consistently high and low performing teams by type of activity. Low performing teams were more likely to have dominant patterns (VE score of 1). Whereas, high performing teams either displayed shared (VE score of 2) or equitable patterns (VE score of 3).

DISCUSSION

Primary activities

We used qualitative methods to identify the primary activities that participant teams engaged in and problems that arose as they completed the crime-solving scenario. We found that all of our teams engaged in higher order thinking processes as they synthesized and interpreted a great deal of data in a relatively short amount of time. Thus our scenario succeeded in eliciting complex higher-order behaviors.

We identified primary activities as a means to help us develop a better conceptual model of the types of activities we want to support with technology. This approach to design is an effective way to help ensure the effectiveness of technological tools [21].

The identified activities were used as a means to examine differences in patterns of interaction between high and low performing teams. We found differences related to how teams shared and synthesized information, and also found differences in verbal equity patterns.

Sharing information: Push and check/clarify acts

When we looked at how teams shared information, we found differences in the proportion of information added by team members without prompting relative to total information transfer acts. High performing team-members *pushed* at higher frequencies than members of low performing teams. They also had lower frequencies of communication acts related to checking, repeating, and clarifying previously added information. These findings replicate previous findings that equated high *push* acts and low *check/clarify* acts with higher levels of activity awareness [8].

Synthesizing information: Use of multiple variables

There were differences between high and low performing teams with regards to how they synthesized information. Higher performing teams used multiple variables (e.g., time, location, etc.) related to the crime scenario to select information to represent visually on their shared artifacts. Low performing teams synthesized all shared information and did not effectively reduce data as they moved from sharing to synthesizing information. This suggests that identifying variables associated with the specific real-world task is important, as combinations of these variables may be an effective way to filter information and reduce the amount of visualized data that users would have to decipher.

Verbal equity: Shifts in authority

High and low performing teams had very different patterns of verbal equity. Overall, high performing teams were more verbally equitable than low performing teams. However, our study demonstrated that verbal equity can be interpreted in different ways and that the types of activities team members engage in may influence verbal equity patterns. When we evaluated verbal equity based on activity rather than overall speech turns, we found shifts in authority (i.e., who controlled most of the behaviors associated with an activity) for members of high performing teams and none of these shifts for low performing teams.

Findings related to how verbal equity fluctuated by activity may help to explain why verbal equity has been associated with group intelligence [28]. It is possible that teams with higher verbal equity make better use of team members as resources and better integrate whatever specialized knowledge or experience different members bring to the table. However, more work needs to be done in order to determine the relationships between verbal equity and the integration of team member expertise and diverse perspectives.

ACKNOWLEDGMENTS

This project is partially funded by the Office of Naval Research and through the Edward Frymoyer Chaired Professorship.

REFERENCES

1. Alifano, C. M. *Fundamentals of criminal investigation.* New York: Worldwide Law Enforcement Consulting Group, Inc., 2006.
2. Barron, B. When smart groups fail. *Journal of the Learning Sciences*, 12(3) (2003), 307-359.
3. Borge, M., & Carroll, J. Using collaborative activity as a means to explore student performance and understanding. In *Proc the International Conference of The Learning Sciences,* ACM Press (2010).
4. Carroll, J.M., Mentis, H., Convertino, G., Rosson, M.B., Ganoe, C.H., Sinha, H. & Zhao, D. 2007. Prototyping collaborative geospatial emergency planning. In *Proc of ISCRAM (2007)*, pp. 105-113.
5. Chaiken, J. M., Greenwood, P. W., & Petersilia, J. R. *The criminal investigation process: A summary report.* Santa Monica, CA: RAND Corporation, 1976.
6. Chin, G., Kuchar, O.A., and Wolf, K.E. Exploring the analytical processes of intelligence analysts. In *Proc. CHI 2009,* ACM Press (2009), 11-20.
7. Convertino, G., Mentis, H. M., Rosson, M., Slavkovic, A., and Carroll, J. M. (2009). Supporting content and process common ground in computer-supported teamwork. In *Proc. CHI 2002*, ACM press (2002), 2339-2348
8. Convertino, G., Mentis, H., Rosson, M.B., Carroll, J.M, Slavkovic, A. & Ganoe, C.H. Articulating Common Ground in Cooperative Work: Content and Process. In *Proc. CHI 2008,* ACM Press (2008), 1637-1646.
9. Convertino, G., Mentis, H.M., Slavkovic, A., Rosson, M.B. & Carroll, J.M. Supporting knowledge sharing and awareness in distributed emergency management planning. *ACM Transactions on Computer-Human Interaction*, (In press).

10. diSessa, A. Metarepresentation: native competence and targets for instruction. *Cognition and Instruction*, 22, 3 (2004), 293-331.
11. Edmondson, A. C. The local and variegated nature of learning in organizations: A group-level perspective. *Organization Science* (2002), 128-146.
12. Greeno, J. G., & Hall, R. P. Practicing representation: Learning with and about representational forms. *Phi Delta Kappan*, 78 . (1997), 361-367.
13. Hogan, K. Relating students' personal frameworks for science learning to their cognition in collaborative contexts. *Science education*, 83, 1 (1999a), 1-32.
14. Hogan, K. Thinking Aloud Together: A Test of an Intervention To Foster Students' Collaborative Scientific Reasoning. *Journal of Research in Science Teaching*, 36, 10 (1999b), 1085-1109.
15. Jordan, B., & Henderson, A. Interaction analysis: Foundations and practice. *Journal of the Learning Sciences, 4*, 1 (1995), 39-103.
16. Kerr, N. L., & Tindale, R. S. Group performance and decision making. *Annu. Rev. Psychol.*, 55 (2004), 623-655.
17. Kozlowski, S. W. J., & Ilgen, D. R. Enhancing the effectiveness of work groups and teams. *Psychological Science in the Public Interest*, 7, 3 (2006), 77.
18. Landis, J. R., Koch, G. G. The measurement of observer agreement for categorical data. *Biometrics* 33 (1977), 159-174.
19. Larkin, J. H., and Simon, H. A. Why a diagram is (sometimes) worth ten thousand words. *Cognitive Science*, 11 (1987), 65-99.
20. Maxfield, M. G., & Babbie, E. R. Research methods for criminal justice and criminology: Wadsworth Pub Co (2010).
21. Norman, D. *The Design of Everyday Things*. New York: Doubleday, 1988.
22. Schafer, W.A., Ganoe, C.H. & Carroll, J.M. Supporting community emergency management through a geocollaboration software infrastructure. *Computer-Supported Cooperative Work: The Journal of Collaborative Computing*, 16 (2007), 501-537.
23. Stahl, G. *Group cognition*. Cambridge, MA: MIT Press, 2006.
24. Suthers, D. Towards a systematic study of representational guidance for collaborative learning discourse. *Journal of Universal Computer Science*, 7, 3 (2001), 254-277.
25. Vygotsky, L. S. *Interaction between learning and development*. In M. Cole, V. John- Steiner, S. Scribner & E. Souberman (Eds.), Mind in Society: The Development of Higher Psychological Processes (pp. 79-91). Cambridge, MA: Harvard University Press, 1978.
26. Warner, N., Burkman, L., & Biron, C. H. Special operations reconnaissance (SOR) scenario: Intelligence analysis and mission planning, No. NAWCADPAX/TM-2008/184, 2008.
27. West, G. P. Collective Cognition: When Entrepreneurial Teams, Not Individuals, Make Decisions. *Entrepreneurship Theory and Practice*, 31,1 (2007), 77-102.
28. Woolley, A., Chabris, C., Pentland, A., Hashmi, M., & Malone, T. Evidence for a collective intelligence factor in the performance of human groups. *Science, 330*, 6004 (2010), 686-688.

Using Low Cost Game Controllers to Capture Data for 6th Grade Science Labs

Sarah Lewis
Stanford University
450 Serra Mall
Stanford California 94305 USA
sarahl@stanford.edu

Ugochi Acholonu
Stanford University
450 Serra Mall
Stanford California 94305 USA
acholonu@stanford.edu

Wendy Ju
Stanford University
353 Serra Mall
Stanford California 94305 USA
wendyju@stanford.edu

ABSTRACT

This paper describes a cooperative design project to develop ways to use Nintendo Wii Remotes as inexpensive data acquisition tools for science. In collaboration with a 6th grade physics instructor and his students, we have developed software tools and curriculum that enable science teachers and students to repurpose gaming technologies to study concepts such as velocity and acceleration. The project involved a year's observation of students' project based learning in a 6th grade physics class, followed by a year of design experimentation to engage students in integrating game controllers into their projects. Using the insights from their observations and suggestions, we created three different Wii Remote-based setups that used the IR camera and the accelerometer to help students glean data from their projects. In this paper, we provide an overview of the project, and then offer data that demonstrates the added value across the material, social, experiential, and temporal aspects of inquiry science activity. We conclude by identifying key design opportunities within this space.

Author Keywords

Education, Wii, Science, Laboratory, Data Visualization, Children, Physics

ACM Classification Keywords

H5.m. Information interfaces and presentation (e.g., HCI): Miscellaneous.

General Terms

Human Factors; Design

INTRODUCTION

The proliferation of interactive devices with embedded processors, integrated sensors and wireless communication capabilities has it possible to gather sensor data from almost any object in our physical world. While designers of products often strive to have data collection, computation and transmission happen invisibly to support people's day-to-day activities, these same technologies can also be designed to bring measured data to the foreground so it can be used to gain insight on phenomena around us. One area in which this design direction is most useful is in science education.

Seeking to lower the barriers to integrating data into our everyday understanding of the world around us, we have been hijacking data from Nintendo Wii Remote game controllers for the purpose of augmenting 6th grade physics labs with visible data. The digital capture of sensor data within the context of in-class labs and projects allows students to see invisible phenomena—such as gravity and acceleration—for which it might be hard to gain an intuitive understanding. In addition, using gaming technologies for science offers the possibility for students to gain a more grounded understanding of the underlying technology and how it might be repurposed.

We hypothesize that sensor technologies found in everyday handheld items such as gaming equipment and cell phones can improve on practices in constructivist "hands-on" laboratory and project-based science learning in four key ways:

- Manipulating ideas via manipulating tools
- Supporting social interaction
- Harnessing everyday and embodied understanding
- Enabling more data, in more classrooms, more often.

The opportunities provided by introducing these new data tools to learning environments are accompanied by a host of challenges to be tackled or designed around. This paper discusses our activities in integrating Wii Remote devices into a 6th grade project based physics classroom. We describe our theoretical approach, as well as activities, findings related to the above hypothesis, and the lessons and design opportunities we encountered in the course of our multi-year engagement on the Wii Science project.

BACKGROUND

Although labs and projects are a cornerstone of modern science education, physics classrooms often lack the tools necessary for "hands on" exploration of physical phenomenon. Below we offer a review of contemporary challenges to integrating data into hands-on learning in classrooms and day-to-day experience.

Lab and Project Activities in Science Education

Hofstein and Lunetta define laboratory activities to be "learning experiences in which students interact with materials and/or with models to observe and understand the natural world." [12] Ideally, lab activities would help students "describe objects and events, ask questions, construct explanations, test those explanations against current scientific knowledge, and communicate their ideas to others identify their assumptions, use critical and logical thinking, and consider alternative explanations" [27].

Constructivism

Laboratory and other "hands-on" activities are of particular importance to advocates of *constructivist* models of education. Although there are different schools of thought within constructivism, generally theories are grounded in the idea that learners learn best when they are able to base their ideas and understandings on a series of personal first-hand experiences. [6][38] Over the last 20 years the turn in cognitive science toward theories of situated [11][22], embodied [21] and distributed cognition [15][30] acknowledges that much of "learning" happens not in the head, but in fact in the body and via arrangements of situations and artifacts in the world around us. Laboratory and project activities can stimulate interest in science by providing opportunities for students to pursue inquiries they have about the natural world, and by framing their prior experiences and intuitions within a more generalizable scientific understanding.

However, while many science teachers learn constructivist theories in education schools and academic researchers have run numerous studies of constructivist methods, Williams and Hmelo note that "this information has had relatively small impact on education practices. We do not, as yet, have a widely accepted theory of instruction or carefully thought out manageable methods of implementation consistent with constructivist theory." [41] Researchers have noted that often integration of new technologies offers opportunities to influence pedagogy, as they open up new practices in the classroom. [26] In the case of wireless gaming devices, we think such new practices may include more pervasive, casual or playful inquiry into everyday phenomena using data and its representations. In this sense, accessible sensors found in everyday devices such as game controllers may enable data-rich constructivist learning activities that were inaccessible without such tools.

Tools of play, tools of science

The Wii Remote's ubiquity in many countries lends it to be a viable tool for both classroom and every-day exploration. The fact that the Wii Remote is mass manufactured means that the components and their associated capabilities are remarkably cheap—at the time of this publication, a battery powered remote with a 3-axis accelerometer, a gyroscope, an infrared camera, a wireless Bluetooth receiver/transmitter as well as seven buttons, a speaker and a pager motor cost less than $30 USD. More importantly, for many children, the Wii Playstation is an everyday household device—Nintendo's survey data indicates 46% of Americans aged 6 to 74 played a Wii or Nintendo DS in the past year [18]—which means that, given well designed software to access its data, the Wii Remote could be for many people as familiar and as ready at hand to appropriate for spontaneous experiments as a measuring spoon. While we have chosen the Wii Remote for this work, we anticipate that the software and activities created can and will be adapted to harness a wide variety of interactive sensing devices currently being brought to market.

Wii Remotes in Education

Currently a wide array of projects are investigating educational uses of the Wii: developing the motor skills of preschoolers [3][13], supporting disabled students in education [31], teaching musical rhythm [5], and, promoting physical activity [12]. In physics, Vannoni and Straulino [39], Somers, et al. [37], and Wheeler [40] have used Wii Remotes in high school and college physics courses to analyze the motion of a pendulum, simple harmonic motion in a spring, and linear displacement on a track, respectively. These have inspired and informed our notions of what is possible in our design activities for earlier physics education.

POTENTIAL BENEFITS OF LOW-COST DATA SENSING

As a research endeavor, this project strives not just to help students learn physics or to only develop tools to support teaching physics, but also to uncover the properties of effective tools for science inquiry. In this sense we hope to inform both theories and practices of effective constructivist learning environments. Below we discuss the four areas in which we hypothesize such handheld gaming technology is well positioned to play a unique role to foster new practices in laboratory and project based learning. These span the material, social, experiential, temporal aspects of inquiry science activity, and gave focus to our design engagement.

Manipulating ideas via manipulating tools

One of the core challenges in designing and deploying project-based curriculum is keeping a focus on the scientific concepts and models motivating the activity. Efforts to use science activities to reinforce specific curricular concepts can tend towards pre-formulated activities which leads learners through a "cookbook" set of instructions [34]. On the other hand, open-ended activities based on student inquiry can at times wind up being only tenuously connected to the scientific concepts they are meant to engage. [20] In both cases, students and instructors can become preoccupied with the materials and procedures of laboratory work—either because they are caught up in following the recipe instructions, or because they are focused on open-ended design issues—to the detriment of meaningful, conceptual-driven inquiry and discovery.

Data aggregation and visualization technologies may be instrumental in keeping the focus of laboratory activities on the broader scientific principles motivating them. Efficient use of technology to collect and analyze data can save time and allows for examination of larger data sets, leaving more time for discussion and reflection on what students were observing. Common measures can be encouraged and visualized across student-driven projects, conceptually unifying diverse arrays of activities. Learning can be assessed by direct queries about their analysis of data produced by their projects over different trials or design iterations, giving more relevant information about their understanding of specific concepts than more typical assessments measuring how well they followed the procedures for the labs or how impressive their projects look on display.

Supporting Social Interaction

Data-driven laboratory activities can illuminate key relationships between natural phenomena and facilitate the process of discussion and analysis that is a critical aspect of the scientific process. Collaboration is a key component of most project or lab based science classrooms. Arrangements in which students work together to inquire, solve problems or design solutions seems particularly effective because they engage students in social talk around science. [24] [32] Data helps enable this process, giving students something concrete and visible to talk about, construct arguments around and come to agreement over, all key components of science itself. [27] For example, researchers on the CoVis project demonstrated the use of *collaborative visualization* to ground social discussion and analysis of observed phenomenal and systems [32]. Mobile, handheld digital data collection devices open up possibilities for new collaborative arrangements in classrooms. Data within more loosely structured "open ended" projects can anchor interactions around core curricular concepts, be those interactions informal conversations with teachers or lab partners or more formal assessments of learning.

The issues of cost and size of equipment are an important to schools in general and to enabling social interaction in particular. Because the per-unit price and storage size of laboratory equipment can dictate the group set-up in a classroom, having equipment be inexpensive and portable makes it easier to have students work in small groups of two to five, considered a cornerstone of cooperative learning [9].

Harnessing everyday and embodied understanding

The importance of grounding understandings in first-hand experience is one of the tenets of constructivist pedagogical approaches. Research shows that in the realm of physics, however, students' naïve interpretation of everyday events can lead to critical misunderstandings of physical principles. Students' everyday experiences, as well as images in movies, cartoons and videogames, may contribute to their misconceptions; discussing at a conceptual level may not correct student's incorrect beliefs, as learners tend to selectively understand or distort information in order to maintain their conceptions. [4] By framing videogame related experiences within the context of a class, and with the presence of measured data, we can provide anchoring experiences [2][4] that would help surface students misconceived intuitions and make them visible for discussion.

Enabling more data, in more classrooms, more often

While biology and chemistry labs have long used sensors to provide students access to real data regarding water quality or chemical compositions in the course of labs and projects, physics classes often have relied on analog manual data collection devices (for example, stop watches), if any data is used at all. This makes it difficult to aggregate data across timescales and classrooms. In addition, specialty 'demonstration' technologies such as constant velocity cars, are often expensive, non-interactive, and limited in capability. The dearth of affordable tools to examine complex concepts related to energy and motion, such as forces, velocity and acceleration, is particularly unfortunate because misconceptions in these areas seem to be particularly robust [23][42].

PROJECT OVERVIEW

The Wii Science project is a multi-year collaborative project funded by the Wallenberg Foundation. The purpose of the project is twofold: 1) to develop activities and software tools that encourage young people in and out of school to repurpose everyday technologies for their own interests and pursuits; and 2) to design activities and software to support scientific inquiry in science classroom labs and projects. Researchers from the engineering and education schools of Stanford University are working in conjunction with a 6th grade physics instructor, Pote Pothongsunan, from Nueva School in Hillsborough, CA, to define the goals and activities. During the first two years we have observed and worked with six classes of students as they conducted hands-on physics projects and lab activities in their science class.

We have used a cooperative design approach on this project, basing our initial design prototypes on observed activity and needs, and framing the instructor and students as co-designers in this engagement. Most of the laboratory and project activities described in this paper build upon longstanding activities at the school, designed with a constructivist pedagogical approach in mind and honed over many years of practice by different teachers. After observing and analyzing the dynamics of these activities during the first year, we worked with the teacher to select activities for which data collection using Wii Remote's accelerometer and IR camera held promise to enhance student engagement and learning.

Methods

We structured our engagement with Nueva school as a cooperative design activity with two distinct phases. In the first phase, we primarily focused on sustained observation of classroom and lab activity in order to understand the design context. In the second phase, we introduced design prototypes to instrument lab activities in the classroom, solicited feedback and design refinements while also observing impact on classroom dynamics and learning. We framed our relationship with the instructors and the students as co-designers of the tools and curriculum. This cooperative design approach is reminiscent of participatory and collaborative approaches outlined by Inkpen [14], Druin, [8] and others working in the realm of classroom technology research and design [34][17].

Participants

All of the participants were students taking a 6th grade physics course with Pote Pothongsunan, our partner instructor at the Nueva School in Hillsborough, CA. Nueva is a private K-8 school with selective admission and a reputation for its special emphasis on constructivist pedagogy and social and emotional learning. Sixth, 7th and 8th grade students use school-issued laptops for their coursework. While we considered several schools as potential partners for this project, Nueva School was selected because the school was able to commit to a multi-year project, because it provided had the needed flexibility in their curriculum to accommodate our design experiments as part of the normal class structure, and because the pre-existing base of common computer hardware would allow us to focus on one version of each design prototype rather than several for each operating system.

OBSERVATION PHASE

During the first phase of the project, we focused on observing the instructor and students in the classroom, understanding the current structure of the course, surveying students about their technology usage and their understandings about their lab activities.

To profile the degree of technological familiarity in the participant population, we constructed a survey that integrated a Learning Ecologies protocol [1] and the Computer Attitude Questionnaire [19]. The results of this survey (see Table 1.) confirmed that most of the students had a high degree of access with and familiarity to both computer and video game technologies. The tech attitude score were calculated by summing the CAQ responses registered on a 5-point Likert scale. The CAQ questionnaire asked questions about attitudes towards technology, allowing students to select along scales that, for example, ranged from enjoying using technology, being comfortable with technology, to avoidance of technology and technology frustration. Both boys and girls scored high in positive attitudes on the questionnaire, with boys slightly more positive about technology than girls.

Table 1. Technology ownership & use in participant population

Devices	Have used	Have in Household	Personally Own
Cell Phone	84%	94%	64%
MP3 Player	94%	94%	90%
Laptop	96%	98%	96%
Desktop	63%	94%	47%
Game Console	84%	62%	46%
Wii	86%	70%	50%
Gaming Handhelds	83%	69%	63%

After conducting a brief Wii Remote orientation activity with students to check their technical understanding and experience with graphing (described in detail below), we then attended classes and labs weekly, documenting visits via field notes, photos and occasionally video. Among the projects we observed were a traditional 'spark timer' lab for students to explore acceleration; a mousetrap car project, in which students worked in pairs to design vehicles powered by a mousetrap's spring mechanism; an 'egg drop' design project in which students worked in pairs to design a contraption to protect an egg as it was dropped from a 40-foot breezeway; and a marble rollercoaster, in which students were given foam tubes, glue, tape, cardboard, cups and wood to build a rollercoaster to meet specific constraints.

We used these observations to inform the design of activities to introduce a data collection into the curriculum.

DESIGN PROTOTYPE PHASE

During the following school year we introduced software prototypes designed to facilitate using Wii Remotes within lab activities. We regularly visited our partner teacher's three physics classes, dropping in weekly during regular class periods, and near daily during lab and project activity sessions. During this phase we more actively sought to identify student's physics misconceptions and opportunities for remediation. We worked with the instructor to introduce our prototypes into the activities, and during the projects and labs worked with students, often making improvements on our designs during the activity itself. We documented our interactions in the classroom through video, pictures, and field notes.

Participants

Fifty-six (30 girls and 26 boys), 6th graders from three physics class (with 20, 20 and 16 students each) at Nueva School taught by our partner instructor. The age range was from 10-12 years old.

Wii Remote Orientation Activity

As in year one, we conducted a classroom activity that helped to introduce ourselves, the project and the Wii system. We used this activity to assess prior understanding of its components and functioning, and to check students' experience with graphs as well as their stance towards viewing the device as a general purpose tool.

Divided into groups of four, students alternately played and observed Nintendo's Wii Tennis game to analyze how the games worked. We asked the class guiding questions to help students make connection between the output generated by the device and the devices components, and asked them to imagine its possible uses beyond gaming. We then showed them real-time data outputted from the Wii and visualized using software we had written in the Processing language. While the previous year we had used Darwin Remote to visualize data, this time we demonstrated the accelerometer sensor data from the Wii using our own software program so that the students could see the code responsible for processing and displaying the data. This was part of an effort to emphasize that the interfaces they would be seeing would be in development, and subject to feedback and corrections.

Students successfully deciphered the many input-output relationships in the Nintendo Wii System, and were able with prompting to deduce many of its components. Despite this, they still had many naïve notions of how it worked. For example, some students thought that some Wii Remotes were more powerful than others based on their color. Although many had mastery over technical terminology, speaking of infrared (IR), Bluetooth, and accelerometers with ease, understanding was shallow. For example, many students knew that the Wii Remote "had Bluetooth," but they did not understand that Bluetooth enabled the device to send sensor data back to the gaming console.

Students had difficulty interpreting the acceleration data, which was visualized on a moving line graph. Their explanations about causal relationships in the graph were centered around position and velocity rather than acceleration. The three axis were confusing, as was the constant 1g measure of gravity. As in the prior year, although they could describe components, students had difficulty generating ideas about other uses for the technology.

As a second part to the original orientation activity, we held a session where we led students through the installation of the Processing application, some introductory interface prototypes, and the pairing of Wii Remotes to their computer. The goal was for each student to have the prototype software on their machines so that they could use it, inspect it or modify it, and would know how to sync the Wii Remote to their laptops. We also issued a survey to assess their current understanding of basic physics principles, and to ferret out some of their misconceptions to consider how these might implicate design.

Mousetrap car

In the mousetrap car activity, students were challenged to build a car based on a mousetrap. The activity itself spanned 8 hours of class time, and took place just after students were introduced to basic concepts of forces. We were able to informally interview the teams about their strategies and design challenges they were encountering. While many correctly identified weight and friction as key issues in the design of their cars, they also echoed common misconceptions that we found earlier in the year.

For example, when trying to decide what material to make the body out of, one student chose a heavy wide board. When asked about why, the student noted that "forces make you go" and that "more weight" would "help it stick to the ground more. So if it sticks to the ground more, it has to move faster." Another student described a similar decision, drawing on his everyday observation that "heavier cars go faster." In their tinkering, few students considered that the only variable they could not control easily was the power of the spring. After discovering that their heavier cars did not move very fast or far, they explained that the "string doesn't unwind fast enough with this weight. Because of friction."

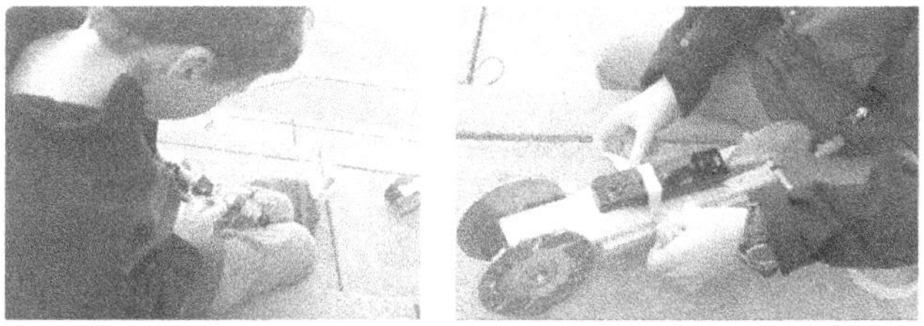

Figure 1. Photos of the stripped down Wii and the WiiMote on a mousetrap car.

Once cars were designed and basically functional, we assisted students in attaching the Wii Remotes so that their car's acceleration could be wirelessly sent to a laptop display. (We intended to introduce the measurement earlier in the design process, but in part because were piloting new tools for the first time, the instructor requested the measurement activity as a separate phase of the students' projects.) As the first team attached the Wii Remote to the top of the mousetrap car, several issues immediately arose. The remote got in the way of the lever arm, and added significant weight to the car, slowing it to a crawl. The graph was barely visible on the vertical scale we had chosen, and the "noise" generated by the Wii Remote's loose masking tape attachment and the bumpy pavement dwarfed the acceleration readings we were after. Several teams became interested in the problem, discovering that they could mount the Wii Remote on the bottom of the car and use more secure mounting methods to get better data. One student in particular became intrigued with taking the Wii Remote apart and powering it with a lighter battery. While this solved much of the weight issues, it raised other issues, such as short battery life. Another team shifted to a rat trap rather than a mousetrap to better host the size and weight of the Wii Remote.

We made numerous changes to the prototype interface and the activity design during this trial, including adding the ability to stop and start the graphing function as well as the ability to more easily save image files. In addition, we made it easier to turn off and on the view of each different axis so that attention could be focused on one axis at a time. One instance when this feature proved critical was during the heated in-class debates about negative acceleration; the acceleration line dipping below zero stirred the most discussion amongst students, with some students expressing understanding, while others lacked accurate explanations. One team was convinced that fact that our graphs showed negative acceleration in this context indicated that our sensing system "wasn't working" and ran several trials to bear out their hypothesis.

Power Punch

In response to some of the misconceptions and design issues uncovered in the mousetrap car activity, we created a new lab activity to enable students to use the Wii Remote to study acceleration more explicitly. Because it was not tied to a larger ongoing project, this lab enabled us to focus the whole lab on measurement data.

The Power Punch lab took place during a single class period, several weeks after the mousetrap car activity. Students were asked to consider what the acceleration graph of a punch would look like. The instructor demonstrated by holding her right hand at her side and thrusting it forward as if hitting a punching bag. The arm was not withdrawn. The example was repeated several times, and the students were asked to draw what they would expect to see on an acceleration graph. These were collected.

Students then were asked to use a Wii Remote to see if they were right. They followed instructions to tape strings to their Wii Remotes, and hang them vertically in a tube; this allowed the effect of gravity to be zeroed out, and for all of the punch's acceleration to be captured on a single axis, simplifying the data. As a student gripped the string and punched, the Wii Remote was vertically displaced within the tube. The interface showed both a bar graph that indicated the acceleration at the current time, and a line graph illustrating the acceleration over time. Students worked in groups of three or four to capture their punches. Each team paired a Wii Remote to one student's laptop, and began conducting trials. Students were given handheld cameras and were asked to video their predictions and their trials.

While one class ran out of time due to pairing issues, the other two classes gathered together after each team had conducted several trials. Students were asked to come to the board and draw their acceleration graphs. When enough were on the board, the instructor asked what could be generalized from these. Students agreed on the general shape of a punch graph, and then as a class began to debate how to map the graph to the actions.

The graph showed a sharp rise, and then a smaller sharp dip below zero, and then a recovery to the zero line. Again students struggled with negative acceleration, sparking engaging conversations. In one class some students claimed that the reversal to the negative must have been when the punch was withdrawn to the punchers side. Others refuted this, because this did not match the action of the assignment or that recorded on the video. In response another student piped up and said "no, it's the up and down of the Wii Remote" indicating the rising and falling of the Wii Remote within the tube. As her hand was moving up and down she hesitated and said, "wait... wait... I almost got it!" Another student exclaimed "wait – we did this! Its moving.. no... Its not.. its.. slowing down!" Because of the shared discussion of the data, we were able to witness firsthand the student's struggles coming to grasp the concepts in question.

Despite that students had studied and graphed acceleration in the months prior and had "done" negative acceleration following their mousetrap car experience, their intuitions related to positional displacement in the direction of motion were the most available to them when considering the graphs. While graphical representations of change in distance over time are difficult to grasp, considering change in change is much more complex. While they "knew" the formulaic answers of how distance, velocity and acceleration were related, the motion of their own arms' displacement was much more readily available than considering change in speed. Like in the mousetrap car project, only a few of the students in all three classes predicted a pattern that included negative values before the activity. However, unlike the graphs of the mousetrap car, no students indicated intuitive understanding of the graphs of their punches' acceleration.

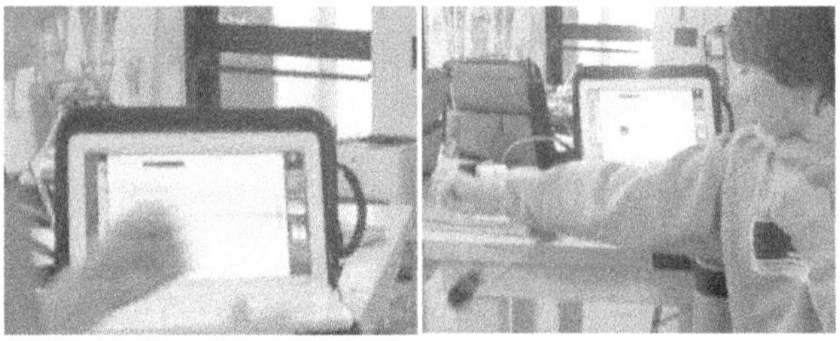

Figure 2. Photos of students engaging in the power punch activity

Roller coaster

The third project with which we engaged was the marble rollercoaster project. The instructor suggested that this design prototype measure velocity rather than acceleration because the activity was tied to a unit on energy formulas that use velocity calculations.

To measure velocity, we decided to use the Wii Remote's IR camera. At first we planned to embed infrared LED lights inside balls for the camera to track. However, it became difficult to balance the batteries inside the balls so that it would roll properly. We then switched to a different strategy – to paint the marbles with retro-reflective paint so that IR lights, mounted on a ring in around the Wii Remote's IR camera, would capture the moment the ball passed. However, it was difficult to get the paint and glass beads to stay on the marble, and, although it worked well in a test environment, when we got into the classroom we picked up lots of interference from the school's security cameras. In the end, we switched to a "photo gate" strategy, placing IR LEDs on clips that students could mount along the track. When the ball passed, it interrupted the camera for a period of time, providing entry and exit points that could be used to calculate the velocity of the ball.

Because one of our goals was getting students to see the Wii Remote as a flexible tool, we spent some time explaining to them the different strategies and what we finally settled on. We presented a very brief Powerpoint on IR light and how the camera works, then showed them how to view IR lights via a cell phone camera and discussed the various strategies we had considered. Then students set about setting up IR lights and Wii Remotes.

During this activity, we noticed that some of the displays the student teams were using differed from those that we had originally designed; when questioned about why the colors and sizes of features in the interface were different, students showed us the places that they had changed our code to improve the interface.

OBSERVATIONS AND FINDINGS

The engagements with our participants allowed us to test and refine our ideas of how handheld gaming technology might foster new and effective practices in laboratory and project-based learning. We review each in sequence:

Manipulating ideas via manipulating tools

Based on a review of the literature that described "cookbook" science [34] in which students followed directions and manipulated equipment according to instructions, one of our own design challenges was to create a system whereby more time was spent on manipulating ideas than manipulating equipment. On the whole, students did spent lots of time manipulating equipment. However, unlike "cookbook" science, these moments often intersected with manipulating ideas. Rudimentary tasks such as pairing Bluetooth or positioning the remote to zero out gravity engaged them in thinking about how the Wii Remote worked as a tool, and led to conversations about syncing and calibration which are fundamental to experimental science. In addition, the presence of real-time data helped students consider why it is necessary to be fussy about the technical mechanics of lab work—for example, proper taping of the sensor leads to less noisy data. The process of collecting scientific data with scientific tools moved to the foreground.

However, the time spent manipulating equipment took away from opportunities to engage students in dynamic discussions of their data and for students to use that data in redesign. In particular, we faced technical issues with pairing of 20 Bluetooth devices with 20 laptops in one room. While we developed work-around procedures to make the system work, the nitpickiness and likelihood of failure would keep these tools from working in a broader set of classrooms without substantial improvement.

The equipment also seemed to have some valence of its own, generating a change in activity in terms of energy and interest. The Wii Remotes newly positioned as tools were intriguing, and the idea of "hacking" a toy into a tool was new and "cool." Students were excited and enthusiastic about using them in their projects; they spent significant time engaging in teamwork to solve problems related to the Wii Remote's use. While we did not intend to have students spend so much time troubleshooting the technical underpinnings of the technology, the repositioning of the students' relationship to the technology fulfilled one of our key project goals.

While capturing and visualizing data was exciting, analyzing its meaning was hard work. Not surprisingly, when students were left to their own devices, they attended more to design aspects of their projects and to collecting data with the Wii Remotes than to analyzing the data they produced. We observed that this was in part related to the structure given to the assignment. While it was exciting to "add" data to previously designed activities, in the future we would like to structure the activities themselves around the data. For example, students could be the more specific, data-driven challenge to build a mousetrap car that reaches a specified acceleration and stops within a given distance, rather than to build a mousetrap car and observe its acceleration pattern. With this change in activity structure, engaging with data becomes part of the fun of the design activity itself. We think the most successful activities will integrate data analysis learning moments into the hubbub of the design and lab activity. If carefully designed, we think this could be done without substantially lengthening the overall activity duration.

Supporting Social Interaction

The Wii Remote's mix of familiarity and complexity seemed to work in favor of student social interaction around both the device and the physics underlying it. Consider the following:

Two students are trying to attach an IR light to the side of their roller coaster so that they can get a measure of velocity as the ball passes the point. One student has positioned the light on the same side of the track as the Wii remote, so that the IR camera cannot see the IR light. Another student is helping but staying quiet. A third is watching in frustration.

B. "No, [it goes] here."

A. "No ... It has to bounce... hold it still"

B. "It can't SEE it." "Move."

A. "Yeah but hold it still, it will [bounce]."

B. "Light doesn't bounce."

A. "Yes it does its IR you cant see it cause its red"

B. "But the sensor has to see it when you swing it." (He makes a move as if playing Wii tennis just before grabbing the IR light clip).

A. "Stop! It can't go like that it will block it!"

B. "But it has to block it!"

A. "It needs to see when it goes by so it can bounce"

The first student has confused two models of tracking IR light – one using retro-reflective paint so that the light will "bounce" off the ball into the camera, and the other using a "photogate" system, so that a steady light is blocked by the ball to trigger a timer. This led to a rich discussion about the nature of light 'bouncing,' waves, how a camera works, the light spectrum, and the misnomer of the 'sensor' bar in the Wii system. It further led to a conversation of binary switches, measurement of time, and instantaneous versus average velocity. The negotiation over tinkering with the tool to measure physical phenomena led to a rich debate and eventually a deeper understanding of related concepts.

Students worked in teams on all projects, and in this vein socially engaging in "science talk" in ways that have been shown to be productive for learning. [24] [32] We followed several teams closely and have noted frequent discussion and argumentation over all aspects of activity. In addition, there was significant cross team fertilization of ideas, as students were free to wander about the space and observe what each other were doing. While we originally planed for each student on a team to have a Wii Remote paired to their own laptop, we were glad that we shifted to a one-laptop-per-team solution. The shared screen facilitated joint attention to data and group conversation – which made considering data more fun and more meaningful.

In addition, students frequently discussed playing various Wii games at home, acted out mock gaming play, and made inside "Wii" jokes while playing with the equipment. We theorize that the Wii Remotes in this case were traversing the different worlds of home and school, serving as "boundary objects" [10] that connected their peer-oriented, home-based play worlds with their new activities in physics class. Several students asked if they could download the software later and use it at home with their own Wii console. Just the possibility that the software tools could be used in the future among friends seemed to add importance to the lab activities, inviting participants to project themselves into a world in which not only did play enter into physics, but physics entered into play.

Harnessing everyday and embodied understanding

Our findings around everyday and embodied intuitions are contradictory. Students have an intuitive sense of the use of the Wii Remote technology due to their experiences in game play. We assumed that these embodied experiences would correctly inform students' intuitions about abstractions related to mathematics and physics [15]. Our observations suggest, however, that for concepts such as velocity and acceleration, the experiences of motion in the body may be misleading. For example, when examining graphs of a the change in a car's velocity over time, most students were readily able to explain negative values as the car's "slowing down." This was despite that their initial predictions of the graph showed no negative values. However, later, when examining the graph of a punch, experienced firsthand, students had difficulty conceptualizing negative values, sometime "remembering" their experience of distance displacement to fit their observation of the graph. For example, in the vignette below, two students are working with the "punch" set up together on a laptop. The instructor passes by :

C. "No she said don't pull [your hand] back!."

D. "I didn't... stop [the graph]"

C. "Yes – look " (Swinging his arm in a play punch to lab partner while pointing to the line sharply dipping below zero on the screen).

D. "Ow. Oh.. but... it [the line graph] kept going. Let me.." (Students set up and same student replicates the punch, this time with arm held out, visibly still)

C. "It went again... it bounced in the tube."

D. "No but.... Ok. it's speed... so it stopped. NO! Its acceleration. But... the speed stopped. But (looking back at the tube)... It fell back... "

C. "(Audible groan). No it didn't...it stopped. Yeah... but... It's here see" (pointing to negative values and then yanking the string up and down).

Instructor. (Overhearing while walking by): "So. Wait. Why is the graph below zero?"

C. "Yeah. Cause it got messed up. He pulled his hand back. Do it again..."

It seems that that watching a car start and stop under its own propulsion outside ones own body gives a clearer overview of forces involved than does the experience of watching a graph of a self generated punch. While students feel themselves generating the punch, they do not feel themselves "stopping" it, as the punch is limited not by muscle action but by the limits of the length of the arm. In this case, students must decouple their intuitive phenomenological understanding of how it feels to punch from the abstraction of "acceleration." We think this hypothesis would be interesting to follow up on in future studies.

Enabling more data, in more classrooms, more often

Although in this early design phase we have yet to implement automated data aggregation and visualization across teams, students were able to generate and visualize more data, in more class periods, more frequently than in the prior year. Already we could see how these led to loud but useful debates (for example, about negative acceleration). By generating data related to the same concepts across several different projects throughout the school year, students encountered more representations of difficult concepts in physics (such as acceleration) in shorter time spans across disparate contexts. Studies indicate viewing multiple representations across various cases is beneficial for conceptual transfer of learning; however, we lack controlled assessment data to prove that students learned more than in prior years.

DISCUSSION

Thus far, we generally confirm our hypothesis that handheld gaming remotes offer specific properties that make them uniquely situated to be useful for science classrooms. Among these properties are the linkages between the devices components and complex concepts in physics, the familiar and social nature of the devices in children's everyday lives, and its capabilities to rapidly, frequently collect, and with software, analyze and visualize large quantities of data for discussion. However, our hypothesis that embodied experiences of game play contribute to conceptual understanding of physics did not play out as we expected. While we conclude that the everyday playful nature of the device makes it accessible and interesting to children, whether or not children's 'embodied' felt experiences of acceleration in game play contribute to or interfere with understanding of acceleration is a matter for further study.

Overall we found that embedding data in student projects provided anchors for integration of diverse design projects within the curriculum, and that when offered the opportunity and some guidance, students will tinker towards abstract concepts in physics as they tinker with familiar tools of its measurement. We recognize that in the case of this project however, the researchers had great influence over students tinkering. It is likely that to a significant degree students' engaged stance towards the inner workings of the technology was enhanced by their collaboration in a technical design research project run by adults engaged in tinkering. As this is relevant to our conclusions, below we further describe this cooperative 'tinkering' stance in our design process, and follow with some conclusions of design opportunities for using handheld game controllers in classroom settings.

Cooperative Design Process

The cooperative design process contributed significantly to both the software outcomes and, we think, student learning. Because we spent significant time in the classroom before any intervention, we, the students, and the staff were familiar with each other and the project. All participants were positioned as part of the design process, each with different roles. Particularly interesting was the students' perceptions of their role in educating researchers. Students were critically engaged in the activities in which they were participating, using the tools but also considering whether activities they were doing were effective for learning. Students felt free to give us feedback on both process and product, as well as to orient us to their expectations in terms of classroom culture. For example, after receiving a list of instructions on how to pair the Wii Remotes, two girls approached and gently told us that at this school "we explore, we don't follow instructions."

Students also gave excellent feedback on the software, pointing out interface issues and aspects that made concepts difficult to understand. Their position as co-designers of the software also seemed to alter their positioning towards the Wii technology itself. Because initial designs were prototyped in an open programming environment, student could read the code before running it, and could make changes and alterations. Several times teams changed sections of code to make things easier to see. Several students spent time watching how data was being read and asked questions about programming.

Students critique was not limited to software and activities, but also extended to the researchers' pedagogical approach. After one particularly complex presentation about infrared light, students had a hard time putting all the pieces together and were frustrated. After some more discussion after class, the teacher assigned them to team up to create a better presentation, so that the researchers could learn how to do it "more kid friendly" next time. Students enthusiastically created detailed Powerpoint presentations, hand drawn comics, animations, movies of action in 3D worlds, and Scratch [33] animations that showed how a Wii IR camera worked and how one could use it to create a photo gate system. Each team presented to researchers a week later, affording another opportunity for us to interview them about the project, and affording both researchers and students the opportunity to "teach to learn" and "learn to teach." Each presentation used vocabulary and analogies that the youth said other kids could relate to. Most students agreed to our request to eventually host these on our web site so that other students could learn from them when the software is released.

While the collaboration was informative for both design and learning, we also ran into familiar "gotchas" in the collaboration process. Institutional time frames that don't match up make workflow difficult. The school is for academically talented students for whom appearing knowledgeable is generally important, and we found it took encouragement to get them to reveal that they might not understand things. In some cases ,it appeared they wanted to please us or the teacher, and so had difficulty expressing mistakes or partially formed ideas rather than an "official" correct answer. As is probably typical, we found that while we were tinkering towards technology and physics, we also were slowly tinkering towards an effective culture of collaboration.

Design opportunities

Several design opportunities present themselves from these findings. First, streamlining the software deployment and computer pairing issues is crucial. Until a teacher can easily pair a classroom of Wii Remotes to a classroom of computers, it will be hard to integrate these activities into school curricula. Along similar lines, it will be very beneficial to social interaction and data-centered reflection to automate the saving and labeling of data output, as as facilitate quick and easy aggregation of the data. Ideally, we would like the teacher to be able to easily bring up anyone's data file to talk about, as well as superimpose results or aggregate results from the whole class on one screen. In addition, we frequently asked students to videotape their trials as they were collecting data. We found this helpful to avoid the "remembering" problem. We would like to integrate video into our tools so that the action and the data could be reviewed side-by-side.

By addressing some of these usability issues, we hope in the next iteration to integrate data measurement into lab and project activities from the outset. This can engage students in considering data in their designs, and make the data more exciting because it would have real impact on design decisions. The same is true with presenting ideas and surfacing misconceptions. Having students present their designs mid-way through would facilitate surfacing misconceptions early on, so that they could more explicitly examine their naïve ideas in light of data that contradicts them. Benchmark break points in projects would provide opportunities for intervention along both these lines.

CONCLUSIONS

We expect this design research, as well as other studies in this vein, will contribute not only to the design and integration of technology into classroom science inquiry practices, but also add fodder to discourse of what makes constructivist "hands-on" learning effective. Recent work has begun to challenge the polarization between creative student-driven "open-ended" exploration and curriculum driven direct instruction. [36] We propose that everyday, low-cost mobile sensor technologies such as game controllers can engage students in student-and-curriculum driven practices that are effective for learning. By engaging kids in manipulating ideas via manipulating tools, by supporting social interaction, harnessing everyday and embodied understanding, and enabling more data, in more classrooms, more often, these tools can promote greater synthesis of the interests of children and the interests of the curriculum [6].

ACKNOWLEDGMENTS

We would like to thank Terry Winograd, Lars Erik Holmquist, and Martin Jonsson for their important contributions to this work. We also thank Pote Pothongsunan and the students and staff at Nueva School for their creativity, energy and patience. We gratefully acknowledge the Wallenberg Foundation for its funding and support.

REFERENCES

1. Barron, B. Learning ecologies for technological fluency: Gender and experience differences. *Journal of Educational Computing Research 31*, 1 (2004), 1-36.
2. Bransford, J.D., Sherwood, R.D., Hasselbring, T.S., Kinzer, C.K., and Williams, S.M. Anchored instruction: Why we need it and how technology can help. (1990).
3. Bryant, J.A., Akerman, A., and Drell, J. Wee Wii: Preschoolers and motion-based game play. (2008).
4. Clement, J. Using bridging analogies and anchoring intuitions to deal with students' preconceptions in physics. *Journal of research in science teaching 30, 10* (1993), 1241-1257.
5. De Bruyn, L., Leman, M., and Moelants, D. Quantifying children's embodiment of musical rhythm in individual and group settings. *The 10th International Conference on Music Perception and Cognition*, (2008).
6. Dewey, J. The child and the curriculum. (1902). Retrieved from http://books.google.com/books.
7. Dillenbourg, P. What do you mean by collaborative learning. Collaborative learning: Cognitive and computational approaches, (1999), 1-16.
8. Druin, A. Cooperative inquiry: developing new technologies for children with children. *Proceedings of the SIGCHI conference on Human factors in computing systems: the CHI is the limit*, ACM (1999), 592-599.
9. Ellis, A.K. and Fouts, J.T. Research on educational interventions. *Eye on Education,* Larchmont, NY, USA, (1997), 29-34.
10. Fujimura, J. Crafting science: Standardized packages, boundary objects, and "translation." In A. Pickering (Ed.), *Science as practice and culture*, University of Chicago Press, Chicago, OH, (1992), 168-211.
11. Greeno, J., Moore, J., & Smith, D. (1993). Transfer of situated learning. In D. Detterman & R. Sternberg (Eds.), Transfer on trial: Intelligence, cognition, and instruction Norwood, NJ: Ablex. (1993), 99-167.
12. Graves, L., Stratton, G., Ridgers, N.D., and Cable, N.T. Comparison of energy expenditure in adolescents when playing new generation and sedentary computer games: cross sectional study. *Bmj 335*, 7633 (2007), 1282.
13. Hill, C.S. Developing psychomotor skills the Wii way. *Science 323*, 5918 (2009), 1169.
14. Hofstein, A. and Lunetta, V.N. The laboratory in science education: Foundations for the twenty first century. *Science education 88, 1* (2004), 28-54.
15. Hutchins, E. *Cognition in the Wild*. MIT press, Cambridge, MA, 1995.
16. Inkpen, K.M. Designing handheld technologies for kids. *Personal and Ubiquitous Computing 3*, 1 (1999), 81-89.
17. Iversen, O.S. and Nielsen, C. Using digital cultural probes in design with children. *Proceeding of the 2003*

conference on Interaction design and children, July, Citeseer (2003), 01-03.

18. Iwata, S. Corporate Management Policy Briefing Semi-Annual Financial Results Briefing for FY ending March 2001. Public presentation, October 29, 2010, Tokyo Japan. http://www.nintendo.co.jp/ir/en/library /events/101029/index.html
19. Knezek, G. and Christensen, R. Impact of new information technologies on teachers and students. *Education and Information Technologies 7*, 4 (2002), 369-376.
20. Krajcik, J. S., Blumenfeld, P. C., Marx, R. W., Bass, K. M., Fredricks, J., & Soloway, E. (1998). Inquiry in project based science classrooms: Initial attempts by middle school students. *The Journal of the Learning Sciences 7*, 313-350.
21. Lakoff, G. and Johnson, M. *Philosophy in the flesh: The embodied mind and its challenge to western thought*. Basic books, 1999.
22. Lave, J. and Wenger, E. *Situated learning: Legitimate peripheral participation*. Cambridge, 1991.
23. Lawrenz, F. Misconceptions of physical science concepts among elementary school teachers. *School Science and Mathematics 86*, 8 (1986), 654-660.
24. Lemke, J.L. Talking science: Language, learning, and values. Norwood. *NJ: Ablex*, (1990).
25. Lunetta, V.N. and Tamir, P. Matching Lab Activities with Teaching Goals. *Science Teacher 46, 5* (1979), 22-24.
26. Means B, Roschelle J, Penuel W, Sabelli N & Haertel G Technology's contribution to teaching and policy: Efficiency, standardization, or transformation? *Review of Research in Education, 27*, (2003) 159-181.
27. National Research Council. *National science education standards: Observe, interact, change, learn*. National Academy Press, Washington, DC, 1996.
28. Pea, R.D. Augmenting the discourse of learning with computer-based learning environments. In E. de Corte, M. Linn, H. Mandl, & L. Verschaffel (Eds.) *Computer-based learning environments and problem-solving*. Springer-Verlag, New York, 1990, 313-343.
29. Pea, R. D.. The collaborative visualization project. *Communications of the ACM, 36(5)*, (1993), 60–63.
30. Pea, R.D. Practices of distributed intelligence and designs for education. In Saloman, G. (Ed.) *Distributed cognitions: Psychological and educational considerations*, Cambridge University Press (1993), 47-87.
31. Pearson, E. and Bailey, C. Evaluating the potential of the Nintendo Wii to support disabled students in education. *ICT: Providing choices for learning: Proceedings ascilite Singapore 2007*
32. Polman, J.L. *Designing project-based science: Connecting learners through guided inquiry*. Teachers College Press, 2000.
33. Resnick, M., Maloney, J., Monroy-Hernández, A., et al. Scratch: programming for all. *Communications of the ACM 52*, 11 (2009), 60-67.
34. Rode, J.A., Stringer, M., Toye, E.F., Simpson, A.R., and Blackwell, A.F. Curriculum-focused design. *Proceedings of the 2003 conference on Interaction design and children, ACM (2003)*, 119-126.
35. Roth, W.M. Experimenting in a constructivist high school physics laboratory. *Journal of research in Science teaching 31, 2* (1994), 197-223.
36. Schwartz, D.L., Lindgren, R., & Lewis, S. Constructivism in an age of non-constructivist assessments. In Tobias, S. & Duffy, T.M. (Eds.) *Constructivist Theory Applied to Instruction: Success or Failure?* Taylor & Francis, New York (2009).
37. Somers, W., Rooney, F., and Ochoa, R. Introductory Physics Experiments Using the Wiimote. *Bulletin of the American Physical Society 54*, (2009).
38. Vygotsky, L., Hanfmann, E.E., and Vakar, G.E. *Thought and language*. (1962).
39. Vannoni, M. and Straulino, S. Low-cost accelerometers for physics experiments. *European Journal of Physics 28*, (2007), 781.
40. Wheeler, M.D. Physics experiments with Nintendo Wii controllers. *Physics Education 46,* (2011), 57.
41. Williams, S.M. and Hmelo, C.E. Guest editors' introduction. *The Journal of Learning Sciences 7,* (1998), 265-270.
42. Zeilik, M., Schau, C., and Mattern, N. Misconceptions and their change in university-level astronomy courses. *The Physics Teacher 36*, (1998), 104.

Effects of Sharing Text Selections on Gaze Cross-recurrence and Interaction Quality in a Pair Programming Task

Patrick Jermann
CRAFT, EPFL, Ecole Polytechnique Fédérale de Lausanne
station 20, CH-1015 Lausanne
Patrick.Jermann@epfl.ch

Marc-Antoine Nüssli
CRAFT, EPFL, Ecole Polytechnique Fédérale de Lausanne
station 20, CH-1015 Lausanne
Marc-Antoine.Nuessli@epfl.ch

ABSTRACT

We present a dual eye-tracking study that demonstrates the effect of sharing selection among collaborators in a remote pair-programming scenario. Forty pairs of engineering students completed several program understanding tasks while their gaze was synchronously recorded. The coupling of the programmers' focus of attention was measured by a cross-recurrence analysis of gaze that captures how much programmers look at the same sequence of spots within a short time span. A high level of gaze cross-recurrence is typical for pairs who actively engage in grounding efforts to build and maintain shared understanding. As part of their grounding efforts, programmers may use text selection to perform collaborative references. Broadcast selections serve as indexing sites for the selector as they attract non-selector's gaze shortly after they become visible. Gaze cross-recurrence is highest when selectors accompany their selections with speech to produce a multimodal reference.

Author Keywords

Dual eye tracking, gaze cross-recurrence, pair programming, grounding, reference, text selection, pointing

ACM Classification Keywords

H.5.3 Information Interfaces and Presentation: Group and Organization Interfaces

General Terms

Experimentation; Measurement.

INTRODUCTION

Our long term goal is to build computational models of collaborative interaction during problem-solving and to support collaborators by mirroring aspects of the interaction back to them [27]. Productive interaction involves collaborators who are aware of each others' actions, beliefs, and intentions and are able to effectively coordinate their actions, knowledge and expertise.

Recent advances in dual eye-tracking (see for instance[4], [23], [14]) suggest that gaze coupling between partners is related to better understanding and more productive interaction. Grounding mechanisms are the source of the coupling, especially, the performance of collaborative reference. The main phenomenon in this area of research is that collaborators' gaze is coupled when they interact about a shared object of interest [25]. The possibility to automatically quantify this coupling through a measure of cross-recurrence opens up new possibilities for the computational modeling of interaction quality.

In this article we present an empirical study that sheds some light on the functions of broadcasting text selection in the context a pair programming task. As we will see, shared text selection is an effective way for programmers to point out portions of the code to their partners and to define the focus of attention for the pair.

BACKGROUND

Interaction quality and gaze cross-recurrence

Interaction quality is a complex construct which combines various aspects of coordination like collaboration flow (do partners react to each other's contributions in coherent way and do they solve the problem by discussing ?), collaborators' efforts to sustain mutual understanding, the degree of division of labor (do both partners participate in the problem-solving and coordinate the nature of their contributions ?), as well as the quality of technical coordination (see [21] and [18]). With the recent advent of desktop eye-tracking methodology, computational interaction models based on gaze behavior are within reach. To be used in an interaction model, raw gaze first has to be aggregated into fixations and then into higer level indicators that reflect cognition and communcation. Many individual features can possibly be derived from collaborators' gaze (e.g. proportion of fixation time on various elements of the workspace, individual sequence of fixations, average direction of saccades) and compared across participants, but a measure that directly models the collaborative aspect of gaze is especially promising in our context.

Cross-recurrence quantification analysis was proposed recently as a generalized method to unveil the interlocking of two interacting people [12]. Authors used the method to analyze the use of language alignment through grammatical sequences [11] or the coupling of gaze in situations of synchronous dialogue [25]. The coupling of the sequence of gaze hits from two collaborators is predictive of a better understanding by the listener [24]. Conversely, a lack of gaze overlap between collaborators predicts misunderstanding in a chat mediated situation ([5],[4]).

In a qualitative study of the data collected for the current study, gaze cross-recurrence has been found to be indicative of good collaboration during collaborative program understanding [18]. An evaluation of the interaction quality following a rating method [21] found that especially the rating dimensions of "collaboration flow" and "sustaining mutual understanding" corresponded to the phenomenon of "looking together". When the collaboration flow is of good quality, partners engage in a coherent exchange of information and keep mutual awareness on what the partner is currently working on. A second dimension of the rating scheme is of interest for the current study, namely "sustaining mutual understanding" that evaluates whether the collaborators efficiently build and maintain common ground [8]. Efficient collaborators use verbal and deictic references to maintain a shared focus of attention, for instance by verbal references to specific parts of the code, and by selecting specific parts of the code in the shared workspace.

Supporting references via text selection

Maintaining a common focus of attention is at the heart of collaborative processes. Mutual understanding stems from the collaborators efforts to ground their conversation (e.g. through backchannel signals, acknowledgments, and references) to make sure their partner has perceived, understood and agreed their message [13]. Referencing and more specifically deictic gestures are central in this grounding process. The increased cross-recurrence that is characteristic of productive interaction stems from the fact that speech and gaze are linked via references. There is a strong relationship between verbal (or written) references and gazed objects: on the one hand, speakers (or writers in a chat-based interaction) will look at the object they will refer to 700 milliseconds (in the case of speech) before making the verbal reference and on the other hand, the listeners (or message readers) will look at the visual reference around 1200ms after hearing the name of the referent [1, 16].

According to recent views, a reference is a composite signal that consists of an indication and a verbal description [6][7]. Two strategies for indicating can be distinguished. Following a directing-to strategy speakers create an indexing site and accompany this indication with a verbal description (e.g. pointing towards an object and saying "that one"). A second strategy for indicating, called placing-for, consists of placing the object of reference inside a predefined indexing site. In this case, indexing sites are longer lived and less speech is necessary for the description, given the conventional agreement about the site's indexical function.

In face to face situations and video-mediated situations, pointing is accomplished by hand and arm gestures, and the lack of visual access to the shared workspace or the imprecision of pointing is compensated by more explicit verbal references (see for instance[20], [15], [3]). The balance between gesturing and speaking follows the principle of least collaborative effort [9], such as the participants in a conversation will combine the means they have at their disposal to minimize the cost of establishing reference, for example by using gestures rather than spoken references if they convey enough information.

The present study

We focus in this contribution on the the sharing of text selection among programmers in the context of pair programming. In pair programming two programmers work together on the same code, performing a range of common software design activities like analysis, design, implementation, review, debugging [28]. Pair programming is usually performed while programmers are co-located and work on the same object. The collaborators adopt the roles of driver (types code at the keyboard) and navigator (planning and monitoring). Spatially distributed flavors of pair programming have been studied as well showing that distance can successfully be overcome and lead to satisfactory results [2].

As in many domains, one of the requirements for the design of distributed pair programming tools is that they support gesturing and deictic references [10]. Not surprisingly, most of the pair programming plugins for standard software development environments offer the possibility to broadcast the pointers [17] or the text selection among collaborators. For instance, with Saros[1] (an Eclipse[2] plugin) all participants can select text to display to their partners. Another example is XPairtise[3], where the roles of driver and navigator are more strongly enforced and where only the driver can highlight text to be displayed to the navigator.

We test two different modalities of sharing the selection among collaborators and compare them to a situation without selection sharing. A shared selection creates a technical interdependence according to which both subjects have to share the control of the selected text. With a dual selections, collaborators can each select different regions of the code which are then displayed to their partners. Dual selection also allows programmers to select two different code elements during comparisons, or to use selection to confirm their partners' reference by selecting the same element.

QUESTIONS AND HYPOTHESES

Question 1 Is selection sharing beneficial for collaboration quality? We are investigating this relationship via a study of gaze cross-recurrence that reflects the extent to which collaborators share a narrow visual focus on the workspace.

H1 Pairs with a good collaboration quality have a higher gaze cross-recurrence than pairs with a poor collaboration quality. As it has been shown by previous studies, we expect that the efforts that collaborators put into coordinating their contributions result in a higher coupling of their gaze.

[1] http://www.saros-project.org/

[2] http://www.eclipse.org/

[3] http://xpairtise.sourceforge.net/

H2 Displaying the collaborators' selection to their partners will help them establish a shared focus of attention and therefore positively affect the gaze cross-recurrence. We hypothesize that the possibility to use text selection as a pointing device makes referring more efficient than through verbal references only.

H3 A shared text selection modality will encourage collaborators to focus most on the same elements (compared to a dual text selection). We speculate that because partners are technically interdependent with regards to the control of the shared selection, this type of selection will be exclusively used to designate elements of the code that constitute the joint focus of attention.

Question 2 What happens during selections? We describe the selection process as a composite signal of gaze fixations and speech activity that takes place in the seconds that precede and follow the creation of a text selections.

H4 Participants' gaze is attracted by the selection target when it appears on their screen.

H5 Selections have a deictic function when they are accompanied by speech. Selectors use the selected screen area as visual indexing sites for their references.

METHOD

In the experiment, pairs of subjects had to solve two types of pair programming tasks. The first task consisted of describing the rules of a game implemented as a Java program of three hundred lines. The only indication that guided the subjects' interpretation was that it is a turn-based arithmetic game. The second type of task consisted of finding errors in the game implementation and proposing a possible fix. The programmers got a few lines of output to analyze the error and had to pinpoint the location of the bug in the code as well as to propose a possible fix.

Subjects

Eighty-two students from the departments of computer science and communication science of the Ecole Polytechnique Fédérale de Lausanne were recruited to participate in the study. They were each paid an equivalent of 20 USD for their participation in the study. The participants were typical bachelor and master students aged from 18 to 29 years old with a median of 23 years old. They had a programming experience from 1 to 13 years with a median of 4 years. The participants were paired into forty pairs without further consideration of their level of expertise, gender, age or familiarity.

Procedure

Upon arrival at the laboratory, subjects had to read and sign a participation agreement form. Then, for the next 3 minutes, the experimenters calibrated the eye-trackers for each of the subjects. This simple procedure consists of fixating the center of nine circles appearing on the screen. Once both subjects were ready, they individually filled a short electronic questionnaire about their programming skills and previous experience. The pretest which followed, consisted of individually answering thirteen short programming multiple choice questions. At the end of the pretest, the pairs received a short explanation about the way text selection worked in the programming editor. Finally, the pairs solved the ten program understanding tasks which overall lasted approximately 45 minutes.

Apparatus and material

Gaze was recorded with two synchronized Tobii 1750 eye-trackers that record the position of gaze at 50Hz in screen coordinates. The eye-trackers were placed backtoback and separated from each other by a wooden screen (see figure 1). The synchronization of the eye-trackers was done by using a dedicated server to log gaze via callback functions from the low-level API of the eye-trackers. The subjects heads were held still with an opthalmologic chin-rest placed at 65 centimeters of the screen. An adaptive algorithm was used to identify fixations and a post-calibration was done to correct for systematic offsets of the fixations with regards to the stimulus (see [22] for details about these procedures).

Figure 1. Experimental setup. Subjects were seated facing each other on opposite sides of a wooden separator.

The JAVA programs were presented in a custom programming editor based on the Eclipse development environment. Text was slightly larger (18pt) than it is usually on computer screens and was spaced at 1.5 lines to facilitate the fixation hit detection at a word level precision. Scrolling was synchronized between the participants, such that when programmers scrolled, their partners' viewport was also updated at the same time. All other highlighting, search and navigation functionalities were disabled in the editor.

Independent variable: selection sharing

We implemented three versions of the same programming editor by varying whether and how text selection is broadcast among the collaborators. There were three modalities for the selection type:

Individual The selection of each participant is held private and is not broadcast to the other participants.

Dual Participants each control their own selection. The selections are broadcast so that all participants see them.

Shared Only one shared selection is available and visible for the two partners. Both can modify it at any time.

Process variables

Interface actions (e.g. mouse events, selections), gaze and audio signals were automatically recorded during the experiments and were sampled at a rate of 200 ms. This resulted, for each pair of a large number of data samples (around 10'000) that served as a basis for the cross-recurrence analyses.

Speech

Audio volume was used as an indicator for speech episodes in the interaction. The volume for each participant was normalized as a z-score to remove differences in volume range due to the specificities of the subjects' voices. Finally, the variable was dichotomized by considering samples with a normalized volume above 0.1 as "spoken" and below 0.1 as "silent". This method is somewhat coarse and sometimes identifies parasite noise as speech (e.g. subjects tapping their fingers on the table). However, with the recorded data this simple method attains similar performance as a speech detection algorithm implemented in PRAAT[4].

Selection

Selections were logged by the shared programming editor. The interaction consists of episodes with and without selection. A selection was considered "spoken" if more than 10% of its duration was spoken and "silent" otherwise.

For each selection, a time-lagged fixation hit probability was computed. The time sample during which the selection was defined was considered as reference time. For 50 samples before and 50 samples after the reference time, we computed the proportion of hitting the selection as the number of fixations that fall inside the selection divided by the number of fixations done during the sample (see figure 3). We also computed the probability to speak as a function of time before and after the onset of a selection (see figure 4).

Gaze cross-recurrence

The extent to which the collaborators S1 and S2 look at the same place at roughly the same time and in the same sequence was measured by the level of gaze cross-recurrence. A cross-recurrence plot like the one in figure 2 is a representation of the time coupling between two time series. The x, y location on the plot correspond at a given time for S1 (on the horizontal axis) and a given time for S2 (on the vertical axis). Points on the diagonal correspond to synchrony. There is a black pixel on the diagonal if S1 and S2 look at the same element exactly at the same time. Points above the diagonal correspond to fixations of S2 that happen after S1 has fixated the element. Conversely, points below the diagonal correspond to S2's gaze leading S1's.

A simple measure for the cross-recurrence rate is the given as the proportion of black points on the diagonals of the cross-recurrence plot. However, a necessary presupposition for the comparison of simple cross-recurrence rates between pairs, is that the number of visual targets is constant across interactions, so that the random baseline for the two collaborators to look at the same object at a given lag is comparable. In cases like pair programming (or more generally with any groupware system) this assumption is violated because the number

[4]http://www.fon.hum.uva.nl/praat/

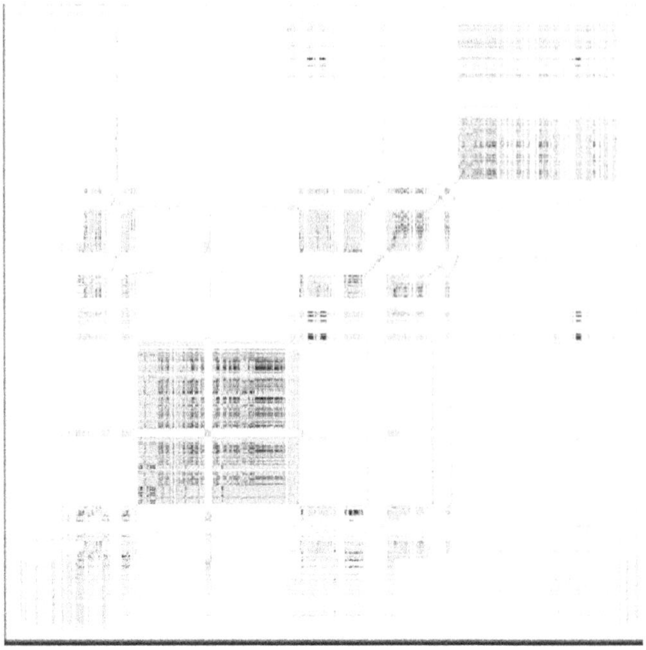

Figure 2. Gaze cross-recurrence plot. Dark dots represent gaze fixations. Grey areas represent opportunities for cross-recurrence. Axes represent time for subjects 1 and 2 respectively. This plot represents cross-recurrence for a duration of 10 minutes.

of objects available for inspection changes constantly (e.g. users change the viewport on the stimulus by scrolling).

Cross-recurrence plots (like the one in figure 2) not only represent the "coupling" of collaborative code exploration, but also show whether the exploration of the program is rather linear (there is almost no off-diagonal activity because regions of code are looked at only once) or iterative (there are marked off diagonal regions that result from the collaborators repeatedly looking at the same regions of the code).

To compensate for the variations introduced by the complexity of the visual stimulus in such a case we computed a zone based cross-recurrence rate that combines one cross-recurrence rate for each zone of the stimulus that is explored. A zone is a collection of small elements that are explored together either because they have a logical link (e.g. lines in a method) or simply because they are co-located on the same region of the screen. In our application domain, we defined zones as JAVA methods. Details of the method are not relevant here, but we invite the interested reader to consult a workshop paper that precisely describes the procedure [19].

Rating interaction quality and level of understanding

In a previous qualitative study [18], we have qualified **interaction quality** by rating several dimension of the interaction following the method proposed by [21]. In this contribution, we simplified the rating scheme and reduced it to a global three-level estimation of interaction quality (Low, Medium and High) that combines the dimensions above. The goal of the rating is to contrast the pairs that "worked well" together, the ones that were "quite ok", and finally the ones that were "very bad". Such a rating is of course too simple to account for the rich nuances of interaction but it has the merit to reflect striking quality differences one notices when watching and listening to the interactions.

Concerning the **level of understanding**, we distinguish between three levels (Good , Medium, Poor). Pairs with a good understanding are able to describe the the rules of the game, including the initial situation (one stack of cards with cards from 1 to 9 and two players), valid moves (players alternate choosing a card), as well as the winning conditions (the first who has three cards that sum up to 15 wins). Pairs with a medium level of understanding only describe partial aspects of the game structure, and often give algorithmic descriptions (e.g. there are numbers in a 'list' and each player has a 'list' of numbers, and the program removes a number) of the program and try to guess the detailed rules from the method names. While following the execution of the program is perfectly valid to orient code exploration, it does not allow them to understand the most difficult aspect of the code (the three cards have to sum up to 15). Pairs who have a poor understanding are not able to describe the functionality of the code and merely describe syntactic features (e.g. there is a loop on a list).

RESULTS

We first report descriptive results about the participants expertise and their distribution into experimental conditions. Second, we describe qualitative results about rating the pairs' quality of interaction and level of understanding. Third, we provide descriptive statistics about the participants' speech and selection. Fourth, we demonstrate the effect of selection on gaze (H4 and H5) and finally we present a quantitative analysis about gaze cross-recurrence and it's relationship with the quality of interaction and the level of understanding (H1, H2 and H3).

Condition and expertise

Forty-one pairs participated in the experiment. Because of various technical problems (participants skipped the pretest, missing audio recording) 40 pairs remain for gaze analyses and 36 pairs for audio analyses. The assignment of 40 pairs into the three experimental conditions resulted in 14 (35%) individual pairs, 16 (40%) dual pairs and 10 (25%) shared pairs.

Participants' score at the individual pretest was used to define levels of expertise. Out of a total of 80 valid pretests, 51 (64%) *Novices* scored below half the range of scores and 29 (36%) *Experts* scored above. The combination of participants into pairs resulted in 21 novice pairs (54%), 9 (23%) mixed ability pairs and 9 (23%) expert pairs.

Novice pairs are somewhat over-represented in the dual condition (13 out of 17 pairs) and expert pairs are slightly overrepresented in the individual condition (6 out of 14). A test of independence however shows that these departures from equiprobability do not reach statistical significance ($\chi^2(4, N = 39) = 8.3, p = 0.08$) .

Interaction quality and level of understanding

Two participants used a shared programming editor to navigate through 300 lines of JAVA source code that implement a simple arithmetic game, and that their task was to explain the rules of the game. Successful interaction has two complementary aspects: finding the solution to the problem and interacting in a coherent and smooth manner.

To describe these two complementary aspects of performance we rated the interactions of 39 pairs during the first question of the collaborative phase with regards to the level of understanding (Poor, Medium, Good) and the quality of interaction (Low, Medium and High). The first question is the most interesting with regards to program understanding because the pairs discover the code for the first time. The time allotted for the question is 10 minutes. Twenty-six pairs did the first question in 10 minutes and 14 pairs took less time. The fastest group finished the question in little over 5 minutes.

Concerning the **level of understanding**, less than half of the pairs managed to identify and correctly explained the gist of the game in the allotted time (N=16, 41% rated *Good*). These successful pairs described the rules of the game (two players have to choose numbers from a stack of numbers from 1 to 9) as well as the conditions for winning the game (the sum of three numbers has to equal 15). The task was more difficult for another half of the pairs who got a shallower understanding of the code that was limited to some aspects (N=18, 46% rated *Medium*). For example, pairs with Medium understanding noticed that the game involved numbers from 1 to 9 but failed to understand that players pick numbers from the same list. Only few pairs were completely overwhelmed by the problem and didn't understand at all what the program was doing (N=5, 13% rated *Poor*).

Concerning the **quality of interaction**, more than a third of the pairs (N=14, 39% rated *High*) collaborate well together, jointly explaining the code by complementing each other's contributions and answering each other's questions. These pairs also display a good coordination of scrolling, with participants negotiating which part of the code they focus on next. Half of the pairs achieve less smooth but nevertheless satisfactory collaboration which includes some division of labor and often the dominance of one subject who is more involved in cognitive aspects of the task (N=19, 49% rated *Medium*). Few pairs (N=6, 15% rated *Low*) encounter difficulties in interaction, with severe coordination issues for scrolling, as well as misunderstandings and disagreements on the way to proceed (e.g. about what method to look at next).

Interaction quality appears to be related to the level of understanding. We see in table 1 that none of the pairs with a poor understanding had a high interaction quality and that most of the pairs who achieved a medium and good understanding also displayed a medium to high interaction quality ($\chi^2(4, N{=}39) = 11, p = 0.03$).

Interaction quality however does not directly predict good comprehension. Naturally, the level of understanding of the pairs is also related to the expertise of the partners as measured by their pretest scores. We see in table 2 that only groups of novices fail to understand the code and that good

	Level of understanding		
Quality of interaction	Poor	Medium	Good
Low	3 (2.54)	2 (-0.46)	1 (-0.93)
Medium	2 (-0.28)	10 (0.42)	7 (-0.28)
High	0 (-1.34)	6 (-0.18)	8 (0.94)

Table 1. Quality of interaction and level of understanding. Numbers in parentheses are standardized residuals corresponding to the chi square test. Residuals bigger than 1.96 are considered statistically significant. One pair was not rated because of a missing audio file.

understanding is mostly achieved by pairs of experts ($\chi^2(4, N = 37) = 16$, p =.003). Mixed ability pairs, i.e. one novice and one expert, achieve medium to good code comprehension.

	Level of understanding		
Pair Composition	Poor	Medium	Good
Novice-Novice	5 (1.4)	12 (0.93)	3 (-1.79)
Mixed ability	0 (-1.04)	4 (0.17)	4 (0.42)
Expert-Expert	0 (-1.10)	1 (-1.54)	8 (2.28)

Table 2. Group composition and level of understanding. Numbers in parentheses are standardized residuals corresponding to the chi square test. Residuals bigger than 1.96 are considered statistically significant. Group composition is missing for three pairs in the sample due to missing pretests.

Speech and selection

As they solve the problem, the two programmers are free to navigate the code and to speak to each other. They can select portions of text which is either held private to themselves (individual condition) or displayed to their partner (dual and shared conditions). We now report descriptive statistics about the amount of speech and selections that happened during the first 10 minutes of the collaborative phase. This corresponds to the timespan for which we rated the interaction as reported in the previous section.

Overall speech and selection rates

For four pairs, some or all of the audio files were missing, hence the statistics were computed on N=36 pairs. Subjects spoke on average for 38% of the time, with a minimum of 7% and a maximum of 59%. The amount of speech is higher for the pairs who displayed a better quality of interaction (F[2,33]=7.3, p=.002), but it does not predict the level of understanding for the pair (F[2,33]=1.56, p=0.23) and does not depend on which condition the pair was in (F[2,33]=2.29, p=0.12). In most pairs, both subjects participated rather equally in the dialogue (the average difference between subjects is equal to m=0.09, sd=0.13).

The selection behavior varies across pairs and subjects. Some subjects select only occasionally (25% of the subjects make 1 to 6 selections during the first ten minutes) whereas others select much more often (25% of the subjects make 32 to 65 selections, that is up to 6 selections per minute). We found that the proportion of time during which some text was selected is higher for high quality interaction than for low quality interaction (F[2,33]=3.83, p=.032), but that this does not depend upon the type of selection (F[2,33]=2.22, p=.12), nor does it vary with the level of understanding achieved by the pair (F[2,33]=1.47, p=0.25).

The fact that speech is a characteristic of good interaction is rather obvious as silent co-presence barely qualifies as productive interaction. More interestingly for our study, it appears that selecting portions of text also participates in good quality of interaction. The statistics about selections and speech were also computed with data covering the whole collaborative phase of the experiment (30 minutes). The direction of the differences between different levels of understanding and between qualities of interaction stays essentially the same when considering only the beginning or the whole interaction.

Selection Precision

The average duration of selections is longer when spoken (m=3.37 seconds, sd=3.71, N=398) as it is when the selector is silent (m=2.05 seconds, sd=3.19, N=217). Also, the number of characters selected is slightly smaller when selectors are speaking (m=20.3, sd=18.0, N=398) than when they are silent (m=22.3, sd=17.5, N=217). Selections are more precise (smaller) when selectors are speaking (SPE) than when they are silent, suggesting that they serve as indexes when accompanied by verbal descriptions. The type of selection (C) does not significantly affect the precision (see table 3).

	Df	logLik	χ^2	df	p
0 Null Model	3	-2726.34			
1 C	5	-2725.49	1.70	2	.43
2 C + SPE	6	-2623.35	204.29	1	< .001
3 C * SPE	8	-2622.65	1.38	2	.50

Table 3. Mixed effect models for selection size. Factors are C=condition and SPE=speech. The user id is used as a random factor to account for the dependence among measures due to repeated measurement of the same subject.

Gaze fixations during selection events

To give a more detailed account of the role of selections in initiating a shared focus of attention, we now describe the gaze of programmers before and during selection events. We distinguish the roles of the *selector* who creates the selection from the role of the *non-selector* who simply attends to the selection.

It is quite obvious that selectors need to fixate the text they are selecting in order to place the caret at the correct position, and then to monitor the position of the caret as they drag the mouse to the end of the selection. Do the non-selectors pay attention to their partners' selections ? In the dual and shared conditions, a change of selection produces a visual stimuli on the non-selectors' screen, which may attract their attention. In the individual condition, non-selectors do not see their partners' selection change and therefore is is unlikely that they would fixate their partners' selection.

We computed the temporal evolution of the probability to fixate the selection for the selector and the non-selector in the three conditions. For each time slot, the probability was obtained by dividing the number of fixations on the selection by the total number of fixations. The resulting curves for dual and shared selections were practically identical and we therefore collapsed the data to simplify its graphical presentation (See figure 3).

Selectors start looking more than chance level at the text they are about to select roughly four to six seconds before the selection is made. The probability to gaze at the selected text culminates at 0.45 for the selector little before the selection is made (200-400 ms) in all conditions. The probability for the non-selector to look at the selection in the dual and shared conditions culminates slightly later (600-800 ms) and with a smaller probability of 0.3. These values are relatively low because the probabilities are computed on short time slots of 200 ms.

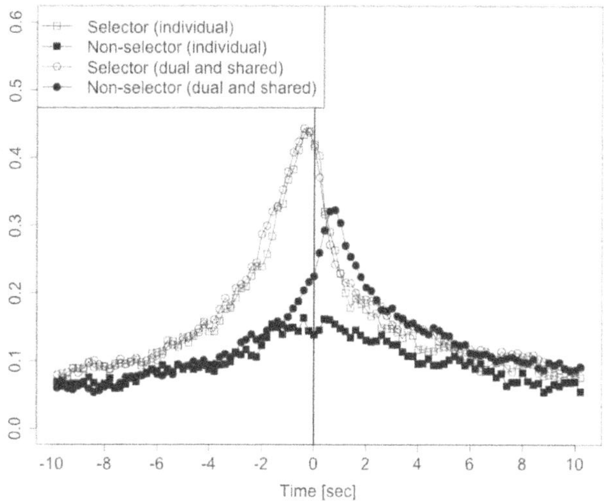

Figure 3. Probability to gaze at own and other's selection for the three modalities of selection (individual, shared and dual). Each datapoint corresponds to a time slot of 200 milliseconds. The probability is the proportion of fixations that fall on the selection during the time slot.

It is interesting to note that the probability for the non-selector to gaze at the partners' selection in the individual condition raises slightly above the baseline at about the time where the selector starts fixating the selection (see figure 3) . Why would people look at invisible selections? This could be explained by the fact that the selection happens in the current zone of shared focus. Hence, the probability to look at it by chance is higher at the moment of the selection rather than just after or just before. Another possible explanation for this phenomenon is that participants accompany verbal references to the code with selections, even though the selection is visible only for themselves. The 'bump' in the curve would therefore correspond to the effect of a verbal reference on a listener's gaze. The evolution of the selector's level of speech around selection events displayed in figure 4 provides some evidence for this hypothesis. The level of speech just before and after the selection is higher for the selectors in the individual condition than for the selectors in the shared and dual conditions.

To sum up, the act of selecting text has an effect on the selector as well as the non-selector's gaze. Selection is accompanied by a simultaneous increase of speech that is more important with individual selection (invisible for the non-selector). These results are compatible with the idea that some visible

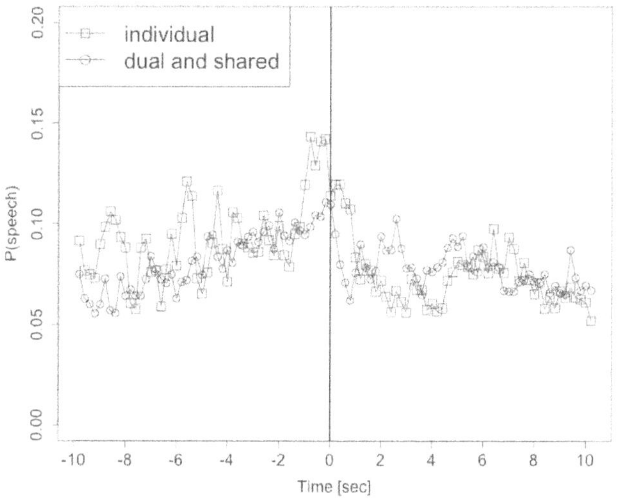

Figure 4. Probability to speak as a function of time for the three modalities of selection (individual, shared and dual). Each datapoint corresponds to a time slot of 200 milliseconds. Time zero corresponds to the onset of the selection.

selections serve as deictic gestures to support reference and that individual selections require more speech from the selector to serve as references.

Gaze cross-recurrence during selection and speech

To further investigate the interplay of the experimental condition with speech and selection we computed filtered cross-recurrence rates for four types of episodes that reflect whether the subjects were selecting text or not and whether they were speaking or not. The episode types were refactored as two independent dichotomous variables "speech" (SPE) and "selection" (SEL).

To compute the cross-recurrence rate by episode type, we proceed by filtering out given cross-recurrence points from the general cross-recurrence plot. For a fixation of S2 to be counted as potentially recurring with S1 in the "selected.spoken" category, the fixation of S2 has to follow the one of S1 and the fixation of S1 has to have happened during a spoken selection.

We compared five mixed-effect models to assess the effect of speech (SPE), selection (SEL) and experimental condition (C) on the level of cross-recurrence inside pairs. The pair identification was used as a random factor to account for the dependence between measures taken from the same pair (for each pair we computed one cross-recurrence rate per type of episodes). Models were fit by using the lmer package and the R statistical framework.

The comparison of the models in table 4 shows that adding the speech factor (SPE) increases the quality of the fit compared to the null model. The selection factor (SEL) further increases the quality of the fit of the model. However, adding the condition (C) alone does not contribute to a better explanation of the cross-recurrence level. Only the interaction of selection and condition (SEL*C) significantly improves the fit of the model. Finally, adding additional interaction terms does not ameliorate the model (SPE*SEL*C). To sum up, it appears that selection affects cross-recurrence levels during selection episodes differently depending on the type of selection.

	df	logLik	χ^2	df	p
0 Null model	3	163.03			
1 SPE	4	169.27	12.49	1	0.0004
2 SPE + SEL	5	172.59	6.63	1	0.01
3 SPE + SEL + C	7	173.92	2.67	2	0.26
4 SPE + SEL * C	9	178.40	8.95	2	0.01
5 SPE * SEL * C	14	181.44	6.08	5	0.30

Table 4. Mixed effect models for cross-recurrence level (factors are SPE=speech, SEL=selection, C=condition)

To further describe these effects we represent the means for the cross-recurrence levels by an interaction plot in figure 5. It appears that dialogue and selection have an additive effect. Selection alone, slightly increases the cross-recurrence as well as speech alone. It seems that selection affects gaze coupling in the same way than speech. However, a more detailed analysis of verbal references would be required to confirm this relationship. The combination of selection and speech with a shared or dual selection modality has the strongest positive effect on cross-recurrence. This most probably corresponds to deictic references where subjects discuss about a common point in the code.

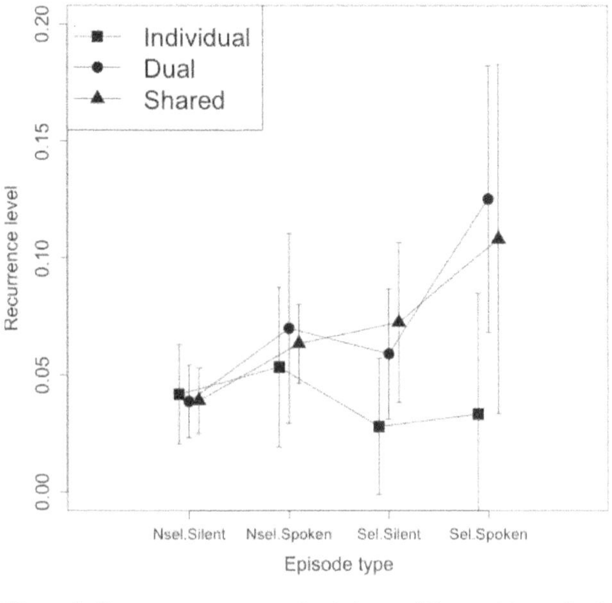

Figure 5. Gaze cross-recurrence levels by condition and type of episode (Nsel=not selected, Sel=selected)

Finally, we see that cross-recurrence is higher for medium and high interaction quality than for low quality but that it does not vary with the level of understanding (see table 5). This result is consistent with our previous findings about the benefits of selection for interaction quality and the relation between gaze cross-recurrence and interaction quality.

Variable	N	ccr	F-test
Quality of interaction			
Low	5	0.0241(0.0296)	
Medium	17	0.0578 (0.0270)	F[2,32]=2.96, p=0.066
High	13	0.0594 (0.0321)	
Level of understanding			
Poor	4	0.0478 (0.0514)	
Medium	16	0.0588 (0.0324)	F[2,32]=0.41, p=0.67
Good	15	0.0496 (0.0241)	

Table 5. Cross-recurrence given quality of interaction and level of understanding. Numbers represent average cross-recurrence values and their standard deviation (in parentheses). Cross-recurrence could not be computed for 5 pairs due to missing data.

DISCUSSION

The two questions we addressed in this contribution concern the general relationship between shared selection and interaction quality, and the anatomy of the selection process. We have gathered evidence that we now discuss as possible answers.

Gaze cross-recurrence, selection and interaction quality

Gaze cross-recurrence is higher for pairs with high interaction quality (H1). Our definition of interaction quality includes several aspects: division of labor, participation symmetry, efforts to sustain shared understanding, as well as the pairs' capacity to agree on the problem-solving strategy. Ratings of good quality were deliberately oriented towards low division of labor and concurrent participation of both programmers in the cognitive aspects of task. Accordingly, good interaction consisted of a smooth and complementary exchange of information between the participants aimed at understanding the program. This type of productive interaction requires participants to 'gaze together' and was sensibly measured by gaze cross-recurrence. Further analyses will benefit from a more detailed rating of the interaction quality, especially focused on grounding efforts, and speech accompanying deictic references. In pair programming tasks which involve the production of code, it is usual that one programmer, called the driver, is more concerned with concrete aspects of the implementation, while the other, called the navigator, is in charge of the regulation of problem-solving. In such cases, a general cross-recurrence rate may not be a valid indicator of interaction quality as programmers focus on different aspects of the task.

We found that gaze cross-recurrence is higher during spoken than silent episodes and also that it was higher during moments with selection than without selection. Furthermore, cross-recurrence is highest during spoken selections, when the selection is visible to all partners (H2). A plausible explanation for the positive effect of speech on cross-recurrence is that participants make references to the code to ground their conversation and thereby look at the same reference sites. The effect of speech on cross-recurrence has to be further investigated, especially by focusing on the effect of verbal references. It is likely that cross-recurrence rates would be higher during verbal references as opposed to any type of speech. Cross-recurrence is also higher during episodes with selections than without selections. The effect of selecting on cross-recurrence might stem from a simple visual pop-up effect (the selection appears on the screen and attracts the attention of the non-selector) as well as from a multi-method reference that combines a verbal description with a pointing gesture. From our analyses we saw that both explanations are plausible and complementary. Gaze cross-recurrence is indeed higher with silent selections that are visible for all collaborators than invisible selections. Gaze cross-recurrence is highest with the combination of a visible selection and speech, suggesting that these selections are purposeful and successful attempts of the selector to direct the non-selector to an indexing site.

We have not found reliable statistical evidence for an advantage of providing programmers with a single shared selection over dual independent selections (H3). Subtle differences exist between shared and dual selection with regards to the precision and the amount of speech that they mobilize, however, further analyses are required to better understand them.

Our findings have confirmed a relationship between gaze cross-recurrence and good interaction quality as well as between gaze cross-recurrence and episodes of referential selection. However, these results do not suffice to establish a causal link between the short term gaze coupling that appears during shared selection and the overall gaze cross-recurrence that is characteristic of good interaction quality. We rather think that is is the sum of all efforts that collaborators put in building and maintaining a shared understanding that eventually results in a high gaze cross-recurrence. Selecting text to establish a shared reference is one way among others to achieve this goal. Pairs in the individual condition who could not share their selection also achieved satisfactory interaction quality, probably through more extensive verbal descriptions of their references.

The rating of the interaction has uncovered a weak link between the level of understanding and the quality of collaboration. It is likely that the expertise of the programmers explains understanding more directly.

Role of selection in multimodal dialogue coordination

Shared and dual text selections efficiently attract the attention (H4). The selectors have a higher probability to look at the selection four to six seconds before the onset of the selection as well as in the 2 seconds that follow it. The maximum probability to fixate the selection is located 200-400 milliseconds before the selection onset. This can be compared with an eye-voice span of 900 milliseconds previously found in a picture description task [16] as well as in a collaborative concept mapping task [26]. The non-selectors respond to this visual signal by gazing at the selection with a maximum probability at around 800 milliseconds after it is initiated. This can be compared with a speech-gaze delay of about 500-1000 milliseconds that was reported in a target identification task [1] and to 1.4 seconds in a concept mapping task [26]. These results suggest that the selection affects gazes in a similar way than spoken verbal references.

Spoken and silent selections are different and may serve different purposes (H5). We have seen in our analyses that spoken selections are more precise than silent selections. This finding suggests that spoken selections serve to direct the listener to a specific element of the code and that the selection span is tightened to serve a deictic function. We also found that the selectors in the individual condition speak relatively more at selection time than selectors in other conditions. This suggests that selectors compensate for the impossibility to display their selections by speaking more during the selection and that these techniques are indeed complementary as proposed by [3]. Larger selections on the other hand may serve to define more broadly the focus of attention of the pair following a placing-for strategy. Other possible uses of the selection include supporting short term memory, for example programmers select a portion of code to lighten their cognitive load, to keep a visual bookmark as a reference in a sequence of instructions, or to highlight the current index in a list of numbers they are adding.

Our results show that selections may serve different purposes depending on whether they are accompanied by speech or not, and depending on their size and duration. These preliminary findings justify a more detailed analysis of selections aimed at establishing a taxonomy. To this end, a joint analysis of selections and verbal content is needed.

CONCLUSION

We have studied the properties of the interaction of two collaborators during a computer program understanding task. High quality interaction, which we defined as tightly coupled interaction in joint problem-solving, is accompanied by a high level of gaze cross-recurrence: the collaborators' gaze fixations tend to focus on the same elements of the code within a short delay of about two seconds. One of the strategies employed by collaborators to build and maintain common ground consists of referring to the objects of interest through a combination of selections and verbal descriptions. It is during moments of spoken selections that collaborators look most at the same program tokens. A selection event provokes a visual response from the non-selectors by attracting their attention on the selected elements of the code. Broadcasting text selections among collaborators therefore appears to be an effective way to support collaborative referencing. The results from this study provide insight into the collaboration processes of multimodal reference and set the way for deeper understanding of the mechanisms that lead to shared comprehension.

ACKNOWLEDGMENTS

We thank the three anonymous reviewers for their insightful comments on the first version of this manuscript. This research was supported by the Swiss National Science Foundation (SNSF) under grants K-12K1-117909 and PZ00P2_126611.

REFERENCES

1. P. D. Allopenna, J. S. Magnuson, and M. K. Tanenhaus. Tracking the time course of spoken word recognition using eye movements: Evidence for continuous mapping models, , , ,. *Journal of Memory and Language*, 38(4):419 – 439, 1998.

2. P. Baheti, L. Williams, E. Gehringer, and D. Stotts. Exploring pair programming in distributed object-oriented team projects. In *In Proceedings of XP/Agile Universe 2002*. Springer Verlag, 2002.
3. A. Bangerter. Using pointing and describing to achieve joint focus of attention in dialogue. *Psychological Science*, 15(6):415–419, June 2004.
4. M. Cherubini, M.-A. Nüssli, and P. Dillenbourg. Deixis and gaze in collaborative work at a distance: a computational model to detect misunderstandings. In *ETRA '08: Proceedings of the 2008 symposium on Eye tracking research and applications*, pages 173–180, New York, NY, USA, 2008. ACM.
5. M. Cherubini, M.-A. Nüssli, and P. Dillenbourg. This is it ! : Indicating and looking in collaborative work at distance. *Journal of Eye-Movement Research*, 3(5):1–20, 2010.
6. H. H. Clark. *Pointing and placing*, pages 243–268. Erlbaum, Hillsdale NJ, 2003.
7. H. H. Clark and A. Bangerter. *Changing ideas about reference*, pages 25–49. Palgrave Macmillan, Basingstoke, 2004.
8. H. H. Clark and S. A. Brennan. Grounding in communication. In L. B. Resnick, J. M. Levine, and S. D. Teasley, editors, *Perspectives on socially shared cognition*. 1991.
9. H. H. Clark and D. Wilkes-Gibbs. Referring as a collaborative process. *Cognition*, 22(1):1 – 39, 1986.
10. D. Cox and S. Greenberg. Supporting collaborative interpretation in distributed groupware. In *Proceedings of the 2000 ACM conference on Computer supported cooperative work*, CSCW '00, pages 289–298, New York, NY, USA, 2000. ACM.
11. R. Dale and M. J. Spivey. Unraveling the Dyad: Using Recurrence Analysis to Explore Patterns of Syntactic Coordination Between Children and Caregivers in Conversation. *Language Learning*, 56(3):391–430, Sept. 2006.
12. R. Dale, A. S. Warlaumont, and D. C. Richardson. Nominal cross recurrence as a generalized lag sequential analysis for behavioral streams. *International Journal of Bifurcation and Chaos,*, 4, 2011.
13. P. Dillenbourg and D. Traum. Sharing solutions: persistence and grounding in multi-modal collaborative problem solving. *Journal of the Learning Sciences*, 15(1):121–151, 2006.
14. D. Gergle and A. T. Clark. See what i'm saying?: using dyadic mobile eye tracking to study collaborative reference. In *CSCW*, pages 435–444, 2011.
15. D. Gergle, R. E. Kraut, and S. R. Fussell. Using Visual Information for Grounding and Awareness in Collaborative Tasks. *Hum.-Comput. Interact.*, Under review.
16. Z. M. Griffin and K. Bock. What the Eyes Say About Speaking. *Psychological Science*, 11(4):274–279, July 2000.
17. C. Gutwin and S. Greenberg. A Descriptive Framework of Workspace Awareness for Real-Time Groupware. *Computer Supported Cooperative Work (CSCW)*, 11(3):411–446, Sept. 2002.
18. P. Jermann, D. Mullins, M.-A. Nüssli, and P. Dillenbourg. Collaborative Gaze Footprints: Correlates of Interaction Quality. In *Proceedings of CSCL 2011*, 2011.
19. P. Jermann and M.-A. Nüssli. Unravelling cross-recurrence: coupling across timescales. In *Duet 2011: Dual Eye Tracking in CSCW*, Aahrus, DK, September 2011.
20. R. E. Kraut, S. R. Fussell, and J. Siegel. Visual information as a conversational resource in collaborative physical tasks. *Hum.-Comput. Interact.*, 18(1):13–49, 2003.
21. A. Meier, H. Spada, and N. Rummel. A rating scheme for assessing the quality of computer-supported collaboration processes. *International Journal of Computer-Supported Collaborative Learning*, 2(1):63–86, Mar. 2007.
22. M.-A. Nüssli. *Dual Eye-Tracking Methods for the Study of Remote Collaborative Problem Solving*. PhD thesis, Ecole Polytechnique Fédérale de Lausanne, 2011.
23. M.-A. Nüssli, P. Jermann, M. Sangin, and P. Dillenbourg. Collaboration and abstract representations: towards predictive models based on raw speech and eye-tracking data. In *CSCL '09: Proceedings of the 2009 conference on Computer support for collaborative learning*. International Society of the Learning Sciences, 2009.
24. D. C. Richardson and R. Dale. Looking to Understand: The Coupling Between Speakers' and Listeners' Eye Movements and its Relationship to Discourse Comprehension. *Cognitive Science*, 29(29):1045–1060, 2005.
25. D. C. Richardson, R. Dale, and N. Z. Kirkham. The Art of Conversation Is Coordination: Common Ground and the Coupling of Eye Movements During Dialogue. *Psychological Science*, 18(5):407–413, June 2007.
26. M. Sangin. *Peer Knowledge Modeling in Computer Supported Collaborative Learning*. PhD thesis, cole Polytechnique Fdrale de Lausanne, 2009.
27. A. Soller, A. Martínez, P. Jermann, and M. Muehlenbrock. From mirroring to guiding: A review of state of the art technology for supporting collaborative learning. *Int. J. Artif. Intell. Ed.*, 15:261–290, December 2005.
28. L. A. Williams and R. R. Kessler. All I really need to know about pair programming I learned in kindergarten. *Commun. ACM*, 43(5):108–114, May 2000.

Micro-coordination: Because We did *not* Already Learn Everything We Need to Know about Working with Others in Kindergarten

Joon-Suk Lee **Deborah Tatar** **Steve Harrison**
Dept. of Computer Science, MC 0106
Virginia Tech
2202 Kraft Dr., Blacksburg, VA 24060
{joonlee, tatar, srh}@vt.edu

ABSTRACT
How is it that groups of people can complete joint tasks without the expected observable markers of "successful" coordination? The relationship between *micro-level, situated* actions and broader outcomes such as opportunities for learning is under-explored. We investigated co-located groups as they played a collaborative, problem-solving game using distributed technology on laptops. There was considerable variety in how groups accomplished the work. Some satisfied groups talked a lot but other satisfied groups did not. Talk was diagnostic of satisfaction but *lack* of talk was not diagnostic of dissatisfaction. In fact, groups that had little or no discourse differed considerably from one another. One kind of group completes the joint tasks very well without observable markers frequently associated with success. Others are less successful in the task goal but manage difficult interpersonal situations.

Author Keywords
Micro-Coordination, Coordination, Qualitative Research

ACM Classification Keywords
H5.m. Information interfaces and presentation (e.g., HCI): Miscellaneous.

General Terms
Design; Experimentation.

INTRODUCTION
How is it that groups of people can complete joint tasks, even excel at joint tasks, without the expected observable markers of "successful" coordination? HCI and CSCW studies of coordination and collaboration often focus on measuring task or process performance [2]. Even in subfields of CSCW where broader outcomes are acknowledged as crucial such as computer-supported collaborative learning, there is a tendency to by-pass the relationship between particular collaborative actions and broader outcomes.

Collaboration is "a coordinated, synchronous activity that is the result of a continued attempt to construct and maintain a shared conception of a problem" (p. 70, [38]). Collaboration consists of coordinative activities and interactions among multiple people working towards a shared solution. Collaboration, then, depends on coordination.

One definition of coordination is "the act of working together harmoniously" (p. 358, [30]). If we confine the definition further by omitting the subjective term "harmoniously," coordination is the act of working together among two or more people. From this point of view, the basic building blocks of coordinative activities are individuals, and the coordination is framed by and within the interactions between the constituting parties.

Many fields investigate coordination. Indeed, we know a great deal about coordination from different perspectives. However, within computer science, "coordination" has come to mean mainly the coordination of information systems and their components. Machine coordination is treated as only the design and enactment of protocols: queuing, locking, layered networking, and so forth. In contrast, human coordination is, at base, how social creatures get social things done in the world [47]. But even here, research approaches the study of coordination from many perspectives. From an organizational behavior perspective, there has been considerable exploration of the idea that "macro-level characteristics of an organizational design affect group structural properties which in turn directly impact performance" (from Pearce & David, 1983, in [25] p. 363). For example, Hossain et al. [25] point out the important role of people with "high social network centrality" in achieving coordinated outcomes in an organization. Valverde and Sole [50] point out that the underlying goals of the community and the underlying hierarchical organization play a key role in shaping organizational dynamics. Hinds and McGrath [24] focus on the ways that structure differentially affects local and geographically distributed teams. Bridging organizational and HCI perspectives, Malone and Crowston [31] describe an area of inquiry they call coordination theory, which defines coordination as "managing dependencies between activities." A number of other thinkers in HCI and information studies concerned with influencing workplace process and distance communication [5, 16, 17, 26, 54] adopt the same approach to the underlying nature of coordination and the set of concerns raised by it. More recently, Herbsleb and his colleagues [7, 22] build on coordination theory to support software engineering and awareness tools. Last, from a systems/game theory point of view, there is a quite elaborated literature on the provability of the relationship between decentralization, communication, and control [11, 48].

Efficiency and dependencies are important components of coordination, but we argue that they do not provide sufficient groundwork to support design in the general case. Even such widely cited papers as Clark and Brennan's "Grounding in Communication" describe properties and conditions of systems rather than the meaning of interactions [9]. A technology can help a person deal with children or old people or customers in a very efficient manner, but leave them feeling angry, alienated, lonely and so forth. A coordinated performance such as a symphony can be made more efficient by speeding up the playback, but loose its experiential point. A traffic light system can be optimized for flow in one direction, but a person who only travels in the other direction on that street can experience the system as unpleasant and unfair. Yet, our theories of coordination do not really address these factors.

A more encompassing approach is found in some of the oldest and most influential work at the juxtaposition of the social sciences and human-computer interaction. First, analogously to Heidegger's distinction between "ready-to-hand" and "present-at-hand" [21], the relationship between collaboration and coordination may be conceptualized as the relationship between the *official* program, that is, the one that people in retrospect give as account of "what they were doing" and the *unofficial* programs, the usually deprecated aspects of managing the interaction that include management of mutual attention, regard and effort. That is, the problem to be solved by interactants could be to a greater or lesser extent the "ready-to-hand" problem of how to engage in an activity well, or the "present-at-hand" problem of how to get through the next few minutes.

This analogy is a psychological one in that it emphasizes what an interactant is thinking about (or capable of thinking about) in the moment. Drawing on anthropology, sociology, linguistics and such more particular approaches as kinesics, ethology, and ethnomethodology, which do not necessarily assume particular cognitive states or structures, Suchman [44,45] draws unflinching attention to those aspects of human coordination that are well described as situated actions. Situated action explanations focus on what we call *micro-coordination*: the tight coupling of behavior to possibility in the moment.

MICRO-COORDINATION

Micro-coordination focuses design on how participants decide who goes next in interaction, what the duration of the action is, what other actions may happen concomitantly, and how they regulate regard and attention, as well as understanding. Micro-coordination lies in the minute details of how we carry out our daily moment-to-moment coordinative activities. It is how we take turns when we talked to our friends. It is two girls playing hopscotch.

Clark long ago said that, in interaction, we seek to have enough understanding of the other for *current purposes* [10]. Much work explores how we come to understand one another, but micro-coordination also includes how we decide on current purposes. In this paper, we, in particular, explore micro-coordination of how young adults contribute (or not) to a group objective, and in-so-doing decide what the objective is.

Measuring Successful Collaboration

There are many ways to measure success in CSCW. With its focus on process—it is, after all, called, "computer-supported *collaborative* work"—it is not surprising that efficiency and optimization are often front-and-center. However, let us consider a sub-area where there are other measures. *Collaborative learning*, a widespread educational innovation [52] wherein groups and pairs of students work together to achieve a common academic goal, has been reported to improve not only students' learning [32,34] but also critical thinking processes [19]. Collaborative learning often revolves around a situation created by technology. Yet, although the notion of collaborative learning originates the works of Vygotsky [51], who advocated the social aspects of developmental learning processes and saw the 'zone of proximal development' as an important site in learning, and of Piaget [35], who viewed inter-subject processes as playing a critical role in cognitive development, the pedagogical advantages in collaborative learning are often demonstrated through studies that employ easily quantifiable metrics such as test scores, class pass/fail ratios, and students' self-reported measures of fun, enjoyment and contentment [i.e., 32,34]. These metrics often illuminate only rudimentary one-dimensional perspectives on success or failure.

While useful in determining broad-brush policy, these studies can, even in their own terms, lead to over-general conclusions and a failure to expose important variation. An increase in average test score can result from a substantial increase in test scores among the top 30% of the class while the rest of the class decreases performance. The same average gain could come from an overall and yet slight increase in test scores from the majority of the students. Large disparities in group performance may be observed between groups assigned to perform the same tasks that hold no distinguishably different traits [3].

Measuring coordination

For years, social psychologists have studied how individuals affect group process and outcome. Behavioral phenomena such as social loafing [27], social traps [36] and process loss [43] have been identified as problems in group performance, as have some personality characteristics [41,42], e.g., excessive dominance can be problematic.

The relationship between group process and task type has also been extensively studied [37,40]. For instance, groups become more active when discussing open-ended problems than those that have only one correct answer [14]. Hackman reports that differences in task type (production, discussion, and problem solving) account for up to 50% of the variance in group outcomes [20]. Carter et al. [6] report a similar correlation between task types (reasoning, mechanical assembly, or discussion task) and group interaction. McGrath classifies group tasks into eight task types and four underlying performance functions on a two-dimensional circumplex schema [33]. In addition to individual traits of agents and task type, group size [18] and the composition [29] are known determinants of group processes and outcomes.

Even though the findings reported from social psychology, organizational literature, small-group research, and group-process research are many, we still do not decisively know what determines diversity in group processes and how group process affects outcomes. For instance, these identified factors—individuals, task type and process, and group size—mutually interact with one another, creating innumerable possibilities that could affect group processes. Finding a correlation between a fixed set of factors and group outcomes becomes impractical [15].

Important details such as non-verbal communication, turn-taking, affective tone, and shifts in attention [3] may seem irrelevant to the questions of interest (e.g. "which technology should I use?", "How shall I design?") but, because they focus on the meaning that the individuals and groups are creating in the moment of use—factors that arguably change in the presence of technology—they may ultimately lead to deeply founded design strategies and highly perspicuous constructs.

Hence, there have been an increasing number of empirical studies that focus less on the superficial attributes of the group processes and that concentrate more fully on the processes and interactions [15]. We build our work along the lines of these studies and investigate coordination in an experimental but *in situ* context, arguing detailed analysis of the unfolding process is important.

MANAGING THE DUAL SPACE

The belief that people are experts in managing group activities with technology (learned it in kindergarten) implies that the requirements are simple extrapolations of the already learned techniques. To the contrary, many tasks involve much more than simple extrapolations. In particular, Barron [4] describes how upper elementary school students solving math problems learn to manage a *dual factor* space: social and cognitive. Pair programming represents another area which requires extension of previously learned skills to manage both spaces. In these cases, people need to manage their internal production of 'computational thinking,' and their social skills in managing group processes. Dual space tasks frequently involve asking a group to perform a task often thought of as belonging to the individual.

Barron did not examine students using digital artifacts. Pair programming, by design, involves only one screen. In the current project, we look at an even more complex situation: a triple space in which people must manage a complex problem solving task (Sudoku), the social space *and* the changing representation on the screen created by the other players. This situation enacts a constellation of three increasingly important properties that often co-exist: (1) participant choice about the definition of "current purposes" inherent in the situation. That is, people may satisfice (in Simon's terms [23]) between goals or sacrifice one. They may not be optimizing. (2) participant choice about mechanisms of engagement with others, that is, people may chose where to direct attention and where *not* to direct attention, (3) tasks in which the effects of particular actions are not known or not known for a considerable lag. Often CSCW research is concerned with whether one player can see what another player is seeing (as in [46]). The assumption is that seeing the action is sufficient to infer that actions meaning. But in these dual or triple spaces, there are two points of failure: the players may not perceive changes in state, or they may not understand the meaning of changes in state.

We videotape, transcribe, and then examine the communicative situation, drawing primarily on interaction and conversation analytic methods that focus on ethnomethodological analyses, that is, seeing how people from a particular culture (U.S. young adults) solve interactional dilemmas. By looking at the moment of interaction, we hope to unveil a range of untold coordinative issues, bring together once stripped away details, and build up foundations for collaborative learning.

Figure 1: Set-up for three Team Sudoku Players

TEAM SUDOKU

Team Sudoku is a multi-user, parallel-distributed form of the Sudoku game. Sudoku presents the player with a 9x9 board with digits between 1 and 9 in some cells. The goal of Sudoku is to fill the board so that each of the nine columns, nine rows and nine distinct 3x3 blocks contain exactly one instance of each digit from 1 to 9. Games are differentiated from one another by the number and location of starting digits. In the computerized form, each distinct game initially contains digits that cannot be written over or changed except by starting a new game, and that are a different color (black) from those that are in play (green).

Team Sudoku provides users three distinct features for manipulating the board. A pen tool enables users to insert entries on the board, and a pencil tool allows users to tentatively mark possibilities (note-entries). Users can delete any entries on the game board with an eraser tool. Team Sudoku is a multi-user collaborative variation of Sudoku in which players have their own computers with their own copies of the shared game board. When one player fills in a number, erases a number, or uses an indicating tool, the results are promptly shared on all players' screens.

THE STUDY

Players were recruited from the Psychology Participant pool, N>1200, at our university, and received extra credit for participation. The advertisement for participation had two components: that the study was about a collaborative game, and that participants needed to have played Sudoku before. Players played in groups of two or three.

The study was conducted in a small room with participants seated in close proximity to one another (Fig. 1). Participants were introduced to one another when they came into the room. After the informed consent process, participants were asked to fill out questionnaires about demographics, prior experiences with Sudoku and with the teammates (usually none). Participants engaged in a system walk-through and an easy warm-up game to learn how the Team Sudoku system worked. After the warm-up session, the groups were asked to work together on two Sudoku puzzles significantly more complex than the warm-up puzzle, in an order counter-balanced across groups. The groups were given 15 minutes to work on each game. After each game, questionnaires asked players about their experiences with the game and with the other players. There was also a short discussion at the end of the study. Video recordings of all the game sessions were collected as well as computer logs and screen shot movies of the games.

PARTICIPANTS

A total of 168 (89 female, 79 male) college students enrolled in the study, in 24 groups of two and 40 groups of three. Participants' age ranged from 18 to 23 (M = 19 SD = 1.13). 17 of 168 reported that their first language was not English, but none appeared to have difficulty because of this. Almost all the participants had prior experience with Sudoku. Four reported that they did not know the Sudoku rules. When asked how often they play Sudoku on a scale of 1 (rarely) to 7 (several times a day), a majority responded that they do not play Sudoku often (M = 2.51, SD = 1.42). But when asked how much they like playing Sudoku on a scale of 1 (not at all) to 7 (very much), a majority responded that they like playing Sudoku (M = 4.74, SD = 1.51). Most participants responded that they had played Sudoku on paper while only a small portion of them had played Sudoku on the computer. Only 6 of 168 reported that they had played a computer version of Sudoku with other people prior to the study.

When only two participants appeared at the agreed time, we ran the game with them, resulting in 24 groups of two. In this paper, we address only the 40 three-person groups.

RESULTS AND CODING

Three video cameras recorded each session. With each camera facing one participant, we were able to ensure that each player's facial expressions as well as bodily gestures were captured in video recordings. Due to the glitches in the recording devices, video recordings for three game sessions were severely damaged and therefore excluded from the analysis.

The 37 15-minute video recordings of the first Sudoku game for triads were transcribed using a slightly modified version of Chafe's prosodic transcription system [8], which focuses on information flow. Six researchers worked on transcribing the sessions, in three different iterations. Transcripts from audio were created in the initial iteration. Descriptions of non-verbal gestures as well as critical changes on the Sudoku board were added in the second phase. Transcripts were then arranged into intonation and conversational turn units. The final transcripts were reviewed for accuracy several times with the log files and screen-captured videos.

Open and axial coding [12] were conducted on the segmented conversational turn units, resulting in a 3-layered hierarchical coding scheme. In total, 20 codes were developed under four main categories and ten subcategories. The four main conversational categories were 'board-related,' 'game-related,' 'off-topic,' and 'other.'

A: this can't be a 4 ((Uses a reference tool to point to a note 4 on a cell 9,4)) *{statement}*

B: It could be a !4,

there's no 4 in that row *{adding dimensionality}*

Excerpt 1: a coding example: statement and adding dimensionality

Board-related utterances refer to specific elements, regions, possibilities, or problems on the Sudoku puzzle on the screen. It has four subcategories: *Statement* represents simple, unelaborated statements or fragmented ideas such as "I don't think a 2 is gonna go right in this spot..." or "Alright let's put a 5, put a 5 there." *Question* refers to incidents in which a participant expresses doubts, asks for confirmation, or demands explanation of elements on the game board such as, "are you sure this one," or "why couldn't it be eight?" *Elaboration* means the participant went a little further to explain reasons for moves, possibilities and problems rather than just stating simple facts. "Because there's an eight in that row already" is an example of *elaboration.*

A particularly interesting sub-category is *adding dimensionality,* a code that captures instances in which participants built ideas on the top of previously presented ones.

An utterance was coded as adding dimensionality if it provided evidence that the person who added the dimensionality had to be giving active attention to the claim that the original person made either by testing its validity or by enumerating its consequences, as in Excerpt 1.

Each of these sub-categories then were again sub-divided into finer categories depending on whether referents were (1) mentioning an element or a region in the puzzle, (2) suggesting possibilities not yet present in the game board such as 4 or 6 in "either 4 or 6 can go in here," or (3) raising a problem as in "this is wrong. Something is wrong here." We do not analyze these in this paper.

Game-related utterances are closely related to the game, but do not refer to any specifics of the game board. This category includes discussion of general game strategy, *game-specific* discourse related to the current puzzle but not to specifics of the puzzle (as in "this puzzle is hard"); *game-general* utterances coded inquiries and comments on Sudoku rules, prior Sudoku experiences, software features and research procedures.

Off-topic included utterances not directly related to the game activities (i.e., "I am hungry.").

Inaudible, regulatory intonations (non-lexical and phrasal backchannels), and non-sentential sounds (laughs…) were coded as *Other*.

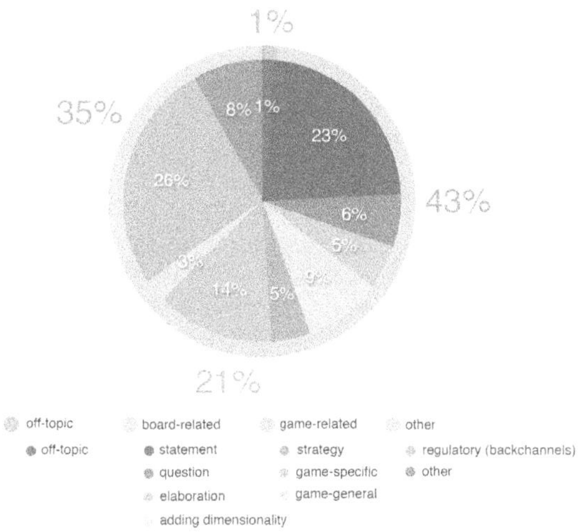

Figure 2: Overall Number of Utterances by Category

Figure 2 shows the distribution of utterances in the top two levels of the coding scheme. Only 1% of the conversation was off topic, suggesting that people were quite engaged in the puzzle solving activities. 26% of the utterances were back channels. 23% were simple board-related statements.

Statistics collected on the coded transcripts include the number of conversational turns and utterances each player made throughout the session. Similarly, a log analyzer was used to gather information on the total number of entries, notes, and deletions that each player made during the game.

The number of correct and incorrect entries for which each player was responsible was also counted at game end-state.

AMOUNT OF ACTIVITY AND SATISFACTION

One of the most obvious differences between groups was in activity level, either through talking or through contribution to the board. The average number of conversational turns/group was 92.8 but the standard deviation was 80.4. 11% of the groups did not have a single utterance by anyone; 24% groups had less than ten conversational turns. The distribution of kinds of utterances (Fig. 3) also differed by group.

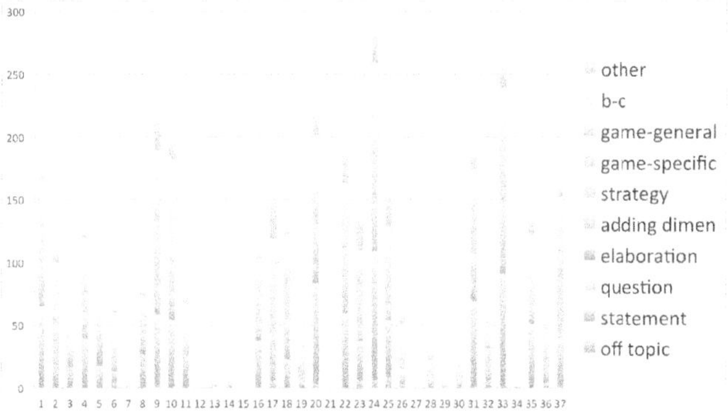

Figure 3: Distribution of Kinds of Utterances by Group

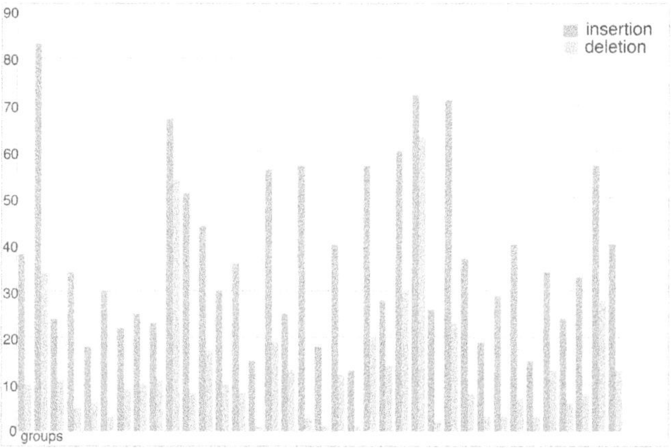

Figure 4: Num. of Game Board Insertions and Deletions by Group

Individuals differed as well as groups. In three groups, two people were responsible for all the discussion. In eight of the groups that had any talking at all, 90% of the turns were taken by two of the players. Overall, the average number of turns/person was 30.9 (SD 29.2).

The number of board entries and deletions by group (Fig. 4) also varied considerably at both the group and individual levels. The board started with 54 blank spaces and 27 pre-filled, un-erasable numbers. The average number of game entries/person was 12.5 (SD 8.9). Three participants never contributed a single number to the game board; ten had no contribution that lasted until the end state. But one group had 83 entries. Some groups had almost as many deletions as entries.

Contributing to discourse was statistically related to contribution to the game board (r= 0.27; p < 0.005). The more a player talked during the game, the more entries the player put on the game board. However, this was by no means an absolute relationship (Fig. 5). Two people contributed above the mean number of utterances, but entered only two-three numbers on the board while others contributed 30-40 entries but never talked.

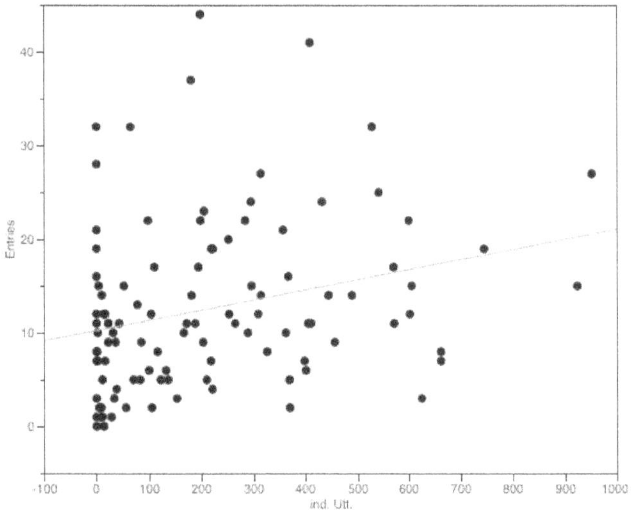

Figure 5: Number of entries by conversational turns by individual (r = 0.27; p < 0.005)

There was also a statistically significant difference in self-reported satisfaction related to amount of discourse in the group. Players were asked to rate how satisfied they were with the group and the way they worked together on a scale of 1 (not at all) to 7 (very much). The number of utterances each player made was significantly correlated with self-reported satisfaction (r = 0.26; p < 0.006). However, there was no correlation between satisfaction rate and number of game board entries (r = 0.01; p = 0.90).

Figure 6 shows a very interesting distribution. Satisfaction level varied more considerably amongst people who spoke very little compared to those who spoke quite a lot. Highly communicative participants tended to be satisfied. There existed no individuals who were highly communicative but fell below the middle of the scale for satisfaction. However, uncommunicative people covered the spectrum of satisfaction.

Adding Dimensionality

Both *amount* and *intensity* of conversation influence how groups felt about their group activities. To investigate how intensely the group maintained focus, we divided the groups into three categories; *adding dimensionality* (AD) provides strong evidence of joint focus across multiple actions on specifics of the puzzle. Board related statements, questions, or elaborations (ST) illustrate fragmented one-time focus. Groups that did not have any board-related conversations were called NO. (As a note, all groups who exchanged less than 10 conversational turns belonged to NO. That is, even when they did talk, they did not talk about the board at hand.)

As we might expect, groups that maintained prolonged joint focus on the puzzle and tried to share and contribute individual ideas on top of the previously shared group knowledge were significantly more satisfied with their group activities and outcome than groups that only shared fragmented ideas and comments. That is, in pairwise t-test (F(2,34)=2.03), AD groups had a significantly higher rate of satisfaction than ST groups (Mean Difference = 0.873; p < .036).

But, curiously, there was a less uniform and consistent difference between AD groups and NO groups than between AD and ST groups. AD and NO had only a marginally significant difference (Mean Dif. = 0.720; p = 0.057). NO and ST were indistinguishable (Mean Dif. = 0.153, p = 0.74.

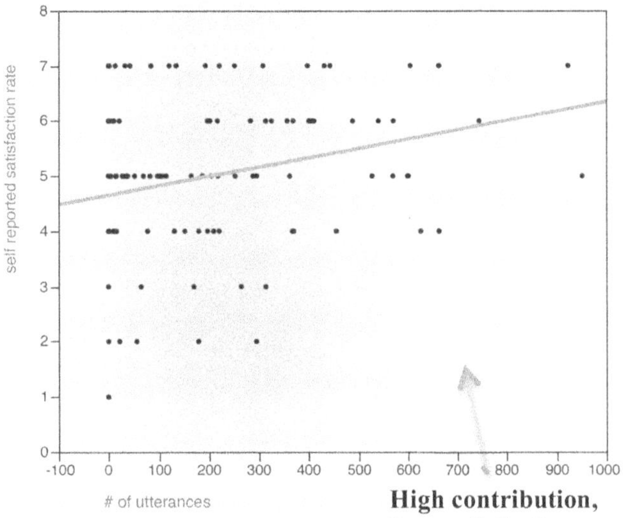

Figure 6: Satisfaction level by number of utterances by individual; the high contribution, low satisfaction quadrant is empty

"SOUNDS OF SILENCE": VARIETIES OF NON-TALK

Thus, from a statistical perspective, we see that groups that talk a lot are more satisfied than groups that do not talk, but that this difference is driven by the fact that groups that talk a lot are not unhappy (dissatisfied) while groups that do not talk a lot may be either happy or unhappy. Furthermore, while depth of conversation is associated with increased satisfaction, lack of depth is not associated cleanly with decreased satisfaction.

These are, by themselves, important findings, but frustrating. They do not lead to clean causal claims and associated design implications (even at the level of saying "talk more and you will be more satisfied"). The immediately observable behavioral outcome (talking/not talking) has asymmetric meaning.

Even studies that focus on behavioral outcomes implicitly brand non-talking as a deteriorative behavior by showing a correlation between the nature and quality of the communication and group outcome [3,4,39]. But in our study, some groups that do not talk much claim satisfaction, thus constituting a reasonable way to engage in joint work. Other groups are both dissatisfied and silent. Following are three examples of kinds of interactions not usually associated with collaborative success. Each of these can be described to a certain extent in terms of high level constructs current in the field. And yet, they strongly suggest alternative constructs that may be more perspicuous.

Alone Together or Together Alone?

Juliana, Stacy and Jason (all names are pseudonyms) were situated in the dual socio-digital space. However, they solved the interactional problem by ignoring the social space. No one chose to utter a word during the whole 15 minutes. Instead, they all were intensely focused on the puzzle-solving activity. Figure 1 displays the intensity of players' focus on the screen. Their eyes remained honed on their screens throughout. Even though they were not verbally communicating in the social space, every move made by one into the game space seemed to immediately be integrated into the others' decision-making processes. This kind of digital interaction has been described as entailing a place into which players project themselves and their willful control.

The way players perceive the changes made by others in the digital space, and the way they perceive the reciprocal interactions are unknown to observers (and could differ amongst interactants). Participants could self-consciously perceive these changes as bits of inter-dependent collaborative efforts projected on to the digital space, or passively take them as external and uncontrollable changes---they may not perceive the activities as collaborative. However actively they perceive the interactions within the digital space or however tightly-coupled these interactions are, the individual players are arguably alone in their social space, having no visible interaction with their teammates. To the third person observer, they were playing the game in absolute solitude.

In Alone Together, Sherry Turkle [49] portrayed people in our current society as becoming more and more detached from face-to-face interactions and increasingly attached to machinery (even emotionally). However, what we were seeing in the case of Juliana, Stacy and Jason was something other than being "alone together." They were "together alone." They were in the same room, playing the same Sudoku game, witness to the material focus of one another. They were highly coordinated. This group did almost as well as some of the other very interactive groups, entering 27/27 numbers in the correct positions. Groups typically made 24 entries during the game and had 5 wrong entries on average.).

Sherry Turkle sees being "alone together" as a distinct and problematic characteristic of today's society in the U.S. But "together alone" may be likened to other highly coordinated performances, such as jazz improvisation, that involve telegraphic or non-existent verbal communication. We do not know the details of what Juliania, Stacy and Jason experienced, but suspect that rather than deserving deprecation, it should be celebrated as a kind of flow or group flow [13]. It is certainly coordination, rather than non-coordination and consistent with collaborative success.

Social Loafing, sort of

Another behavior seen in less communicative participants is to engage in off-task activities. Eden (group 89) was the quiet member of a group that had process difficulties. The other two members were voluble and at odds with one another. Eden constantly checked his phone, read text messages and occasionally texted during the session. Eden was not totally indifferent; he took part in the group conversation occasionally, and placed a number of entries onto the game board. But he fell into the quiet end of the spectrum. His behavior, taken in isolation, for the most part was analogous to what social scientists would call social loafing. The classical social loafing model explains the loafing behavior as people working less hard when they are working in a group as opposed to when they are working alone [27,28]. Lack of accountability is one factor traditionally associated with social loafing. Yet this is not an exact description of Eden. Eden's distracted behavior was perfectly visible to all. He was not fully engrossed with making the task at hand work, and found other things to do, as we might check our emails during meetings or listen to the radio while driving.

The meaning of Eden's behavior is evidently different than the meaning of Juliana, Stacy and Jason's quietude. It seemed that Eden was defining the situation as not requiring his full attention. He is setting a different standard than we see in most groups for "good enough" participation. Eden is not exhibiting the surface level characteristics that would make him a good collaborator. In this case, we do not know whether his allocation of attention is a good choice on his part.

The Simply Lost or Process Loss?

An example of another kind of less communicative player was found in group 87. Joan appeared to be less experienced in playing Sudoku than her partners. While the other two made 40 and 13 entries, she made only 1. Also, while her teammates, Hardy and Sam, took 43 and 61 conversational turns respectively she took only 9. She responded to questions directed to her with low content replies such as "mm" and "yeah," or "what?" However, she appeared to be paying attention. She continually used a software feature to demarcate a screen area on which she was focusing, presumably either to show the group that she was working on the puzzle or to aid and maintain her focus on the game. At [9:54], she said, "so five would go here?" to get a confirmation for her guess. No one replied and she never put in the number (which was correct). Toward the end of the game, when Sam looked at her to check if she was OK, she said, "yea-h- Sudoku is exactly not my game." She was simply lost and overwhelmingly left alone.

Barron reported a similar kind of behavior in her work through an example in which two students ignore a third student who was proposing a correct solution for the group problem. Barron turns analytic attention to an occasion in which smart groups fail [4].

We build on this to propose a new question. When two people ignore a third person and that third person has an idea that could lead to the correct answer, we normally consider this process loss for the group. But what if the third person does *not* have a good idea?

Collaborative Sudoku as well as the math problem solving task in Barron's example is a disjunctive activity in that the outcome depends on the group recognizing the best player, getting that player to share unique information and avoiding process loss [1]. To maximize group performance and efficiency, it is logical to exclude a less effective player from the group activities. From an educational point of view, this is a poor outcome because it deprives students like Joan of opportunities to learn. It may also be poor outcome from a social point of view. Joan's group does not behave as though inclusion/participation is particularly important in their definition of the situation.

Current Purposes, or How Process Loss Arises

It would be easy to conclude that Joan's team should include her. However, we draw a contrastive example by looking more at Eden's group.

The other two members of group 89 talked quite a bit but experienced difficulty conveying their ideas to each other. As soon as the game started, upon inserting 5 in cell (1,1), Adam said "everybody gots to saw that ..right?" As it turns out, this was an ambiguous query. It could refer either to what people saw on the board, or whether 5 was the right entry for cell (1,1). However, Bob and Eden both acknowledged Adam's inquiry with "oh yeah" and "yeah" respectively. Then, Bob asked Adam "how do you know that?" Bob elaborated by asking, "are you just guessing?" Even after Bob's elaboration, Adam answered back that he knew that everyone saw the same thing because the researcher told them they would during the walk-through session. This breakdown soon got repaired by help from Eden, who rephrased Bob's initial question for Adam.

Bob's behavior—incrementally refining his initial question—is in accordance with the principle of least collaborative effort [8]. Bob was filling in enough to help Adam understand easily. Yet, his judgment about what was "enough" information for Adam was not in fact enough.

Later in the game, Adam became confused by all the notes Bob was entering on the board and suggested that everyone should only place only one number in the cell by assigning big numbers to one player, the first small note to the second player, the second small note to the third player. In fact, the proposed strategy would not work because there was no way in the software of assigning a note in a particular order to a player. Any one who enters a note into a cell first becomes the owner of the first note. Bob tried to explain the difficulty, unsuccessfully.

Upon meeting with misunderstanding, Bob stopped trying to explain the difficulty and instead suggested another alternative to simplify the display. He asked the group to divide the board into sections so that each player could work on their own section. This strategy would mean that Bob could use notes his way in his cells and Adam could use notes differently. NB, like Adam's strategy, this one could not really work, at least not for long, because of the intertwined nature of the game.

From the point of view of an outside observer, Bob had a better grasp of the game play situation than Adam. He questioned Adam's baseless guesswork at first. He tried to explain issues of process. But Bob compromised his initial strategy of using notes to capture the possible numbers that could go into a cell because Adam did not understand it. Adam did not end up "simply lost" like Joan. Bob did not ignore him. Neither did the group maximize its potential achievement in the game. As we have seen, Eden opted out. The current purposes of the collaborative game play move, in effect, away from achievement towards lowering active disagreement.

DISCUSSION AND CONCLUSION

We investigated co-located groups as they played a collaborative, problem-solving game using distributed technology on laptops. There was considerable variety in how the groups accomplished the work. Some satisfied groups talked a lot but other satisfied groups did not. Talk was diagnostic of satisfaction, but *lack* of talk was not diagnostic of dissatisfaction. Additionally, groups and individuals that had little or no discourse differed considerably from one another. However, one kind of group completes the joint tasks very well without observable markers frequently associated with success. Another kind of group demonstrates problems with process but some components of these problems may represent rational choices for the participant. A third kind of group is marked by inequity—but the contrastive example shows that the design implications depend on the priorities of the setting and participants (and designers).

CSCW is like chemistry before the periodic table. We need descriptive categories for phenomena that are fine-grained enough to inform decision about how to support particular designerly values, but what seem like small differences in the situation make a huge difference in outcomes. Is it the absence of phlogiston or the presence of oxygen? Our examples are important not because of frequency but because they capture variation in the human responses to immediate conditions. That variation includes behaviors that can be interpreted as desirable or undesirable, depending on precisely what the goals are for the interaction.

In fact, to be useful, studies of micro-coordination need to incorporate a variety of conditional outcomes of different sorts. Beyond contextualizing the micro-coordination phenomena, they should set the user of the analysis's frames of interpretation. That is, they are not footnotes to results but starting points for exploring how competing (and perhaps conflicting) values will frame investigations and design results.

This argument supports our contention that the relationship between *micro-level, situated* actions and broader outcomes—including but not limited to—opportunities for learning is under-explored. A key question that follows from this analysis is: "What descriptive categories of behavior constitute the coordination and collaboration from which higher level constructs such as 'collaborative learning' emerge in novel CSCW/CSCL situations?"

We do not "put this question to bed," but we:

---remind researchers and designers that it is centrally important to CSCW research,

---remind researchers and designers that one reason global measures may fail to inform is that they may ignore micro-coordination, and

---draw attention to variety in human behavior that merits design focus in CSCW work.

The assumption that people learned everything about how to collaborate productively in kindergarten [53] itself assumes that interactive technology does not place its own game-changing and possibly problematic demands on cooperative work. We note that there would be little need for research in CSCW if this were true.

Simple behavioral or design lessons such as "talk more" risk interfering with legitimate, productive styles of interaction and papering over differences between the skills required in CSCW settings and those learned in kindergarten.

ACKNOWLEDGMENTS

We thank Nouf Alaloula, Candace Lohr and Traci Luzi who helped us running the study. We also thank Stacy Branham and Meg Kurdziolek for comments on an earlier draft of this paper. This work was supported by NSF Grant. IIS-1018607 HCC-Small.

REFERENCES

1. Aronson, E., Wilson, T., & Akert, R. (1994). *Social Psychology: The heart and the mind*. Harper Collins
2. Bannon, L. & Schmidt, K. (1990) CSCW: four characters in search of a context, *Studies in computer supported cooperative work: theory, practice and design*, North-Holland Publishing Co.
3. Barron, B. (2000) Achieving coordination in collaborative problem-solving groups, *The Journal of the Learning Sciences*
4. Barron, B. (2003) When smart groups fail, *The Journal of the Learning Sciences*
5. Bowers, J. & Churcher, J. (1988) Local and global structuring of computer mediated communication: Developing linguistic perspectives on CSCW in COSMOS, In Proc. of CSCW
6. Carter, L., Haythorn, W., Meirowitz, B., & Lanzetta, J. (1951) The Relation of Categorizations and Ratings in the Observation of Group Behavior, *Human Relations*, 4. 239-254
7. Cataldo, M., Wagstrom, P., Herbsleb, J.D., & Carley, K. (2006). Identification of coordination requirements: Implications for the design of collaboration and awareness tools. In Proc. of CSCW
8. Chafe, W. L. (1993) Prosodic and Functional Units of Language. In J. Edwards & M. Lampert (Eds) *Talking Data*, pp. 33-44, Lawrence Erlbaum Associates
9. Clark, H. H. & S. E. Brennan (1991) Grounding in communication. In: L. B. Resnick, J. Levine, and S. D. Teasley (eds.): *Perspectives on socially shared cognition*. Psychology Press, pp. 127–149.
10. Clark, H. H., & Wilkes-Gibbs, D. (1986). Referring as a collaborative process. Cognition, 22(1), 1-39.
11. Conitzer, V. & Sandholm, T. (2004) Communication complexity as a lower bound for learning in games. In Proc. of International Conference on Machine Learning
12. Corbin, J. & Strauss, A. (2008) *Basics of Qualitative Research 3ed*, SAGE.
13. Csíkszentmihályi, Mihály (1990), Flow: The Psychology of Optimal Experience, Harper and Row
14. Deutsch, M. (1951) Task structure and group process. *American Psychologist*, 6, pp. 324-325.
15. Dillenbourg, P., Baker, M., Blaye, A. & O'Malley, C. (1996) The evolution of research on collaborative learning. In E. Spada & P. Reiman (Eds) *Learning in Humans and Machine: Towards an interdisciplinary learning science*. pp. 189- 211. Elsevier
16. Dykstra, E.A. & Carasik, R.P. (1991) Structure and support in cooperative environments: the Amsterdam Conversation Environment, *Journal of Man-Machine Studies*, 34, pp. 419- 434.
17. Fitzpatrick, G. & Welsh, J. (1995) Process support: inflexible imposition or chaotic composition? *Interacting with Computers*, 7(2) pp.167-180.
18. Frank, F. & Anderson, L. R. (1971) Effects of Task and Group Size Upon Group Productivity and Member Satisfaction. *Sociometry*, 34(1), pp. 135-149

19. Gokhale, A. (1995) Collaborative learning enhances critical thinking, *Journal of Technology Education*, 7(1)

20. Hackman, J. R. (1968) Effects of task characteristics on group products, *Experimental Social Psychology*, 4(2)

21. Heidegger, Martin (2000), *Being and Time*, J. Macquarrie & E. Robinson (trans), Blackwell

22. Herbsleb, J.D., & Mockus, A. (2003). Formulation and preliminary test of an empirical theory of coordination in software engineering. In Proc of European Software Engineering Conference and ACM SIGSOFT Symposium on the Foundations of Software Engineering

23. Herbert A. Simon (1996), *The Sciences of the Artificial*, MIT Press

24. Hinds, P. & McGrath (2006) Structures that work: social structure, work structure and coordination ease in geographically distributed teams. In Proc of CSCW

25. Hossain, L., Wu, A., & Chung, K. (2006) Actor Centrality Correlates to Project Based Coordination. CSCW

26. Kaplan, S.M., Tolone, W.J., Bogia, D.P., & Bignoli, C. (1991) Flexible, active support for collaborative work with Conversation Builder. In Proc. of CSCW

27. Karau, S. J., & Williams, K. D. (1993). Social loafing: A meta-analytic review and theoretical integration. *Personality & Social Psychology*, 65(4), 681- 706.

28. Kraut, R. (2003) Applying social psychological theory to the problems of group work, In (Carroll, J.M. Ed.) *HCI Models, Theories and Frameworks: Towards a Multidisciplinary Science*. Morgan-Kaufmann

29. Laughlin, P. R. & Johnson, H. H. (1966) Group and individual performance on a complementary task as a function of initial ability level. *Journal of Experimental Social Psychology*. 2(4) pp. 407- 414

30. Malone, T. & Crowston, K. (1990), What is coordination theory and how can it help design cooperative work systems? In Proc of CSCW

31. Malone, T. & Crowston, K. (1994) The interdisciplinary study of coordination. *ACM Computing Surveys*, 26(1)

32. McDowell, C., Werner, L., Bullock, H. E., & Fernald, J. (2006) Pair programming improves student retention, confidence, and program quality, *Communications of the ACM*, 49(8), pp.90-95

33. McGrath, J. (1984) *Groups: Interaction and performance*, Prentice Hall

34. Mendes, E., Al-Fakhri, L., & Luxton-Reilly, A. (2006) A replicated experiment of pair-programming in a 2nd-year software development and design computer science course, In Proc. of SIGCSE

35. Piaget, J. (1932) *The moral judgment of the child*. Free Press

36. Platt, G. (1973) Social traps. *American Psychologist*.

37. Poole, S.M., Seibold, D.R., & McPhee, R.D. (1985) Group decision-making as a structurational process, *Quarterly Journal of Speech*. 71(1) pp. 74-102

38. Roschelle, J. & Teasley, S.D. (1995) The construction of shared knowledge in collaborative problem solving. In C.E. O'Malley (Ed), *Computer-Supported Collaborative Learning*. pp. 69-197. Springer-Verlag

39. Sfard, A. & Kieran, C. (2001) Cognition as Communication: Rethinking Learning-by-Talking Through Multi-Faceted Analysis of Students' Mathematical Interactions. *Mind, Culture, and Activity*.

40. Shaw, M. (1981) *Group Dynamics: The psychology of small group behavior*. McGraw-Hill

41. Smith, R.J. & Cook, P. E. (1973) Leadership in Dyadic Groups as a Function of Dominance and Incentives. *Sociometry*. 36(4), pp. 561-568

42. Sorenson, J.R. (1973) Group Member Traits, Group Process, and Group Performance. *Human Relations*.

43. Stroebe, W. & Diehl, M. (1994) Why Groups are less Effective than their Members: On Productivity Losses in Idea-generating Groups. *European Review of Social Psychology*. 5. pp. 271-303.

44. Suchman, L. (1987). *Plans and situated actions*. Cambridge Univ. Press.

45. Suchman, L. (2007). *Human-machine Reconfigurations: Plans and situated actions*. Cambridge Univ. Press.

46. Tatar, D., Foster, G., Bobrow, D., (1991) Design for Conversation: lessons from Cognoter, International Journal of Man-Machine Studies, 34(2), pp. 185-209

47. Tatar, D., Lee, J.S. & Alaloula, N (2008) Playground games: a design strategy for supporting and understanding coordinated activity, In Proc. Of DIS '08

48. Tripakis, S. (2001) Undecidable Problems of Decentralized Observation and Control. CDC'01

49. Turkle, S. (2011) *Alone Together: Why We Expect More from Technology and Less from Each Other*. ReadHowYouWant

50. Valverde, S. & Solé, R. V. (2006) Self-Organization and Hierarchy in Open Source Social Networks. *Santa Fe Institute Working Paper: #06-12-053*

51. Vygotsky, L. (1978) *Mind in society: The development of higher psychological processes*. Harvard Univ. Press.

52. Wiener, H. S. (1986) Collaborative Learning in the Classroom: A Guide to Evaluation. *College English*

53. Williams, L.A. & Kessler, R.R. (2000) All I really need to know about pair programming I learned in kindergarten, *Communications of the ACM*, 43(5)

54. Winograd, T. & Flores. F. (1986) *Understanding Computers and Cognition*. Ablex Publishing Corp.

See Friendship, Sort of: How Conversation and Digital Traces Might Support Reflection on Friendships

Victoria Schwanda Sosik[1*], Xuan Zhao[2*], Dan Cosley[1]
[1]Information Science, Cornell University
301 College Ave., Ithaca, NY 14850
[2]Communication, Cornell University
Kennedy Hall, Ithaca, NY 14850
{vls48, xz298, drc44}@cornell.edu

ABSTRACT
Inspired by conversational visualization tools and the increasing enactment of relationships in social media, we examine how people reflect on friendships and how social data and conversation may affect this. We asked 28 people to reflect on their relationship with a close friend either alone, alone but with access to Facebook's "See Friendship" page, or with the friend using their See Friendship page. Observation and interviews revealed a rich array of practices around why, when, and how people reflect on friendships; that both friends and data make reflection more positive, more focused, and more fun; that those are not necessarily good things; and that third parties are a common theme. These findings suggest a number of design considerations, including supporting different types of reflection, aligning the interface with important moments and content useful for reflection, and carefully considering the fidelity of the visualization and data presented.

Author Keywords
Social media, lifelogging, visualization, friendships.

ACM Classification Keywords
H.5.m. Information interfaces and presentation (e.g., HCI): Miscellaneous.

INTRODUCTION
Researchers have made increasing use of "digital traces"—data generated as a by-product of people's online activity—to study social processes such as collaboration in Wikipedia and to build systems that leverage these data. For instance, credit card transactions [24] and social media content [22] have been used to both help people understand themselves and to help researchers understand human behavior.

In tools such as text messaging, email, discussion forums, and Facebook, these digital traces go beyond the individual and capture the communication that is an important part of expressing and developing relationships with others [29]. Thus, a natural question is to explore how technology might leverage these traces of communication to help people better understand their relationships with others.

Visualizations of workgroup activity (e.g., [8,16]) and individual email and chat archives (e.g., [28, 30]) are one such tool that may give people insight into how they interact with co-workers and friends. However, these tools are not widely used. And even for tools like Friendwheel[1] that are more commonly used, it is hard to evaluate them. Do they help people reflect on, or even improve, their relationships? Or, like much reminiscing in Pensieve [22], are they just a moment's diversion?

Following Sellen and Whittaker's critique of lifelogging [25], we argue that these systems do not spend enough time considering end uses. Technical challenges such as ubiquitous capture, opportunities provided by easily-computable features like authorship and timestamps, and aesthetic considerations that contribute to engagement are all important in system design. But without attention to how these tools and data support people's needs, practices, and values in reflecting on relationships, they are unlikely to succeed. Current work also focuses on supporting reflection by individuals, but reflection is often a shared activity that should be supported.

In this paper, we study these practices, needs, and values, with the goal of informing the design of tools to support them. We brought 28 people to our lab (14 individuals, 7 pairs), gave some of them access to Facebook, asked them to reflect on a close friendship, and interviewed them afterwards. We focused on three main questions: 1) *How, and why, do people reflect on their relationships?* 2) *How do digital traces affect these practices?* and 3) *How does reflecting with others affect the experience?*

RELATED WORK
"Reflection" is a slippery term, used to mean many things [23]. We follow Lindley et al. [18] in using the definition developed by educational development researcher Jennifer A. Moon. This definition draws on the discussion of reflection in several disciplines, characterizing it as a process that involves pulling together and trying to make

CSCW 2012, February 11–15, 2012, Seattle, Washington, USA.

[*] Sosik and Zhao are co-first authors.
[1] http://thomas-fletcher.com/friendwheel/

sense of unstructured material. Reflection is a key component of both personal and professional development and helps to generate awareness of one's self and environment. Though it is often used in counseling when there are deficits, it is useful even when there are not problems to address [21].

Storytelling, through private journaling or listening and contributing to stories with others [15], is often linked to reflection. So is reminiscing, which can help people work through past events and serve social functions such as relationship maintenance [31]. While people can reminisce about a wide array of topics, they often reminisce about and with other people [5].

We aim to build on this work by better understanding specific practices and outcomes that might inform the design of technologies that support reflection. This leads to our first research question:

RQ1: How do people currently reflect on their friendships? When does this happen, what do they think about, and how do they feel about the experience?

Reflection is often supported by environments that provide a space and material to engage with [21], and system designers have increasingly used digital traces to provide these environments. While [4] finds that reminiscing about positive events using cognitive imagery boosts happiness more than using memorabilia, systems commonly use photos as a starting point (e.g., [26]) since they help people share and reflect on experiences [10]. Digital representations of physical objects can help families tell stories about their memories [27] and text-based social media has also been used to encourage reminiscing [22]. And more digital traces are coming, as personal informatics and lifelogging systems like MyLifeBits [11] gather vast amounts of information.

The question then becomes what to do with these data. Sellen and Whittaker point out that lifelogging researchers should explore potential uses of these systems, and that more data isn't necessarily better [25]. Li et al. also argue that personal informatics systems should help people collect and reflect on personally relevant information [17]. These systems are often used in unexpected ways. For instance, conversational visualizations (e.g., [28,30]) often prompt stories about people's pasts, even when this was not the tool's intended goal. Other work has explored how image and GPS data [14], SenseCam images taken 18 months prior [18], and other social media can promote different types of remembering and reminiscing [22].

The increasing prevalence of systems for reflection and digital traces of relationships, combined with our limited understanding of how and why these data might support reflection, led to our second research question:

RQ2: How does access to data about friendships affect the process and experience of reflecting on friendships?

Much of the lifelogging and visualization work in CSCW and HCI focuses on interfaces for individuals. Yet other people also play a key role in reflection, serving as both reasons and partners for reflecting on the past. As Halbwachs writes: "The individual memory, in order to corroborate and make precise and even to cover the gaps in its remembrances, relies upon, relocates itself within, momentarily merges with, the collective memory." [13] In this kind of collective reminiscing, people involved in the same events try to construct a shared representation, in which different opinions, feelings, and emotions are negotiated and communicated [20].

This reflection through conversation has a dual role: it both furthers goals such as identity management, affinity seeking, and image confirmation [6], while serving as a fundamental constituent of the relationship itself [7]. For example, self-disclosure through reflecting on past events both serves the function of uncertainty reduction [3] and becomes an important part of the relationship history [29]. These conversations also teach people how to reflect on relationships: when mothers and children reminisce together, it supports the child's understanding of the past and of other people's perspectives [9].

Thus, reflection is doubly social: it is often both *about* and *with* others, and a fundamental part of relationships. This, plus the opportunity we see for designing tools that go beyond individuals, led to our third research question:

RQ3: How does reflecting with a friend affect the process and experience of reflecting?

METHODS

We explored these questions through observing participants during a reflection task and interviewing them about their reflection practices, both during the task and in everyday life. At the beginning of each interview session, we observed participants completing a task where they were asked to think about a close friendship for five minutes. The instructions were deliberately broad, choosing "think" over "reflect" or "reminisce" because we didn't want to influence how people approached the task. The task also helped to ground the interviews by giving participants a recent experience of reflecting to draw on.

There were three variations of this task, which allowed us to observe and ask questions about how access to data and conversation with a friend impact reflecting on friendships. Seven participants completed the task as described above (*single/no data*). Seven others were asked to use Facebook's See Friendship page when thinking about their friendship (*single/data*). Finally, seven pairs of friends were asked to explore their See Friendship page and think about their friendship together (*pairs/data*). To make data collection more manageable, we didn't have a *pairs/no data* variation; our hope was that questions we asked about reflecting in everyday life would give us information about how people reminisce together without using digital traces.

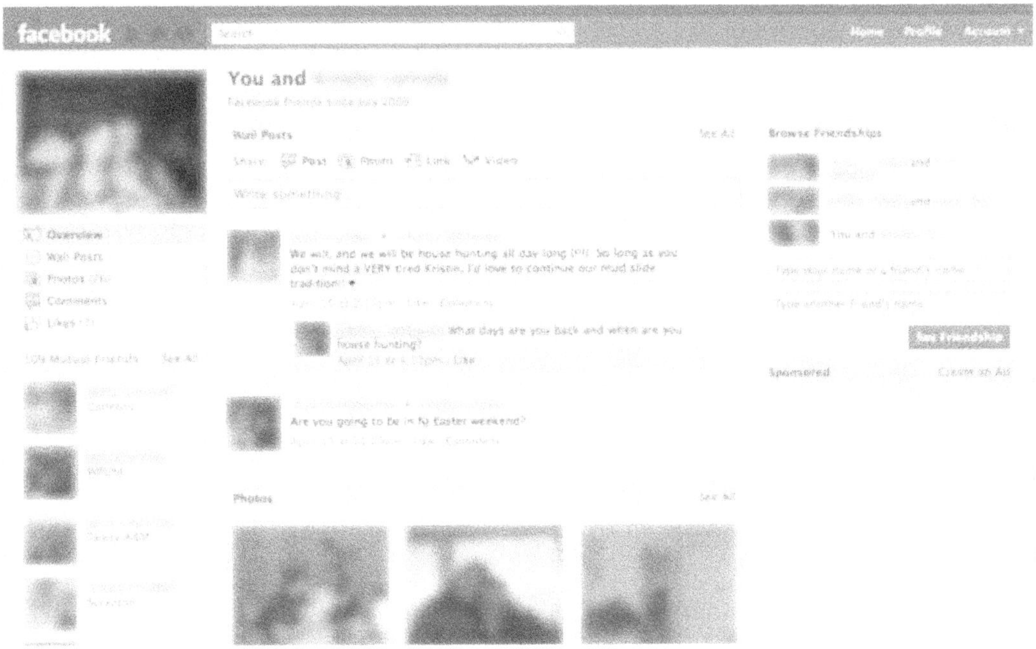

Figure 1. The top portion of the See Friendship page between two Facebook friends, which shows recent activity between the friends including wall posts, comments on each other's posts, and mutual events, photos, friends, and likes.

We chose See Friendship (see Figure 1) as our interface to digital trace data because it is an existing tool in a widely used social network. It gathers different media shared by two people, including wall posts and comments between them, recent photos, and mutual events, liked topics, and friends to "[tell] the story of friendships"[2]. People can use See Friendship with any Facebook friend and can access any two people's See Friendship page if they are friends with one and have access to both users' profile pages.

After the task, we video recorded in-depth, semi-structured interviews that lasted about 40 minutes. We first asked participants what they thought we meant by "think about your friendship", the types of things they thought about during the task and the experience of doing it, and how they think about their friendships in their daily life. We then asked them to draw on their everyday experiences to talk about how their reflection would have been different if they had done the two other task variations. Finally, we asked why and how they used the See Friendship page in daily life and how well it represented their friendships. We interviewed pairs/data participants together.

We recruited 28 participants from a large Northeastern US university (20 female, 8 male; median age 20; 16 White/Caucasian, 8 Asian, 3 Hispanic/Latino, 1 Black or African-American) who received course credit and were entered into a lottery for five $50 Amazon gift cards. We asked them to select a close friend they interact with at least once a month both on Facebook and face-to-face. If this friend was local, we asked if they would want to participate together. We recruited pairs in this way until we reached seven pairs. Fourteen others were randomly assigned to complete one of the two single task variations. Participants completed the Interpersonal Solidarity Scale (ISS), a 20-item measure of closeness in dyadic relationships [33], one week prior to and immediately after the interview. Our original plan was to use this scale to see how the task affected their feelings about the friendship, and whether there would be differences between the task variations. However, through our interviews it became clear that this interpretation of ISS outcomes might not be appropriate, a topic we will return to in the discussion.

To analyze the data, we used the constant comparative method [12]. Two researchers independently partially transcribed all videos and divided the data into chunks, which we organized into themes using concept charting [19]. We chose to conduct one analysis across all data, rather than separate analyses for each task variation, because participants seamlessly interwove discussion of the task with talking about their everyday practices around reflecting on relationships. Although we primed people with the different variations, participants had reflected on relationships in all three ways (without data, with data, and with a friend) in their everyday lives and drew on these experiences. Thus, many of our themes were supported across all variations; we call out cases where themes are primarily supported by evidence from participants in one task variation.

RESULTS

We now lay out these themes, organized around our three main research questions. Participant numbers are noted after each quote (1-7 did the single/no-data variation; 8-14 did the single/data variation; and pairs 15-21 did the pair/data variation, with the partners noted as 'a' or 'b').

[2] http://blog.facebook.com/blog.php?post=443390892130

How people reflect on their friendships

Participants described reflection as a complex set of activities: both spontaneous and intentional, both specific and general, both fun and awkward.

Reflection is both spontaneous and intentional

As in [23], we found reflecting on friendships was often unplanned and spontaneous, triggered by random cues such as common interests, related events, or online or offline co-presence with a friend. Some participants mentioned that daily use of Facebook—such as looking at posts, pictures, comments and likes—also sparked thinking about a friendship without explicitly planning to reflect on it. Reflection tends to be more explicit and intentional when there are problems such as arguments, or potential changes in the relationship because of life events.

"We talk about our problems but we don't really talk about our friendship. It's assumed to be OK...we both know we get along very well, we won't sit around and say I love you...we only have conversations about our relationship when bad things happen." (15-a)

"I don't usually intentionally think much, but during this time of year when everyone is about to leave the campus, it makes me think more about the relationship." (7)

Reflection is both specific and general

During the task and in daily life, people thought about their friendships on two levels: both about specific shared events in the past and about connections between these events and the development of their friendship. Thinking about "how we met" and the timeline of relationship development happened across all task variations.

"I started with when I first met her in middle school, and we got closer after middle school, so I went on and thought about how we were in the same class, and in high school she sat in front of me so we always talk...I guess the timeline is important because this is essentially how the relationship formed in a sequential manner...different events that bond you and make you closer." (2)

Reflections from those without See Friendship were more chronological and structured, starting from the beginning of a relationship and leading to recent events. In contrast, See Friendship's reverse chronological ordering led participants to start with the present. Reflecting on the evolution of friendships also included future events, particularly in the face of predictable changes such as graduation.

"[During the task] I thought about what he'll be doing in the future...I thought about what kind of things I could do with him in the future, and then I realized he's not gonna be here next year, it makes me realize, oh maybe I should talk more about him in the past." (7)

Reflection is fun, valuable, and sometimes awkward

Participants in all variations described reflection as valuable for friendships. Reflecting together helps friends value their friendship more, increases trust, and signals that they care about each other. Also, it's "fun". When reflecting alone, they realize how much they value the friendship and how good friends they are, which makes them feel happy.

However, for some participants reflection is an awkward, "touchy-feely" experience that they don't seek out in daily life. It can also be bittersweet.

"We became good friends through a really tough time with another friend who we are both close with...so reminiscing is somewhat bittersweet because we are still dealing with the repercussions from that." (15-b)

Since we used See Friendship as a trigger for reflection in the task, some participants described the experience as surprising because they don't normally look at past records on Facebook. For example, we observed them talking about unexpected Facebook interaction frequencies between them and their friends while they were trying to match that record with their offline interactions.

How data affects reflecting on friendships

As with their general reflection practices, participants painted a complex picture of how data and See Friendship were used in reflection. Funny content provides serious information, data sharpens but limits reflection, and See Friendship is accurate but incomplete and misleading.

Humor and media sharing can signal closeness

Participants often interacted with their friends through wall posts, messages and chat. Unsurprisingly, they use messages and chat for more personal, deep conversations since these channels are private. Wall posts were most often used for sharing media such as links to YouTube videos or articles, or for humorous content such as inside jokes.

"That's a lot of how we interact over Facebook, like 'oh I found this song and I thought you would like it' and she posts it on my wall." (13)

"When you're writing on someone's wall...it's just a short little comment that someone's going to see and you just want it to be something funny that you can laugh at in the library when you're taking a break and that's it." (16-b)

These "silly" elements, however, often helped people think about the evolution of their friendship.

"I noticed how the language has changed between each other...it used to be one short sentence which is kind of formal and now it's like a random video and we know the other person will like it...it shows we have a deeper understanding of the other person." (15-b)

See Friendship is mostly used to filter content

All participants were aware of the See Friendship page before the study, but used it "almost never" or "rarely". The most common use was as a filter to easily find a specific conversation, comment, or photo with a particular friend.

"I usually use the See Friendship page to look back on a comment, because it's easier to narrow down than going through my wall." (16-a)

However, once there, participants would sometimes use See Friendship to reflect in an unplanned way.

"If she wrote on my wall and I forgot what I wrote, then I would press See Friendship, which used to be See Wall-to-wall, and look what I had said previously…then there would be pictures also, which I may at that point start looking at those because they caught my attention." (2)

Many participants likened See Friendship to the See Wall-to-Wall feature that it replaced. See Wall-to-Wall was much like See Friendship, but only displayed wall posts. Some participants missed See Wall-to-Wall because it was both easier to use as a content filter and it felt less "creepy".

"There was the Wall-to-Wall feature before…that was better, it felt less dirty when you looked at it, but also…it was easier to [track conversations]." (18-b)

See Friendship is accurate, limited, and misleading

About two-thirds of participants felt that See Friendship is accurate and can represent the "overall tone" of a friendship. Attending events together, having pictures tagged together, posting inside jokes on each other's wall, and having a lot of Facebook interaction signifies closeness.

"I feel like [See Friendship] is a pretty accurate depiction of our relationship as friends…more just like having fun, and having fun in terms of us being friends instead of trying to fit into a bigger social scene…it's just between us, so…all the nonsense is inside jokes that we have." (2)

"I think [See Friendship] shows that we're together a lot, and people assume…we're close because of that." (18-b)

Some participants also felt that the See Friendship page helped them see the progression of their friendship through changes in their activity patterns.

"It's funny that there's a physical map of it almost, it can tell you the day…that we became Facebook friends, and how our conversations changed, and how we started talking more." (15-b)

However, even participants who felt that See Friendship was accurate saw it as limited and incomplete.

"It would be an accurate representation, it just wouldn't be a complete representation…there are things you talk to your friends about that you wouldn't post on Facebook because you don't want it to be public." (2)

One-third of our participants felt that See Friendship was not accurate and may misrepresent friendships. For instance, asymmetric Facebook activity doesn't necessarily mean a one-way friendship. Facebook was also described as "superficial", missing the personal communication that contributes to friends being close to each other. This communication often happens during "mundane", daily interactions that are not captured on Facebook.

"You definitely wouldn't get the evenness, or maybe the depth either of the friendship, because a lot of things that end up on Facebook are superficial." (16-b)

"There are a lot of things that are mundane that you do, that are quite important to the experience in general, just not quite exciting enough to say anything about…to make it worthy of a Facebook post." (10)

Facebook content also tends to be positive, with pictures of fun events or the humor that dominates wall posts, and therefore See Friendship under-represents negative events or feelings. Its representativeness also differs for different kinds of friends; long distance friendships were thought to be better represented because a higher percentage of overall interaction with them would be via Facebook.

Data focuses, but limits reflection

In the task, participants using See Friendship focused on exploring pictures and videos, wall posts, and mutual friends. They explored content chronologically, starting with the most recent, and visual elements appeared to get the most attention. This content served to remind people of events and activities, focusing their attention while reducing cognitive effort to reflect, at least for some participants. However, as with [4], participants described drawbacks to this reduction of effort. The triggers led some people to focus on just what was captured and not the deeper, more serious, and more personal aspects of their friendship.

"[It's] pretty good at reminding you of exactly what happened, what day you went, what was said...but it's bad at depicting the essence of the experience…it might actually limit the way you recall certain things." (10)

Likewise, the biases in what See Friendship captures led people away from mundane and negative events.

"[Without See Friendship] I would think more about personal stuff, like when I'm sad, and traumatic events…those events that make us closer together." (12)

As described earlier, a common way people approached the instruction to "think about your friendship" was by focusing on its development. Participants using data to reflect were less likely to talk about friendship development, but when they did, they would often use the data as a kind of friendship timeline to tell stories about what was going on in their friendship at the time of the posts.

"There were some insinuations of us being mad at each other, and having just gotten over it." (18-b)

"We'll go from like some really funny inside joke, to like hearts, so clearly we had just made up." (18-a)

People having access to data also remarked more often on patterns the data reflected, such as the changes in tone or asymmetry in frequency of Facebook posting between themselves and the friend they selected for the task. This was true whether they knew about this asymmetry before completing the task or whether it was surprising and only realized after viewing their data.

Facebook's present focus and public nature affect its utility
For some participants, Facebook was not an effective tool for reflection because it privileges new content, though others found value in taking the effort to review the past.

"Facebook is always updating and always moving forward, forward, forward...there's no facility in Facebook to suddenly bring back memories." (21-a)

"[It] plays a role in [thinking about things we've done in the past that make us closer]...I think back to the pictures and it helps me have a better memory of what we actually did together, I was just doing that the other day." (5)

The differing levels of public-ness of various channels in Facebook also affected its utility. Participants felt that more private data, such as Facebook messages and chats, text messages, and other instant messenger logs, would be much more representative of their friendships. Some thought that it would be interesting to include this content on a private page just for themselves and their friend.

However, others were concerned about Facebook becoming the hub for this personal content and didn't have any desire for See Friendship, or a private version, to better represent their friendships. For some participants this lack of desire was less about Facebook, and more due to a feeling that strong friendships don't require or shouldn't have records.

"I don't think [Facebook] should have so much information that it's more accurate than you two hanging out together. If [it] knew more, it would take away from your friendship a little bit, everyone would know what it's like." (5)

How conversation affects reflecting on friendships
Participants engaged in both solo and mutual reflection in their daily life, and these modes are each useful in different ways. Interestingly, reflecting with other people, versus reflecting alone, led to some of the same kinds of tradeoffs as reflecting with data. Solo reflection is deeper, and often more general, but mutual reflection builds the relationship and stimulates reflection. Third parties also play an important role in reflecting on friendships.

Solo reflection is deeper and more structured
Participants said that reflecting alone leads to deeper reflection and more general evaluation of the friendship as a whole, while reflecting together often stops at the level of specific events. Just as data focuses participants' reflections, conversations about events can be very detailed, but they rarely turn into a reflective evaluation of the friendship unless the pairs intend to talk about these issues.

"When I talk to her and talk about things we've done in the past...just talk about how fun they were and how stupid they were...I also think about these things on my own, but when I'm talking to her I was not trying to connect that to any sort of emotional...if I were thinking about our friendship I'll more think about us as friends as opposed as things we've done as friends." (2)

Reflecting alone also appears to be more structured than reflecting with a friend, perhaps because people influence each others' thoughts through conversation.

"If we are in the same room and talking, it'll be more about what's happening now and what's current, as opposed to if I was thinking about my friendship with [a] by myself, I could start from the beginning...go back and from the beginning, talk about how we moved sequentially." (21-b)

Reflecting together can confirm relationships
The pair experience was described as "stimulating" and "fun". Participants also enjoyed the emotional experience of the conversation, such as when they shared laughter together. When reflecting together, friends also confirm each other's thoughts about the friendship, which was considered valuable.

"One nice thing about this is her confirming my beliefs about it...if I'm thinking this on my own it'll be like this is what I think and what I always thought, but I have no idea how she feels about it. A friendship is not a one-way street." (15-b)

Another participant said that talking actually helps to build the friendship.

"I think they have different functions....when I talk about memories and experiences with my friends, we'll have a fun time...which can really reinforce our relationship and make us more intimate." (12)

However, just as data leads to a focus on positive events, reflecting together might lead people away from saying negative or critical things.

"When we talk about it, we'll want to enjoy the moment so we won't talk about other sad stuff together. It'll be more positive than thinking on my own...I won't talk to her like, remember last time you cried?" (12)

Third parties play a role in reflecting on friendships
Mutual friends are often part of thinking about a friendship. For example, reflection on a friendship is often triggered by thinking about mutual friends or a group of friends with the same background (e.g., high school friends).

"When you share the same social circle, mutual friends come up a lot when you talk about stuff...a lot of times when you are reflecting on your own friendship, it's an extension of discussion of friendships with others." (10)

For some participants, See Friendship is used entirely from the third party perspective. For instance, awareness of publicity and concern for privacy influence people's decisions about Facebook activities.

"I just keep it in mind that it is a public area...you see others' pages and you make inferences so I thought about

how others might see my pages. With all my wall posts, there is an expectation that other people could see it." (6)

Consistent with this notion that Facebook is more intended for third parties, some people said they don't mind others accessing their See Friendship page. Even if displaying the data to third parties might risk a distorted view, most participants are not concerned about it, because mutual friends who have access to the page are supposed to have a better understanding of how they interact in real life.

"I think if our friends see us in real life as opposed to virtual like on Facebook, they'll understand it's mutual." (16-a)

However, people do think about others' reactions to public evidence of friendships.

"Lately I get nervous because I have been posting too many things on your wall." (15-b)

"Yeah some of our friends are sensitive about who's friends with whom, so that's why we are trying not to put it in people's faces that we are close." (15-a)

Even though some people think that See Friendship does not accurately represent their friendships, they still use it to explore relationships between others.

"I tend to be interested in...other people's friendships ...mostly because I want to put mine in context." (21-a)

"We definitively check other people's see friendship page... it's natural because you want to know other people and it's there". (17-b)

Checking others' See Friendship might be simply triggered by Facebook's News Feed and link suggestions, but more often people are driven by curiosity to learn about others and get a sense of what their relationships are like.

"Yeah, [I use it] to see what pictures they had together and what they say on each other's walls." (17-a)

"Especially when they are in a relationship, you'll be curious about what they write to each other...I feel when I look at their pages, I'm definitely making assumptions about people...if they have many pictures together you might think they are really close and hang out a lot, or they know each other for a long time." (17-b)

DISCUSSION

Participants painted a nuanced picture of their practices around reflecting on friendships, and both digital traces and conversations with others change the ways people reflect and the value they get from reflecting. In this section, we discuss how these results might inform the design of tools that support reflection. We first explore how some of our themes suggest possible design moves, then turn to a more general discussion of how our results shed light on decisions that any tool in this space must address.

Data and people trigger reflection, but differently

Results showed that both having social media data and talking with a friend change the reflection process by focusing the experience, making it more fun, and bringing up experiences that might otherwise be forgotten. However, recent and positive experiences are privileged because social media data are associated with positive and sometimes superficial interactions. Similarly, when talking with friends, more details are filled in about a specific event, but the focus is on positive experiences because this kind of collective reminiscing supports relationship maintenance and individual well-being.

Systems can leverage this idea that data and conversation don't necessarily direct people to focus on the same "specific" and "positive" events to encourage different types of reflection. Social media triggers can be used to help people reflect on particular events, while the system could prompt conversations about the mundane with friends. The non-personalized text prompts in Pensieve [22] refer to mundane events like cooking and sunglasses, and might be well-suited for this sort of reflection.

Reflection as sensemaking and storytelling

Conversation and data both support a certain kind of sensemaking: when friends are trying to figure out what a wall post means and telling stories and laughing about it, they are compensating for and filling in gaps left by digital traces to create a more complete picture of events in the relationship and, sometimes, how it has evolved. This conversation leads to enriched social and emotional experiences around reflection that can help build friendships, adding to the value of reflection.

But individual reflection without data triggering is also necessary and beneficial for personal growth and reflection, mostly because of the negative memories that occur in the process [20]. Our results also align with findings that although pictures can lead to more vivid memories, encouraging free recall of events by using mental imagery is more effective in helping them recreate the same feelings or emotions as when their memory initially formed [4].

This suggests that systems could explicitly support storytelling as a form of reflection [15], allowing people to create narratives that connect multiple pieces of data and add context that is missing from what is explicitly captured. The system might even include algorithmic support for telling these stories, suggesting related content from both one's own and one's friends' digital traces. Allowing for both private and shared stories is important. Private stories allow people to work through negative emotions and add meaningful content that would not be appropriate to share in a semi-public system like Facebook. Others could be shared, allowing friends to create the bonding experiences and "fill in the gaps."

The embeddedness of friendships

Finally, people often try to relate one relationship to another and understand them in a wider social context. Reflecting on a particular friendship is often accompanied by thinking about another friendship; some memories are better shared among a group of friends than between two people; and seeing or talking to mutual friends (both face-to-face and through the Facebook interface's links to other See Friendship pages) can trigger reflection on a friendship.

Third parties also come up in the discussion of whether digital traces such as See Friendship accurately portray a relationship. And though people sometimes felt that these digital traces presented incomplete or misleading views, they do seem to believe they can "see the friendship" of others. They explore others' See Friendship pages to learn and make inferences about their relationships, and compare those relationships to their own. Meanwhile, they consider third parties, and the semi-public nature of Facebook content, when thinking about what to post and to whom.

This probably does not surprise sociologists, but was something we did not expect because of our focus on particular friendships. Thus, tools should explicitly use these third-party relationships to structure and support reflection (this might be part of the secret to Friendwheel's success, for instance). In the relational context, allowing partners to create a "designed" public presentation of their relationships might support relationship development, comparison with others, and privacy management.

General considerations and questions

We now turn to a more general discussion of how our findings highlight questions, tensions and tradeoffs to consider when designing for reflection in this space.

Choosing appropriate levels of representativeness

The fact that See Friendship misses the day-to-day and personal interactions that make up much of a friendship, and focuses but limits how people think about friendships, leads to questions of how to represent a friendship through digital traces, and to what extent representativeness is necessary or desired in a tool aimed at simulating reflection.

Participants thought that private communication like SMS and IM would make a collection of trace data more reflective of a friendship because these media capture more day-to-day and personal interaction. Still, these would miss the face-to-face time spent with friends that was the most important gap for many participants. The face-to-face and the mundane matter, as with SenseCam images supporting connection, insight, interpretation, and awareness of change [18].

A straightforward design implication would be to capture more data, but, like Sellen and Whittaker [25], we question whether perfect representation would encourage reflection. Likewise, imposing structure on the trace data, though useful for some kinds of reflection (like timelines used to think about the evolution of a relationship), may fail to stimulate reflection in the way that messy, unstructured material begs to be made sense of [21]. The gaps themselves add value, providing occasions for joint meaning-making [13] as well as a level of ambiguity that can help relational partners maintain face [1]. Thus, we caution against trying to provide a "perfect picture" of a friendship, and based on our results, suggest supporting a variety of media, levels of detail, opportunities for individual and joint reflection, and so on, as a design goal.

Supporting both reflection and social comparison

The question of representativeness leads naturally to the question of who a digital trace record is designed for. Participants sometimes had strong feelings about See Friendship only being for themselves, or only for others. If the page is just for the two friends, then there is less concern about capturing more private communication, but none of our participants thought that it would be a good idea for the public See Friendship page to display more personal communication.

Further, they did not necessarily want it to be private. Being able to see third parties' digital traces of interaction, especially mutual friends, can support better understanding of one's own relationships, even though it is also sometimes seen as "dirty" and "creepy". Ironically, the ability to filter out activity that makes See Friendship a useful tool for finding content from a particular friend is likely what makes it seem less acceptable when used with third parties—somewhat like advertisers' aggregation of an individual's behavior across multiple web sites.

Technical approaches such as fine-grained privacy controls would be one approach to the problem, although they would likely suffer from classic problems: people are willing to give up their privacy cheaply and are often bad at using privacy interfaces. An alternate approach would be to recognize that there are many purposes for digital trace data and thus provide multiple tools and representations. Then the answer isn't to change See Friendship—it has its own uses, and for us it was simply a convenient, real interface that contained enough digital traces to support our task. Instead, the answer becomes to build appropriate environments for reflection.

Providing effective environments for reflection

This raises the question of where, and when, systems should be situated to encourage reflection. We saw several examples of how the norms around Facebook affected how participants used See Friendship to think about their relationships. The humor and positivity of Facebook content contributed to considering more positive events and aspects of friendship; the idea that Facebook is for recent events sometimes prevented people from using it to look back; the fact that See Friendship replaced See Wall-to-Wall may have influenced people's use of See Friendship as a content filter; and third-party use sometimes caused people to consider what kinds of content to post.

Thus, the system's interface, the content it contains, and its history and norms contribute to how one might use digital traces to support reflection. They also affect how one might integrate reflection into the system. We already argued that

See Friendship itself shouldn't change. But people are in fact triggered to reflect on relationships through their use of Facebook, and this could be more explicitly supported.

Interfaces that encourage reflection could also be integrated into other tools such as email, SMS, or IM clients. These archives of content could support reflection by bringing back elements of the past that are relevant to current content, supporting grounding, reflection, and conversation about past activity. Another option is to aggregate across media in a separate system. The Intel "Museum of Me"[3] creates a faux art exhibition that represents a Facebook user by aggregating their publicly available data. Integrating this with other traces and providing users with tools to curate their own collections, tell stories, and make meanings about their relationships might be useful. There are downsides to asking people to go to a separate site—it is more effort and less spontaneous—but that is one of the many tradeoffs afforded by this rich space.

Measuring Success Beyond "He Liked It"

These tradeoffs raise one final question. See Friendship was useful for filtering content and stalking third parties, but less useful for supporting reflection on friendships. But what does it mean to be useful for reflection, and how can we measure these outcomes? For instance, we found that after the interview, pair/data participants felt significantly closer to their chosen friend than single/no data participants according to the ISS scale of dyadic closeness. This means conversation and data are great for reflection, right? Or maybe reflecting together imposed social pressure to score their relationship higher (which is why we did not make any strong claims about this in the results).

A more general concern is that closeness may not be the right measure. Sometimes reflecting on a relationship might lead to a realization that it should change, or end. But it's hard to measure outcomes of reflection such as self-awareness and personal growth. Existing studies, including this one, are often exploratory, and/or focused on the design goals of the system. At some point we will need to move toward evaluations that go beyond "people liked it" and directly address the actual needs and practices that have come out of these studies. People want to reflect on both events in and arcs across relationships, do sensemaking and storytelling around the data and about the relationship, search for specific content and browse generally across archives of activity, reflect both with others and on their own, and think about their relationships as situated in their wider network of friends.

Thus, systems should set design goals that align with these practices and values, and evaluations should focus on them. These evaluations should also reach out beyond the lab. Reflection is both intentional and spontaneous, and usually more an ongoing activity than a specific task. This affects both tool design and tool evaluation, and suggests that both should be in it for the long haul. How can tools encourage repeated use over time? How can they help both researchers and users know that they are valuable? And how do they work when integrated into everyday life?

Limitations

Despite the need for long-term, natural evaluation, we too conducted a lab study. We also focused on close friendships, partly because they are important but understudied compared to romantic or family relationships, and partly because friendships often have more Facebook activity, which we needed in order to use the See Friendship page as our source of digital trace data. We recruited mostly co-located friends because of our desire to study everyday reminiscing and interview pairs together, but friendships at a distance may make use of social media for reflection more often, or in different ways. The pair methodology helped us see how people reflect together, but probably limited our participants to friends in good standing. Our participants were college students, and age affects how people reflect on the past [32], conceptualize friendship and use digital traces. And finally, although we saw no differences in how people responded based on gender or cultural background, these were not our focus, there might very well be differences that could be drawn out by studies that explicitly focus on those dimensions.

CONCLUSION

Still, we hope we have provided useful insights to build upon. We identified a number of practices and values that talking with others and digital trace data support in how people reflect on their relationships. Our findings around the role of storytelling and sensemaking align with other work around reflection on digital trace data, suggesting that this is a key element to support. Both the parallel effects of data and people on the character of reflection and the prominent role of third parties were surprising to us and hopefully useful to designers. Finally, we hope that our discussion of the issues around representativeness, goals, and evaluation, informed by our data, can nudge future work and designs in directions that will lead to better tools and, ultimately, better experiences for people as they seek to understand themselves and their relationships.

ACKNOWLEDGMENTS

We thank NSF for supporting this work under grant IIS 0835451 and a Graduate Research Fellowship.

REFERENCES

1. Aoki, P.M., Woodruff, A. (2005). Making space for stories: Ambiguity in the design of personal communication systems. In *Proc. CHI 2005.*
2. Baxter, L. (1992). Interpersonal communication as dialogue: A response to the "Social Approaches" forum. *Commun Theor*, 2, 330–337.
3. Berger, C., Gardner, R., Parks, M., Schulman, L., Miller, J. (1976). Interpersonal epistemology and

[3] http://www.intel.com/museumofme

interpersonal communication. In *Explorations in interpersonal communication*. Sage, 149–171.

4. Bryant, F., Smart, C. et al. (2005). Using the past to enhance the present: Boosting happiness through positive reminiscence. *J Happiness Stud, 6*, 227–260.
5. Cosley, D., et al. (2009). Using technologies to support reminiscence. In *Proc. BCS HCI 2009*.
6. Daly, J., Wiemann, J. (Eds.). (1994). *Strategic interpersonal communication*. Lawrence Erlbaum.
7. Duck, S., Pond, K. (1989). Friends, Romans, countrymen, lend me your retrospective data: Rhetoric and reality in personal relationships. In C. Hendrick (Ed.), *Close relationships*. Sage, 3–27.
8. Erickson, T., et al. (1999). Socially translucent systems: Social proxies, persistent conversation, and the design of "Babble". In *Proc. CHI 1999*, 72–79.
9. Fivush, R., Nelson, K. (2006). Parent-child reminiscing locates the self in the past. *Brit J Dev Psych*, 24, 235–251.
10. Frohlich, D., Kuchinsky, A., Pering, C., Don, A., Ariss, S. (2002). Requirements for photoware. In *Proc. CSCW 2002*, 166–175.
11. Gemmell, J., Aris, A., Lueder, R. (2005). Telling stories with MyLifeBits, In *Proc. ICME 2005*, 1536-1539.
12. Glaser, B.G., Strauss, A.L. (1967). *The discovery of grounded theory: Strategies for qualitative research*. Aldine Publishing Company, Chicago.
13. Halbwachs, M. (1925/1992). *The Collective Memory*, Harper & Row, New York.
14. Kalnikaite, V., Sellen, A., Whittaker, S., Kirk, D. (2010). Now let me see where I was: Understanding how lifelogs mediate memory. In *Proc. CHI '10*.
15. Kenyon, G.M., Ruth, J.E., Mader, W. (1999). *Restorying our lives: Personal growth through autobiographical reflection*. Praeger, Westport, CT.
16. Leshed, G., et al. (2009). Visualizing real-Time language-based feedback on teamwork behavior in computer-mediated groups. In *Proc. CHI 2009*.
17. Li, I., Dey, A., Forlizzi, J. (2010). A stage-based model of personal informatics systems. In *Proc. CHI*, 557–566.
18. Lindley, S.E., Glancy, M., Harper, R., Randall, D., Smyth, N. (2011). "Oh and how things just don't change, the more things stay the same": Reflections on SenseCam images 18 months after capture. *Int J Hum-Comput St*, 69, 311–323.
19. Lofland, J., Lofland, L. (1994). *Analyzing social settings: A guide to qualitative observation and analysis*. Wadsworth, Belmont, CA.
20. McLean, K.C., Lilgendahl, J.P. (2008). Why recall our highs and lows: Relations between memory functions, age, and well-being. *Memory* 16, 751–762.
21. Moon, J.A., (1999). *Reflection in Learning and Professional Development*. Routledge Falmer, Oxon.
22. Peesapati, S.T., Schwanda, V., et al. (2010). Pensieve: supporting everyday reminiscence. In *Proc. CHI 2010*.
23. Ricoeur, P. (2004). *Memory, history, gorgetting (Trans Blamey and Pellauer)*. University of Chicago Press.
24. Schwarz, J. Mankoff, J., Matthews, H.S. (2009). Reflections of everyday activities in spending data. In *Proc. CHI 2009,* 1737–1740.
25. Sellen, A., Whittaker, S. (2010). Beyond total capture. *Commun ACM*, 53, 70–77.
26. Shen, C., Lesh, N.B., Vernier, F., Forlines, C., Frost, J. (2002). Sharing and building digital group histories. In *Proc. CSCW 2002*, 324–333.
27. Stevens, M., Abowd, G.D., Truong, K.N., Vollmer, F. (2003). Getting into the Living Memory Box: Family archives & holistic design. *Pers Ubiquit Comput,* 7.
28. Tat, A., Carpendale, S. (2006). CrystalChat: Visualizing personal chat history. In *Proc. HICSS 2006*.
29. Taylor, D., Altman, I. (1987). Communication in interpersonal relationships: Social penetration processes. *Interpersonal processes: New directions in communication research,* 257–277.
30. Viégas, F.B, Golder, S., Donath, J. (2006). Visualizing email content: Portraying relationships from conversational histories. In *Proc. CHI 2006*.
31. Webster, J.D. (1993). Construction and validation of the Reminiscence Functions Scale. *J Gerontol*, 48, 256–262.
32. Webster, J.D., McCall, M.E. (1999). Reminiscence functions across adulthood: A replication and extension. *J Adult Dev,* 6, 73–85.
33. Wheeless, L.R. (1978). A Follow-up Study of the Relationships Among Trust, Disclosure, and Interpersonal Solidarity. *Hum Commun Res*, 4, 143–157.

The Material Practices of Collaboration

Daniela K. Rosner
School of Information, UC Berkeley
Berkeley, CA 94720 USA
daniela@ischool.berkeley.edu

ABSTRACT

Drawing on a three-month bookbinding apprenticeship, this paper examines how people's coordination work is tightly bound up in material practices, the union of material arrangements and social relations. Through the construction of a book, I reveal how sensitivities to delicacy, flexibility and delay emerge through detailed engagements with the book, the binders and the workshop environment. From small adjustments of the hand, to the coordination and exchange of materials and tools, the accomplishment of each task rests on how digital and age-old resources are woven into everyday collaborative practice. This approach extends how CSCW frames and mobilizes the material to recognize materials as compositional elements, surfaces and flows. It also contributes to conversations on digital materiality by emphasizing the temporality of material practice. Thus, I use the bookbinding workshop as a resource for understanding the ways materials, techniques, and relationships are continually re-bound in a digital age.

Author Keywords
Handwork, skill, apprenticeship, material culture, digital materiality, material, material practice, craft, physicality.

ACM Classification Keywords
K.4.0 Computers and Society: general.

General Terms
Design, Human Factors.

INTRODUCTION

"Materiality is our physical engagement with the world, our medium for inserting ourselves into the fabric of that world, and our way of constituting and shaping culture in an embodied and external sense." [25:11] —Lynn Meskell

"In employing this term [materiality] I am not just trying to discuss materials and their processual properties [...] I am attempting to engage with the manner in which the material properties of things profoundly affect human conduct, both enabling and empowering people's lives and constraining them."[40:3]—Christopher Tilley

As material culture scholars, Meskell and Tilley illustrate the concept of materiality does not entail one set of ideas or approaches to the study of culture. Indeed a homogeneous and coherent theory of materiality may never fully surface. Yet over the last few decades, the concept of materiality has gained considerable currency in a variety of fields, including anthropology, sociology, archeology, museum studies, and even CSCW. By emphasizing the *ordering* capacity of things—the ways in which things enable and constrain action—researchers have used the concept of materiality to avoid the idealism that people interact in the world however they wish, independent of non-human actors [40].

For CSCW the lack of definitional clarity has helped sustain two analytical shortcomings. For one, materiality is taken as tantamount to physicality, a conflation that assigns material to a distinct realm of embodied or tangible interaction. As recent work has begun to address [4,7,30], treating material practice as a special case of CSCW places materiality a long way from the digital and risks overlooking important players in collaborative work. This treatment exposes the *trope of immateriality* [4] wherein digital information is denied its material form.

A second concern for CSCW is how we have elevated artifacts over the material—"the stuff things are made of" [18:1]. While we have usefully highlighted the social and functional roles of artifacts (paper, books, tools) [6,8, 11,13,14,38], we have also overlooked the constituents (the grain of paper or shine of plastic) and their continued mixing, changing, combing, and dissolving over time. As Suchman [36] and others have noted, treating artifacts as uniform actors belies their emergent and constituent nature. This view advances an *object-bias* wherein materials are attended to as fixed forms rather than as heterogeneous enactments. As we will see, this bias conceals the temporality of material with which we might effectively conceptualize collaborative practice.

Bringing together perspectives from CSCW [7,30,36], cultural anthropology [18,19,26,40], and STS [2,20,28], I offer material practice as an alternative analytical lens on collaborative work. In particular, I extend anthropologist Tim Ingold's notion of *circulatory flows* [18]—"the generative fluxes of the world of materials"— to suggest that materials not only enable and constrain action, they also unfold through collaborations with people, workspaces, and even each other. As I elaborate later, this perspective acknowledges "material" as part of human interactions in three ways: (i) as compositional elements; (ii) as surfaces; and (iii) as spatial-temporal flows. Thus I weave together an

CSCW'12, February 11–15, 2012, Seattle, Washington, USA.

understanding of material arrangements and social practices to consider how materials come to frame and constitute human action and understanding. Through this lens material is understood as *more* than the physical, encompassing the breadth of interwoven constitutive elements, and underscoring their formative and transformative nature [18,19].

The material practice perspective makes two central contributions to the CSCW literature. First it broadens our understanding of collaborative work by taking into account a heterogeneity of interactions. For example, it allows us to recognize what might appear to be individual activity as constituently collaborative, developing among materials, people, and workspaces. Second, this view advances discussions of digital materiality by emphasizing the emergent and improvisational nature of material relations. Collaborations are not fixed in time but extend over a broad range of temporal and spatial configurations. Together these contributions provide conceptual scaffolding for moving beyond the trope of immateriality and object-bias to consider what Miller calls "the large compass of materiality" [26:4].

In this paper I examine material practices through a three-month bookbinding apprenticeship. By exhibiting prolonged engagements with digital and non-digital elements, bookbinding illuminates the technical particularities of material. This approach draws on autoethnographic methods in HCI (*e.g.*,[1,15]) and Lave's recent account of apprenticeship in critical ethnographic practice as "*learning to do what we are already doing*" [21:156]. I thus use my own binding practice to understand the ways seemingly individual craft practices are actually part of collaborations with the book, the workshop and the binding trade, more broadly. Through the construction of a book, I reveal how sensitivities to delicacy, flexibility and delay emerge through detailed engagements with, and awareness of, particular qualities of the book: the grain of leather, the stiffness of cord and the evenness of glue. From small adjustments of the hand, to the coordination and exchange of materials and tools, the accomplishment of each task rests on how digital and age-old resources are woven into everyday collaborative practice. It is by taking part in multiple material interactions that I began to uncover the temporal patterning of cooperative work.

BACKGROUND

To set the stage for an analysis of material practices, I briefly examine how CSCW and craft scholars perceive the material. Specifically, I review key themes in the CSCW literature of relevance to this work—*handwork*, *paper*, and *systems design*—and basic notions of embodiment and material engagement. This review is necessarily partial, but is meant to foreground issues of long-standing interest to CSCW that motivate our theorizing of the material.

CSCW & materiality

A rich and varied literature in CSCW is already oriented toward the close examination of the material settings for collaboration. This work examines how tools, artifacts, and machinery are brought to bear in the practical accomplishment of a range of cooperative tasks, including passing and handing surgical implements [38], operating a steel plant [8], the codification of soil samples [13], the arrangement of clutter in the home [39], and the communication of knitwear design specifications [11]. Here the material refers primarily to the tools of the trade—drills, suction instruments, slabs of steel. While these studies attribute agency to people, other work has viewed humans and non-humans as symmetrical social actors, the actor-network approach [20] being perhaps the most familiar to CSCW. This work begins to push at the boundaries of what is considered material, but it rarely looks beyond the artifact to its constitutive relations.

Closely related to this work, a second theme in CSCW concerns the use of books, paper and physical documents. This includes Harper and Randall's [14] descriptions of flight strips in air-traffic control, Berg's [3] discussions of paper as a bedside technology, Mackenzie's [21] analysis of task cards in programming, and Sellen and Harper's [34] discussion of paper in office work. Here materiality is not connected to the digital or infrastructural layers of CSCW. Rather materials are enrolled circuitously: when a particular communicative breakdown arises [23], a request for information is made [34], or defects in operations emerge [3]. Thus, the material qualities of practice are considered critical only to some aspects of action and not others.

A third strand of CSCW research consists of the designer's perspective on material. Here we find Büscher's [6] extensive research on what she terms *palpable computing* helpful for considering how computing might be "available to the senses" through visibility, deconstruction, understandability, coherence, stability, user control and difference. Dix and others [10,41] have similarly attended to "physicality" by exploring the way artifacts, tools, and appliances can inform the design of more "novel digital and hybrid digital–physical artefacts" [10:1]. Although the concept of *affordance* (*e.g.*,[27]) has usefully called attention to the ways in which physical objects structure and inform practice, it has been treated with some caution in CSCW, as it sensitizes designers to the sociomaterial dimensions of artifacts as a matter of a perception rather than a matter of situated material engagement [16,21]. These explorations of "digital-physical artifacts" also maintain an ontological separation between atoms and bits, furthering the familiar trope of immateriality.

Altogether this prior work highlights the breadth of interest in material as well as some challenges for its theorizing. A growing number of CSCW scholars are working to overcome these analytical hurdles by looking beyond individual artifactual actors. Rattenbury *et al.* [30], for example, address the temporality of the material by turning to the metaphor of plastic, a concept they use to describe how mobile devices are integrated into everyday patterns of activity. Plastic time describes the temporal and spatial rhythms of "unplanned, opportunistic" interaction and how they fit into surrounding events. Their work thus makes an appeal to concepts of materiality, which this work seeks to extend in more depth.

In another promising analysis, Chalmers and Galani offer the idea of "seamful interweaving"—the process by which perceivable differences between technological constituents become less important than "*the quality of interaction with the whole*" [7:244]. In their study of mixed reality system they found that people's understanding of the system emerged as part of interconnections between multiple media. Emphasizing the importance of heterogeneity, they suggest designers attend to the diversity of actors in different "modes" of interaction. The material practice approach advanced in this paper furthers this view by suggesting we not only design for *perceptions* of seamfulness; we should also design for *processes* of seamfulness: the ongoing capability of those seams to perform, mix and flow.

Materials in Craft and Design

Just beyond CSCW, several scholars of craft and design consider the kinds of social, emotional, and political processes at play in material interactions [9,21,29,31,32,35]. They observe structural qualities that are often not immediately "visible" and become accessible only through continued practice [17,21,32]. In a broad examination of embodied knowledge, Schön [32] develops the idea of *reflective conversation* with the materials to describe how the designer frames and imposes order on a given situation. Through a generative cycle of material interaction, the architectural studio becomes a craft-based learning environment that provides insights for educational reform. Materials are collaborators in the craft process, enabling artisans to construct, enact, and reaffirm their identities [21].

Furthering the centrality of material collaboration, McCullough embraces the possibilities of "traditional notions of practical, form-giving work" [24:19] by urging technology designers to become sensitive to the properties of their medium. In recent dispositions on craftwork in modern society, Sennett [35] and Crawford [9] similarly make the case for working more with the hands, extolling the virtues of "the spirit of craftsmanship" [35:286]. They maintain that professionals bear witness to an increasingly "rationalized" and management-driven workplace that inhibits artistic pride and accountability. However, whereas Sennett celebrates the open source movement in which he finds Linux programmers the modern embodiments of Medieval craftsmen, Crawford takes a hard stance against "cubicle life," implying that often "there isn't anything material being produced" [9:127]. In light of modern technologies, Sennett and Crawford thus take opposing sides regarding the trope of immateriality.

The present discussion of material practice confronts these debates by building on concepts of plasticity and "seamfulness," to conceptualize how heterogeneous interactions come about. By framing material as neither static nor uniform, we begin to move beyond the analytic separation of our digital actions from their material seams. In the following section I seek to further ground this approach in ethnographic work by turning to the practice of bookbinding.

METHOD

To study a binding workshop, I organized my ethnographic inquiry through an apprenticeship. This auto-ethnographic approach follows from prior CSCW research that employs the author as research subject by constructing a reflexive autobiographical account of the author's experience. This work includes examinations of a naval tactical command and control system [1] and embodiment while horseback riding [15]. My methodology draws most closely on anthropological approaches to the study of craft skill, such as Ingold's [17] sawing of wood, Prentice's [29] employment in a garment factory, and work by Lave [21] and others that suggests apprenticeship gives way to valuable insights into technical and social behavior. As compared to a course, apprenticeship imparts tacit skills (physical, economic, social) "through long-term observation and experience," [9:xii]. Anthropologists have long employed embodied subjectivity as an instrument of ethnographic inquiry, "theorizing not only what work *means* to people, but also what it *does* to them" [29:55]. Through continued engagement with materials and tools, my work became a gateway for my social inclusion in the workshop and in my understanding the particularities of the binders' practice.

I visited a bookbinding workshop in the UK for an average of three days per week over three months, and attended binding classes at a second workshop in the US one day per week for an additional four months. I also conducted one-to-two hour semi-structured interviews with 13 key participants: five professional binders, five hobbyist binders, and three customers. Informed by CSCW research where the observation of a given context has been given primacy over the talk about it [38], I built up an account of my practice by taking part in and documenting ongoing bookbinding activi-

Figure 1: (left to right) Sean prints gold letters on a spine; Ellen, an assistant, & Peter examine mottled pages; the binders at work.

ties through co-present and video-mediated observation. Handwritten jottings, digital photos and bits of bound and unbound material also served to record my interactions. In effect, I attended to not only what is seen or heard, but also to my own reflexive account of learning the practice.

In the following sections I introduce my fieldwork materials by following the trajectory of books in the bindery. There books develop from parts and pieces into encased archival objects through a series of discrete activities: folding, sawing, sewing, pressing, gluing, chopping, rounding, backing, lining, paring, staining, covering, and finishing. Performed sequentially, these activities also form the backbone of my exposition. Specifically, I work my way from the detailed use of materials and tools to their situated use in the collaborative environment of the workshop. I then show how each stage of binding has temporal and collaborative qualities, sometimes between the person, resource and tool, and sometimes with the wider setting of the workshop and those working in it. It is by examining these forms of collaboration that I open up some different ways of thinking about digital tool use and, in doing so, reflect on material practice.

FIELDWORK

On my first visit to the workshop I met Sean, the owner and operator of the bindery, and Peter, his long-time business partner.[1] While Sean is a loquacious character, Peter is more reserved and disciplined, attending to the task at hand and leaving most of the client relations to Sean. The materials around Sean seem to echo his liveliness. Book spines, tattered covers, and newly printed theses are stacked on tables and shelves, and colorful papers and cloths hang out of drawers. The bindery, divided into two rooms, enables Sean and Peter to work separately, following the long-practiced separation of *forwarding* (Peter's binding) from *finishing* (Sean's decoration).[2]

The workshop now represents a disappearing site in the book binding industry. Much like workshops of the 19th and early 20th centuries, it mostly serves local patrons and bookbinding hobbyists—enthusiasts seeking to learn more about the trade. Despite the continued presence of these visitors, the bulk of the workshop's income comes from a neighboring university where library books need constant repair and student theses require binding.

Within the last five years a few things have changed. New binding jobs have decreased due to a proliferation of online self-publishing companies (*e.g.* lulu.com or shutterfly.com), which offer cheap products in small quantities and in less time than hand binding. It is through these developments that journals, once the workshop's "bread and butter" work, became almost entirely digitally produced. In addition to new books, repair and restoration work has declined by virtue of a downturn in clientele, such as secondhand book dealers who face increasing competition by e-reader and online book markets.

Alongside these shifts, new tools have entered the workspace. A laptop connected to wireless Internet gives Sean immediate access to business inquires and customer correspondence. Word processing software enables the design and printing of labels for book spines. And a mobile phone service provides a means of coordinating jobs in between personal tasks. If one binder misses a call on his phone, the call is automatically routed to the other binder's phone, and vice versa, until the call is picked up. This pragmatic digital presence extends to the workshop's website, which describes the binders' expertise and workmanship. It also led me to the workshop.

Beginnings of a Book

To consider the dynamics of material practice, I first turn to a passage from my field notes that describes the seemingly individual activity of sawing along the edge of folded and nested pages to create the book spine (see Figure 2).

> *I insert my saw into the spine of the text block, angling it backward as I pull it across the sections of the spine. I stop. The saw does not want to move back up the sections. Instead, it wavers, and the sections waver with it. I readjust the saw in my hand, curving my thumb around top of the handle, aligning my body over the block. I pull down, hit the bottom of the spine, and reinsert the teeth at the top once more. I repeat: pull down, realign, pull down. Aware that I am only sawing in one direction, I try to move the saw up the groove on the block. The block begins to wobble, and I stop. "Not deep enough," Sean says, leaning down to check how far the groove has come. I reinsert the saw at the top and apply more downward force. The groove looks thick and contorted; far messier than the thin mark Sean created a few inches to the left.*

As this excerpt suggests, my experience sawing into a book spine follows a coarsely defined trail, reflecting what Ingold [17] has called the *processional* quality of tool use in reference to sawing a plank of wood. As an intervention, sawing is one of the first steps in bookbinding: grooves are created along the edge of pages that will be sewn along the spine. As a collaborative process, sawing creates holes for other hands to insert a needle and thread. As a spatial-temporal process, sawing becomes a successive stage in the lifecycle of the book: catalogues produced by a company, collected by an enthusiast, and now arranged by me for rebinding.

Figure 2: Sawing along edge of folded and nested pages that are held together in a wooden press.

[1] This and all following names of individuals are pseudonyms.

[2] Some empirical materials have been presented in [31].

In this respect, sawing begins to unveil a set of different relations around handwork practice of relevance to CSCW. It is easy to see this detailed engagement as individual, i.e., cutting through thin layers of brittle coated paper involves two hands and a saw. Yet, as we will soon observe, sawing reveals itself as part of an intricate array of social and material activities beyond this immediate context. Sawing presents a possibility: the beginnings of a book.

Materials

Materials reveal their itinerary to the binder as part of, not separate from, the unfolding of skill. After creating saw grooves, *cords* (thick string) are inserted along those grooves and a needle and thread pass around the cords to secure the gathered pages (see Figure 3a). In the next example from my field notes, Peter demonstrates how to fray the ends of cords so that they eventually lie flat under the cover:

> *Peter frays the cords that adhere the sections of the 18th century book. As his knife moves along the cord, he is sensitive to how his thumb creates resistance with the knife, grooming the material down to a thin, flexible form. As it is worked, the crisp end thus gradually looses its shape, turning flat, malleable, and increasingly thin. "Feel the ends," he instructs, taking a moment to let me rub the material. The cord has a silky texture. As Peter continues, a small cloud of beige material builds around the knife, obscuring my view of his hands. Peter stops again to fold the end of the cord over the book's spine, pressing it flat against the bare cover board. Some fuzz has fallen to the floor and I can see the cord's remains: a fine wisp. The once tight, brittle form is now a delicate lock of thread. Peter hands me the knife: "Your turn."*

Fraying a cord is one of the first techniques I learned at the bindery because it highlights some of the ways in which materials hold the book together. On older books, cords are used to secure the pages by creating thick bands along the spine, which threads are sewn around (see Figure 3a). To ensure the book's strength and smooth look, the cord's middle must remain strong (securing the pages), while its edges must become weak (so that they lie flat and imperceptible under a cover board). As such, the cord's properties must be changed: its round shape turned flat, its brittleness made smooth and flexible, and its solid mass converted into a cloud of fuzz. Peter is attending to each of these changes by pressing his thumb between the cord and paring knife, a small hand tool used to thin leather knife (Figure 3b). He concurrently monitors the knife's movement and the cord's tactile qualities to respecify the book's look and durability.

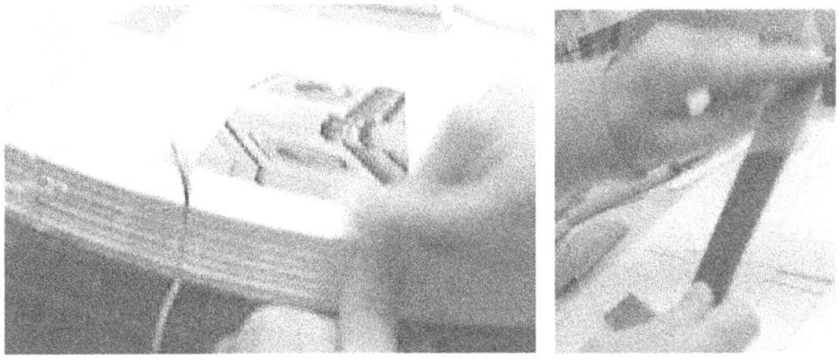

Figure 3: (a) Fray a cord inserted into sawn grooves. (b) paring knife: the metal blade is uniquely worn in by the binder.

The ability to manipulate material is therefore *not* an all-encompassing skill. A material may give the binder hints as to how it should be sawed, sewed or pressed, but it will challenge and surprise the binder, too. Consequently, much like Schön's [32] notion of *reflective conversation,* materials are often described as *having a say* in the binding process; and sometimes they even need convincing. "*Persuade the sections out*" was Peter's way of telling me to separate the sections of the text block while I rounded a spine. Similarly, when an assistant wanted to set letters on a spine, he asked: "*Does it want to be capital?*" Thus, though materials are inherently oriented toward performing one way or another, binders can negotiate a way forward through careful use of tools.

Yet Peter's work involves additional concerns beyond the book. He is aware of my presence, asking me to take part in actively monitoring the cord myself. He is also attending to his next job (a stack of theses that await new bindings) and the subsequent work for this book (pressing and then handing it to Sean). Fraying cords involves interweaving these seemingly discrete activities. Like the sawing that came before, it is not a solitary event; rather it is entrenched in the broader spatiotemporal arrangements in the workplace.

Before the next stage of binding, let us first briefly consider the relevance of this work to CSCW. For starters, we see how the binders engage the particularities of material. By identifying the delicate or intricate we might similarly interact with specificities of the digital. When we talk of e-readers, for example, to what extent do we invoke the metal case, the processor, the e-reader software, the digital file, or all of the above? The ambiguity of these terms and how we refer to our computational devices, suggests an ambivalence toward their digital particularities and an understanding of the digital as metaphor [11]. Designing for how materials affect our interactions means attending to the material properties of digital content: the ways digital elements mutate and degrade over time, how they get encoded and stored as well as how people fine-tune their configurations.

We also recall from the interplay between knife and leather that materials have a "say" in the process. The materials tell us they are not passively confined to the things made from them but have their own propensities for mixing, mutating, swelling, or shrinking. In this sense, materials are not imbued with agency but exhibit agency by rising above other material activity. The cloud of fuzz is no longer a cord but a part of the formation of a flexible and flat wisp. This suggests we consider how digital materials have an equal say in work practices, and how our interactions sometimes preclude listening. In the following section, we see that how tools also figure into these material assemblies sheds further light on the collaborative possibilities of human skill.

Tools

The tools of bookbinding tend to resemble common household implements: scissors, knives, rulers, hammers, and so on. They also reflect the breadth of techniques involved in

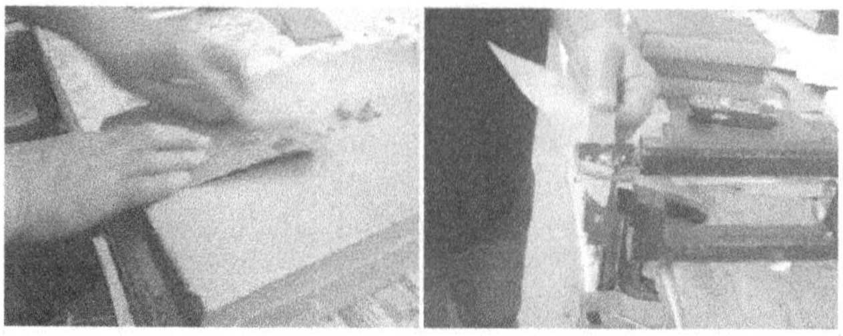

Figure 4. Using (a) "paring knife" and (b) "paring machine"

binding, much like Svensson *et al.*'s ecology of surgical instruments "suited to the specifics of particular interventions and procedures" [38:44]. For example, the bookbinding hammer has a rounded rather than flat face so that it does not indent the paper (while "*rounding*" a spine). Each tool is put to use in order to accomplish a particular task—sharpen a corner, trim an edge, fray a cord. Next we see how a round brush is used to apply glue to a piece of cloth that will soon be attached to the book cover.

> *"Splunge!" Peter instructs, glancing over my shoulder. "Let your brush dance across the page." My left hand (holding the cloth) jiggles with each paint stroke. I move the brush more quickly, but it pulls at the surface. "Hold the page still. Don't let it move," Peter directs. I readjust the position of the cloth with my right forefinger and continue to paint, paying close attention to the thickness of the glue across the surface. Peter's voices reemerges: "not too thick!" The glue refuses uniformity. The brush coats parts of the surface that I was not aiming to cover, unevenly distributing the glue across the surface. "Here, here and here," Peter points, calling attention to bits of dry cloth, areas where my brush had not traveled. Frustrated, I scrape the surface with the brush, changing my brush marks from dots into lines. I carefully lift the cloth and remove the newsprint below.*

In the above excerpt, glue is worked into a piece of cloth with the goal of creating an evenly coated surface. Peter urges me to use the brush as a spring, allowing the bristles to push back at my hand and my hand to respond in kind. This rhythmic motion, or "*splunging*," disperses the glue one gesture at a time in even dot-like patterns. When I use the brush as paintbrush instead, smearing the canvas with long strokes, the surface becomes rough and uneven, eventually resulting in visible bumps along the cover. In Peter's words, such work is akin to "*building a castle on top of sand*": the next steps of the binding process may be executed flawlessly, but the book will still collapse.

Here my interactions with the brush, glue and book reveal something more about Peter's direction. By pointing out the look of the surface, the feel of the spring, and the pace of my movement, Peter is sensitizing me to the various elements of binding. Like the fraying and sawing that came before, *splunging* is entangled with the next stages of binding as well as my role in the workshop. Once again we observe my brushwork as not a static or solitary achievement, but as embedded in materials distributed over time. In this routine activity we find the ingredients of intra-activity [2].

These apparently simple instruments, and their use while binding, also highlight the ways in which different tools become more or less tool-like through their situated use in collaborative environments. While the *tool* has long been contrasted with the *machine* [24], neither concept refers to a particular set of devices in the bindery. Rather, these concepts are evocative of certain values embedded in different devices at different times. Recall Peter's paring knife (Figure 3b)—the tool he used to fray the cords along the book spine. The knife is a standalone metal blade designed for thinning (or "*paring*") leather, *e.g.*, that will cover a box or book. The *paring machine* (Figure 4b) is also designed for thinning leather, but it is attached to a bench, requiring the binder to move the material rather than the tool. Despite its name, the paring machine has few conventionally machine-like qualities: it is simple and lightweight, has no moving parts, and is not mechanically or electrically powered. For a novice, the machine is more difficult to use than the knife and cannot fray cords or sprinkle paint. The machine serves one purpose, remains in one spot, and is one of a kind in the workshop. The knife, by contrast, serves multiple purposes, moves around the workshop, and is one knife among many. Each binder not only has his own knife, but the metal blade is often so thoroughly worn in that using another binder's knife is uncomfortable or infeasible.

The difference between machinery and hand-tools is thus attributed to how they enable or constrain the specialized needs of the binder. The machine designed for cutting large stacks of paper (appropriately called a *guillotine*), serves additional purposes, such as handing off material (see Figure 5). By virtue of its weight and size, the guillotine becomes a stable and predictable location in the bindery, making its flat surface suitable for exchanging unfinished books. Sean stacks sewn books for Peter to re-cover while Peter stacks bound books for Sean to decorate. Yet this use of the

Figure 5: The guillotine is used for handing-off unfinished books between the binders (left) and cutting the pages (right).

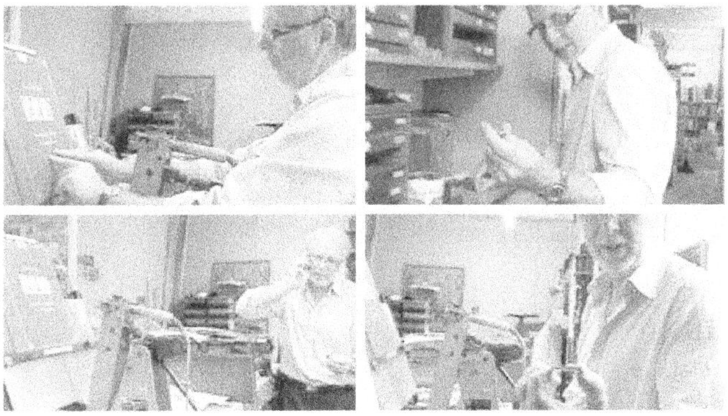

Figure 6: Sean arranges decoration for an album cover.

guillotine is transitory because the machine is frequently required for cutting paper. Like the paring instruments, the guillotine emphasizes the layered spatio-temporal quality of collaborative work.

It is the *un-sharable, mobile* character of the paring knife, and the *sharable, immobile* character of the paring machine and guillotine, that suggest some interesting possibilities for flexibility and stability in CSCW. Designing digital tools for un-sharability might entail the design of software that can become "worn in": the more it is used the more it becomes assigned to one person or another. Designing for immobile devices involves adjusting material properties (weight, size, plasticity) in response to a given situation: a device that changes its weight based on human proximity—e.g., becoming stationary when it nears a small child. By attending to the temporal aspects of tooling, we might rethink sociomaterial possibilities for flexibility and ownership.

Workshop

After binding, but before delivery, a book is given to a "finisher"—the person who applies text and decorative elements to the cover (such as clasps and gold leaf). Most often forwarding is done by Sean, who decorates the cover while keeping an eye and ear on the work around him. In the next example, Sean is deciding how he wants to decorate a wedding album:

> *Sean: Oh I'll—I'll tell you what we use. No, no, no, no, no. They're lovers, they're in love. They're getting married. We need something unique. [Phone rings] Good morning, [removed] binders... Yeah we can do, no problems at all. Yeah, we can do that.... Well I'm here 'til half past seven tonight... Friday I'm here 'til have past four, so we're here quarter to say quarter to 8 til half past, til half past four . Okay, super, thank you. Bye. Like that? Fancy that?*
>
> *Me: That's nice.*
>
> *Sean: Of course it is. And they're flying away together!*

In this typical exchange between Sean and me, Sean is able to flexibly integrate a range of activities into the task at hand: a new customer's phone call, an old customer's wedding album, and my (dubious) assistance to this work (see Figure 6). Sean points to the location on the cover he wants printed, removes a few decorative metal elements from the drawer, and hands me both to consider. When his mobile phone rings, this flow of activity is not broken; instead his humor inserts pause and delay. The pause reflects other workshop arrangements such as how the laptop is pulled out from under the bench to check email at 9:00, 11:00, and 1:00 each day. Email, or as Sean aptly calls it, "the post," is limited to certain places and times even though wireless Internet is continually available throughout the workshop. This somewhat paradoxical combination of limitation and access, efficiency and delay, is critical to preserving Sean's awareness of workshop activities.

Sean's work at the blocking machine also reveals how coordination takes place among actors inside the workshop as well as outside it: the customers and the standardized production of decorative metal elements. This spatial distribution of work is evident on several counts, as when Sean runs into trouble while using word-processing software to create a new label for an older book:

> *Sean finds a serif font to match the original label, noting, "it just looks right." After typing the title, he struggles to find a tool that allows him to add a line underneath it and tells me that his son usually helps. As he talks, he moves the mouse over a "tools" menu, then "format" menu, then the "tools" menu again. Finding nothing, he returns to the keyboard and inserts dashes one by one. The next day Sean shows me the printed label. Individual dashes have been replaced with a solid line and the font is bold and modern, no longer matching the original book. I ask Sean why the font has changed. With some delight, he explains that his wife fixed the label on their home computer that evening, a computer with different fonts.*

Here we find Sean is less familiar with the software than other instruments, such as the blocking machine. He has trouble finding digital resources to create a desired effect (the solid line) and enrolls human resources outside the workshop to help out (his son and his wife). But people are not the only actors shaping the printed result. Sean encodes his work in a particular file format (.doc) that depends on font files stored on his laptop. When Sean copies the file to his home computer, it is unable to access the same font, and instead links to another. The .doc file therefore spatially stabilizes some aspects of Sean's work and not others.

As we assess implications for CSCW, we find a few key aspects of Sean's workshop activity. First, his insertion of pauses and delay inspires other ways of thinking about the pace of workplace activity. For example, enabling our email

Figure 7: Sean checks email at his computer.

clients to receive mail for certain durations and times (hours of the day, days of the week) suggests ways we might accommodate a range of undervalued actions, such as lingering, hesitation, dwelling, and patience. We also find that the spatial stabilization and visibility of digital font shapes Sean's desired results. Similarly, the encoding of data in JPEG file formats entails perceptually indistinguishable changes that result in irretrievably lost information [4]. Digital information thus deals with similar material constraints to that of leather or glue—in this case constraints of storage. The limitations then offer different possibilities for how the digital is produced, maintained and shared. Like leather and cords, digital properties transform over time, sometimes becoming unusable. Given Sean's restorative intentions, collaborative software might also selectively visualize this complexity—indicating cross-platform shifts and the spatial stability of dependencies and file encodings.

Before we leave the workshop, consider one last concern. Each instrument in the workshop perilously left around the bindery, including the laptop, accumulates grease, dirt, paint, and even intricate patterns of glue (see Figure 8). Though visitors often comment on the beauty of these marks, the binders see them as simple traces of production. The temporal quality to these traces, though seemingly inconsequential, is central to how materials effectively communicate their provenance to the binders. By considering the interplay between different material elements—how work environments leave traces on materials, which reciprocally leave traces on the materials themselves—we might produce more meaningful interaction histories that consider the distinctive rhythms of collaborative work.

THE BINDERY AS COLLABORATIVE SYSTEM

We have seen so far how the bookbindery is an archetypical workshop, inviting us to reconsider how we understand the long-term prospects for CSCW technology—in both non-office work environments and our own practices as systems designers. The unfolding of skill occurs as materials reveal their itinerary to people through, and as part of, collaborations with the workshop environment. But what does this mean for CSCW? How might this formulation of tools, as something materially salient but socially unremarkable, enable us to understand computing?

To begin with, we found the binders engage the particularities of material and those materials have a "say" in the process. Becoming sensitive to delicacy of a digital file, like a cord or a piece of leather, might involve identifying the fragile, or the intricate, by acknowledging the interplay between constituent computational processes. This activity illustrates *material-material collaborations*, or how consistent elements (digital and non-digital) collaborate to convey their intricacies, such as frailty, firmness or pushiness.

When tools come into play, we saw how they demonstrate a bounded sharable and mobile character that affects their flexibility and use in the workplace. The specific limitations of tools (the unsharable knife and immobile machine) suggest design opportunities for the spatially inflexible or temporally unsharable wherein a digital tool is assigned to one person or another through continued wear and use. This observation suggests taking seriously how different elements become more or less tool-like through their situated integration with people in *material-human collaborations*.

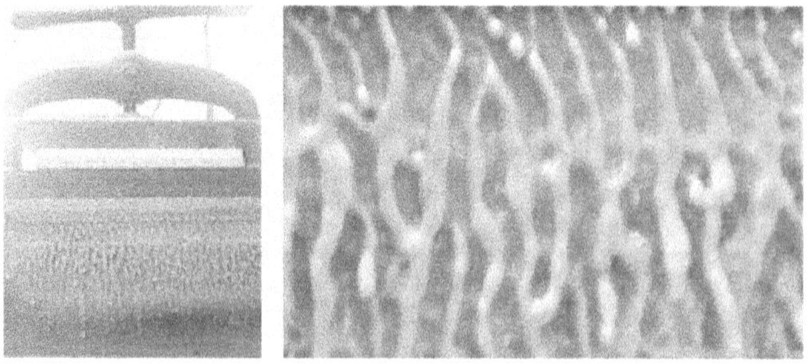

Figure 8: Traces of glue left on the side of the press

As we examined the larger rhythms of workshop activity, we observed the patterned pauses of integrating different resources into work—both inside and outside the workshop. Like Sean's metaphor of the "post," this suggests we might design for the productive combination of limitation and access by enabling email clients or social networking sites to reveal materials for particular times and durations. We also found that the degree to which these materials and their properties stabilize emerges through ongoing practice. As the materials move and interact they leave traces on their surroundings workspaces, which equally shape the materials themselves. Digital tools may allow for the communication of varying amounts of inscription and stability. By tracing material across time, they could foreground the generative processes and evocative histories of interaction. This productive interplay between the workspace and its material constituents exposes *material-workspace collaborations*.

These multiple forms of collaboration that emerged in the bindery prompt us to think critically about the temporal patterning of work and how our materials help to configure their unfolding rhythms. As our personal and professional landscapes exhibit increasing signs of busyness, how we perceive the passage of time might be shaped not only by the design of our software or services, but also by the traces they leave behind. Instead of distinguishing the digital from the physical, this work suggests we consider the vast range of material practices. What might appear to be an individual activity—Peter's cord fraying or Sean's typesetting—is tightly interwoven with the tools, people, and workspaces with which one works. Collaborations are not fixed in time but consisted of a spread of events. In the diverse practices of binding we find a different view of work—one that emphasizes the active processional character of material.

THE CIRCULATORY FLOWS OF MATERIAL PRACTICE

In sum, this work demonstrates how material continues to be a valuable resource for reflecting on the design and use of technologies to support collaboration. It is as information technologies become part of our daily lives that the coordination of digital materials becomes increasingly important, particularly in such relatively non-digital contexts as a handcraft workshop. How we consider such technologies in light of human-material collaborations ultimately affects the cultural histories woven into the things we produce. As designers, we must imagine new techniques for coping with modern rhythms of collaboration. In order to better account for these practices, let us now follow Orlikowski [28] in considering the multiple roles that digital technology as material might play. As she points out,

> *It should be quickly evident that a considerable amount of materiality is entailed in every aspect of organizing, from the visible forms — such as bodies, clothes, rooms, desks, chairs, tables, buildings, vehicles, phones, computers, books, documents, pens, and utensils — to the less visible flows — such as data and voice networks, water and sewage infrastructures, electricity, and air systems. [28:1436]*

With few exceptions (*e.g*, [37]), CSCW has approached the material through objects, its most "visible form," rarely framing material practice as anything other than artifactual practice. Yet as we saw with the blocking machine and laptop, not only do tools, workspaces and people influence the work at hand, they have collaborative qualities through which meaningful skills are produced. But as I type at the keyboard now, where is the material? Is it the keyboard and mouse, the cursor, the operating system, the sentence structures and words?

The answer this work suggests is that each of these components is material. Not only am I interacting with the physical constraints of my environment (keyboard, laptop, chair, room, air), my work is highly circumscribed by the operating system, the software, and the data and meaning around which particular functions (such as copy/paste or send) are put to use. Moreover, as Levy aptly notes, *"digital materials, too, need to be properly tended*" [21:119]. For instance, even when written, this document will continue to evolve and dissolve as it passes through many hands and forms.

Materials in this sense are not stable. They are instead interwoven with the "generative fluxes" of human and nonhuman interaction [18]. To overcome the limitations of our object-bias and its trope of immateriality, I propose we approach materials in three ways. First, we should understand materials as *compositional elements*—the matter and substances that make up our environments (presses, leather, glue, word-processing software). This attribute exposes collaborations among constituent properties, *e.g.*, the interplay between fluctuating properties of the cord (round and flat, solid and wispy). Second, we should recognize materials as *surfaces*—the interfaces at which different substances interact and combine (benches, cutting machines, digitally encoded dependencies). As surfaces, materials facilitate interaction between different elements, *e.g.*, the guillotine's emergence as a medium for exchange. Third, we should view material as caught up in *spatial-temporal flows*—textures of activity continually reconfigured across space and time. Materials as flows stress the circulatory character of their properties wherein materials entwine with workspaces to become the medium through which elements move and mix, *e.g.*, the word processing file did not stabilize all elements of work but revealed the temporal and spatial instability of its properties. As such, materials are active inhabitants whose properties transpire and mutate depending on the currents of surrounding activity [18].

While I have referred to "digitally-mediated" practice in this paper, I have done so with a grain of salt. It is through this lens, or the language of mediation, that we begin to loose sight of the emergent character of materials and their diverse arrangement in social practice. Tools should not be designed to passively facilitate or streamline the process between what one intends to do and what one does. Such technological mediation does not play out so smoothly in practice. As has been long discussed within the CSCW community [36] plans for tool use do not exist purely in the mind, but are enacted and realigned through practice. Furthering this view, the present material practice perspective suggests that we consider how not only artifacts, but also data and digital tools, perform as materials—how they resist and accommodate action as well as form, transform, and evolve.

Thus the tools through which people configure objects are not uniform but made up of different active interstitial elements. In a recent analysis, Schmidt and Wagner compare different accounts of material in CSCW to argue that they often presuppose a "mentalist" notion of artifacts as "*simple vehicles of 'information'*" [33:1]. One focus of their critique is activity theory as understood through Vygotsky's concept of "psychological tools." They claim that through the reification of mental processes "*any notion of materiality is eradicated from the concept of tool*" [33:3]. Looking to material practice, we no longer view materials as inert substrates stably inscribed with perceived characteristics.

This study instead urges us to attend to the temporality of material. It is in the emergent patterns of material activity that we recognize the formative techniques and practices that hold lasting personal and cultural value. Returning to the generative currents of practice, this approach extends our understanding of collaborative work—dismantling digital and non-digital binaries, and drawing attention to the "circulatory flows" of practical work [18]. From raw stuff to the broader landscapes of interaction, we find that the digital is no exception. In Blanchette's words, "*Computing, it turns out, is material through and through*" [4:1].

ACKNOWLEDGEMENTS

I would like to send a special thanks to Alex Taylor for his intellectual mentorship. I am also grateful to the researchers at MSR Cambridge for their support, Melissa Mazmanian, Morgan Ames, Jenna Burrell, Silvia Lindtner, Susan Wyche and my anonymous reviewers for their feedback, and my prodigious participants for welcoming me into their world.

REFERENCES

1. Aoki, P. M. "Back stage on the front lines: perspectives and performance in the combat information center." *Proceedings CHI'07*. (2007) 717–726.

2. Barad, K. "Posthumanist performativity: Toward an understanding of how matter comes to matter." *Signs*. (2003) 801–831.
3. Berg, M. "Lessons from a dinosaur: Mediating IS research through an analysis of the medical record." *Proceedings of the IFIP TC9 WG9*. (2000) 487–506.
4. Blanchette, J. F. "A material history of bits." *Journal of the American Society for Information Science and Technology,* 62,6.(2011) 1042–1057.
5. Brown, J. S, and P. Duguid. *The social life of information*. Harvard Business Press. (2002)
6. Buscher, M., M. Kristensen, and P. H Mogensen. "Making the future palpable: notes from a major incidents future laboratory." *International Journal of Emergency Management* 5(1). (2008) 145–163.
7. Chalmers, M., and A. Galani. "Seamful interweaving: heterogeneity in the theory and design of interactive systems." *Proceedings of DIS '04.* (2004) 243–252
8. Clarke, K. et al. "Dependable red hot action." *Proceedings ECSCW'03*. (2003) 61–80.
9. Crawford, M. B. *Shop class as soulcraft: An inquiry into the value of work*. Penguin Press. (2009)
10. Dix, A. "First steps in physicality." Preface to Physicality. (2006) 257–274.
11. Dourish, P. and M. Mazmanian. "Media as Material: Information Representations as Material Foundations for Organizational Practice." Working Paper for the *Third International Symposium on Process Organization Studies,* Corfu, Greece. (2011)
12. Eckert, C. "The communication bottleneck in knitwear design: Analysis and computing solutions." *CSCW* 10,1 (2001) 29–74.
13. Goodwin, C. "Professional vision." *American anthropologist* 96, 3, (1994) 606–633.
14. Harper, R., and D. Randall. *Rogues in the Air: An Enthnomethodology of Conflict in Socially Organised Airspace*. (1992)
15. Höök, K. "Transferring qualities from horseback riding to design." *Proceedings of NordiCHI'10*. (2010) 226–235.
16. Hutchins, E., and T. Klausen. *Distributed cognition in an airline cockpit*. Cambridge University Press, New York, NY. (1996)
17. Ingold, T. "Walking the plank: meditations on a process of skill." *Defining technological literacy: towards an epistemological framework New York, Palgrave Macmillan*. (2006)
18. Ingold, T. "Materials against materiality." *Archaeological Dialogues* 14, 1. (2007) 1-16.
19. Joyce, R. A. (2008a), 'Practice in and as Deposition', in B. Mills and W. Walker (eds), *Memory Work: Archaeologies of Material Practices*. Santa Fe: School of Advanced Research Press, 25-39.
20. Latour, B. Drawing things together. In M. Lynch & S. Woolgar (Eds.), *Representations in scientific practice*. Cambridge, MA: MIT Press. (1990) 19–68.
21. Lave, J. 2011. *Apprenticeship in critical ethnographic practice*. University of Chicago Press.
22. Levy, D. M. *Scrolling forward: Making sense of documents in the digital age*. Arcade Publishing. (2001)
23. Mackenzie, A., and S. Monk. "From cards to code: How extreme programming re-embodies programming as a collective practice." *CSCW* 13, 1 (2004) 91–117.
24. McCullough, M.. *Abstracting craft: The practiced digital hand*. The MIT press. (1998)
25. Meskell, L. *Object Worlds in Ancient Egypt: Material biographies past and present*. Berg Publishers (2004)
26. Miller, D. *Materiality*. Duke University Press. (2005)
27. Norman, D. A. *The psychology of everyday things*. Basic books. (1988)
28. Orlikowski, W. J. "Sociomaterial practices: Exploring technology at work." *Organization studies* 28,9, (2007) 1435-1448.
29. Prentice, R. "Knowledge, Skill, and the Inculcation of the Anthropologist: Reflections on Learning to Sew in the Field." *Anthropology of Work Review* 29, 3 (2008) 54–61.
30. Rattenbury, T., D. Nafus, and K. Anderson. "Plastic: a metaphor for integrated technologies." *Proceedings of Ubicomp '08*. (2008) 232–241.
31. Rosner, D.K., and A.S. Taylor. "Antiquarian answers: book restoration as a resource for design." *Proceedings of CHI'11* (2011) 2665–2668.
32. Schön, D. A. "The architectural studio as an exemplar of education for reflection-in-action." *Journal of Architectural Education (1984-)* 38, 1 (1984) 2–9.
33. Schmidt, K. and I. Wagner. "Coordinative artifacts in architectural planning." *Proceedings of COOP '02*. (2003) 257-274.
34. Sellen, Abigail J., and Richard H. R. Harper. *The myth of the paperless office*. MIT Press. (2003)
35. Sennett, Richard. *The craftsman*. Yale University Press. (2008)
36. Suchman, L. A. *Plans and situated actions*. Cambridge University Press. (1987)
37. Star, S.L., and K. Ruhleder. "Steps towards an ecology of infrastructure: complex problems in design and access for large-scale collaborative systems." *Proceedings of CSCW'94* (1994) 253–264.
38. Svensson, M., C. Heath, and P. Luff. "Instrumental action: the timely exchange of implements during surgical operations." *ECSCW'07* (2007) 41–60.
39. Swan, L., A.S. Taylor, and R. Harper. "Making place for clutter and other ideas of home." *ACM TOCHI* 15, 2, (2008) 1–24.
40. Tilley, C. "Materiality in materials." *Archaeological Dialogues* 14, 1, (2007) 16–20.
41. Vyas, D. M., D. K. J. Heylen, A. Nijholt, and A. Popescu-Belis. "Physicality and Cooperative Design." in, *MLMI 2008, Utrecht, The Netherlands, September 8-10, (*2008) 325.

Beyond Data Sharing: Artifact Ecology of a Collaborative Nanophotonics Research Centre

Gerard Oleksik
Instrata Ltd.
12 Warkworth Street
Cambridge, CB1 1EG, UK
geoleksik@instrata.co.uk

Natasa Milic-Frayling
Microsoft Research
7 J J Thompson Avenue
Cambridge, CB3 0FB, UK
natasamf@microsoft.com

Rachel Jones
Instrata Ltd.
12 Warkworth Street
Cambridge, CB1 1EG, UK
racheljones@instrata.co.uk

ABSTRACT
Scientific communities have long been concerned with the design and implementation of effective infrastructures for data access and collaborative scientific work. Recent studies have shown an increase in collaborative data generation and reuse. However, further improvements require a deeper understanding of the social and technological circumstances under which they emerge. To that effect we conduct *in-situ* observation study of a Nanophotonics Research Centre. We consider the *artifact ecology* that evolved from the Centre's common experimentation and data platform, the scientific practices, and the intricate interactions with digital artifacts that arise from the researchers' activities. We uncover the use of progress *summaries* for collaborative data interpretation and knowledge sharing. By studying this reputable collaborative scientific environment we (1) identified the factors that led to its functional and effective artifact ecology and (2) propose expansions of tools and services to improve it further. The latter include effective support for contextual search, browsing, and flexible viewing of information artifacts based on relevant parameters and properties.

Author Keywords
Data sharing, collaborative work, artifact ecology, information management, eScience.

ACM Classification Keywords
H.5.m. Information interfaces and presentation (e.g., HCI): Miscellaneous. H.5.3 Group and Organization Interfaces: Computer-supported cooperative work.

General Terms
Human Factors; Design.

INTRODUCTION
Over the past decades we have witnessed rapid adoption of digital technologies in all aspects of human endeavor which continue to shape individual and collaborative work practices. Scientific environments are no exception. Contemporary empirical methods have led to an explosion in 'digital objects' which are now considered primary forms of evidence in the discovery process [10]. Various scientific disciplines are producing repositories of unprecedented size and complexity. Thus, a considerable effort has been put in providing infrastructure for data sharing and collaboration. Advances in cyber infrastructure, collaboratories, and eScience have led to a notable increase in collaborative data generation and reuse [3, 6, 13]. However, further progress is dependent on supporting not only data access but the entire process of scientific inquiry. That includes a range of individual and team practices, from running experiments to preparing scientific publications. Through that process, the collected data is continuously sifted and imbued with meaning, changing its form and becoming embodied in various types of artifacts such as sketches, inscriptions, notes, records, and intermediary reports that enable communication and reuse of information.

While most of the studies have considered the role of specific artifacts, such as the lab notebook [8, 15, 16] or shared electronic databases [4], less attention has been given to the inter-relationship among the scientific artifacts that emerge throughout the scientific discovery and knowledge sharing. Similarly, the studies of collaboratories examine the support for data access, contextualization through metadata and annotation, and social processes of real-time collaborative analysis and brainstorming [6]. However, they do not seek to understand the social and technological circumstances of the artifacts that emerge during such interaction, nor the contexts of their creation and the roles they fulfill.

We propose observations of the entire *artifact ecology* that arises in a scientific environment. The artifact ecology encompasses the technical infrastructure, tools, individuals, and interactions that evolve through the exchange of digital artifacts in a specific locality or a digital space. We illustrate this notion through a case study that involves *in situ* observations of a leading high-tech Nanophotonics Research Centre (NPRC). Since its inception in 2007, the Centre continues to embrace information technologies to optimize scientific processes. The recognition of the

Centre's success and its strong orientation towards collaborative projects, made it particularly attractive for the study.

Our analysis of NPRC shows that, even within a collaborative environment that comprises highly cohesive teams, one has to provide beyond simple access to common data and metadata. Indeed, it is essential to support effective interaction around a chain of digital artifacts that emerge during the scientific process and fulfill various needs of individuals and teams. This is exemplified by the progress *summaries* and practices of collective data interpretation that were embraced by the NPRC researchers and form an essential part of the NPRC intricate artifact ecology. Furthermore, through the study we uncover the factors that shape this effective artifact ecology and outline a set of recommendations for increasing its utility. We suggest including contextual search, browsing, interlinking, and viewing of the data and artifacts based on different context parameters and properties. In this regard, the study plays an important role, underscoring that efforts in developing shared scientific infrastructures and collaborative environments must take the view of the entire artifact ecology rather technology or practices alone.

In the following section we discuss the relevant insights from the literature on scientific practices and artifacts. We follow by describing the study methodology and discuss the artifact ecology at NPRC. We elaborate on the factors that shaped the collaborative environment and design recommendations for improving its effectiveness. We conclude with reflections on future research directions.

BACKGROUND AND RELATED RESEARCH

Artifact ecology could be considered as a specific instance of the *information ecology*, defined by [11] as '*a system of people, practices, values and technologies in a particular local environment*'. Introducing information ecology was important to move away from the prevalent preoccupation with *information technologies* to a more comprehensive view of the entire ecosystem where technology plays a specific role but is, by no means, the only factor. While the change to the ecology metaphor was helpful to broaden the scope of considerations, the reference to 'information' turned out to be rather under defined. By observing that information is, to a large degree, encoded and transferred through information artifacts, we propose a more concrete notion that enables us to describe and study contemporary scientific environments—the *artifact ecology*. We focus on understanding the ecology of artifacts that arise from a specific technical infrastructure and working practices of scientists who produce, share, reuse, and interact through digital artifacts.

This orientation provides a good anchor for empirical studies. We fully recognize the importance of information exchanges through verbal or online communication that is less traceable. Thus, we adopt observation methods that are comprehensive but focus on the characteristics and factors involved in developing artifact ecologies that are effective in collaborative scientific settings. In the following section we first review the insights about scientific practices and environments from related research.

Scientific Practices and Information Artifacts

Van House et al. [18] state that '*scientific practices are designed to translate local knowledge into global, personal into universal*'. This process of universalizing knowledge is an inherently social enterprise. Birnholtz, and Bietz [2] illustrate how adopted ways of gathering and validating shared data bind the researchers into distinct communities of practice. For example, they report a clear distinction between experimentalists, who collect data to test theoretical hypothesis, and theoretical modelers, who use data to validate and refine their models.

Latour [7], on the other hand, differentiates between the scientific work conducted within the laboratory and the reports communicated to the scientific community, illustrating a complex, multi-stage social journey of data as it travels from the laboratory experiments to the written paper. This path is paved with various types of scientific records and graphical output from scientific machines. However, while record keeping is a central element of scientific endeavor, unlike medical documentation which is rigorously prescriptive, there are no clear and universal rules and ways of creating and managing scientific records. Shankar [14] argues that a 'good' scientific record keeping is an evolutionary process of trial and error that unfolds in the context of institutional rules and codes of conduct. It is an essential part of researchers' initiation into a scientific community and its practices. According to Shankar [14], the scientific record stands as an intermediary between the raw data and the formal scientific paper which reports facts to the community. She is careful to point out that data sets are not scientific records since raw data in an archive is of limited value without contextualizing explanation, arguing that the more '*annotation, augmentation, deletion and imposed structure*' are added to raw data, the more that data moves towards record, '*increasing the amount of tacit knowledge it represents*'.

As part of the scientific discovery process, the lab notebook emerges as a lynchpin of the scientific record keeping where researchers keep daily records of progress, developing thoughts, findings, and details of experiments they have run [8, 15, 16]. Lab notebooks may also fulfill a legal function and serve as a proof of discovery in patent claims. Yeh et al. [16] and Mackay et al. [8] draw attention to the heterogeneous information types that scientists physically cut and paste, including X-ray images, photographs and computer printouts. Mackay et al. [8] describe biologists' paper lab notebooks as '*extremely multi-media documents*'. While they provide an important record and rich body of contextual information, these lab notebooks have traditionally been a paper artifact. Consequently, the information contained within them has been hard to access [15]. Furthermore, the highly personal nature of the data recording in some lab notebooks and a lack of information of what the notebook may contain hinders the reuse by others [15].

Context, collaboratories and knowledge sharing

Data sharing is at the heart of collaborative science. Collaboratories enable teams of distributed scientists to collaborate on scientific problems using tools for shared data access, data analysis, and communication. Bly [3] defines a collaboratory as '*a system which combines the interests of the scientific community at large with those of the computer science and engineering community to create integrated, tool-orientated computing and communication systems to support scientific collaboration*'. While this presents opportunities for scientific advancement, Olson et al. [13] also see it as '*a challenge to human organizational practices*'. Drawing on insights from over 10 major collaboratory projects, they report that pre-specifying data sharing rules, and having a clear understanding of the common benefits, are essential for the success of a collaboratory. Effective collaboratories can improve the training and education of new researchers, enable participants to form, maintain and expand their social networks, and thus lead to new collaborations.

While data sharing is a pivotal aspect of a collaboratory, research has shown that, in order to be truly sharable, the scientific datasets need to be contextualized with information regarding experimental conditions and setup, documentation, personal notes, and other aspects that are often transmitted only within the social knowledge networks [2]. Metadata, in particular, has been described as a stumbling block in the description efforts as researchers may '*lack time, vocabulary and [...] broader frameworks*' of metadata standards to utilize [18].

Chin and Lansing [6] describe the Biological Sciences Collaboratory (BSC) that supports data contextualization by allowing researchers to attach user defined metadata to datasets. It enables capture of transient and intermediate forms of knowledge through written or audio notes and annotations on data items. Finally, BSC integrates with audio and video conferencing to support real time collaboration around data and support social aspects of scientific analysis.

Considering the factors that affect reuse and sharing, Faniel and Jacobsen [5] highlight the varying importance of different forms of context to earthquake engineering researchers who are assessing the reusability of colleagues' data. They found that engineers first assess the relevance of the colleagues' data based on the parameters they wish to study. Once the data is deemed relevant, the researchers consider the understandability and validity of the data. That requires information on how the experiment was run, under what conditions and constraints, and how are those constraints addressed. Without such information researchers tend to reject the data rather than risk misinterpreting and deriving wrong results.

At the same time, research by Bly [3] shows that scientists can be reluctant to share data for fear of losing their 'monopoly rent' on that data. Vertsi and Dourish [17] found that the methods of producing and acquiring data in the scientific collaboration influence the manner in which the data is shared. Comparing the cultures of two robotic space exploration teams, the authors found a different sense of data ownership. A collective and interdependent research approach adopted by one team engendered a notion that data is owned by the group rather than an individual. On the other hand, the more independent research of the second group, where researchers have to compete for equipment, time, and resources, led to the feeling that data is personally earned by individuals and therefore owned by them. Thus, Vertsi and Dourish [17] contend that the circumstances of data production feed into the 'data economy' in which scientific data flows and strongly influences how scientists' approach data sharing.

In summary, the existing research has focused on specific characteristics of the scientific environments including scientific records and record keeping practices, specific types of artifacts such as notebooks, a trust issue in data sharing, and the use of metadata for contextualization. We aim to understand the interdependencies of technologies, practices, and artifacts that emerge as part of the scientific activities. In that vein, we conducted in-situ observations of NPRC, a reputable collaborative research environment, as described in the following sections.

STUDY DESIGN

The conducted study is part of our research program focused on understanding information needs of scientists and requirements for developing supportive environments. It was designed as exploratory and undirected, yet scoped to:

- Capture processes and collaborative practices
- Understand the inter-relationship of technology and practices that emerge through the user interactions and the produced information artifacts
- Identify opportunities to improve the experience and the effectiveness of the collaborative environment.

In this section we provide details about the NPRC study setup and methodology.

Environment

Research and Learning Objectives

The Nanophotonics Research Centre (NPRC) engages in the science of nanophotonics, exploring how new materials can be created in which the interaction between light and matter is fundamentally altered to produce useful new effects. Research involves theoretical and experimental explorations of innovative approaches to assemble nano-chunks of matter into sophisticated structures and create nano-materials with emergent properties that are novel, i.e., not observed in their constituents.

The nano-technology research landscape is highly competitive and fast moving. Labs with considerable investments in the state-of-the-art technologies have an advantage. In contrast to large establishments that comprise the main stream nano-material research, the observed Centre is associated with the University and combines research and teaching. With moderate investments, it has evolved into a nimble and creative environment that continues to impress with its innovative and disruptive approaches.

Experiments are at the very core of the Centre's activities, providing data that is used to generate or illuminate theory. Thus, a relatively large amount of time is spent setting up and conducting experiments in the laboratories equipped with sophisticated laser technologies that are applied to specially produced materials referred to as 'samples'. The experiments are carefully controlled and the results of each material scan are captured digitally for further analysis.

The observed research lab is also a learning environment, which plays a role in establishing the work practices. The research leader explained that he optimized the experimentation workflow to enable rapid circulation of information and his frequent contact with the staff and students. He introduced practices that foster collaboration and collective inquiry. The regular contact with students allows him to observe progress and validate results in a timely fashion, *"preventing them from 'treading water' unnecessarily"*. Furthermore, through group meetings he can pool the expertise of the group to address a specific problem and, at the same time, maximize the reach of his own teaching.

Personnel

The NPRC is headed by a professor with many years of experience in industry and academia. Consisting of 5 post-doctoral students, 11 PhD research students, and 5 support staff (3 at the beginning of the study), the Centre is a highly advanced and dynamic scientific environment. It takes part in the EPSRC-funded UK Nanophotonics Portfolio and covers projects in five distinct areas: meta-materials, nano-assembly, semiconductor microcavities, elastometric polymer opals, and plasmonics. At the Centre, the staff is trained to use the state-of-the-art technologies and apparatuses that are essential for nanophotonics research.

Infrastructure

The Centre stores its data on a server shared with other groups within the University. This server is configured to provide two network spaces, R drive and O drive. R drive hosts folders of individual researchers, containing experimental data and resources such as written work and sample information. Although all the researchers have their own folder space, the Centre fosters an open access policy, so that researchers have complete access to each other's resources. O drive stores shared information such as group workbooks for the projects, notes from meetings, and archived folders.

Each staff member has an HP Compaq tablet PC. They use IE or Firefox as a web browser and Microsoft Outlook for email. The Centre runs Microsoft Windows Vista and MS Office 2007. The tablet PCs communicate wirelessly with the server although some information is stored on the tablet itself, such as items dropped to the desktop. The computers in the Lab are disconnected from the University network. Each experimental setup has its own computer to control the experiment and experimental data is stored directly onto the computer. From there it has to be manually copied to the file space of the researchers' network.

Information technology

Software used by researchers comprises standard office productivity tools and specific tools for scientific data analysis and experiment control:

- *MS OneNote* was adopted from the start of the Centre to serve as a lab book instead of standard paper notebooks. In fact, OneNote has been used in multiple ways: as an electronic lab-book for record keeping, a collaboration tool, and a multi-purpose information management tool. Shared OneNote sessions are set up in meetings and project level note books are used to pool information from sub-projects into central repositories.
- *Igor* is the sole analysis package used in the lab. The package is highly extensible and researchers' code tools and commands used to run and analysis experiments.
- *MS PowerPoint* is used to produce summaries of data and analysis to present in group meetings. PowerPoint is also used for presentations and production of diagrams for papers.
- *Groove* is used to catalogue samples and equipment and their location and link to relevant information about them. Groove is also used as a shared calendar and instant message communication tool.
- *Endnote* is used by some members of the group for references.

The Centre's research leader describes the process of selecting lab software as being akin to Darwinian evolution. His goal is to achieve a minimal set of software to support the work, ensuring that all the members of the staff are skilled in using the software packages and can exchange information effectively. Continuity and reliability of the software is a key aspect. Thus he chooses software providers who can provide a reasonable assurance of ongoing support for extended periods of time.

Practices

In order to process data and circulate information efficiently, the research leader has cultivated work practices that optimize data collection and analysis and support research validation through regular discussions and knowledge exchange. Each research group meets bi-weekly. They present significant outcomes from the previous two weeks and engage in the discussion and interpretation of the experimental results. Throughout the

ID	Participants	With the Lab
P1	Professor – Founder of the Centre	30 months
P2	Post Doc – Multiple project	30 months
P3	Post Doc – Multiple projects	30 months
P4	PhD Student – Nano group	22 months
P5	PhD Student – Nano group	18 months
P6	PhD Student – Nano group	22 months
P7	PhD Student – Engineering group	22 months
P8	PhD Student – Nano group	30 months
P9	Post Doc – Multiple projects	22 months

Table 1. Study participants

meeting, the research leader offers feedback and advises each researcher on the next steps in experimentation and analysis. This provides research directions until the following meeting. Over time, the data, the research questions, and the investigative approaches become more refined. The findings crystalize based on the experimental evidence and become the building blocks of a theory and the basis of scientific papers.

Study Participants

We selected participants according to two aspects: the membership of a specific research group and the seniority and length of the time spent with the centre (Table 1I). In order to understand how data was collected by individual scientists and discussed collectively, we focused on the largest research team that worked closely together, P3-P7. The remaining participants were selected according to the seniority and the length of time spent with the Centre. We expected these factors to correlate with the experience and complexity of assignments that individuals undertake. Our objective was to cover a broad spectrum of practices in order to gain a full understanding of them and associated issues.

Method

Our engagement with NPRC spanned more than 12 months, involving several exploratory projects. The observation study described in this paper was timed to capture typical scientific activities and, thus, help us understand the core factors that shaped the Centre scientific environment. The primary method of our research was *in situ* observations of the work place followed by interviews with each participant.

In situ Observations and Interviews

The bulk of the study data was collected during the two-week period of embedded observations within the research centre. Observations were conducted in three locations: the laboratory for nanophotonics experimentation, the main space for the group meetings—the research leader's office, and the shared office space for PhD students. We conducted five observations, of research experiments in the laboratory with individual study participants (each between 60 and 90 minutes) and five observations of group meetings in which they took part (each between 60 and 120 minutes).

During the experiment observations we paid particular attention to the data collection and note taking practices. In the observations of group meetings we focused on the type of information artifacts that were used and the nature of presentations, discussions, and other interactions that took place. In between the observations of experiments and meetings, our researcher was based in the shared student office and observed working and communication practices therein. Both the laboratory and the group meeting observations were video recorded for further analysis. When reviewing the videos we focused on the actions that were important to our study of the artifact ecology, i.e. the creation, use and reuse of data and artifacts, and associated collaborative practices.

Interviews lasted between 60 and 90 minutes and covered all aspects of the participants' work, including how and where they stored information, what collaborative and communication methods they used, and how they run the experiments in the Lab environment.

Additional Interviews

As we embarked on the analysis of collected data, we uncovered a systematic practice of creating short digests of recent progress, here referred to as *summaries*. The summaries were primarily prepared in advance of the group meetings. In light of this finding we returned to the Centre and conducted a series of semi-structured interviews to solicit further information. Since the observed behavior was consistent across participants, we interviewed two participants from the original sample (P4 and P5, see Table 1) and sought out another researcher (P9) who was not part of the original sample.

Data Analysis

We used Thematic Coding [9] to analyze the data collected in interviews. This was a highly intensive process since we recorded and had transcribed over 15 hours of interviews. We used the software package Atlas.ti (http://www.atlasti.com) to help with data processing. Throughout the coding process, two researches discussed and refined the emerging codes. Over several sessions, the codes were physically copied and clustered on A1 sheets to identify the emerging research themes, concepts, and categories.

We also captured over 5 hours of video footage of meetings and lab observations. The embedded researcher reviewed video data, in conjunction with field notes taken at the time of observations, to compile evidence of artifact creation, handling, and use in the laboratory and meeting environments and to understand the steps involved in such practices.

STUDY FINDINGS

In order to characterize the artifact ecology of the NPRC, we focused our analysis on the use of technologies, communication among the team members, and creation of

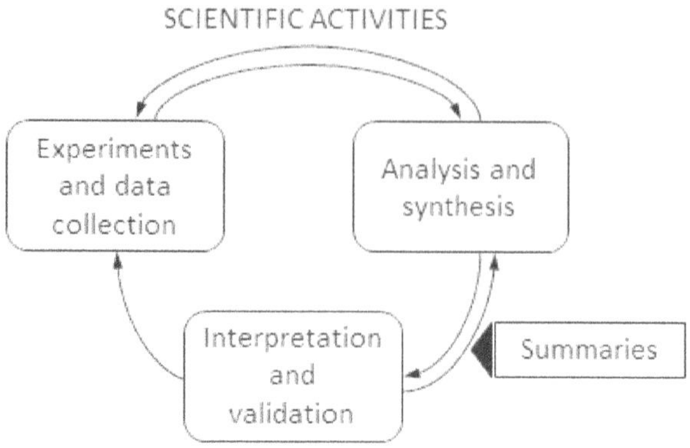

Figure 1. Three aspects of the scientific work—experiments, analyses, and interpretation are interconnected and applied in an iterative fashion. *Summaries* provide a progress status and facilitate information distillation and knowledge consolidation.

information artifacts support specific aspects of the scientific work. We uncovered three coherent patterns of activities that reveal intricate interconnection of technologies, practices, and artifacts. We refer to them as: (1) experiments and data collection, (2) analysis and synthesis, and (3) interpretation and validation activities around the findings. They are, in part, determined by the practices enforced by the research leader in the Centre, as described in the previous section, and by the personal styles and preferences of individual researchers.

The patterns bear resemblance to information life-cycle stages, described in the previous literature [1], that include complex interrelationships between stages and involve information eddies and sub-cycles within larger 'multi-loop' cycles. Similarly, we found that the researchers iterate across different types of activities to support a specific investigation (Figure 1). Indeed, the activities are interrelated; experiments are run to produce data; data is analyses and the outputs synthesized; the results of the analysis are validated within group settings. Along the way, the data and observations are recorded, creating a trail of digital artifacts that enable the scientific discovery. We describe each of these patterns of activities by reflecting upon the technologies, user practices, and artifacts that are involved. They all come together to form the artifact ecology of the Centre.

Action 1: Experiments and data collection

Raw scientific data is generated through experiments which involve manual calibration of the delicate lab equipment and fine level tuning via computer software. Researchers use a remote desktop facility to control the experiments from their tablet PCs which they carry around almost continually whilst at the Centre (Figure 2a). The tablets host the OneNote electronic notebook and Igor, the data analysis software. During our observations, we witnessed researchers selecting experimental data to cut and paste into their lab notebook, and adding context through handwritten notes and sketches, as the following examples illustrate (Figure 2b).

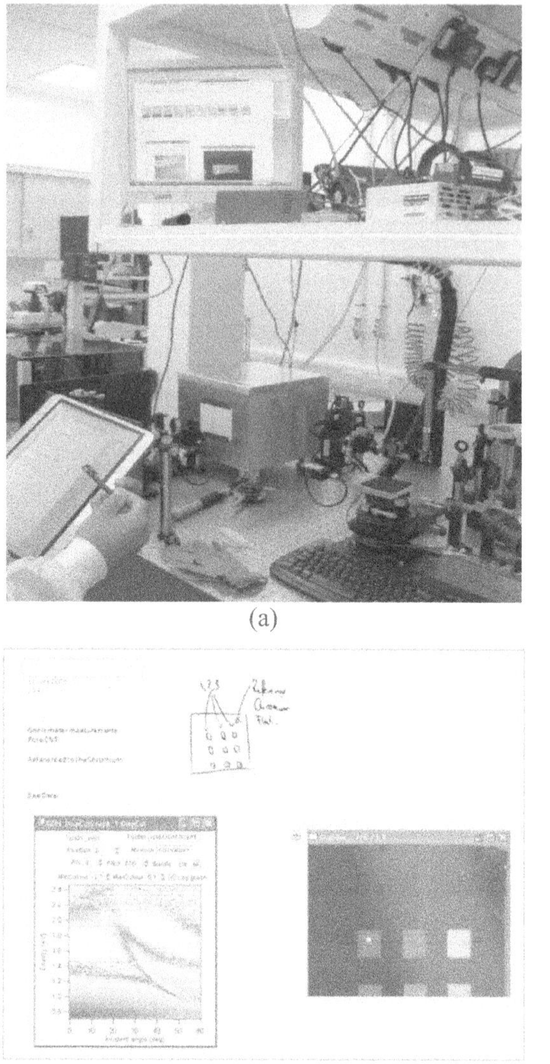

(a)

(b)

Figure 2. (a) Lab set-up, with the tablet and PC and the Lab computer. (b) Notes taken during experiment set up. P6 had scanned a material sample and, unsure as to why the signal was noisy, pasted the results into OneNote.

Example 1. We observed P4 performing a typical instrument calibration exercise as he set up an experiment over the course of a morning. After physically adjusting equipment on the lab bench, he began performing test scans on a dummy material sample to prepare for the final experiment. By doing so he was able to isolate background experimental noise. Before running the first dummy scan, P4 created a folder in the file system to hold the resulting data and named it using the current date. He repeated the dummy scan a number of times, and adjusted the equipment between scans to improve the signal. He saved all the data to the folder, including scans which produced poor results. He copied the final scan, in which equipment was well calibrated, into the lab notebook and saved for future reference.

Example 2. P5 applied a similar procedure while setting up his experiments. We then observed activities during the experiment as he performed a large number of scans, changing one parameter each time, such as angle or intensity of the light beam. Using file names that corresponded to the discrete parameter values, P5 saved each scan into a data folder together with information captured by the data analysis tool Igor. Prior to running the experiment, P5 created a table in his notebook. Each time he saved a scan, he also entered the name of the corresponding file into the table. He also added further details about the experiment setup, such as power level parameters, that could not be captured adequately in the data folders. He stated that this information would be important for interpreting raw data at a later time

Filtering and contextualization. Lab observations revealed variations in the individual practices of record keeping from saving only final scans to making notes on each scan or copying results from multiple intermediary scans. However, the purpose remained the same: to capture key information and images from the experiments and provide contextualizing notes that can serve as information sources and *aide-mémoire* when conducting further analysis. Through the interview discussions we learnt more about the selective capture of data at this early stage in the discovery process. Indeed, only a small percentage of digital artifacts, e.g., images and measurements were pasted into electronic lab-books.

P4 elaborated: *"It's only the [readings] that say something or could potentially say something. It's not that important if it's not everything, but it's something that I would like to know, at least at some stage, that everything's going okay and that everything was referenced properly and normalized".* Thus, P4 is prospectively filtering and recording data that enable him to verify the soundness of the experiment set-up retrospectively.

P5 remarked about an issue they commonly face, i.e., the similarity of the artifacts that are produced by the experimentation software. His selection criteria are thus the differentiating aspects of the data that most clearly supported his argument. In that respect, the lab notebook fulfilled the role of an intermediary buffer, where data and images are kept until they are needed.

Action 2: Analysis and synthesis

The researchers in the Centre analyze properties of the sample materials to isolate interesting reactions and phenomenon. In the study we observed them post-processing and fitting raw data to make it comparable and then looking for causal relationships among different parameters. The researchers present these relationships through graphs produced with analysis and visualization software. Part of their tasks is to look for the meaning in the graphs and organize them in a coherent summary prior to the group meetings (see Figure 3 for example summary slides). That is typically accomplished by reusing images already gathered in the lab notebook and pasting them directly into the PowerPoint slides or by generating new images using the analysis software.

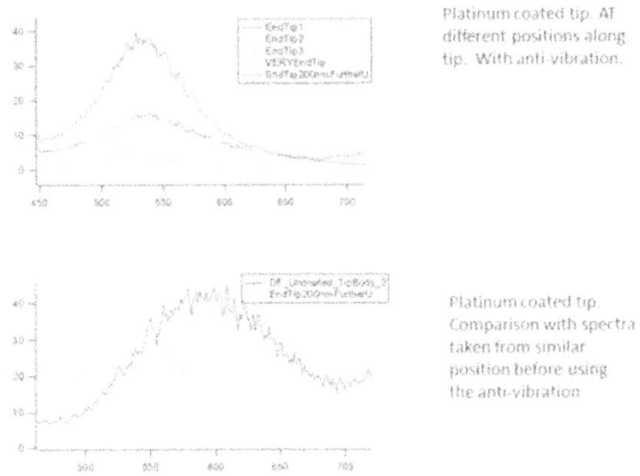

Figure 3. Example summary slide from P8, including graphs generated using Igor analysis software and observation notes.

P6 speaks of the use of a summary to tell the story of his experiment results: "*This is my sample, and in this experiment, this is how my sample behaves and I probe it here and here* [indicating different points on a graph] [...] *and these graphs show this kind of thing* [...] *So it's important results all the way through and you're telling a story, trying to—did it show how it fits into your theory and your understanding of it."*

While there are variations amongst the participants, e.g., in the number of slides they use for summaries, all the summaries were highly selective and sparse in the textual content, primarily containing graphs and images. P4 reasoned why they were produced in such a way: "*I guess the reason is because it's just an internal meeting. Everyone knows what we're doing... so I won't show them all the data that I've taken previously that makes up part of the whole picture. I'll just show them the latest bit of data that I took, like this week, this is what I'm thinking about, this is what I'm talking about."* Thus, minimal contextualization of summaries is an artifact of the common ground developed within the group. At the same time, the summaries facilitate and reinforce the shared knowledge within the group.

Furthermore, summaries represent incremental steps in the ongoing development and refinement of the research projects. They drive the discussion of developing ideas and can range from carefully outlined arguments to presentation of data that is still tentative and raw. This is emphasized by P9, a post-doctoral researcher, who draws attention to the rawness of the data: '*Really the figures are done very quickly...quite raw in fact. It's more to discuss than really to make a formal thing... in a meeting you want to see the data in its form and discuss a little bit... it's really low level processing, the starting process.'* The research leader (P1) pointed out that, over time, data presented in meetings becomes increasingly refined, approaching the format of data and information used in papers.

Action 3: Interpretation and validation.
During fortnightly meetings, researchers gather in the research leader's office to present the progress of the previous 2 weeks. The summaries play a pivotal role by encapsulating the progress and introducing the 'raw material' for discussion. Since summaries do not 'speak for themselves', researchers use them as an aid to articulate information about experiments, hypotheses, findings, and outstanding questions. At the same time the research leader (P1) asks extensive and probing questions about the experimental setup, collected data, and observations to establish the validity of the data and findings.

This process frequently requires researchers to refer to additional resources such as their lab-book pages or raw data on their tablet PC. Speaking about this, P5 states: *"Sometimes we realize that we didn't put in something important, well, not important, but something that came into discussion which is not in the PowerPoint. Maybe it was old data that we already discussed and that is interesting in this moment. Maybe it's something a bit different, that you didn't imagine that you would talk about."*

Throughout the meeting, the research leader takes notes on behalf of the group, recording conclusions, action points and sketches to illustrate concepts or describe possible experimental setups. He cuts and pastes data images from summary slides into the meeting notes, where he annotates and contextualizes them with handwritten text. Meeting notes act as a tool for explanations, and become a record of key conclusions drawn through collective interpretation (Figure 4, centre). They serve as a mechanism for the group coordination after the meeting since researchers use them to check the tasks that have been assigned to them.

DISCUSSION

Our findings illuminate the complex nature of the artifact ecology that emerges within a collaborative scientific environment. Scientific work produces a chain of interrelated, mutually constitutive artifacts which support the proper interpretation of scientific data, and the ongoing crystallization of scientific findings. Artifacts are interrelated in the contexts of their creation and the circumstances of use: lab notes taken during experiments later give critical context to experimental data; summaries, drawing on lab notes, synthesize intermediary findings for group discussion; during meetings summary images are embedded in meeting notes that record group interpretations. Data, such as graphs and microscope images, are used and reused from one artifact to the next, contextualized in new ways as fresh meanings and interpretations emerge. The importance of the experimental data is prominent but more striking is the fine interplay between various elements: the data store and access, the selection of technologies to support practices, the activities that characterize various aspects of the scientific discovery, and the digital artifacts that emerge playing different roles, as the means of capturing relevant data, communicating information about raw data, capturing emerging ideas or validated findings, and recording consolidated knowledge and planned actions. Here we reflect upon the factors that have shaped the environment and therefore contributed to the productivity and the recognition of the Centre for its research excellence.

Infrastructure and information technology. According to the research leader, the tools such as MS OneNote, MS PowerPoint, and Igor are selected to optimize the reusability and sharing, striking the balance between the richness of the feature set versus accessibility and full adoption across the team. The choice of applications enabled effective embodiment of various information types, from ephemeral inscriptions to scientific records that are an essential part of the discovery process. As different applications offer unique affordances and use different formats, there is a disconnect among them that needs to be bridged. Fortunately, generic facilities, such as clipboard that supports copy/paste actions, enabled easy movement of information across and helped with the common interoperability problem.

Open access policy and group meetings. The research leader created a collaborative research environment with high standards of scholarly ethics. By fostering openness at all levels, from data sharing to idea exchange, he addresses a key challenge of the creative scientific work: uniting the personal and collective discovery. The activities depicted in Figure 1, naturally involve information artifacts that support personal and collective work. Our findings point to three prominent types of artifacts: personal lab notebook that provides a 'thinking space' for individuals, the summaries that instigate the collective dialogue, and the shared lab note-book that records the consolidated group knowledge (Figure 4). The transition from the individuals' information spaces to the collective spaces occurs during group meetings, through discussions supported by the summaries. That leads to consolidated findings that are captured in the meeting notes and, thus, increase a common understanding of the specific research topic. Figure 4 depict the flow of data and information, from personal notebooks to consolidated knowledge in shared meeting notes.

Administration of common practices. The observed types of artifacts and practices show a fine balance between the uniformity required to establish a common ground of the team and the individuality with which practices are applied in concrete instances. For example, there is a wide variety of styles in organizing personal notebooks, resulting from personal preferences and styles of working. Yet, the applied practices generate sufficient commonality to optimize the collective good.

Expansion of the Artifact Ecology

We noted several critical aspects of the observed artifact ecology that could be improved by introducing a combination of cross-application middleware and new technologies and allowing the users to adapt them to the specific purposes.

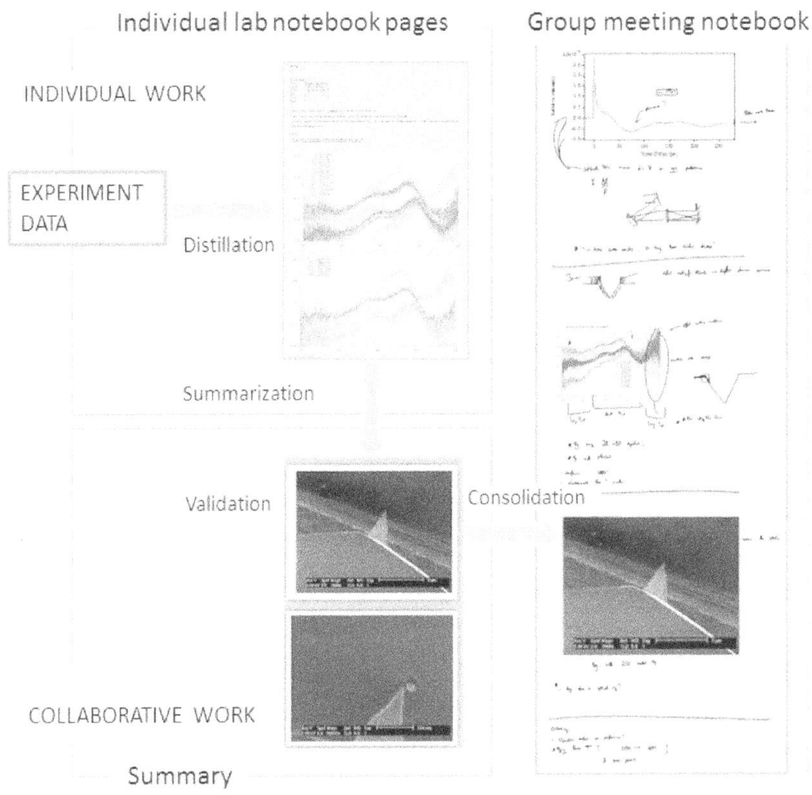

Lab Notebook
- On-going record of scientific discovery progress
- Scratchpad for ideas
- Area where data is filtering and contextualized
- A means for the research leader to keep track of progress and leave notes and annotations

Summary Artifact
- Synthesis of ideas
- A means of sharing data and project progress with the group
- A basis for discussion and the social processes of scientific knowledge making
- An aid to teaching – presented and discussed within the group, maximizes the extent of teaching and instruction across multiple teams at the same time
- A means for the leader to validate the continual stream of data and conclusions drawn by researchers.

Shared Meeting Notes
- A record of key decision points and conclusions
- A means of recording goals and assigning tasks
- Shared resource that all group members can return to and be aware of group activity
- Contextualization of summary data by linking and embedding.

Figure 4. Usage of information artifacts from personal to collaborative work space: a graph from P4's lab notebook (upper left) and a slide from P8's summary document are both discussed at the meeting, annotated and pasted into the common meeting page. The table shows the types and roles of digital artifacts that shape ecology of the Lab.

Reusability and automation of content aggregation. Our observations highlighted reusability of the data representations as key to the information flow. Currently, a manual selection and extraction through the copy and paste facility enables the users to delineate parts of the content that are of interest and use across software applications. and can be used across software applications. Automating the selection and extraction process across multiple experiments would considerably increase productivity and, possibly, expand the range of captured data.

Furthermore, the researchers are in need of tools for crafting collated information into new representations to support personal and group analyses and information sharing. Software applications such as MS OneNote and MS PowerPoint were appropriated to meet some of these needs. However, such applications need to be integrated with other functions and resources. For example, to facilitate easy access to the supporting raw data, it is necessary to leverage PowerPoint summaries in the contextual data search and automate hyperlinking to the raw data files, including the related data samples and experiment records in OneNote.

Artifact organization and access. As the ideas progress and empirical data is analyzed, the specific line of exploration is represented through multiple digital artifacts that are linked to the findings and represent a record of the decisions and conclusions. The current support for organizing and accessing information artifacts is not optimal. Many of the transient but important artifacts, such as summaries and graphs from the Igor software, do not fit neatly within the standard file organization structure. The research leader articulated the problem as a need to connect related artifacts and enable different views on the information space that comprises different formats (MS Power Point, MS OneNote, Igor Graphs, etc.). He suggested 'pivoting and linking'. Linking is now enabled in three ways: (1) hyperlinking from one document to another, (2) embedding one document into another, and (3) collocating artifacts in the same folder and directory or the same OneNote file.

One of the approaches to gather and persist collections of related resources is through the use of tagging [12]. Tagging information artifacts, from images and segments of OneNote pages to slide decks and OneNote files, would provide alternative views and new associations among information items. Furthermore, tagging enables the same artifact to be included in different collections, allowing an item to occur in multiple contexts. The current OneNote tagging facility is optimized for annotation and association of individual pages in notebooks but insufficient to accommodate collections of artifacts across applications.

Study Limitations

The bulk of our findings are derived from a two-week detailed observation of common practices. For that reason, we missed activities that normally crown the scientific discovery, i.e., the preparation of scientific publications. It would have been instructive to observe the practices and evolution of digital artifacts from the notes and summaries to a published scientific article.

CONCLUSION

In this paper we introduce the notion of the artifact ecology to capture essential aspects of scientific discovery and scope effective empirical studies of collaborative research environments. We argue that the sole focus on technologies for data access and sharing limits the potential impact of attempts to improve scientific collaboration. Our research shows that successful collaborative research involves intricate interconnections of technical infrastructure, tools, and purposefully created digital artifacts that emerge in various stages of the scientific discovery and fulfill individual and collective needs of the researchers. The digital artifacts fulfill the essential functions of providing the means of capturing and contextualizing experimental data, recording emerging ideas or validated findings, and documenting consolidated knowledge and planned actions.

We conducted a comprehensive study of the Nanophotonics Research Centre and investigated the artifact ecology that evolved within its research and teaching environment. We highlight the role of transient summaries that draw from individual scientists' observations and synthesize intermediary findings for group discussions. Thus, they serve a critical role of binding the individual and collective discovery. Together with the personal and project lab notebooks, the summaries form a body of research material that should be equipped with contextualized search, linking, and browsing to optimize reuse and sharing of collected data.

The presented case study is the first to illustrate our approach and will be complemented with further studies of artifact ecologies across scientific environments.

ACKNOWLEDGMENTS

We would like to thank Professor Jeremy Baumberg, the Director of the Nanophotonics Research Centre at the University of Cambridge and his team who generously gave their time and enthusiastically shared information about their research practices.

REFERENCES

1. Baker, K. S., and Millerand, F. Infrastructuring ecology: challenges in achieving data sharing. In *Collaboration in the New Life Sciences*. Parker, J., Vermeulen, N., and Penders B. (eds), (2009) Ashgate.
2. Birnholtz, J. P., and Bietz, M. J. Data at work: supporting sharing in science and engineering. In *Proc. of GROUP '03*. ACM Press (2003), 339-348.
3. Bly, S. Special section on collaboratories, *Interactions*. ACM Press (1998), 5, 3, 31-32.
4. Buneman, P., Chapman, A., and Cheney, J. Provenance management in curated databases. In *Proc. of SIGMOD*, ACM Press (2006), 539-550.
5. Faniel, I., and Jacobsen, T. Reusing Scientific Data: How Earthquake Engineering Researchers Assess the Reusability of Colleagues' Data. *Computer Supported Cooperative Work*, (2010) 19, 3-4, 355-375.
6. Chin, G., and Lansing, C. S. Capturing and supporting contexts for scientific data sharing via the biological sciences collaboratory. In Proc. CSCW'04, ACM Press (2004), 409-418.
7. Latour, B. *Science in Action*, Harvard University Press, Cambridge MA, 1998.
8. Mackay, W. E., G. Pothier, C., Letondal, K. Begh., and H. E. Srensen. The Missing Link: Augmenting Biology Laboratory Notebooks. *Proc. of UIST '02*, ACM Press (2002), 41-50.
9. Miles, M. B., and Huberman, M. A. *Qualitative Data Analysis*, (1994) SAGE.
10. Monteiro, M., Reconfiguring Evidence: Interacting with Digital Objects in Scientific Practice. *Computer Supported Cooperative Work*. (2010) 19, 3-4, 335-354.
11. Nardi B. A., and O'Day', V. L. *Information ecologies: Using technology with heart*. (1999) MIT Press.
12. Oleksik, G., Wilson, M. L., Tashman, C., Mendes Rodrigues, E., Kazai, G., Smyth, G., Milic-Frayling, N., and Jones, R. Lightweight tagging expands information and activity management practices. In *Proc. of CHI '09*, ACM Press (2009), 279-288.
13. Olson, G. M., Teasley, S., Bietz, M. J., and Cogburn, D. L. Collaboratories to support distributed science: the example of international HIV/AIDS research. In *Proc. of SAICSIT '02* (2002), 44-51.
14. Shankar, K.. Order from chaos: The poetics and pragmatics of scientific recordkeeping. *J. Am. Soc. Inf. Sci. Technol.* (2007) 58, 10, 1457-1466.
15. Tabard, A., Eastmond, E., and Mackay, W. E., From Individual to Collaborative: The Evolution of Prism, a Hybrid Laboratory Notebook. In *Proc. of CSCW '08*, ACM Press (2008), 569-578.
16. Yeh, R., Liao, C., Klemmer, S., Guimbretière, F., Lee, B., Kakaradov, B., Stamberger, J., Paepcke, A., ButterflyNet: a mobile capture and access system for field biology research, In *Proc. CHI '06*, ACM Press (2006), 571-580.
17. Vertesi, J. and Dourish, P. The value of data: considering the context of production in data economies. In *Proc. of CSCW '11*, ACM Press (2011), 533-542.
18. Van House, N. A., Butler, M. H., and Schiff, L. R. 1998. Cooperative knowledge work and practices of trust: sharing environmental planning data sets. In *Proc. of CSCW '98*. ACM Press (1998), 335-343.

Collaboration in Open-Source Hardware: Third-Party Variations on the Arduino Duemilanove

David A. Mellis & Leah Buechley
MIT Media Lab
75 Amherst St., Cambridge, MA 02142
{mellis, leah}@media.mit.edu

ABSTRACT
This paper looks at collaboration in open-source hardware: physical goods whose digital design files are shared for others to make or modify. Through research into nine variations on the Arduino Duemilanove (an electronic circuit board) and interviews with their developers, we explore the process and outcome of open-source hardware development. We find a structure that differs substantially from that of most open-source software projects, involving many small-scale collaborations rather than a centralized process. We discuss three possible reasons for this structure: differing component selections, the investment required for prototyping, and the lack of software collaboration tools.

Author Keywords
open-source hardware, collaboration, electronic circuit boards, Arduino, version control

ACM Classification Keywords
K.5.1 [Legal Aspects of Computing]: Hardware/Software Protection.

General Terms
Documentation, Economics, Legal Aspects

INTRODUCTION
Recently, the philosophy and principles of open-source software have begun to be applied to the design and production of physical products. This practice of open-source hardware involves sharing the original design files for an object in a way that allows it to be modified or reproduced by others, including for commercial use. The recently drafted open-source hardware statement of principles [6] explains it this way: "Open source hardware is hardware whose design is made publicly available so that anyone can study, modify, distribute, make, and sell the design or hardware based on that design." Open-source hardware has been perhaps most-widely adopted in the domain of electronic circuits, both by producers of do-it-yourself kits (e.g. Adafruit Industries) and of mass-manufactured devices (e.g. Chumby). These companies publish schematics and layout files for circuit boards and computer-aided design (CAD) files for enclosures or other mechanical parts. Others can study and modify these designs to create their own versions of a product or to contribute improvements back to the original manufacturer.

We see these activities as a form of distributed collaboration, enabled by the internet and by the increasing accessibility of fabrication technology. This paper explores the nature of such open-source hardware collaboration through a prominent example, the Arduino microcontroller development platform. Here, we examine the nine variations on the Arduino Duemilanove (an electronic circuit board) that were included a comprehensive list published in 2009 by Make Magazine [8]. By reviewing online information about these variations and through present-day interviews with their developers, we form a model of open-source hardware collaboration. We find that its structure differs substantially from that of open-source software, emphasizing multiple alternatives from small-scale partnerships rather than centralized public processes. In this work, we are drawing partly on our own experience as developers of Arduino and of one of the variations discussed here (the LilyPad Arduino).

In the next section, we briefly review related work. Then, we introduce the Arduino platform and analyze the changes found in the third-party variations of its circuit board. This is followed by information about developer motivations and processes gleaned from our interviews. We then sketch a model of the collaboration found in this community and speculate on the ways it is shaped by available tools and processes.

RELATED WORK
There's a long, established body of research that discusses open-source software (e.g. [3]). Only recently, however, has this kind of attention been focused on the application of open-source to hardware. For example, [4] surveys a group developing an open-source electric car conversion kit, detailing their background and motivation. In another work [5], we developed a new product – an open-source FM radio – in order to explore possibilities for user customization and construction of consumer electronic

Figure 1. The Arduino Duemilanove (left) and variations: (top row) Boarduino, Bare Bones Board, Freeduino, iDuino; (bottom row) Illuminato Genesis, LilyPad Arduino, Seeeduino, Seeeduino Mega, Sanguino.

devices. Our paper [1] about the LilyPad Arduino discusses further variations on that product's hardware.

Open-source hardware can also be seen as an example or enabler of technological appropriation [2] and user-driven innovation [9]. By providing design files for others to modify and build from, it allows them to adapt technology to their own circumstances or needs. This blurs the division between producer and consumer in ways similar to those discussed in the theories of Eglash and von Hippel.

THE ARDUINO PLATFORM AND VARIATIONS

The Arduino platform consists of both microcontroller-based circuit boards and the software for programming them. It is widely used by designers, artists, computer programmers, and other electronics hobbyists. Both the source code for the Arduino software and the original design files for the Arduino hardware are published under open-source licenses. Arduino has become one of the better known examples of open-source hardware, featured, for example, in a Wired Magazine article [7] on the subject.

The standard, official version of the Arduino hardware was, at the time of the Make Magazine list, the Arduino Duemilanove (shown in Figure 1). This board is sold pre-assembled, includes USB connectivity for communication with the Arduino software, and has female headers (sockets) for connecting electronic components or wires. The nine variations on the Duemilanove included in the list are also shown in Figure 1. Two (the Seeeduino and the Seeeduino Mega) were produced by the same company, but each of the others originates from a different group of developers. Eight of the nine boards (all but the iDuino) continue to be available for purchase from their original producers. All of the boards can be programmed using the Arduino software, allowing them to benefit from the Arduino documentation and user community.

The differences between the variations and the original Arduino hardware can be grouped into five major categories:

- aesthetics: e.g. PCB color and shape, component layout, and additional LEDs.
- form factor: e.g. four of the variations can be inserted into a solderless breadboard.
- assembly: five of the variations come as kits to be soldered together by the end user, using larger through hole components instead of surface mount parts.
- processor: three variations include a different processor than that used on the standard Arduino board.
- other functional variations: e.g. omission of on-board USB connectivity, alternative power connections.

It is interesting to note that many of these variations offer alternative functional or aesthetic design choices as opposed to simple improvements or added functionality. These kinds of modification don't lend themselves to contribution back to the original design because they reflect a different (and incompatible) approach than that taken by the Arduino hardware. Still, together they provide a useful range of products to the Arduino community, an example of the open-sourcing of hardware designs leading to distributed development of a platform's offerings.

DEVELOPER MOTIVATIONS AND PROCESS

In order to gather additional information for this paper, we requested interviews with the developers of the Arduino variations. Five responded, four by email and one by phone. We asked questions about topics including motivation, collaborators, communication methods, software design tools, the prototyping process, and financial arrangements. Below we present quotes and information from the interviews, supplemented with data gleaned from public websites. We also draw on our own experience in developing the LilyPad Arduino.

The motivations for many of the Arduino derivatives stemmed from functional requirements for the hardware itself. The Sanguino website explains: "We needed a more powerful microprocessor, but we were reluctant to leave the warm bosom of the Arduino community." The creator of the Bare-Bones Board wanted "low-cost boards that would fit into breadboards." The Seeeduino has "13 changes like [surface-mount microcontroller], 2.54 [mm] pitch pin, mini USB and etc." We created and commercialized the LilyPad Arduino to make it easier for people to attach electronics to fabric. The developers of the Freeduino had more varied motivations; one explains: "the Arduino team had just released the Diecimila [the predecessor of the Duemilanove], but not the accompanying reference design.... D____... was angry at the lapse in open-sourceness and wanted cheaper versions for his students.... I... was mainly interested in doing the PCB design as a sort of education exercise."

In contrast with open-source software, where development tends to be done publicly with anyone able to contribute, much of the development of the Arduino variants was done privately by select collaborators. For example, the Boarduino was "just L____." The developer of the Bare Bones Board worked with "students, co-teachers, and a couple of other electronic suppliers / hobbyists." A developer of the Freeduino described the roles this way: "roughly, D____ was 'marketing,' T____ was 'manufacturing,' and I was 'engineering.'" Interestingly, the three had "no previous relationships; we met on the Arduino forum." Three developers worked on the Illuminato Genesis as part of a commercial partnership. The Seeeduino boards were developed by a company (Seeedstudio) based on "complaints / suggestions to the Arduino Diecimila." We went to an existing company, SparkFun Electronics, to commercialize the LilyPad Arduino.

Communication processes vary across the collaborations. Some of the teams were distributed, like the Illuminato Genesis developers – who coordinated using phone calls – and the Freeduino developers. In this latter case, "communication was almost exclusively by email, with the freeduino web site eventually being set up as a drop-box for design files." The developers of the Bare-Bones Board also "mostly emailed gifs of files, or actual files back and forth." The Seeeduino developers "collaborate with wiki and dropbox [file sharing], project management basing [sic] on Excel." The other developers didn't mention use of software for project management.

Development of the variations involved different prototyping processes. The Boarduino, for example, "took about 2 [iterations]!" For the Freeduino, "N____ had all the prototypes made (100 of each [of four] style[s]) and distributed bare boards to each of the team members.... all four boards worked." The developer of the Bare-Bones Board also mentioned mailing boards to collaborators. The company producing the Seeeduino has a "quick board house able to generate PCB in 24 hours, then our RnD tech will help solder the prototype." We received prototype hardware from SparkFun during the development of the LilyPad Arduino.

Seven of the nine variations (all but the Bare-Bones Board and Illuminato Genesis) were designed using the same circuit layout software (Eagle) as the original Arduino board. Some of the developers started from the original Arduino design files in creating their variations; others simply recreated them from scratch using the originals as a reference (in the words of the Boarduino developer: "I only looked at the schematic to make sure it was compatible"). None of the projects make regular public use of a software version control system (like Subversion or Git), although the Sanguino used an online version control system to publish the finished design files.

The design files for the Arduino variants tended to be published, if at all, only when they were finished and the board had been produced. As a result, the boards have very few public versions (to date). Three of the variations (the Boarduino, Illuminato Genesis, and Seeeduino Mega) appear to have had only a single public release and all but the Freeduino have had five or fewer. Interestingly, though, over half of the variations were themselves the basis for further variations, typically by the same developer or manufacturer.

In all but two of the cases (the LilyPad Arduino and the Freeduino), the Arduino variations were designed and developed by the same people or company that eventually made and sold the boards. The money invested for prototyping can therefore be seen as an investment in the expectation that it will be made up with sales of the finished boards. In the other two cases, one person did the initial conceptual development and initial versions of the product (LilyPad Arduino) or the final hardware design (Freeduino) but another party handled the cost and logistics of manufacturing the prototypes and boards. In both cases, all or almost all of the eventual revenues from sales of the board went to the manufacturer, not the designer. As the designer of the Freeduino explains it, "As far as I know, N____ is the only team member who spent real money, and the only one to have seen any real income from the project." In the case of the Illuminato Genesis, the board was never intended as a source of income. Instead, it was sold at or below cost as a promotion for the engineering consulting services of the company making it.

DISCUSSION: COLLABORATION STRUCTURE AND INFLUENCES

These variations on the Arduino circuit board present a very different portrait of open-source collaboration than that seen in most open-source software projects. It is an ecosystem of many small groups or companies providing alternative offerings within a product space. Individual products undergo few iterations; instead, their designs are used as the basis for new alternative variations. In this model, open-source collaboration means increasing the number of choices offered to users rather than improving the functionality of a single, central option. This may be partially a result of the relatively simple design of the Arduino hardware but it also reflects the nature of physical products. With software, the functionality and appearance of a program can be customized by the user after it's been downloaded; with hardware, user control typically requires a choice of products. As a result, making an alternative version of an open-source hardware design can serve as a positive contribution to the community, in contrast to software where divergent code bases are often seen as resulting from arguments or differences among developers.

Besides the value of increasing the choice of products available to consumers, there are a number of aspects of hardware development processes and tools that seem to promote the decentralized collaboration structure found in this example of open-source hardware. We discuss three of the most important in the following paragraphs, using our personal experience and knowledge to make some connections that may not be immediately obvious from the variants themselves. Still, we think they serve as a good illustration of the influence of these factors on open-source hardware collaboration. Here, we discuss these issues in the context of electronic circuit boards but we think they also apply to the development of other kinds of open-source hardware.

Agreeing on the components to use in a hardware design is critical to enabling collaboration between developers. There are many practical obstacles; for example, certain components may not be available in a given country or a company may already stock alternative versions of a part. A particularly pronounced split is between the smaller surface-mount components that are used for machine-assembled circuits (e.g. the Arduino Duemilanove, LilyPad Arduino, Seeeduino, Seeeduino Mega, and Illuminato Genesis) and the larger through-hole components favored for manual assembly (e.g. on the Bare-Bones Board, Boarduino, iDuino, and Sanguino). It's difficult for someone to make or test a change to the design of a board if it requires them to first acquire a new set of components or redesign large portions of the circuit to use the components they already have. In order to easily collaborate, therefore, individuals need to agree on and have access to a particular set of components and assembly processes.

The constraints of manufacturing make it more difficult and costly to test design revisions, limiting the frequency of iteration and the ability to integrate modifications from many contributors. Additionally, the money required to make a product emphasizes the financial and business side of the development process, aspects which can often be postponed or sidelined in open-source software development. This need to invest financial resources in the development process may encourage someone to make and sell their own version of the hardware, rather than contribute improvements back to a product in which they have no monetary stake. For example, the Seeeduino is similar in both functionality and production to the original Arduino Duemilanove. Its manufacturer didn't suggest their specific improvements to the Arduino project but instead uses them as a means of distinguishing their products in the marketplace.

Finally, unlike software, hardware doesn't have mature tools or techniques for tracking and integrating changes using free or low-cost tools. While existing version control systems can be used for hardware designs, they simply store subsequent versions of a file without providing mechanisms for understanding the differences between them. This makes it harder to examine or combine changes between multiple versions of a design, complicating collaboration. Another difficulty is the necessity of tracking the version of a design that was used to make a particular physical product, so that problems with the hardware can be diagnosed with reference to its design.

CONCLUSION

In examining these variations on the Arduino Duemilanove, we've sketched a model of collaboration in open-source hardware. It is very different from that typically seen in open-source software, involving multiple small-scale collaborations rather than many people working on a single project. We identified three possible reasons for this structure: the complication of sharing components, the investment required for prototyping, and the lack of mature software tools for collaboration. Still, despite these challenges, we think this case study shows some of the exciting and evolving possibilities of open-source hardware collaboration.

ACKNOWLEDGEMENTS

Thanks to the makers of the variations for responding to our questions.

REFERENCES

1. Buechley, L. and Hill, B.M. 2010. LilyPad in the wild: how hardware's long tail is supporting new engineering and design communities. DIS '10. ACM, New York, NY, USA, 199-207.
2. Eglash, R., Appropriating Technology: An Introduction. in Eglash, R., Croissant, J.L., Di Chiro, G., and Fouche, R. (eds.) *Appropriating Technology: Vernacular Science and Social Power*, University of Minnesota Press, 2004.
3. Feller, J., Fitzgerald, B., Hissam, S., and Lakhani, K. (eds.). 2007. *Perspectives on Free and Open Source Software*. MIT Press. Cambridge, MA.
4. Malinen, T., Mikkonen, T., Tienvieri, V., and Vadén, T. 2010. Open source hardware through volunteer community: a case study of eCars -- now!. MindTrek '10. ACM, New York, NY, USA, 65-68.
5. Mellis, D.A., Gordon, D., and Buechley, L. 2010. Fab FM: the design, making, and modification of an open-source electronic product. TEI '11. ACM, New York, NY, USA, 81-84.
6. Open-Source Hardware Statement of Principles and Definition. http://freedomdefined.org/OSHW
7. Thompson, C. 2008. Build It. Share It. Profit. Can Open Source Hardware Work?. Wired Magazine 16, 11 (October 2008).
8. Torrone, P. 2009. The definitive guide to open source hardware projects: Arduino. http://blog.makezine.com/archive/2009/12/arduino-open-source-hardware-2009.html
9. von Hippel, E. and Katz, R. 2002. Shifting Innovation to Users via Toolkits. Management Science 48, 7 (July 2002), 821-833.

Computer Support for Collaborative Data Analysis: Augmenting Paper Affinity Diagrams

Gunnar Harboe **Jonas Minke** **Ioana Ilea** **Elaine M. Huang**
University of Zurich
Zurich, Switzerland
{harboe,minke,ilea,huang}@ifi.uzh.ch

ABSTRACT
The traditional paper-based affinity diagram is a powerful tool for collaborative qualitative data analysis, but the present paper-based process has limitations. In this work we describe how users work with paper-based affinity diagrams as uncovered through a set of interviews with professionals who use the method. We also present an early prototype system to provide computer support for paper-based affinities.

Author Keywords
Affinity diagram, augmented paper, augmented reality

ACM Classification Keywords
H5.m. Information interfaces and presentation (e.g., HCI): Miscellaneous.

INTRODUCTION
Affinity diagramming is a powerful method for performing large-scale qualitative data organization and analysis, commonly used within CSCW and HCI as well as in other fields such as business and anthropology. Originally formulated by Kawakita to assist in brainstorming and planning [6], the method was adapted as a way of analyzing interview and observational data by Beyer and Holtzblatt and integrated into the Contextual Design process [1].

Affinity diagramming is often used to help understand the role of technology in everyday life. The affinity diagramming process itself, however, is typically done with minimal technological support, relying largely on a paper-based procedure in which individual observations or data items are recorded on paper cards or sticky notes. The items are organized on a physical wall based on their "affinity" to one another in an iterative fashion to create successively higher-level categories of data. This method is well suited for team-based data analysis, and the collaborative aspect of the method is often emphasized as one of its important characteristics. (For a fuller explanation of the affinity process, see the books on Contextual Design [1] [3].)

Although computational tools to support the analysis of large qualitative data sets exist, many researchers and practitioners still rely on the traditional paper method because of the benefits it offers. Perhaps most importantly, paper notes allow participants to collaborate with multiple points of interaction and to build a shared awareness of the work in ways that have proved difficult to achieve with digital systems.

Nevertheless, foregoing computer support also has as number of drawbacks. For example, as an affinity diagram grows, it becomes increasingly unwieldy to manipulate and hard to search. The diagram exists in only one copy in one location, and archived versions lose many of the benefits of the live diagram. Additional work is usually required to turn the results into computerized form.

For these reasons, we are investigating ways to offer computer support for the affinity diagramming process while maintaining the benefits of current practices and artifacts. We are approaching the project in an iterative, user-centered fashion, seeking to understand current practices and their context, then developing a series of prototypes and bringing them back to users for feedback. This note reports on our initial data gathering and first round of prototyping.

RELATED WORK
Although numerous papers mention using the affinity diagramming method, few describe the process in sufficient detail to guide design of supporting tools. However, Curtis et al. [2], and Holtzblatt, Wendell and Wood [3] do provide detail on actual affinity practice. Additionally, Judge et al. describe a user study observing the diagramming stage of the process [4]. We take these accounts of the method as our starting point against which we can compare the practices reported by our participants.

A number of tools exist for creating affinity diagrams on a computer or digital display, such as GUNGEN [11], PathMaker[1], StickySorter[2] and the affinity tools by Koh and Su [9] and by Judge et al. [5]. Some of these are desktop systems that impose many or all of the disadvantages

[1] http://www.skymark.com/pathmaker/tour/brain.asp

[2] http://www.officelabs.com/projects/stickysorter/

mentioned above. Others require customized, expensive technology and impose extra overhead on users.

The Designers' Outpost, although geared towards the architecture of websites rather than the affinity diagramming process, similarly attempted to offer computer augmentation to interaction with paper notes [7] [8]. However, their method relies upon a dedicated interactive screen as the working surface, which would impose acute space limitations if applied to the affinity diagramming process.

The literature on augmented paper describes various attempts to add digital enhancements to paper or use paper artifacts as a computer interface (see Luff et al. [10] for an overview). Of some particular interest is the work by Vyas, Nijholt and van der Veer [12], who tagged sketches and other design artifacts with visual markers to support additional collaborative annotation and communication around them.

METHOD

Our work to date involved initial interviews with affinity diagram practitioners, followed by the development of prototypes demonstrating particular design concepts, one of which we tested with another group of participants in a series of user tests that also involved additional interviews. We first describe the interview process and discuss the findings related to current affinity diagramming practices from *all* the interviews, before presenting the prototypes.

Interviews

We first conducted a set of semi-structured interviews with four professionals in the areas of usability and technology design to learn about their practices for creating affinity diagrams. All four participants work at different companies and institutions, and use the affinity diagramming method in their jobs. Being recruited from our social networks, they had collaborated previously in affinity diagramming exercises with each other and with some of the authors, and we therefore recognize that their practices are not necessarily representative of affinity diagramming in general. Interviews were conducted either in person or over the phone, and lasted between 30 and 60 minutes.

Following the development of the Affinity Note Finder prototype, three additional interviews were conducted with professionals recruited from three different local usability and consulting firms. The interviews were held in conjunction with a user test of the prototype, but before the participants had tested it or had it explained to them, and lasted up to 30 minutes. The practices these participants reported differed from that of the first group in significant ways. Both of the studies involved small numbers of participants, in part because of the early stage of the work, and in part because of the difficulty of recruiting participants who had used affinity diagramming in practice and were available for telephone or onsite interviews. We acknowledge that our study findings may not be representative, but still believe them to be valuable for exposing practices and generating ideas.

FINDINGS

Space does not permit a full account of what we found in the interviews, so we describe some general aspects of what our participants told us about how they work that have important implications for the design of computer tools to support their practices, and focus specifically on the issues that motivated the Affinity Note Finder prototype.

General Trends

All participants followed broadly the same process for doing affinities. All created them manually with paper sticky notes on the wall; some had investigated computerized alternatives and found them unsatisfactory: "It's not so easy with a software, because it's very structured and you need to do things in a certain way." (P4) "Paper is much more efficient. [...] There is this issue of physicality and tangibility in paper that cannot be replicated in software." (P3) Most worked on the affinity diagrams as part of a group, although one participant reported sometimes creating affinity diagrams by himself.

The main differences were in the scale of the affinity diagrams created. Some participants talked about diagrams with 50–100 or up to 200 notes, and others routinely worked with diagrams of up to 1800 or 1000–2000 notes. In practice, around two thousand notes appears to be the upper limit for the size of diagram it is feasible to work with, and these larger diagrams were often created iteratively, starting with some fraction of the data and then adding additional batches of notes as the diagramming progressed ("It's the only way you can do it" (P3)).

These participants reported much more difficulty finding notes within the affinity, as well as manipulating and rearranging the diagram. Participants working on smaller affinities generally worked on smaller teams and did not have the same level of organizational support for the process. They could not see themselves working on a larger diagram because the schedule did not permit: "You have to fight like a lion to really do the interviews, because everyone says it takes too much time. And then you have to do the analysis in the speed of light, because otherwise the project is over." (P6)

Another important difference was the process of creating the items. Some participants (typically those working with larger diagrams) would type notes on the computer and print them out on paper, while others wrote them by hand directly onto the sticky notes. On the typed notes it was common to include additional information about the item (e.g. a number, the source of the item, or the person responsible for the note), while those writing the notes by hand did not report making these annotations.

Locating Notes

One of the most critical issues to arise from our interviews was the challenge of searching for notes in the affinity diagram. Because affinity diagramming consists of moving related notes together, locating the relevant notes is a crucial step in the process. As the number of notes increases, so does the time required to locate or identify relevant notes. From the interviews, we identified a number of dimensions to this problem.

Sometimes the target is a definite note or group of notes, and the problem is to locate it physically on the wall. Participants typically first rely on their spatial memory and orientation to attempt to find these: "You remember physically and spatially where a topic is emerging and so when you get a new post-it that seems it goes with something you have seen before, you have the spatial clue about where it is in the room." (P3) This is often a general sense rather than the ability to pinpoint it precisely: "It's much more likely I'll remember on what wall it is, rather than the exact position." (P1) However, even if the participant is looking in the right place, the note(s) may have been moved, perhaps by another member of the team: "Sometimes you get a Post-It that looks like it goes in a place you remember and you go over there and someone moved it." (P6)

The other problem is that the participant may have only a hazy recollection of the note, or a general idea of what he or she is looking for. "Often you just have a vague idea about the note, or a piece of a story about it, or an idea you had while reading about it." (P2) In this case, the participant may fail to recognize the right note even when it is found.

When spatial orientation fails, participants reported using two other approaches to locate the notes they were looking for. One way is to simply scan the wall, hoping to find them. However, it can be easy to overlook one note among many. The other approach is to ask for help: "You have the wisdom of the group that emerges, that's the second source of assistance in placing the notes. You can ask the team if someone has seen the note." (P3) "Sometimes people know where it is, sometimes they don't." (P2)

CONCEPT PROTOTYPES

Key themes and issues were extracted by informal analysis, and transcribed from the initial interviews. We identified the issue of locating notes as one of the most common and frustrating problems, and designed and implemented the Affinity Note Finder prototype to address it.

Affinity Note Finder

The design concept for the Affinity Note Finder is to allow users to locate notes by text search using an augmented reality interface on a mobile device. The design assumes that the text of the notes is available to be searched, and relies on 2D barcodes that encode unique ID numbers for each item to locate the notes.

A prototype of this concept was implemented as a Flash-based web application running on a Microsoft tablet computer with a webcam. We also created a database that held the unique ID and text of each note. Using the tablet, the user enters a search string, and is presented a checklist with the text of every note that contains the words in the search string. The user selects the note or notes she is interested in locating. Using the tablet's webcam, she can then hold up the tablet and "pan" across the wall to see the sticky notes. When the barcode of a selected sticky note is in the frame, the application recognizes it and highlights the barcode on the tablet view in bright orange (Figure 1). In this way, the user can quickly locate all of the notes of interest without having to scan the text of the notes on the wall for the correct ones.

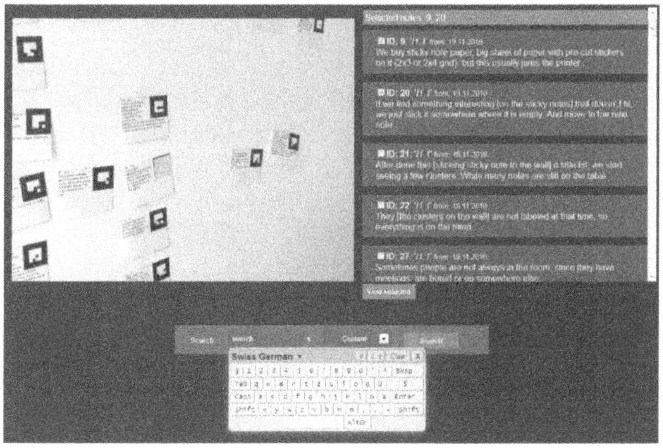

Figure 1: Affinity Note Finder, with viewfinder frame, list of notes matching search, and search field and soft keyboard.

User Tests

We conducted a small-scale user evaluation of the Affinity Note Finder with the three participants from the second round of interviews. Following the interviews about their existing affinity diagramming practices, we described the prototype to them and instructed them in how to use it. We provided them with a sample set of 200 notes and asked them to try using the prototype to start an affinity diagram. The total length of each session was about one hour, and was audio-recorded and transcribed.

Participants were generally quite positive regarding the prototype concept. They found that they were able to locate notes with relative ease and speed, and saw potential value in the tool for creating affinity diagrams.

The main stumbling block with the prototype for these participants was that they, unlike our initial set of interview participants, all used handwritten sticky notes for their affinities. This presented a mismatch between the design and their practices, as the prototype assumed that the notes came from typed data that could be readily stored in a database. These participants also tended to work with smaller affinities than our initial set, which may make support for search practices less crucial, although the participants did not indicate this.

Participants also had issues with the clunky form-factor of the tablet, wishing for a sleeker, lighter device, and noted the delay in the responsiveness of the barcode reader. However, the biggest complaint was that keyword search alone was not sufficient for finding the notes to locate.

They all wanted to be able to search for a concept or topic and get back all the related items.

Participants appreciated that the prototype did not remove the need to interact with the actual notes, stating that the spatial and social awareness of the diagram is an important part of building a cognitive model of the data. They were leery of possible "improvements" that would automate away too many steps in the process.

DISCUSSION

The similarities and variations in how affinity diagramming is currently practiced carries important lessons for the design of supporting computer tools. Despite the availability of digital solutions, all participants relied on paper notes on the wall. This has led us to an approach that modifies the physical diagram itself as little as possible, relying on 2D barcodes on the notes to capture the digital model of the diagram.

One issue we did not explicitly address in this work was the preparation of the physical notes for use with the Affinity Note Finder. Barcodes may be printed along with the note or attached later as a sticker. If users are already typing their data into notes, the creation of a database of items can be made relatively transparent to the user. However, as our evaluation indicated, it will also be important to find a lightweight way to convert handwritten notes to a computer-readable format so computerized searching and other features are made possible. We are currently working on approaches to support handwritten notes.

Search is a promising point for computer support, because it becomes increasingly difficult in large diagrams, and because small diagrams are often associated with a need for utmost speed in the analysis. The benefit of the approach we have taken is that it does not interfere with current practices: the system is strictly optional, and the work can be completed without it just as before.

In terms of the specifics of the design, improvements are needed in the interaction and performance of this prototype, and it needs to be deployed on a smaller, more convenient device before it is suitable for real use. More fundamentally, we need to rethink the search concept to support fuzzier, more conceptual categories. Techniques based on ontology systems may come into play. We are also exploring ways to support users' social and spatial search strategies using the history of the diagram.

CONCLUSION AND FUTURE WORK

Users still prefer a paper-based process when doing affinities, but that does not mean that there is no room for or benefit of computer support in the method. By examining current practices, we have identified problems, limitations, and frustrations faced by those working with affinity diagrams. These form the motivation for the Affinity Note Finder, as well as other planned tools to support and augment the affinity diagramming process.

In addition to iterating upon the Affinity Note Finder prototype, we are also designing tools to support other issues identified in our research. In particular we are exploring how people archive completed affinity diagrams, the limitations to existing methods of archiving, and how these saved versions are used and shared. We are developing tools to improve the archiving process and resulting digital artifacts.

REFERENCES

1. Beyer, H. and Holtzblatt, K. *Contextual design: defining customer-centered systems*. Morgan Kaufmann Pub, 1998.
2. Curtis, P., Heiserman, T., Jobusch, D., Notess, M., and Webb, J. Customer-focused design data in a large, multi-site organization. *Proceedings of the SIGCHI conference on Human factors in computing systems: the CHI is the limit*, ACM (1999), 608–615.
3. Holtzblatt, K., Wendell, J.B., and Wood, S. *Rapid contextual design: a how-to guide to key techniques for user-centered design*. Morgan Kaufmann, 2005.
4. Judge, T.K., Pyla, P.S., McCrickard, D.S., Harrison, S., and Hartson, H.R. Studying Group Decision Making in Affinity Diagramming. (2008).
5. Judge, T.K., Pyla, P.S., McCrickard, D.S., and Harrison, S. Using Multiple Display Environments for Affinity Diagramming. .
6. Kawakita, J. The original KJ method. *Tokyo: Kawakita Research Institute*, (1991).
7. Klemmer, S.R., Newman, M.W., Farrell, R., Bilezikjian, M., and Landay, J.A. The designers' outpost: a tangible interface for collaborative web site. *Proceedings of the 14th annual ACM symposium on User interface software and technology*, (2001), 1–10.
8. Klemmer, S., Newman, M., Farrell, R., Meza, R., and Landay, J.A. A Tangible Evolution: System Architecture and Participatory Design Studies of the Designers 'Outpost. *NCSTRL. UCB/CSD-00 1117*, .
9. Koh, B. and Su, R. Interactions for Addressing Shortcomings Encountered when Physically Creating and Manipulating Large Affinity Diagrams. http://www.benjaminkoh.com/AffinityTool.html.
10. Luff, P., Heath, C., Norrie, M., Signer, B., and Herdman, P. Only touching the surface: creating affinities between digital content and paper. *Proceedings of the 2004 ACM conference on Computer supported cooperative work*, ACM (2004), 523–532.
11. Munemori, J. and Nagasawa, Y. GUNGEN: groupware for a new idea generation support system. *Information and Software Technology 38*, 3 (1996), 213–220.
12. Vyas, D., Nijholt, A., and van der Veer, G. Supporting cooperative design through "living" artefacts. *Proceedings of the 6th Nordic Conference on Human-Computer Interaction: Extending Boundaries*, ACM (2010), 541–550.

A Reference-Based Scoring Model for Increasing the Findability of Promising Ideas in Innovation Pipelines

Anbang Xu and Brian P. Bailey
Department of Computer Science
University of Illinois
Urbana, IL 61801
{xu26, bpbailey}@ illinois.edu

ABSTRACT

Idea pipelines enable open innovation within organizations but require the evaluation teams to assess large numbers of ideas. To help filter promising ideas, community voting is often included as part of the pipeline but the outcome of the voting rarely aligns with the ideas selected by the team. To address this problem, we introduce a new scoring model for increasing the findability of promising ideas within idea pipelines. In the model, each participant need only score a subset of the ideas, ideas are scored independently, and the individual scores can be aggregated. We tested the model on an authentic data set and found our model filters ideas chosen by an evaluation team better than community votes.

Author Keywords

Idea pipeline; innovation; reference-based scoring.

ACM Classification Keywords

H.5.3 [Information Interface and Presentation]: Group and Organization Interfaces – Evaluation/methodology.

General Terms

Algorithms; Design; Human Factors.

INTRODUCTION

An idea pipeline enables a model of open innovation within organizations [2, 8]. Each cycle of the pipeline begins with community ideation on a business problem, where the community is formed from employees, consumers and/or the public. Idea proposals, or just *ideas*, are collected and managed via a collaborative idea management system. An idea proposes a new product or service and its rationale. Ideation may result in a few hundred to tens of thousands of ideas in a short time, which need to be evaluated efficiently.

A key challenge of open innovation is therefore not idea generation, but idea *selection*. To address this challenge, organizations form dedicated teams charged with evaluating ideas. We use the phrase *promising ideas* to refer to the ideas initially selected by an evaluation team to receive consideration at the front end of a pipeline. These ideas will be refined and further filtered with a few ideas progressing to implementation [1]. However, manually considering a very large set of ideas is impractical for an evaluation team.

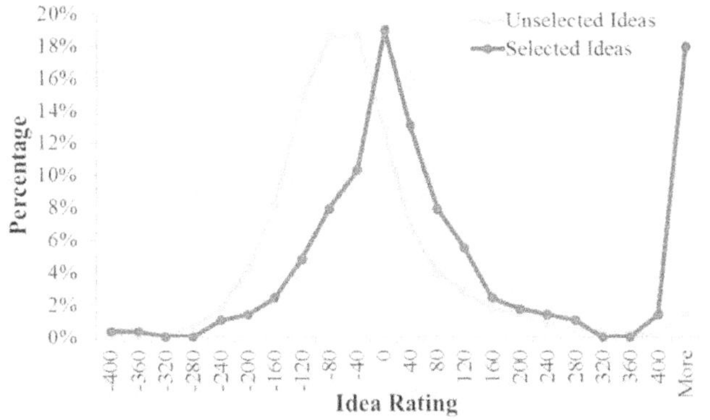

Figure 1. The distribution of votes for 10,000 ideas on MyStarBucksIdea.com (see Data Set). The red (dark) line represents ideas selected by the evaluation team while the green (light) line denotes the unselected ideas. The large overlap demonstrates that community votes are poorly aligned with the idea selections of the team.

One common solution has been to include interaction for community voting within idea management systems [1]. The rationale is that the evaluation team can use community input to help identify ideas that deserve consideration, e.g., many votes for an idea could signal potential for market adoption. The typical voting model allows users to rate the ideas independently and displays the sum with the idea [4]. For example in one popular system, MyStarBucksIdea.com, users may cast a "thumbs-up" (+1) or "thumbs-down" (-1) vote on each idea with the sum displayed near each one.

Unfortunately, the theory and implementation of this voting model make it unreliable for filtering promising ideas. For instance, user votes are susceptible to information cascades [10, 16], users typically vote for only a few ideas, which makes aggregation less reliable [11], and the presentation algorithm can disadvantage ideas submitted early as they are pushed out of view [1, 13]. As a result, evaluation teams report dismissing community votes in their decision making process [1]. Figure 1 shows this mismatch for one pipeline.

In this paper, we introduce a novel scoring model for increasing the findability of promising ideas at the front end of idea pipelines. The key elements are (i) each participant need only score a subset of the ideas, thereby scaling to larger data sets; (ii) each idea is scored independent of the others, removing the cognitive burden of comparison; and (iii) the individual scores can be reliably aggregated. The model works by inserting a *reference* idea into each idea set rated by participants and adjusts all scores relative to it.

The model was evaluated using ideas collected from an authentic idea pipeline. Results show that our model filters promising ideas better than community votes and can be realized with low cost and time delay. Our scoring model can therefore serve as useful input to an evaluation team, in addition to other indicators or criteria they may consider.

RELEVANT THEORY

There are two categories of scoring methods for eliciting value judgments of items: independent and comparison scoring [14]. *Independent scoring* asks respondents to rate their degree of favor or disfavor with attributes of items [5]. Many examples appear in social media, e.g., with ratings of "thumbs up / down". Advantages of independent scoring include that it makes few assumptions about behavioral decisions and it is straightforward to implement. However, respondents can become inconsistent in their responses, especially when there is insufficient information for evaluation (e.g. is a book with a torn cover worth $20?) [9]. Also, the aggregation of individual ratings can be unreliable if each respondent does not rate all of the items [7, 17]. This is problematic for idea management systems where each user typically scores only a fraction of the ideas [1].

Comparison scoring asks respondents to directly compare two or more items. Advantages include the results can be aggregated to form a global ranking and respondents can evaluate items by weighing attributes that would otherwise have insufficient evaluability information [9]. Researchers have advocated using comparison scoring for ranking items in online communities [17]. However, comparison scoring increases cognitive demands especially when no one item is objectively better than the others [14]. In such situations, respondents use cognitive heuristics to simplify decision making and may become inconsistent in their responses [6, 18]. As the number of comparisons can grow non-linearly with the number of items, this method does not scale well for large data sets. This is problematic for idea management systems in which thousands of ideas may be contributed.

In this work, our research goal is to combine the simplicity of independent scoring with the ability to aggregate the results of comparison scoring and scale to large data sets.

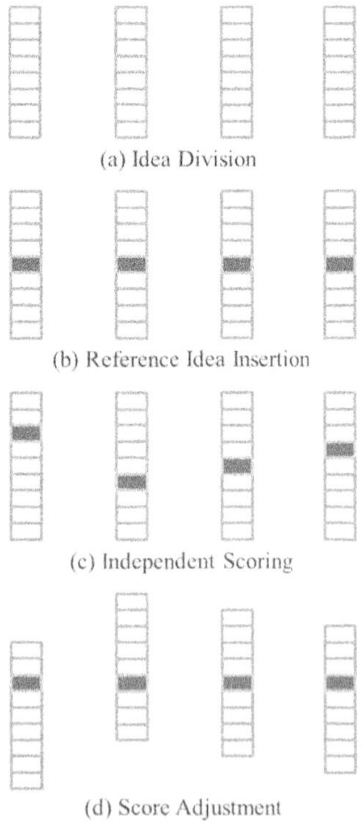

Figure 2. The scalable reference-based scoring model.

A SCALABLE REFERENCE-BASED SCORING MODEL

We introduce a scoring model for improving the findability of promising ideas at the front end of idea pipelines. Our model allows global aggregation of individual idea scores, yet requires each user to rate only a subset of the ideas. This is achieved by inserting a *reference* idea into each idea group and adjusting all scores relative to it.

Figure 2 shows the process of the scoring model. First, we randomly divide all ideas into m groups of n ideas obtaining $\{\{I_{11},\ldots,I_{1n}\},\ldots,\{I_{m1},\ldots,I_{mn}\}\}$. A pre-selected reference idea is then replicated and inserted into each group. Each group is presented to a group of users for rating. In the first phase, at least ten users should rate the ideas in their assigned group in order to consider the ratings stable [13]. Users are unaware of the reference idea and cannot view the ratings of other users. The score for each idea is normalized against the reference idea in the corresponding group as follows:

$$S(I_{ij}) = \mu(I_{ij}) - \mu(\phi_i), \quad i = 1, \ldots, m, \; j = 1, \ldots, n,$$

where $\mu(I_{ij})$ and $\mu(\phi_i)$ denote the average score of the idea I_{ij} and the reference idea ϕ_i in the ith group respectively. The adjusted scores can be interpreted as how much better or worse each idea is relative to the reference idea.

EVALUATION

To test our scoring model, we applied it to a set of publicly accessible ideas collected from a popular idea management system, MyStarbucksIdea.com. This system implements an independent scoring model where users can vote for or against ideas via interaction. Ideas propose ways to improve the products or services of Starbucks, a global retailer of coffee and related products. A vote is cast as thumbs up (+1) or thumbs down (-1) and the sum is shown with the idea. An evaluation team from the organization periodically reviews ideas from the categories and selects a few ideas for consideration in the pipeline. This task is challenging given that every category receives many thousands of ideas.

Data Set

We collected 10,000 recent ideas on MyStarBucksIdea.com in Dec. 2010 spanning all product and service categories.

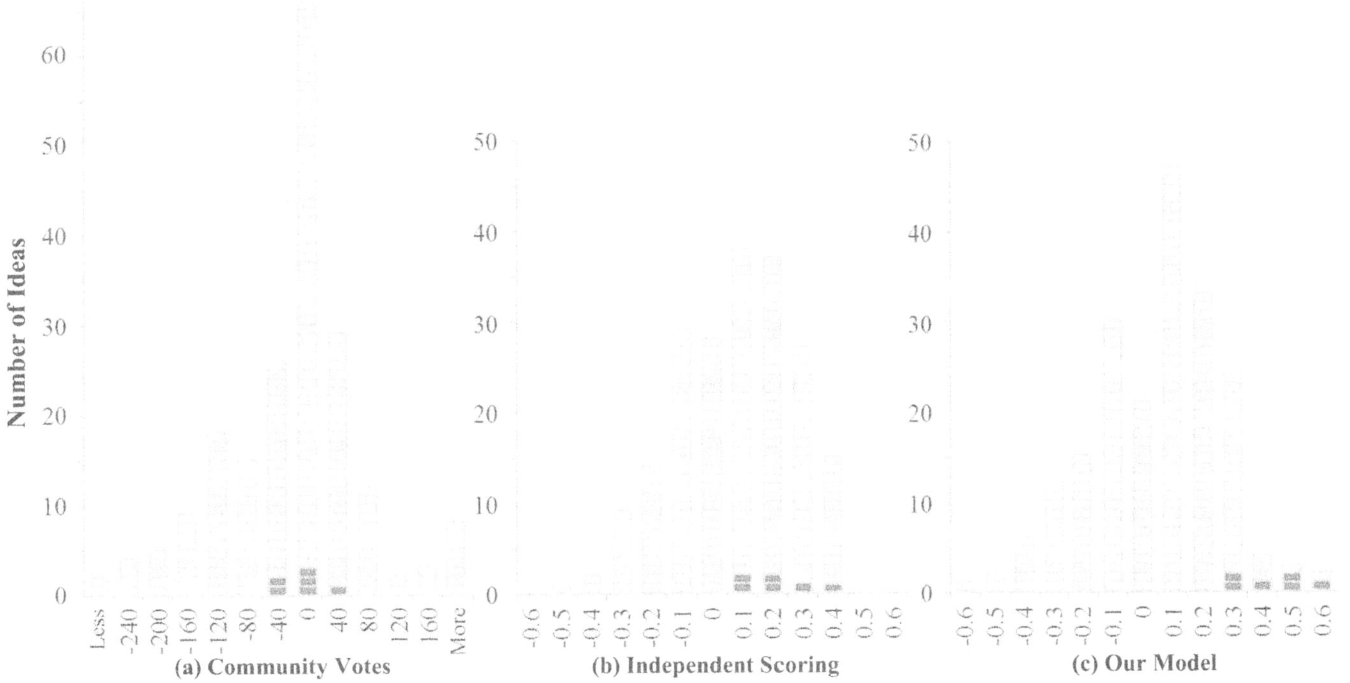

Figure 3. The distributions of scores for our sample of ideas based on (a) Community Votes, (b) Independent Scoring — the results of our experiment without the adjustment and (c) reference-based scoring — the results of our experiment with the adjustment. The key outcome is that the ideas selected by the evaluation team (the red/dark rectangles) received a more favorable ranking with our model than with community votes or independent scoring.

The community ratings and status of ideas were collected three months later. We categorized the ideas as *not selected* or *selected*. The latter set were the ideas deemed worthy of review by the evaluation team (i.e., *the promising ideas*) and we included the status of 'under review', 'reviewed', 'in the works', and 'launched' in this set. If an idea is selected by the evaluation team, it cannot receive additional votes on the site. The proportion of 'not selected' and 'selected' ideas was 97% and 3% respectively. From this set, we sampled 200 ideas; 194 (97%) from 'not selected' and 6 (3%) from the 'selected' set for testing our model.

Realization of Scoring Model

The 200 ideas were randomly divided into twenty groups of ten ideas. Since the scoring model does not have specific assumptions about the reference idea, an idea whose length was equal to the median length (61 words) was chosen as the reference and inserted into each group. The experiment was conducted on Amazon's Mechanical Turk. Participants were paid $0.15 for scoring a group of ideas. The scoring interface included two options: *vote against* (-1), and *vote for* (+1) and each idea was rated independently. To avoid external effects, we did not provide interaction to allow the ideas to be accessed within the idea management system. To increase robustness of the ratings [13], each group was scored by fifteen participants. The presentation order of the ideas in a group was randomized each time it was shown to reduce order effects. After scoring the ideas, participants were asked for demographic information, their familiarity with Starbucks, and frequency of purchases at Starbucks.

The geographic distribution of participants was USA (50.4%), India (28.1%), UK (2.9%), Canada (0.8%) and Other (17.8%). Familiarity with Starbucks was Very Familiar (43.5%), Somewhat Familiar (35.4%), Somewhat Unfamiliar (19.9%), and Unfamiliar (1.2%). The frequency of purchases was Daily (11.8%), Weekly (29.3%), Monthly (26.8%), Quarterly (22.8%), and Never (9.3%). Overall, the majority of participants in our study were familiar with Starbucks and purchased items at least once a month.

Results

The experiment was completed within 24 hours by 267 participants. The range of all scores in our experiment was [-0.6, 0.6]. The mean and standard deviation (SD) of the reference idea scores in the twenty groups were .04 and 0.12 respectively and ranged from -0.17 to 0.23. The mean and SD of all idea scores were .08 and .19 respectively (Fig. 3b) and, after the adjustment, were .04 and .22 (Fig. 3c). An interesting outcome of our scoring model is that all of the 'selected' ideas received scores that placed them in the top 17% of the sample (Fig. 3c). In contrast, community votes ranked these same ideas only in the top 74% of the sample (Fig. 3a), thereby increasing the likelihood that they could be missed by evaluators. Also, four of the selected ideas would not have been ranked in the top 17% via independent scoring (Fig. 3b). Applying the adjustment for the reference idea improved separation of the selected / unselected ideas.

In sum, results show that an evaluation team could use our model to narrow their focus to a smaller pool of ideas. As shown in Fig. 3c, this set has a higher concentration of the promising ideas than the set produced with community voting. The other ideas that appeared in this top cluster may also represent a missed opportunity by the evaluation team, but testing the veracity of this claim is left for future work.

DISCUSSION AND FUTURE WORK

Our realization of the scoring model utilized Mechanical Turk to recruit participants for rating ideas. However, the model could be easily realized using any user community, e.g., contributors to an idea management system or the employee base of a large organization.

The community voting model used within idea management systems typically allows for a rolling vote, i.e., votes can be cast at any time. In contrast, our model separates the *collection* of ideas from the *scoring* of ideas. We believe this separation is beneficial because it better aligns the idea workflow with recommended brainstorming practices [12] and the scoring model can be performed by evaluators with minimal cost or time delay. In addition, the evaluation team need not rely solely on the results of our model. For example, the outcome of our model could be imported into a visualization tool (e.g. see [15]) that allows evaluators to visually explore ideas based on this and other attributes such as topic similarity, comments, and community votes.

Our model ranks ideas based on how they compare to a reference idea, but how the choice of a different reference idea affects the outcome is not currently known. It would also be interesting to test how the use of *multiple* reference ideas affects the outcome. Comparing the outcomes of the model with different and/or multiple reference ideas offers interesting opportunities for further research.

In realizing our scoring model, we chose a single criterion for evaluating ideas (vote for / against) as this mimics the criterion used for community voting on the existing site, thereby supporting comparison of the results. However, the literature on idea evaluation indicates that specifying multiple criteria such as 'strategic fit' and 'feasibility' may allow ideas to be judged more effectively [3]. It would be interesting to study how the use of multiple criteria affects the results of the scoring model. Future work should also offer a more thorough theoretical and empirical comparison of reference-based, independent, and comparison scoring.

Finally, the purpose of our scoring model is to assist an evaluator team in quickly narrowing a large space of ideas to a smaller subset for closer scrutiny. The use of our model cannot guarantee that the best ideas are identified, as this choice remains a human and inherently uncertain decision.

CONCLUSION

The large number of ideas funneled into idea pipelines has created the challenge of knowing *which* ideas to pursue. Evidence shows the commonly used method of community voting is ineffective for identifying promising ideas. This paper has introduced a scalable referenced-based scoring model for quickly filtering promising ideas. In the model, each user only needs to score a subset of the ideas; each idea is scored independent of the others; and the scores can be reliably aggregated for comparison. A test of the model using ideas collected from an authentic pipeline shows that our model filters promising ideas better than community votes. We believe this work offers a useful tool for helping evaluators identify quality ideas in innovation pipelines.

ACKNOWLEDGENT

This work was supported in part by the National Science Foundation under award no. IIS 06-43512.

REFERENCES

1. Bailey, B.P. and Horvitz, E., What's Your Idea? A Case Study of a Grassroots. Innovation Pipeline within a Large Software Company. In *CHI*, (2010), 2065-2074.
2. Chesbrough, H. *Open Innovation: The New Imperative for Creating and Profiting from Technology*. Harvard Business School Press, 2003.
3. Cooper, R.G. and Brentan, U.d. Criteria for Screening New Industrial Products. *Industrial Marketing Management*, *13*, 3, (1984), 149-156.
4. Cosley, D., Lam, S.K., Albert, I., Konstan, J.A., & Riedl, J., Is Seeing Believing? How Recommender Interfaces Affect Users' Opinions. In *CHI*, (2003), 585-592.
5. Eagly, A.H. and Chaiken, S. Attitude Structure and Function. In Gilbert, D., Fiske, S.T.& Lindzey, G. eds. *Handbook of Social Psychology*, New York, 269-322.
6. Fischhoff, B. Value Elicitation: Is There Anything in There? *American Psychologist*, *46*, 8, (1991), 835-847.
7. Hacker, S. and Ahn, L.v., Matchin: Eliciting User Preferences with an Online Game. In *CHI*, (2009), 1207-1216.
8. Holtzblatt, L. and Tierney, M, Measuring the Effectiveness of Social Media on an Innovation Process. *CHI*, 2011, 697-712.
9. Hsee, C.K. The Evaluability Hypothesis: An Explanation for Preference Reversals between Joint and Separate Evaluations of Alternatives. *Organizational Behavior and Human Decision Processes*, *67*, 3, (1996), 247-257.
10. Hullman, J., Adar, E., & Shah, P., The Impact of Social Information on Visual Judgments. In *CHI*, (2011), 1461-1470.
11. Kostakos, V., Is the Crowd's Wisdom Biased? A Quantitative Analysis of Three Online Communities. In *Intl Conf on Computational Science and Engineering*, (2009), 251-255.
12. Osborn, A.F. *Applied Imagination: Principles and Procedures of Creative Problem Solving*. Charles Scribner's Sons, New York, NY, 1963.
13. Otterbacher, J., Helpfulness' in online communities: a measure of message quality. In *CHI*, (2009), 955-964.
14. Phillips, K.A., Johnson, F.R., & Maddala, T. Measuring What People Value: A Comparison of "Attitude" and "Preference" Surveys. *Health Services Research*, *36*, 7, (2002), 1659–1679.
15. Riedl, C., S, W., JM, L., & H., K., Exploring Large Collections of Ideas in Collaborative Settings through Visualization. In *Proceedings of 20th Annual Workshop on Information Technologies and Systems*, (2010).
16. Salganik, M.J. and Watts, D.J. Web-Based Experiments for the Study of Collective Social Dynamics in Cultural Markets. *Topics in Cognitive Science*, *1*, (2009), 439-468.
17. Sarma, A.D., Sarma, A.D., Gollapudi, S., & Panigrahy., R., Ranking Mechanisms in Twitter-like Forums. In *Proc. ACM Conference on Web Search and Data Mining*, (2010), 21-30.
18. Slovic, P. The Construction of Preference. *American Psychologist*, *50*, 5, (1995), 364–371.

The Power of the Ask in Social Media

Rick Wash
Communication Arts and Sciences
Michigan State University
wash@msu.edu

Cliff Lampe
School of Information
University of Michigan
cacl@umich.edu

ABSTRACT

Social computing and social media systems depend on contributions from users. We posit the existence of a latent demand for contribution: many users want to contribute but don't. We then test a simple interface that can induce these users to actually contribute: we display a popup window asking users to contribute. In a real-world randomized field experiment, we found that asking them to contribute right now is ineffective, but reminding the users to contribute actually leads to approximately a 23% increase in contributions with no reduction in quality. However, this effect wanes as users habituate to the popups.

Author Keywords

power of the ask, social media, social computing, discussion

ACM Classification Keywords

H.5.3 Information Interfaces and Presentation: Group and Organizational Interfaces

INTRODUCTION

The real promise of social media systems is that rather than simply consuming content, as on a traditional website, users can interact with website content and with other users who are also consuming content. For this to happen, users must *contribute* to social media systems; they must take the time to leave comments, to participate in the discussion, and to collaborate with others.

However, contribution can't be taken as a given. Contributing to a social media system requires effort. Typing information into a text box takes up valuable time. Packaging information for contribution by deciding how to phrase things isn't always straightforward. Participating in a discussion requires even more time because users must first read and comprehend the discussion that has happened to this point. For these reasons and others, users often choose not to contribute to online social media systems [7].

Even when users have sufficient motivation to contribute to social media systems, they still suffer two additional problems. First, which system should they contribute to? Choosing which social media system to participate in is a difficult undertaking. And second, when should this contribution happen? Users could contribute when they first visit a site. They could wait until they've thought about it more before contributing. Users often choose to wait, expecting to contribute later but never actually getting around to it.

To overcome these problems, we suggest a simple mechanism inspired by research in philanthropy: *the power of the ask* [1]. Explicitly asking is considered one of the most powerful tools for charitable fundraising [1]; all charities employ this technique as part of their fundraising work. By asking, a social media system can signal that it values user contributions, helping to overcome the "which system?" problem. And explicitly asking users to contribute can help overcome the urge to procrastinate and actually make a contribution now. On Wikipedia, suggesting users edit specific content has lead to increases in participation [3]. We propose that the much of the behavioral benefit can be achieved by simply asking for contributions.

We examine the "power of the ask" in the context of social media systems by conducting a randomized field experiment on an existing social media system: the Great Lakes Echo. The Echo is an online news service run by the Knight Center for Environmental Journalism. It currently uses the Wordpress blog engine. The Echo has original reporting from student journalists on various environmental issues in the Great Lakes region. In addition, users discuss the news in the form of comments on stories. This is a fairly typical news site with a community of readers engaging in discussion.

THEORETICAL BACKGROUND

Contribution problems are not unique to social media systems. These two challenges listed above are shared with another similar situation: charitable giving. Charities report that exactly these two challenges cause people to contribute less money than the charities would like. Often people seem to have a *latent demand* for giving to charities: they are willing to contribute but do not because they can't decide which charity to give to, and because they procrastinate the actual act of giving [1]. Despite these problems, though, millions of dollars a year are contributed to charities. How do charities overcome these problems?

Many charities engage in fundraising activities. These activities are expensive, but (hopefully) end up leading to a large increase in donations. One of the most popular and effective strategies is also among the simplest: ask people to contribute to your charity. The *power of the ask* is that by simply approaching potential donors and asking for a contribution, you solve the two problems mentioned above. The charity has solved the "which charity" problem; the donor should donate

CSCW'12, February 11–15, 2012, Seattle, Washington, USA.

to the charity that asked them for money. It also has solved the "when to donate" problem; the donor can easily make a donation now, as they are being asked [2, 1].

Charities and social media systems are both instances of what economists call *public goods* [10]. In general, it is difficult to motivate people to contribute to the creation of public goods. When we rely on voluntary contributions for creating a public good, we often find that the good is *underprovided*; not enough people contribute despite the widespread benefits of the good [12]. Social psychologists call this problem *social loafing*; when working in groups, people usually exert less effort than they would if they were working individually, hoping that others will pick up the slack [6].

Applying social science findings to design better social media systems is not always straightforward [8]. Ling et al. [9] attempted to apply a number of findings from social psychology (including suggestions from the social loafing work of Karau and Williams [6]) to design online communities, and had very mixed results. Therefore, it is worthwhile to replicate the *power of the ask* in this online setting; because it is computers doing the asking instead of people it is unclear how well it will work.

METHODS

To study the effects of *ask*ing in a social media context, we conducted a randomized field experiment on the Great Lakes Echo[1], an environmental journalism website run on the WordPress blogging platform. Each visitor on the site during the study period was randomly assigned to one of three conditions. This assignment was stored in a permanent browser cookie to ensure that upon return visits, they see the same version of the site.

The first of our three conditions is our control condition, *No Ask*. In this condition, we use the Wordpress default: on the bottom of the page that contains the full article is a form where a user can write a comment on the article. Its not really a "No Ask" condition; the title of the form instructs users to "Please Leave a Comment." This is a form of asking, but it is not as explicit as a popup. We suspect that an explicit popup asking users for comments is closer to the ideal of a human being soliciting contributions as they do in charity fundraising because it interrupts the user and forces them to consider the request. Additionally, an explicit popup may invoke a feeling of the computer as a social actor [11].

The remaining conditions vary the immediacy of the ask. This tests the idea that asking is a way to overcome procrastination; if there truly is a latent demand for contributing but users procrastinate entering comments, then we should be able to detect that with these conditions. In the *Immediate* condition, we ask users for an immediate comment. The users are presented with a popup window that asks them to "Please leave a comment"; the popup contains the comment form and a "Leave a comment" button. It also contains a "No Thanks" button that simply dismisses the popup. In the *Reminder* condition, we ask users to leave a comment later. The popup says "When you are finished reading this article, please go to the bottom of the page and leave a comment." There same two buttons exist on this popup, but the "Leave a Comment" button just automatically scrolls the page down to the commenting form, and focuses the comment textbox.

In both conditions, the popup window appeared 500ms after the document was fully loaded. We did some preliminary tests that involved a) immediate popups like this, b) 5-30 second delays before displaying popups, and c) detecting scrolling and displaying the popup 5 seconds after scrolling to the bottom of the news story. All of the options other than a) involved serious confounds. If the initial delay for b) was too low, then the popup appeared before completing the reading of the article – effectively the same as a). But if the delay was high, then a large number of people closed the window and never saw the popup. Individual reading speeds vary widely, and no timing worked well. We didnt want different conditions to have different rates of popup display, so b) didnt work. We tried c) as a way to adjust to reading speed. However, different readers have different resolution screens and browsers, so the bottom of the story appearing on the screen varies widely also.

In the end, we decided that we had no way to properly control for reading speed and screen resolution, as we cannot measure these for all readers of the news site. We decided to use a cleaner experimental design – everyone gets the popup while reading – to focus on the more theoretical questions at the expense of some amount of external validity. We plan to explore timing of asking as a future research questions; this is actually a really interesting question because asking users to contribute on stories they read a day or two ago might actually lead to greater insight and participation. Few users return to previous days posts to comment, but appropriate asking or reminders may actually produce higher quality discussion after readers have had some time to think about the story. Of course, too much time and people forget or stop caring.

Users are randomly assigned to one of the three conditions (No-Ask, Immediate, Reminder) upon arriving at the site. Only comments from other users in the same condition are displayed to a user. This avoids a potential confound: comments cause more comments. If one condition causes people to contribute and everyone saw those comments, then users in other conditions might also comment in response, artificially inflating the quantity of comments for other conditions. To avoid this, we isolate the conditions. The downside to this is floor effects; we might receive so few comments that we cannot differentiate the conditions. By running the experiment for multiple weeks, we hoped to get enough contributions to accurately measure any differences that exist.

The study ran for 10 weeks, from Feb 15, 2010 to Apr 29, 2010. During the study period, Echo news staff posted 140 news stories to the Great Lakes Echo. They continued posting news stories in their normal fashion, and were instructed not to do anything differently during the study period.

RESULTS

During the 10 week study period, the Great Lakes Echo received approximately 19,967 unique readers, or approxi-

[1] http://www.greatlakesecho.org

Table 1. Number of Comments submitted, per condition

Condition	*# Comments*
No Ask	83
Immediate	81
Reminder	102

Table 2. Estimated Rate of Change per week, by condition.

Condition	*Slope*
No Ask	-0.52
Immediate	0.07
Reminder	-0.85

Differences are *not* statistically significant.

mately 2000 per week. About 1700 of these 2000 weekly readers were new and had not seen the site previously during the experiment. These readers viewed 36,773 full news stories on the Echo site. Like most news sites, the Echo has many readers who simply browse headlines (not included in these numbers) or read a very small number of stories (included). These readers submitted a total of 266 comments during the experiment.

We believe our site represents a very common class of social websites and that this sample size is similar to the population size of many small websites. However, this is actually a fairly small sample size (266 comments) to be dividing up across 3 conditions and 10 weeks. In situations like this, any result that achieves statistical significance is likely to be an overestimate, as only overestimates will be large enough to achieve statistical significance [4]. Therefore, we focus our analysis on our estimates of the size of the effect, recognizing the limits this places on our claims.

Table 1 contains the breakdown of these comments by condition. The first thing to notice is that asking for an Immediate comment was not effective; it produced basically the same number of comments as not asking at all. However, reminding the user to comment did lead to a 23% increase in the number of comments submitted.

While an extra 20 comments is not a lot, it does represent a noticeable increase in the number of comments. Since these readers were looking at the same news stories at the same time, and the readers were randomly assigned to conditions, we believe that this can be interpreted as our popup causing a 23% increase in participation. Additionally, it does not appear that a single individual contributed enough comments to alter the results; no one contributed more than 8 comments during the experiment, and the vast majority of commenters (179 out of 209) only contributed a single comment during the study.

Contributions Wane Over Time

In addition to this immediate effect, we have contribution data over time. The experiment ran for 10 weeks, and we can look at how contributions varied over those 10 weeks, and see how time and exposure to popups might change the effect of the treatments.

The first thing to note is that each week did not necessarily have the same number of news stories posted to the site; it varied from a low of 10 stories in a week to a high of 17, with a median week having 13 news stories. Interestingly, the number of news stories per week had very little correlation with the number of comments contributed in each condition.

Figure ?? shows how many comments were contribution in each week for each condition. The number of comments varied widely. The second week of the study had the reminder condition with 19 comments, more than twice of the other two conditions, which each had 7. But then the third week showed a reversal, with the Reminder condition only having 6 comments but Immediate and No Ask having 10 and 11 respectively. Despite this variance, all three conditions show a downward trend, and seem to be converging. The only exception is the Immedate comment condition, which has its highest weekly total of 13 contributions in the final week, which breaks from its otherwise downward trend.

Table 2 shows our estimates of the slope of each of those 3 regression lines. For example, we estimate that the Reminder condition loses 0.85 comments per week that it is active on the site. Because we have so few data points (10 weeks x 3 conditions) and the weekly variance in the number of comments is large, and a downward trend was observed in our control condition, we cannot confidently claim that this downward trend exists. Still, our best estimates indicate that indeed there is a dropoff in the effectiveness of the popups over time, and that all three conditions are converging to approximately the same number of comments, on average.

Quality of Comments

When asking for money, charities don't need to worry about the quality of the contribution; one person's $5 is the same as anyone else's $5. However, when social media systems ask for contributions of information, quality is often a top concern. More contributions don't really help if those contributions are uninformative or off topic. When asked, users may contribute whatever first pops into their head, rather than thinking deeply and making a substantive comment. However, reminding users to contribute in the future may prompt them to think about comments they might make as they read. Reminders may actually *increase* the quality of comments because they have more time to think about it.

After the experiment was completed, we asked 4 Great Lakes Echo journalists go through all 266 comments that were submitted during the experiment and rate the *quality* of each comment on a scale of 1-5 stars. The average quality across all 4 raters was used as the quality score for each comment. The inter-rater reliability (Cronbach's alpha) across raters was 0.82. The journalists did not know which condition the comments were from when they rated them. Table 3 shows the average quality of a comment in each of the three conditions. These differences were fairly small; an average different of 0.1 on a 1-5 point scale. Additionally, there was little evidence of quality decreasing over time. This indicates that explicitly asking users to comment does not materially change the overall quality of comments.

DISCUSSION

Our results suggest that using popups to remind users to participate in a social media site can indeed increase participation. We suspect that reminders serve as a *prompt* for users, prompting them to think about what they might have to contribute. This occasionally leads users to come up with valu-

Table 3. Average Quality of Comments per Condition.

Condition	*Quality*
No Ask	3.29
Immediate	3.40
Reminder	3.27

Differences are *not* statistically significant.

able contributions they otherwise wouldn't have. However, users need time to think about their contribution between the prompt and the contribution form. Asking users to comment *right now* doesn't work any better than not asking at all.

Additionally, users appear to habituate to popups like this fairly quickly. After only 10 week, all three conditions were identical, and reminders seemed to no longer have any effect. This suggests that reminders should be used judiciously, and only used for short periods of time and for special purposes where contribution is particularly important. However, the majority of users (and the majority of commenters) on the site were first-time visitors; it is not clear how this habituation process works.

LIMITATIONS

As a small, special purpose news site, the Great Lakes Echo does not receive a large quantity of readers. There are many similar sites that exist right now, and better understanding small, special purpose sites is important because they may be different than extremely large websites like Facebook and Wikipedia. However, studying this type of website is difficult because the small sample size limits explicit hypothesis testing, and therefore limits our ability to make strong claims. Additionally, the fact that the effects of our intervention diminish over time makes it difficult to gather more data by extending the timeframe of the study. That said, the 40% improvement in the first few weeks and the 23% improvement overall represents a very large effect that warrants further study. Most social science attempts at design have found much smaller effects. For example, famed social psychologist Robert Cialdini found "large" effect sizes of 20-35% in his study of hotel towel reuse [5]. For some behaviors, like home energy conservation, changes in the 5-10% range are considered large [13].

CONCLUSION

By testing *the Power of the Ask* in a field experiment on a social media system, we have been able to show that asking users to contribute content is effective, at least initially, in generating more comments, though its effectiveness extinguishes over time. Contributions solicited directly from users showed no differences in quality based on expert ratings. Few social media systems actively guide user contribution by directing attention through asking for participation. Our field experiment has high external validity in measuring the effects of this real-world intervention. Our results here suggest this may be an effective method for increasing contribution to social media systems.

Acknowledgements

We thank the Great Lakes Echo for allowing us to conduct this research on their site.

REFERENCES

1. J. Andreoni. Philanthropy. In S.-C. Kolm and J. M. Ythier, editors, *Handbook of Giving, Reciprocity and Altruism*, pages 1201–1269. North Holland, 2006.
2. J. Andreoni and A. A. Payne. Do government grants to private charities crowd out giving or fund-raising? *American Economic Review*, 93:792–812, 2003.
3. D. Cosley, D. Frankowski, L. Terveen, and J. Reidl. Suggestbot: using intelligent task routing to help people find work in wikipedia. In *Proceeding IUI '07 Proceedings of the 12th international conference on Intelligent user interfaces*, 2007.
4. A. Gelman and D. Weakliem. Of beauty, sex and power. *American Scientist*, 97(4), 2009.
5. N. J. Goldstein, R. B. Cialdini, and V. Griskevicius. A room with a viewpoint: Using normative appeals to motivate environmental conservation in a hotel setting. *Journal of Consumer Research*, 35:472–482, 2008.
6. S. Karau and K. Williams. Understanding individual motivation in groups: The collective effort model. In M. E. Turner, editor, *Groups at Work: Theory and Research*, chapter 4, pages 113–131. Lawrence Erlbaums Associates, Mahwah, NJ, 2001.
7. A. Kittur and R. E. Kraut. Harnessing the wisdom of the crowds in wikipedia: Quality through coordination. In *CSCW 2008: Proceedings of the ACM Conference on Computer-Supported Cooperative Work*. ACM Press, New York, 2008.
8. R. Kraut and P. Resnick. *Evidence-based social design: Mining the social sciences to build online communities.* MIT Press, Cambridge, MA, Forthcoming.
9. K. Ling, G. Beenen, P. Ludford, X. Wang, K. Chang, D. Cosley, D. Frankowski, L. Terveen, A. M. Rashid, P. Resnick, and R. Kraut. Using social psychology to motivate contributions to online communities. *Journal of Computer-Mediated Communication*, 10(4), 2005.
10. A. Mas-Colell, M. D. Whinston, and J. R. Green. *Microeconomic Theory*. Oxford University Press, 1995.
11. C. Nass and Y. Moon. Machines an mindlessness: Social responses to computers. *Journal of Social Issues*, 60(1):81–103, 2000.
12. P. Samuelson. The pure theory of public expenditure. *The Review of Economics and Statistics*, 36(4):387–389, November 1954.
13. P. W. Schultz, J. M. Nolan, R. B. Cialdini, N. J. Goldstein, and V. Griskevicius. The constructive, destructive, and reconstructive power of social norms. *Psychological Science*, 18:429–434, 2007.

Collaborative Workflow for Crowdsourcing Translation

Vamshi Ambati, Stephan Vogel, Jaime Carbonell
Language Technologies Institute, Carnegie Mellon University
5000 Forbes Avenue, Pittsburgh, PA 15213
{vamshi,vogel,jgc}@cs.cmu.edu

ACM Classification Keywords
K.4.3 Organizational Impacts:
Computer-supported collaborative work]

General Terms
Design; Human Factors.

Author Keywords
Language translation, Collaborative workflow, Crowdsourcing, Amazon Mechanical Turk

ABSTRACT
In this paper, we explore the challenges involved in crowdsourcing the task of translation over the web, where remotely located translators work on providing translations independent of each other. We then, propose a collaborative workflow for crowdsourcing translation to address some of these challenges. In our pipeline model, the translators are working in phases where output from earlier phases can be enhanced in the subsequent phases. We also highlight some of the novel contributions of the pipeline model like assistive translation and translation synthesis that can leverage monolingual and bilingual speakers alike. We evaluate our approach by eliciting translations for both a minority-to-majority language-pair and a minority-to-minority language-pair. We observe that in both scenarios, our workflow produces better quality translations in a cost-effective manner, when compared to the traditional crowdsourcing workflow.

INTRODUCTION
Large-scale parallel data generation for new language-pairs requires intensive human effort and availability of experts. For most language-pairs, the paucity of expert translators or lack of access to even bilingual speakers makes it immensely difficult and expensive to build statistical machine translation systems that use large amounts of parallel data to train mathematical models for language translation. Therefore, only a small fraction of the world languages have automatic translation systems. If we can reliably use crowdsourcing for obtaining translations for low-resource language pairs, the cost of building translation systems for most languages can be significantly reduced.

Crowdsourcing, a term that has been popularized recently, is the process of farming out tasks to a large user population on the Internet. These tasks broadly belong to the language or vision community, where for a number of tasks it is either impossible or challenging and time-consuming for computers to complete them, whereas only requires a few seconds for a human to complete. For example, identifying a person in a photograph, tagging a video for a particular event, flagging an email as spam, identifying the sentiment of a written text, spotting characters in an image are still some of the challenging research problems to computers. With the advent of online market places like Amazon's Mechanical Turk[1] and systematic micro-payment mechanisms, crowdsourcing is becoming feasible and easy to conduct.

Recent work has seen a rapid adoption of crowdsourcing and Mechanical Turk for research tasks, especially in the language processing community [9]. In this paper, we conduct all our crowdsourcing experiments on Amazon's Mechanical Turk. Crowdsourcing translation involves posting tasks which are typically one or more sentences in the source language to be translated to a target language. We provide detailed instructions for both completion of the task and its evaluation. Mechanical Turk also has a provision to seek annotations from qualified workers from a specific location with a specific success rate in their past tasks. We set the worker qualification threshold to 85%. Similar to Callison-Burch [4], we post the input sentences as images in order to discourage workers (also called turkers) from copy-pasting the input into existing translation services. In the rest of the paper, we refer to this workflow as a *traditional crowdsourcing workflow*.

However, as the nature of the task grows in complexity it is to be understood that finding large number of users that are skilled to complete the task becomes difficult in the crowd. Language translation is one such example of a cognitive task that spans skill levels in at least two different languages. While most tasks on Mechanical Turk require monolingual speakers, the requirement of bi-linguality drastically reduces the potential size of suitable turkers on a crowdsourcing platform. In this paper, we discuss the problems with the traditional crowdsourcing approach and propose a collaborative workflow that is amenable to crowdsourcing for translation. Our main motivation for the workflow is to involve both bilingual and monolingual speakers to cost-effectively elicit quality data. In particular, we focus on involving 'weak' bilingual

[1] http://www.mturk.com/mturk/

speakers; those that are non-experts and require assistance in completing a full sentence translation. The rest of the paper is organized as follows: We discuss related work in crowdsourcing and translation in Section 2. In Section 3, we discuss in detail some of the challenges with crowdsourcing for translation. Section 4 details our collaborative workflow for translation in the crowd. We conclude with experiments and future work.

RELATED WORK

Crowdsourcing has thus far been explored in the context of monolingual tasks that involve eliciting a discrete annotation label. Less has been explored to date for analyzing the feasibility of Mechanical Turk for eliciting structural annotations; for example, a summary of an article, translation of a sentence into another language, sequential labeling, syntactic analysis of a sentence, etc. Some recent research has looked at obtaining translations via crowdsourcing, in particular for low-resource languages [1]. Callison-Burch [4] has explored feasibility studies for evaluating the translation output. In both these studies, authors have assumed availability of bilingual speakers for translating a sentence and follow the workflow of eliciting multiple sentence translations independently from users. Recently, researchers have also looked at protocols to involve monolingual speakers collaborating with a translation system to produce translations [5]. Their protocol, however, requires the availability of an intermediary translation system for both the languages. Truly low-resource language pairs with no seed data may not be candidates for such a workflow.

Aside translation, there is general work in the area of designing collaborative workflows for effective crowdsourcing. Bernstein et al.[3] discuss a word processor that can crowdsource and involve humans for completing writing tasks. They introduce an interaction pattern called "find-fix-verify" for integrating crowdsourced human contributions directly into user interfaces. Little et al.[6] discuss a tool to perform iterative human computation algorithms on Mechanical Turk. Crowdforge is a framework for performing complex tasks in a crowdsourced manner [2].

CHALLENGES IN CROWDSOURCING TRANSLATION

In particular, the following three aspects make the task of translation using the crowd more challenging.

- **Large label space:** The input, a sentence in a source language, can be translated into some finite number of meaning-preserving sentences in the target language and a very large number of invalid translations under the target language vocabulary. With such an indefinitely large output space of possible annotations for any given input, it becomes difficult to evaluate the translation quality. Even with the availability of a set of gold standard translations, it is difficult to evaluate the quality of an annotator due to natural variations in the style of their translations which could result in a lexically different, yet valid translation. As an example, consider the translations into English provided by three different turkers which look different at the word-level, but preserve the meaning.

  Spanish: Me alegra mucho que hayas podido venir

  - I am so glad you could come
  - I 'm very happy you were able to come
  - I am glad you could make it

- **Availability:** The availability of bilingual speakers for translation is relatively more difficult when the languages are low-resource or have low-presence on the Web (e.g. Urdu, Thai, etc) than it is to find for high-resource languages (e.g. Chinese, Arabic, Spanish, etc). This also makes it difficult to seek multiple translations, for purposes of quality assurance.

- **Low quality:** Available translators for most languages are non-linguist bilingual speakers and therefore the quality of translation is typically low. Unlike tagging images or flagging spam, translation is a complex cognitive task that requires specific language skills like reading, understanding and writing in multiple languages.

- **Cost:** One of the approaches to getting quality data in crowdsourcing is repeated labeling. In the case of translation, repeatedly obtaining translation for an entire sentence in the wake of high costs and unavailability of translators becomes difficult and less appealing.

COLLABORATIVE WORKFLOW

In this section, we discuss the methodology and the three phases of our collaborative workflow. The desired characteristics of our collaborative workflow are three-fold:

- **Verifiable**: We want to improve the verifiability of crowdsourcing for complex outputs like in the case of translation, by breaking down the complex task into meaningful subtasks. For example, while it is difficult for multiple translators to agree upon a sentence translation, consensus can be reached upon when translating at word level, which may in turn be used to check validity of sentence translations.

- **Diversity**: Along with bilingual speakers, we want users of monolingual nature also to be part of our workflow, as it is relatively easier to find the latter. For example, while there are more than a billion Chinese speakers, only a very small portion of them may be able to translate from English into Chinese.

- **on-experts**: We want our workflow to not only be robust to low quality inputs, but also be able to assist non-expert translators in providing better translations. Bilinguals, efficient in translation of the entire sentences are few in number, but a major portion of speakers can translate individual words with high accuracy.

Figure 1 shows our collaborative translation pipeline. We conduct our workflow on Mechanical Turk as well, but unlike unlike the traditional workflow for crowdsourcing translation, here the translators are working in phases where the output from earlier phases is enhanced in the subsequent phases.

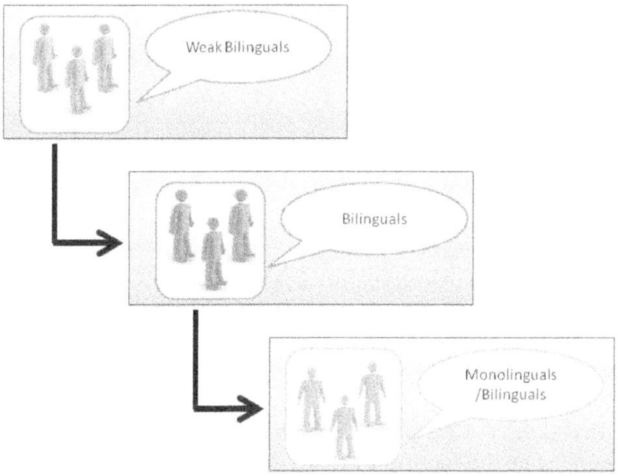

Figure 1. Our three phased collaborative workflow for translating in the crowd - 1. Lexical translation , 2. Assistive translation, 3. Monolingual synthesis

Phase 1: Context-sensitive Lexical Translation

In the first phase, we focus on translations at the word/phrase level. We first, identify content words in the input sentence and crowdsource for collecting their translations. This task can be repeated a large number of times as it is cheaper to translate a single word than an entire sentence. Unlike translation at the sentence level, this can also be verified easily by a simple lexical comparison.

We designed the task so that the user can also see the sentence that the word is in and translate the word in its context. We also observe that turkers converge on a translation much faster when required to translate within the context of an input sentence than when asked to translate out-of-context.

Phase 2: Assistive Translation by Weak Bilinguals

In the second phase, we now collect complete sentence level translations. The turker is required to translate the entire sentence into a target language by preserving the meaning. However, in this phase, we require the translators to use vocabulary gathered from Phase 1 in order to translate certain words in the sentence. As part of a post-verification process, we ensure that the turkers indeed use one of the potential translations for the words in the sentence. As translating a word is not an expensive task when compared to entire sentence translation, we can repeat the word translation task more number of times until reach a sufficient level of inter-translator agreement and only then, proceed to Phase 2.

We observed that breaking the translation task into two different phases enables us to not only control spammers and increase verifiability of the task, but also engage non-expert translators, who may require some guidance in completing a translation.

Phase 3: Target Synthesis by Monolingual Speakers

In the final phase we do not require bilingual speakers, but only monolingual speakers of the target language. The task in this phase is to construct a new translation by synthesizing a translation from among the multiple translations produced in Phase 2. We also allow for post-editing of the translation for spelling and grammar errors.

For example, consider the multiple translations for the Spanish sentence below. We observe that typically there are missing words, mis-spelt words, non-translated words and overall incorrect grammar. We also notice that while there is no evidently better translation among the multiple translations, a meaningful and a complete translation can be synthesized from them. This is similar in spirit to multi-engine machine translation [7].

Spanish: lo tomar desde la parada de taxis

- i'll climb it from the taxi stop
- i'll take it from the taxi rank
- i will have it from the taxi rank

In this phase, a turker is only shown the multiple translations from Phase 2 and is required to guess and select the correct translation. Redundancy among the translations gives sufficient evidence to even a monolingual speaker to guess the correct intent of the source sentence, although he does not speak the source language. Once the intent and context of the sentence is understood, the turker can either select the best suitable translation or synthesize a new translation from the alternatives provided. One can also obtain multiple translations in this phase, although we observe that usually a single solution is sufficient as the monolingual speakers do a good job of constructing the right sentence from the alternatives.

EVALUATION

Baseline

Our baseline is the traditional setup for crowdsourcing translation as described in the introduction section, where sentences were translated by independently working turkers and a majority agreement was conducted to select the best translation. For the baseline, we obtained translations from 5 different turkers and, similar to Ambati et al.[1], use a fuzzy matching algorithm for comparing two sentences and computing majority agreement. The fuzzy matcher has an internal aligner that matches words in the sentences given and scores them separately based on whether the match was supported by the exact match or the fuzzy match. The scores are then combined to provide a global matching score. If the score is above a threshold, we treat the sentences to be equivalent translations of the source sentence.

Preliminary Results

We obtain translations for two language pairs using our workflow and compare it with the traditional crowdsourcing workflow. Firstly we pick Telugu-English language pair, where the source language is a minority and the target language is a majority language. This represents a scenario where availability of bilingual speakers is scarce, but obtaining users for target language is quite easier. We also try a new language pair Telugu-Hindi, where it is extremely difficult to find experts that speak both the languages, although it is relatively

Method	Language	BLEU
Baseline	Telugu-English	21.22
Collaborative	Telugu-English	27.82
Baseline	Telugu-Hindi	18.91
Collaborative	Telugu-Hindi	20.9

Table 1. Evaluation of quality under different workflows

easier to find weak bilingual speakers, who, given enough word level assistance, can perform a decent job of translation. The target language, Hindi, is linguistically a richer language than English, with greater scope for grammatical errors due to gender, number inflections on nouns and verbs. For both language-pairs we translated 100 sentences each using both workflows and compared with the available gold-standard translations that were obtained from experts. As shown in Table 1, we compare the gold-standard match using automatic translation evaluation metric: BLEU [8].

From Table 1, we can see that the collaborative workflow proposed in this paper performs much better for obtaining translations in a crowdsourcing paradigm, when compared to a traditional crowdsourcing setup of farming the task to multiple independent turkers. We also observe that our collaborative workflow enables quicker turn-around time for translations as it fosters participation of weak-bilinguals and monolingual speakers, which is a greater portion of the population than pure bilingual speakers.

Cost Factor

When working with crowd data we would like to extract annotations that are of highest possible quality using non-experts. This is typically achieved by requesting annotations from multiple turkers and computing agreement statistics, which helps in accounting for natural variability of translators and reduces human error. However, repeating a task multiple times comes at a cost, and in this section we argue that our collaborative workflow while providing better quality and faster turn-around times, is still cost-effective.

For instance the cost of obtaining translations from the crowd using baseline approach for 100 sentences was $100 * (5 * 0.10) = 50$USD, where each sentence was translated by five different turkers for 10 cents each. The cost for our three staged process was $100 * (5 * 5 * 0.01 + 3 * 0.05 + 3 * 0.02) = 41$USD , where the first phase of word translations was done by five turkers, sentence translation by three and monolingual synthesis by three turkers at prices of 1 cent per word (avg 5 words per sentence), 5 cents per sentence, 2 cents per monolingual repair respectively. We see a 20% savings in cost when using our workflow as compared to the baseline workflow.

CONCLUSION

Crowdsourcing is increasingly being adopted by researchers in order to elicit annotations over the Internet. In this paper we proposed a novel collaborative workflow for language translation. Our three-phase workflow involves breaking the atomic task of sentence translations into three stages - word translation, assisted sentence translation and translation synthesis. We showed that collecting translations using our collaborative workflow has several advantages over the traditional crowdsourcing approach of independently obtaining multiple translations. We evaluated our approach on two language pairs and showed that the overall quality of translations has improved at lowered costs.

Acknowledgement

This material is based upon work supported by, or in part by, the U.S. Army Research Laboratory and the U.S. Army Research Office under contract number W911NF-10-1-0533.

REFERENCES

1. V. Ambati, S. Vogel, and J. Carbonell. Active learning and crowd-sourcing for machine translation. In *Proceedings of the LREC 2010*, Malta, May 2010.
2. R. E. K. Aniket Kittur, Boris Smus. Crowdforge: Crowdsourcing complex work. Technical report, Human-Computer Interaction Institute, SCS, Carnegie Mellon University, January 2011.
3. M. S. Bernstein, G. Little, R. C. Miller, B. Hartmann, M. S. Ackerman, D. R. Karger, D. Crowell, and K. Panovich. Soylent: a word processor with a crowd inside. In *Proceedings of the 23rd UIST*, UIST '10, pages 313–322. ACM, 2010.
4. C. Callison-Burch. Fast, cheap, and creative: Evaluating translation quality using Amazon's Mechanical Turk. In *EMNLP 2009*, pages 286–295, Singapore, August 2009. Association for Computational Linguistics.
5. C. Hu, B. B. Bederson, and P. Resnik. Translation by iterative collaboration between monolingual users. In *Proceedings of the ACM SIGKDD Workshop on Human Computation*, HCOMP '10, pages 54–55. ACM, 2010.
6. G. Little, L. B. Chilton, M. Goldman, and R. C. Miller. Turkit: tools for iterative tasks on mechanical turk. In *Proceedings of the ACM SIGKDD Workshop on Human Computation*, HCOMP '09, pages 29–30, New York, NY, USA, 2009. ACM.
7. S. Nirenburg and R. Frederking. Toward multi-engine machine translation. In *HLT '94: Proceedings of Human Language Technology*, pages 147–151, Morristown, NJ, USA, 1994. ACL.
8. K. Papineni, S. Roukos, T. Ward, and W.-J. Zhu. Bleu: a method for automatic evaluation of machine translation. In *ACL 2002*, pages 311–318, Morristown, NJ, USA, 2002.
9. R. Snow, B. O'Connor, D. Jurafsky, and A. Ng. Cheap and fast – but is it good? evaluating non-expert annotations for natural language tasks. In *Proceedings of the EMNLP 2008*, pages 254–263, Honolulu, Hawaii, October 2008.

Collaborative Design of an Oceanographic Event Logger

Brian Lindseth
Department of Sociology
Science Studies Program
University of California, San Diego
blindseth@ucsd.edu

Karen Baker
Graduate School of Library and Information Science
University of Illinois, Urbana-Champaign
karensbaker@gmail.com

ABSTRACT
We report on an in-progress project to design a new field instrument used to link data collection and preservation practices across the gaps separating groups of oceanographic scientists engaged in interdisciplinary collaborations. Oceanographic cruises provide an important means for collecting data as an input for specific scientific investigations and for longer term efforts to make a wide range of environmental field data available for future scientific investigators. For both of these tasks, there is the need to perform the invisible work of identifying and resolving potential gaps and consistency issues in the data in order to make the data usable. The event logger system was designed to address these issues by associating every measurement on two organization's scientific cruises with a latitude, longitude, and time stamp. It is the finding of this ethnographic analysis that the event logger system has been successful to the extent that the design process has been able to incorporate a diverse range of voices into an open and collaborative activity.

Author Keywords
Collaborative design, information infrastructure, invisible work, oceanographic research.

ACM Classification Keywords
H.5.2 User Interfaces: User-Centered Design, Prototyping; H.5.3 Group and Organization Interfaces: Computer-supported Cooperative work;

General Terms
Design, standardization.

INTRODUCTION
We provide an account of an event logger system deployed recently on a series of oceanographic research cruises. Each of these cruises brings together a variety of scientists interested in collecting data in the waters off the coast of Southern California to investigate a wide range of research questions. In addition to the data being used to answer specific research questions, there is an imperative to render the data interoperable across the contexts in which it was collected so that it can provide a resource for future, potentially larger scale research questions.

At the level of specific investigations, measurements must be associated with a specific time and place in order to be meaningful. Seemingly small differences in establishing the exact sequence and location of measurements become progressively more difficult to reconcile as the ship data return to land and are carried by investigators into their labs. Bringing attention to this invisible work and enlisting a broader range of actors to the task of ensuring the accuracy and usability of data at the level of specific scientific projects has been a design target for the event logger.

Another design goal of the event logger system has targeted issues inhibiting efforts to bring together data collected by different scientific organizations as resources for future scientific collaborations. As different organizations' cruises employ very different kinds of sampling strategies, measurements made in different contexts are tagged in different ways—sometimes associated with a fixed grid of stations and sometimes with moving masses of water that are followed by the ship. In the contexts of these different kinds of cruises, the event logger provides a common way of locating measurements in time and space in a shared, annotated log so that data generated by different organizations can be rendered commensurable more easily. The event logger was designed in order to minimize under-recognized post cruise data management work and to facilitate efforts to render data collected on these cruises interoperable across organizational divides.

DESIGN: SETTING, SYSTEM AND PROCESS
It is very important for measurements generated within a given team of scientists to be linked with a definite time and place where they were taken in order for these measurements to be usable. Traditionally, this information has been recorded by hand by different cruise personnel according to different conventions. Further, details of time and place can sometimes be omitted in the chaotic conditions of taking measurements in the middle of storms at sea or amidst make shift efforts to address equipment malfunctions that threaten to delay sampling schedules and prevent the collection of valuable data. Even under the best of conditions, a cruise member documenting the time of a

measurement could draw the time from one of two global positioning satellite systems (GPS)—potentially configured differently in the GPS' receiving equipment—or from any one of a bevy of unsynchronized shipboard computer clocks. Even with all notations in place then, discrepancies in the timing of measurements can emerge because of the availability of multiple possible inputs.

Traditionally, the work of addressing these gaps and discrepancies takes place after the cruise ends among graduate students, data managers and cruise and scientific support personnel. For many of the scientists leading the research, this work is often invisible [2,6,7,18,19]. As cruise experiences fade in memory and resurface less frequently in conversational encounters with time, such discrepancies become progressively more difficult to resolve as the links between measurement data and the contexts in which they were taken become more and more attenuated. One data manager commented on many scientists' tendency to take the work of resolving gaps and inconsistencies in the data for granted: "All that. . . metadata work [of] going to many people [who had been on the cruise] to resolve inconsistencies, that step's often taken for granted, and it gets harder as collaborative science grows. And yet, it's not budgeted in terms of the pressure from the PI. 'Well certainly you can get this processing done in a week.' Whereas they're not counting the day and a half that it takes to do that bookkeeping that hasn't been done." In the same interview, this data manager contextualized this problem in terms of the growth of scientific collaborations: "In the past they [specific people working in data management roles] had it done because they used to work with investigators for years. And they had all these coordination mechanisms passively agreed upon. When you have a new cruise like this with a new team, none of that is in place. And so the burden on someone like L. handed a notebook [full of cruise data and asked to resolve problems in the data] like that [when she] wasn't on the cruise, is tremendous." The event logger was designed in order to facilitate this invisible, post-cruise work by associating each measurement with a definite time and place as the measurement is made on the cruise.

The scope and impact of this kind of post cruise work in making the data usable grow when more than one team of scientists is interested in using the same data. Oceanographic cruises are composed of investigators with different disciplinary and institutional backgrounds and with a variety of research interests brought together by a shared interest in describing and understanding the marine system off the California coast. Perhaps unsurprisingly, the data collected by different scientific teams and particularly across organizational boundaries require extensive work to be rendered commensurable. Research focused on the social dimensions of large scale Cyberinfrastructure projects in the U. S. context and eScience projects in the European context [2,3,4,9,17] describes precisely this kind of work.

Assisting in rendering data generated on cruises interoperable across divisions separating larger scale organizational contexts is second design goal for the event logger. Differences in the sampling strategies of California Cooperative Oceanic Fisheries Investigations (CalCOFI) cruises and a subset of the Long Term Ecological Research Network's (LTER) California Current Ecosystem (CCE) cruises provides an illustration of the kinds of problems encountered in rendering data interoperable across organizational boundaries.

CalCOFI cruises build on a sampling pattern that was first established in the years following World War II and that was based on the original mission of the CalCOFI project--to understand the collapse of sardine populations. There are a number of stations extending out from the California coast in a grid, the majority of stations roughly 40 nautical miles away from the next station. Typical cruises in the summer and fall collect samples at, or "occupy," seventy five of these stations over eighteen days. For CalCOFI participants, stations are generally referred to by the number of the line running perpendicularly away from the coast and then the number of the station along that line. 90.60 is station 60 along line 90. Sometimes, however, these stations take on less formal names as part of the experience of each cruise. In order for the data collected on CalCOFI cruises to be meaningful in comparison to other samples that are part of a given study, it is very important that they be associated with the precise time and location—or formal station name—where they were taken. Established much more recently, the Long Term Ecological Research Network's (LTER) California Current Ecosystem (CCE) project began joining CalCOFI's cruises in 2004 as part of an effort to build on the decades of data collected by CalCOFI. In addition to accompanying CalCOFI scientists on cruises following a station based sampling strategy, the CCE site engages in "process" cruises that do not follow the long standing station-based sampling pattern established by CalCOFI. Instead these CCE cruises follow masses of water

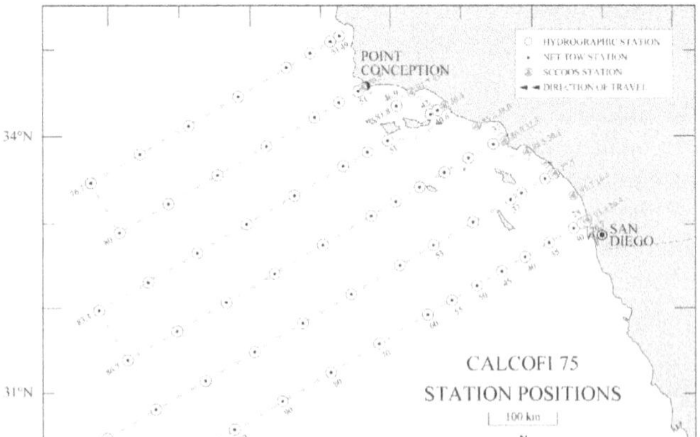

CalCOFI station based sampling pattern.

for several days and take a variety of samples in a series of four to six sampling periods or "cycles."

By associating each measurement—whether from CCE process cruises or CalCOFI station based cruises—with a precise latitude, longitude, and time, the event logger was designed to render these measurements interoperable across these organizations and sampling strategies. In the process, the event logger could provide a mechanism for storing measurements that might have fallen through the cracks of CalCOFI's station based approach to sampling. One CalCOFI cruise participant noted the inaccessibility of data that did not fit neatly into the organization's station-based sampling with its standard station names: "CalCOFI's always been focused on stations, so anything between the stations has been ancillary or extra. And it's not—it's not reported by CalCOFI or stored in their databases for public consumption. You know, it's all on a DVD somewhere. . . but it's not easy to get at".

What does the event logger system look like? The system is made up of two or more tablet computers—at least one placed in the lab area of the ship and one on the bridge. Both scientific support personnel and bridge personnel interface with a custom program on the computers in order to associate planned measurements with latitude and longitude and a time stamp as the measurements take place. An event log is produced as an output, a list of each measurement that has taken place on board the cruise. It is a sequential, digital record in a standard format that can be accessed by all cruise participants. Together, the event logger and the event log were designed to span the flow of data - from measurements in the field to specific scientific investigations and a shared data repository. The standard time and location allow for translation of measurements across organizational boundaries, and a unique identifier (the event number) allows commensurability to be enacted at the level of the database, establishing relations across research organizations and ultimately enabling queriability. In this context, the event logger was designed as a way of distributing data management work [11,12]. Instead of relegating the work of cleaning up the data to post cruise data users, the work of "keeping the data clean" – organizing and relating the data - begins at the source of the

Sampling pattern for a LTER CCE 'process' cruise superimposed on a map of CalCOFI stations.

data itself in measurements on board cruises. In extending post-cruise reconciliation efforts into the cruise, the event logger functions to distribute this work over time and a wider set of actors [10,11,12,14].

FINDINGS

The central finding of this project so far has been the importance of an open and collaborative design approach to the ongoing success of the event logger as a socio-technical system [17]. Although the event logger was designed as part of an effort to highlight and distribute invisible data management work, it was initially defined primarily in technical terms as a 'lightweight' system impacting a relatively narrow range of cruise participants. As the system was implemented and met with occasional resistance and breakdowns, the design team quickly adjusted its approach and attended in greater detail to the working environments of the cruise [8,10,11,12,13], soliciting the feedback from a much wider range of cruise-based personnel than were initially considered. In incorporating a large number of cruise personnel into the study as designers and not merely as less involved support personnel [6,7,14], the event logger system gained support and achieved a greater degree of success. In order to take advantage of this larger circle of designers, a greater degree of the system's functionality was made configurable. On one cruise this allowed greater flexibility in associating measurements with organizational settings.

The initial resistance of some bridge personnel was unanticipated and provided a prompt to solicit interviews with ship-based personnel and initiate an ethnographic study in order to determine how the system was being used, and not being used, in practice. One of the things we found was that the event logger was initially disproportionately supported by a few scientific support personnel already convinced of the system's value. One research participant had the following to say about the crew's initial reaction to the event logger: "So first it was rough going, and the crew. . .didn't seem very happy with it at first. It took them a while to adjust to it because it's not replacing something that they've already been doing. It's just another added feature. . . Ultimately (chuckle) a few of the mates are like so are you taking the event logger with you? (chuckle) So it's like, oh sorry guys. I mean it is a little bit more of a extra duty for them." Although this input was not the glowing review that the design team had hoped for, it provided a key opportunity to include the voices of a range of cruise personnel into the design of the event logger as a more open and collaborative process [1,6,7,14].

One cruise member, for example, suggested that the event logger become more integrated with the ship's already existing logging mechanism: "So if it can ultimately get integrated with a bridge log, that would be easier to do or instead of having for them to write stuff out, maybe if there was a keypad up there and then like they can add in their own comments, like oh we're having a fire drill today or something like that." Although the functional division separating the role of the bridge from the rest of the ship would make implementation of this suggestion difficult, it called attention to the need to approach bridge personnel as an active part of the event logger system—effectively widening the initial design conception of the people affected by the event logger system. Once the crew were approached directly as part of a dialog about the future place of the event logger, they have been much more responsive to the positive role that it can play for scientists, scientific support personnel, and data managers.

In implementing the insights gained from a more open and collaborative approach, the event logger has become a success story. Crew member responses to occasional technical issues provides an important indicator of the impact of adopting a more open and collaborative approach to the design of the event logger. Whereas early technical malfunctions were sometimes seen as an opportunity to ignore the event logger for the remainder of the cruise, more recent problems have been met by efforts to improvise fixes. When problems were encountered with the tablet computers on one cruise, the event logger software was installed on a laptop that became the de facto interface for the event logger system. Now the event logger is not only an accepted component of these cruises,

In going forward, the design team hopes to resolve the impact crew turnover has on the event logger system. Turnover is not only one of the biggest remaining issues for the event logger system but also a reminder of the importance of viewing the event logger as a system that is both technical and social in nature. As new crew members focus initially on their duties, overlap in staff has been important in introducing new personnel to the event logger system in ad hoc training sessions initiated by other cruise participants. As the design team formulates back ups to these ad hoc training sessions, it will be important to include the new crew members as potential participants in an open and collaborative design process.

ACKNOWLEDGEMENTS

Thanks to Geof Bowker, Florence Millerand, David Ribes, and members of the LTER and Ocean Informatics communities at the Scripps Institution of Oceanography.

REFERENCES

1. Baker, K.S., Jackson, S.J., and Wanetick, J.R. Strategies supporting heterogeneous data and interdisciplinary collaboration. Proceedings of HICCS 06 (2005).
2. Baker, K.S., and Millerand, F. Articulation work supporting information infrastructure design. Proceedings of HICCS 07 (2007).
3. Bietz, M.J., Baumer, E.P.S., and Lee, C.P. Synergizing in Cyberinfrastructure Development. Computer Supported Cooperative Work 19 (2010), 245-281.
4. Bowker, G.C., Baker, K.S., Millerand, F., and Ribes, D., Toward Information Infrastructure Studies. International Handbook of Internet Research. J. Hunsinger, L. Klastrup, and M. Allen, Eds. Singer, New York, (2010).
5. Bowker, G.C. Memory Practices. MIT Press, Cambridge, MA, (2006).
6. Bratteteig, T. Making change: dealing with relations between design and use. PhD Thesis, University of Oslo, Norway, (2003).
7. Clement, A. Looking for the designers: Transforming the 'invisible' infrastructure of computerised office work. AI & Society 7, 4 (1993), 323-344.
8. Dourish, P. Where the Action Is. Cambridge, MA: MIT Press, (2001).
9. Edwards, P., G. C. Bowker, S. J. Jackson, and R. Williams. An Agenda for Infrastructure Studies. Journal for the Association of Information Systems 10, 5 (2009), 364-374.
10. Halverson, C. A. and Ackerman, M.S. 'Yeah, the Rush ain't here yet – Take a Break': Creation and use of an artifact as organizational memory. Proceedings of HICCS 03 (2002).
11. Hollan J., E. Hutchins, D. Kirsh. Distributed Cognition: Toward a New Foundation for Human-Computer Interaction Research. ACM Transactions on Human Computer Interaction 7, 2, June (2000), 174-196.
12. Hutchins, E. Cognition in the Wild. MIT Press, (1995).
13. Kaptelinin, Victor, Nardi, B. Acting with Technology: Activity Theory and Interaction Design. Cambridge, MA: MIT Press, (2006).
14. Kanstrup A.M. and Bertelson, P. Participatory IT Support. PDC 2006 – Proceedings of the 9th Participatory Design Conference (2006), 87–94.
15. Lee, C. Boundary Negotiating Artifacts. Computer Supported Cooperative Work 16 (2007), 307-339.
16. Ribes, D. and Lee, C. 2010. Sociotechnical Studies of Cyberinfrastructure and e-Research. Computer Supported Cooperative Work, 19, (2010), 231-244.
17. Star, S.L. and Ruhleder. K. Steps towards an ecology of infrastructure. Computer Supported Cooperative Work, Chapel Hill, (1994), 111-134.
18. Star, S.L. and Strauss, A. Layers of silence, arenas of voice: the ecology of visible and invisible work. Computer Supported Cooperative Work 8 (1999), 9-30.
19. Suchman L. Making Work Visible. Communications of the ACM. 38, 9, September (1995), 56-64.

Inflo: Collaborative Reasoning with Open Calculation Graphs

Jonathan Lung
Department of Computer Science
University of Toronto
LungJ@cs.toronto.edu

Steve Easterbrook
Department of Computer Science
University of Toronto
sme@cs.toronto.edu

ABSTRACT
Inflo is a web tool that introduces new ways to collaboratively construct and deconstruct logical arguments drawn as visual dataflow graphs. *Inflo* graphs are dynamic: nodes are logical propositions that can contain computations based on other nodes. *Inflo* nodes and graphs have URLs, permitting sharing via blogs, e-mails, papers, etc. People can collaboratively construct, refine, and adapt/reuse arguments by making changes to shared nodes. By combining community-curated nodes and using *Inflo*'s nodes for computation, back-of-the-envelope calculations can rapidly be made.

Author Keywords
collaboration, knowledge curation, decision making

ACM Classification Keywords
K.4.3 Organizational Impacts: Computer-supported collaborative work

MOTIVATION AND GOAL
Decision making involves evaluating quantitative and/or qualitative factors of each option. Examples include choosing a credit card and picking sustainable food sources. Relevant factors may be hard for an individual to grasp by design (e.g., credit card fees) or innate complexity (e.g., carbon footprints). However, stronger arguments may be built if individuals can contribute sub-arguments from areas of their expertise [4].

Support for complex comparisons is limited. Lists of pros and cons can be used. Back-of-the-envelope calculations might be scrawled on paper or captured in a spreadsheet. Complex calculations may be coded as algorithms where underlying facts and assumptions are hidden. Carbon calculators and university rankings are examples where some or all *factors* are known, but *algorithms and/or inputs* are private.

Visual argument tools like gIBIS and Compendium [1, 2] can handle such arguments, but do not support quantitative analysis or may be too formal for general use. These tools also lack some collaboration features described in Table 1. Open wikis (e.g. Wikipedia) and on-line spreadsheets permit collaboration but are not geared for arguments.

One of this paper's authors compared CO_2 emissions from printing a document versus reading it on-screen using 39 axioms and 15 logical inferences, motivating *Inflo* as a way to show these (along with references) so others could understand, disagree with, and refine the analysis. Our goals were similar to features of contested collective intelligence (CCI) systems identified by De Liddo and Buckingham Shum [3].

Spreadsheets and wikis do not handle knowledge reuse well (see Table 1). In science and maths, new discoveries usually build on previous findings or use previously developed analytical tools. Citations provide *traceability* but not *reuse* because knowledge chunks (such as steps in a calculation or a proof) cannot be *executed* in new contexts. Software-supported decision making may be helped by the equivalent of a programmer's software library. This allows bug fixes (corrections and improvements) in components (logical propositions) to propagate. For example, corrections to our carbon footprint calculation could "patch" copies reused in other contexts, e.g., adapted to cities with different energy mixes or in a comparison of a laptop to iPad.

DESIGN
We built *Inflo*, an HTML5 web app for collaborative reasoning based on argumentation diagrams, to address these problems. Wikipedia is the result of a community collectively curating information; *Inflo* is a body of collectively curated *executable* knowledge. Here we cover *Inflo*'s design and capabilities, a scenario, and future work. *Inflo* has been undergoing small-scale public beta testing since April 2011 by people not involved with its development. Feedback, including from a physicist and a teacher, has prompted design changes and new features. We also hired someone to model parts of Berners-Lee's *How Bad Are Bananas* to identify usability problems. The approach and scenarios sections describe *Inflo* as it exists at the time of writing, unless otherwise specified.

Nodes: Building blocks of arguments
Inflo displays arguments as directed acyclic graphs with each connected subset of nodes drawn as a tree (Fig. 1 depicts a single tree). Each node represents a logical proposition such as "the height of the Empire State Building is 381m tall". Nodes have content that evaluates to a value (e.g., 381 m), a title (e.g., Height of the Empire State Building), and a description field that can be used to explain the content (e.g., providing a hyperlink to the source for the height). In this example, the node's content was a numeric literal, but it

Table 1. Comparing *Inflo*, spreadsheets, and wikis

Functionality	*Inflo*	Spreadsheet	Wiki
Reuse	Individual nodes and graphs can be reused, maintaining history and dependencies. Supports branching.	Templates, copy-paste cell formulae & and contents. May not capture all dependencies.	Templates
Provenance tracing	Individual node author and data source as first class metadata	File-level edit history	Edit history and footnotes
Navigation & storytelling	Follow semantic links, hyperlinks, graph collapsing	Tabular scrolling, hyperlinks	Linear, hyperlinks
Data semantics	Node names, dimensional analysis, implicit conversions	Usually none (e.g., a cell with "50" is meaningless without context)	N/A
Relationship visualization	Forwards, backwards traceability; related info is spatially collocated	Related info may be dispersed within one or over more sheets	N/A
Rationale	Node title, information sources, justifications are first class entities	Cell annotations	Talk page

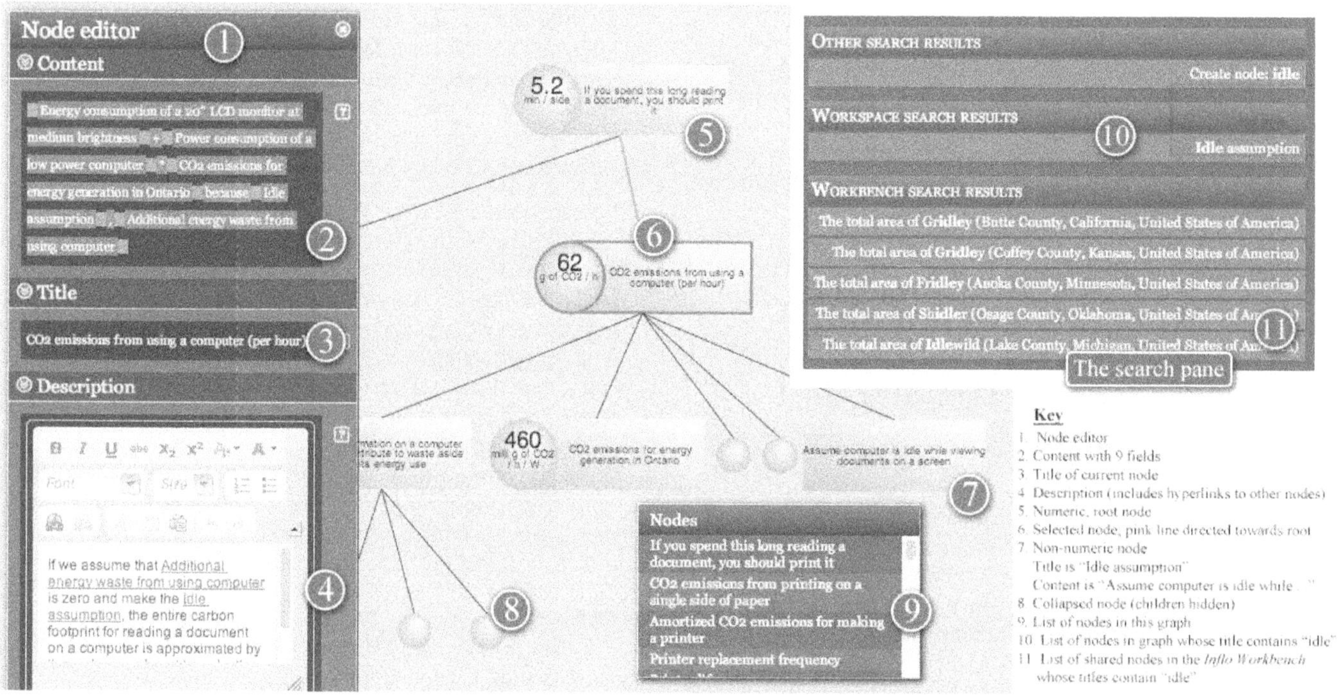

Figure 1. A sample argument shown as an *Inflo* graph and a search window.

could have contained string literals, nodes referenced by title (automatically creating a parent-child relation), and function calls[1]. *Inflo* draws node C as a child of node P iff P depends on/refers to C. Types of references could include because of and contradicts C. Thus, leaves in the tree are axioms; collaboration can be used to dissect these further. Unreferenced and formerly referenced nodes are roots in the forest.

To aid sound reasoning, *Inflo* works with units and alerts users when a dimensional mismatch occurs (e.g., trying to compute 3 m + 2 m/s). Implicit unit conversions may help user comprehension. For example instead of showing the result of 1 N / 9.8 m/s^2 as 1 N*s^2/m, *Inflo* will show 1 kg. Users can use the generic unit "?" to bypass dimensional analysis when using pre-existing formulae that include units. The "?" is propagated towards the root as a reminder that units have not been fully specified.

To avoid burdening users with syntax, few restrictions are placed on node titles (e.g., # of -ve/+ve ions) and units (e.g., 3 C++ books/student). To achieve this, instead of using an automated tokenizer for parsing, users divide a node's content into "fields" using the tab key or mouse (e.g., entering "3 m/s[tab]/[tab]2 s" results in 3 m/s / 2 s).[2] Any field whose contents are an exact match to a node title or function name are visually colour-coded and treated as node references and function calls, respectively.

Users need not remember titles exactly or the syntax of function calls; an *Inflo*-specific autocomplete widget (Fig. 1 search pane) proposes choices with hints on usage. E.g., typing "arct" shows a dropdown with arctan x. When a node

[1] *Inflo* supports user-defined functions written in JavaScript.

[2] Tokenizing is only performed on numeric literals to determine the numeric value and units, using "*" and "/" as delimiters, .

is referenced by title, the tree is redrawn with the referenced node as a child of the referring node. This creates spatial locality for related ideas for navigating and retracing steps during exploration. Nodes referenced more than once are drawn multiple times. Cycles in an argument diagram are sufficient for circular logic, so cycles are forbidden. Thus, *Inflo* arguments are stored as DAGs, but shown as forests.

Example use

The following example was chosen for its simplicity and mix of semantic and numeric values rather than its representativeness of *Inflo* arguments. Consider a theatre selling child tickets for $5 to those under 18 years old and $10 to everyone else. An *Inflo* model could be constructed as follows: First, create a node titled Patron age with content value whose units is "years" (e.g., 16 years). Next, create another node Ticket type with content if Patron age < 18 years then General else Child. The value of Ticket type will evaluate to the string literal General or Child. Lastly, create Ticket price with content if Ticket type = General then 10 dollars else 5 dollars.

Arguments that do not take advantage of *Inflo*'s automated reasoning can also be constructed. Consider three nodes: Mortal premise with content All men are mortal, Socrates' manliness with content Socrates is a man, and Socrates' mortality with content Socrates is a mortal because Mortal premise , Socrates' manliness. *Inflo* will use the supplied conclusion, Socrates is a mortal, as the node's value and automatically draw connections to the referenced nodes. *Inflo* warns users when and where it cannot automatically propagate reasoning, allowing manual updates.

Navigation

Spatial navigation of *Inflo* graphs is similar to the tree/outline view common to file managers. Clicking a node selects it and brings up the node editor (see Fig. 1); a pink line from each visual instance of a selected node is drawn towards the root to show the nodes it influences. *Inflo* supports two methods for managing complex graphs: node collapsing and isolation. Double-clicking nodes collapses them into nondescript circles and hides their children, allowing users to ignore parts of a graph or to emphasize others thus hiding low-level details; this is akin to code-collapsing in an IDE. The node isolation button creates a new workspace with the selected node as the root for focusing on a sub-argument, hiding complexity around and above the node. Users can explore graphs by double-clicking on nodes, panning, scrolling, and zooming.

Versions & URLs: Cornerstones of collaboration

When a node or one of its descendants is changed, a new version is created. Each version of a node has a unique web URL; these URLs are the cornerstones of *Inflo*'s collaborative capabilities. The base URL is of the form http://server/, which points to the *Inflo* web application; this is followed by a URL query string indicating to the web app the unique id of a node and the version to be retrieved. The most obvious advantage to using this scheme is that existing tools that deal with http:// links handle *Inflo* graphs, including blog software, e-mail, and browser bookmarks.

Based on the URL query string, *Inflo* loads the requested node and all its dependencies from a central database. Similarly, a forest of nodes can be retrieved by getting a URL for a particular "view" of a graph. There is no built-in concept of authorization; possessing a node's URL is sufficient for access. Following a link to a graph loads an editable copy. Because a link was provided to specific versions of nodes and edits result in new versions being created, other users following the same link will see the original. Edited graphs can still be shared with others through *Inflo*'s built-in tools or by using conventional link-sharing methods.

The history of a graph or its nodes can be viewed using *Inflo*'s history browser. In a future revision of *Inflo*, users loading an older copy of a graph will be shown an on-screen notification informing them of newer versions of a graph. Likewise, users can also be shown that newer versions of subgraphs exist without affecting the existing view.

Inflo Workbench: Integrated node manager

The *Inflo Workbench* is an *Inflo*-aware collaborative bookmarking system for tracking nodes. Nodes added to the *Inflo Workbench* are not publicly searchable by default, but may be changed on a case-by-case basis. In addition to its collaboration features, *Inflo Workbench* fetches node metadata using node URLs and supports drag-and-drop with *Inflo*.

Opportunistic reuse

There are several ways to reuse nodes within *Inflo*. One way is to drag-and-drop a node's URL onto a graph; sources of the drag-and-drop operation include blog posts, an e-mail links, the *Inflo Workbench*, or a node from *Inflo* running in another window. Since every node has a unique URL, all or parts of a graph can be reused as needed: *Inflo* takes care of node dependencies, so each node can be treated as a discrete, exportable unit. Therefore, users can take advantage of modularity without explicit planning for reuse. Nodes can also be reused by selecting them from the *Inflo*-specific autocomplete widget. This widget searches through functions; nodes in the current workspace; and the user's private collection and all publicly shared nodes in the *Inflo Workbench*. This permits opportunistic reuse of work from others *and* taking advantage of community updates (see below).

Inflo supports basic model merging when conflicts arise. Conflicts occur when a graph contains a different version of a node being imported (either directly or as a dependency). To avoid logical inconsistencies, only one version of a node may exist in a graph at a time. Unused dependencies are removed from the graph rather than forming new trees. Users may choose to convert all instances to either the existing version or the one being imported. *Inflo* never updates versions of nodes without the user's explicit action.

In many or all programming languages and spreadsheets, variable/cell names in a namespace/sheet are unique. *Inflo* node titles need *not* be unique; importing a node with an already-used title does not result in a conflict. No equivalent of variable name shadowing occurs; the autocomplete widget shows all matches with the same title, albeit indistinguishably. Users may opt to drag and drop a node into a field to set the content as desired. However, confusion may still arise. Fortunately, "refactoring" a title is simple; changing the title of a node in the node editor updates all references.

Storytelling

Sometimes, it is necessary to explain why a particular argument or calculation was used. Wikipedia uses wiki (talk) pages for discussions without cluttering the main entry. In addition to providing references, *Inflo*'s description field can serve a similar purpose. Because descriptions can include hyperlinks, including links to other nodes in the graph (which will shift the focus if clicked), it is possible to create narratives about individual nodes and entire graphs (*Inflo*'s help system, another *Inflo* graph, is an example). As software code comments can help explain a codebase, so can the storytelling aspect of *Inflo* be used to help explain a graph.

SCENARIO

Since *Inflo* incorporates the capabilities of both spreadsheets and wikis into one package, it has many applications. A scenario is presented here to illustrate how *Inflo*'s collaborative features create new opportunities and ways for collectively curating knowledge. In this example, a back-of-the-envelope calculation is created, refined, and extended collaboratively.

Back-of-the-envelope calculation

Jono wonders how the carbon footprint of printing compares to reading a document on his low-power desktop computer. With no answer to be found, he begins a calculation in *Inflo*. He first searches *Inflo* for the carbon footprint for printing, but finds nothing suitable. So, he searches the web for information about the manufacture and power consumption of printers. He builds an *Inflo* tree of CO_2 emissions for single-sided printing.

Next, Jono tries to find the carbon footprint of a typical low-power desktop. This information is not yet in *Inflo*, but the local utility company, which shares many nodes with facts about itself such as the number of employees, shares a node with CO_2 emissions per kWh generated. Using that node and a wattmeter, Jono measures his computer's power consumption and derives hourly CO_2 emissions for his computer use.

Jono concludes that reading on his computer at one page per minute produces the same emissions as printing the page. Surprised, he blogs about it. Instead of explaining the entire argument with prose, he drags the root node into his WordPress blog post, creating a link back to his reasoning.

Across the country, Sam, a reader of Jono's blog, is dubious about the analysis. Were CO_2 emissions from paper transport considered? Because of the spatial locality of related concepts in *Inflo* graphs, Sam quickly finds the relevant section, fixes the omission, and clicks "share". Readers of Jono's blog still see Jono's original graph, but also, via an unintrusive popup, that a new version exists.

Elsewhere, Pat, an employee at the local utilities company, updates the CO_2 emissions per kWh node to to reflect lower emissions due to newly-installed wind turbines. Although Pat is unaware of Jono's blog post and Sam's update, people viewing those graphs are notified of the existence of the updated node and have an opportunity to load the latest changes and see the results. Thus, as with software library patches, changes can easily trickle downstream if the API (the node's units) is unchanged.

A year later, Leo wonders about the environmental impact of buying an iPad 3 and cancelling his magazine and newspaper subscriptions. Though unable to find a comparison of the iPad against print media, he does find the latest copy of Jono's analysis via the *Inflo Workbench*. Leo finds the calculation of the CO_2 emissions for paper within Jono's graph; deciding it will be useful for other comparisons, he publicly shares it in the *Inflo Workbench*. He then drags it into his own *Inflo* analysis of the iPad 3, quickly getting an answer to his question.

CONCLUSIONS AND FUTURE WORK

Inflo provides a collaborative environment for organizing information into small, reusable, and traceable chunks. Though the number of user-exposed actions is small – text/calculation entry, spatial & temporal navigation, search, and drag-and-dropping of nodes – it is capable of supporting several different workflows and is generic enough to find uses in a wide variety of domains.

The core collaborative and interactive aspects of *Inflo* have been implemented, but many features are still envisioned. The current implementation of *Inflo* has an architecture designed for extension through the use of plug-ins and APIs allowing third-party developers to build on this work. One of the primary envisioned uses of *Inflo* is as an open carbon calculator; the ability to link to live data sources such as current power consumption has been proposed to support this. Such an addition would be useful in other domains such as business intelligence and logistics.

Because *Inflo* provides a new way of communicating and collaborating, we plan to use it as a platform for exploring how to convey knowledge provenance and trust in decision-making tasks.

ACKNOWLEDGEMENTS

This research was made possible through the generous support of the Business Intelligence Network.

REFERENCES

1. J. Conklin and M. L. Begeman. glbis: A hypertext tool for exploratory policy discussion. *CSCW*, pages 140–152, 1988.
2. J. Conklin, A. Selvin, S. B. Shum, and M. Sierhuis. Facilitated hypertext for collective sensemaking: 15 years on from gibis. *HYPERTEXT*, pages 123–124, 2001.
3. A. D. Liddo and S. B. Shum. Cohere: A prototype for contested collective intelligence. *CSCW Workshop: Collective Intelligence In Organizations*, 2010.
4. A. K. Rantilla and D. V. Budescu. Aggregation of expert opinions. *Hawaii International Conference on System Sciences*, pages 1–11, 1999.

Predicting Creativity in the Wild: Experience Sample and Sociometric Modeling of Teams

Priyamvada Tripathi **Winslow Burleson**
School of Computing, Informatics, and Decision Systems Engineering
Arizona State University
{Pia, Winslow.burluson} @asu.edu

ABSTRACT
Relationships between creativity in teamwork, and team members' movement and face-to-face interaction strength were investigated "in the wild" using sociometric badges (wearable sensors), electronic Experience Sampling Methods (ESM), the KEYS team creativity assessment instrument, and qualitative methods, in academic and industry settings. Activities (movement and face-to-face interaction) and creativity of one five-member and two seven-member teams were tracked for twenty-five days, eleven days, and fifteen days respectively. Paired-sample t-test confirmed average daily movement energy during creative days was significantly greater than on non-creative days and that face-to-face interaction tie strength of team members during creative days was significantly greater than for non-creative days. The combined approach of principal component analysis (PCA) and linear discriminant analysis (LDA) conducted on movement and face-to-face interaction data yielded a model that predicted creativity with 87.5% and 91% accuracy, respectively. Computational models that predict team creativity hold particular promise to enhance Creativity Support Tools.

Author Keywords
Creativity Support Tools (CST), Sociometric Modeling, Experience Sample Method, Wearable Computing.

ACM Classification Keywords
H.5.3 Group and Organization Interfaces

General Terms
Human Factors; Measurement.

INTRODUCTION
Understanding how to foster creative capacity is among the most important goals of our society in preparation for the future. While there are many definitions of creativity, there is broad consensus that creativity is the creation of anything that is useful and original [32]. Creativity takes place through the unfolding of moment-to-moment activities in natural environments. This investigation studies the relationship between group activity characterized through team members' movement and face-to-face interactions within teams, and creativity in research and development teams in industry and academia. Group activity was tracked through sensor data from sociometric badges [25]. A social science survey instrument KEYS [2][5] was implemented through electronic ESM and Day Reconstruction Method [21] to capture self-reported creativity and was supplemented with expert-coded creativity measures. Statistical methods, machine learning, and qualitative approaches were used to analyze and validate the relationship between group activity (movement and face-to-face interaction) and everyday creative and non-creative events. This investigation contributes to the basic science of creativity and to the empirical methodologies that assess creativity. Providing movement and face-to-face interactions as a means of continuously sensing creativity accurately, with minimal human input, this research contribute to the design of CST.

Three studies ranging in duration from two to four weeks were conducted over a two-year period in leading research and development laboratories. These laboratories had similar spatial environments, consisting of a room with cubicles facing walls and a central collaboration space. All participants had regular working hours and the environment encouraged hands-on, real time interaction towards development of artifacts. To explore initial variables of interest, a pilot study was conducted with five participants over 25 days. Encouraged by the trends discovered in the pilot study, two further experiments were conducted with two, seven member teams, for 11 and 15 days, respectively.

The framework based on these studies paves the way for automated CST based on team activity [47] [48]. This framework combines existing qualitative methods of studying group creativity in context [4] with sensor-based data. The research was conducted in natural work place settings and advances the use of sensor data to support human creativity and teamwork.

BACKGROUND

Assessment of Creativity
Aimed at measuring creativity, several divergent thinking tests have been designed that test for fluency or rate of ideation in individuals. Some early tests proposed to test creativity were Guilford's Structure of Intellect (SOI) divergent production tests [19], and Torrance's Tests of

Creative Thinking (TTCT) [51]. A limitation of these parametric approaches is that they may measure only one aspect of creativity and may only work in controlled laboratory conditions. Alternate approaches have focused on the creative qualities of the process and outcome or final products, e.g., the creative product semantic scale [8] and Amabile's consensual assessment technique (CAT) [2].

CAT can be employed to address domain specific creativity and also be extended for analysis of team creativity. CAT relies on the inter-rater reliability between these expert judges to evaluate levels of creativity in processes and products. Amabile has also developed the KEYS scale based on her componential model of creativity [3] [5] that measures a variety of factors such as affect, rewards, and motivation, and asks the participants to self report on creativity (on a Likert scale) and to explain what they did throughout the day in an open ended question format. This scale addresses individual, team, and context variables concurrently, with checks and cross checks to ensure consistency and accuracy of responses.

Group Creativity Research

Work on creativity has largely focused on individual creativity. However, in recent years, there has been an increased interest in studying team creativity within organizations. An important observation is that it is not very clear how individual creativity is linked to team creativity [43]. Researchers have often dealt with this conundrum by focusing on individual creativity alone, or on team creativity alone, or on processes of interactions between team members [6][43][48][50].

Group creativity can be conceived as an additive or disjunctive property of individual creativity [43]. If it is additive, then each individual member's creativity adds up to the final creative output of the team. If it is disjunctive, the most creative ideas which may come from one or more individuals are adopted by the team. Team creativity may also manifest itself as a weighted combination of individual contributions. Amabile, in her componential model of creativity, has pointed out that intra-individual factors such as organization incentive for innovation, resources made available, and external pressure can impact individual creativity [2]. Taggar [50] found that in addition to creativity relevant skills, domain relevant knowledge, and intrinsic motivation at the individual level, there might be group related processes that are relevant to creativity. Amabile's KEYS scale [5] quantifies such variables in a reliable manner suitable for measuring team creativity.

Sensors for feedback and the display of group behavior [13][25] have provided automated support for group performance. These tools employ sensors in laboratory environments and focus on single modality, such as speech [28]. Several CSTs have also been developed that aim to improve group creativity. Most of the studies in CSTs center on the comparisons of an experimental group that uses the CST system versus a nominal group (set of individuals not acting as a group) or a control group that does not use the system [31]. Studies tend to focus on quantifying interactions and using them as a measure of creativity and productivity.

Interactions and Movement in Group Creativity

Network communication strength and the types of communication modalities within a team are additional behavioral factors that may impact group creativity [26]. While there is a belief that face-to-face interaction strength is central to the understanding of social networks in relation to creativity, there is insufficient empirical evidence to indicate strong relationship between face-to-face interaction and creativity. Tie strength (weak, strong) is a function of the amount and quality of interactions, emotional intensity, and reciprocity that takes place between two individuals [17]. Zhou *et al.* [55] found that employees exhibited greater creativity when their number of weak ties was neither too low, nor too high (an intermediate level exhibited greatest level of creativity). Perry-Smith and Shalley [42] showed that weak ties rather than strong ties are beneficial for creativity among research scientists. In contrast, Obstfeld [34] showed that engineers with strong ties are more creative. These studies show a complex, inconclusive, and possibly domain specific relationship between tie strength and creativity.

Research has also investigated the nature of the structure of social networks, within teams, that is most supportive for creativity [35]. Burt [10] claims that a network with several structural holes (many disconnected individuals) may be more creative. Burt hypothesizes that members who are closer to these structural holes are exposed to a greater diversity of perspectives, which has a positive impact on creativity. On the other hand, Perry-Smith and Shalley [42] claim that a dense network with all members strongly connected to each other provides an opportunity for free interchange of information and hence greater creativity.

Most research conducted on the relationship between movement and creativity is in the exercise sciences where brief period of activity such as walking on the treadmill is followed by creativity assessment questionnaires [30][49]. These studies have established that physical activity in humans is linked to their creativity. However, research is needed to understand how individual movement in the work environment is related to creative production.

Sensor Based Approach to Group Creativity Research

Recent advancements in sensor based pattern recognition with applications such as face recognition [53] and gait recognition [27] demonstrate the power of detecting low level signal streams and recognizing relevant patterns from them. Sociometric badges [39], used to capture movement, speech, and location, are an interesting recent example. They are a form of "environmentally aware computing" allowing capture of person's location, presence, and elements of the environment [38]. HCI research has leveraged such sensors using speech, and artifacts to study interactions within members of groups [13][16][37].

Burleson et al.; Choudhary; Kapoor et al.; Kim et al.; Olguin-Olguin et al.; and Pentland [9][11][22][25][37] [41] have conducted empirical studies that use physiological sensing and wearable computing to understand and predict high level behavioral constructs such as affect, activity and creative output. Methods from affective computing have been able to distinguish affective state with 81% accuracy throughout everyday activities [22] while machine learning tools that incorporate Human Eigen behaviors and Coupled Hidden Markov Models (CHMMs) have been shown to account for 96% of the variance of behavior of typical individuals [15].

Assumptions and Challenges in Analyzing Group Data

Group research is a challenging task [45]. The most difficult challenge from a statistical perspective lies in analyzing data from groups [20][24]. Data gathered from individual participants in group studies is often interdependent, which limits the use of several statistical tools for analysis. Yet, employing many of these techniques can be valid in group analysis as long as observations are shown to be independent. A foremost technique to show independence is correlation analysis [20] [12][19][23][33]. In the investigations reported here, calculation of intraclass coefficients confirmed the assumption of independence of data to be valid.

INSTRUMENTS AND METHODS

The following instruments and methods were approved by Institutional Review [52].

Sociometric badges: wearable sensors, worn as a pendant around the neck, recorded network data (Infra Red pings) at 17 Hz, body movements (2D accelerometer) at 50 Hz and ambient audio, not used in the present studies, using embedded speaker at 8 kHz. Badges track location and analyze elements of participant's social interaction through bi-directional infrared transceiver, accelerometer, and low-resolution microphone analysis. No personally identifiable data is recorded which ensures privacy of subjects. The raw data from the sensors are extracted into meaningful features that may correlate with team members' characteristics. Badges are equipped with triaxial accelerometers that give the value of movement in X, Y, and Z directions. The mean and standard deviation of movement energy for each participant for each day was calculated. Movement energy gives a measure of the intensity of individual movement that includes the effect of variation in signal around the three axes in the accelerometer [37]. It may also be classified into various types of physical activity such as walking, running, and sleeping [44].

Calculating Face-To-Face Tie Strength: Infrared signals in the sociometric badges provide a measure of face-to-face interaction. Badges record presence and duration of other badges when they are in direct line of each other (IR signal cone of height $\leq$ 1 meter and radius r $\leq$ h tan Θ where $\Theta = \pm 15°$) [37]. We counted the number of pings for each badge and constructed adjacency matrix for the data. Cells in the adjacency matrix represent the number of pings recorded for each badge with all other badges. This matrix was first made symmetric with respect to the minimum number of pings recorded for each pair. Subsequently, the adjacency matrix was used to generate face-to-face tie strength for each day (Total pings/Detected Number of Badges) for each participant. The badges have been extensively validated over several studies [7][25][40][37].

KEYS Scale: was used to obtain daily measures of creativity. The KEYS survey is designed to assess the perceived stimulants and obstacles to creativity in organizational work environments. Items of KEYS scale address negative and positive aspects of the environment. It is widely recognized as the current standard for measuring team creativity and innovation within organizational work environments [4]. The survey has fifteen questions, two of which are open-ended responses. A 7 point Likert scale is used for each of the questions. One measure is self-rated creativity that is extracted from the report of team creativity. The variable assesses member reports of creativity being experienced by the team. For the open ended questions, participants were asked to 1) "In a few words, briefly describe the major work you did on the assigned project pertaining to this study today, or the major activities you engaged in that were relevant to the target project" 2) "Briefly describe ONE event from today that stands out in your mind as relevant to the target project, your feelings about this project, your work on this project, your team's feelings about this project, or your team's work on this project."

CODE	EVENTS	CREATIVE (1/0)
11_P6_D4	Work on Cholecystectomy [sic] scene. Made a minor breakthrough today. A physics asset of a gall bladder model seemed to interact well. I pursued that lead with Cord and as it turned out I managed to create with his help a very nicely interacting model of the gall bladder.	1
12_P6_D4	Besides this I spent the day adding another layer to the connective tissue.	0

Table 1. A sample of coding combined narratives from events. CODE value represents Event Number_ParticipantID_Day. Note: This participant previously described adding the layer to connective tissue as a routine task.

KEYS requires an expert judge to rate the participants' reports by assigning numerical value for the level of creativity (0 or 1) in addition to the self-reports through the questionnaire. It has been shown to be reliable when the rating is conducted with one or more expert judges. Expert is defined as a person knowledgeable about domain.

In this investigation, the method described by Amabile et al. [4] was followed to obtain "expert coded creativity." The descriptions from the open-ended questions were combined together to form open-ended narratives for each participant. Unique instances of completed actions were extracted from the narrative for each participant to identify individual 'events.' The KEYS coding protocol defines creative thought as any of the following: (1) a discovery, insight, or idea; (2) the act of searching for a discovery, insight, or idea; (3) solving a problem in a non-rote way; or (4) the act of searching for a problem solution in a non-rote way. Events that had any of these were labeled 1 and events that did not have any of these were labeled 0. Table 1 illustrates the process through an example.

The basic assumption of KEYS is that psychological perceptions of work environment by the team members play a vital role in their creativity. The underlying model [1] identifies three components within the individual that have an effect on creativity, including individual's intrinsic motivation, his or her thinking style, and domain-relevant knowledge. The KEYS scales have been validated over several studies and are reported to have high validity and reliability [2].

EXPLORATORY EXPERIMENT

A pilot study explored whether there are correlations between individual activity and self-reported team creativity in a small group. A combination of quantitative and qualitative data for a team of individuals over an extended period of time was collected. These individuals worked in an industry research environment that required high levels of information technology and creativity in an industry setting. Creativity was measured through an online survey that had a combination of scale-rated responses and open-ended questions that allowed participants to describe their day-to-day experience of creativity. A multi-methodological approach was used to explore the relationship between data obtained from the sensed activity (movement and face-to-face interaction) [39] and levels of creativity collected via electronic ESM [4]. The results of this study informed our hypotheses for subsequent experiments.

Participants: A team of five people (2 females, 3 males; mean age = 32.4 years, range= 26-38 years) participated in a five-week study (total 25 working days). All participants had undergraduate degrees in engineering and two had post-graduate degrees (1 MBA and 1 MS). The team was involved in software coding and research in a leading industrial research and development laboratory in the United States. All participants were part of a single team engaged in highly creative research and development activities. The participants were selected because they worked in a tightly knit single location laboratory advancing IT research. The members conduct the majority of work in this laboratory in a highly interactive manner. No rewards were given to participants in this study. The head of this department was contacted via email and they in turn put the experimenter in contact with the team that volunteered for the study. All participation was voluntary and participants had the option to opt out at any time.

Materials and Procedure: This study used sociometric badges and the KEYS daily questionnaire. The study was conducted at a remote site with a team involved professionally in software coding projects. The experimenter shipped the badges to the remote site at the beginning of the study. Participants were required to charge the badge on their own every night by plugging them into computers via a USB cable that was provided.

All participants were informed that the investigation was on workflow issues in teamwork. This was largely done to avoid any bias on the part of the participants towards creativity. All participants were given a unique participation ID through which they corresponded for the duration of the study. The participants were also informed that their responses would remain anonymous and evaluated by researchers unaffiliated with their work environment. The participants were ensured that the data would not be shared with the supervisors directly and only anonymized aggregate analysis would be presented to audiences.

Before the experiment began, subjects were requested to answer an initial demographic questionnaire. During the study, each subject wore a sociometric badge. The subjects were requested to wear the badges throughout their workday (9 am to 5 pm) during the experimental period. At the end of the day, subjects were requested to answer a daily questionnaire. The data collection protocol occurred for 25 days and provided us with an extensive sampling of creative, non-creative episodes and the activity profiles associated with it. A reminder was sent at 4:15 pm everyday with the survey link via email to each participant. The data was downloaded only once at the end of the study when the badges were shipped back. Except for initial clarification on how badges worked and debriefing, there was no interaction between the experimenter and the participants.

Data Analysis and Results

KEYS and Sociometric Badges data were analyzed.

KEYS Daily Questionnaire Data: While there are 15 questions in the KEYS survey, this analysis focused on three questions that dealt with self-rated creativity, expert-coded creativity, and measures of team interaction (other variables in the KEYS survey are beyond the scope of current investigation). Out of 125 expected responses (25 days *5 participants), 96 daily surveys were received, and the average response rate was 76.8% with a standard deviation of 23%. From the surveys, the value for self reported creativity was obtained (Likert Scale: 1 – 'not at all', 7 – 'extremely'). In addition to the scaled responses, the KEYS instrument and its methodology provide the opportunity for expert coding of creative and non-creative events. For each survey response, the narratives from the two open ended questions were combined. The participants' combined narratives ranged from 462 words to 2348 words with a mean of 53 words per entry.

Sociometric Badges Data: The five badges were collected at the end of the 25-day period. While the mean and standard deviation for four participants was obtained over all days successfully, one of the badges failed to record any data and the remaining four failed to record face-to-face interaction data. Due to the remote nature of the study and the lack of time stamps, the exact time and duration of wearing and taking off the badges could not be determined.

Correlation Results: Pearson correlation coefficient values obtained for all major variables. The significance value was set at 0.1 as this was an exploratory study with a low N. There was a significant large correlation ($r = 0.91$) between self-rated creativity and movement of the participants. There was a significant medium correlation ($r=0.77$) between speech and expert-coded creativity. There was a significant correlation ($r=0.88$) between degree (KEYS scale) and expert-coded creativity. There was a significant negative correlation ($r = -0.82$) between movement and hours spent with team (KEYS scale).

Summary: Participants' self-rated creativity was highly correlated with their daily movement energy. There was low correlation between expert-coded creativity and movement and between expert-coded creativity and self-reported creativity. The number of people a team member meets had medium correlation with expert-coded creativity. The data indicated a few interesting trends. First, participants feel more creative when they move more. Second, they are generally more creative when they are meeting more people in the team and feel more connected.

MAIN EXPERIMENT I

Experiment I employed the pilot study methodologies and procedures to investigate the following two hypotheses:

- **H1.** *Average daily movement energy of team members during days with above average self-rated creativity is significantly greater than the average daily movement of days with below average self-rated creativity*
- **H2.** *Average face-to-face tie strength of team members during days with above average expert-coded creativity is significantly greater than the average face-to-face tie strength of team members of days with below average expert-coded creativity*

with $p < 0.05$ accepted as statistically significant.

Methods

Seven participants engaged in creative research were observed for two work weeks (11 days) during regular work hours (9 am to 5 pm). The mean age of participants was 24.7 years (range = 24–32 years), and 4 out of 7 participants were men. The sample was highly educated, 4 out of 7 participants were college graduates engaged in postgraduate work, and 3 were senior undergraduates. All participants were recruited via email and signed consent form for voluntary participation prior to the start of the study. Approval was also obtained from the laboratory head, prior to the start of the study. No rewards were provided for participation in the study. Recruited participants worked together as a team in a Carnegie Research I University in information technology rich environments. For 11 days, the experimenter visited the laboratory each morning to ensure that the participants' badges were worn at 9 am. The experimenter observed activities throughout the day and at 5 pm requested the participants to turn the badges off.

Data Analysis and Results

KEYS Daily Questionnaire Data: Out of total 77 (11 days *7 people) daily online surveys, the number of surveys completed was 58. The mean response rate was 75% with a standard deviation of 19%. From the survey, the value of self-rated creativity was calculated. Expert-coded creativity scores were obtained by analyzing the narratives. Participants' combined narratives ranged from 63 words to 516 words with a mean of 290 words for each participant.

Sociometric Badge Data: For each day, participants' movement energies were calculated and face-to-face interaction recorded. The adjacency matrix thus obtained was made symmetric with respect to the lowest number of signals (or pings) that were recorded. The average number of pings was calculated for each participant for each day.

Experimental Data: The following four variables: (1) self-rated creativity; (2) expert-coded creativity; (3) movement energy; and (4) face-to-face tie strength were analyzed. The creativity data was mean split in two ways based on 1) self-rated creativity and 2) expert-coded creativity. K-Means clustering showed that the ratio of inter-cluster distance to intra-cluster distance was high ($R=0.94$) which validated the choice of mean split. For each of these two measures of creativity, the days that had values for creativity higher than the mean were labeled creative while those days that were at or below the mean value were classified as non-creative.

H1 Result: A paired-samples t-test was conducted to test H1. This t-test [$t(36) = 3.132$, $p < 0.005$] confirmed, the hypothesis that average daily movement energy during days with above average creativity ($M = 1.31$, $SD = 0.04$) was significantly greater than the average daily movement of days with below average creativity ($M = 1.29$, $SD = 0.03$). The eta-squared statistic (0.21) indicated a large effect size.

H2 Result: A paired-samples t-test was conducted to test H2. The t test [t (21) = 1.05, p > 0.1] showed no significant difference between average face-to-face tie strength of team members during days with above average expert-coded creativity (M = 9.4, SD = 10) and the average face-to-face tie strength of team members (M = 6.3, SD = 7) for days with below average expert-coded creativity

Correlation Data: There was a significant correlation between face-to-face interaction and both self-rated creativity (r=0.45) and expert-coded creativity (r=0.45). A significant correlation (r=0.66) was also found between movement and self-rated creativity.

Summary: Results confirm H1, average movement for creative days is significantly higher than for non-creative days. H2 was not confirmed. Face-to-face interaction was highly correlated with expert-coded creativity and movement was highly correlated with self-rated creativity.

MAIN EXPERIMENT II

Experiment II built on results from Experiment I, using the same methodologies, procedures, and hypotheses.

Seven participants engaged in creative research were observed for two work weeks (15 days) during regular work hours (10 am -5 pm). They engaged in research intensive creative work in an information technology (IT) rich environment. The mean age of participants was 27.4 years (range = 23–32 years) and 6 out of 7 participants were men. Our sample was highly educated, 4 out of 7 participants were college graduates engaged in postgraduate work, and 3 were senior undergraduates. All participants were recruited via email and signed consent forms for voluntary participation prior to the start of the study. Approval was also obtained from the laboratory head prior to the study and no rewards were provided for participation.

Materials and Procedure: Experiment II followed Experiment I protocols, adding ESM reports to understand face-to-face interaction relationships with creativity. At the end of each hour (from 11 am - 5 pm), participants received an SMS request: "For the last hour, you were Creative 1 or Non-creative 2 and Meeting 1 or not meeting 2 (respond 1 1 if creative and meeting and so on)". Qualitative observations by an expert coder provided descriptions of events, people involved, actions, movement, and meetings.

Data Analysis and Results

KEYS Daily Questionnaire Data: Out of a total of 105 (15*7) daily surveys, the number of surveys completed was 76. The open-ended narratives were coded to obtain scores for expert-coded creativity for all participants for each of the 15 days. Participants' combined narratives ranged from 293 words to 1663 words with a mean of 973 words.

Sociometric Badge Data: Accelerometer data from the badge of each participant was downloaded every day. By using the same formula used in our previous studies, we calculated a movement energy array that was later used to give us mean and standard deviation of movement energy for each day. The average face-to-face tie strength was calculated for each participant across 15 days.

Experimental Data: We obtained the following four variables for each participant for 15 days: (1) self-rated creativity (2) expert-coded creativity (3) movement energy (4) average face-to-face tie strength. The data was mean split in two ways based on 1) self-rated creativity and 2) expert-coded creativity. For each of these two measures of creativity, the days that had values for creativity higher than the mean were labeled creative while those days at or below the mean value were classified as non-creative.

H1 Result. A paired-samples t test was conducted to test H1. The t test [t (23) = 6.49, p < 0.001] confirmed that average daily movement energy during days with above average self-rated creativity (M = 1.37, SD = 0.07) is significantly greater than the average daily movement of days with below average self-rated creativity (M = 1.24, SD = 0.09). This was a large effect (eta-squared = 0.36).

H2 Result. A paired-samples t test was conducted to test H2. The t test [t (41) = 2.36, p < 0.01] showed average face-to-face tie strength of team members during days with above average expert-coded creativity (M = 2.69, SD = 4.01) is significantly greater than the average face-to-face tie strength of team members for days with below average expert-coded creativity (M = 0.9, SD = 2.1). The eta-squared statistic (0.11) indicated a large effect size.

Correlation Data: Pearson product-moment correlations between all major variables in the study were calculated. Self-rated creativity was weakly, but significantly correlated with expert-coded creativity (r = 0.25). In addition, movement and self-rated creativity were significantly correlated (r = 0.55). Face-to-face interaction had significant correlation with both self-rated creativity (r = 0.20) and expert-coded creativity (r = 0.25).

SMS Data: A total 99 hours of data was collected for 1 hour intervals of self-reported daily activity indicating whether meetings or non-meetings were occurring and whether or not these hours were creative. We summed across all days for four variables: (1) Creative and Meeting (2) Creative and Not meeting (3) Non-creative and Meeting and (4) Non-creative and Not meeting. We found that people reported to be creative while they were meeting (165 hours) more than twice than when they reported to be not creative while meeting (71 hours). The correlation between self-rated creativity and creative and meeting reports was significant (r = 0.82, p<0.01), and there was significant negative correlation between reports of non-creative and non-meeting and self-rated creativity (r= -0.58, p<0.05).

Summary: A significant difference was found between team member movements for creative days and non-creative days. Creative days were also shown to have higher face-to-face interaction than the non-creative days. Participants' SMS reports indicated that episodes of meeting one or more team members were twice as likely to be creative than non-creative. Moreover, across fifteen days, there was a significant correlation between meeting episodes and self-reported creativity. People were two times more likely to report non-creative events when not in meetings. Overall, results show that participants in a small group are likely to be more creative when they are more active, in terms of both movement and face-to-face interaction.

COMPUTATIONAL MODELING OF TEAM CREATIVITY

Statistical learning techniques and pattern recognition techniques on a validated subset of features available from the sociometric badges and labeled events were employed for the development of the computational models, following methods developed by Olguin et al. [36][37]. Olguin-Olguin et al. [37] have developed computational techniques for studying the relation between activity measured through sociometric badges and several variables like performance in healthcare environment and studying productivity in IT domains. These techniques employ signal processing techniques to extract relevant features from the data stream that correlate with social signals and measures of performance. Pentland employed eigenvector representation to study the variance of behavior of individuals [39]. They showed that there was limited amount of behavior variance across days for individuals implying high predictability.

With data from Experiments I and II, standard linear regression [14] was used to study relationships between activity-network profiles and the creativity class. Subsequently, Naïve Bayesian Classifier (NBC) [14] were employed. A third approach, a combination of principal component analysis (PCA) [14] for dimensionality reduction and linear discriminant analysis (LDA) [14] for classification based on approaches developed for face recognition by Li et al. [29], was then used to develop a deterministic approach to computational modeling of creativity. Maximum Likelihood Estimation (MLE) was used as the training approach. Matlab 2009® algorithm implementations, *glmfit* for linear regression, NaiveBayes.fit and predict for NBC and classify function for LDA, were used.

Procedure for Computational Modeling Approaches

Data from Experiments I and II provided day-to-day team members' activity and overall creativity scores. The data sets were combined and the days were divided into two classes: creative and non-creative based on the mean split of reported creativity measures. The movement data was divided based on self-rated creativity while the face-to-face interaction (or network pings) data was divided based on expert-coded creativity. The corresponding measures were chosen to classify the data based on the results from Experiments I and II. Overall 182 hours of data per subject (participant N=7, for 26 days) totaling 1274 hours of data was collected. The activity as measured through accelerometer (X, Y, and Z) and network pings from IR were considered for analysis.

For face-to-face quantification, the average IR ping information for the day for each participant was considered for the computational model. As each experiment had 7 participants, there was 7x7 matrix of face-to-face network pings as sensed by the IR sensor for each day. For every day, the frequency of pings for every pair of participants, which could be understood as network edge strength in the team's network, was calculated. In the team network, participants are the node and the edges represent face-to-face interactions. Of the 26 days worth of network data, 14 were labeled creative and 12 were labeled as non-creative according to expert-coded creativity. The 7x7 matrix of IR ping frequency for each day was linearized into a 49x1 vector representing pings per day for all possible person-person interactions. The creativity class (creative or non-creative) for each vector was known. This matrix was employed to train pattern recognition algorithms to assess expert-coded creativity, measure in Experiment I and II.

For movement analysis, the accelerometer readings were sampled at 50,000 readings per day with 3 measures per reading (X,Y,Z), to define a representative sample of activity profile for each day. The day-activity matrix was assembled by linearizing the accelerometer activity into a vector and then assembling the individual vectors into a matrix. For each vector, a class of creativity (creative or non-creative) was known. This matrix was employed to train pattern recognition algorithms to assess creativity.

For each of the three approaches, an 80/20 train/test paradigm was employed. Algorithms for movement data and network ping (face-to-face interaction) data were trained individually as they provided related but distinct information and related to different measures of creativity. In the analysis of face-to-face interactions, the core idea was to classify the entire day as being creative or non-creative for the whole team. This computational engine was tuned to gestalt creativity classification for an entire day and hence provided complementary information to the movement data based classifier that provided per-day per-person ratings. The network ping based classifier was geared towards assessing the team's everyday creativity.

Results from Computational Modeling Approaches

PCA was applied for dimensionality reduction and LDA for classification as a means of achieving high accuracy and fast computation results. The energy of the eigenvalues indicated 7 dimensions were sufficient to cover 95% of variance with the movement data; PCA was used to reduce the dimensionality of the data from 150,000 to 7. LDA was then used as the classification technique. In the case of face-to-face interaction strength, 3 dimensions were sufficient to represent 95% of variance in PCA, hence dimensionality was reduced to 3 and LDA was performed.

For movement data, linear regression showed the lowest classification accuracy of 45.2%; the fit was not high or significant. NBC showed an accuracy of 70.2%. The NBC fit performed significantly better than linear regression achieving accuracies of about 70% for both movement and face-to-face interaction data. The combined approach of PCA and LDA showed an accuracy of 87.5% for per-day per-person data as measured through the movement stream and 90.9% for face-to-face interaction.

Additional endeavors (see [52]) using reduced dimensionality data for linear regression and NBC showed slight improvements (47.1% and 71% classification accuracy). This suggests the superiority of the PCA/LDA approach in obtaining accurate classification. The results for face-to-face interaction data were analogous, with the PCA/LDA combination achieving the highest recognition accuracy of 90.9%, NBC achieving 71.2% and linear regression achieving an accuracy of 44.5%.

Discussion of Computational Modeling Approaches

While the results are based on a limited data set and require further validation, it is encouraging to note that computational engines can be designed to ascertain creativity from sensor data. PCA and LDA analysis yielded close to 92% accuracy. While we cannot imply causality to this result, the fact that linear approaches give encouraging results opens up several possibilities for analysis of creativity in an automated fashion. The two approaches NBC and PCA-LDA combination both have unique advantages and requirements. NBC can be very successful in developing long-term trends and patterns and can be employed in a formative fashion. The PCA-LDA combination can actually give the highest accuracy as it removes noise from the original data. Noise may have contributed to low accuracy in the results of linear regression. We trained on data from two studies, suggesting this approach may be somewhat robust and generalizable.

DISCUSSION

This investigation shows there is a significant relationship between (1) individual movement and self-rated creativity and (2) face-to-face interaction and expert-coded creativity.

Specifically, daily movement energy for creative days was significantly higher than the movement energy of the non-creative days for team members. In terms of face-to-face interaction, in Experiment I, while no significant difference between face-to-face interaction for creative and noncreative days classified on the basis of expert-coded creativity was found, the trend in significance encouraged further exploration in Experiment II, using sms based ESM to gather participants report on their ongoing behavior [54]. Participants reported the highest number of both creative and meeting and noncreative and not-meeting episodes. The third highest number was creative and not-meeting. The least reported variable was not creative and meeting. This suggests that participants were generally more creative when they were meeting and generally more non-creative when they were not meeting. However, an important component of overall team creativity is a combination of team and individual creativity. Reports of being creative and not-meeting tend to be on the same days participants had also reported to be creative and meeting. Teams were far more creative on days in which the members met. Team members also reported to be personally more creative after active interactions with other team members. In Experiment II, face-to-face tie strength was significantly greater in the creative days than that of non-creative days.

These results show a strong correlation between movement and self-rated creativity. Prior studies have found that exercise or a physical activity of some kind enhances cognitive performance [49] and physical activity is correlated with creativity [30]. While the results of these prior studies were based on questionnaire data implemented on the middle aged or elderly populations, the presented research is the first effort of its kind to employ a multi-methodological approach that confirms the relationship between sensed movement data with creativity.

In the KEYS scale, there are two variables namely individual creativity and team creativity. Interestingly, there was 94% correlation between reported scores of team creativity and individual creativity. This might be because individual participants had no prior definition of creativity or basis of differentiating between the two variables. This raises the question, "What, exactly, do the personal creativity and team creativity variables represent in the KEYS scale?" The results show that how participants feel about their own creativity (self-reported personal creativity) may be the same as how they rate their team as being creative (team creativity). It must be noted that the creativity score obtained by an expert that is based on their descriptions is not necessarily correlated with their creativity self-reports. This could be because these measure two different facets of creativity.

Several key questions need to be answered with respect to the nature of the following question: how much and how often team interactions should occur for the team to be more creative? To provide clues to some of these questions, the role of degree (number of team members meeting each other) in both the experiments was explored and found in both cases to have no significant [$t(36) = 1.55, p > 0.12$; $t(20) = 0.23, p > 0.8$]. The means in the two cases in both the experiments were almost equivalent (Non Creative: M = 1.81, SD = 1.68; M = 1.67, SD = 1.8; Creative: M = 1.24, SD = 1.38; M = 1.52, SD = 1.5). Thus it is not the number of people a team member meets with, but rather the quality of face-to-face interaction (or the time spent with the team members) that influences creativity.

The computational modeling results show the feasibility of developing an automated system for creativity based on team members' activities. Linear regression analysis did not yield high accuracy but the Bayesian modeling and the combined PCA and LDA approach had high recognition accuracies. Principal component analysis showed that 7 dimensions encompassed close to 95% variation in the underlying data from movement data and 3 dimensions encompassed 95% variation in the face-to-face interaction data. The analysis of principal dimensions and the weights of the individual units showed that individuals with highest creativity were given the highest weight and individuals with the lowest creativity where given the lowest weight.

CONCLUSION

Computational modeling of team creativity has several benefits: (1) it allows automated evaluation and prediction of creativity; (2) it paves the way for software and programs that support creativity; (3) it allows development of guidelines and procedures towards creativity in teams and within organizations; (4) it enhances theoretical understandings of creativity and its relationship to team member activity.

The key findings of these studies were: (1) days in which the team is highly creative are also the days in which the teams' members meet more often, and (2) days in which team members report to be highly creative have higher levels of movement among team members than the days they report to be non-creative. Through a multi-methodological approach that coupled sensor based analysis, wearable computing, and creative behavior assessment this investigation helps us better understand the nature and mechanisms of team creativity in the wild.

ACKNOWLEDGMENTS

We thank Teresa Amabile, Leo Burd, Mary Czerwinski, Kanav Kahol, Taemie Kim, and Sandy Pentland for advice and support in conducting this research.

REFERENCES

1. Amabile, T. (1993). Motivational synergy: toward new conceptualizations of intrinsic and extrinsic motivation in the workplace. *Human Resource Management Review, 3*(3), 185-201.
2. Amabile, T. (1996). *Creativity in context*: Westview Press, Boulder, CO.
3. Amabile, T. M. (1983). The social psychology of creativity: a componential conceptualization. *Journal of Personality and Social Psychology, 45*(2), 357-376.
4. Amabile, T. M., Barsade, S. G., Mueller, J. S., & Staw, B. M. (2005). Affect and creativity at work. *Administrative Science Quarterly, 50,* 367-403.
5. Amabile, T. M., Conti, R., Coon, H., Lazenby, J., & Herron, M. (1996). Assessing the work environment for creativity. *Acad. of Mgt. J., 39*(5), 1154-1184.
6. Bain, P., Mann, L., & Pirola-Merlo, A. (2001). The innovation imperative. *Small Group Research, 32*(1), 55–73.
7. Basu, A. 2002. Conversational scene analysis. Doctoral dissertation. MIT.
8. Besemer, S. P., & O'Quin, K. (1993). Assessing creative products: Progress and potentials. In S. G. Isaksen (Ed.), *Nurturing and Developing Creativity: The Emergence of a Discipline* (pp. 331-349). Norwood, New Jersey: Ablex Publishing Corp.
9. Burleson, W., Picard, R., Perlin, K., & Lippincott, J. (2004). A platform for affective agent research. Wkshp. on Empathetic Agents, 3rd. Int. Joint Conf. on Autonomous Agents and Multi-Agent Sys.
10. Burt, R. S. (2004). Structural holes and good ideas. *American Journal of Sociology, 110*(2), 349-399.
11. Choudhary, T. 2004. Sensing and modeling human networks. Doctoral dissertation. MIT.
12. Christensen, R., & Bedrick, E. J. (1997). Testing the independence assumption in linear models. *Journal of the American Statistical Assoc., 92,* 1006-1016.
13. DiMicco, J. M., & Bender, W. (2007). Group reactions to visual feedback tools. In Y. de Kort, B. J. Fogg, W. IJsselsteijn, B. Eggen & C. Midden (Eds.), *Persuasive Technology* (Vol. 4744, pp. 132-143): Springer Berlin / Heidelberg.
14. Duda, R., Hart , P., & Stork, D. (2000). *Pattern Classification* (2 ed.). NY: Wiley Interscience.
15. Eagle, N. (2005). *Machine Perception and Learning of Complex Social Systems*. MIT.
16. Farooq, U., Carrol, J. M., Ganoe, C. H. 2007. Supporting creativity with awareness in distributed collaboration. *ACM Group*.
17. Granovetter, M. (1973). The strength of weak ties. *American Journal of Sociology, 78*(6), 1360-1380.
18. Griffin, D., & Gonzalez, R. (1995). Correlational analysis of dyad-level data in the exchangeable case. *Psychological Bulletin, 118,* 430-439.
19. Guilford, J. P. (1956). The structure of intellect. *Psychological Bulletin, 53*(4), 267-293.
20. Hoyle, R., Georgesen, J., & Webster, J. (2001). Analyzing data from individuals in groups: The past, the present, and the future. *Group Dynamics: Theory, Research, and Practice, 5*(1), 41-47.
21. Kahneman, D., Krueger, A., Schkade, D., Schwarz, N., Stone, A. (2004). A survey method for characterizing daily life experience: the day reconstruction method science, *306* (5702), 1776-80.
22. Kapoor, A., Burleson, W., & Picard, R. W. (2007). Automatic prediction of frustration. *International Journal of Human-Computer Studies, 65*, 724-736.

23. Kenny, D. A., & Judd, C. M. (1996). A general procedure for the estimation of interdependence. *Psychological Bulletin, 119*, 138-148.
24. Kenny, D. A., Mannetti, L., Pierro, A., Livi, S., & Kashy, D. A. (2002). The statistical analysis of data from small groups. *Journal of Personality and Social Psychology, 83*(1), 126–137.
25. Kim, T., Chang, A., & Pentland, A. S. (2007). Enhancing organizational communication using sociometric badges. Paper presented at the IEEE 11th Int. Symp. on Wearable Computing.
26. Kraut, R. E., Egido, C., & Galegher, J. (1988). Patterns of contact and communication in scientific research collaboration. *CSCW*.
27. Lee, L., & Grimson, W. E. (2002). Gait analysis for recognition and classification. 5th IEEE Int. Conf. on Automatic Face and Gesture Recognition (FG'02).
28. Leshed, G. (2009). Automated language-based feedback for teamwork behaviors. Doctoral dissertation. Cornell University.
29. Li, J., Zhao, B., & Zhang, H. (2009). Face recognition based on PCA and LDA combination feature extraction. In *1st. Int. Conf. on Inf. Sci. and Eng*.
30. Malone, H. N. (1989). The relationship between traits of creativity and physical activity in the elderly. (Unpublished thesis). Ohio State University.
31. Massetti, B. (1996). An empirical examination of the value of creativity support systems on idea generation. *MIS Quarterly, 20*, 83-97.
32. Mayer, R. E. (1999). Fifty years of creativity research. In R. J. Sternberg (Ed.), *Handbook of Creativity*. NY: Cambridge University Press.
33. Moritz, S. E., & Watson, C. B. (1998). Levels of analysis issues in group psychology. *Group Dyn.: Theory, Research, and Practice, 2*, 285-298.
34. Obstfeld, D. (2005). Social networks, the tertius iungens orientation, and involvement in innovation. *Administrative Science Quarterly, 50*, 100-130.
35. Ohly, S., Kase, R., & Skerlavaj, M. (2010). Networks for generating and for validating ideas: The social side of creativity. *Innovation: Management, Policy & Practice, 12*, 41-52.
36. Olguín-Olguín, D., Kam, M., & Pentland, A. S. (2010). Quantifying the effects of centrality and tie strength on performance in face-to-face networks. Workshop on Information Networks, New York, NY.
37. Olguin-Olguin, D., Gloor, P. A., & Pentland, A. S. (2009). Capturing individual and group behavior with wearable sensors. *AAAI Spring Symposium*.
38. Pentland, A. (2005). Socially aware computation and communication. *IEEE Computer* (March), 63-70.
39. Pentland, A. (2007). Automatic mapping and modeling of human networks. *Physica A: Statistical Mechanics and Its Applications, 378*(1), 59-67.
40. Pentland, A. (2008). *Honest Signals*. Cambridge, Massachusetts: The MIT Press.
41. Pentland, A. (2009). Reality mining of mobile communications: Toward a new deal on data. *The Global Information Technology Report*, 75-80.
42. Perry-Smith, J. E., & Shalley, C. E. (2003). The social side of creativity: A static and dynamic social network perspective. *Academy of Management Review, 28*, 89-106.
43. Pirola-Merlo, A., & Mann, L. (2004). The relationship between individual creativity and team creativity: aggregating across people and time. *Journal of Organizational Behavior* 25, 235–257.
44. Ravi, N., Dandekar, N., Mysore, P., & Littman, M. L. (2005). Activity recognition from accelerometer data. In *The Seventeenth Conference on Innovative Applications of Artificial Intelligence (IAAI)*, Pittsburg, Pennsylvania, July 2005.
45. Saddler, M. S., & Judd, C. M. (2003). Overcoming dependent data: A guide to the analysis of group data. In M. A. Hogg & R. S. Tindale (Eds.), *Blackwell Handbook of Social Psychology: Group Processes*. Oxford, UK: Blackwell.
46. Scott, S. G., & Bruce, R. A. (1994). Determinants of innovative behavior: a path model of individual innovation in the workplace. *Academy of Management Journal, 37*(3), 580-607.
47. Shneiderman, B. (2003). *Leonardo's Laptop: Human Needs and the New Computing Technologies*. Cambridge, MA: The MIT Press.
48. Shneiderman, B., Hewett, T., Fischer, G., Jennings, P., Czerwinski, M., Kules, B., et al. (2006). Creativity support tools, NSF wkshp. *Int. J. HCI, 20*(2), 61-77.
49. Singh-Manoux, A., Hillsdon, M., Brunner, E., & Marmot, M. (2005). Effects of physical activity on cognitive functioning in middle age: Evidence from the Whitehall II Prospective Cohort Study. *American Journal of Public Health, 95*(12), 2252.
50. Taggar, S. (2002). Individual creativity and group ability to utilize individual creative resources: a multilevel model. *Acad. of Mgt. J., 45*(2), 315–330.
51. Torrance, E. P. (1974). *The Torrance Tests of Creative Thinking-Norms-Technical Manual Research Edition-Verbal Tests, Forms A and B-Figural Tests, Forms A and B*. Princeton, NJ: Personnel Press.
52. Tripathi, P. (2011). Predicting creativity in the wild: Doctoral dissertation. ASU.
53. Turk, M., & Pentland, A. (1991). Eigenfaces for recognition. *J. of Cog. Neurosicence, 3*(1), 71-86.
54. Weisner, R., Ryan, G., Reese, L., Kroesen, K., Bernheimer, L., & Gallimore, R. (2001). Behavior sampling and ethnogr. *Field Methods, 13*(1), 20-46.
55. Zhou, J., Shin, S., Brass, D., Choi, J., & Zhang, Z. (2009). Social networks, personal values, and creativity. *J. of Applied Psych., 94*(6), 1544-1552.

ConvoCons: A Tool for Building Affinity Among Distributed Team Members

Michael A. Oren
Iowa State University
1620 Howe Hall, Ames, IA 50011
mikeoren@gmail.com

Stephen B. Gilbert
Iowa State University
1620 Howe Hall, Ames, IA 50011
gilbert@iastate.edu

ABSTRACT

In this paper we present the result of a user interface designed to increase social affinity between two remote collaborators working on design tasks. The results suggest that the tool is successful in creating an overall affinity that is 14.6% higher than the control group without adding a significant difference in task completion time. Affinity is measured with a framework with demonstrated inter-rater reliability using codes assigned to specific conversational patterns and video recorded interactions. This research approach provides a platform for future work codifying affinity and trust among larger numbers of remote collaborators.

Author Keywords

Social Affinity, Distributed Teams, Collaboration, Social Interface Design

ACM Classification Keywords

H5.m. Information interfaces and presentation (e.g., HCI): Miscellaneous.

INTRODUCTION

For modern office workers, an all too common problem in the globalized workforce tends to be a case of feeling misunderstood by fellow employees, disconnected, or even embattled with an individual who is supposed to be on the same team. While part of this problem stems from clashes of cultures and personalities, components of the problem are present in any team setting. However, distributed team arrangements enhance this problem as workers are unable to have the water cooler chats that help them build social affinity bonds. In this paper, we adapted Nardi's framework for affinity and define "social affinity" as the "convergence of thoughts, actions, or ideas" [24]. Using this definition, it can be inferred that a group that lacks affinity will have group members that are more likely to work independently from one another and more likely to enforce personal space.

Increasing globalization has heightened the need for remote collaboration with a distributed workforce where team members may have little information about the individuals with whom they work and no opportunities to learn about their colleagues' expertise through informal face-to-face communication [37]. While instant messaging (IM) and other computer mediated communication tools may allow for some opportunities for colleagues to learn about one another's background and expertise, the barriers of time zones and limited opportunities for incidental conversation with remote colleagues often prevent these informal dialogues. This situation results in the hidden cost that team members may not be aware of expert knowledge another team member may have. There is also the more salient cost that remote collaborators have an impaired ability to form social affinity bonds that are critical to the creation of social capital and the type of social creativity required by modern product design teams [12, 31].

Much of the work of computer supported cooperative work has examined making the experience more comparable to natural interactions [30, 34], increasing the efficiency of work [6], or improving the flow of project-specific information [25]. Similarly, the design of groupware systems has so far focused primarily on either all participants sharing the same workspace [11, 21] or participants having a shared workspace with personal workspaces that serve to test ideas individually and these personal spaces are often visible to collaborators [32, 33, 35].

For our particular project, we were interested in using privileged information to encourage incidental conversation and affinity building among remotely located strangers working on design tasks, extending our work on the co-located version of this problem [26, 27]. In previous research on co-located collaboration, Oren and Gilbert provided a possible solution design solution called ConvoCons (conversational icons) with which social affinity was 40% higher in the experimental group compared with a control [27]. Furthermore, Aragon demonstrated that simple computational systems could be used in an applied work environment to increase social bonds and collaboration [1]. Theory suggests that by encouraging individual awareness of partner-privileged information, it will increase the sharing of additional information outside of the elements the design solution presents to collaborators [14, 24, 36]. The contributions of this paper include design guidance for interfaces that promote awareness of privileged information and a tool for promoting social affinity among remote collaborators.

CSCW 2012, February 11-15, 2012, Seattle, Washington, USA.

In this research, we had three research questions: (Q1) How can we promote awareness of privileged information in the interface during remote collaboration? (Q2) Are ConvoCons effective at promoting incidental conversations between remote collaborators? (Q3) Does our design solution result in increased observable signs of affinity as measured through behavioral and conversational cues?

ConvoCons

A ConvoCon, or conversational icon, is a semi-transparent visual interface element that appears for a brief time on top of an existing interface, somewhat like notification alerts from calendar or email software [27]. However, ConvoCons are different in two key ways. First, they are designed specifically not to interfere with the current task; they do not afford any interaction. They are not clickable or closeable; they disappear on their own. They do not interfere with clicking/touching UI elements underneath them. Second, their content, which can be text or media, is chosen to spark conversation. This content may be unrelated to the task at hand. While this design approach may seem to be an apt definition of "distraction" for some readers, the aforementioned success at increasing affinity by 40% without a statistically significant difference in completion time makes them worth further research and development [27].

Overview of Sections

As we used an iterative pilot study to evaluate elements of the interface and refine the final study, several insights into the design of interfaces with privileged information came to our attention. As these insights were critical to the final design of the remote ConvoCon study, we have chosen to detail this approach as part of addressing Q1. In particular, we see this iteration history as having application in the design of systems in which differing domain expertise may lead to different display configurations even as all collaborators work within the same software application. Following our discussion of the design of remote ConvoCons, we address Q2 and Q3 by presenting the results of a study comparing a control and experimental group based on self-reported metrics, performance metrics, and observed social affinity. Finally, we discuss the implications of these results, how they might be generalized, and several limitations that exist both in our experiment and in the ConvoCons system more generally.

Q1 PROMOTING AWARENESS OF PRIVILEGED INFORMATION

By "privileged information" we mean information that only one team member possesses. In the specific case, that information may be a simple fact that is known by one person. In the general case, privileged information includes deep knowledge of a domain that only one member possesses based on expertise, e.g. a neurosurgeon's knowledge when in a surgical team as the only neurosurgeon. In our research context, we adopt the following logic model based on previous research: incidental conversation increases affinity among partners [24, 27], which increases sharing of privileged conversation [14, 24, 31, 36]. While we had previously succeeded in increasing the social affinity of co-located groups, we found that the approach used in the co-located condition was ineffective when working with remote dyads [27]. We attempted to resolve this by utilizing research that explains how technology can define an individual's social expectations as well as work that explored establishing coordination policies outside of traditional social protocols [19, 23]. In addition, we were able to utilize previous research into design and placement of web advertisements to try to alleviate problems of banner blindness by varying the color of the ConvoCons so they would be salient while at the same time matching the style of the content the users were working with [18, 20].

Individuals who lack social affinity will be less likely to share privileged information, which acts as a tangible form of social capital [13, 31]. Privileged information may also not be shared because individuals assume expertise will be shared. and experts assume that other individuals have the same information as they do. Increasing individuals' awareness of these disconnects may reduce these problems, although the evaluation of this question is beyond the scope of this paper. Finally, it should be noted that individuals who have high affinity may also have reduced sharing of privileged information due to an assumption that somebody in agreement with and similar to oneself must share the same information.

As expressed in design teams, privileged information may include technical details about the implementation that engineers are aware of, which they may withhold from designers or not realize need to be shared. On the reverse side of the equation, designers may have critical information about the aesthetics and interaction that might seem intuitively obvious unless they are aware of information gaps.

In examining this problem, we defined the audience as strangers collaborating remotely for the first time with no knowledge of physical appearance, skill set, or expertise. We chose to have participants collaborate via voice communication but not video to minimize the effect of stereotypes based on appearance.

We evaluated the interaction within a multitouch, multiplayer tangram puzzle interface developed internally that made collaborators aware of where their partners were touching in accordance with the recommendation by Kellogg and Erickson [17] for transparency of actions within collaborative applications. Tangram puzzles require a high cognitive load while requiring no interface beyond direct manipulation and thus minimizes the possibility of poorly designed interface elements being the cause of conversation [26]. Partners worked with touch screens in separate rooms, linked by voice using Skype.

Our goal in discussing the iterative design process in this section is to make other designers and researchers aware of seemingly intuitive designs that failed in testing. These iterations helped us better refine the design constraints for a system intended to promote knowledge of privileged information, which was a research question that emerged from the failure of the initial remote prototype.

Design Process

To evaluate whether our design promoted awareness of privileged information, we used a multiple phase iterative design process to explore different design options given our context. These phases included brainstorming sessions with the research team, informal feedback from colleagues, and examining the effectiveness of the design with participants through pilot studies with each pilot phase consisting of 2-3 dyads. Through this iterative process we examined layout on the screen to promote awareness, different ways to promote knowledge of privileged information, and different ways of making users aware that they do no have all available information. In this context, the privileged information consisted of the question or answer to children's jokes or riddles, e.g.:

Q. Why did Donald Duck go to college?
A. He wanted to be a wise quacker.

Because participants are generally aware of the paired question-answer joke paradigm, we anticipated that seeing just the question or just the answer singly might suggest that their collaborator had the missing information. Even without the participants being aware of the privileged information, we hoped the initial reading of one part might stimulate conversation due to a natural desire to avoid social awkwardness when one person talks and the other does not respond within a culturally dependent timeframe [4]. While jokes may seem overly casual or unrelated to a task, they offer a simple paradigm with which to analyze a privileged information interface that could be generalized to task-related information [14].

We setup the following design constraints due to the larger needs of the research project:

1. The system had to use the same joke/riddles that had been used in the previous co-located experiment [27].
2. The design could not *force* awareness of information in continuing with the design goals of ConvoCons as an unforced and unobtrusive system.
3. At least 50% of participants had to be able to make the connection during either the study or in the exit interview that a partner possessed a different fragment of information.
4. Participants could not be given all available information (e.g. both the question and the answer)
5. The design had to be low bandwidth, in keeping with the goal of making them as unobtrusive as possible.

In exit interviews, participants had to indicate some awareness of privileged information when asked, "At any time, did anything that appeared on your screen differ from your partners' screen?" or "For the questions that appeared

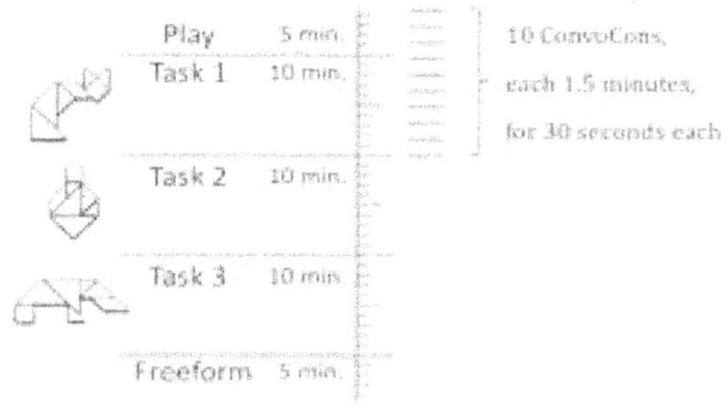

Figure 1 A sample timeline showing tasks and ConvoCon appearance.

on the screen, were you aware of the answers?"For all iterations, ten ConvoCons appeared at the first touch for a duration of thirty seconds each with a minute in between the disappearance of one ConvoCon and the appearance of the next one. The total duration of ConvoCons was thirteen minutes (see Figure 1). We chose to disable them midway through to see if effects from ConvoCons would continue after they stopped appearing.

First Iteration

In the first iteration (Figure 2), the system gave one person the question half of a riddle or joke (unrelated to the tangram puzzles) while the collaborator received the answer half. Participants were told neither that the messages would be appearing nor the significance of the messages. The messages did not allow interaction and did not interfere

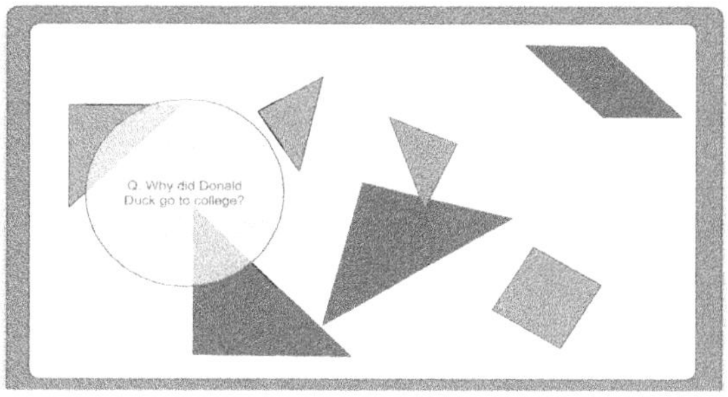

Figure 2 Iteration 1 with the message left-aligned and no indication of a second half.

with the tangram interface beneath them.

Dyads used the tangram interface for approximately 25 minutes and experienced these messages for the first 10 minutes of that time; we experimented with the placement of the information—left, center, and right side to see if that would affect the likelihood of collaborators discussing the information. We also manipulated the presence of a half circle at the top center of the screen with the content of the other participant's message displayed upside down.

From this iteration, we learned that participants were most likely to discuss the information when the text was placed on the left. We thought that placing it in the center, on top of the work, might increase their awareness and thus the number of conversations associated with the jokes and riddles. However, center alignment tended to result in banner blindness. Informal interviews after the study indicated that participants chose to ignore the center-aligned text in favor of focusing on the work at hand. Since participants were from Western cultures, the failure of the right aligned configuration was unsurprising although in cultures where text is right aligned, the optimal placement may be different.

Exit interviews also uncovered that regardless of layout, individuals in both groups believed they had the same information on their screen as their collaborator. Those with the half-circle indicating part of the content of their collaborator had noticed the half-circle but assumed they could pull down the answer/question from the half-circle and wrongly assumed the inability to do so was due to a software bug. Given these results, we observed that the first design failed at design constraints 3 and 6.

Second Iteration

The decision was made to run a new round of pilot studies with just the subtle change of making the half circle containing the text of the other participant as a dashed circle instead of a solid circle in an attempt to indicate lack of ownership of the ConvoCon content (see Figure 3).

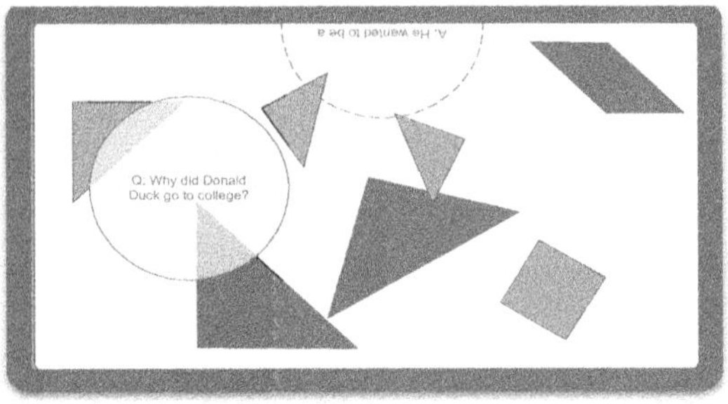

Figure 3 The layout for the second iteration, with second half indicated as "other" by dotted line.

While this minor tweak tested slightly better than the solid half-circle, participants were still unlikely to begin discussing the content in the same manner as the co-located groups had in our previous experiment [27]. Furthermore, exit interviews still indicated that participants believed their collaborator shared the same content they did and that there was no difference in terms of the text shown.

Ultimately this design also failed to meet design constraints 3 and 6, but we also observed a failure to meet constraint 4 in some cases where the answer to the joke or riddle was a single word that participants could read upside down.

Final Iteration

The failure of the second design led us to begin rethinking our approach to making participants aware of their collaborator's privileged information. Instead of displaying the content as solid text, we began to explore the use of varying the opacity of the content as a means of indicating privileged information. With this in mind, we developed three primary designs to test in the pilot phase. Before moving to the pilot phase we ran the mockups of the previous designs and the new mockups by colleagues and several strangers in an attempt to get more feedback on what worked and what did not for each design. Based on informal polling, we decided to eliminate a design in which the primary content fades (see Figure 4).

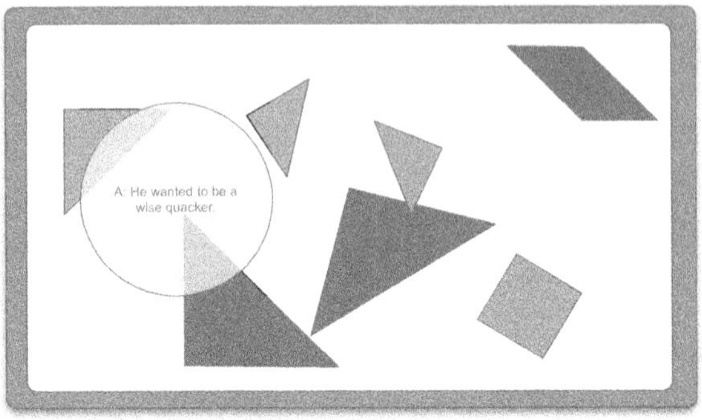

Figure 4 Stage three design with fading text eliminated via informal polling.

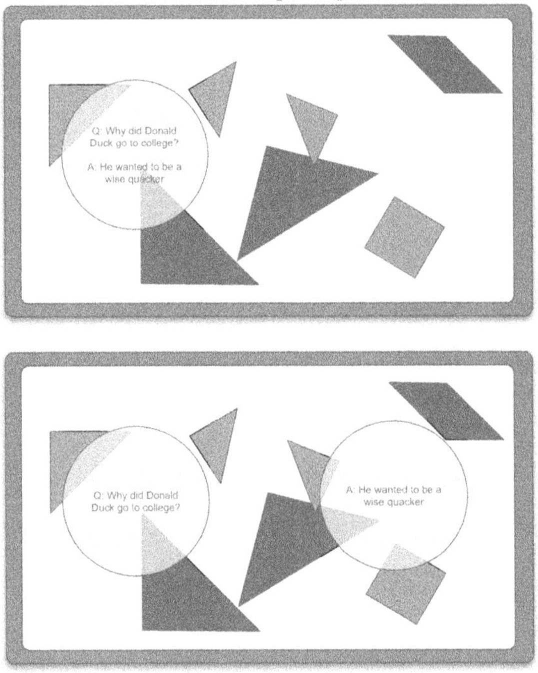

Figure 5 The new designs evaluated in the pilot studies.

Figure 5 shows the two new designs that were evaluated in this round. Both of these new designs provide participants with both halves of the information but fade out the information that belongs to their partner. In addition, we explored swapping which piece of information a participant owned—before one person always owned the question half and the other always owned the answer half. In this round, the design where both the question and answer were in the same bubble with the other half faded tested the most successfully and resulted in discussions being prompted.

Exit interviews also indicated that this last design was successful in making participants aware of privileged information, addressing Q1.

This final design (Figure 5, top) satisfied all six design constraints, including constraint number 4 since we found that even with half the characters showing with a single word answer, participants could not easily determine the answer individually.

Additional Observations

In some cases, it was apparent that one participant noticed the information while the other participant either failed to notice the text or chose to ignore their partner. Failing to notice may be related to research into road signs showing that some individuals do not attend to textual information while working on another task [3].

Q2 & Q3: Improving Social Affinity

To evaluate the effectiveness of our system in stimulating conversations and improving social affinity between remote collaborators, we first pre-tested 50 participants using the form board test and a subset of Goldberg *et al*'s AB5C personality test [2, 9, 15, 16]. Since the reliability of AB5C is evaluated on each subsection, in addition to the big 5 factors, we chose to only use the aspects of personality relevant to our study, specifically: sociability (μ=2.79; σ=0.69), creativity (μ=3.46; σ=0.51), friendliness (μ=3.59; σ=0.63), leadership (μ=3.40; σ=0.57), gregariousness (μ=3.21; σ=0.63), assertiveness (μ=3.68; σ=0.41), cooperation (μ=3.33; σ=0.48), and ingenuity (μ=3.80; σ=0.43). Individuals with high spatial ability and high sociability scores were paired with individuals who scored low to ensure all dyads were balanced on both of these scales. Dyads were then randomly assigned to either the control group or the experimental group and Student T-Tests (α=0.05) were run to ensure that no significant difference existed on any personality aspect or on spatial abilities between groups. Effect sizes reported were calculated by dividing the means by the standard deviation. Participants also indicated their previous experience with multitouch systems such as the iPhone (a mean score of 3, σ=1.05 on a 5-point Likert scale) and computers, and no significant differences appeared between groups on these measures. All participants came from the psychology department's participant pool and had a mean age of 19.6 (σ=3.09).

Methods

Having minimized the impact of individual variance affecting the results, we then attempted to schedule participants for the follow-up study to complete the tasks. We faced some difficulty with participants failing to respond for the follow-up study or failing to show up. However, we were still able to successfully run nine control dyads and ten experimental dyads (for a total of 40 participants, a 20% attrition rate). To ensure participants did not meet before the start of the experiment, we had one participant enter the lab on the second floor and the other enter on the first floor. The process of starting requiring mutual touch was done to ensure accuracy of task timing and to make sure both participants were ready to begin the task. Aside from piece movements, participants' touch points were transmitted and displayed as circles on the interface to allow for translucence of action [10].

The researcher simultaneously gave both participants the following instructions via a 3-way Skype audio call: "For the study you will be participating in today, you will be using a multitouch device that allows multiple hand and finger inputs. For this study, you will be working with a person in another location with whom you can communicate through Skype. Please wear the headset at all times. The application you will be working on is a virtual version of tangrams, where there are pieces that you use to complete a puzzle. You will have 5 minutes where you will play with the system and figure out how to manipulate the pieces. After that you will be given the first of three puzzles that you will complete. There is no time limit on the puzzles, so take as much time as you need to complete it to your satisfaction. After all three puzzles are completed, you will have up to 5 minutes to build anything you want with the pieces. When you are ready to begin, you will both need to touch the screen—you can touch and hold until the other person touches his/her screen." Both the control group and the experimental group received these exact instructions. In addition, the term "partner" was specifically avoided in the instructions, as we did not want to reduce the possibility that participants would compete with one another by priming them for collaboration using the term "partner."

Participants had five minutes, or until they were satisfied, to learn how to use the tangram application ("Playtime"). Next, they were given the first of three puzzles with no time limit. Participants worked together to solve a puzzle (with the silhouette of the desired shape shown to both participants) using a shared set of seven pieces. For puzzle tasks, completion was determined when participants successfully filled in the silhouette of the shape they were building (multiple correct solutions existed). While using this networked multitouch tangram application, participants were free to move as many pieces as they chose. If both users touched a piece, the piece changed to orange and would not move until one participant ceded control. After all three puzzles had been completed, the participants were given up to five minutes to create anything they wanted with the pieces ("Freeform") and could stop when they were satisfied with their creation. During all activity, the experimenter was silently present in the 3-way conference call. Participants' audio and touchscreen interactions were recorded as video.

Upon completing all tasks, participants then completed a short exit survey based on Convertino's survey to assess common ground [5]. The exit survey also asked them to rate their prior familiarity with their partner and all participants indicated that their partner had previously been a stranger. The video was categorized based on two overall constructs: the type of **behavior** (9 codes) and type of

conversation (16 different codes) using the affinity-coding technique defined by Oren and Gilbert, which has interrater reliability of 90% (Cohen's k=.612) for behavioral tags and 90.7% (k=.708) for verbal tags [27, 28]. Each five-second block of video received one code related to dyad behavior and one related to dyad conversation. The total number of affinity related blocks were then calculated and divided by the total number of blocks for each task. The overall affinity score is based on two parts: the proportion of affinity conversation and the proportion of affinity behavior (all affinity blocks / all blocks that exhibited some conversation or behavior). Affinity is calculated independently for each task, looking only at the instances of behavioral and verbal affinity in the given task.

RESULTS

A significant limitation of this study was lost data that arose from network issues and problems with the commercial screen recording software that worked well during pilots. We ultimately had only four control dyads and four experimental dyads (16 participants total) for the detailed video analysis. We excluded the majority of dyads due to empirical evidence suggesting that the affinity of the rejected groups was likely affected by bonding due to network bugs that forced different communication to solve the puzzle. However, some of the groups had to be removed due to simple data loss of network connections preventing communication and recording of conversations. Despite this loss of data, we believe the findings of the detailed video analysis present an accurate view of the overall trend. The dyad compositions were two male-male dyads and two male-female dyads in the control group; with three male-male dyads and one female-female dyad in the experimental group. Participants could identify one another's gender via the voice communication but were unaware of any other traits of their collaborator. No significant differences existed among the demographics or spatial ability between the dyads in the control group and the dyads in the experimental group—this was examined using the Student T-Test both at the dyad unit of analysis and at the individual participant level of analysis. Additionally, no significant difference existed between the dyads where usable data was obtained and the larger sample population.

Completion Time—Log Data

Some dyads from the full sample are not included in this analysis due to the network issues; below we report results separately from both the full sample data set and the eight dyads where no factors have contaminated the data, the final sample set. The data from the full sample is reported as the results indicate some possible downsides of ConvoCons and are reported here in case they represent a trend that was not statistically significant in the reduced sample due to the small sample size. Including the Playtime and the Freeform task, there was a marginally significant difference (p=.08, r=.37) between the experimental group (n=7 dyads; μ=27.85 minutes, σ=4.43) and the control group (n=7 dyads; μ=22.51 minutes, σ=8.54) when examining the entire sample. Within the final sample, there was no significant difference (r=.31) in completion time between the experimental group (n=4 dyads; μ=26.72; σ=4.44) and the control group (n=4 dyads; μ=21.69; σ=9.84). Since one concern was that ConvoCons and the incidental conversations might distract groups from the work at hand, we calculated the mean completion time just for the three puzzles to look at just the effects of ConvoCons on work efficiency. Looking at the full sample, there was a marginally significant difference (p=.057, r=.35) puzzle completion time between the experimental group (n=7; μ=21.62 minutes; σ=3.14) and the control group (n=7; μ=17.45; σ=7.35). There was no significant difference (r=.31) for the final sample in time spent on the three puzzle tasks between the experimental group (n=4; μ=20.88 minutes; σ=3.62) and the control group (n=4; μ=16.60 minutes, σ=8.48). In the full sample, no single task indicated a significant difference in completion time between the experimental and control group. However, Play time was marginally significantly longer (p=.066, r=.53) when looking at the final sample between the experimental group (n=4; μ=3.11 minutes; σ=0.91) and the control group (n=4; μ=2.16; σ=0.59).

Exit Survey

In the full sample, the experimental group reported significantly higher (experimental μ=4.05; σ=.39; control μ=3.72; σ=.75; p=0.048; r=.27) feelings of "shared task understanding" as well as a marginally significant higher feeling of "role understanding" (experimental μ=3.75; σ=0.55; control μ=3.39; σ=0.55; p=.063; r=.31) with both metrics coming from Convertino's survey on assessing common ground, which utilizes a 5-point Likert scale [5]. All other survey metrics were non-significant.

In the final sample, we analyzed the data on both the individual level as well as comparing on paired dyads. Comparison by dyadic units follows the recommendation of

Individual		Time	Amount of Work	Quality	Task 1	Turns
n=8	Experimental	3.25 (.71)	3.75 (.47)	3.63 (.92)	3.375 (1.06)	0.25 (0.46)
n=8	Control	3.75 (.71)	4.00 (0)	4.25 (.46)	4.13 (.64)	0.75 (0.46)
		p=.09 | r=-.33	p=.074 | r=-.35	p=.054 | r=-.39	p=.054 | r=-.40	p=.024 | r=-.48
Dyadic						
n=4	Experimental	3.25 (.29)	3.75 (.29)	3.63 (.25)	3.375 (.85)	0.25 (0.29)
n=4	Control	3.75 (.29)	4.00 (0)	4.25 (.29)	4.13 (.48)	0.75 (0.29)
		p=.025 | r=-.65	p=.067 | r=-.52	p=.008 | r=-.75	p=.088 | r=-.48	p=.024 | r=-.65

Table 1 Exit Survey results indicating the control group self-reported higher on their assessment of time-efficiency, amount of work, quality of work, Task 1 satisfaction, and use of turn-taking strategy.

	Play	*Task 1*	*Task 2*	*Task 3*	*Freeform*	*Total*
ConvoCons (n=4)	8.25 (6.40)	8.00 (4.24)	5.25 (4.27)	4.50 (.58)	7.25 (2.99)	6.65 (1.53)
Control (n=4)	0 (0)	0 (0)	0.75 (.96)	1.50 (2.38)	1.75 (1.26)	0.80 (.67)
p-Values	.021	.005	.043	.025	.007	<.001
Effect Size (r)	.67	.80	.59	.65	.77	.93

Table 2 Means and standard deviations of incidental conversations over all tasks indicate a higher frequency in the experimental (ConvoCons) group.

[22]. In the comparison based on individual units, we found marginally significant differences between the experimental and control group on ratings of time efficiency, amount of work, the quality of work, the satisfaction with their work on Task 1, and self-reported use of the turn-taking strategy (significant) with higher scores in the control group.

Incidental Conversations

In calculating the frequency of incidental conversations, we did not count all conversational labels that we classified as signs of affinity—only the tags that were not related to work were counted (e.g. "playful conversations" and "talking about partner"). There was a significant difference between the frequency of incidental conversations between groups across all tasks, with a higher frequency count seen in the experimental group. Overall, there was a significant difference between groups thus supporting the idea that ConvoCons increase the frequency of incidental conversations for remote collaborators (see Table 2).

Affinity Metrics

In reading the following graphs it should be noted that, per the method in Figure 1, ConvoCons typically stopped appearing between the end of Task 1 and the middle of Task 2. In addition, the puzzles used for each task, presented in a consistent order, were intended to go from simplest to solve to hardest to solve. All Student T-Tests were conducted with an $\alpha=0.05$.

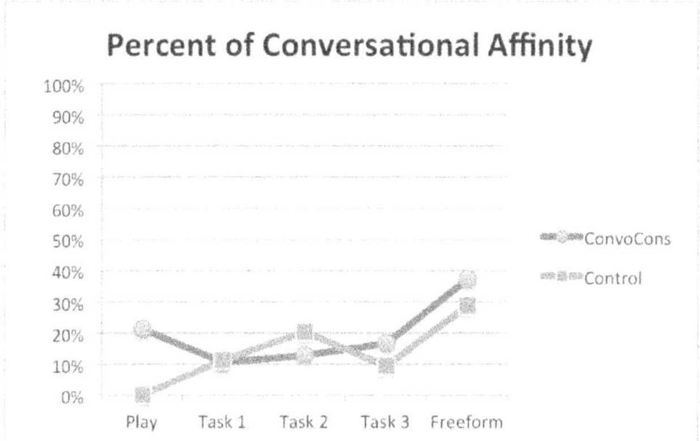

Figure 6 ConvoCons serve as an early conversation starter for groups and the conversational affinity increases steadily (after an initial drop when switching from play to work).

Figure 6 presents the percentage of conversational affinity across all tasks. As expected from the literature on ice breakers that providing a shared framework for conversation allowed participants to begin incidental conversations at an early stage, resulting in a 21% increase in conversational affinity which was statistically significant at $p=.031$; $r=.63$. However, outside of Task 3 ($p=.021$; $r=.52$), no statistically significant difference was seen in conversational affinity between the experimental and control groups. Taking the mean across all tasks (not seen in the graph), there was a marginally significant difference ($p=.097$; $r=.32$) between the experimental group with a mean of 17.68% affinity ($\sigma=6.14\%$) and the control group with a mean of 13.90% affinity ($\sigma=5.10\%$).

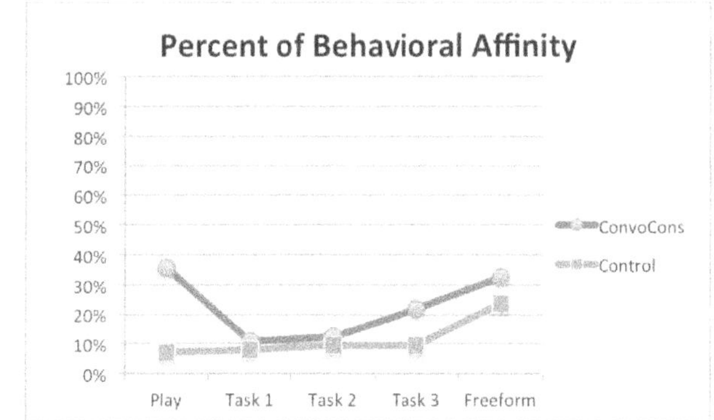

Figure 7 Behavioral affinity begins almost 30% higher for the experimental group and remains slightly higher during the work tasks (after an initial drop) and ends about 10% higher than the control group.

Figure 7 shows the measured behavioral affinity across all tasks. To the researchers, this is the more important question since our ultimate goal for ConvoCons is to enable individuals to work with one another in a collaborative manner. One of the more interesting findings in this study is that the experimental group actual began with significantly higher behavioral affinity ($p=.033$; $r=.62$), which stands in contrast to findings from the co-located study [27]. This initially high affinity, which we suggest stems from participants' building on to each other's creative designs during play, falls drastically when the work begins. A statistically significant difference in behavioral affinity is seen again in Task 3 ($p=.021$; $r=.67$). Taking the mean score across all tasks results in a significant difference ($p=0.013$; $r=.72$) between the experimental group with a mean of 22.57% affinity ($\sigma=7.35\%$) and the control group with a mean of 11.52% affinity ($\sigma=1.76\%$).

Figure 8 displays the composite, overall affinity across all tasks. Playtime and Task 3, both had statistically significant differences between the experimental and control groups (p=.003; r=.72 and p=.002; r=.85); additionally, the Freeform task had a marginally significant difference between groups (p=0.099; r=.46). The mean across all tasks was statistically significant (p<0.001; r=.94) with the experimental group having a mean of 32.06% affinity (σ=3.90%) compared to a mean of 17.46% affinity (σ=2.33%) for the control group.

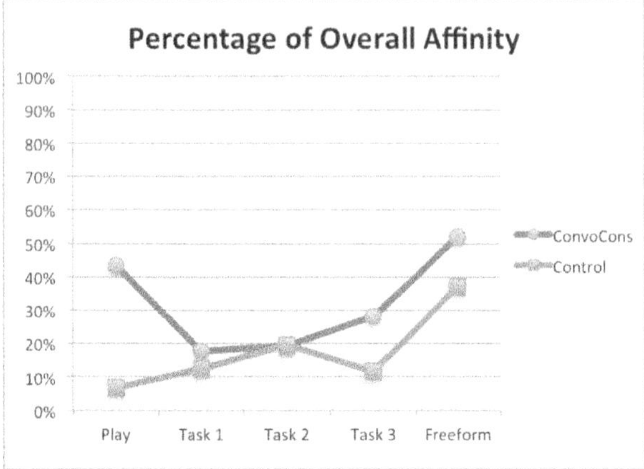

Figure 8 The experimental group starts out with just over 35% higher affinity, due to the increased conversational and behavioral affinity occurring due to ConvoCons. There is a drastic decrease in affinity when the puzzle tasks begin, but the affinity of the experimental group grows during each task and ends nearly 25% higher than the control group in the Freeform task. Across all tasks there was a mean difference of 14.6% (p<0.001; r=.94) between the groups.

DISCUSSION

Through an iterative design process, we determined some of the basic visual elements that contribute to the discovery of privileged information within an interface. While an additional study still needs to be conducted to ensure that this approach will lead people to share more privileged information, the results of the iterative design process have at least shown the potential for indicating privileged interface information in a subtle way to collaborators. A qualitative assessment also suggested that this design approach will lead to participant conversations about the privileged information, which our previous research has shown leads to participants having more conversations in general (both work and non-work related) without a negative affect on performance as measured by completion time. We suggest that this approach of presenting both halves of privileged information but fading it out can be generalized to other projects needing to promote awareness of privileged information—whether that information is text (such as previous work experience), images (such as a design), or another visual medium.

The large drop in affinity conversation and behavior may be due to participants' switching from play to work. It may be because the play phase, combined with the ConvoCons, served as an icebreaker period and the drop in affinity is similar to the drop seen when moving from icebreakers to actual work. Or, it might be due to a combination of these two factors. There is some evidence that the decrease is related to a change from play to work, however, since the majority of behavioral affinity in the play task came from participants' building off of one another's designs rather than working in close proximity or in cooperative turn taking. Similarly, there is only a very small drop in frequency of incidental conversation from play to the first task, which suggests that the drop in conversational affinity is due to increased work-related conversations.

While the exit survey for the full sample must be considered carefully, the responses do suggest that the ConvoCon group members were able to establish stronger bonds of affinity and form a greater understanding of working with their partners. In looking at the final sample, the results suggest that the control group felt that they were generally more efficient at accomplishing good quality work. There is no evidence that this is true when examining their completion times, although we do see evidence of efficiency in the faster completion times seen in the full sample. However, the finding of groups with higher affinity performing less efficient work is unsurprising as previous research on remote collaboration showed a similar result when comparing videoconferencing to teleconferencing, with videoconferencing still being recommended as a tool to help bond individuals at the first team meeting [7, 8]. While the experimental group is potentially less efficient, there are other potential benefits to increased affinity such as recognizing the strength of collaborators and the build up of social capital that can produce more efficient work over a longer period of time [31].

Limitations of Findings

Due to the low sample size, some non-significant results may have been found to be significant, had we been able to collect a larger sample. However, as seen from the reported effect sizes, many of the results are medium to large and the most important finding, that overall affinity is higher in the experimental group shows a strong effect (near 1). Some results, such as the significant result for "shared task understanding" in favor of the experimental group, had low effect sizes, though, and should be interpreted cautiously until further evidence is available. It should be noted that the participants from the full sample that were removed from the analysis were interrupted by network lag while working, which led to both longer completion times and bonding over the network frustration. This bonding over technology frustration has been observed in other studies [26, 29]. Due to the difficulty in quantifying that mitigating factor as a covariate in analysis, we excluded the data.

However, one finding that is clear is that control group participants perceived work as more efficient and that work was of higher quality. This lower rating in the experimental group may be due to negative side effects of increased affinity and conversation or to a latent property of the distracting effect of the ConvoCons themselves. In either case, this finding, in combination with longer completion times for the ConvoCon dyads, which was significant in the full sample (although perhaps due to network lag), suggest a cost to efficient work practice when building affinity. Thus, for tasks where efficiency is critical, the use of a solution similar to ConvoCons may be ill-advised. In creative tasks where efficiency is less critical and affinity bonds are necessary for productive collaboration, a similar approach may help distributed teams function better.

Implications for Practitioners

While the results presented above derived from a controlled experiment, the findings from both the design of interfaces for privileged information and building affinity can be generalized for practitioner use. First, in the case of interfaces where collaborators will necessarily require different information being displayed based on their expertise, such as the ad-hoc teams created to respond to national disasters, other users should be given some indication of information that they do not have. We have shown several approaches to this indicator. Showing a portion and fading the remaining information appeared to be most effective.

Also, while the tangrams task is fairly simplistic, the work involves a high cognitive load. This may partially explain the slowdown in work observed from the study, while tasks that require lower cognitive load may see a smaller delay from the conversational intervention. These conjectures, however, will require additional studies for confirmation.

While the results varied in significance and tended toward medium effect sizes for building affinity, the large effect size (r=.93) of the overall affinity across all tasks does provide strong evidence that subtle interface manipulations can successfully increase social affinity among team members. Furthermore, the particularly large gap in initial affinity provides support that such manipulation might be most effective at the onset of remote collaboration. Integrating subtle user interface elements into remote meeting software may help teams build the initial affinity they need without the expense of expensive site visits or time-consuming ice breakers. While there is evidence that use of user interface elements may also come with a cost in increased time, further research is needed to determine if the affinity bonds formed during work are more stable than those formed through pre-work icebreakers and perhaps worth the relative costs in time.

CONCLUSION

We have presented the design of user interface elements to encourage awareness of privileged information and in future work, we plan to test whether or not increased awareness of privileged information within the user interface will increase sharing of privileged information given to participants prior to the start of the study. One element of the design that needs to be improved in the future is the inclusion of both graphical and textual information to increase the salience of indicators and reduce the possibility of one individual's ignoring the information while the other attends to it.

Despite the aforementioned limitation, the results of this study do suggest that ConvoCons can be used to increase incidental conversation. Additionally, there is evidence that ConvoCons have an initial impact on conversational and behavioral affinity as well as a significant effect on overall affinity. We believe that the aforementioned change to the system, which may increase awareness of the ConvoCons, will result in heightened effectiveness of ConvoCons in terms of increasing conversations and all affinity metrics.

Finally, as the results of this study also indicated that the affinity bonds associated with ConvoCons may decrease work efficiency, we plan to conduct future work that attempts to decrease affinity bonds to improve efficiency. We hope that over time we can categorize the optimal range of affinity for various types of tasks.

ACKNOWLEDGMENTS

We thank the Air Force Research Laboratory for their support. We thank Tony Milosch and Kate Longley for technical assistance and helping manage the participants.

REFERENCES

1. Aragon, C.R., et al., *A tale of two online communities: fostering collaboration and creativity in scientists and children*, in *Proceeding of the seventh ACM conference on Creativity and cognition*2009, ACM: Berkeley, California, USA. p. 9-18.
2. Bäckström, M., F. Björklund, and M.R. Larsson, *Five-factor inventories have a major general factor related to social desirability which can be reduced by framing items neutrally.* Journal of Research in Personality, 2009. **43**(3): p. 335-344.
3. Brewer, K.A., L.L. Avant, and W.F. Woodman, *Addendum to Perception and Interpretation of Advance Warning Signs on County Roads*, 1985, Iowa Department of Transportation.
4. Collins, R., *Sociological Insight*1992, New York, NY: Oxford University Press.
5. Convertino, G., et al. *A multipleview approach to support common ground in distributed and sychronous geo-collaboration.* in *CMV '05*. 2005.
6. Cutkosky, M., J. Tenenbaum, and J. Glicksman, *Madefast: collaborative engineering over the Internet.* Communications of the ACM, 1996.
7. Dubé, L. and G. Paré, *Global Virtual Teams.* Communications of the ACM, 2001. **44**(12): p. 71-73.
8. Egido, C., *Video conferencing as a technology to support group work: a review of its failures*, in *Proceedings of the 1988 ACM conference on Computer-supported cooperative work*1988, ACM: Portland, Oregon, United States. p. 13-24.
9. Ekstrom, R.B., et al., *Kit of Factor-Referenced Cognitive Tests*, O.o.N. Research, Editor 1976, Educational Testing Service: Princeton, NJ. p. 281-285.

10. Erickson, T. and W. Kellogg, *Social Translucence: Using Minimalist Visualizations of Social Activity to Support Collective ....* Designing Information Spaces: The Social Navigation Approach, 2003.
11. Esenther, A. and K. Ryall, *RemoteDT: Support for Multi-Site Table Collaboration.* Proc. Int. Conf. Collaboration Technologies (CollabTech), 2006.
12. Fischer, G., et al., *Creativity Support Tools: Report From a US National Science Foundation Sponsored Workshop.* International Journal of Human-Computer Interaction, 2006.
13. Goffman, E., *The Presentation of Self in Everyday Life*1959, Garden City, NJ: Doubleday.
14. Goffman, E., *Role-Distance*, in *Life as Theater: A dramaturgical sourcebook*, D.E. Brisset, C., Editor 1975, Aldine Publishing Company: Chicago, IL. p. 123-132.
15. Goldberg, L.R., et al., *The international personality item pool and the future of public-domain personality measures.* Journal of Research in Personality, 2006. **40**: p. 84-96.
16. Hofstee, W.K.B., B. de Read, and L.R. Goldberg, *Integration of the Big-Five and circumplex approaches to trait structure.* Journal of Personality and Social Psychology, 1992. **63**: p. 146-163.
17. Kellogg, W.A. and R.T. Erickson, *Social Translucence, Collective Awareness, and the Emergence of Place.* Proceedings of CSCW2002, 2002.
18. Langheinrich, M., et al., *Unintrusive customization techniques for Web advertising.* Computer Networks, 1999. **31**(11-16): p. 1259-1272.
19. Latour, B., *Where are the missing masses? The sociology of a few mundane artifacts*, in *Shaping Technology*, W.B.J. Law, Editor 1992, MIT Press: Cambridge, MA. p. 225-258.
20. Lohtia, R., N. Donthu, and E.K. Hershberger, *The Impact of Content and Design Elements on Banner Advertising Click-through Rates.* Journal of Advertising Research, 2003. **43**(04): p. 410-418.
21. Maher, M. and J. Rutherford, *A model for synchronous collaborative design using CAD and database management.* Research in Engineering Design, 1997.
22. Mizruchi, M.S. and C. Marquis, *Egocentric, sociocentric, or dyadic? Identifying the appropriate level of analysis in the study of organizational networks.* Social Networks, 2006. **28**(3): p. 187-208.
23. Morris, M., et al., *Beyond" social protocols": multi-user coordination policies for co-located groupware.* Proceedings of the 2004 ACM conference on Computer supported …, 2004.
24. Nardi, B., *Beyond Bandwidth: Dimensions of Connection in Interpersonal Communication.* Computer Supported Cooperative Work (CSCW), 2005.
25. Neff, G., B. Fiore-Silfvast, and C.S. Dossick, *A CASE STUDY OF THE FAILURE OF DIGITAL COMMUNICATION TO CROSS KNOWLEDGE BOUNDARIES IN VIRTUAL CONSTRUCTION.* Information, Communication & Society, 2010. **13**(4): p. 556 - 573.
26. Oren, M. and S. Gilbert, *ConvoCons: Encouraging Affinity on Multitouch Interfaces.* Lecture notes in computer science, 2009. **5612**: p. 651-659.
27. Oren, M. and S. Gilbert. *Building Better Design Teams: Enhancing Group Affinity to Aid Collaborative Design.* in *Design, Computing, and Cognition.* 2010. Stuttgart, Germany.
28. Oren, M.A. and S.B. Gilbert, *Framework for measuring social affinity for CSCW software*, in *Proceedings of the 2011 annual conference extended abstracts on Human factors in computing systems*2011, ACM: Vancouver, BC, Canada. p. 1387-1392.
29. Riche, Y., et al. *Hard-To-Use Interfaces Considered Beneficial (Some of the Time).* in *CHI.* 2010. Atlanta, GA.
30. Robertson, T., *Cooperative work and lived cognition: A taxonomy of embodied actions.* … on Computer Supported Cooperative Work, 1997.
31. Schmid, A., *Affinity as social capital: its role in development.* Journal of Socio-Economics, 2000. **29**(2): p. 159-171.
32. Scott, S., *Territory-based interaction techniques for tabletop collaboration.* UIST 2003 Conference Companion, 2003.
33. Scott, S. and S. Carpendale, *Investigating Tabletop Territoriality in Digital Tabletop Workspaces.* eng.uwaterloo.ca, 2006.
34. Scott, S., K. Grant, and R. Mandryk, *System guidelines for co-located, collaborative work on a tabletop display.* Proceedings of the eighth conference on European Conference on Computer-Supported Cooperative Work, 2003: p. 159-178.
35. Tuddenham, P. and P. Robinson, *Distributed Tabletops: Supporting Remote and Mixed-Presence Tabletop Collaboration.* Horizontal Interactive Human-Computer Systems, 2007. TABLETOP '07. Second Annual IEEE International Workshop on, 2007: p. 19-26.
36. Vetere, F., S. Howard, and M. Gibbs, *Phatic Technologies: Sustaining Sociability through Ubiquitous Computing.* First International Workshop on Social Implications of …, 2005.
37. Warkentin, M.E., L. Sayeed, and R. Hightower, *Virtual Teams versus Face-to-Face Teams: An Exploratory Study of a Web-based Conference System*.* Decision Sciences, 1997. **28**(4): p. 975-996.

Facilitating the Reuse Process in Distributed Collaboration: A Distributed Cognition Approach

Syavash Nobarany[1], Mona Haraty[1], Brian Fisher[2]

[1]Department of Computer Science
University of British Columbia, Vancouver, Canada
{nobarany, haraty}@cs.ubc.ca

[2]School of Interactive Arts and Technology
Simon Fraser University, Surrey, Canada
bfisher@sfu.ca

ABSTRACT
Facilitating the reuse process and enabling unanticipated reuse can improve efficiency of distributed collaboration. However, supporting the reuse process in complex and dynamic contexts, where future use of information is difficult to predict, is challenging. Collaborative analytics exemplifies such a context. We employed distributed cognition theory to design a collaborative visual analytics system, called AnalyticStream, for facilitating the reuse of analysis outcomes. In contrast with the commonly used detail-oriented approach to applying distributed cognition, we performed a high level analysis of the design situation and we identified the cognitive processes that could be distributed over people to facilitate their collaboration. We examined some of the ideas derived from the theoretical analysis, by designing a simple reminding process through recommending relevant pieces of analysis, as well as a mechanism for attention management through allowing users greater control over their shared activity streams. A mixed-methods study of AnalyticStream showed that suggesting relevant artefacts facilitated discovering and consequently reusing them, and provided context-relevant awareness of other analysts' activities.

Author Keywords
Distributed cognition; reuse; collaborative visual analytics; distributed collaboration; reusability.

ACM Classification Keywords
H.5.3 Group and Organization Interfaces: Computer-supported cooperative work.

General Terms
Human Factors; Design.

INTRODUCTION
Distributed collaboration heavily relies on reuse of shared artefacts. Artefacts generated by some users may become an input for other users to perform their tasks and to build new artefacts based on them. Sometimes, especially in organizational settings, the reuse process is planned and the artefacts generated for reuse are expected to be well documented and hence reusable by other users. Moreover, in a planned reuse scenario, collaborators know which resources are available to them. However, in large-scale collaboration often opportunities for reuse are hard to plan for, and these unanticipated opportunities are eventually missed. Unanticipated reuse plays a prominent role in collaborative systems [15,20]; however, knowing which artefacts should be shared with others is challenging, especially when people are not aware of how their contributions may be helpful to others [15,21].

In collaborative analytics, human reasoning is the valuable resource that is shared and reused. However, only a fraction of reasoning turns into products that are widely distributed. The absence of support for collaboration and reuse of the analysis process and products inhibits analysts from efficient cooperation and engaging in collaborative sensemaking processes [13,31]. Supporting collaboration in visual analytics tools have been a subject of study over the last few years [11,13,32,33]. However, there has been little emphasis on supporting reuse of reasoning artefacts (e.g. hypotheses, evidence and causal relations).

We approached this problem by analyzing distributed collaboration through the lens of distributed cognition theory, and we investigated how the distribution of memory and attention processes can provide a platform for supporting unanticipated reuse in large-scale collaborative systems. We applied the proposed theoretical perspective in the design of a collaborative visual analytics system called AnalyticStream. We designed a simple socially distributed reminding process through recommending pieces of analysis that are relevant to the user's workspace, as well as a mechanism for attention management through allowing users greater control over their shared activity streams. The specific contributions of this work are as follows:

1. Introducing a non-traditional approach to applying distributed cognition theory to the design of CSCW systems.
2. Applying the proposed approach to the design of a collaborative visual analytics system called AnalyticStream.
3. Collecting qualitative and quantitative data about under- or unexplored design ideas resulted from adopting the proposed approach.

CSCW'12, February 11–15, 2012, Seattle, Washington, USA.

In the following sections, first, we provide an overview of the collaborative analysis process to describe the context of our design. Then, we briefly explain how distributed cognition theory shaped the design of AnalyticStream, and we conclude with a mixed-methods study of AnalyticStream.

COLLABORATIVE VISUAL ANALYTICS

Visual Analytics is defined as "the science of analytical reasoning facilitated by interactive visual interfaces" [31]. A typical use case of visual analytics systems in the context of intelligence analysis is supporting analysts "to piece together information buried in disparate data—including immigration records; patterns of travel; telephone calls; and names, affiliations, and locations of suspected terrorists—to enable them to spot an emerging attack before it can be executed" [31]. Similar use cases can be found in other analytical processes such as scientific research where researchers piece together theories, previous findings, and new data to explain a phenomenon or to make predictions.

Collaborative analytics systems are designed to provide the required infrastructure for efficient analytical collaborations and collaborative sensemaking processes. In the collaborative analytics process, analysts engage in the intertwined processes of sensemaking and sensegiving to address a problem more accurately and more comprehensively. Analysis processes and products should be externalized to enable collaborative processes. Traditionally, analysts use paper notes, concept maps, and other reasoning and argumentation diagrams for this externalization [18]. Recently, reasoning support systems such as Analyst's Notebook [35], Scalable Reasoning System [25], and Oculus SandBox [34] support an extensive set of analytical methods. However, these systems do not provide specific mechanisms for facilitating reuse of analysis' outcomes.

The analytics process involves seeking relevant resources followed by extraction, marshalling and summarizing relevant pieces of information and analysis. This process often involves the reuse process in the form of building upon the previous findings. The cycle of reuse starts with sharing of the analysis findings, and continues with the discovery of them by other analysts or the same analyst at another time, understanding them, integrating them in the current analysis and ultimately sharing the outcome. Every step of the reuse cycle presents challenges and needs to be supported by collaborative analytics systems.

ADOPTING A DISTRIBUTED COGNITION APPROACH

As was stated by Simon [29], "...solving a problem simply means representing it so as to make the solution transparent". Looking through a theoretical lens enables perceiving and representing the problem space differently. We applied distributed cognition theory [16] to investigate how analysts, reasoning artefacts, and user interface elements take part in various cognitive processes to form a distributed cognitive system. Cognitive processes are the processes by which the cognitive system's input is transformed, reduced, elaborated, stored, recovered, or used [22]. Learning, remembering, attention, reasoning and problem solving are some of the cognitive processes that may happen as a cognitive system operates.

From the distributed cognition perspective, a cognitive process is delimited by functional relationships among the elements that participate in it [16]. A cognitive process can be distributed across people, through time, or across internal and external representations. In this section, we demonstrate how distributed cognition theory can inform and shape the design of collaborative analytics systems. Our approach to applying distributed cognition theory is slightly different from the detail-oriented approach that is commonly used in HCI and CSCW research [10,14]. In the detail-oriented approach, a researcher performs a detailed analysis of how information is propagated through the cognitive artefacts and actors, and how its representation is transformed in the process. This analysis helps the researcher to identify breakdowns in the system and design new representations or workflows to address it [10]. Our approach, while similar in nature, focuses on higher-level analysis of collaborative workflows through identifying various cognitive processes that can be distributed over people, time and artefacts to facilitate the collaboration. In our approach, the collaborative system is considered as a cognitive system, which needs to perform various cognitive processes such as remembering, attention, reasoning and learning to achieve its goals. Therefore, the design of a collaborative system involves identifying the cognitive processes that can help the cognitive system succeed, and designing the infrastructure required for an efficient distribution of these processes.

A collaborative analytics system can be seen as a cognitive system composed of analysts, reasoning artefacts and tools that are used to represent, communicate and manipulate the artefacts. Analysts' mental resources normally constitute a significant part of a distributed cognitive system and are responsible for complex or creative computations and coordination of cognitive resources (including themselves). They also act as part of the distributed memory of the system. However, they externalize the information stored in their memory to be able to cope with their complexity and volume. The externalized reasoning artefacts (e.g. evidence, notes, comments, causal networks, hypotheses, etc.) can be stored, shared, retrieved, and reused by other actors in the system.

As discussed earlier, first we need to identify the cognitive processes that should be supported to achieve the goal of the system, which is facilitating collaborative reasoning and reuse of reasoning artefacts in collaborative analytics systems. One approach is to identify such cognitive processes based on how an individual achieves this goal. If we consider reuse of one's own knowledge or work, memory processes are the most apparent cognitive processes that should be explored. We are constantly reusing our knowledge or work, because we remember the

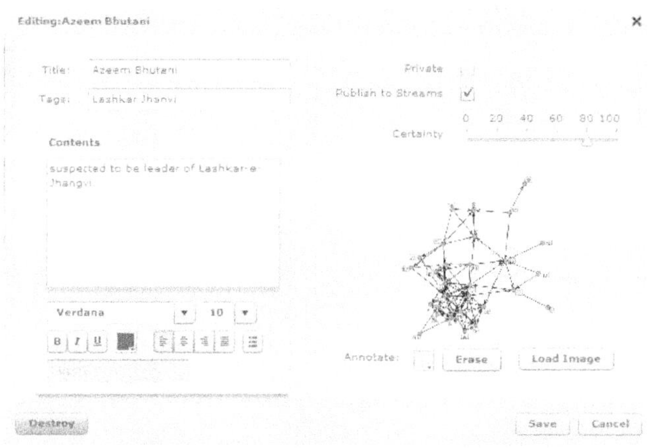

Figure 1. UI for creating and editing a piece of analysis

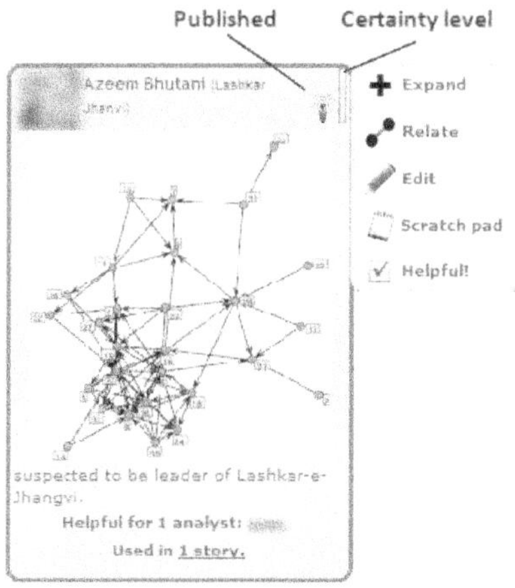

Figure 2. Visual representation of a piece of analysis

relevant ones, intentionally or unintentionally, when we need them.

Looking closely, we see that some of the knowledge that is reused has been intentionally memorized or kept carefully, because we had anticipated the future reuse. We pay attention to the pieces of information that are deemed to be helpful in future, and we can only remember and reuse what we have noticed or attended to. After remembering the relevant experience or piece of information, we need to find a way to apply the previously acquired knowledge to the current situation. Decontextualization and recontextualization of the knowledge require reasoning [1]. In the context of collaborative analytics, reuse of analysis strategies, methods, and heuristics requires the process of recontextualization. In this work, for the sake of simplicity, we focused on facilitating the reuse of products of analysis, and in the next sections, after a brief overview of AnalyticStream, we describe the social distribution of attention and memory processes in AnalyticStream.

OVERVIEW OF ANALYTICSTREAM

AnalyticStream is a collaborative visual analytics system that provides an environment for evidence filing and marshalling. Analysts can share and schematize their pieces of analysis, build cases and tell stories to communicate their analysis. AnalyticStream is designed to support early-stage sharing and reuse of analysis outcomes. Often, sharing the outcomes of the analysis process is postponed to the end of the project or milestones and most of the intermediate outcomes of the analysis do not reach a publishable state. Several benefits are associated with the sharing of ideas and outcomes in the early stages of analysis and research, including early identification of flaws in the analysis process, refining the ideas and incomplete hypotheses, accelerating the review of available information, and avoiding missing of the important sources of information.

Using AnalyticStream, analysts can create sequences of pieces of analysis that are generated by various analysts to convey their line of reasoning. The *piece of analysis* is the basic unit of analysis in AnalyticStream; it includes a title, rich text contents and possibly an image/visualization that can be annotated (Figure 1 and 2). A piece of analysis can be used to represent a fact, an assumption, an entity, a relation, or any other type of artefact that analysts may want to externalize or record. A piece of analysis can be expanded to a sequence of pieces of analysis. We call this sequence the *story* of the piece of analysis; however, the *story* may be just a group of pieces related to the expanded piece and the semantic relations between the pieces and the story is arbitrary. For example, Figure 3 shows the story of "Azeem Bhutani", a person that is represented by a piece of analysis. In this example, the story is a sequence of events and other information related to the person's activities. Analysts can also create relations between pieces; these explicit relations are shown in the Graph view (Figure 3, bottom). In addition, analysts can edit the pieces, add them to their personal scratchpad (Figure 4, bottom-left), or mark them as helpful (Figure 2) to praise or thank the producer of the piece, as a basic incentive mechanism.

The main workspace is the tabbed area shown in Figure 3. Each tab represents the story of a piece of analysis using a multiple-coordinated view approach to enable both sequential marshalling using Narrative view (Figure 3, top) and relation-oriented interaction using the Graph view (Figure 3, bottom). Document-Viewer (Figure 4) is a permanent tab that provides an environment for reading documents during the analysis process. The user interface components that contribute to the social distribution of attention and memory processes are explained in the following sections.

SOCIAL DISTRIBUTION OF MEMORY PROCESSES

The externalized artefacts should be accessible by the other analysts to enable the reuse process. Rudimentary support for sharing and reuse of artefacts can be provided by supporting storage and retrieval of them. Looking through the lens of distributed cognition, to facilitate the reuse process the system should support various processes that are associated with memory such as memorizing, remembering, reminding, and perhaps even forgetting.

As discussed earlier, reusing one's own work and knowledge is only possible because we remember the

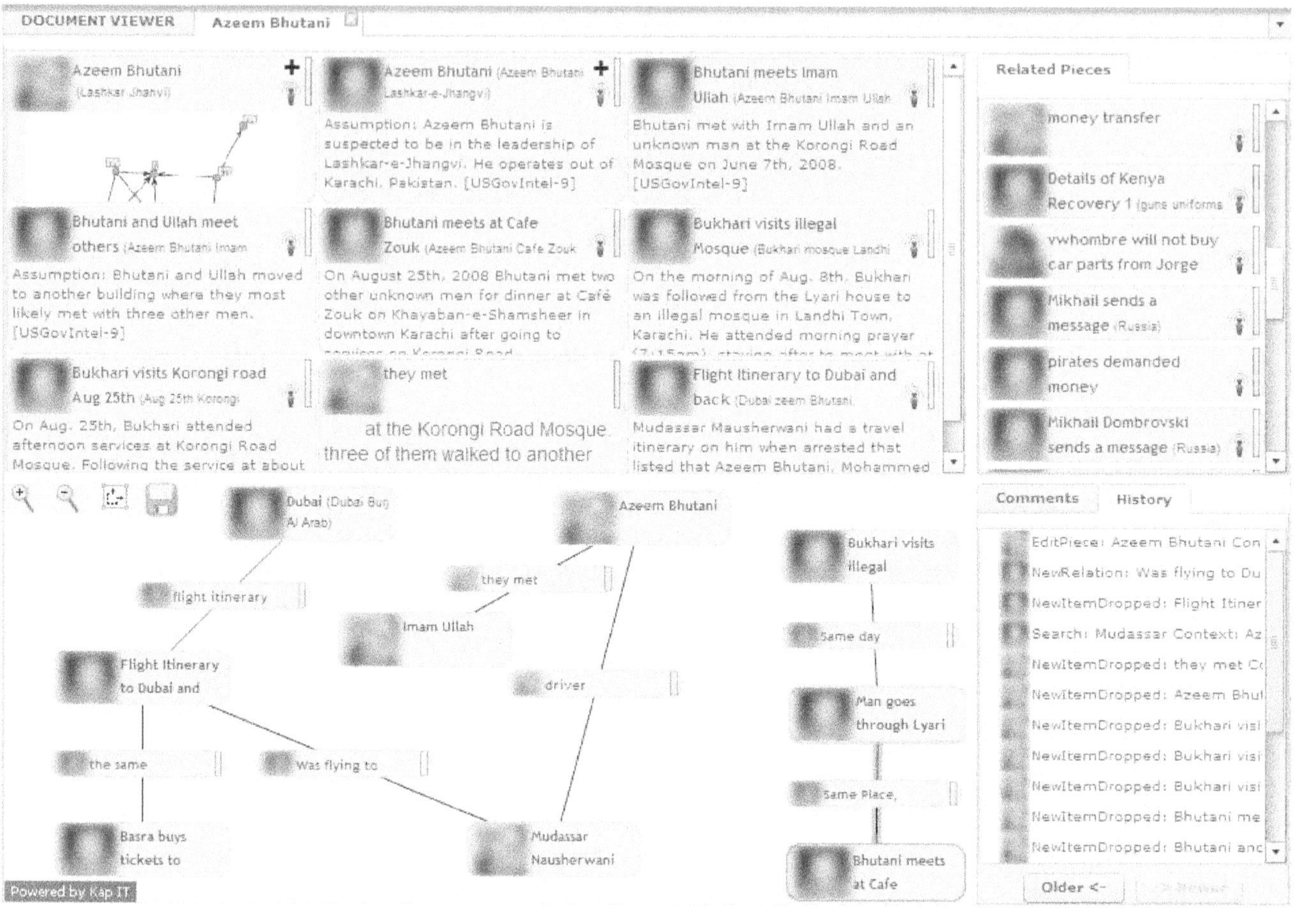

Figure 3. Representation of the story of a piece of analysis ("Azeem Bhutani") using Narrative view (top), Graph view (bottom), Related-Pieces panel (top-right), History panel and Comments panel (bottom-right).

relevant previous experiences and works. Supporting the aforementioned memory processes can facilitate various collaborative workflows. Memorizing (storage) and active remembering (retrieval through search or browsing) processes are supported by all collaborative systems; however, there has been little work on supporting the forgetting and the reminding processes, mainly because the need for them is less apparent. For example, recording (memorize) the entire user interactions can be desirable, because it enables users to navigate through their interaction histories to find and reuse sequences of interactions. Forgetting mechanisms can be designed to handle the unbounded interaction logs efficiently. The simple strategy that is often used is to eliminate the old data, which is not desirable when designing for unanticipated reuse. Cognitive theories of human memory architecture and processes can inform the design of these mechanisms. For example, based on the Schema theory of cognition, forgetting occurs when certain pieces of information get integrated and lose their individual identity [3]. In a collaborative system, this integration may occur over several users' interaction histories over a period of time. Looking at the design space through the lens of distributed cognition theory enables us to transform the design problem by bringing it to the cognition domain and subsequently enables applying other theories of human cognition to solve it.

Various history recording and navigation mechanisms are proposed to enable the reuse of one's own previous works [12,17,26]. Allowing users to replay, manipulate, or simply continue the steps taken by other users enables a greater level of reuse in collaborative systems. However, finding and managing activity sequences is challenging, and various related privacy issues should be addressed. Efficient recording and automatic integration of activity history are exciting but challenging research problems that we postpone for future research.

AnalyticStream provides the basic mechanisms for interacting with activity history. The History panel (Figure 3, bottom-right) shows the activities related to the pieces that are visible in the main workspace (the Narrative or the Graph view). Each item presents the name of the user, the related piece, and the name of the action performed (e.g. adding pieces to the story, creation of the piece, edits, etc.). Moreover, clicking on the user name or profile picture displays the activities of the user. Despite providing basic history navigation mechanisms, we decided to focus on the less explored mechanisms for supporting the distribution of memory and attention processes. The Activity-Stream panel

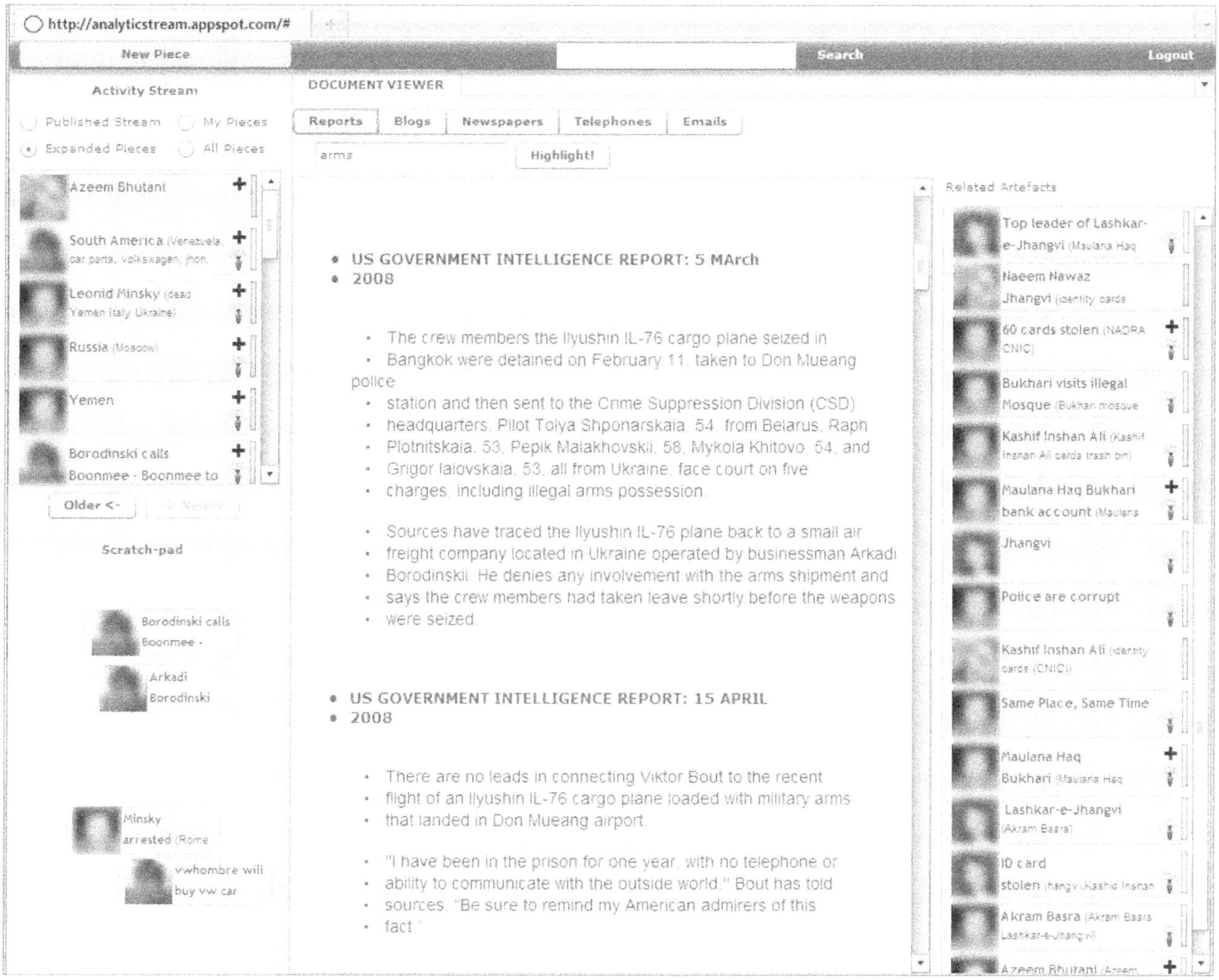

Figure 4. Initial AnalyticStream user interface: The left sidebar includes the Activity-Stream panel (top) and the Scratchpad (bottom-left). The Document-Viewer includes a reading area and its right sidebar shows the relevant pieces.

(Figure 4, top-left) provides a coarse-grained history and is considered as an awareness mechanism, which will be discussed in the section on the distribution of attention.

In a collaborative analytics system, the reuse process starts with searching for other analysts' findings. This process may be ineffective when the analysts are not aware of the items that others have stored. To generate a query, analysts must know enough to know what is not known and which of the many unknowns can be understood from the other analysts' findings. Finding out about all relevant abstractions and entities is challenging when the analysts do not know what to ask [8]. Due to the exploratory nature of the analysis process, the discoverability is a prominent problem. The analytics process deals with vague situation models, which makes it near impossible to ask the right questions.

Looking through the lens of distributed cognition, this challenge can be addressed by extending its analogous process of reusing one's own experiences and prior knowledge. Storing an item in a shared repository can be seen as the process of memorization of an item by a group; therefore, reusing it requires remembering. Information can be retrieved from memory in two different ways: The first one is actively trying to remember something that we are aware of having in our memory, and the second one is being reminded about the artefacts and processes that are related to the current context, which happens frequently in our daily lives. Reminding process often happens when a situation or a change in the external world, triggers a related memory; thus it is often a process distributed over the artefacts, times and one's (internal) memory. Schank's theory of reminding [27] posits that when we process events as they happen, we need to find specific episodes in memory that are closely related to the current input; however we do not consciously look for them, because we are not explicitly aware of their existence. In a collaborative system, the system can assist users by reminding them about other users' products that are related to the user's current task. We hypothesize facilitating the social distribution of reminding process through automatic recommendations creates opportunities for reuse.

Related-Pieces panel (Figure 3, top-right) automatically suggests the pieces of analysis that are related to the analyst's workspace. Previous research has shown that content similarity and collaborative filtering algorithms can be effective for similar purposes [5]. In this study for the sake of simplicity and due to the small number of subjects, we only used content similarity as a measure of relevance for generating suggestions. To assess content similarity, AnalyticStream generates a query based on the contents of the pieces of analysis in an analyst's workspace and searches the repository of pieces to find related pieces. The search is automatically performed whenever the workspace is updated; for example, adding a piece to the workspace or removing or editing it triggers the search process. We used Stanford Named Entity Recognizer [7] to extract the entities from the pieces of analysis and give them more weight in the search process to improve the relevance assessment. Similarly, in the Document-Viewer (Figure 4) the pieces that are related to the reading area are suggested to the user. In this case, the query is generated based on the visible text in the Document-Viewer and scrolling the page triggers the generation of suggestions. We hypothesize that these suggestions improve the discoverability of the pieces of analysis, which can facilitate the reuse process. During the course of this study, we found out that a similar approach has been evaluated in a case study with one analyst, which showed a high rate of reuse in the single-user scenario [28].

Additionally, AnalyticStream provides a scratchpad (Figure 4, bottom-left) to drag and drop pieces to and from other components such as the Related-Pieces panel, the Narrative and the Graph views, etc. The scratchpad supports organizing the pieces spatially and was aimed at providing a personal space like a desktop. Through the lens of distributed cognition theory, the scratchpad acts as an extension of short-term memory that helps a user to keep track of his analysis during a session as well as between sessions. However, due to its personal (non-collaborative) nature, analysing its role is out of the scope of this paper.

SOCIAL DISTRIBUTION OF ATTENTION PROCESSES

Attention is a cognitive process that serves various purposes. It helps us to select a target item from distracters and enables the ongoing awareness of the environment [19]. Attention can be socially distributed in a collaborative analytics system. Socially distributed attention mechanisms have been subject of research under the name of awareness. User awareness in a collaborative system is defined as the way users perceive their collaborators and what they are doing, without direct communication [6].

From the point of view of distributed cognition theory, awareness is a distributed attention mechanism in which users' behaviour attracts other users' attention to the extent that makes them aware of their behaviour. In a collaborative analytics system, sharing of attention among several analysts can facilitate the coordination between analysts.

Analysts should be able to share their attention, i.e. to let others know of their foci of attention, and actively attract other analysts' attention to tasks, artefacts and people of interest. Analysts as elements of the distributed cognitive system should be able to find out about the foci of attention of other elements of the system as well as the foci of attention of the cognitive system (or subsystem) that they are part of. Awareness helps analysts to coordinate their activities based on the common or related goals, for example, by devoting their cognitive resources to the common foci of attention. Supporting awareness is essential for facilitating collaborative sensemaking processes [24]. However, recognizing awareness as one of the attention mechanisms that can enhance the flow of information in a complex cognitive system helps to explore and examine new interactions and workflows in collaborative systems. In AnalyticStream, the Activity-Stream panel (figure 4, top-left) provides awareness about recently created or edited pieces. Additionally, it serves as a browsing mechanism for finding pieces of analysis. Similar to a social network stream, the Activity-Stream panel makes analysts aware of the foci of attention of other analysts and helps them to better allocate their cognitive resources.

Privacy and Attention

The concept of privacy has been defined in various ways in social science literature. Parent [23] reviewed several previously proposed definitions and based on them, he proposed a new definition that describes privacy as "the condition of a person's not having undocumented personal information about himself known by others" or in other words "the absence of undocumented personal knowledge about a person". However, this definition does not capture nuances of this concept. The definition suggests that if personal information is documented somewhere, it does not matter if others know it or not. This issue is challenged by recent privacy researchers. Boyd introduced the concept of privacy and security through obscurity [4], which implies that one can put her/his personal information in a public or shared space, while maintaining some level of privacy. Boyd underscored the difference between something being public versus something being announced to others.

The concept of privacy by obscurity suggests that privacy is not just about the existence of information in a public place, but also strongly interrelated with the availability of information to others, awareness of the availability, and the amount of attention that it receives. The design of collaborative systems should aim at providing mechanisms that enhance discoverability and availability of information and foster sharing of the potentially useful information while maintaining collaborators' privacy.

In AnalyticStream, a piece of analysis may have one of the following privacy states: private, public, or published. Private pieces are only visible to the analyst who produced them. Public pieces are visible to all analysts, but they do not show up in the default view of the Activity-Stream panel (hence unpublished). Finally, published pieces are visible to all the analysts and show up in the Activity-Stream panel (Figure 4, top-left). The Activity-Stream panel provides 4 different modes for browsing through pieces of analysis: browsing through one's own pieces, expanded pieces, published pieces, and all pieces. The creators of pieces of analysis mark them as published, when they want to make other analysts aware of them. The default mode of the Activity-Stream shows the published pieces so that analysts become aware of the latest important activities of other analysts. An important cost of information sharing is the cost incurred by the recipients of the information which is their attention. Therefore, devising new attention management mechanisms can help to balance the trade-offs in sharing [2,30].

METHODS

As part of the evaluation of AnalyticStream, we were interested in understanding how recommendations affect participants' reuse behaviour and how participants compare it with search. Moreover, as a secondary goal we were interested to see how the shared activity stream and the enhanced privacy settings affect sharing behaviours.

We used a mixed methods design to collect and analyze qualitative and quantitative data. The qualitative data, collected through interviews and participants' diaries, are the core of the study, which were complemented by quantitative data derived from Likert-scale questions. A controlled lab study could allow for methods such as think-aloud that can provide a clear sense of user behaviours; however, we decided to allow participants to conduct analysis in their comfort zones and at times that work for them to enable them to engage in the analysis process. Moreover, the collaboration in natural settings cannot happen in a one or two-hour session and we wanted the participants to get involved in analyzing the dataset, so that the collaboration and the reuse process occur naturally. Although we did consider using simple datasets that can be analyzed by untrained users, we decided to use a complex realistic dataset to enhance the ecological validity of the study.

Task and Dataset

Participants were given a text corpus including five large document sets related to illegal arms dealing. The dataset was acquired from the Visual Analytics Science and Technology (VAST) contest 2010 [9] and contained intelligence reports, emails, blog posts, telephone transcripts, and news articles. The participants were asked to provide a forensic analysis of illegal arms dealing. In particular, we asked them to find the hidden plot in the data, which involved summarizing and making sense of the activities that happened in each country with respect to illegal arms dealing and the associations among the involved players, based on a synthesis of the information from the different sources (reports, emails, etc.).

Participants

A total of 6 participants (3 females), between 25 and 38 years of age, with science and engineering backgrounds were recruited by calling for volunteers through emails to visual analytics research groups and researchers of a North American university. The participants should have been able to participate in a collaborative analysis of a complex realistic dataset and deal with uncertain or missing data, in multiple analysis sessions.We did not have access to intelligence analysts, but we had the opportunity of recruiting a group of visual analytics researchers who had experience performing analytical tasks in the VAST challenge and/or in visual analytics courses. As a result, our subjects were familiar with typical visual analytics tools, tasks, and processes.

Procedure

Participants were asked to use AnalyticStream for multiple sessions to make sense of the dataset. Initially, we asked them to use the system for a specific amount of time in every session, but later we noticed that because of not being in a lab environment, we cannot dictate the details of their participation. Therefore, we did not specify any timing for their participation, and some of them started their analysis process several days later than others, which is normal for a distributed collaboration. Especially because we primarily focused on collecting qualitative data, it was desirable for us to have participants in different situations, i.e. different levels of experience with analytics tasks and starting analysis with different numbers of pieces of analysis available to them. Participants were asked to fill out a semi-structured diary during and after each analysis session. After the experiment period, participants were asked to fill out a post-test questionnaire, to reflect on the overall experience and evaluate various features of the system. Finally, based on the collected data, we interviewed them to disambiguate or validate our uncertain interpretations of diaries and answers to open-ended questions.

RESULTS AND FINDINGS

Memory Distribution Mechanisms

Just being exposed to the artefacts produced by self or others can remind people of related information. One participant mentioned using this strategy actively by browsing other participants' products: *"I tried to remember some parts using [one of the participant's] stories and some pieces created by a new guy. But still after these 5 sessions, the topic and the written reports are hard to absorb for me and I can't remember events very well..."*.

Participants were asked to assess the usefulness of the two main memory distribution mechanisms: Active retrieval using search and passive retrieval (or reminding) using recommendations. All participants found recommendations to be useful for finding other analysts' pieces of analysis and 4 (out of 6) of them found search to be useful for this purpose (Figure 5). Since we anticipated the helpfulness of both mechanisms, additionally, we asked the participants to compare the helpfulness of the two mechanisms. Overall, most of the participants (4/6) found recommendations more useful than search for finding other analysts' pieces of analysis (Figure 6).

Figure 5. Usefulness of and search for finding other participants' pieces of analysis

One of the participants explained her preference for recommendations, as follows: *"I wasn't looking for a specific thing; I read related artefacts during reading documents; I guess search would be more useful later in my analysis process"*. The dataset was designed to be analyzed by several analysts over a long period; therefore, during this study participants were mostly in the initial phases of analyzing the dataset, where they had an ambiguous model of the problem space, and they could not distinguish the key entities in the dataset. The recommendations that referred to the entities in the workspace, as one participant said, helped to *"relate some events that the reports didn't connect"* and identify the entities that require further investigation. This benefit of recommendations can be realized in a variety of collaborative systems that deal with complex problems where collaborators have to deal with constantly changing data and situations.

Another participant explained his usage of search, as follows: *"I use the search [...] to find pieces I know exist."* Even in these situations, sometimes as he reported, recommendations worked as a substitute for search: *"I was going to search for [a piece] but it turned out it was already listed [in the Related-Pieces panel]"*. The only participant who found recommendations less helpful than search was the least active participant of the study (based on the number of interactions with the system). This suggests that the more analysts engage in their analysis, the more recommendations become helpful; because when analysts are focused on their analysis, they may spend less time exploring others' analysis products. Investigating this hypothesis is left for future work.

One of the participants found recommending relevant artefacts useful for connecting subplots when analysts work on different subplots, and the subplots had something in common. This was one of the main anticipated benefits of recommendations. In distributed collaboration, often, implicit or explicit division of labour makes collaborators focus on a specific set of resources and the resources connected to them (similar to exploring research literature through citations). In such situations missing relevant

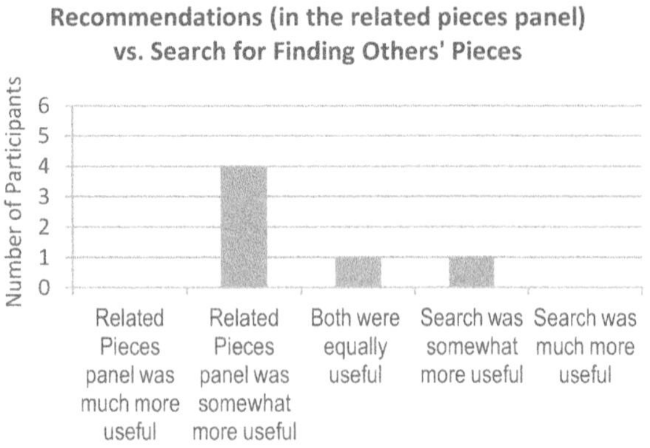

Figure 6. Comparing usefulness of recommendations vs. search for finding other participants' pieces of analysis

resources is easy and unsolicited recommendations can help to solve this problem.

According to usage logs, all participants browsed through the recommendations and read many of the recommended pieces. This can be considered as an indicator of reuse; every instance of reading relevant pieces has potentially helped an analyst to develop his understanding of the information space. For example, one of the participants mentioned that by seeing other analysts' relevant pieces, he noticed: *"We had common hypotheses and there were pieces that added new info to what I knew."* This statement also shows that the recommendations can be employed as a context-based awareness mechanism, as another participant said: *"[I] used related artefacts to know what others analyze and what they discovered."* Additionally, we reviewed the usage logs to find if any explicit instance of reuse has occurred, and we found that the more active half of the participants (3/6) explicitly reused the recommended pieces of analysis in building stories.

We also asked the same questions regarding the reuse of *own* pieces of analysis. However, participants' responses were equally divided between search and recommendations. One explanation is that the analysis process was not long enough for participants to forget about the pieces that they have created earlier. The major advantage of recommendations over search is evident when users cannot ask the right questions. Being aware of the existence of the pieces and remembering specific information or keywords related to them allows for effective search.

In sum, the study showed that the recommendations were particularly helpful when the participants did not know what to look for or even were not aware of the existence of helpful pieces of information.

Attention Distribution Mechanisms

Usage logs showed that all participants browsed through the activity stream right after logging in. Interviews indicated that browsing through the shared activity stream served two purposes. First, it helped remembering their own activities, which exemplifies the distribution of refocusing attention and remembering over time. Second, browsing through the activity stream helped them become aware of others' activities, which exemplifies the distribution of attracting and paying attention across people and over time.

As discussed earlier, understanding the effects of enhanced privacy settings requires a focused study in ecologically valid settings where analysts care about the consequences of sharing. Nevertheless, we looked at how participants used the privacy settings, and we found that the two most active participants used the public (unpublished) privacy level. Content analysis of the public pieces revealed two usage patterns: first, creating helper pieces or relations that did not have an independent meaning, but were generated to explain or comment on other pieces, and second, creating pieces that were considered to be less important or less relevant to the participants' main line of reasoning. These pieces may be helpful to other analysts or may become helpful later and sharing them creates opportunities for unanticipated reuse.

All participants used the published mode of sharing pieces of analysis, which was the default mode and only one participant created private pieces. In realistic settings, people are more concerned about when and with whom they share pieces of information as well as about consequences of sharing them [2]. This suggests that in-depth investigation of the effects of the enhanced privacy/attention settings requires a higher level of ecological validity, which is left for future research.

In addition, allowing participants to mark helpful pieces worked as another mechanism for attracting other participants' attention. Originally, this feature was designed to provide an incentive for creating and sharing valuable pieces of analysis. As a side benefit, as one of the participants said: *"It helps in emphasizing the better posts"*, which suggests that marking as helpful was used to signal valuable pieces and attract other analysts' attention.

In sum, the study showed that the attention distribution mechanisms can help users to make their products available without necessarily attracting other analysts' attention, and to attract attention only to helpful pieces of analysis.

SUMMARY AND CONCLUSION

Looking through the lens of distributed cognition theory helped us gain a different understanding of the design space of collaborative systems. Rather than focusing on explicit requirements for a collaborative analytics system, we analyzed how various cognitive processes can be distributed over collaborators and how the system can facilitate the distribution of these processes.

One approach to employing distributed cognition theory for designing a collaborative system is to consider it as a cognitive system and identify the cognitive processes that can be socially distributed to support the goals of the collaborative system. Using this approach, we identified several possibilities for facilitating the reuse process through supporting the social distribution of memory and attention processes. Then we analyzed how user interface components can augment and support the social distribution of memory and attention processes. Implicit division of labour can be facilitated through enhancing shared attention and awareness mechanisms. Awareness of others' efforts can help collaborators to reuse each other's products and avoid redoing. Additionally, collaborators should be able to attract each other's attention to their products and processes as a method for initiating or enhancing collaborative work.

We focused on the use of recommendations as a distributed reminding process, through which analysts are reminded of other analysts' products that are related to the current workspace. This study showed that suggesting the relevant artefacts facilitated discovering them and helped participants to identify the key entities based on their occurrence in multiple pieces of analysis. Additionally, the Relevant-Artefacts panel provided context-based awareness of other analysts' activities. The study showed that public (unpublished) privacy level was used for sharing seemingly unimportant pieces or supplementary pieces. However, further research in realistic settings is needed to understand how enhancing control over attention and awareness affects sharing and reuse.

In sum, AnalyticStream enables the reuse process when users are not aware of the availability of useful shared artefacts or do not have a clear model of their information space to ask right questions. Moreover, AnalyticStream provides attention management mechanisms to allow collaborators share their products and decide about attracting others' attention to them. The design process and evaluation of AnalyticStream helped to develop an understanding of how the proposed approach to applying distributed cognition theory can be implemented in the design of collaborative systems. Future research is needed to further test the generalisability of our findings and the applicability of the proposed approach in different design situations.

ACKNOWLEDGMENTS

This work was supported by NSERC, and the GRAND NCE.

REFERENCES

1. Ackerman, M.S. and Halverson, C. Organizational Memory as Objects, Processes, and Trajectories: An Examination of Organizational Memory in Use. *Computer Supported Cooperative Work (CSCW) 13*, 2 (2004), 155-189.
2. Ackerman, M.S. The Intellectual Challenge of CSCW: The Gap Between Social Requirements and Technical Feasibility. *Human–Computer Interaction 15*, 2 (2000), 179.
3. Ausubel, D.P., Novak, J.D., and Hanesian, H. *Educational psychology: A cognitive view*. Holt Rinehart and Winston, 1978.

4. Boyd, D. Facebook's Privacy Trainwreck: Exposure, Invasion, and Social Convergence. *Convergence 14*, 1 (2008), 13-20.
5. Cosley, D., Frankowski, D., Terveen, L., and Riedl, J. SuggestBot: using intelligent task routing to help people find work in wikipedia. *Proceedings of the 12th international conference on Intelligent user interfaces*, ACM (2007), 32-41.
6. Dourish, P. and Bellotti, V. Awareness and coordination in shared workspaces. *Proceedings of the 1992 ACM conference on Computer-supported cooperative work*, ACM (1992), 107-114.
7. Finkel, J.R., Grenager, T., and Manning, C. Incorporating non-local information into information extraction systems by Gibbs sampling. *Proceedings of the 43rd Annual Meeting on Association for Computational Linguistics*, Association for Computational Linguistics (2005), 363-370.
8. Fischer, G. Cognitive View of Reuse and Redesign. *Software, IEEE 4*, 4 (1987), 60-72.
9. Grinstein, G., Plaisant, C., Scholtz, J., and Whiting, M. IEEE VAST 2010 Challenge. 2010. http://hcil.cs.umd.edu/localphp/hcil/vast10/index.php.
10. Halverson, C.A. Activity Theory and Distributed Cognition: Or What Does CSCW Need to DO with Theories? *Comput. Supported Coop. Work 11*, 1-2 (2002), 243-267.
11. Heer, J. and Agrawala, M. Design Considerations for Collaborative Visual Analytics. *Proceedings of the 2007 IEEE Symposium on Visual Analytics Science and Technology*, IEEE (2007).
12. Heer, J., Mackinlay, J., Stolte, C., and Agrawala, M. Graphical Histories for Visualization: Supporting Analysis, Communication, and Evaluation. *IEEE Transactions on Visualization and Computer Graphics 14*, 6 (2008), 1189-1196.
13. Heer, J., Viégas, F.B., and Wattenberg, M. Voyagers and voyeurs: Supporting asynchronous collaborative visualization. *Commun. ACM 52*, 1 (2009), 87-97.
14. Hollan, J., Hutchins, E., and Kirsh, D. Distributed cognition: toward a new foundation for human-computer interaction research. *ACM Trans. Comput.-Hum. Interact. 7*, 2 (2000), 174-196.
15. Holmes, R. Unanticipated reuse of large-scale software features. *Proceedings of the 28th international conference on Software engineering*, (2006), 961–964.
16. Hutchins, E. *Cognition in the Wild*. The MIT Press, 1996.
17. Kadivar, N., Chen, V., Dunsmuir, D., et al. Capturing and supporting the analysis process. *IEEE Symposium on Visual Analytics Science and Technology*, (2009), 131-138.
18. Kirschner, P.A., Buckingham-Shum, S.J., and Carr, C.S. *Visualizing Argumentation: Software Tools for Collaborative and Educational Sense-Making*. Springer, 2003.
19. LaBerge, D. Attention, Awareness, and the Triangular Circuit. *Consciousness and Cognition 6*, 2-3 (1997), 149-181.
20. Lutters, W.G. and Ackerman, M.S. Beyond Boundary Objects: Collaborative Reuse in Aircraft Technical Support. *Computer Supported Cooperative Work (CSCW) 16*, 3 (2006), 341-372.
21. Marshall, C.C. Toward an ecology of hypertext annotation. *Proceedings of the ninth ACM conference on Hypertext and Hypermedia*, ACM (1998), 40–49.
22. Neisser, U. *Cognitive Psychology*. Prentice Hall, 1967.
23. Parent, W.A. Recent Work on the Concept of Privacy. *American Philosophical Quarterly 20*, 4 (1983), 341-355.
24. Paul, S.A. and Morris, M.R. CoSense: enhancing sensemaking for collaborative web search. *Proceedings of the 27th conference on Human factors in computing systems*, (2009), 1771–1780.
25. Pike, W., Bruce, J., Baddeley, B., et al. The Scalable Reasoning System: Lightweight visualization for distributed analytics. *Information Visualization 8*, 1 (2009), 71-84.
26. Robinson, A.C. and Weaver, C. Re-Visualization: Interactive Visualization of the Process of Visual Analysis. *Workshop on Visualization, Analytics & Spatial Decision Support*, (2006).
27. Schank, R.C. *Dynamic Memory Revisited*. Cambridge University Press, 1999.
28. Shrinivasan, Y.B., Gotzy, D., and Lu, J. Connecting the dots in visual analysis. *IEEE Symposium on Visual Analytics Science and Technology*, (2009), 123-130.
29. Simon, H.A. *The Sciences of the Artificial - 3rd Edition*. The MIT Press, 1996.
30. Simon, H. Designing Organizations for an Information-Rich World. In *Computers, communications, and the public interest*. 1971, 37-72.
31. Thomas, J.J. and Cook, K.A. *Illuminating the Path: The Research and Development Agenda for Visual Analytics*. National Visualization and Analytics Ctr, 2005.
32. Viegas, F. and Wattenberg, M. Communication-Minded Visualization: A Call to Action. *IBM Systems Journal 45*, 4 (2006).
33. Viegas, F.B., Wattenberg, M., van Ham, F., Kriss, J., and McKeon, M. ManyEyes: a Site for Visualization at Internet Scale. *IEEE Transactions on Visualization and Computer Graphics 13*, (2007), 1121–1128.
34. Wright, W., Schroh, D., Proulx, P., Skaburskis, A., and Cort, B. The Sandbox for analysis: concepts and methods. *Proceedings of the SIGCHI conference on Human factors in computing systems*, ACM (2006), 801-810.
35. i2 Analyst's Notebook. http://www.i2inc.com/products/analysts_notebook/.

Analyzing the Structure of the Emergent Division of Labor in Multiparty Collaboration

Noriko Suzuki
NICT
2-2-2 Hikaridai Seika-cho
Soraku-gun Kyoto
619-0288, Japan
nrk_suzuki@nict.go.jp

Tosirou Kamiya
Osaka Univ.
8-1-1 Aomatani Minoh
Osaka 562-8558, Japan
tosirou.kamiya@gmail.com

Ichiro Umata
NICT
2-2-2 Hikaridai Seika-cho
Soraku-gun Kyoto
619-0288, Japan
umata@nict.go.jp

Sadanori Ito
NICT
2-2-2 Hikaridai Seika-cho
Soraku-gun Kyoto
619-0288, Japan
sadanori.ito@nict.go.jp

Shoichiro Iwasawa
NICT
2-2-2 Hikaridai Seika-cho
Soraku-gun Kyoto
619-0288, Japan
shoichiro.iwasawa@nict.go.jp

ABSTRACT

In our daily life, the interactive roles of leaders, followers, and coordinators tend to emerge from multiparty collaboration. The primary purpose of this study is to automatically predict the leading role in multiparty interaction by ubiquitous computing techniques. Even though the leading role has been predicted for an entire task, there has been little focus on evaluating how roles are reorganized during a task. To find the verbal and nonverbal cues that might predict roles, we asked neutral third parties to select the participant playing the leading role in an assembly task. We examined the correlation between behavioral data gathered during a task and third-party evaluations of the leading role player in terms of temporal alterations. The preliminary results suggest that task-oriented utterances and verification behaviors regarding progress status contribute to the prediction of the emerging and reorganized leader. Moreover, we discuss the implications of our findings for the design of applications that can enhance multiparty collaboration.

Author Keywords

Nonverbal Behaviors; Multiparty Interaction; Emergent Leader; Third-party Evaluation.

ACM Classification Keywords

H.5.3 Information Interfaces and Presentation: Group and Organization Interfaces—*Evaluation/methodology*

General Terms

Human Factors; Design; Measurement.

INTRODUCTION

Group work occurs within countless everyday activities: learning or experimental trials in schools, company training, social services, and even camping. Conventional studies of group dynamics focus on the prediction made for the entire interaction of interactive roles, i.e., the work of leaders, followers, and coordinators [1; 2, etc.]. On the other hand, few studies have analyzed the emergence and reorganization of interactive roles in multiparty interaction, with Kato being a notable exception *et al.* [4].

The purpose of this study is to develop a method that can automatically predict the leading role player in multiparty interaction by ubiquitous computing techniques. This paper focuses on how verbal and nonverbal behaviors contribute to natural leader emergence and reorganization in interaction. The leader plays an important role in the development of teamwork or task performance in group activity. Some conventional studies of multiparty conversations with positionally fixed participants have pointed out the crucial

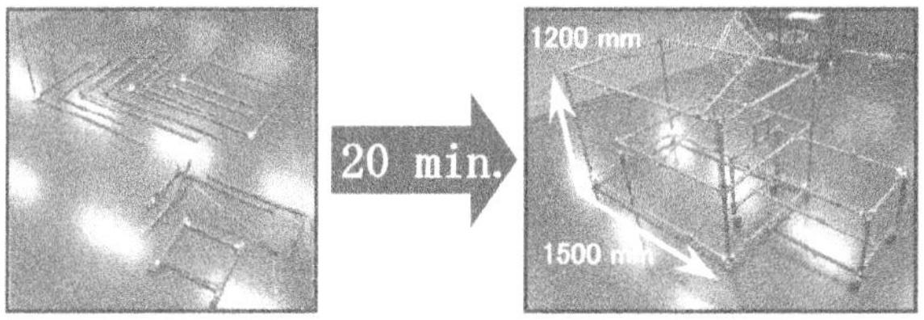

(a) Materials used in the task of assembling a structure: twelve kinds of components (left) and completed figure (right).

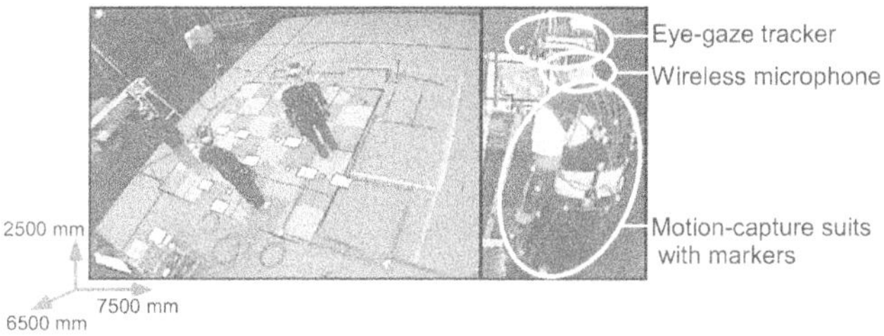

(b) Large-structure assembly task in shared physical space (left) and devices worn by participants (right).

Figure 1. Materials used in assembly task: twelve components (upper left) and completed figure (upper right), large-structure assembly task in shared physical space (lower left), and devices worn by participants (lower right)

role played by verbal and nonverbal behaviors in the process of natural leader emergence [7, 3]. However, few research works have captured and analyzed the nonverbal behaviors of participants in teamwork while they are actively moving, due to the difficulty of regarding the changes in distance or position among participants as a factor in predicting the roles in positionally fixed tasks.

In this study's task, people assembled a large structure consisting of pipes. No participant was assigned a particular role. As the participants moved in a shared physical space to assemble the structure, their gaze, speech, motion, and position data were captured by sensors. The captured data were analyzed to investigate the relationships between verbal/nonverbal behaviors and natural leader emergence. First, we examined these relationships with a triad because it is the minimum unit in multiparty interaction.

In our previous analysis results, we found no significant difference regarding the leading role in a task from the self-evaluations of the participants [8]. To examine the co-occurrence relation between an observer's judgment and verbal/nonverbal behaviors in the task, we asked neutral third parties to select the participant with the leading role in the assembly task.

This paper presents a third-party rating experiment in which 22 people participated. The raters selected the leader role in the assembly task while watching a movie of the task activity. We also report the correlation between the results of third-party evaluations and the coding/measuring results of verbal/nonverbal behaviors to identify useful parameters for predicting the emergence and reorganization of leadership. These useful findings might help to reduce the costs of capturing and analyzing multiparty interaction. Furthermore, we discuss the implications of our findings for the design of applications that can enhance multiparty collaboration.

TASK OF ASSEMBLING A LARGE STRUCTURE

We focused on how both verbal and nonverbal behaviors help us examine emerging leadership through group work while the participants are moving. A preliminary experiment was conducted on the task of assembling a large structure in a shared physical space while checking a picture of the completed structure. The large structure consisted of pipes assembled into "pipe furniture" as this group task ' s target object. This approach is based on a previous TV-cart assembly task [5].

Figure 1(a) (upper left) shows twelve types of components, and Fig. 1(b) (upper right) shows the picture of the completed structure (PCS) used in this experiment. Gaze, speech, and distance among participants were captured within a space of 7500 × 6500 × 2500 (mm) (width/depth/height) (Fig. 1)(b) (lower left)). Each participant wore an eye-gaze tracker attached to a cap, a close-proximity microphone, and optical markers on a body suit for the motion capture device (Fig. 1)(b) (lower right)).

Two groups (C1 and C2), each consisting of three participants, took part in this preliminary experiment. Before the task, the participants had never met each other. No participant was assigned a particular role, such as leader or manager. At the start, all participants shared equal status.

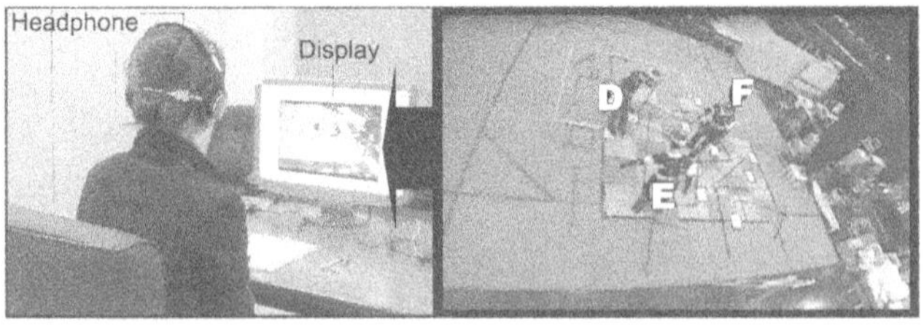

Figure 2. Third-party rating experiment (left) and movie scene used for third-party evaluation (right)

Group C2 successfully assembled the large structure in just over 13 minutes, but group C1 failed to complete the task within 20 minutes.

We obtained the following findings from previous analysis results [8, 9]: (1) the self-evaluation results of the participants in the task did not show any significant difference regarding the leading role, (2) the qualitative analysis results suggest that the participant who notices assembling errors might become the leader, and (3) the quantitative analysis results also suggest that task-oriented utterances and verification behaviors might contribute to the emergence of a leading role. However, it remains unclear how these results might be used for actually predicting emergent leaders during the task.

METHOD OF THIRD-PARTY EVALUATION

We conducted a third-party rating experiment on predicting the emergent leader to investigate the relationship between an observer's judgment and the participants' verbal/nonverbal behaviors.

Participants

Twenty-two people from 20 to 38 years old were recruited as raters. They did not take part in the task of assembling a large structure.

Rating task

We used movies that recorded the task of assembling the large structure (Fig. 1 (lower left)). The raters watched the movies of both C1 and C2 groups. In the rating experiment, the order of watching the movies was counterbalanced between the two groups. Each movie was evenly split into thirds: early, middle, and final phases. This was done for two reasons: first, the two groups took different durations to complete the task, and second, each group assembled the pipes in different orders or phases. The raters could watch the same movie three times.

Procedures

Each rater was assigned to a computer with headphones (Fig. 2) and told that they would watch a movie of an assembly task and then select the task's leader. After receiving the instructions, they practiced and became familiar with selecting the leader from among three participants by viewing a short sample movie. Next they watched the movies and answered a post-experiment questionnaire. The raters wrote the number of the participant who emerged and led the task's work

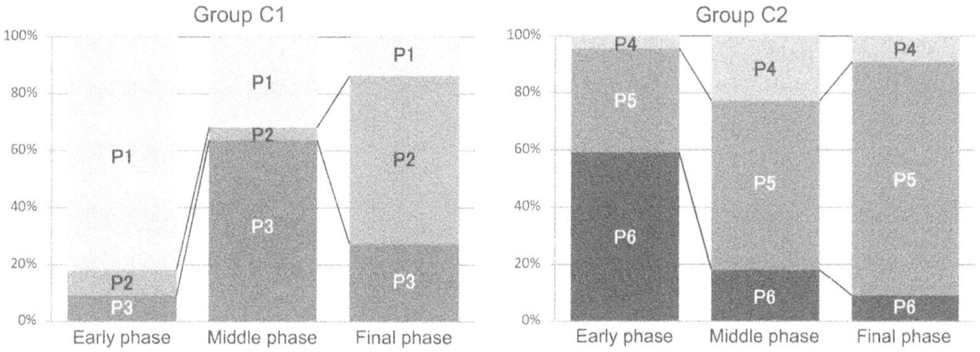

(a) Results of third-party evaluation for emergent leadership with temporal alternations

Group C1

	Early phase			Middle phase			Final phase		
	P1	P2	P3	P1	P2	P3	P1	P2	P3
P1	—	>*	>*	—	n.s.	<*	—	<*	<*
P2		—	n.s.		—	<*		—	>*
P3			—			—			—

* $p < 0.001$

Group C2

	Early phase			Middle phase			Final phase		
	P4	P5	P6	P4	P5	P6	P4	P5	P6
P4	—	n.s.	<*	—	<*	>*	—	<*	n.s.
P5		—	<*		—	>*		—	>*
P6			—			—			—

* $p < 0.001$

(b) Results of multiple comparisons to third-party evaluation for emergent leadership

Figure 3. Results of third-party evaluation for emergent leadership with temporal alterations: groups C1 (upper left) and C2 (upper right), and results of multiple comparisons to third-party evaluation for emergent leadership: groups C1 (lower left) and C2 (lower right)

by asking for other participants' cooperation. The raters did not comment on their own selection criteria or determination method.

Hypotheses

In this experiment, we assumed the following hypotheses on predicting emergent leaders:

(a) **Reorganization of leadership:**
Interactive roles, including leader, might emerge and be reorganized in the task.

(b) **Relationship to verbal/nonverbal behaviors:**
Verbal and nonverbal behaviors might contribute to the emergence and reorganization of such interactive roles as leadership.

RESULTS

Third-party evaluations

Figure 3 (upper) shows the third-party evaluation results for emergent leadership with temporal alterations in the assembly task. The bar graph indicates the percentage of the raters' responses that select each of the three participants as leader of the group; here, participants were labeled for group C1: P1, P2 and P3; for group C2: P4, P5 and P6. For example, participant P1 was selected by 82% of the raters as the leader in the early phase of group C1, participant P2 by 9%, and participant P3 by 9%.

Cochran's Q test was performed on the third-party evaluation results in each phase. There were significant differences in the ratios of potential leaders in every phase of both groups ($p < 0.05$). This result suggests that the ratios of the participant who was predicted to be the leader were significantly higher than those of other participants.

Figure 3 (lower) shows the results of multiple comparisons of the third-party evaluations, whose raters selected the emergence and reorganization of the leadership. There were significant differences in potential leaders in every phase of both groups ($p < 0.001$): P1 > P2 = P3 (early phase), P3 > P1 $\simeq$ P2 (middle phase), and P2 > P3 > P1 (final phase) in group C1, and P6 > P5 $\simeq$ P4 (early phase), P5 > P4 > P6 (middle phase), and P5 > P4 = P6 (final phase) in group C2. These results suggest that the reorganization of leadership is as follows: from P1 to P3 and then from P3 to P2 in group C1, and from P6 to P5 in group C2. Therefore, hypothesis (a) was supported.

Table 1. Correlation coefficient between results of third-party evaluation of emergent leadership and verbal/nonverbal behaviors

Verbal/nonverbal behavior	Correlation coefficient	
Frequency of task-oriented utterances	0.484	*
Amount of task-oriented utterances	0.735	*
Frequency of all utterances	0.300	
Amount of all utterances	0.631	*
Frequency of visual contact with PCS closer	0.270	
Amount of visual contact with PCS closer	0.417	⋆
Frequency of visual contact with PCS	-0.111	
Amount of visual contact with PCS	0.095	
Total moving distance	-0.138	
Distance to other participants	-0.237	
Frequency of facing each other	0.181	
Frequency of overlapping utterances	0.022	
Amount of overlapping utterances	-0.047	
Frequency of gaze to others	0.122	
Amount of gaze to others	-0.072	
Frequency of mutual gaze	-0.112	
Amount of mutual gaze	0.068	
Frequency of gaze to components	0.244	
Amount of gaze to components	0.042	
Frequency of joint attention to components	0.029	
Amount of joint attention to components	0.046	
Frequency of joint attention to PCS	0.108	
Time of joint attention to PCS	0.070	

PCS: picture of completed structure
$* : p < 0.05, \star : p < 0.10$

Relationship with verbal and nonverbal behaviors

We calculated the correlation matrix between the third-party evaluation results for emergent leadership and the measured results of the verbal/nonverbal behaviors in the assembly task. These co-occurrence relations might indirectly provide hints about both the selection criteria of the raters and useful parameters for predicting emergent leaders in the task.

Table 1 shows the correlation coefficients and p-values using the Fisher r-z transform. The emergent leadership might have a positive correlation with (i) both the amount and frequency of the task-oriented speech and (ii) the total amount of speech. Moreover, it might have a weak positive correlation with (iii) the amount of close visual contact with the picture of completed structure (PCS). Close visual contact with PCS in the assembly task was regarded as verification behavior for the task status. The results suggest that these factors might provide a link between someone's judgment and the participants' verbal/nonverbal behaviors. Accordingly, hypothesis (b) was supported.

These results also might show the possibility that the following parameters are useful for predicting emergent and reorganized leaders in a cooperative task: (i) both the amount and frequency of speech with/without content and (ii) the amount of verification behavior for the task status.

CONCLUSION

We captured, analyzed, and evaluated verbal and nonverbal behaviors in group collaboration in an effort to find a method for automatically predicting the emergent division of labor. To examine the co-occurrence relation between someone's judgment and verbal/nonverbal behaviors in an assembly task, we asked neutral third parties to select the participant taking the leading role in the task.

The following findings might contribute to the development of a method to predict the emergent division of labor, including the roles of leaders, followers, and coordinators:

- Leadership typically emerges and gets reorganized in group work.
- Two parameters, the amount and frequency of task-oriented speech and the amount of verification behavior, are useful for predicting the person who takes the leader role in group work.

These findings could help to reduce the costs of capturing and analyzing multiparty cooperation. We will conduct an assembly task using more groups with simpler equipment than in our first trial. Using these data, we will investigate again the effectiveness of our findings for predicting leaders.

In our preliminary multiparty cooperation task, we created groups of strangers without checking their capacity for assembly tasks or spatial cognition ability. In future work, we will conduct a similar task and control the familiarity among participants or address their task adequacy.

If we could make a model of the structure of interactive roles, including leaders in multiparty cooperation, and then automatically predict these roles from captured data, such an approach would be useful to inform the design of future collaborative systems: (1) face-to-face cooperation support systems that enhance the emergent division of labor through visualization of the status of interactive roles, or that optimize the performance and the contribution among participants; (2) evaluation systems that control multiple cameras according to the detection results of the key person in multiparty cooperation, or that conduct comparative quality evaluation between remote and face-to-face meeting in terms of the emergent division of labor; and (3) communication robot systems that participate in and activate multiparty conversation [6, etc.].

The authors thank Kazumi Asai, Takugo Fukaya, Hiroaki Noguchi, Naho Orita, Dr. Kohei Suzuki, and Tetsushi Yamamoto for their technical support. This work was partly supported by funds from a Grant-in-aid for Scientific Research (C) (Grant No. 20500247 and No. 23500338).

REFERENCES

1. L. Carter, W. Haytorn, B. Shriver, and J. Lanzetta. The behavior of leaders and other group members. *The Journal of Abnormal and Social Psychology*, 46:589–595, 1951.
2. D. R. Forsyth. *Group dynamics, fifth edition*. Wadsworth, Cengage Learning, 2009.
3. D. Jayagopi, S. Ba, J. Odobez, and D. Gatica-Perez. Predicting two facets of cosial verticality in meetings from five-minute time slices and nonverbal cues. In *Proceedings of ICMI2008*, pages 45–52, 2008.
4. H. Kato, T. Nishimori, and T. Mochizuki. A design of collaborative learning in terms of supporting emergent division of labor. In *Proceedings of CELDA2005*, pages 309–316, 2005.
5. S. C. Lozano and B. Tversky. Communicative gestures benefit communicators. In *Proceedings of CogSci2004*, 2004.
6. Y. Matsuyama, H. Taniyama, S. Fujie, and T. Kobayashi. Framework of communication activation robot participating in multiparty conversation. In *Proceedings of AAAI Fall symposium, dialog with robots*, pages 68–73, 2010.
7. K. Otsuka, J. Yamato, Y. Takemae, and H. Murase. Quantifying interpersonal influence in face-to-face conversations based on visual attention patterns. In *Proceedings of CHI2006*, pages 1175–1179, 2006.
8. N. Suzuki, T. Kamiya, I. Umata, S. Ito, and S. Iwasawa. Verbal and nonverbal behaviors in group work: a case study of leadership through the assembling process. In *Proceedings of ICCS2008*, pages 262–265, 2008.
9. N. Suzuki, T. Kamiya, I. Umata, S. Ito, and S. Iwasawa. Nonverbal behaviors in cooperative work: a case study of successful and unsuccessful team. In *Proceedings of ICCS2010*, pages 448–449, 2010.

Awareness as an Antidote to Distance: Making Distributed Groups Cooperative and Consistent

Taemie Kim
Accenture Technology Labs
50 W San Fernando St 1200
San Jose, CA 95113
taemie.j.kim@accenture.com

Pamela Hinds
Stanford University
475 Via Ortega, Huang 207
Stanford, CA 94305
phinds@stanford.edu

Alex (Sandy) Pentland
MIT Media Lab
20 Ames St. E15-383
Cambridge, MA 02142
pentland@media.mit.edu

ABSTRACT
Sociometric feedback visualizes social signals among group members to increase their awareness of their communication patterns. We deployed the Meeting Mediator, a real-time sociometric feedback system to groups participating in two rounds of a social dilemma task: in one round, all members were co-located and in the other round, the members were geographically distributed. Laboratory results show that the sociometric feedback successfully increases the speaking time and the frequency of turn transitions of groups that are initially distributed and later co-located, and also leads to a higher cooperation rate, increasing the overall earnings of these groups. In addition, the sociometric feedback helps groups have a more consistent pattern of behavior before and after a change in their geographic distribution.
Therefore, the sociometric feedback influences the communication patterns of distributed groups and makes them more cooperative. Furthermore, the sociometric feedback helps groups sustain those patterns of communication even after a change in geographic distribution.

Author Keywords
Sociometric feedback, distributed collaboration, cooperation, consistency in behavior

ACM Classification Keywords
H.5.3 Group and Organization Interfaces: Computer-supported cooperative work

General Terms
Experimentation; Design; Measurement

INTRODUCTION
Communication is an essential component of successful group collaboration. A group needs to properly communicate to define their goals, designate tasks, and accomplish their goals. Therefore, measuring communication patterns of groups can give us insight into the processes of group work [12]. Moreover, real-time feedback based on these measurements provides us the opportunity to influence communication styles, which may improve the performance of groups.

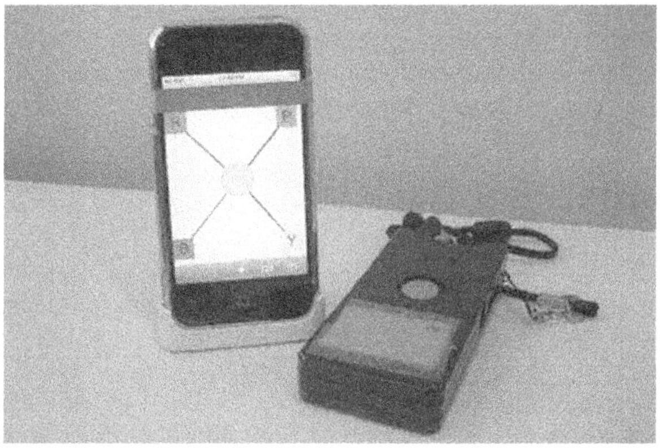

Figure 1. The Meeting Mediator system. The sociometric badge measures the group's communication patterns (right). The processed data is visualized on personal displays facing each subject (left).

The ability to provide feedback on a group's communication pattern can be especially valuable for geographically distributed groups. In distributed groups, the functionality of social signals is hindered, making it difficult for groups to coordinate their communication [17]. The lack of social signals makes it difficult for group members to understand the current state of the group communication, and how individuals should behave accordingly. Additionally, the lack of feedback expressed through social signals among the group members makes it difficult for group members to reflect on their behavior. Hence, real-time feedback on group's communication patterns may help distributed groups have an accurate understanding of their current style of communication so that they can adjust their behavior to improve performance.

Meeting Mediator introduced in [10] is an example of such a real-time sociometric feedback system that measures and visualizes the communication patterns of groups (Figure 1). The Meeting Mediator has a persuasive interface in order to encourage groups to follow a certain norm. The real-time visualization of communication patterns informs groups how much they deviate from the norm. Using this system, the authors of [10] showed that persuasive sociometric feedback can change group communication patterns. They also found that this influence was stronger for distributed groups compared to co-located groups, making the communication pattern of distributed groups more like that of co-located groups. However, the authors did not find any change in performance in a problem-solving task.

Researchers have taken various approaches to changing groups' communication patterns by providing real-time feedback. A fun example of Basu *et al.* is the use of an actuator to increase the intensity of lighting on under-participating individuals to emphasize their presence [1]. DiMicco *et al.* measured the speaking time of each participant and visualized it as a bar graph on a shared screen with the intent to balance the amount of participation [6]. They showed that feedback effectively makes the over-participators speak less, but does not make the under-participators speak more. They did not find any effects on objective performance measures of the task. Leshed *et al.*'s work is one of the few that examined distributed collaboration. They showed language-based feedback on a chatting system using a peripheral visualization [13]. This made participants express more agreement toward each other and focus more on their language use.

All of the aforementioned examples focused on influencing the communication patterns of groups, with no measurable impact on group performance. Our aim is to influence both the communication patterns and the resulting performance of task-oriented groups. We examine whether distributed groups *communicating* in a style more like co-located groups also *perform* as well as co-located groups. To test this hypothesis, we deployed the Meeting Mediator system on groups performing a social dilemma task.

RELATED RESEARCH

Social Dilemma Task and Distributed Collaboration

A social dilemma task is a mixed-motive task often used in social psychology to measure the level of cooperation. A social dilemma can be defined as a situation in which a group of people must decide between maximizing selfish interests or maximizing collective interests [11]. It is generally more profitable for the individual to maximize selfish interests, but if all do so, all are worse off than if everyone had maximized collective interests. The performance of the group is measured as the sum of earnings of all members.

In many social dilemma experiments, researchers find that cooperation is not a natural choice when selfish interest is in conflict with the group's interest. This is especially true for geographically distributed groups. Researchers such as Rocco [20] and Bicchieri and Lev-on [2] found that trust breaks down in computer-mediated communications, undermining cooperative behavior. They found that it is extremely difficult for distributed groups to establish and maintain trust and cooperation compared to groups communicating face-to-face. Bos *et al.* further explored how different modes of communication affect trust and cooperation [4]. They discovered that text-based communication was associated with the lowest level of cooperation, followed by audio and video. Face-to-face communication displayed the highest level of cooperation. The cooperation level of groups that communicated via audio and video developed more slowly and vulnerably increased as they repeated the studies over a long period of time. Hence, we see that in distributed communication mediated by computers, the limited modality of communication delays the development of trust and the trust that is developed is easily broken. Out of the variety of communication methods, we chose to use audio as our medium of communication for distributed groups. We chose audio as it is seems to be a good representative of the current state of synchronous distributed communication, as it is still the most common medium and has similar temporal patterns of trust development with video conferencing [4].

Overcoming Distribution Effects

There have been efforts to overcome the effects of distribution in social dilemma tasks. Providing opportunities for the members to socialize before the tasks has proven to be consistently helpful for cooperation, whether the socializing is face-to-face [20] or mediated by a computer [23]. Orbell and Kragt found that offering a chance to have task-related discussions greatly increased the level of cooperation compared to groups that did not get any chance to talk [18]. This was due to the fact that discussions often led to shared commitments about cooperation. Not all members kept their promises, but having a commitment made group members more likely to follow through with cooperative decisions. Nguyen and Canny found that correcting the spatial distortions of eye gaze can improve the level of cooperation even more, making video conferencing groups have essentially equal performance as groups that are co-located [15].

MEETING MEDIATOR SYSTEM

The Meeting Mediator has two components: sociometric badges that detect the communication patterns and mobile phones that display that information to the group members.

Measuring group communication patterns

The Sociometric badge (Figure 1, right) is an electronic sensing device that collects and analyzes social behavioral data [16]. When worn around the neck, it can (i) extract speech features in real-time to measure non-linguistic social signals, (ii) measure body movement using a 3-axis accelerometer, and (iii) send and receive information over radio to and from different users for time synchronization. Non-linguistic social signals exclude information contained in speech content, but include information on how speech is spoken, such as speaking speed, pitch, and turn-taking patterns.

Visualization on mobile phones

The phone visualization was designed for collaboration settings in which active and balanced participation and frequent turn transitions are beneficial to the group performance. Each of the four participants is represented by a colored square in the corner of the screen (Figure 2). In the study, the square colors were identical to the color of each participant's badge and seat. We display each member's speaking time through the thickness of the line connecting the central circle with each member's corner. Balance in participation is displayed

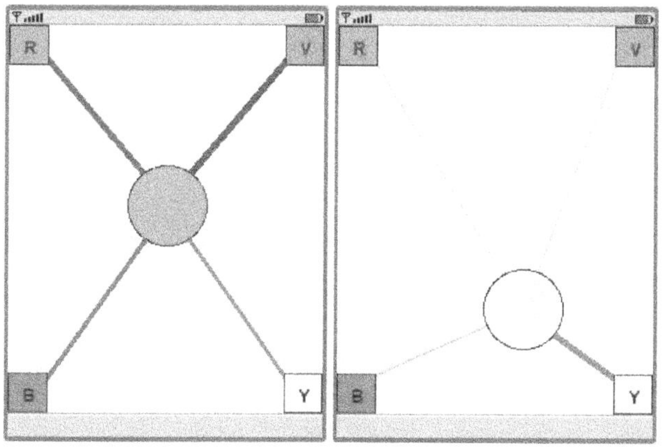

Figure 2. Feedback visualization for a four person group. An example of a visualization of a group when every one's participation is balanced with frequent turn transitions and (left) one person is dominating the conversation with infrequent turn transitions (right).

through the location of the circle: the more a participant talks, the stronger they pull the circle closer to their corner. Lastly, the color of the central circle gradually shifts between white and green to indicate the frequency of turn transitions. Green corresponds to frequent turn transitions, which can be a predictor of the group interactivity level. The data is accumulated throughout the meeting, showing the accumulated communication patterns from the start of the meeting to the current time. The devices are on the table facing each user, intended to be in the periphery of the user's attention. The display updates gradually so that it does not require constant attention from the user.

HYPOTHESES

Effect of Feedback on Communication Patterns

Researchers have found that providing feedback on participation balance can change the communication patterns of groups. Terken and Sturm found that under-participators speak more and over-participators speak less when given feedback on their speaking ratio [21]. Kim *et al.* found that the Meeting Mediator reduced the behavioral differences between co-located and distributed groups in problem solving meetings [10]. They saw that feedback on the whole group's communication pattern increased awareness about the group including the members that are not in the same room. Increased awareness seemed to have helped the distributed group to behave more like co-located groups.

The Meeting Mediator in Figure 2 provides a persuasive sociometric feedback: it encouraged participants to speak more, be balanced in participation, and to have frequent turn transitions. Information about how much the group deviates from the norm will encourage groups to behave closer to the norm. We believe that this effect of the sociometric feedback will be minimal for co-located groups but significant for distributed groups. Our reasoning follows. First, distributed groups have a stronger need to reconstruct the functionality of social signals. Co-located groups already have enough channels for members to provide feedback on each other's behavior. Examples of feedback include staring, looking bored, or even a kick underneath the table in extreme cases. For distributed groups, these channels are limited, making it harder for group members to understand the current balance or the interactivity level of the group or their role in it. Hence, sociometric feedback will have a greater impact on distributed groups. The second reason we think the sociometric feedback should have a stronger effect on distributed groups is that there is more room for improvement in distributed groups. Van der Kleji *et al.* found that distributed groups took fewer turns and had more silence [22], which may mean more opportunity for improvement. Hence, we might see a stronger effect of sociometric feedback on distributed groups compared to co-located groups. With the restoration of the functionality of the social signals, the behavior of distributed groups may become more like co-located groups.

> Sociometric feedback increases the speaking time, balance in participation, and the frequency of turn transitions, especially in distributed groups (H1)

Effect of Feedback on Group Performance

We believe that the increase in speaking time, participation balance, and the frequency of turn transition will result in a higher cooperation level. Orbell and Kragt found that having a chance to talk increased the cooperation level [18], and Nguyen and Canny improved the cooperation rate by correcting the visual cues in video communication. Prior work seems to hint that there is a causal relationship between communication patterns and performance. Hence, we question if more speaking, balanced participation, and higher number of turn transitions will build stronger trust among members during the conversation, leading to higher cooperation levels.

Again, we believe that the effect of feedback on performance will be stronger in distributed groups. This hypothesis will be supported if a relationship is present between communication patterns and performance. If so, the larger changes in communication patterns will result in larger change in performance. Moreover, there exists a ceiling effect in the cooperation level for co-located groups. Bos and his colleagues [4] discovered that there is very little headroom for improvement for groups collaborating face to face: the group's cooperation level is close to maximum even in their first encounter. However, for distributed groups with only audio communication, Bos found that the cooperation rate was lower than 70% of the maximum, allowing 30% headroom for improvement. Hence, we posit that sociometric feedback will increase the level of cooperation, and the size of the effect will be greater for distributed groups.

> Sociometric feedback increases the cooperation level, especially in distributed groups (H2)

METHODS

Experimental Setup

To test the effect of feedback, we ran a laboratory study where four-person groups participated in a social dilemma task. The study had a control setting in which no feedback

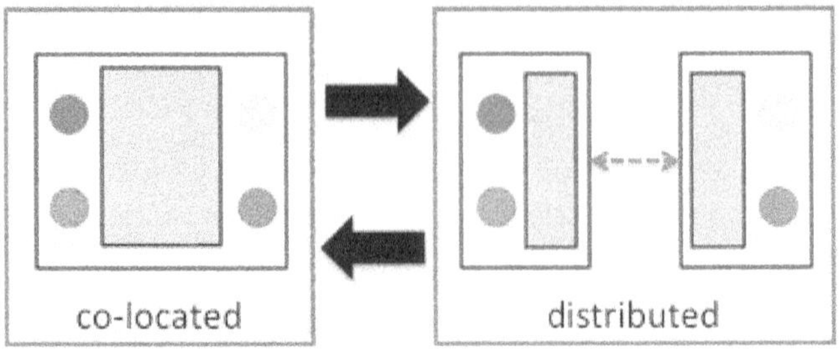

Figure 3. The change in geographic distribution between the two rounds. The sequence was counter balanced.

Performance and Survey analysis

	# of groups w/o Feedback	# of groups w/ Feedback
co-located first	14	9
distributed first	13	9

Sociometric Data Analysis

	# of groups w/o Feedback	# of groups w/ Feedback
co-located first	8	9
distributed first	8	9

Table 1. Number of four-person groups included in the analysis.

was provided and an experimental setting with the Meeting Mediator as the sociometric feedback. In the experimental condition, all four participants received the feedback on mobile phones. In the control setting, even though no feedback was given to the participants, their communication patterns were still measured by the sociometric badges. Also given the consent of all participants, the session was video recorded using two webcams in the corner of the rooms. Additionally, participants were verbally informed of the norm that they should follow: more speaking, balance in participation, and frequent turn transitions. Therefore, in both control and experimental conditions, participants were aware that they were being observed and measured, and that they should follow a specific norm to improve their performance. The only difference was that the experimental conditions had the Meeting Mediator, which indicated how much the group was deviating from that norm.

Each group participated in two rounds: once with all group members co-located in one room and once separated into pairs in two different rooms (Figure 3). Half of the groups were co-located in the first round and distributed in the second round (co-located first). For the other half of the groups, they had to participate in the first round separated into two rooms with no knowledge of who was in the other room and later moved into one room (distributed first). None of the groups were aware that their geographic distribution would change after the first round.

Participants

The data set includes 45 groups of four subjects each for a total of 180 participants (99 male, 81 female, mean age=29.4, SD=10.0). Subjects were recruited individually on multiple university campuses and through Internet message boards. Every effort was made to keep subjects from having prior knowledge of one another. Due to equipment failure, one of the badges did not collect audio data in the first few experiments. The sociometric data collected of these sessions were ignored. In addition, the performance data of these sessions in the feedback conditions were ignored, as the feedback presented using this badge would not have been accurate. However, the performance data of the no-feedback condition sessions were included in the analysis as the decisions of the subjects were not affected by the badge malfunction. The total number of groups included in the analysis is shown in Table 1.

Tasks and Procedures

All groups performed two rounds of the social dilemma task. To provide a social dilemma situation, we created a conflict between maximizing collective interests and selfish interests: all subjects were told that the goal of the task was to maximize group earning, but the payoff structure was dependent on personal performance. Each subject was given sixteen $1 bills, of which they could invest any partial amount to the group fund and keep the rest for themselves. The total money gathered in the group fund was increased 50% by the experimenters and divided equally among the four participants regardless of how much each subject invested. Hence, investing all $16 to the group fund would help increase collective interests, but keeping all $16 would maximize personal earnings given a set of decisions of the other participants. However, if all participants were to keep all their money, all participants would earn 50% less than what they would have earned if everyone invested all. The instruction sheet had a sample calculation table and the experimenter confirmed that all subjects comprehended the situation and the consequences of their decisions.

Once all participants understood the problem and the goal of the task, each group was given up to 10 minutes to discuss their group strategy. Badge data collected during these discussions were analyzed as we hypothesized that the communication patterns of these discussions would predict the individual private decisions made by the participants after the discussion had ended. After the discussion time, participants were asked to turn away from each other to put their contribution decisions into two envelopes (one labeled *group* and the other labeled *keep*) and then handed both envelopes to the experimenter so that individual decisions were not known to the other participants. Once all the envelopes were collected, the experimenter announced the total amount in the group fund and the amount to be distributed. The individual contribution amounts were never revealed.

In both co-located and distributed settings, the earnings were dependent on the decisions of all four participants, requiring all participants to collaborate to maximize their group or individual earnings. All subjects received the average of their earnings in the two rounds. After each round, the total amount in the group fund was announced to all participants. Therefore in the second round, the subjects knew the total group fund amount of the first round, though they did not know the amount invested by each individual.

Initially we considered using each round as an independent data point in analyzing the effect of feedback. However, we found a strong relationship between the first and second rounds: the communication patterns and the performance of the second round was strongly dependent on that of the first round (especially since the result of the first round was announced before starting the second round). Naturally, the second round's data was dependent on the geographical condition of the first round, therefore it could not be considered as independent data points. Therefore, the data of the two rounds were combined in the analysis of H1 and H2: the average value of the two rounds was used for the analysis of both the groups' communication patterns and their performance. We label the two different sequence conditions as "co-located first" and "distributed first", and the analysis includes the data from both rounds. Though we merge the two rounds for the analysis of H1 and H2, we report the relationship between the two rounds later in the paper.

Measures

Communication Pattern Measures

Using the sociometric badges, we observed multiple aspects of the groups' communication patterns. The main focus is on the three features that are directly addressed by the Meeting Mediator: speaking time, balance of speaking time, and the number of turns per second. Additionally, the sociometric badge provided information such as duration of discussion, body movement energy, speech energy, speaking speed, and average turn length. We calculate the group-level measures based on individual-based measures. We used group level measures in the analysis as members' actions within a group are highly dependent on each other. Details follow.

- We define an individual's speaking time as the fraction of time during which an individual speaks, regardless of interruptions or overlap speech from others. The group's *speaking time* is the fraction of time that one or more person is speaking.
- The *balance of speaking time* is the standard deviation of the speaking time between members. Lower values correspond to more balanced speaking time.
- We define a turn as any one continuous stream of speech from an individual, regardless of interruption or overlap from other participants. A turn ends either by an interruption caused by another participant that resulted in the speaker to stop speaking or a significant length of silence. We measure the number of turns each person had and sum that number to measure number of turns of a group. *Frequency of turn transitions* is the normalized value over the duration of the discussion.
- Each group was given up to 10 minutes of discussion in both rounds. However, many groups chose not to use the whole 10 minutes. We measure the *duration* of their discussion in each round.
- We define *movement energy* as the average amount of body movement, i.e. the amount of gesturing during conversation. We use the average of the individual values as the group measure.
- We measure the *speech energy* using the variation in volume. High speech energy tends to make people sound more expressive [19]. We use the average of the individual values as the group measure.
- *Speaking speed* is measured by approximating the number of voiced segments per speaking time [5]. Higher number of voiced segments indicates faster speech. We use the average of the individual values as the group measure.

Performance Measures

Level of *cooperation* is measured by the amount contributed to the group fund. Each individual had two chances to invest \$0 to \$16 to the group fund. The average of the two values is used as the individual measure of cooperation. The group measure is the sum of the four individual values, which ranges from \$0 to \$64.

Another measure of performance is the level of *defection*. Defection is the difference in the amount that a member promised from the amount that they actually invested. Before making individual decisions, groups were given the opportunity to discuss their strategy. At this time, most group members verbally expressed how much they would put in the group fund. For most groups, this amount was the same for all group members. 33 out of the 34 groups verbally expressed that all members would invest equal amounts of money into the group fund. 27 groups came to the consensus that all members would invest the full \$16 to the group fund. However, not all members kept their word and the amount of *defection* is the difference between the amount that the participants promised and the actual amount that they invested. The amount of defection has a strong negative correlation with the cooperation level. The relationship is not a perfect linear relationship due to the six groups that decided that all members should invest the same amount but decided on a partial amount. For example, if the group came to a consensus that all members would invest \$10 out of the \$16 into the group fund and kept their promise, the defection value would be zero. However, the cooperation rate would be \$40 out of the maximum of \$60. We used the sum of the individual defection values as the group measure, which ranges from \$0 to \$64. The defection amount is \$0 when all members kept their promises independent of how much the promise was, and the defection amount is \$64 when all group members promised to invest the full amount but everyone ended up investing \$0.

RESULTS

Effect of Feedback on Communication Patterns

We see clear differences in communication patterns between the controlled and experimental conditions. First, we examine the overall speaking time of groups. The feedback increased the speaking time of groups by 36% (mean=46% without feedback and 63% with feedback, $F(1,32)=8.06$ $p<.05$). Hence, we see that feedback successfully encouraged subjects to speak more. This was true in both groups that were co-located first (12% increase, $F(1,15)=1.67$, $p=.22$) and groups that were distributed first (21% increase, $F(1,15)= 10.31$,

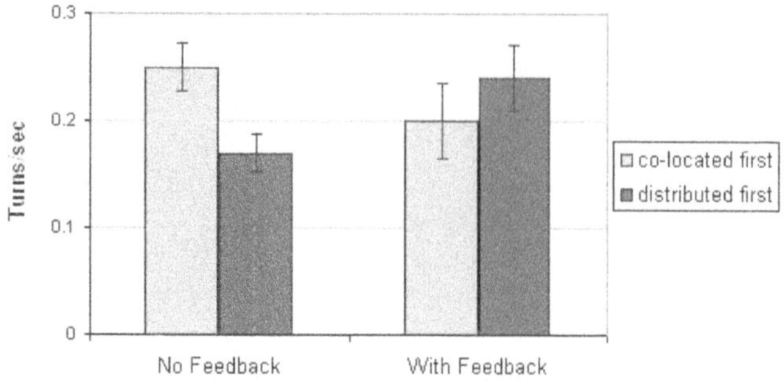

Figure 4. Frequency of turn transitions of groups in the four conditions (N=8,8,9,9). Feedback increased the frequency of turn transition for groups that were distributed first.

p<.05) but the difference was significant only for groups that were distributed first. The main effect of geographical distribution was not significant (F(1,30)=1.51, p=.23) nor was the interaction effect (F(1,30)=0.47, p=.49).

Secondly, we observed the balance of speaking time among the group members. Unfortunately, we did not find any significant effect of feedback on this variable. The standard deviation among the normalized speaking time among members was 0.16 for groups without feedback and 0.18 for groups with feedback (F(1,32)=0.84, p=.37). The main effect of geographical condition was not significant (F(1,30)=0.18, p=.67) nor was the interaction effect (F(1,30)=1.08, p=.31). Hence, we see no effect of feedback on speaker balance.

Lastly, we observe the frequency of turn transitions within the group. We did not find a significant relationship overall (mean=0.21 turns/sec without feedback and 0.21 turns/sec with feedback, F(1,30)=0.02 p=.87, excluding outliers). However, if we only look at groups that were distributed first, groups with feedback tended to have more frequent turn transitions (mean=0.17 turns/sec without feedback and 0.24 turns-/sec with feedback, F(1,14)=3.39 p=.087, Figure 4). There was a significant main effect for geographical distribution (F(1,30)=11.48, p<.05), and a significant interaction effect (F(1,30)=8.29, p<.05). Therefore, the results show that sociometric feedback did not have much of an effect on groups that were co-located first, but increased the frequency of turn transitions in groups that were distributed first. As can be seen in Figure 4, there was no significant difference between groups that were distributed-first and groups that were co-located first when feedback was provided.

Effect of Feedback on Performance

The main question of interest is if this change in behavior results in a change in the level of cooperation. We examined the total amount of money invested in the group fund as a measure of cooperation. The maximum amount of contribution of an individual is $32 which is when the participant fully invested their $16 into the group fund both rounds. In the control condition, the cooperation level was significantly lower for individuals in groups that were distributed first (Mean = $27.85, $23.29 for co-located-first and distributed-first respectively). But when feedback was provided we see that there was a significant increase in the cooperation level in groups that were distributed first (Mean = $26.64, $28.69 for co-located-first and distributed-first respectively, $X^2(3,176)=10.17$, p<.05, Figure 5). Hence, the sociometric feedback helped distributed-first groups to perform as well as co-located-first groups. The main effect is not significant for either feedback (F(1,176)=2.43, p=.12) and geographical condition (F(1,176)=0.86, p=.35), but the interaction effect is significant (F(1,176)=6.02, p<.05). This result also holds in the *group level*, but the difference is not significant due to the lack of power ($X^2(3,41)=3.67$, p=.30).

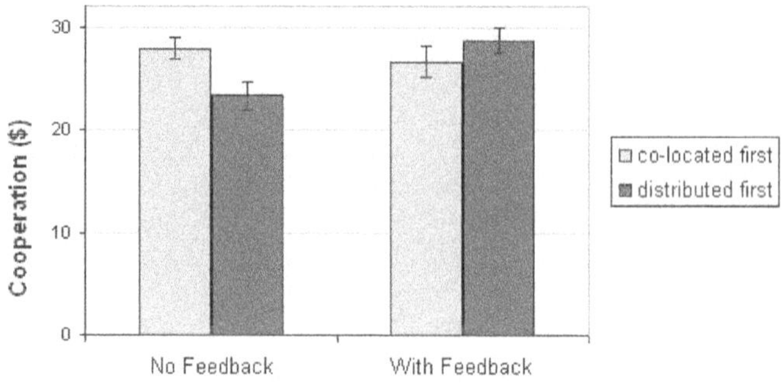

Figure 5. Cooperation level of individuals in groups in the four conditions (maximum value is $32 per individual, N=52,56,36,36). Feedback significantly increased the cooperation level for individuals in groups that were distributed first.

Interpretation of the Effect of Feedback

The effectiveness of the sociometric feedback can be explained in two ways. First, the visualization guided the subjects on which norm they should follow. The Meeting Mediator did more than merely providing an accurate reflection on their behavior. The Meeting Mediator interface deployed persuasive design methodologies making subjects aware of which direction a change should occur. Secondly, having real-time measurements and a visualization of those measurements may have increased the subjects' awareness of their communication patterns. As the subjects knew that they were being measured, they might have been more conscious of how they spoke and interacted with others. This consciousness may have made the groups more likely to follow the communication norm they wish to follow. Therefore, providing guidelines on which norm to follow and making the subjects more conscious about their communication patterns seem to have made the subjects communicate in a way more similar to the desired norm.

In summary, the change in communication patterns and performance of distributed-first groups was in a direction making them behave more like co-located-first groups.

FEEDBACK AND CONSISTENCY OF BEHAVIOR

In addition to the effect of feedback that we hypothesized, we found an additional effect of feedback that was not expected. As mentioned earlier, we initially intended the two rounds of the social dilemma study to be two independent data points, but soon found that the second round was strongly

	w/o feedback	
	co-located first	distributed first
Speaking Time	0.27	0.02
Balance Speaking Time	0.03	0.01
# of Turns/sec	0.02	0.01
Duration	0.09	0.08
Body Movement Energy	0.15	0.19
Speech Energy	0.28	0.00
Speaking Speed	0.26	0.05

Table 2. The consistency of pre-change and post-change behavior (R^2) without Feedback. Values listed are the amount of variance in the second round's data predicted by the first round's data, N=(8, 8). Without feedback, the pre-change behavior does not predict the post-change behavior.

	w/ feedback	
	co-located first	distributed first
Speaking Time	0.66	0.49
Balance Speaking Time	0.12	0.05
# of Turns/sec	0.58	0.02
Duration	0.88	0.28
Body Movement Energy	0.46	0.62
Speech Energy	0.59	0.48
Speaking Speed	0.62	0.06

Table 3. The consistency of pre-change and post-change behavior (R^2) with Feedback. Colored cells are R^2 values with $p<.05$, N=(9, 9). With feedback, the pre-change behavior predicts the post-change behavior.

dependent on the first round. This finding inspired us to closely examine the relationship between the two rounds.

To test the relationship between the pre-change and the post-change behaviors of each group, we measured the correlation coefficient between the two round's sociometric data. The correlation coefficient (R) tells us how much the post-change behavior is dependent on the pre-change behavior. We are interested in understanding how much of the post-change behavior can be explained by the pre-change behavior (R^2). Hence, this R^2 value informs us how consistently each group behaves in the two rounds. We did not compare the absolute values of group means as there could be differences caused by the repeated nature of the study (e.g. all groups might talk less in the second round as they have already discussed their strategy before). Instead, we examined the relationship of a group's first round behavior compared to other groups, and see how much of that relationship holds in the second round (e.g. if a group was more talkative than other groups in the first round, would the same group also be more talkative than other groups in the changed condition?).

If we suppose that groups performed the two rounds in the same geographical condition, we would have expected a strong consistency of between-round behavior. This phenomenon can be explained by the concept of social entrainment, the persistence of social "rhythms" over time [9]. When groups become entrained to a certain style of behavior, they show a consistent style of behavior in their subsequent encounters. Sometimes this entrainment effect is strong enough that it persists even though the external conditions have changed significantly. Based on Kelly *et al.*'s work, groups only need a few minutes to be entrained to a style of behavior which can be observed in their following sessions. Some authors even argue that lasting patterns can appear as early as the first few seconds of a group's life [7].

Groups Without Feedback

We compared the sociometric measurements of the first round (pre-change behavior) to that of the second round (post-change behavior). In the control condition, we found no significant correlation in any of the sociometric measures (none of the R^2-values are significant in Table 2). This result holds for both co-located-first groups (left column) and distributed-first groups (right column). Hence, there is no evidence of between-round consistency in groups that did not receive feedback. The change in geographic distribution seems to have disrupted the entrained behavior, hindering groups from sharing consistent behavior between the first and second round.

We use speaking speed as an example to interpret this result. In the initial round, each group developed their own style of behavior: some groups spoke faster, while other groups spoke slower. Results show that the groups who spoke faster than other groups in the first round did not necessarily speak faster in the second round. In other words, observing the pre-change behavior did not predict the same group's post-change behavior. Hence, the behaviors developed in co-located settings did not carry over to when the groups were later distributed. And vice versa for the distributed-first groups. It seems that the change in their geographical condition is so disruptive that the groups develop a whole new style of behaviors when the geographic distribution changes and they encounter a new group context.

Groups With Feedback

We observe, however, a very different pattern when feedback is provided. With feedback, a strong consistency is found in the groups' behavior between the first and second round. In Table 3, we see statistically significant correlations between round 1 and round 2 in many of the sociometric features. The pre-change behavior predicts 46% to 88% of the post-change variance (R^2).

The consistency in behavior is observed in both co-located-first groups (left column) and distributed-first groups (right column). Comparing the two conditions, we see that the consistency is weaker for distributed-first groups when compared to co-located-first groups: almost all measures in the co-located-first condition show a significant correlation between round 1 and round 2 (Table 3, left column) whereas less than half of the features show a significant correlation in the distributed first condition (Table 3, right column). McGrath speculated that one would find such a result saying that a group's entrainment may be hindered in distributed settings due to the response lags and the loss of nonverbal cues [14]. Hence, we can posit that the level of entrainment in the initial round was weaker for groups that were distributed than for groups that were co-located, resulting in the between-round consistency being weaker. This result is in line with Bos *et al.*'s work, in which they found that distributed-first groups had faster adjustment to their new setting, whereas the co-located-first groups continued to keep signs of their old behavior [3].

Interpretation of Consistency of Behavior

We use an analogy to help talk through possible interpretations of this finding. First we present the analogy and later we will use it as a means of discussing alternative interpretations. Let's say we conduct a between-subject study on the amount of salt usage in cooking. In the control condition, we ask subjects to cook a dish in which salt is a critical ingredient. Subjects come back the next day and cook the same dish. Often the amount of salt used on the second day is not exactly the same as the amount used previous day. In the experimental condition, subjects perform the same task, but we intervene with the salt usage on both days: we inform the subjects on the negative impact of sodium. As a result of this intervention, we find that subjects in the experimental condition tend to use less amount of salt compared to the control group, meaning that the overall average shifted to a lower amount. However, we notice an unexpected phenomenon: the subjects also show stronger between-trial consistency in the amount of salt that they use. The amount of variance between the two days is much smaller in the experimental condition. The intervention did not reduce the variance among subjects, but it reduced the within-trial variance per subject.

Coming back to the sociometric data, we found in testing H1 and H2 that sociometric feedback changes the communication patterns of groups and the change is in a direction benefiting the performance. Here, we find that feedback not only shifts the behavior of all groups, it also increases the consistency of behavior between the two rounds of each group. We would like to note that this effect is not the result of feedback eliminating the between-group differences. In fact, often the variation among groups with feedback is larger than that of groups without feedback (in the speech energy case, there is a 44% increase). Our results are showing that the between-round relationship of each group is quite strong, validating that each group's unique style of behavior persists even when there is a change of geographical distribution. As can be seen from Table 3, the feedback increased the consistency in multiple dimensions of communication, including speaking time, body movement, and speech energy.

We explain two possible explanations for these results. First, the feedback may reduce the gap between co-located and distributed conditions by reconstructing the functionality of social signals, thus making distributed collaboration feel not so different from when the group was co-located. The decreased gap between co-located and distributed settings may have eliminated the need to adjust to the new post-change condition, making the transition between the two settings more subtle, almost as if they were constantly in a co-located condition. The subtleness of the transition may have allowed groups in the second round to transfer their entrained behaviors from the earlier round. Connecting it to the salt analogy, a more similar environment of cooking (i.e. a similar sized saltshaker) may have helped subjects use similar amounts of salt in the two trials. Secondly, the feedback may have increased the members' awareness on their communication patterns. A real-time visualization of the communication patterns make members more aware of how they are communicating, perhaps resulting in more conscious decisions about how they behave. Going back to the salt example, one may have originally put little thought into the amount of salt used, but now that the experimenter has brought attention to salt, the subjects may choose to make a more conscious effort in deciding how much salt is used, resulting in a more consistent amount of salt used on both days.

	w/o Feedback	
	co-located first	distributed first
Cooperation	\$58.3→\$53.1	\$50.2→\$43.0
Defection	\$2.0→\$10.9	\$9.8→\$21.1
	w/ Feedback	
	co-located first	distributed first
Cooperation	\$52.1→\$54.4	\$59.7→\$55.2
Defection	\$1.2→\$9.6	\$4.3→\$8.9

Table 4. The average pre-change and post-change performance of groups. Groups without feedback have significantly lower cooperation rate in the second round than the first round. Feedback reversed this tendency so that the drop of performance is not significant even when the groups face change in geographic distribution.

Consistency of Behavior and Performance

For performance, we find strong between-round consistencies for all conditions regardless of the sociometric feedback. Without feedback, the R^2 of cooperation was 0.81 for co-located-first groups, 0.58 for distributed-first groups. With feedback, R^2 was 0.66 for co-located-first groups and 0.62 for distributed-first groups ($p<.05$ for all conditions). Hence, groups that performed high in the first round tended to perform high in the second round as well. This is not surprising as revealing the first round's results would either significantly strengthen or weaken trust among the members.

We start to see an effect of feedback when looking at the change of absolute values in cooperation between the two rounds. We find that the level of cooperation drops in the second round compared to the first round for most groups. We think that this finding was mainly driven by two factors: (i) the fact that the subjects knew that the second round was the final round and (ii) the change in geographic distribution. Knowing that the second round was the final round, some of the subjects defected from their promises more than the first round, as there were no consequences. In some cases, we saw subjects intentionally cooperated in the first round in order to create trust only to earn more money on the second round through defection. In addition, the change in geographical conditions may have hurt the trust built up in the previous condition, as impressions of one another may have changed following the change of the communication medium. Therefore, we saw a significant drop in the second round's cooperation level in groups without feedback. When feedback is given, this drop in cooperation rate tended to be smaller than groups without feedback (the average drop was

\$6.2 for group without feedback and \$2.2 for groups with feedback, $F(1,43)=2.3$, $p=.13$, Table 4, first rows). It is interesting to mention that, when provided feedback, co-located-first groups' cooperation actually increases (from \$52.1 to \$54.4), reversing the last-round-defection tendency.

The interpretation of performance is clearer as we examine the amount of defection (Table 4, second rows). For groups without feedback there is a significant increase in defection for both co-located first and distributed-first groups: increment of \$8.1 for co-located-first groups ($t(12)=-2.4$, $p<.05$) and an increment of \$11.3 for distributed-first groups ($t(13)=-2.8$, $p<.05$). However, for groups with feedback, the increment still exists but is no longer significant: increment of \$8.4 for co-located-first groups ($t(8)=-1.5$, $p=.17$) and an increment of \$4.6 for distributed-first groups ($t(8)=-1.9$, $p=.09$). Therefore, groups tended to defect less when provided feedback.

DISCUSSION

Effect of Feedback on Communication and Performance

We find that sociometric feedback changed the communication patterns in groups that were distributed first, which resulted in groups achieving higher performance. This effect seems to hint that there is a strong relationship between the pattern of communication and the performance of the group. To closely examine this relationship, we examined all the features of communication detected by the Sociometric badges. The most apparent and consistent relationship that we find is that the frequency of turn transitions has a positive correlation with cooperation ($R=0.37$, $p<.05$, $N=34$). This result indicates that groups in which members took more speaking turns tended to have higher cooperation. Hence, when the sociometric feedback increased the frequency of turn transitions, it may have resulted in increasing the cooperation level of the group as well.

The relationship between frequency of turn transitions and cooperation is especially interesting when we analyze the content of speech during the conversation. Surprisingly, the verbal content of the conversation did not predict the level of cooperation that we observed. As mentioned earlier, we saw that 33 out of the 34 groups came to the consensus that they would invest equal amounts into the group fund. However, only 20 out of the 33 groups kept their promises. One or more members in the other 13 groups decided to break their promises. Hence, listening to what the group members were saying did not predict the outcome, but rather, we can predict how much the group is going to put in the group fund just by counting the number of turn transitions.

Feedback and Consistency of Behavior

When groups are faced with a change in geographic distribution, they are forced to make significant adjustments in the way they communicate. As groups make this adjustment, they drop their previously developed behavior and develop new patterns of behavior. When real-time sociometric feedback is provided to groups, however, we see consistency in behavior before and after the change, which suggests less adaptation to the new context. Although future research is needed, we suspect that the feedback made the group members more aware of and committed to their communication behaviors established during round one.

Limitations

In previous studies, researchers have often conducted multiple, ten to thirty, trials to observe the temporal change in group cooperation levels [20]. However, due to the large number of trials in these studies and limited funding, each trial had a very small payoff (often less than a dollar), which can easily reduce the motivation to make realistic decisions. As a tradeoff, we limited ourselves to two trials, so that a single decision could make up to a \$22 difference in their final payment. Even with this relatively high stake in decision-making, many of the participants mentioned that the amount was rather small to persuade them to deceive their group members, and stated that their decision might have been different if the amount was larger. Another reason we decided to limit the number of trials in our studies was the fact that initial phases of cooperation are when the biggest need for improvement in group processes exists. Bos *et al.* [4] found for advanced communication technologies, such as audio and video, the level of trust is low in the first few rounds but gradually reaches that of face-to-face as rounds are repeated. Having said that, our study still suffers from having only two trials because it limited our ability to examine the effect of feedback over a longer period of time.

Another limitation to our approach is the fact that our rounds were consecutive. Unlike our study, many of the prior studies of social entrainment have days or weeks in between studies which may have weakened the entrainment effect. Moreover, our experiment only included two rounds, thus not allowing us to learn the long-term effects of entrainment. Our findings are also limited to a single task type. Hernes found that social entrainment is not observed when tasks change [8], a finding that we are curious to explore from the viewpoint of communication patterns and feedback. We leave many of our questions to future work.

CONCLUSION

Sociometric feedback helps groups to be aware of their communication patterns and which communication norms they might follow. We deployed real-time sociometric feedback to groups participating in two rounds of a social dilemma task in different geographical conditions: once with all members co-located and once with the members distributed. Results show that the sociometric feedback successfully increased the speaking time, the frequency of turn transitions, and the level of cooperation in groups that were distributed first. In addition, while inspecting the between-round change of behavior, we found that feedback also increased the between-round consistency of each group even though there were significant changes in their geographical conditions.

In summary, we found that sociometric feedback can not only help distributed groups to have a communication pattern which leads to higher performance, but it can also help groups to sustain that pattern of behavior even when they oscillate between being co-located and distributed, as many distributed groups do. The sociometric feedback appears to successfully reconstruct some of the functionality of the lost social signals in distributed collaboration, improving the performance of distributed groups.

ACKNOWLEDGEMENTS
We would like to thank Camille Doykan for helping us conduct the lab studies. Additionally, Sarah No, Daniel Olguin Olguin, and Ben Waber helped greatly in polishing ideas and writing this paper.

REFERENCES
1. S. Basu, T. Chouhdury, B. Clarkson, and A. Pentland. Towards measuring human interactions in conversational settings. *Proceedings of the IEEE International Workshop on Cues in Communication*, 2001.
2. C. Bicchieri and A. Lev-On. Computer-mediated communication and cooperation in social dilemmas: an experimental analysis. *Politics, Philosophy and Economics*, 6:139–168, 2007.
3. N. Bos, J. Olson, A. Cheshin, Y.-S. Kim, and N. Nan. Traveling blues: The effect of relocation on partially distributed teams. *Proceedings of the ACM Conference on Human Factors in Computing Systems*, pages 1917–1920, 2005.
4. N. Bos, J. Olson, D. Gergle, G. Olson, and Z. Wright. Effects of four computer-mediated communications channels on trust development. *Proceedings of the ACM Conference on Human Factors in Computing Systems*, pages 135–140, 2002.
5. T. Choudhury and S. Basu. Modeling conversational dynamics as a mixed memory Markov Process. *In Proceedings of IEEE Conference on Neural Information Processing Systems*, 2004.
6. J. M. DiMicco, A. Pandolfo, and W. Bender. Influencing group participation with a shared display. *In Proceedings of the ACM Conference on Computer Supported Cooperative Work*, Nov. 2004.
7. C. J. G. Gersick. Time and transition in work teams: Toward a new model of group development. *Academy of Management*, 31:9–41, 1988.
8. T. Hernes. Effects of media of communication and collaboration in structural change: insights from a computer-mediated research group . *Human Resource Development International*, 3:69–87, 2000.
9. J. R. Kelly and J. E. McGrath. Effects of time limits and task types on task performance and interaction of four-person groups. *Journal of Personality and Social Psychology*, pages 395–407, 1985.
10. T. Kim, A. Chang, L. Holland, and A. Pentland. Meeting mediator: Enhancing group collaboration using sociometric feedback. *Proceedings of the ACM Conference on Computer Supported Cooperative Work*, 2008.
11. S. Komorita. Interpersonal relationsions: Mixed-motive interaction. *Annual Review of Psychology*, 46:183–207, 1995.
12. R. Kraut, R. Fish, R. Root, and B. Chalfonte. Informal communication in organizations: Form, function, and technology. In S. Oskamp and S. Spacapan, editors, *Human reactions to technology: Claremont symposium on applied social psychology*, pages 145–199. Sage Publications, 1990.
13. G. Leshed, D. Perez, J. H. Hancock, D. Cosley, J. Birnholtz, S. Lee, P. McLeod, and G. Gay. Visualizing real-time language-based feedback on teamwork behavior in computer-mediated groups. *Proceedings of the ACM Conference on Human Factors in Computing Systems*, 2009.
14. J. E. McGrath. Time matters in groups. In J. Galegher, R. E. Kraut, and C. Egido, editors, *Intellectual teamwork: Social and technical foundations of cooperative work*, pages 23–61. Psychology Press, 1990.
15. D. Nguyen and J. Canny. Multiview: Improving trust in group video conferencing through spatial faithfulness. *Proceedings of the ACM Conference on Human Factors in Computing Systems*, pages 1465–1474, 2007.
16. D. Olguin Olguin, B. Waber, T. Kim, A. Mohan, K. Ara, and A. Pentland. Sensible organizations: Technology and methodology for automatically measuring organizational behavior. *IEEE Transactions on Systems, Man, and Cybernetics. Part B: Cybernetics*, Feb. 2009.
17. G. M. Olson and J. S. Olson. Distance matters. *Human-Computer Interaction*, pages 139–178, 2000.
18. J. Orbell and A. Kragt. Explaining discussion-induced cooperation. *Journal of Personality and Social Psychology*, 54:811–819, 1988.
19. A. Pentland. *Honest Signals*. MIT Press, 2008.
20. E. Rocco. Trust breaks down in electronic contexts but can be repaired by some initial face-to-face contact. *Proceedings of the ACM Conference on Human Factors in Computing Systems*, pages 496–502, 1998.
21. J. Terken and J. Sturm. Multimodal support for social dynamics in co-located meetings. *Personal and Ubiquitous Computing archive*, 14, 2010.
22. R. van der Kleij, J. M. Schraagen, P. Werkhoven, and C. K. W. D. Dreu. How conversations change over time in face-to-face and video-mediated communication. *Small Group Research*, 40:355–381, 2009.
23. J. Zheng, N. Bos, J. Olson, and G. Olson. Trust without touch: jump-start trust with social chat. *Proceedings of the ACM Conference on Human Factors in Computing Systems*, pages 293–294, 2001.

Distributed Scientific Group Collaboration across Biocontainment Barriers

Jane Li [1,2]
[1] CSIRO ICT Centre, Australia
[2] University of Technology, Sydney, Australia
PO Box 76, Epping, NSW 1710, Australia
Jane.Li@csiro.au

Toni Robertson
University of Technology, Sydney, Australia
PO Box 123, Broadway, NSW 2007, Australia
Toni.Robertson@uts.edu.au

Christian Müller-Tomfelde
CSIRO ICT Centre, Australia
PO Box 76, Epping, NSW 1710, Australia
Christian.Mueller-Tomfelde@csiro.au

ABSTRACT
This paper reports the findings from a field study of distributed scientific collaboration within a national animal health laboratory. Collaboration in this setting is challenged by the need for biosecurity – there are physical containment barriers between scientists and work groups and movement of people and other physical objects across the barriers requires extensive security procedures. The aim of the field study was to understand how the scientists communicate across the barriers, particularly how they share information and collaborate on its analysis. The findings reveal that the collaboration issues relate not just to the challenges caused by the containment barriers but also to the need for collaboration support between the scientists and their work groups irrespective of the barriers. The paper explains how these findings informed the design of the collaboration platform being installed and how more generic requirements of supporting collaboration over distance were configured and extended to meet the specific requirements of a very particular local setting.

Author Keywords
Distributed teams; scientific collaboration; human-work interaction design

ACM Classification Keywords
H.5 Information interfaces and presentation (e.g., HCI): Miscellaneous. H.5.3 Group and Organization Interfaces: Synchronous interaction, Computer-supported cooperative work

General Terms
Design; Human Factor

INTRODUCTION
Supporting robust and flexible communication and the sharing of different kinds of information between people working in different places are fundamental to CSCW research. The complexity of scientific collaboration, the coordination work it relies on and the increasing need for scientists to collaborate with other groups and over distance have made this a particularly rich domain for investigation. Sharing a wide variety of data and collaborating on its review and analysis are central to scientific research. Computer-supported systems have been developed to enable scientists to work with each other, with a range of research facilities and with shared data repositories [e.g. 6, 8, 9, 13, 14]. These systems and their applications have been explored in various domains including the physical sciences, biological and health sciences, earth and environmental sciences and social science [e.g. 11, 15, 17, 20].

Our particular concern in this paper is scientific collaboration in the Australian Animal Health Laboratory (AAHL) that is part of the Commonwealth Scientific and Industrial Research Organisation (CSIRO), Australia's national science agency. AAHL is one of the most sophisticated laboratories in the world for the safe handling and containment of infectious micro-organisms. It plays a vital role in maintaining Australia's capability to quickly diagnose exotic, new and emerging animal diseases and to prevent the economic impact of livestock disease outbreaks. AAHL provides a wide range of laboratory services, including diagnostic services (agent identification and characterisation), histology, protein and nucleic acid sequencing, cell culture and microscopy. There are also facilities for the housing and handling of laboratory and large animals. It has ongoing research programs in developing the most sensitive, accurate and timely diagnostic tests to support eradication campaigns in the event of disease outbreaks. AAHL also undertakes research to develop new diagnostics tests, vaccines and treatments for animal diseases of national importance.

Collaboration within AAHL is similar to other scientific collaboration in that it is driven by the need to share data as well as knowledge about the data across different work groups [6, 14]. This means that there are basic requirements for robust and flexible communication support, the ability

CSCW'12, February 11–15, 2012, Seattle, Washington, USA.

to access and share different kinds of files from a range of sources, to look at images and other data in these files together and to annotate or otherwise capture the shared understandings that characterise successful interaction [28].

However, AAHL is a biosecurity laboratory with very sophisticated biocontainment facilities. These containment facilities are fully enclosed physical spaces designed to ensure the safe housing and handling of animals and any micro-organisms the animals may be infected with. Scientific staff move in and out of the containment areas through a range of airlock doors that require specific containment practices of them. For example, they are required to wear personal protective clothing before moving into containment areas; they must change out of their protective clothing and take compulsory showers on exit; any equipment leaving the containment areas needs to be decontaminated. These practices pose additional and particular challenges to effective communication and data sharing between staff working inside the containment area and staff working outside, particularly in the context of an emergency animal disease outbreak. The scientists are working within the same building. But the containment barriers act to "distance" individual scientists and work groups from those on the other side of the barrier by imposing very specific constraints on physical movement and the sharing of information within the building.

The AAHL management recognised that an effective collaboration platform could support communication and the efficient sharing of information within and between different work groups. This has led to the "Biosecurity Collaboration Platform" project which involves the design team from CSIRO ICT Centre and design representatives from AAHL. There are three stages in the project: a field study to understand the collaboration practices of the scientists at AAHL, an iterative design process to fit the platform to the specific requirements of this setting and a longitudinal evaluation of the platform in use. At the time of writing the major component of the platform, a shared workspace, has been installed on each side of the main containment barrier. A longitudinal evaluation of its use is in progress. In this paper we present the findings of the field study, describe how these findings informed the overall design approach and how this approach was organised and used in the first phase of the collaboration platform implemented in the laboratory.

Distributed scientific collaboration has been widely explored in the CSCW literature, particularly in the context of laboratories or institutes which are nationally or internationally distributed [e.g. 8, 11, 15, 17, 20]. Finholt and Olsen reviewed scientific collaboration systems in various domains and identified three core capabilities for technologies to support scientific collaboration: linking people with people, linking people with information and linking people with facilities [8]. These capabilities require technologies to support, enable or mediate not only audio-video communication, but also the collaborative analysis of information from various resources, including instruments, and from specific work environments [8, 20]. These latter requirements echo well-established findings from early media space research. Heath, Luff and Sellen, for example, argued that participants in collaborative work needed the flexibility to align their attention towards the focal point of their activity – whatever and wherever that is [12]. They emphasized the importance of providing different forms of access to other participants and their local environments and flexibility of interaction with the various artefacts that drive or are otherwise involved in the collaboration.

Over recent years shared digital workspaces and multi-display technologies have been developed to provide rich support for both the sharing of data and its analysis in distributed collaborations [e.g. 4, 5, 19, 29]. These technologies enable the concurrent display of a number of different information streams including live video streams of participants and a range of data including video data, still images and other documents. To date the uses of these technologies in scientific collaboration have been mostly explored at a research prototype level and for generic scientific collaborations [e.g. 5, 21, 29], such as our prior research in designing the prototype of Blended Interaction Space in which interactive groupware is incorporated into video-mediated collaboration space [e.g. 5, 19, 21]. The current project extends this prior work and other related research to the design and development of these technologies in a challenging scientific work environment.

A more recent trend in CSCW research is attention to the development of CSCW technologies that can be used across highly variable local settings without compromising the integrity of local practices. This has been explored from various perspectives, including investigations of the use of specialised coordination artefacts designed to enable the coordination of cooperative activities, such as collaboration in different work domains [e.g. 25, 26]; the use of shared or common information spaces across contexts and communities of practice through an ongoing process of mutual interpretation of single items of information within those spaces [e.g. 3, 22, 24]; and the effect of technology standardisation across different local settings [e.g. 7, 10]. For example, Schmidt et al. identified two categorically different relationships between studies of work practice and the technology design these might inform [25]. They differentiated between studying "*specific* settings for the purpose of 'developing' *specific* technologies for that setting" (p. 9, original emphasis) and studies for the purpose of "developing more or less generic or standardised building blocks that can be combined and recombined endlessly" [25]. A closely related approach to the challenges of variability in local practices is to extend traditional design arguments for flexibility and tailorability of local systems to a broader notion of configurability that includes developing our understandings of the range of things that might need to be configured when technologies are appropriated into specific settings [e.g. 1, 2]. The current project contributes to this important development within CSCW through its recognition of both, the generic and site specific requirements of the research setting that have guided the shaping of the design process and the development stages of the collaboration platform at AAHL.

The paper is organised as follows. A brief description of the research methods leads to two sections that present the major issues that emerged from the field study data. The first focuses on the work of AAHL and the second on collaboration between the scientists. From there, the paper reports how these findings shaped the design of the collaboration platform including how the more generic requirements of information sharing and collaboration 'over distance' shaped the first stage of the platform design while the local requirements caused by the very specific kind of work at AAHL and the physical containment barriers shaped the second and third stages. The paper ends with a discussion of how more generic requirements of supporting collaboration over distance were configured and extended to meet the specific requirements of a very particular local setting.

RESEARCH METHOD

As the first stage of our research, we conducted a field study at AAHL to understand the collaboration practices in this laboratory. We intended to use this understanding as a basis for informing and guiding the design of the collaboration platform. The field study included a focus group meeting with twenty scientists and twelve semi-structured interviews during four site visits. It was undertaken by two researchers from the design team over a period of two months. Participants were asked about their work and how it was accomplished within the AAHL. They were also asked about their expectations of collaboration technologies and their collaboration practices, particularly how information artefacts were arranged and shared in and between groups in different work situations. The focus group and interviews were audio recorded and transcribed. Visits to the containment area were important parts of the site visits. Field notes were taken by the researchers during the visits. The physical setup of the workspaces was documented through photographs and notes.

Because of the biosecurity regulations we were not able to go into the most secure containment area at all. This part of the containment facility is being replaced and further observation of this environment and the work done in it will be part of future analysis and design activities around the work practice of AAHL. Even so there were particular constraints on getting data collection materials, such as the camera, audio recorder and notes, out from the parts of the containment area we could enter. The notes we took inside were scanned and sent to us by email. A digital camera that AAHL scientists kept inside the containment area for general purposes was used and photos were sent to us by email. Our audio recorder had to be decontaminated and posted to us later. This gave us important insights into the information sharing issues faced by the scientists and some of the current strategies and resources they used to work around them.

Transcriptions and field notes were analysed using thematic coding in NVivo software. Four major, closely related issues were identified in the data. Two were concerned with defining aspects of this particular local setting: the physical work setting, including the containment barriers, and the roles, responsibilities and practices of the different workgroups within AAHL. The other two were concerned with aspects of collaboration within AAHL: collaboration issues between and within different workgroups and issues of information sharing between individuals and groups.

Further analysis identified three broad collaboration requirements that needed to be supported by the collaboration platform. These were reviewed with the AAHL design representatives, including two senior specialist scientists, a project officer and an IT manager. They were then mapped to three design distinct stages of technology development. The first addresses the more generic requirements that would be common to many settings where distributed collaboration is required. The other two address specific requirements of the particular setting that relate to the biosecurity work of AAHL.

THE WORK OF AAHL

The work of AAHL is vital to protect Australian from the threat of exotic and emerging animal diseases. Various groups of scientists in the laboratory work together to deliver diagnostic and research services in animal health. AAHL has large, microbiologically secure, physical containment facilities. The practices and equipment in the physical containment level 3 facilities, known as PC3, are designed for work with hazardous micro-organisms where there is a risk of serious infection to humans and animals. The physical containment level 4 facilities, known as PC4, are the highest level of physical containment available and is only accessible via PC3. PC4 practices and equipment are designed for work with even more dangerous micro-organisms which could pose a high risk of life-threatening disease. PC4 is the area we were not able to physically enter during the field study.

The physical setting

Figure 1 shows the different physical work areas established by the physical containment barriers. These are located on the same floor of the main building. The general office area is outside the containment areas and includes offices, meeting rooms, lecture theatres, canteen, and reception and so on. Each staff member has a workspace and a dedicated personal computer in this general office area, including those who spend most of their time working in the containment areas. The containment areas include both the PC3 and PC4 facilities. These facilities are fully enclosed spaces, separated from the general office area by a corridor with a range of airlock doors. There is a change in/shower out facility between PC3 and the general office area. Before entering PC3, staff need to change their own clothing and wear clean, standard laboratory clothing which includes underwear, overalls, polo shirts and sneakers. A full three-minute shower must be taken before changing back to their own clothing when exiting the secure area. There are three laboratory suites, a large animal facility and an area of canteen and meeting rooms in PC3. Each of these is separated from the other by airlock doors. The three suites, research, diagnostics and microscopy, are the major laboratory work areas of AAHL. Each suite is configured to multiple rooms for equipment and for the particular group to conduct their work. Rooms within each suite are separated by normal doors. The large animal facility includes rooms for animal accommodation. It is maintained by animal technicians and allows scientists to conduct studies on animals, for example trial a vaccine. Canteen and common meeting room facilities are available in PC3. The canteen is the only window area where staff in PC3 can see the outside world.

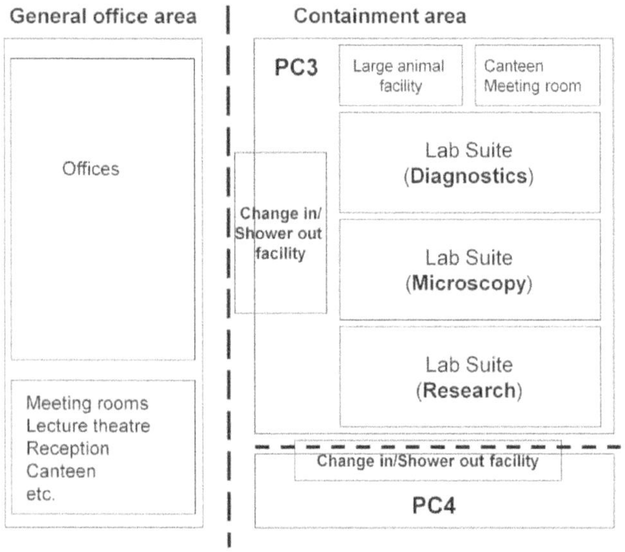

Figure 1. The physical layout of the work areas at AAHL

PC4 is a smaller area that is separated from PC3 by a second physical containment barrier. The scientists in PC4 change their PC3 clothing and wear fully encapsulated suits with their own oxygen supply. When they leave the PC4 they are required to have a chemical shower and then a regular shower before changing back to their PC3 clothing and re-entering PC3.

Work groups

The core work of AAHL is conducted by three major scientific work groups - diagnostics, research and microscopy. The responsibilities of each work group are described below.

Diagnostics group

The diagnostics group provides diagnostics services for a range of animals and animal diseases, such as equine influenza, foot-and-mouth disease and other emergency animal diseases of national importance. This work group includes diagnostics scientists and diagnostics management team. Diagnostics scientists work in PC3 to undertake tests using cell culture, virus and pathogen identification techniques, and optical microscopy. Their results include text or table-based reports, pathology images and microscopy images. The diagnostics management team (e.g. veterinary officers), working in the general office area, is responsible for preparing and delivering text-based reports to the clients who submitted samples, based on analysis of the results from the diagnostics scientists and the microscopy group within the containment area.

Research group

The research group conducts research to develop improved diagnosis, vaccines and anti-viral drug targets from molecular, cellular and animal levels. Some research scientists need to spend most of their work time in the containment areas. Their work can include, for example, using genetic sequencing facilities and techniques, such as gel electrophoresis, to generate genetic sequences of pathogens, from copies of genetic materials, and reporting these data in table-form in a document such as an Excel worksheet and recording the digitized sequencing gel images. Other research scientists spend most of the time working in the general office area though sometimes they need to enter the containment area for observations of tests and studies. They undertake scientific research in the investigation of interactions between animals and viruses as early outbreak detection tools. Data involved in their work include the genetic sequence data and various analysis results such as graphs based on software and web-based analysis tools.

Microscopy group

The microscopy group uses advanced electron microscopy equipment and expertise to provide microscopy diagnostic services and research capability. Most of microscopy scientists spend most of their time in the microscopy suite in PC3. However, as with the other work groups, the team leader needs to complete management and coordination work in the general office area in addition to engaging with the work inside the containment areas.

COLLABORATION WITHIN AAHL

The diagnostics and research work in AAHL often involves collaboration between scientists from different groups and from different sides of the containment barriers. In this section we describe these collaborations and the collaboration and information sharing issues that we identified from the study.

Collaboration within and between groups

Collaboration within and between groups at AAHL is a mix of concurrent, sequential, partly within and partly between groups, partly co-located and partly distributed, sometimes involving conversation and often involving discussions of data. Figure 2 shows the distribution of work groups across the main containment barrier, the approximate number of staff in each groups and interactions between and within groups. We describe the collaborations around diagnostics, research and microscopy work in this section.

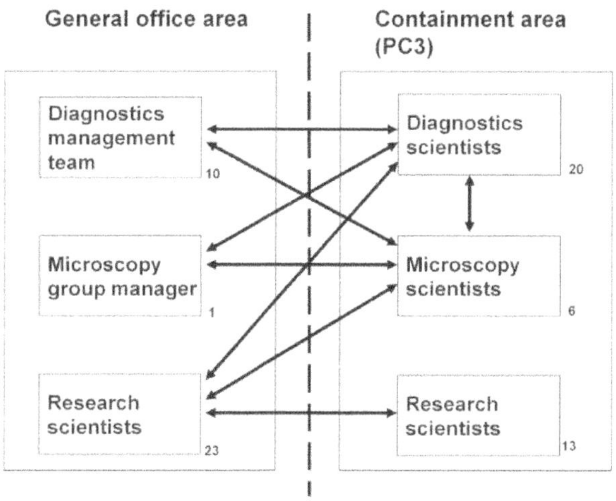

Figure 2. Overview of the work groups and interactions between them

Diagnostics collaboration

There is a standard procedure in handling samples and diagnostics requests received from clients. Figure 3 illustrates this diagnostics procedure, the data generated by each related group and the information sharing process.

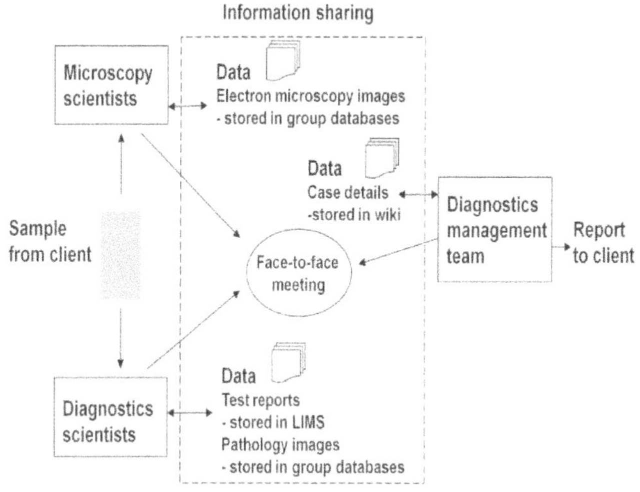

Figure 3. Diagnostics collaboration between related work groups

Samples that arrive at AAHL are tested by diagnostics scientists and examined by microscopy scientists in PC3. This is followed by a group discussion meeting between these scientists and the diagnostics management team. Participants bring paper printouts to this meeting and use them to collaboratively interpret the tests and microscopy results. During the meeting the diagnostics management member leads the case introduction and discussion, diagnostics scientists and microscopy scientists then contribute their points of view based on their results. After the meeting the diagnostics management team generates a report for the client.

Text-based case details and reports are maintained in a web wiki by the diagnostics management team, usually the veterinary officers, for all related groups to access. There is a shared information system, Lab Information Management System (LIMS), where diagnostics scientists record the text-based diagnostics test results and reports. Related diagnostics management team members, microscopy scientists and research scientists can access this system. Test-related pathology images are stored in the databases belong to the diagnostics scientists. Digital and scanned microscopy images are stored in databases which can only be accessed by the microscopy team members.

The diagnostics work is a group effort based on individual work and collaborative analysis. The data generated by different teams contribute to the coordination of this process. The results and status of the diagnostics process need to be communicated and understood by groups involved not only during the face-to-face meeting, but also before the meetings. For example microscopy scientists might need to access LIMS and refer to the diagnostic test results when making their microscopy diagnosis decisions. The analysis conducted by the diagnostics management team relies on the accurate interpretation of various diagnostics results.

Research collaboration

Research in AAHL involves collaboration between research scientists on both sides of the main containment barrier and microscopy and diagnostics scientists in PC3. Research scientists in the general office area need to understand the results of the tests conducted inside PC3 to modify their research directions or methods. In turn, the results of this work will guide scientists inside PC3 to adjust their test settings. For example, the research scientists in the general office area work on new tests for viruses or new drugs at a RNA molecular level. They need results from scientists in P3 including microscopy results to see drug effects in cells and animals and diagnostics results to identify a virus or to see the effect of drug treatment. They also work closely with research scientists in PC3 for genetic sequence data in cell engineering and animal model studies. At times they need to go into PC3 to observe data that needs to be viewed in real-time and in situ, such as fresh sequencing gel images, and to work with scientists in PC3 to build shared understandings of the meaning of the results.

Microscopy collaboration

Microscopy scientists interact with diagnostics and research groups in two processes that often take place in parallel: communicating microscopy results to related groups and understanding other groups' data to make appropriate decisions on microscopy diagnosis. There are also situations when microscopy scientists in PC3 need to consult the microscopy group leader who sometimes works at the general office area. Data involved in the microscopy collaborations can be microscopy diagnostics results and saved digital and scanned images. There are also discussions of images from fresh sample slides under a microscope when the microscope scientists have particular interesting findings to share, or need input from others, based on the fresh samples. By sitting together to discuss real-time microscopy images, microscopy scientists can move the slide to show areas-of-interest, get other scientists' feedback to make adjustments before recording the digital image and effectively decide on further investigation of the sample.

Collaboration issues

Scientists on different sides of the main containment barrier use telephones for quick discussions and email for sharing data via attachments. Face-to-face meetings have been the usual means for communication and sharing information. This requires staff to spend time and effort going through security procedures to cross the containment barriers. To avoid multiple "change-in" and "shower-out" and the resulting interruptions to workflow, organised group meetings are regularly held in the general office area, either early in the morning or late in the afternoon, that is before or after staff work in the containment areas.

The effort required to cross the barriers affects the ways that these scientists are able to discuss the details of the data effectively. For the diagnostics collaboration the issue of concern is the capacity for real-time interaction and data sharing between the diagnostics management team, diagnostics scientists and microscopy scientists. This is critical to AAHL's delivery of timely diagnostics tests to identify and characterise infectious agents, particular during an emergency animal disease outbreak. Another particular concern is that the discussions around real-time laboratory data such as fresh sample images under a microscope can be especially difficult when the microscopy group leader or other related scientists in the general office area are not able to go inside PC3 in time.

While the containment barriers pose physical constraints on collaboration, these are further complicated by the need to share information, in the form of test results and other kinds of data produced by and used in the work of AAHL, between different groups. That is, there are collaboration difficulties caused by the physical separation and access to shared data that impacts access to other scientists and to the work of the presentation and shared interpretation of the data. Data from different workgroups, on both sides of the containment barrier, need to be shared to coordinate the different work practices and processes and to ensure timely progress in each group's activities. The three core capabilities that Finholt and Olsen [8] identified as being necessary for supporting scientific collaborations, access to others, to information and to facilities also apply within the AAHL. Our findings showed that support for the sharing of data and its analysis would greatly facilitate not only quick diagnostics and similar tasks but also the general and ongoing collaboration between the work groups. These issues are explored in more detail in the following section.

Information sharing issues

The field study identified a number of issues with information sharing practices including: shared data repositories, shared visualisations, accessing remote computing resources, accessing real-time scientific images and the particular challenges of working in PC4. The first three are issues related to the difficulties of sharing information between groups and in their group discussions. The last two are mainly caused by the containment barriers.

Shared data repositories

Each work group has its own data repositories which can usually be accessed only by group members. For example, microscopy images are stored in databases which can only be accessed by the microscopy team members. There are necessary data access security rules and configurations for each repository. As described above, there is a shared Lab Information Management System (LIMS) for text-based diagnostics results. Staff can also log on to the intranet to access web-based animal monitoring data, such as animal video from the large animal facility and animal physiologic information from telemetry monitoring facilities in PC3. However these common shared repositories do not include a range of other data involved in various intergroup discussions or meetings, such as microscopy images or image results from sequencing gel.

Even when a common repository, such as LIMS is available, some results can be difficult to understand by other work group members if explanations are not provided with them. One of the diagnostics scientists commented:

"Our results are entered in and then that is available to anyone ... If there are any contentious results, it is very difficult for LIMS to describe it because the duty veterinary officer only sees the yes or no, positive or some sort of value. If there is any question, that cannot be recorded in LIMS, where in our hand-written and notes sheets – the results can be recorded."

Shared visualizations

Documents are sometimes exchanged by email and then discussed by telephone across the main containment barrier. In face-to-face meetings people usually bring printouts of related documents. We identified familiar issues with communication breakdown when participants could not see a common representation of a relevant file, particularly when images and graphs were involved [e.g. 23]. Group discussions also often require simultaneous viewing of multiple documents.

Accessing remote computing resources

Even when scientists meet in face-to-face meetings and bring documents with them, there are still situations when they require access to data that are not readily accessible on a data server, for example the data being processed on individual computers or instrumental computers. One of the research scientists commented:

"Generally we just bring paper notes and a pen and sit and talk. A lot of time it was not a major problem, but quite often in the middle of something someone says: 'Oh I saw that happen when I was doing that.' 'Oh what did it look like?' "I got that image here somewhere.' "

Accessing real-time scientific data

Microscopy scientists (e.g., the leader of the microscopy group) in the general office area can access their databases for stored microscopy images during discussions with microscopy team members working in PC3. However, at times there is a need for scientists to look together at real-time scientific images from fresh samples or results from fresh samples. This is currently not always possible as all those involved need to coordinate their on-going work in order to meet in PC3 at the right time.

PC4 work

For scientists working in PC4 it is currently particularly difficult to share data in real-time with scientists outside PC4 (in either the general office area or in PC3). There is a major challenge to enable scientists wearing fully encapsulated suits within PC4 to effectively communicate and share information with their colleagues outside PC4. This challenge is very specific to the biosecurity work of AAHL and of a higher order to those facing other parts of the laboratory. We have not yet been able to develop clear understandings of the collaboration issues specific to PC4 work and how they might be affected by the functionalities introduced in the first two stages of the platform design and development. PC4 work will be addressed separately in the final stage of development.

INFORMING THE DESIGN

The ultimate goal of the design is to enable information from various data resources (e.g. microscopes) and work areas (e.g. PC4) to be shared and discussed by individual scientists or groups of scientists who are on different sides of the barriers. The proposed solution is to use integrated communication and shared digital spaces over the AAHL network for various collaboration needs [18].

In our analysis of the findings of the field study we identified three broad collaboration requirements that needed to be met within AAHL, the specific local setting of the project: general group discussion, specialized real-time scientific data discussion, e.g., microscope images and those that need to be viewed 'in situ' and in real-time, and collaborative work in PC4. The first requirement is to enable a group of scientists in PC3 to communicate and share data with a group of scientists in the general office area. The second is to support collaboration during real-time scientific data consultation. The third is to support scientists working in PC4 to share their information with scientists outside PC4. While the first is relatively common to scientific meetings between distributed groups, the second and third are specific requirements for collaboration within the local setting of AAHL because of the work it does and the physical setting in which the work is done.

These three requirements have been mapped to three 'scenarios' of cooperative work. We understand that the term 'scenario' has different meanings within participatory design and interaction design. But it is used here because it is the term that the AAHL participants use and that is used within the project. These scenarios have driven the iterative design and development of the collaboration platform. Figure 4 maps the three scenarios to the collaboration within AAHL. The final platform will consist of components to support these three scenarios. Each scenario is addressed in a distinct design stage of the technology development. To date, the design for the first scenario which is the major component of the collaboration platform has been developed and implemented and is currently under evaluation.

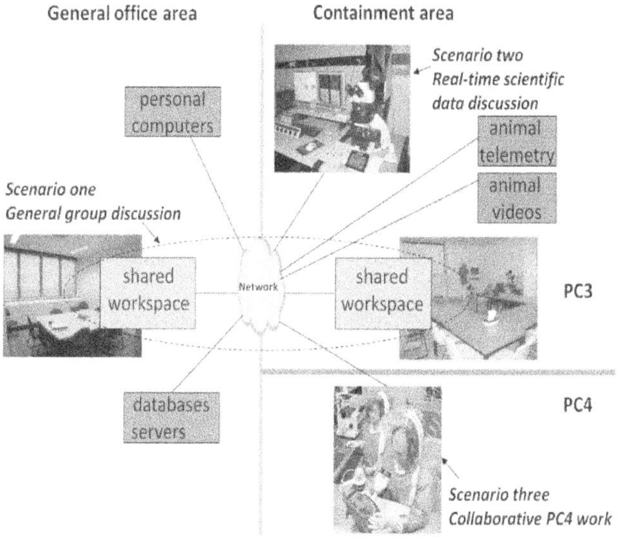

Figure 4. Three design scenarios to drive the design of the collaboration platform

General group discussion

This scenario supports two groups of scientists to share information and access to a range of data resources in their distributed group meetings across the main containment barrier. Given the complexity of the information sharing involved in the group discussion including access to data, shared visualization and the need to interact with multiple resources, face-to-face group meetings within AAHL as a solution for physical separation still have collaboration issues. For example, they require support for flexible visualization beyond that which enables only the sequential presentation of pre-prepared single documents.

We have introduced two shared workspaces to support distributed group meetings, one in PC3 and another in the general office area. Each workspace is connected to the AAHL network and various data resources, such as real-time animal monitoring videos and animal physiologic monitoring information from the large animal facility in PC3 area, databases (e.g. LIMS) and desktops of computers which run specific applications (e.g., microscope). Different group members can access their data resources using their existing access credentials.

Each shared workspace has high-resolution, large displays so that multiple digital information and remote participants can be displayed and clearly seen by a group of participants. Enabling this shared visualisation in a multi-display environment and over the network supports simultaneous viewing of multiple data resources and synchronous interaction with the shared applications. Also the displays and high quality video cameras which are placed in their designed positions enable nearly 'life-size' video-conferencing communication between the two distributed groups. Appropriate integration of video-conferencing space and shared digital space has been one of the key design considerations of the shared workspace.

AAHL management has decided that this shared workspace is to be a shared facility for the different workgroups. One shared workspace is located in a small common meeting room in the general office area and another is in a large common meeting room close to the canteen in PC3. Different group meetings in AAHL have different settings in terms of the number of participants, the purpose of the meeting, the ways of presenting information and interaction activities (e.g., verbal communication or interacting with digital information). The shared workspace needs to provide not only common functionalities for different group meetings but also flexibility for these variations [16]. According to our interview participants, each workspace needs to cater for up to four participants. Our design considerations included the physical setting of the shared workspace, the size and position of the displays and the position of the cameras. Our study also showed that participants need to be able to make adjustments to the information spaces on the displays as well as their view of their separated colleagues so they can tailor the workspace to the demands of particular activities of the meetings. For example, the participants can use all of the display space for multiple data visualization when focusing on data sharing, or use some to show life-size, high-definition video of remote participants when the conversation is less data-focused.

Real-time scientific data discussion

This scenario specifically supports individual scientists sitting in front of their workstations in PC3 to share real-time scientific information from their instruments with staff working outside. For example, a microscopy scientist working on samples slides in PC3 can share images from the microscope computer screens with the microscopy specialist or research scientists in the general office area. Individual scientists sitting at their personal computer or a group of scientists at the shared workspace on the other side of the containment barrier can interact with the shared microscopy images and the associated application windows. They can see and talk to the scientist in PC3 while looking at the image of the current microscope slide. The advanced electron microscopes are specific and expensive instruments. The hardware and software interfaces to the microscope computers need to be carefully assessed during the design phase to minimize the interference with microscopy work. Therefore, these instrument computers are solely set up to share their desktops to the shared workspace, e.g., outside the containment area, rather than being used to display workspaces themselves. Such use would compromise the operation of these dedicated workstations. Also suitable solutions to integrate audio-video communications between individuals or individual and multiple scientists need to be addressed to support this scientific data discussion in addition to the real-time image sharing.

Collaborative PC4 work

The ability to enable real-time sharing of various data types would greatly facilitate PC4 work. The higher level containment constraints have a practical impact on any potential technology especially the selection and installation of appropriate hardware. A new PC4 facility has been planned at AAHL and the design of the collaborative PC4 work will be part of the overall new PC4 design process. The ultimate goal is to allow data from PC4, such as live microscopy images, to be shared on the shared workspaces in PC3 and the general office area.

DISCUSSION

The use of collaboration technology within AAHL was proposed as a way to reduce the complexity of coordinating distributed activities in collaborative diagnostics and research work and to improve data sharing processes. The findings of the field study demonstrate how collaboration within AAHL is affected not only by the physical containment barriers but also the challenges of sharing information between different groups. We identified physical constraints posed by the containment barriers that are, in many ways, very similar in kind to those faced by people who need, for example, to cross town or otherwise expend extra effort in order to collaborate with people who separated by physical distance. We also identified issues with information sharing that rely on standard communication methods (e.g. email, telephone and face-to-face meetings) for supporting the coordinative process. These, too, are in many ways similar in kind to those faced in settings where collaboration involves developing shared understandings of various and multiple kinds of data. But while these issues might be partly common to other distributed groups, their particular expression within the work in AAHL was also shaped by the specific biosecurity requirements of the setting; that is, by the actual work done by AAHL and the actual physical containment that entailed.

This implies that while there are two broad requirements for providing successful technology support for collaboration in AAHL, these will need to be configured and extended by those posed by the particular work the laboratory does. One broad requirement is access to a "distributed" shared workspace on each side of the main containment barrier, so that staff do not need to cross the barrier to communicate and collaborate with each other. The second is support for the availability of data, including evolving experimental results, for shared viewing and analysis between individuals and workgroups, irrespective of where they are. We found no current need for the development of further shared data repositories but a strong requirement for technologies to support collaboration during the interpretation and analysis of data. These data are in various existing repositories with different access requirements that are required by the work of AAHL.

The initial stage of platform development, the shared workspace, will not solve all the collaboration issues within AAHL. This is reflected by the design of the multi-stage development process. The shared workspace, appropriately configured, can be a generalisable solution for distributed group meetings. However, the local requirements of specific kinds of real-time scientific data discussion, collaborative PC4 work and the appropriate integration of these design components, still need to be addressed to meet the challenges of scientific collaboration and collaborative laboratory work in AAHL.

Schmidt et al. identified two categorically different relationships between studies of work practice and the technology design these might inform [25]. The first are work practice studies of specific settings for the purpose of developing specific technologies for that setting and the second are studies for the purpose of building generic technologies that can be combined and re-combined in different settings. Our study was of the first kind. But by including the discussion of how the findings of the study actually informed the design process we have been able to show how the actual technologies developed can be hybrids. Generic collaboration platforms, with configurable spatial arrangements and functionalities can be extended by capabilities developed in response to the specific requirements of the work of the local setting. Over time we might also understand if and how those requirements, specific to the local setting, shift and reshape when more generically available technologies are provided to support collaborative work over various kinds of distance.

CONCLUSION AND FUTURE WORK

Two shared workspaces featuring multiple displays and supporting information sharing and nearly life-size video-conferencing have been installed at AAHL, allowing scientists to collaborate in real-time across the containment barrier between the general office area and PC3. Early findings suggest that this can be an effective collaborative workspace. Staff have indicated their appreciation of the capacities to share and interact with multiple data resources and the availability of high quality audio and video. Future work includes the design of technology to support the remaining two scenarios, real-time scientific data discussion and collaborative PC4 work, that were developed from the findings of the field study. The effectiveness of the platform will then be evaluated during a longitudinal user study when the system is fully developed and is closely integrated into AAHL's collaboration practices.

Through the work presented in this paper we have been able to explore the collaborative practices, particularly information sharing, in scientific collaborations between different groups and over the "distance" of physical containment barriers in a biosecurity laboratory. Our findings have contributed to the design of a collaboration platform for this environment that can resolve common communication issues over distance while still supporting those that arise out of the specific work and physical environment of AAHL. As such they have broader implications for other scientific collaboration settings where information and practice need to be coordinated across other local settings.

ACKNOWLEDGEMENTS

This work is part of a National eResearch Architecture Taskforce (NeAT) project, supported by the Australian National Data Service (ANDS) through the Education Investment Fund (EIF) Super Science Initiative, and the Australian Research Collaboration Service (ARCS) through the National Collaborative Research Infrastructure Strategy Program. We thank other members of the technical team from CSIRO ICT Centre for their contributions and Alex Hyatt and Martyn Jeggo from AAHL for their supports.

REFERENCES

1. Balka, E., Wagner, I. and Jensen, C.B. Reconfiguring critical computing in an era of configurability. In *Proceedings of the 4th decennial conference on Critical computing: between sense and sensibility*, ACM Press (2005), Aarhus, Denmark, 79-88.
2. Balka, E., Bjorn, P. and Wagner, I. Steps toward a typology for health informatics. In *Proceedings of the Computer Supported Cooperative Work (CSCW'08)*, ACM Press (2008), San Diego, CA, USA, 515-524.
3. Bannon, L. and Bodker, S. Constructing common information spaces. In *Proceedings of the fifth conference on European Conference on Computer-Supported Cooperative Work* (*ECSCW'97*), Lancaster, UK, 81-96.
4. Biehl, J.T., Baker, W.T., Bailey, B.P., Tan, D.S., Inkpen, K.M. and Czerwinski, M. Impromptu: a new interaction framework for supporting collaboration in multiple display environments and its field evaluation for co-located software development. In *Proceeding of the twenty-sixth annual SIGCHI conference on Human factors in computing systems (CHI '08)*, ACM Press (2008), New York, NY, USA, 939–948.
5. Broughton, M., Paay, J., Kjeldskov, J., O'Hara, K., Li, J., Phillips, M. and Rittenbruch, M. Being Here: Designing for Distributed Hands-On Collaboration in Blended Interaction Spaces. In *Proceedings of the 21st Australasian Conference on Computer-Human Interaction (OzCHI'09),* ACM Press (2009), Melbourne, Australia, 73-80.
6. Chin, G.J. and Lansing, C.S. Capturing and supporting contexts for scientific data sharing via the biological sciences collaborator. In *Proceedings of Computer Supported Cooperative Work (CSCW'04),* ACM Press (2004), Chicago, USA, 409-418.

7. Ellingsen, G. and Monteiro, E. Seamless Integration: Standardisation across Multiple Local Settings. *Computer Supported Cooperative Work*, vol. 15, no. 5-6 (2006), 443-466.
8. Finholt, T.A. and Olson, G.M. From laboratories to collaboratories: A new organizational form for scientific collaboration. *Psychological Science*, vol. 8, no. 1 (1997), 28-36.
9. Finholt, T.A. Evaluation of electronic work: Research on collaboratories at the University of Michigan. *SIGOIS Bull.*, (December 1995), 49–51.
10. Fitzpatrick, G., Kaplan, S.M. and Parsowith, S. Experience in Building a Cooperative Distributed Organization: Lessons for Cooperative Buildings, In *Proceedings of 1st International Workshop on Cooperative Buildings, Integrating Information, Organization, and Architecture*, Springer-Verlag (1998), 66-79.
11. Fraser, M., Hindmarsh, J., Best, K., Heath, C., Biegel, G., Greenhalgh, C. and Reeves, S. Remote Collaboration Over Video Data: Towards Real-Time e-Social Science. *Computer Supported Cooperative Work,* vol. 15, no. 4 (2006), 257-279.
12. Heath, C., Luff, P. and Sellen, A. Reconsidering the Virtual Workplace: Flexible Support for Collaborative Activity. In *Proceedings of the Forth European Conference on Computer Supported Cooperative Work (ECSCW'95)*, Kluwer Academic Publishers (1995), Stockholm, Sweden, 83-99.
13. Henline, P.: Eight collaboratory summaries. *Interactions,* (May 1998), 66–72.
14. Jirotka, M., Procter, R., Rodden, T. and Bowker, G.C. Special Issue: Collaboration in e-Research. *Computer Supported Cooperative Work,* vol. 15, no. 4 (2006), 251-255.
15. Lee, C.P., Dourish, P. and Mark, G. The human infrastructure of cyberinfrastructure. In *Proceedings of Computer Supported Cooperative Work (CSCW'06)*, ACM Press (2006), Banff, Alberta, Canada, 483-492.
16. Li, J. and Robertson, T. Physical space and information space: studies of collaboration in distributed multidisciplinary medical team meetings. *Behaviour and Information Technology*, Vol. 30, No. 4 (2011), 443-454.
17. Mark, G., Abrams, S. and Nassif, N. Group-to-group distance collaboration: examining the "space between". In *Proceedings of the 8th European Conference of Computer-supported Cooperative Work (ECSCW'03)*, Helsinki, Finland, 99 – 118.
18. Mueller-Tomfelde, C., Li, J. and Hyatt, A. An Integrated Communication and Collaboration Platform for Distributed Scientific Workgroups. In *Proceedings of 13IFIP TC13 Conference on Human-Computer Interaction (Interact'11)*, Springer (2011), Lisbon, Portugal, 248-258.
19. O'Hara, K., Kjeldskov, J. and Paay, J. Blended interaction spaces for distributed team collaboration. *ACM Transactions on Computer-Human Interaction (TOCHI)*, vol. 18, no. 1 (2011), article 3.
20. Olson, G.M., Zimmerman, A. and Bos, N. *Scientific Collaboration on the Internet,* The MIT Press, 2008.
21. Paay, J., Kjeldskov, J. and O'Hara, K. BIS i: a blended interaction space. In *Proceedings (extended abstracts) of the 2011 annual conference on Human factors in computing systems (CHI'11)*, ACM Press (2011), Vancouver, Canada, 185-200.
22. Reddy, M.C., Dourish, P. and Pratt, W. Coordinating heterogeneous work: information and representation in medical care. In *Proceedings of the seventh conference on European Conference on Computer-Supported Cooperative Work (ECSCW'01)*, Kluwer Academic Publishers (2001), Bonn, Germany, 239-256.
23. Robertson, T., Li, J., Hansen, S. and O'Hara, K. Collaboration within different settings: a study of co-located and distributed multidisciplinary medical team meetings. *Computer Supported Cooperative Work*, vol. 19, no. 5 (2010), 483-513.
24. Schmidt, K. and Bannon, L.J. Taking CSCW Seriously: Supporting Articulation Work. *Computer Supported Cooperative Work*, vol. 1(1-2) (1992), 7-40.
25. Schmidt, K., Wagner, I., and Tolar, M. Permutations of cooperative work practices: a study of two oncology clinics. In *Proceedings of the Conference on Supporting Group Work (Group'07)*, ACM Press (2007), Florida, USA, 1–10.
26. Schmidt, K. and Wagner, I. Ordering Systems: Coordinative Practices and Artifacts in Architectural Design and Planning. *Computer Supported Cooperative Work*, vol. 13, no. 5-6 (2004), 349-408.
27. Sonnenwald, D.H. Expectations for a scientific collaboratory: a case study. In *Proceedings of the international ACM SIGGROUP conference on Supporting group work (GROUP'03)*, ACM Press (2003), New York, NY, USA, 68–74.
28. Suchman, L. *Human-Machine Reconfigurations. Plans and Situated Actions*, 2nd Edition, Cambridge University Press, 2007.
29. Wigdor, D., Jiang, H., Forlines, C., Borkin, M. and Shen, C. WeSpace: the design development and deployment of a walk-up and share multi-surface visual collaboration system. In *Proceedings of the 2009 annual conference on Human factors in computing systems (CHI'09)*, ACM Press (2009), Boston, MA, USA, 1237-1246.

Remote and Alone: Coping with Being the Remote Member on the Team

Benjamin Koehne*, **Patrick C. Shih***, **Judith S. Olson**
Department of Informatics
University of California, Irvine
Irvine, CA 92697-3440 USA
bkoehne@uci.edu, patshih@ics.uci.edu, jsolson@uci.edu

ABSTRACT
Geographically distributed work has become a popular way to work. Past CSCW research has shown that remote workers rely on innovative communication platforms but still face challenges being remote. Research has also provided organizational and managerial strategies to bridge the distance gap. Our study in contrast investigates how individuals develop strategies to cope with the daily challenges of working remotely and alone, and what managers can do to help them. We interviewed seventeen individuals involved in remote work about their experiences, identifying unique challenges and their workarounds. Our interview results suggest that, although people may work alone, the process of conducting distributed work is actually very social. Individual remote workers establish a unique kind of work rhythm, visibility management for evaluation, social support infrastructure, and personal connection as a part of their coping strategies to balance their professional and personal lives.

Author Keywords
Distributed Teams; Individual Remote Worker; Visibility Management; Best Practices.

ACM Classification Keywords
H.5.3. Group and Organization Interfaces: Computer Supported Cooperative Work, Organizational Design.

General Terms
Human Factors; Management.

INTRODUCTION
Geographically distributed work has become a global phenomenon. The formation of distributed teams has become common business practice [5]. A report by the Gartner Group, a research company investigating the global IT industry, estimated that 41 million corporate employees worldwide worked in distributed settings for at least one day per week in 2008 [11]. Recent developments in information and communication technology for collaborative work processes have enabled many employees to work from any location without requiring a physical office. Many companies benefit from the reduced costs associated with allowing people to work from home. However, working alone from remote locations also presents a variety of challenges on individual employees and, we find, their teammates. Given the growing number of remote team workers, a closer look at individual remote workers' perspectives and their daily routine practices and challenges can offer important insights.

Past literature in CSCW has suggested best practices on how to mitigate the issues inherent in collaboration across distance [15, 19, 20]. However, research has focused mostly on analyzing communication patterns and process outcomes. Our study aims at complementing this research by contributing an understanding of how individual remote workers cope and what their managers can do to help them.

RELATED WORK
Distributed teams have been the focus of extensive research in organizational science and CSCW for more than two decades [15, 20, 25]. This work recommends enabling remote workers with innovative communication platforms (*e.g.*, [3]), recognizing the downsides of computer-mediated communication (*e.g.*, [1]), and providing organizational and managerial strategies to bridge the distance gap (e.g., [19]). Our study extends the previous literature by understanding how individual remote workers adapt their personal and professional lives to accommodate for challenges of distance work, and how managers can aid them.

In their review of distributed teams research, Martins *et al.* and Powell *et al.* stress the importance of investigating distributed team member characteristics and interpersonal team processes such as affect management, social integration of team members, and the social context of distributed teams and individual team members [15, 20]. Our study explores these previously under-researched areas.

Olson and Olson synthesized past studies on the effects of geographical distances on workgroups [18, 19]. They found that in spite of the availability of advanced information and

* These authors contributed equally to this work, and are listed in alphabetical order.

telecommunication technologies, inherent effects of collaborating over distance continue to linger. Specifically, persistent factors such as culture, time zones, management styles, and trust continue to have influence over collaboration outcomes. Table 1 presents a summary of organizational strategies to mitigate challenges in distributed collaboration.

Team Challenges	Organizational Strategies
Collaboration Readiness	Organizations should implement incentive structures that support a mix of competition and cooperation
Technology Readiness	Organizations should provide sufficient technical support to enable remote workers to conduct their work
Common Ground	Organization should maintain a common base of shared knowledge and vocabulary for geographically distributed teams.
Nature of the Work	Organizations should structure tasks so that interdependence is reduced
Management & Decision Making	Organization should provide good leadership. Team members should feel that decisions are made fairly and clearly
Culture	Organizations should promote awareness of cultural differences
Time Zone	Organizations should adjust work shift hours in order to allow overlapping work time to accommodate time zone issues
Visibility & Presence	Awareness tools should be provided to indicate availability of remote workers and to increase their sense of presence across distributed teams
Coordination & Communication	Organizations should have clearly defined distributed work processes and communication plans
Social Support Network	Enterprise social networking and knowledge management tools should be provided to enable easy expertise identification

Table 1. Organizational Strategies to Overcome Distributed Team Challenges.

Olson and Olson defined three classes of distributed work topologies that could exhibit distinct characteristics due to their differing setups [18]. Using a team of four to illustrate, the three classes of topologies are:

- Hub and spoke: 3-1
- Hub-to-hub: 2-2
- Fully distributed: 1-1-1-1

Most of the literature focuses on the hub-to-hub configuration in which there is critical mass represented at the headquarters and the remote hub centers. For example, Hinds and McGrath conducted a longitudinal study on globally distributed teams in the hub-to-hub configuration and found that informal hierarchical structure was most effective in inducing smooth communications [8].

O'Leary and Mortensen [17] presented one of the few studies of individual remote workers. Interestingly, the authors found that while a hub-to-hub configuration created tensions across subgroups, individual remote workers did not. The authors further suggested that isolates may serve a beneficial role for the team by strengthening the need for overall information sharing and explicitly confronting conflict.

We build our analysis on the concept of coping, pioneered by Lazarus and Folkman in the field of psychology [12, 13]. We look at individual actions of remote workers as coping strategies to investigate the different ways of dealing with being alone. Nurmi extended Lazarus and Folkman's concept of coping and undertook a qualitative examination of teams with some dispersed members [16]. The study found that general coping strategies that are typically employed to ease long distance collaboration (*e.g.,* using synchronous and asynchronous CMC and traveling) can result in *more* stress for the remote members. Consequently, individual workers need to develop strategies to cope with the coping strategies that are in place. In contrast to O'Leary and Mortensen's findings [17], Nurmi suggests avoiding isolates in a team, by having at least two members at a location for social support. Clearly there are tradeoffs—social support vs. the possibility that they will become an in-group.

Tang *et al.* conducted interviews of globally distributed team members in the hub-to-hub configuration to study their work rhythms and strategies of getting around time zone issues [24]. Given the wide variety of environmental and contextual differences in the way individual remote workers operate in their surroundings, the same strategies that resulted from the hub-to-hub setting may not generalize to the hub and spoke or the fully distributed setup. Very few studies have focused on understanding the personal affect of remote workers who work alone at a distance. In general, we believe that individual remote workers would encounter the same or even more challenges than the remote workers working in the hub-to-hub setting. Venolia *et al.* saw an opportunity to address the "out of sight, out of mind" problem for the remote members and created a tool to sustain their social presence at the hub site [26]. We share a similar perspective with these authors, and our study details various facets of sociotechnical issues that individual remote workers face. Previous studies did not put much focus on individual accounts of remote work in actual daily work settings. This study provides personal perspectives to provide a more accurate account of individual remote work and to provide best practices for managers and team members. Studies on multicultural teams [2] and individual work rhythms also informed our approach [9, 22].

METHODS

To explore a broad range of personal experiences of remote workers working in global teams, we conducted a total of seventeen semi-structured interviews with individuals working in a wide range of industries. Table 2 shows the demographics of the seventeen interview participants and the context of their work.

Participants were recruited using connections to industries and a snowball sampling methodology. Potential participants qualified for the study if they fit into one of the following categories:

1. The company does not provide them a physical office. The participant works primarily from home or at a client site, and occasionally travels to the company (*P2*, *P3*, *P4*, *P8*, *P9*, *P10*, *P11*, *P12*, *P13*, *P15*).

#	Gender	Industry	Company Size	Job Role	Experience	Work Setting	Work Type (Continuous- vs. Project-based)	Work Location	Remote Collaboration
P1	F	IT	Small Start-up	UX Engineer	5 years, always remote	Home	Continuous & Project	US (CA)	China, Europe, US (CA)
P2	M	IT	Small Start-up	Founder and President	1 year, always remote	Home	Continuous	US (CA)	India, US (CA)
P3	M	Software	Small Start-up	Founder and President	8 years, always remote	Home	Continuous & Project	Estonia	Estonia, Philippines
P4	M	Entertainment	Small Start-up	Founder and President	8 years, always remote	Home	Continuous & Project	Estonia	Australia, Canada, China, Estonia, France, Netherlands, Singapore, UK
P5	F	IT	1,000-9,000	Sr. UX Designer	3 years	Office (80%)	Continuous & Project	US (CA)	Germany, India, US (CA, NY)
P6	M	IT	1,000-9,000	Sr. UX Designer	4 years, 1 year remote	Home	Project	US (CA)	Germany, India, US (CA, NY)
P7	M	Software	1,000-9,000	Director, Product Marketing	14 years	Office (80%)	Continuous & Project	US (CA)	Asia, Australia, New Zealand, Sweden, UK, US
P8	M	Software	1,000-9,000	Vice President, Product Marketing	19 years, gradually became remote	Home	Continuous & Project	UK	Australia, Austria, Germany, Russia, US (CA, MN),
P9	M	IT	> 10,000	Sr. Researcher	13 years, always remote	Home	Project	US (MN)	Netherlands, US (IA, NY)
P10	F	IT	> 10,000	Sr. Researcher	15 years, 10 years remote	Home	Project	US (CA)	UK, US (CA, TX, NY, PA, DC)
P11	F	Financial Services	100-500	Sr. Pricing Application Analyst	2 years, always remote	Home	Project	US (WI, IL), or Client Sites (50% travel)	Czech Republic, France, Germany, Netherlands, Switzerland, UK, US (CA, IL, PA, UT)
P12	M	Financial Services	100-500	Lead Configuration Engineer	5 years, always remote	Home	Project	Spain	France. Switzerland, UK, US (CA),
P13	M	Financial Services	100-500	Project Manager	2 years, always remote	Home	Project	US (FL)	China, Czech Republic, Germany, India, UK, US (CA, IL, PA, TN)
P14	M	Cosmetics	> 10,000	Human Resource Information System Project Manager	5 years, 1 year remote	Hub Office	Project	Mexico	Argentina, Brazil, France, Mexico, Pakistan
P15	F	Environmental Services	Small Start-up	Partner	2 years, 1 year remote	Home	Continuous & Project	Mexico	France
P16	M	Software	> 10,000	Sr. Researcher	2 years, always remote	Hub Office	Continuous & Project	US (CA)	China, US (ME, WA)
P17	M	Computer Hardware	1,000-9,000	Global Product Marketing Manager	1 year	Office (80%)	Continuous & Project	US (CA)	China, Japan, UK, US (CA)

Table 2. Demographics of Interview Participants.

2. The participant has a physical office at the company but chooses to work primarily from home (*P1*).
3. The participant works as a remote team member at a hub office. The managers, team members, customers, and all other project-related personnel are dispersed in other locations. The participant works from the office for the sole purpose of utilizing physical resources and technological and network infrastructures provided in an office (*P14*, *P16*).
4. The participant works at an office, but a significant number of team members are remote. We included this category in order to verify the remote worker practices with the collocated person who offers support (*P5*, *P7*, *P17*).

All interviews were conducted on the phone or over VoIP by two interviewers and lasted approximately 40 minutes to 1 hour. Participants were not compensated. The interview protocol covered questions about the nature of work, performance evaluation, the planning and decision-making process, common ground, collaboration readiness, technology readiness, and trust. The interviews were semi-structured to allow the interviewees to interject personal perspectives and other reflections on working in distributed teams. A particular emphasis was put on a personal experiences and concrete examples of their use of technology and their social network.

Interviews were audio-recorded and transcribed. We used open-coding techniques to discover patterns and recurring themes [23]. The cross-referenced themes allowed us to develop our understanding of the social context of our participants and their individual workplace configurations. Our coding thus focused on individual solutions developed by our participants and their managers rather than processes implemented at the organizational level. Through the personal accounts conveyed during the interview sessions, we believe we can best understand the complex relationship between groups and remote workers.

RESULTS: COPING STRATEGIES

In the following sections, we use selected quotations to illustrate the emergent themes from the interviews. We discuss our findings in the format of individual coping strategies [12, 13, 16] as reported by our study participants. We present our findings in the following categories:

1. How individual remote workers deftly adapt their work rhythms to accommodate for coordination and time zone issues.
2. How individual remote workers manage to remain visible in order to allow effective communication, and how they strategically maintain their visibility so that they are evaluated fairly at performance evaluation.
3. How individual remote workers cope with their social needs and the type of personal social infrastructure they create in order to balance their professional and personal lifestyles.
4. How individual remote workers use their personal connections to smoothly transition into distributed work.

Work Rhythms and Time Zone Issues

Remote team members report explicit attention to organizing their workdays. All but two participants talked about the setup and attendance of meetings with their team members. Meeting schedules to a large extent anchored the organization of the employees' workday. For individual remote workers, all too often they do not have the same leverage as collocated workers to set meeting times and agendas. *P15*, a founding partner of a French start-up company who is now working remotely in Mexico, discusses a case where she is less flexible to meeting time changes than her collocated colleagues:

> *"They are usually late. I'm not, because I have it scheduled. But as they are working together, and they have a meeting that lasts longer than the other, and they see each other, it's okay for them to be late, like ten or twenty minutes. For me, it's difficult because it's early; I woke up early and I organized all my day according to this." (P15)*

Individual remote workers find they have to adapt to the more flexible and *ad-hoc* meeting environment of their collocated team members.

Time zone issues also presented a major challenge for all of our participants and resulted in many adjustments of their typical work rhythms. Individual remote team members were often asked to adapt, to accommodate to the time zone of the majority. For instance, *P11*, a senior pricing application analyst located in the US but who mainly works on projects based in Europe, explained to us that due to the time zone differences, she has to spend additional time in the morning to catch up with her colleagues about what had been done during what for her was overnight.

> *"When I'm sleeping a lot of stuff happens. So I have no idea what's happening. I have to adjust my work hours to start at 7 AM instead. . [...] When I come in everyday, I will have an email exchange, where someone will have been working with the client in the morning already and say, "Hey, what have you done? What have you communicated?" [...] They finish their stuff. They log off." (P11)*

Time zone issues also required the individual remote workers to be more explicit in emails, to explain everything in more detail to prevent questions in order to reduce turnaround time. *P6*, a user experience designer at a large IT company who is currently working from home, noted the following when talking about email exchanges with his colleagues:

> *"It basically creates a 24-hour [response] cycle. You have to learn to be as efficient as possible in your communication so that they [the work colleagues at the hub site] can move forward [...]. You cut down on the back and forth as much as possible." (P6)*

A lot of work during the day is concerned with continuous communication across different time zones and locations. The explicit and fast emailing style defines a typical, fast paced work rhythm of our participants.

The findings related to different time zones are consistent with previous literature [24]. Additionally, in order to battle uncertainties from a distance, we found that individual remote workers often employ careful planning and strategizing in advance. The earlier example showed scheduling as a daily work component. On top of that, 12 out of 17 participants spend a considerable amount of time working ahead of actual meetings. They want to be as prepared as possible in order to achieve the desired meeting outcome. The following sentiment by *P14*, a project manager at a large cosmetics company who works from a remote hub office away from all of her team members, provides an example for this coping strategy:

> *"What they expect from me is to be prepared. That's the thing I learned with starting to work remotely; you need to either have a presentation ready or, like, know every point that you want to talk about. So you won't miss something. When you are not working remotely you can always forget something and then go back: 'Oh, you know what, I forgot about that. What should we do?' You can't do that when you work remotely." (P14)*

Working alone remotely means a considerable preparation overhead that becomes part of the daily workday. Being well prepared is not only necessary for the individual remote team members to perform any distributed tasks; it is also often expected from them—more so than from collocated team members. It is much more difficult for remote members to clarify discussions after meetings unlike collocated members who can easily do so in face-to-face conversations. Three quarters of the participants reported that it was helpful to finish administrative tasks such as emails, calendar scheduling, and to-do lists at a set time during the day—most often in the early morning hours or the previous evening.

When working remotely means working at home and at times that are normally part of one's home life, they have to balance personal and work life in novel ways. Our participants reported many benefits of remote team work, such as the freedom to arrange their personal workday in the way they desire. For instance, *P10* stated the following:

> *"I have a lot of flexibility. So, all the family issues and some health issues I've had over the last three or four years, I've been able to do all kinds of accommodations and keep my job and keep working at basically a full salary in a way that would have been extremely difficult to do if I have to go into a 9-to-5 office."(P10)*

Work-life balance for remote workers has often been a one-sided tale. Studies found that remote work creates more flexibility [7] and higher productivity [6] because it allows more freedom for the remote workers to plan their work and personal life. Our findings confirm previous findings but they also show that the issue is often more complex. Our participants mentioned the ability to be "flexible" in the face of fast changing needs. Coping with work-life balance and time-zone issues simultaneously demands careful strategizing. Getting a child dressed and off to school immediately before an important meeting or milestone deadline can be another stressor. Working at a physical office often creates a routine to help structure a person's workday. However, remote workers who work from home often do not have a clean separation of work from private life. They have to be extra cognizant of their priorities and consciously organize their workday in order to keep a coherent schedule and maintain a healthy work-life balance.

Visibility & Evaluation

Visibility within their team and the company they work for in general was a universal concern for our participants. They have to generate different strategies to make their voices heard and to establish a remote presence. A core strategy to maintain visibility was described as "over-communication" by *P6*:

> *"It's one of those things where you really do need to be online, have your instant messenger up so that people know that you're at your desk, because they have no other way to really gauge that. If they need to get a hold of you, they can't walk over to your desk. So you have to advertise that [the availability] electronically and virtually. Really doing that and really over communicating in the sense of maybe sending out status updates a little bit more often just to show people what you're working on. And in meetings, speaking up, chiming in. Even if it's sometimes just to say 'yes that's sounds good. I agree with what you guys are saying. That's great.' " (P6)*

Remote workers need to learn to communicate many of the actions that are easily observable in a collocated office work context. The previous quote also highlights that communicating one's availability on a regular basis is particularly important. The remote worker's goal is to avoid the appearance of being unreachable.

Being remote requires remote workers to pay close attention to communication channels such as chat and email in order to manage visibility. However, the extra communication for visibility purposes can also cause disruptions to the normal workflow and overall work rhythm. Emailing caused too many disruptions for *P10*, a senior researcher at a large IT company who is currently working from home:

> *"I got distracted checking for email too much. So, I've now changed my email client so it only gets updates once an hour." (P10)*

Mark *et al.* compared the work fragmentation caused by interruptions between collocated workers and distributed workers in the hub to hub configuration, and found that collocated people encounter more interruptions than their distributed colleagues [14]. In our study, we found that remote team members who work alone and away from the critical mass face even greater stress in having to manage their visibility while not getting overwhelmed by the constant interruptions. A manager who can understand and respect a remote worker's work style can greatly help mitigate such a distraction. *P13*, a project manager at a financial services company who worked as a developer before he stepped into the managerial role, shed light on this issue:

> *If I was a developer or a programmer, then maybe I would turn that [the instant messenger] off, because I would need a solid period of time when I couldn't be interrupted. [...] You can't always be available because of the type of work that you're - where you have to be concentrating. [...] I try not to instant message people on the team, unless absolutely necessary. We definitely use it. But I think everybody knows and respects people's heads-down time as well. (P13)*

In addition to making themselves visible, they established a supportive relationship with their project managers. For instance, in a project described by *P9*, a senior researcher who works for a large IT company from home, the manager would make sure to let remote collaborators present their own work during meetings as well as specifically point out their contributions and availability. *P15*, a partner at a small start-up, actively sends out email accolades to recognize the employee contributions:

> *"We try to sometimes over-recognize what people do, just to make sure that they are feeling okay and they're keeping involved." (P15)*

P16, a senior researcher at large software company who works from a hub office away from all his team members, pointed out to us that having a close contact person to co-manage some of the visibility aspects was of great value. However, it also represented additional work for the collocated workers to provide support for the remote workers:

> *"So, I feel very supported socially by my colleagues up there kind of looking out for me. Now, is it inconvenient for them? I think yes. Do they complain about it? I think yes, but not to me." (P16)*

The concept of "paying one's dues" by picking up more workload as a remote worker is prevalent, as *P9*, a senior researcher at a large IT company, described:

> *"If there is some last minute thing and people need to scramble around and talk to people or make equipment work, they're the ones who are doing it. And so, you need to figure out as a remote worker, 'How do I pay my dues to the group?' [...] You don't want to be a free rider just because you're a thousand miles away."(P9)*

For remote workers, visibility needs to be maintained and supported by explicit social processes. Remote workers do not share the benefit of brief social interactions that often occur naturally in collocated office settings. *P8*, vice president of product marketing at a software company, shared the following strategy:

> *"I strongly believe that every email should have a please and a thank you in it [...] if you get negative team feelings, they grow*

because there's not a chance to respond to each other. You don't get the ability to physically interact to confront it." (P8)

Issues related to visibility also surfaced in their performance evaluations. This is an important time for all team members, but can be especially critical for remote workers. When asked about evaluations, our participants stated concerns about fair representation of their contributions. Since our participants did not always have the opportunity to point out their contributions directly to the management chain, all of our participants (except for those who founded their own companies) developed a careful way of representing themselves. Often, the participants would try to positively influence their own evaluations by fostering elaborate communication with their evaluators. For instance, managers who are the principal evaluators need to be kept up to date even more frequently when the worker is remote. Over-emphasizing the communication of results and achievements turned out to be another strategy:

> *"[...] You have to play the game a little bit, sending out specific emails and saying, 'Oh yes, this was a great win here. Look what we did. Good job team. Thanks for working on this.' We kind of congratulate each other a little bit and call out specific contributions."(P6)*

Our participants often discussed their achievements publicly and used that as a strategy to make their contributions more visible for evaluation purposes. In one case, *P6* described a company-wide reward system that allowed team members to send out automated congratulatory messages while copying the recipient's manager on the message. Having a system that actively supports and encourages the celebration of positive project outcomes can help elevate individual contributions and mitigate disadvantages of being remote.

Evaluation and incentive structures provided by the company itself have been adopted in different ways by our participants. Many organizations do not evaluate productivity by the work hours spent on the project, but rather by results. Project results are reviewed by managers and also indirectly by customers. When remote workers work closely with specific customers, this can be an opportunity for direct evaluation. Since peer evaluation doesn't work for somebody working mostly alone, customer evaluation represents an alternative form of feedback that makes the remote worker's achievements visible to the team.

Another way for companies to identify contributions of remote workers is to provide assignments of clearly-defined work items. When possible, dividing up a project into clearly separated work elements can help mitigate evaluation issues for remote workers. For instance, in a project described by *P13*, a project manager who works for a financial services company from home, it became apparent that one of the team members did not carry out his assigned work items. The issue was discovered relatively early in the project due to the clear separation of responsibilities. At the end of the project, team members, remote or not, can be evaluated based on their specific contributions.

While email is universally mentioned as a communication medium, it is also used as a repository of past discussions. Recommendations and ideas generated by an individual remote team member were often overlooked, sometimes leading to costly errors or ultimately to project failures. Therefore, our participants reported that they often take extra time to create summary meeting notes, and decisions made in emails were archived for the purpose of clarification. In the case of *P11*, well-maintained communication trails were used as evidence to avoid taking blame for negative developments in the project:

> *"In case something happens you have an email to save you. You have: 'I said this and this is the decision that came up in this meeting and this is what happened.' So you have the emails to conclude everything." (P11)*

Based on our results, individual coping strategies that suit the unique work environments and work styles of the remote workers are essential for them to remain visible. Evaluation has previously not been considered as a motivating factor for managing visibility in global teams. Our results show the importance of this connection and how establishing a remote presence through communication trails can solve some of the related problems.

Establishing Personal Social Support Infrastructure

The lack of social interaction can pose serious issues for the remote workers. If remote workers are not able to successfully adapt to a remote work style, they often suffered degraded work performances, as well as lowered motivation and personal satisfaction levels. *P3*, a founder of a small start-up that does not have a physical office space, shared with us an experience with his previous employee:

> *"We had one person that used to work for us and he was not getting tasks done because he was just, I think, lacking enough social interaction from being at home [...] The thing about it is he's actually a very - knowing the stuff he's done, he's very competent and talented. So, it really was just coming down to he couldn't be in an environment - because I think he was an extrovert, he couldn't be in such a work environment where he wasn't getting enough of that. And so, he ended up taking a job which was more a level of interaction, working in an office and the whole type of thing." (P3)*

P11 also shared similar experiences:

> *"I actually have a coworker started working remotely for a half a year and quit because he cannot justify the remote working structure. He enjoyed seeing people every day, going to an office every day, and that's why he found another job which he can go to the office every day." (P11)*

The need of social interaction with people emerged as a common thread in our interviews. Ten out of 17 participants mentioned having to cope with the feeling of wanting more people interactions. This is a result of the fact that an individual remote worker spends the majority of the day working alone or working with strangers. One effective strategy is to utilize nearby friend and family networks in order to remain connected to people.

"The flip side of working remote is - not feeling connected to anything. I was born in [location name], I grew up here, I went to school here. I have lots of friends and colleagues physically here. I have to make the effort, but I can get that kind of action, which I think for somebody who's in the middle of nowhere that would be a lot harder." (P10)

The ability to keep their well-being in tact by interacting socially with other human beings and sharing their experiences is often acquired through many years of practice working in the remote setting. Not many companies include training on how to work remotely. As *P1*, a user experience engineer working at a small software company emphasizes:

"You have to have the understanding of what working remotely entails, you know, what 'working remotely' really means." (P1)

Most distributed team training programs emphasize teleconferencing software tool usage and distributed team process models [27], and neglect coaching on remote work style and visibility management. *P7*, a product marketing director at a software company remarked:

"Our culture is you're not going to get a whole lot of handholding. You just figure it out." (P7)

Personal Connections

Fourteen out of 17 participants rely on their personal connections to identify personal mentors as a successful transition strategy. These mentors are people who have prior experience working in remote locations and have acquired the know-how to deal with the wide ranging issues that occur in being an individual remote worker. *P10* told us about being nervous during the first few months at a new job that involved her working alone from home and travelling to the headquarters office once every few weeks. She sought advice from a personal mentor who provided her not only with general support, but also essential advice. She was told that when she was at headquarters she should focus on building personal connections and when she was back home she should concentrate on work that did not need personal interaction. The remote worker and her mentor continue to engage each other for advice, which made her overall transition to becoming a remote worker much easier.

P6 also sought out coworkers, albeit strangers, to help coach him on the necessary transitions into distributed work:

"One of the things that I did before I started working remotely was I just pinged a lot of the other folks that do work remotely. [...] I pinged them and I just said, 'Hey, I know you've been working remotely for a couple of years now. I'm going to start next month. Any tips, pointers, advice how to make it work, etcetera?' 'Anything you can offer?' I got back a lot of really great feedback." (P6)

Participants also mentioned that they depended on personal contacts who are part of the core teams to keep them up-to-date on news and politics. *P14* commented on a situation in which things worked against his favor because he did not ask the personal contacts about the political situation on the status of a decision prior to an important meeting:

"It happened because I didn't understand the relationships between some people so I got screwed somehow. And next time you understand that if you want to get that guy's approval you first talk to that one and that one because they have a big influence in this one." (P14)

P9, a senior researcher at a large IT company, also emphasized the importance of collocated team members on distributed work:

"If you're actually being hired into a job where you're going to be a telecommuter, make sure that you have a chance to interview with your colleagues and not just your management chain. Because your colleagues will - they can, you know, make it easy or they can make it very, very hard." (P9)

Past work on distributed teams found that establishing a contact person who is responsible for communication among hub sites is critical to successful collaboration across distance [4, 8, 19]. Our finding suggests that it may be useful to have an official liaison who would provide constant meeting notes and feedback. It is essential to have a trusted insider who is able to provide more sensitive information or to represent the remote employee on his/her behalf.

Research has found that by making the work of the remote person as independent as possible, which decreases the amount of communication needed to synchronize, distributed teams are able achieve high performance output [19, 21]. Today, many distributed teams have begun to adopt this modular project management style. However, the independent nature of the tasks also makes individuals indispensable because they the only people responsible for the tasks. An individual remote worker who assumes that role is often required to be constantly available because the results of their work are heavily relied upon. One participant said this created a need to have a viable backup. In case of a technology breakdown, which occurs fairly frequently, or other personal emergencies, it becomes essential to trust in the co-workers to represent the remote member. While individual remote workers can rely on a coworker to cover for them, they can also rely on established personal connections as alternative options of backup support in case of needs:

"Even though [we] don't actually work together right now, we keep up with each other talking about twice a week. Usually if something breaks on one of us, the other person will know about it." (P10)

Countless distributed team studies have been conducted in the past, but few have focused on the need for social support as detailed in this paper. To our knowledge, no tools have been built to support such needs. The need for a social infrastructure stood out as one of the primary themes worthy of future investigation. Although our participants all noted that the transition to becoming an individual remote worker is a very difficult journey, they have also noted that when they succeed, the experience is an invaluable one:

"In the beginning it may be hard for me, but it takes time to adapt. And once you pass a certain time period it is hard to go back. I don't know if I'm at that point yet, but it's close to getting there that I'm not sure I can go back to the corporate

setting where you have to be there at certain times, certain hours." (P11)

BEST PRACTICES

We provide best practices emerged from the reported coping strategies for teams with individual remote members in the following two main categories: best practices that confirm findings discussed in current CSCW literature (see Table 1) and best practices that are novel additions to the literature. These best practices can serve as guidelines for both team managers and remote team members.

Best Practices: Confirmation of Existing Literature

- **Plan for extra communication overhead**

  What a remote worker can do: To plan a daily agenda, individual remote workers need to consider additional time spent on (over-)communication. It can be beneficial to limit the amount of interruptions by dealing with email only at set intervals and to deal with administrative work at one time of the day. Conference calls should be scheduled with additional buffer time to accommodate for *ad-hoc* agenda changes occurring at the hub location.

  What a manager can do: The whole team should accommodate for flexible meeting times and share accurate and timely information of the teams' activities. Ad-hoc schedule changes should be kept to a minimum.

- **Greater team awareness of time zone issues**

  What a remote worker can do: Very early or late meeting times caused by time zone differences can be unavoidable. It can be beneficial to explicitly create and follow task transition processes at the end of the workday to reduce communication problems with co-workers and customers. A well-defined status update protocol can further reduce time spent on catching up with the status of the work of other team members.

  What a manager can do: Managers can ease the negative impacts of time zone issues by scheduling global team meetings only if the presence of the remote worker is absolutely required. Minor issues should be coordinated using asynchronous tools. Having a well-defined structured work hand-off process helps team members to collaborate across time zones.

- **Prepare for meetings**

  What a remote worker can do: It is more difficult to convey messages effectively when attending meetings from a remote location. It is also difficult to address conflicts in efficient ways. To cope with these issues, for remote workers, especially careful preparation of discussion topics and individual conversations with individual participants before the actual meeting are often necessary to limit possible unplanned and difficult-to-control developments.

  What a manager can do: Assign a contact person for remote workers to create more awareness of remote members during actual meetings. If possible, meeting agendas and related documents should be distributed before the meeting to allow remote workers to prepare for unexpected events.

- **Expose tacit activities to raise awareness**

  What a remote worker can do: It can be beneficial to develop a work style based on much more explicit communication. Communication that would often be conducted in a tacit manner in collocated work environments needs to be explicit in distributed team contexts. In order to maintain a general status of higher visibility with other team members, availability needs to be signaled continuously and explicitly using instant messaging, email and other technologies. It is particularly important for remote workers to portray the impression that they are available and easy to reach. Visibility also needs to be addressed on a social level. Courtesy in digital communication for instance creates a more social form of communication.

  What a manager can do: Team managers can strive for higher team cohesion and minimize conflicts by promoting an open communication culture in the team. Implementing specific ICT that broadcasts activities and group interaction, such as instant messaging, document management systems and weekly newsletters about activities can also increase team awareness. Remote workers need to be explicitly kept on the group awareness horizon by having them present progress or specifically introducing their remote presence in meeting contexts. Managers should also provide enough room for social interaction of employees to develop a social awareness that can easily get lost in remote relationships with individual remote team members.

- **Plan for a healthy work and life balance**

  What a remote worker can do: It requires personal organizational skills from the remote worker and a good sense for timing and agendas to retain a healthy personal life when working at home or on the road. It takes time to develop a daily work rhythm that allows for a clear separation of personal and professional life. Individual remote workers need to consider the impact on family life and friend circles. Working alone requires a high degree of self-motivation and commitment to the job. Building a social network of colleagues can be just as important as communicating with colleagues from work to find help and support in times of crisis and without the presence of co-workers.

  What a manager can do: Managers should consider the difficult work-life balance that many remote workers are facing and provide sufficient space for personal activities.

Best Practices: New Insights

- **Create visibility for evaluation**

  What a remote worker can do: If possible, communicating very specific work assignments can make contributions more apparent and reduce the problem of visibility to a large extent. Customers can play an important role in the evaluation process by providing feedback about their experiences with individual remote workers in customer feedback channels. Keeping the project manager up-to-date with even more specific status updates than would be necessary in collocated teams also improves visibility of individual contributions. Remote workers should not be reluctant to talk about success publicly in the team. Keeping records of actions taken during the project is important to justify invisible actions to the core team and manager.

What a manager can do: Managers need to look into different measures to evaluate remote workers. The result of specifically assigned work tasks should be combined with input from customers and other co-workers. Providing remote workers with means to document their work process in details is essential to allow for transparency and visibility. Having a searchable and documented history affords proof of contributions to a project for evaluation purposes.

- **Establish a personal trustee**
  What a remote worker can do: Remote workers can greatly benefit from a personal contact at the core team who can be trusted with representing the individual remote team member's interests. The personal contact can act as a delegate to better represent the team member's voice and facilitate activities for the individual remote member that can only be done in person on-site.

  What a manager can do: Simply *assigning* a trustee is insufficient. Ideally, a trustee relationship develops over a longer term and is based on previous work experiences between colleagues. Managers can support the development of trustee relationships by giving employees room to share work and personal experiences. Company-wide social activities and enterprise social media can help employees to connect and share experiences.
- **Establish mentorship relationships**
  What a remote worker can do: Besides establishing a trustee in a distributed team, an experienced remote worker can take on the mentorship role during active project work or before the project assignment to coach employees to become successful remote members.

  What a manager can do: The organization can maintain a network of mentors and individual remote members who will act as a social support group in case of needs. A buddy system can also be implemented when an employee is about to transition into distributed work
- **Account for the impact on the collocated members**
  What a remote worker can do: Remote workers need to realize that there is overhead necessary for the core team to continuously integrate remote team members. Maintaining visibility and cohesion of all team members requires additional work to which everyone, including the management, must commit substantial resources. Being appreciative of this fact can make a remote worker's effort to stay visible in the team easier and creates a mutually trusting and understanding relationship.

  What a manager can do: It can make a big difference if the company culture actively promotes distributed work as a viable working style. Companies that operate an IT infrastructure that provides the fundamental technical framework for remote work, such as VPN and flexible firewall rule sets, can create beneficial groundwork for the successful development of distributed teams. Additionally, the cost of maintaining an active relationship with remote workers needs to provide collocated workers with benefits. Creating a healthy balance is the task of the team manager.
- **Provide relevant training for both remote workers and the collocated workers who will support them**
  What a remote worker can do: Team members should discuss the implications of remote work for the team as a whole as well as for the individual remote team members.

  What a manager can do: The provisions of training resources, in particular for social impacts, are necessary to help the remote workers transition into becoming an effective team member. Without the proper human infrastructure, technology alone will not be able to overcome the persisting issues inherent in distance collaboration. However, collocated team members also need to be aware of team's configuration and they need to learn to incorporate remote members better into daily work processes.

CONCLUSION AND FUTURE WORK

There is a wealth of literature on distance collaborations. However, most prior work focuses on enabling remote workers with innovative communication platforms, understanding the effects of computer-mediated communication, and providing organizational and managerial strategies to bridge the distance gap. Very little research has focused on the coping strategies of individual remote workers. Our work builds on existing work by interviewing seventeen people involved in remote work across a variety of business sectors, company sizes, and job functions.

The concept of coping strategies allowed us to analyze remote worker's daily work practices from a personal perspective. While we validated past results on distanced collaboration such as time zone issues and visibility management, we also uncovered previously understudied dimensions. Arguably one of the most striking findings is expressed in the area of evaluation which turned out to be a great concern for remote workers who coped with skillful creations of a virtual presence.

There needs to be support for allowing remote workers to connect with people who could become potential mentors, friends, and activity partners. Within the corporate intranet level, remote workers need to be able to identify employees with past experience with distributed work. In the public domain, there needs to be a platform designed specifically for remote workers to connect with other remote workers in the same situation, perhaps located in the same geographical region, so they can interact, socialize, share experiences and problem-solving strategies in order to sustain a healthy remote work lifestyle.

Globally distributed work almost always involves cross-cultural collaboration which can have a strong impact on remote workers in particular. Cultural concerns were raised during the interviews, but a detailed discussion was beyond the scope of this study. In future work, we plan to focus specifically on cultural factors that individual remote workers need to cope with every day.

ACKNOWLEDGMENTS

This project is supported by Google Inc. We thank our participants for their openness to share their personal experiences working as distributed team members.

REFERENCES

1. Bly, S. A., Harrison, S. R., and Irwin, S. Media spaces: Bringing people together in a video, audio, and computing environment. *Communications of the ACM* 36, (1993), 28–46.
2. Connaughton, S.L. and Shuffler, M. Multinational and multicultural distributed teams. *Small Group Research* 38, 3 (2007), 387 -412.
3. Erickson, T., Smith, D. N., Kellogg, W. A., Laff, M., Richards, J. T., and Bradner, E. Socially translucent systems: social proxies, persistent conversation, and the design of "Babble". *Proceedings of the ACM Conference on Human Factors in Computing Systems* (1999), 72-79.
4. Galbraith, J.R. *Designing complex organizations*. Addison-Wesley Longman Publishing Co., Inc., 1973.
5. Gibson, C.B. and Cohen, S.G. *Virtual teams that work: creating conditions for virtual team effectiveness*. John Wiley and Sons, 2003.
6. Hartman, R.I., Stoner, C.R., and Arora, R. Developing Successful Organizational Telecommuting Arrangements: Worker Perceptions and Managerial Prescriptions. *SAM Advanced Management Journal* 57, 3 (1992), 35.
7. Hill, E.J., Miller, B.C., Weiner, S.P., and Colihan, J. Influences of the Virtual Office on Aspects of Work and Work/Life Balance. *Personnel Psychology* 51, 3 (1998), 667-683.
8. Hinds, P. and McGrath, C. Structures that work: social structure, work structure and coordination ease in geographically distributed teams. *Proceedings of the ACM Conference on Computer Supported Cooperative Work* (2006), 343-352.
9. Jackson, S.J., Ribes, D., Buyuktur, A., and Bowker, G.C. Collaborative rhythm: temporal dissonance and alignment in collaborative scientific work. *Proceedings of the ACM Conference on Computer Supported Cooperative Work* (2011), 245–254.
10. Johansen, R. *Groupware: Computer support for business teams*. The Free Press, 1988.
11. Jones, C. Teleworking: the quiet revolution (2005 update). *Gartner Group Publication 122284*.
12. Lazarus, R. S. Towards better research on stress and coping. *American Psychologist* (2000), 665-673.
13. Lazarus, R.S. and Folkman, S. *Stress, appraisal, and coping*. New York: Springer, 1984.
14. Mark, G., Gonzalez, V.M., and Harris, J. No task left behind?: Examining the nature of fragmented work. *Proceedings of the ACM Conference on Human Factors in Computing Systems* (2005), 321–330.
15. Martins, L.L., Gilson, L.L., and Maynard, M.T. Virtual teams: what do we know and where do we go from here? *Journal of Management* 30, 6 (2004), 805 -835.
16. Nurmi, N. Coping with coping strategies: How distributed teams and their members deal with the stress of distance, Time Zones, and Culture. *Stress and Health* 27 (2011), 123-143.
17. O'Leary, M.B. and Mortensen, M. Go (con)figure: subgroups, imbalance, and isolates in geographically dispersed teams. *Organizational Science*, 21.1 (2010), 115-131.
18. Olson, G.M., Olson, J.S., and Venolia, G. What still matters about distance. A talk presented at the *Human-Computer Interaction Consortium* (2009).
19. Olson, G.M. and Olson, J.S. Distance matters. *Human-Computer Interaction* 15, 2 (2000), 139.
20. Powell, A., Piccoli, G., and Ives, B. Virtual teams: A review of current literature and directions for future research. *The DATA BASE for Advances in Information Systems* 35, (2004), 6–36.
21. Ramesh, V. and Dennis, A.R. The object-oriented team: Lessons for virtual teams from global software development. *Proceedings of the Hawaii International Conference on System Sciences* (2002), 212- 221.
22. Reddy, M. and Dourish, P. A finger on the pulse: Temporal rhythms and information seeking in medical work. *Proceedings of the ACM Conference on Computer Supported Cooperative Work*, (2002), 344-353.
23. Strauss, A.C. and Corbin, J. *Basics of qualitative research: techniques and procedures for developing grounded theory*. Sage Publications, Inc., 1998.
24. Tang, J.C., Zhao, C., Cao, X., and Inkpen, K. Your time zone or mine?: A study of globally time zone-shifted collaboration. *Proceedings of the ACM Conference on Computer Supported Cooperative Work* (2011), 235–244.
25. Townsend, A. M., DeMarie, S. M., and Hendrickson, A. R. Virtual teams: Technology and the workplace of the future. *The Academy of Management Executive* 12, 3 (1998), 17-29.
26. Venolia, G., Tang, J., Cervantes, R., et al. Embodied social proxy: Mediating interpersonal connection in hub-and-satellite teams. *Proceedings of the ACM Conference on Human Factors in Computing Systems* (2010), 1049–1058.
27. Warkentin, M. and Beranek, P.M. Training to improve virtual team communication. *Information Systems Journal* 9, 4 (1999), 271-289.

As if Being There: Mediated Reality for Crime Scene Investigation

Ronald Poelman[1], Oytun Akman[2], Stephan Lukosch[1], Pieter Jonker[2]
[1]Delft University of Technology
Faculty of Technology, Policy and Management
Systems Engineering Section
Jaffalaan 5, 2628 BX Delft, The Netherlands
[2]Delft University of Technology
Faculty of Mechanical Engineering
BioMechanical Engineering
Mekelweg 2, 2628 CD Delft, The Netherlands
{r.poelman, o.akman, s.g.lukosch, p.p.jonker}@tudelft.nl

ABSTRACT
This paper presents a novel mediated reality system designed to support collaboration between crime scene investigators during a first analysis on a crime scene, remotely supported by expert colleagues. Requirements elicited from interviews and interactive sessions with practicing crime scene investigators, provided the design criteria for a head mounted display capable of real-time map-making for spatial collaboration. The resulting system is evaluated in a staged crime scene experiment in which lay investigators collaboratively solve a spatial problem with remote experts. The results show that our novel approach to remote spatial interaction with the physical scene enables investigators to tackle current issues on site in collaboration with experts at a distance.

Author Keywords
Mediated reality, augmented reality, collaborative spatial analysis.

ACM Classification Keywords
H.5.1 Multimedia Information Systems; H.5.3 Group and Organization Interfaces; I.2.10 Vision and Scene Understanding; K.4.3 Organizational Impacts

General Terms
Human Factors; Design; Measurement.

INTRODUCTION
Crime scene investigation in the Netherlands is primarily the responsibility of the local police. For severe crimes, a national team supported by the Netherlands Forensic Institute (NFI) is called in. Initially capturing all details of a crime scene is of prime importance (so that evidence is not accidently destroyed). NFI's Department of Digital Image Analysis uses the information collected for 3D crime scene reconstruction and analysis. This process is currently costly in time and required expertise.

Figure 1 Mediated reality head mounted device in use during the experiment in the Dutch forensic field lab.

This paper reports on the results of a project between TU Delft and the NFI in which the potential of mediated and augmented reality for future crime scene investigation is explored. This paper focuses in particular on real-time alignment of physical and virtual environments and interaction with the environment using mediated and augmented reality to support collaborative spatial analysis on location. To this purpose a novel mediated reality system for collaborative spatial analysis on location (see Figure 1) has been designed, developed and evaluated[1]. This system supports collaboration between crime scene investigators (CSIs) on location and expert colleagues at a distance.

The design and evaluation of the mediated reality system is the focus of the paper in which five phases are distinguished: (1) requirement capture from international experts, (2) initial design of a mock-up system, (3) evaluation of mock-up by practitioners, (4) design of the mediated system, and (5) evaluation of the mediated reality system for collaboration. After discussing related work the remainder of the paper discusses the above five phases in

[1]Please note that consideration of the implications of such new technology on the organization itself as discussed in [16] are beyond the scope of this project

more detail and finishes with conclusions and directions for future work.

RELATED WORK

In most of the western countries, when a severe crime is committed, the crime scene is digitalized by either photogrammetry or laser scanning methods [7]. Some of the digitalized data is used for communication purposes, some for archiving and some for analysis. The most common analyses are; line of sight determination, reconstruction of ballistic trajectories, blood pattern analysis and reconstruction of crime scenes.

In most current practice worldwide, CSIs synchronous communication during spatial analysis is limited to voice or in rare cases video. In augmented reality virtual data is spatially overlaid on top of physical reality. With this technology the flexibility of virtual reality can be used and is grounded in physical reality [1]. Mediated reality refers to the ability to add to, subtract information from, or otherwise manipulate one's perception of reality through the use of a wearable computer or hand-held device [15].

Neither mediated reality or augmented reality is currently deployed for CSI. Augmented reality is however deployed in other domains. Fighter pilots, e.g., use a head mounted display (HMD) to display spatial information about the environment [4]. Surgeons use similar systems to overlay the patient with Magnetic Resonance Image (MRI) data during operations [5].

The GestureCam [13] system allowed a remote expert to influence the view of a novice wearing an HMD for spatial workplace collaboration. However, the technological means for superimposing more tight interaction were not available during their experiments. Many further attempts at mediated reality and augmented reality systems have been conducted over the last years; MARS, ELMO, BARS, etc [6, 11, 8]. The pose of the system is either extracted by global positioning system (GPS) and/or inertia tracking or pre-created scene elements such as markers. Interaction with the scene is with a device or with markers.

Standard approaches for vision-based hand gesture tracking employ hand segmentation and model fitting [17,21]. These algorithms require either a static camera or a static background, supply 2D information.

PHASE 1: REQUIREMENTS FOR SUPPORTING SPATIAL ANALYSIS FOR CRIME SCENE INVESTIGATORS

Structured interviews with five international experts in the area of 3D crime scene reconstruction define the requirements for support to be designed. The experts (from the USA (1), UK (1) and the Netherlands (3)), are each responsible for national crime scene investigation in their own countries, and have all had many years of experience in this domain.

The interview sessions with each expert individually start with a brief introduction to the notion of augmented reality followed by pre-defined open questions on current work practices. i.e. 'how is the current 3D reconstruction pipeline structured in your organization'. An open discussion on tool support in the future with all experts follows.

Each individual interview lasts approximately 1 hour, the open session lasts ½ hour, notes are taken of all sessions. All notes are verified by the interviewees individually.

The results of these interviews are analyzed by 2 researchers and verified with the NFI. The results show a particular interest for current challenges in spatial reconstruction and the interaction with the reconstruction data.

The interviews identify the following current challenges:

- *Time needed for reconstruction*: data capture, alignment, data clean-up, geometric modelling and analyses are manual steps.
- *Expertise* required to deploy dedicated software
- *Complexity*: Situations differ significantly.
- *Time freeze*: Data capture is often conducted once after a scene has been contaminated.

The four requirements (R1-R4) for the support to be designed, as discussed with the experts in the open discussion at the end of the interviews are:

(R1) *Contactless augmentation alignment (no markers on the crime scene):* The first investigator whom arrives on a crime scene has to keep the crime scene as untouched as possible. Technology that involves preparing the scene is therefore unacceptable.

(R2) *Remote connection to and collaboration with experts:* Expert crime scene investigators are a scarce resource and are not often available at location on request. Setting up a remote connection to guide a novice investigator through the crime scene and to collaboratively analyze the crime scene has the potential improve the investigation quality.

(R3) *Bare hands gestures for user interface operation:* The hands of the CSIs have to be free to physically interact with the crime scene when needed, e.g. to secure evidence, open doors, climb, etc. Additional hardware such as data gloves or physically touching an interface such as a mobile device is not acceptable.

(R4) *Lightweight head-mounted display (HMD):* It became clear that the investigators whom arrive first on the crime scene currently carry a digital camera. Weight and ease of use are important design criteria. Experts would like those close to a pair of glasses.

In conclusion, the experts agree that the reconstruction process needs to be more accurate, simpler and repeatable. Furthermore, there are important restrictions on the mediated reality support to be designed.

PHASE 2: MOCK-UP DESIGN

The first mediated reality collaborative support system is designed to meet the requirements identified in the first phase of design. In the mock-up design the emphasis is on marker less tracking, hand gesture interfacing and a lightweight HMD.

The mock-up consists of a off-the-shelf video HMD (cf. Figure 2) with strapped-on webcams running an adapted version of PTAM [12] and a color based hand tracker relying on colored finger caps. Collaboration is supported by cloning the HMD's view on a desktop.

Figure 2 Mock-up HMD Design

PHASE 3: MOCK-UP EVALUATION

The third phase of design entails evaluation by practitioners, practicing NFI and Police crime scene investigators. The mock-up was demonstrated in two sessions, each 1,5 hour long, each with 30 practitioners. The main goal of the sessions is to acquire early feedback from potential users on the system design.

To this purpose the practitioners are asked to evaluate the design of the mock-up, reflecting on fulfillment of the initial requirements, the capabilities, usability, and work practice.

In our mock-up, the tools are organized according to a generic personal computer program i.e. WIMP interface. The practitioners preferred a tool organization that is equivalent to their current physical workflow, i.e. not open a menu with all functions available, but only the options that are available corresponding the task at hand. With respect to design of interaction the practitioners agreed that the interface should include as little information as possible. Thus, CSIs preferred an as clean as possible interface not showing all the additional information we proposed.

With respect to capabilities, quick 3D scene mapping was considered the most important application, especially in the early phase of crime scene investigation when the crime scene is still untouched. In the orientation phase of investigation, as few investigators as possible enter the crime scene. These investigators have to notify their colleagues which can be quickly and visually updated on the scope of the crime. The temporal aspect of a degrading crime scene can therefore be captured. More direct analysis, such as; scene tagging and on the spot spatial collaboration were ranked next, especially the knowledge of previous actions of colleagues placed on a timeline received a lot of votes. Scene tagging is used to notify colleagues of important facts, to indicate change or to prepare for further investigation. Spatial collaboration refers to the interaction with colleagues on spatial problems on the crime scene itself. Crime scene investigators normally have to wait for experts to conduct spatial analyses such as; ballistics, blood pattern analysis or line of sight analysis. In conclusion, our system was positively received, but it also became apparent that investigators would not like to wear it all the time and that they would like to be able to block external interference.

PHASE 4: DESIGN OF MEDIATED REALITY SYSTEM

Figure 3 depicts the mediated reality system designed on the basis of the initial requirements and the evaluation of the mock-up by practitioners. The mediated reality system consists of 4 main components[2]: Pose estimation module (PE), Dense 3D map maker (MM), Hand tracker (HT), Networked 3D engine (NE).

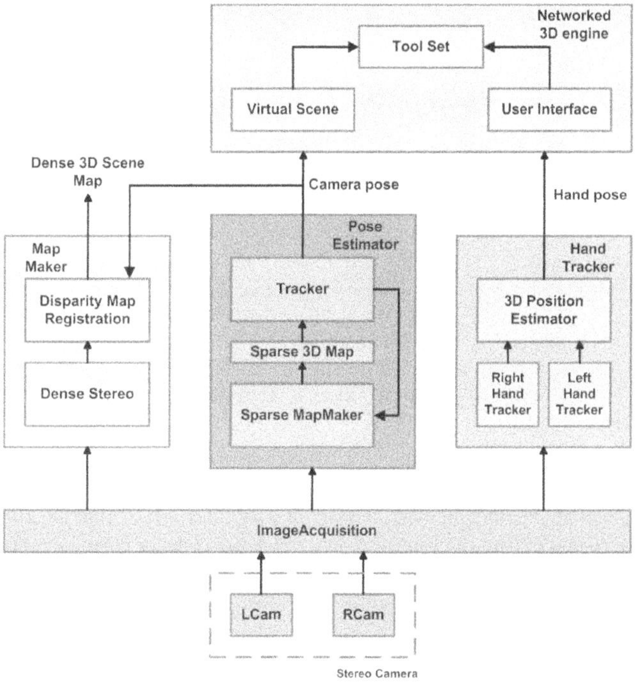

Figure 3 Overall system design

The 3D pose (position and orientation) of the user is calculated by the PE module in real time. The estimated pose is utilized by the mediated reality system to render virtual objects into the scene. The MM module uses the pose information and the stereo images to calculate a dense 3D map of the scene in near real-time. The HT module runs independently from the other modules and scans the input image for gestures. This module also has real-time

[2] Modularity allows developers to independently modify parts of the system to address new tasks or hardware setups.

performance and reflects the relative position of the hands in relation to the HMD. The NE takes care of all the rendering, networking and scene management.

The video see-through of a modified Carl Zeiss Cinemizer OLED (cf. Figure 4) for displaying content fulfills the requirement for a lightweight HMD. Two Microsoft HD-5000 webcams are stripped and mounted in front of the Cinemizer providing a full stereoscopic 720p resolution pipeline. Both cameras record at ~30hz in 720p, images are projected in our engine, and render 720p stereoscopic images to the Cinemizer. The weight of the Cinemizer is ~115 grams and the attached stereo rig ~65 grams. Thereby, addressing requirement R4. The system runs on an i7 quad core laptop with Linux. To support +25 frames per second tasks are divided over multiple cores: one core analyses both image streams, one runs the 3D engine, and one core generates depth maps.

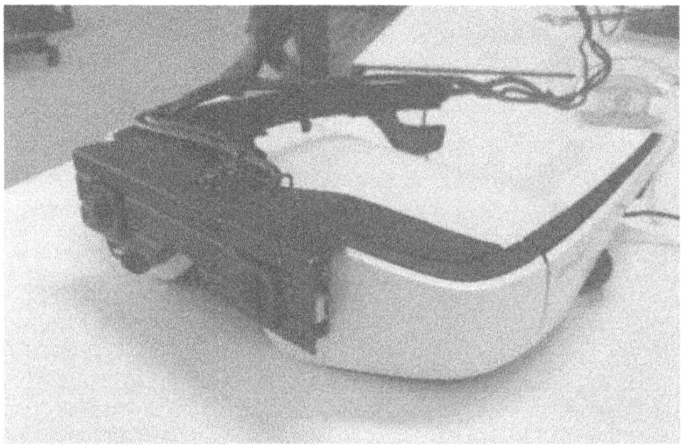

Figure 4 Head mounted display, modified Cinemizer OLED (Carl Zeiss) with two Microsoft HD-5000 webcams.

Pose Estimation (PE)

Robust real-time pose estimation is one of the most crucial parts of an augmented reality system. The 3D pose of the camera in the physical world is needed to render virtual objects correctly on required positions. A heavily modified version of PTAM (Parallel Tracking and Mapping) [12] in which a single camera setup is replaced by a stereo camera setup enables 3D natural feature matching and estimation based on natural features. Stereo camera and natural feature tracking relaxes problems that are evident in single camera setups such as lack of scale and lack of absolute 3D metric information and lack of speed (current technology supports real time processing). Natural feature tracking is less time consuming than marker tracking: features do not, need to be physically placed into a scene. Natural features are distributed across a scene, enabling accurate tracking, making occlusion is less of a problem. A sparse metric map (cf. Figure 5) of the environment is created that can be used by other modules or directly used in 3D modeling software fulfilling the requirement on contactless augmentation alignment (R1).

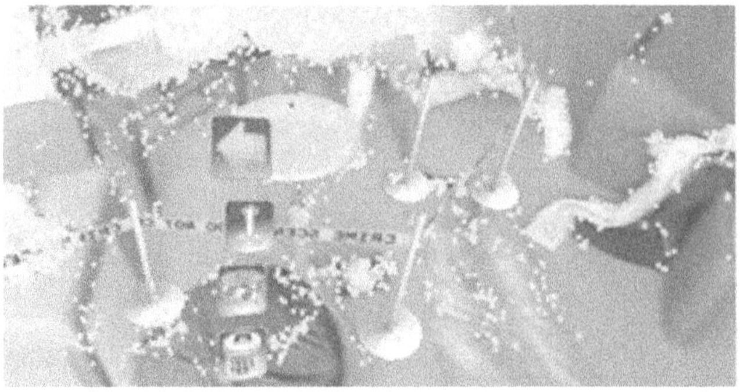

Figure 5 Sparse 3D feature map generated by the pose estimation module.

Dense 3D Map Maker (MM)

A dense 3D map of the crime scene provides a detailed copy of the crime scene enabling detailed analysis. Pose information provided by the PE module is used to construct a 3D map of the scene. A continuous stream of disparity maps are generated while the user moves around the scene. Each new disparity maps is registered (combined) using the pose information from the PE module to construct or extend the 3D map of the scene. The point clouds are used for occlusion and collision checks, and for snapping digital objects to physical locations. The dense maps are created at full 720p resolution. (Note that the PE which uses a quarter of the resolution). A dense map is generated every key frame (0,5-2 seconds) and stored as a point cloud. The time and processor friendly block matching algorithm is used to generate the depth maps, quick enough to be effectively used. Again, the requirement on contactless augmentation alignment is fulfilled (R1).

Hand Tracking (HT)

An innovative hand tracking system is the answer to support our requirement on bare hands gestures for user interface operation. This hand tracking system, utilizes our stereo camera rig to detect the hand movements in 3D. The cameras are part of the HMD and an adaptive algorithm has been designed to determine whether to rely upon on the color, disparity or on both depending on the lighting conditions. This is the core technology to fulfill the requirement on bare hand interfacing (R3).

Networked 3D Engine (NE)

The OGRE [10] render engine instruments connectivity between users at different locations. Thereby, it supports our requirement on a remote connection to and collaboration with experts (R2). The server-client architecture enables all image streams, camera track pose estimations, dense maps and interactions with the scene to be uploaded to the server, the HMD wearer and remote clients to receive their information from the server. The identity of the users and their access rights, known to the system, determine user access privileges.

Further optimization of the engine to meet the requirement R2 on collaboration, include a 3D graphical user interface (opposed to the default 2D interface), a stereoscopic pipeline to render virtual content on top off stereo image streams, and network options that enable remote spatial oriented collaboration. Both the remote expert and HMD wearer can add and remove artifacts from the scene. Their interface, however, is different, the mediated reality system wearer has stereoscopic first person view and the expert has a free 3D navigable view on the scene. Interaction between two users is synchronous and turn-based: one user must complete his/her actions before the other can perform new actions. The mode of interaction with the engine differs: the HMD wearer uses his/her hand to navigate the graphical user interface and the remote expert uses mouse and keyboard.

The mediated reality system design in phase 5 makes use of the Hand Tracker, Pose Estimation, Map Maker and Networked 3D Engine modules. It heavily relies on the rendering engine for scene management, 3D rendering and filling tasks. In more detail; the inner system consists of three parts: the virtual scene, the user interface and the tool set. The Virtual Scene is a collection of necessary 3D information for the mediated reality system. It contains the dense map of the scene as well as the virtual artifacts that CSIs have placed. All of this information is stored to be linked to a position in the real room. The virtual scene is rendered in overlay with the real crime scene, using the camera position from the PE. The user interface allows users to select and use tools, and supports some basic widgets, like menus slider bars, text labels and icons. It translates the 3D in formation from the hand tracker into click and drag events which trigger the widgets and control the CSI tools. The events are quite similar to mouse events from WIMP interfaces, except that they also contain 3D information. On the one hand, CSIs need to move their hands freely without triggering unintended events. On the other hand, gestures have to be intuitive and easy to make.

Gesture-based interaction design

To address requirement R3 on bare hand gestures our vision based hand tracking distinguishes three types of gestures: Left hand thumb-up, left hand thumb-down, and right hand thumb-down. The orientation of the hand, and the 3D position are used to both draw the interface elements and the gesture recognition.

A menu surrounding the hand appears when the left hand thumb-up is detected (cf. Figure 7). The menu sticks to the hand and is locked in space until the posture changes and the thumb points downwards options can be selected. The right hand, as a pointing device, is used to select objects in the virtual scene. Effectively, recasting is used to determine with which scene point to interact.

Figure 6 shows the gestures distinguished with the defining hand postures. A click is done by moving the left or right recognized segmented hand forward quickly, and moving it backward again. The direction of movements of the segmented hand is continuously monitored to recognize this gesture. When the pointer moves only in a forward direction, the path over which it is moving is tracked. As soon as it has moved forward, and backward more than halfway along the same path, this is registered as a click at the furthest point of the path. If anywhere in this sequence the segmented hand deviates more than a pre-defined angle from the path, the event is not recognized as a click. In this way both small and big gestures are recognized, as long as the direction of the movement is right.

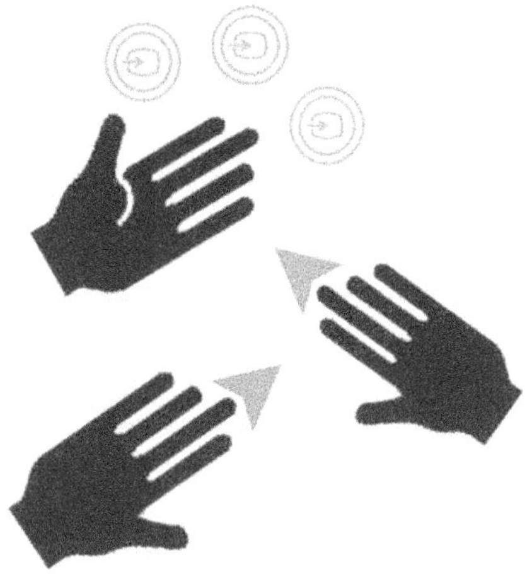

Figure 6 Types of hand postures which are recognized by the hand

Tool Set for CSI

The user interface and the virtual scene are general-purpose parts of the mediated reality system. They can be used for CSI, but also for any other mediated reality application. The Tool Set, however, needs to be tailored for the application domain. The current mediated reality system supports following tasks for CSIs (identified as requirements scene mapping in phase 3): recording the scene, placing tags, loading 3D models, bullet trajectories and placing restricted area ribbons. Figure 7 shows the corresponding menu attached to a user's hand.

The above tools are based on generic functions to store real-world data (video streams, measurements, photos), import data from other sources (photos, databases, the internet) and change the virtual scene (placing tags). By offering the above tools, we enable the collaboration between the novice on the crime scene and the guiding. Thereby, we further address our requirement (R2) on the remote collaboration with experts.

Figure 7 Graphical user interface options menu

PHASE 5: EXPERIMENTAL EVALUATION OF OUR MEDIATED REALITY SYSTEM FOR COLLABORATION

This section focuses on the experimental evaluation of the extent to which our mediated reality system supports collaborative spatial analysis on location, i.e. allowing the spatial specialist to be virtually there and collaborate with an investigator on location. Communication processes such as exchange of knowledge relevant for the task at hand, argumentation processes, coordination processes and motivational processes, rely on symmetric individual contributions for collaboration.

Communication processes are important to ensure a common ground within a group. Establishment of common ground in collaborative processes, in which co-workers mutually establish what they know, is key to our proposed system. Important characteristics of collocated synchronous interactions are assumed to support grounding. [2]. Multimodal channels for communication enable multiple ways to convey complex messages and provide redundancy. Furthermore, shared local context allows for mutual understanding. The balance in participants' roles in communication, group management and task management is considered as a good indicator in collaboration. Meier and Spada [21] consider that the quality in collaboration for learning is linked to the symmetry of the interaction. This position is leading to the evaluation of our system.

Technology supported collaboration is rarely tested in a multidimensional and generic way. Evaluation of our mediated reality system that provides novel additional communication possibilities requires an evaluation method that measures a broad range of collaboration aspects. Spada et al.'s [20] evaluation method for computer supported collaborative learning (CSCL) tools fulfills the bill. This method compares and assesses collaboration in collaborative learning tasks along nine qualitatively defined dimensions covering five aspects of a collaboration process, namely: communication, joint information processing, coordination, interpersonal relationship and motivation. Burkhardt et al. [2] claim that the indicators exploited by observers in Spada et al.'s approach to assess collaboration are underspecified. Burkhardt et al.'s method relies on the subjective evaluation of 7 dimensions (cf. Table 1) on a 5-grade Likert-like scale supported with a training session [2]. Burkhardt et al.'s approach, however, neglects to capture the observables from the collaborative situation (a bird's eye view), making it difficult to track back assessment value to the original data.

Adapting Burkhardt et al.'s assessment procedure to make observable indicators underlying the evaluation explicit is the approach taken to evaluate our mediated reality system.

Dimensions	Definition	Indicators
1. Fluidity of collaboration	It assesses the management of verbal turns, of actions (tool use) and of attention orientation.	Fluidity of verbal turns, Fluidity of tools use (style, menu), Coherency of attention orientation
2. Sustaining mutual understanding	It assesses the grounding processes concerning the artefact (problem, solutions), the investigators actions and the state of the mediated reality disposal (e.g., activated functions).	Mutual understanding of the state of the analysis, Mutual understanding of the actions in progress and next actions, Mutual understanding of the state of the system (active functions, open documents)
3. Information exchanges for problem solving	It assesses analysis ideas pooling, refinement of ideas and coherency of ideas.	Generation of analysis ideas (problem, solutions, past cases, constraints), Refinement of analysis ideas, Coherency and follow up of ideas
4. Argumen-tation and reaching consensus	It assesses whether or not there is argumentation and decision taken on common consensus.	Criticisms and argumentation, Checking solutions adequacy with analysis constraints, Common decision taking
5. Task and time management	It assesses the planning (e.g. task allocation) and time management.	Work planning, Task division, Distribution and management of tasks interdependencies, Time management
6. Cooperative orientation	It assesses the balance of contribution of the actors in analysis, planning, and in verbal and graphical actions.	Symmetry of verbal contributions, Symmetry of use of graphical tools, Symmetry in task management, Symmetry in analysis choices
7. Individual task orientation	It assesses, for each contributor, its motivation (marks of interest in the collaboration),	Showing up motivation and encouraging others motivation, Constancy of effort put in the task, Attention orientation in

	implication and involvement (attention orientation).	relation with the analysis task

Table 1 Dimensions and indicators of our method, adopted from Burkhardt et al. [2]

Our method is based on Burkhardt et al. [2] which again is based on Spada et al.'s [20] and extends the assessment procedure with experts observing and evaluating the collaboration [2]. The method targets a design task but is general enough to be adapted to our spatial analysis task, which uses the dimensions from Table 1. The questions with positive valence and negative valence are balanced for each indicator. With respect to a good spatial analysis, the questions distinguish "good" collaboration and "low quality" collaboration. An example positive question related to dimension 3 "Information exchanges for problem solving": Do the investigators improve the spatial analysis by having their shared ideas available, pooled and coherent? Or the negative version: Is there miscommunication because refinement during the analysis takes place and is pooled? In total 28 questions are formulated for the seven dimensions. The questions are formulated to fit the spatial analysis task. The same set of questions is posed to the layman, the expert and the observers. Our interest, of course, is to see if there is coherence on the questions for all participants and what the qualitative interviews of the observers would bring. Furthermore, all interaction with the system is logged for further analysis, i.e. video, interpretation of the system and results of the spatial analysis.

THE EXPERIMENT

A staged crime scene at the NFI's Lab is the setting for our experiment. The Lab itself is designed to train investigators in as realistic as possible scenarios.

The crime scene

Two separated rooms are used for the experiment, 1) a room in which the expert resides monitored by the observers (cf. Figure 8) and 2) a physical crime scene for the wearer of the HMD (cf. Figure 1).

The subjects

In total, 3 observers, one expert and 1 layman with only limited background in CSI participate in the experiment.

The set-up

The layman has the mediated reality Head Mounted Device in room 2. The expert is positioned behind a large projector screen in room 1 where he can see the video stream from the head mounted device, the 3D model being created by the vision tracker and the interactive elements put there either by himself using a generic keyboard and mouse, or by the layman using our gesture-based interface. The expert and the novice can communicate via an audio channel which was established using voice over IP. From behind the expert, the observers can see both the actions from the experts as well as from the layman through the projection.

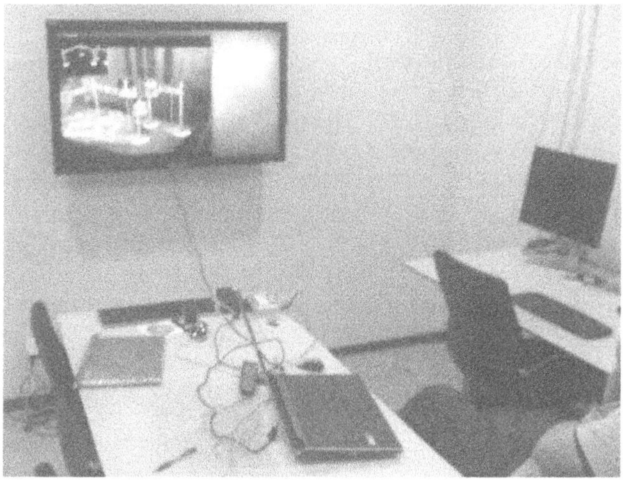

Figure 8 Tagged crime scene viewed by the observer

The observers

The observers are familiar with crime scene investigation and work at the NFI. Their age is between 25 and 55. They are not familiar with the capabilities of our Mediated Reality system.

Experimental Procedure

The layman, facilitated by the expert, conducts 3 spatial tasks:

1. Tagging a specific part of the scene with information tags;
2. Using barrier tape and poles to spatially secure the body in the crime scene;
3. A bullet trajectory analysis with ricochet, from the body to the side wall bounced by the back wall.

The tasks are based on real world spatial problems and would normally be conducted either with physical means or otherwise with 3D offline reconstructions. They were created and designed during interactive sessions with crime scene investigators and validated with experts described earlier in this paper.

The experiment is introduced by showing how the system works, a small trial period and the experiment itself. After the experiment, the observers are requested to answer the questionnaire and conduct a group discussion on the seven collaboration dimensions in the questionnaire. The total time of the experiment and the group discussion is approximately two hours.

During the experiment, the video streams, the interactions of the users with the system and the audio are logged. After the experiment, the seven dimension collaboration questionnaires are used to discuss the experiment with the observers, the expert and the layman.

EVALUATION RESULTS

The results of our experiment are presented along the seven collaboration dimensions (cf. Table 1).

Fluidity of collaboration

One of the first quotes from an expert is: "what's the protocol for interaction?" From his perspective, there is no clear protocol in place to support the fluidity of verbal turns except listening to the audio line. Nevertheless the attention of both the expert as well as the layman is rated high, the gaze of the layman perfectly guides the shared focus. One observer notes: "having the expert present in the scene as a virtual camera with tracked hands would give him an identity in the scene which I currently miss". The actions themselves are coordinated well and the verbal communication dominates the actions.

The expert view consists of the HMD wearer view and a free camera view. The free camera can be placed anywhere in the scene and then shows the scene from this perspective. Experts can select one of these views as their main view. The screen in Figure 7, e.g., shows the HMD wearer view as the main view while the free camera view is shown in small in the top-left corner. The preference of the remote expert is to follow the view of the HMD wearer and to not focus on the free camera. Experts expressed the fact that with the free camera view the connection between them and the lay investigator is too decoupled.

Sustaining mutual understanding

All participants strongly agree that our system supports mutual understanding. The actions are visible to both participants and the visual feedback provide a clear mutual understanding of the state of the analysis. Furthermore, our system provides feedback on active and non-active items that are visible to the users of the system. One remark from the observers is that the expert had a better overview due to the free camera view, i.e. when needed he is able to virtually walk around. But as mentioned before, the expert preferred the HMD wearer view. In general, we observed that very few communication was needed to acquire mutual understanding.

Information exchange for problem solving

The limited tasks did not provide a clear understanding of this dimension. The team members jointly followed up on their ideas but no clear problem solving was involved in the tasks. Information exchange was very picture oriented. i.e. "behind the table", "don't cross the uttermost right ribbon", "if you look slightly to the left", etc.

Argumentation and reaching consensus

Again, all participants strongly agree that our system supports argumentation and reaching consensus. The strong visual feedback quickly leads to consensus, as it supports instant hypothesis testing to rule out other possibilities. The observers agree that the instant visual feedback on the state of the spatial analysis is convincing. Disagreement on the placement of object was settled by getting a better angle on the problem location real time. When we ask the expert why he so readily agrees he replies: 'there is not much arguing about something you can both see'.

Task and time management

The task division and planning naturally follows from the different tasks in the experiment. All participants agree on this dimension. During the second task the expert, e.g., simultaneously works on the barrier tapes and poles. According to the observers this is really interesting, as this clearly shows how one can jointly work on a scene. To not collide in each other's work one starts at the back and the other in the front just as if both are physically in the room.

One observer remarked that our mediated reality system probably influences the entire investigation sequence (chain). Quote 'when the process is this fast, even the judge will probably want to use the data as soon as it is available' On average a 3D reconstruction from a crime scene takes a few weeks. Our system in comparison reduces this time tremendously.

Cooperative orientation

After the initial discussion on the interaction protocol, there is clearly symmetry in the experiment. The expert remarks that the same visual focus aligns their cooperative effort. Although the layman remarks that knowing that somebody can see exactly what you see and not vice versa put some stress on the interaction relation. However, all vote for a "strong agree" on this dimension.

Individual task orientation

Both participants motivate each other during the analysis. All participants rate this high. Again, the layman remark that being observed all the time results in some stress.

Further topics

During the interviews many other topics surface that are not directly related to the above dimensions but are nevertheless interesting for understanding collaboration in mediated reality.

Privacy

Within the experiment, the privacy of the HMD wearer turned out to be a major concern. Literally every move is recorded, if someone missed something it can be retraced, etc. One investigator remarked: 'I consider this somewhat privacy intruding but based on our car GPS they know where we are all the time which took some getting-used-to too'. Another one remarked: 'Some specialist teams already have mounted cameras specifically used for their protection'. Compared to the above, our system not only records the investigation but also allows someone else to look at what you do from a remote location. This was considered somewhat eerie.

A lot of the crime scene investigators that are the first to arrive on a crime scene handle the case from experience.

When they are asked to write a report about their on-going investigation they are generally incomplete in their reporting (according to the observers). Quote "when they are asked to write about researching a certain trace they will tell you but never write that down". They prefer not to be bothered with desk work and the team has to trust their experience. Recording their activity can be either positive or negative. When they do not have to write everything down, every move is monitored. If the recording is perceived as a tool to monitor their work, it will encounter resistance. According to the observers, only with new recruits it will be possible to change the way of working.

Furthermore, because our research is aimed at the "pre-assessment on location", we do not specifically focus on investigators such as judges and court options. According to the observers a judge would appreciate the option to review the research of an investigator, the record of an investigation. Again privacy is at stake here but according to the observers it may improve the quality of the research in the end.

Virtual Presence

During our experiment it became clear that the presence of the expert is not experienced. In particular, when the expert creates or moves objects in the scene without verbal indications, disconnect between both participants occurs. There is a need to raise collaboration awareness to indicate the status of the other or where he is looking at, etc? Kuzuoka et al. [13] address this by depicting the camera asleep to show that nobody is watching. Our mediated reality system supports a whole new range of interaction and indicates a need for new mechanisms to achieve virtual presence.

Remote Presence

Another side of presence is related to the remote expert. Kallinikos [9] argues that 'while a closed circuit TV (CCTV) camera can show events in distant parts of the city it can never replace the sense of being there'. Sørensen and Pica [19] explain that there is devaluation on the natural communication. Within our experiment the experts also remark that some investigators still would like to see the location with their own eyes. In our system the virtualized interaction results in only only one or two predominant human senses Kallinikos [9]. Further experiments are needed to explore how to support experts in their presence on the location and to understand what they miss when they use our mediated reality system with respect to be physically there?

Making up reality

Latour [14] argues that a great deal of work goes into the construction of what he terms immutable mobiles: '[...] you have to invent objects which have the properties of being mobile but also immutable, presentable, readable and combinable with one another, [...]' One of the observers is also crime scene investigation trainer and liked to know if it was possible to setup a scenario, not for real investigation but for pure training purposes. He, e.g., asked: "can you inflict virtual injury on a dummy or actor?" Looking at the capabilities of the movie industry it seems possible, however, that it is currently still a manual procedure that uses pre-scanned objects, high dynamic range imagery and considerable render time. With the current system virtual objects stand out from real objects.

CONCLUSION

This paper presents a novel mediated reality system that builds a 3D map of the environment in real-time, allows remote users to virtually join and interact together in shared augmented space with the wearer of the HMD, and uses bare hand gestures to operate the 3D multi-touch user interface. The mediated reality system designed and developed within this project, together with experts in the field and the NFI, explores novel technologies to improve crime scene investigation. The resulting mediated reality system supports a lightweight head-mounted display (HMD), contactless augmentation alignment, and a remote connection to and collaboration with expert crime scene investigators.

Evaluation of the use of the mediated reality system on collaboration between an expert and a layman, is based on 7 dimensions adapted from Burkhardt.

The results show a need for more support to identify whose turn it is and who wants the next turn, etc. The demands are similar to other teleconferencing systems that use floor control mechanisms to avoid conflicts or establish an interaction protocol [3]. Additionally, the results show the need to represent the expert in the scene to increase the awareness of working in a team and to counterbalance the feeling of being observed.. Knowing the expert's focus and current activity could possibly help to overcome this issue. Whether traditional patterns for computer-mediated interaction [18] support awareness in mediated reality or rather new awareness forms need to be designed, is future research.

In conclusion, our approach to remote spatial interaction with the physical scene tackles current issues in crime scene investigation, and identifies needs for further research. The communication support of our current system needs further thought, especially the virtual presence of the expert in relation to the layman, privacy and security. One option that is currently being explored is to integrate a next version of our system in a pilot system currently being deployed by the Dutch Police in which officers are equipped with video monitoring equipment with strongly encrypted video streams. Security is a requirement for future system design.

On the technical side, making better use of an inertia tracker in conjunction with our vision tracker would hopefully circumvent the weakness of not being able to walk around quickly or large distances. Furthermore the depth maps our system generates are currently not merged, fusing the maps and creating a surface model probably results in easier to use and more precise data. Recognizing more complex hand gestures would enable more complicated interaction with the scene, upscaling the resolution with faster algorithms are therefore high on the list. One possibility to support walking more freely would be to port our algorithms to a more mobile platform, something that can be worn on a belt.

ACKNOWLEDGMENTS

Funded by Pieken in de Delta, Provincie Zuid-Holland, Gemeente Den Haag. www.csithehague.com

REFERENCES

1. R. Azuma, A Survey of Augmented Reality. Presence 6, Vol 4, 355-385, 1997
2. J. Burkhardt, F. Détienne, A. Hébert, L. Perron, S. Safin, P. Leclercq, An approach to assess the quality of collaboration in technology-mediated design situation, European Conference on Cognitive Ergonomics: Designing beyond the Product - Understanding Activity and User Experience in Ubiquitous Environments, 1-9, 2009
3. H. Dommel, and J.J. Garcia-Luna-Aceves, Floor control for multimedia conferencing and collaboration, Journal of Multimedia Systems, Vol. 5, 23-38, 1997
4. E. Foxlin, Y Altshuler, L. Naimark, M. Harrington. FlightTracker: A Novel Optical/Inertial Tracker for Cockpit Enhanced Vision. Proceedings of the 3rd IEEE/ACM International Symposium on Mixed and Augmented Reality, p. 212-221, 2004
5. H. Fuchs, M. Livingston, R, Raskar. Augmented Reality Visualization for Laparoscopic Surgery. Proceedings of the First International Conference on Medical Image Computing and Computer-Assisted Intervention, 934-943, 1998
6. T. Höllerer, S. Feiner, T. Terauchi, G. Rashid, D. Hallaway, Exploring MARS: Developing Indoor and Outdoor User Interfaces to a Mobile Augmented Reality System, Computers and Graphics, 23(6), Elsevier Publishers, 779-785, 1999
7. B. Jenkins, Laserscanning for forensic investigation, Business and technology trends in capturing and managing existing-conditions data for engineering/construction/operations, Spar Point Research LLC, Vol 3, No 21, 2005
8. S. Julier, Y. Baillot, M. Lanzagorta, D. Brown, L. Rosenblum. BARS: Battlefield Augmented Reality System, In NATO Symposium on Information Processing Techniques for Military Systems, 9-11, 2000
9. J. Kallinikos, The age of flexibility. Sweden: Academia Adapta, 2001
10. F. Kerger, OGRE 3D 1.7 Beginner's Guide, Packt Publishing, 2010
11. K. Kiyokawa, Y. Kurata, H, Ohno. ELMO: A Head Mount Display for Real-time Image Synthesis, ACM SIGGRAPH, 177-178, 2001
12. G. Klein, D. Murray, Parallel Tracking and Mapping for Small AR Workspaces, In Proc. International Symposium on Mixed and Augmented Reality, 225-234, 2007
13. Kuzuoka, H., T. Kosuge, GestureCam: Platform for Augmented Reality Based Collaboration International Conference on Artificial Reality and Telexistence, 1994
14. B. Latour, B. Visualisation and Cognition: Drawing Things Together, Culture Technique 14: 1-32, 1985
15. S. Mann, W. Barfield. Introduction to Mediated Reality, International Journal of Human-Computer Interaction, 205-208, 2003
16. P. K. Manning, The Technology of Policing: Crime Mapping, Information Technology, and the Rationality of Crime Control. New York University Press, 2008
17. M. Schlattman and R. Klein. Simultaneous 4 gestures 6 DOF real-time two-hand tracking without any markers. In Proc. VRST 2007, 39-42, 2007
18. T. Schümmer, and S. Lukosch, Patterns for Computer-Mediated Interaction, John Wiley & Sons, Ltd. 2007
19. C. Sørensen and D. Pica, Tales from the police: Rhythms of interaction with mobile technologies. Information and Organization, Elsevier Ltd. 15:125-149, 2005
20. Spada, H., Meier, A., Rummel, N., and Hauser, S. 2005. A new method to assess the quality of collaborative process in CSCL. In Proceedings of Computer Supported Collaborative Learning, 622-631, 2005
21. R. Y. Wang and J. Popovic. Real-time hand-tracking with a color glove. ACM Transactions on Graphics, 28(3), 2009

Social Coding in GitHub: Transparency and Collaboration in an Open Software Repository

Laura Dabbish, Colleen Stuart, Jason Tsay, Jim Herbsleb
School of Computer Science and Center for the Future of Work, Heinz College
Carnegie Mellon University
5000 Forbes Ave., Pittsburgh, PA 15213
{dabbish, hcstuart, jtsay, jdh}@cs.cmu.edu

ABSTRACT
Social applications on the web let users track and follow the activities of a large number of others regardless of location or affiliation. There is a potential for this transparency to radically improve collaboration and learning in complex knowledge-based activities. Based on a series of in-depth interviews with central and peripheral GitHub users, we examined the value of transparency for large-scale distributed collaborations and communities of practice. We find that people make a surprisingly rich set of social inferences from the networked activity information in GitHub, such as inferring someone else's technical goals and vision when they edit code, or guessing which of several similar projects has the best chance of thriving in the long term. Users combine these inferences into effective strategies for coordinating work, advancing technical skills and managing their reputation.

Author Keywords
Transparency; awareness; coordination; collaboration; open source software development; social computing.

ACM Classification Keywords
H5.3. Information interfaces and presentation (e.g., HCI): Group and organization interfaces.

General Terms
Human Factors; Design.

INTRODUCTION
The internet has become increasingly social in the last ten to fifteen years, but the productivity implications of these changes remain unclear. We can track a person's moment-by-moment status updates on Facebook, location on Foursquare, and updates on Twitter, blogs, and wikis. These applications all have a common set of important functionality. Users can articulate an interest network of people or things by defining a set of individuals or artifacts (like blogs or RSS feeds) to pay attention to. In doing so, users immediately subscribe to a stream of events and actions other individuals take. Thus the social web provides an unprecedented level of transparency in the form of visibility of others' actions on public or shared artifacts. The question remains, however, what benefits this transparency provides, particularly in the large scale (i.e. across a community).

Previous work on awareness has explored the value of activity information for small groups [7, 12]. This work has found that notifying members of actions on shared artifacts helps them maintain mental models of others activities [11] and avoid potential coordination conflicts [20]. However, activity awareness has largely been examined in the context of well-defined small groups within organizations. Online, individuals participate in large-scale, ill-defined communities that often have hundreds if not thousands of members. Transparency of others' actions in this type of setting may have very different benefits as a function of the larger scale and the fact that interactions are no longer embedded in an organizational context.

Visible cues of others' behavior on a social website are likely to support a variety of interpretations about their motivations and the community more generally. People are social creatures and make inferences about others from what they observe (e.g., [27]). Surfacing information about people's actions on artifacts is no longer a technological challenge. What is more interesting, and less understood, is what people are able to infer from such a collection of information, and how these inferences help them carry out their collective work. In this research we were interested in the collaborative utility of activity transparency in a large community engaged in knowledge-based work. We address the following two research questions to advance our understanding of transparency in online social sites:

(1) *What inferences do people make when transparency is integrated into a web-based workspace?*

(2) *What is the value of transparency for collaboration in knowledge-based work?*

In order to address these questions, we examined a successful social site called GitHub (GitHub.com), a code-hosting repository based on the Git version control system. GitHub is an iconic example of a knowledge-based workspace. This site integrates a number of social features that make unique information about users and their activities visible within and across open source software projects. We interviewed light and heavy users of the site, having them walk us through a typical session and describing their activity within projects. We found that they made a rich set of inferences from the visible information, such as inferring someone's technical goals based on actions on code. Developers combined these inferences into effective strategies for coordinating projects, advancing their technical skills and managing their reputation. In the next sections we consider related research, describe the GitHub context and our study, present the results of our interviews, and finally discuss implications of our findings.

THE VALUE OF AWARENESS

Previous work on collaboration and awareness suggests that providing visibility of actions on shared artifacts supports cooperative work in a variety of ways. More recent work has shown the utility of social tools and systems for relationship management in the workplace. However, these literatures have not yet articulated the value of integrating social networking functionality with activity awareness.

Collaboration and awareness

Collaborators who are physically collocated have some level of awareness of each other's activities because of frequent opportunities for interaction [17, 24]. The affordances of collocation, documented through careful field study of software developers [14, 24] and other knowledge-based workers include: overhearing, shared visual space, and shared memory of discussion around artifacts [11, 17, 24]. These affordances support awareness of others' work state and expertise, both useful for coordinated action in collaborative projects [2, 12, 17].

Awareness systems attempt to provide distributed collaborators with the same type of mutual knowledge [11]. These systems have taken various forms with a variety of foci, including informal social awareness to support casual interaction [11], structural awareness of group member roles and status, and workspace awareness of actions on shared artifacts [2, 12, 18]. The theory of social translucence suggests these types of awareness systems are useful because they can make socially significant information visible, support awareness of collaborators' behavior, and make the viewer accountable for that information [8].

For the most part, however, collaborative awareness tools have been designed for and evaluated within small groups. It is unclear to what extent they scale across a wider range. Previous work on awareness and software development has indicated a tradeoff between specific awareness of a very small set of developer actions, versus general awareness across a project as a whole, noting the effort required to proactively provide status information (e.g. [13]).

In addition, collaborative awareness systems have typically utilized momentary notification of the most recent activity as opposed to a history of actions on shared artifacts. Only a handful of systems have attempted to provide visualizations of activity over long periods of time (e.g. history flow system which visualizes collaborator edits to Wikipedia articles [26]). We do not yet understand how these types of activity traces influence collaborative action, particularly in online production settings like Wikipedia where hundreds or thousands of collaborators can be involved on an article.

Social computing and software development

Social computing technologies such as micro-blogging, activity feeds, and social annotations, facilitate lightweight interactive information sharing within the web browser. Social computing technologies shift the focus of interaction to individual contributors and their activities with electronic artifacts. Individuals articulate their interests, likes and dislikes, as well as their social network [4]. When combined with information visualization techniques, these tools may help individuals make sense of activity and contribution on a much wider scale.

Previous work on social media for work purposes has shown that systems like Facebook and LinkedIn are useful for maintaining weak tie relationships and bridging organizational boundaries [6, 21]. And organization internal social networking sites like Beehive in IBM support similar types of boundary spanning activities in an organization [6]. At the same time, these systems have been integrated with work artifacts in a limited way (e.g. bookmarks in [16]).

When social computing technologies are used in a software development context, there is an opportunity to leverage articulated social networks and observed code-related activity simultaneously to support the type of awareness previous only available to collocated teams (e.g. in systems like [9, 18, 19]). Software engineering is only beginning to make exploratory use of social computing technologies to enhance collaboration. For example, tagging [22], searchable graphs of heuristically linked artifacts [3], and workspace awareness [9, 18, 19] have shown some promise for supporting coordination in software development. However, the utility of these technologies has been examined in isolation from the rich ecology of open software development [23]. We know relatively little about how developers actually adopt and adapt these tools in the process of their work, and when and how they improve coordination and performance.

METHOD

Research Setting

In order to address our research questions, we examined collaboration among users of a large, open source software hosting service GitHub [10]. GitHub provides a set of "social coding" tools built around the Git version control system (http://git-scm.com/) and incorporates social functionality that makes a developer's identity and activities visible to other users. The GitHub site is unique in that it makes user identities, internal project artifacts and actions on them publicly visible across a wide-community.

People
On the GitHub site, developers create profiles that can be optionally populated with identifying information including a gravatar (an image representing them throughout the site), their name, email address, organization, location, and webpage. A developer's profile is visible to other users and displays all the repositories that person is working on and a list of their latest activities on the site (see Figure 1).

Code Artifacts
GitHub currently hosts over one million code repositories, and has 340,000 registered contributors [10]. While a majority of the projects on GitHub are single-developer code dumps, many are active multi-developer projects of significant scale that have been running for some time. Each repository on GitHub has a dedicated project page that hosts the source code files, commit history, open issues, and other data associated with the project. Developers can create permanent URLs to link to specific lines within a code file. This functionality allows information about artifacts within the site to flow outside of the GitHub community to the web at large.

Actions
Actions in GitHub occur when a person changes an artifact or interacts with another person through the site. These actions can be code-related, communication, or subscription. Actions on code or associated with code include committing, forking and submitting a pull request. Project owners can make *commits*, i.e. changes to the code, by directly modifying the contents of code files. Developers without commit-rights to a project must fork a project, creating a personal copy of the code that they can change freely. They can then submit some or all of the changes to the original project by issuing a pull request. The project owner or another member with commit rights can then merge in their changes. Developers can also communicate around code-related actions by submitting a comment on a commit, an issue, or a pull request.

The record of all action information combined with user subscription allows activity updates to flow across the site. Subscription actions include *following* and *watching*. Developers can 'follow' other developers and 'watch' other repositories, subscribing them to a feed of actions and communications from those developers or projects (Figure 2) with frequent updates for active projects.

Actions on artifacts also become artifacts themselves, as the history of user actions on code artifacts is recorded over time. The feed presents a recent history of following, watching, commit, issues, pull requests, and comment actions. Visualizations on the site, such as the network view, provide access to the history of commits over time across all forks of a particular project (see Figure 3).

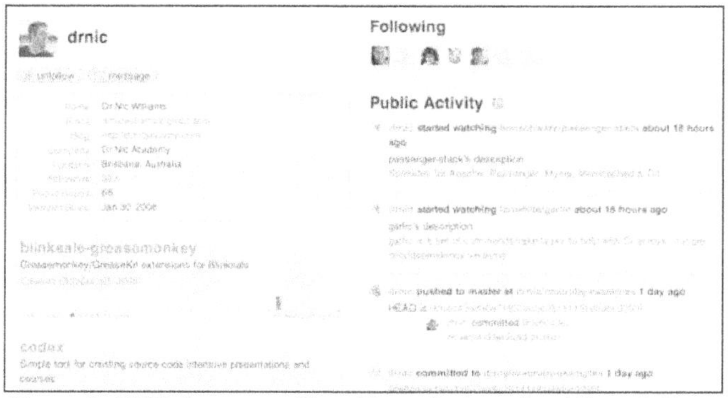

Figure 1. GitHub user profile with projects and public activity

Figure 2. Feed of actions on code artifacts

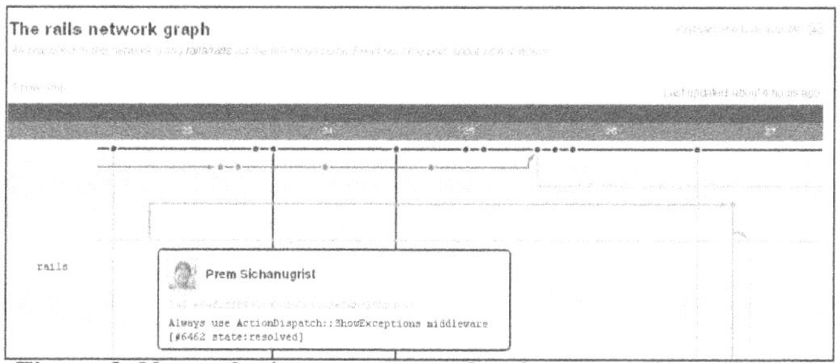

Figure 3. Network view: sequence of actions on code artifacts

To get a sense of how visible information on GitHub influenced the nature of collaboration and interaction, we interviewed a set of developers who use GitHub. We first examined the types of inferences they made based on the visible information in the site, and next examined what types of higher-level activities these inferences supported.

Data Collection
We conducted a series of semi-structured interviews with 24 GitHub users. Our goal in these interviews was to document and understand in more detail the different ways GitHub functionality was used by our participants. We solicited participants via email and conducted our interviews in person or via phone. Participants were chosen for equal representation across peripheral and heavy users (with greater than 80 watchers on at least one of their OSS projects). This was done because we thought that serious and hobby users might have different purposes and strategies, and very different information loads. Table 1 summarizes the 24 participants in our sample.

	Hobbyist	Work use: non-SW org	Work use: SW org
Peripheral users	P2, P7, P10, P18, P23	P6, P12, P16, P24	P5, P17
Heavy users	P11, P15, P21, P22	P3, P4, P9, P14, P19	P1, P8, P13, P20

Table 1. Summary of interview participants.

Participants were asked to walk us through their last session on GitHub, describing how they interpreted information displayed on the site as they managed their projects, and interacted with other users' projects. Remote participants shared their screen during the interview using Adobe Connect so we could ask specific questions about data on the site and users could demonstrate their activities on the site. Interviews lasted approximately 45 minutes to one hour. These interviews were then transcribed verbatim to support further analysis. The interviews, videos and field notes supported our analysis process.

Data analysis

We applied a grounded approach to analyze the transparency related inferences in our interview responses [5]. We first identified instances of these types of inferences in five interview transcripts. For each example analyzed, we identified what information was made visible by the GitHub system, what inferences the participant was making based on that information, and the associated higher-level goal. We then conducted open coding on these responses, comparing each instance with previously examined examples and grouping examples that were conceptually similar. This process revealed categories of transparency related inferences and higher level behaviors these inferences supported. We used this first set of categories to code the remaining interviews, revealing additional categories and refining our original coding scheme to represent the dataset as a whole. We repeatedly discussed the codes and transcripts in a highly collaborative and iterative process. We continued this process until the interviews no longer revealed new behaviors not captured in our existing set of categories (theoretical saturation).

RESULTS

Our analysis revealed that individuals made a rich set of inferences based on information on GitHub. These inferences were a function of four sets of visible cues (summarized in Table 2).

Recency, volume, and location of actions signaling commitment and interests

As with other low-cost hosting sites, GitHub has a mix of projects that are little more than code dumps and serious projects that continue to receive attention and effort. There is also a mix of hobbyists who make occasional contributions and move on, and dedicated developers who provide project stewardship over the longer term. Our interviewees often used the recency and volume of activity as a signal of commitment or investment at the individual and project level.

Visible information about other developers' actions influenced perceptions of their commitment and general interests. Recent activity gave a sense of the level of investment in a project. The feed of developer actions across projects helped other developers infer their current interests. One respondent described following a friend to stay up to date on what he was up to through his commits (P16). The amount of commits to a single project signaled commitment or investment to that project, while the type of commits signaled interest in different aspects of the project.

Visible Cues	Social Inferences	Representative Quote
Recency and volume of activity	Interest and level of commitment	*"this guy on Mongoid is just -- a machine, he just keeps cranking out code." (P23)*
Sequence of actions over time	Intention behind action	*"Commits tell a story. Convey direction you are trying to go with the code ... revealing what you want to do." (P13)*
Attention to artifacts and people	Importance to community	*"The number of people watching a project or people interested in the project, obviously it's a better project than versus something that has no one else interested in it." (P17)*
Detailed information about an action	Personal relevance and impact	*"If there was something [in the feed] that would preclude a feature that I would want it would give me a chance to add input to it." (P4)*

Table 2. Visible cues and the social inferences they generated.

Recent activity signaling project liveness and maintenance

As with many open source hosting sites, dead and abandoned projects greatly outnumber live ones that people continue to contribute and pay attention to. It can be tedious to figure out which are which, yet it is important to do so, since one does not want to adopt or contribute to a dead or dying project. In GitHub, developers described getting a sense of how 'live' or active a project was by the amount of commit events showing up in their feed.

> *"Commit activity in the feeds shows that the project is alive, that people are still adding code."* (P16)

Users also relied on historical activity to make inferences about how well the project was managed and maintained. Lots of open pull requests indicated that an owner was not particularly conscientious in dealing with people external to the project, since each open pull request indicates an offer of code that is being ignored rather than accepted, rejected or commented upon (P11).

Sequence of actions conveying meaning

Visible actions on artifacts carried meaning, often as a function of their sequence, or ordering with respect to other actions. When considering the actions of an individual developer, they signaled intentions, competence and experience. In the project context, actions on code and who carried them out allowed others to make inferences about the structure of the project and collaborator roles.

Commits conveying developer intention

At the lowest level, commit information connected with other commits, comments, or issues conveyed meaning or intention behind actions. Several respondents were able to look at a sequence of commits and infer what the developer was trying to accomplish with their changes (e.g. P1, P13, P9, P21, P11). Linking commits and issues similarly communicated the reasoning behind a change to the code.

History of activity signaling competence

At the developer level, information about past commits, number of projects created (versus forked), and activity in those projects all fed into perceptions of developer skill. Several respondents noted that GitHub profiles now act as a portfolio of work and factor into the hiring process at many companies (P3, P9, P13, P8, P17), in part because they provide a sense of a developer's work style and pace.

History of activity signaling project structure and roles

Developers also seemed able to use the history of actions on code to make sense of a project's evolution over time or history. The active public record of who contributed what aspects of the code when, meant developers were able to describe how a project got into its current state, who originally founded the project, what happened across different releases, and who was responsible for what areas of the code. Developers described using this commit history information to infer other's expertise with parts of a project. Respondent P1 indicated that he would look at who made changes to which file to find who had expertise on a piece of the system (essentially inferring who knows what from the record of activities on the project).

Attention signaling community support

Visible cues about who was attending to something served as an important signal of community support (or lack thereof). Developers interpreted activity traces of attention (following, watching, and comment activity) as an indicator that the community cared about that person, project, or action. Signals of attention also seemed to lead to developer attention to that person, artifact or event.

Attention signaling action or artifact importance

Respondents used signals of other users' attention to a feed item as indicators that an artifact or action was important. In particular, comments on a commit suggested the commit was interesting, controversial, or worth looking at (P17). Actions signaling attention to a project or person (watching or following) similarly signaled it or they were interesting in some way and prompted developers to look more closely. Inferences about who would see a particular action also influenced perceived value of engaging in that action. Inference of the size of a potential audience was cited as a motivation to contribute. Respondents indicated the number of forks or watchers of a project signaled that 'lots of other people will benefit from this change' (P13) or that 'someone would find this useful' (P16). The size of the potential audience was also frequently cited as a reason for using GitHub in the first place, based on general community interest in other forums such as mailing lists.

Attention signaling developer status

The number of followers a developer had was interpreted as a signal of status in the community. Developers with lots of followers were treated as local celebrities (e.g. dhh). Their activities were retold almost as local parable; our interviewees knew a great deal about them and paid attention to their actions (P20).

Attention signaling project quality

Visible information about community interest in the form of watcher and fork counts for a project seemed to be an important indicator that a project was high quality and worthwhile. Several respondents indicated using the number of watchers of a project or forks of a project as a signal that a project had community interest, and so was likely to be good or of interest. As one developer put it:

> *"The way you know how useful something is, is how much community there is behind it."* (P23).

These signals of attention, at the same time, put pressure on developers since their visible actions affected attributions about project quality. Several respondents indicated an awareness of being watched, noting that updates about their changes would 'flow to everyone watching' (P13) and that 'everyone can see what you're doing' (P1). In some cases they inferred the identity of this audience (e.g. users of their project) based on who they knew was watching or had forked the project noting for example "people are watching because they depend on it." (P4).

Action details signaling personal relevance

Certain properties of actions in the feed signaled potential personal impact. These inferences were highly dependent on the developer's own work and interests, rather than the community at large.

Actions signaling contribution opportunities

Several respondents inferred contribution opportunities from action information they would see in the feed. For example, one respondent described continually watching the feed for issue submissions or comments on commits (P9), both representing a chance for him to add something to the code or to the ongoing discussion.

Actions signaling potential problems

Respondents also inferred potential problems from commit events they would view in the feed or in the recent commit list. These inferences were based on cues that a commit was connected with specific files on a project, or had comments suggesting the change would affect their own projects (P16, P19). Comments on a commit also signaled a potentially contentious or problematic change (P1).

SOCIAL INFERENCES INFORMING JOINT ACTION

The social inferences that individual developers made based on visible cues of others' behavior fed into three types of higher-level collaborative activities: project-management, learning through observing, and reputation management.

Project management

All of the developers we interviewed had GitHub projects they were primarily responsible for, either because they were owners of the project or centrally involved in development. Certain types of social inferences described above supported project management activities.

Recruiting developers

Several of the developers we talked with actively recruited others (or were recruited by others) to contribute to a project more heavily. This recruitment was fueled by visible information about the other developers' competence and investment in the project. For example, P8 watched commits occurring in the various forks of his project to identify skilled and committed developers who could contribute more actively. In some cases this was based on past successful contributions to the project and observed commitment. For example P2, a newer member of GitHub was 'recruited' by a project owner after submitting several good commits. The project owner began sending him tasks such as requests to address incoming issues. Intense interest in the project, inferred from a high volume of commit actions in a short period of time, sent a strong signal that a contributor was invested in the project, and could be trusted to contribute more centrally (P17 & P21). In the cases observed this perceived investment seemed to translate into trust, with project owners granting commit rights, allowing new members to influence project vision, and sometimes even turning over ownership to the newcomer after they had demonstrated high levels of investment (P2, P8, P11, P17, P21, P22).

Identifying user needs

Transparency also supported identification of user skills and needs. Here the term user refers to other developers who make use of a particular project in their own work, becoming dependent on that project for certain functionality [23]. Developers inferred user needs by watching their activity in forks (personal copies) of the project (P3, P6, P9, P13, P11). For example, one developer described awareness that users were forking his project to deal with various incompatibilities with a new version of another piece of software they used in concert. He was made aware based on their activity in the forks, which incompatibility issues were particularly problematic for his users (P9).

> *"I saw somebody trying to use it with Rails master I'm like well crap I don't know if it works with Rails master so let me check. So that type of stuff has been useful just to get a sense of the kinds of things people might like to see, you know?" (P9).*

In almost all cases these user modifications represented innovations that extended the project in interesting ways, making it compatible with other systems or more generally useful (P3, P21, P9, P13, P11).

Although observable behavior in the forks provided information about user needs, developers often sought direct interaction with users to get feedback on their needs. Several developers mentioned also posting information about a change (using a direct URL to the code) into a project mailing list (P3, P4, P11). In many cases this was to get user input or buy in for a new design decisions that would go into the next release of a project (e.g. P11). Users would also contact developers directly to let them know about a change they wanted to make to the code or an issue they were having with the project (P1, P3, P9, P11). These interactions helped surface user needs but were also seen as a nuisance in some cases when responses were sought in a private channel such as e-mail rather than a public channel where everyone could observe the interaction.

Managing incoming code contributions

Perhaps the most important project management activity developers engaged in on GitHub was managing incoming code contributions. As noted above, users and other developers could submit changes to a project by forking the project and then making a pull request (a request that the changes be merged back into the master branch). Developers were constantly making decisions about what code to accept back into the project (P1, P2, P4, P8, P9, P11, P16, P19, P21). For very large and popular projects, owners dealt with many pull requests per day (P1, P8, P22). As noted above, they described making inferences about the quality of a code contribution based on its style, efficiency, thoroughness (e.g. were tests included?) and in some cases the submitter's competence (P8, P11, P22). Some developers indicated prioritizing requests that were tied to issues or integrated a feature that users had been requesting (P11, P21). Not all of the projects on GitHub used the pull request mechanism. In some cases because of legacy reasons, patches to a project had to be sent to a mailing list (P14, P24) for approval, where the community would chime in on their acceptability. Interestingly in this way, the GitHub pull request mechanism centralized control over changes by allowing managers to bypass a public mailing list notification and discussion mechanism.

Visibility across forks (or copies) of a project took the pressure off of project owners to accept all changes, and allowed niche versions of a project to co-exist with the official release. Thus contributors could build directly on each other's work, even if the project owner did not approve of the changes. As one developer put it:

"I can ignore bad changes but know that the network of experimenters can continue." (P13)

The cross-fork visibility also meant that project owners could proactively solicit changes from developers as they were working, and use the transparency to track the status of ongoing changes by others. Several respondents indicated using the network view (Figure 3) to identify the leading wave of changes to their project, or the newest code (P9, P11, P21). As noted above, they could see what people were trying to do with their code (P1).

"I would look at this [network] view and actually find folks who had uploaded a patch and say, 'Hey are you planning on sending that back to [my project], this is what I think of it, here's some changes you could make, here's some suggestions,' and that kind of got the ball rolling." (P8)

In some cases, the changes would not be submitted back because the person did not finish doing what they had intended to with the project (P1, P11). Here respondents described pinging the developer to solicit a pull request (P21, or receiving a ping P2), or asking when they would finish the change. In some cases, if the change was novel or useful enough, the project owner would take over the code and finish it themselves (P11).

As with user needs, in many cases, project owners needed to directly communicate around a code contribution. This was sometimes an attempt to solicit and motivate changes as described above. More often, however, this interaction consisted of negotiation around incoming pull requests. There was a clear sense that project owners had a view of the trajectory for the project, and there was a need for others to get buy in before making changes (P1, P9, P16). Project owners would often see potential problems that a code submission would cause with other parts of the code, or with changes they wanted to make in the future. In both cases their reaction was based on implicit knowledge about code organization or their future plans for the code (their 'vision' for the project as they often called it):

"I could tell that was actually going to cause some serious problems down the road, so I just responded. I always thank them because it's a big help when people contribute back, but it wouldn't work so I kind of explained to him why it didn't work." (P19)

This information was not transparent to submitters and could only be elicited through direct communication around the code. Similarly the developer's reasoning behind a change or the organization of a code submission was not always clear to the project owner. In some cases, several rounds of comments around a pull request were required to establish shared understanding of what the developer was trying to accomplish and why (P16). The inline interaction with code supported negotiation around a submission so that in some examples, the developer submitting a change would be able to modify the code he had submitted to address concerns a project owner might have about potential conflicts or conformity to project style norms.

Managing dependencies with other projects

Cross project visibility allowed project owners to proactively manage the dependencies their code had with other projects. Project owners were in almost all cases 'users' of the code of many other project owners, meaning changes to those projects would affect the functioning of their own project (P8, P9, P16, P19). Because of this, they attended closely to change events from projects they were dependent on. They watched for commit events in the feed, and reported paying special attention to new releases (which likely contained new features they could make use of) and changes to files they knew their project used (P8, P9, P16).

"[Popular website] their entire engineering team uses [My Project], and so they keep an eye out for any changes as well, because when I do a release, it breaks something then I essentially broke [Popular website]'s entire development for a day or something." (P19)

In some cases, they were watching for changes they knew were coming because they had heard about them in other forums (mailing lists, blogs etc.), or had discussed them directly with project owners or other developers (P9).

When changes occurred that affected their code, developers often directly contacted the project owner or contributor who had made a specific change (P9) or joined in on discussion about a proposed change (P19). For example, one project owner showed us a case where a third party chimed in on the discussion around a pull request someone else had submitted because the change affected functionality his company depended on (P19).

Developers would also handle conflicting or problematic changes by directly modifying the dependent project to address the problem (P9, P16, P20). Transparency supported this behavior because the code artifacts of the dependent project were open and accessible, and the visibility of changes meant the project owner knew exactly why something was no longer working. The project owners in this case were users of others projects, and then had to lobby and negotiate with the dependent project owner to get their changes accepted (e.g. P9).

Learning from others

Interestingly, the transparency on GitHub supported learning from the actions of other developers. Being able to watch how someone else coded, what others paid attention to, and how they solved problems all supported learning better ways to code and access to superior knowledge.

Following rockstars

Developers in our sample described following the actions of other developers because they deemed them particularly good at coding. They referred to these developers with thousands of followers as 'coding rockstars' (P20) and reported interest in how they coded, what projects they were working on, and what projects they were following. In most cases this was because these developers were deemed to have special skill and knowledge about the domain (P17, P20) in part as a function of their large following.

Watching watching

Developers also reported interest in which projects other users were looking at, and described certain users as acting almost as curators of the GitHub project space (P1, P4, P18, P16, P22). As one developer put it:

> *"I follow people if they work on interesting projects, [then] I'm interested in the projects they're interested in." (P4)*

Certain developers were deemed to have a knack for finding useful projects in a particular interest area:

> *"This guy has good taste in projects. He curates for me. Watching him is like watching the best of objective C that GitHub has to offer." (P16).*

This interest in finding the 'hottest' new projects through what others were watching highlighted the importance that GitHub users seemed to place on novelty more generally.

> *"I learn about new projects and new technologies way faster than ever before and it's just encouraged me to get dialed in to a bunch of different tech communities I never would have had access to before." (P4)*

Identifying new technical knowledge

Developers were also interested in watching the actions of other developers and other projects to find new technical knowledge. In some cases other projects served as a resource to see how other developers had solved a similar problem to theirs (P17, P23). Developers were also interested in watching development over time within projects that were similar in nature to their own.

> *"When I find a project that solves a problem that I had and I'm going to continue to have then I will watch it" (P19).*

By watching these projects and getting updates on the changes they made as they happened, they learned how their technical 'neighbors' were approaching related problems, informing their own development (P5, P16).

Direct feedback

Developers also learned from others through direct interaction. Through comments on pull requests, developers got feedback about their code from more experienced developers. This was sometimes comments about 'good form' or the 'right' way to do things in terms of coding style or what was normative. This was also feedback about code correctness or more efficient ways of writing the same code (e.g. P1). These interactions helped improve the quality of the code submissions.

Communication also supported learning about another developer's project and getting help with attempts to build on that project (P16). Some developers were extremely forthcoming with this type of help, checking their IRC channels and issue requests constantly to find and address those in need (e.g. P11, P19, P22). For some, this was an opportunity to grow a potential contributor, and project owners saw this as a process of ramping up users to eventually become full-fledged contributors (e.g. P8, P6).

Managing reputation and status

The public visibility of actions on GitHub led to identity management activities centered around gaining greater attention and visibility for work.

Self-promotion

Visibility for work was recognized as a valuable aspect of the GitHub community (P13, P16). The developers we interviewed talked about the positive utility of visibility, which led to increased use of a project, extension by others, ideas from a broader audience and exposure for other projects created by the owner (P16).

At the same time, self-promotion, active attempts to gain additional visibility for work, was recognized as a somewhat distasteful activity and something the developers said they wouldn't do (P17). Regardless, many developers consciously managed their self-image to promote their work through consistent branding (giving their project and blog the same name, or using the same Twitter handle and GitHub user id), and by publicizing their work on other platforms outside of GitHub (P9, P19, P17, P23). As one user noted:

> *"I think a lot of people that use GitHub are trying to promote themselves. This is very self-promotional. It's like I have this project, you will be interested in it" (P16).*

The attention associated with self-promotion was motivating for some of the developers we talked to. One developer noted that watchers kept him working on something he might have otherwise abandoned:

> *"Watching lets me know someone cares" (P17).*

Social capital, identity and recognition

Because watching was recognized as a signal of project quality, it carried meaning as a sign of community approval for a project as well. Several developers we talked to mentioned watching a friend's project to increase their 'social capital' on the site, or promote their work (P23). This was also done explicitly by posting projects to external sites such as HackerNews, a common source of information for developers in the GitHub community, or suggesting a project for RailsCast. Projects featured there were known to receive a boost in watchers. The reciprocal visibility of actions in GitHub meant that a certain amount of face management was associated with behavior on the site. Developers did not want to offend others by, for example publicly rejecting code contributions from long time contributors (P9, P21), or not following someone who followed them (P9, P16).

Being onstage

Many of the heavy users of GitHub expressed a clear awareness of the audience for their actions (P1, P6, P13). This awareness influenced how they behaved and constructed their actions, for example, making changes less frequently (P6), because they knew that 'everyone is watching' (P1) and could 'see my changes as soon as I make them' (P13). There was a concern to get things right because of how public changes to the code would be. One developer contrasted his heavily watched project with a niche project, noting that he could be more experimental in the niche project because no one was watching (P21). Another developer directly compared it with the pressure of performing:

> *"I try and make sure my commit messages are snappy and my code is clean because I know that a lot of people are watching. ...It's like being on stage, you don't want to mess up, you're giving it your best, you've got your Hollywood smile"* (P4).

DISCUSSION

Three interesting themes cross-cut the observations in our data about the value of visibility and transparency in the GitHub community: the micro-supply chain ecosystem on GitHub, the value of observation versus direct interaction, and the affordances of attention signals.

Visibility across micro-supply chains

We found that transparency in GitHub allowed work to progress and projects to evolve to become more general as a function of micro-supply chain management. Because all artifacts are visible on the GitHub site, users of a particular project can access its contents, and are made aware of changes to the project on a continuous basis. This awareness and visibility supported direct feedback and interaction between project owners and their users, creating what we refer to as a "micro supply chain." Visibility between the supplier (project owner) and consumer (user) meant that the owner could infer more clearly who their user base was, how they were using the project, and when they were having problems. Consumers were notified about changes to the product, meaning they could anticipate problematic modifications and provide immediate feedback about them. Once notified, consumers could directly communicate with the project owner about changes being made to discuss their consequences or request adaptations that would suit their needs. But they could also directly modify the product and customize it to suit their needs with or without direct communication, if they so desired. In contrast to relatively static and sequential supply chain relationships, what emerged was a far more interactive producer-consumer relationship, characterized by reciprocal dependencies [25].

Communication occurs at the limits of transparency

Communication generally seemed to be a response to the limits of transparency, when the information and inferences afforded by transparency were insufficient for the purpose at hand. Users interacted when conflicts arose between two dependent projects, or when negotiating modifications to pull requests. In each case, communication seemed to happen when transparency broke down -- there was certain information developers could not directly observe.

People seemed to work independently until certain events brought them together, making the dependency more salient, such as when a potentially problematic change would show up in the feed, or when a pull request would create problems for other aspects of the code. Direct communication functioned in these cases, much as mutual adjustment, allowing individuals to directly share unobservable information about their rationale (why they were doing what they were doing), and plans (what they were planning to do next), and negotiate mutually compatible solutions to a conflict. These negotiations were supported by direct communication interactions in code comments, IRC channels, campfire, mailing lists, and a variety of other web-based communication tools.

Thus although passive activity traces of others' behavior are powerful in some ways, they are limited when joint action is required. In part this is because of the lack of feedback or interactivity these visible traces provide. Our results suggest these traces support knowing what someone has done, and who might be looking at something, at the individual level, and when new collaborative actions introduce new dependencies, two-way communications are required.

Signals of attention

Visible signals of attention provided notification of other developers' behavior on the GitHub site. Interestingly, these signals of attention seemed to help users manage the downsides of transparency across a large-scale network. Visible cues of what others were watching or commenting helped developers find 'interesting' or 'useful' projects and events (in their words). These signals, when aggregated, also gave some users higher status because they indicated community approval or admiration. As one user put it, "I'm kind of giving them some token of my attention. I'm saying, I like what you're doing" (P23). Signals of attention functioned to provide awareness of what other users cared about or were looking at. This awareness is one aspect of social translucence as described by [8].

These signals of attention also in some cases motivated behavior, giving developers a feeling that someone cared about what they were doing. This connects with the notion of accountability in social translucence and collective effort. This affordance of transparency relates to research investigating how working with others affects one's own productivity through social pressure (e.g., [15]), the flow of ideas [1] and help. Our findings suggest that the visibility of actions might act to facilitate information flows and help-giving, both of which have important implications for the quantity and quality of work.

CONCLUSION

In this work we examined how individuals interpreted and made use of information about others' actions on code in an open social software repository. We found that four key features of visible feedback drove a rich set of inferences around commitment, work quality, community significance and personal relevance. These inferences supported collaboration, learning, and reputation management in the community. Our results inform the design of social media for large-scale collaboration, and imply a variety of ways that transparency can support innovation, knowledge sharing, and community building.

ACKNOWLEDGEMENTS

This research is supported by the Center for the Future of Work at Carnegie Mellon University's Heinz College and by the National Science Foundation under award: CNS-1040801.

REFERENCES

1. Azouley, P., Graff Zivin, J.S., & Sampat, B.N. The diffusion of scientific knowledge across time and space. *NBER Working Paper Series* (2011).
2. Bardram, J. E. & Hansen, T. R. Context-based workplace awareness. *Computer Supported Cooperative Work (CSCW) 19*, 2 (2010), 105-138.
3. Begel, A., DeLine, R., & Zimmerman, T. Social media for software engineering. In *Proc. FoSER 2010*, IEEE Computer Society (2010), 33-38.
4. boyd, d.m., & Ellison, N.B. Social network sites: Definition, history, and scholarship. *Journal of Computer-Mediated Communication, 13*, 1 (2007), article 11.
5. Corbin, J.M., & Strauss, A.L. Basics of qualitative research. London, UK: Sage Publications, 2008.
6. DiMicco, J., Millen, D., Geyer, W., Dugan, C., Brownholtz, B. & Muller, M. Motivations for social networking at work. In *Proc CSCW 2008,* ACM Press (2008), 711-720.
7. Dourish, P. & Bellotti, V. Awareness and coordination in shared workspaces. In *Proc. CSCW 1992*, ACM Press (1992), 107-114.
8. Erickson, T., & Kellogg, W. Social translucence: An approach to designing systems that support social processes. *TOCHI 7*, 1 (1999), 59-83.
9. Froehlich, J., & Dourish, P. Unifying artifacts and activities in a visual tool for distributed software development teams. In *Proc. ICSE 2004*, IEEE Society (2004), 387-396.
10. Github: Social Coding, http://github.com/, accessed March 17, 2011.
11. Gross, T., Stary, C., & Totte, A. User-centered awareness in computer-supported cooperative work systems. *Int. J. of HCI, 18*, 3 (2005), 323-360.
12. Gutwin, C., Greenberg, S., & Roseman, M. Workspace awareness in real-time distributed groupware: Framework, widgets, and evaluation. In *Proc. HCI on People & Computers,* Springer-Verlag (1996), 281-298.
13. Gutwin, C., Penner, R., & Schneider, K. Group awareness in distributed software development. In *Proc CSCW 2004*, ACM Press (2004), 72-81.
14. Ko, A.J., DeLine, R., & Venolia, G. Information needs in collocated software development teams. In *Proc ICSE 2007*, IEEE Computer Society (2007), 344-353.
15. Mas, A., & Moretti, E. Peers at work. *American Economic Review, 99*, 1 (2009), 112-145.
16. Millen, D., Feinberg, J., & Kerr, B. Dogear: Social bookmarking in the enterprise. In *Proc. CHI 2006*, ACM Press (2006), 111-120.
17. Olson, G., M., & Olson, J.S. Distance matters. *Human-Computer Interaction 15* (2001), 139-178.
18. Omoronyia, I., Ferguson, J., Roper, M. & Wood, M. Using developer activity data to enhance awareness during collaborative software development. *Computer Supported Cooperative Work (CSCW) 18*, 5 (2009), 509-558.
19. Sarma, A., Maccherone, L., Wagstrom, P., & Herbsleb, J. (2009). Tesseract: Interactive visual exploration of socio-technical relationships in software development. In *Proc. ICSE 2009*, IEEE Computer Society (2009), 23-33.
20. Sarma, A., Z. Noroozi, & Htreetreeoek, A. (2003). Palantír: raising awareness among configuration management workspaces. In *Proc ICSE 2003*, IEEE Computer Society (2003), 444-454.
21. Skeels, M.M., & Grudin, J. When social networks cross boundaries: A case study of workplace use of Facebook and LinkedIn. In *Proc. GROUP 2009*, ACM Press (2009), 95-103.
22. Storey, M.A., Ryall, J., Singer, J., Myers, D., Cheng, L.T., & Muller, M. How software developers use tagging to support reminding and refinding. *IEEE TSE 35*, 4 (2009), 470-483.
23. Storey, M., Treude, C., van Deursen, A., & Cheng, L.T. The impact of social media on software engineering practices and tools. In *Proc. FoSER 2010*, ACM Press (2010), 359-363.
24. Teasley, S. Covi, L. Krishnan, M. & Olson, J. Rapid software development through team collocation. *IEEE TSE 28*, 7 (2002), 671–683.
25. van de ven, A.H., Delbecq, A.L., & Koenig, R. Determinants of coordination modes within organizations. *American Sociological Review*, (1976).
26. Viegas, F., Wattenberg, M., & Kushal, D. Studying cooperation and conflict between authors with *history flow* visualizations. In *Proc CHI 2004*, ACM Press (2004), 575-582.
27. Weiner, B. *Human Motivation: Metaphors, Theories and Research*, Newbury Park, CA: Sage Publications, 1992.

DiscoTech: A Plug-In Toolkit to Improve Handling of Disconnection and Reconnection in Real-Time Groupware

Banani Roy[1], T.C. Nicholas Graham[1], and Carl Gutwin[2]

[1]School of Computing, Queen's University
Kingston, ON, K7L 3N6
{broy, graham}@cs.queensu.ca

[2]Computer Science, University of Saskatchewan
110 Science Place, Saskatoon, SK, S7N 5C9
carl.gutwin@usask.ca

ABSTRACT

Disconnection and reconnection are common problems for users of synchronous groupware, but these problems are not easy for developers to handle because of the wide range of scenarios and timeframes that must be considered. We have developed a new toolkit called DiscoTech that helps programmers deal with disconnection. The toolkit is based on five design dimensions that determine how stored information can be manipulated as the system waits for an absent user to rejoin, and how information should be replayed upon reconnection. DiscoTech provides a plug-in architecture to handle a wide variety of behaviours that developers may need during disconnection; these plug-ins range from fully generic tools to customized strategies with full knowledge of the groupware application. We present the design of the DiscoTech toolkit, show examples of its use, and provide evidence that it covers a broad range of situations, imposes minimal performance overhead, and is easy for programmers to learn. DiscoTech handles a wider range of issues than previous toolkits, without requiring undue effort, and provides a practical way to improve the real-world usability of synchronous groupware.

Author Keywords

Real-time groupware; toolkits; disconnection; reconnection.

ACM Classification Keywords

H.5.3 [Information Interfaces and Presentation]: *CSCW*

General Terms

Human Factors; Design; Experimentation.

INTRODUCTION

Collaborators in synchronous groupware frequently become disconnected from the session (e.g., because of power failure, network outage, network latency, or explicit departure). Disconnections can range in duration from a few seconds (e.g., due to network congestion) to hours or days (e.g., stowing a laptop while flying). Disconnected participants lose track of the ongoing collaboration, and when they rejoin the session, they can have difficulty understanding both the state of the workspace and the current activities of other people. Previous work in CSCW has shown the kinds of problems that disconnection can cause, and has proposed several solutions for handling reconnection [13], late entrance (e.g., [4,15,17,19]), periods of asynchrony [23,24], or network faults [14].

However, existing techniques handle only a limited number of disconnection and reconnection situations, and there is little support for dealing with different lengths of disconnection, user-level concerns such as summarization, and application-level requirements for changes made to stored data during an absence. As a result, developers must have a deep understanding of the issues underlying disconnection, and must write a great deal of code to handle different scenarios. Recently, a general framework of disconnection was proposed [13], showing that there are several recurring patterns in the way that disconnection and reconnection can be handled, and suggesting that this service would be an ideal candidate for a toolkit approach.

We have developed such a toolkit – called *DiscoTech* – that simplifies developer tasks in handling disconnection and reconnection, based on an analysis of user-level questions that need to be answered on reconnection (what happened during the absence, what is the state of the workspace, and what is happening now). These questions are formalized in a design space with five dimensions that specify how messages can be processed in different disconnection scenarios. The different strategies on the five dimensions are implemented as plug-ins in DiscoTech's component architecture, which allows developers to handle a wider range of disconnection and reconnection requirements than have been seen in any previous toolkit. The architecture allows three types of plug-ins: *fully generic*, which address standard issues such as message format, sampling, and ordering in the data that is queued during a disconnection; *partially generic*, which are parameterized to allow tuned behaviour (e.g., to allow re-ordering with priority for certain message types); and *customized*, which allow application-dependent transformations of data based on the systems specific needs (e.g., changing movement data to a 'heat map' representation). Different plug-ins and parameters provide support for disconnections of different lengths and for different usage scenarios. The goal of DiscoTech is to make it simple for the groupware programmer to handle standard cases, but also to make it possible to handle more complex cases when required.

Our initial evaluations of DiscoTech show that it succeeds in three important design areas. First, we demonstrate the coverage of the toolkit by showing how policies from previous work (including latecomer support) are handled by DiscoTech. Second, we show that the toolkit is easy for developers to learn and use by reporting on tutorial sessions with four programmers. Third, we provide empirical evidence that DiscoTech adds minimal overhead for connected clients, and that memory use is appropriately constrained when people are disconnected.

Our work makes two main contributions. The design space provides a set of concepts to show the range of solutions for handling disconnection, and identifies a number of specific strategies that can be implemented as plug-ins. The DiscoTech toolkit itself provides an architecture and model for using and composing individual plug-in solutions, and our evaluations show that the toolkit has broad coverage, is easy for developers to use, and performs well. DiscoTech provides a wider range of solutions to the problem of disconnection than exist in any previous toolkit, without causing undue programmer effort or performance penalties. The libraries for DiscoTech are freely available (at [7]) and work with any .NET language.

RELATED WORK

Overview of the disconnection problem

Issues of robustness, fault tolerance, network disconnection, and late joiners have been investigated for some time (e.g., [1,3,5,11,16,29]), but the user view of groupware disconnection has not been widely considered. Gutwin et al. [13] recently provided an overview of the problem from this perspective, stating two main factors for handling disconnection: the time scale of the absence, and the phase of the disconnection (specifically identifying a disconnection, determining what to do during the absence, and determining what to do on reconnection.)

Time scale is important in these decisions because users want different kinds of information depending on how long they have been away; therefore, duration of absence can be used as the basis for adapting storage behaviour.

The high-level design presented by Gutwin et al. included this conceptual architecture and several example systems, but did not go into detail about the range of techniques that could be used in handling disconnection and reconnection, or about development infrastructures that could allow the disconnection problem to be dealt with in an efficient and general fashion by groupware programmers.

Techniques for handling aspects of disconnection

Strategies for dealing with disconnection issues have been explored in research on individual systems and toolkits. The range of techniques seen in previous literature was part of the motivation for a plug-in architecture for the DiscoTech toolkit, and many of the techniques described below have been used to inform the design of DiscoTech's specific plug-ins. We do not cover some basic issues, such as identification of disconnection, or reestablishing a network connection (although these are handled by the toolkit). In addition, we consider fault tolerance for data (e.g., data replication [21]) and consistency maintenance for replicated models (e.g., [27]) to be outside the scope of DiscoTech. These issues are important but can be handled by other modules in the overall groupware architecture. Strategies for handling disconnection include:

- *Persistence.* Maintaining a persistent state for the shared environment allows that state to be sent to users after a disconnection. This strategy is used for place-based groupware (e.g., TeamRooms [26]) and for the virtual worlds used in games (e.g., World of Warcraft).
- *State recovery.* Even in groupware systems that are not place-based, the state of documents or workspaces can be stored at a central location and sent to a reconnecting user (e.g., the YCab framework [3]). In pure state-recovery systems, no event-based information (such as awareness events) is stored. In some systems (e.g., DOORS [24]), event-based information exists when users are connected synchronously, but events are not stored during periods of asynchrony.
- *Store-and-forward.* In this approach, events are queued at a central server and are sent to the receiver upon request (e.g., XTV [5] or Chung et al.'s latecomer service [4]). Unlike state-based systems, state is reconstructed at the receiver using forwarded events.
- *Replay.* On reconnection, queued events from store-and-forward systems are delivered to the receiver and can be replayed – both to reconstruct state, and to provide an understanding of what happened during the absence. For example, DreamObjects [19] allows playback of some or all of the queued events, and a system by Manohar and Prakash provided a 'video-player' interface that allowed playback to be paused or fast-forwarded [20].
- *Type-based selection.* A few systems select what messages to send after a reconnection, based on the message type. For example, WebArrow [12,18] only sends chat messages after reconnection, not voice.
- *Discarding old state-update events.* Some event-based systems recognize that certain events only update state variables (e.g., a temperature from a sensor), and discard all but the most recent of these events [8].
- *Reordering.* Some games priorize state updates for nearby avatars ahead of those for distant avatars [2], or move important messages (e.g., deaths and spawns) to the front of the queue.
- *Coalescing and chunking.* When messages are batched at the sender, some systems reduce space requirements by aggregating several messages into one (e.g., ReConMUC [1]) or converting incremental updates into a larger single updates (e.g., change multiple draw messages into a single polyline) [24].

- *Compression.* Batched updates can be compressed using libraries such as zlib (e.g., XTV [5], ReConMUC [1], or Chung's latecomer system [4]).
- *Continuation while disconnected.* When a connection is lost, some systems such as DISCIPLE [16] allow a mobile client to work offline. These systems are similar in approach to groupware that supports both asynchronous and synchronous work (e.g., DOORS [24]), but applies the idea to network disconnection.
- *Content-based filtering.* The volume of messages stored for a particular receiver can in some cases be reduced by selecting only those messages that match certain patterns (e.g., keywords in an IRC client [1]).

Latecomer support

The existing CSCW toolkits that are closest to our work are those that deal with the 'latecomer' problem that has been considered since the earliest groupware systems (e.g., [4,19 ,20,28]). Toolkit approaches to the latecomer problem can generally be divided into those that provide state-based recovery (e.g., Habanero [17] or Suite [9]), those that provide replay-based recovery (e.g., Chung et al.'s accommodation service [4] or XTV [5]), and those that combine both approaches (e.g., DreamObjects [19]).

Although there are often different issues at play in supporting latecomers versus disconnected users, many of the ideas are similar – and in fact some researchers have noted that absences in the middle of a groupware session can also be thought of as 'latecomers' (e.g., [4]). However, no groupware toolkit has addressed these concerns in a way that provides both flexibility and simplicity for the application programmer. In order to fill this need, we designed the DiscoTech toolkit.

DESIGN DIMENSIONS FOR DISCONNECTION

The overall goal of handling disconnection is to help collaborators rejoin and continue the collaborative work session as smoothly and seamlessly as possible. This involves three main questions from the user's perspective:

- *What happened during the absence?* The returning user needs to 'catch up' on important events and changes that have occurred during the absence.
- *What is the state of the workspace?* The user needs to understand the current state of the collaboration artifacts, both in order to interpret changes and to understand the overall state of the collaboration.
- *What is happening now?* The user needs information about current activities in order to smoothly re-integrate into the group's activity. For example, the user needs the last few messages of a chat conversation in order to restart their participation in the conversation.

These needs involve competing goals: the user wants to get as complete an understanding as possible of the missed events, but reconnection data must be delivered as quickly as possible if the user is to rejoin the collaboration in a timely fashion. This implies, for example, that in many cases the events cannot simply be replayed in their original form (since this would take too much time); in addition, this means that the transmission time of stored messages after reconnection must be minimized.

From these user-level requirements, we identify five dimensions along which groupware messages can be manipulated or altered during or after a disconnection.

1. Message Format: changing the way messages are represented and packaged, primarily to reduce volume.

- *Compression*: using lossless compression techniques (such as Zip or GMC) to reduce message size; some lossy techniques also apply (e.g., re-encoding JPEGs).
- *Aggregation*: repackaging to incorporate several individual events per message. For example, sending multiple telepointer locations per message saves the overhead of identifying each event as a telepointer.
- *Chunking*: adding together several events to create a single larger event. For example, changing a set of character-by-character typing events into a single chat message event; or coalescing several pixel edits into a larger bitmap region event.

2. Sampling: selecting a subset of the stored messages based on a particular property. Sampling techniques imply that some messages are deleted from the queue.

- *Sampling by priority or type*: selecting messages based on an explicit priority designation in the message, or on an implicit designation based on message type. An example of the latter approach is to select messages that involve changes to the model and discard awareness messages (e.g., telepointer movement).
- *Sampling by time*: messages may be selected either by time period (e.g., randomly retain one message per second, to show the distribution of events), or by time cutoff (e.g., retain the last ten seconds of activity).
- *Sampling by count*: similar to time sampling, but using the number of messages rather than time as the governing structure. This approach might retain every Nth message, or just the most recent N messages.

3. Pacing: changing the temporal spacing of a stream of messages, primarily to reduce the time needed for the user to interpret events on reconnection.

- *Uniform speedup*: message timestamps can be uniformly altered to decrease playback time; for example, events could be replayed at double speed.
- *Non-uniform time change*: times can be altered to achieve specific purposes, such as removing gaps in the message stream, or reducing less important sequences.
- *Quick-as-possible playback*: in extreme cases, events can be played with no time delay – that is, messages are processed directly one after another.

4. Ordering: changes to the order of messages in the queue, without removing any messages. As with sampling, decisions are made based on properties of the message data.

- *Priority*: some messages may be considered as more important and can be moved to the front of the queue.

Examples include important game events (e.g., hits), or messages that are important for causal processes.

- *Size*: if small messages can be processed faster, it may be useful to collect them at the front of the queue.
- *Recency*: in a standard queue, recent messages would arrive last after reconnection; in situations where messages do not have causal dependencies, however, recent messages could be delivered first. For example, a chat system might show the recent parts of an ongoing conversation, and then gradually fill in earlier parts.

5. Transformation: changing the content or representation of messages, either to reduce size or interpretation time. Transformations are often paired with visualizations that show the information in a way that is different to the original presentation.

- *Averaging*. Some messages (such as position or movement events) can be combined through averaging (e.g., showing the average location of an avatar over one-second intervals, rather than at each movement).
- *Summarization*. Messages can be summarized without changing the basic data representation. For example, text chat could be replaced with a shorter text summary.
- *Representation*. Messages can be processed to create a completely new representation. For example, the text of a chat conversation could be replaced with information about participants' activity level; similarly, telepointer movements could be replaced with a 'heat map' showing overall activity. Transformations can also convert event updates to state structures (e.g., converting movement messages to a 'game frame' containing every avatar location).

PLUG-IN ARCHITECTURE

Guided by this design space, we have created the DiscoTech architecture. DiscoTech's goals are:

- *Ease of Use:* Groupware developers should be able to use the architecture without having to substantially modify it or their application. The architecture should be available as a usable toolkit with a simple API.
- *Expressiveness:* The architecture should support a wide range of disconnection/reconnection behaviour, as captured in the design space above.
- *High Performance:* Applications using the architecture should not pay a major performance penalty, and any penalty should be predictable and quantifiable.

We have realized these goals through a plug-in architecture that has been implemented within the DiscoTech toolkit. DiscoTech is based on an earlier design [13], but is novel in that it deals with disconnection issues using plug-ins. Groupware developers can use DiscoTech as a networking API that provides built-in disconnection handling. Developers stream their application events via the DiscoTech API, and events are propagated via the network to other clients. In case of network outages, events are queued on a server, and sent to the disconnected client upon reconnection. Developers can easily select among available strategies in the DiscoTech API for dealing with disconnection, or can develop custom plug-ins.

Ease of Use through the DiscoTech toolkit

DiscoTech allows groupware developers to easily add disconnection handling to their application. Developers simply route their application's events through the toolkit. Similarly to other middleware solutions, DiscoTech broadcasts the application's events to all other clients. DiscoTech handles disconnection and reconnection events by constantly queuing application events in case of disconnection, and by automatically providing catch-up functionality when the client reconnects.

Figure 1 shows how applications interact with DiscoTech. The current implementation uses a client/server architecture in which the application sends events to DiscoTech via its API. DiscoTech then propagates the events to other clients (via its *Sender* module). Events received from other clients are queued on an event queue, and are forwarded to the application via a call-back. DiscoTech therefore propagates events for applications, providing the network functions usually provided by a middleware such as GT [6] or by raw socket communication. DiscoTech has no knowledge of event semantics; events are simply viewed as serializable objects that can be queued or sent over a network.

DiscoTech provides a server (Figure 2) whose primary function is to broadcast messages from each client to all of the other clients. Incoming events for client i are read by a Receiver component, which then enqueues the message on each client's Event Queue. A Sender process for each client waits for new messages to arrive on the Event Queue, and sends them to the client.

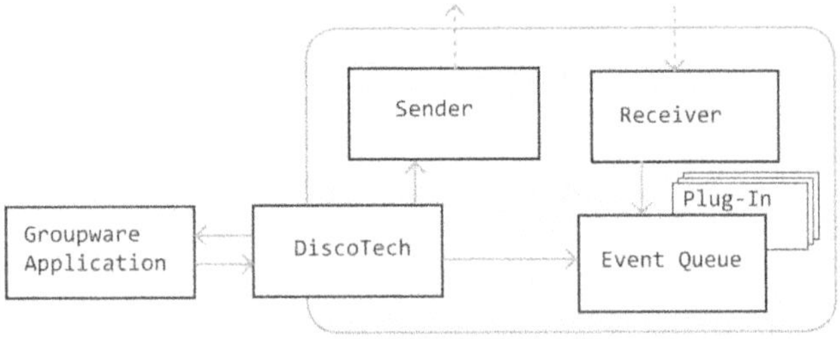

Figure 1: DiscoTech client

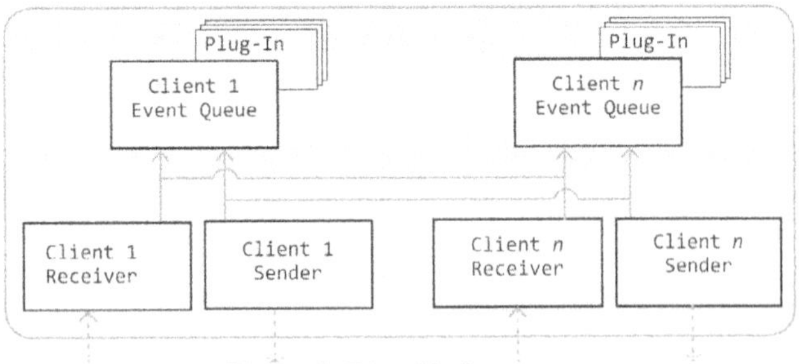

Figure 2: DiscoTech server

If a client disconnects, its sender/receiver pair attempts to reestablish connection. In case of a brief network disruption, the connection might be reestablished immediately. In a longer disconnection (e.g., a computer being powered down for the weekend), the connection may take hours or days to reestablish. In the meantime, events are queued so that they can be sent to the client upon reconnection. During longer disconnections, the contents of the event queue must be modified in order to reduce space requirements and to avoid the need for lengthy data transmission following reconnection. The groupware developer can configure the techniques used to reduce the space requirements of the server-side event queue. Two techniques are used: (1) the data stored on the event queue is reduced through the approaches discussed in the design space (e.g., compression, aggregation, and sampling) and (2) messages can be compressed using standard techniques as part the network transmission process.

Following reconnection and receipt of data, the client controls how the data is sent to the application. Events can simply be forwarded to the application directly, or can be modified to help the user re-establish context. For example, the client's plug-ins may reorder events so that highest priority events are processed first, or may adjust playback to show missed activity at double speed.

Expressiveness through Plug-ins

Application programmers can use the DiscoTech toolkit as-is, selecting among a set of predefined compaction and replaying behaviours. This allows easy addition of disconnection handling – all that the developer needs to do is route the application's events through DiscoTech.

This approach limits disconnection handling, however, to behaviours that can be programmed without knowledge of the underlying semantics of the events. For example, the following generic behaviours are possible with the toolkit:

- Compression – using standard libraries such as zlib
- Truncation – the last *k* events (or *k* seconds of events)
- Sampling – discarding all but a subset of events
- Accelerated playback of events

However, many interesting behaviours require knowledge of the semantics of the events themselves, such as:

- Aggregation of multiple events to a single event conveying the same information
- Discarding events which are superseded by later events
- Transforming events into a summary representation

DiscoTech uses a plug-in mechanism to open the toolkit,, allowing programming of custom disconnection behaviours. Plug-ins can be attached to either the server or client-side event queues. Plug-ins are periodically invoked by the toolkit (as triggered by timer interrupts or by the queue reaching a threshold size), and may arbitrarily modify the contents of the queue. Plug-ins fall into three categories: *generic, partially generic* and *custom*.

Generic Plug-ins: Generic plug-ins, as described above, provide functionality that can be implemented with no knowledge of events' semantics. Events are considered to be generic objects, tagged with a time stamp specifying when the event originated at the source client. The toolkit provides a set of generic plug-ins, providing simple and useful disconnection behaviour. Generic plugins are parameterized by the type of message on which they should operate (e.g., awareness messages only), and by the timeframe in which they should operate.

Partially Generic Plug-ins: The toolkit provides plug-ins that must be parameterized by the application programmer to adapt them to the event types used by the application. For example, a *chunker* combines groups of events into coarser-grained events. This plug-in could transform individual keystroke events from a chat system into a single event, or could coalesce line-segment events into a poly-line for a drawing program. While the aggregation behaviour is generic, the specifics of how a set of events are transformed into a single event are application-specific. Users of this plug-in must parameterize it by providing the implementation of a *Chunk* method that takes a list of events and combines them into a single event. In DiscoTech, this plug-in is implemented as an abstract class, requiring the application programmer to create a concrete subclass that implements the *Chunk* function.

As a second example, the *AggregateToState* partially-generic plug-in allows a sequence of events to be collapsed into a single state update event, possibly involving a significant change in form. As we shall see, *AggregateToState* can be used to convert a sequence of line drawing commands to a single bitmap image, or a sequence of telepointer move events to a matrix representing a heatmap. This plug-in must be customized with the underlying data structure (e.g., the bitmap) and with a method that applies events to the data structure (e.g., drawing the line on the bitmap).

Partially generic plug-ins significantly extend the expressiveness of the toolkit. The cost to the application programmer is that he/she must understand the functionality of the plug-in well enough to provide the code customizing it for the application's event types.

Custom Plug-ins: Some functionality is so dependent on the underlying event types that no generic behaviour is possible. For example, a sequence of moves in a chess game might be summarized using standard chess notation, or a sequence of video frames might be converted through image analysis to a summary of the video's content.

These three plug-in types represent a progression from the simplicity of full genericity to the power of custom components. This allows developers to choose the degree to which they wish to engage with the toolkit – if standard behaviour is acceptable, there is little for developers to learn. If they wish to have sophisticated, custom behaviour, the toolkit makes it possible.

High Performance through Light-Weight Operation

While disconnection handling can greatly improve the usability of groupware applications, it must not unreasonably reduce application performance. DiscoTech is designed to provide minimal overhead during normal connected state, and to provide developers with hooks to manage resource consumption during disconnected states.

Application events sent from one client to another pass through the DiscoTech server, which broadcasts them to other clients. This message broadcasting architecture is widely used in groupware implementation (e.g., GT [6], or many commercial games). DiscoTech adds the overhead of queuing events on the server rather than sending them directly. When a client is connected, however, events can be removed from the queue as soon as they are added. As shown below, the overhead of the queue is minimal compared to the cost of sending messages over the network.

When a client is disconnected, the server enqueues its messages until the client reconnects. This can lead to unbounded memory use, as there is no limit to the length of disconnection. Server-side plug-ins allow the developer to reduce queue size with a variety of pruning and compaction techniques. Through parameters on these plug-ins, the developer can control how aggressively these algorithms are applied – e.g., how often they should be invoked and how much data should be retained.

Following reconnection, the queued data is sent to the reconnected client. As the event queue grows, so does the bandwidth required to transmit these events. Bandwidth requirements are controlled through two mechanisms. First, as described above, developers can control the amount of data stored on the event queue. Second, the network module can minimize transmission time by delivering the queue as a whole, and by using compression to reduce size.

Later in the paper, we present evaluation results showing that DiscoTech indeed imposes minimal overhead during normal connected operation, and provides hooks for control over resource requirements during disconnection.

DETAILS OF PLUG-IN IMPLEMENTATION

The main novelty of DiscoTech is its plug-in approach to handling disconnection and reconnection. Plug-ins are classes that descend from the abstract base class *DTPlugin*, and are all designed around a similar pattern – plug-ins have access to the queued events, and can perform manipulations on that queue depending on the algorithm built into the plug-in. We have implemented plug-ins to correspond to all of the types detailed in the design space, including reformatters, resamplers, re-orderers, re-pacers, and transformers (see descriptions above).

A plug-in's 'main' method is called *ApplyPlugin*. When invoked by the toolkit, this method applies the plug-in's algorithms to the event queue. Plug-ins have two properties: *EventQueue*, which links to the event queue that is to be manipulated; and *Timeframe*, which specifies the time period for which the plug-in is to operate. In addition, certain plug-ins have additional properties (e.g., the *TimeBasedTruncator* plug-in takes an argument on creation to determine the age at which events will be deleted from the queue). Last, plug-ins all have a method that carries out the desired actions on the given queue (this method is specific to the plug-in type).

Application programmers can use the built-in generic plug-ins (e.g., the *Truncator*) without any customization. For the partially generic plug-ins, such as the *Chunker* plug-in (see above), the programmer needs to redefine the behaviour of the *Chunk()* method. For a custom plug-in, the programmer creates a new class that inherits the abstract base class *DTPlugin*. With custom classes, programmers can arbitrarily change the content of the event queue.

Multiple plug-ins can be applied to the event queue (e.g., to provide different treatment for old versus new events). Each plug-in must therefore be capable of recognizing event types generated by other plug-ins. For example, if chunking introduces a new event type into the event queue to represent the newly 'chunked' data, other plug-ins must be capable of dealing with that event type.

USING THE DISCOTECH TOOLKIT

DiscoTech is implemented in C#, and can be used in any .NET project by including DiscoTech's client-module or server-module libraries with the client or server application. There is a clean separation between the application and DiscoTech's components; the application only interacts with the toolkit's *Disco* component (which acts as a mediator between the application and DiscoTech). At the simplest level of use (i.e., generic plug-ins only), developers need only learn the DiscoTech APIs in order to pass events through the Disco instance; disconnection and reconnection behaviour is handled transparently. Programmers instantiate DiscoTech with details of the server IP address and port, and then define two event handlers to receive command and data messages.

The programmer also needs to specify the set of plug-ins they want to use: e.g., to use the 'HeatmapTransformer' plug-in between 60 seconds and 10 minutes of disconnection, the following lines are used:

```
DTPlugin hm = new HeatmapTransformer(60,600);
Disco.AddPlugin(hm);
```

For sending a message over the network, the programmer uses the following call:

```
Disco.SendMessage(message);
```

where 'message' is a string or an event object. The receiver will get the message via the event handler mentioned above.

EXAMPLES USING DISCOTECH

We show two examples – a chat system and a paper-reviewing application – that demonstrate a range of strategies for handling disconnection, and show that DiscoTech supports both low-cost generic behaviours as well as application-specific behaviour when needed.

Text Chat Application

In this simple chat system (Figure 3), users type messages and press Send to propagate the chat to all users. The application uses two event types: one to send the content of a chat message, and one to send an 'is typing' awareness message. When a client is disconnected, these messages are queued on the server; for long disconnections, messages are transformed to take up less space according to the following rules:

- Events less than 10 seconds old are preserved as-is.
- Chat messages older than 10 seconds are chunked into a single message (using the partially-generic *Chunker* plug-in)
- Awareness events older than 10 seconds are removed from the queue (using the generic *Truncator* plug-in).
- Chat messages older than 10 minutes are replaced with a 'chat frequency' event that counts the number of chat messages from each user. This uses a custom plug-in requiring knowledge of the application's event types.

On reconnection, messages are replayed at the client according to the following rules:

- 'Chat frequency' events are passed to the client, which highlights users' icons based on number of messages (this is application-specific behaviour).
- Chunked chat messages are passed to the client so that they can be immediately shown in the chat pane. This is default behaviour requiring no plug-in.
- Newer chat messages are replayed at double speed (using the generic *Speedup* plug-in) until the playback catches up. The order and timing of the messages matches their original input, but the timeline is compressed. This allows users to see the rate at which messages were originally typed, but faster.

Despite its simplicity, this example illustrates much of the power of the DiscoTech architecture. It is easy to configure the server to limit the amount of information that is stored, an approach that allows a client to be disconnected indefinitely. A custom plug-in is used to create the chat frequency event, but if developers prefer not to create this plug-in, the generic truncation plug-in could be used to discard old chat messages. This shows that developers can choose between simple behaviour with generic plug-ins, or extended behaviour with custom plug-ins.

The reconnection plug-ins are used to help users regain context. Here, highlighting user icons gives a general picture of who was active during the disconnection. Older chat messages are simply posted to the window, while newer messages are played back at the relative rate they were originally typed.

The plug-ins used in this application are parameterized by thresholds such as the age at which awareness messages should be discarded, or the age at which double-speed

Figure 3: Chat application

playback should be used on the client. These parameters are simple properties that are set through the DiscoTech API.

Collaborative Paper Reviewing System

Our second example is a system used by groups of authors to review and comment on a paper draft (Figure 4). The application allows real-time text highlighting, whiteboard-style annotations, and addition of typed comments, and also provides telepointers to convey gestures. The application also shows a summary of comments in a separate window.

Clients send a stream of events specifying the current position of each user's mouse pointer. Clients also send events capturing users' markup operations, such as adding a comment or an annotation.

Although this application is substantially different from the chat system, the programmer handles disconnection in a similar fashion. All editing operations must be preserved on the server event queue. If the disconnection is lengthy (>10 minutes), the partially generic *AggregateToState* plug-in is used to combine all edit events into a single event that conveys the current state of the annotations. The handling of telepointer events depends on the length of the absence:

- The last 60 seconds of telepointer events are stored as-is and replayed with the *Speedup* plug-in;
- For longer disconnections, telepointer events are transformed to a heatmap display (Figure 4) which shades the document according to the number of telepointer events in each area. A custom plugin (*HeatmapTransformer*) converts telepointer events into the heatmap data structure.

These examples show common ways in which disconnection behaviour is handled by DiscoTech. A small number of plug-ins allows a wide range of application behaviour across different application types. Plug-ins provide general solutions to common problems that recur across applications (e.g., truncation of awareness events, accelerated replay, or shifting to a state representation as the length of the disconnection increases).

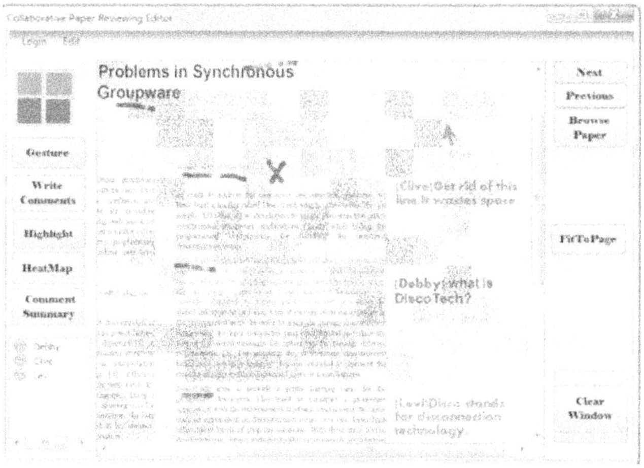

Figure 4: Reviewing application showing heatmap.

EVALUATION OF DISCOTECH

We have performed three evaluations of the DiscoTech framework. As discussed earlier, our key claims are that DiscoTech is *expressive,* supporting a wide range of disconnection behaviours; that DiscoTech is *easy to use,* with a plug-in architecture that hides the disconnection handling infrastructure, but still provides customizability; and that DiscoTech is *performant,* demanding only modest overhead in feedthrough times and memory use.

Expressiveness

DiscoTech can reproduce a wide variety of policies and strategies seen in previous work. In the following list, we show how several earlier approaches, including latecomer support, are accomplished using DiscoTech.

- *Maintain model state.* We provide the partially-generic 'aggregate-to-state' plug-in, which can convert model updates to a single state representation. Although not a purely state-based approach, this plug-in allows developers to come arbitrarily close to this behaviour.
- *Store-and-forward.* DiscoTech provides this policy natively through its queues, although not all updates will be forwarded (i.e., if pruned by another plug-in).
- *Event replay.* This is possible with the generic 'Speedup' plug-in. One earlier system provided a 'VCR-style' interface for replay [4]; we do not supply this specific interface, but the Speedup plug-in could easily support a replayer with 'pause' and 'fast-forward' controls.
- *Selection filtering.* DiscoTech supports filtering with generic plugins (which are parameterized by message type); more complex filtering (e.g., by message content [1], and the "freshest data" policy [8]) can be achieved through custom plug-ins.
- *Reordering.* This policy is part of the DiscoTech design framework, but must be implemented as a custom plug-in.
- *Coalescing, chunking, and compression.* We handle these strategies through partially-generic plug-ins such as the 'Chunker' described above. In addition, the full queue is compressed before delivery (upon reconnection).
- *Working while disconnected.* Although DiscoTech's conceptual architecture supports this policy, we currently uses a client-server architecture, so working while offline is not possible; however, a peer-to-peer version of DiscoTech (in development) will support this approach.
- *Latecomer support.* Support for latecomers is built into DiscoTech; we implement this by creating an extra client at system startup that is considered to be always disconnected. When a late entrant joins, we copy the extra client's queue to the new entrant and send it to them. Note that whatever policies are in place for disconnected clients will also affect the late entrant – e.g., they may receive a summary representation of chat rather than all of the text. This is different from schemes that guarantee the sending of a full model, but our approach provides more flexibility for the application programmer – we believe that what is sent to a late entrant should be an application-level decision, which can be achieved with DiscoTech.

Ease of Use

To obtain early feedback on ease of use, we solicited opinions of four software developers not associated with this project. Two developers were undergraduate research interns, and two were graduate students. All were familiar with the concepts of groupware and with development using C#, but none had programmed disconnection handling in a groupware application. Each was asked to carry out a one-hour tutorial which showed how to convert a single-user drawing application into a multi-user version including disconnection handling. We observed each developer as they worked through the tutorial, and then conducted a semi-structured interview after the session.

All four developers were able to complete the tutorial in one hour, correctly adding multi-user functionality to the application and experimenting with a variety of disconnection behaviors by swapping plug-ins. All reported that they found the toolkit's API straightforward, and that DiscoTech would be a suitable candidate for future projects. One participant commented that "The API is really generic… Since there is only one method call and a callback, it is very straightforward." Others stated "I would use DiscoTech because I don't want to reinvent the wheel." and "I would use DiscoTech. It does [it] all for me." While this was far from a comprehensive study, it does provide encouraging feedback that people with strong programming background and familiarity with groupware can learn the DiscoTech concepts quickly, and see value in it for programming disconnection behavior.

Performance

In order to characterize the overhead of using DiscoTech, we tested its effect on an application's feedthrough time and memory requirements. In both cases, we used the canonical groupware example of a shared drawing program.

To test *feedthrough time,* we ran a drawing program under two conditions: with and without disconnection handling enabled. In the "no disconnection handling" condition, DiscoTech's server-side queue was removed, and the server simply forwarded incoming events to all clients, thus simulating a traditional message broadcasting architecture. In both conditions, a "sender" client was automated to inject a new random drawing command every 2,000 ms, over a total of 200 seconds. Between one and four additional "receiver" clients received these drawing events. Feedthrough time was measured as the time from the event being sent by the sender client to the time that the message was received by a receiver client. A local area network was used between the client and server computers with ping times not exceeding 1 ms.

The results of this experiment are shown in Figure 5, which shows that feedthrough time increases with number of clients, but that the impact of DiscoTech's message queuing on feedthrough time is negligible.

To characterize DiscoTech's *overhead when a client is disconnected,* we tested the same drawing program, with

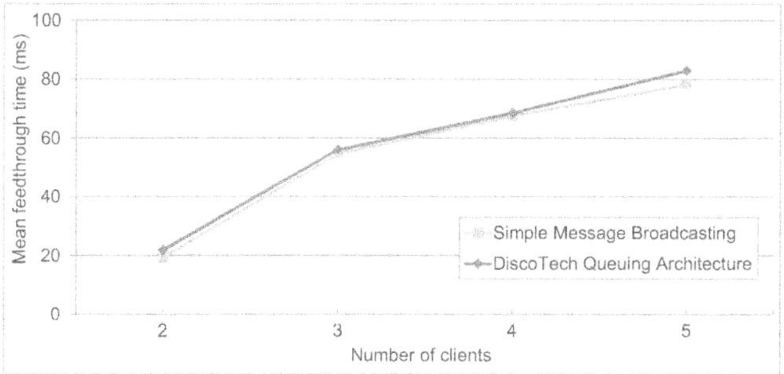

Figure 5: DiscoTech feedthrough time

one "sender" client, one connected "receiver" client, and one disconnected "receiver" client. In this scenario, the server must use its event queue to store information allowing the disconnected client to be brought up to date following reconnection.

The application transmitted two forms of events: telepointer movement events, and drawing commands. We measured server-side storage use under two conditions. The "without compaction" condition measured the space required to store the telepointer and drawing messages as-is, with no attempt to compress them to a smaller size. The "with compaction" condition used partially generic plug-ins to reduce storage size: (1) Drawing events: any drawing events occurring over the last ten minutes are represented in the queue as sent by the client; older drawing events are applied to a special bitmap message (using an *AggregateToState* compactor). (2) Telepointer events: the last minute of telepointer events are stored as sent by the client; events between one and ten minutes old are averaged to provide at most one event per five seconds (using an *Averager* compactor), and events older than ten minutes are converted to a heatmap (using *AggregateToState*).

Each condition was run for 12 hours (720 minutes). The results are summarized in Figure 6. In the "without compaction" condition, memory use climbed steadily over time. This is as expected, as events are continuously added to the event queue. Interestingly, even after 12 hours of disconnection, only 15 MB was required to store data from the drawing program. This hints that even with no compaction, small-group shared workspace groupware applications such as a drawing program can sustain lengthy disconnections with acceptable overhead.

In the "with compaction" condition, memory usage reaches a steady state after approximately one hour, at approximately 0.4 MB. This indicates that the aggregation to state strategy works well, where individual events are retained to allow progressive update (e.g., through double-speed replaying), while a full state snapshot allows aggregation of large numbers of events. The limitation of space to 0.4 MB also allows considerably faster reconnection than under the "without compaction" condition, as less data needs to be transmitted to the client.

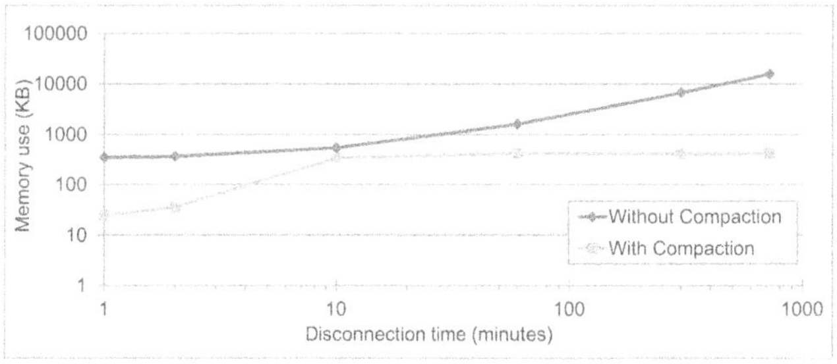

Figure 6: Memory use during disconnection (log-log plot)

This shows that with the use of parameterized plug-ins, DiscoTech can have modest and bounded storage requirements when handling disconnection. These results depend very much on the kind of application being tested. Our drawing surface was limited to 500 x 500 pixels; a larger drawing surface would have required more storage space. Similarly, trying to save the full contents of a video chat on a server would require considerably more storage. Nevertheless, for small-group shared-workspace groupware applications, this test indicates that storage requirements are well within the capacities of modern hardware.

CONCLUSIONS AND FUTURE WORK

Handling user-level disconnection and reconnection issues in synchronous groupware is difficult for developers. To simplify this support, we developed DiscoTech, a toolkit that covers a wider range of policies than any previous infrastructure, but that is easy to understand and imposes only minimal performance costs. DiscoTech's main novelty is that it addresses disconnection problems with a plug-in architecture, which provides both simple use in basic cases, as well as full customizability for experts. DiscoTech is based on a new representation of the design space that characterizes the types of behaviour that applications might need to exhibit as a consequence of disconnection. Our initial evaluations of DiscoTech indicate that it can cover a wide range of policies introduced in previous work, that it is easy for developers to learn, and that it does not impose major performance penalties during both connected and disconnected operation.

Our next steps with DiscoTech fall into three main areas. First, we will carry out further work on mechanisms for composing and timing the plugins. Currently the programmer must decide when different plugins will operate, and there is no system support for helping people schedule plug-ins and determine how different plug-ins will work together. In order to work on data that has already been manipulated by another plugin, all data must be tagged with a flag indicating whether the effects of the previous plugin can be reversed. We plan to explore other ways of dealing with this issue, such as with a timeline manager that can schedule and apply the plugins.

Second, we will test peer-to-peer versions of DiscoTech. The current toolkit places most of the responsibility for handling disconnection at the server – particularly during long disconnections. While this is a reasonable division (since servers are less likely to disappear than clients), we are interested in a more distributed or peer-to-peer version of the architecture that uses strategies from fault-tolerant computing, and that will allow clients to continue work while disconnected (e.g., in multi-player games).

Third, we will carry out additional tests to further evaluate DiscoTech's ease of use and performance in realistic situations. We have made the toolkit freely available ([7]) in order to gather feedback from the CSCW development community, and we plan to build several further groupware applications in order to test DiscoTech's performance with short-term outages (e.g., caused by network jitter), long-term absences, and custom plug-in scenarios. We are also interested to see how frequently the different plug-in types are used in practice, and whether a small number of plug-ins can cover a large majority of use cases for the toolkit.

ACKNOWLEDGEMENTS

This research is supported by NSERC through the Strategic Grants program and the GRAND NCE.

REFERENCES

1. Alves, P. and Ferreira, P. ReConMUC: Adaptable consistency requirements for efficient large-scale multi-user chat. *Proc. CSCW 2011*, 553-562.
2. Brockington, M. Level-Of-Detail AI for a Large Role-Playing Game, *AI Game Programming Wisdom*, S. Rabin ed., Charles River, 2002, 419-435.
3. Buszko, D., Lee, W. and Helal, A. Decentralized ad-hoc Groupware API and Framework for Mobile Collaboration. *Proc. Group 2001*, 5-14.
4. Chung, G., Dewan, P. and Rajaram, S. Generic and Composable Latecomer Accommodation Service for Centralized Shared Systems. *EHCI 1998*, 129-147.
5. Chung, G., Jeffay, K., and Abdel-Wahab, H. Dynamic Participation in Computer-based Conferencing System, *Journal of Com. Comm.* 17, 1 (1994), 7-16.
6. de Alwis, B., Gutwin, C. and Greenberg, S. GT/SD: performance and simplicity in a groupware toolkit. *EICS 2009*, 265-274.
7. DiscoTech Website: http://equis.cs.queensu.ca/?page_id=797 and http://hci.usask.ca/research/view.php?id=42.
8. Dix, A. Cooperation without (reliable) communication: Interfaces for mobile applications. *Dist. Sys. Eng.* 2 (1995), 171-181.
9. Dewan, P. and Choudhary, R. Primitives for Programming Multi-User Interfaces, *UIST 1991*, 69-78.
10. Edwards, W. Flexible conflict detection and management in collaborative applications. *Proc. UIST 2007*, 139-148.
11. Fraga, J., Siqueira, F., Favarim, F. An adaptive fault-tolerant component model. *WORDS 2003*, 179-186.
12. Graham, T.C.N., Kazman, R. and Walmsley, C. Agility Experimentation: Practical Techniques for Resolving Architectural Tradeoffs. *Proc. ICSE 2007*, 519-528.
13. Gutwin, C., Graham, T.C.N., Wolfe, C., Wong, N. and de Alwis, D. Gone but not Forgotten: Designing for Disconnection in Synchronous Groupware. *Proc. CSCW 2010*, 179-188.
14. Hall, R., Mathur, A., Jahanian, F., Prakash, A. and Rassmussen, Ç. Corona: A Communication Service for Scalable, Reliable Group Collaboration Systems. *Proc. CSCW 1996*, 140-149.
15. Illmann, T., Thol, R. and Weber, M. Transparent Latecomer Support for Web-Based Collaborative Learning Environments. *Proc. CSCL 2002*, 540-541.
16. Ionescu, M., Krebs, A. and Marsic, I. Dynamic Content and Offline Collaboration in Synchronous Groupware. *Proc. CTS 2002*
17. Ionescu, M. and Marsic, I. Latecomer and Crash Recovery Support in Fault Tolerant Groupware. *IEEE Distributed Systems Online* 2, 7, 2001.
18. Long, B., Dingel, J. and Graham, T.C.N. Experience applying the SPIN model checker to an industrial telecommunications system. *Proc. ICSE 2008*, 693-702.
19. Lukosch, S. Transparent Latecomer Support for Synchronous Groupware. *Proc. CRIWG 2003*, 26-41.
20. Manohar, N.R. and Prakash, A. The Session Capture and Replay Paradigm for Asynchronous Collaboration. *Proc. ECSCW 1995*, 149–164.
21. Narasimhan, P., Moser, L. E. and Melliar-Smith, P. M. Eternal: a component-based framework for transparent fault-tolerant CORBA. *Softw., Pract. and Exper.* 32, 8 (2002), 771-788.
22. Navarre, D., Palanque, P. and Basnyat, S. Usability Service Continuation through Reconfiguration of Input and Output Devices in Safety Critical Interactive Systems. *Proc. SAFECOMP 2008*, 373-386.
23. Pinelle, D., Dyck, J. and Gutwin, C. Aligning Work Practices and Mobile Technologies: Design for Loosely-Coupled Mobile Groups. *Mobile HCI 2003*, 177-192.
24. Preguica, N., Martins, L., Domingos, H. and Duarte, S. Integrating Synchronous and Asynchronous Interactions in Groupware Applications. *CRIWG 2005*, 89-104.
25. Roseman, M. & Greenberg, S. Building Real-time Groupware with GroupKit, a Groupware Toolkit. *ACM ToCHI*, 3, 1(1996), 66-106.
26. Roseman, M. and Greenberg, S. TeamRooms: Network Places for Collaboration. *Proc. CSCW 1996*, 325-333.
27. Sun, C. and Ellis, C. Operational transformation in real-time group editors: issues, algorithms, and achievements. *Proc. CSCW 1998*, 59–68.
28. Vogel, J., Mauve, M., Geyer, W., Hilt, V., Kuhmünch, C. A generic late-join service for distributed interactive media. *Proc. ACM Multimedia 2000*, 259-267.
29. Vogel, W. Object Oriented Groupware using the Ensemble System. *Proc. ECSCW OOGP* 1997, 23-26.

Towards Multi-Domain Collaboration Toolkits

Jacob Bartel
Computer Science Department
University of North Carolina
Chapel Hill, NC 27514 USA
+1 919 962 1890
bartel@cs.unc.edu

Prasun Dewan
Computer Science Department
University of North Carolina
Chapel Hill, NC 27514 USA
+1 919 962 1823
dewan@unc.edu

ABSTRACT
A multi-domain collaboration toolkit hides heterogeneity of user-interface toolkits and associated domains from both programmers and end users of collaborative, widget-synchronizing, applications. We have developed such a system for the stand-alone, Eclipse, and web domains; and the AWT, Swing, SWT, and GWT single-user toolkits associated with these domains. Several new concepts are supported to meet these requirements including a widget server allowing a distributed widget client to manipulate widgets on an interactive device, flexible widget synchronization, flexible placement of widget listeners, "piping" centralized non-interactive replicas communicating with interactive user replicas, factory-based retargeting of the user-interface toolkit, and a new process architecture.

Author Keywords
Heterogeneity; distributed user-interfaces; user-interface toolkits; web; multi-device interfaces

ACM Classification Keywords
D.2.2 [Software Engineering] Tools and Techniques –user interfaces

General Terms
Design; Performance

INTRODUCTION
All forms of computer systems, such as hardware systems, programming/command languages, and operating/ database systems, exhibit some degree of heterogeneity, which can be defined as the existence of different concrete mechanisms for implementing the same abstract concept. Heterogeneity has led to efforts to hide aspects of it from users of these systems. These efforts have had two main goals. First, allowing developers to create a single unifying implementation of some functionality for heterogeneous systems. Second, allowing heterogeneous systems to work together or interoperate with each other.

This paper focuses on unifying and interoperating collaboration capabilities that hide heterogeneity of user-interface toolkits and associated domains such as standalone and web applications. The unifying capabilities would allow collaboration toolkits built on top of different user-interface toolkits/domains to share some or all of their code. The interoperation mechanism would allow heterogeneous widgets, and ideally, also widget compositions, to be synchronized with each other. The unifying and interoperation goals can be met independently. However, we consider both goals in this paper, because, as we see below, a common set of concepts can be used to address both of them.

A more intriguing goal is to create a *cross fertilizing* heterogeneous toolkit. The requirement was first articulated in the context of the work of Heering and Klint[1] to unify command, programming, and debugging languages into a single "monolingual environment". As Heering and Klint argue, even if it is not possible to develop a practical unified system, the attempt to integrate systems in different domains can lead to a cross fertilization in which crucial features found in one domain are incorporated as useful features in another domain.

In the rest of the paper, we expand on what it means to achieve these three main goals, and describe a first-cut system for realizing them

SCOPE
Before we can discuss our solution, we need to better describe the problem and solution requirements. We begin by explaining the terms *user-interface toolkit*, *domain*, and *collaboration*.

Single-User Layers and Toolkits
In general, the I/O of a single user is processed by several user-interface layers. A *framebuffer* treats the screen of the user as a two dimensional array of pixels, allowing higher layers to (a) access and manipulate these pixels, and (b) intercept keyboard and mouse events. A *window system* divides the screen into smaller regions, called windows, allowing drawing of text and images in a window and interception of window-specific events, such as typing and mouse clicks in a window or resizing and movement of a window. A *user-interface toolkit* is a layer above the

window system that divides windows into finer-grained abstractions such as text-boxes, sliders, and menus, and allows interception of widget-specific events such as typing and commitment of text in a text-box. A *view* is a layer between the toolkit and the semantic component of an application, called the *model*. The view composes widgets into a user-interface, and keeps the model and user-interface state consistent.

User-interface toolkits can create stand-alone or plug-in widgets in some applications. We shall refer to each environment in which widgets are created as a *domain*. Our work is currently restricted to Java applications, and addresses four popular Java toolkits: AWT, Swing, IBM's SWT, and Google's GWT. Together, these define three domains: the (desktop) stand-alone, (browser) web, and Eclipse domains. AWT and Swing support both stand-alone widgets and web-browser plug-in widgets in an applet. SWT supports both stand-alone widgets and plug-in Eclipse widgets. GWT supports plug-in (web) browser widgets by converting Java to AJAX-based JavaScript We have not yet fully targeted toolkits developed for mobile computers. We have developed single-user support for the Android toolkit, but not collaboration support, because certain Java features on which our implementation currently depends are missing in Android. However, the concepts described here should work for mobile user-interface toolkits.

In all of these toolkits, the client and user-interface toolkit layer run in the same process and hence host. Each toolkit (a) supports calls to instantiate or change a widget and associate a widget with observer or *listener* client objects, and (b) each announces widget events to interested listeners. All of them assume a single user views and manipulates each widget. In the rest of the paper, we shall assume this model of a single-user user-interface toolkit.

Collaboration Tools

A collaboration tool allows sharing of abstractions in one or more user-interface layers. There are unique advantages and disadvantages of sharing each layer [2]. In particular, sharing the user-interface toolkit layer allows non WYSIWIS (What You See is What I See) collaboration, and does not require special abstractions designed for collaboration. Sharing the framebuffer or window layer forces near-WYSIWIS collaboration. Sharing higher layers (a) does not allow sharing of toolkit events not intercepted by the higher layers, such as scrolling and incremental changes to a text field widget; and (b) constrains the abstractions that can be used to create the view and/or model. Thus, for each user-interface toolkit, it is important to offer a collaboration tool that allows sharing of its widgets.

A *layer-independent collaboration tool* offers general synchronization mechanisms such as remote procedures and shared objects [3, 4], which can be used by application programmers to manually intercept and share events/calls of one or more layers among different users. A *layer-dependent collaboration tool*, on the other hand, understands the events and calls of the layer on which it depends, and provides automatic sharing of events/calls of these layers, possibly using abstractions of a layer-independent tool. By a *collaboration toolkit*, we mean a layer-dependent collaboration tool that automatically shares events/calls of one or more user-interface toolkits.

The applications supported by a collaboration toolkit are *collaboration-aware* or *collaboration-transparent* based on whether they are aware that they are being used by multiple users. It is possible to support collaboration transparency at all layers. NetMeeting and Suite [5] are examples of desktop/window and model sharing systems, respectively, that support collaboration-transparent applications. It is also possible to transparently make individual single-user applications collaborative without changing them – for example, as shown in [6], Microsoft Word and PowerPoint. Any tool that provides tailoring of collaboration functionality supports collaboration-aware applications. As we see below, the cross fertilization goal requires a small amount of collaboration awareness in the application. Therefore, rather than using the dichotomy of collaboration awareness and transparency to evaluate the automation of our tool, we use the "proportional effort" requirement given below.

Requirements of Multi-Domain Collaboration Toolkit

As mentioned in the introduction, ideally a multi-domain collaboration toolkit should support unification, interoperability, and cross fertilization. Below, we refine these abstract goals by outlining specific requirements such a toolkit should meet.

Unification: It should offer a single set of mechanisms for sharing widgets of each of the target user-interface toolkits in each of the domains in which these toolkits can be used. This requirement was personally motivated by a collaboration system we have worked on for several decades. We have had to continuously port it to the single-user toolkit "most in fashion" at that time. In particular, we have created versions of it for Motif, UIL, HTML, AWT, and Swing. Each of these resulted in a different code base. As it is was difficult to keep multiple code bases consistent, only one of these toolkits was supported at one time. This is not a problem if newer user-interface toolkits supersede previous ones; however, this is not the case today. For instance, there is no consensus today on whether AWT, Swing or SWT should be used to create standalone user-interfaces for a Java application. More important, as mentioned above, different plug-in domains offer different toolkits.

The problem of creating separate implementations of a collaborative system for each popular user-interface toolkit is not peculiar to our project. Consider an IM tool. Today we see independent implementations of it in web user interfaces (e.g. Gmail), in the Eclipse environment (e.g. Jazz [7]), and, of course, on the desktop (e.g. Windows

Live Messenger) as a stand-alone tool. An even more serious problem is that no collaboration toolkit has been built so far for the relatively new SWT and GWT toolkits. A single collaboration toolkit layered on top of Swing, AWT, GWT and SWT, supporting all of the domains in which these user-interface toolkits can operate, would solve the above two problems.

Compatibility: Such a collaboration toolkit must bridge the gap between both the target user-interface toolkits and domains. One way to bridge the domain gaps is to use the cross fertilization idea to make all domains equal from the point of a collaboration toolkit. This approach has been used in [8] to make web browsers directly communicate events with each other, much as stand-alone replicas in current collaboration toolkits do. However, it is not practical to change web browsers, and more important, violate web constraints. Therefore, we include the following broader compatibility requirement: The collaboration toolkit must follow domain constraints.

Cross fertilization: Cross fertilization to the web domain is consistent with the general view that the web is a liability for collaboration, though recent work has shown that this is not the case in many situations[9, 10]. We go a step further and suggest that it is, in fact, an asset, in that many aspects of it should be included in other domains. In particular, in all domains, it should be possible, as in web applications, to:

(a) *centralize communication* through a central server, as such communication provides more ordering guarantees, which can be exploited in replica consistency algorithms[11]; and does not require the user computer to accept connection requests, disallowed by certain firewalls. As centralized communication adds network latency to remote response times, it should be done only for those widgets such as text for which such guarantees are important.

(b) *centralize computation* in a central server, for several reasons. Certain resources, such as some files and databases, may not be available to stand-alone applications on a user computer. In addition, the computation may be expensive, and thus carried out faster on a powerful server than a slow user computer. Furthermore, certain computations such as file writes and email sends are not idempotent, that is, yield the same result regardless of how many replicas carry them out. As centralized computation adds network latency to response times, it should be done only when it is essential or beneficial.

(c) *use a generic program to join* a session so that all users in the session are not responsible for installing and keeping up-to-date application-specific code, which can be a heavyweight and error-prone task.

Begole et al[12] have shown that these are essential features when application code runs in a web browser, and we argue here that they are important convenience features in other domains.

Interoperation: It should be possible to support real-time collaboration among collaborators using different single-user toolkits and domains. Increasingly, the same application is being implemented in different domains (e.g. Microsoft's Word and Google Docs's web version of it, and the Google Map/Translate implementations on the web and various mobile devices). In various scenarios (some of which are given in [13, 14]), a group of collaborators may wish, or be forced, to use different domains and associated user-interface toolkits, and thus, have a need for such interoperation.

Multiple widget-compositions: Often different domains offer different widget-compositions for the same application (e.g. Google translate) that make use of the unique capabilities and constraints of the domain. However, synchronizing different widget compositions seems fundamentally at odds with collaboration toolkits. To illustrate, consider the classic case of an integer value being represented by a slider in one user-interface and a textbox in another. Synchronizing two different widget types directly requires a way to translate from one to another, which in turn, implies that it is implemented in a layer above the user-interface toolkit.

However, it is possible to use the following observation to relax the requirement in current collaboration toolkits that only identical widget-composition can be synchronized. The widget compositions may differ, not because the same abstraction is displayed by different types of widgets, but because certain user-interfaces (a) contain optional widgets not displayed in other interfaces, and/or (b) provide different layouts and composition of common widgets. Therefore, allowing collaboration among multiple (but not arbitrary) widget compositions is another requirement.

Controlled retargeting: As collaborators may interact from different domains, associated with different user-interface toolkits, and may also have different preferences for the user-interface toolkit, the programs run by them should be able to control which user-interface toolkit is used to create the user-interface. This requirement distinguishes our work from a multi-platform user-interface toolkit, such as AWT, which provides a logical layer that is targeted automatically at multiple physical user-interface toolkits offered by different platforms.

Proportional programming effort: The requirements above imply several customization capabilities, which increase programming overhead. This effort should be proportional to the amount of customization desired by the application. In particular, applications that wish the traditional semantics supported by existing collaboration toolkits should require no collaboration awareness.

No performance penalty: A collaboration toolkit meeting these requirements and targeted at a particular user-interface toolkit and domain should be able to offer the same performance as one designed for that user-interface toolkit and domain.

No superfluous constraint: The system must impose only those constrains required by the domains. In particular, it should not force two processes to (a) centralize a computation, if the computation can be safely replicated, and (b) centralize a communication, if it is possible for it to be safely done directly.

TECHNICAL CONCEPTS

To explain how we address these requirements, we start with an overview section describing the process architecture, and then individually address some of the components of the architecture.

To concretely understand the architecture and other concepts, let us consider an application, inspired by Google Translate, that allows English-speaking users to study Chinese by viewing together the translations of a collaboratively composed sequence of English words. It comes with two user-interfaces (Figure 1), a small and a large user-interface. The small user-interface presents, in a single column, two text fields for displaying an English phrase and its translation, and a button for performing the translation. The large user-interface uses text areas instead of text fields as the two text components, provides an extra button to clear these widgets, and lays widgets in a matrix rather than a column. The small user-interface has been developed for the mobile and Eclipse domains, where screen space is an issue, and the large one for other domains. The two interfaces are implemented by the classes, ASmallGUI and ALargeGUI, respectively.

Process Architecture

Like traditional collaboration toolkits, our system assumes that a user in a collaborative session runs some local process that joins the session and creates and manipulates local widgets for that user. Corresponding widgets created by different local processes in the same session are kept consistent with each other. Therefore, like other collaboration toolkits, we will refer to these processes as (local) *replicas*, even though they are not required to run the same code. Each replica has a module called a *widget server* module, which is provided by our collaboration toolkit. A widget server is like a window server in a network window system, distributing the user-interface toolkit rather than the window layer. This, it accepts remote calls from a widget client to create and update widgets, and sends widget events to the latter. The widget server module can execute as part of (a) a *generic session joiner*, provided by our toolkit, in which case it receives remote calls to both create the initial user-interface and make updates to it in response to remote actions, or (b) a program executing application specific-code such as ASmallUI and ALargeUI, in which case it receives calls only to update the user interface in response to remote actions.

For each kind of user-interface, a separate *piping replica* process is created, so named, because instead of making calls in a single-user toolkit, it directs them to the session server, which in turn forwards them to regular replicas to remotely create and update their user-interfaces. Thus, in this example, two piping replicas are created, for the small and large interfaces, respectively. As we support the web domain, we assume that each collaborative application is installed on some web server. In addition, we assume that existence of a *session server*, which (a) allows users of the application to form one or more sessions, (b) creates piping replicas for each session, (c) centralizes communication of information among replicas, and (d) and stores session state downloaded into latecomers.

All centralized processes must be located on well-known hosts. In our implementation, they all run on the machine hosting the web server. It is attractive to combine them all in one central process to reduce the startup costs. A session server and piping replica are separate because they execute toolkit-defined and application-defined code, respectively. A web server and other processes are separate because a web server can execute external code only when a web browser referencing that code connects to it; and we support sessions in which no web browser is involved.

Let us continue with the example to illustrate and further refine the architecture above. Assume that programmer Alice has just finished creating the latest version of the code. She installs it on a well known directory, *translator*, at a web server, www.univ.edu, associated with this application. In addition, she installs it as a plug-in in the Eclipse environment.

To join a new session with the application, she starts a local replica that makes the following call:

VirtualToolkit.join(joinDescription, replicaId, false, false)

All four arguments are passed by the local call to the remote session server. The two Boolean arguments indicate that by default, the communication between widget replicas is direct and the listeners of the widgets are replicated. "replicaId" is an optional argument, and is used by the local replica to register with the session server an address that can be used by other replicas to communicate with it directly. The join description consists of three parts: a web server address, and an application, session, and UI description, as shown below:

www.cs.univ.edu/~translator/?session=test1&kind=small

Here ~translator, session=test1 and kind=small are the application, session, and UI descriptions, respectively. The UI description is passed to the session server so that it can connect it to the appropriate piping replica. In response to (a) the first join request, the session server

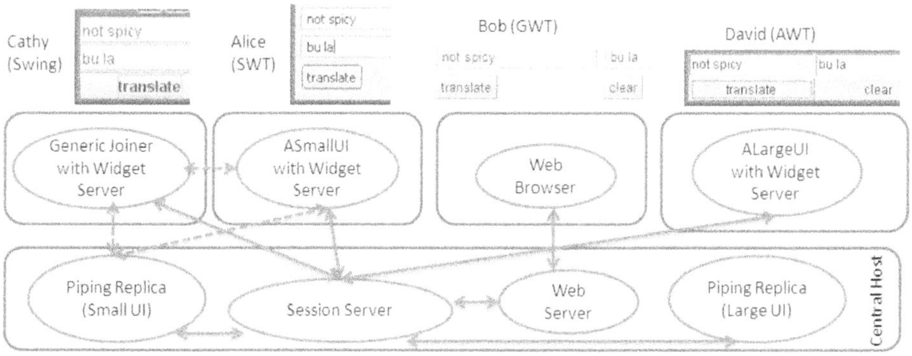

Figure 1 User Interfaces and Physical Process Architecture in Example Session

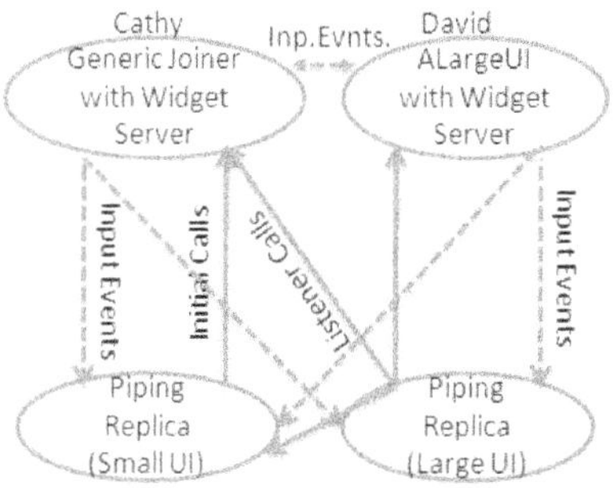

Figure 2 Logical Call/Event Flow

creates a new object to represent the session; and (b) all join requests, the requesters are added to the session object, and the replica address of the joiner, if provided, is sent to existing session members with registered replica addresses.

On the creation of a new session, the session server also starts the two piping replicas for the two user interfaces. A piping replica for a particular kind of user-interface executes the same code as a corresponding user replica, creating the same user-interface, and also has a replica address to communicate with the session server. A configuration file specifies the program(s) that the piping replicas run, runtime arguments to the program(s), and the widgets whose listeners they centralize. In our example, it states that for all widgets, the centralized listeners are located in the piping replica created for the large interface.

Alice next asks Bob, Cathy, and David to join her in testing the new version, communicating the session URL to them. David is on the file system referenced by the web server, so he simply runs the installed code on his machine to create a replica, binding it to AWT and the large interface. The other users are on separate file servers and have not installed the software. This is not a problem for Bob, who interacts through the web browser, which uses the web protocol to download code compiled into JavaScript by GWT, and binds it to the large interface. Cathy creates a stand-alone user-interface, and is also able to use a generic application, the generic session joiner mentioned above, and binds it to Swing and the small interface. David is behind a firewall that prevents incoming connections, so he does not provide a replica address when joining the session. As Bob uses a web browser, he too does not provide such an address. The other two users, not behind firewalls, provide such addresses, which are used to connect them to each other and the two piping replicas. Figure 1 shows the user interfaces and process architecture created for the resulting session, in which multiple users, single-user toolkits, widget compositions, and domains are involved. The dashed lines indicate connections among replicas. Such connections are not shown for the piping replica for the large interface to avoid further cluttering the figure. David and Bob's replicas have no such connections as they have not registered replica addresses.

Factory-based Retargeting

A collaboration toolkit supporting both replication and centralization of widget listeners must trap and distribute events and calls of the underlying user-interface toolkit. Like several previous works, we have developed an abstract user-interface toolkit layer that is mapped to multiple target user-interface toolkits, which allows us to meet the unification requirement by implementing the trapping/distribution support in this layer. There have been two main approaches for such abstraction.

One approach is to create a declarative re-targetable user-interface tool such as an XML-based system [15]. However, this approach fundamentally changes the way developers program, thereby also restricting the set of supported user-interfaces. For instance, it does not allow a program to dynamically add widgets in response to user input.

Another approach is to create a procedural abstract layer and require the programmer to use appropriate subclasses of it to choose the appropriate concrete implementation. This approach has been used in WAHID[13] to map abstract scrollbars and menus to different concrete implementations of them in a stand-alone application and a sketching tool. In a single-inheritance language, the class inheritance approach works only when the target widgets are not related by an inheritance hierarchy, as in the case of the scrollbar and menu widgets. For example, it cannot support a container widget that is a subclass of a component widget, as the former would have to now be a subclass of an abstract container class. Therefore, we have developed an alternate solution based on using (programming) interfaces, and two interface-based design patterns: a) factories [16], that is, objects that create other objects, and (b) abstract factories[16], that is, objects that select among different factories.

We have created an abstract widget interface hierarchy based on the class hierarchy of Swing widget classes. For instance, we have created interfaces, VirtualContainer and VirtualComponent, which declare the public methods of Component and Container, respectively; and made VirtualContainer a subtype of VirtualComponent. For each target toolkit, we have created *proxy toolkit classes* that delegate to corresponding classes of the toolkit. For instance, we have created the proxy toolkit classes SwingContainer and SWTContainer to provide the Swing and SWT implementations, respectively, of the VirtualContainer interface.

Competing *toolkit-specific factories* are created for different versions of toolkit abstractions in different target toolkits, and are assigned to abstract factory classes, which are used, via static methods, to instantiate toolkit abstractions. For instance, in our example, the following call is used to instantiate the translate button:

ButtonSelector.*createButton*("translate")

It invokes the static method. createButton() on the abstract factory, ButtonSelector, which returns an instance of the abstract interface VirtualButton.

Abstract factories are initialized by functions that choose the toolkit, which in turn results in them being assigned the concrete factories of the chosen toolkit. For instance, if the Swing toolkit is chosen, then the abstract factory, ButtonSelector, is assigned an instance of the factory, SwingButtonFactory. Thus, the call given above asks the instance of SwingButtonFactory to create a button, which, in turn, returns an instance of the proxy class SwingButton. An operation such as addActionListener() or setName() on the proxy class (SwingButton) delegates to the corresponding operation provided by the target toolkit class (JButton). The proxy toolkit classes not only delegate to target toolkit classes, but also, as we see below, distribute toolkit events among collaborators and interpose toolkit-provided proxy listeners between widgets and their application-defined centralized listeners (Figure 3).

Requiring developers to type toolkit abstractions using interfaces and instantiate them using factories is arguably good programming practice, yet *none* of our target Java target toolkits define a factory or even an interface for *any* widget. We might have also ignored them in our API had they not offered a way to support controlled retargeting, a side effect of which is the ability to create better designed programs, consistent with the argument of Heering and Klint that the exercise of trying to unify a set of computer systems can result in enhancement of individual members of the set. To allow developers to use familiar APIs, we have built adapters that translate calls of an existing user-interface toolkit to our abstract toolkit-independent top layer (Figure 3). To use them, developers must change the name of the top-level package in their imports of classes/interfaces provided by the existing toolkit.

Not all of our target toolkits support the same set of abstractions. How one translates between heterogeneous toolkit abstractions is an issue that modern multi-platform toolkits [15] have addressed and is, thus, beyond the scope of our research. In our current implementation, if a target toolkit does not support the equivalent of a supported abstraction or operation, we simply return a null object or do nothing when the abstraction is instantiated and the operation is invoked, respectively. If an application uses some functionality that is common to a subset of the target user-interface toolkits, then our implementation is able to bind it to all of these toolkits without loss of functionality. An important implication of this guarantee is that existing programs bound to some target toolkit would suffer no loss of functionality when they are ported to our abstract layer and then targeted back at the original toolkit. A more robust system would implement missing functionality.

Our factory-based approach allows toolkit API calls to be redirected to another process rather than a target toolkit. To do such redirection, the redirector must set the target "user-interface toolkit" to an address that represents the remote process. In response, the call sets the abstract factories to *factories* rather than toolkit-specific factories. These factories return, not toolkit proxy objects, but *forwarder objects*, which forward calls to the target process (and store local un-displayed state). This feature is used by the piping replicas to forward calls to the session server. Thus, when the translator program is run by a piping replica, ButtonSelector.createButton() returns an instance of ForwarderButton, which forwards setActionListener() and other calls to the session server.

In summary, we support a three layered approach for abstracting the user-interface toolkit. The top layer defines widget interfaces, factory interfaces, and abstract factory classes, which define the API used by the programmer. The second layer provides, for each target user-interface toolkit and the forwarder "user-interface toolkit," implementations of the factory and widget interfaces defined by the topmost layer. This layer references instances of the actual classes of the target toolkits.

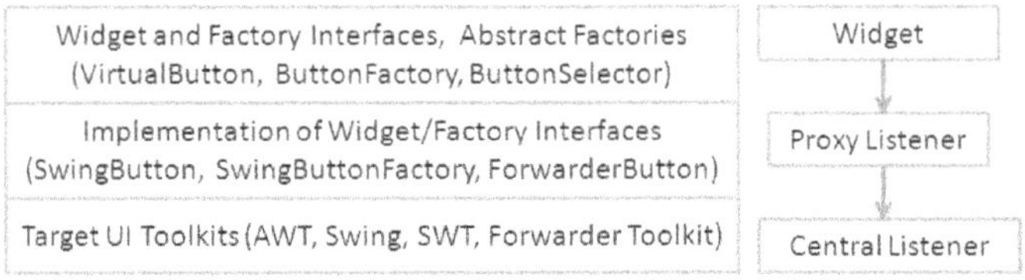

Figure 3 Layers and Modules Processing Calls/Events

Widget Servers and Piping Replica Clients

Systems such as X[17] and NeWS[18] have shown the usefulness and possibility of distributing the window layer. An interactive computer runs a special local process, called a *window server*, which manages the windows on that computer, and accepts connections from multiple, possibly remote, processes, called *window clients*. A window client can ask a window server to create windows on the computer it manages, and is sent user events associated with these windows. This is called the *inverted server* architecture as the local machine hosts a server, and remote machines the clients.

As mentioned above, we distribute the user-interface toolkit layer, which seems like a simple variation of the idea of distributing the window layer, where the main difference is in the types of the objects on the user's computer and the events that are fired by these objects. Using the window system inverted server terminology, we will use the terms *widget server* and *widget client* to refer to a module that serves and issues, respectively, remote requests to create and manipulate toolkit abstractions. As in the case of a window system, the widget server runs in a process on the user's computer, while a widget client is a remote process.

However, there are some subtle related differences between the motivations for and nature of the distribution of the window and toolkit layers. One difference has to do with the number of user-interface servers on a user's computer. A window system running on a user's computer provides a single process serving all possible window clients that wish to create windows on that computer. Our approach, on the other hand, creates a separate widget server process on a computer for each remote widget client process that creates (synchronized) widgets on that computer.

In a network window system, the single window server is guaranteed to be up before any of its window clients starts, and allows connections to be made to it by clients. Moreover, a client can be on an arbitrary host, and pushes requests to a server. In our context, a piping replica is a client. It is located on a well known host, and is started when a session is created. The server is typically started after this client, when its user joins the session. Furthermore, to respect firewall restrictions, it is not guaranteed to allow inward connections. Therefore, we interpose a central process, the session server, between the server and the piping replicas, which accepts connections from both. The calls of the piping replicas are piped to the session server instead of a target toolkit, which stores them. Later, when a widget server joins a session, it pulls these calls. Any subsequent call made by the piping client is immediately sent to the widget server, again through the session server.

Remote window systems differ on where event processing code is executed. X [17] requires events to be passed back to the window client that made the API calls, while NeWS [18] allows the client to download some event-processing code, written in a special language, into the window system. Our user-interface toolkit model requires us to support listener-based event handling, which means deciding where event processing is done reduces to locating the listeners, discussed next.

Flexible Listener Placement

Like traditional single-user toolkits, we allow a widget to be bound to a local listener. In addition, we allow it to be bound to a central listener in a piping replica, as shown in the call below:

```
translate.setCentralizedComputation(true);
```

which centralizes the listener for the translate button, as it accesses a database located only on the central host.

How the widget-listener binding is done depends not only on the listener location but also on whether a user-interface is created in response to requests issued by a local application replica or a central piping replica. Thus, we have four cases: (1) local replica, local listener; (2) local replica, central listener; (3) piping replica, central listener; (4) piping replica, local listener. The first case is the traditional approach, and can be supported directly by associating the listener with the target toolkit widget. In the other cases, the widgets and listeners are in different address spaces, and in the last two cases, the binding is being made in one process, the widget server, by another process, the piping replica.

Consider case (2). When the local replica makes the call to bind a widget to a local (application-defined) listener, the proxy class that intercepts this call binds the widget to a toolkit-defined *proxy listener*, which forwards received events to the piping replica that hosts the central listener for that widget (Figure 3). Case (3) is similar except that the call to bind the widget to the central listener is invoked by the remote piping replica, through the session manager. This call does not send a listener object to the replica. Instead, it sends a directive to bind the widget to the toolkit-defined proxy listener.

Case (4) is the most difficult, as a listener must be created in the local replica in response to a request from a remote process. One approach, which we support, is to make the requesting process instantiate the listener and send a copy to the widget server. However, the listener may have location-specific references and thus, in Java's terminology, not be serializable. Moreover, this approach does not allow listeners for different widgets to share objects, as copies rather than references of objects are shared. Therefore, our collaboration toolkit allows the application to bind a widget, not only to a listener, but also a factory that returns a listener. The toolkit uses the factory to obtain the real listener. When a piping replica makes such a binding call, it sends a copy of a factory rather than that of a listener. The widget server uses this copy to obtain the listener. The factory can construct the listener locally and, optionally, bind it to parts of listeners constructed by previously sent factories. This approach is illustrated in the following code, where the translate button is associated with a listener factory:

```
translate.addActionListener(new ATranslateListenerFactory(from,
to).createActionListener());
```

Here, "from" and "to" are the text components containing the original and translated text, respectively. A factory can be expected to be serializable as its job is relatively simple. As we see from the call above, a factory or listener may have references to widgets, which are not normally serializable. We define special "serialization" procedures for them that send their global ids, which are de-serialized by mapping them to the corresponding widgets installed in the local process.

Case (4) requires the widget server to access application-defined (listener/factory) classes. If the underlying RPC system allows classes of objects to be sent along with objects, then this is not an issue. However, the ones we use in our implementation – GWT RPC for communication between web clients and servers and RMI for all other communication - do not currently include this capability. This is not a problem in the GWT case as it allows client-side classes to be specified at the web server, which are automatically compiled and downloaded in the browser. In the RMI case, we use a network loader to obtain such a class, if such an operation does not cause access violations, and centralize the listener otherwise. Creating application-defined factories increases program burden, and dynamically sending them and loading their classes over the network increases the time required to create a user-interface. These problems are consistent with extensible network window systems such as NeWS, which allow only certain kinds of code to be executed in the window system, and incur the cost of creating and sending event handlers.

A widget event can go to a local listener (case 1 and 4) without the need for an intermediary. Yet, even in these cases, we interpose a proxy between the two, which forwards events to the local listener, and also implements widget synchronization, discussed below.

Synchronization

One challenge in automatically synchronizing different widget composition is determining the correspondence between widgets in these compositions. The traditional approach is to assume that identical widget compositions are created by identical replicated code, and use the order in which widgets are created to determine the correspondence. We use a more general approach in which the creation order is used by default, unless the programmer explicitly names the widgets, in which case the name is used to resolve the correspondence. The standard Swing setName() method is also provided by our toolkit to name the widgets:

```
translate.setName("translate")
```

Unlike the Swing toolkit, our synchronization approach requires the name of a widget to be unique.

A toolkit such as ours that supports replication and centralization must support the following synchronization invariants. (a) An event sent to a listener in one process must also be sent to all corresponding replicated listeners in other processes. For instance, in our example, when the user presses the clear button, the event should be sent to all replicated listeners of the widget. (b) A state-changing API call made by a centralized listener must be invoked on all widget servers in the user replicas. Thus, in our example, when the listener in the large UI piping replica sets the text of the "to" widget, the call should be forwarded to all user replicas. (c) Corresponding local toolkit calls made by listeners in different replicas must return the same value. For instance, when the translate button is pressed, the replicated listeners in different replicas must see the same state in the "from" and "to" text widgets.

We support three coupling modes that offer these invariants. In all of these modes, each change to a widget causes the widget and event to be stored in a global buffer. The buffer is sent to all remote (piping and user) replicas whenever a proxy listener (Figure 3) forwards an event to an application-defined listener. In the default/action/incremental coupling mode, no other event/action events/all events cause buffer transmission. We have included these coupling modes to show the range of existing coupling modes [5] that can be supported in our collaboration toolkit. They subsume those offered by current collaboration toolkits, and thus help meet the no superfluous constraint requirement.

On receiving an input event, an interactive replica makes an equivalent call to update the local widget, and also forwards it to local listeners of the event. Thus, when a user edits the "from" text component, the resulting input event, when transmitted to another interactive replica, causes the corresponding local "from" component to be updated with the edited value. The calls made by a centralized listener are sent to all interactive replicas. A replica ignores an event or call referencing a widget that does not exist in its user interface.

Synchronization events and calls are sent to the session manager by the piping replicas through the forwarder user-interface toolkit (Figure 3). These are buffered in the session object in the session manager for replicas that join the session late. While compression techniques [19] can be applied to them, we have not so far provided them in our implementation. Buffered actions are separated into the initial calls for creating the user interface, which are forwarded to generic session joiners, and the subsequent actions, which are forwarded to all replicas. The initial calls received from different piping replicas are kept in separate buffers as these replicas create different user interfaces. All subsequent events and listener calls are kept in a single global buffer. All calls made before the first synchronization input event is received are considered initial calls. A piping replica generates no input events but receives all synchronization events. The synchronization events received by only one of these replicas are stored in the global buffer. Moreover, a call made by a listener in a piping replica in response to a synchronization event is stored in the global buffer only if the (a) the listener is centralized, determined by the API call given earlier, and (b) the replica is responsible for centralizing it, determined by the configuration file, also mentioned earlier.

Figure 2 illustrates and summarizes the logical flow of events and API calls among the interactive and piping replicas. As Cathy joins the session with a generic session joiner, the piping replica for the small user interface sends it calls to create the interface. David's replica does not receive such calls from the piping replica to create the large interface, as he joins the session with a custom replica that makes local calls to create it. As the listener for the translate button is centralized in the large piping replica, the calls issued by the listener to update the "to" widget are sent to all other (user and piping) replicas. Finally, each user replica sends input to all other replicas.

This logical flow does not reflect the physical flow of messages discussed in earlier sections, which may involve the session manager. It is involved in delivery of (a) all communication to interactive replicas such as David's that have not registered addresses, (b) all calls made by piping replicas, and (c) all latecomer input events.

DISCUSSION

Our abstraction of the target user-interface toolkits and implementation of the sharing mechanisms in terms of this abstraction allows us to meet the unification requirement.

By allowing communication to be centralized in the session server, and some listeners to run on a central machine, we ensure that constraints of our target domains are not violated, thereby meeting the compatibility requirement. Moreover, by allowing processes that can do so to execute listeners locally and communicate directly with each other, we meet the no superfluous constraint requirement. By allowing generic programs to be used to join collaborative sessions and allowing programmers to determine if computation/communication is centralized or replicated allows us to meet the cross fertilization requirements. By allowing programs to also choose the target user-interface toolkit, we meet the controlled retargeting requirement.

By allowing synchronization among heterogeneous compositions of widgets of different target toolkits, we meet the requirements of interoperation and multiple widget-compositions. Modulo a few extra levels of indirection (proxy widgets and listeners), we support the existing functionality and communication and computation architectures of these toolkits. Our preliminary performance measurements show, not surprisingly, that these indirection levels cause un-measurable changes to the performance. Thus, we meet the performance requirement.

The functionality unique to our collaboration toolkit is optional. Defining a configuration file, listener factories and overriding of the communication, centralization, and coupling modes is necessary only if the semantics supported by traditional stand-alone collaboration toolkits, which are replicated, is unacceptable. Thus, arguably, we meet the proportional effort requirement.

Dynamic binding of an application program to a concrete user-interface – also called *plasticity* [20] - is the goal of several collaborative and non collaborative systems. As mentioned earlier, a particularly relevant example of a procedural system supporting this idea is WAHID [13]. However, it is not a collaboration toolkit, and thus does not meet any of our other requirements. There are numerous examples of previous collaboration toolkits such as [3, 8, 12]. However none of these supports heterogeneous domains or user-interface toolkits.

Several other forms of collaboration tools meet one or more of our requirements. Like us, Cooperative Teresa [14] allows synchronization of heterogeneous widget compositions. However, it is targeted only at the web domain. More important, it shares the view rather than the user-interface toolkit layer. As mentioned before, a higher-level tool such as this one supports a non standard and restrictive programming paradigm, and does not allow certain useful coupling modes that can be implemented only in a collaboration toolkit. Some model-based [4] or layer-independent[21] tools support multiple communication and/or computation architectures. One difference between these systems and ours is that the former assume all computation can be safely replicated, and support multiple architectures only for performance.

As mentioned before, sharing of each layer provides a unique set of advantages and disadvantages. For instance, as also mentioned before, sharing of a layer higher than the user-interface toolkit allows more divergence in the synchronized widget compositions, and also, in view-sharing systems such as Cooperative Teresa, allows automatic generation of these compositions. Thus, our system has several disadvantages that collaboration toolkits suffer in general. As mentioned before, the unique advantages and disadvantages of sharing each layer are discussed in depth in [2].

In summary, no other system meets all of the requirements our toolkit was designed to meet. More strongly, none of them supports: a generic session-joining program in domains other than the web, programmer-controlled retargeting of an entire user-interface toolkit, widget-grained control over whether communication and computation is centralized, and no superfluous constraints.

Novel Mechanism	Supported Requirements
Factory-based retargeting	Unification, controlled targeting
Widget server	Generic session joining tool, listener centralization, latecomer
Synchronization modes	No extraneous constraints
Flexible listener placement	Widget-grained computation centralization/replication, no extraneous constraints
Piping replicas	Computation centralization, Generic session joining tool, Hetero. widget compositions
Process architecture	All requirements

Table 1 Novel Mechanisms vs. Requirements

The novelty of a system must be judged not only by the requirements it meets but also the mechanisms it offers. Table 1 identifies the major novel mechanisms and the collaboration requirements they support. Some of these mechanisms have applications beyond collaboration. Factory-based retargeting can be used to create plastic single-user interfaces, and piping replicas could be used for monitoring user-interface activity.

Perhaps more important than the novel aspects of our collaboration toolkit are the requirements themselves, which, for the first time, define what it means to support a collaboration toolkit that can be targeted at multiple domains and associated user-interface toolkits. In particular, they show that web features can be an asset rather than a liability in collaboration toolkits.

Experience with our system is necessary to refine our requirements and identify alternative mechanisms to meet them. It would be useful to identify: (a) other uses of some our mechanisms, (b) support for multi-language user-interface toolkits, (c) how collaboration functions other than widget synchronization, such as concurrency control, operation transformation, awareness, and collaborative undo can be added to our mechanisms, (d) practical ways to attach our adapters to existing code, without any modification to it, and (e) adapt our requirements and mechanisms to higher-level collaboration tools exhibiting heterogeneity.

ACKNOWLEDGEMENTS

This research was funded in part by NSF grants IIS 0712794 and IIS-0810861.

REFERENCES

1. Heering, J. and P. Klint, *Towards Monolingual Programming Environments.* ACM Transactions on Programming Languages and Systems, April 1985. **7**(2).
2. Dewan, P., *Architectures for Collaborative Applications.* Trends in Software: Computer Supported Co-operative Work, 1998. **7**: p. 165-194.
3. Roseman, M. and S. Greenberg, *Building Real-Time Groupware with GroupKit, A Groupware Toolkit.* ACM Transactions on Computer-Human Interaction, 1996. **3**(1).
4. Wolfe, C., T.C.N. Graham, W.G. Phillips, and B. Roy. *Fiia: User-Centered Development of Adaptive Groupware Systems*. in *ACM EICS*. 2009.
5. Dewan, P. and R. Choudhary, *Coupling the User Interfaces of a Multiuser Program.* ACM Transactions on Computer Human Interaction, March 1995. **2**(1).
6. Sun, C., S. Xia, D. Sun, D. Chen, H. Shen, and W. Cai, *Transparent adaptation of single-user applications for multi-user real-time collaboration.* ACM Transactions on Computer Human Interaction, 2006. **13**(4).
7. Cheng, L.-T., S. Hupfer, S. Ross, and J. Patterson. *Jazzing up Eclipse with collaborative tools.* in *Proceedings of the OOPSLA workshop on eclipse technology eXchange*. 2003.
8. Greenberg, S. and M. Roseman. *GroupWeb: A WWW Browser as Real Time Groupware*. in *Proc. CHI*. 1996: ACM.
9. Gutwin, C., M. Lippold, and N. Graham. *Real-Time Groupware in the Browser: Testing the Performance of Web-Based Networking.* in *Proc. CSCW.* 2011: ACM.
10. Shao, B., D. Li, T. Lu, and N. Gu. *An operational transformation based synchronization protocol for Web 2.0 applications*. in *Proc. CSCW*. 2011.
11. Nichols, D., P. Curtis, M. Dixon, and J. Lamping. *High-Latency, Low-Bandwidth Windowing in the Jupiter Collaboration System*. in *UIST*. 1995.
12. Begole, J., Rosson, M., and Shaffer, C. *Flexible collaboration transparency: supporting worker independence in replicated application-sharing systems*. in ACM Transactions on Computer Human Interaction, 1999. **6**(2).
13. Jabarin, B. and N. Graham. *Architectures for Widget-Level Plasticity*. in *Proc. DSV-IS*. 2003.
14. Paternò, F. and I. Santos. *Designing and Developing Multi-User, Multi-Device Web Interfaces.* in *Proc. CADU*. 2006: Springer.
15. Bishop, J. *Multi-platform User Interface Construction – a Challenge for Software Engineering-in-the-Small.* in *Proc. ICSE*. 2006.
16. Gamma, E., R. Helm, R. Johnson, and J. Vlissedes, *Design Patterns, Elements of Object-Oriented Software*, Reading, MA.: Addison Wesley, 1995.
17. Scheifler, R.W. and J. Gettys, *The X Window System.* ACM Transactions on Graphics, Aug. 1983. **16**(8).
18. Gosling, J. *"SunDew?: a distributed and extensible window system.* in *Proceedings of an Alvey Workshop on Methodology of window management,*. 1986.
19. Chung, G., P. Dewan, and S. Rajaram. *Generic and composable latecomer accommodation service for centralized shared systems* in *Proc. IFIP Conference on Engineering for Human Computer Interaction, Chatty and Dewan, editors.* 1998: Kluwer Academic Publishers.
20. Calvary, G., J. Coutaz, David Thevenin, Q. Limbourg, L. Bouillon, and J. Vanderdonckt, *A unifying reference framework for multi-target user interfaces.* Interacting with Computers, 2003. **15**(3).
21. Chung, G. and P. Dewan. *Towards dynamic collaboration architectures*. in *Proc. ACM CSCW*. 2004.

CoRED – Browser-based Collaborative Real-Time Editor for Java Web Applications

Janne Lautamäki, Antti Nieminen, Johannes Koskinen, Timo Aho, and Tommi Mikkonen
Tampere University of Technology
Korkeakoulunkatu 10, FI-33720, Tampere, Finland
{janne.lautamaki, antti.h.nieminen, johannes.koskinen, timo.aho, tommi.mikkonen}@tut.fi

Marc Englund
Vaadin Ltd.
Ruukinkatu 2-4, FI-20540, Turku, Finland
marc.englund@vaadin.com

ABSTRACT
While the users of completed applications are heavily moving from desktop to the web browser, the majority of developers are still working with desktop IDEs such as Eclipse or Visual Studio. In contrast to professional installable IDEs, current web-based code editors are simple text editors with extra features. They usually understand lexical syntax and can do highlighting and indenting, but lack many of the features seen in modern desktop editors. In this paper, we present CoRED, a browser-based collaborative real-time code editor for Java applications. CoRED is a complete Java editor with error checking and automatic code generation capabilities, extended with some features commonly associated with social media. As a proof of the concept, we have extended CoRED to support Java based Vaadin framework for web applications. Moreover, CoRED can be used either as a stand-alone version or as a component of any other software. It is already used as a part of browser based Arvue IDE.

Author Keywords
Development tools, collaboration architectures, Vaadin.

ACM Classification Keywords
D.2.3.c. Program editors. D.3.2.h. Development tools. H.5.3.c. Computer-supported cooperative work. J.8.s. Web site management/development tools.

General Terms
Design, Experimentation.

INTRODUCTION
It is widely recognized that communication problems are a major factor in the delay and failure of software projects [2]. Numerous tools and methods have been proposed to solve issues in different phases of projects, starting from capturing requirements and ending at customer documentation. One of the most promising approaches to communication problems is offered by agile methods that advocate close and frequent communication between the client and the developers. In reality, this is often implemented in the form of a team that shares the same premises, encouraging frequent informal communication.

While the software development community is already struggling with communication issues, the emerging practice of global software engineering is raising even more challenges: Software work is undertaken at geographically separated locations across national boundaries in a coordinated fashion, involving both real time (synchronous) and asynchronous interaction [13]. This emphasizes the need for timely, precise and uniform forms of communication across the planet. Then, since the development takes place at the global scale, also the necessary communication should take place at such scale.

In almost any other field, the recent standard answer to global communication problems has been the World Wide Web, or simply the Web. Indeed, in a relatively short time, the Web has become the platform for all types of applications that enables real-time collaboration in forms and scale that would have been difficult to imagine a few decades ago. Recently, the collaborative capabilities of the Web have been further enriched with a new invention – social media. Facebook, Linkedin and other services enable us to be in contact with the friends, colleagues, and enthusiasts of different topics in real time all over the planet.

While the users of completed applications are heavily moving from desktop to browser, the majority of developers are still working with desktop IDEs such as Eclipse or Visual Studio. At present, most of the available web-based code editors are just text editors with some extra features like code highlighting, indentations and collaboration clued on top and they are not yet as usable as the best of the desktop editors. However, the web editors offer their own possibilities. For example, real-time collaborative editing sits very naturally in the environment. In addition, we get the general web-based application benefits like automatic distribution, installation and updating of applications [9] and independence on the development environment. Steps towards the direction are also proposed in [1, 14].

In this paper, we describe an experiment where the collaborative capabilities of the Web in general and the features of social media in particular are harnessed to help solving some of the communication problems of software development. As a concrete technical contribution, we introduce the browser based editor CoRED[1] (Collaborative Real-time Editor) intended for collaborative real-time editing of Java based source codes. CoRED contains highlighting, indentation, semantic error checking and some code completions. In addition, we present a number of features inspired by social media services, which we believe will be helpful for developing software applications. To the best of our knowledge, the similar set of functionalities is not offered by any of the previously existing web-based code editors.

We have selected Java and Vaadin [6] as the target language and framework, meaning that CoRED is an editor initially aimed for those two. Nevertheless, it can be extended for other environments with reasonable amount of work. The web applications based on Vaadin are implemented just like desktop Java applications. Because of the strong typing and good tool support in Java it is possible to augment CoRED with many features. These features include semantic error checking and code completion. This could just be dreamed of for weakly typed dynamic languages like JavaScript.

The rest of this paper is structured as follows. In the next section, we give an overview to the Vaadin framework, to the Ace editor, and to Java Developer Kit (JDK) which we are using as a base of our work. We also give a brief introduction to Arvue IDE which is going to use our editor as a building block. After this, we describe the technology behind our solutions and discuss the collaborative features. Moreover, we explain how CoRED could be extended for different frameworks. Then, we compare our editor with other code editors available in the web. Towards the end of the paper, we draw some final conclusions.

BACKGROUND

In this section, we give brief introduction to tools we are using in CoRED. We also show Arvue IDE as an example because it is going to be the first actual web application using CoRED. Tools we are using are the Vaadin framework, Ace editor, and Java Developer Kit (JDK). As a framework, Vaadin is obviously the lowest layer of our architecture. Vaadin is used for communicating over HTTP(S) and for making a separation of concerns between the client and the server [18]. On the client side, we use Ace

[1]CoRED is available for testing at http://jlautamaki.virtuallypreinstalled.com/CoRED

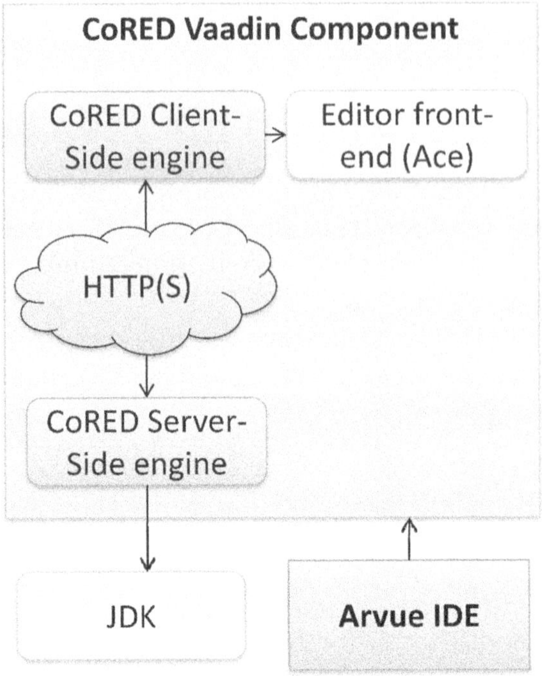

Figure 1. Architecture of CoRED Vaadin component and Arvue IDE using it.

editor as a front-end, and on the server side JDK as a tool for analyzing the source code. Vaadin also offers us a way for packaging the whole CoRED as a deliverable component as presented in Figure 1. CoRED can be used as a part of Vaadin based application like Arvue IDE or as it is.

Arvue

Arvue[2] is a cloud based IDE and hosting solution for the users who need a simple web-based tool for implementing and publishing Java based Vaadin applications. The basic philosophy of Arvue is to create applications "in the web for the web". In other words, the goal is to implement web applications in the web and publish them with minimal effort. No other tool except the browser is needed, implying that no installation is necessary in any phase of the development.

Applications are created in the browser-based visual editor that contains both the GUI (see Figure 2) and the code editor. On the GUI side, the user can create a new GUI just by dragging and dropping elements and layouts. The created GUI is then converted to source code and it can be further modified with the code editor (namely CoRED). Arvue is a round trip tool between the GUI and the text editor, meaning that same GUI edits can be done from both of the editors. The code editor is also used to implement features behind the GUI. Finally, the new application can effortlessly be deployed to a cloud type environment, which

[2]Arvue@dev.vaadin.com wiki. http://dev.vaadin.com/wiki/Arvue

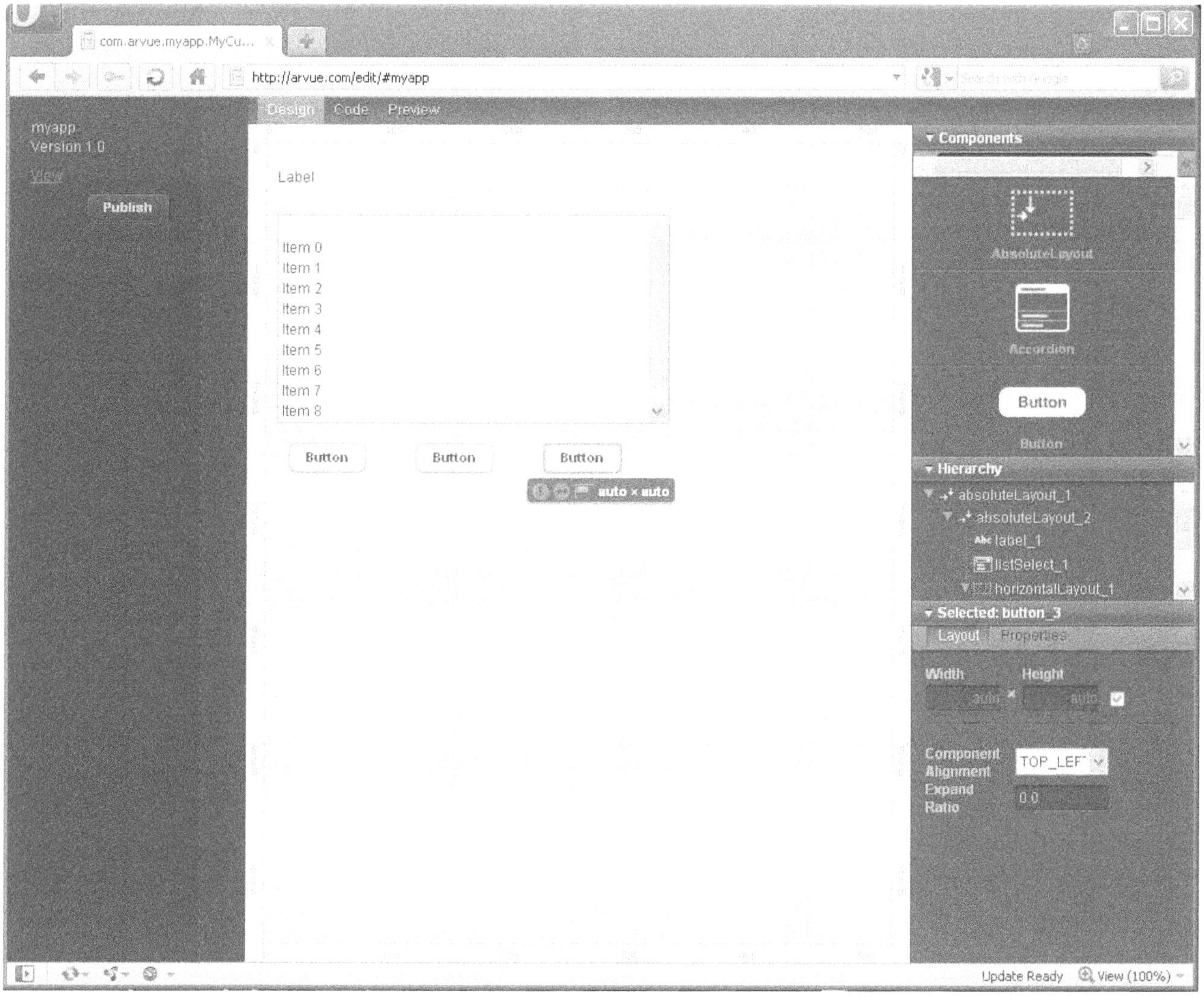

Figure 2. Arvue IDE with the graphical UI editor tab opened.

scales up by starting more server instances when needed. Every server is able to host multiple applications, which share many resources while not interfering with each other.

Arvue utilizes the Vaadin framework in its implementation. While editing is done inside a browser, most of the processing is carried out on the server side, as is common in Vaadin based system. For example, the server side of the CoRED utilizes JDK for semantic error checking and it also eases the implementation of code completion. Furthermore, our code editor is implemented as a custom Vaadin component whose client side is a Google Web Toolkit (GWT) [12] widget. Additionally, the client side widget uses JavaScript based Ace editor for basic editor capabilities.

The Vaadin Framework

Vaadin is an open source framework for developing Rich Internet Applications (RIA) using the Java programming language. The Vaadin framework relies extensively on the facilities of GWT [12]. GWT is an open source development system that allows the developer to write AJAX applications [10] in Java and then compile the source code to JavaScript which can be run on all browsers. In the Vaadin framework, GWT is used for compiling the client side engine and for communication between the client and the server.

From the developer perspective, individual Vaadin applications are implemented similarly to Java Standard Edition desktop applications. However, instead of usual UI libraries like AWT, Swing or SWT, the developer has to use the specific set of Vaadin UI components and the framework knows how to use the browser as a view. In addition, new custom made UI components can be implemented. In this case the client side of the customized UI component can be either developed in Java and then compiled with GWT or written directly with JavaScript. The use of any combination of Java and JavaScript is also possible. Thus, this enables us to use readily made JavaScript applications as a part of the Vaadin client side component.

Java Developer Kit (JDK)

Usually, Java applications run on top of a Java Runtime Environment (JRE) and are only compiled using a Java bytecode compiler included in developer kits like the Sun JDK[3]. However, this is not enough in order to develop the code editor applications, which can create other new applications on the fly. Instead, we need to run the application on the developer kit. JDK contains the necessary tools for compiling, executing, debugging and documenting the programs. Furthermore, it includes `tools.jar` package, which contains useful Sun specific APIs for compiling, diagnosing, and parsing the source code.

For our purposes, JDK provides a couple of very useful features: JavaCompiler[4] is an interface for invoking Java compiler from the program. The compiler generates complete error and warning diagnostics during compilation (for example, error messages) and they can be collected using DiagnosticCollector. In addition, by extending ClassLoader and StandardFileManager, the source and destination of compilation can be redirected. Finally, the offered API contains TreePathScanner[5] that can be used for processing source code. The scanner visits all the child tree nodes of the source code and can, thus, be used for finding Classes, Methods, Variables and other kinds of Java structures.

Ace

Ace[6] is an open source code editor written using JavaScript. It can be easily embedded in any web page and it has support for several different programming languages, including Java. Ace offers a lot of basic text editor features such as undo/redo, search/replace, and customization of appearance using themes. It also implements many features important specifically for programmers like syntax highlighting and automatic indentation.

It is easy to extend the behavior of Ace without editing its source code. It is possible, for example, to implement your own keyboard handler. Another feature important to us is that Ace supports markers for showing code errors. Also custom markers like underlining are possible. Moreover, Ace offers information useful in integrating the editor into a broader framework. For example, the position of the cursor in screen coordinates is needed for displaying a suggestion box at a suitable position.

ARCHITECTURE OF CORED

In CoRED, most of the hard work such as checking code errors and generating code suggestions is done on the server side. The client side editor does the interaction with the user. CoRED utilizes the Vaadin framework to tie these two sides together.

Separation of concerns

Both the client side and the server side of CoRED are designed to be easily customizable. Most of the features of the editor, such as error checking or code suggestions are implemented as replaceable and extendable components. A part of the CoRED architecture is presented in Figure 3. The main component, CollaborativeCodeEditor, and its client side counterpart act as glue between the server side components and the front-end editor. For example, when the user needs code suggestions, the main CoRED component requests suggestions from the server and then displays a widget for the user for selecting among the suggestions. The suggestions are generated by server side suggester components, and the selected suggestion is finally sent to the front-end editor.

The front-end editor component is typically a wrapper for a third-party JavaScript code editor. We have implemented a prototype component with three possible choices for the front-end editor: Ace, CodeMirror[7] and Eclipse Orion[8]. Wrapping a JavaScript editor inside a Vaadin GWT component was quite straightforward using JavaScript Native Interface (JSNI)[9] calls. Eventually, we chose Ace as our front-end editor because of its good support for indentation, syntax highlighting and customizable markers among other things.

CoRED has a possibility for flexible component add-ons. For example error checking and code completion components can be added by simply implementing the corresponding interfaces. Next we present the implemented components in detail.

Error Checking

Error checker is an example of component for extending CoRED. For checking errors, there are basically two possible approaches. First, we may use our own or third party library for parsing and error searching. Second, it is possible to compile the code from source to bytecode and then get compiling diagnostics.

For our implementation, we decided to use the latter solution with Java SE Development Kit (JDK). This way

---

[3]JDK File Structure for Windows. http://download.oracle.com/javase/6/docs/technotes/tools/windows/jdkfiles.html

[4]Java Compiler (Java Platform SE6). http://download.oracle.com/javase/6/docs/api/javax/tools/JavaCompiler.html

[5]TreePathScanner (Compiler Tree API). http://download.oracle.com/javase/6/docs/jdk/api/javac/tree/com/sun/source/util/TreePathScanner.html

[6]Ace – Ajax.org Cloud9 Editor. http://ace.ajax.org/

[7]CodeMirror. http://codemirror.net/

[8]Orion – Eclipsepedia. http://wiki.eclipse.org/Orion

[9]Coding Basics - JavaScript Native Interface (JSNI). http://code.google.com/webtoolkit/doc/latest/DevGuideCodingBasicsJSNI.html

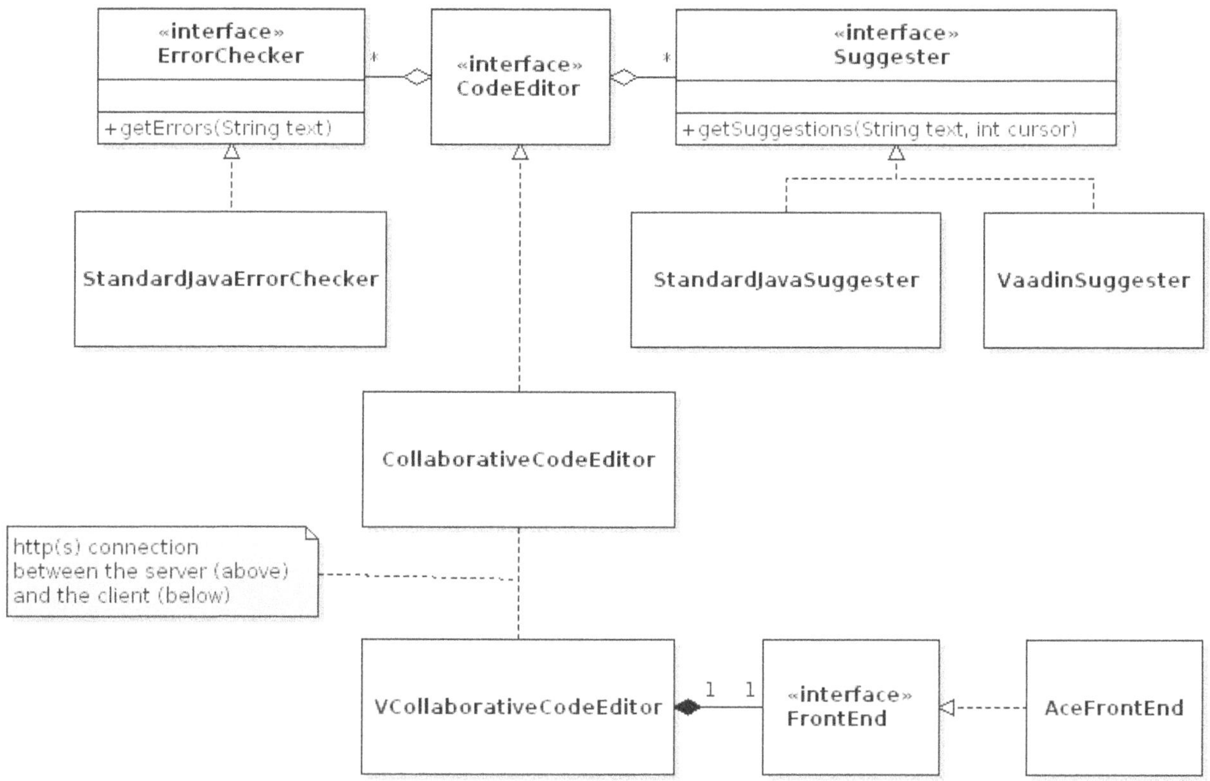

Figure 3. A part of the CoRED class hierarchy.

we get all-inclusive error and warning diagnostics from JavaCompiler and we do not need to stumble with the parser-compiler incompatibility. However, a basic problem with compiling is its consumption of computing resources. If we use a third party library or some kind of separate incremental parser like in Eclipse SDK for error checking, we could have better changes to tune the balance between efficiency and accuracy. However, we think that the approach is sufficient for our prototype.

In error checking, our basic procedure is to first compile the code and then ask for compiling diagnostics. Error diagnostics offered by JDK contain all the information needed for the message to user: in addition to the actual error message, line and column numbers are available. For efficiency reasons we do not save the files but only compile in memory. Furthermore, we compile only when we assume that the user wants the errors to be checked. In practice we wait for a while after the last edit and compile when user is in an idle state planning the next modifications. No compilation is done during code editing and even during the compilation the user interface is not blocked.

With just a few users, the compiling happens in the blink of an eye and most of the delay is caused by network communication. However, with multiple users, the continuous compiling is an efficiency problem. To make the system more scalable we compile less frequently when the number of users increases. In practice this is implemented with a separate worker thread for compilations.

Suggestions and Code Completions

While editing the source code, the code editor also suggests possible code completions. The suggestions can be invoked in two ways, by using a special key combination or by typing a dot after, e.g., an interface or an object name.

In either case, the server side client analyzes the code with all the implemented suggestion components. In fact, we have implemented two different suggestion components: one for standard Java suggestions and another for Vaadin specific ones. Based on the cursor location in the text the components resolve suitable suggestions. In addition to the actual inserted text, each suggestion includes a visible name of the suggestion and a longer description. These are passed to the editor and then shown to the user as seen in Figure 4.

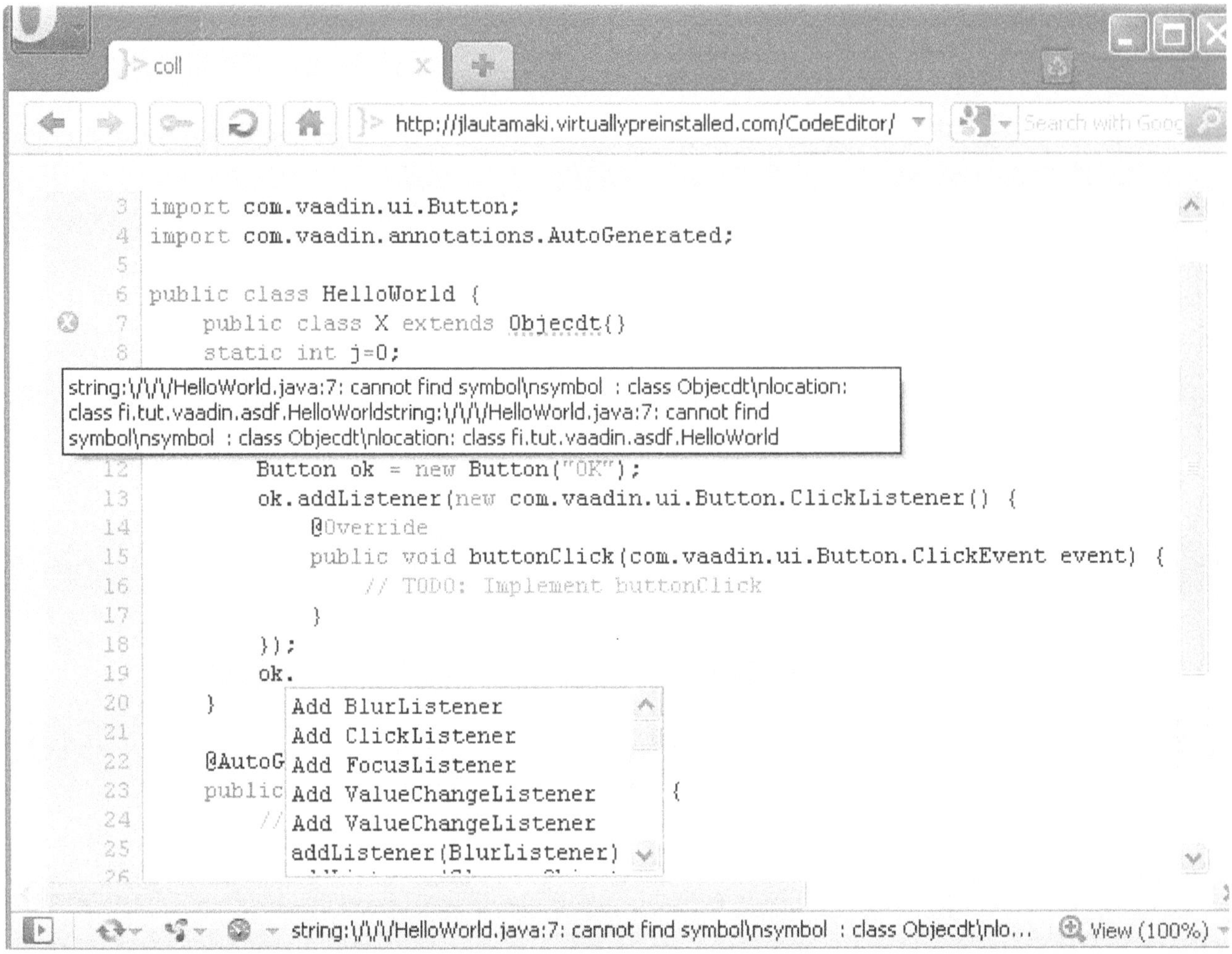

Figure 4. CoRED with generated listener, error tooltip and suggestion box opened (last two cannot normally be opened simultaneously)

To help resolving the suggestions, we use tools offered by JDK. With TreePathScanner it is possible to build a tree of classes, methods, variables or other parts of Java syntax. The currently visible variables, their types and methods, and the visibility scopes can be tracked down. To calculate the suggestions, the whole document is scanned with linear time operation. A suggestion may be related to a class originating from an imported package. For resolving those suggestions, we load the class and use reflection[10] to ask for its public methods and variables.

Collaborative features

It is natural to consider web applications as multiuser applications. The main requirement for a multiuser application is the shared data [11]. When all the users are connected to the same system it seems only reasonable to assume that in addition to interacting with the system, they are communicating with each other. In our case collaboration means simultaneous editing of code document and some features inspired by social media.

Collaborative editing

For collaborative editing, we decided to use Neil Frasers

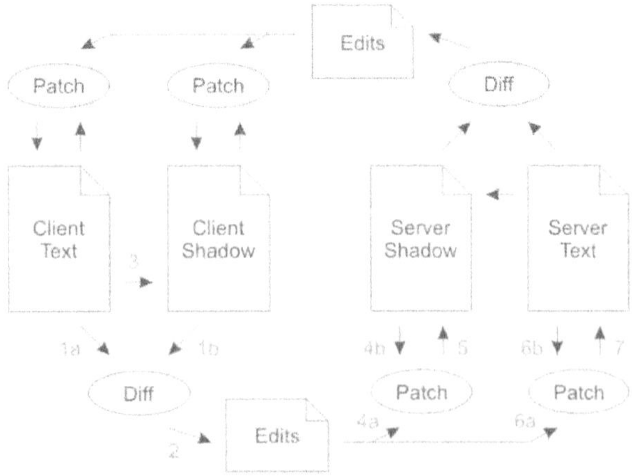

Figure 5. Neil Fraser's Differential synchronization with shadows [11]

[10]Reflection (Java SE Documentation) http://download.oracle.com/javase/6/docs/technotes/guides/reflection

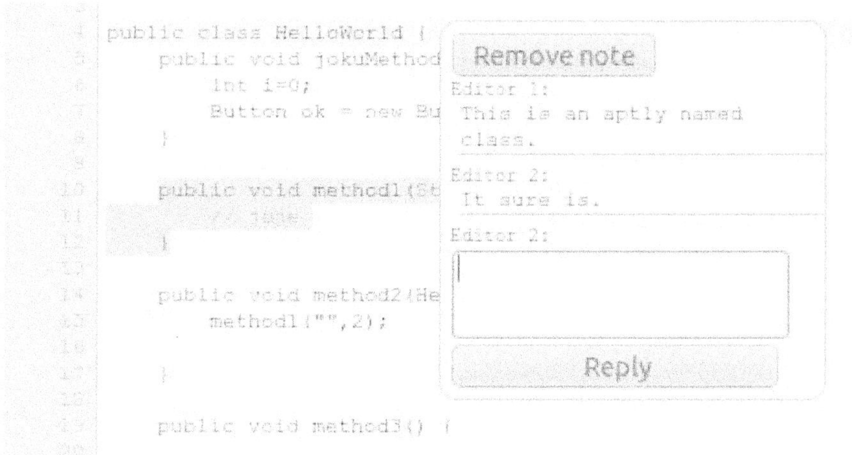

Figure 6 . A note related to "HelloWorld" and a reply in CoRED. The method called "method1" is locked by another editor.

Differential Synchronization with shadows [5]. It is a robust and convergent collaborative editing algorithm with open source implementations available on various languages, including Java and JavaScript.

The basic idea of Differential Synchronization is the following: the server stores the shared document, and each client has a separate shadow copy of the document both on server and client side, along with the copy they are editing (Figure 5). When a client changes its document, the differences between the newly edited document and the latest shadow are calculated using Myer's algorithm [8]. A patch (made using Bitap matching algorithm [18]) containing the differences is sent to the server. The patch is used both for keeping the server side shadow in sync, and for applying the changes to the shared document. The algorithm is symmetrical in a sense that the changes made to the shared document by other clients, is communicated to the client in the same way as the changes from the client to the server.

Differential synchronization is relatively easy to implement and it meets three basic demands often set for collaborative editing [16]: Firstly, it has high responsiveness. The edits can be done locally and only the differences are delivered to the server. Therefore the local actions are as quick as in a single-user editor. Secondly, it has high concurrency rate and multiple users can simultaneously edit any part of the document. Finally, it is able to hide communication latencies to some extent. Naturally, when latencies grow the conflict rate rises.

In addition to differential synchronization, there are plenty of ways to implement collaborative editing. One approach would be to lock the document or a subsection of the document before editing. A drawback with the locking approach is that a user must wait for the lock to be confirmed by a server, resulting to a loss in usability [15].

Another commonly used technique in collaborative editing is Operational Transform (OT) [3, 4, 7], used in e.g. Ethercodes[11] and Google Docs[12]. In OT, each *operation* (insert, delete, etc.) is recorded and sent to other clients who then transform the operation to take into account all the concurrently executed operations. In practical use, the OT implementations must deal with quite a large number of different editor actions including cut, paste, auto-corrections, auto-indentation, and suggestions, which may make the implementation problematic [5].

Features inspired by social media

In addition to plain collaboration in the form of writing code collaboratively, there are also some features inspired by social media. Perhaps the most obvious feature is the option to write comments in a fashion normally associated with text rather than code, as demonstrated in Figure 6. When some text is selected ("HelloWorld" in the figure), a popup is shown that allows the user to add a note referring to that text. When a user places the cursor on top of an existing note, the note popup is shown. Other users can reply to the original note, thus extending the note to a discussion, as also shown in Figure 6.

The notes reside in their original logical positions even though the document is modified. The start and the end positions of a note are marked with a *marker*. When a user inserts (or deletes) text before a marker, it is moved forward (or backward). The positions of markers are kept in synchronization similarly to the differential synchronization algorithm by sending, along with the text differences, also the position changes of markers from the client to the server and back.

---

[11] EtherCodes: Online Collaborative Code Editing. http://gigaom.com/collaboration/ethercodes-online-collaborative-code-editing/

[12] Google Docs. http://docs.google.com/

In CoRED, it is also possible to lock portions of the document to be edited only by one editor. For example, if a user wanted to make changes to a specific function without anybody interfering, he/she could lock a function by selecting the function and clicking a "Lock for me" button in a popup that showed up after selecting. After locking, the locked area is shown as grey for other users and they are unable to edit it although they can still add notes to it. Like notes, locks also have a start marker and an end marker which retain their logical positions.

The locking requests are sent to the server, and if no one else had an overlapping lock, the lock is granted. Users are disallowed to do any operations that would modify (or delete) a portion locked by another user. Such actions are already blocked on the client side, but the validity of edits is also checked on the server side. The additional server side check is needed because a lock may have been granted to editor A while editor B was editing the same part of the document. Thus, when B sends its modifications to the server, they are discarded.

Performance considerations

The most time-consuming operation on the server side CoRED is the compiling of the edited Java source code. The result of the compilation is needed to present the user with error messages and code suggestions.

In our brief experiments, when running the server on a laptop containing Core 2 Duo processor, the compilation of a typical Java file with a couple of hundreds of lines, took tens of milliseconds. For sufficient user experience, the compilation needs to be done at most once a second, which could be managed on quite modest hardware.

Another heavy operation is applying patches to the collaborative document. The resource consumption of patching depends on the density of edits done on the document. It should be noted that there is a practical usability limit on how many people can edit the same document simultaneously, which is most likely a more constraining factor than the performance of patching. In our brief tests where a few people edited the same document simultaneously, there were no performance issues.

Editing multiple documents can be done on separate instances of CoRED, which could easily be distributed on multiple server machines if needed. Consequently we do not presently consider this as a major performance bottleneck.

CUSTOMIZING THE EDITOR

CoRED can be customized and extended in several ways. As mentioned, it is possible to use new error checkers and suggesters instead of, or in addition to, the existing components. For example, it is possible to use CoRED for another language than Java by implementing custom suggesters and error checkers, and changing the syntax highlighting and indentation of the front-end editor.

Suggestions

In case of Java based frameworks, it is possible to use our Java suggester. The required jar files of the target framework just have to be added to classpath. If the need for special suggestions related to a specific framework arises, it is possible to create custom suggesters by implementing the Suggester interface in Figure 3.

For example, when developing for Vaadin framework, there is often a need to add an anonymous listener for an UI component, such as ClickListener for a button. We have developed a Vaadin specific suggester, which is to be used in addition to the standard Java suggester. It generates empty skeletons for anonymous listeners where applicable. For example, let us assume that there is a Vaadin Button called myButton defined in the scope of the cursor. When the user types "myButton.", one of the suggestions is to add an anonymous ClickListener. An illustration of the above case can be seen in Figure 4. The anonymous skeletons are created using Java reflection. Similar suggesters can be easily developed for other Java frameworks.

The suggestion feature is not limited to Java language, although we have not implemented any non-Java suggesters. It is possible to develop arbitrary suggesters for any language. However, creating a useful suggester for a dynamically typed language such as JavaScript is more difficult.

Error checking

As our error checker relies on the Java compiler, it can be used with any Java-based framework as long as the correct libraries are in the classpath. The standard Java error checking is most likely sufficient for most Java projects. Although it is possible to create custom error checkers by implementing the ErrorChecker interface (Figure 3).

Once again, things get more difficult with non-Java frameworks. Error checkers can be created for any language but CoRED offers no support for non-Java ones. The Ace editor we use as a front-end, contains a JavaScript error checker that is not a part of the CoRED architecture.

Front-end editor

Ace, the front-end editor used in CoRED, is highly customizable. It offers the possibility to change its appearance and define custom highlighting rules in separate configuration files. Ace already contains the files for the most popular languages such as JavaScript, HTML, XML, PHP, C++. Thus, adapting the front-end to be used for developing for other languages than Java is very simple.

If Ace, for some reason, does not meet our requirements, it is even possible to use another front-end, leaving the rest of CoRED intact. The front-end component must implement the FrontEnd interface (Figure 3). The interface defines the methods needed for the editor, including setting and getting the editor text, changing the cursor position, setting callbacks for changes, displaying error markers, and so on.

RELATED WORK AND COMPARISON

CoRED is not the first in the field of collaborative browser-based code editors. The first collaborative editor was presented as early as 1968 in the demo, retrospectively named as "The Mother of All Demos"[13]. Naturally, the demo in 1968 did not work on the browser. One of the first collaborative editors runnable in a browser (using Java Applets) was REDUCE [17]. The Web 2.0 phenomenon introduced the browser-based collaborative editors to a larger audience. One of the most successful was Writely that later evolved to Google Docs. The step from a text editor to simple code editor is quite short, and currently lots of browser based collaborative code editors are available.

Most of the browser based code editors have some of the same features as CoRED, but none has exactly the same ones. Many of the competing editors like CodeMirror and Ace are aimed for only code editing, not for creating applications. Like in the desktop world, also in the web there are wide variety of different languages and frameworks. Thus, it is virtually impossible to create one IDE that would support the whole project from writing the code from scratch to publishing it for all of the frameworks. As CoRED is a part of Arvue IDE, our goal is exactly the whole process from beginning to deploying to the web. Akshell[14] has the similar kind of framework approach. It allows a developer to implement both the client and the server with JavaScript. The system also takes care of deploying. In addition, Orion project by Eclipse community limits the frameworks that the user can use. Orion is still in a proposal phase but it looks promising.

When comparing the features of other editors, most code editors have code coloring and indenting available for several different programming languages. To the best of our knowledge, there is only one other example of the browser based editor with code completion and error checking. The editor, named WWWorkspace[15], uses Eclipse as a back-end. As our editor has probably some scalability issues because of JDK, one can only imagine the situation with a massive editor like Eclipse. Like CoRED, WWWorkspace is also using strongly typed Java language. Most of other code editor examples are aimed for weakly typed dynamic languages like JavaScript. JavaScript has its own good sides, but it is virtually impossible to do semantic checking for weakly typed interpretive language.

As a further comparison, CoRED can be easily extended to support any Java based framework. As a downside, CoRED is heavily dependent of the server side and it cannot be used in offline mode like, for example, Google Docs.

FUTURE WORK

Since we are still working with the editor, it is obvious that numerous directions to future work exist. To begin with, introducing support for other phases of development work, such as requirements or project management, would be natural extensions. Then, also these tasks could be turned collaborative as well as more closely linked with development activities. Currently, we assume that these features come from environments that use CoRED as a component.

Another obvious direction for future work is to perform the series of usability studies in order to find out how programmers wish to use the facilities of the system. This could take place in the form of a coding camp, where students would take part in the experiment, and provide feedback on the system. Based on the results, we can then further refine the implementation and focus on parts that provide most support for the actual development work. In addition, the results of such studies could also help us to identify more potentially useful features that are commonplace in social media but not widely applied in software development.

Finally, in order to gain experiences from a larger user base, we are going to publish CoRED in the open Vaadin Directory[16] as a re-usable add-on for all the Vaadin Community. CoRED can be used as a component of other Vaadin projects or as a stand-alone application. It will also be used as a part of the IDE called Arvue. Currently, Arvue is in an early alpha stage. The other components are going to be the graphical designer for generating user interfaces and the capability to save applications to Git version management. In addition the developed applications can be published directly to the offered cloud. Arvue is mostly designed for creating small Vaadin applications and for testing purposes, but there is no obvious reason why it could not be used more generally.

CONCLUSION

In this paper, we described the browser based editor CoRED intended for collaborative real-time editing of the Java based source codes. We extended the system to offer some Vaadin framework specific features for developing the web applications in the web. As editing features, CoRED contains highlighting, indentation, semantic error checking and code completion. As a combination, this set of features is unique when compared with other browser based code editors. CoRED is going to be published in the Vaadin Directory as a re-usable add-on. It will also be used as a part of the web based IDE called Arvue.

CoRED is built to be modular and many of its parts can be replaced or extended. In this paper, we gave a small summary of what kind of modifications are needed to extend CoRED to different frameworks. In the case of Java

---

[13] Wikipedia – The Mother of All Demos. http://en.wikipedia.org/wiki/The_Mother_of_All_Demos

[14] Akshell. http://www.akshell.com/

[15] WWWorkspace. http://www.willryan.co.uk/WWWorkspace/

[16] Directory – vaadin.com. http://vaadin.com/directory

based frameworks, just small additions for the suggestion component and error checker are needed. However, for non-Java frameworks more laborious modifications are needed and the benefit of using CoRED is smaller. Fortunately, communication from client to server and collaborative features should work without problems in frameworks of all kind.

As a further contribution, we discussed on how the web applications should be developed and made a small comparison between our editor and other web based code editors available. As a piece of future work it would be interesting to do more experimentation on the usability as well as the scalability of our system.

REFERENCES

1. Begel, A., DeLine, R., and Zimmermann, T. Social media for software engineering. In *Proceedings of the Workshop on Future of Software Engineering Research*, pp. 33–38. Santa Fe, NM, USA, 2010.
2. Curtis, B., Krasner, H., and Iscoe, N. A Field Study of the Software Design Process for Large Systems. Communications of the ACM 31(11), pp. 1268–1287. 1988.
3. Davis, A. H., Sun, C., and Lu, J. Generalizing operational transformation to the standard general markup language. In *Proceedings of the 2002 ACM conference on Computer supported cooperative work*, pp. 58–67. New York, NY, USA, 2002.
4. Ellis, C. A., and Gibbs, S. J. Concurrency control in groupware systems. In *Proceedings of the 1989 ACM SIGMOD International Conference on Management of Data*, pp. 399–407. Portland, OR, USA, 1989.
5. Fraser, N. Differential Synchronization. In *Proceedings of the 2009 ACM Symposium on Document Engineering*, pp. 13–20. New York, NY, USA, 2009.
6. Grönroos, M. Book of Vaadin. Uniprint. 2011.
7. Ignat, C-L., and Norrie M. C. Customizable collaborative editor relying on treeOPT algorithm. In *Proceedings of the eighth conference on European Conference on Computer Supported Cooperative Work*, pp. 315–334. Norwell, MA, USA, 2003.
8. Myers, E. W. An O(ND) difference algorithm and its variations. Algorithmica 1(1), pp. 251–266. 1986.
9. O'Reilly, T. What is Web 2.0: Design Patterns and Business Models for the Next Generation of Software. O'Reilly. 2005.
10. Paulson, L. D. Building rich web applications with Ajax. Computer 38(10), pp. 14–17. 2005.
11. Patterson, J. F., Hill, R. D., Rohall, S. L., and Meeks S. W. Rendezvous: an architecture for synchronous multi-user applications. In *Proceedings of the 1990 ACM conference on Computer-supported cooperative work*, pp. 317–328. New York, NY, USA, 1990.
12. Perry, Bruce W. Google Web Toolkit for Ajax. O'Reilly Short Cuts. O'Reilly, 2007.
13. Sahay, S. Global Software Alliances: The Challenge of 'Standardization'. Scandinavian Journal of Information Systems 15, pp. 3–21. 2003.
14. Storey, M-A., Treude, C., van Deursen, A, and Cheng, L-T. The impact of social media on software engineering practices and tools. In *Proceedings of the Workshop on Future of Software Engineering Research*, pp. 359–364. Santa Fe, NM, USA, 2010.
15. Sun. C. Optional and Responsive Fine-Grain Locking in Internet-Based Collaborative Systems. IEEE Transactions on Parallel and Distributed Systems 13(9), pp. 994–1008. 2002.
16. Sun, C., Jia, X., Zhang, Y., Yang, Y., and Chen, D. Achieving Convergence, Causality-Preservation, and Intention-Preservation in Real-Time Cooperative Editing Systems. ACM Transactions on Computer-Human Interaction 5(1), pp. 63–108. 1998.
17. Sun, C., Jia, X., Zhang, Y., Yang, Y., and Zhang, Y. REDUCE: a prototypical cooperative editing system. In *Proceedings of the Seventh International Conference on Human-Computer Interaction*, pp. 89–92. 1997.
18. Sun, W. Manbed, U. Fast text searching with errors. Communications of the ACM, 35(10), pp. 83–91. 1992.

To Talk or Not to Talk: Factors that Influence Communication around Changesets

Adrian Schröter[†], Jorge Aranda[†], Daniela Damian[†], and Irwin Kwan[‡]
University of Victoria, Canada[†], Oregon State University, USA[‡]
schadr@acm.org, jaranda@uvic.ca, danielad@cs.uvic.ca, and irwink@ieee.org

ABSTRACT

Building tools to help software developers communicate effectively requires a deep understanding of their communication dynamics. To date we do not have good comprehension of why developers talk to each other as a result of *some* events in the life of their projects, and not of others. This lack of knowledge makes it difficult to design useful communication models and support systems.

In this paper, we narrow down the study of communication behaviour to focus on interactions that occur as a result of a particular kind of project event: the submission of a changeset to the project repository. In a case study with the IBM® Rational® Team Concert™ development team we investigate which factors influence developers to request information about a changeset to their product. We identify several such factors, including the development mode in which the team is operating, the background and recent performance of the author of the changeset, and the risk that the changeset poses to the stability of the product. Incorporating these factors into recommender systems may lead to improvements in their performance.

Author Keywords

Information Sharing, Communication, Software Teams

ACM Classification Keywords

D.2.9 Software Engineering: Management—*Programming teams*; K.6.3 Management of Computing and Information Systems: Software Management—*Software development*

General Terms

Human Factors,Management

INTRODUCTION

For all but the most trivial programs, software development today is a collaborative activity. The members of software teams must coordinate and communicate, often intensely, if their projects are to reach a satisfactory conclusion. Previous research has shown that communication among developers has a profound influence on several aspects of software development [14, 22].

Despite this acknowledged importance of communication in software teams, our understanding of communication behaviour is still very limited. Ko *et al.* [15] point out that developers often require information about the work output of their peers. We know little about why developers act upon this requirement. What causes developers to seek information in some cases, but not in others? There are a multitude of potential factors: the closeness of their peers' work with their own, the expertise of the developers, their physical proximity, their level of workload, and even, perhaps, the time of day. By identifying which factors actually influence the likelihood that a developer will request information about the events surrounding her, we might better understand the nature of software-centric information-seeking behaviour. This increased understanding allows us to develop improved recommender systems that enable developers to coordinate their activities efficiently.

For this study we decided to investigate information-seeking behaviour around changesets for the purpose of identifying guidelines that can improve the applicability and usefulness of recommender systems. A study of changesets is generic enough to be applicable in many settings, but particular enough to be informative about detailed patterns of behaviour. We report on a field study that used a mixed-methods approach (participant-observation, surveys, and interviews) to understand what technical, social, and process-based factors influence whether a developer will seek information about a changeset or not. We investigated communication in the IBM Rational Team Concert (RTC) project, which is distributed across North America, Europe, and Asia, and in which communication is linked to changeset data. The RTC project presents unique opportunities for research on communication in software teams not only because it takes place within a development environment in which a significant fraction of communication is recorded in technical artifacts, but also because the team is tasked with the goal of developing these artifacts themselves. The challenge of effective team communication is particularly present in the RTC project team.

In the remainder of the paper we present the motivation and background for our study, and then describe our study design. We present in detail the results of our analysis of the data, and distill a number of technical, process and social factors that we identified as influencing developers' information-seeking behaviour. We conclude by discussing the implications of our findings on the design of collaborative systems.

BACKGROUND AND MOTIVATION

This research builds upon the growing body of work that studies coordination and communication in software organizations, which have long been recognized as playing central roles in leading software projects to success, e.g. [7, 16].

Our research group gained the opportunity to study the IBM Rational Team Concert (RTC) development team and the software artifacts produced by this team over several years. The RTC team maintains and cross-links all of their software and process artifacts using the very tool they produce. Partly due to its distributed nature, and partly due to its open source origins, the team's emphasis on written and archivable electronic communication results in a wealth of data for analysis.

Our previous investigations of the RTC project repositories revealed a significant relationship between gaps in communication structures and build success [22]. Therefore we proposed a recommendation system that allows team members to learn about who they should talk with in order to avoid build failures [20]. This recommendation system should focus on changesets and analyze significant differences between code dependencies and team communication structure to identify anti-patterns that the developers should attempt to break. The basis for this principle is derived from Conway's Law [6] and by the model of socio-technical congruence proposed by Cataldo *et al.* [4,5]. The model compares the communication network to the code dependency network and derives insights with respect to productivity from the gaps between those networks.

In order to build a good recommendation system, however, one needs to go beyond providing valuable information. As Murphy and Murphy-Hill show [18], we need developers to trust the recommender system: delivering the right recommendation at the right time is one important way to build such trust. Unfortunately, recommender systems often fall short on this front, saturating the developer with recommendations they neither need nor want, or presenting recommendations at inappropriate times. It is therefore important to know when developers actually need information, and what factors influence them to seek information. There are many potential factors that could change the likelihood that developers would want to obtain further information, and we do not have a sense, other than our intuition, to learn which factors are actually important and which are not.

Related work has examined factors that influence communication among software developers. For instance, while APIs are intended to reduce coordination complexity among development teams, they also introduce barriers that hinder communication between teams by obscuring dependencies [8,9]. Software architecture, organizational structure and project age are also factors that influence communication and the awareness that developers have of each other's work [10]. Processes, in particular, are often used to influence the communication among team members to reduce information overload [12], and geographic distance has been shown to affect communication, but its effects vary between projects [13,21]. Nakakoji *et al.* [19] distilled the current knowledge about communication among developers into a set of guidelines to design tools and processes that facilitate effective expertise communication. Those studies, and to our knowledge, literature in software engineering in general, only address communication on a project-wide level. However, to fully understand, and thus offer actionable knowledge to developers, we need to know what influences an individual developer's information-seeking behaviour. We surveyed literature to compile a list of possible information-seeking triggers spanning change-related (such as code metrics), developer-related (such as experience level) and process-related (such as peer reviews) factors.

Therefore we pursue to answer the following **research question:** *What factors influence whether a developer will decide to seek information about a changeset in her project?*

STUDY DESIGN

To address our research question, we complement our previous analysis of the RTC electronic repositories with rich qualitative data from interviews and observations, considering that much information on a project's lifecycle is not recorded in its repositories [1]. We focused on studying what factors cause a developer to seek information about a changeset, since changesets are the smallest units of change to a project that directly impact other developers.

Our research question called for a mixed methods empirical study. Therefore, we collected data about the team's information-seeking behaviour from three different sources. First, the first author of this paper (Adrian) was embedded in a subteam of the RTC team as a participant-observer for four months. Second, we deployed a survey with the entire development team to validate some of the findings from the observations. Third, we conducted interviews with the developers from one component team to obtain richer information about their communication behaviour.

Study Setting

Rational Team Concert is a scalable and extensible team collaboration platform that integrates source code management, issue tracking, and planning tools. The RTC platform uses a client-server architecture, with the server acting as a central data repository. The team also uses RTC to develop RTC, and in this way RTC is a self-hosting project. This helps the RTC team become aware of issues with the product before customers.The project follows a large scale iterative development process that emphasizes transparency [11]. It defines six-week iteration cycles, which are separated into planning, development and stabilization activities. A project management committee formulates the goals and features for each release at the beginning of each iteration, and the output of this process is assigned to the teams in the form of work items. The work items and nearly all documentation are publicly available.

The RTC development team has over 100 developers distributed across multiple sites in North America, Europe and Asia. The RTC development team is subdivided into several teams that manage a component each, such as the source code system or the web user interface. To communicate with each other, especially across different geographical locations, the developers extensively use RTC's own issue and task management system. A particular characteristic of the RTC development environment—and one that made this study of communication behaviour around changesets possible—are explicit traceable links between work tasks, associated changesets, and developers' online comments about these tasks and changesets[1].

Data Collection

We used a mixed methods approach to answer our research question. We obtained data from three sources: participant observation, a survey, and a set of interviews with RTC team members.

Participant-Observation

The first author of this paper (Adrian) joined one of the RTC development sites in Europe for a four-month period in the Fall of 2010. He was involved as an intern with this development team helping with minor bug fixes, feature development, and testing, and thus was in a position to directly participate in the project development and communication activities. Our data collection opportunities were thus much richer than in typical observations conducted over shorter periods of time, or that do not involve active participation in the project. During his period as a participant-observer, Adrian kept a daily activity log, recording any information of relevance to the communication behaviour of his team.

The observation period coincided with the months prior to a major release and during which the team focused on extensive testing rather than new feature development. As such, the majority of our observations are concerned with activities around testing the integration of RTC with other IBM Rational products, and it offered the experience of collaborating with many developers from different teams and across the remote sites. Finally, in the one month following the release, Adrian also participated in the development of a feature for the upcoming version of the product.

The team in which he was embedded had the responsibility to develop the task management and the planning components of RTC. There were ten developers at the site, including two novices that had recently joined the team and eight experienced developers. The team includes RTC's three senior project management members, who play a major role in planning the entire product's architecture and development.

Interviews

We conducted interviews with ten developers of the RTC team to inform our observational findings. The setting for the interviews was slightly unusual, and beneficial from a research perspective, since the first author's participant-observation allowed him to develop working relationships during his stay at the team, and to delve into a discussion of complex communication issues without needing to spend time understanding the basic context of the team.

In the interviews, we requested developers to provide details into their communication dynamics through a narration of "war stories" that directly related to communication among developers. "*War stories*" are events that left an impression on the respondent. War stories emphasize specific events that they witnessed or took part in [17]; their narrative is particularly powerful at uncovering the elements of the stories that are relevant to the respondents. The interviews lasted between thirty minutes and one hour, and they were conducted at the end of the observation period.

Survey

To complement the insights we obtained from the observations and interviews, we deployed a survey with the entire RTC team at the end of our observation period. The survey was designed iteratively and piloted with a European team, and intended to collect input about which factors increase the likelihood of a developer requesting information about a changeset from the changeset author. The items we included in the survey were in the categories of code-related, developer-related and process-related items. Each category included 14 items, as shown in Table 1. *Code-change related* items describe the changeset delivered or the code that the changeset modifies or affects. *Developer-related* items relate to the developers that delivered a changeset, the developer requesting the information, and their relation to each other. Finally, *process-related* items relate to the development phase in effect when the changeset was delivered, and to items relating to process requirements or practices. For each of the three categories, the survey asked the developers to rank each item in the category according to how strongly it increases their likelihood of requesting information about a changeset.

We initially formulated our list of items from an analysis of the current literature on coordination and communication, as well as from our own previous research. We then refined the list of items through piloting and discussions with the development team. An initial version of the survey included fifty-nine items; the refined list had forty-two. Besides reducing the number of items in our list, the pilot survey led us to add several process-related items, as well as to change the format of the question (the initial survey had a battery of questions with Likert-scale answers; the final survey asked respondents to rank each item in comparison to the rest in its own category).

We deployed the survey through a web form, and invited the entire distributed RTC development team to participate. We sent a reminder one month later to increase the response rate. We obtained 36 responses to the survey; approximately a 25% response rate. Of the 36 respondents, 26 are located in North America, 5 are located in Europe, and 5 are located in Asia. Furthermore, 22 of the respondents are developers, 5 team leads, 5 component leads and project management committee, and 4 respondents withheld their information.

[1]Changesets in RTC are created in a developer workspace; each changeset consists of several changes to code files.

Survey Items	Interview Quotes (I)/Participant Observation Quotes (O)	Mean Rank
Release endgame	(O) *"Adrian, in the endgame we only do minimal changes. Is your change minimal?"*	3.79
To review the change	(I) *"I often lack sufficient understanding of the part of the code I'm reviewing."*	5.00
To approve the change	—	5.11
Late milestone	—	5.14
During iteration endgame	(O) *"Adrian, in the endgame we only do minimal changes. Is your change minimal?"*	5.42
Obtain a review for the change	(O) *"It is demotivating to get a reject, thus I talk to my reviewer beforehand."*	5.55
Obtain an approval for the change	(O) *"I already fixed it, but I need to convince my team lead to give me approval."*	5.72
Related work item has high severity	—	6.00
Verify a fix	(I) *"Often I need to ask how I can tell that a change-set actually fixed the bug."*	6.37
Topic of work item the change is attached to	—	7.64
Priority set by your team lead	—	8.55
Role of the committer (e.g. developer)	—	9.00
Early in an iteration	(I) *"... there are weeks I sometimes don't talk to my colleagues at all."'*	11.24
Early milestone	—	12.10

(a) Process-related items and quotes

Survey Items	Interview Quotes (I)/Participant Observation Quotes (O)	Mean Rank
Author is inexperienced	(O) *"Adrian, please put me always as a reviewer on you change-sets."*	2.60
Author recently delivered sub-standard work	(I) *"She just changed teams and still needs to get used to this component."*	3.04
Author is not up to date with recent events	(I) *"After you return from vacation we ensure you follow new decisions."*	3.15
You do not know the change-set author	(I) *"I'd be very irritated if someone other than [...] would touch my code."*	5.09
Author is currently working with you	(O) *"We sometimes discuss changes we made to brag about a cool hack."*	5.56
Author part of same feature team	—	6.00
Author part of your team	—	7.00
Worked with author before	—	7.77
Busyness of yourself	(I) *"If I see a problematic change-set, I'll ask for clarifications even if I'm busy."*	8.05
Busyness of the author	(I) *"If I need to know why an author made that change I just contact him." [Even if he is busy.]*	8.55
Met in person	(I) *"I've worked with him for 5 years now but never even met him."*	9.57
Physical location	(O) *"Here, America or Asia, I don't care, I ping them when they are online."*	10.14
Author is experienced	—	11.00
Author recently delivered high-quality work	—	11.09

(b) Developer-related items and quotes

Survey Items	Interview Quotes (I)/Participant Observation Quotes (O)	Mean Rank
Changed API	(O) *"Adrian, why did you change that API?"* [The RTC team avoids changing API.]	2.84
Don't know why code was changed	(O) *"I don't see a reason why you changed that code, you sure you needed to?"*	3.00
Affects frequently used features	(I) *"Before I ok a fix [even to a main feature], I ask if there is a workaround."*	4.10
Complex code	—	4.89
Introduced new functionality	—	6.14
Is used by many other methods	(O) *"Why did you fix this part? The bug is not in this part of the code, it is used and tested a lot."*	6.41
Your code was changed	(I) *"I'd be very irritated if someone other than [...] would touch my code."*	6.42
Stable code was changed	(O) *"Why did you fix this part? The bug is not in this part of the code, it is used and tested a lot."*	6.62
Change unlocks previously unused code	—	7.42
A bug fix	—	8.61
A re-factoring	(O) *"I separate a re-factoring from a fix so that people can ask me questions about the fix."*	9.15
Frequently modified code was changed	(I) *"I like to know where the 'construction sites' of the project are."*	10.35
Code is used by few other methods	—	10.96
Simple code was changed	—	12.57

(c) Code-change-related items and quotes

Table 1: This table (in three parts) summarizes the data we collected from our three data sources: 1.) our participant-observer's log-book; 2.) survey responses from 36 developers situated around the world; 3.) interviews with 10 developers. These items are ranked by their average rank. Whenever possible, we provided quotes from interviews (I), or quotes from the participant-observation period (O) to exemplify the items.

Analysis

For our data analysis, we transcribed the interviews, and then coded both the interviews and the participant-observation notes. From the codes we created categories, which we cross-referenced to the survey rankings. We used an open coding approach, during which we assigned codes to summarize incidents in sentences and paragraphs of the transcribed interviews that relate to our research question.

We calculated the ranking of the survey items for each category by calculating the mean over all ranks given by developers to a survey item (see Table 1). Table 2 shows the distribution of the rankings for each survey item.

During our analysis, we derived a set of factors affecting communication behaviour based on our list of survey items and qualitative data from our interviews and observations. Whenever possible, we triangulated our findings using all our data sources. We tried to ensure that all of our findings were supported by at least two data sources; none of the findings we report were challenged by any of our data sources.

FINDINGS

The evidence collected from our survey, interviews, and participant observation allowed us to derive seven factors that affect communication behaviour in software organizations, which we outline below. In the remainder of this section, text in italics refers to survey items that can be found in Table 1. Text in italics and around quotation marks denotes interview fragments.

Development Mode

One of the strongest findings from our study was the effect of the development mode that the team is in on its communication behaviour. Developers and managers alike give much importance to the development mode they are in, namely (1) normal iteration, and (2) endgame.

The normal iteration mode mainly consists of work that can be planned by the developer. This work tends to be new feature development, or modifications to existing features. Most of the planning for it has been laid out in advance; furthermore, each developer individually knows what features have been assigned to her, and can plan ahead to meet her obligations. In contrast, the endgame mode mainly consists of work that is coming uncontrollably in short intervals from others. As a result of integration and more intense testing, defects crop up more rapidly and need to be addressed more quickly. Beyond allocating time for endgame activities, there is very little in this development mode that can be planned in advance.

The RTC team switches between the two modes in each iteration. Of the six weeks of a regular iteration, four weeks are assigned to normal iteration mode and two weeks to endgame. However, as deadlines approach, there are occasional special iterations that consist mostly of endgame-like work. In this manner, the same detailed pattern of alternation between normal iteration and endgame within an iteration is reproduced at a higher level, as shown in Figure 1.

We identified the same pattern with respect to the amount of changeset-related interactions in the team. We found that the mode in which the team is currently in is an important factor determining whether developers will feel a need to communicate about changesets. Being in endgame mode increases the need for developers to communicate about a changeset, whereas being in normal mode decreases the need to request information about it.

The first author of this paper experienced both modes during his participant-observer time with the RTC team. He joined the team in a release endgame phase, which was characterized by fixing bugs that were reported by testers, and he helped by fixing minor bugs as well as setting up servers for testing. When the team released the project, it switched gears, and in the decompression after the endgame he had the opportunity to develop a feature for the product. The differences in the patterns of interaction between the two modes were distinctly clear, for him and for his peers. During the endgame mode, developers were essentially "on demand," available to fix whatever bugs were discovered. Later, during the normal iteration mode, they experienced far more autonomy and control over their time, and began working on activities that

Process-related items
Release endgame
To review the change
To approve the change
Late milestone
During iteration endgame
Obtain a review for the change
Obtain an approval for the change
Related work item has high severity
Verify a fix
Topic of work item the change is attached to
Priority set by your team lead
Role of the committer (e.g. developer)
Early in an iteration
Early milestone
Developer-related items
Author is inexperienced
Author recently delivered sub-standard work
Author is not up to date with recent events
You do not know the change-set author
Author is currently working with you
Author part of same feature team
Author part of your team
Worked with author before
Busyness of yourself
Busyness of the author
Met in person
Physical location
Author is experienced
Author recently delivered high-quality work
Code-change related items
Changed API
Don't know why code was changed
Affects frequently used features
Complex code
Introduced new functionality
Is used by many other methods
Your code was changed
Stable code was changed
Change unlocks previously unused code
A bug fix
A re-factoring
Frequently modified code was changed
Code is used by few other methods
Simple code was changed

Table 2: This table contains the distribution of ranks for each survey item. The leftmost point of each sparkline represents the amount of respondents that ranked the item first; the rightmost point represents the amount that ranked it last (14th). No survey item received the same rank from more than ten respondents.

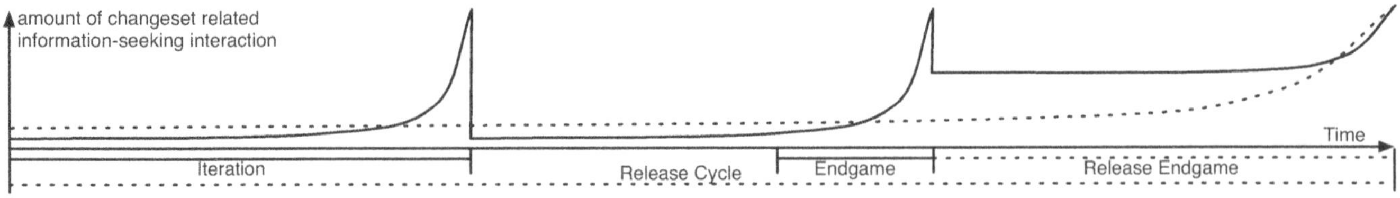

Figure 1: The pattern of information-seeking interactions throughout several iterations of a release cycle. Every release cycle consists of a number of iterations; each iteration includes an endgame phase. Changeset-based interactions are more frequent during endgame phases and during the last iteration of the release cycle.

were less demanding of an interaction back-and-forth, and especially less demanding of keeping track of the changesets committed by their peers. In our interviews, developers almost unanimously pointed to the separation of the two types of modes, describing the differences in the type of communication in each, and identifying the autonomous *vs.* uncontrollable, inside *vs.* outside influence.

This is not to say that developers do not communicate while they are in normal iteration mode, but that the nature of their communication seems to be different. In normal iteration mode, developers communicate less about concrete changesets, but they communicate more about high level ideas: for instance, they raise questions about how a feature fits into the existing architecture or general tactics to implement a feature, about how much of it actually needs to be implemented or can be reused from other libraries, and so forth. Generally, however, the amount of communication decreases in normal iteration mode. As a developer commented in one of our interviews, *"during feature development iterations there are weeks I sometimes don't talk to my colleagues at all."*

In contrast, the endgame mode is characterized by bug reports and last minute feature requests—that is, by work coming into every developer's desk uncontrollably. Changesets become first class concerns during this mode because each change threatens the stability of the product: developers need to evaluate whether the changeset actually improves the product instead of making things worse. Therefore, they develop a habit of reviewing each other's changesets to assess the risk they pose to the project's stability.

Our survey data provides significant support for this finding. In Table 1a, we can see that overall, for the RTC development team at large, there is a greater likelihood to request information during product-stabilizing phases, such as *during the release endgame*, and a lesser likelihood to request information when working towards an *early milestone*. The former was ranked as the most important of the process-related items in our survey; the latter was ranked as the least important. All the survey items that refer to a late stage in the iteration or in the project lifecycle were ranked highly, and all the items that refer to an early stage were ranked lowly. This finding resonates especially with the team we interviewed.

Perceived Knowledge of the Changeset Author

One key determinant for a developer to seek information about a changeset consists of what the developer knows about the background of its author. Several aspects of the author's background seem to be important: the quality of her recent work, her level of experience, and her awareness of recent team events or decisions.

First, these factors are important in part because they point to potential problems with the stability of the product. If a changeset author has *recently delivered sub-standard work*, other developers will want to ensure that the new changeset will not deteriorate their product, and therefore they will try to find more information about it.

Similarly, when the author is *inexperienced*, or is not *up to date* with recent team events for any reason, the risk of introducing problems into the product increases. One developer that interacts frequently with a newly founded team told us that *"most of the work that I need to review is of very low quality and needs several iterations before it is up to our standards."* Novices, generally speaking, face a ramp-up problem that takes a significant amount of time to overcome [3]. This was the case with Adrian's work, too: his first changesets were subjected to more scrutiny due to his unfamiliarity with the code base.

The survey data backs up these observations. The three top items in Table 1b consist of factors related to an unfavourable perception of the background of the changeset author. In comparison, the two least important items in that table refer to favourable perceptions of said background.

In essence, these items point to the relevance of trust in software development teams. For developers, trust in the skills of their colleagues is important. If this trust is not-established (for instance, if a developer does not know the changeset author), developers are more likely to check the changeset and request information to ensure that the modifications were truly necessary and appropriate. But when trust exists (that is, when the author has a good record of delivering high-quality work, or is known to be an experienced team member), the need to seek information about a changeset decreases.

Common Experience and Location

Shared work experiences affect the likelihood of information-seeking behaviour in the RTC distributed team. This is partly related to the trust and perception issues discussed above, but also to the establishment of interpersonal relations and to the intertwining work responsibilities and expectations.

According to our interviews, this is the case particularly for senior team members. Although they work in a globally distributed team, they have managed to establish personal relationships with developers at many different sites. Through continuous interaction and through social events, they have learned more about each other, and thus feel more comfortable to initiate contact with them. Junior team members, in contrast, know very few of their teammates globally, and since they simply do not have these interpersonal connections with the rest of their team, it is less important to them whether they know the author of a changeset when needing to contact them.

Generally speaking, despite the lack of opportunities to build personal relationships with off-site people, for most developers sharing common experiences makes it easier to contact teammates to request information. One team lead told us: *"I have one or two contact people in each team we usually work with whom I ask for information and then often enough get referred to the right person in their team."*

Our participant-observation data confirm this. At one point, Adrian needed to set up and test a specific component in the RTC product. The development team in charge of that component was located on a different site. However, since Adrian had previously had the opportunity to establish relationships with some of the developers of that team through a previous research study, it was easier for him to contact them and ask for help in his setup task.

Our survey data corroborate these observations. It suggests that the developers that form relationships (on a personal or work level) with other developers gave more emphasis on previous experiences with them. For instance, it made a difference whether the developers *are currently working together* (Table 1b). Additionally, whether they have shared work experiences seems to be a more determinant factor than having *met in person* or sharing the same *physical location*.

This last finding would seem to indicate that the RTC team has managed to overcome obstacles created by geographical distance. Developers state that the physical location of a changeset author is not an important factor to seek more information about the changeset. Nevertheless, we should note two things. First, this finding merely points out that developers have no greater need to inform themselves of work output of their remote peers than of their local peers; it says nothing about the ease with which such information is acquired. Second, the RTC team has determined to carry out as many of its interactions as possible through textual, electronic media. This neglects the natural advantages provided by proximity in favour of uniform accessibility of interactions, no matter the physical location of the interlocutors.

Risk Assessment

A central factor at the heart of the decision to seek information is a concern with the quality of the product and components developed by the team at large. Both managers and developers share this concern. Because of it, every team member is constantly evaluating whether there are significant risks involved in accepting a changeset and including it into the final product. This concern is greatest close to releases or major milestones, and less important when the team is in normal iteration mode.

Developers request information more frequently about changesets that touch on code that has a high customer impact. According to our interviews and observations, code parts with a high customer impact are those that are directly related to frequently used features or changes to the API that might be used by customers to customize the RTC product. In the case of the impact of API changes, there is an extensive knowledge exchange in the jazz.net forums between customers and developers about how to use the API to build extensions to RTC, which gives developers plenty of information about the possible impact of API changes to the customers. Consequently, changesets that modify code that has less impact on the customer are of less concern and less likely to be discussed. For example, when scanning fixes to reported bugs, developers perform a risk assessment to determine whether the bug fix is even needed. In the words of one team member, *"with every tenth bug fix you introduce another bug to the system, so unless the bug does not have a workaround and is something most customers would experience, we give it low priority."*

The ranking of items in Table 1c provides additional insights into the kinds of changesets that carry a risk for developers. A *changed API* comes at the top of the list, code that *affects frequently used features* comes third, immediately followed by changes to *complex code*, changes that *introduced new functionality*, and changes to code that *is used by many other methods*.

Work Allocation and Peer Reviews

In the later stages of the development cycle, developers have two process-based constraints that prompt them to interact with their peers. First, they need their peers to review their changesets before they are included in the product. Second, they need an approval to start working on a task (a triaging process needs to take place so that developers are allocated to the most important work items).

In the changeset review process, there are two ways the changeset author and the reviewers interact. Either the changeset author submits his changeset for review, or the changeset author discusses the changeset with the reviewer before submitting it for review. The main discriminant between meeting with the reviewer to discuss the changeset before submitting it or submitting without prior discussion seems to be whether the reviewer and the author are co-located.

Adrian's mentor during his time with the RTC team explained: *"It is very demotivating to get a changeset rejected, that's why we usually try to discuss things before and then the reviewing just becomes all about quickly testing and accepting the changeset."* Of course, this does not prevent an already discussed changeset from being rejected, but it signals that the process-based constraint is not as strict as to forbid discussions about a changeset between authors and reviewers in the interest of an unbiased code review.

In the case of developers seeking approval to start working on a task, the process is similarly flexible. The approval is supposed to be issued before the developer begins work on the task. However, we observed several times that developers performed quick fixes, and later went to their team leads to acquire approval for the fixes they had already performed.

Several items in our survey point to the importance of information-seeking around the processes of approval and peer review. In Table 1a, the second- and third-highest items were information needed because the respondent needed *to review the change* or *to approve the change*. The need to *obtain a review for the change* or to *obtain an approval for the change* were of moderate importance. *Verifying a fix* was not judged as important by our respondents.

Type of Change

The three main reasons for a developer to commit a changeset are to (1) do feature development, (2) fix bugs, and (3) refactor. Among them, feature development seems to be the one that prompts developers to seek information the most. In our survey (Table 1a), code that *introduced new functionality* is ranked fifth among the code-change related factors, while changes that consist of *a bug fix* and *a refactoring* ranked far lower on the same list.

This may be due to the fact that feature development has less tool support than bug fixing (which is supported by debugging tools and automated test frameworks) and refactoring (which is essentially an automatic process today). The limited tool support and the inherently difficult nature of the task itself makes changesets that introduce new functionality more difficult to understand or assess. Hence, developers are more likely to request information about them.

Business Goals vs Developers' Pride

Senior team members (managers and team leads among them) often ask about the purpose and the real need of a changeset in order to minimize unpleasant surprises that might be introduced with further code changes, and simply to have an economically feasible product. One senior development lead told us: *"often I need to stop my developers from fixing every little bug otherwise we would never be able to ship."*

Although every team member is concerned with the quality of their product, a more realistic, business-oriented perspective seems to be more prominent in the senior team members' information-seeking behaviour: they may request clarifications on the business case of changesets or work items if they are not immediately clear in the existing documentation.

More junior team members, however, do not have this concern. They express their pride in the actual product and want it to be as bug free as possible. A developer commented to us: *"I want to be proud of what I deliver and I am fairly certain if we don't fix it now it will come back to haunt us because it might upset some customers."* Not only does this lead the developer to try to convince her manager that including changesets for seemingly unimportant fixes is valuable, it also makes her information-seeking behaviour different with respect to that of the more senior team members. Broadly speaking, managers will be more interested in seeking clarifications as to the business case of a work item if it is not clear in its description, while developers will not care as much about this.

RECOMMENDER SYSTEM DESIGN GUIDELINES

Nakakoji *et al.* [19] formulated nine design guidelines for systems supporting information-seeking in software teams. Some of them deal with minimizing the interruptions experienced by the developers who are asked for information, while others refer to enabling the information-seeker to contact the right people. Our findings help us refine Nakakoji *et al.* guidelines:

Guideline #1: *Recommender systems should adjust to the development mode.* Our first finding strongly suggests that a developer's information needs can dramatically change between development modes. When in normal iteration mode, developers act upon planned work and can therefore anticipate the information they need, but in endgame mode, developers react to unplanned incoming work, such as bug reports or requests for code reviews.

Many tools, such as Codebook [2] and Ensemble [23] provide information and recommendations in a fixed way. Codebook enables developers to discover other developers whose code is related. In contrast, Ensemble provides a constant stream of potentially relevant events for each developer. In the Codebook case, this might lead to extra overhead in endgame mode when developers frequently need to search for information instead being automatically provided, whereas Ensemble might overload developers during the feature development mode by providing a constant stream of information.

To avoid overwhelming or reducing overhead further for developers, recommendation systems should either automatically adjust to the development mode or feature customizable templates that can easily be switched.

Guideline #2: *Recommender systems should account for perceived knowledge of other developers.* Our second and third findings unveiled factors that trigger developers to seek information about a changeset that are not related to its code. Instead, developers pay close attention to the experience level as well as the quality of previously delivered work to determine whether to talk to the changeset owner.

Traditional recommender systems in software engineering focus on the source code to determine useful recommendations, e.g. Codebook [2] and Ensemble [23]. This might lead to providing developers with information about changes that are of little interest due to the trust placed in more experienced developer.

But because developers often look beyond source code and perform an additional step, namely considering the changeset owner's experience and recent work, information solely created from source code might miss interesting instances where novices to the code made inappropriate changes.

Recommender systems might report issues that are of less importance due to the substantial experience of the changeset owner.

Implementing filtering mechanisms based on author characteristics such as experience and quality of previously delivered work can help developers focus on the information that is important to them.

Guideline #3: *Recommender systems should assist in non-implementation tasks such as code reviews and risk assessment.* We observed, as described in the fourth, fifth, and sixth findings, that developers are highly engaged in discussions when performing risk assessments or reviews of changesets.

In software engineering, most recommendations are focused on providing information to support concrete tasks such as bug fixes or re-factorings, but not for tasks such as reviews. To provide information for non coding tasks, recommender systems should be configurable to display relevant information beyond the tasks that they are intended to support, so that developer can easily access the information provided by recommender systems when performing code reviews or risk assessments.

Guideline #4: *Recommender systems should account for business goals.* Our last finding points to internal conflicts within teams and among developers caused by the desire to create a flawless product under the restriction of a set of business goals such as shipping the product on time. Thus, developers often need to be reminded that they must focus their efforts on fulfilling business goals rather than on polishing the product as they see fit. Existing recommenders that use code-related metrics such as quality or productivity may shift attention away from fulfilling business goals.

To support developers in focusing on business goals, systems supporting the information-seeking behavior of developers should be able to prioritize information related to tasks that are mission-critical to the organization, helping the team focus its attention on the most relevant problems for the upcoming release.

THREATS TO VALIDITY

Our survey asked the developers to rank a pre-defined list of items in terms of the influence they may have on their information-seeking behaviour. In doing so, we attempted to reach a compromise between the survey length and survey response rate. This bias poses a threat to our findings due to the possibility that we were missing important items. We mitigated it by developing the survey iteratively by piloting and discussing it with one of the development teams to identify the most important items, and by relying on our other two sources of data to triangulate our findings.

We had the chance to interview ten developers, which represent a fraction of the development team at large. These ten developers were all located at the same site. As a result of this, our interview data could be biased and unrepresentative of the RTC team at large. However, we are confident that this threat is minor, due to the mix of developers we interviewed, including novices, senior developers, and team members that had been part of the group since its beginning. Furthermore, triangulation with our observations and survey responses increases our confidence in our findings. However, we plan to interview team members from other locations to minimize the cultural (national and local corporate culture) bias that might have been introduced by focusing the interviews on one location.

Our data come exclusively from the IBM RTC development team, and the extent to which our results are valid for other companies is not clear without replications. The RTC development team has more than one hundred members, it interacts with a number of customers, and it is in the process of integrating its product with others. These are all forces that shape communication dynamics. However, their interaction patterns seem to be similar to those of other globally distributed teams that need to synchronize work across multiple time zones.

CONCLUSION AND FUTURE WORK

Coordinating work among developers is a keystone of successfully shipping a software product [13, 16]. To fully understand how developers coordinate, it is necessary to understand the factors that influence their communication behaviour. Among our findings, we saw that the current phase in the development process and worker experience were two major factors that influenced whether developers communicate about a change. Tools providing information and research on coordination in software engineering should consider and incorporate our list of factors in order to help developers interact more effectively.

Many recommendation systems focused on creating awareness among developers about changsets using information generated from source code. We found that developer's information seeking behavior is influenced by factors that go beyond source code. Especially information about changeset owners as well as the process consistently informs developers decisions to seek information about a changeset or not. This lead us to propose four guidelines suggesting to incorporate these non technical factors in a recommender system to improve their usability and flexibility. For future work, we are currently implementing a recommender system to help developers investigate changesets, and we plan to investigate the effect of implementing our proposed guidelines on the usefulness and adoption of our recommender system.

REFERENCES

1. J. Aranda and G. Venolia. The secret life of bugs: Going past the errors and omissions in software repositories. In *Software Engineering, 2009. ICSE 2009. IEEE 31st International Conference on*, May 2009.

2. A. Begel, Y. P. Khoo, and T. Zimmermann. Codebook: discovering and exploiting relationships in software repositories. In *Proceedings of the 32nd ACM/IEEE International Conference on Software Engineering - Volume 1*, ICSE '10, pages 125–134, New York, NY, USA, May 2010. ACM.

3. A. Begel and B. Simon. Struggles of new college graduates in their first software development job. In *Proceedings of the 39th SIGCSE technical symposium on Computer science education*, SIGCSE '08, pages 226–230, New York, NY, USA, 2008. ACM.
4. M. Cataldo, J. D. Herbsleb, and K. M. Carley. Socio-technical congruence: a framework for assessing the impact of technical and work dependencies on software development productivity. In *Proceedings of the Second ACM-IEEE international symposium on Empirical software engineering and measurement*, ESEM '08, pages 2–11, New York, NY, USA, 2008. ACM.
5. M. Cataldo, P. A. Wagstrom, J. D. Herbsleb, and K. M. Carley. Identification of coordination requirements: implications for the design of collaboration and awareness tools. In *Proceedings of the 2006 20th anniversary conference on Computer supported cooperative work*, CSCW '06, pages 353–362, New York, NY, USA, 2006. ACM.
6. M. E. Conway. How do Comittees Invent? *Datamation*, 14(4):28–31, 1968.
7. B. Curtis, H. Krasner, and N. Iscoe. A field study of the software design process for large systems. *Commun. ACM*, 31:1268–1287, November 1988.
8. C. R. B. de Souza, D. Redmiles, L.-T. Cheng, D. Millen, and J. Patterson. How a good software practice thwarts collaboration: the multiple roles of apis in software development. In *Proceedings of the 12th ACM SIGSOFT twelfth international symposium on Foundations of software engineering*, SIGSOFT '04/FSE-12, pages 221–230, New York, NY, USA, 2004. ACM.
9. C. R. B. de Souza, D. Redmiles, L.-T. Cheng, D. Millen, and J. Patterson. Sometimes you need to see through walls: a field study of application programming interfaces. In *Proceedings of the 2004 ACM conference on Computer supported cooperative work*, CSCW '04, pages 63–71, New York, NY, USA, 2004. ACM.
10. C. R. B. de Souza and D. F. Redmiles. The awareness network, to whom should i display my actions? and, whose actions should i monitor? *IEEE Transactions on Software Engineering*, 99(PrePrints), 2011.
11. R. Frost. Jazz and the eclipse way of collaboration. *IEEE Softw.*, 24:114–117, November 2007.
12. S. R. Fussell, R. E. Kraut, F. J. Lerch, W. L. Scherlis, M. M. McNally, and J. J. Cadiz. Coordination, overload and team performance: effects of team communication strategies. In *Proceedings of the 1998 ACM conference on Computer supported cooperative work*, CSCW '98, pages 275–284, New York, NY, USA, 1998. ACM.
13. J. D. Herbsleb, A. Mockus, T. A. Finholt, and R. E. Grinter. An empirical study of global software development: distance and speed. In *Proceedings of the 23rd International Conference on Software Engineering*, ICSE '01, pages 81–90, Washington, DC, USA, 2001. IEEE Computer Society.
14. P. Hinds and C. McGrath. Structures that work: social structure, work structure and coordination ease in geographically distributed teams. In *Proceedings of the 2006 20th anniversary conference on Computer supported cooperative work*, CSCW '06, pages 343–352, New York, NY, USA, 2006. ACM.
15. A. J. Ko, R. DeLine, and G. Venolia. Information needs in collocated software development teams. In *Proceedings of the 29th international conference on Software Engineering*, ICSE '07, pages 344–353, Washington, DC, USA, 2007. IEEE Computer Society.
16. R. E. Kraut and L. A. Streeter. Coordination in software development. *Commun. ACM*, 38:69–81, March 1995.
17. W. G. Lutters and C. Seaman. The value of war stories in debunking the myths of documentation in software maintenance. *Information and Software Technology*, 49(6):576–587, 2007.
18. G. C. Murphy and E. Murphy-Hill. What is trust in a recommender for software development? In *Proceedings of the 2nd International Workshop on Recommendation Systems for Software Engineering*, RSSE '10, pages 57–58, New York, NY, USA, 2010. ACM.
19. K. Nakakoji, Y. Ye, and Y. Yamamoto. Supporting Expertise Communication in Developer-Centered Collaborative Software Development Environments. In *: Finkelstein, A., van der Hoek, A., Mistrik, I., Whitehead, J. (eds.) Collaborative Software Engineering*, 2010.
20. A. Schröter, I. Kwan, L. D. Panjer, and D. Damian. Chat to succeed. In *Proceedings of the 2008 international workshop on Recommendation systems for software engineering*, RSSE '08, pages 43–44, New York, NY, USA, 2008. ACM.
21. T. Wolf, T. Nguyen, and D. Damian. Does distance still matter? *Software Process*, 13:493–510, November 2008.
22. T. Wolf, A. Schroter, D. Damian, and T. Nguyen. Predicting build failures using social network analysis on developer communication. In *Proceedings of the 31st International Conference on Software Engineering*, ICSE '09, pages 1–11, Washington, DC, USA, 2009. IEEE Computer Society.
23. P. F. Xiang, A. T. T. Ying, P. Cheng, Y. B. Dang, K. Ehrlich, M. E. Helander, P. M. Matchen, A. Empere, P. L. Tarr, C. Williams, and S. X. Yang. Ensemble: a recommendation tool for promoting communication in software teams. In *Proceedings of the 2008 international workshop on Recommendation systems for software engineering*, RSSE '08, pages 2:1–2:1, New York, NY, USA, 2008. ACM.

Conflict Detection and Resolution for Product Line Design in a Collaborative Decision Making Environment

Xiaoqing Frank Liu
Missouri University of Science and Technology
Rolla, Missouri
fliu@mst.edu

Eric Christopher Barnes
Missouri University of Science and Technology
Rolla, Missouri
ecbyt7@mst.edu

Juha Erik Savolainen
Danfoss Power Electronics
Gråsten, Denmark
JuhaErik.Savolainen@danfoss.com

ABSTRACT

Ensuring that the non-functional requirements (NFRs), of a system are satisfied is an essential task in software development. However, this task is complicated by the fact that many NFRs conflict with each other from multiple perspectives. It is essential to resolve conflicts collectively in a collaborative decision making process since stakeholders often disagree on how conflicts should be resolved. In this paper, we describe a method for dividing high-level NFR conflicts within a product line into more manageable sub-problems. Stakeholders make use of an argumentation based collaborative decision support system to determine which design alternatives provide the best trade-offs between NFRs. Finally, we present an empirical study in which the aforementioned system was used to resolve a single instance of an NFR conflict across 3 members of a product line. It shows that the system is effective in resolving conflicts in a collaborative decision process.

Author Keywords

Collaborative Software Development, Computer-Mediated Communication, Participatory/Cooperative Design Collaboration Architectures

ACM Classification Keywords

D.2.2 Computer Aided Software Engineering

General Terms

Design, Experimentation, Human Factors

INTRODUCTION

One of the most important factors in the software design phase is ensuring that the system supports the satisfaction of its non-functional requirements (NFRs). Each functional component contributes in some way to the overall satisfaction of the systems NFRs. Therefore, prudent developers must keep NFRs in mind when they make design decisions regarding these components, taking into account how their choices affect NFR satisfaction. Unfortunately, this is not always easy to accomplish. Many NFRs have inherent conflicts with each other, in which measures taken to support one NFR will have a detrimental effect on another. Failure to understand these NFR conflicts can easily cause developers to overemphasize certain NFRs over their opponents. In order to resolve NFR conflicts, developers must make design decisions which strike a tradeoff between conflicting NFRs that satisfies the various stakeholders of the system.

Often these stakeholders have different ideas about which NFRs are most important in a software system, and will disagree on which design alternatives contribute to a quality product. Such disagreements can complicate the design process, unless the decision making process is supported by a system geared towards managing opposing viewpoints. A collaborative argumentation system was developed which has the ability to capture stakeholders rationale, and support the decision making process. In this system, stakeholders present their rationale in the form of arguments and evidences. This allows them to benefit from each other's experiences and understanding before attempting to select design alternatives. When a decision is reached, the rationale captured by the system can always be viewed at a later time, allowing developers to understand the reasoning behind the decision [1]. Our paper describes a framework for identifying NFR conflicts in a software product line, organizing them, and supporting their resolution through collaborative decision making.

RELATED WORKS

Conflict Resolution Oriented Decision Support

There has been much research into decision support systems, especially those which attempt to address conflicts among stakeholders. Mark Klein proposed a method for conflict resolution in which conflicts are organized into a hierarchy. Each class of conflict may have pointers to conflict resolution strategies, which contain advice for resolving the conflict and preconditions for that strategy [2]. Another framework, proposed by Jin Guilin, divided conflicts into 3 categories: design, resource, and process conflicts. In order to resolve design conflicts, each design team defines their own set of design objectives, with a set of variables that contribute to that objectives completion. Fuzzy math is used to determine which design variables provide the best contribution to design goals with the least cost of conflict resolution [3].

Philosopher Stephen Toulmin proposed a model of argumentation which has inspired a large family of computer-based conflict resolution methods [4]. The first such method was gIBIS, which displayed arguments, issues, and positions in a graph [5]. HERMES is a decision support tool which organizes arguments and evidences into a hierarchy [6]. Evidences in this system are specific arguments which attach themselves to conflicting argument in order to provide one with more concrete proof. The system then can use the weights of all arguments to find the most favored alternative. Chenn-Junn Huang developed an argumentation system which automatically parses arguments, assesses their quality, and sends feedback to users depending on their calculated skill level [7].

NFR Conflict Analysis

Poort developed an influential method of NFR conflict analysis called non-functional decomposition (NFD)[8]. NFD allows users to trace NFRs to the system architecture in order to examine NFR conflicts. Chi-Lun Liu developed a process of defining NFRs and detecting conflicts. The model makes use of NFR, module, and value ontologies to define NFRs. The framework has an included set of rules to detect NFR conflicts, which are addressed by users through the use of the adjustment direction ontology to define what NFRs will be adjusted and why[9]. Xu et. all proposed a method for determining NFR satisfaction by modeling partial state charts for design alternatives to satisfy the NFRs[10]. The design alternatives are then combined into a cohesive design which is then analyzed in terms of NFR support. NFR conflict detection can be performed by examining several composed designs to determine which NFRs are violated and whether this correlates with the satisfaction of others.

OUR PROPOSED FRAMEWORK

The proposed framework applies existing NFR conflict analysis techniques to detect and organize NFR conflicts and support their resolution with a web-based decision support system. The framework is geared for use in product lines, as it is structured in a way that supports knowledge and design sharing among individual products. An overview of the process is provided in Figure 1. The framework takes a functional hierarchy of the product line as well as a list of high level NFRs that the product line must satisfy. Conflict detection and analysis is then performed to create a conflict hierarchy. The hierarchy is composed of instances of the conflict as it manifests itself in the various functional components of the product line. Because product members are often aimed at different customers and applications, there may be divergence in terms of which NFRs are more important to stakeholders. Therefore, conflict instances must be addressed on a product-by-product basis.

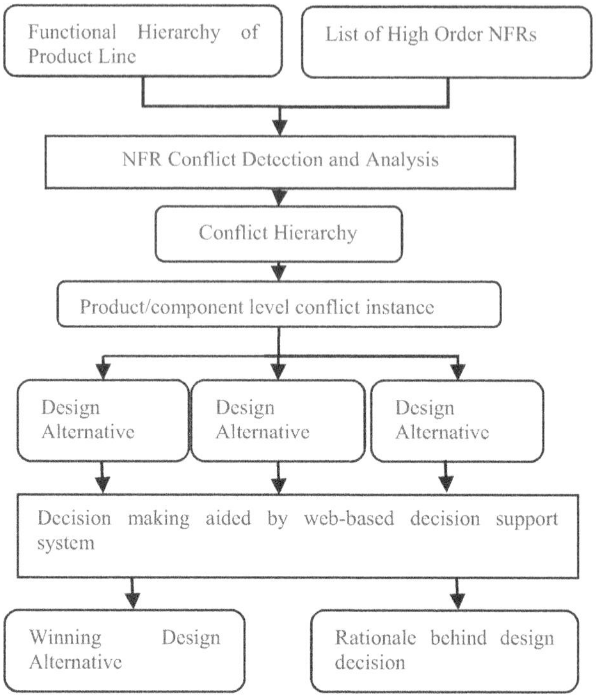

Figure 1. Framework Overview

Stakeholders examine each conflict instance and determine whether they wish to resolve the instance with a design decision. When resolution is desired, stakeholders propose several design alternatives which attempt to strike a tradeoff between the NFRs of the conflict instance. The process of alternative selection is supported by an argumentation-based decision support system. Once a design alternative has been selected, stakeholders may move on to the next conflict instance and resolve it in the same manner. The rationale captured by the decision support system may be reviewed by stakeholders to guide other decision design decisions throughout the product line. When the process is concluded, stakeholders will have a set of concrete design decisions which strive to ensure the satisfaction of the conflicting NFRs.

NFR CONFLICT ANALYSIS IN PRODUCT LINES

In order to properly address NFR conflicts, stakeholders must possess a clear representation of the NFRs themselves. Our proposed framework makes use of earlier work [11] which involves mapping NFR conflicts to a hierarchy based on the functional architecture of the system. This provides stakeholders with a comprehensive view of the conflicts as they manifest themselves throughout the system, as well as flexibility in terms of what level of detail they want to work at. This section is devoted to the explanation of this process, the conflict hierarchy it creates, and how the process is extended to the case of product lines.

Creation of Product Line Level NFRs

The language used in this framework defines NFRs as consisting of 3 elements: quality attribute, functionality, and constraint. The quality attribute describes the quality factor of the NFR, the functionality describes which functional component must support the quality attribute and constraint defines in what way that the quality attributes should be satisfied. This can be described in natural language by phrasing NFRs as follows: *Quality Attribute* of *Functionality* shall/must be *Constraint.* For instance, consider the following example of an NFR defined in the canonical form:

The *response time* of *basic search* should be *fast.*

here, *response time* is the quality attribute, *basic search* is the functionality, and *fast* is the constraint.

This canonical form of creates a systematized language for defining NFRs which lends itself to the creation of the hierarchy used by our framework. Stakeholders use this form to draft a set of high-level NFRs that represent all possible NFRs that members of the product line should satisfy. It is important to note that not all NFRs drafted will be important to the stakeholders of each product. This variance is an essential aspect of product lines and will be dealt with in the conflict resolution phase of the process.

NFR Conflict Detection

Once the NFRs of the product line have been defined, the next step is to determine which NFRs conflict with each other. This is accomplished by using a set of rules regarding which quality attributes conflict with each other. The following is an example of such a rule set, in which 'O' denotes the absence of a conflict between two NFRs, and 'X' denotes the presence of NFR conflict:

	Maturity	Reliability	Fault Tolerance	Time Behavior	Efficiency
Maturity	O	O	O	X	X
Reliability	O	O	O	X	X
Fault Tolerance	O	O	O	X	X
Time Behavior	X	X	X	O	O
Efficiency	X	X	X	O	O

Table 1. Sample rule set for quality attribute conflict detection

In this example the time behavior and efficiency quality attributes conflict with the maturity, reliability, and fault tolerance quality attributes. An important factor to consider is that not all paradigms will have the same rule set for quality attribute conflicts. It is important to devise a set that adequately describes the relationship among quality attributes in a particular product line.

The NFRs are examined to determine if any of them contain conflicting quality attributes. If any are detected, a conflict is created containing the identifiers of the NFRs in conflict, as well as the relationship among them. For instance, consider the following NFRs

NFR1 The Maturity of the system should be high

NFR2 The Reliability of the system should be high

NFR3 The Efficiency of the system should be high

If applied to the rules set in table 1, conflicts would be detected between both NFR 1 and 3, and NFR 2 and 3. This could be described in two possible ways. Once could create a single conflict which encapsulates all 3 NFRs, such as:

C1:NFR1, NFR2 vs. NFR3

which indicates that both NFR1 and NFR2 are in a conflict with NFR3. The following is also a possible result, in which 2 conflicts are created as opposed to 1:

C1:NFR1 vs. NFR3

C2 NFR2 vs. NFR3

Both approaches have their advantages and disadvantages. As with quality attribute conflict rules, determining the degree of isolation in conflicts depends greatly on the nature of the product line. It may also vary from product to product, in which case it may be preferable to create all possible combinations of conflicts (such as creating all 3 of the example conflicts), even if it results in redundancy. However as the number of NFRs rises this could inject a large amount of confusion and work into the conflict resolution process.

After stakeholders organize NFR conflicts, they now have a defined set of problems to consider. At this point, these high level conflicts are generally too abstract to be resolved with design decisions. However, if broken up into a subset of more detailed problems, these conflicts become easier to manage.

Creation of a Functional Hierarchy for Conflict Refinement

The NFRs in conflict can be subdivided in terms of the *functionality* they pertain to, in order to provide stakeholders with more manageable portions of the problem. Stakeholders can solve these lower level conflicts to recursively deal with the bigger issue. Before this can be done, stakeholders need an organized perspective on the functionalities of the product line.

In order to create such a view, the NFR conflict analysis framework [12] takes the functional requirement hierarchy of the system and the conflict set to derive a conflict hierarchy. In order to get the most benefit from the architectural homogeny of product lines, we propose that stakeholders draft a single functional hierarchy for the entire product line. This creates an additional complication: how do we ensure that the feature variability of individual products are preserved? One possible approach to this issue was proposed by Savolienen and Kuulesa [12], in which the requirements of the product line were decomposed into a logical AND tree. Each child node in the tree partially defines the meaning of the parent. Each node contains an ordered list of numbers which correlate to the importance of that node in supporting its parent within each product. These numbers can range from 0 to 9, with 9 representing maximum contribution and 0 representing no contribution. Additionally, no node may have a higher priority than its parent for a given product in its list.

An example of such a hierarchy is given in Figure 2, which represents a set of requirements for a product line containing members A, B, and C. REQ 1 represents the entire system, while its direct children REQ 1.1, REQ 1.2, and REQ 1.3 represent high level subcomponents. In particular REQ 1.3 is of interest, as it is not implemented in product B (as denoted by its priority of 0 in the priority list). As a result, REQ 1.3's children, REQ 1.3.1 and REQ 1.3.2, are also not implemented for product B, and also have priorities of "0" for that product.

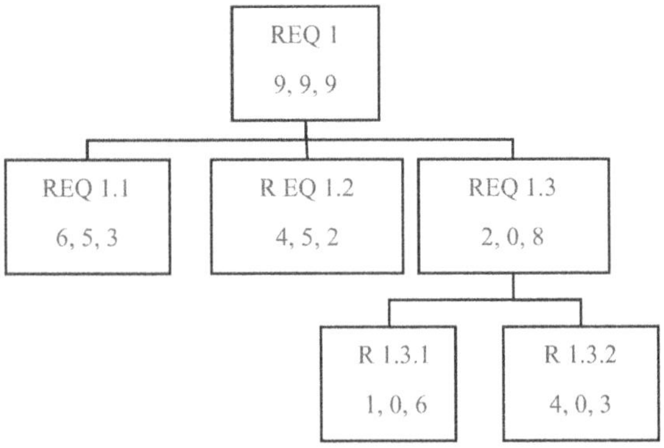

Figure 2. Example Requirement Hierarchy for Product Line (Product Priorities given in order A, B, C)

Mapping Conflict to Functional Hierarchy

With a list of NFR conflicts along with a functional hierarchy of the product line, it is possible to combine these two artifacts to create a conflict hierarchy. This hierarchy will provide stakeholders with instances of the conflict at varying degrees of detail. It is structured in a way that reflects the architecture of the product line, allowing stakeholders to perceive the role that each conflict instance plays in the overall conflict.

The method of mapping is as follows: for each node in the functional hierarchy, a corresponding node is created in the conflict hierarchy. This conflict node, or conflict *instance,* contains all information in the conflict being mapped as well as the name of the functionality it is being mapped to. This results in a conflict hierarchy with an identical structure to the functional requirement hierarchy. The process is visualized in Figure 3, where conflict C1 is mapped to a search engine and its functional components. This results in the creation of 3 conflict instances.

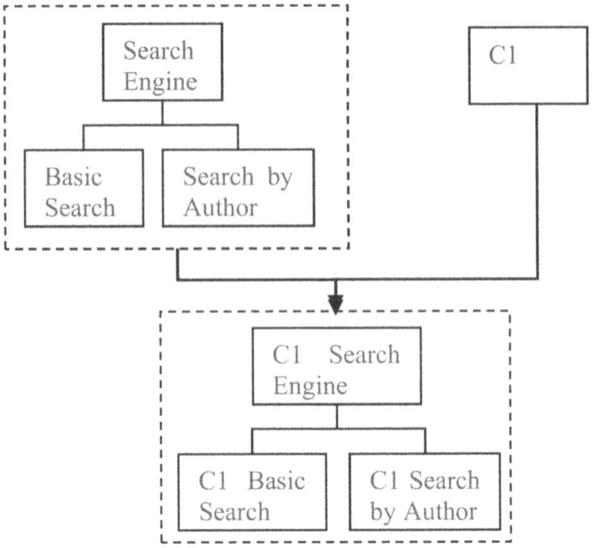

Figure 3. Mapping NFR Conflict to Functional Hierarchy in order to create Conflict Hierarchy

NFR CONFLICT RESOLUTION

Conflict Instance Evaluation

It is an accepted fact that the members of a product line must satisfy NFRs differently [13]. Some products may not need to satisfy certain NFRs as stringently as others, and may not even have to satisfy them at all. This is in part because each product has its own sets of stakeholders who have diverse needs that the product must satisfy. Therefore, when attempting to resolve NFR conflicts in a product line, one must examine the conflicts on a product by product level. At this stage in the process, the stakeholders of each product examine the conflict hierarchy in the context of their own product.

In particular, they must decide which conflict nodes must be resolved with a design decision. There are many reasons to avoid resolving a conflict node, these include:

1. The NFRs contained in the conflict node are considered to be unimportant to this product.

2. The functionality contained in the conflict node is considered to be unimportant to the resolution of the overall NFR conflict

3. The conflict node takes place at a level of detail too abstract to be resolved with a single design decision. The conflict will be resolved in the nodes children, recursively solving the conflict for this node.

4. The conflict node's parent has already been resolved with a design decision. No further resolution is necessary.

In general this process works best when stakeholders work from top to bottom. That is, stakeholders consider the higher level conflict instances first before evaluating their children. Stakeholders do not necessarily need to examine all of the lower level nodes, as this can be unnecessarily time consuming.

Design Alternatives for Conflict Resolution

When stakeholders locate a conflict instance node that they would like to be resolved with a design decision, many different design alternatives could be presented. Each alternative strikes a different tradeoff among the conflicting NFR. As a result, stakeholders will most likely disagree over which tradeoff is ideal, often preferring those which favor NFRs they perceive as important. Such disagreements are a natural factor in NFR conflict resolution, and need to be addressed by any attempt at decision making. Ideally, stakeholders would be aided by a decision support system geared towards conflict resolution. The system would allow users to share their rationale and knowledge, providing each with a better understanding of their fellow stakeholders concerns. This understanding could be used to determine which design alternative strikes the best NFR tradeoff for all concerned.

A COLLABORATIVE DECISION SUPPORT SYSTEM FOR CONFLICT RESOLUTION

An argumentation-based collaborative decision support system was developed [14] based on Toulmin's model of argumentation. Because the system is accessible over the internet, stakeholders who are geographically dispersed are not omitted from the decision making process. This decision support system aims to aid stakeholders in reaching a consensus by managing their disagreements in a constructive manner. A useful feature of this system is the ability to use rationales posted to calculate a *favorability factor which is a quantification of the general popularity of a given position.* We propose that stakeholders use this system in support their decision regarding which design alternative to choose for the resolution of a given conflict instance.

Structure of the Decision Support System

The decision support system was developed based on the client-server architecture. The client component of the system allows users to post their rationale in the form of arguments and evidences, view the rationales collected by the system in a user-friendly interface, as well as make use of a chat box and drawing pad to communicate with other online users. The server component of the system maintains a database of rationale posted to the system, accepts rationale postings from clients, and maintains fuzzy inference engines to calculate the favorability factor.

The rationale tree is comprised of projects, the issues those projects face, positions or design alternatives to resolve these issues, and arguments and evidences which provide the rationale behind each position. The role of each and how they apply to this framework will now be described.

Project- This is the overall project, which has one or more issues which are to be resolved through collaborative decision making. Stakeholders can instantiate as many projects as needed. Project in the context of this framework corresponds to either the product line, or individual products.

Issue – This is a design problem or complication that a particular project faces. The solution to this issue is to be found through collaborative decision making. In the context of our paper, issues correspond to conflict instances which stakeholders wish to resolve with a design decision. When stakeholders identify such an instance, they attach it to their project in the form of an issue.

Position – This is a potential solution to a given issue. In the context of this framework, it is a design decision which attempts to resolve a given conflict instance. When stakeholders draft a potential design alternative, they attach it to the conflict instance it's intended to resolve. As stakeholders view the rationale posted by their peers, they expand their knowledge base and understanding of the problem domain. As a result, they may become inspired to draft and propose a new design alternative which attempts to incorporate their newfound knowledge and address the concerns of their fellow stakeholders. Therefore, stakeholders should be allowed to add positions to the system while the argumentation process is underway.

Argument – This is a concise statement of support or attack, and can be attached to both positions and other arguments. Arguments attached to positions contain a rationale which partially explains a stakeholders support or lack of support for that position. Arguments attached to other arguments attempt to reinforce or contradict the statement made by that particular argument.

An argument is either supporting or attacking depending on its *weight*, a number ranging from -1 to 1. Negative weights indicate attack, while positive weights indicate support. The magnitude of the weight reflects the degree of support or attack. Another element of the argument is the *priority*, which reflects the importance and authority of the stakeholder posting the argument. This value ranges from 0 to 1, with 1 indicating the highest degree of authority. Priority can be used to ensure that arguments coming from important stakeholders have a greater degree of influence on the rationale tree.

Evidence- This is another form of rationale which is attached to arguments. Evidence consists of a reference to more concrete proof that an argument is valid. Evidences have two values associated with them, the degree of support and degree of attack. Both values range from 0 to 1, and the sum of both cannot exceed 1. The degree of support indicates the posters confidence level that the evidence is true. A degree of support approaching 1 indicates a very high level of confidence in the evidence. Conversely, a degree of support closer to 0 indicates a low level of confidence that the evidence is true. The degree of attack operates in much the same way, with values around 1 indicating a high level of confidence that the evidence is false and 0 indicating a low level of confidence that the evidence is false. Although we use the term "weight of attack" here, evidence cannot directly attack arguments. The weight of support and attack for an evidence item only reflects the degree to which the evidence supports an argument. If users wish to use evidence to disprove an argument, they must first make a counter-argument and attach their evidence to that.

As with arguments, evidences are posted by stakeholders during the decision making process in order to provide the rationale behind their preferences.

The Rationale Tree

These elements compose a structure which will be referred to as a rationale tree. A representation of a sample rationale tree can be seen in Figure 4. In this figure, squares correspond to nodes in the tree, and edges indicate a parent/child relationship. The system allows users to determine where they wish to focus their viewpoint by clicking on a node in the rationale tree to collapse or expand its children.

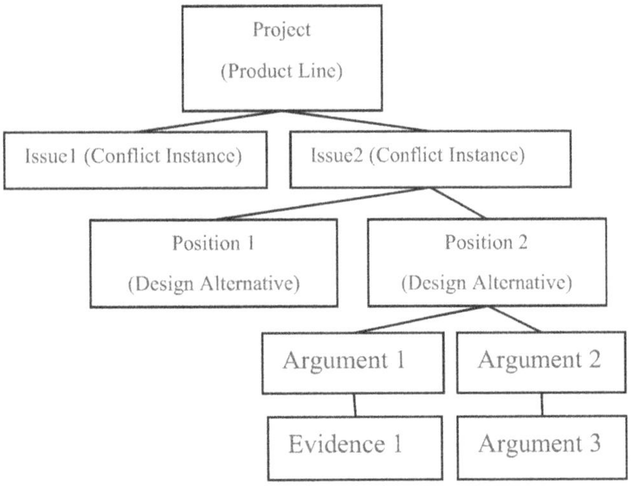

Figure 4. Sample Rationale Tree

Reduction of Arguments

The combined weights of all arguments and evidences for a given issue can be used to evaluate which position, or design alternative, is receiving the most support in terms of rationale. Because many arguments and all evidences are not directly tied to positions, the system must be able to trace these rationales to their position of origin as well as preserve their original intent.

Several approaches were developed to reason with argumentation, such as formal logic [15] and probabilistic methods [16]. Sillence [15] proposed a logic model where dialogs are represented as recursive graphs. Both rhetoric and logic rules are used to manage the dialog and to determine when the dialog has reached closure. Carofiglio uses a probabilistic method to model argumentation with belief networks [16].

Our system makes use of a fuzzy logic to reduce all arguments to a single level and connect them directly with the positions they are traced to. Fuzzy logic was chosen for argument reduction for two primary reasons. First, fuzzy linguistic terms translates well to natural language, using terms such as "medium support" or "indecisive" which are simple to understand and utilize. The second is that fuzzy logic is useful for handling uncertainty, a driving factor in any attempt to sort through multiple viewpoints regarding positions with uncertainty. This reduction is based upon 4 fuzzy heuristic rules:

Rule 1 If argument A2 supports argument A1 and Argument A1 supports position P1, then argument A2 supports position P1

Rule 2 If argument A2 attacks argument A1, and argument A1 supports position P1, then argument A2 attacks position P1.

Rule 3 If argument A2 supports argument A1 and argument A1 attacks position P1, then argument A2 attacks position P1

Rule 4 If argument A2 attacks argument A1 and argument A1 attacks position P1, then argument A2 supports position P1.

These rules are expanded to a set of 25 fuzzy inference rules which take into account the degree of support or attack. These rules are provided in the matrix in table 2. In this table SS stands for strong support, MS stands for medium support, I is indecisive, MA stands for medium attack, and SA stands for strong attack. For example the shaded cell in figure 2 represents the rule "If argument A1 is SA, and argument A2 is MA responding to A1, then A2 can be reduced to MS at A1's level".

	SS	MS	I	MA	SA
SS	SS	MS	I	MA	SA
MS	MS	MS	I	MA	SA
I	I	I	I	I	I
MA	MA	MA	I	MS	MS
SA	SA	MA	I	MS	SS

Table 2. Fuzzy Association Rules for Argument Reduction

Fuzzy linguistic terms, such as *Strong Support*, are characterized by fuzzy membership functions In order for the system to make use of these rules, it must be able to use the weight of argument to determine its membership in the fuzzy set. This is accomplished by the use of a piecewise trapezoidal/triangular membership function. The trapezoidal membership function for strong attack is (-1, -1, -0.8, -0.6), medium attack is (-0.8, -0.6, -0.4, -0.2), indecisive is a triangular function of (-0.3, 0, 0, 0.3), medium support is (0.2, 0.4, 0.6, 0.8), and strong support is (0.5, 0.8, 1, 1). These membership functions are displayed in the graph in Figure 5, with the x axis representing the weight of a given function and the y axis representing its degree of membership to the fuzzy sets. These rules are used in the process of reducing all arguments to a single level, the level of arguments responding directly to a position. This allows the system to calculate the relative favorability of a position.

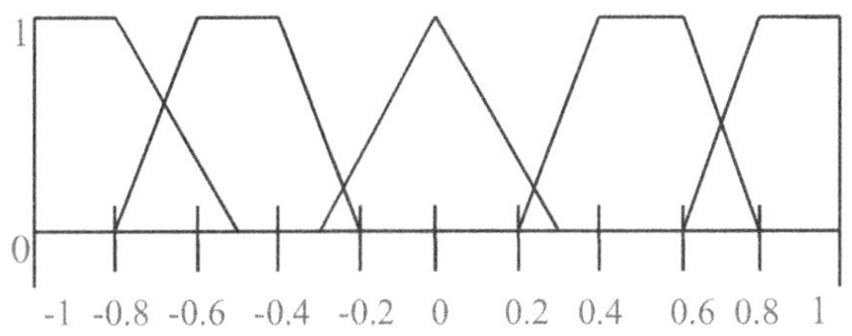

Figure 5: Fuzzy Membership Function

For instance, suppose argument A has a weight of -0.7 and is attached to argument B which has a weight of 0.6. We wish to reduce argument A up to argument B"s level, applying rule 3 of our fuzzy heuristic rules. To do this, we first determine Argument A"s membership in the fuzzy set as given by the trapezoidal functions as seen in figure 6. In figure 6 the x axis corresponds to an arguments weight, while the y axis corresponds to the degree of membership to each member of the fuzzy set.

$F_{SA}(A) = F_{SA}(-0.7) = 0.67$
$F_{MA}(A) = F_{MA}(-0.7) = 0.5$
$F_{I}(A) = F_{I}(-0.7) = 0$
$F_{MS}(A) = F_{MS}(-0.7) = 1$
$F_{SS}(A) = F_{MS}(-0.7) = 0$

As well as Argument B"s membership in the fuzzy set:

$F_{SA}(B) = F_{SA}(0.6) = 0$
$F_{MA}(B) = F_{MA}(0.6) = 0$
$F_{I}(B) = F_{I}(0.6) = 0$
$F_{MS}(B) = F_{MS}(0.6) = 1.0$
$F_{SS}(B) = F_{MS}(0.6) = 0.33$

Next, all nonzero fuzzy membership values for A and B are compared. Each comparison correlates to an activated fuzzy association rule in figure 2. The minimum of each comparison is taken to produce 4 weights.

$W_1 = \text{Min}\,[F_{MA}(A), F_{SS}(B)]$
$= \text{Min}\,[F_{MA}(-0.7), F_{SS}(0.6)]$
$= \text{Min}\,[0.5, 0.33]$
$= 0.33$
$W_2 = \text{Min}\,[F_{MA}(-0.7), F_{SA}(0.6)]$
$= \text{Min}\,[0.5, 1.0]$
$= 0.5$
$W_3 = \text{Min}\,[F_{SA}(-0.7), F_{SS}(0.6)]$
$= \text{Min}\,[0.67, 0.33]$
$= 0.33$
$W_4 = \text{Min}\,[F_{SA}(-0.7), F_{MS}(0.6)]$
$= \text{Min}\,[0.67, 1.0]$
$= 0.67$

Each weight is multiplied by the fuzzy value of fuzzy rule activated by its original comparison. For instance, W_1 activates the rule comparing MA and SS, which results in an MA (0.5). These are added together and divided by the sum of all weights:

The new weight of the reduced argument A is found by multiplying each weight by the fuzzy value and dividing this by the sum of all weights:

$$WA = \frac{W_1(MA) + W_2(SA) + W_3(MA) + W_4(MA)}{W_1 + W_2 + W_3 + W_4}$$

$$WA = \frac{0.33*-0.5+0.5*-1+0.33*-0.5+0.67*-0.5}{0.33 + 0.5 + 0.33 + 0.67}$$

$$WA = -0.59$$

The result is the new de-fuzzified weight of the inferred relationship from reduction of arguments A and B.

Favorability Factor

After all arguments have been reduced to the sub-position level, where they all are directly attached to some position, it is possible to calculate the favorability factor. To do this, the system takes the summation of every argument, multiplied by the priority of their poster to provide the favorability factor. This can be performed at any point in the decision making process to take a snapshot of which alternative has the most support from arguments and evidences, and is probably the most favorable among stakeholders.

Decision Making and the Rationale Tree

The completed rationale tree provides stakeholders with a good overview of the concerns of their peers, along with new insights and perspectives on the problem domain. Armed with this new knowledge, stakeholders are better prepared to collaborate and decide which design alternative will be implemented. Once a decision is reached, stakeholders can move on to the next conflict instance and resolve it in the same way. However, the rationale tree is not discarded, as it contains many uses in the software design process:

- This tree provides stakeholders with a detailed description of the factors that have motivated the design of the product so far. This can serve as a useful reference when the time comes to actually implement these decisions.
- Much of the rationale applies to other conflict instances within this product. This rationale can be

reused or referenced to cut down on the work involved in the resolution of such instances.

- The tree can also be used by the stakeholders of other products when trying to resolve similar conflict instances. While there is some expected variation in the NFRs of the members of a product line, they are not completely heterogeneous. Stakeholders may find that the rationale behind one accepted design decision mirrors their own concerns. They may then quickly resolve to implement the same or a similar decision in their own product. This promotes code and design artifact reuse among products, an important aspect of product line design.

EXPERIMENTAL ANALYSIS OF DECISION SUPPORT SYSTEM

We have conducted an experiment which involves the use of this framework in the conflict analysis and resolution of a product line. The experiment centers on a hypothetical software development firm which is trying to create a product line of software security suites. In particular they are concerned the resolution of a particularly important conflict in their product line. The aim of the experiment was to verify the usefulness of the web-based decision support system when used by stakeholders to resolve NFR conflicts. A graduate-level software engineering class consisting of 19 students participated in this experiment. The class was chosen due to the fact that the discussion of software metrics and requirements covered in the class could be tied to the concerns of the hypothetical stakeholders. These participants participated in argumentation as if they were the stakeholders of the security suite product line.

Architecture of Hypothetical Product Line

The security suite product line, which is the focus of the empirical study, is designed to allow administrators to manage a central database of security policies which are enforced by the security suite. It is comprised of 3 major functional components:

- The *architect* - an interface which administrators use to add, remove, and modify policies in the central policy database.
- The *enforcer* -monitors specified resources and prevents the violation of security policies on local machines. Users need the permission of the enforcer to utilize the monitored resources
- The *librarian*- queries the central policy database to provide the enforcer with the policies it must enact.

The architect and central policy database sit on a relatively secure server under the supervision of network security personnel, while the enforcer and librarian exist on every client machine intended to be monitored by the security suite.

The NFR Conflict

The experiment focuses on 3 NFRs that the product line must satisfy

NFR1 – The efficiency of the system must be high

NFR2 – The security of the system must be high

NFR3 – The variability between products must be low

NFR1 reflects the idea that the product line must be relatively lightweight, as it is used for many interactions of the system. Efficiency in this case refers to both the use of time and resources that the system incurs. NFR2 represents the ability of the system to resists attempts at infiltration. In this case it aims to ensure that access control is strict. NFR3 is a concern that the developers have that in order to maximize code and design artifact reuse between products, there must not be too much variation among them.

A conflict exists between these 3 NFR: the security requirement conflicts with the efficiency requirement as any additional security protocols use up time and system resources. Attempts to reduce the workload of the system and increase efficiency can also potentially incur security risks. Over-specification of the system in order to support either of these NFRs will cause it to diverge too much from other members of a product line, limiting the developer's ability to reuse code and design artifacts.

For the purpose of this experiment, we focus on a single instance of this conflict which is located in the *librarian* component. In particular, we are concerned with how the librarian fetches security policies. In order to address this issue, participants in the experiment need to understand the needs of the stakeholders of each product.

The Product Line Members

The product line consists of 3 members, each member being deployed in a different environment. While they provide the same type of functionality, they must reflect the different needs of their respective environment and customer stakeholders. The products and their environments are as follows:

School Product –This product is aimed at K-12 public school networks. The stakeholders of the school product were primarily concerned with the efficiency of the suite, as many schools are constrained in terms of system resources. Security was a concern, but did not need to be as strict due to the low cost and risk of a security breach. The school product provides participants in the experiment with a base case for understanding the conflict.

Military Product – This product is aimed at military customers, for use in networks deployed in the field. The risk of a security breach in a military application is very high, and the cost could incur the loss of human life.

Therefore, security was of utmost importance. However, stakeholders deployed in mission critical situations have real-time requirements which should not be delayed by the suite. This is complicated by the fact that the connection to the central policy database may be interrupted as a result of a hostile environment. The military product provides participants with an example of a high-stakes NFR conflict, where the need to satisfy both is very high.

Corporate Product – This product is intended for use in large-scale business networks. Corporate networks possess a high risk and cost for security breaches, although they are abundant in terms of system resources. The corporate product has an additional functional requirement not found elsewhere in the product line which the librarian must interact with. The corporate product provides participants with an example of how the feature variability of a product line affects design alternatives.

All three products have their own set of 3 design alternatives, which possess some similarities which may be used for code reuse and reinforce low product variability if certain alternatives are chose.

Process of Experimentation

In the first phase, participants were asked to review the problem documentation and consider the objectives of the stakeholders in the product line. These stakeholders included the developers and managers of the firm attempting to design the product line, as well as the various customers they were marketing their products towards. They then voted on which design alternative best addresses stakeholder concerns for each of the 3 products. The voting process took place for a period of 1 week and the results reflect the knowledge base of participants before argumentation. After voting had concluded, participants were provided with login information and instructions for the use of the argumentation-based collaborative decision support system. They were instructed to post the rationale behind their decisions made in phase one and engage in argumentation to determine the best design alternative to their knowledge. All participants were given an equal priority of 0.5. The argumentation process took place over the course of 2 weeks, resulting in 280 arguments and evidences being collected from the participants. At the conclusion of the argumentation period, participants were asked to review the complete rationale trees before participating in another survey. This second survey again asks the participants for their favored design alternatives, as well as the effect that argumentation had on their degree of confidence in their original selection. This voting process took place for a period of 1 week and the results reflect the impact of the collaborative decision support system on the opinion of participants.

Analysis of Results

The results of the first and second surveys are compared in figures 6 through 9. For both the school and corporate products, the amount of support for the most popular alternative increased. This indicates that the argumentation process helped some participants to get behind the winning alternative. For the military product, popular opinion was split on the best alternative, with half favoring alternative 1 and the other half favoring 3. For both the school and military products, twice as many participants had their original choices reinforced as those who had their opinions changed. These results show that the argumentation system is effective in promoting a better understanding of the NFR conflict domain, as the majority of stakeholders have had it influence their opinion in some way.

Table 3 displays the favorability factor of each alternative, calculated via fuzzy reduction at the conclusion of the argumentation process. Negative values result from a given alternative receiving more attacking arguments than supportive ones. In each product, the Alternative with the highest favorability also had the highest degree of votes in the second survey. For the school product, Alternative 2 won with 11 votes and a favorability factor of 0.77. For the military product, Alternatives 1 and 3 tied for the most votes in Survey 2. However, Alternative 3 had a greater degree of supporting arguments, resulting in a favorability factor of 2.695 as opposed to Alternative 1's favorability factor of 1.261. For the corporate product, Alternative 3 is the only one with a positive favorability factor, totaling at 1.473. This corresponds to its victory in Survey 2, with 10 votes. The correlation between the favorability factors calculated by the argumentation and the results of the surveys reflect the effectiveness of the system at gauging user opinion.

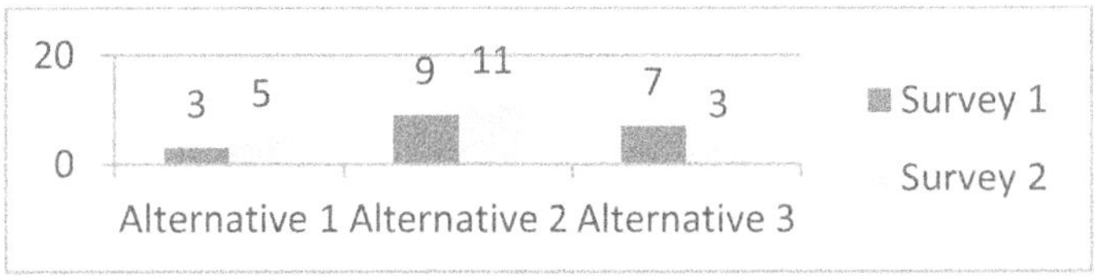

Figure 6. Alternative Voting Results for School Product

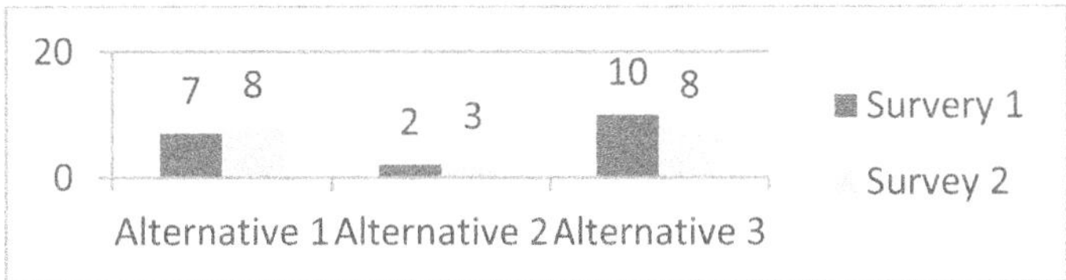

Figure 7. Alternative Voting Results for Military Product

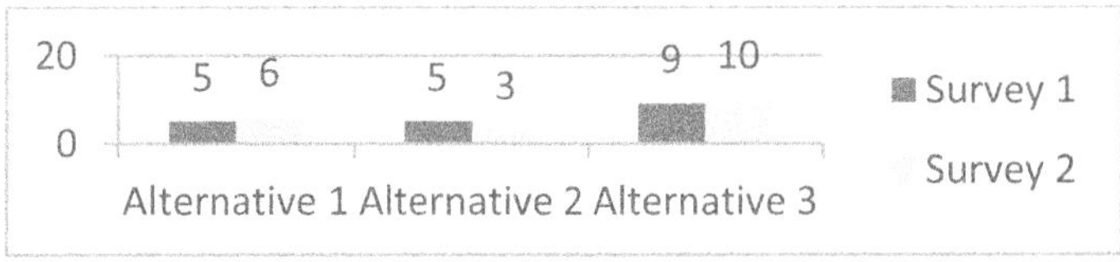

Figure 8. Alternative Voting Results for Corporate Product

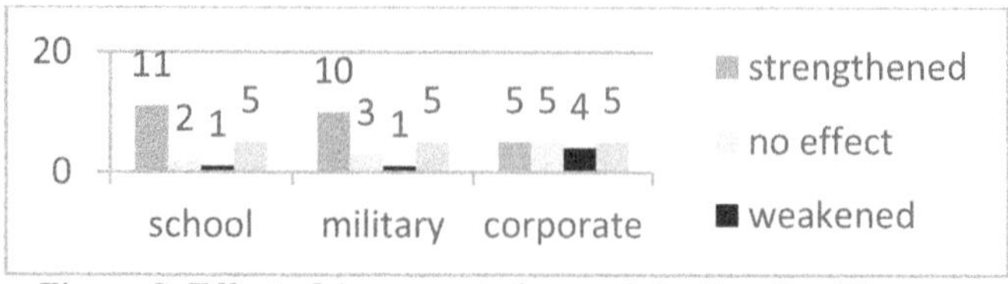

Figure 9. Effect of Argumentation on Selection Confidence

	Alternative 1	Alternative 2	Alternative 3
School	-3.2	0.77	0.73
Military	1.261	0.495	2.695
Corporate	-0.448	-0.620	1.473

Table 3. Calculated Favorability Factors

DISCUSSION AND CONCLUSIONS

While the empirical study discussed in this paper was based around the problem of NFR conflict in software engineering, the issue of quality attribute conflict within product line design can manifest itself in a variety of paradigms. Such applications will be explored in future research to determine the flexibility of our approach.

Conflict detection and resolution are essential in software product line design since their stakeholders often have conflicting viewpoints about their requirements and design. The conflicts should be resolved collectively in a collaborative decision making process to discover the best trade-offs based on collective determination. This paper presents a framework for design conflict resolution for software product lines in a collaborative decision making process supported an argumentation based collaborative decision support system. The results of the experiment show that the argumentation based collaborative decision support system is effective at assisting stakeholders in decision making.

REFERENCES

1. Tyree, J., and Akerman. A., Architecture Decisions: Demystifying Architecture. *IEEE Software* (2005) vol. 22 (2) pp. 19- 27.
2. Klein, M., Supporting Conflict Resolution in Cooperative Design Systems. *IEEE Transactions on Systems, Man, and Cybernetics,* Vol. 21.
3. Guilin, J., Baosheng, Y., Rong, Z., A Conflict Resolution Algorithm Considering Design Objective Optimization in Collaborative Design. *Proc. 16th International Conference on Industrial Engineering and Engineering Management,* IEEE (2009), pp. 20-23.
4. Toulmin, S. E., *The Uses of Argument.* Cambridge, UK, University Press, 1958.
5. Conklin, J., Begeman, M.L., gIBIS: A Hypertext Tool for Exploratory Policy Discussion, *ACM Transactions on Information Systems,* Vol.6, No. 4, (1998) pp. 303-331.
6. Papadias, N., HERMES: Supporting Argumentative Discourse in Multi Agent Decision Making". *Proc. 15th National Conference on Artificial Intelligence (AAAI-98)* (1998) pp. 827-832.
7. Huang C. J. et al, Implementation and Performance of an Intelligent Online Argumentation Assessment System. *International Conference on Electrical and Control Engineering,* (2010) pp. 25-27.
8. Poort, E., Peter H.N., Resolving Requirement Conflicts through Non-Functional Decomposition. *IEEE Conference on Software Architecture,* (2004).
9. Liu, C., Ontology based Conflict Analysis Method in Non-functional Requirements. *IEEE/ACIS 9th International Conference on Computer and Information Science* (2010).
10. Xu, L., Hendrickson, S., Hettwir, E., Ziv, H., Hoek, A., Richardson, D., Towards Supporting the Architectural Design Process Through Evaluation of Design Alternatives. *Proc. ISSTA workshop on Role of Software Architecture for Testing and Analysis,* (2006) *ACM* New York, NY, USA.
11. Sadanam V., Liu, F., Analysis of Conflicts among Non-functional Requirements using Integrated Analysis of Functional and Non-functional Requirements. *31st Annual International Computer Software and Applications Conference,* 24-27 (2007), pp. 215-218.
12. Kuulesa, J., Savolienen J., Requirements Engineering for Product Families. *Proc. International Conference on Software Engineering,* (2000) pp. 61-69.
13. Nguyen, Q., Non-Functional Requirements Analysis Modeling for Product Lines. *ICSE Workshop on Software Engineering, IEEE* (2009) pp. 56-61.
14. Liu, F. Raorane, S., Leu, M.A., Web Based Intelligent Collaborative System for Engineering Design. *Collaborative Product Design and Manufacturing Methodologies and Applications*, Springer, London, UK, 2007 pp. 37-58.
15. Sillence, J., Intelligent Argumentation Systems: Requirements, Models, Research Agenda, and Applications. In Allen Kent (Ed.), *Encyclopedia of Library and Information Science,* Marcel Dekker, New York, pp. 176-217.
16. Carofiglio, V., Modeling Argumentation with Belief Networks. *Proc. of the 4th Workshop on Computational Models of Natural Argument*, 2004.

On the Perceived Interdependence and Information Sharing Inhibitions of Enterprise Software Engineers

Alicia M. Grubb
Department of Computer Science
University of Toronto
Toronto, ON, Canada
amgrubb@cs.toronto.edu

Andrew Begel
Microsoft Research
Redmond, WA, USA
andrew.begel@microsoft.com

ABSTRACT
Software teams often have trouble coordinating shared work due to poor communication practices. We surveyed software engineers (N=989) at Microsoft to investigate three rarely explored aspects of coordination: (1) how an engineer's perception of dependence is predicted by his organizational characteristics, (2) how this perception differs when the dependence varies by the kinds of shared work artifacts, and (3) how the work group range affects the likelihood that an engineer will share information about work artifacts with another. Our results indicate that engineers tailor their communications about shared work for each group of intended recipients. This suggests that many existing coordination tools that rely on automatic mining and visualization of engineering activities have prevented senders from controlling the distribution of information about their work, and may have overestimated the receivers' abilities to comprehend it.

Author Keywords
Coordination; Enterprise software development; Awareness; Communication

ACM Classification Keywords
K.4.3 Organizational Impacts: Computer-supported cooperative work

General Terms
Human Factors

INTRODUCTION
Large-scale software engineering requires coordination between engineers who build and ship a software product. Effective coordination relies on communication between individuals who are dependent on the status and content of the shared work artifacts (e.g., source code, bugs, tests, documentation, and project schedules). Prior research has shown that necessary communication is inhibited by physical, technical, cognitive, social, and organizational factors, which leads to coordination breakdowns that can threaten the viability of a project [14, 18, 34].

Quantifying the mismatch between actual communication and suggested communication (by relating people to their shared work [12]) can help indicate possible coordination problems (e.g., build failures [35]) which may be fixed by increased (or decreased) communication [17, 26, 28, 41, 49]. If employed successfully, better *communication strategies* should improve team performance [1].

We tried to employ this extensive body of research to make sense of observations of inter-team coordination in large-scale software development at Microsoft, and noticed three gaps. First, studies suggest that if engineers communicated properly with one another along dependency lines, it would avoid problems [12, 35]. But, we find that this picture to be too simplistic; not all engineers are the same. The activities associated with some job functions involve many more dependencies than others. Likewise, an engineer's departmental affiliation and tenure in the company influences the number and depth of dependencies [9, 25]. Differences in dependencies may have significant effects on associated coordination and communication needs.

Second, software modularity at all levels (e.g., methods, classes, libraries, components, applications, etc.) isolates teams of engineers from one another [19], and creates an *asymmetry* in many engineers' perceptions of their dependencies. To an engineer using a software library, it is obvious that he depends on the library's team. However, the library team may be completely unaware of his existence unless he chooses to contact them. One will not (and cannot) communicate with a dependent that one does not perceive to exist.

Third, social biases and organizational culture can interfere with an engineer's willingness to share information about his work with outsiders, even direct dependents. The amount of information an engineer is willing to share is inversely related to his *work group range* to the other person. People on the same team trust one another much more, and consequently share much more information, than people who work in different corporate departments. Ingroup bias and confidentiality requirements may be the source of these inhibitions. A belief that outsiders would not even be able to comprehend your information (i.e. the illusion of transparency) may also play a role.

In our study, we investigated three research questions:

> RQ_1: Does an engineer's organizational characteristics (measured by job function (developer, tester, project manager (PM)), management role (manager or individual contributor (IC)), department, years of experience in the software industry, and years of experience in the company) predict whether an engineer perceives that he depends on or is dependent upon shared artifacts from engineers on other teams?
>
> RQ_2: How does an engineer's perception of his dependencies differ with the kinds of shared artifacts, and how much?
>
> RQ_3: How does *work group range* (measured on a scale from no one, to my team, and to the entire company) affect the likelihood that an engineer will share information about work artifacts with another? Does this likelihood vary by artifact type?

We surveyed software engineers (N=989) at Microsoft, a large U.S.-based software company, on their perceptions of interdependence and communication between engineers. Our findings on interdependence mainly agree with previous research at Microsoft [7, 36], but reveal several significant differences. As we thought, our data indicates that engineers' perception of their dependencies varies significantly by their organizational characteristics and the direction of the dependency. In addition, among many work artifact types, we see significant signs of an asymmetry in dependency perception.

We found that the most widely shared work artifacts are specifications and release schedules. Among developers, code changes (checkins) are surprisingly the most *narrowly* shared work artifacts. Our analysis revealed that with every type of work artifact we asked about, engineers who perceive that they depend on others are both permitted, and willing, to share information more widely than those who do not. We expected to find the reverse—if you reported that others depend on you, you would be more likely to share—but did not. Finally, irrespective of dependencies, developers and requirements and project engineers felt more comfortable sharing information than they were permitted, but testers felt less comfortable.

Our findings and analyses suggest engineers customize the information they share according to the organizational characteristics and work group range of their chosen recipients. In the Implications section, we explore how the automation inherent to many existing coordination support tools may in fact thwart this customization ability, and places undue burden on receivers to comprehend the import of a generic, untargeted message. Many of these tools do not allow senders to control the recipients of their messages at all, which further inhibits communication. We believe that a new generation of communication and coordination support tools operating with a mixed-initiative approach to message customization and recipient targeting could enable senders to increase their information sharing with a comfortable sense of control.

RELATED WORK

There is inherent risk in depending on others to develop software; they may not deliver on their promises. Managing the risk and ensuring a successful outcome, then, requires discovering, maintaining awareness of, and communicating effectively with one's dependencies.

Dependence Discovery

Since Conway, we have known that software teams organize the architecture of their software similarly to their own organization [13]. Thus, software analysis methods are often used to derive technical dependency networks and relate them to their authors [16]. However, more complete socio-technical dependency network discovery derives additionally from an understanding of software process, organizational culture, and workflow [11]. Here, empirical methods that mine software repositories are used to uncover how team members coordinate their work around various kinds of work artifacts, such as bugs [12], checkins [38], and emails [4].

While the dependence network shows where communication should occur, it does not show where it *does* occur. Cataldo quantified this difference using a measure called socio-technical congruence [12], and along with others, showed that the magnitude of the congruence difference correlates with coordination problems and project failures [11, 35, 51].

The existence of a so-called *socio-technical congruence gap* illustrates that many engineers have difficulty identifying (and communicating with) their dependencies. Our work seeks to discover how organizational factors can help predict whether engineers perceive that they have dependencies on one another.

Dependence Awareness

Engineers gain awareness of their dependencies's actions during daily activities. At a high level, daily work varies by job function, management role, departmental affiliation, and tenure within the company. Developers communicate with colleagues and dependents about software code quality through code reviews [43], about software code changes through push-based notification mechanisms [32, 22], and learn about code ownership and responsibility through the exploration of revision control systems and bug databases [6, 23]. Testers wait for project managers (PMs) to send them specifications for their features before they can write testing plans [5, 36]. Then, they must wait for developers to finish writing the code and notify them before they can run their tests and report bugs. PMs depend on one another to coordinate work between dependent teams by maintaining awareness of the status, scheduling, and any changes to work artifacts on which their own team depends. They conduct regular meetings with other PMs and developers to prioritize bugs and to coordinate component completion schedules [2].

Despite much communication, engineers' awareness of their dependencies remains incomplete. For example, both developers and PMs may stay unaware of testers' work until the tester finds and reports a bug. Testers reporting bugs in a build may have difficulty discovering which developers among a large set should be made aware of a problem, and resort to inefficient email broadcasts to notify them [3]. Requirements gathering activities challenge many PMs, due to the difficulties in discovering and communicating with *all* relevant stakeholders [37] and the dynamic and unpredictable dependencies between projects with changing requirements [15]. Creating and enforcing strict APIs between component modules hinders developers from observing and communicating about shared work that spans the boundary [19]. If developers are not contacted by users of the modules they own, they may lack awareness of the existence or needs of their dependent developers.

Zooming in, some software team practices such as daily standup meetings (common in Agile software methods), can improve awareness of imminent dependencies (e.g. when one engineer is blocking another from getting work done). Coordination tools, such as configuration management systems, dependency and conflict awareness visualizations, and collaborative IDEs, support communication, work artifact management, and task management [46]. Recommender systems can help engineers discover others who are working on similar projects to them, so that they might discover and stay aware of one another's progress [40, 53]. These tools are often intended for individual developers, leaving other job functions, management levels, and experience levels understudied and under-supported.

Our study identifies how engineers with various organizational characteristics perceive their dependencies on work artifacts beyond software code and APIs. The prevalent asymmetry of this dependence, along with an engineer's organizational characteristics, affects his visibility into and understanding of those dependencies [44, 42]. Our survey uncovers these work artifact dependence asymmetries and explores how these might affect the perception of dependence.

Communication Inhibitions

Even when engineers are aware of their dependents, they may not wish to share information about their work with them. Inhibitors to communication include geographic separation [30, 31, 39], information overload [32], low social capital [33] and lack of trust [5, 10, 31, 52], organizational separation [13, 19], and personality [48]. Communication difficulties in software teams resemble those in many other kinds of product development organizations [9], therefore advice on improving coordination through increased cross-functional communication may be applicable to software organizations as well [1, 21].

Prior work rarely discusses communication inhibitors in *enterprise* software development. The perceived confidentiality of one's work artifacts will inhibit the distribution of information about the artifact to recipients. The specific sensitivity of the work artifact will inversely affect the acceptable communication range, i.e. a more sensitive work artifact will be shared with fewer people than a less sensitive or public one. A prevalent desire for a team to speak with one voice and control its message to outsiders may inhibit sharing information that is unfinished, or not yet approved by management. Likewise, individual team members may not feel empowered to speak on behalf of the team, preferring that an official team liaison mediate communication with outsiders [36]. As teams isolate themselves from others, they may easily demonstrate social biases where they mistrust others — something which is equally likely in open source software teams [47] — or perceive that their dependents do not know enough to understand the information that they requested. Our survey uncovers the diversity and range of these enterprise-oriented communication-inhibiting factors on engineers with varying organizational characteristics.

RESEARCH CONTEXT

At Microsoft, engineers fall mainly into one of three job functions: developer, tester, and project manager (PM) [36]. Developers are responsible for writing the software code and fixing bugs. Testers create test harnesses, write and execute blackbox and end-to-end scenario-based test suites, and report bugs. PMs elicit requirements from customers to create high-level design specifications and coordinate work between the developers, testers, and PMs of other teams according to the product's release schedule.

The smallest workgroup at Microsoft is the *feature crew*, in which a developer, a tester, and a PM create, develop, and maintain a feature in the product. *Feature crews* may be organized hierarchically or grouped according to the coupling of their features, but ultimately report to a *team* consisting of development, test, and PM leads and managers. The entire set of *teams*, along with general managers, architects, and liaisons to sales and marketing form a *product group*, ranging in size from 100 to 5,000 people. *Product groups* are then organized into *departments*, each of which housing a suite of products.

Engineers at Microsoft coordinate their work with one another using a variety of communication methods, including face-to-face and computer-mediated team meetings, emails, instant messages, phone calls, and via entries in work item (bug) databases [7].

METHODOLOGY

Our research was conducted using a web-based survey over a period of 8 days in the summer of 2010. An invitation was emailed to 3,000 software engineers (with at least one year of tenure at Microsoft), randomly selected from a much larger population of around 28,000 engineering employees from around the world. Responses were anonymous, but respondents could identify themselves (separate from their survey submissions) to enter a raffle for a prize of US$250. The survey contained 40 questions, though in this paper, we only analyze questions relating to interdependence and information sharing.[1]

In preparing the survey, we prototyped our questions through a series of pilot surveys and followup interviews (in which we discussed the wording of the questions). We adapted lists of work artifacts from the previous work at Microsoft [7]. All questions with lists allowed the respondents to select

[1] We encourage other researchers to replicate our study. Please contact us for a copy of the questionnaire.

Table 1. Response Rate and Sample Distribution by Job Function[2]

	Total	PMs	Devs	Testers	Other
Total Sampled	3000	1000	1000	1000	0
Responses	989	247	327	376	39
Response Rate	33%	24.7%	32.7%	37.6%	–
Percent of Sample	–	25%	33%	38%	4%

"Other," and include a qualitative response. We analyzed these "Other" responses for completeness, but they were not frequently used by the respondents.

Demographics

The survey began with a set of demographic questions to determine the respondent's organizational characteristics. Respondents were asked to indicate their job function (PM, Developer, Tester, Other), their management role (Individual Contributor (IC), Lead, Manager, Other), department within the company, the number of years of professional software engineering experience they had, and the number of years they had worked at Microsoft.

We received 1052 responses, of which 63 were invalid (empty or duplicate). This resulted in 989 valid responses, for an overall response rate of 33% (see Table for response rates by job function). Overall, respondents reported that they worked at Microsoft for an average of 6.01 years (SD = 4.3), and as professionals in the software industry for 10.03 years (SD = 6.59). Although both means are positively skewed, the individuals in our sample report a fair amount of experience, and have spent several years working in the software industry before joining Microsoft. Years of experience at Microsoft is strongly correlated with years experience in the software industry ($r = 0.52$, $p < 0.001$). For the remainder of our analysis, we will only use years of experience at Microsoft.

PMs were the most experienced, followed by developers and then testers, both at Microsoft and as software engineers. From our sample of 989 participants, 774 respondents reported working as individual contributors, 158 were either leads or managers, 39 reported working as both an individual contributor and a lead/manager, and 18 reported working in another role (e.g. architect or executive). Managers have four years, on average, more experience at Microsoft than individual contributors, but a similar number of years as software engineers. The distribution of respondents' departments within our sample is consistent with the distribution of software engineers across the organization.

Statistical Methodology

Throughout the Results section, we examine various relationships within the dataset. The dataset is quite large and the majority of the variables are ordered or dichotomous variables. We used t tests to evaluate whether two sub-populations of our sample had significantly different means, and whether the slope of our regression lines differed significantly from zero.

[2] *Other* responses were excluded from analysis when split across job function.

We used ANOVA (Analysis of Variance) to test for significantly different means in more than two subgroups. We minimally used CHI-Square (χ^2) because its sensitivity is problematic with large samples. Throughout the analysis, we used three forms of regression: linear regression for continuous dependent variables, binary logistic regression for dichotomous dependent variables, and ordered logistic regression for categorical dependent variables.

Terminology

We introduce two terms: *iDepend* – the respondent perceives that he depends on work done by others outside his team, and *oDepend* – the respondent perceives that individuals from outside his team depend on him for his work. We also list the 20 work artifact types for which at least one engineer in Microsoft reported a dependency: API Definitions, Binaries, Bug Fixes, Bug Reports, Build Information, Checkin Messages and Source Code Diffs, Source Code, Delivered features, Documentation, Schedules (Feature, Release, and Product/Shipping), Specifications (Design, Development, Implementation, Product, Test, and Other), Team-specific Engineering Standards, Team Meeting Notes, Tests, Test Results, Work Items, Work Item Priorities, and Work Status.

In our understanding, the concepts of *work artifact* and *information about a work artifact* are indistinguishable. When an engineer sends a message to another, sometimes it is a simple artifact (e.g. source code in a repository, binaries in a build, specifications on a web site), and sometimes it is a deliberate act of communication (e.g. an email sharing status meeting notes, an IM checking up on a task request). But, it is often both at the same time. For example, writing a checkin message might be considered sharing information about code, but the source code diff contained in the checkin is code. The reduction of a buggy program to a simple test case to include in a bug report is simultaneously an act of communication and an artifact. Bug reports contain structured fields describing the problem, while unstructured fields record acts of communication between the engineers who worked on it. Thus, in this paper, we use the terms *sharing artifacts* and *sharing information about artifacts* interchangeably.

We operationalize the notion that individuals share their work information (the status and content of the shared work artifacts) to specific audiences within Microsoft. We measure sharing through a set of proxies corresponding to various work information types (including artifacts and status) using a scale called *work group range*. This scale ranges from (0) no one, (1) their feature crew, (2) their team, (3) their dependents and those that depend on them, (4) their whole product team, (5) their department, or (6) the entire company. We combine these proxies to create a *sharing metric* instrument to understand with what work groups engineers share confidential and non-confidential information. We also use the same *sharing metric* to evaluate the difference between the information that engineers are permitted to share vs. what they report feeling comfortable sharing.

Table 2. Logistical Regression Analysis of Perception of Inter-team Dependencies

(Q1) I depend on the work of people outside my team.					
iDepend	Coeff	OddRatio	Std Coeff	z	$P > \|z\|$
Developer	-1.09	0.34	0.60	-3.83	0.000
Tester	-1.30	0.27	0.53	-4.70	0.000
Manager	0.45	1.57	1.20	1.73	0.083
Years-Exp.	0.08	1.08	1.40	3.09	0.002
Intercept	1.88			6.52	0.000
Number of Observations=899			Log likelihood=-420.1809		
			Null Model Log likelihood=-456.0344		

(Q2) People outside my team depend on work that I personally do.					
oDepend	Coeff	OddRatio	Std Coeff	z	$P > \|z\|$
Developer	-1.01	0.37	0.62	-3.52	0.000
Tester	-1.32	0.27	0.53	-4.75	0.000
Manager	0.49	1.64	1.22	1.85	0.064
Years-Exp.	0.08	1.09	1.40	3.07	0.002
Intercept	1.87			6.47	0.000
Number of Observations=899			Log likelihood=-415.4851		
			Null Model Log likelihood=-448.9960		

RESULTS

Interdependence

We asked respondents about their perception of interdependence with two Yes/No questions: (Q1) "I personally depend on the work of people outside my team." (Q2) "People outside my team depend on the work that I personally do." 78.8% of respondents said they were dependent on others outside their team, and 79.7% said that others depended on their work. Only 67.4% of respondents said yes to both questions (bi-directional dependencies). Q1 and Q2 are moderately correlated ($r(911) = 0.37$, $p < 0.0001$).

We were interested in learning whether our respondents' organizational characteristics could predict whether they perceived having a dependency. The null hypothesis is that the likelihood of having inter-team dependencies does not vary by organizational characteristics. We explored this relationship using logistic regression. Q1 and Q2 were coded as dichotomous dependent variables. Any respondent who indicated that the question was not applicable ("N/A") was coded as blank.

The organizational characteristics likely to correlate with perceived interdependence are job function (PMs, Developers, Testers, Other),[3] management role (Yes (Lead or Manager) or No (IC)), department, and years of experience (minimum 1 year). We removed department from the analysis because there was no significant variation.

In Table 2, we report significant variables and their significance levels for the regressions of Q1 and Q2. The log odds of years of experience and job function were significant in both models; this allows us to reject our null hypothesis. PMs have a significantly higher likelihood than Developers ($\chi^2(1) = 14.69$, $p = 0.0001$) and Testers ($\chi^2(1) = 22.08$, $p < 0.0001$) of reporting that they are dependent on engineers outside their team. Perceiving an external dependence also varied by years of experience ($\chi^2(1) = 9.53$, $p = 0.002$); greater years of experience increase a respondent's likelihood of depending on others. PMs have a significantly higher likelihood than Developers ($\chi^2(1) = 12.41$, $p = 0.0004$) and Testers ($\chi^2(1) = 22.53$, $p < 0.0001$) of perceiving that others depend on their work. Engineers with more experience have an increased likelihood as well ($\chi^2(1) = 9.44$, $p = 0.002$). We did not find any significant interaction effect between years of experience and job function.

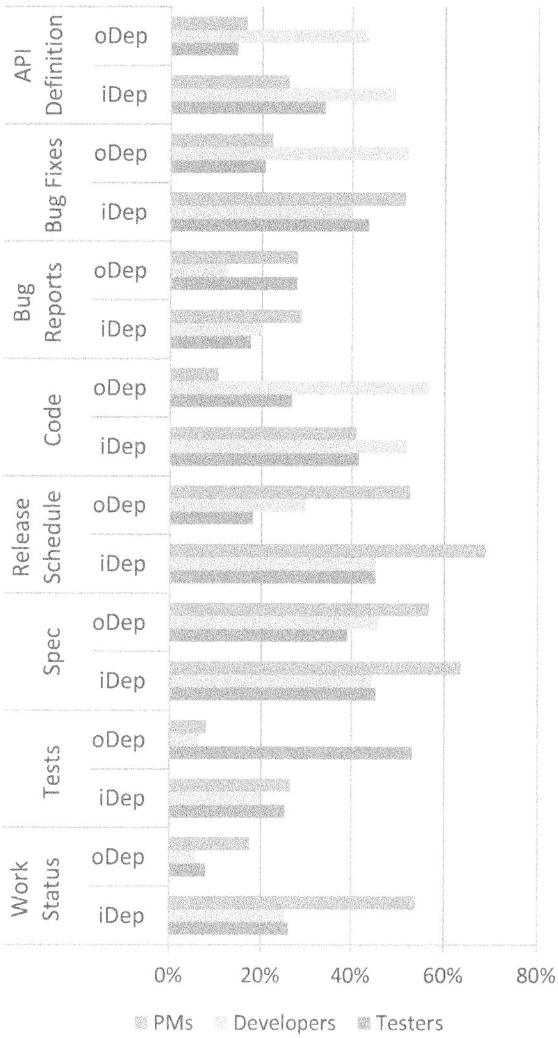

Figure 1. Artifact dependency as a percentage of respondents with dependencies divided by job function.[5]

Shared Work Artifacts

Next, we investigated how an engineer's perception of his external dependences on different types of shared work artifacts varied by his organizational characteristics. We asked respondents (Q3) "Which kind(s) of work artifacts from engineers outside your team do you depend on?" and (Q4) "For which

[3] *PM* was selected as the omitted category. *Other* was removed due to extremely low sample size.

[5] Some work artifact types listed in the question (selected by very few respondents) were omitted to make the plot easier to read.

kind(s) of work artifacts do engineers outside your team depend on you?" Respondents could choose any number of artifacts from a list we supplied (see Terminology section), and/or choose to write in their own artifact type. Our null hypothesis is that the distribution of perception of dependence between different shared work artifact types does not vary by a respondent's organizational characteristics.

We first explored which shared work artifacts were reported as the most common dependencies. For each work artifact type, we calculated the percentage of respondents who reported being dependent upon an engineer outside their team, and the percentage of those who reported that an engineer outside their team was dependent on them. Respondents reported that they depended most on others for release schedules and specifications, while others were most dependent on them for specifications and source code.

Figure 1 shows these shared work artifacts split by job function. Each row consists of two sets of three bars representing the percentage of the respondents who report being dependent on that artifact (iDepend) and the percentage of respondents who report that others depend on them for the artifact (oDepend). Each of the three bars represents the results for respondents with one of the job functions. When divided by job function, we observe striking variations in most of the dependencies. These variations are significant, and enable us to reject our null hypothesis.

In this figure, one can additionally see distinct asymmetries in the direction of each work artifact type's dependencies. 53.85% of PMs report that they depend on other engineer's work status, but only 17.41% report that others depend on their work status. These differences are larger for developers (iDepend: 25.38%, oDepend: 5.81%) and testers (iDepend: 26.06%, oDepend: 7.98%). For almost every work artifact type and job function, oDepend is less than iDepend. The exceptions for developers are bug fixes, and code, which makes sense, since writing code and fixing bugs are their main job tasks. Testers report that more people are dependent on them for bug reports and tests, matching their job tasks.

Information Sharing

In this section, we look at the factors that influence how widely engineers share information about their work artifacts. In an enterprise work environment, there are rules about sharing information with other teams. Some features are considered *sensitive* (i.e. secret), and should not be talked about with people who are not privy to the secret. Most features are *non-sensitive*, which Microsoft often advertises to the public long before a product ships.

We asked respondents four questions that covered whether they were permitted to share and comfortable with sharing information about *sensitive* and *non-sensitive* work artifacts. One instance of the question read, "What are the work groups to which you are *allowed* to share each of the following work artifacts that are related to this *sensitive* feature?"[6] Three

Table 3. Mean & Standard Deviation of the work group range (0-6) to which engineers were allowed to share and comfortable with sharing information about sensitive and non-sensitive features. Higher values indicate wider sharing. Each of the 8 sections reports the statistics for a different subsample. The four questions are labeled (Q5) AS: allowed-sensitive, (Q6) CS: comfortable-sensitive, (Q7) AN: allowed-non-sensitive, and (Q8) CN: comfortable-non-sensitive.

	Mean	Std. Dev.		Mean	Std. Dev.
Entire Sample			**iDepend = Yes**		
(Q5) AS	3.017	1.279	(Q5) AS	3.091	1.264
(Q6) CS	3.089	1.283	(Q6) CS	3.155	1.252
(Q7) AN	3.865	1.442	(Q7) AN	3.942	1.404
(Q8) CN	3.850	1.472	(Q8) CN	3.924	1.431
PMs			**iDepend = No**		
(Q5) AS	3.098	1.337	(Q5) AS	2.767	1.310
(Q6) CS	3.190	1.308	(Q6) CS	2.893	1.396
(Q7) AN	3.969	1.401	(Q7) AN	3.653	1.543
(Q8) CN	3.947	1.453	(Q8) CN	3.642	1.583
Developers			**oDepend = Yes**		
(Q5) AS	3.088	1.315	(Q5) AS	3.059	1.289
(Q6) CS	3.278	1.325	(Q6) CS	3.150	1.272
(Q7) AN	4.054	1.414	(Q7) AN	3.935	1.424
(Q8) CN	4.059	1.406	(Q8) CN	3.914	1.459
Testers			**oDepend = No**		
(Q5) AS	2.916	1.202	(Q5) AS	2.894	1.233
(Q6) CS	2.877	1.202	(Q6) CS	2.916	1.322
(Q7) AN	3.645	1.459	(Q7) AN	3.669	1.473
(Q8) CN	3.613	1.509	(Q8) CN	3.670	1.487

variants substituted *comfortable with* for *allowed to* and *non-sensitive* for *sensitive*. We label these (Q5) allowed-sensitive (AS), (Q6) comfortable-sensitive (CS), (Q7) allowed-non-sensitive (AN), and (Q8) comfortable-non-sensitive (CN). Each of the representative work artifacts were rated by respondents on our *work group range* scale and combined into a single *sharing metric* value for each of the four questions (see Terminology section). We accommodated missing data in the *sharing metric* to ensure that missing responses would not positively skew our results. The resulting distributions approximate to being continuous and normal.

The mean and standard deviations of the *sharing metric* and subpopulations are reported in the 8 sections of Table 3. Notice that respondents indicated that they were allowed ($t(750) = 17.94$, $p < 0.0001$) and comfortable ($t(739) = 16.73$, $p < 0.0001$) sharing non-sensitive features much more widely than sensitive ones. Additionally, there was a significant effect for perceiving that one had external dependents in all cases (AS: $t(802) = 2.87$, $p < 0.01$, CS: $t(770) = 2.25$, $p < 0.05$, AN: $t(765) = 2.23$, $p < 0.05$, CN: $t(769) = 2.14$, $p < 0.05$). Those who say they depend on the work of people outside their team (iDepend) share to a wider audience than those who say they do not have outside dependents. However, when the respondent perceives that others depend on his work, there is a significant effect only in the comfort-sensitive and allowed-non-sensitive cases (CS: $t(770) = 2.01$, $p < 0.05$, AN: $t(765) = 2.02$, $p < 0.05$). Overall, respondents who perceive that others depend on their work (oDepend) share more widely than those who do not.

Splitting the data by job function shows that PMs and developers reported being allowed to share work artifacts with a wider audience than testers. There was a significant effect

[6]Italics were in the original question.

Table 4. Artifacts (and their means) that are shared the most widely and most narrowly by role. Increased values indicate wider sharing.

	Most Widely Shared		Most Narrowly Shared	
PM	Release Schedule	4.26	Source Code	2.77
	Specifications	4.24	Checkin Msg.	2.81
	Feature Schedule	4.18	Test Suites	2.95
Dev	Release Schedule	4.24	Meeting Notes	2.71
	Specifications	4.24	Test Suites	2.98
	Binaries	4.18	Source Code	3.00
Test	Release Schedule	3.79	Meeting Notes	2.53
	Bugs Fixes	3.77	Source Code	2.69
	Bug Reports	3.69	Checkin Msg.	2.71

for job function in all but the allowed-sensitive case: (CS: $F(2, 790) = 8.07$, $p = 0.000$, AN: $F(2, 785) = 6.65$, $p = 0.002$, CN: $F(2, 788) = 7.43$, $p = 0.001$).

To further understand the relationship between organizational characteristics, the perception of interdependence, and our *sharing metric*, we performed linear regressions for each of the four questions (AS, CS, AN, and CN). AS is not significant. In both the CS and AN models, there is a statistically significant difference between PMs and testers, and between developers and testers. In the CN model, there is a statistically significant difference between developers and testers. For the CS, AN, and CN models, a management role and years of experience are also statistically significant, albeit with smaller standardized effect sizes than job function. Years of experience has the largest standardized effect size. The descriptive statistics indicate that comfort levels contribute to the significant effect between PMs and testers, and between developers and testers. Thus, developers and PMs are more comfortable sharing both sensitive and non-sensitive artifacts than they are permitted. Testers, however, are allowed to share more widely than they feel comfortable with. There may be an interaction effect between job function and the perception of interdependence that requires further data to validate.

Next, we analyzed which artifacts were shared to the widest and most narrow work group range. The results are shown in Table 4. Respondents of any job role were willing to share release schedules with the widest range of recipients. PMs shared code and checkin information with the most narrow audience. Developers shared team meeting notes and test suites with the most narrow audience, and testers minimally shared team meeting notes and code.

After asking about these hypothetical information sharing situations in our survey, we asked, using Yes/No questions, whether respondents had ever not been allowed to or felt uncomfortable sharing information about a sensitive or non-sensitive feature in response to an explicit information request. If they had, we asked them to explain why. 33.2% of respondents report having been asked for work-related information that they were not *allowed* to share. Fewer (25.1%) reported being asked for information that they did not feel *comfortable* sharing. We triangulated their answers by analyzing the long-form "why" follow-up question. Using an iterative card-sorting technique, we categorized the respondents' reasons into 5 groups: (A) the sensitivity of the request (e.g. confidentiality, legal issues, preventing leaks to the press), (B) uncertainty as to whether the information should be shared (e.g. response should come from management), (C) the information was too preliminary (e.g. draft or incomplete work), (D) mistrust of the requestor (e.g. request is too vague, requestor has no "business need," requestor may have "malicious intent."), and (E) would not understand (i.e. the requestor lacks the background or technical expertise/depth to understand the information).

DISCUSSION

The results and analysis of the survey support several conclusions. First, answering RQ_1, PMs are more likely than developers or testers to perceive that they have dependency relationships with outside teams. This is an expected result, given that PMs function as project engineers and are responsible for coordinating their team's work with others. Second, engineers with more work experience are more likely to perceive that they have dependency relationships with outside teams. This is consistent with an earlier finding [36] that junior engineers are insulated from outside teams by a team lead who handles much of the inter-team communication. We did not find significant correlations of dependence perception with a management role or departmental affiliation.

The third result, answering RQ_2, showed that overall, engineers of all job functions report that they depend the most on specifications and release schedules. This result initially surprised us, but when the dependencies were split by job function, more familiar rankings appear for developers — they feel most dependent on code and API definitions. The split does not change the ranking for testers and PMs. This makes sense for PMs, who coordinate work between teams, however for testers, it confused us. After we interviewed a few testers, however, we found that they must wait for specifications from PMs before they can begin designing their test suites, and are extremely sensitive to the release schedule because much of their work cannot proceed until the developers have finished programming new features. Indeed, the fourth most dependent work artifact for testers is source code. Continuing with the opposite dependence direction, engineers of all job functions feel that others depend on them mostly for specifications and code. When broken down by job function, PMs provide specifications and schedules, developers provide code and bug fixes, and testers provide tests and specifications. This result also agrees with the literature.

We noticed that some of the dependency numbers were quite low. For example, only 6.42% of developers report that others depend on them for tests. Since at Microsoft, testers write the integration and acceptance tests, while developers write unit tests, this indicates that either very few developers perceive that anyone depends on them to write unit tests, or that very few engineers depend on the results. A followup interview revealed that developers are expected to be responsible for their own unit tests, and rarely expect others to read, write or run them.

Another set of low numbers for developers was for bug reports. Only 20.18% say they depend on others' bug reports, and only 12.54% say that others depend on theirs. Since developers are the only engineers knowledgeable enough to file bugs against the source code, this may indicate they do not find bug reports to be useful for telling one another about buggy code. Developers told us in followup interviews that when they may suspect a bug in another team's code, they feel that they are likely missing something important. It is better to leave "buggy" code alone, than risk causing a new problem by changing it. They would also rather visit another developer in person to tell them about a bug than file a bug report.

Our last results answer RQ_3, and focus on the willingness to share information about shared work artifacts with a variety of audiences. When the feature to be shared was sensitive (for which respondents were told that they should be concerned about confidentiality), engineers mainly refrained from sharing information further than their immediate dependencies. When the feature was not sensitive, they could share with their entire product team.

A surprising result is that engineers who perceive that they depend on others feel comfortable sharing information about work artifacts with a *larger* range of recipients than those who say they do not depend on anyone. Might this suggest that engineers at this company are altruistic? Perhaps they share with others to set an example for, and thus encourage, the people they depend on to share more information. We expected the inverse, that engineers would only share more widely when they knew that people on other teams were depending on them for information. This will require further exploration at Microsoft (and at other companies) to understand the engineers' sharing motivations.

Considering job function, we found that developers and PMs are more comfortable sharing information about their work artifacts than they are permitted to by their organization. Testers, however, reported the opposite; they are permitted to share with a wider audience than with whom they feel comfortable. Two possible explanations came to mind. (1) If testers are reporting news of problems with the product, sharing that news widely might harm its reputation. (2) Testers may lack enough confidence in their own abilities and activities to reveal their ideas about work artifacts, and fear they might receive a poor response from their more accomplished and experienced PM and developer co-workers. Followup interviews revealed that testers' lack of confidence was the most likely explanation.

Finally, more engineers than we expected reported being apprehensive or not allowed to share information when asked. One-third of all respondents reported they were not permitted to share information after being explicitly asked, and one quarter felt uncomfortable doing so. Our long answer followup question indicated that confidentiality, uncertainty in one's authority, and unfinished information were the primary reasons to avoid sharing work artifacts with outsiders. Particular product features may be embargoed to small teams during early phases of development. This helps to prevent early designs from being revealed and possibly misconstrued as final product guidance by others at the company, or by outsiders. In addition, we had anticipated that social biases like ingroup bias and the illusion of transparency might affect how much sharing with which an individual would be comfortable, and we saw that in this question's other two categories of responses as well.

Implications

We hypothesize that engineers are tailoring their information sharing behavior to the organizational characteristics and work group range of the possible recipients of their communication. We ask the question, then, is this behavioral mediation deliberate, and how does it change in response to evolving organizational contexts? Studies of product innovation have found correlations of product success to increased cross-functional communication and violation of established barriers to communication because they allowed team members to combine their perspectives in a highly interactive and iterative way [21]. Researchers have hoped that communication behaviors could be shaped with appropriate communication practices and new tools. Prior work in communication tools aimed at software engineers incentivizes changes in communication behavior through tool use. For instance, Palantir [45], FastDash [8], and Syde [29] promote early, source code change conflict resolution communication by notifying engineers when they are working on the same file. Common repository-based notification systems attempt to keep engineers up-to-date on other engineers' changes through frequent emails, IMs or even new Web 2.0 technologies. Passive notification systems, such as Codebook [6] or GitHub [24], record repository changes in a persistent context-dependent newsfeed that may be accessed by interested engineers at their leisure.

When these tools are viewed from an enterprise perspective, we notice that their displays commonly require the recipients of information to make sense of automatically mined information presented in a form familiar to participants in the project, but often unknown, overwhelming, and/or irrelevant to outsiders. In addition, all of these systems presuppose that any and all engineers with an interest in the information will already have appropriate security credentials to see it. Tools such as TagSEA [50] and James [27] integrate tagging and microblogging into the IDE, enabling developers to broadcast their information to all, but do not give the sender control over who receives his message. Our study's results indicate that awareness tools should enable engineers to customize the message about their work to be more salient to those whom they *choose* to send it. Enabling the sender to tailor his message to be more salient for a particular audience, however, requires that the sender do more work than current practice typically presumes.

While engineers already use non-automated information sharing tools such as email and IMs, a semi-automated approach could help in a number of ways. To help engineers identify potential interested recipients, a system could use Socio-Technical Congruence [12] to discover probable, and potentially unknown, external dependents and enable the engineer to investigate their organizational characteristics, including whether they have access to the original software repository in which the artifact originated. To help engineers craft an appropriate message, a system might indicate which recipients are most strongly tied to the sender. These recipients would be permitted to receive more detailed information on the rationale behind a change, or a frank assessment of a project's likelihood for shipping on time (which our probe surveys show would be closely guarded secrets). The system could group recipients by various organizational characteristics, since they often share particular information needs. For example, when a developer informs engineers of his checkins, other developers will read the source code diffs to review the effects on the code, but testers may simply care how much closer this checkin brings the project to the time where they may begin black box testing the software component. In addition, since some interested recipients have more seniority, more power, or tighter deadlines than the others, a tool that visually represented dependents' relative organizational characteristics could also help the engineer to craft an appropriate message to each.

Threats to Validity

Construct Validity: The dependency relationships reported by the respondents are the respondents' *perceptions* of their dependencies, not their actual dependencies. Dependency relationships were not verified, as respondents were not asked to identify them. Respondents selected work artifact types from a list (with an "Other" option) generated through past studies at Microsoft and verified through preliminary surveys and interviews. We operationalized engineers' sharing through measuring the *sharing metric* on the *work group range* scale. We believe this is the best approximation, thus far, of this concept, and encourage other researchers verify its validity.

Internal Validity: Our results about organizational characteristics may be confounded with demographic factors that we did not collect (e.g. age, gender, native language, or country of origin). Years of experience and the ratio of interdependent work involved per job role may be confounded, thus we required participants to have at least one year of employment. Survey participation was voluntary and anonymous, though some may have answered solely for the US$250 draw. No invited participant shared a common manager with the research team. We believe that participants answered sensibly to the intermittent long answer questions in the survey. All questions were optional, allowing respondents to complete only part of the questionnaire. Although the number of respondents answering each long answer question did drop slightly towards the end of survey, those who completed the survey appear to have given their answers some thought. Thus, we believe respondents either answered truthfully, or did not answer at all. We triangulated our results by correlating the results of oDepend with a rephrased version of oDepend at the end of the survey.

External Validity: This study is based on a single large US-based software company, so the results may not a priori generalize to other large software companies. However, studies of other large enterprise software companies [52, 20] show that they share a similar work environment, and would likely have similar results to ours. Microsoft's communication culture maintains a significant reliance on email, even as it enables contextualized communication within software repositories (e.g. source code and bugs [6]) and begins to experiment with Web 2.0 communication technologies. Since Microsoft is an enterprise-level, profit-oriented organization, observations and analyses of open-source community information sharing and altruism may have limited explanatory power here.

FUTURE WORK AND CONCLUSIONS

In this paper, we reported on a survey we conducted to understand three gaps in inter-team coordination. First, we learned that an engineer's job function and years of experience are significant determinants of his perception of dependency. Second, we found that these dependencies differed significantly by work artifact, and were always asymmetric. Third, we found that organizational rules, along with the type and sensitivity of particular shared work artifacts mediate the work group range to whom an engineer is willing to communicate. We also discovered a surprising result that begs further study. Engineers at this company appear to be altrustic because they report that they share more widely when they depend on information from others. Why? As Grudin asked about calendars [25], what are the social factors that incentivize or inhibit engineers at this enterprise company from sharing information with colleagues?

The results have important implications for tool designers, guiding them to explore ways in which information sharing tools can enable engineers to share their work artifacts automatically, yet be able to select the intended recipients and make the message salient for each. We hope that as new tools are introduced with increased understanding of the effects of organizational characteristics, dependency perception, and attitudes around information sharing, they can help make inter-team coordination function better.

ACKNOWLEDGEMENTS

We thank the HIP team at Microsoft Research, Steve Easterbrook, and our anonymous reviewers for the contributions to our study. We thank our study participants for their time.

REFERENCES

1. Ancona, D. G., and Caldwell, D. F. Bridging the boundary: External activity and performance in organizational teams. *Administrative Science Quarterly 37*, 4 (1992), pp. 634–665.

2. Anvik, J., and Murphy, G. C. Reducing the effort of bug report triage: Recommenders for development-oriented decisions. *IEEE TSEM 20*, 3 (2011).

3. Aranda, J., and Venolia, G. The secret life of bugs: Going past the errors and omissions in software repositories. *Proc. ICSE '09*, 298–308.

4. Bacchelli, A., Lanza, M., and Robbes, R. Linking e-mails and source code artifacts. *Proc. ICSE '10*, 375.

5. Begel, A. Effecting change: coordination in large-scale software development. *Proc. CHASE '08*, 17–20.

6. Begel, A., Khoo, Y. P., and Zimmerman, T. Codebook: Discovering and Exploiting Relationships in Software Repositories. *Proc. ICSE '10*.

7. Begel, A., Nagappan, N., Poile, C., and Layman, L. Coordination in large-scale software teams. *Proc. CHASE '09*, 1–7.

8. Biehl, J. T., Czerwinski, M., Smith, G., and Robertson, G. G. Fastdash: a visual dashboard for fostering awareness in software teams. *Proc. CHI '07*, 1313–1322.
9. Brown, S. L., and Eisenhardt, K. M. Product development: Past research, present findings, and future directions. *The Academy of Management Review 20*, 2 (1995), pp. 343–378.
10. Casey, V. Developing trust in virtual software development teams. *J. Theor. Appl. Electron. Commer. Res. 5* (August 2010), 41–58.
11. Cataldo, M., Mockus, A., Roberts, J. A., and Herbsleb, J. D. Software Dependencies, Work Dependencies, and Their Impact on Failures. *IEEE TSE 35*, 6 (2009).
12. Cataldo, M., Wagstrom, P. A., Herbsleb, J. D., and Carley, K. M. Identification of Coordination Requirements: Implications for the Design of Collaboration and Awareness Tools. *Proc. CSCW '06*, 353–362.
13. Conway, M. E. How Do Committees Invent? *Datamation 14*, 4 (1968), 28–31.
14. Curtis, B., Krasner, H., and Iscoe, N. A Field Study of the Software Design Process for Large Systems. *Comm. ACM 31*, 11 (1988), 1268–1287.
15. Damian, D., Kwan, I., and Marczak, S. *Collaborative Software Engineering*. Computer Science Editorial Series. Springer-Verlag, May 2010, ch. Requirements-Driven Collaboration: Leveraging the Invisible Relationships between Requirements and People.
16. de Souza, C. R., Quirk, S., Trainer, E., and Redmiles, D. F. Supporting collaborative software development through the visualization of socio-technical dependencies. *Proc. GROUP '07*, 147–156.
17. de Souza, C. R., and Redmiles, D. F. The Awareness Network, To Whom Should I Display My Actions? And, Whose Actions Should I Monitor? *IEEE TSE 37* (2011), 325–340.
18. de Souza, C. R. B., and Redmiles, D. An Empirical Study of Software Developers' Management of Dependencies and Changes. *Proc. ICSE '08*.
19. de Souza, C. R. B., Redmiles, D., Cheng, L.-T., Millen, D., and Patterson, J. How a good software practice thwarts collaboration: the multiple roles of apis in software development. *Proc. FSE '04*, 221–230.
20. DiMicco, J., Millen, D. R., Geyer, W., Dugan, C., Brownholtz, B., and Muller, M. Motivations for social networking at work. *Proc. CSCW '08*, 711.
21. Dougherty, D. Interpretive barriers to successful product innovation in large firms. *Organization Science 3*, 2 (1992), 179–202.
22. Fritz, T. Determining Relevancy: How Software Developers Determine Relevant Information in Feeds. *Proc. CHI '11*.
23. Fritz, T., and Murphy, G. C. Using information fragments to answer the questions developers ask. *Proc. ICSE '10*, 175–184.
24. Github, I. Github social coding, 2011. Available at: http://www.github.com.
25. Grudin, J. Groupware and social dynamics: eight challenges for developers. *Comm. ACM 37* (January 1994), 92–105.
26. Gutwin, C., Greenberg, S., and Roseman, M. Workspace awareness in real-time distributed groupware: Framework, widgets, and evaluation. *Proc. HCI on People and Computers XI '96*, 281–298.
27. Guzzi, A., Pinzger, M., and van Deursen, A. Combining micro-blogging and ide interactions to support developers in their quests. *ICSM, Early Research Achievements Track* (2010), 1–5.
28. Halverson, C. A., Ellis, J. B., Danis, C., and Kellogg, W. A. Designing task visualizations to support the coordination of work in software development. *Proc. CSCW '06*, 39–48.
29. Hattori, L., and Lanza, M. Syde : A Tool for Collaborative Software Development. *Proc. ICSE '08*, 235–238.
30. Herbsleb, J. D., and Grinter, R. E. Splitting the Organization and Integrating the Code: Conway's Law Revisited. *Proc. ICSE '99*, 85–95.
31. Hinds, P., and McGrath, C. Structures that work: social structure, work structure and coordination ease in geographically distributed teams. *Proc. CSCW '06*, 343–352.
32. Holmes, R., and Walker, R. J. Customized awareness: recommending relevant external change events. *Proc. ICSE '10*, 465–474.
33. Jiang, H., and Carroll, J. M. Social capital, social network and identity bonds: a reconceptualization. *Proc. C&T '09*, 51–60.
34. Kraut, R. E., and Streeter, L. A. Coordination in Software Development. *Comm. ACM 38*, 3 (1995), 69–81.
35. Kwan, I., Schroter, A., and Damian, D. Does socio-technical congruence have an effect on software build success? a study of coordination in a software project. *IEEE TSE 37* (May 2011), 307–324.
36. LaToza, T. D., Venolia, G., and DeLine, R. Maintaining mental models: a study of developer work habits. *Proc. ICSE '06*, 492–501.
37. Lim, S., Quercia, D., and Finkelstein, A. StakeNet: using social networks to analyse the stakeholders of large-scale software projects. *Proc. ICSE '10*, 295–304.
38. Maalej, W., and Happel, H.-J. From work to word: How do software developers describe their work? *Proc. MSR '09*, 121–130.
39. Mockus, A., Fielding, R. T., and Herbsleb, J. D. Two case studies of open source software development: Apache and mozilla. *ACM TOSEM 11*, 3 (2002), 309–346.
40. Mockus, A., and Herbsleb, J. D. Expertise browser: a quantitative approach to identifying expertise. *Proc. ICSE '02*, 503–512.
41. Omoronyia, I., Ferguson, J., Roper, M., and Wood, M. Using developer activity data to enhance awareness during collaborative software development. *Journal of CSCW 18* (2009), 509–558.
42. Poile, C. *Asymmetric dependence and its effect on helping behaviour in work groups*. PhD thesis, University of Waterloo, 2010.
43. Rigby, P. C., and Storey, M.-A. Understanding broadcast based peer review on open source software projects. *Proc. ICSE '11*, 541–550.
44. Safayeni, F., Duimering, P. R., Zheng, K., Derbentseva, N., Poile, C., and Ran, B. Requirements engineering in new product development. *Comm. ACM 51* (March 2008), 77–82.
45. Sarma, A., Noroozi, Z., and van der Hoek, A. Palantír: raising awareness among configuration management workspaces. *Proc. ICSE '03*, 444–454.
46. Sarma, A., Redmiles, D., and van der Hoek, A. Categorizing the spectrum of coordination technology. *IEEE Computer 43* (2010), 61–67.
47. Sinha, V. S., Mani, S., and Sinha, S. Entering the circle of trust: developer initiation as committers in open-source projects. *Proc. MSR '11*, 133–142.
48. Sodan, A. C. How much do technical scientists really cooperate? *ACM SIGCAS 36*, 2 (June 2006).
49. Teasley, S. D., Covi, L. A., Krishnan, M. S., and Olson, J. S. Rapid Software Development through Team Collocation. *IEEE TSE 28*, 7 (2002), 671–683.
50. Treude, C., and Storey, M.-A. How Tagging Helps Bridge the Gap Between Social and Technical Aspects in Software Development. *Proc. ICSE '09*.
51. Wolf, T., Schroter, A., Damian, D., and Nguyen, T. Predicting build failures using social network analysis on developer communication. *Proc. ICSE '09*, 1–11.
52. Wu, A., DiMicco, J. M., and Millen, D. R. Detecting professional versus personal closeness using an enterprise social network site. *Proc. CHI '10*.
53. Xiang, P. F., Ying, A. T. T., Cheng, P., Dang, Y. B., Ehrlich, K., Helander, M. E., Matchen, P. M., Empere, A., Tarr, P. L., Williams, C., and Yang, S. X. Ensemble: a recommendation tool for promoting communication in software teams. *Proc. RSSE '08*, 2:1–2:1.

A Sociotechnical Exploration of Infrastructural Middleware Development

Charlotte P. Lee[1], Matthew J. Bietz[2], Katie Derthick[1], Drew Paine[1]
[1]University of Washington, 423 Sieg Hall, Seattle, WA 98195, USA
[2]University of California, Irvine, Donald Bren Hall 5042, Irvine, CA 92697, USA
{cplee, derthick, pained}@uw.edu, mbietz@uci.edu

ABSTRACT

While previous CSCW research has noted that computer scientists have their own research interests pertaining to cyberinfrastructure development projects, most have focused on the research imperatives of scientists. This qualitative, interview-based study investigates the perspective of computer scientists developing middleware software for cyberinfrastructures at two supercomputing centers. This paper examines how technologists develop and sustain middleware applications over time by leveraging expertise and partnering with different research domains in order to achieve long-term infrastructural goals.

Author Keywords

Cyberinfrastructure, sustaining development, software, infrastructure, qualitative methods

ACM Classification Keywords

H.5.3 Computer-supported cooperative work

General Terms

Human Factors, Design

INTRODUCTION

As part of ongoing explorations in CSCW investigating how complex, large scientific cyberinfrastructures are created and sustained over time, this qualitative, interview-based study of computer scientists at two supercomputing centers investigates *how middleware developers sustain long-term research agendas over time*. Scientific cyberinfrastructure development necessarily requires collaboration between domain scientists and computer scientists (who we here crudely group with developers and engineers). A common finding is that the collaboration between scientists and computer scientists (also referred to as technologists or developers) is contentious or difficult [8,11]. However, more problematic is the trope to also paint the already over simplified domain vs. computer scientist division as embodying a split in long vs. short-term concerns. Previous CSCW research has explored the sometimes difficult negotiations of cyberinfrastructure collaborators that work according to different temporal scales [9], for example the fast pace and shorter temporal frames of developers vs. the slower pace and longer temporal frames of information managers [5]. We find that similar to information managers and domain scientists, middleware developers are also constrained by the short time frames provided by government project funding which inevitably are not long enough for more than initial infrastructure development.

Cyberinfrastructures (CI) and eScience refer to the computational and communication infrastructures that support scientific work. Large-scale, distributed cyberinfrastructures are sociotechnical systems that offer new opportunities to conduct increasingly complex and data-intensive research that will answer some of society's most pressing environmental, health, and energy problems. The field of CSCW has increasingly considered the challenges of these complex systems [4,10] because a great deal of sociotechnical innovation occurs first in the scientific realm, making the study of scientific work a harbinger of new ways of working.

The importance of middleware, software that lies between the network and the application, is well accepted in the world of CI and is frequently considered by its developers to itself constitute infrastructure [3]. For our paper, we look at middleware as software systems that may include some end-user applications, but that primarily functions at a lower, back-end layer. Understanding how to support middleware development will shed light on how to support other large-scale, long-term cyberinfrastructures designed to support innovation, both inside and outside of the scientific milieu.

LITERATURE REVIEW

Infrastructures are inherently relational - they are embedded in networks of connections to other systems and infrastructures [11]. Similarly, rather than being systems cyberinfrastructure can be thought of as "networks or webs that enable locally controlled and maintained systems to interoperate more or less seamlessly" [2]. At the same time, the concept of cyberinfrastructure has expanded to include the notion of virtual organizations. The variety of terms used to describe CI illustrate the difficulty of talking about a complex, multi-faceted phenomena.

In line with the historical accounts provided by Edwards et al. [2], Lee et al. [7] found that cyberinfrastructure-in-action requires a hybrid of old and new organizational forms. When describing the on-the-ground business of creating and maintaining cyberinfrastructure, the notion of *human infrastructure* continues to be a useful lens; *human infrastructure* is the collaborative partnerships of various researchers, technologists, and others who develop and maintain the software, hardware, tools and applications of CI. *Human infrastructure is a more complex and heterogeneous form of organization that encompasses a multitude of collaborative forms including organizational structures, distributed teams, and personal networks.*

Synergizing is "a broad concept that includes strategic collaborative undertakings in pursuit of greater combined effects than individuals, groups, or organizations could effect on their own" [1] and is one way in which human infrastructure functions to enact CI. Bietz et al. [1] find that much of the work of developing CI involves creating and managing these relationships. The synergizing lens provides a conceptual link between global infrastructure creation and the local day-to-day work of systems development. The notion of synergizing highlights the process by which CIs come to exist and that CI requires the active coordination and collaboration of both the technical and social aspects of creating infrastructure. We use the notions of human infrastructure and synergizing in order to understand middleware as part of larger sociotechnical arrangements.

RESEARCH SITES AND METHODS

Distinct from typical approaches that study particular domain-specific projects, this research focuses on how resources transcend and cross cyberinfrastructure project collaborations. We investigated two of the United States' premier supercomputing organizations, the National Center for Super Computing Applications (NCSA) at the University of Illinois Urbana-Champaign and the San Diego Supercomputer Center (SDSC) at the University of California, San Diego, in order to discover commonalities across these two institutions that might be generalizable to similar computing organizations. These research sites afford a perspective that focuses on software that can support myriad cyberinfrastructures.

Both SDSC and NCSA work with multiple scientific communities coming from various academic disciplines. Each project is funded individually, directly from the NSF or another funding body, with group leaders responsible for writing grants. CI developers at NCSA and SDSC typically are involved with multiple projects at a given point in time. These projects can range in size from two or three people up to the hundreds of people involved in projects like TeraGrid (www.teragrid.org).

We interviewed 20 participants at NCSA in spring 2009 and 12 participants at SDSC in summer 2009, for a total of 32 interviews. Interviews were semi-structured to ensure both consistency across interviews, but to also allow for deeper questioning to elicit new insights. Participants in this study included upper-level management, principal investigators on grants, staff computer scientists and programmers, and domain scientists who work with NCSA or SDSC on CI development. Most of our participants work on software rather than hardware development. Interviews were semi-structured, were scheduled for an hour, and lasted between 15 and 86 minutes (median: 56 min.). Interviews were recorded and transcribed for analysis. Data were analyzed using a grounded approach. We began with a closed coding scheme based on the interview protocol and then iteratively created a codebook including open codes based on new discoveries. Finally a series of memos were generated to further identify and develop thematic relationships.

FINDINGS: SUSTAINING MIDDLEWARE DEVELOPMENT

Cyberinfrastructures tend to be funded from either the base level of hardware and network development or from the top level of funding from the particular domain science or sciences. This has created an interesting tension regarding the creation of middleware in cyberinfrastructure. Identified by some as the cyberinfrastructure layer [3], middleware receives comparatively little direct funding. Given the transformational aspirations of NSF research funding, iterative and somewhat incremental improvements of middleware are not considered to be innovative enough to warrant funding.

Most of the work of the centers is funded from "soft" money, that is, funding for relatively short-term projects, often directed toward a specific application domain. Many of our participants find that a significant amount of their time is spent developing new proposals to stay funded. The gap between the need for long-term cyberinfrastructure and the reality of short-term funding for developers is recognized [2]. The contribution of this research is showing how computer scientists address the challenge of developing middleware and researching middleware development beyond short time horizons.

Our research finds that participants are very strategic in terms of how they: synergistically seek collaborators (individuals, groups, and organizations), including hiring individuals who bring both code and the expertise for building and using that code; use legacy code as a stepping stone to move towards more advanced middleware software; re-scope and rename middleware as funding sources and projects change; and insert into and sometimes customize middleware for different domain-specific cyberinfrastructure efforts. How these different activities contribute to sustainable middleware development is discussed below using representative examples from our data.

Leveraging Sociotechnical Resources

As noted earlier, human infrastructure is a hybrid of organizational forms. These organizational forms are also constantly in flux, changing shape in accordance to demands on the virtual organization [7]. In the soft money environment at our research sites, attempts to slow or control the flux often involved trying to keep development teams together despite projects beginning and ending and despite projects differing in their scope and scale. Having experience and prior investment in one area can lead to continued funding to pursue similar topics. Often one project is an explicit continuation of one that came before. Some projects receive continuing funding or structure the project to be funded in phases.

Just as common, however, are informal threads that connect projects over time. In most cases, new projects are proposed specifically because they allow an individual or group to continue working in the same or a similar vein. One PI was able to leverage his expertise to help get a new grant using the same technology in a different way: *"Because of my track record there... we had the expertise, we had the hardware, we knew how to [set up the systems]...we got another grant"* (Paul, Project Lead). We see here the human infrastructure working to maintain some organizational stability by leveraging the principal investigator's expertise. This representative example shows how expertise is leveraged with and through middleware development. Expertise is used to synergistically control flux in human infrastructure—keeping a team together in the face of the end of project funding.

However, human infrastructure not only works to maintain stability, but also to support innovation, by bringing in new sociotechnical resources. One participant told us about recruiting a specific computer scientist to work at the center. *"I was a very strong supporter of bringing Jerry here... And then I invited him to be part of our team so that we could get access to his [Application X]."* Hiring Jerry was a way to bring both his expertise and his technology into the organization.

Jerry recounted the same story in his own words. He talks about developing middleware for his previous job: *"So [Middleware Y] had a life there as part of the Collaboratory. It was inside our [Application X] that we had built there, so there was about a year left of funding on that project going when I came here, so I as the PI brought some of the funding with me."* When Jerry arrived at his new job, he realized that his new project, while in a very different domain, had some of the same requirements as his earlier project. Even though the state of the art was moving away from the approach used in Middleware Y, the new technologies were *"not ready for prime time."* Middleware Y would do what they needed and was stable, and even though it didn't use the latest technologies, it would set the project up for an easier transition to the new technologies when the time came: they would *"be aligned with where we think things are going next."* In other words, Jerry was hired with the understanding that he would bring useful expertise and usable middleware with him. Furthermore, there was an understanding that his software would be a functional stop-gap to fulfill urgent workflow needs.

In the above example we see planning for technological obsolescence of Jerry's Middleware Y, with the understanding that newer underlying technologies would be necessary to sustain the larger system. At the same time, there is more at work than simple retrieval of knowledge or trading on specialized knowledge. Instead, human infrastructure synergistically sustains middleware development by leveraging sociotechnical networks [6] comprised of people and technology—in other words, how people enlist human resources and convenient, appropriate technologies in order to do more with less.

Advancing Research to Accomplish Infrastructure

From an institutional perspective, cyberinfrastructure can be scoped in different ways; for example, modeling and analytical tools and even computing resources may or may not be considered part of the CI, depending on disciplinary needs [12]. The middleware that our study participants develop, however, is generally considered to be foundational for cyberinfrastructure. For our participants, the goal of cyberinfrastructure is to provide an infrastructure in the traditional sense of a plug-and-play technology (at least from the user's standpoint). For the developers in our study, the infrastructural vision — the loftiest goals of cyberinfrastructure — resides on the continued iterative development of middleware.

As middleware receives comparatively little direct funding, it may at first seem that the push to appeal broadly to different application domains is purely an economic decision, but there is also a larger goal to create software that would be broadly useful. As domain scientists would like other scientists to build on their discoveries, so too would computer scientists: *"So we made a decision early on that we wouldn't focus in a discipline like astronomy or earth sciences or business, but we would try to build an environment, a cyberinfrastructure or infrastructure that could support a breadth of applications"* (Mick, Project Lead). The ultimate goal is to build an infrastructure that is broadly useful, or generalizable, across domains.

Developers and managers find ways to drive middleware development—perpetuating the advancement of their software—by attaching them to new, non-computer science, domain-specific scientific research questions. This entails finding different application domains in which their middleware can be applied.

So I used to work a lot on bioinformatics. I worked on it for two years, and then suddenly it disappeared from the radar of the funding agencies. And then, I couldn't raise funding, so then, I had to move to other domains. But the technology was the same, so I could reuse it. Just having, if I had focused only on bioinformatics, right now I would really struggle, right? But having that flexibility of moving from project to project, and building enough preliminary results to propose to new things is to our advantage. (Paul, Project Lead)

The group lead found that he would have to attach his research to different application domains in order to get funded. Even though he was continuing his own research in the same area, working on multiple projects gave him the flexibility to target different grant areas and therefore different funding sources.

The other thing that I do is I go out and I look for new opportunities to fund applications that can drive our development because my model is kind of a unique one. ....To make [Software] viable and exciting to researchers in the application domains, I have collaborations with computer science departments, graduate schools, the library information sciences, bioinformatics groups that are developing new data management analysis and visualization techniques that we feed into this development environment. So there's big research and big technology going on here. We do big development, and we point that at big time applications... I'm looking for applications that can help fund this development and some of this research. (Mick, Project Lead)

As with other scientists, these computer scientists need to find and excite collaborators and funders about their research. A primary motivator for these computer scientists is furthering their own middleware development research. As noted earlier, the middleware layer is sometimes thought of as not just being part of the infrastructure but as being the infrastructure. The goal of advancing middleware, from the perspective of our participants, is the larger goal of creating infrastructure itself.

CONCLUSION

Unlike in other research [5], the developers in our study did not live natively or comfortably within short-term "project time." The difference may be attributed to particular organizational configurations that may or may not support developers who are truly computer *scientists* with a research orientation as opposed to engineers. While our participants' notion of "infrastructure time" was not on the scale of many decades as with ecologists, our research shows computer scientists engaging in elaborate and strenuous synergistic activities in order to sustain their software development research agenda well beyond the lifetime of projects.

The scale and scope of CIs is beyond the traditional core of CSCW and we are still struggling to find concepts that do justice to their complexity while still being comprehensible. The first challenge of being able to support scientific CIs is to understand how they are formed and maintained. Computer scientists that develop CI middleware (considered by some to be the most important technical layer) engage in simple, everyday activities to sustain future research and development including hiring people with particular technical expertise, using readily available and easily supportable appropriate technologies, and adapting software to be useful to a larger user base. Middleware developers strategically work towards expanding the scale of their middleware across domains in order to combat the short-term funding provided by funding agencies. Mobilizing human resources through synergistic activities is yet another way to maintain some semblance of stability in the face of constant flux. If middleware is indeed a key technical layer, cyberinfrastructures will benefit from additional research seeking to understand and support CI middleware development.

ACKNOWLEDGEMENTS

This research supported in part by NSF Awards OCI-0838601, IIS-0712994, and IIS-0954088. Thanks to our participants, Silvia Lindtner, and our anonymous reviewers for their assistance and feedback.

REFERENCES

1. Bietz, M. J., Baumer, E. P. S., & Lee, C. P. Synergizing in Cyberinfrastructure Development. Computer Supported Cooperative Work (CSCW), 19, 3-4 (2010), 245-281.

2. Edwards, P. N., Jackson, S. J., Bowker, G. C., et al. (2007). Understanding Infrastructure: Dynamics, Tensions, and Design (Workshop Report).

3. Hey, T., & Trefethen, A. E. Cyberinfrastructure for e-Science. Science, 308, 5723 (2005), 817-821.

4. Jirotka, M., Procter, R., Rodden, T., et al. Special Issue: Collaboration in e-Research. Computer Supported Cooperative Work (CSCW), 15, 4 (2006), 251-255.

5. Karasti, H., Baker, K. S., & Millerand, F. Infrastructure Time: Long-term Matters in Collaborative Development. Computer Supported Cooperative Work (CSCW), 19, 3-4 (2010), 377-415.

6. Latour, B. Science In Action. Harvard University Press, Cambridge, MA, 1987.

7. Lee, C. P., Dourish, P., & Mark, G. The Human Infrastructure of Cyberinfrastructure. In Proc. CSCW, ACM (2006), 483-492.

8. Olson, J. S., Hofer, E., Bos, N., et al. A theory of remote scientific collaboration. Scientific Collaboration on the internet (2008), 73-97.

9. Ribes, D., & Finholt, T. A. The Long Now of Technology Infrastructure: Articulating Tensions in Development. Journal of the Association for Information Systems, 10, 5 (2009), 375-398.

10. Ribes, D., & Lee, C. Sociotechnical Studies of Cyberinfrastructure and e-Research: Current Themes and Future Trajectories. Computer Supported Cooperative Work (CSCW), 19, 3 (2010), 231-244.

11. Star, S. L., & Ruhleder, K. Steps Toward an Ecology of Infrastructure: Design and Access for Large Information Spaces. Information Systems Research, 7, 1 (1996), 24.

12. Wheeler, B. E-Research Is a Fad: Scholarship 2.0, Cyberinfrastructure, and IT Governance. In The Tower and The Cloud: Higher Education in the Age of Cloud Computing. R. N. Katz, Ed. Educause, 2008, 108-117.

Proximity: a Measure to Quantify the Need for Developers' Coordination

Kelly Blincoe
Computer Science Department
Drexel University
Philadelphia, PA, USA
kelly.blincoe@drexel.edu

Giuseppe Valetto
Computer Science Department
Drexel University
Philadelphia, PA, USA
valetto@cs.drexel.edu

Sean Goggins
College of Information, Science and Technology
Drexel University
Philadelphia, PA, USA
sgoggins@drexel.edu

ABSTRACT
We describe a method for determining coordination requirements in collaborative software development. Our method uses "live" data based on developer activity rather than relying on historical data such as source code commits which is prevalent in existing methods. We introduce proximity, a measure of the strength of the work dependencies that lead to coordination requirements among members of a software development organization. Our proximity measure relies on a tool which captures the interactions of a developer with her IDE. It quantifies the similarity between records of interactions of developers as they work on their assigned tasks. We describe an algorithm that measures proximity between pairs of tasks or pairs of developers. Through an empirical study on an open source project that routinely records environment interaction data, we show how proximity accurately determines coordination requirements. The proximity measure thus enables proactive detection of coordination requirements and makes possible real time intervention and coordination facilitation via management-, design- and team-related decisions.

Author Keywords
Awareness, Proximity, Management, Coordination Requirements, Socio-Technical, Task Context, Tools.

ACM Classification Keywords
H5.3. Information interfaces and presentation (e.g., HCI): Group and Organization Interfaces.

1. INTRODUCTION
The coordination of concurrent activities by multiple developers remains problematic for software development organizations [18]. Software engineering pioneers such as Parnas [20] and Brooks [2] recognized the importance of efficiently managing work dependencies and coordination overhead arising within a development team. Such dependencies are becoming more critical as software organizations become larger and more distributed [3,13,14].

Dependencies between tasks often result in Coordination Requirements (CRs) among team members. Cataldo et al. [4,6] introduced a framework to detect and quantify CRs between pairs of software developers by identifying the technical dependencies between software artifacts modified during their assigned tasks. This formalization of CRs led to the definition of Socio-Technical Congruence (STC) in software development. STC is an index that measures the degree to which actual acts of coordination mirror coordination requirements. Empirical studies suggest that high levels of STC are beneficial: when coordination activities focus on the empirically identified CRs, productivity is likely to improve [4,6,25].

Current methods for detecting CRs and calculating socio-technical congruence have two serious drawbacks. First, CRs are identified by mining the source control repository of the project for changes to artifacts committed by a developer. This type of data is typically available only towards the end of the development work for a task. Second, for each file committed to a source code repository, a developer may have consulted several other files. Knowledge of this source code reference behavior is inaccessible from commit records.

Without a "live" view of activities, CRs and STC are not actionable devices for managing coordination in software projects. Several potential applications for such a live view have been discussed. Ehrlich et al. have elaborated a way to rank CRs in a project, enabling prioritization of those whose resolution can improve STC the most [11]. Valetto et al. proposed a set of management-, design-, and team-related decisions that can be used as alternatives to resolve CRs; each with its associated costs and risks [27]. These and other techniques require the ability to detect, analyze and manipulate CRs as they emerge.

CSCW 2012, February 11–15, 2012, Seattle, Washington, USA.

To surface CRs in a timely way, we introduce a measure we call proximity, which characterizes the similarity of working sets of artifacts employed by developers as they work. Proximity can be applied to pairs of tasks as well as pairs of developers who carry out those tasks.

To measure proximity, we need to record developers' actions on artifacts as they occur. Several such recording frameworks exist. Because of its popularity, we focus on the Mylyn framework (formerly Mylar) [16,17]. By means of a field study, we show how our proximity measure detects CRs at least as accurately as other methods such as that described in Cataldo et al. [4,6] We also show that it can detect CRs substantially earlier than other methods. Thus, proximity can provide enhanced support to the management of coordination in software projects.

The rest of the paper is organized as follows: in Section 2 we discuss related work; in Section 3 we present our method, including the data we use and our proximity algorithm; in Section 4, we describe in detail the setting, method and results of our empirical study; in Section 5, we discuss the significance of our contributions; finally, in Section 6, we offer some concluding remarks.

2. RELATED WORK

In the course of any non-trivial software project, it is paramount to be able to manage work dependencies. If such dependencies are not recognized early, they must be reconciled later. This often leads to lower product quality and developer productivity [5,14,25].

The design literature, beginning with Parnas' recognition of the workflow implications of modularization [20], focuses on ways to streamline the technical dependencies between modules as a way to maximize task parallelism [25,26]. In software, such technical dependencies are often derived from a syntactic analysis of the code base. As an alternative to identify technical dependencies, Gall et al. introduced the notion of logical coupling based on the "files changed together" heuristic [12] which aims at identifying semantic relationships that may not manifest in the syntax of the programmatic implementation of the software product. Whereas syntactic dependencies exist a priori with respect to a project and an organization, logical couplings reflect accumulated empirical evidence about how the development work unfolds in the project.

The shift from studying technical dependencies *per se* to exploring the complex interplay they have with organizational structure and project dynamics continues in recent research on the socio-technical aspects of software engineering. For example, several field studies show how information hiding may hamper the ability of development team members to coordinate with one another by decreasing awareness of important work decisions [3,13]. Herbsleb et al. [15] argued for a systematic framework to satisfy, as opposed to try to reduce, work dependencies by explicitly computing and orchestrating the coordination needs of a project. Works on CRs and STC in software development are part of this thread of research [4,5,6].

The study of Coordination Requirements

Cataldo et al. [4,6] describe STC as an index based on the alignment between team interactions and technical dependencies. Conway [7] was the first to describe the possibility of such an alignment. STC measures the extent to which CRs and coordination behavior are aligned in practice. STC is expressed as a simple ratio between CRs that are satisfied by actual acts of coordination and the set of outstanding CRs between developer pairs. Those CRs can be identified according to the following formula:

$$CR = TA \times TD \times TA^t$$

In this formula [6], TA is a people-by-task matrix representing task assignments, and TA^t is its transpose. TD is a task-by-task matrix capturing the work dependencies between tasks. Those are established by considering the technical dependencies occurring between artifacts involved in those tasks. According to this formula, a CR between two developers Alice and Bob can be represented graphically as in Fig. 1. Arc TD_{ab} represents a technical dependency between software artifacts S_a and S_b. These artifacts are involved in tasks to which Alice and Bob, respectively, are assigned (denoted by arcs TA_a, TA_b).

Among the methods for computing technical dependencies, Cataldo et al. offer empirical evidence that logical coupling obtained by tracking files that have been historically checked in together provides a more reliable representation of the technical dependencies relevant for CR detection than syntactic coupling does [5]. However, logical dependencies are computed based on past project history and are only visible after work is completed. Even when syntactic dependencies are chosen, as done by Ehrlich et al. [11], they only become fully known following a commit.

In prevalent CR detection methods, the association of developers to artifacts they work on becomes visible only after code is committed. That limits the potential of CRs as a means to support coordination as the development work unfolds. Our research aims to close that gap.

Applications of Coordination Requirements

Awareness [10] is one of the ways used to conceptualize coordination. A recent work shows that, for a software engineer, the most important form of awareness is locating and keeping up to date with other developers whose work is relevant to her own [1]. Examples of systems that try to achieve that by employing abstractions similar to

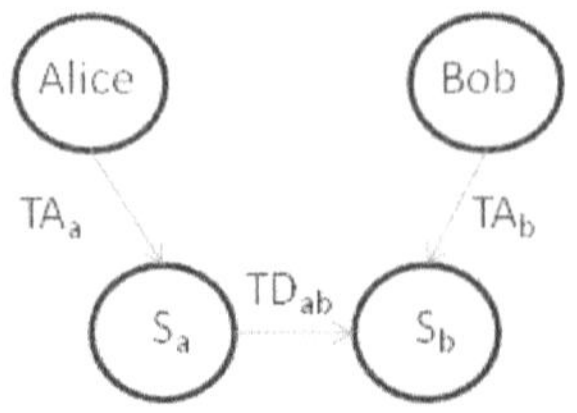

Figure 1. Representation of a Coordination Requirement.

CRs include Ariadne [8], EEL [19], Tesseract [23], and Codebook [1]. Those systems offer various mechanisms including visualization of socio-technical networks (Ariadne and EEL), dashboards (Tesseract), and query and search facilities (Codebook) to try to identify and show important work relationships within a team. All of those systems rely upon the commit logs in the source code repository to establish technical dependencies among artifacts. They use these dependencies to compute transitive relationships between developers. Therefore, these approaches suffer from the same drawback we mentioned earlier, that is, they are hampered in their ability to detect CRs and provide timely awareness support. Among them, the work most similar to our approach is EEL because of the way it combines the concepts of working set and CRs. However, our proximity measure aims at bypassing reliance on any specific conceptualization of technical dependency relationships and removing the reliance on post-mortem data.

There are other awareness approaches in collaborative software development that have tried to leverage live workspace information. For example, Palantír uses notifications to keep a developer abreast with what happens in her colleagues' workspaces [22]. Notifications relate only to changes occurring to the same artifacts a developer has in her own workspace. Palantír thus provides each developer with timely information about any arising same-artifact conflicts which can be seen as a narrow subset of CRs. CollabVS is another awareness system that uses notifications. Compared to Palantír, it has an expanded model of interest. The CollabVS model captures additional conflicts by considering a subset of syntactical dependencies between artifacts [9]. It issues instantaneous warnings to developers as an individual instance of conflict emerges, but it does not offer a model for quantifying the strength of CRs. By introducing the proximity measure, we contribute such a model and can draw a complete and explicit view of coordination across the whole team.

3. TASK CONTEXT AND PROXIMITY

Task Context

The main goal of our research is to identify CRs accurately and early enough to enable decisions on how to best resolve those work dependencies. For example, if Alice and Bob are assigned to tasks that require extensive negotiation and synchronization around interdependent software artifacts, early design decisions to refactor those dependencies and modify modularization can be taken to improve Alice's and Bob's productivity.

We look to capture meaningful data from development work as it happens in order to build an incremental record of the development activities carried out on the working set of artifacts for a task. Several facilities of this kind have been described in the literature [21,24]. Here we focus on Mylyn, a tool that captures the interactions of a developer with her IDE and constructs a data structure called a "task context" [16,17]. Mylyn is an Eclipse plugin whose goal is to provide an individual developer with a task-centric interface. It adapts the Eclipse GUI and focuses its presentation on what is most relevant for that developer in the context of the task she is performing. To achieve that, Mylyn stores significant GUI events, such as software element manipulation, artifact consultation, or the issuing of IDE commands in a *task context event*. Those events are weighted according to a model of interest that takes into account – among other things – action type, frequency of interaction, and a decay factor [16]. Mylyn task contexts therefore characterize a task in terms of its working set, the relative importance of artifacts in the working set, and the nature of the interactions with those artifacts. Since this kind of data is of general significance, Mylyn has started to extend to a number of other prominent development environments besides Eclipse.

A sequence of task context events in Mylyn is therefore a list of IDE interactions by the developer described in an XML dialect. The pertinent information associated to each action includes:

- Kind: type of interaction (selection, edit, etc.)
- Structure Handle: a unique ID that identifies a software artifact.
- Start Date: a timestamp
- End Date a timestamp

We are interested in only selection and edit events. Selection events are captured when a developer opens a file in the Eclipse IDE. Additional selection events can be captured whenever a developer navigates to a class, method or field defined in that file. Edit events are captured as the developer makes changes to those file locations.

The Mylyn structure handle provides more granularity than simply file names. It identifies the file name, class name and even the name of the class element (method or attribute) when available. We can thus choose to consider artifacts at different granularity levels allowing us to determine if two developers were working on the same area of code within a large file. This level of granularity is not available when looking only at commit information.

Note that the original purpose of Mylyn task contexts is to support the work of an individual developer during a single task or to allow a single developer to easily switch between tasks without loss of focus. Instead, we use that same information to support a collaborative goal. We want to detect areas in the project that are relevant for the coordination of concurrent tasks by looking at the amount of overlap between the working sets of the developers assigned to those tasks. To achieve that, we introduce our proximity measure which applies to task contexts and, by extension, to tasks and developers.

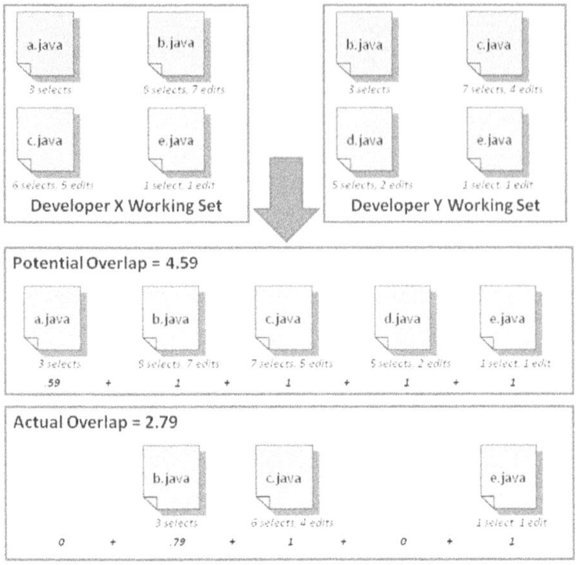

Figure 2. Proximity Algorithm.

Proximity

Proximity is a relative measure that conveys the amount of similarity between the development activities recorded in any two working sets. A working set can be construed at different levels simply by aggregating context events appropriately. To compute proximity between developers, each developer's working set will include all task context events produced for all tasks carried out by that developer during a time frame of interest. To compute the proximity of tasks, the working set of a task includes all context events produced for that task by all developers who worked on that task.

When calculating proximity between two working sets, our algorithm considers all actions recorded for each artifact in each working set in order to apply a weight to that artifact's proximity contribution. There are several types of actions captured by Mylyn. For this study we consider only select and edit actions. Other actions used within Mylyn, such as prediction, propagation and manipulation, were purposely left out of our algorithm. Since these event types are specific to Mylyn, including them would make the replication of our experiments and findings outside of the Mylyn framework difficult. Manipulation actions represent information that developers can explicitly provide to Mylyn to emphasize the importance (or lack thereof) of a given artifact for the task at hand. Prediction and propagation events occur when Mylyn itself "suggests" other artifacts, which are not included in a developer's working set, but appear to be structurally relevant.

We base our weights on the factors that Mylyn itself uses when computing its Degree-Of-Interest (DOI) model for each artifact present in a task context [16]. The DOI provides Mylyn with a way to prioritize the presentation of elements in its task-based interface. The factors used in the Mylyn DOI model are 1 for select events and 0.7 for edit events where higher values indicate higher interest. Those factors have been extensively validated in practice by the Mylyn user community.

Since edit events in the GUI are always preceded by at least one selection event, our algorithm weighs an edit overlap as 1.7. An edit overlap occurs when both developers edit the same artifact. Each developer contributes 1.7 to the overlap score for a total score of 3.4, which is the maximum score for an overlap. In a mixed overlap, one developer edits the artifact while the other developer selects or views the same artifact. In this case, one developer provides a score of 1.7 for the edit event and the other developer provides a score of 1 for the selection event for a total score of 2.7. In a selection overlap, neither developer edits the artifact, but both developers select and view the artifact. In this case, each developer contributes a score of 1 for a total score of 2. We then calculate our weights as percentages of the maximum possible overlap score:

- Edit overlap: $1.7 + 1.7 = 3.4$, $3.4/3.4 = 1$
- Mixed overlap: $1.7 + 1 = 2.7$, $2.7/3.4 = .79$
- Selection overlap: $1 + 1 = 2$, $2/3.4 = .59$

With those weights we compute two scores: an actual overlap and a potential overlap. Actual overlap is the intersection of the two working sets. Potential overlap is the union of the two working sets representing the maximum similarity score had there been perfect overlap between the two sets. Our proximity measure is the ratio between the actual overlap and the potential overlap. Fig. 2 shows the results of our algorithm on two sample working sets. The actual overlap includes files B, C and E since these three files are included in both working sets. B has an overlap score of .79 since working set X edited the file while working set Y only selected the file. C and E have an overlap score of 1 since both working sets edited these files. The Potential overlap includes all five files since we are now taking the union of the two sets. B, C, D and E each have an overlap score of 1 since at least one of the working sets edits each of these files. File A has an overlap score of .59 since only selection events exist for this file.

As a final step of our algorithm, we apply a scaling factor where we consider the total number of events recorded within all working sets. The scaling factor is the ratio between the number of overlapping events for each pair and the average number of overlapping events computed across all pairs in the population. The rationale for this scaling factor is to place greater weight on those pairs engaged in complex development activities, where coordination is likely to be more necessary, than for pairs involved in simple tasks. When performing a complex task, a developer is likely to spend a lot of time on the task and will therefore create many context events. Conversely, a developer completing a task via a trivial change will likely produce a small number of events.

Research Objectives

This study explores the extent to which our proximity measure enables the detection and management of CRs between software developers. Having introduced the semantics of proximity and its measurement technique, we now state our main research objectives:

Research Question RQ1: to what extent are the proximity relationships obtained with task context information (aggregated at the developer level) analogous to CRs determined using information about artifact commits and technical dependency relationships? RQ1 speaks to the feasibility of detecting CRs by leveraging developers' working sets and their overlap, thus bypassing the analysis of technical dependencies between artifacts.

Research Question RQ2: can CR detection based on task contexts and proximity provide more accurate results than current methods? RQ2 speaks to the ability of leveraging the detailed information offered by task contexts to improve precision, recall, or both in detecting CRs.

Research Question RQ3: can the data provided by task contexts support the detection of CRs significantly earlier than current methods? RQ3 speaks to the possibility of supporting timely decisions on how to handle CRs as they form in the project and has immediate consequence on coordination management practices and technologies.

4. CASE STUDY - MYLYN

We carried out an empirical study on the open source project which developed the Mylyn framework itself. Contributors to the Mylyn Eclipse plugin use Mylyn for their work and conventionally publish the task context data in the project's Bugzilla repository (code contributions without attached context data are often rejected). Sixty-nine other projects in the Eclipse community alone report freely available Mylyn task contexts. We selected the Mylyn project because it provides the largest amount of and most complete task context information.

Data Collection and Preparation

We collected development data over eight releases of Mylyn (v2.0 - v3.3). These releases span almost three years, from December 2006 until October 2009. Mylyn data is captured as an attachment file to a Bugzilla entry (which denotes a development task). Our analysis focuses on the 1,970 Bugzilla entries which contain such attachments during the study period. For those tasks, we also collected all code commits recorded in the project's SVN repository and all patch description files. Patch descriptions are attached by those developers who contribute code but do not have commit privileges and report the diff information for all artifacts that were modified as part of a patch. They are thus semantically equivalent to commits. Work on Mylyn during the study period involved 51 distinct developers who attached task context data (context attachers) and 8 distinct developers who committed code (committers). Each release has between 10 and 32 distinct context attachers and 4 to 6 distinct committers.

We compiled three data sets, summarized in Table 1. For the first data set, DS1, we looked at the activity of the group of committers. Each Bugzilla task may have one or more context attachments. We expanded the contexts attached to the 1,970 tasks to enumerate the 588,796 selection and edit events contained within. The majority of these events relate to Java source code files. Some pertain to .class, .jar, and other file types which are by-products, rather than objects, of development work. We thus focused only on the 450,747 context events dealing with Java source code artifacts.

We similarly filtered the SVN commits to include only java files, yielding 27,074 commits of individual artifacts over the same time period. Most of the commits, 25,135 or 92.8%, were linked directly to 1,835 unique tasks via the Bugzilla task IDs conventionally inserted by developers in their commit comments. We then intersected those 1,835 tasks for which we have commit data with the 1,970 tasks which have context data attachments. This resulted in 1,127 tasks which have both context data attached and associated commit records. This set includes 10,647 artifact commits and 450,757 context events.

Upon further examination of DS1, we noticed that a number of file changes reported in commits for a given task were not matched by any edit events in that task's context data. In the time period considered, we identified 6,507 commits out of 10,647 that are not matched by any proof of editing of the same file in the associated task contexts by the developer who committed the change. One reason is that, although it is customary to submit context when committing a change for a task, Mylyn developers do not always abide to this convention. Another reason is that the developer who commits a change is not always the developer who contributed it. We split DS1 in two: DS1-a includes the 4,140 commits for which we have matching events within task contexts; DS1-b includes the other 6,507 commits.

Data Set		Actors	Artifact info	Context info	Matching artifact commit and context info
DS1	DS1-a	8 committers	4,140 SVN commits	450,757 task context events	YES
	DS1-b		6,507 SVN commits	450,757 task context events	NO
DS2		34 patch contributors	1,387 patch file edits	345,521 task context events	YES
DS3		DS1-a and DS2 combined			YES

Table 1. Data sets.

Since looking at just commit data, as in DS1, would limit our analysis to the few developers with commit privileges, we compiled a different data set. DS2 considers the patch description files attached to Bugzilla records. Those files contain data on 7,196 java file changes spanning 936 tasks. Mylyn contexts attached to those tasks yield 345,521 context events for java artifacts contributed by 47 developers. Again, we match the patch description files retrieved from Bugzilla to task context events, leaving 1,387 file changes with associated task context data contributed from 34 different developers.

It is important to notice that DS1 and DS2 are disjoint. There is only a single developer, common to both sets. This ensures there are no overlapping pairs of developers among the two sets. Therefore, DS1 and DS2 represent complementary analyses over the full picture of the project activity. The 1,387 patch file changes in DS2 represent substantially different development work from what is captured in DS1. The one common developer is responsible for 219 changes in DS2, and a manual inspection revealed that only 11 of those 219 changes overlap with commits made by the same developer in DS1 (5%).

Finally, we combined DS1-a and DS2 into a third data set DS3, which incorporates all records of file changes (either via commit traces or patch diff files) and all context events.

Results of the Field Study

RQ1: Is Proximity a Good Proxy for Coordination Requirements?

We started our analysis with DS1-a. We used the 4,140 commits in that set to calculate CRs between committers according to the method described by Cataldo et al. As recommended in [4,6], to define technical dependencies between software artifacts, we used the "files committed together" heuristic introduced by Gall [12] which defines logical coupling between artifacts. We then computed our proximity scores for the same set of committers. Initially, since Cataldo's method calculates CRs at the file level, we considered only the file associated with each context event and ignored the finer-grained information made available by Mylyn at the method and attribute level. Since releases are a logical unit of concurrency for tasks in an open source project, we looked at work in each release separately. DS1-a yielded 70 pairs of committers across all eight releases.

First, we checked that higher values of proximity correlate with the likelihood of a CR by performing a point-biserial correlation with a binary vector denoting the presence of CRs. We then performed a Spearman correlation between the count of CRs for each pair and their proximity scores. We chose to use a Spearman correlation because both the CR counts and proximity scores are not normally distributed. Both tests were statistically significant and provided us with strong positive correlations, as shown in Table 2. Moreover, we observed that 46 of the 70 pairs of committers had some CR, and 43 of those 46 pairs (93.5%) have proximity > 0. Conversely, of the 24 pairs with no CRs, seven present a proximity score of 0.

Test	Unit of Work	p-value	rho
Spearman	File	2.4e-11	0.69
Point-biserial	File	4.9e-07	0.55
Spearman	Granular	6.8e-09	0.62
Point-biserial	Granular	8.8e-06	0.49

Table 2. DS1-A: CR V PROXIMITY CORRELATIONS

We repeated these tests by computing proximity at the finest granularity level for artifacts reported in Mylyn context events. Our expectation was that analysis of contexts at finer granularity would yield less proximity and lower levels of correlation with CRs calculated with Cataldo's method. The results shown in Table 2 are in line with those expectations, but correlations between proximity and CRs are still strong and significant. Of the 46 CR pairs, 42 (91.3%) have proximity > 0. Therefore, the additional granularity removes proximity from one of the 43 pairs with proximity when looking at file level granularity. Eight pairs have a granular proximity score of 0.

These findings seem to confirm that proximity is a valid proxy for CRs. However, DS1-a contains rather homogenous commit and context data: artifacts that are committed are likely to show up prominently in select and edit actions within the task contexts of their respective committer. Therefore, we performed analogous tests on DS1-b. In this data set, the CR and proximity analyses are performed on two completely distinct sets of artifacts since recorded context events do not align with the artifacts that were committed. However, since we are still looking at manifestations of the work done by the same developers within the same set of tasks, we speculated that proximity scores should remain a good indicator of CRs. The results of our tests on DS1-b, in Table 3, show strong and statistically significant positive correlations. Among the 75 developer pairs showing up in this data set, 33 have a CR, and all 33 pairs have a proximity score > 0 at both the file and granular level of analysis. Of the 42 pairs with no CRs, 10 of the pairs also have a proximity score of 0 at the file level and 14 at the more granular level. These results show that the proximity relationship can capture CRs by examining working set information even when that information is partial.

We then moved our analysis of RQ1 from the restricted core group of Mylyn committers of data set DS1 to the

Test	Unit of Work	p-value	rho
Spearman	File	8.7e-09	0.60
Point-biserial	File	1.1e-08	0.59
Spearman	Granular	2.5e-07	0.54
Point-biserial	Granular	1.8e-07	0.55

Table 3. DS1-B :CR V PROXIMITY CORRELATIONS.

Test	Unit of Work	p-value	rho
Spearman	File	< 2.2e-16	0.55
Point-biserial	File	< 2.2e-16	0.54
Spearman	Granular	< 2.2e-16	0.57
Point-biserial	Granular	< 2.2e-16	0.55

Table 4. DS2 CR V PROXIMITY CORRELATIONS

larger group of project contributors represented in data set DS2. DS2 yielded 277 developer pairs; of which 37 have CRs. Of these, 28 (75.7%) have file-level proximity > 0 and 24 (64.9%) have granular proximity > 0. Of the 240 pairs with no CRs, 206 also have a proximity score of 0 at the file level and 222 at the granular level. Table 4 shows strong positive correlations that are also statistically significant.

Our largest data set, DS3, which combines DS1-a and DS2, includes a total of 347 developer pairs. The correlation results for this data set are shown in Table 5. Using DS3, we further investigated the relationship between CRs and our proximity measure by means of a regression model. We employed a zero-inflated negative binomial regression (zinb) since the CR count is highly skewed and presents many zeroes (264 out of 347 developer pairs have no CRs). The zinb model is statistically significant (χ^2=161.69, df=2, p < 2.2e-16). Results from the regression are shown in Table 6 for both the count and the excess zeroes portions of the model (white and grey rows, respectively). In particular, a one-unit increase in proximity (a large increase in the proximity scale) causes a 2.20-times increase in the log of expected CR count. That is an expected ~9-times increase in CRs for each one-unit increase in proximity. To investigate the influence of the select events in defining our proximity metric, we recomputed proximity including only edit event overlaps. We then ran the same zinb regression and obtained a new model. This new model captures only direct edit conflicts and is, therefore, similar to what could be observed with tools like Palantír. It is still statistically significant (χ^2=157.17, df=2, p < 2.2e-16). We then compared the AIC scores of the new model and our original model of Table 6. We found that our original model has considerably better support since it has a lower AIC. The difference in the AIC scores is 4.51416. Thus, our original proximity model is almost 10 times as likely as the edit event-only model to minimize information loss.

We conclude that the proximity measure is a valid proxy to CRs determined using information about artifact commits and technical dependency relationships.

RQ2: How Accurate is Proximity in Determining Actual Coordination Requirements?

To investigate RQ2, we first reviewed how developer pairs with CRs match against pairs with proximity >0, and conversely how developer pairs with no CRs match against pairs with proximity = 0 in terms of precision and recall. Results at the granular level are reported in Table 7. We assume here that CRs detected with the Cataldo et al. method are the ground truth.

Test	Unit of Work	p-value	rho
Spearman	File	< 2.2e-16	0.68
Point-biserial	File	< 2.2e-16	0.66
Spearman	Granular	< 2.2e-16	0.68
Point-biserial	Granular	< 2.2e-16	0.66

Table 5. DS3 CR V PROXIMITY CORRELATIONS

Considering all proximity scores > 0 as indicators of CRs may cast a net that is too wide. A sensitivity analysis to understand the impact and appropriateness of different proximity thresholds will be part of our future work. However, conceptually, a threshold of 0 seems sensible. The lowest possible CR score of 1 indicates that a developer pair worked on only one pair of dependent files. The lowest proximity score of 0.01 also indicates (at least) one artifact overlapping in the developers' working sets. Since CRs computed according to Cataldo et al. are themselves only an approximation of ground truth, we then proceeded to manually examine some of the mismatches. Our goal was to determine if proximity is conducive to identify actual CRs more accurately by weeding out either false positives or false negatives of that method.

For potential false positives, we reviewed the four cases in DS1-a where developer pairs with CRs had granular proximity=0. The record of changes made by each pair of developers held in the relevant task contexts determined that in each case the developers operate on a totally disjoint sets of files and all of the recorded code changes were in areas of those files that appear unrelated to one another. An example is provided by the single CR that exists between developers 6 and 7 in release 3.2. Developer 6 committed BugzillaClient.java, while developer 7 committed BugzillaTaskEditorPage.java. The changes by developer 6 involve a character encoding method that is private to the BugzillaClient class. Developer 7 added a new section to the Mylyn task editor. Although we could ascertain those changes were semantically unrelated, the two involved files had been historically changed together by other developers often enough to cause a logical dependency to be established by the CR detection algorithm. We noticed analogous incidents in the other three cases in DS1-a. Those CRs are therefore false positives of the traditional method that our proximity algorithm correctly eliminates.

	Estimate	Std. Error	Z	p-value
(Intercept)	5.22	0.37	14.17	< 2.2e-16
Proximity	2.20	0.51	4.33	$< 10^{-4}$
Log(theta)	-2.01	0.14	-14.53	< 2.2e-16
(Intercept)	2.32	0.30	7.61	$< 10^{-13}$
Proximity	-106.49	33.18	-3.21	< 0.01

Table 6. ZINB REGRESSION: CR V PROXIMITY

Data Set	# of pairs	Precision	Recall
DS1-a	70	42/58 = 0.72	42/46 = 0.91
DS1-b	75	33/61 = 0.54	33/33 = 1
DS2	277	24/40 = 0.6	24/37 = 0.65
DS3	347	70/100 = 0.7	70/97 = 0.72

Table 7. PRECISION AND RECALL (GRANULAR)

Moving to potential false negatives, we examined the 16 pairs of committers in DS1-a that present some amount of granular proximity but have no CR. We were able to recognize two distinct types of behavior in this set. In one case, involving developers 3 and 7 during release 3.3, proximity contributions came exclusively by selection and mixed overlaps. The pair had seven mixed overlaps and six selection overlaps. Meaning that developers 3 and 7 viewed 13 of the same artifacts, of which seven were edited at some point by either developer 3 or developer 7, but no single artifact was edited by both developer 3 and developer 7. Since there were no overlapping commits, the traditional CR method does not allow for a CR to be detected. However, since we have the advantage of knowing not only what files are edited but also what files are consulted by a developer in the process of completing a task, our algorithm picks up what is likely to be an actual work dependency. Developer 3 and developer 7 repeatedly examined the same area of the software code base and consulted each other's code during their work for release 3.3.

The remaining 15 developer pairs we examined represent an even more interesting case. In each of these cases, the developers edit from 1 to 67 of the same artifacts (17 on average). CRs could not be established in any of these cases because at least one of the developers did not commit her changes. However, task contexts prove that those developer pairs were at one time engaged in development on the very same artifacts - the epitome of a Coordination Requirement. It is likely that in some cases, the two committers became somehow aware of the overlap and decided to avoid conflicts by having one of the two merge all changes and commit on behalf of both. Evidence of such a scenario may be recorded in the archived communications for the Mylyn project, which we intend to mine in the future.

All cases examined in DS1-a turned out to be false positives or negatives of the traditional CR detection method. More importantly, they highlight drawbacks of that method's reliance on post-mortem information and dependency conceptualizations. We conclude that proximity-based CR detection can be more accurate than existing methods.

RQ3: Does Proximity Provide Timely Detection of Coordination Requirements?

Finally, we set out to investigate whether proximity is an early indicator of CRs. The context events we use are, by their nature, antecedents to code commits. It is important to notice that, although the study described in this paper is retrospective, a method for analyzing CRs based on proximity and task contexts does not need to be. All

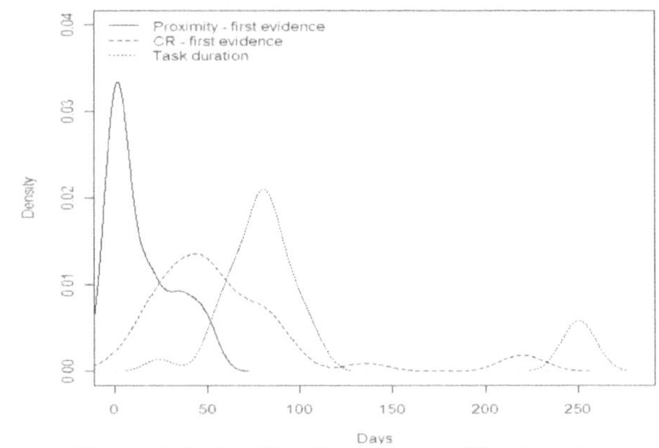

Figure 3. DS1-a Timeliness Probability Density

context events are recorded in real time. Therefore, a tool could gather context data as it is created by all developers and compute proximity on the fly. We discuss such a tool in Section 5. Here, our analysis focuses on how early proximity produces evidence of work dependencies between tasks. The earlier the evidence, the more actionable it is in supporting decisions aimed at resolving CRs as they form. For this analysis, we used the two data sets for which we have task context data associated with file changes (DS1-a and DS2). We considered all pairs of developers who present some CR and have granular proximity >0. There are 36 such pairs in DS1-a and 18 in DS2.

We obtain the time when the first contribution to the proximity score occurs by examining the timestamps for the first overlapping event recorded in all tasks contexts for the two developers for that release. We then compare the first proximity event with the first day of concurrent work by that pair during that release. For perspective, we also considered the day in which the first CR is identified for the same pairs. Fig. 3 shows the probability density functions of proximity detection, CR detection and task duration for data set DS1-a. The difference in the timeliness of recognition of work relationship shown is evident. Similarly distributed probability densities were seen in DS2. We found that in DS1-a the first evidence of proximity is detected on average 14.2 days after parallel work begins. In DS2, it takes 6.2 days. The first CR detection happens in DS1-a 60.7 days on average after the beginning of concurrent work by a pair (a delay of 46.5 days). In DS2, the first CR is detected 17.9 days after the concurrent work begins (11.7 days later). We also compared our findings with the duration of the concurrent work intervals by the same pairs in the various releases. In data set DS1-a, concurrent work intervals last 102 days on average, whereas in DS2, they last 31.4 days on average. The average "advance notice" provided by proximity is 87.8 and 25.2 days, respectively, showing that proximity significantly improves the timeliness of CR detection.

5. DISCUSSION

Our results suggest that CRs can be determined accurately based exclusively on the similarity of task contexts. Our proximity measure adequately models the presence and intensity of CRs independently of any conceptualization of technical dependencies. Unlike methods which rely on data that is available after work has been completed, we rely on data that is accessible while development is underway.

Implications for Tools

Many tools exist for enhancing developer awareness, and several of them leverage information about CRs [1,8,9,23]. Many of these tools strive to identify all technical dependencies that exist in a software project and provide a comprehensive view of project coordination needs. Since our method provides a novel approach to the identification of CRs, it could be incorporated into those awareness tools and provide them with the benefits outlined above.

To explore our design implications, we developed a prototype that calculates proximity of tasks using the described algorithm. The tool leverages a shared central database which communicates with client components hosted within the individual IDEs and automatically stores context information for the team. Existing IDEs can push context to the database as events occur. This allows proximity relationships to be continuously updated as development is underway with no effort on the part of the developers. An early observation from using this prototype is that the use of selection events can allow for a proximity relationship to appear even before any code modification begins. For example, if a developer starts to consult source files that are likely involved in some task, she can be provided with a list of tasks (and developers) with high proximity. A tool using task context information and proximity is not only timelier, but it can also be richer and more accurate. It captures the entire working set involved in a task and follows the evolution of that working set throughout the task duration, tracking how heavily each artifact is actually used.

The timeliness and comprehensiveness that our proximity measure provides is not currently available in other awareness tools for software engineering. Palantír and CollabVS provide timely CR detection, but only observe a narrow subset of CRs and do not measure their severity. Our measure can alert developers of CRs before the majority of work has been completed. A tool using our measure could facilitate developer coordination much earlier in the development cycle. This could allow developers to negotiate design decisions and code changes to reduce technical dependencies. Early detection of CRs can significantly reduce the amount of rework required when conflicts are determined later in the development process and can even help avoid duplicate work.

The method described can also be incorporated in a decision support tool. For example, it can provide a dynamic view of Socio-Technical Congruence to inform real-time decisions on aspects like task assignment, scheduling, team composition, or design refactoring [27]. A further implication of our work is the ability to rank detected CRs based on the corresponding proximity scores. Previous methods of CR detection support rank only as a simple count of CRs occurring within a pair of developers [27]. Our rank is based instead on two components: the amount of weighted overlap in the working sets of the pair and the number of overlapping context events as compared to the average number across the population. This way of ranking CRs can help de-emphasize trivial development activities and their impact on coordination.

Finally, while the analysis presented in this paper focuses on detecting CRs between pairs of individuals, proximity can easily be applied at other levels such as tasks, projects or teams. This can be accomplished simply by aggregating context events appropriately. For example, to compute the proximity of teams, each team's working set would include all context events produced by all members of that team. This provides the ability for awareness tools to easily display coordination needs at different aggregation levels. This enables the construction of visualizations, dashboards or reports oriented towards a variety of roles including individual developers, team leaders and project managers.

Threats to Validity

A general caveat is that our findings derive from a single project. In this case study, the number of developers involved and the number of CRs are relatively moderate in size. Our findings should be corroborated by additional empirical studies to ensure that our approach works for other projects and projects of different scales. Another limitation can derive from performing our analysis at the release level. When considering concurrent work at finer-grained temporal units, the outlook on CRs and/or proximity may differ. To properly investigate how sensitive our findings are with respect to this issue, a project with a high density of CRs would make for the best follow-up case study. Another limitation, as mentioned earlier, is that we have considered any level of proximity >0 as an indicator of possible CRs. A sensitivity analysis is the next logical step.

Finally, there may be issues of repeatability. Although Mylyn is widely adopted in open source as well as industrial settings, its consistent use by all developers during all of the project activities is not guaranteed. A commercial version of Mylyn (Tasktop Dev) is available for the Visual Studio IDE. Other commercial-grade facilities (such as Cubeon for the Netbeans IDE) offer similar features, but we cannot assume that they record the exact same IDE interactions. However, it is likely that any facility similar to Mylyn can provide the data our proximity algorithm needs which is – at a minimum – data about the developer, task, timestamp, filename and path for artifact selection and edit events.

6. CONCLUSION

We introduce a proximity relationship that can be used to infer CRs between developers as they form. We describe the algorithm for measuring proximity based on task context information. This context information details activities of developers within their IDEs and is obtained using existing tools. We show that proximity provides an earlier indication of CRs and overcomes known drawbacks in current CR detection methods. Proximity is promising as a foundational measure for building more accurate and useful representations of developer coordination. These advances improve the quality and timeliness of management, design and team coordination decisions.

ACKNOWLEDGEMENT

Special thanks to Dave Berry for his help with the initial data mining, to Gail Murphy for initial discussions, advice and encouragement, and to Patrick Wagstrom for his feedback and suggestions. This work was partially supported by the NSF through grant no. CCF-0916891.

REFERENCES

1. Begel, A., Phang, K.Y., and Zimmerman, T. 2010 Codebook: Discovering and Exploiting Relationships in Software Repositories. Proc. ICSE 2010.
2. Brooks, F.P. 1995. The Mythical Man-Month: Essays on Software Engineering. Addison Wesley. Reading, MA.
3. Cataldo, M., Bass, M., Herbsleb, J., and Bass, L. 2007. On Coordination Mechanisms in Global Software Development. Proc. ICGSE 2007, 71-80.
4. Cataldo, M., Herbsleb, J.D., and Carley, K.M. 2008. Socio-Technical Congruence: A Framework for Assessing the Impact of Technical and Work Dependencies on Software Development Productivity. Proc. ESEM 2008, 2-11.
5. Cataldo, M., Mockus, A., Roberts, J. A., and Herbsleb, J. D. 2009. Software dependencies, work dependencies, and their impact on failures. IEEE Transactions on Software Engineering. 35, 6, 864-878.
6. Cataldo, M., Wagstrom, P.A., Herbsleb, J.D., and Carley, K.M. 2006. Identification of Coordination Requirements: Implications for the Design of Collaboration and Awareness Tools. Proc. CSCW 2006.
7. Conway, M.E. 1968. How do committees invent. Datamation. 14, 4, 28-31.
8. de Souza, C.R., Quirk, S., Trainer, E., and Redmiles, D.F. 2007. Supporting collaborative software development through the visualization of socio-technical dependencies. Proc. of the 2007 international ACM conference on Supporting group work. 147-156.
9. Dewan, P. and R. Hegde. 2007. Semi-Synchronous Conflict Detection and Resolution in Asynchronous Software Development. Proc. E-CSCW 2007. p. 159-178.
10. Dourish, P., and Bellotti, V. Awareness and Coordination in Shared Workspaces. Proc. CSCW 1992: p. 107-114.
11. Ehrlich, K., Helander, M., Valetto, G., Davies, S., and Williams, C. 2008. An analysis of congruence gaps and their effect on distributed software development. Proc. STC 2008.
12. Gall, H., Hajek, K., and Jazayeri, M. 1998. Detection of logical coupling based on product release history. Proc. ICSM 1998.
13. Grinter, R.E., Herbsleb, J.D., and Perry, D. E. 1999. The geography of coordination: dealing with distance in R&D work. Proc. of the international ACM SIGGROUP conference on Supporting group work.
14. Herbsleb, J.D. and Grinter, R.E. 1999. Splitting the organization and integrating the code: Conway's law revisited. Proc. ICSE 1999, 85-95.
15. Herbsleb, J.D., Mockus, A., and Roberts, J.A. 2006. Collaboration in software engineering projects: A theory of coordination. Proc. ICIS 2006.
16. Kersten, M. and Murphy, G.C. 2005. Mylar: a degree-of-interest model for IDEs. Proc. AOSE 2005, 159-168.
17. Kersten, M. and Murphy, G.C. 2006. Using task context to improve programmer productivity. Proc. FSE 2006.
18. Kraut, R. and Streeter, L. 1995. Coordination in software development. Communications of the ACM. 38, 3, 69-81.
19. Minto, S. and Murphy, G.C. 2007. Recommending emergent teams. Proc. MSR 2007.
20. Parnas, D.L. 1972. On the criteria to be used in decomposing systems into modules. Communications of the ACM. 15, 12, 1058.
21. Rothlisberger, D., Nierstrasz, O., Ducasse, S., Pollet, D., and Robbes, R. 2009. Supporting task-oriented navigation in IDEs with configurable heatmaps. Proc. ICPC 2009, pp. 253–257
22. Sarma, A., Noroozi, Z., and van der Hoek, A. Palantír: raising awareness among configuration management workspaces. Proc. ICSE 2003.
23. Sarma, A., Maccherone,L., Wagstrom, P., and Herbsleb, J. 2009. Tesseract: Interactive visual exploration of socio-technical relationships in software development. Proc ICSE 2009, 23-33.
24. Singer, J., Elves, R., and Storey, M.-A. 2005. Navtracks: Supporting navigation in software maintenance, Proc. ICSM 2005, pp. 325–335.
25. Sosa, M.E., Eppinger, S.D., and Rowles, C.M. 2004. The misalignment of product architecture and organizational structure in complex product development. Management Science. 50, 12, 1674-1689.
26. Sullivan, K.J., Griswold, W.G., Cai, Y., and Hallen, B. 2001. The structure and value of modularity in software design. Proc. FSE 2001, pp. 99-108.
27. Valetto, G., Chulani, S., and Williams, C. 2008. Balancing the value and risk of socio-technical congruence. Proc. STC 2008.

Software Reuse Through Methodical Component Reuse and Amethodical Snippet Remixing

Susan Elliott Sim[1,2], Rosalva Gallardo-Valencia[1], Kavita Philip[3], Medha Umarji[1], Megha Agarwala[4], Cristina V. Lopes[1], Sukanya Ratanotayanon[5]

[1]Department of Informatics
University of California, Irvine
{ses|rgallard|lopes}@ics.uci.edu
medha1@gmail.com

[2]Department of Management Science and Systems
SUNY – Buffalo
susanell@buffalo.edu

[3]Department of Women's Studies
University of California, Irvine
kphilip@uci.edu

[4]Teachers College,
Columbia University
ma3037@columbia.edu

[5]Faculty of Science and Technology
Thammasat University
sratanot@gmail.com

ABSTRACT
Every method for developing software is a prescriptive model. Applying a deconstructionist analysis to methods reveals that there are two texts, or sets of assumptions and ideals: a set that is privileged by the method and a second set that is left out, or marginalized by the method. We apply this analytical lens to software reuse, a technique in software development that seeks to expedite one's own project by using programming artifacts created by others. By analyzing the methods prescribed by Component-Based Software Engineering (CBSE), we arrive at two texts: Methodical CBSE and Amethodical Remixing. Empirical data from four studies on code search on the web draws attention to four key points of tension: status of component boundaries; provenance of source code; planning and process; and evaluation criteria for candidate code. We conclude the paper with a discussion of the implications of this work for the limits of methods, structure of organizations that reuse software, and the design of search engines for source code.

ACM Classification Keywords
H5.m. Information interfaces and presentation (e.g., HCI): Miscellaneous.

General Terms
Experimentation, Human Factors, Measurement

Author Keywords
Science and technology studies; software development; tools and methods; inclusive design; feminist

INTRODUCTION
Software developers apply various tools and methods to ensure that they deliver products that are satisfactory to the user, on time, and on budget. There is a plethora of books that provide advice on how to do this, covering topics such as use design patterns, Scrum, frameworks, user-centered design, test-driven development, programming languages, and so on. Despite all the advice available, a remarkable number of projects do not succeed, finish late, or are cancelled altogether. Why does this still happen?

Part of the answer lies in the nature of software methods themselves. Turning knowledge about how projects in the past were successfully completed into prescriptions of how others ought to do requires details of the experience to be abstracted or excluded. Consequently, every method has assumptions and ideals built into it. By the same token, there are assumptions and ideals that lie outside of the method.

In a deconstructionist analysis of information systems development methods, Truex, Baskerville, and Travis [27] identified a privileged "methodical" text and a marginalized "amethodical" text. The former is expressed explicitly in the prescription. The latter is implied by what is omitted or lies outside of the method. They found that the methodical text idealizes logical decomposition, consistency, and goal determination. The amethodical text idealizes creativity, social constructivism, and human independence.

In this paper, we apply this analytical approach to software reuse, a practice that seeks to make use of existing work artifacts, such as components, frameworks, and source code, in order to deliver software more effectively. It has long been an ideal of software engineering to create new systems from existing components to the largest extent possible while maintaining high quality standards. This impulse has led to the emergence of component-based software engineering (CBSE). This discipline is concerned with designing components and libraries to be reusable as-is, identifying and isolating reusable components from an existing code base, and making a searchable repository of components [6, 17, 21, 23].

Our analysis begins with examining the prescriptions from books and papers on CBSE to identify the privileged methodical text. As a deconstructionist analysis, the focus is on assumptions and ideals, which leads to a characterization that is less nuanced than the advice found in the texts. To make this distinction obvious, we shall refer to our characterization as "Methodical CBSE."

From there, we identify an amethodical text, i.e. assumptions and ideals that are left out or dismissed by the prescriptions. We shall refer to this characterization as "Amethodical Remixing," to highlight the similarities to contemporary remix culture and practices. To be clear, we are not implying that there is no method in remixing, only that remixing lies outside of Methodical CBSE.

Empirical data on software reuse draws attention to four key points of tension between methodical and amethodical software reuse: the status of component boundaries; provenance of source code; planning and process; and evaluation criteria for candidate code. The data that we used come from four studies: an exploratory survey, a quantitative survey, a laboratory experiment, and field observations. While results from the exploratory survey and laboratory experiment have been described in detail elsewhere, the meta-analysis in this paper is entirely new.

We discuss the implications of our findings for three areas: the limits of methods, structures for organizations that reuse software, and tools for software reuse.

RELATED WORK

In this section, we provide a brief introduction to components and software reuse. We use this review of related work to illustrate the methodical and amethodical distinction.

When building software of any significant size, the project needs to be divided into parts, or components, to make the problem more tractable. Software engineering promotes the use of established methods, best practices, and sound principles for designing components. Some examples include:

- High cohesion—functionality that is grouped inside a component should make sense together [29].
- Low coupling—a component should not have too many dependencies on other modules [29].
- Information hiding—a component should hide implementation details and provide a stable interface to reduce complexity for other programmers.

Subsequent work by CSCW researchers has picked up on uses of components that lie outside the design methods.

Grinter pioneered the study of "recomposition," the work of putting components together after they have been decomposed [10]. Recomposition is affected not only by the design of the components, but how the organization is structured and dependencies among people who have worked on the components. At the same time that engineering principles advocate using components to hide information from other developers, roles evolve in organizations solely for the purpose of coordinating and communicating information.

Building on Grinter's research, De Souza and Redmiles investigated the role of application program interfaces (APIs) in coordination [5]. An API is the face of a component, an agreed-upon set of procedures for accessing the functionality inside a component. As a coordination mechanism, APIs are both artifact and protocol. Previous research, primarily in software engineering, have focused on the artifact aspect and yielded recommendations for good design of APIs. De Souza and Redmiles's focus is on the protocol aspect, which draws attention to how developers communicate and coordinate through APIs.

Our work extends this line of research on components. This prior work studied the role of components while they were under development within a single organization. Our research looks at the role of components in software reuse, which occurs after the components have been finished and usually consumed in an organization other than where they were created. In this context, there is a greater emphasis on finding the components and evaluating them, because there tends not to be communication between creators and consumers.

The aim of software reuse is to facilitate the construction of new systems using existing components and artifacts to the largest extent possible. Even at the first NATO Software Engineering Conference in 1968, McIlroy envisaged a world where software was built from standardized components that could be purchased commercially from a competitive marketplace [16]. Brooks in his essay, "No Silver Bullet," has posited that buying components rather then building software may result in an order of magnitude improvement in software processes [2].

Research into component-based software engineering (CBSE) has yielded prototypes and principles [23]. Tools include repositories for components, ontologies for categorizing components and facilitating search, and programs for identifying and extracting components in existing source code. Process prescriptions include methods for de novo software developing and for designing with components. New software should be developed with future reuse in mind and APIs standardized from the outset.

Despite the appeal of these ideals, CBSE has found only limited traction outside of academia. We have yet to see a commercial component marketplace and previous attempts to standardize interfaces were viewed as too complex [11]. It can be difficult to know all the requirements for a system before creating the design [19]. Nevertheless, developing software with the help of components can save time, money, and heartache, which is why there are ongoing attempts to improve software reuse.

APPROACH

In this section, we describe the work of Truex, Baskerville, and Travis [27] to lay the groundwork for our analysis of CBSE methods.

Historically, the term "method" referred to how something was accomplished and gradually the meaning became amended with "and how you ought to do it too." The prescriptive connotation is the one attached to systems development methods. As such, methods are not just procedures, but also a normative statement of values.

Privileged Methodical	Marginalized Amethodical
1. Systems development is a managed, controlled process.	2. Systems development is a random opportunistic process driven by accidents.
3. Systems development is a linear, sequential process.	4. Systems development is simultaneous, overlapping, and there are gaps.
5. Systems development is a replicable, universal process.	6. Systems development occurs in completely unique and idiographic forms.
7. Systems development is a rational, determined, and goal-driven process.	8. Systems development is negotiated, compromised, and capricious.

Table 1: Methodical versus Amethodical

Truex et al. performed a postmodern deconstruction to information systems development methods to identify privileged and marginalized meanings. The privileged interpretation in systems development was "methodical," that is, a view of the world as ordered, rational, and logical. The marginalized interpretation was "amethodical," a view of the world as capricious, random, and socially ordered. The term amethodical does not mean without procedure or careless, but rather, beside or outside of method.

Characterizations of methodical and amethodical are found in Table 1 above. Each row in the table contains a pair of opposing statements. The values on the left were implied by the methods and the values on the right were absent and excluded.

Others have made similar observations. In their study of software process improvement projects, Teixeira and Cukierman found that successes were used as evidence of the effectiveness of the technology or method, but that failures were attributed to non-technical factors, such as people, culture, and politics [26]. Where decomposition emphasizes the methodical, Grinter's recomposition emphasizes the amethodical. De Souza and Redmiles's artifact and protocol distinction also aligns with the characterization of methodical and amethodical.

To be clear, the assumptions and ideals associated with the methodical text are not fixed. A number of software process methods, such as Computer-Aided Software Engineering (CASE) [7] and the Capability Maturity Model (an approach to increasing software quality through quantitative management) [20], privilege process and control. While others, such as Extreme Programming, Scrum, and Agile methods [14], privilege negotiation and adaptation. This fluidity is illustrated by the Agile Manifesto[1], a declaration of values regarding software process. It states:

> *We are uncovering better ways of developing software by doing it and helping others do it. Through this work we have come to value:*
>
> *Individuals and interactions over processes and tools*
>
> *Working software over comprehensive documentation*
>
> *Customer collaboration over contract negotiation*
>
> *Responding to change over following a plan*
>
> *That is, while there is value in the items on the right, we value the items on the left more.*

Here, the left-right order is opposite from the list in Table 1.

In practice, software developers are not purely methodical or amethodical. They are constantly picking and choosing between design considerations and social constraints. Nevertheless, identifying what is missing or left out will help researchers question their assumptions and what is taken for granted.

TWO TEXTS

In this section, we begin by sketching out two texts, Methodical CBSE and Amethodical Remixing, that have been identified through deconstructionist analysis of software reuse methods.

Methodical CBSE

Methodical CBSE idealizes components, accepted engineering principles, planning and predictability, consistency of the architecture, and software quality. To reiterate, Methodical CBSE is the privileged text that is found in the prescriptive methods for software reuse. It is an ideal and as such unlikely to be observed empirically.

[1] http://agilemanifesto.org/

Since it is based on a close reading of methods, it has the same assumptions and ideals that were identified by Truex et al. for systems development methods.

Amethodical Remixing

At the margins of Methodical CBSE lies a set of amethodical assumptions and ideals. This is software reuse without components, without careful planning, and without the use of quality metrics. Also constructed from a close reading of methods, this position is a marginalized text. In contrast to CBSE, there are no prescribed methods for remixing.

We use the term "remixing" to label this text, because it bears a strong resemblance to the creative practices that has emerged around digital media. New works are constructed by taking parts of existing music, video, and/or images, and combining them in novel ways. For example, DJ Earworm is known for creating mashups, a piece of music that is a creative and novel combination of pieces (or "samples") from multiple songs [22]. His most popular works are his annual "United State of Pop" retrospectives where he samples from the 25 most popular songs from the previous year and creates a single mashup with them. While mashups are a gray area in intellectual copyright law, the practice is becoming accepted by fans and artists. In 2010, a radio station in London, UK hosted a "Summertime Ball" at Wembley Stadium [9]. DJ Earworm was invited to create a mashup of songs from fifteen featured artists, which included Justin Bieber, Ludacris, and Rihanna. He debuted this new work on the same stage as the other performers, signifying the acceptance of remixing as a creative art.

Having identified these two texts, we now turn to empirical data to describe practices.

METHOD

For the meta-analysis presented in this paper, we draw on data from a series of studies that we conducted to better understand how programmers search for, find, and use source code on the web. We began with an Exploratory Survey (Study 1) in 2006 to characterize the breadth of search behaviors. The results from this first study motivated the subsequent studies. We noticed trends in what participants were searching for and the tools that they were using to perform the searches. We conducted a Laboratory Experiment (Study 3) to examine this relationship more closely. When we analyzed the data from this and other experiments, we realized that studying search behaviors on assigned tasks led to limitations in our conclusions. Consequently, we undertook Field Observations (Study 4), where we collected data on the searches that software developers performed as they worked. Finally, a follow-on Quantitative Survey (Study 2) was conducted in 2010.

The work presented in this paper is a novel synthesis of results from all four studies. Study 1 and Study 3 have been published elsewhere. The two remaining studies are new. Study 2 has not been published at all and only a preliminary analysis from Study 4 has been published.

Combining data from diverse studies with heterogeneous subjects strengthens our results, because doing so allows us to triangulate a phenomenon [13]. A key concept in triangulation is that weaknesses of a particular research design or metric can be buttressed by another with different characteristics. Consequently, consistent findings from diverse studies buoy our confidence in the conclusions. By the same token, a behavior appearing consistently among participants with different expertise levels and backgrounds lends credence to the resilience of the phenomenon under study.

Study 1: Exploratory Survey

We fielded an online survey that asked participants about their habits when searching for source code on the web [28]. The survey questions can be found at http://www.drsusansim.com/research/cscw2012/. We solicited participants through a variety of newsgroups, web sites, and our own social network. A total of 69 participants responded to our survey and contributed 58 anecdotes about how they searched. A majority of the developers that responded to our survey were programmers in Java (54), C++ (58) and Perl (32). More than half of the participants (37) had contributed to an open source project. Most of the participants (41) had experience working on small teams with 1 to 5 people.

Our analysis here relies primarily on the data from one question. We asked for a free-form description of a search that they had performed previously. The question read:

> *Please describe one or two scenarios when you were looking for source code on the Internet.*
>
> *(Please address details such as: What were you trying to find? How did you formulate your queries? What information sources did you use to find the source code? Which implementation language were you working with? What criteria did you use to decide on the best match?)*

Study 2: Quantitative Survey

Subsequently, we conducted another online survey on the same topics with some modifications. This study was less exploratory; armed with the results from the first study, we were able to formulate closed ended questions that collected data on the frequency of different activities. The questionnaire had 22 multiple choice questions related to the motivation and search target of Internet-scale source code search, as well as the tools and selection criteria used to look for source code snippets, software components, and open source projects. The survey questions can also be found at the above URL.

We specifically sought data from professional software developers. We solicited participants from two conferences of professional developers, Agile Open SoCal (Southern

California), and SoCal Code Camp. A total of 26 professional developers participated in our questionnaire. They had on average 13.8 years of development experience. Forty percent of participants indicated that they look for source code at least once per week.

Study 3: Laboratory Experiment

Using lessons learned from Study 1, we designed a laboratory experiment in which we evaluated the effectiveness of search engines on various combinations of search targets and search intentions [24]. Each participant was given a search problem and was asked to conduct the search on five different search engines. The sites that we used were one general-purpose search engine (Google), three code-specific search engines (Koders, Krugle, and Google Code Search), and one project hosting site (SourceForge). The problems specified a goal, a search target, a programming language, the intention behind the search, and a scenario to link together the first four parts. The search target was either a snippet or a component and the intention was reuse or reference example.

Participants were permitted to make as many queries as they wished. When they were satisfied with their search results, we asked them to judge the relevance of the first ten matches returned (P@10).

Thirty-six participants were recruited for this study. Their average age was 27 and on average they had 4 years of professional programming experience. All had experience searching for source code on the web and had used multiple programming languages.

Study 4: Field Observations

We conducted a field study over four weeks at Anonymous, a small software company that develops software for banks, telecommunications companies, government, and other organizations. The company has achieved CMM level 3 and its processes are certified as ISO 9001-compliant. All 25 developers who were working on implementation tasks at the time of our study participated.

We collected data in two ways: daily self-reports and direct observation. Each day, developers were given a form to record their searches for source code. We periodically interviewed these developers to obtain more detailed information about the searches. We also shadowed 12 of the developers for one day each. We took notes on their activities, with a particular attention to their code searches. After each search, we asked questions about the goal of the search, their expectations, how they evaluated the matches, and how they were going to use the source code selected. Using these two methods, we collected data from 218 distinct search sessions.

RESULTS

We found four key areas where Methodical CBSE and Amethodical Remixing were in conflict: status of component boundaries; provenance of source code; planning and process; and evaluation criteria for candidate code.

In practice, a developer does not follow a method verbatim. It is impossible to do so, because information has been left out. Enactments of methods necessarily move away from their abstract descriptions. How far removed is an empirical question.

Methodical CBSE	Amethodical Remixing
Components	Snippets
Repositories	Web pages, email, forums
Controlled and planned	Ad hoc
Correctness and consistency	Reputation and appearance

Table 2: Methodical CBSE and Amethodical Remixing

The following is a scenario provided by a participant in Study 1 that describes component reuse.

> *Usually I try to find libraries or frameworks that I can integrate in my own projects. Therefore I start like one would search for a product to buy example: once I looked for a library that could read even broken html so I started to look for html parsers. There were many of them so secondary project goals contributed to narrow down the search. On that occasion I wanted to extract some information from a well known website so the data model to represent the html was important. I ended up with a library called Tagsoup that did exactly what I needed: reading html repairing broken html during reading and storing it into an easily utilized standardized format (W3C DOM). After I found that library my project was done within hours where I before that estimated days. Almost all of that spared time was because of the DOM data model that only Tagsoup provided (i.e. of the product I had found at that time). Oh btw I almost always look for Java code.*

The developer had a set of requirements and when the search turn up many possible candidates, he used other project requirements as selection criteria. A component was found and used without modification. However, this reuse was not planned from the beginning of the project.

This next scenario came from the same study and describes snippet remixing.

> *Looking for a base-64 encode/decode function implemented in C++. Google searches didn't turn up anything useful. Because I was writing a web server I knew that Apache would be doing something similar so I went straight to the source code and dug through by hand to find the function I needed.*

The developer reached into the source code for an existing project, pulled out a single function, and inserted the code into his own project. This kind of software reuse is farther removed from Methodical CBSE.

In the remainder of this section, we will discuss the four points of tension in detail.

Status of Component Boundaries

In Methodical CBSE, component boundaries are inviolate. Examples of components include classes, libraries, application program interfaces (APIs), packages, and open source projects. While the size of a component varied, they all had in common a well-defined conceptual boundary that was enforced by constructs in the programming language.

Components are meant to be used as-is, because, according to conventional wisdom, delving into a component to modify the source code would quickly eliminate any efficiency gains. Mili, Mili, and Mili further argue against modifying components during reuse, writing:

> *With modification, the changes are often unanticipated or poorly planned. ...modifying reusable components may defeat both the quality and the productivity advantages of reuse.* [17]

In contrast, Amethodical Remixing frequently works with units that do not obey component boundaries or the advice to not modify. It was not unusual to search for a few lines of code, such as a loop, code block, or example. These snippets were often modified, so that they could be used. Frequently, the snippet is consulted as a reference and implemented from scratch. A close cousin to this practice is copying, pasting, and modifying the snippet to work in the new project. CBSE is critical of snippet remixing, as Sametinger wrote:

> *Today reuse is still done by grabbing some pieces of code, studying and trying to understand them and then modifying and integrating them. The term code scavenging applies to this scenario. The abstraction level of reusable components has to rise in order to considerably improve productivity. The reuse of plain source code should be the exception.* [23]

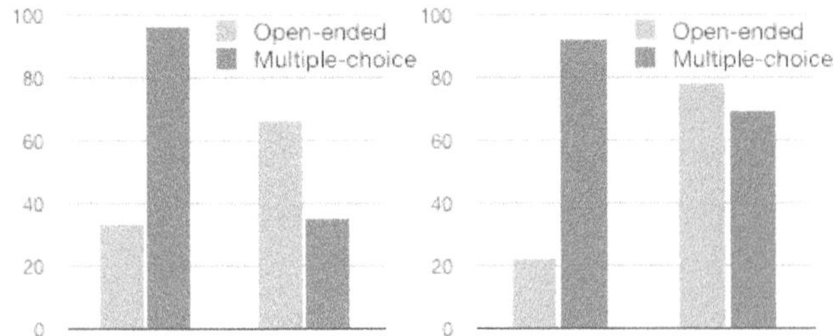

Figure 1: Comparing Data from Open-Ended versus Multiple-Choice Questions

In the Exploratory Survey, we found that 22% of the scenarios provided described searches for snippets and the remaining 78% were for components. These categories were used to create the response options for the multiple-choice questions in the Quantitative. In terms of search targets, 92% reported searching for snippets and 69% were seeking components.

Initially, we found that the intention behind two thirds of the searches were for code to reuse as-is and the remaining one third was for reference examples. In the Quantitative Survey, 96% of the participants had performed searches for reference examples, while only 35% of them were looking for code to reuse as-is.

These findings are summarized in Figure 1. The quantitative changes should not be interpreted as trends as the open-ended data sum to 100 and the multiple-choice data do not. However, they do show the differences from allowing participants to choose what kinds of searches to describe and explicitly asking about particular kinds of searches. This shift is indicative of a marginal practice that has been brought into the light. When we asked explicitly about code searches that seek reference information and snippets, the rates of self-reporting increased significantly. At the same time, reports of searches for components and as-is reuse decreased.

In the Field Study, we found that 76% of the searches were to solve knowledge problems. Developers were trying to understand how to do something (38%), to refresh their memory (24%), and to acquire abstract knowledge (14%). Less than 10% of the searches were to download a component or to determine the suitability of a component. Results from our Field Study are shown in Figure 2.

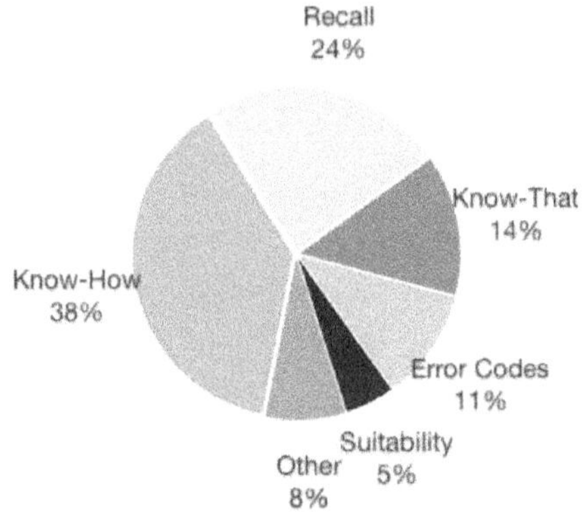

Figure 2: Types of Problems Solved by Code Search

Taken together, these results show that source code is being used as more than functionality, that is, as computation. Source code is being used as a kind of knowledge, specifically knowledge that can be used to make computational machines. In this respect, component boundaries are incidental and not sacred.

When source code-as-computation travel, they require metrology, i.e. scaffolding to make them work when they travel to contexts [15]. Adjustments need to be made to the surrounding software project by adding statements to access components, variables to hold data, and function calls written. In contrast, source code-as-information requires no such scaffolding. Example snippets are powerful because they are solutions to problems that are expressed in a specific context, rather than general principles. Therefore, additional effort is not required to make the abstract knowledge concrete.

Provenance of Source Code

In fine art, the provenance of a work denotes not only the original creator, but also the historical sequence of owners. Being able to trace the provenance of a work increases one's confidence in its authenticity. We use a similar definition here. The provenance of source code pertains not only where it came from, but also how it arrives in one's possession. Search engines play an important role in the provenance of source code, because each one indexes a distinct set of resources.

In Methodical CBSE, components for reuse come from repositories. Sametinger gives an overview of desirable characteristics.

> *A component repository is a database for the storage and retrieval of reusable components. It contains software components with all relevant information about them, including their design, history, interactions with other components, classification (for retrieval) and documentation.*

Within a company or a hypothetical component marketplace, write access to the repositories is controlled by the authorities. In open source repositories, write access is also controlled, but web sites such as SourceForge, Tigris.org, and Google Code permit anyone who is interested to create a repository for a new project or potential component.

In Amethodical Remixing, snippets for remixing can come from anywhere. The growth of technologies to support a participatory World Wide Web has made it possible for diverse authors to contribute material on topics as varied as the quality of information. People wrote about what mattered to them and for software developers this was often source code. They blogged about good practices, wrote tutorials for new tools and techniques, and participated in discussions. Many of these writings contained source code. Consequently a wealth of code snippets can be found on tutorials, blogs, wikis, forums, and mailing lists.

The following example from the Exploratory Study illustrates the agility and ingenuity of developers when they use multiple tools and resources to find code.

> *Looking for the way to get connection details out of a WiFi card in Windows XP for a Visual C++ application. Searched Google for various combinations of keywords with limited success. (Most places were trying to sell me code for thousands of dollars.) Had more luck with Google News searching the Microsoft developer newsgroups. Someone had posted a small code snippet which gave me clues as to where the API documentation was. I used that to write something from scratch.*

The diverse provenance of source code is confirmed by results from our Laboratory Study. The P@10 metric indicates the precision of the first ten results, and indicates the proportion that participants judged to be relevant. Overall, Google was the most effective; participants judged 50% of the first ten matches as relevant to the scenario. The remaining search engines had P@10 scores ranging 0.29-0.37. This difference was statistically significant at $p < 0.001$. When we looked further, we saw that there was an interaction effect. Google did especially well on searches for snippets, but worse on searches for components. In contrast, Koders and Krugle did better on searches for components. This effect was also statistically significant at $p < 0.001$. This effect can be explained by looking at the design of these search engines.

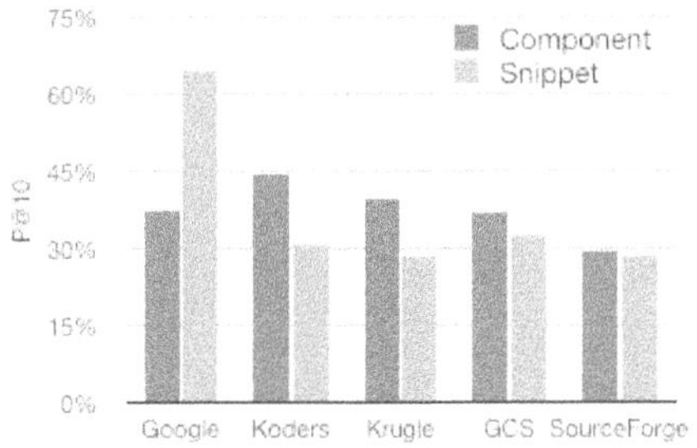

Figure 3: Interaction Effect Between Search Engine and Type of Search Target

Google indexes web sites omnivorously, including news sites, forums, blogs, and tutorials. When a snippet is encountered, Google indexes it along with the rest of the page, which more readily matches terms in search specifications.

Code-specific search engines, such as Koders and Krugle, index the contents of code repositories and project hosting sites. In other words, these search engines contain only components. The matches that they return tend to be entire source code files, which point the way to the larger component or project.

Planning and Process

Planning and control of risk are fundamental engineering principles. According to Methodical CBSE, the decision to use components is a conscious choice and the selection criteria for components should be based on principles, requirements, and quality. Furthermore, the decision to reuse components should be made when the component is developed, as Sametinger wrote:

> *Software process models and software reuse interact in two ways. First, a model may or may not encourage developers to consider the reuse of existing components (design with reuse). Second, the resulting products (anything from design documents to source code) will turn out to be more or less reusable (design for reuse).* [23]

In contrast, Amethodical Remixing idealizes spontaneity and adhocracy. Software developers do not always have a pre-defined notion of the component or code snippet that they want or even the task to be done. Decisions to remix snippets are made after seeing the snippet. Sometimes they are searching to see what is available. For instance, during the development of the Science Activity Planner, the requirements phase "included many Web 'shopping trips' to search for open source components that fit customer requests" [18].

In the Quantitative Survey, we asked how often they searched for source code on the web. All of them reported doing it and nearly one third did so every day.

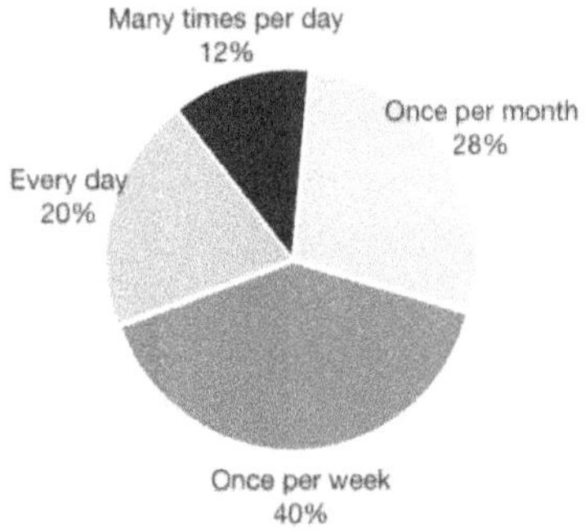

Figure 4: Frequency of Searches for Code on the Web

In the Field Study, nearly all of the 218 searches were for reference and snippets. One person in the study was looking for a component. He performed a series of 15 searches over a day and had not yet made a final selection. So, searches for components to reuse as-is were infrequent, but memorable, and searches for snippets to consult were frequent, but not mentioned. These finding corroborate the idea of privileged and marginal practices in software reuse.

Evaluation Criteria for Candidate Code

In Methodical CBSE, components that are correct and consistent should be preferred. Criteria for evaluation include requirements compliance, component quality, architecture compliance, licensing, price, and support [3]. Mili, Mili, and Mili give the following equation to characterize the cost effectiveness of reuse.

$$\begin{gathered} \mathit{Search} + (1-p)\,\mathit{ApproxSearch} \\ + (1-p)\,q\,\mathit{Adaptation} \leq \\ (p + (1-p)\,q)\,\mathit{Development} \end{gathered}$$

where p is the probability that the component is found in the database, q is the probability that a satisfactory approximation of the component can be found, *Search* is the cost of performing an exact search on the repository, *ApproxSearch* is the cost of performing an approximate search, *Adaptation* is the cost of adapting the component to its host environment, and *Development* is the cost of developing the component from scratch [17]. Note that the cost of evaluating the suitability of component is not included nor is the cost of comprehending how to use the component. The two terms that capture the cost of searching only includes the effort of issuing and executing the query. The existence of such an equation clearly illustrates that CBSE expects software reuse to be predictable and quantifiable.

In Amethodical Remixing, non-quality criteria, such as reputation and appearance, are foregrounded. Open source projects were judged based on number of users, activity level on the project, friendliness of forums, and availability of documentation. Recommendations from personal friends, Internet acquaintances, and trusted blogs were important. The following excerpt from the Exploratory Study illustrates the importance of social factors when searching for source code and programming knowledge.

> *I am looking for a "how to do it" which is best incorporated in a section of code often example code. How to search? In short I would never rely on a "code search engine". This idea is just plain silly. Sort of ivory tower. If you want to find something usable you have to look for "people already using it."*

The appearance of a web site was also taken into consideration. Participants did not like web sites that had poor graphic design and too many advertisements. During the Laboratory Study, search sessions lasted on average 6 minutes, including the time to form and revise queries. In other words, decisions about relevance were made quickly and by necessity relied on some factors that could be assessed through a rapid visual inspection. As one participant wrote, "I decided on the best match based on whether I understand the example code."

On average, more time was spent looking for snippets (426 seconds) than for components (325 seconds), a difference that was statistically significant with $p < 0.05$. Searches for reference took longer (417 seconds) than for as-is reuse (334 seconds) as well.

DISCUSSION

Limits of Methods

Methods are generalized prescriptions for how to do something. Like models, they necessarily leave out details in an attempt to focus on the activities that were key to success. As abstractions, they leave out contextual information, and as Truex et al. pointed out, the most obvious omission is the influence of people, both positive and negative.

The incompleteness of methods is not necessarily a problem, because people do not use static procedures the way that machines do. As Suchman showed, plans are used as resources for action. Plans are generative, rather than scripts to be followed [25].

Problems do arise when marginalized methods are the most common practices of software developers. In CBSE methods, remixing practices are at best absent, and at worst criticized using terms such as "code scavenging." If software engineering research has little to say to the 92% of developers who are remixing snippets, they run a real risk of becoming irrelevant to practitioners. In a previous study, we interviewed software developers about the software process that they use [8]. The first reaction of all of them was that they don't use any software process. This was clearly not the case, because their teams had established procedures for producing software. But participants in the study felt that they were not using a process, because they were not following a prescribed, formalized process. The same may be occurring with software reuse, with developers selecting themselves out as potential beneficiaries of leading edge research.

Organizational Structures

According to Conway's Law, the structure of a software system reflects the organization that was responsible for its construction [4]. Grinter's and de Souza and Redmiles's findings regarding components and APIs supported this idea. Grinter found that groups working on tightly coupled components had greater need for informal communication changes [10]. Furthermore, groups that were geographically distributed found it more difficult to work on tightly coupled components. Gradually, the architecture of the system was changed to make the coupling looser. De Souza and Redmiles [5] observed that while APIs are supposed to reduce communication needs between developers through information hiding, API producers and consumers still needed to coordinate their efforts.

Typically, consumers of finished components do not communicate with the producers and the two parties are not located in the same organization. Working with a finished component suggests that little communication is necessary to coordinate work. However, other kinds of information exchange are necessary for consumers to become aware of a component and to learn how to use it.

Component consumers tend to rely on documentation, the web, and their own social network to find information about the component. Consequently, we would expect to see a relationship between adoption of a component within a developer's social network and adoption of a component by that developer's project.

Sometimes an organization will task an individual to be an expert in a particular library, framework, or API, in order to compartmentalize the knowledge that is needed. In such cases, a wrapper or Façade design pattern may be placed around the component. This will isolate the code and allow the assigned developer to be a gatekeeper or point of coordination for the component.

Design Implications

Many CBSE tools have already been created, and most of these have been published in the software engineering literature. There is room for improvement in code-specific search engines and project hosting sites, such as the ones used in our Laboratory Experiment. Despite being designed to locate components, their P@10 scores were only 0.29-0.44. Changing how results are ranked may help with this. A common strategy in information retrieval is to rank higher the documents with more matches to the search keys. But a source file with the most matches may not be the most desirable. Source code may need to be ranked using a different metric, such as code quality, popularity, or level of activity.

Some early work on tools for snippet remixing has been done [1, 12], but there are still many possibilities to explore. For instance, repositories that treat snippets as first-class objects and search engines that make use of the fact that searches for code are often searches for knowledge. Snipplr and Smipple are two web sites that allow users to submit snippets, tag them, and rank each other's submissions. StackOverflow was popular among participants in all of our studies. The question-and-answer format is an effective way to organize knowledge. We are doing initial work to analyze the structure of discourse around code snippets for the purpose of building a better snippet search engine.

CONCLUSIONS

Methods are a necessary part of engineering, and software engineering is no exception. Consequently, it is important to understand their limitations and how work is accomplished with them. In this paper, we performed a deconstructionist analysis on methods for Component-Based Software Engineering to identify a privileged text, which we called "Methodical CBSE," and a marginalized text, which we called "Amethodical Remixing." We used data from four empirical studies to highlight points of tension between them.

We found that remixing, i.e. the reuse of code snippets, was marginalized in practice as well in relation to component reuse. On surveys, developers tended to report searches for snippets when queried using multiple choice questions than open ended questions. Subjects in a laboratory experiment found that Google, which indexes a variety of web pages, returned more relevant results than search engines designed specifically to search for code. Our field study found that searches for snippets are performed everyday and quickly forgotten, but searches for components were rare but memorable. Finally, candidate source code returned by a search engine were judged based on reputation and appearance, rather than quantitative measures of quality.

Gaps between methodical and amethodical texts are expected. But a large gap between practice and prescriptive methods is an opportunity for both CSCW and software engineering researchers.

ACKNOWLEDGMENTS

Thanks to the UCI Narrative Reading Group for the ongoing intellectual stimulation and social support, but especially for excellent feedback during the early stages of this work. This research was possible due to their generosity in sharing their time and work with us. This material is based upon work supported by the NSF under Grant No. IIS-0846034. Any opinions, findings, and conclusions or recommendations expressed in this material are those of the authors and do not necessary reflect the views of the NSF.

REFERENCES

[1] Brandt, J., Guo, P.J., Lewenstein, J., Dontcheva, M., and Klemmer, S.R., "Two Studies of Opportunistic Programming: Interleaving Web Foraging, Learning and Writing Code," in *Proceedings of the 27th international conference on Human factors in computing systems* Boston, MA, pp. 1589-1598, 2009.

[2] Brooks, F.P., "No Silver Bullet-- Essence and Accidents of Software Enginering," *IEEE Computer,* vol. 20, pp. 10-19, 1987.

[3] Chen, W., Li, J., Ma, J., Conradi, R., Ji, J., and Liu, C., "An Empirical Study of Software Development with Open Source Components in the Chinese Software Industry," *Software Process: Improvement and Practice,* vol. 13, pp. 89-100, January 2008.

[4] Conway, M.E., "How Do Committees Invent?," *Datamation,* vol. 14, pp. 28-31, 1968.

[5] de Souza, C.R. and Redmiles, D.F., "On the Roles of Apis in the Coordination of Collaborative Software Development," *Computer Supported Cooperative Work,* vol. 18, pp. 445-475, 2009.

[6] Frakes, W. and Terry, C., "Software Reuse: Metrics and Models," *ACM Computing Surveys,* vol. 28, pp. 415-435, 1996.

[7] Fugetta, A., "A Classification of Case Technology," *IEEE Computer,* vol. 26, pp. 25-38, 1993.

[8] Gallardo-Valencia, R.E. and Sim, S.E., "Enacting Software Processes through Prescription and Improvisation," in *ACM Crossroads*. vol. 14, p. 3 (8 pages), 2007.

[9] Global Radio. Summertime Ball 2010 - the Party of the Summer! - Capital Fm. Available from: http://www.capitalfm.com/music-showbiz/summertime-ball/, Last accessed November 18.

[10] Grinter, R.E., "Recomposition: Coordinating a Web of Software Dependencies," *Computer Supported Cooperative Work,* vol. 12, pp. 297-327, 2003.

[11] Henning, M., "The Rise and Fall of Corba," *ACM Queue,* vol. 4, 2006.

[12] Holmes, R. and Murphy, G.C., "Using Structural Context to Recommend Source Code Examples," in *Proceedings of the 27th International Conference on Software Engineering.,* New York, NY: ACM Press, pp. 117-125, 2005.

[13] Jick, T.D., "Mixing Qualitative and Quantitative Methods: Triangulation in Action," *Administrative Science Quarterly,* vol. 24, pp. 602-611, 1979.

[14] Larman, C. and Basili, V.R., "Iterative and Incremental Development: A Brief History," *IEEE Computer,* vol. 36, pp. 47-56, 2003.

[15] Latour, B., *Science in Action.* Cambridge: Harvard University Press, 1988.

[16] McIlroy, M.D., "Mass Produced Software Components," in *Software Engineering: Report of a Conference Sponsored by the Nato Science Committee, Garmisch, Germany, 7-11 Oct. 1968*, Peter Naur and Brian Randell, Eds.: Scientific Affairs Division, NATO1969.

[17] Mili, H., Mili, F., and Mili, A., "Reusing Software: Issues and Research Directions," *IEEE Transactions on Software Engineering,* vol. 21, pp. 528-562, 1995.

[18] Norris, J.S., "Mission-Critical Development with Open Source Software: Lessons Learned," *IEEE Software,* vol. 21, pp. 42-49, 2004.

[19] Nuseibeh, B., "Weaving Together Requirements and Architectures," *IEEE Software,* vol. 34, pp. 115-119, 2001.

[20] Paulk, M.C., Weber, C.V., Curtis, B., and Chrissis, M.B., "The Capability Maturity Model: Guidelines for Improving the Software Process," Addison-Wesley Publishing Company, 1994.

[21] Prieto-Díaz, R., "Implementing Faceted Classification for Software Reuse," *Commun. ACM,* vol. 34, pp. 88-97, 1991.

[22] Roseman, J., *Audio Mashup Construction Kit: Extremetech.* Wiley, 2006.

[23] Sametinger, J., *Software Engineering with Reusable Components*: Springer, 1997.

[24] Sim, S.E., Umarji, M., Ratanotayanon, S., and Lopes, C.V., "How Well Do Search Engines Support Code Retrieval on the Web?," *ACM Transactions on Software Engineering and Methodology,* vol. 21, 2012.

[25] Suchman, L.A., *Plans and Situated Actions: The Problem of Human-Machine Interaction*: Cambridge University Press, 1987.

[26] Teixeira, C.A.N. and Cukierman, H.L., "Why Do Software Process Improvement Projects Fail?," *Interdisciplinary Studies in Computer Science,* vol. 18, pp. 24-32, 2007.

[27] Truex, D., Baskerville, R., and Travis, J., "Amethodical Systems Development: The Deferred Meaning of Systems Development Methods," *Accounting, Management, and Information Technology,* vol. 10, pp. 53-79, 2000.

[28] Umarji, M., Sim, S.E., and Lopes, C.V., "Archetypal Internet-Scale Source Code Searching," in *4th International Conference on Open Source Systems*, Milan, Italy, p. 7, 2008.

[29] van Vliet, H., *Software Engineering: Principles and Practice, Third Edition*: John Wiley & Sons, 2008.

Information Needs for Integration Decisions in the Release Process of Large-Scale Parallel Development

Shaun Phillips
University of Calgary
Department of Computer Science
phillist@ucalgary.ca

Guenther Ruhe
University of Calgary
Department of Computer Science
ruhe@ucalgary.ca

Jonathan Sillito
University of Calgary
Department of Computer Science
sillito@ucalgary.ca

ABSTRACT
Version control branching allows an organization to parallelize its development efforts. Releasing a software system developed in this manner requires release managers, and other project stakeholders, to make decisions about how to integrate the branched work. This group decision-making process becomes very complex in the case of large-scale parallel development. To better understand the information needs of release managers in this context, we conducted an interview study at a large software company. Our analysis of the interviews provides a view into how release managers make integration decisions, organized around ten key factors. Based on these factors, we discuss specific information needs for release managers and how the needs can be met in future work.

Author Keywords
Parallel development; release management; version control; integration; decision support; team meetings

ACM Classification Keywords
D.2.9 Software Engineering: Management

General Terms
Management

INTRODUCTION
Software engineering decision support qualifies the process of decision-making through the different stages of the software life-cycle [14], but decisions can only be as good as the information they are based upon. Version control systems are generally considered to be a vital information source in development projects [1, 17]. Version control *branching* refers to the parallelization of development in a version control system. With branching, different software development teams or individual developers can work in separate branches or "copies" of a code base. The decision to branch is typically motivated by the need to prevent workflow disruption, and reduce overall cycle-time, by having teams stabilize their development in isolation before integrating with their organization. *Integrations* involve merging code, resolving merge conflicts, and compiling and testing the merged code.

Different organizations use different numbers and arrangements of branches. As an example, Figure 1 depicts the branching model used by our interview participants' organization. In this model, developers are assigned to teams that make code changes primarily in the feature branches. Staging branches are used for integrating work from several related feature branches in preparation for further integration in the mainline branch. In addition to integrating code up the tree, code also flows downward to ensure that development teams do not operate on out-of-date code bases.

As a release approaches, decisions need to be made around what integration work will be required. Though previous research has looked at various aspects of planning and managing releases (e.g., [15]), the focus of our ongoing research is on understanding information needs for managing releases in a branched context. The interview study reported in this paper aims to identify current approaches and challenges around release management in branched projects, including identifying the information needs of release managers making integration decisions.

From our analysis of the interview data we have identified ten decision factors that are important considerations when making integration decisions and derived several key information needs. We discuss the extent to which these information needs are met by the participants' organization and how they can be implemented in future work.

Several aspects of this study are relevant to the CSCW community. First, the use of version control requires coordination between potentially 1000s of individuals and this complexity demands considerable computer support. Second, while version control is generally considered in the scope of software engineering, it is also required by many organizations that require co-development of other intellectual goods. Finally, this work considers version control from the perspective of key individuals in an organization who are supported by technology and captures practices and problems that have evolved over time.

RELATED WORK
Release management and version control integration are topics well-represented in academic literature. Exploring where

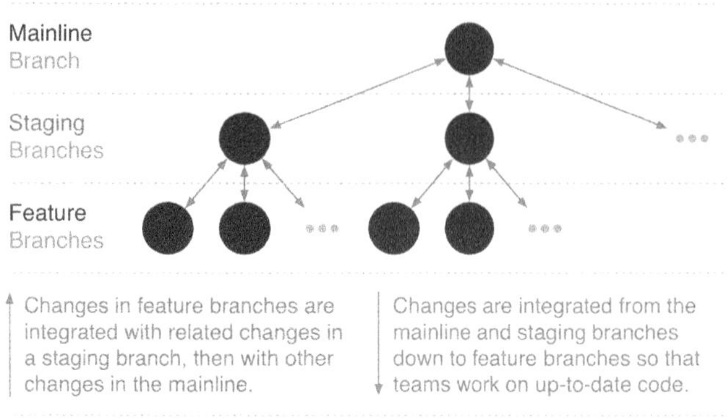

Figure 1. Branching model used by the software company in our study.

these areas intersect is a key contribution of this study. Findings from our interviews show that there are opportunities to improve integration decision-making with software support. Previous work has shown these findings to be applicable to other organizations; for example, Wright and Perry's case study on the Subversion project [21] discussed how certain integration decisions delayed the 1.5 release of the product.

Several studies have explored merging at the code level, for example, the paper from Mens [9]. Current high-level merging practices (such as merge frequency in an organization) were explored in our broad 2010 user survey [12]. The impact of some merging practices was explored by Perry and Votta in an observational case study of large-scale parallel development [11]. A key finding from the study was that development parallelism was higher in the organization than anticipated by tool builders. While merging practices are an important consideration in this study, the focus is on the higher-level decision making process for releasing branched products, of which the practices are one of many factors.

Our study builds on existing release management literature by addressing concerns and information needs for parallel environments. Previously, Sassenburg has briefly discussed how collaborative efforts can impact release decisions [18]. Ruhe has produced extensive work on release processes [15], though the book does not explicitly address issues that are unique to parallel environments. Walrad et. al. have considered how release maintenance can benefit from branching [20] (e.g., creating branches specifically for release purposes), but this differs from our study in that we are focused on product development in branches and the associated release concerns.

Many studies have examined planning in software development projects, such as that from Rönkkö et. al. [13]. Here, we are concerned with integration decisions—an aspect of planning in branched projects. These decisions are usually reached collaboratively between branch representatives and other release stakeholders. Saarelainen et. al. note that group decisions such as these are widely used both in private and public organizations and attitudes towards them are generally positive or neutral [16]. One widely recognized method to improve the effectiveness of group decisions is the use of Group Decision Support Systems. The systems combine computer, communication, and decision technologies to support group activities [8]. Similarly, this paper attempts to better understand the information needs for computer support required for group decision-making towards integration decisions in large-scale parallel software development.

While previous research has studied information seeking for decision support in various contexts including the daily information needs of software developers [7], to the best of our knowledge, no work has looked at the information seeking behaviour of release managers as they make plans for integrating source code from different teams. In this context, release managers need timely information from individuals working on different teams, possibly with similarities to command and control situations where the concept of individual, intragroup, and intergroup "situational awareness" is central [19]. The information seeking process has been conceptualized to include activities identifying, seeking, and retrieving needed information [6] as well as sense-making [10]. The goal of our study is to build on this previous work by studying these information seeking activities in the release planning context.

METHODOLOGY

Organization Information

Our study involved semi-structured interviews with an unaffiliated software organization of roughly 1000 developers. Development teams are organized in the hierarchy depicted in Figure 1: developers are divided amongst 15 product units, or major components, and each product unit is composed of feature teams. Developers on the same team tend to be colocated, but the teams themselves may not be in close proximity (some are in different geographic regions).

The flagship product, approximately 100 million lines of code, has been in development for more than ten years and has undergone several major releases, generally in a two-year cycle. Each product unit has a release team which is part of a larger release organization. Development teams will collaborate with their release team to establish schedules, verify release quality criteria, and assess integration risk. This information is then communicated in release organization meetings to determine overall project strategy, status, and risk. Many different project stakeholders will attend the meetings throughout the release cycle and their input is one of many information sources that must be considered when making complex integration decisions.

Participants

Seven practitioners (P1...P7) in the target organization, with industry experience ranging from 6 to 17 years, participated in our study. P1 and P2 are both release managers who develop release schedules, coordinate development teams, and support the version control and test systems; P3, P4, and P5 manage and lead teams of developers and testers, perform cross-team coordination for end-to-end product scenarios, and are responsible for delivering and integrating their features with the rest of the product group; P6 and P7 develop the product software and perform the actual integrations and testing.

Table 1. Factors identified in our analysis.

Categories	Factors (Subcategories)
Branch Evolution	Code Churn, Conflicting Changes
Branch Health	Bugs & Bug Counts, Feature Completeness, Test Runs & Results
Project Awareness	Dependencies, System Architecture, Infrastructure
Project Traffic Control	Branch Organization, Code Flow

Study Design
Each interview was conducted one-on-one by the first author of this paper. The interviews were one hour in length and the audio was recorded and transcribed verbatim. The interviews were semi-structured in that they were initiated with broad questions stemming from our branching and merging survey [12], but allowed to flow as they delved into the participants' integration experiences, and to what extent these experiences have affected their product releases. We specifically targeted participants with different responsibilities in order to capture the diverse perspectives and information needs of those involved in integration and release decisions.

Analysis
To analyze the transcribed interview data we first performed open-coding to identify concepts and passages in our data of particular analytic interest [4]. We next grouped these codes into categories and subcategories with the goal of understanding our participants' integration decision making and information needs. These categories and subcategories are discussed in detail in the next section.

FINDINGS
Given the extensive use of branches in the participants' organization, integration work is an important part of the development process. If an integration results in code with serious problems (e.g., does not compile or run) the product is said to be "on the floor" (P1). The time taken to perform an integration, called its latency, has proven difficult for our participants to predict. Latency ranged from a day to many weeks. Even though our participants' organization incorporates integration costs into its release plans, integration issues continue to result in significant release delays. One particular incident, where over a dozen branches were integrated into the mainline branch in a two-week period, resulted in the project "being on the floor for 45 days" and "threw our schedule totally out of whack" (P1). After that incident, "everyone realized that obviously code flow and scheduling have to be best friends" (P1).

Our analysis has identified ten factors that capture what our participants have learned about making integration decisions. These factors are organized into four categories: branch evolution, branch health, project awareness, and project traffic control. The categories and factors are listed in Table 1 and described in the remainder of this section.

Branch Evolution
In a branched project, branches are changed in parallel and paying attention to these changes is important for planning how and when to integrate. If the amount of change being introduced is large or the changes are in some way incompatible, the integrations may be particularly problematic.

Code Churn
When planning integration work, our participants consider the amount of code churn, which is the total number of lines of code changed and not yet integrated, as a gross measure of how difficult an integration will be. Broadly speaking, the more different two branches are the more likely that there will be integration problems that are difficult to diagnose.

When dealing with thousands of changes across dozens of branches on a daily basis, it is not feasible to throughly examine the impact of individual changes, but code churn is used to make a "high level assessment of risk" (P6) for integration decisions. Indeed, "the biggest [integration] cost is the payload that each integration is bringing into a common branch. The larger the payload...the more chances that something will not work well" (P5) and it was "always the case that a lot of code changes meant a lot of latency" (P1). That is, larger amounts of churn have resulted in longer integrations and increased pressure on the release schedule.

The volume of changes that have to be integrated is also a function of the number of branches being integrated over some period of time, and this number tends to increase towards the end of project milestones—the last chance for significant changes before a release date. When planning integrations, P2 considers how many branches have "significant payload" (or code churn) to integrate at the end of a milestone, because he has found that even integrating four branches with significant changes in one day is "almost impossible to do" without breaking the mainline.

If at any time there is an integration problem that delays subsequent integrations, the volume of changes that need to be integrated in a potentially short amount of time grows as the delay continues. This "mounting pressure" (P2) increases the likelihood of additional integration problems. For example, if an integration results in "a major performance regression" our participants do not allow integrations from other branches until "a root cause analysis on the regression" is completed. A decision then needs to be made about whether to continue delaying integrations to avoid the problem getting "compounded by more code getting piled on top of it" (P2), backing out the integration that resulted in the regression, or allowing the known regression to remain in the mainline. In any given situation, it is difficult to know which option introduces more risk to the schedule.

Being able to view where pressure is building in the project can help influence better integration decisions; in particular, with integration effort estimation and when to sacrifice quality to relieve the code churn pressure. If detected with enough warning, steps can be taken to mitigate risk through stricter integration regulation, particularly when close to a release date.

Conflicting Changes

Conflicting changes are incompatible code modifications—they can be literal, such as changes to the same line of code, or they can be subtle, for example, when "two functions got added with the exact same name in different branches, except one was 'virtual public' and the other 'public virtual'" (P7). These more subtle conflicts are not detected by the version control system during a merge and "are the harder ones that cost more" (P7).

In branched development environments, conflicting changes typically are not discovered until branches integrate. This latency can cause conflicts to build up and be compounded, increasing the risk of delays. The integration policy of the organization attempts to mitigate these risks by first requiring branches to integrate downstream (for example, from the mainline into a staging branch), resolve any conflicts and test, before integrating upstream. This process ensures that any conflicts are fixed locally in the branch before being shared with the rest of the organization.

This process breaks down, however, when several branches attempt to integrate within a short time period. These situations can arise when, due to scheduling or business demands, branches must integrate by a certain date. A branch's initial downstream integration can take several days to complete, and in that time other branches will integrate upstream, forcing the branch to take another downstream integration to absorb the latest changes. As described by P3:

> "Then I submit, and I come up with a bunch of merge conflicts, because of all of a sudden other people have checked in [to the mainline]. Well, at that point, what do I do? The best that I can hope for is resolve the merge conflicts, try and do a build, and then just hope for the best. Or I start the whole integration process over again, in which case I never finish."

Individual branches being integrated may be in good states, but when conflicts are resolved on-the-fly, there is a greater risk of defects. The threat to the release schedule in this case is the "hoping for the best." The code base is far too complex to accurately predict whether conflicts were resolved correctly without running the test suite. But if strict adherence to the downstream before upstream integration policy is required, there can be even greater delays. A key integration decision in this context is choosing an ordering for integrations that can reduce the amount or severity of conflicts. To gather information on conflicts to help with integration planning, P7 often performs a mock integration several days prior to the merge date in order to see "how many conflicts" there are and whether "anything looks bad."

For higher-level integration ordering decisions, a broader view of the project is required. Within the organization, the code base is structured in such a way that directories roughly correspond to development teams or branches. As a result, different parts of the code are expected to be modified in different branches. Our participants consider a large volume of change outside of these directories to indicate the potential for conflicting changes; a situation P2 described as "a storm waiting to happen, there is a convergence zone." To minimize risk, this information can be used to create a more effective integration ordering.

Branch Health

Some considerations around code churn and conflicts, as discussed above, may encourage frequent integrations, however our participants tended to delay integrations based on issues related to *branch health*. Problems in a branch, if integrated up, result in those problems being spread to other branches, impacting the work of other teams and the stability of the mainline. Our participants are concerned with three aspects of branch health in particular: (1) bugs and bug counts, (2) feature completeness, and (3) test runs and results.

Bugs and Bug Counts

The participants frequently identified bugs as a key input to integration decisions; in particular, estimating when a branch will be ready to integrate for scheduling purposes. In this case, the bugs are those that are open in a branch before it integrates. Bug information was used differently by different participants.

Participant P3, a development lead, can not assess which individual bugs in the different branches are "more risky." Across the project there can be hundreds or thousands of open bugs depending on the point in the development cycle. A deep consideration of what the bugs mean is infeasible, so instead he is simply concerned with the number of open bugs for each branch as a predictor of which "branch is at a greater risk of not making it because there is more [expected] churn, so there is more things that could go wrong." P2, a release manager, also uses the number of open bugs as a predictor of future code churn:

> "You take any 30 bugs...some will be small, some will be big, and they will average out in code churn dispersion. So [near a release date], we are pretty good just by looking at bug count and directly correlating that to risk, in terms of how much more stabilization there is going to be, and do we need to move our milestone out. Bug count is really what drives a lot of those decisions."

It is important to note that P2 distinguishes between the time periods close to release dates and during development milestones. Development milestones, also known as coding milestones, are the periods of work where new features tend to be introduced (roughly corresponding the alpha stages of the release). At development milestones, the bug counts tend to be very large and the association with churn is not very accurate—likely because they are accompanied by millions of lines of code in new development. Near release dates, however, typically only bug fixes are integrated (and are heavily regulated) and the association with churn is more accurate. But in general, predicting the impact of bugs on the release schedule remains a "gut feel" (P2).

It may seem unwise to have active bugs during integrations as the defects will be propagated to other branches, "but in reality [there are] always bugs when integrations happen" (P7). There are many reasons to integrate features that have bugs;

for example, if a branch with a dependent feature needs the code (even if incomplete) or would be at risk for delaying the release schedule. The justification is summarized by P4:

> "The style we choose is to let people integrate with exceptions as long as we discuss it and we understand the risk on the schedule, and we approve it. The other side would be, 'no, you cannot integrate unless you fix everything', we do not do that. This latter style makes the predictions you are asking about easier, but at the same time we can miss opportunities. You can end up cutting a feature prematurely from an integration."

Within the organization, bugs are an important input to integration decisions as they can be associated with future code churn. This risk assessment supports the difficult integration decision to either delay an integration because of open bugs, or permit the integration with defects in order to not delay the product or fail to deliver certain features to customers.

Feature Completeness

Feature development in our participants' organization is parallelized among many branches (see Figure 1). Work on these features is broken down into "work items" (P5) and a branch schedule details when those work items should be completed. Tracking progress on work items "provides a sense of completeness" or a measure of the "maturity" (P5) of the code in a given branch; a branch with many outstanding work items, "might still be in a state where nothing is really working" (P5).

In addition to preferring to not integrate code until there are no open bugs, our participants prefer to integrate code once "the work items are complete and no bugs are pending" (P5). However scheduling issues, such as plans around end-to-end testing of product scenarios that require the integration of code across multiple branches, may force features to be integrated before completion to work out any broad integration problems as development progresses.

Knowledge about the "schedule and completeness" (P7) of the features in a branch being integrated is used to estimate "how many integrations you need after your [first] integration" (P4) in order to completely integrate the features. Determining the number of subsequent integrations needed is mostly based on the velocity of work being completed in the branch. Because there are significant costs associated with integrations themselves—in this project, an integration takes 24-48 hours if there are no problems—P4 has found that estimating the number of future integrations is a useful input to scheduling decisions.

While tracking work items is a typical way to track progress in development projects, the distinction to make in branched development environments is that this data needs to be considered, and presented effectively, at the branch level.

Test Runs and Results

Testing was often raised as an important consideration by the interview participants. Of course, there are many testing considerations in the software release process. And like feature completeness, tracking test results is a typical way to measure progress and quality. But here, our primary consideration is the relationship between testing and integration decisions in a parallel development environment. The testing that occurs during an integration "is how I am going to judge the success or failure of the integration" (P3).

However, the time to stabilize during an integration is unpredictable, which complicates scheduling decisions. For an integration to be complete, the branch must be healthy and stable, but "given that the feature [branch] is good, we do not actually know the mainline will be good once it gets in" (P6). We have previously discussed a severe 45 day delay that occurred when many branches integrated in a short time period. In that situation, the majority of the 45 days was spent stabilizing the mainline branch. A contributing factor to this stabilization unpredictability is that "if you are under resource constraints, it is possible your branch will only run 5% of the actual tests versus the [mainline] running 100% of the tests" (P7). In other words, because the full test suite contains hundreds of thousands of tests that would take over a week to execute, teams must settle on running a subset of the suite in their branches. So one of the causes of the delay was that different branches run different sets of tests, and when a greater proportion of the tests are run after an integration, the outcome is not predictable.

The strategy taken by the organization to reduce integration stabilization time and force more predictability into the release process has been to redefine the integration tests. The original integration test suite consisted of about 500 tests that had been slowly accumulating over the course of 8 years. Recently, the 500 tests have been replaced with 24 new integration tests that represent important end-to-end customer scenarios, which all feature branches have some stake in. Great importance is placed on the tests not being "flaky" (P1), in that there is confidence that a failure during an integration represents a true product bug. The new approach has so far led to fewer major integration problems than the previous approach, but it has not yet been used through a full release cycle.

Integration decisions involving testing are typically about how much time to plan for stabilization, and the actions that can be taken to reduce the stabilization time. Our participants would appreciate more information about the testing being done on each branch to help estimate the stabilization costs for the integrations. While they have found that these costs can be minimized by optimizing the tests that are run during integrations, this remains a difficult problem for their organization.

Project Awareness

Project awareness covers knowledge of the system under development and its supporting infrastructure. Because the participants' system is extremely large and complex, it is infeasible for those making integration decisions to possess system-wide, in-depth technical knowledge. Instead, the interviews identified three important high-level considerations: the dependencies between branches, where the development in each branches is situated in the system architecture, and the reliability of the project's infrastructure systems.

Dependencies

Awareness of dependencies, and especially *new* dependencies, was frequently cited as a factor in integration decisions; in particular, in how much time to plan for an integration. To estimate the time required to integrate a feature branch through a staging branch and into the mainline, an important consideration is how that code will affect the branches at each step, and how other branches will affect it, so a branch dependency becomes a scheduling dependency:

> "Parallel development exercises your ability to think about the bigger picture. Now, you cannot just sit in your office and say, 'The feature is going to be done and integrate on that day.' No, you have to go and look around to figure out what are other teams integrating that depends on you, or what you depend on them, so that [the mainline] is not on floor once everybody meets there. So you need to do dependency analysis and be very familiar with each others schedules." (P5)

Part of the problem is that defects caused by dependency changes may require significant effort to fix and may force design changes, which can cause stabilization times to balloon. In fact, changes in APIs that are used by several features have been a "good portion" (P1) of the most disruptive release delays in the project. P6 describes the implications of dependency failures encountered during merges:

> "Functional dependencies can cause a long tail of bugs to be fixed, and can have bugs that require the involvement of many teams. So when a behaviour is changed, there is no way to change it back. But if you broke somebody, then you start having to negotiate between the people who needed the change and the people who needed it to not have happened."

A "long tail of bugs" refers to quality issues that arise long after the integration is complete. Such issues are more likely when dependency information is unavailable or not used during integration planning. Dependency analysis is challenging for our participants because the project has thousands of components in the feature branches and the dependency graph "is like a hairball" (P2). However, our participants have found that performing frequent (about once every two weeks) and early integrations can help identify dependencies between code being changed in different branches. Frequent integrations have helped add greater predictability to integration planning as the risk of long stabilization times is reduced:

> "Part of the problem that we were having when doing integrations every milestone or so, is that you do not figure out your dependencies or your dependents until really late in the product cycle, when many things are coming together and everyone is trying to determine what were the resulting dependencies. So by doing a lot more integrations often, we weed out some of these dependencies as we go, instead of creating a large amount of debt that we end up having to pay all together." (P5)

System Architecture

From the participants' experience, where a branch's source code changes are in the system architecture can strongly influence the outcome of an integration. P2 describes the system architecture as a "layer cake," with the most fundamental features comprising the bottom layer. In terms of risk during integrations, "the lower the payload in the stack, the more chances that something will not work well" (P5). In this project, the lower layers have had a "humongous impact" on the release schedule by "blasting [out] code that was putting people completely on the floor" (P1).

The key integration decision in this case is to determine an effective ordering for branch integrations. The organization attempts to mitigate the risk of destabilization by identifying the features in the lower layers and encouraging those branches to integrate first. This approach, in theory, allows the fundamental features to stabilize in the mainline branch and be absorbed into the features branches before those feature branches integrate, giving them time to adjust to any breaking dependency changes. The approach is further described by P2:

> "We also recognize that for teams higher up in the cake to be productive, it is best that the [lower layers] get a head start, and it is best that their milestones are offset from the others. So in the broader milestone, we take half of the teams and say, 'you guys are going to try and hit halfway in the milestone' and then the rest of the layer cake, 'you are going to hit at the end.'"

The architecture information is most useful during development milestones, because "towards the end of a product cycle, that assessment is less important because each branch ought to be working on bug fixes" (P3). Nevertheless, a broad understanding of system architecture supports integration decisions by providing guidance on how to better regulate the integrations—particularly, to avoid a situation where a low-level branch integrates after several high-level branches and breaks their integrations after-the-fact.

Infrastructure

Infrastructure systems—version control, build, and test—are the backbone of any integration, and the participants stressed the importance of keeping them "rock solid" (P5). The problem is that infrastructure adds another dimension to integrations that can have a significant impact on their outcome. These additional concerns are described by P6:

> "In the case of integrations, there is a much broader class of things that will go wrong, and I think we have much more trouble predicting the probability that those things will happen. We have build tools issues, we have compiler issues... [There are] more different sources of breakage."

While the infrastructure is there to support integration activities, it can also derail an integration if there is any instability. This problem is exacerbated when developers have little knowledge of the systems involved in the integration and how to troubleshoot them. For instance, P7 discussed how a complex problem with the build system caused a great amount of frustration:

> "There were race conditions in the build system. So, it is possible you do an integration, you build fine and it looks good. Then you build on better hardware, and because stuff gets parallelized more, you end up in the race conditions in the build system. The [merge] was easy, but you're getting regressions from the build system and tracking these down and reproducing them is nearly impossible."

Awareness of the infrastructure supporting integrations is an important factor in costing integrations. Having some measure of confidence in the reliability of the infrastructure systems, and the capabilities of those using them, allows one to adjust the planned length of integrations accordingly.

Project Traffic Control

Integration is fundamentally about moving code changes between branches with the goal of taking work done in parallel and combining it into one code base that can be released. The way branches are organized defines paths for the flow of changes between branches and integration policies determine how frequently code flows along those paths.

Branch Organization

Branch organization is a fundamental component of integration decisions, as branch structure in the version control system defines how code will flow between the branches. For example, knowing how many integrations are required to get a feature into a dependent branch across the organization is a valuable planning aid, because "there is a cost, a fixed cost, from going from branch-to-branch" (P1). That is, for every integration, there is a minimum amount of time and effort that must be spent merging, building, and testing.

> "Even if a feature branch wanted to integrate, it would take them a few weeks before that code actually got up to [the mainline]. And of course, it would have to go down the other side so it could be a month or more before other teams saw the code." (P1)

The organization has used several different branch topologies over 10 years. In 2005, there were 3 branches with 150 developers working in each. In this model, the branches were constantly broken because of the large amount of churn happening on a daily basis. By 2010 the pendulum had swung the other direction, and there were 25 branches underneath the mainline, with even more feature branches underneath those. However, our participants found that with this model the cost to propagate code became overwhelming because of the fixed integration costs multiplied by the large number of branches. The model in use today is depicted in Figure 1, which has 15 branches under the mainline with feature branches underneath those—and it has so far "had the best of both worlds...[and] worked really well" (P1).

By optimizing the branch structure, the goal is to reduce the overall amount of integrations while not sacrificing the benefits of branching. The decision to create a particular structure with features being developed in particular branches is typically done at the beginning of a release cycle. However, decision makers must also be prepared to adjust the structure on-the-fly:

> "When features are in different branches, validating a lot of [customer scenarios] is harder because you can not get features to interact with each other as they are in different branches. So sometimes we end up delaying this type of work until a time when they come together....which introduces uncertainty into the product because you are getting this data a lot later than you would have liked to." (P5)

A key observation from P3's experience is that important end-to-end customer scenarios can be difficult to verify in a branched development environment, which creates uncertainty about the product quality from a release perspective. P3 went on to discuss a potential solution: "We tend to have branches across organizational boundaries, but we are trying to have some of those branches be across end-to-end scenarios...so that we facilitate this type of testing earlier on in the product cycle." P6 echoed support for this new branching model, believing that it is "a dramatically lower cost than any other option."

So, in order to make effective integration decisions, particularly around release scheduling, a clear understanding of the branch organization is required. Similarly, decision makers must be prepared to alter the branch organization on-the-fly to mitigate risk to the release schedule.

Code Flow

The flow of code between branches proved to be significant concern for the interview participants. The problem is that infrequent integrations lead to unpredictability, particularly in stabilization costs. This finding was hard-earned by the organization: "One of our learnings from the last release, was that teams that had the most trouble, the least predictability of getting their code into [the mainline], were the ones furthest separated from [the mainline] in terms of integrations" (P2). The integration decision in this case is determining how frequently branches should perform upstream and downstream integrations. P5 discusses the historical implications of this decision for the organization:

> "We had the pendulum at the two extremes: one where we were not [validating the results of our integrations] and it was cheaper, but we would break things in [the mainline], and then we swung it too much the other way where our integrations would be very expensive and teams would not want to pay for them, so they would delay doing integrations until as late as possible, and there would be a huge amount of integrations in a short amount of time. And everything would be on the floor because of all of these things coming together."

The consequences of having a large amount of code integrated together at once have been detailed in the discussion on code churn, and they can be severe—a 45 day delay was the worst reported case. The difficult integration decision in this context is to determine the ideal integration frequency given the practical constraints in the development environment. P5 continues on to describe the outcome of this decision for the organization:

> "We have tried to put the pendulum somewhere in the middle where the size of the integrations and validations are smaller, and we are encouraging teams to do integrations more often to avoid the big integrations at the end. We are not fully done because not all the systems are in place, but I would say it has gotten a bit better than it was in the past."

Regardless of the strategy being used, in order to make integration decisions, it is important to know how frequently integrations are happening to and from various branches. If any branch is "stale" (P4), not having integrated up or down for a long time, then there is greater chance for destabilization and a delay in the schedule because "that branch is going to have a much harder time integrating up" (P5). In these cases it can take a branch "two weeks to absorb whatever has been changing around them" (P3).

It is clear that code flow is a critical input to making effective integration decisions. It is important for decision makers to be aware of how frequently integrations are occurring between branches, and if any branches are introducing risk in the project by going stale. Plans should be adjusted based on this feedback to make the release schedule more predictable by encouraging integrations to and from branches that are trending towards staleness.

INFORMATION NEEDS

Despite many years of experience, integration decisions continue to be challenging for our participants. In the previous section we discussed 10 factors that are important in the participants' integration decision making process. In this section we discuss specific information needs implied by those factors and the extent to which those needs are met in the target organization.

Buse and Zimmerman have noted that there is significant research into information needs of developers, but a deficit in understanding the needs of managers [3]. Hence, the novelty of these information needs does not stem from the information itself, as many tools readily provide the data. Rather, the novelty is uncovering how the data can be processed, abstracted, and displayed to promote effective decision making for release management. For example, in a release meeting in our participants' organization where dozens of team representatives are present, we need to determine what information should be presented, and in what manner, to quickly facilitate good integration decisions.

Predicting Storms

It is valuable to identify conflicting changes as early as possible as they are a major source of integration risk. Early warnings of impending conflicts can be achieved by executing mock, or temporary, merges and builds between branches, which would identify the location and scale of conflicting code. This approach is similar to the speculative analysis proposed by Brun et. al. [2]. As each pair of branches needs to be continuously mock-integrated, the process should be automated and executed in manner that would not seriously degrade the performance of the version control system. Currently, such a system does not exist in the organization; P7 does perform mock-integrations on an ad-hoc basis, but the resulting conflict information is used for managing his personal workload. Ideally the data should be project-wide, generated close to real-time, and presented in a single view that is appropriate for large collaborative meetings.

The next concern is where and when the conflicts will meet. The conflicts represent impending storms (destabilization) and the challenge is to predict the point where they will materialize. Two pieces of information are required: the integration paths between branches and the branch integration schedules. The paths describe how code is intended to flow through the branches, such as the depiction in Figure 1. The schedules are the dates and times of each branch's intended upstream and downstream integrations. This information is typically communicated in meetings and added to internal wikis; however, the data is not accessible to other tools.

To more accurately predict collision points, teams should enter their (often changing) integration plans into a tool that can be leveraged by the mock-integration system. Alerts could then be provided about when, in which branch, and with what severity integration problems may occur. Such a system could promote better cooperation as teams can work together to alleviate the integration problems before they arise, or adjust their schedules to accommodate increased integration effort at future collision points.

Detecting Pressure

Pressure reflects the amount of code churn that has built up in a branch. The greater the volume of code, the more likely a branch will encounter integration problems. That is, as the amount of change grows between any two branches, even if separated by intermediate branches, then there is an increasing risk to the release schedule. Like a dam ready to burst, the large amount of code in the originating branch threatens to wash out the target.

Pressure can be prevented from rising to unacceptable levels by making good decisions about when to integrate and also when to back-out integrations that are causing delays. Code churn data is available from the version control system, but there is no system in place that effectively visualizes churn across all branches so that potential problems can be easily recognized in release meetings. Currently, last integration dates for each team are tracked on a wiki, but this data is input manually and can only provide a rough estimate of how much change has occurred. Precise churn data may be a better predictor of risk and can be frequently and automatically extracted.

Monitoring Feature and Dependency Flow

To make informed integration decisions, two key considerations are which features are currently in each branch and where are their dependencies. However, the version control system used by the organization monitors code flow only at the change-level, and because features can consist of thousands of individual changes, it is tedious to determine if a branch contains a particular feature in its entirety. There is no mechanism to associate multiple changes to the high-level concept of a *feature*.

Late in the release cycle, tracking changes individually is usually not a problem. Questions in release meetings tend to be around whether certain branches contain certain bug fixes, which are usually single changes. But in development milestones, there is a large amount of code churn and changes flow rapidly between branches. During this time, questions in release meetings are more likely to be about which branches contain a particular feature X, as well as which branches contain the feature dependencies of X. Answering these questions can quickly put branch test results into context (e.g., failures might be expected if certain features are not present), and can help facilitate efficient integration planning by knowing when and which branch to pull code from to have features meet and be tested.

Because these questions involve high-level abstractions of code flow, the solution must enable the association of a set of code changes to a revision of a feature. The idea is to streamline code flow analysis in release meetings by moving away from developer-centric per-change analysis to release-centric per-feature analysis. Such a tool would remove tedious version control log parsing, or having to build and run the product to see which features are present.

Tracking Health

Tracking test results, bugs, and task completion is the usual way to measure project health. But in branched software development, these metrics must be considered at the branch level. For example, due to resource constraints, individual branches in the organization do not run the entire test suite. Rather, branches run a subset of tests that are (believed to be) the most relevant to the features being developed in them. However, this practice creates blind spots for the release organization. The pass rate may be 100%, but if the branch is only running 1% of the test suite there is a large degree of uncertainty. When that branch integrates and a greater proportion of the test suite is run against its features, bugs can be discovered and significantly lengthen stabilization times.

The organization generally tracks metrics at the branch level. However, these metrics tend to be spread across many different systems—each with its own reporting mechanism. In a release meeting where status must be communicated quickly, this limitation slows information finding and integration decision making.

The ideal solution is to combine all branch metrics into a single view that can be expanded to reveal specific details. For example, in Figure 1, each branch could be coloured in a manner to suggest their overall health based on a weighting of the tracked metrics. Then, in a release meeting, attention can be drawn to the branches that are creating risk in the project.

THREATS TO VALIDITY

While the interview participants in our study act in a diverse set of roles, they nevertheless work in the same organization using many of the same tools and processes. The benefit of having participants from the same organization is that we are able to deeply explore experiences from several different perspectives, but it may be the case that the experiences are shaped by the particular organizational culture.

Efforts were made to increase validity by initiating the interviews with questions resulting from prior work [12]. Nevertheless, care should be taken when generalizing our findings. The organization is very large, as is the product under development. The problems encountered in this environment may not occur in smaller companies, or may not occur to the same degree.

FUTURE WORK

From our experience, the lack of information support experienced by our participants is not unique. In many software development organizations, the necessary data may be available; however, the information is dispersed and is not processed and visualized in a way that is useful for release management. Nevertheless, a systemic review of existing tools is needed to broadly understand the extent that tools support release management in branched development projects. Such an endeavor is part of a larger effort to implement our ideas in an industry setting. We have begun work with another large organization, one that is encountering similar integration challenges to those described in this paper, by developing a tool that incorporates the described information needs and is measured statistically for effectiveness.

Future contributions to CSCW research will consider how organizations can manage branching of any intellectual product. We expect branch evolution and branch health to be concerns in any product that requires people to work in parallel. Awareness is already well studied in CSCW [5], but here we introduce the notion of project awareness as essential to managing branches in version control. Project traffic control considers how work is organized to facilitate awareness and collaboration within large teams, and why it is important to constantly monitor it for ineSfficiency. As with our findings, the information needs of those managing software projects also applies to those managing other products. Predicting storms, detecting pressure, monitoring flow, and tracking health are all general concepts. While our emphasis on software engineering may be domain-specific, these concepts outline a framework for considering and researching version control branching as a general CSCW activity.

SUMMARY

We have conducted an interview study focused on how our participants make branching and integration decisions while managing releases. We found that making these decisions is complex and requires considering many factors such as code churn, potential conflicts, bug counts, and dependencies between branches. We also identified several information needs that can support integration decision-making in a branched context by helping release decision makers predict storms of conflicts, detect pressure building up from non-integrated changes, monitor code flow between branches, and track branch health.

More generally, we found that parallel development with version control branching can have a significant impact on the ability to release software on time. The interview participants in this study experienced many such delays, some several weeks in duration. For businesses, tool makers, and researchers, a key message to take away from this paper is that branching, while beneficial for some aspects of collaborative software development, leads to complex integration decisions with significant costs. These considerations should be incorporated into their work to ensure the results are useful and relevant in industry settings.

ACKNOWLEDGMENTS

We would like to express our appreciation to our seven interview participants for their generous sharing of knowledge and experience, and to Dr. Saul Greenberg for his valuable feedback. This study has been funded through the Natural Sciences and Engineering Research Council of Canada (NSERC) discovery grants 250343-07 and 341367-07.

REFERENCES

1. Barcellini, F., Détienne, F., Burkhardt, J.-M., and Sack, W. A socio-cognitive analysis of online design discussions in an open source software community. *Interact. Comput. 20* (January 2008), 141–165.
2. Brun, Y., Holmes, R., Ernst, M., and Notkin, D. Speculative analysis: exploring future development states of software. In *FSE/SDP workshop on Future of software engineering research*, FoSER '10, ACM (2010), 59–64.
3. Buse, R., and Zimmermann, T. Information needs for software development analytics. Tech. rep., Microsoft Research, 2011.
4. Corbin, J., and Strauss, A. *Basics of Qualitative Research*, 3rd ed. SAGE Publications, 2008.
5. Gutwin, C., and Greenberg, S. The importance of awareness for team cognition in distributed collaboration. In *Team Cognition: Understanding the Factors that Drive Process and Performance*, APA Press (2004), 177–201.
6. Hansen, P., and Jrvelin, K. Collaborative information retrieval in an information-intensive domain. *Information Processing and Management 41*, 5 (2005), 1101 – 1119.
7. Ko, A., DeLine, R., and Venolia, G. Information needs in co-located software development teams. In *International conference on Software Engineering*, ICSE '07, IEEE Computer Society (Washington, DC, USA, 2007), 344–353.
8. Limayem, M., Banerjee, P., and Ma, L. Impact of gdss: opening the black box. *Decis. Support Syst. 42* (November 2006), 945–957.
9. Mens, T. A state-of-the-art survey on software merging. *Software Engineering, IEEE Transactions on 28*, 5 (may 2002), 449–462.
10. Paul, S., and Reddy, M. Understanding together: sensemaking in collaborative information seeking. In *Computer supported cooperative work*, CSCW '10, ACM (New York, NY, USA, 2010), 321–330.
11. Perry, D., Siy, H., and Votta, L. Parallel changes in large scale software development: an observational case study. In *International Conference on Software Engineering* (apr 1998), 251–260.
12. Phillips, S., Sillito, J., and Walker, R. Branching and merging: an investigation into current version control practices. In *International workshop on Cooperative and human aspects of software engineering*, CHASE '11, ACM (2011), 9–15.
13. Rönkkö, K., Dittrich, Y., and Randall, D. When plans do not work out: How plans are used in software development projects. *Comput. Supported Coop. Work 14* (October 2005), 433–468.
14. Ruhe, G. Software engineering decision support—a new paradigm for learning software organizations. In *Advances in Learning Software Organizations*, vol. 2640 of *Lecture Notes in Computer Science*. Springer, 2003, 104–113.
15. Ruhe, G. *Product Release Planning: Methods, Tools and Applications*. CRC Press, 2010.
16. Saarelainen, M.-M., Koskinen, J., Ahonen, J., Kankaanpaa, I., Sivula, H., Lintinen, H., Juutilainen, P., and Tilus, T. Group decision-making processes in industrial software evolution. In *International Conference on Software Engineering Advances*, IEEE Computer Society (2007), 78–.
17. Sack, W., Détienne, F., Ducheneaut, N., Burkhardt, J.-M., Mahendran, D., and Barcellini, F. A methodological framework for socio-cognitive analyses of collaborative design of open source software. *Comput. Supported Coop. Work 15* (June 2006), 229–250.
18. Sassenburg, H. A multi-disciplinary view on software release decisions. In *International workshop on Workshop on interdisciplinary software engineering research*, WISER '06, ACM (2006), 45–52.
19. Sonnenwald, D., and Pierce, L. Information behavior in dynamic group work contexts: interwoven situational awareness, dense social networks and contested collaboration in command and control. *Information Processing and Management 36*, 3 (2000), 461 – 479.
20. Walrad, C., and Strom, D. The importance of branching models in scm. *Computer 35* (September 2002), 31–38.
21. Wright, H., and Perry, D. Subversion 1.5: A case study in open source release mismanagement. In *ICSE Workshop on Emerging Trends in Free/Libre/Open Source Software Research and Development*, FLOSS '09, IEEE Computer Society (2009), 13–18.

Interactional Identity: Designers and Developers Making Joint Work Meaningful and Effective

Judith M. Brown
Psychology &
Computer Science
MMJBrown@gmail.com

Gitte Lindgaard
Psychology
Carleton University,
Ottawa, Canada
Gitte_Lindgaard@carleton.ca

Robert Biddle
Computer Science &
Cognitive Science
Robert_Biddle@carleton.ca

ABSTRACT
We studied collaborating interface designers and software developers engaged in multidisciplinary software creation work. Twenty-one designers and developers in 8 organizations were interviewed to understand how each specialist viewed team interactions. We also shadowed most participants as they worked on novel software projects with user interface design challenges. A grounded theory analysis of interview transcripts showed that designers and developers construct unique identities in the process of collaborating that provide meaning to their artefact-mediated interactions, and that help them to effectively accomplish the work of creating novel software. Our model of interactional identities specifies a number of aspects of joint project work in which an interactional identity is expressed. We suggest these identities are constructed to bridge a gap between how designers and developers were taught to enact their roles and the demands of project-specific work.

Author Keywords
Collaboration; interactional identity; design; development

ACM Classification Keywords
H.5.3 Information Interfaces and Presentation (e.g., HCI): Theory and models

General Terms
Design; Theory

INTRODUCTION
Collaboration is purposeful joint action that creates shared understanding leading to the development of shared goals and visions of a group's desired outcomes. Collaboration can also be about making direct progress on a group's outcomes. Collaboration is an increasingly important part of many complex activities since these often cannot be accomplished by a single individual or the skillset of a single discipline.

Software creation work is a complex, creative, artefact-rich, multidisciplinary, and highly collaborative activity. When we began our research we wanted to understand what meaning shared design artefacts (e.g. sketches, lists, documents, and so on) had for software team members as they engaged in the early, open-ended, influential stages of software creation work, sometimes called the concept design stage. To focus our research we studied interaction designers and developers because they held key roles on the team and because their work was highly interdependent. Our aim was to understand the collaborative work of designers and developers in depth in order to contribute to the development of better tools that would support their collaborations.

In the course of this research we discovered that software designers and developers construct project-specific *identities* that appear to 1) imbue talk- and artefact-mediated interactions with meaning and 2) provide direction to their team interactions to make them effective. This paper argues for the existence of, and elaborates on, this pervasive and valuable conceptual tool that we have named *interactional identity*. This cognitive tool appears to be an essential, but largely unexplored, aspect of collaborative work that enables social interactions. This paper provides evidence for the existence of interactional identities and explores aspects of this identity.

BACKGROUND
Understanding collaborative work is an active research area crossing many domains; collaboration has been studied to meet business aims, to support and sustain community organizations, and to ensure positive health-care outcomes. Here we investigate collaboration from the perspective of collaborators, studying it to contribute to the large body of research on the creation of better software products. However, because our research investigates a conceptual, cognitive tool that collaborators in general would likely use, our research is of potential relevance to multiple domains.

A large body of research exists on identities because identities are an aid to understanding an individual's actions, thoughts and even feelings [2]. We focus on interactional identities at work, which are an important aspect of the overall identity of many adults. We show that such identities are meaningful to those who construct them because they help that individual to make sense of their team interactions. As such, we suggest that these constructs satisfy a personal need for a sense of self and a sense of self in relation to others. Similarly, we will show that these identities are also used by individuals to structure and direct their interactions with other team members, and as such they influence the outcomes of collaborative work. In short, such identities satisfy psychological needs and guide goal-directed interactions.

One strand of research uses social identity theory [27]. Of particular relevance are studies of the relationship between shared identity constructs meaningful to software workers. Fidel and Garner asked which shared identities were strongest in computer professionals when they surveyed 125 computer professionals with master's degrees. Focusing on the impacts of organizational identity and professional identity on personal identity they found that "Computer workers with advanced degrees have some elements of a professional identity, but show little evidence that this identity conflicts with or supersedes their identity as corporate employees" ([10], p. 122). Carmel focused more on the influences on developers' professional identities [6]. He studied developers in six countries and investigated how national identities contributed to the professional identities of software developers in each of these countries. He found that professional identities of software developers are influenced by "national myths".

Some other work, taking a different tack on the study of groups [19], has addressed *enacted* identities. Brown studied engineers' identities in the workplace and showed these are deliberately influenced by employer actions and actively shaped by engineers in response to many factors in their professional and personal lives [3]. Kilker studied 26 student software teams and found that team members enact either technology-centric or socially-centric 'design identities' when interacting with each other [13]. Turkle and Papert found computer programmers created their own personalized "style of working", reflecting concrete "ways of knowing" [28]. Their work showed that cultural identities of "those who compute" are commonly rejected and replaced by more personalized identities. Collectively, this line of research suggests that enacted identities, which are shaped by many factors, are the most relevant identity in workplace settings.

Our work is grounded in cultural-historical psychology and more specifically activity theory, which provides a sociocultural and historical lens. We use rigorous methods for data collection and analysis [1, 23], and focus on enacted identities constructed in the context of real project work in organizational settings. In an activity-theoretical framework [30, 9, 8, 31] identities are understood as cognitive tools that can be used within an activity system. Identities are also often seen as being constructed in the process of engaging in an activity, or as an outcome of an activity [5]. Work on identity from an activity-theoretic perspective often makes connections between identity and artefact use. For example, Vagän suggested "A sociocultural perspective is needed to capture how the incorporation of artifacts provides people with tools of agency and identity; how artifacts mediate, expand, and limit action; and how they work as tools for individual's identities in cultural worlds." ([29], p. 45).

We studied the enacted identities of designers and developers, which we have called "interactional identities" from an activity-theoretic perspective. To date these identities have only been studied in very broad terms [3, 13, 28]. We aim to show how they are expressed in the context of activities, why they are created, the aspects in the workplace and an individual's life that influence an interactional identity's nature, their variation across a discipline, the nature of interactional identities as they change over time, and their use in actual artefact-mediated team interactions.

METHOD

Eight organizations in eastern Canada that developed software for a global or Canadian market participated in this research. At each organization we identified a particular team and software project as our focus of interest. The teams we selected were multidisciplinary and co-located and working on projects in the early open-ended stage, which required significant amounts of team interaction. This mostly occurred face-to-face, but some of it occurred through electronic means. The teams varied with respect to the products they were designing, their processes (waterfall, Scrum and XP), their organizational culture, and their market, but they all created successful and deployable software. A typical team comprised 7 people; the smallest was 3 and largest was 37. Twenty-one designers and developers, at least one designer and developer from each team, volunteered for this research. Many of the designers and developers were also team leaders. The role of the designers on the team varied greatly, from a graphic designer with responsibility for screen design to a user experience designer with much broader responsibilities. Their years of experience in the discipline ranged from 2 to 40 years. The developers were mostly computer science university graduates, although one was a trade school graduate and another was self-taught. Their years of experience in the discipline ranged from 3 to 22 years. In all cases, the team's most salient desired outcome was the creation of the completed interactive software, which would be produced by their collective skills.

The primary researcher (and co-author) was a psychologist with a background in software development and interaction design. We were able to observe 14 of the 21 participants in our study at work (i.e., 67%). We first followed the designer for several days and then the developer, choosing days where the project work we were focusing on was their top priority. At all organizations we took notes and photographs of computer-generated and hand-drawn artefacts since these were prominent in interactions; we have described these artefacts in [4]. Our observation period spanned 93 days in total across all organizations, but we observed only on 23 of these days when the project work we were tracking was our participants' top priority. We conducted 21 interviews, each lasting approximately one hour. The interviews were the primary source of data for this analysis; other data served to confirm and enhance understanding. We asked questions about their project, their team, the team's process, the artefacts they used to support communication within the team, the end product, and also about their interactions with their fellow designer (or developer). We also asked about project tensions and their resolution. We then transcribed our interview.

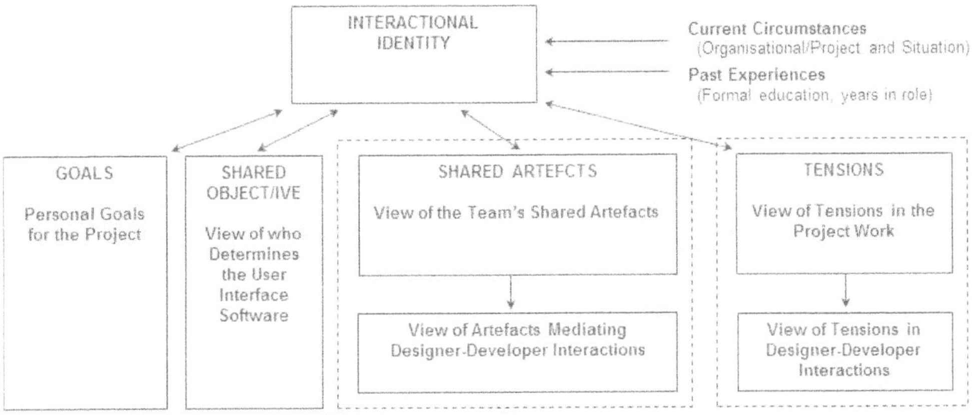

Figure 1. A model of interactional identity showing six aspects of a designer or developer's team work in which it is expressed, and influences on its specific incarnation for an individual: previous experiences, current circumstances and desired outcomes. The 6 categories were 6 of 21 categories that were the outcome of the open coding step. The higher-level category 'interactional identity' was the outcome of the axial coding step.

Grounded theory was used because it is very suitable for exploratory work, and for analyzing interview data and producing theories about the meaning participants ascribe to their actions. We followed the guidelines of Strauss and Corbin [26], but substituted Strauss's 'theory' of action, which provides the underlying perspective for Strauss and Corbin's approach, with an activity-'theoretic' perspective on action. This allowed us to use grounded theory from an activity-theoretical perspective, and to make our basic preconceptions overt (i.e. that our analysis would address subjects engaging in activity, and would assume that interesting aspects of this activity were their goals, their tools, and so on). At the heart of the grounded theory method is the method of constant comparison. Analysts, staying close to the data, create carefully defined codes and then higher-level categories that they constantly refine, combine, or break up as they test emerging theories. Therefore the categories or theories that emerge are a true reflection of the analyst's perspective and the data that were collected. This analysis introduced a variation to the standard use of grounded theory in that it was used to generate a theory about people engaged in interactions, but it also produced knowledge about individual variation within this theory. That is, we identified a cognitive strategy used by all individuals, but then also analyzed individual variations in the use of this strategy. Throughout, Atlas.ti was used to aid with coding more than a thousand quotes, and comparing, counting, and finding data subsets. The study was designed to follow standards for social validity, subjectivity, reflexivity, and the adequacy and integrity of the data and analysis [21].

THE INTERACTIONAL IDENTITY CONCEPT

The derivation of the concept *interactional identity* was the major outcome of the grounded theory analysis. The first step, the open coding step (a systematic reading of an initial set of transcripts) produced 15 saturated categories. As a simple example of an action in this step, a quote such as "My goal for this project is to ensure that my fellow team members converge on a design concept quickly." would suggest the creation of a category 'Personal Goal'. As we found other quotes expressing a participant's personal goals for the project (from the same participant and others), we would code these similarly. After coding all of the transcripts the category 'Personal Goal' was saturated and then the category served as a tag or container to collect all of these similar quotes together. Fifteen other saturated categories were produced in this manner.

In the axial coding step we produced a large spreadsheet to reflect on the quotes for each participant across all the categories. We began to see that 8 of the 15 categories reflected similar patterns in how people made sense of their work environments. As we explored the interview and observation data, the commonalities appeared stronger, with people exhibiting a pattern of behaviour and perspective that brought coherency to several different aspects of their work with others on their projects. We identified this as a higher-level category that we labeled 'interactional identity'. The quotes in each of the 8 categories (the aspects exhibiting coherency) reflected how the individual viewed their collaborative work. This new unifying theoretical concept then became the central interest of the analysis. Consequently, 7 categories of no particular relevance to this concept were dropped. We present 6 of the remaining 8 categories here, dropping two more that were insufficiently distinctive.

Figure 1 shows our model of 'interactional identity'. The 6 categories each show a way in which an individual's 'interactional identity' is reflected. Each category identifies an individual's 'view', by which we mean not only a passive opinion, but the active way they engage. An individual's interactional identity was reflected in their comments about their personal goals for the project, and their view of who determines the user interface software (the team's shared object). It was also reflected in an individual's view of the team's shared artefacts. These were design artefacts that were used to support interactions. It was also reflected in their view of tensions in the team's project work, which are an inevitable aspect of software creation work. Some of the aspects that moderate an individual's interactional identity are their past experiences and current circumstances.

Once we were sure of this relationship, we re-analyzed the

data to find a way to concisely express an individual's interactional identity. We therefore created a descriptive phrase for each participant's interactional identity. This reflected what a participant said (usually 'between the lines'), about who they were when interacting with others on the team. When reviewing relevant quotes, we paid particular attention to unusual verbs (e.g. bind) or occasional analogies (e.g. "It's like being a movie director"). We then further distilled the descriptive phrases to a *handle* that fit with all the quotes in all six categories. Using the descriptive phrase and re-examining an individual's data we would try out and then frequently discard handles, until we found one that was completely satisfactory in the sense that it fit all the data tagged with the six categories and also our observations. The handles, not intended to be stereotypes, had the negative consequence of reducing the data and losing some richness for readers of this work, but handles are succinct and memorable and help with presenting results, such as our analysis of identities by years of experience beginning on page 7.

The next sections contain two detailed case studies: developer Wil and designer Owen [1], and we later outline others. In all these cases we use the four main categories shown in Figure 1 (Goals, Shared Objective, Shared Artefacts, Tensions) to document how an identity formed a coherent approach to project activity. This serves two purposes: it provides evidence for an 'interactional identity' as a distinct theoretical construct, and demonstrates how we identified the specific interactional identity of each individual.

DEVELOPER WIL'S INTERACTIONAL IDENTITY

Wil was one of three developers on a project team and was responsible for implementing the product, supervising a junior programmer, and liaising with a third programmer who was designing a database for the back end. He had 22 years of experience as a developer. Wil's project was in a constant state of flux. No one, not even the clients, could clearly specify the requirements, since these were constantly evolving. Part of the envisioned application may not even have been feasible, and on top of this, there were complex political issues related to the product's effect on the marketplace.

In interactions with others on his team Wil saw himself as a 'binder' or someone whose actions cause two elements to cohere or stick together in a coherent whole. In Wil's case the two elements to be bound were a variety of different artefacts, such as a mock-up of the user interface, a story of user interaction, or a database schema. The glue that caused the two elements to stick together was the program code he wrote and rigorously tested using a suite of test cases he also coded. In effect, by 'binding' artefacts that were produced by other team members, Wil produced the software. When Wil codes and writes test cases to test his code, he works from artefacts that other team members have created.

Goal: Wil's personal goal was to create the required functionality and test that it works as it should. This is a large and consuming task.

> Interviewer: How do you know when your goal in the project is achieved?
> Wil: ...when I can execute the app[lication]...We write tests ...to test ...each unit of work—like an object or a data access—so [that] ...at a certain level we know that it works—the functionality's been achieved.

Shared Object/ive: In Wil's view, each team member is responsible for certain aspects of the project and producing certain artefacts. He relies on, and expects that, others will do their job and produce the artefacts he needs to produce the code to generate the application (the team's shared object/ive). For example, he sees the designer as the person responsible for discerning important business and client issues, and the person who will specify, through suitable artefacts, the look, feel, and functionality of the user interface and the user stories that capture how the user interface will be used. Wil says the designer "gathers the business requirements from meetings with the client and [also the] documentation from them. He gathers the requirements and fleshes that out into [a list of written down] user stories." Wil sees the designer as a buffer between himself and the turbulent business world, and their client's ever-changing response to it.

Shared Artefacts: For Wil, artefacts play an important role. Shared artefacts represent a kind of high-level map that indicates the "path" someone else wants to take with their aspect of the work. These maps can indicate what a client or interaction designer wants in terms of the product. They play a strong role in guiding what Wil codes.

Wil is aware that certain artefacts (e.g., the mock-ups) require client approval and are more unstable relative to other team-produced shared artefacts, revealing his need for stable artefacts. He avoids unstable artefacts to prevent recoding. In Wil's view, new artefacts are created from others. In the following quote, Wil discusses mock-ups, stories, and database schemas in relation to the code that he must write.

> Wil: The main stakeholder is the client. They ...provide the ideas and their vision of what they want the application to do and what it looks like.

> Wil: During the estimating of the effort, [The designer] would do a walk-through of the mock-ups [guided by the stories] so that we [the developers] understand what's required. ...From that meeting we get a lot of knowledge to help us in designing it [the structure of the software]. ...And [the database analyst] ...he's at those meetings as well, to get an understanding.
> Interviewer: He seems to always have his database schema in front of him and is always considering the implications to that schema.
> Wil: Right. Exactly. Cause he'll use the mock-ups, as well [as the stories], to come up with the [database] schema. And ...on the developer's side, we do the same thing ...[Using] his [database] schema [artefact #1] and the user stories [artefact #2] ...we try to create the [software] objects that'll *bind* those two [artefacts] together.

As Wil sees it, new artefacts are created from old ones by 'binding,' an unusual verb he used that caught our attention.

[1]All personal and organizational names used in this paper are pseudonyms.

Wil saw stories and mock-ups as artefacts that he would bind through the software objects he created, which would produce the desired software. In Wil's view, sequences of binding actions (by himself and other developers, whom Wil also sees as binders) complete the application.

Tensions: One of Wil's aims was to protect himself from project tensions. Tensions arose in Wil's work when artefacts changed, because this created a tension between what others required and what he had coded. Wil wanted to remain productive and to focus on the work of binding. He appeared to find that the project moved forward when team members agreed on the key artefacts (e.g., stories and mock-ups).

> Sometimes, a picture is ...far easier for people to understand, [it] makes it clearer. It's always at a high level-right?—[the] relationship between objects, or relationships between pages—like navigation, ...or what's gonna be displayed on the page. Things like that. ...sometimes you wanna just ..., brainstorm through it to see if it makes sense. And then, once you've ...decided on a particular path then, ...everybody lines up on the same page.

Wil protected himself from wasted effort by coding the more stable parts of the application first. For instance, he understood that the mock-up was volatile and the stories were more stable, so he relied more on stories and he coded using the stories (i.e., the behavioural aspects of the user interface) before coding using the visual aspects of the user interface, which were captured in the mock-up.

Discussion of the 'Binder' Identity as Conceptual Tool: Wil's case was like all others analyzed in that all of the data coded by the six categories in the model together indicated one singular identity. Wil's goal was to make sure the application worked. He saw shared artefacts as things that team members produced (because each team member had responsibilities for different aspects of the the user interface) and things that he used in his 'binding' work, which produced tested software. Tensions arose within the team when shared artefacts were not stable. In particular, for Wil, unstable artefacts meant that he would have difficulty achieving his personal goal of ensuring the application worked.

Wil's identity as binder provided an additional meaning to his interactions beyond that of just being a developer. He used this identity to shield himself from much of the project's turmoil. It allowed him to focus on producing the quality code the team required. He looked at artefacts in terms of their potential to enter into his binding work, and he looked at producers of artefacts as agents in that process. This was a positive way of making sense of his work and likely also provided him with motivation and a sense of well-being in the challenging circumstances in which he found himself. Wil's identity also helped him to be effective because it gave him a way of assessing the work of others in the workplace, and helped him to prioritize which artefacts he should rely on first for his work (i.e. stable artefacts). Wil's identity likely arose out of his previous experiences (in particular knowledge of binding processes in another context, and also 22 years of experience as a developer), the current project circumstances, and his genuine desire to contribute to the success of the project.

DESIGNER OWEN'S INTERACTIONAL IDENTITY

Owen was a lead game designer and chief technology officer in his organization. He had 11 years of experience in design work. He was one of five people creating a game for an established client. The successful completion of this project would require a significant amount of creativity from all the team members and the coordination of the work output of 6 different types of designers and 2 developers. Owen's interactional identity of 'movie director' shines through in the aspects of Owen's work identified in the model depicted in Figure 1. However, unlike most other participants (e.g. Wil), Owen was conscious of his interactional identity, Owen represents the extreme case of someone who was more self-aware in this respect.

Goals: One of Owen's goals in his work as lead game designer was to find "the central motif" for the game. As Owen said, "The main thing in design is the concept, or the motif, and at this point [the very early stages of design] I have no idea what that's going to be". Another of Owen's goals was to motivate people so that they cared about their work. He also encouraged the team to explore and be creative. To do this, on occasion, he would deliberately make himself look foolish to allow others to take risks.

> You often have to, ...help them [the team] ...break out of their shell by doing it yourself first. ...like that example I gave, "Do it really, really loud, and then do it really, really soft." If I do that, and I take the risk of looking foolish, then you [someone who sees Owen taking risks] are more comfortable [taking risks]. If I don't think I'm getting enough [risk taking], if I ...make a real fool out of myself in front of everyone, [then] it's easier for the actor to do that [to be more creative]. I found that worked really, really well, working even on the design [of the game].

Owen was unique in his description of making progress in design work through the initiation of exercises to promote risk-taking and creativity. This and Owen's talk of motifs and actors evoked the creative arts.

Shared Object/ive: The team's shared object was the interactive game that they would jointly create. Owen believed that as a lead game designer he must hold an opinion about everything. Consequently, he relinquished control over parts of the game, but "offered opinions", because "if you don't offer an opinion, they get frustrated ...It's very similar to what a *movie director* has to do". "I learned this, actually, believe it or not, when I was in film school". Using his past experience with film and an analogy with movie directing, Owen explained his interactions with the team as follows:

> The [movie] director has to have an opinion. If the director comes in and says, "Just give me something groovy"—an expression I learned from my film school days—that's what you don't wanna do [give vague directions]. ... [Directors] direct every little thing, but they can't *do* anything. The same thing ...happens in game design.

In Owen's view, the team had a shared objective (creating the game), but he played a strong role in helping individuals "play their part" by providing strong opinions about their work. Owen used an analogy to the work processes of hardware designers and film directors to describe his team interactions. Although he claims his movie director experiences in film school was influential, we still checked to see if this identity "shone through" strongly in all of the categories in the interactional identity model and in his behavior at work.

Shared Artefacts: Owen sees artefacts as elements around which dramatic creative events unfold under his leadership. In one story he told us he organized a game enactment in the office with the designer, writer, and developer to explore variations for the "voice" of the in-game characters. This worked particularly well because the setting of the game was a virtual office. In the description below, the team used a representation of the in-game characters created by the artist and Owen's office space as the stage, for an enactment of the game. Owen valued the shared artefacts because they encouraged fun and exploration, which helped with game design.

> So we [the game development team] put together a simple prototype concept—just take the [in-game] characters around the [real] office, and do some silly event around them. ...We had me and [the developer] and [the writer] and [the graphic designer]. They [all the characters in the game] were all in there [in the reenactment]. [The graphic designer] just drew them. It was fun. I told [the writer] "Just try different voices, ways of doing each of the things for each of the people [characters]. ...Don't worry about being consistent; just expand [explore different voices]".

Tensions: Owen sees tensions within the team as creative opportunities. For example, Owen described a tension between the contents of his game design document, which contained the game mechanics, and the team's mis-understanding of it. His view was that resolving these tensions resulted in the creation of a 'motif' (i.e., the central idea of the game), which, once identified, would serve to motivate the team to continue their work.

> We now get this tension, because for some reason they feel that what I wrote down in my first draft [of the design document] is ...cold or brilliant. ...And they don't get it. And ...they struggle and try to ...understand it. And they're not [understanding it] 'cause there's a lot of problems with it. ...Through iteration [of the game design] and through discussion [with the team], my ideas start to clarify. At some point, what magically emerges is this concept, or this motif, that everyone suddenly grabs onto and gets. ...It becomes this unifying aspect...that everyone rallies behind.

He also described the work of creating games as a dramatic process that had a built-in tension between the forces of expansion and contraction. "Initially everything expands [and] expands ...as new ideas get thrown in the mix. And I keep trying to incorporate those ideas. ...As soon as my mental framework moves from adding to taking things away, I know it's near[ly] finished." At other times, Owen discussed design work in terms of cycles of abstraction and 'concretization'. "There's holes, it's horrible. And at this point what I try to do, is we try to start reducing it down to something concrete again. So I started concrete, went abstract, and then go down to concrete". Owen's theory about design in general was that it was inherently imbued with tension and drama, but that this was a good thing because these helped the team create the game.

Discussion of the 'Movie Director' Identity as Conceptual Tool: Owen's personal goal was to find the central motif for the game, which would energize the work of the team. He contributed most towards the advancement of the team's end objective by keeping the team motivated, encouraging creativity, and providing opinions about everything. He saw shared artefacts as things that the team used in dramatic reenactments of the game play or elements around which the drama of game design unfolds. Tensions were inherent in game design and seen positively as part of a natural and dramatic process that produces a game.

Owen's 'movie director' identity served as a cognitive tool to help Owen respond to unique project circumstances, collaborate, and achieve shared project goals. We described how Owen's project required significant amounts of creativity and coordination. From the perspective of this challenge, it made sense that Owen would see himself as a 'movie director', since no one else on the team had particular responsibility for keeping the team motivated and keeping the creative output high. This was an identity he crafted for himself, because it drew on his skill set, filled a need of the team, and because he was very invested in the success of the project. It provided additional meaning to his interactions, made his work more interesting and pleasurable, and contributed to his sense of self-worth (because movie directors play a central and critical role). Owen's identity was also effective because by using it he could draw on techniques for motivating the team and augmenting their creativity. In this way the team produced better games more effectively. Owen's identity was a response to the current project circumstances, his previous experiences, and his strong desire for the project to succeed.

Using grounded theory we discovered that an individual's interactional identity was reflected in certain aspects of the talk in interviews and an individual's collaborative, artefact-mediated team interactions. In both case studies, the specific interactional identity was reflected in the unique way that Owen or Wil brought meaning to their work (their purpose), their view of the role of shared artefacts, interactions with project team members, and their view of project tensions. Owen and Wil's interactional identities were confirmed through their behavior. Owen worked with others as he understood a movie director would interact with his cast and crew. Wil's interactions with others on the team also corroborated his interactional identity as binder—he was particularly attentive to artefacts, was annoyed when they were unstable, avoided meetings where volatile artefacts were being produced, and wrote application and test code while referring to multiple artefacts. Although both identities were self-evident in the sense that the designer and developer's behavior was explained by the interpretation of their interview data, neither

Designer handles	Descriptive phrase	Yrs.
Incorporator	Incorporates their design work with the work of others.	2
Pioneer	Leads the way in terms of valuing/gathering user needs.	2
Negotiator	Negotiates with others to arrive at design decisions.	6
Closer	Closes in on a design 'deal' that is agreeable to all stakeholders, including himself.	8
Reformer	Reforms organizational structure to achieve greater compliance to design standards.	10
Movie director	Acts as a director of a cast and crew in rehearsal mode for production of a movie.	11
Quality advocate	Advocates for product quality.	11
Steward	Acts as the team's steward for producing useful software for his product's target audience.	12
Facilitator	A facilitator of a distributed, problem-solving activity.	13
Teacher	Engages others in courseware production through teaching.	33
Artist-in-business	Uses his art to achieve business goals for the team.	40
Elder	Sees software-creation work evolving over time.	40+

Figure 2. Designers' Interactional Identities by years of experience. A dashed horizontal line separates more and less experienced developers.

Developer handles	Descriptive phrase	Yrs.
Assembler	Assembles parts from others and produces parts of his own to build a product.	3
Catalyst	Acts as catalyst in team to ensure changes in product meet team objectives (e.g. usability).	7
Problem solver	Seeks satisfactory solutions to difficult software problems.	10
Practitioner	Reliably and professionally delivers and expects a high standard of work in the team.	10
Historical anomaly	Holds unique position in software work; is misunderstood. Must constantly explain role.	15
Training advocate	Advocates training concepts, uses training techniques to deliver this message to the team.	17
Enabler	Provides team members with adequate means, opportunity, or authority to do their work.	19
Pragmatist	Helps the team establish & meet achievable goals.	20
Binder	Aims to develop software that binds together the work of others to create something that is functional.	22

Figure 3. Developers' Interactional Identities by years of experience. A dashed horizontal line separates more and less experienced developers.

identity was overt in their behavior. The interviews revealed the meaning behind their actions and therefore more strongly reflected their interactional identity.

EXPERIENCE AND INTERACTIONAL IDENTITY

Nineteen other interactional identities were identified. Designer interactional identities are shown in Figure 2 and developers' in Figure 3. To provide more of a sense of the diversity of these interactional identities, we very briefly present two more identities, this time selecting a less-experienced designer and developer.

Kate was a designer with two years' experience in charge of the design of a user interface for a product to be used in the financial sector. Her organization had a software development- and profit-focused culture. The financial analysts at her organization "on the business side" had a strong role in determining what would be built and how it would be built. Designers were seen as graphic artists who were a part of the development team "on the software side" and were individuals whom the developers could approach for help. Only the financial analysts had contact with end users. Kate had become an advocate for change in how software was designed precisely because her organization still had a software development and profit-focused culture and not a user-centered design culture. She experienced a high degree of frustration in her work, and responded by finding subversive and creative ways to reach her clients and end users (the business side discouraged this) to determine the right software to develop and to ensure that it was properly developed. Kate's identity of 'pioneer' shone through in the various categories shown in Figure 1. a) Goal: to design an effective user interface that fits how end users would use this interface in the context of their work over long periods of time, an objective clearly in conflict with the company culture. b) Shared objective: designing the user interface software is the interaction designer's responsibility, but it can't be designed properly without access to clients and end users; once designed, developers build it; c) Shared artefacts: are tools for exploring ideas. She uses many such artefacts in her work with others on the team, and with clients and end users when she can reach them. d) Tensions: according to Kate, should be resolved directly and not avoided. However, her meetings with the developers, where Kate and other people on the team presented their concerns, were generally very unsatisfactory experiences for Kate. Kate had huge difficulties engaging the developers (who were inexperienced as well) in caring for, or adhering to, her designs. She struggled with how to be an effective designer within an organization that valued business and development over design and that does not give power to the designers. Once in sheer frustration with the developer group, she recommended her design group hire a user interface developer themselves and have him join the group of developers. This developer would implement only the changes she wanted. In her sheer tenacity and refusal to accept the status quo in her organization, Kate saw herself as a pioneer, someone who ventures into unknown or unclaimed territory to settle; or someone who opens up new areas of thought, research, or development. She particularly wanted to transform the workplace to better meet user needs.

May was a developer with 7 years of experience. She was the lead designer on a project that involved developing a feature for an established graphical user interface product. Her organization was in a state of flux, having recently been acquired. May worked with different types of designers on every project, but did not understand their different skillsets. May's identity of 'catalyst' shone through in the various categories shown in Figure 1. a) Goal: to produce the feature in a timely manner and to produce something that was usable and consistent with the feel of the product in its entirety. Her goals therefore overlapped significantly with the designer who was responsible for the feature's look and feel, which would inevitably spark debates. b) Shared Objective: according to May the designer was responsible for producing the initial proposal for the user interface and the developer and other stakeholders shape and alter it (sometimes significantly) with their responses. c) Shared artefacts: are things that facilitate change and afford feedback. "Once you see it, you can pick other issues with it..." d) Tensions: May sees tensions as issues to be addressed. She told us many stories about problems that occurred during the implementation of the feature, including that the design as specified could not be built due to the choice of terminology, the choice of controls and approach to consistency issues. May presented herself as a catalyst in the sense that she saw herself as a person who caused important changes to take place. She acted as a catalyst within the team to ensure changes in the product were made so that it was consistent, usable, and well-implemented.

Overall, we found that identities did tend to differ with the total number of years of experience. More experienced designers were able to relinquish control of the design of the user interface. They were also more likely to view and use artefacts as a mechanism for collaboration and coordination of the work rather than a tool for completing a specific role-related task. In general we found that more experienced designers and developers constructed interactional identities that took into consideration the social aspects of their work, in the sense that they showed a greater understanding of their own contribution in the context of the contribution of others on the team.

DISCUSSION

Our research began with a question about the meaning that design artefacts had for designers and developers in their collaborative work. Our focus on concrete team projects, rather than the study of design or development work in general, was fortunate because it revealed an interesting cognitive construct that was pervasive amongst our participants and associated with concrete activity. We have identified a number of ways that an interactional identity is utilized. Interactional identities explain the unique way each of our participants imbued mediational artefacts with additional meaning. Interactional identities were also influential in other important aspects of our participant's work such as how they viewed and resolved tensions within their teams, how they framed interactions with other team members, and their strategy for advancing their collaborative work.

Our data suggests these identities bridge a gap between how designers and developers were taught to enact their roles and the demands of project work. Because undergraduate education often does not emphasize the topic of multidisciplinary interactions, one way we interpret these identities was that participants constructed them to make sense of their role in the context of multidisciplinary work. Viewed in this way interactional identities are a sort of 'glue' that fills a gap between the contributions of other team members and an individual's own contributions, because they suggest new actions that will make the team work successful. They can also be understood as a component of articulation work, in that the construction and use of an interactional identity to fill in gaps in the work and to organize work can help with "putting together tasks, task sequences and task clusters" [25]. For example, the binder organizes his work by collecting completed artefacts from other team members and binding them, and the movie director keeps the work on learning games productive by ensuring that creative team events happen regularly. We also noticed the interactional identities we analyzed were positive ways of seeing project work and positive ways of creating an identity, thereby satisfying a personal need for a sense of self and a sense of self in relation to others. Further, interactional identities appear to work in conjunction with roles, which are an individual's responsibilities that are generally understood by other team members and are closely linked with that person's training. However, in contrast to roles, interactional identities are more personalized, situated, relational and private.

The particular interactional identity that is adopted appears to be a personal response based on an individual's background, their perception of the project situation, and their understanding of the group's desired outcome. We have shown that there is considerable variation in the interactional identities that are constructed within each of the disciplines we studied. This variation appears to be greater for interaction designers than developers (a number of these identities had an underlying sense to do with practical construction) and we hypothesize this is due to the non-standardized training that interaction designers receive in comparison to the standardized ACM curriculum for computer scientists that most developers are influenced by in their post-secondary education. Still, we find the amount of variation within each discipline remarkable.

Our results suggest that individuals become better at constructing more efficacious interactional identities with experience. Since we have found that interactional identities are associated with specific projects, and we know that individuals work on many projects over the years, the opportunity for constructing new interactional identities would present itself regularly. It therefore makes sense that individuals would become better at constructing such identities over time.

Cultural-historical psychology and more specifically activity theory suggests that the construction of an artefact is an important way of externalizing one's ideas. Similarly, artefact consumption is an important way of internalizing the ideas of others. We suggest that in addition to these mechanisms individual artefacts and sets of artefacts are also imbued with additional meaning because they are attached to the expression of an international identity. For example, we have seen that Wil understands artefacts as elements that are bound by his code, and that Owen sees artefacts as an important element in the dramatic design activity of his team. This means that in practice Wil and Owen have additional undisclosed criteria for artefacts that are used in team interactions. For Wil, artefacts must be 'bindable' entities, and for Owen they must support dramatic action. An individual's view of artefacts was also linked to their experience in that, in general, less experienced participants tended to view them as some sort of specialized tool (e.g. as an aid to solving their problems), whereas more experienced participants viewed them as collaborative aids (e.g. as an aid to facilitating group work). Our work on shared artefacts used in small multidisciplinary teams is complementary, but distinct, from work on standardized boundary objects that bridge communities of practice [24], and also work on boundary negotiating objects used in large projects involving entire departments [14]. We have not studied interactional identities in these wider contexts.

This research also contributes to a theoretical understanding of identities in interaction. Identities have been studied from many different perspectives such as psychology, anthropology and organizational studies. Regardless of the disciplinary or theoretical approach, work on identity has helped to capture the notion of one's distinctiveness from others as well as one's affinities to others. This makes 'identity' a relational concept that is particularly relevant when studying individuals engaged in collaborative work [11]. We have distinguished between identity constructs that are shared cultural artefacts, such as organizational identities, and we focused on enacted identities. We think the relationship between these other types of identities and enacted identities is an interesting and open issue. We have understood enacted identities as cognitive tools created by individuals to support their group interactions. Lemke also highlighted the cognitive aspect of identities expressed in interactions and called them "evaluative stances towards interaction" [15].

Our work on interactional identity as a theoretical concept can be compared to other activity-theoretic or socio-cultural work on identity. Crafter and de Abreu studied the identity of one student in a classroom setting, and found that her identity was constructed and reconstructed in response to belonging to, and engaging with, communities of practice [7]. Roth, studying several workers in a fish hatchery emphasized the dialectical nature of the concept of identity, and how it could be understood relationally with other aspects of an activity system. He concluded that 'identity' is best understood in relation to the other people who are engaged in an activity, mediating artefacts, and other aspects of an activity [22].

Mokros and Lemke both called for an extensive examination of this type of identity [20, 15]. Our results provide a name for the type of identity that emerges in group interactions and clearly specifies some ways this identity is manifested. Also, while foundational work theorized about the development of such identities [16], we have begun to look for patterns in the types of identities that emerge over time. Our research contributes an understanding of how such identities are tied to activities, how they come to be, their benefits, and how they develop as specialists become more experienced.

Our method for discovering interactional identities is similar to a very general method suggested by Bucholtz who has proposed that a focus on talk and artefact use can help in revealing intentional, habitual or non-conscious identities [5]. It also has a similarity to the methods proposed by Holland et al. who suggest looking for identities in the context of figured worlds [12] and Wortham, who suggests analyzing interview data to find identities through the way individuals position themselves in narratives [32].

Knowledge of interactional identities could be valuable when designing collaborative systems, in the same way that collaboration personas [18] or collaboration patterns [17] can inform design. We know that interactive identities are enacted through use of a diverse set of artefacts that are created then used in collaborative work. Several practical implications for design follow from this observation. Firstly, tools that create or manipulate artefacts could be designed for specific interactional identities. For example, for the 'closer' designer, a mock-up of the future user interface is also a proposed deal that the business person and developer could agree on (or not). The 'closer' might be better supported if they could easily record points of contention and agreement and access visualizations of such. The 'enabler' developer might like to see blockages and interventions made more explicit and 'trackable'. An interactional identity may involve a perspective on tools and their purposes that goes beyond simple functionality, and carries rich semantic and affective overtones about the nature of the work. Secondly, general design guidelines for collaborative tools that support the enactment of interactional identities could be posited. For example, tools that support a secondary level of notation for working with artefacts such as tagging, highlighting, and linking artefact parts could support the enactment of a wide range of interactional identities. Finally, tool designers might consider whether they are primarily designing for less experienced or more experienced individuals. More experienced collaborators may appreciate tool sets with links between shared artefacts, and easy ways to collaborate with other team members. Less experienced team members may work best in more task-focused environments. Moreover, tools might be designed to scaffold transitions between these perspectives.

CONCLUSIONS

We studied designers and developers collaborating to create software. Using grounded theory we discovered and explored the concept of *interactional identity*. We showed interactional identities are constructed in the process of engagement in design activity. We showed they are expressed in the way designers and developers describe their goals, view their team's object/ive, view their team's shared artefacts, and understand and resolve project tensions. We showed that these identities were valuable cognitive tools that provide meaning to our participants' talk- and artefact-mediated interactions with other team members, and provide direction to their team interactions to make them more effective.

Interactional identities are cognitive tools that are pervasive in highly collaborative, multidisciplinary, creative work. We suggest such identities may be common in other types of work with similar properties such as many other types of design work (architectural design, mechanical design and so on), and that it is possible they exist in all forms of collaborative work. Knowing that such identities exist can help individuals to consciously select and develop more meaningful and effective identities. It could also help individuals involved in creating better tools for supporting team interactions, since an important finding is that interactional identities are enacted through the use of shared artefacts. This suggests that tools that support such interactions need to be designed with this in mind.

Acknowledgments

We gratefully acknowledge the support of our participating organizations, their employees, our reviewers, GRAND NCE, and NSERC for the Cognos Industry Research Chair grants and SurfNet grants.

REFERENCES

1. P. A. Adler and P. Adler. *Observational techniques*, pages 377–392. Handbook of qualitative research. Sage Publications, 1994.
2. B. E. Ashforth and G. E. Kreiner. Dirty work and the challenge of constructing a positive identity. *The Academy of Mgmt Review*, 24(3):pp. 413–434, 1999.
3. A. Brown. Engineering identities. *Career Development International*, 9(3):pp. 245–273, 2004.
4. J. Brown, G. Lindgaard, and R. Biddle. Collaborative events and shared artefacts. In *Proc. Agile*. IEEE, 2011.
5. M. Bucholtz. Identity and interaction: A sociocultural linguistic approach. *Discourse Studies*, 7(4-5):585–614, 2005.
6. E. Carmel. Narratives that software nations tell themselves: An exploration and taxonomy. *Communications of the Association for Information Systems*, 17(1):pp. 851–872, 2006.
7. S. Crafter and de Abreu Guida. Constructing identities in multicultural learning contexts. *Mind, Culture, and Activity*, 17:102–118, 2010.
8. H. Daniels. *Vygotsky and Research*. Routledge, 2008.
9. Y. Engeström. Activity theory as a framework for analyzing and redesigning work. *Ergonomics*, 43(7):960–974, 2000.
10. K. Fidel and R. Garner. Computer workers: career lines and professional identity. *SIGCAS Comput. Soc.*, 20:118–123, August 1990.
11. K. Gergen. *The Saturated Self: Dilemmas of Identity in Contemporary Life*. Basic Books, 2nd edition, 2001.
12. D. Holland, W. L. Jr., D. Skinner, and C. Cain. *Identity and Agency in Cultural Worlds*. Harvard Press, 1998.
13. J. Kilker. Conflict on collaborative design teams: Understanding the role of social identities. *Technology and Society Magazine, IEEE*, 18(3):12 –21, Fall 1999.
14. C. P. Lee. Boundary negotiating artifacts: Unbinding the routine of boundary objects and embracing chaos in collaborative work. *Computer Supported Collaborative Work*, 16(3):pp. 307–339, 2007.
15. J. Lemke. Across the scales of time: Artifacts, activities, and meanings in ecosocial systems. In *The Fourth Congress of the International Society for Cultural Research and Activity Theory*, 1998.
16. J. Lemke. Identity, development and desire: Critical questions. In *American Educational Research Association Conference*, 2011.
17. D. Martin and I. Sommerville. Patterns of cooperative interaction: Linking ethnomethodology and design. *Trans. Comput.-Hum. Interact.*, 11:59–89, March 2004.
18. T. Matthews, S. Whittaker, T. Moran, and S. Yuen. Collaboration personas. In *CHI 2011*, pages 2247–2256. ACM, 2011.
19. J. McGrath, H. Arrow, and J. Berdahl. The study of groups: Past, present, and future. *Personality and Social Psychology Review*, 4:95–105, 2000.
20. H. B. Mokros, editor. *Interaction and Identity*. Transaction Publishers, 1996.
21. S. L. Morrow. Quality and trustworthiness in qualitative research in counseling psychology. *Journal of Counseling Psychology*, 52(2):250–260, 2005.
22. W.-M. Roth. Emotion at work: A contribution to third-generation cultural-historical activity theory. *Mind, Culture, and Activity*, 14:40–63, 2007.
23. J. A. Smith. *Semi-structured interviewing and qualitative analysis*. Rethinking methods in psychology. Sage, 1995.
24. S. L. Star and J. R. Griesemer. Institutional ecology, 'translations' and boundary objects. *Social Studies of Science*, 19(3):pp. 387–420, 1989.
25. A. Strauss. The articulation of project work: An organizational process. *The Sociological Quarterly*, 29:163–178, 1988.
26. A. L. Strauss and J. M. Corbin. *Basics of qualitative research: Techniques and procedures for developing grounded theory*. Sage, 1998.
27. H. Tajfel and J. Turner. *The social identity of intergroup behavior*, pages 7–24. Psychology of intergroup relations. Nelson Hall, 1985.
28. S. Turkle and S. Papert. Epistemological pluralism: Styles and voices within the computer culture. *Signs*, 16(1):pp. 128–157, 1990.
29. A. Vagän. Towards a sociocultural perspective on identity formation in education. *Mind, Culture, and Activity*, 18(1):43–58, 2011.
30. L. S. Vygotsky. *Mind in society*. Harvard Press, 1978.
31. J. V. Wertsch. *Mind as action*. Oxford Press, 1998.
32. S. Wortham. *Narratives in Action: A strategy for Research and Analysis*. Teachers College Press, 2001.

Operational Transformation for Orthogonal Conflict Resolution in Real-time Collaborative 2D Editing Systems

Chengzheng Sun, Hongkai Wen, Hongfei Fan
School of Computer Engineering, Nanyang Technological University, Singapore

ABSTRACT
Operational Transformation (OT) is commonly used for conflict resolution in real-time collaborative applications, but none of existing OT techniques is able to solve a special type of conflict—orthogonal conflict, which may occur when concurrent operations are inserting/deleting an arbitrary number of objects in different dimensions of a two-dimensional (2D) workspace, such as spreadsheet documents. This paper is the first to identify and solve the orthogonal conflict problem by extending OT with a new capability of resolving 2D conflicts. Extending OT from one- to two-dimensional conflict resolution is fundamental to the theory and application of OT, and technically challenging as well because 2D orthogonal conflict is different from but intimately related to the one-dimensional positional shifting conflict and necessitates new and integral solutions for multi-dimensional conflicts. In this paper, we present formal definitions of orthogonal conflict, pseudo-code description, design rationale analysis, and correctness verification and complexity analysis of the 2DOT solution.

Author Keywords
Conflict Resolution, Operational Transformation, Real-time Collaborative Spreadsheet and Table Editing.

ACM Classification Keywords
H.5.3 [**Information Systems**]: Group and Organization Interfaces – Synchronous Interaction, Theory and Model.

General Terms
Algorithms; Theory.

INTRODUCTION
Operational Transformation (OT) is a technique for conflict resolution in collaborative computing systems, and a subject of continuous research in CSCW in past decades [1-4, 6-17]. In recent years, OT has been increasingly adopted as a core collaboration technique in industrial applications, e.g. Google Wave [17] and Docs[1], IBM OpenCoWeb[2], Novell Vibe[3], and Codoxware[4], which are creating a new wave of OT research and application.

Spreadsheets and word processors (with table functions) are among the most widely used computer software applications, and they are commonly used by data and knowledge workers in finance, business, and government organizations, as well as ordinary people in their daily lives. The need for real-time collaborative editing of spreadsheets and table-based documents has long been recognized and stimulated research and development efforts from both academia and industry [8,12,16]. Representative collaborative spreadsheet tools include Google Spreadsheet[5], eXpresso[6], etc. However, these collaborative tools lag in functionality far behind their desktop counterparts, such as Microsoft Excel[7] and Open Office Calc[8].

Modern single-user spreadsheet tools are capable of supporting comprehensive functionalities on two-dimensional (2D) tables with an arbitrary number of rows and columns. Inserting and deleting cells, rows, or columns are common operations in these applications, but supporting such operations in real-time collaboration is a challenge. One special characteristic of such operations is they have *global effect* ranges that cover not only the cells inserted or deleted directly by an operation (the *direct effect range*), but also those cells whose positions are shifted due to the execution of such an operation (the *indirect effect range*). Dynamic positional shifting of existing cells in a table may lead to inconsistencies if operations are generated concurrently and executed in different orders. Those technical obstacles are part of the reasons why existing collaborative spreadsheet tools (e.g. Google Spreadsheet) are unable to support many editing functionalities available in desktop spreadsheet tools (e.g. Microsoft Excel).

OT was originally invented to resolve positional shifting problems and maintain consistency while allowing concurrent operations to be executed in different orders [3,11,14]. Existing OT techniques are able to resolve positional shifting problems if concurrent operations are targeting objects in a single or hierarchical linear address space, like a sequence of cells in the same row/column, a sequence of rows/columns in the same table. However, none of existing OT techniques has ever addressed the *orthogonal operation conflict* problem, which occurs when concurrent operations are inserting or deleting objects (e.g. cells, rows, and columns) in orthogonal dimensions of a 2D workspace –

[1] http://en.wikipedia.org/wiki/Google_Docs
[2] https://github.com/opencoweb/coweb#readme
[3] http://en.wikipedia.org/wiki/Novell_Pulse
[4] https://www.codoxware.com
[5] http://spreadsheets.google.com/lv
[6] http://www.expressocorp.com/
[7] http://office.microsoft.com/enus/excel/default.aspx
[8] http://www.openoffice.org/product/calc.html.

a common phenomenon in collaborative spreadsheet applications. Two operations are orthogonal if their dimensions are different, e.g. one is to insert a cell in a row, and the other is to insert a cell in a column. Two orthogonal operations conflict if they are concurrent and have overlapping effect ranges.

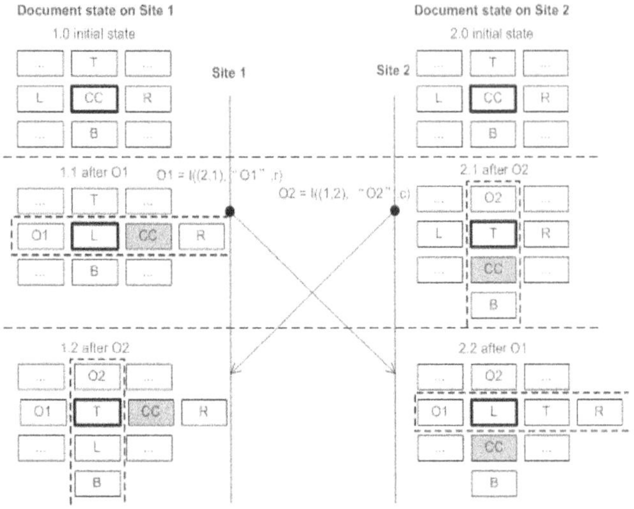

Figure 1 Conflicts between concurrent orthogonal operations in a 2D table. The effect range of each operation is highlighted in a dashed frame in the document after its execution. The critical cell position is highlighted by a box with thicker edges. The current position of the old critical cell is indicated by a shaded cell.

As shown in Figure 1, O1 is to insert a cell, denoted by [*O1*], at position (x_1, y_1) in *row*-x_1, O_2 is to insert a cell, denoted by [*O2*], into position (x_2, y_2) in *column*-y_2. These two operations are orthogonal as their operational dimensions are different, and there is a shared *Critical Cell* (denoted as [*CC*]) at (x_1, y_2) in their effect ranges. These two operations are generated concurrently and executed in different orders at the two sites. Due to the orthogonal nature of the two concurrent operations, the final results at the two sites are inconsistent: the old critical cell [*CC*] is shifted right to (x_1, y_2+1) by O_1 at site 1, but down to (x_1+1, y_2) by O_2 at site 2; the new cell at (x_1, y_2) is [*T*] at site 1, but [*L*] at site 2. Generally, concurrent orthogonal operations may result in inconsistent tables: old critical cells in their overlapping effect ranges are moved to different positions, and different new cell are moved into old critical cell positions in overlapping effect ranges.

Orthogonal conflict is a special 2D conflict problem: it involves critical cells at the intersection of the effect ranges of two orthogonal conflict operations, and those critical cells are shifted in different dimensions. No prior OT techniques can solve this problem because they are essentially one-dimensional (1D) in the sense that they work only if operations are targeting and shifting objects in the same 1D addressing space [3,6,7,9,11], or in a hierarchy of multiple 1D addressing spaces [2,12]. Another subtle aspect of orthogonal conflict is that it may occur in indirect effect ranges of concurrent operations. In Figure 1, the critical cell (x_1, y_2) is not directly inserted by O_1 or O_2, but indirectly affected by their shifting effects. Such indirect conflict relationships cannot be detected by conflict detection techniques that rely on the condition in which concurrent operations directly target common objects [13]. Orthogonal conflict may occur whenever two concurrent operations are inserting/deleting *any number of* cells, including a *full row or column,* in different dimensions.

This paper contributes a novel 2DOT solution to resolve orthogonal conflict problems in real-time collaborative 2D document editing applications. The rest of this paper is organized as follows. First, basic concepts and relations in orthogonal conflict resolution are defined. Then, combined effects for two orthogonal conflict operations are described. Next, the 2DOT solution for resolving conflicts among an arbitrary number of operations is discussed. Furthermore, a comprehensive example is used to illustrate how various 2DOT technical components work together. This is followed by theoretic verification of correctness and time complexity analysis of the 2DOT solution. Then, the 2DOT work is compared to related work, and future work is discussed. Finally, main contributions in this paper are summarized.

BASIC CONCEPTS AND DEFINITIONS

In this paper, a spreadsheet or table-based document is modeled as a 2D workspace consisting of multiple rows and columns; each row or column contains a sequence of cells; and each cell contains values, formulas, etc. A row (or column) in the 2D space is labeled by a sequence number from 0 to M − 1 (or N −1), where M (or N) is the maximum number of rows (or columns) in the 2D workspace.

Real-world spreadsheet applications (e.g. Microsoft Excel) may provide end-users with a rich set of operations. This work, however, focuses on two primitive ones: insert and delete of cells, as they are representative and specially related to the orthogonal conflict problem addressed in this paper. For the sake of clarity and simplicity, the direct effect range of an operation is restricted to a single cell, but the issues and solutions reported in this paper can be generalized to operations that insert/delete *any number* of cells (e.g. a full row or column). Two primitive operations are defined:

1. I(*p*,*c*,*dim*): insert a cell *c* at position *p* in dimension *dim*.
2. D(*p*,*dim*): delete the cell at position *p* in dimension *dim*.

The parameter *p* is a pair (*x*, *y*), where *x* and *y* represent the cell's row and column sequence numbers, respectively; *c* represents a cell object; and *dim* can take one of two values: *row* for a row-oriented operation, which has position shifting effects from *left-to-right* (for insert) or from *right-to-left* (for delete) in the target row; or *col* for a column-oriented operation, which has position shifting effects from *top-to-bottom* (for insert) or from *bottom-to-top* (for delete) in the target column. The dot notation is used to refer to the type and parameters of an operation *O*: *O.type* can be either *I* or *D*; O.*p* refers to the *p* parameter, and *O.p.x* and *O.p.y* refer to the coordinates in (*x*, *y*), respectively; *O.c* refers to the *c* parameter; and *O.dim* refers to the *dim* parameter.

The *Effect Range* of operation *O*, denoted as *ER*(*O*), is the set of cells directly or indirectly affected by the execution of *O*. If *O* is row-oriented, *ER*(*O*) includes all cells at or on the right of position *O.p* in the target row; if *O* is column-oriented, $ER(O)$ includes all cells at or below position $O.p$ in the target column. Two operations are overlapping if their effect ranges have shared cells, as defined below.

Definition 1: *Overlapping Relation* "#". Given two operations O_a and O_b, they have an overlapping relation, denoted as $O_a\#O_b$, *iff*: $ER(O_a) \cap ER(O_b) \neq \{\}$.

Following Lamport [5], the causal (partial) ordering relation of operations is defined in terms of their generation and execution sequences as follows.

Definition 2: *Causal Ordering Relation* "→". Given two operations O_a and O_b, generated at sites i and j, O_a is causally ordered before O_b, denoted as $O_a \rightarrow O_b$, *iff*: (1) $i = j$ and the generation of O_a *happened before* the generation of O_b; (2) $i \neq j$ and the execution of O_a at site j *happened before* the generation of O_b; or (3) there exists an operation O_x, such that $O_a \rightarrow O_x$ and $O_x \rightarrow O_b$.

Definition 3: *Concurrent Relation* "||". Given two operations O_a and O_b, they are *concurrent*, denoted as $O_a || O_b$, *iff*: neither $O_a \rightarrow O_b$ nor $O_b \rightarrow O_a$.

In real-time collaborative editing systems, operations with causal relationships are executed in their causal order according to the causality preservation requirement in [10]; but concurrent operations may be executed in any orders at different collaborating sites.

Definition 4: *Orthogonal Relation* "⊥". Given two operations O_a and O_b, they are *orthogonal*, denoted as $O_a \perp O_b$, *iff*: $O_a.dim \neq O_b.dim$.

If orthogonal operations O_a and O_b are concurrent and their effect ranges are overlapping, their execution in different orders may result in inconsistent states (see Figure 1). Such a relationship is called *orthogonal conflict* (or *2D conflict*), as defined below.

Definition 5: *Orthogonal (or 2D) Conflict Relation* "⊕". Given two operations O_a and O_b, they have an *orthogonal conflict* relation, denoted as $O_a \oplus O_b$, *iff*: (1) $O_a \perp O_b$; (2) $O_a || O_b$; and (3) $O_a\#O_b$.

Definition 6: *Parallel Operation Relation* "//". Given two operations O_a and O_b, they are parallel, denoted as $O_a // O_b$, *iff* they are not orthogonal.

Two parallel operations are overlapping if they are performed in the same row or column. If two parallel and overlapping operations are concurrent, their execution in different orders may result in inconsistent document states [1,2,9,14]. Such a relationship between the two operations is called *1D conflict*, which is defined below.

Definition 7: *1D conflcit Relation* "⊘". Given operations O_a and O_b, they have a *1D conflict* relation, denoted as $O_a \oslash O_b$, *iff*: (1) $O_a // O_b$; (2) $O_a || O_b$; and (3) $O_a\#O_b$.

Definition 8: *Compatible Relation* "⊙". Given operations O_a and O_b, they are *compatible*, denoted as $O_a \odot O_b$, *iff*: neither $O_a \oslash O_b$ nor $O_a \oplus O_b$.

Figure 2 is used to illustrate operation relations defined in this section. For four operations O_1, O_2, O_3 and O_4, their positional relationships in a 2D workspace are shown in Figure 2 (a), and their causal relationships are illustrated in Figure 2 (b). In Figure 2 (a), O_2 is illustrated as a column-oriented operation, but O_1, O_3, and O_4 are all row-oriented. Therefore, O_2 is orthogonal with O_1, O_3, and O_4, i.e. $O_1 \perp O_2$, $O_3 \perp O_2$, $O_4 \perp O_2$, according to Definition 4; and O_1, O_3, and O_4 are parallel operations, i.e. $O_1 // O_3 // O_4$, according to Definition 6. Moreover, O_1 is overlapping with O_4 and O_2, i.e. $O_1\#O_4$ and $O_1\#O_2$, but O_3 is not overlapping with any operation, according to Definition 1.

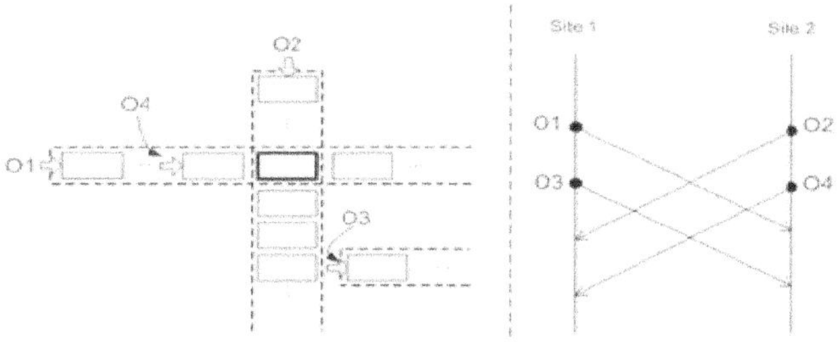

Figure 2 (a) Positional relations among four operations in a 2D table. (b) Operation causal relations in a time-space diagram.

In Figure 2 (b), the four operations have the following causal and concurrent relationships: $(O_1 \rightarrow O_3) \; || \; (O_2 \rightarrow O_4)$, according to Definitions 3 and 4. Conflict/compatible relations among these four operations can be derived from considering both the positional and causal relation scenarios in Figure 2 (a) and (b) together. Among the three pairs of orthogonal operations, only one pair is orthogonally conflicting, i.e. $O_2 \oplus O_1$, according to Definition 5. This is because O_2 is concurrent and overlapping with only O_1, but is causally before O_4 and not overlapping with O_3. Among the three parallel operations, only one pair is *1D conflicting*, i.e. $O_1 \oslash O_4$, according to Definition 7. This is because O_1 is concurrent and overlapping with only O_4, but O_1 is causally before O_3, and O_4 is not overlapping with O_3.

In summary, causally-related operations are compatible and their execution order is constrained by their causal relationships [3,5]. Concurrent operations may be compatible (if non-overlapping) or conflicting (if overlapping). Compatible concurrent operations can be executed in any orders and achieve consistency without special treatment. Conflict (1D/2D) concurrent operations may cause workspace inconsistency if they are executed in different orders. The focus of this paper is to devise new 2DOT techniques to resolve 2D orthogonal conflicts and to adapt existing 1DOT techniques in 2D workspace.

RESOLVING CONFLICT BETWEEN TWO OPERATIONS

Combined Effect for Orthogonal Conflict Operations

From the example scenario in Figure 1, it can be observed that, after executing O_1 and O_2 on the same 2D document at two sites separately, two document states are produced, each preserving the effect of one operation only. Based on these two states, one can envisage a merged document state that combines the effects of the two orthogonal conflict operations, as shown in the final document states at both sites in Figure 3.

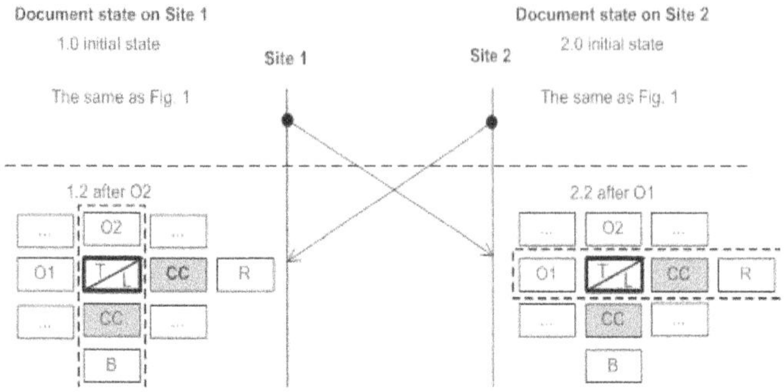

Figure 3 Combined effect of two orthogonal conflict operations.

In the merged document state, effects of both operations are preserved as if each operation was executed alone, except that the critical cell position (x_1, y_2) becomes a special *Multi-Version* (MV) position capable of hosting two cells, denoted by [*T*/*L*], where *L* is shifted into this position by O_1 and *T* by O_2. This combined effect is termed as the *Union Effect*, as defined below.

Definition 9: *Union Effect (UE)*: Given two orthogonal conflict operations O_a and O_b defined on the same 2D document, their union effect consists of the following:

1. an MV position is created at the interaction of the effect ranges of O_a and O_b;
2. effects of O_a (or O_b) are the same as if O_a (or O_b) was executed alone on the 2D document state on which O_a (or O_b) was defined; and
3. cells outside effect ranges of O_a and O_b are untouched.

This union effect is intuitive for users to understand as it retains the original effect of an operation as if the operation was executed alone, and it is capable of preserving all users' work even in the face of conflict. The 2D union effect is also compatible with the 1D union effect achieved by the basic OT technique for insert and delete operations in a linear (1D) workspace [10,14], and hence well suited for OT support, which will become clear late in this paper.

Required Properties of the Multi-Version Position

One key element of the union effect is the creation of an MV position to accommodate the two cells shifted into by two orthogonal conflict operations. The implementation of the MV position is required to preserve the following properties:

1. **Uniqueness and Fixed Location:** An MV position is a *unique* location in the 2D workspace. This location is fixed in the sense that it cannot be changed by operations, though cells in this MV position can be shifted by operations according to OCOD (see below).
2. **One Cell One Dimension (OCOD):** Each cell place in the MV position belongs to one specific dimension. When a new MV position is created, it has two initial cell places: one is occupied by the current cell located at this position and the other is vacant for new contents. A vacant cell place can be filled by directly inserting a cell into it or indirectly shifting a cell into it. When an existing MV position falls into the effect range of an operation *O*, only one cell place belonging to *O*'s dimension will be affected. If the cell place in *O*'s dimension is occupied, then that cell will be shifted out of the MV position. If the cell place in *O*'s dimension is vacant, then the position shifting effect of *O* will not propagate beyond the MV position, which means those cells beyond the MV position in the indirect effect range of *O* will not be affected.
3. **Multi-Version Single-Display (MVSD):** A MV position maintains two cells internally, but displays only one cell on the user interface. The determination of which cell to display must be consistent across all sites. There exist various ways to implement this MV property. For example, the MVSD technique in [13] can be adapted to support the MVSD property. Suitable user interfaces can be provided for users to select (i.e. commit to) one cell among the two cells in an MV position. After the selection, the MV position is removed and the location becomes a normal one.

The feasibility of preserving the above properties has been experimentally tested in our designing and implementing real-time collaborative spreadsheet tools and word processors [12,13,16]. The rest of the paper will assume these properties for the MV cell are supported by underlying MV implementation mechanisms, without further elaborating their technical details.

Achieving the Union Effect

In OT-based collaborative systems, it is the operations, not the documents that are propagated among collaborating sites. To incorporate the orthogonal conflict solution in the OT framework, it is necessary to devise techniques to achieve the union effect *incrementally* by (1) executing one (local) operation as-is to produce one intermediate 2D document, and (2) executing the other (remote) operation in a *transformed* form that merges its effect into this intermediate 2D document to achieve the full union effect.

In Figure 3, for example, when O_2 arrives at site 1, O_1 has been executed with effects of inserting a new cell [*O1*] at (x_1, y_1), shifting cell [*L*] into the critical cell position (x_1, y_2), and shifting the old critical cell [*CC*] to position (x_1, y_2+1). To achieve the union effect of O_1 and O_2 under this 2D document state, the following steps can take place to process O_2 (a similar process occurs in processing O_1 at site 2):

1. *create* an MV position at location (x_1, y_2), which hosts the existing cell [*L*] in its row-dimension cell place and leaves its column-dimension cell place vacant;
2. *copy* cell [*CC*] at position (x_1, y_2+1) and *insert* it to position (x_1+1, y_2) in the column dimension, which will shift the following cells one position downwards; and
3. *execute* the original O_2 to insert a new cell [*O2*] at position (x_2, y_2), which will shift cell [*T*] into the MV position (x_1, y_2), but will not shift the cells below the MV position because the MV position has a column-dimension vacant place for cell [*T*], which effectively blocks the shifting effect downwards, thanks to the OCOD property of the MV position.

As the effect achieved in the above process is only part of the union effect for two orthogonal conflict operations, the term *Partial Union Effect* is used to refer to this part of the union effect. Also, all actions involved in the above process, i.e. creating an MV position, copying and inserting the critical cell, and executing the original operation, can be determined by the parameters of the two conflict operations.

```
PU(Oa, Ob) {
  if (Oa.dim = row && Oa.type = I && Ob.type = I) {
    1. create an MV position at (Oa.p.x, Ob.p.y);
    2. copy the cell at position (Oa.p.x, Ob.p.y+1) and
       insert it to position (Oa.p.x +1, Ob.p.y) in the
       dimension of Oa; and
  } else { // other cases are omitted for conciseness }
  execute the original Oa;
}
```

The *Partial Union* procedure, $PU(O_a, O_b)$, is defined to achieve the partial union effect of O_a on top of O_b's effect: The full union effect of two conflict operations O_a and O_b can be achieved by $O_b \circ PU(O_a, O_b)$, or $O_a \circ PU(O_b, O_a)$, where "$\circ$" denote the execution of an operation or procedure, as stated in the following proposition.

Proposition 1: Given two orthogonal conflict operations O_a and O_b, defined on the same 2D document state S, we have:

$$S \circ O_b \circ PU(O_a, O_b) = S \circ O_a \circ PU(O_b, O_a),$$

Proof: It follows directly from UE and PU definitions.

One corollary of this proposition is that using the PU procedure to execute two orthogonal conflict operations in different orders will achieve the same union effect, which is the basis to ensure convergence in 2D OT transformation functions (to be discussed in late sections).

RESOLVING CONFLICTS IN ARBITRARY OPERATIONS

In real-time collaborative editing systems, multiple operations may be generated with arbitrary concurrency and positional relationships, resulting in complex conflict scenarios, as illustrated in Figure 2. In this section, the orthogonal conflict solution is extended from two to multiple operations, and both 2D and 1D conflict resolution solutions are integrated in the same OT framework.

Adopting Existing OT Control Algorithms

An OT system consists of generic control algorithms and domain-specific transformation functions [3,7,9-12]. OT control algorithms ensures conditions governing operation execution and transformation [14,15]. One important condition is that operations with causal relationships must be executed in their causal orders; concurrent operations may be executed in any order [14,15]. There exist various distributed techniques to achieve causally ordered message delivery or operation execution [3,7,10,14,15,17].

Another important condition is that a pair of operations must be *context-equivalent* (i.e. defined on the same document state) before being transformed with each other [10,11,14,15]. Violation of this condition was the root of a major algorithmic flaw in the first OT system [3,11]. Various OT control algorithms, such as adOPTed [9], Jupiter[7], GOT/GOTO [10,11], and COT [15], have been proposed to ensure the context-equivalency condition.

As causal and context relationships among operations are generic and independent of document types or dimensions (1D/2D). Existing solutions to them can be directly adopted for supporting orthogonal conflict resolution in collaborative 2D document editing systems. In this work, we focus on the design of OT transformation functions that are special to orthogonal conflict resolution. In particular, we design special *IT (Inclusion Transformation)* functions that re-define an operation on a 2D document by including the impact of another operation [10,11]. Such transformation functions for orthogonal conflict resolution can be combined with any OT control algorithm that requires only *IT* functions (e.g. COT [15], adOPTed [9], Jupiter[7], and Google Wave OT [17], etc).

Representing Partial Union Effects

The *PU* procedure would have been adequate to solve orthogonal conflicts if two orthogonal conflict operations O_a and O_b are always executed one after the other, without interleaving with other operations in-between. In unconstrained collaborative computing environments, however, execution of two orthogonal conflict operations may be interleaved with executions of arbitrary operations. Consider the scenario in Figure 2. When O_1 arrives at site 2, it must be transformed against concurrent operations O_2 and O_4 in sequence [17]. In transforming O_1 against O_2, their orthogonal conflict relation can be detected and resolved by invoking $PU(O_1, O_2)$ to achieve the partial union effect for O_1. However, as O_2 is not the only concurrent operation that has been executed before O_1 at site 2, O_1 has to be further transformed against O_4 (to resolve potential conflict with O_4) before its execution. Therefore, the partial union effect of O_1 has to be recorded inside O_1, which may be further transformed and performed later. Mechanisms are needed to represent partial union effects within operations and to execute an operation with partial union effects properly.

Parameters of an operation are the places to record transformation effects on an operation so that execution of the transformed operation can achieve the desirable effect. Normal positional parameters of an operation, however, can only record positional shift effects caused by 1D conflict operations targeting in the same dimension, but cannot record partial union effects. Therefore, it is necessary to add a new operation parameter, called *Partial Union Effect Record* (*pur*), to record the partial union effect of an operation O with respect to another conflict operation.

Definition 10: Partial Union Effect Record (*pur*). A *pur* is a tuple of three elements, i.e. $pur = (mv, sc, dc)$, where:

1. *mv* records the MV position for this partial union effect;
2. *sc* records the position of the source cell that is to be copied for realizing this partial union effect;
3. *dc* records the position of the destination cell to insert the copied *sc* cell.

As an operation may be transformed with multiple orthogonal conflict operations, a *Partial Union Effect Record List* (*purl*) is needed to keep track of all records accumulated in transformation. We use the term *Internal Parameter* to refer to the new parameter *purl* in an operation, and the term *External Parameter* to refer to the normal positional parameter of an operation.

Executing Operations with Partial Union Effects

```
PUX(O) {
  1. for each pur in the purl of O, create an MV position
     at each pur.mv position;
  2. for each pur in the purl of O, copy the cell at
     position pur.sc and insert the copied cell at position
     pur.dc in the same dimension of O; and
  3. execute O according to its external parameters.
}
```

To execute an operation O with the internal parameter *purl*, a *Partial Union effect eXecution* (PUX) procedure is devised.

The *PUX* procedure is an extension of the *PU* procedure for handling multiple partial union effects: creating *multiple* MV positions (Step 1), and copying *multiple* source cells and inserting them into destination cells (Step 2). Inside each of the two steps, a loop is used to handle multiple records in the *purl*, but the order of handling these records is insignificant. The reasons for this order-independency are: (1) multiple MV positions can be created in any order since each MV position is unique (a property of an MV position) and the creation of an MV position has no positional shifting effect on any cell in the document; (2) source and destination cells can be copied and inserted in any order because the positional shifting effect caused by destination cell insertions can always be absorbed by existing MV cells, thanks to the OCOD property of the MV cell. By definition, the effect achieved by $PUX(O_a)$ is the same as that by $PU(O_a, O_b)$, as stated in the following proposition.

Proposition 2: Given two orthogonal conflict operations O_a and O_b, defined on the same 2D document state S, we have:

$$S \circ O_b \circ PU(O_a, O_b) = S \circ O_b \circ PUX(O_a),$$

Proof: It follows directly from PUX and PU definitions.

Furthermore, it is important to point out that among the three steps in the *PUX*, only the last two steps may cause positional shifting effects along the dimension of O in the 2D document, and their overall effects are fully captured and represented by O's external parameters. Therefore, when transforming an operation O_x against O, we only need to examine the impact of O's external parameters on O_x.

Transforming External Parameters

To transform operation O_a against O_b, we must consider O_b's impact on O_a's external parameters. Three cases can be differentiated. First, O_a and O_b are compatible, i.e. $O_a \odot O_b$, so no change is made to O_a's external parameters. Second, O_a and O_b are 1D conflicting, i.e. $O_a \oslash O_b$, so the positional parameter of O_a must be adjusted according to the impact of O_b. The *1D Conflict Resolution (1DCR)* function is defined to achieve this. The *1DCR* function invokes the *NIT* (*New IT*) function to do the real work. The *NIT* function encapsulates the address conversion between 2D to 1D according to operation dimensions, and the invocation of suitable existing 1D *IT* functions according to operation types. We leave the definition of 1D *IT* functions unspecified because there are a variety of existing 1D *IT* functions (e.g. [3,9,10, 13]) to choose from and any suitably matching 1D *IT* function can be used.

```
1DCR (Oa, Ob) {
   Oa.p := NIT(Oa.p, Ob.p, Oa.dim, Oa.type, Ob.type);
   return Oa;
}
NIT (p1, p2, d, t1, t2) {
   if (d = row) { // row-oriented
      if (t1 = I && t2 = I) p1.x := IT_II(p1.x, p2.x);
      else {// other cases are omitted for conciseness }
   } else {// column-oriented
      if (t1 = I && t2 = D) p1.y := IT_ID(p1.y, p2.y);
      else {// other cases are omitted for conciseness }
   }
   return p1;
}
```

Third, O_a and O_b are 2D conflicting, i.e. $O_a \oplus O_b$. In this case, a *pur* is created to record the partial union effect, which can be achieved by the *2D Conflict Resolution (2DCR)* function defined below. For conciseness, the *2DCR* definition assumes O_a is a row-oriented *Insert* while O_b is column-oriented *Insert* (definitions for other cases can be derived by following the same ideas illustrated here).

```
2DCR (Oa, Ob) {
   pur := new PUR; // create an empty pmr record
   if (Oa.dim = row && Oa.type = I && Ob.type = I) {
      pur.mv := (Oa.p.x, Ob.p.y);
      pur.sc := (Oa.p.x, Ob.p.y+1);
      pur.dc := (Oa.p.x+1, Ob.p.y);
   } else { //other cases are omitted for conciseness }
   if UniqueMVCheck(pur.mv,Oa,Ob) then Record(pur, Oa)
   return Oa;
}
```

In *2DCR*, a subroutine *UniqueMVCheck*(*pur.mv*, O_a, O_b) is invoked to check whether the MV position *pur.mv* is already in O_a or O_b. Only if the *pur.mv* does not exist in O_a and O_b, the new *pur* is recoded in O_a by calling *Record* (*pur*, O_a). This check is to ensure the uniqueness of an MV position in the 2D space. Actually, the OT control algorithm (e.g. COT), which ensures context-equivalence of transformed operations, also plays a role in enforcing MV uniqueness: if an operation is orthogonally conflicting with multiple operations at the same critical cell position, only one MV position will be created at this position regardless of the order of operation execution.

Transforming Internal Parameters

To transform operation O_a against O_b, it is also necessary to examine O_b's impact on internal parameters of O_a as well. The purpose of this transformation is to adjust O_a's internal parameters according to the positional shifting effect of O_b. Among three cell positions, *mv*, *sc*, and *dc*, in an internal parameter *pur*, only the *sc* and *dc* cells are subject to positional shifting effects of other concurrent operations. To illustrate the positional shifting effect on source and destination cells and to motivate key technical elements in transforming internal parameters, consider the scenario in Figure 4. There are five operations with following causal and positional relations: $O_1 \parallel (O_2 \rightarrow O_3 \rightarrow O_4 \rightarrow O_5)$; O_1 is orthogonal with O_2, O_3 and O_5; O_1 and O_4 are performed on the same column; O_2 and O_3 are performed on the same row; O_5 is performed on a parallel row; O_1 is orthogonally conflicting with O_2, O_3, and O_5, and 1D conflicting with O_4. When O_1 arrives at site 2, it needs to be transformed against O_2, O_3, O_4 and O_5 in sequence, which is determined by the control algorithm (e.g. COT).

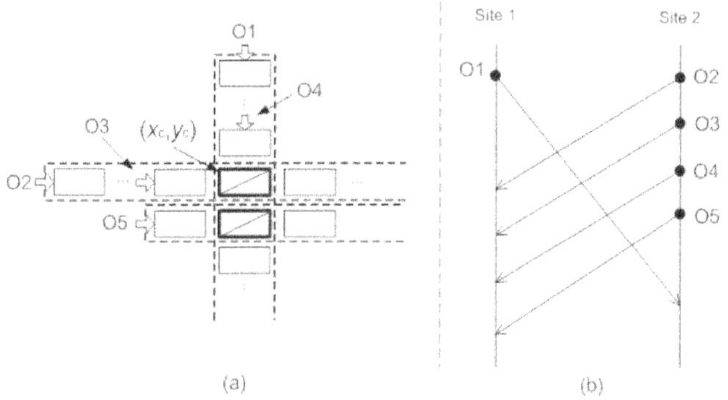

Figure 4 A scenario for illustrating transformation of source and destination cells in a *pur*.

The following steps occur at site 2. First, O_1 is transformed against O_2, and a *pur*-1 is created to resolve their orthogonal conflict and recorded in O_1. Then, O_1 is further transformed against O_3, which records no new *pur* in O_1 due to the MV uniqueness check. However, O_3 has positional shifting effects on the source cell *pur*-1.*sc* in O_1, so the position *pur*-1.*sc* should be adjusted according to the shifting effect of O_3. This adjustment is essentially resolving a 1D conflict between an internal parameter (*pur*-1.*sc)* of O_1 and O_3, and can be achieved by invoking the *NIT* on *pur*-1.*sc* against $O_3.p$.

Next, O_1 is transformed against O_4, which has positional shifting effects on not only O_1's external parameter (which can be resolved by the *1DCR* function), but also on the internal destination cell *pur*-1.*dc* which falls in the effect range of O_4. The shifting effect on *pur-1.dc* is also a 1D conflict relation between an internal parameter (*pur*-1.*dc)* of O_1 and O_4, and can be resolved by invoking the *NIT* on *pur*-1.*dc* against $O_4.p$ as well.

Finally, O_1 is transformed against orthogonal conflict operation O_5, and a new *pur*-2 is created and recorded in O_1 since it is unique. There is one thing special: O_5 has no shifting effect on the destination cell *pur*-1.*dc*, even though the effect range of O_5 covers *pur*-1.*dc*. This is because *pur*-1.*dc* has become an MV position in the new *pur*-2, due to orthogonal conflict resolution between O_1 and O_5. The *pur*-1.*dc* cell is always inserted in the same dimension as its hosting operation O_1 (see the definition of *PUX*), and hence must be orthogonal to the dimension of O_5. So, O_5 cannot shift *pur*-1.*dc* due to the ODOC property of an MV cell.

By analyzing all cases in this example, we can derive the following general conditions for a source/destination cell of an operation O_a to be affected by the positional shifting effect of another concurrent operation O_b:

1. the source/destination cell of O_a falls in the effect range of O_b (e transforming O_1 against O_3, and against O_4, in the above example), and
2. the source/destination cell is not an MV position (e.g. transforming O_1 against O_5 in the above example).

The positional shifting effect to source and destination cells is essentially a 1D conflict, stated as a proposition below.

Proposition 3. Given two operations Oa and Ob defined on the same 2D state, the positional shifting effect of Ob on Oa's an internal source/destination cell is a 1D conflict.
Proof: It follows directly from Definition 7.

Based on the general conditions for detecting positional shifting effect on internal parameters and the 1D conflict nature of such effects, the *Internal Parameter Transformation* function *IPT*(O_a, O_b) is devised, which uses the same *NIT* function based on an existing 1D *IT* to resolve this 1D conflict. One detail in invoking the *NIT* function is worth noting: the operation type for the source/destination cell position is *P* (for Pointer), which is neither *I* (for Insert) nor *D* (for Delete) because 1D *IT* functions for *P* against *I*/*D*, *i.e. IT_PI* and *IT_PD*, are different from *IT_II*, or other *I*/*D* combinations. The extra condition NOT($O_a \oplus O_b$) is to ensure a source cell is not adjusted by O_b if it is orthogonally conflicting with O_a and hence is responsible for creating the current *pur* under exam.

```
IPT(Oa, Ob) {
  pl := Oa.purl;
  for (i = 0; i < |pl|; i++) {
    if pl[i].sc is in ER(Ob) but not an MV in Ob and
                                    NOT (Oa ⊕ Ob )
   then pl[i].sc:=NIT(pl[i].sc, Ob.p, Ob.dim, P, Ob.type)
     else  if pl[i].dc is in ER(Ob) but not an MV in Oa
   then pl[i].dc:=NIT(pl[i].dc, Ob.p, Ob.dim, P, Ob.type);
   }
   return Oa;
```

2DIT Function for Resolving 1D and 2D Conflicts

Based on the component solutions, a *2D Inclusive Transformation* (*2DIT*) function is defined to provide an integrated solution for resolving both 1D and 2D conflicts.

```
2DIT (Oa, Ob) {
          if Oa ⊘ Ob then Oa := 1DCR (Oa, Ob);
          else if Oa ⊕ Ob then Oa := 2DCR (Oa, Ob);
          Oa := IPT (Oa, Ob);
          return Oa;
}
```

The *2DIT* function requires the two input operations O_a and O_b to be context-equivalent, but may have arbitrary positional relationships in the 2D document. The *2DIT* function first transforms O_a's external parameters by invoking *1DCR* to resolve 1D conflict, or *2DCR* to resolve 2D conflict, and then internal parameters by invoking *IPT* to resolve 1D conflict with internal position parameters.

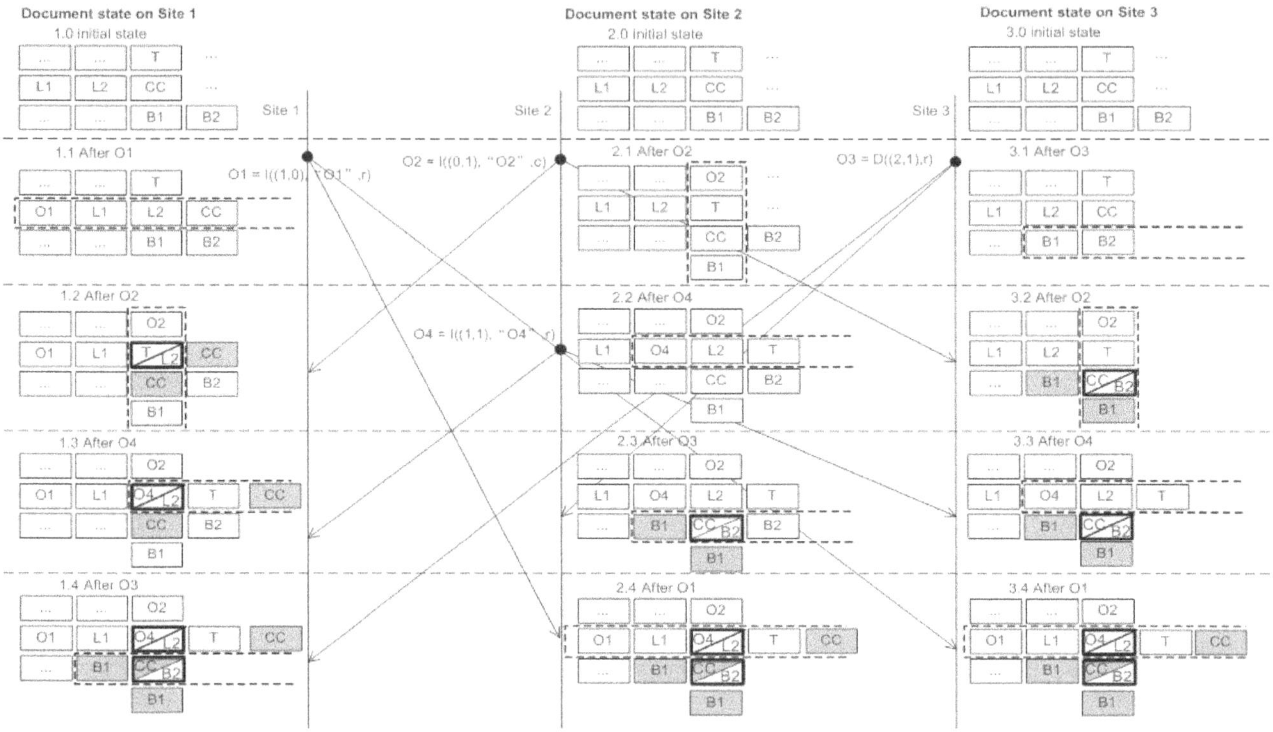

Figure. 5 A comprehensive example for illustruting the working of the 2DOT solution.

A COMPREHENSIVE EXAMPLE

In this section, one comprehensive example is used to illustrate how all components in the *2DOT* solution work together to resolve 2D and 1D conflicts. The illustration assumes that, in each invocation to $2DIT(O_a, O_b)$, O_a and O_b are *context-equivalent* ensured by the companion OT control algorithm (e.g. COT [15]). A 3-site collaborative 2D editing scenario is shown in Figure 5. Based on the positional and causal relationships of the four operations, their conflict relations can be derived: $O_1 \oplus O_2$, $O_2 \oplus O_3$, $O_1 \oslash O_4$, and all other pairs are compatible. Main steps in processing each operation at all sites are explained below.

Site 1: in order of O1, O2, O4, and O3

1. O_1 is executed as-is.
2. To process O_2, $2DIT(O_2, O_1)$ is invoked. Due to $O_2 \oplus O_1$, $2DCR(O_2, O_1)$ is invoked, which creates *pur-1* =(*mv*(1, 2), *sc*(1, 3), *dc*(2, 2)) in O_2. Then, $IPT(O_2, O_1)$ is invoked but does not change O_2. $PUX(O_2)$ is invoked to create an MV at *pur*-1.*mv* with content [*/L2*], copy cell [*CC*] from *pur-1.sc* to *pur-1.dc*, and insert [O_2] at position $O_2.p$ = (0, 1), which shifts cell [*T*] into the MV position, resulting in [*T/L2*].
3. To process O_4, $2DIT(O_4, O_1')$ is first invoked, where O_1' = $2DIT(O_1, O_2)$. Due to $O_4 \oslash O_1'$, $1DCR(O_4, O_1')$ is invoked to shift $O_4.p$ from (1, 1) to (1, 2). Then, $IPT(O_4, O_1')$ is invoked but has no effect as O_4 has no internal parameter. Finally, $PUX(O_4)$ is invoked to insert [O_4] at the MV position (1, 2), which changes the MV content from [*T/L2*] to [O_4/*L2*].
4. To process O_3, $2DIT(O_3, O_1)$ is first invoked but makes no change to O_3 since $O_3 \odot O_1$. Second, $2DIT(O_3, O_2')$ is invoked, where O_2' = $2DIT(O_2, O_1)$. As $O_3 \oplus O_2$, $2DCR(O_3, O_2')$ is invoked to create *pur*-2 = (*mv*(2, 2), *sc*(3, 2), *dc*(2, 1)) in O_3, Third, $2DIT(O_3, O_4')$ is invoked, where O_4' = $2DIT(O_4, O_1')$. Since $O_3 \odot O_4$, neither *1DCR* nor *2DCR* is invoked, and $IPT(O_3, O_4')$ makes no change to O_3. Finally, $PUX(O_3)$ is invoked to create an MV position at *pur*-2.*mv* with content [*CC/*], copy cell [*B*1] from *pur*-2.*sc* to *pur*-2.*dc*, and delete [O_3] at the cell at $O_3.p$ = (2, 1), which shifts [*B*2] into the MV position, resulting in [*CC*/*B*2].

Site 2: in order of O2, O4, O3, and O1

1. O_2 and O_4 are executed as-is in sequence.
2. To process O_3, $2DIT(O_3, O_2)$ is first invoked, which in turn invokes $2DCR(O_3, O_2)$ due to $O_2 \oplus O_3$, and creates *pur*-3 = (*mv*(3, 2), *sc*(3, 2), *dc*(2, 1)) in O3. Second, $2DIT(O_3, O_4)$ is invoked but makes no change to O_3 since $O_3 \odot O_4$ and O_4 has no effect on *pur*-3 in O_3. Finally, $PUX(O_3)$ is invoked to execute O_3.
3. To process O_1, $2DIT(O_1, O_2)$ is first invoked, which in turn invokes $2DCR(O_1, O_2)$ due to $O_1 \oplus O_2$, and creates *pur*-4 = (*mv*(1, 2), *sc*(2, 2), *dc*(1, 3)). Second, $2DIT(O_1, O_4)$ is invoked, which in turn invokes $1DCR(O_1, O_4)$ due to $O_1 \oslash O_4$, and does not change $O_1.p$; $IPT(O_1, O_4)$ shifts *pur*-4.*dc* = (1, 3) to (1, 4) as the *pur*-4.*dc* falls in the effect range of O_4, and *pur*-4.*dc* is not an MV in O_4. Third, $2DIT(O_1, O_3')$ is invoked, where O_3' = $2DIT(2DIT(O_3, O_2), O_4)$. Since $O_1 \odot O_3$, neither *1DCT* nor *2DCR* is invoked, and $IPT(O_1, O_3')$ does not change O_1, though *pur*-4.*sc* = (2, 2) falls in the effect range of O_3', because O_3' has an MV at *pur*-4.*sc* which was created in $2DIT(O_3, O_2)$. Finally, O_1 is executed by invoking $PUX(O_1)$.

Site3: in order of O3, O2, O4, O1

1. O_3 is executed as-is.

2. To process O_2, $2DIT(O_2, O_3)$ is first invoked, which in turns invokes $2DCR(O_2, O_3)$ due to $O_2 \oplus O_3$, and creates *pur*-5 = (*mv*(2, 2), *sc*(2, 1), *dc*(3, 2)). Finally, O_2 is executed by $PUX(O_2)$.
3. To process O_4, $2DIT(O_4, O_3')$ is first invoked, where $O_3' = 2DIT(O_3, O_2)$. Since $O_4 \odot O_3$, neither *1DCT* nor *2DCR* is invoked, and $IPT(O_4, O3)$ does not change O_4 either since O_4 has no internal parameter. Finally, O_4 is executed as-is by $PUX(O_4)$.
4. To process O_1, $2DIT(O_1, O_3)$ is invoked, which makes no change to O_1 since $O_1 \odot O_3$ and O_1 has no internal parameter. Then, $2DIT(O_1, O_2')$ is invoked, where $O_2' = 2DIT(O_2, O_3)$. As $O_1 \oplus O_2$, $2DCR(O_1, O_2')$ is invoked to create *pur*-6 = *mv*((1, 2), *sc*(2, 2), *dc*(1, 3)) in O_1. Next, $2DIT(O_1, O_4')$ is invoked, where $O_4' = 2DIT(O_4, O_3')$. Since $O_1 \oslash O_4$, $1DCR(O_1, O_4')$ is invoked, but makes no change to O_1 as $O_1.p$ is at the left side of $O_4'.p$. $IPT(O_1, O_4')$ changes *pur-6.dc* from (1, 3) to (1, 4) since *prm-6.dc* falls in the effect range of O_4' and is not an MV in O_4'. O_1 is executed by $PUX(O_1)$.

From the final document states at three sites, we see consistent results have been achieved by using *2DIT* functions under the control of a COT-like algorithm.

CORRECTNESS AND COMPLEXITY ANALYSIS

One assumption: *2DIT* functions are used under the control of the COT algorithm for consistency maintenance only. We only need to verify the correctness of *2DIT* functions with respect to *CP1* (Convergence Property 1) because other criteria, such as *CP2* (*Convergence Property* 2), and *IP1-3* (*Inverse Properties* for supporting group undo), are irrelevant to *2DIT* under this assumption [15]. Another assumption is that the *1DIT* functions adopted by *2DIT* functions are able to preserve *CP1*, which is easy to achieve [3,9,10,11,14,15]. Thus, the following theorem establishes the correctness of *2DIT*.

Theorem 1: Given two operations O_a and O_b defined on the same 2D document state, if $O_a' = 2DIT(O_a, O_b)$, and $O_b' = 2DIT(O_b, O_a)$, then we have:

$$S \circ O_a \circ PUX(O_b') = S \circ O_b \circ PUX(O_a')$$

Proof: For the given pair of operations O_a and O_b, they may have three possible conflict/compatible relationships: compatible, 1D conflict, or 2D conflict. We show that the theorem holds in all cases. In the compatible case, the theorem holds trivially. The 1D conflict case covers both external and internal parameters because the positional shifting effects on internal parameters are 1D conflicts according to Proposition 3. In this case, the theorem holds because of the *CP1*-preserving property of 1D *IT* functions (by assumption) adopted by *2DIT* to resolve 1D conflict for both external parameters (in *2DCR*) and internal parameters (in *IPT*). In the 2D conflict case, $2DIT(O_a, O_b)$ invokes $2DCR(O_a, O_b)$ to record the partial union effect in the internal parameters of O_a, and the transformed O_a' will be executed by invoking $PUX(O_a')$. According to Proposition 2, the effect of $PUX(O_a')$ is exactly the same partial union effect achieved by $PU(O_a, O_b)$, i.e.

$$S \circ O_b \circ PUX(O_a') = S \circ O_b \circ PU(O_a, O_b).$$

Following the same reasoning, we can derive:

$$S \circ O_a \circ PUX(O_b') = S \circ O_a \circ PU(O_b, O_a).$$

By Proposition 1, the theorem holds in the 2D conflict case as well. Thus the theorem holds for all cases.

For OT time complexity, a common measurement is the number of transformation function invocations for each operation to be executed [14]. From the assumption that *2DIT* functions are used under the control of COT, which has a linear time complexity (with respect to concurrent operations) for consistency maintenance [15], we derive the same linear time complexity for the 2DOT solution in terms of *2DIT* function invocations. A *2DIT* invocation may include one *1DIT* call for transforming external parameters, plus additional *1DIT* calls for transforming internal parameters (source/destination cells) due to orthogonal conflict, which is bounded by the number of concurrent operations as well. So, the time complexity of the *2DOT* solution in terms of *1DIT* function invocations is $O(n^2)$, where n is the number of operations that are concurrent or context independent with the operation to be executed. More work is needed for real performance measurement and evaluation of 2DOT in the future.

Some caveats for theoretic verification of OT correctness and complexity analysis. Theoretic verification plays an important but limited role in validating an OT solution since verification criteria (e.g. *CP1-2, IP1-3*) cover only a restricted part of a complete OT solution, and not all criteria are relevant to every OT solution. Many aspects of an OT solution do not lend themselves well to rigorous description and verification, and can be more effectively addressed by real implementation and benchmarking [14]. Worst case time complexity rarely matters in real-time collaborative sessions since the degree of concurrency is often small and a transformation function call is cheap [14]. In reality, time efficiency of a real OT system has much more to do with its practical implementation than theoretic complexity. More comprehensive discussions on the facts and myths related to OT correctness and complexity can be found in [14].

COMPARISON TO RELATED WORK

Conflict resolution has been explored in a wide range of collaborative systems. Floor control, locking, and serialization were commonly used conflict prevention and resolution strategies for supporting collaborative work [4], but they were found too restrictive for collaborative work that require concurrent and free interactions [2,3,10,13]. Due to its lock-free and unconstrained interaction properties, OT is particularly suitable for supporting real-time collaboration over the Internet [1,7,9,11,12,14-17].

To the best of our knowledge, there exist only two prior work directly related to applying OT to collaborative spreadsheet/table editing systems [8,16]. In [8], transformation functions were defined for operations with 2D addresses, rather than 1D addresses as in most other OT systems. A set of spreadsheet operations were derived from a public domain spreadsheet system *sc*, which include: *insert* (full rows/columns), *delete* (full rows/columns), and *set*, *format*, and *copy* the cell value in a spreadsheet. Concurrent semantics for the set of operations were defined and transformation functions were proposed to resolve linear positional shifting conflicts (or 1D conflicts) among concurrent operations. 2D orthogonal conflicts, however, may occur among concurrent operations inserting or deleting *any number of* cells, including a full row/column of cells, but this 2D conflict issue was not addressed in [8].

In [16], a 2D table is represented as a sequence of rows (row-based) or columns (column-based); and 1D OT techniques (control algorithms and transformation functions) are directly used to support operations on tables. In a row-based table representation, cells belonging to the same row can be addressed by their indexes in the row, but cells belonging to the same column are scattered among multiple rows. Consequently, row-oriented operations can be processed efficiently, but column-oriented operations are inefficient as they have to be decomposed into multiple operations targeting individual cells. The reverse is true for column-based representation. This 1D hierarchical approach works reasonably well when the table size (the number of cells in a row or column) is relatively small (e.g. tables in word processor documents), but it does not scale well to tables with a very large number of rows/columns, like Microsoft Excel spreadsheets (with 64K rows or columns). Moreover, the technique in [16] was unable to resolve the orthogonal conflict issue either.

2DOT provides a solution to orthogonal conflict, but it alone is not a complete solution to supporting collaborative 2D applications. 2DOT needs to be integrated with suitable OT control algorithms like COT [15], and with other transformation functions like those from [8, 16] to provide a comprehensive OT solution to collaborative 2D systems. In our future work, 2DOT will be extended to handle data schemas (or constraints) and support group undo in real-time collaborative spreadsheet editing sessions.

CONCLUSIONS

In this work, we have contributed a novel OT technique for resolving the orthogonal conflict problem in collaborative 2D document editing systems. This work is the first to identify, formalize and solve the orthogonal conflict problem in real-time collaborative systems. The extension of OT from 1D to 2D conflict resolution is fundamental to the theory and practical application of OT, and represents an important advancement to the state-of-the-art of OT.

When OT was originally invented to solve the 1D positional shifting problem in concurrent inserting/deleting characters in a string, few people predicted such primitive capability would evolve into a tech for supporting a range of real-world collaborative applications. 2DOT was invented to resolve orthogonal conflict (2D positional shifting problem) in spreadsheets, but we anticipate potential application of 2DOT to any collaborative computing problem that can be modeled as concurrent operations inserting/deleting objects in multi-dimensional workspaces. Future exploration will discover more applications as well as limitations of OT.

ACKNOWLEDGEMENT

The authors wish to thank anonymous expert reviewers for their insightful and encouraging comments and suggestions.

REFERENCES

1. Agustina, C. Sun, and D. Xu,"Operational transformation for dependency conflict resolution in real-time collaborative 3D design systems," *ACM Conf. on CSCW*, 2012, Feb. 2012.
2. J. Begole, M. B. Rosson, and C. A. Shaffer, "Flexible collaboration transparency: supporting worker independence in replicated application-sharing systems," *ACM Transactions on Computer-Human Interaction,* 6(2), pp. 95-132, 1999.
3. C. A. Ellis and S. J. Gibbs, "Concurrency control in groupware systems," *ACM SIGMOD Conf.*,1989, pp. 399-407.
4. S. Greenberg and D. Marwood, "Real time groupware as distributed system: concurrency control and its effect on the interface." *ACM Conf. on CSCW*, pp.207–217, Oct. 1994.
5. L. Lamport, "Time, clocks, and the ordering of events in a distributed system," *CACM*, 21(7), pp. 558-565, 1978.
6. D. Li and R. Li, "Transparent sharing and interoperation of heterogeneous single-user applications," *ACM Conf. on CSCW*, 2002, pp. 246-255.
7. D. A. Nichols, P. Curtis, M. Dixon and J. Lamping, "High-latency, low-bandwidth windowing in the Jupiter collaboration system," *ACM Symp. on UIST*, 1995, pp. 111-120.
8. C. Palmer and G. Cormack, "Operation transforms for a distributed shared spreadsheet," *ACM Conf. on CSCW*, 1998, pp. 69-78.
9. M. Ressel, et al, "An integrating, transformation-oriented approach to concurrency control and undo in group editors," *ACM Conf. on CSCW*, 1996, pp. 288-297.
10. C. Sun, X. Jia, Y. Zhang, Y. Yang, and D. Chen, "Achieving convergence, causality preservation, and intention preservation in real-time cooperative editing systems," *ACM Transactions on Computer-Human Interaction,* 5(1), pp. 63-108, 1998.
11. C. Sun and C. Ellis, "Operational transformation in real-time group editors: issues, algorithms, and achievements," *ACM Conf. on CSCW*, 1998, pp.59-68.
12. C. Sun, S. Xia, D. Sun, D. Chen. H.F. Shen and W. Cai: "Transparent adaptation of single-user applications for multi-user real-time collaboration," *ACM Transactions on Computer-Human Interaction,*13(4), pp. 531 – 582, Dec. 2006.
13. D. Sun, S. Xia, C. Sun and D. Chen, "Operational transformation for collaborative word processing," *ACM Conf. on CSCW, 2004,* pp. 437-446.
14. C. Sun,"OTFAQ: Operational Transformation Frequent Asked Questions and Answers," http://cooffice.ntu.edu.sg/otfaq,2011.
15. D. Sun, and C. Sun, "Context-Based Operational Transformation in Distributed Collaborative Editing Systems," *IEEE Transactions Parallel Distributed Systems*, 20(10), pp. 1454-1470, 2009.
16. S. Xia, D. Sun, C. Sun, and D. Chen, "A collaborative table editing technique based on transparent adaptation," *Intl. Conf. on CoopIS*, 2005, pp. 576 - 593.
17. D. Wang and A. Mah, "Google Wave Operational Transformation",*http://www.waveprotocol.org/whitepapers/ operational-transform*.

Operational Transformation for Dependency Conflict Resolution in Real-time Collaborative 3D Design Systems

Agustina, Chengzheng Sun, Dong Xu
School of Computer Engineering, Nanyang Technological University, Singapore
{Agustina, CZSun, DongXu}@ntu.edu.sg

ABSTRACT
Conflict resolution is one major challenge in real-time distributed collaborative 3D design systems, which allow concurrent collaborative work on shared 3D documents. Operational Transformation (OT) is a core conflict resolution technique in a range of real-world collaborative systems. No existing OT technique is, however, capable of resolving conflicts among objects with dependency relations, i.e. an update of one object may propagate to other connected/dependent objects, which is commonly used in 3D or complex graphic design systems. This paper contributes a novel OT solution with such a capability for collaborative 3D design systems. This work is the first to extend OT capability to dependency conflict resolution, and OT application scope from 1D/2D to 3D applications, thus advancing the state-of-the-art of OT in both theory and practical application. The proposed solution has been theoretically verified for its correctness in detecting dependency conflicts and achieving consistent results, and implemented in the CoMaya collaborative design system.

Author Keywords
Concurrency control; consistency maintenance; dependency conflict resolution; operational transformation; real-time collaborative 3D design systems.

ACM Classification Keywords
H.5.3 [**Information Interfaces and Presentation**]: Group and Organization Interfaces – Synchronous Interaction.

General Terms
Algorithms; Theory.

INTRODUCTION
The process of creating 3D digital media contents for movies, scientific explorations, product simulations, etc. is very complex and lengthy. It typically involves collaboration from a group of designers with different roles or expertise and possibly at geographically dispersed locations. This collaboration process can be supported by real-time collaborative 3D design systems, which allow multiple geographically dispersed people to edit shared 3D documents at the same time over computer networks [1].

Such systems will increase not only the efficient use of human and financial resources, but also the productiveness, quality, and competitiveness of the work of 3D designers.

To achieve good responsiveness in Internet environments, nearly all real-time collaborative editing systems [1,2,8,9,21] adopt a *replicated* architecture, i.e. shared documents and the application are replicated at all sites in a collaborating session. Advanced collaborative editing systems support the notion of *unconstrained* collaboration [17], i.e. multiple users can *freely* and *concurrently* interact with the local copy of the application and document. One core issue in supporting unconstrained collaboration over distributed and replicated documents is conflict resolution in the face of concurrent operations [4,6,15,17].

In collaborative document editing, two operations conflict if they are concurrent and their executions in different orders result in inconsistent document states. Conflicts can be prevented by prohibiting concurrency (e.g. by locking or floor-control) [3,6,10], or resolved by concurrency control techniques (e.g. serialization [7,8,22] and *Operational Transformation* (OT) [4,16,17,18,20]). Early collaborative 3D (virtual environments) systems adopt either locking (e.g. in blue-C [11], Mu3D [5], etc.), or serialization (e.g. in Avocado [22], DIV [7], etc.) for achieving document consistency. Prohibiting concurrency contradicts with the objective of unconstrained collaboration, thus it is not an option for advanced real-time collaborative editors [21]. Serialization allows concurrency and is able to ensure document *convergence*, but unable to achieve *intention preservation* [17]. OT, on the other hand, is able to resolve conflicts and maintain consistency (achieving both *convergence* and *intention preservation*) in unconstrained collaborative environments. OT was originally invented for supporting collaborative editing of plain text documents [4], and was later extended for supporting any linearly addressable objects (e.g. office productivity documents) and for resolving conflicts among concurrent operations on overlapping objects [21]. OT has been increasingly adopted as the core real-time collaboration technique by industrial collaborative applications, including SubEthaEdit[1], Google Wave/Docs[2], IBM OpenCoWeb[3], and Codoxware[4].

---

[1] http://www.codingmonkeys.de/subethaedit/
[2] http://en.wikipedia.org/wiki/Google_Docs
[3] https://github.com/opencoweb/coweb#readme
[4] http://www.codoxware.com

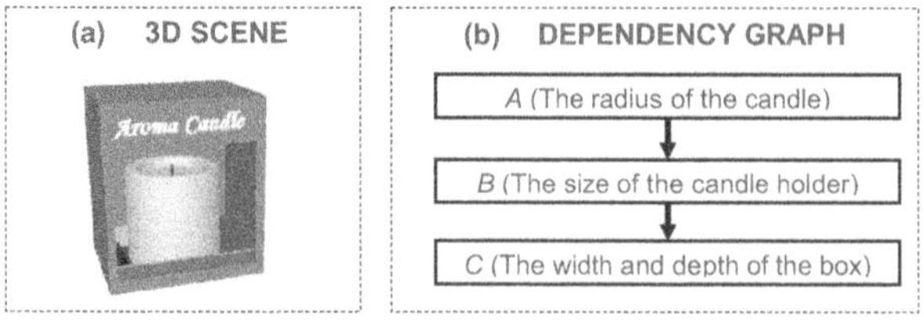

Figure 2. Dependency relations of an aroma candle.

From the point of view of conflict resolution, state-of-the-art OT techniques are capable of resolving conflicts caused by concurrent operations on: (1) *address-dependent* objects (e.g. concurrent insert and delete on a sequence of characters [16]); and (2) *overlapping* objects (e.g. concurrent updates on the same attribute of the same object [21]). However, existing OT techniques are restricted to supporting documents with *attribute-independent* data objects, i.e. an update of the attribute value of one object has no impact on the attribute value of another object. The attribute-independent object model is suitable for plain or rich text documents for office productivity tools (e.g. Word, PowerPoint, etc.), but unsuitable for complex graphic documents (e.g. 3D documents supported by design tools like Autodesk Maya, 3ds Max, etc.)

To support comprehensive 3D graphic functionalities (e.g. modeling, rigging, animation, deformation, etc.), professional 3D design applications map high-level 3D objects into internal graphic objects (called *g-objects*), and organize them into a *Dependency Graph* (*DG*) [13,22]. Many 3D design applications provide multiple user interfaces (UIs) to allow end-users to manipulate 3D-objects (which are then mapped into operations on internal g-objects), and directly manipulate the internal g-objects. In a DG, nodes represent g-objects, and arrows represent *attribute-dependency* relationships among connected g-objects: when the attribute of one g-object is changed (by any means), the changed attribute value will propagate from this g-object to all downstream g-objects (if any) in the DG.

For example, the 3D model of an aroma candle in Figure 1a has, among others, three internal g-objects with the attribute dependency relationships as shown in Figure 1b: g-object C (representing the width and depth of the box) depends on g-object B (representing the size of the candle holder) that depends on g-object A (representing the radius of the candle). Under such dependency relationships, a change to the radius of the candle (by a user from the 3D or g-object UI) will also change the size of the holder and then the width and depth of the box. These dependencies capture the interdependent relationships among related objects and are useful in fitting the candle to the candle holder and box. However, with such attribute-dependency relationships among g-objects, concurrent operations may conflict with each other even if their target g-objects are not overlapping.

To illustrate this special conflict problem in collaborative DG-based 3D design systems, consider the concurrency scenario using the 3D model in Figure 1. Suppose two users intend to modify different aspects of the model

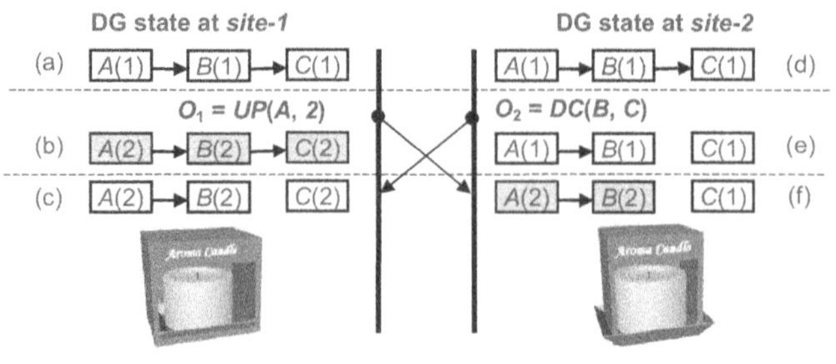

Figure 1. Dependency conflict in a DG.

concurrently: one is to make the candle fatter, and the other is to change the box design for containing multiple candles and to this end, this user has to first remove the dependency relation of the box with the candle holder. Although the two users are modifying different aspects of the same model, their actions happen to be conflicting due to the internal dependency relation of the targets, as explained below. Let $N(x)$ denotes node N with an attribute value x and $\rightarrow$ denotes a connection (attribute-dependency relationship), the initial DG state is: $A(1)\rightarrow B(1)\rightarrow C(1)$ (Figure 2a and d). To achieve their purposes, the two users generate two operations concurrently: O_1 is to increase the radius of the candle by updating the attribute value of node A from $A(1)$ to $A(2)$, which is propagated to downstream nodes, and O_2 is to remove the dependency of the candle holder with the candle by removing the connection between nodes B and C. After executing the two operations in different orders: (1) O_1 followed by O_2 (at *site-1*), the DG becomes $A(2) \rightarrow B(2)$ and $C(2)$ (Figure 2c), with the candle and its holder still fit into the box; and (2) O_2 followed by O_1 (at *site-2*), the DG becomes $A(2) \rightarrow B(2)$ and $C(1)$ (Figure 2f), with the candle holder no longer fits to the box. Clearly, the two candle models are different due to inconsistent final DGs: $C(2) \neq C(1)$. This means O_1 and O_2 conflict with each other even though they do not share any common target object! Their conflict is due to the attribute-dependency relationship among their target objects: nodes B and C (targets of O_2) are depending on node A (the target of O_1). This kind of conflict is named as *Dependency Conflict*.

In unconstrained collaborative editing environments, operations with arbitrary *causal-dependency* (or concurrency) relations can be generated to target objects with arbitrary *attribute-dependency* relationships. Conflict resolution and consistency maintenance (achieving both convergence and intention preservation) in such environments is a new challenge that has never been addressed by prior work [1,5,8,11,15,17]. In this paper, we contribute a novel OT technique for dependency conflict resolution in collaborative DG-based 3D design systems.

The rest of the paper is organized as follows. First, we define the basic object and operation models in a DG. We then discuss the dependency conflict relations and detection conditions, and define the combined effects for conflict and compatible operations. Afterwards, we present the OT solution for dependency conflict resolution. Finally, we summarize the main contributions and future work.

OBJECTS AND OPERATIONS IN A DG

Object Dependency Relations

A DG is composed of a collection of nodes (representing g-objects) and arrows (representing attribute-dependency relations among g-objects), as defined below.

DEFINITION 1. Dependency Graph. *A dependency graph DG is represented as a tuple* $(\mathcal{N}, \mathcal{A})$, *where* $\mathcal{N}$ *is a set of nodes, and* $\mathcal{A}$ *is a set of arrows and* $\mathcal{A} = \{(S, D) \mid S, D \in \mathcal{N}\}$.

The attribute-dependency relation of two nodes in the DG is defined as follows.

DEFINITION 2. Dependency Relation. *Given two nodes, A and B, in a DG =* $(\mathcal{N}, \mathcal{A})$, *i.e.* $A, B \in \mathcal{N}$, *A and B have an* attribute-dependency *relation or simply* dependency *relation, denoted as DR(A, B), iff:* (1) $A = B$; (2) *there is an arrow from A to B, i.e.* $(A, B) \in \mathcal{A}$; *or* (3) *there is a node X* $\in \mathcal{N}$, *such that DR(A, X) and DR(X, B).*

From the graphic point of view, a pair of nodes, *A* and *B*, has a dependency relation if there is a sequence of arrows from node *A* to node *B*. Terms such as dependency relation, arrow, and connection mean the same thing and are used interchangeably in this paper. The notation $DR(A, B)^d$ is used to indicate the *distance d* (i.e. the number of arrows) between two dependent nodes *A* and *B*. A node can be regarded as self-dependent, i.e. $d = 0$. The dependency relations among nodes in Figure 2a are: $DR(A, A)^0$, $DR(B, B)^0$, $DR(C, C)^0$, $DR(A, B)^1$, $DR(B, C)^1$, and $DR(A, C)^2$.

For simplicity and clarity in discussing dependency conflict resolution, we assume: (1) each node has only one attribute (hence a node may have only one input arrow but multiple output arrows); and (2) a node always propagates the input attribute value as-is (i.e. without making any change to it). According to Definition 1 and 2, and above assumptions, a *valid* DG must meet three conditions: (1) there is no *dangling arrow* in the DG; (2) there is no more than one input arrow to each node; and (3) dependent nodes have the same attribute value. In real systems, however, each node may have multiple attributes (and thus multiple input arrows), and may apply an internal function to transform the input value (received from an upstream node) into a new output value (to be propagated to downstream nodes). The discussions and solutions presented in this paper are generalizable to systems which allow multiple attributes per node and functional transformation at each node.

Operations in a DG

G-objects in a graphic design system can be addressed in various ways, provided they are unique and consistent for the same replicas [1,15]. For clarity, g-objects in our examples are identified simply by using unique alphabets.

In attribute-independent graphic editing systems, there are three basic operations: a *Create* operation creates a new g-object, a *Delete* operation removes an existing g-object, and an *Update* operation changes the attribute value of a g-object [15]. DG-based graphic design systems also have these operations, but the *Update* operation has an additional effect of propagating the change of an attribute value to all dependent g-objects. DG-based graphic design systems have two additional basic operations: a *Connect* operation establishes a dependency relation of two g-objects, and propagates the attribute value of one g-object (the *source*) to another g-object (the *destination*), which may further propagates the value to downstream g-objects (if any); and a *Disconnect* operation removes the dependency relation of two g-objects. It is worth highlighting that a *Disconnect* cannot reverse the effects of a *Connect* because a *Disconnect* can only remove a dependency relationship established by a *Connect,* but cannot eliminate the attribute value propagated by a *Connect*. All operations except *Update* may change the structure of a DG; *Update* may only change attribute values of DG nodes.

A general requirement for a DG operation is that its execution must transform a valid DG state into another valid DG state. To ensure that the execution of a DG operation will lead to a valid DG state, certain specific conditions must be met for an operation to be generated from and/or executed on a document state. For example, a *Delete* operation must not target an object with any connection because otherwise the execution of the *Delete* operation will lead to an invalid DG state with dangling arrows. Such conditions are called operation *preconditions*. In single-user 3D design systems, operation preconditions are enforced by the underlying system: when a user is to generate an operation, the underlying system will check the current DG state to see whether the preconditions of the operation are met. If so, the operation will be generated and executed successfully; otherwise, the generation will fail and have no effect on the DG state. As we will explain later, operation preconditions play an important role in detecting and resolving dependency conflicts.

The execution effect of an operation on the DG state can be specified as a set of *postconditions*, which capture the changes to the DG state. One general postcondition for all operations is the resulting DG state must be valid. Postconditions can be used to evaluate preconditions for follow up operations and detecting potential conflicts as well. In the following, we give precise specifications of the five DG operations, together with their preconditions and postconditions, on the initial DG state $G = (\mathcal{N}, \mathcal{A})$.

1. ***X* := *CR*(*g*)**: *Create* a new g-object *g* and return the identifier *X*.
   a. ***Pre-CR***: none.
   b. ***Post-CR***: a new g-object *g* with the identifier *X* is added into the DG, i.e. $G = (\mathcal{N} \cup \{X\}, \mathcal{A})$.
2. ***DL*(*X*)**: *Delete* an existing g-object *X*.
   a. ***Pre-DL***: *X* must exist in the DG and have no input/output connection, i.e. $(X \in \mathcal{N}) \wedge (\forall(S, D) \in \mathcal{A}\ (S \neq X \wedge D \neq X))$.
   b. ***Post-DL***: *X* is removed from the DG, i.e. $G = (\mathcal{N} \setminus \{X\}, \mathcal{A})$.
3. ***UP*(*X*, *v*)**: *Update* the attribute value of a g-object *X* with *v*.

a. ***Pre-UP***: X must exist in the DG and have no input connection, i.e. $(X \in \mathcal{N}) \wedge (\forall(S, D) \in \mathcal{A}\, (D \neq X))$.
b. ***Post-UP***: attribute values of X and its downstream g-objects are updated with value v, *i.e.* $G = (\mathcal{N}', \mathcal{A})$ where $\mathcal{N}' = \{Y \mid (Y \in \mathcal{N}) \wedge (DR(X, Y)^d \rightarrow Y.v = v)\}$.

4. ***CN(S, D)***: *Connect* the source g-object S to the destination g-object D.
   a. ***Pre-CN***: S and D must exist in the DG and D must not have any input connection, i.e. $(S, D \in \mathcal{N}) \wedge (\forall(X, Y) \in \mathcal{A}\, (Y \neq D))$.
   b. ***Post-CN***: a connection from S to D is established and the attribute value of S is propagated to D and its downstream g-objects, i.e. $G = (\mathcal{N}', \mathcal{A}')$, where $\mathcal{N}' = \{Y \mid (Y \in \mathcal{N}) \wedge (DR(S, Y)^d \rightarrow Y.v = S.v)\}$ and $\mathcal{A}' = \mathcal{A} \cup \{(S, D)\}$.
5. ***DC(S, D)***: *Disconnect* the source g-object S from the destination g-object D.
   a. ***Pre-DC***: S and D must exist in the DG and a connection between S and D must also exist, i.e. $(S, D \in \mathcal{N}) \wedge ((S, D) \in \mathcal{A})$.
   b. ***Post-DC***: the connection from S to D is removed, i.e. $G = (\mathcal{N}, \mathcal{A} \setminus \{(S, D)\})$.

The above operation notations capture only essential parameters for discussing dependency conflict resolution. In real systems, DG operations may carry additional parameters required by the application. In the absence of concurrency, a precondition met at the local site when an operation was generated can also be met when this operation is executed at a remote site. In the presence of concurrency in real-time collaboration, however, a precondition met at the local site may be violated at a remote site due to the execution of other concurrent operations. Due to different execution orders of concurrent operations, the same operation may succeed in one execution order but fail in another order, leading to inconsistent document states.

DEPENDENCY CONFLICT RELATION AND DETECTION

Conflict Definition

Operations in collaborative design systems may have dependency conflict/compatible relations as defined below.

DEFINITION 3. *Dependency Conflict Relation "⊗".* *Given two DG operations,* O_1 *and* O_2*, they have a* Dependency Conflict Relation*, denoted as* $O_1 \otimes O_2$*, iff*: (1) O_1 *and* O_2 *are defined on the same DG state*; (2) *targets of* O_1 *and* O_2 *have dependency relations*; *and* (3) *different execution orders of* O_1 *and* O_2 *result in different DG states, i.e. different DG structures and/or g-objects values.*

DEFINITION 4. *Compatible Relation "⊙".* *Given two operations,* O_1 *and* O_2*, they have a* Compatible Relation*, denoted as* $O_1 \odot O_2$*, iff they do not have a dependency conflict relation, i.e.* $\neg(O_1 \otimes O_2)$.

The overlapping conflict relation, as defined in [15], can be viewed as a special case of the dependency conflict relation since the overlapping g-objects targeted by concurrent operations can be viewed as self-dependent g-objects with a zero distance dependency relation (i.e. $DR(A, B)^0 \leftrightarrow A = B$).

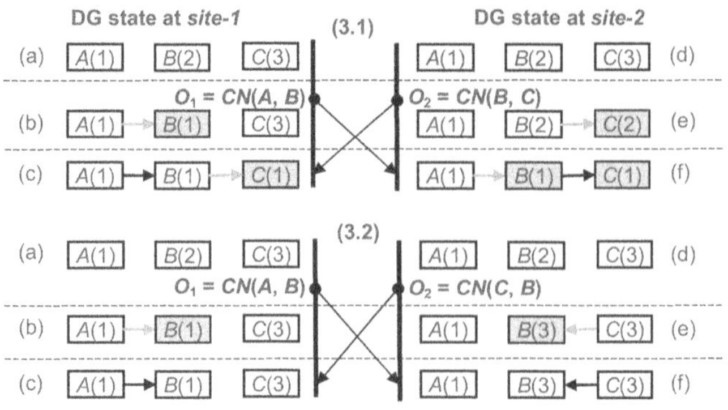

Figure 3. Concurrent operations with common targets: (3.1) compatible relation; and (3.2) conflict relation.

Target-dependency is a necessary but insufficient condition for two operations to have a dependency conflict relation. To illustrate, consider the scenario in Figure 3.1: two connect operations, $O_1 = CN(A, B)$ and $O_2 = CN(B, C)$, are generated concurrently by *site-1* and *site-2*, respectively, over an initial DG state: $A(1)$, $B(2)$, and $C(3)$ (Figure 3.1a and d). Regardless on which orders operations are executed, O_1 followed by O_2, or O_2 followed by O_1, the DG becomes $A(1) \rightarrow B(1) \rightarrow C(1)$ consistently after both operations have been executed as shown in Figure 3.1c and f. In this case, the two operations are compatible even though they share one common target g-object B (thus being dependent).

Consider a similar scenario in Figure 3.2 with the same initial DG state but slightly different parameters for O_2, where $O_2 = CN(C, B)$. Suppose these two operations are executed in the order of O_1 followed by O_2 (at *site-1*). After the execution of O_1, the DG becomes $A(1) \rightarrow B(1)$, $C(3)$ (Figure 3.2b). The execution of O_2 failed due to the *precondition* that the destination g-object cannot have any existing input connection as specified in *Pre-CN*, thus the DG cannot be changed by O_2 (Figure 3.2c). Now suppose these two operations are executed in the reverse order of O_2 followed by O_1 (at *site-2*). After the execution of O_2, the DG becomes $A(1)$, $B(3) \leftarrow C(3)$ (Figure 3.2e). The execution of O_1 also failed due to the violation of the same precondition *Pre-CN* and the DG cannot be changed by O_1 either (Figure 3.2f). After both operations are executed, the dependency relation and attribute value of B are clearly different on different execution orders. In this case, the two operations conflict due to a shared g-object B.

To summarize, in both Figure 3.1 and 3.2, the two operations share a common (thus dependent) target g-object B, but they conflict only in the case of Figure 3.2. The inconsistent result (thus conflict) was caused by the failure of one of the operations due to a precondition violation. Preconditions are useful hints for conflict detection, but precondition-violation alone is neither necessary nor sufficient for determining whether two operations conflict.

	$CR(g_2)$	$DL(X_2)$	$UP(X_2, v_2)$	$CN(S_2, D_2)$	$DC(S_2, D_2)$
$CR(g_1)$	$\odot$	$\odot$	$\odot$	$\odot$	$\odot$
$DL(X_1)$		$\odot$	$\odot$	$\otimes \leftrightarrow DR(X_1, S_2)^0$ or $DR(X_1, D_2)^0$	$\odot$
$UP(X_1, v_1)$			$\otimes \leftrightarrow DR(X_1, X_2)^0$	$\odot$	$\otimes \leftrightarrow DR(X_1, S_2)^d$
$CN(S_1, D_1)$				$\otimes \leftrightarrow DR(D_1, D_2)^0$	$\otimes \leftrightarrow DR(D_1, S_2)^d$
$DC(S_1, D_1)$					$\odot$

Table 1. Conflict relations and detection conditions

There are subtle scenarios, in which precondition-violating operations may not conflict, and precondition-satisfying operations may conflict. The next section provides precise and theoretically verified conflict detection conditions between every pair of the five DG operations.

Conflict/Compatible Relations

Based on comprehensive analysis, we summarize the conflict/compatible relations between all pairs of DG operations in Table 1. Some pairs of operations are always compatible because either their targets do not (or cannot) have any dependency relation (e.g. a *CR* with all other operations) or their executions in different orders always result in the same DG state (e.g. a pair of *DL*s). Some other pairs may be either compatible or conflicting, depending on the dependency relations of their targets and whether their executions in different orders result in the same or different DG states. There are five such pairs: *DL-CN*, *UP-UP*, *UP-DC*, *CN-CN*, and *CN-DC*, of which precise conflict conditions are filled in the corresponding cells of Table 1.

We have conducted theoretical verification on the conflict conditions for every pair of operations. Due to space limitation, only the proof for a pair of *UP* and *DC* is presented here to show the basic ideas and methods of our verification. First, we introduce Lemma 1 which establishes some necessary conditions for an *UP* to conflict with another operation generated from the same DG state.

Lemma 1: Given an $UP(X_1, v)$ and any operation O with a target X_2 generated from the same DG state $G = (\mathcal{N}, \mathcal{A})$, they are conflicting only if X_1 is overlapping with or on the upstream of X_2, i.e. $DR(X_1, X_2)^d$, where $d \geq 0$.

Proof: First, for an $UP(X_1, v)$ to conflict with O, their targets must have a dependency relation according to Definition 3. Second, it is impossible for their targets to have a dependency relation other than X_1 is overlapping with or on the upstream of X_2, i.e. $DR(X_1, X_2)^d$, where $d \geq 0$. Otherwise, X_1 would have an input connection, i.e. $\exists Y \in \mathcal{N}$ $((Y, X_1) \in \mathcal{A})$, which contradicts with the *Pre-UP* for generating $UP(X_1, v)$. Hence, the lemma follows.

Theorem 1: An $UP(X, v)$ conflicts with a $DC(S, D)$ defined on the same DG state $G = (\mathcal{N}, \mathcal{A})$ *iff* X is overlapping or on the upstream of S, i.e. $UP(X, v) \otimes DC(S, D) \leftrightarrow DR(X, S)^d$.

Proof: First, we show the theorem holds for $UP(X, v) \otimes DC(S, D) \longrightarrow DR(X, S)^d$. From the precondition that $UP(X, v)$ conflicts with $DC(S, D)$, we derive X is overlapping or on the upstream of S, i.e. $DR(X, S)^d$, where $d \geq 0$, by Lemma 1. Second, we show the theorem holds for $DR(X, S)^d \longrightarrow UP(X, v) \otimes DC(S, D)$. In case $UP(X, v)$ is executed before $DC(S, D)$: (1) $UP(X, v)$ will update X and its downstream with value v and result in $G_1 = (\mathcal{N}_1, \mathcal{A}_1)$ where $\mathcal{N}_1 = \{Y \mid (Y \in \mathcal{N}) \wedge (DR(X, Y)^d \rightarrow Y.v = v)\}$ and $\mathcal{A}_1 = \mathcal{A}$; and (2) $DC(S, D)$ will only remove the arrow (S, D) from $\mathcal{A}$ and result in $G_1' = (\mathcal{N}_1', \mathcal{A}_1')$ where $\mathcal{A}_1' = \mathcal{A} \setminus \{(S, D)\}$ and $\mathcal{N}_1' = \{Y \mid (Y \in \mathcal{N}) \wedge ((DR(X, Y)^d \vee DR(D, Y)^d) \rightarrow Y.v = v)\}$ because $DC(S, D)$ has split X's downstream nodes (in G_1), which share the same attribute value as X, into two groups: (a) nodes from X to S (due to $DR(X, S)^d$), expressed by $DR(X, Y)^d$, and (b) nodes from D and downwards (due to the connection (S, D)), expressed by $DR(D, Y)^d$. In case $DC(S, D)$ is executed before $UP(X, v)$: (1) $DC(S, D)$ will remove the arrow (S, D) from $\mathcal{A}$ and result in $G_2 = (\mathcal{N}_2, \mathcal{A}_2)$ where $\mathcal{N}_2 = \mathcal{N}$ and $\mathcal{A}_2 = \mathcal{A} \setminus \{(S, D)\}$; and (2) $UP(X, v)$ will update X and its downstream nodes, up till S due to $DR(X, S)^d$, and result in $G_2' = (\mathcal{N}_2', \mathcal{A}_2)$, where $\mathcal{N}_2' = \{Y \mid (Y \in \mathcal{N}) \wedge (DR(X, Y)^d \rightarrow Y.v = v)\}$. From the fact that $(DR(D, Y)^d \rightarrow Y.v = v)$ is in G_1' but not G_2', we have $G_1' \neq G_2'$ and conclude $UP(X, v)$ and $DC(S, D)$ conflict under the condition $DR(X, S)^d$ by Definition 3. The theorem holds under all circumstances.

COMBINED EFFECTS OF CONCURRENT OPERATIONS

General Requirements on Combined Effects

The following three general requirements are imposed on the combined effects of concurrent operations, with or without dependency conflicts:

1. ***Convergence***: combined effects must be identical at all sites, in terms of attribute values of all g-objects and their dependency relations in the DG.
2. ***Intention-confined effect***: combined effects should be confined by user-generated operations; namely, no changes can be made to dependency relations or attribute values of g-objects in the DG, unless such changes are initiated by user-generated operations.
3. ***Aggressive effect preservation***: combined effects should preserve effects of compatible operations fully, and effects of conflicting operations as much as possible.

These requirements are not a replacement for the general consistency requirements for collaborative editors in [19]. The first requirement is a specialization of the *convergence property* in [19]: covering not only the value part of g-objects but also the structure of the DG. The second and third requirements together define a special form of the *intention preservation* property in [19]: changes made to the DG must be initiated by user-generated operations and as much operation effects as possible should be preserved even in the face of conflict, which is desirable in real-time collaborative working environments with optimistic concurrency control strategies [4,6,15,20]. The *causality preservation* property in [19] should also be preserved in collaborative 3D design systems, but is not listed here as it is irrelevant to defining combined effects of operations.

Combined Effects for DG Operations

Guided by the general requirements on combined effects, we define six concrete combined effects for operations in Table 1 as follows.

1. ***CE1***: the combined effect for compatible operations is the union of the effects of all operations, which can be achieved by executing compatible operations in any causality-preserving order.
2. ***CE2***: the combined effect for conflicting *DL* and *CN*, i.e. $DL(X) \otimes CN(S, D)$, is: (1) the target X is deleted, which preserves the effect of $DL(X)$; and (2) there exists no connection from S to D (as one of them must overlap with X and has been deleted) but the attribute value of S has been propagated to D (if it is not the target of $DL(X)$), which preserves part of the effect of $CN(S, D)$.
3. ***CE3***: the combined effect for conflicting *UP*s, i.e. $UP(X, v_1) \otimes UP(X, v_2)$, is the attribute value of the overlapping target X and its downstream are updated with either v_1 or v_2, depending on the priority between the two *UPs*. This is a case that a conflict is resolved by priority and only one operation effect is preserved.
4. ***CE4***: the combined effect for conflicting *UP* and *DC*, i.e. $UP(X, v) \otimes DC(S, D)$, is: (1) the attribute value of X is updated to v and propagated to its downstream g-objects (including S and D), which preserves the full effect of $UP(X, v)$; and (2) the connection from S to D is broken, which preserves the effect of $DC(S, D)$. This is a case that all conflicting operations effects are preserved.
5. ***CE5***: the combined effect for conflicting *CN*s, i.e. $CN(S_1, D) \otimes CN(S_2, D)$, is: only one connection is successful, depending on the priority of the two *CN*s. This is another case that a conflict is resolved by priority and only one operation effect is preserved.
6. ***CE6***: the combined effect for conflicting *CN* and *DC*, i.e. $CN(S_1, D_1) \otimes DC(S_2, D_2)$, is: (1) a connection from S_1 to D_1 is established, and the attribute value of S_1 is propagated to its downstream g-objects (including D_1, S_2 and D_2), which preserves the full effect of $CN(S_1, D_1)$; and (2) the connection from S_2 to D_2 is removed, which preserves the effect of $DC(S_2, D_2)$. This is another case that all conflicting operations effects are preserved.

Various priority schemes can be used in the priority-based resolution for $UP \otimes UP$ and $CN \otimes CN$ cases. For example, priorities can be based on a total ordering of operations [17]. To facilitate total ordering and concurrency checking, operations are time-stamped with state vectors [17].

OT-BASED DEPENDENCY CONFLICT RESOLUTION

Basic Idea

From the point of view of consistency maintenance, the basic idea of OT is to transform an operation defined on one context (i.e. a document state) into another operation defined on a new context, so that the transformed operation can be correctly executed on the new context and achieve document consistency in the face of concurrent operations [16,17]. This basic OT idea can be applied for consistency maintenance in the face of concurrent operations with dependency conflict relations.

To illustrate this, consider again the scenario in Figure 2, in which operations are always executed in their original forms and different execution orders of the two dependency conflicting operations O_1 and O_2 result in inconsistent DG states. This problem can be resolved if a remote operation is transformed against the other concurrent operation in such a way that the transformed operation can achieve the same and correct combined effect. For the scenario in Figure 2, the combined effect for a pair of *UP* and *DC* operations should be the *CE4*, which preserves effects of all operations. We observed that the effects of O_1, when generated at its local *site-1* (Figure 2b), are to update the attribute value of not only g-object A, but also the two dependent g-objects: B and C. However, these effects cannot be fully achieved if O_1 is executed (as-is) on a different DG states at *site-2*, where C is no longer depending on A (the target of O_1) due to the prior execution of O_2 (Figure 2e). To achieve the full effects of O_1 on the new DG state, an additional *UP* operation should be performed on C. From the OT's point of view, O_1 should be transformed (against O_2) into a list of two operations: one is the original *UP* operation on g-object A and the other is a new *UP* operation on g-object C. The execution of the transformed O_1 would achieve the full effects of O_1. At *site-1*, O_2 should be transformed (against O_1) as well; but this transformation does not change O_2. In this way, a consistent and correct combined effect *CE4* can be achieved at both sites: the candle and its holder are resized and fit into the resized box. This combine effect is also a desirable one because the user at *site-2* can directly rescale only the width of the box to achieve the objective of fitting multiple candles in the box.

Transformation Control Algorithm

An OT system consists of generic control algorithms and domain-specific transformation functions [16,17]. OT control algorithms determine the correct order and conditions for operation transformations and executions, while transformation functions perform the actual transformation of an operation against another operation according to the types and parameters of the operations. One important condition is that for two operations to be transformed with each other, they must be defined on the same document state (i.e. *context-equivalent*) [12,18]. The violation of this condition has been well known as the root problem of some prior OT algorithms.

Past research of OT has devised various transformation control algorithms that preserve the context-equivalency condition, e.g. adOPTed [14], GOT/GOTO [16,17], Jupiter [12], COT [18], etc. These control algorithms are independent of application domains and can be directly adopted for supporting dependency conflict resolution. We designed our transformation functions based on two requirements imposed by control algorithms: (1) the transformation functions are *Inclusion Transformation* (IT), which is to include the impact of the reference operation [16,17]; and (2) the transformation functions preserve the *Convergence Property 1* (CP1), i.e. applying O_x followed by $O_y' = T(O_y, O_x)$ on a DG state G achieves the same effect as applying O_y followed by $O_x' = T(O_x, O_y)$ on the same G [16]. COT and Jupiter are example of control algorithms that impose only these requirements and any of them can be adapted (i.e. to call the *LOT* function defined in the next sub-section, instead of the *T* function) and integrated with the dependency conflict resolution presented in this paper.

Transformation of Lists of Operations

OT-based dependency conflict resolution may transform an operation into a *list of operations* (*LO*) in resolving dependency conflict, as seen in the previous example. To facilitate transformations at the *LO* level, i.e. transforming one LO_1 against another context-equivalent LO_2, a list OT function *LOT* is defined in the pseudocode form as follows.

Algorithm-1: *LOT(LO₁, LO₂)*

```
1:  var LO1' := [ ];
2:  Repeat until LO1 = [ ]:
3:     if LO2 = [ ] then { LO1 := LO1' + LO1; return; }
4:     else{
5:        Remove Ox from LO1, where Ox is the first element in LO1;
6:        Remove Oy from LO2, where Oy is the first element in LO2;
7:        LOx := T(Ox, Oy);  LOy := T(Oy, Ox);
8:        LOT(LOx, LO2);
9:        LO1' := LO1' + LOx;   LO2 := LOy + LO2;  }
10: LO1 := LO1';
```

In *LOT*, the following repeats until LO_1 becomes empty. If LO_2 is empty, it inserts LO_1', which is the transformation result so far, in front of LO_1 and returns (1.3); otherwise, it removes the first element O_x from LO_1 and O_y from LO_2 (1.5, 1.6). Then, it transforms O_x against O_y and O_y against O_x by the transformation function $T(O_x, O_y)$ (see the next section for *T* function definition), which return LO_x and LO_y, respectively (1.7). Afterwards, the *LOT* function is recursively invoked to further transform LO_x against the remaining operations in LO_2 (1.8). After the recursive call, LO_x stores the transformation result of O_x against all operations in the initial LO_2, and LO_2 stores the transformation result of all operations but O_y in the initial LO_2 against O_x. Then, LO_x is merged with LO_1' (i.e. $LO_1' = LO_1' + LO_x$) and LO_y, which is the transformed value of the first element of the initial LO_2, is inserted in front of the transformed LO_2, i.e. ($LO_2 = LO_y + LO_2$) (1.9). Finally, after all operation in LO_1 has been transformed (i.e. when LO_1 becomes empty), LO_1' overwrites LO_1 (1.10), so LO_1 contains the transformed operations against LO_2.

There are two things that we should point out. First, the *LOT* function not only transforms LO_1 against LO_2, but also transforms LO_2 against LO_1, which is necessary to ensure the context-equivalency of later transformations. Second, for the concurrency/context checking, all operations in *LO* share the same state/context vector [17,18].

Transformation Functions

Algorithm-2: *T(Oₓ, O_y)*

```
if type(Ox) = DL and type(Oy) = CN then
    LO := Tdlcn(Ox, Oy);
else if type(Ox) = CN and type(Oy) = DL then
    LO := Tcndl(Ox, Oy);
else if ... // other cases are omitted for conciseness
return LO;
```

The transformation function $T(O_x, O_y)$ in Algorithm-2 transforms O_x against O_y in such a way that the effect of O_y is included in O_x (i.e. *IT* [16,17]). The transformation function has the following precondition and postcondition:

- ***Pre-T***: O_x and O_y are context-equivalent.
- ***Post-T***: an operation O is included in the returned *LO* only if its precondition is satisfied after sequentially executing other preceding operations in *LO*; and the execution of O_y followed by all operations in *LO* achieves the combined effects defined in *CE1–CE6*.

The postcondition also implies that any operation with a precondition violation would not be included in *LO* and has no impact on subsequent executions and transformations. This is important for ensuring the correctness of the transformation.

The following basic strategies are used in designing the transformation function: assume O_y has been executed, assess the impact of O_y on the DG state and derive what should be executed to achieve the combined effects of O_x and O_y according to *CE1–CE6*. Based on the types of O_x and O_y, function $Tpq(O_x, O_y)$ is invoked to transform O_x to achieve a suitable combined effect. In each $Tpq(O_x, O_y)$: (1) if $O_x \otimes O_y$ (see Table 1 for conflict detection conditions), O_x is transformed into a list of operations that can jointly achieve the suitable combined effect according to *CE2–CE6*; (2) if $O_x \odot O_y$, then O_x is transformed into $[O_x]$ in case that its preconditions are met, or [ ] in case that its preconditions are violated (so O_x should not have any effect in later executions or transformations), according to *CE1*.

According to Table 1, conflicts may occur only for five pairs of operation types. For each pair of operation types, *p* and *q*, two transformation functions *Tpq* and *Tqp* need to be defined for handling two different orders of execution. Since pairs *UP-UP* and *CN-CN* need only one function for each case, a total of *eight* transformation functions cover all conflict resolution cases. For the compatible pairs, there are four cases that involve precondition violations and require the operation to be nullified so that it will not affect subsequent transformations. The pseudocode of the transformation functions are defined in Algorithm-3.

Algorithm-3: Transformation Functions

Tdlcn(DL(X), CN(S, D)):

```
if DL(X) ⊗ CN(S, D) then return [DC(S, D), DL(X)];
else return [DL(X)]; // for DL(X) ⊙ CN(S, D)
```

Tcndl(CN(S, D), DL(X)):

```
if DL(X) ⊗ CN(S, D) then {
    if S ≠ X then return [ ]; // i.e. D = X
```

```
    else return [UP(D, S.v)]; }
else return [CN(S, D)]; // for CN(S, D) ⊙ DL(X)

Tupup(UP1(X1, v1), UP2(X2, v2)):
if UP1(X1, v1) ⊗ UP2(X2, v2) then {
    if HigherPriority(UP1, UP2) then return [UP1(X1, v1)];
    else return [ ]; }
else return [UP1(X1, v1)]; // for UP1(X1, v1) ⊙ UP2(X2, v2)

Tupdc(UP(X, v), DC(S, D)):
if UP(X, v) ⊗ DC(S, D) then return [UP(X, v), UP(D, v)];
else return [UP(X, v)]; // for UP(X, v) ⊙ DC(S, D)

Tdcup(DC(S, D), UP(X, v)):
  return [DC(S, D)]; //for both ⊗ and ⊙ relations

Tcncn(CN1(S1, D1), CN2(S2, D2)):
if CN1(S1, D1) ⊗ CN2(S2, D2) then {
    if HigherPriority(CN1, CN2) then
        return [DC(S2, D2), CN1(S1, D1)];
    else return [ ]; }
else return [CN1(S1, D1)]; // for CN1(S1, D1) ⊙ CN2(S2, D2)

Tcndc(CN(S1, D1), DC(S2, D2)):
if CN(S1, D1) ⊗ DC(S2, D2) then
    return [CN(S1, D1), UP(D2, S1.v)];
else return [CN(S1, D1)]; // for CN(S1, D1) ⊙ DC(S2, D2)

Tdccn(DC(S1, D1), CN(S2, D2)):
  return [DC(S1, D1)]; //for both ⊗ and ⊙ relations

Tdldl(DL1(X1), DL2(X2)):
if X1 = X2 then return [ ]; //Pre-DL violation
else return [DL1(X1)];

Tupdl(UP(X1, v), DL(X2)):
if X1 = X2 then return [ ]; //Pre-UP violation
else return [UP(X1, v)];

Tupcn(UP(X, v), CN(S, D)):
if X = D then return [ ];     // Pre-UP violation
else return [UP(X, v)];

Tdcdc(DC1(S1, D1), DC2(S2, D2)):
if(S1 = S2 and D1 = D2) then return [ ]; //Pre-DC violation
else return [DC1(S1, D1)];

//Details for transformation functions Tcrcr, Tcrdl, Tdlcr, Tcrup,
//Tupcr, Tcrcn, Tcncr, Tcrdc, Tdccr, Tdlup, Tdldc, Tdcdl, and Tcnup
//are omitted because they handle pairs of compatible operations
//whose pre-conditions are always satisfiable in execution, and hence
//always return the original operation.
```

The combined effect for a pair of concurrent $DL(X)$ and $CN(S, D)$ should be *CE2* in both execution orders. (1) The *Tdlcn* function handles the case that $DL(X)$ is executed after $CN(S, D)$. If conflict is detected, $DL(X)$ is transformed into a list of two operations: $DC(S, D)$ to remove the connection from S to D for satisfying the *Pre-DL*, and then $DL(X)$ to delete the target X. Otherwise (compatible), it returns $[DL(X)]$. (2) The *Tcndl* function handles the case that $CN(S, D)$ is executed after $DL(X)$. In case of conflict, it returns an empty list [ ] if $S \neq X$; else it returns an $UP(D, S.v)$ to propagate the value of S (i.e. $S.v$) to D. Otherwise (compatible), it returns $[CN(S, D)]$.

The combined effect for a pair of concurrent *UP* is *CE3*. Only one *Tupup* function is needed. In case of conflict, it returns $[UP_1(X_1, v_1)]$ if $UP_1(X_1, v_1)$ has a higher priority than $UP_2(X_2, v_2)$; else it returns [ ]. In case of compatible, it returns $[UP_1(X_1, v_1)]$. The combined effect for a pair of concurrent $UP(X, v)$ and $DC(S, D)$ is *CE4*. (1) The *Tupdc* function handles the case that $UP(X, v)$ is executed after $DC(S, D)$. If conflict, it returns a list of two operations: the original $UP(X, v)$, followed by a new $UP(D, v)$ to propagate the attribute value v to D. If compatible, it returns $[UP(X_1, v)]$. (2) The *Tdcup* function handles the case that $DC(S, D)$ is executed after $UP(X, v)$. It returns $[DC(S, D)]$ regardless whether the two operations conflict or not.

The combined effect for a pair of concurrent *CN* operations is *CE5*. Only one *Tcncn* function is needed. In case of conflict, if $CN_1(S_1, D_1)$ has a higher priority than $CN_2(S_2, D_2)$, it returns a list of two operations: $DC(S_2, D_2)$ to break the connection from S_2 to D_2, followed by $CN_1(S_1, D_1)$; else it returns [ ]. In case of compatible, it returns $[CN_1(S_1, D_1)]$. The combined effect for a pair of concurrent $CN(S_1, D_1)$ and $DC(S_2, D_2)$ is *CE6*. (1) The *Tcndc* function handles the case that $CN(S_1, D_1)$ is executed after $DC(S_2, D_2)$. If conflict, it returns a list of two operations: $CN(S_1, D_1)$, followed by an $UP(D_2, S_1.v)$ to propagate the attribute value of S_1 to D_2 and its downstream. If compatible, it returns $[CN(S_1, D_1)]$. (2) The *Tdccn* function handles the case that $DC(S_2, D_2)$ is executed after $CN(S_1, D_1)$. It returns $[DC(S_2, D_2)]$ regardless whether the two operations conflict or not.

The combined effect for other pairs of operations is *CE1* as they are compatible pairs. However, based on *Post-T*, operations with precondition violations must be nullified. The *Tdldl*, *Tupdl*, *Tupcn*, and *Tdcdc* functions handle the cases where two operations are always compatible but the preconditions may be violated under certain conditions: if preconditions are violated, these functions return an empty list; otherwise, they return the original operation. It should be pointed out that in *Tdlcn* and *Tcncn*, the *DC* is not to undo the conflicting operation *CN* (thus move *backward* to an old *DG* state) as in some serialization approaches like [8], but to move *forward* to a new *DG* state that meets the precondition for the *DL* and *CN*. In fact, undoing *CN* cannot be achieved by simply removing the connection because it requires eliminating the value propagation effect as well.

Convergence property of Transformation Functions

For any pair of DG operations O_x and O_y, their combined effect is defined by *CE1*–*CE6*, regardless of their execution orders. Let G be a *DG* state, $O_x' = T(O_x, O_y)$ and $O_y' = T(O_y, O_x)$. The T function is required to preserve the following *Convergence Property*:

$$G \circ O_x \circ O_y' = G \circ O_y \circ O_x',$$

which means applying O_x followed by O_y' on a state G achieves the same effect as applying O_y followed by O_x' on the same G (i.e. TP in [4], TP1 in [16], and CP1 in [18]).

We have conducted theoretical verification on the convergence property for every pair of DG operations. Due to space limitations, we only include the proof of one pair, $UP(X, v)$ and $DC(S, D)$, to show the basic ideas that can be applied to the proof of other pairs of operations.

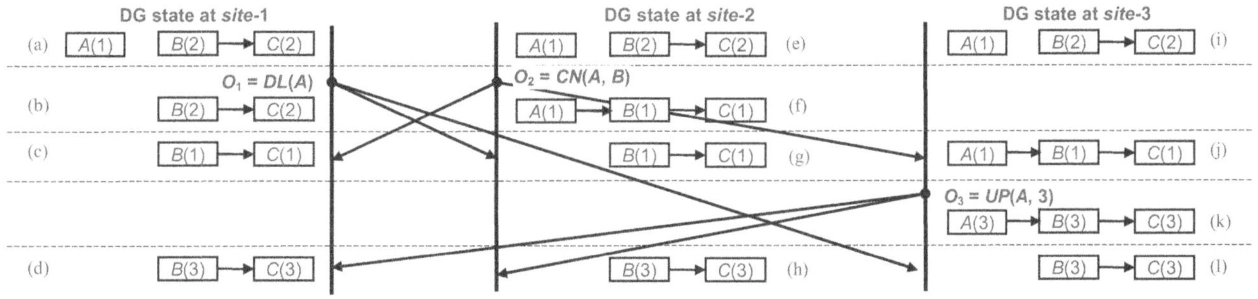

Figure 4. An example of dependency conflict resolution.

Theorem 2: Given two operations, $O_x = UP(X, v)$ and $O_y = DC(S, D)$, defined on the same state $G = (\mathcal{N}, \mathcal{A})$, the convergence property $G \circ O_x \circ O_y' = G \circ O_y \circ O_x'$ is preserved for $O_x' = Tupdc(O_x, O_y)$ and $O_y' = Tdcup(O_y, O_x)$.

Proof: It is trivial (so details are omitted) to show convergence is preserved when O_x and O_y are compatible, i.e. $O_x \odot O_y$, since their preconditions are always satisfied in execution according to *Pre-UP*, *Pre-DC*, and Theorem 1. So, we only show convergence is preserved when they are conflicting, i.e. $O_x \otimes O_y$. From Theorem 1 and $O_x \otimes O_y$, we derive $DR(X, S)^d$. According to the definitions of *Tupdc* and *Tdcup*, we have $O_x' = [UP(X, v), UP(D, v)]$, and $O_y' = [DC(S, D)]$, respectively. In the following, we show that the states produced by executing O_x and O_y in different orders are the same under the condition $DR(X, S)^d$.

For the execution sequence $G \circ O_x \circ O_y'$: (1) O_x will update X and its downstream nodes, and result in $G_1 = (\mathcal{N}_1, \mathcal{A}_1)$, where $\mathcal{N}_1 = \{Y \mid (Y \in \mathcal{N}) \wedge (DR(X, Y)^d \rightarrow Y.v = v)\}$ (by *Post-UP*), and $\mathcal{A}_1 = \mathcal{A}$; (2) *Pre-DC* for O_y' must be met as (S, D) is in $\mathcal{A}_1$ and hence in $\mathcal{A}$, so O_y' will only remove the arrow (S, D) from $\mathcal{A}$ and result in $G_1' = (\mathcal{N}_1', \mathcal{A}_1')$, where $\mathcal{A}_1' = \mathcal{A} \setminus \{(S, D)\}$ (by *Post-DC*), and $\mathcal{N}_1' = \{Y \mid (Y \in \mathcal{N}) \wedge ((DR(X, Y)^d \vee DR(D, Y)^d) \rightarrow Y.v = v)\}$ because $DC(S, D)$ has split X's downstream nodes (in G_1), which share the same attribute value as X, into two groups: (a) nodes from X to S (due to $DR(X, S)^d$), expressed by $DR(X, Y)^d$, and (b) nodes from D and downwards (due to (S, D)), expressed by $DR(D, Y)^d$.

For the execution sequence $G \circ O_y \circ O_x'$: (1) O_y will remove the arrow (S, D) from $\mathcal{A}$ and result in $G_2 = (\mathcal{N}_2, \mathcal{A}_2)$, where $\mathcal{N}_2 = \mathcal{N}$ and $\mathcal{A}_2 = \mathcal{A} \setminus \{(S, D)\}$ (by *Post-DC*); and (2) O_x' contains two sub operations and their preconditions (*Pre-UP*) must be met since O_y removes but not add an arrow from/into the *DG*: (a) $UP(X, v)$ will update X and its downstream nodes, up till S due to $DR(X, S)^d$, and result in $G_2' = (\mathcal{N}_2', \mathcal{A}_2)$, where $\mathcal{N}_2' = \{Y \mid (Y \in \mathcal{N}) \wedge (DR(X, Y)^d \rightarrow Y.v = v)\}$ (by *Post-UP*); (b) $UP(D, v)$ will update D and its downstream nodes, expressed as $DR(D, Y)^d$, and results in $G_2'' = (\mathcal{N}_2'', \mathcal{A}_2)$, where $\mathcal{N}_2'' = \{Y \mid (Y \in \mathcal{N}) \wedge ((DR(X, Y)^d \vee DR(D, Y)^d) \rightarrow Y.v = v)\}$ (by *Post-UP*).

By comparing G_1' and G_2'', we have $G_1' = G_2''$, so the theorem holds when $O_x \otimes O_y$. Therefore, the theorem holds under all circumstances.

AN INTEGRATED EXAMPLE

The OT-based dependency conflict resolution presented in this paper has been used in the CoMaya real-time collaborative 3D design system [1]. In this section, we use the *classic dOPT-puzzle* scenario [16], as shown in Figure 4, to illustrate how the whole system works. Three operations, $O_1 = DL(A)$, $O_2 = CN(A, B)$, and $O_3 = UP(A, 3)$, are generated by *site-1*, *site-2*, and *site-3*, respectively, with the causal relations $O_1 \parallel (O_2 \rightarrow O_3)$. The initial DG states at all sites are: $A(1)$ and $B(2) \rightarrow C(2)$ (Figure 4a, e, and i). The processing of each operation at all three sites is as follows.

Site-1 in the order of O_1, O_2, and O_3 (Figure 4b – d):

1. O_1 is executed as-is and results in $B(2) \rightarrow C(2)$.
2. When O_2 arrives, $LOT([O_2], [O_1])$ is invoked and results in $[O_{2a}]$ where $O_{2a} = UP(B, 1)$, by *Tcndl* due to $O_2 \otimes O_1$. The execution of O_{2a} results in $B(1) \rightarrow C(1)$.
3. When O_3 arrives: (a) $LOT([O_1], [O_2])$ is first invoked to bring $[O_1]$ to the same context as O_3 (the key step to resolving the *dOPT-puzzle* [16]), which results in $[O_{1a}, O_1]$, where $O_{1a} = DC(A, B)$, by *Tdlcn* due to $O_1 \otimes O_2$; and (b) $LOT([O_3], [O_{1a}, O_1])$ is then invoked, which first results in $[O_3, O_{3a}]$, where $O_{3a} = UP(B, 3)$, by *Tupdc* due to $O_3 \otimes O_{1a}$, and then these results are transformed with $[O_1]$ into $[O_{3a}]$ by *Tupdl* due to $O_3 \odot O_1$, $O_{3a} \odot O_1$, and *Pre-UP* violation for O_3. The execution of O_{3a} results in $B(3) \rightarrow C(3)$.

Site-2 in the order of O_2, O_1, and O_3 (Figure 4f – h):

1. O_2 is executed as-is and results in $A(1) \rightarrow B(1) \rightarrow C(1)$.
2. When O_1 arrives, $LOT([O_1], [O_2])$ is invoked and results in $[O_{1a}, O_1]$ (see step 3(a) at *site-1*). The execution of O_{1a} followed by O_1 results in $B(1) \rightarrow C(1)$.
3. When O_3 arrives, it is processed in the same manner as in step 3 at *site-1* and results in $[O_{3a}]$. The execution of O_{3a} results in $B(3) \rightarrow C(3)$.

Site-3 in the order of O_2, O_3, and O_1 (Figure 4j – l):

1. O_2 is executed as-is and results in $A(1) \rightarrow B(1) \rightarrow C(1)$.
2. O_3 is executed as-is and results in $A(3) \rightarrow B(3) \rightarrow C(3)$.
3. When O_1 arrives: (a) $LOT([O_1], [O_2])$ is first invoked and results in $[O_{1a}, O_1]$ (see step 3(a) at *site-1*); and (b) $LOT([O_{1a}, O_1], [O_3])$ is then invoked and results in $[O_{1a}, O_1]$ due to $O_{1a} \odot O_3$ and $O_1 \odot O_3$. The execution of O_{1a} followed by O_1 results in $B(3) \rightarrow C(3)$.

The final DG states at all sites are the same: $B(3) \rightarrow C(3)$, as shown in Figure 4d, h, and l.

CONCLUSIONS AND FUTURE WORK

In this paper, we have contributed a novel OT technique to resolve dependency conflicts in DG-based real-time unconstrained collaborative 3D design systems. This work is the first to extend OT capability from *address*-dependency to *attribute*-dependency conflict resolution, and OT application scope from 1D/2D to 3D applications, thus advancing the state-of-the-art of OT in both theory and practical application.

Main elements of the contribution include: (1) formal definitions of attribute-dependency conflict relations, detection conditions, pre- and post-conditions for five generic primitive operations – *Create, Delete, Connect, Disconnect, and Update* – on a general DG model; (2) definitions of both general and operation-specific requirements on combined effects of concurrent operations that ensure convergence and preserve operation effects in the face of conflicts; (3) OT transformation techniques and functions for resolving attribute dependency conflicts and achieving required effects; and (4) theoretical verification of conflict conditions and the correctness of the proposed solution. The proposed solution has been implemented in the CoMaya collaborative 3D design system.

The OT-based dependency conflict resolution technique in this paper is designed for supporting five primitive graphic operations on a general DG model. Like other OT solutions based on primitive operations (e.g. character insert/delete), combined effects at the primitive operation level may not always meet the user needs when multiple primitive operations are considered together. In real world collaborative systems (e.g. CoMaya), user interactions may generate *compound* operations, each of which is composed of multiple primitive operations. Additional conflict resolution mechanisms are required to support complex semantics of compound operations in the face of conflict. We are in the process of extending the dependency conflict resolution technique from primitive to complex compound operations and incorporating creative conflict resolution in collaborative design process [19]. Another future work is to support group undo in the face of dependency conflicts.

ACKNOWLEDGEMENT

This work is partially carried out at BeingThere Centre sponsored by the Singapore NRF and Interactive & Digital Media Program Office, MDA; and partially supported by the Agency of Science, Technology and Research of Singapore under SERC Grant 0821010018. The authors wish to thank anonymous reviewers for their insightful and constructive comments and suggestions.

REFERENCES

1. Agustina, F. Liu, S. Xia, H.F. Shen, and C. Sun. CoMaya: incorporating advance collaboration capabilities into 3D digital media design tools. *Proc. ACM CSCW 2008*, 5–8.
2. J. Begole, R. Smith, C. Struble, and C. Shaffer. Flexible collaboration transparency: supporting worker independence in replicated application-sharing systems. *TOCHI*, 6(2), 1999, 95–32.
3. P. Dourish. Consistency guarantees: exploiting application semantics for consistency management in a collaboration toolkit. *Proc. ACM CSCW 1996*, 268–277.
4. C.A. Ellis and S.J. Gibbs. Concurrency control in groupware systems. In *ACM SIGMOD Record*, 18(2), 1989, 399–407.
5. R. Galli and Y. Luo. Mu3D: a causal consistency protocol for a collaborative VRML editor. *Proc. ACM Web3D-VRML 2000*, 53–62.
6. S. Greenberg and D. Marwood. Real time groupware as distributed system: concurrency control and its effect on the interface. *Proc. ACM CSCW 1994*, 207–217.
7. G. Hesina, D. Schmalstieg, A. Fuhrmann, and W. Purgathofer. Distributed Open Inventor: a practical approach to distributed 3D graphics. *Proc. ACM VRST 1999*, 74–81.
8. C. Ignat and M. Norrie. Draw-Together: graphical editor for collaborative drawing. *Proc. ACM CSCW 2006*, 269–278.
9. R. Li, and D. Li. Transparent sharing and interoperation of heterogeneous single-user applications. *Proc. ACM CSCW 2002*, 246–255.
10. J. Munson and P. Dewan. A concurrency control framework for collaborative systems. *Proc. ACM CSCW 1996*, 278–287.
11. M. Naef, E. Lamboray, O. Staadt, and M. Gross. The blue-c distributed scene graph. In *Proc ACM. IPT/EGCE Workshop 2003*, 125–133.
12. D.A. Nicholas, P. Curtis, M. Dixon, and J. Lamping. High-latency, low-bandwidth windowing in the Jupiter collaboration system. *Proc. ACM UIST 1995*, 111–120.
13. K.P. Picott, B. McPherson, W.D. Angus, and I.V. Nagendra. System and method for using dependency graphs for the control of a graphics creation process. United State Patent No. 5,808,625, 1998.
14. M. Ressel, D. Nitsche-Ruhland, and R. Gunzenhauser. An integrating, transformation-oriented approach to concurrency control and undo in group editors. *ACM CSCW 1996*,288–297.
15. C. Sun and D. Chen. Consistency maintenance in real-time collaborative graphics editing systems. *TOCHI*, 9(1), 2002, 1–41.
16. C. Sun and C. A. Ellis. Operational transformation in real-time group editors: issues, algorithms, and achievements. *Proc. ACM CSCW 1998*, 59–68.
17. C. Sun, X. Jia, Y. Zhang, Y. Yang, and D. Chen. Achieving convergence, causality preservation, and intention preservations in real-time cooperative editing systems. *TOCHI*, 5(1), 1998, 63–108.
18. D. Sun and C. Sun. Context-based operational transformation in distributed collaborative editing systems. *TPDS*, 20(10), 2009, 1454–1470.
19. D. Sun, C. Sun, S. Xia and HF Shen. Creative conflict resolution in collaborative editing systems. *Proc ACM CSCW 2012.*
20. C. Sun, H. Wen and H. Fan. Operational transformation for orthogonal conflict resolution in collaborative two-dimensional document editors. *Proc. ACM CSCW 2012.*
21. C. Sun, S. Xia, D. Sun, D. Chen, H.F. Shen, and W. Cai, Transparent adaptation of single-user applications for multi-user real-time collaboration. *TOCHI*, 13(4), 2006, 531–582.
22. H. Tramberend. Avocado: a distributed virtual reality framework. *Proc. IEEE VR 1999*, 14–21.

Creative Conflict Resolution in Collaborative Editing Systems

David Sun
EECS, University of California Berkeley, USA

Chengzheng Sun
Nanyang Technological University, Singapore

Steven Xia
Sybase Pte Ld, Singapore

Haifeng Shen
Flinders University, Australia

ABSTRACT
Conflict is common in collaboration, and may have both negative and positive effects on collaborative work. Past research has focused on controlling negative aspects of conflict by preventing, eliminating or isolating conflicts, but done little on exploring positive aspects of conflict. In this paper, we contribute a novel *creative conflict resolution* (CCR) approach to address these issues in real-time collaborative editing systems. In addition to maintaining consistency, the CCR approach is able to create new results from conflicts, generate alternative solutions based on collective effects of conflict operations, and support users to choose suitable conflict solutions and conflict resolution policies according to their needs. The CCR approach provides not only a new way of resolving conflicts in real-time collaborative editing systems, but also a framework for supporting a range of existing conflict resolution strategies. Techniques and user interface issues related to the CCR approach and a prototype implementation are discussed in this paper.

ACM Classification Keywords
H.5.2 [Information Interfaces and Presentation]: Group and Organization Interfaces - Collaborative computing.

General Terms
Algorithms; Design; Theory

INTRODUCTION
Conflict is a common phenomenon in collaboration between people, and conflict management is one of the central concerns in designing collaborative applications [5, 7]. Conflict may have both negative and positive effects on work [5], so conflict management for collaborative applications should not only control negative aspects but also explore positive aspects of conflict. Real-time collaborative editing systems are a class of collaborative applications that allow geographically dispersed people to view and edit shared text, graphics, or multimedia documents at the same time over the Internet [1, 3, 9, 10, 12, 15, 16, 19]. In these systems, conflict may occur when users simultaneously change the content of shared documents [2, 7, 8, 18, 20]. A main negative effect with concurrency-related conflicts is data inconsistency. Past research has focused on controlling such negative effects by restricting users in their interaction with the system or imposing system-solutions on users, but done little on exploring positive aspects of conflicts. To put existing conflict resolution approaches in perspective, we provide a taxonomy of representative approaches according to their way of maintaining consistency as follows.

Conflict prevention maintains consistency by prohibiting users from doing concurrent work, thus preventing conflict. Techniques for supporting this approach include floor-control and locking [8, 9, 15, 16]. Conflict prevention is suitable for supporting inherently sequential interactions in some collaborative work, but too restrictive for collaborative work requiring concurrent and free interactions [3, 18]. In contrast to conflict prevention, conflict resolution supports concurrent work, allows conflict to occur and resolves conflict to achieve consistency. Various conflict resolution approaches have been proposed to achieve different consistency effects.

One approach is *eliminative* conflict resolution that achieves *null-operation-effect* consistency [18]: no conflict operation may have a final effect on the shared object. It is eliminative since the effects of all conflicting operations on the shared object are eliminated. This approach can be supported by *undo* [19] or *rollback* [7, 8] that can reverse operation effects or restore prior object states when conflict is detected.

Another approach is *arbitrative* conflict resolution that achieves *single-operation-effect* consistency: a single conflict operation may have the final effect on the shared object. It is arbitrative since, whenever conflict occurs, the system makes arbitration among conflict operations to choose one "winner" to affect the shared object. This approach can be supported by serialization techniques that can achieve the same effect as if all operations were executed in a total order (e.g. by using undo/redo) [10, 11, 19]. Both eliminative and arbitrative approaches achieve consistency at the price of losing concurrent work in the face of conflict.

Still another approach is *preservative* conflict resolution that achieves *all-operations-effect* consistency and can be supported by the multi-versioning technique [18]: when the same object is updated by concurrent operations in conflicting ways, the system creates multiple versions of the object to isolate the effects of conflict operations. It is preservative since, in addition to maintaining consistency, concurrent work is preserved in the face of conflict. The capability of preserving concurrent (conflict) work helps collaborators better understand the conflict and coordinate their activities accordingly.

CSCW'12, February 11-15, 2012, Seattle, Washington, USA.

All existing conflict management approaches, from preventive, eliminative, arbitrative, to preservative approaches, focus on controlling negative effects of conflict (e.g. data inconsistency), but are incapable of creating desirable results for circumstances in which concurrency-related conflicts constitute a natural part of and play a positive role in collaborative work, as illustrated below.

Conflict in cooperation. Users of some collaborative applications will often jointly manipulate shared objects, and may want their concurrent work automatically combined in the final result. For example, as shown in Fig. 1 (a), two users re-size a common graphic object by dragging different handlers in different directions. One desirable combined effect of these two operations could be the object size being changed in both directions, as shown in Fig. 1 (b). In existing conflict resolution approaches, however, these two operations are viewed strictly as non-cooperative conflict operations since they are concurrent and updating the same object in different ways [13, 18]. Such conflicts are actually generated from cooperating work, so their effects should be combined in the final result. Unfortunately, none of existing approaches is able to offer this combined effect: no size change would occur in the eliminative approach; the object size is changed in only one direction in the arbitrative approach; two versions of the object created and each version's size changed in one direction in the preservative approach.

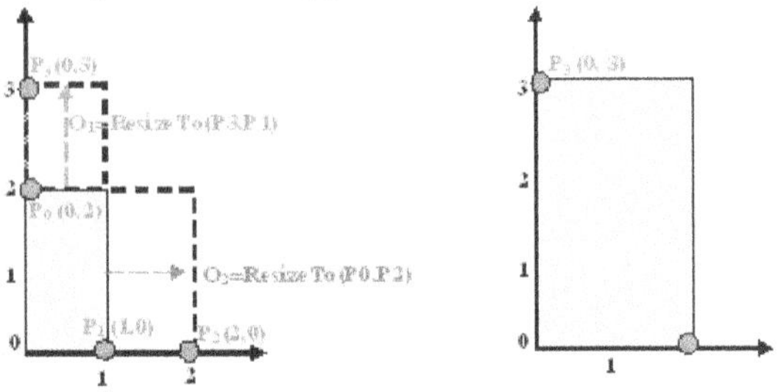

(a) Two concurrent resizing operations (b) A desirable combined effect

Figure 1. Combined effects for cooperating operations.

Conflict in competition. Combined effects of conflict operations could be mandatory in dealing with conflicts in competitive work. Some multi-user games are designed to support users to compete for common objects, and the result of competition conflicts must be determined by combining conflict actions according to game rules (or physical laws). In a multi-player soccer game, for example, players are actively competing for a soccer ball. When two players kick the same ball simultaneously from different directions, the ball must fly in the direction determined by combining the two competing kicks, as shown in Fig 2 (a). However, such a combined effect is not achievable by existing approaches: the ball would not be affected by any competing kick under the eliminative approach; or fly in a direction determined by a single competing kick, shown in either Fig. 2 (b) or (c), under the arbitrative or preservative approach.

Conflict in exploration. Combined effects of conflict operations could be inspirative in explorative work. Digital media design processes, such as digital film making, animation, etc., are creative and explorative in nature, and are typically characterized by a broad design space [1]. This design space

(a) Collective effect of two kicks (b) Individual effect of one kick (c) Individual effect of one kick

Figure 2. Combined effects for competing actions.

can be better explored if multiple designers are allowed to simultaneously explore multiple alternatives and experiment different ideas on shared objects. In such cases, conflicts related to concurrent explorative operations are not really harmful but could be positive stimuli to designers: inspiring them with new alternatives and better understanding of the design space. As a simple yet generalizable example, suppose three designers are concurrently experimenting with different coloring of a shared object (e.g. a cloth, or curtain under design), by issuing operations O_1, O_2, and O_3, to change the color from the original *Yellow* to *Red*, *Blue*, and *Green*, respectively. These experimental actions could be combined to create new effects unintended by individual designers yet still useful in inspiring new design alternatives, as shown in Table 1. Under such circumstances, the system could create multiple alternative solutions based on conflicting operations and provide suitable interface for users to decide on a final solution. If users do not wish to be involved in conflict solution, or do not mind which solution is chosen, the system can always support automatic selection of alternative solutions and ensure system consistency. Clearly, none of existing conflict resolution approaches is able to create new effects that combine conflicting operations and allow users to participate in the process of conflict resolution.

Combined Effects	Combining Operations
White	$\{O_1, O_2, O_3\}$
Magenta	$\{O_1, O_2\}$
Yellow	$\{O_1, O_3\}$
Cyan	$\{O_2, O_3\}$
Red	$\{O_1\}$
Blue	$\{O_2\}$
Green	$\{O_3\}$
Yellow (original color)	$\{\ \}$

Table 1. Combined effects for explorative operations

In summary, in cooperative, competitive, or explorative work, it is useful or even necessary under certain circumstances to combine and create new effects from conflict operations, rather than eliminating or isolating them. In this paper, we propose a novel *Creative Conflict Resolution* (CCR) approach with such a capability. In addition to offering system-decided conflict solutions, the CCR approach allows users to decide on suitable solutions according to their needs – a knowledge that is generally unknown to the system. Moreover, the CCR approach also supports a range of existing conflict resolution approaches and allows users to tailor the system's conflict resolution strategies to meet different collaboration needs.

The rest of this paper is organized as follows. First, the notion of conflict adopted in this work is defined and discussed.

Next, key ideas and technical components of the creative conflict resolution approach are presented. Then, sections are devoted to detailed discussions on algorithms for conflict detection, techniques for creating new results and maintaining alternative solutions, and interface techniques to support users in deciding on conflict solutions and strategies in a prototype implementation. Furthermore, similarities and differences between the proposed approach and early representative object versioning and merging approaches are discussed. Finally, main contributions and future work are summarized.

CONFLICT DEFINITION

There exist widely-varying notions of conflict [2, 4, 5, 6, 8, 14, 17, 18, 20, 24]. In this work, we adopted a notion of conflict that refers to *situations in which concurrent operations are updating common objects in different ways* [13, 18, 23]. This notion of conflict is independent of application semantics. For study of application-defined or semantics-related conflicts, the reader is referred to [4, 5, 6, 14, 17, 24].

We consider real-time collaborative object-based editing systems, where a data object can be a character, word, line, a rectangle, a circle, an image, and so on, which may make up big paragraphs, pictures, and diagrams. Each object has a collection of attributes, such as type, size, position, color, etc., which can be set to various attribute-specific values. There are three classes of basic editing operations: (1) *Create* operations for creating objects of any type and setting initial attribute values; (2) *Delete* operations for removing existing objects; and (3) *Update* operations for changing attribute values of existing objects. These basic operations can model main functionalities of a wide range of commercial word processors, computer-aided design and digital media design tools. Without losing generality, we assume each basic operation may target only a single object.

We aim to support unconstrained real-time collaboration: multiple users may freely edit any objects at the same time [18]. A replicated architecture is adopted: shared objects are replicated at all collaborating sites. Local operations are executed immediately after generation and instantly propagated to remote sites for notification. Operations may be generated concurrently, and concurrent operations may conflict with each other if they produce different results when executed in different orders [18]. In this work, a precise conflict definition is adopted from the GRACE system [18], as given below.

DEFINITION 1. *Conflict relation "⊗".* Two operations O_1 and O_2 conflict with each other, expressed as $O_1 \otimes O_2$, *iff*: (1) they are concurrent, denoted as $O_1 \parallel^1 O_2$; (2) they target the same object; (3) they target the same attribute; and (4) they set the attribute to different values.

If a pair of operations are not in conflict, they are compatible. Under Definition 1, conflict may occur only among concurrent *Update* operations. A *Create* operation cannot conflict with any other operation because no concurrent operation can target the same object being created by this *Create* operation. A *Delete* can be modeled as a special updating operation that sets a *Visibility* attribute of an object to *False* (which was initialized to *True* by a *Create* operation). When the special *Visibility* attribute of an object is set to *False*, it becomes invisible to users, so no future operations can be applied to this object; but all information about this object may still be kept internally for supporting *undo* [22] (an *undo* operation may set this *Visibility* attribute value back to *True*). Under this model, a *Delete* operation does not conflict with any other operation because concurrent *Delete* operations targeting the same object always set the special *Visibility* attribute to the same *False* value, so they are compatible by Definition 1; a normal *Update* operation can never change the *Visibility* attribute of an object so it cannot conflict with a concurrent *Delete* operation either. When a normal *Update* operation and a *Delete* operation concurrently target the same object, the object attribute will be changed by the *Update* but the object will become invisible (the effect of the *Delete*). Meanwhile, involved users are notified about the hidden combined effects between a *Delete* and an *Update*. If the *Delete* operation is undone late, the object will be restored and the attribute changed by the *Update* will become visible. In the rest of this paper, we will focus on conflict resolution among concurrent *Update* operations.

[1] In this paper, $O_1 \parallel O_2$ denotes that O_1 and O_2 are concurrent; and $O_1 \rightarrow O_2$ denotes that O_2 is causally dependent on O_1. For formal definitions of operation causal-dependency/concurrency, the reader is referred to [18].

BASIC IDEAS AND TECHNICAL COMPONENTS

One basic idea of the CCR approach is to create new results by *synthesizing* the effects of conflict operations. Based on collective effects of conflict operations, multiple alternative results can be created. The CCR approach offers users with both default (auto selection) and alternative solutions, provides interface support for users to decide on suitable solutions according to their needs, and ensures consistent creation and selection of solutions across all collaborating sites.

In real-time unconstrained collaboration environments, operations may have arbitrary conflict relationships, and may be executed in different orders at different sites. To support the CCR approach in such environments, we divide the CCR system into three components. The first one is the *conflict detection* component that is responsible for detecting conflicts and determining a consistent set of conflict operations. Conflict conditions, as given in Definition 1, are generic in the sense they are independent of operation types (e.g. Create, Delete, or Update), object types (e.g. line, circle, square, etc), attribute types (e.g. color, position, size, etc.). These and other conditions (see the Section on *conflict detection*) can be checked by a generic conflict detector which is able to detect concurrency, and check the equality of object identifiers and attribute types and values.

The second is the *conflict synthesization* component that is responsible for performing synthesization on concrete conflict operations and creating multiple synthesized conflict solutions. In contrast to the conflict detection component, the conflict synthesization component must have the knowledge of the type and representation of object, attribute and value. This component contains a collection of synthesization methods (or synthesizers) that can be applied to different object attributes. These synthesizers may be built-in or user-provided application-specific synthesizers.

The third is the *conflict management user interface* component that provides user interface support for: (1) *conflict notification* – users are notified of when and where (which objects) conflict has occurred and whom (which users) are involved; (2) *conflict solution selection* – users can browse alternative conflict solutions and make decisions on which one to accept; and (3) *conflict resolution strategy customization* – users can customize the system to take suitable conflict resolution approaches under different circumstances. In the following sections, the three basic CCR components are discussed in detail one by one.

CONFLICT DETECTION

Infrastructure requirements

To facilitate conflict detection, the conflict detection component at each site maintains a log of operations executed so far. In addition, there must be mechanisms for capturing concurrency relationships among operations, e.g. state/context-vectors [19, 22]. Such infrastructure is commonly required by most consistency maintenance or undo techniques in collaborative editing systems [2, 3, 10, 12, 18, 22, 20]. No additional infrastructure is required when the conflict detection scheme is integrated with these existing techniques.

Detecting conflict operations

We assume causally dependent operations are executed in their causal orders, but concurrent operations (including conflict operations) may be executed in any order [19]. For each causally ready operation O, we need to detect a set of relevant conflict operations that may have impact on the execution effect of O. A naive solution to this problem is to search the log to find a set of operations that conflict with O, but this solution works only in simplistic scenarios. We first describe this solution, then discuss its problems and extend it to a sophisticated one.

DEFINITION 2. *Conflict Set.* Given a causally ready operation O and a log L which contains all operations executed before O, the Conflict Set of O under L, denoted as $CS(O)$, contains O plus every operation $O_x \in L$[2] such that $O_x \otimes O$.

ALGORITHM 1. *DetectCS(O, L): CS*

1. $CS := \{O\}$;

2. for each $O_x \in L$ *do: if* $(O_x \otimes O)$, $CS := CS \cup \{O_x\}$;

To illustrate, consider a simple scenario shown in Fig. 3-(a), with two conflict operations $O_1 = Update(id_x, Color, Blue)$ (to change the color of object id_x to *Blue*), $O_2 = Update(id_x, Color, Red)$ (to change the color of object id_x to *Red*). Suppose O_1 is executed before O_2. After executing O_1, the color is changed to *Blue* and $L = \{O_1\}$. When O_2 arrives, $DetectCS(O_2, L)$ is invoked to get $CS(O_2) = \{O_2, O_1\}$. $CS(O_2)$ will then be passed to the synthesization component, which will apply a suitable color synthesizer (see the next section) to create a synthesized color *Magenta* based on $CS(O_2)$. If O_1 is executed after O_2, the algorithm will detect $CS(O_1) = \{O_1, O_2\}$ and pass it to the synthesization component, which will create the same synthesized color *Magenta* since $CS(O_1) = CS(O_2)$. This solution works well as long as all operations in the CS *mutually* conflict.

[2] For notation convenience, the log L is treated as a set (of operations) in this paper. In real implementation, L can be implemented as a list or a set [22].

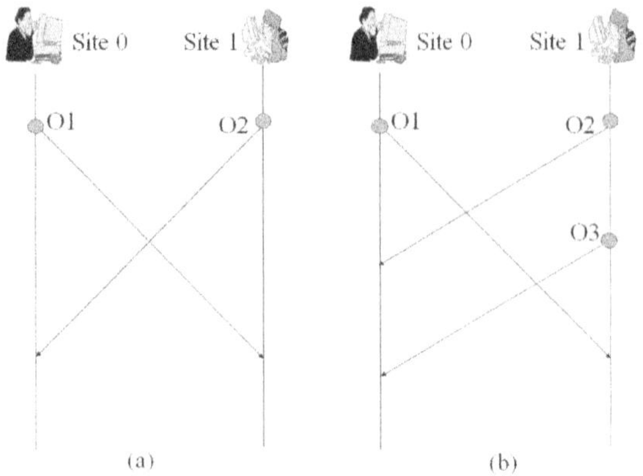

Figure 3. Concurrent operations may not mutually conflict.

However, complication occurs when a group of operations do not mutually conflict. There exist arbitrarily complex situations in which operations may not mutually conflict, but a simple scenario would illustrate the point. As shown in Fig. 3-(b), there are three operations with the following causal dependency relationships: $O_1 \parallel (O_2 \rightarrow O_3)$. Suppose $O_3 = Update(id_x, Color, Green)$, and O_1 and O_2 are the same as those in the prior scenario. According to Definition 1, we have $O_1 \otimes O_2$ and $O_1 \otimes O_3$, but O_2 and O_3 are not conflicting since they are not concurrent. At site 0, after executing O_1, the object color is changed to *Blue* and $L = \{O_1\}$. When O_2 arrives, the DetectCS algorithm is invoked to detect and pass $CS(O_2) = \{O_2, O_1\}$ to the synthesization component, which will create a synthesized color *Magenta* based on $CS(O_2)$. Next, O_3 arrives, and the algorithm will detect and pass $CS(O_3) = \{O_3, O_1\}$ to the synthesization component, which will create a synthesized *Cyan* color based on $CS(O_3)$. After executing all three operations at site 0, the object is changed to the *Cyan* color.

At site 1, after executing O_2 and O_3 in sequence, the object color is changed to *Blue* and then to *Green*, and $L = \{O_2, O_3\}$. When O_1 arrives, the DetectCS algorithm is invoked to find O_1 is conflicting with both O_2 and O_3, and then passes $CS(O_1) = \{O_1, O_2, O_3\}$ to the synthesization component, which will create a synthesized color *White* based on $CS(O_1)$. The *White* color is different from the *Cyan* color at site 0, and the reason for this inconsistency is that $CS(O_1) \neq CS(O_3)$.

In this example, the correct synthesized color should be *Cyan* at both sites. This is because O_2 and O_3 are causally related and their combined effect is solely determined by O_3 – the last operation in the sequence. When O_1 arrives at site 1, it should be synthesized only with O_3 – the *effective* conflict operation, rather than with both O_3 and O_2.

Detecting effective conflict operations

To capture the set of conflict operations that should have effects on the synthesized result, the notion of *Effective Conflict Set* is defined below.

DEFINITION 3. *Effective Conflict Set.* Given a causally ready operation O and a log L that contains all operations executed before O, the *Effective Conflict Set* of O under L, denoted as $ECS(O)$, contains O plus every operation $O_x \in L$ that meets the following conditions: (1) $O_x \otimes O$; (2) there exists no O_y in L such that $O_y \otimes O$ and $O_x \rightarrow O_y$. Furthermore, no two operations in $ECS(O)$ are identical, i.e. to set the same value to the same attribute of the same object.

For the example in Fig. 3-(b), when O_1 arrives at site 1, we have $L = \{O_2, O_3\}$ and $ECS(O_1) = \{O_1, O_3\}$. O_2 is excluded from $ECS(O_1)$ because there exists an $O_3 \in L$ such that $O_2 \rightarrow O_3$ and $O_3 \otimes O_1$.

PROPOSITION 1. *All effective conflict operations in $ECS(O)$ are mutually conflicting.*

Proof: It follows directly from Definitions 1 and 3.

According to Definitions 2 and 3, we have $ECS(O) \subseteq CS(O)$ for any operation O in the same log. Therefore, if $CS(O)$ has been obtained (e.g. by using Algorithm 1), the following algorithm can be used to get $ECS(O)$.

ALGORITHM 2. *DetectECS(CS): ECS*

1. $ECS := \{\ \}$;

2. for each $O_x \in CS$ *do:*

(a) $isEC := true$;

(b) for each $O_y \in CS$ *do:*
if $O_x \rightarrow O_y$, $isEC := false$ *and break inner loop;*

(c) if $isEC = true$, $ECS := ECS \cup \{O_x\}$ *// union operator "∪" eliminates redundant elements in ECS.*

Basically, Algorithm 2 gets the *ECS* by removing those operations from CS that are causally before any operation in CS. This is achieved by using two `for` loops to check every O_x against every other O_y in CS to see whether $O_x \rightarrow O_y$, and to decide whether O_x should be included in or excluded from ECS. Algorithm 2 could be optimized, but this simple and intuitive form is used here for easy verification of correctness. The following theorem establishes the equivalence between the ECS set determined by Algorithm 2 and the $ECS(O)$ specified in Definition 3.

THEOREM 1. *Given an operation O and a log L that contains all operations executed before O. The ECS set determined by Algorithm 2 is equivalent to the $ECS(O)$ in Definition 3.*

Proof: We first show that every operation in ECS obtained by Algorithm 2 meets all conditions as specified in Definition 3. It is trivial to assert that every operation in the input parameter CS (obtained from Algorithm 1) conflicts with O, which implies every operation in ECS obtained from Algorithm 2 conflicts with O. Then, for any O_x in ECE, it is impossible to have an O_y in CS (and in L) such that $O_x \rightarrow O_y$, because Algorithm 2 would have excluded O_x from ECS in Step 2-(b). Finally, no two operations in the ECS could be identical since the union operator "∪" ensures the uniqueness of operations in the ECS. In anther direction, we show that every operation in $ECS(O)$ by Definition 3 must be included in ECS obtained by Algorithm 2. This is true simply because of the exhaustive search of L by Algorithm 1 and of CS by Algorithm 2.

The following theorem establishes that if operations are executed in their causal orders (concurrent and conflict operations can be executed in any order) and Algorithm 2 is used for determining the ECS, a consistent set of effective conflict operations will be detected at all sites after executing the same group of operations – a necessary condition for creating consistent combined effects from conflict operations.

THEOREM 2. *Under causally-ordered operation execution, for any pair of conflict operations O_x and O_y, if $L(O_x) = L(O_y)$, then $ECS(O_x) = ECS(O_y)$, where $L(O)$ is the set of operations in the log immediately after executing O (O is in $L(O)$), and $ECS(O)$ is determined by applying Algorithm 2.*

Proof: Based on the given conditions, we first make the following derivations: (1) from causally-ordered operation execution, we derive there exists no O_z in either $L(O_x)$ or $L(O_y)$, such that $O_x \rightarrow O_z$ or $O_y \rightarrow O_z$; (2) from $L(O_x) = L(O_y)$, we derive $O_y \in L(O_x)$ and $O_x \in L(O_y)$; and (3) based on the previous two derivations and $O_x \otimes O_y$, we derive $O_y \in ECS(O_x)$ and $O_x \in ECS(O_y)$.

Then, we show $O \in ECS(O_x) \Rightarrow O \in ECS(O_y)$. Since both O and O_y are in $ECS(O_x)$, it must be that $O \otimes O_y$ (by Proposition 1). It is impossible to have an O_z in $ECS(O_y)$ (and in $L(O_y)$) such that $O \rightarrow O_z$. Otherwise, it must be that $O_z \otimes O_x$ (since both O_z and O_x are in $ECS(O_y)$ and by Proposition 1); combined with $O \rightarrow O_z$, O would be excluded from $ECS(O_x)$, which contradicts to the precondition $O \in ECS(O_x)$. Following the same reasoning, it can be shown that $O \in ECS(O_y) \Rightarrow O \in ECS(O_x)$. Thus the theorem follows.

For example in Fig. 3-(b), after executing O_3 and O_1 at site 0 and site 1 in different orders, respectively, we have $L(O_3) = L(O_1) = \{O_1, O_2, O_3\}$, and $ECS(O_3) = ECS(O_1) = \{O_1, O_3\}$, which provide consistent ECS sets for creating a identical synthesized *Cyan* color. The reader may use arbitrarily complex scenarios to verify the ECS consistency under the conditions of Theorem 2.

CONFLICT SYNTHESIZATION

After detecting a set of effective conflict operations, the conflict detection component passes the set to the conflict synthesization component, which applies suitable synthesization methods to conflict operations to create combined results.

Synthesization methods

Different operations and attributes may require different synthesization methods. The same type of operation and attribute may be synthesized in different ways to achieve different effects. The choice of a particular synthesizer depends on the suitability of the synthesized effects for the application. A CCR-based system may provide alternative synthesizers for users to choose from and may even allow users to define and supply their own synthesizers. The CCR approach itself is independent of concrete synthesizers.

In this section, we define several synthesization methods and discuss their application to some common conflict scenarios. The goal here is to demonstrate the basic ideas of synthesization and how useful synthesized effects can be achieved in this framework, rather than being comprehensive, as synthesization methods necessarily vary with the context of use.

Additive synthesis method

The additive synthesis method adds the effects of conflict operations together in the final effect. This method is generally applicable to attribute types that are represented by numeric values, and their added values make sense in the application, such as color, font size, sound volume, some animation effects, etc. Additive synthesizers are useful for supporting collaborative exploration.

To give a concrete example, consider the color synthesization. It is well known that any visible color can be obtained by mixing three primary colors: *Red, Green*, and *Blue*, and represented as a tuple *(R, G, B)*, where each element may take a value from 0 to 255. The additive color synthesizer can be defined by adding corresponding elements of two tuples.

SYNTHESIZER 1. *Additive Color Synthesizer* $\overset{color}{\oplus}$.

Given two[3] colors $C_1 = (R_1, G_1, B_1)$ and $C_2 = (R_2, G_2, B_2)$, $\overset{color}{\oplus}$ can be used to create a synthesized color C_s as follows:

$$\begin{aligned} C_s &= C_1 \overset{color}{\oplus} C_2 = ((R_1 + R_2) \bmod 256, \\ &\quad (G_1 + G_2) \bmod 256, (B_1 + B_2) \bmod 256) \end{aligned}$$

All synthesized colors in Table 1 can be obtained by applying this additive color synthesizer.

The additive method can also be used to synthesize conflict operations in competition, e.g. competing kicking operations (or forces) in games. In a 3-dimensional multi-player game space, a force can be represented by a vector $F = (f_x, f_y, f_z)$, where f_x, f_y, f_z represent the force elements in dimensions x, y, z, respectively. When the same object (e.g. a ball) is kicked by two players from different directions, the moving direction of the object will be determined by the combination of the two competing forces, which can be achieved by using the following synthesizer.

SYNTHESIZER 2. *Additive Force Synthesizer* $\overset{force}{\oplus}$.

Given two forces $F_1 = (f_x^1, f_y^1, f_z^1)$ and $F_2 = (f_x^2, f_y^2, f_z^2)$, $\overset{force}{\oplus}$ can be used to create a synthesized force F_s as follows:

$$F_s = F_1 \overset{force}{\oplus} F_2 = (f_x^1 + f_x^2,\ f_y^1 + f_y^2,\ f_z^1 + f_z^2)$$

By applying the force synthesizer to the multi-player soccer game scenario in Fig. 2, the naturally combined effect of two competing operations, shown in Fig. 2 (a), can be achieved.

Following the same idea as the additive synthesis method, an alternative *average* synthesis method can be used to define synthesizers that compromise the effects of conflict operations in the final result. Corresponding to the additive synthesizers for color and force, two average synthesizers can be defined by simply taking average on each added value of the tuple elements. A collaborative system may be equipped with alternative synthesizers for the same attribute type for users to choose from. In real system implementations, we also need to consider whether synthesized values are valid in the application. For example, the addition or average of two valid font sizes may be invalid (unavailable in a particular application). Some compromising measures (e.g. using the closest font size) may be used to handle such situations.

[3]All synthesizers in this section are defined using two conflict operations, but can be extended to more than two operations.

Delta synthesis method

The delta synthesis method adds delta changes made by conflict operations in the final result. It is suitable for attribute changes expressed in delta values and useful for achieving desirable combined effects of cooperating operations.

The size of a 2-dimensional object can be determined by positions of two points – the left-top and right-bottom points of the object, and represented by coordinates of these two points as a tuple $((LX, TY), (RX, BY))$. A resize operation on an object can be expressed by the object's original and new sizes. When two resize operations conflict, the following delta synthesizer can be used.

SYNTHESIZER 3. *Delta Size Synthesizer* $\overset{size}{\Delta}$.

Given two conflict resize operations O_1 and O_2, which change the size of the same object from S_0 to S_1 and from S_0 to S_2, respectively, where

$$\begin{aligned} S_0 &= ((LX_0, TY_0), (RX_0, BY_0)) \\ S_1 &= ((LX_1, TY_1), (RX_1, BY_1)) \\ S_2 &= ((LX_2, TY_2), (RX_2, BY_2)) \end{aligned}$$

$\overset{size}{\Delta}$ can be used to create a synthesized size S_s as follows:

$$S_s = S_1 \overset{size}{\Delta}_{S_0} S_2 = ((LX_s, TY_s), (RX_s, BY_s)),$$

where

$$LX_s = (LX_1 + LX_2 - LX_0);\ TY_s = (TY_1 + TY_2 - TY_0);$$

$$RX_s = (RX_1 + RX_2 - RX_0);\ BY_s = (BY_1 + BY_2 - BY_0).$$

The expression for each synthesized size coordinate (e.g. LX_s) can be transformed into a different form:

$$\begin{aligned} LX_s &= (LX_1 + LX_2 - LX_0) \\ &= (LX_1 - LX_0 + LX_2 - LX_0 + LX_0) \\ &= \Delta LX_1 + \Delta LX_2 + LX_0 \end{aligned}$$

Clearly, the synthesized result is the addition of the two delta changes to each original coordinate. This size synthesizer can be used to achieve the combined effects of the two cooperating operations in Fig. 1 (b).

Creating and maintaining alternative synthesized effects

Binary selection

For n effective conflict operations, there exist 2^n different combinations in which each operation may or may not be a member (*binary selection*). Taking each of these combinations as an input to a synthesizer, one synthesized effect can be created. Given a synthesizer and n operations, a total of 2^n alternative synthesized effects can be created. The eight synthesized colors in Table 1 can be created by applying binary selection over three conflict color operations and using the additive color synthesizer. Binary selection provides a scheme for creating multiple synthesized effects from effective conflict operations. The remaining issue is how to represent those synthesized effects in the system.

Synthesized Multi-Version

In [18], the *Multi-Version* (MV) scheme was invented to support preservative conflict resolution: when multiple conflict operations update the same object, multiple versions of this object are created to isolate the effects of conflict operations. We call this multi-versioning scheme as *Isolated Multi-Version (IMV)* due to its isolation nature of handling conflict operations. The essence of the CCR approach is to combine conflict operations (for creating new effects), rather than isolating them, which seems to be opposite to what the IMV scheme supports. However, the basic idea of multi-versioning is independent of conflict resolution approaches: it is a generic mechanism for representing object versions. By applying this multi-versioning idea and binary selection to the CCR approach, we devised a new multi-versioning scheme to accommodate synthesized effects in multiple versions.

SCHEME 1. *Synthesized Multi-Version (SMV).* Given n effective conflict operations targeting the same object, 2^n versions of the target object, numbered from 0 to $2^n - 1$, will be created by binary selection and synthesization. These 2^n versions include one special version (numbered by 0) for retaining the original object, n conflict-isolated versions (numbered by $2^0, 2^1, ..., 2^{n-1}$) based on individual operations, and $(2^n - n - 1)$ conflict-synthesized versions based on different combinations of conflict operations.

Synthesized Multi-Version Single-Display

In [23], the *Multi-Version Single-Display* (MVSD) technique was proposed to maintain all information for multiple versions outside the document but create (inside the document) and display (on the user interface) only one version at a time. We call the original MVSD scheme as *Isolated MVSD* (or IMVSD for short) since it supports isolated versions only. In IMVSD, information about multiple versions is maintained in an operation history buffer (the same as the log of operations used in the CCR system); consistent single-display is ensured by using a priority-based scheme to uniquely select the same version for display at all sites. By applying the single-display idea to the SMV scheme, we devised the following *Synthesized Multi-Version Single-Display (SMVSD)* scheme.

1. *Multi-version information maintenance.* In addition to the log of operations maintained in the conflict detection component, the synthesization component maintains an *Effective Conflict Sets Buffer* (ECSB) for saving all detected ECSs. Each ECS is associated with the object involved in the conflict. As operations have been saved in the underlying log, the ECSB contains just references to, rather than copies of, the corresponding operations in the log.

2. *Consistent single-display version selection.* The default single-display version can be the synthesized version based on all effective conflict operations (i.e. Version $2^n - 1$) or any other version pre-selected by users. Due to the uniqueness of each version number, consistency of the default version is guaranteed, which is simpler and more flexible than the priority-based scheme in [23].

3. *Dynamic creation of alternative versions.* Alternative versions of an object are created on-demand by the user via the CCR user interface (see the next section). When a user selects a particular version for display, the relevant group of conflict operations will be extracted from the corresponding ECS in the ECSB to create the synthesized effect, which is then applied to the object in the document. Users may browse alternative versions asynchronously at different sites, but committing to a selected version is synchronized across all sites to ensure consistency.

CCR UI ISSUES AND PROTOTYPE IMPLEMENTATION

In previous sections, we have focused on system mechanisms for detecting conflicts and creating alternative solutions. In this section, we discuss issues in supporting users to make final decisions on conflict solutions and select conflict resolution policies. The following discussions are based on a prototype implementation of the CCR approach in the CoWord real-time collaborative word processor [21, 23].[4]

Conflict notification and alternative awareness

The CCR user interface should support conflict notification and alternative awareness. When conflict occurs, users should be notified of the conflict by audio and/or visual cues, and provided with further information about the operations and users involved in the conflict. Moreover, users should be provided with awareness information about alternative solutions of conflict. Multi-versioned objects (as alternative conflict solutions) should be visually distinguishable from other normal objects on the UI.

In the prototype system, when conflict occurs, a special tone is generated and the affected object is flashed for a few seconds to notify users. To be distinguishable from normal objects, a multi-versioned object is highlighted with shadows. As shown in Fig. 4 (a) and (b), the block representing the conflict detection component is shadowed since it has been resized by conflict operations. When a user moves the mouse over a shadowed object and clicks, a pop-up window, anchored to the affected object, will be displayed (Fig. 4 (a)), which gives detailed information about the conflict. The default display version is based on all three effective conflict operations, as indicated by the checks in all selection boxes associated with these conflict operations.

Alternative solutions browsing and selection

The CCR user interface should support users to browse alternative solutions, and decide to commit to a specific solution according to their needs at any time. In the prototype system, a user can check or uncheck any selection box to view any version. For example, by un-checking the box associated with the operation generated by "Judy", a new version of this object will be created and displayed, as shown in Fig. 4 (b). In this new version, the object size is reduced from the bottom

[4]A video demonstrating the CCR in CoWord can be found at http://www.youtube.com/watch?v=84zqbXUQIHc.

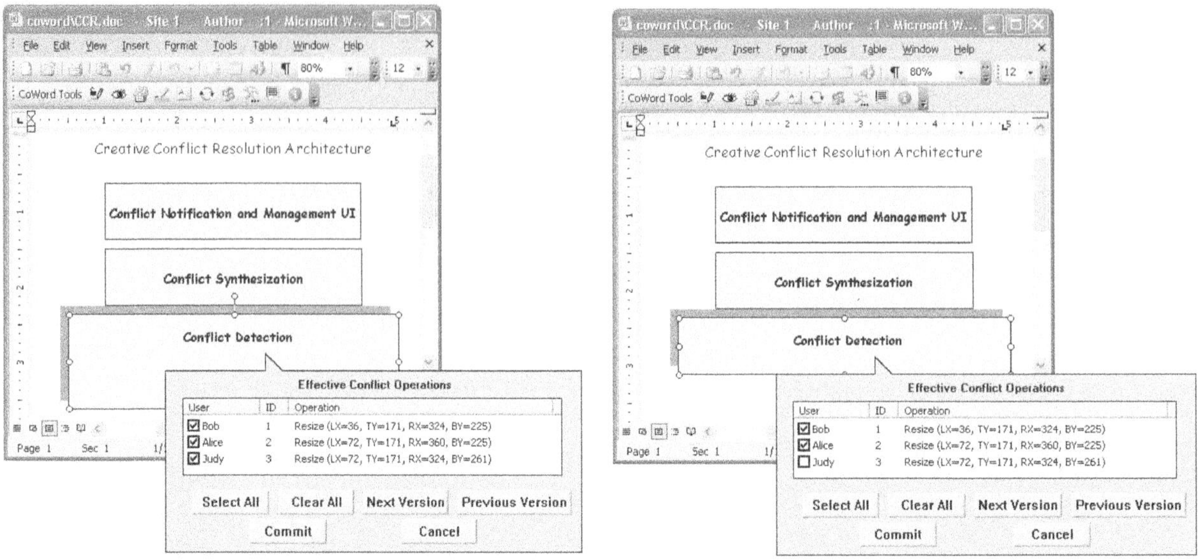

(a) A synthesized version based on three conflict operations (b) A synthesized version based on two conflict operations

Figure 4. UI features for displaying and managing multi-versioned objects in the CoWord prototype implementation.

due to the exclusion of the third operation in synthesization. During the solution browsing process, newly synthesized effects are performed on the local document and displayed on the local UI. If multiple users wish to view and discuss alternative solutions together, they could switch the system into a single-view mode [23].

When the user clicks the "Commit" button, the selected version is committed and a message is propagated to remote sites to commit display versions to the same selected version. After committing to a selected version, a multi-versioned object becomes a normal object without a shadow at the UI. A multi-versioned object may be implicitly committed to the displayed version when a user performs an operation, that is causally after all effective conflict operations, on this object. With default version selection and implicit commitment mechanisms in place, users have the flexibility to be or not to be involved in conflict resolution in the CCR framework.

Conflict resolution approach customization

No single conflict resolution approach can meet all collaboration needs [5, 18], so it is desirable for one system to have the capability of supporting multiple conflict resolution approaches and allowing users to select suitable approaches according to their needs. The CCR approach is unique in providing the mechanism and interface to support such a capability. In the following, we explain why this is achievable by CCR and show how it is implemented in the prototype.

Different conflict resolution approaches are capable of achieving different effects: the eliminative conflict resolution (ECR) approach achieves the "null-operation-effect"; the arbitrative conflict resolution (ACR) approach achieves the "single-operation-effect"; the preservative conflict resolution (PCR) approach achieves the isolated "all-operations-effect"; and the CCR approach achieves the synthesized "all-operations-effect". By analyzing the effects achievable by these approaches, we made the following observation: CCR effects cover all PCR effects, which cover all ACR effects; and the ECR effect is equivalent to the CCR Version 0 effect, as expressed below:

OBSERVATION 1. *$E_{ccr} \supset E_{pcr} \supset E_{acr}$, and $E_{ccr} \supset E_{ecr}$, where E_x denotes the set of effects achievable by conflict resolution approach X.*

Furthermore, by analyzing techniques for supporting these conflict resolution approaches [2, 7, 8, 9, 15, 10, 11, 19, 18, 23, 20], we made the following observation:

OBSERVATION 2. *A conflict resolution technique that is able to support approach X can also support approach Y if $E_x \supset E_y$, but is unable or difficult to do so if $EC_Y \supset EC_x$.*

Observations 1 and 2 together suggest that mechanisms for supporting the CCR approach can be used to build a general conflict management framework capable of supporting a range of conflict resolution approaches.

In the prototype implementation, a conflict management UI panel (Fig. 5) is provided for users to select a specific policy from the following list: (1) creative conflict resolution, which is implemented by the full set of synthesized versions (as discussed in previous sections); (2) preservative conflict resolution, which is implemented by a subset of synthesized versions corresponding to isolated individual conflict operations; (3) arbitrative conflict resolution, which is implemented by single conflict-isolated version; (4) eliminative conflict resolution, which is implemented by the original object version (Version 0); and (5) preventive conflict management (PCM), which is implemented by the single-actor mode [23]: only one user can update the document at a time.

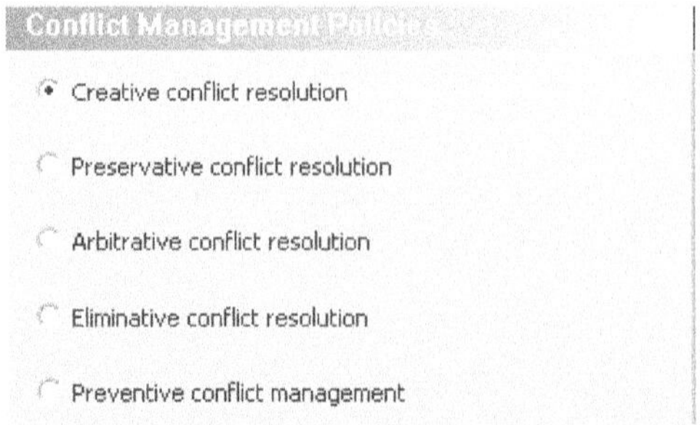

Figure 5. UI panel for managing conflict resolution policies in CoWord.

Conflict notifications using special audio and visual effects are available for all approaches except PCM (which does not allow conflict to occur). If CCR is chosen (the default), user interface features for managing multiple versions are exactly what were discussed before. If PCR is chosen, when a user clicks a multi-versioned object involved in conflict, the pop-up window is similar to that in Fig. 4, except that only a single selection box can be checked at a time, and only n conflict-isolated versions are available for selection. If ACR or ECR is chosen, the pop-up window gives only information about conflict operations, but only a system-decided single version is accessible to users. Under this framework, users may change conflict resolution approaches during a collaboration session at any time.

Finally, we offer some general guidelines for implementing the CCR approach and the flexible conflict management framework in real collaborative applications. The CCR approach can be implemented in any collaborative applications that need them. One way of building collaborative applications is by the Transparent Adaptation (TA) approach [21], which converts single-user interactive applications into multi-user collaborative tools without changing the source code of the original application. A TA-based collaborative application consists of three layers: the top layer is the *single-user application* which provides conventional functionalities and interface features; the middle layer is the *transparent adaptor* which provides application-specific collaboration capabilities and bridges the top layer and the bottom *generic collaboration engine* layer, which provides generic collaboration mechanisms for consistency maintenance, undo, etc. To incorporate the CCR approach into a TA-based collaborative application (as we did in implementing the CCR in CoWord), it is recommended to integrate the generic conflict detection component inside the generic collaboration engine so it can be re-used in different applications, to implement the conflict synthesization component in the transparent adaptor since the adaptor has the necessary application and operation knowledge to carry out the synthesization work, and to integrate the CCR UI component within existing single-user application UIs. With the CCR approach integrated with the TA approach, implementation of the flexible conflict management framework is straightforward.

DISCUSSIONS

Conflict resolution and management are issues explored in a wide range of collaborative systems, as well as in a variety of areas of computer science, such as operating systems, databases, and distributed systems. As such, terminologies like conflict, object, version, and merging are often shared in the literature. However, each problem domain has its own specific and often subtly different definitions for these terms, and comes with its own unique challenges and calls for different technical solutions. In this section, we compare the CCR approach with early work on object versioning and merging in collaborative applications. Due to space limitation and the diversity of collaborative applications, this comparison has to be selective and focus on key similarities and differences between compared approaches.

An object merging framework was proposed in early 90s [14]. This framework focused on flexible policies for merging multiple versions of an object to a common state. In [14], a document object (e.g. a journal article, or a program source code file) may evolve into multiple versions when it is duplicated and separately manipulated by co-workers for *a period of time without synchronization*, and conflicts are resolved at a late time when multiple versions are merged into a common one. Such kind of collaboration is commonly known as *non-real-time* (or asynchronous) collaboration, which is different from the *real-time* (or synchronous) collaboration in which co-workers' updates on the shared object are *instantly propagated to each other for synchronization* and conflicts are resolved in real-time – the focus of the CCR approach. Another key difference is that the object versioning and merging occurred at the coarse-grained document object level in [14], but at the fine-grained object (e.g. a character, a line, or circle inside a document) level in the CCR approach. In [14], conflicts can be defined by users according to specific object types and other needs, which may cover *syntactic* conflicts, such as updates on overlapping texts in a text file object, as well as *semantic* conflicts, such as changes to the same production in a Yacc grammar document object. In the CCR approach, however, conflict is pre-defined (Definition 1) but generic as it is independent of operation/object/attribute types or application semantics. The CCR approach and the work in [14] have distinctive sets of technical issues and solutions, which stem from their different object, version and conflict definitions and differences between real-time and non-real-time collaboration. The CCR approach and the work in [14] (and similar early work on object merging and conflict resolution [24]) are also complementary: the CCR focuses on combining conflict operations on fine-grained objects in real-time collaboration, whereas the work in [14] focused on merging conflict operations on coarse-grained objects in non-real-time collaboration.

Operational Transformation (OT) is well-known for its capability of merging the effects of fine-grained concurrent operations in the same document in real-time collaborative editing systems [2, 7, 19, 22, 20]. However, the basic OT technique does not have the capability of merging the effects of conflict operations in the same fine-grained object. Prior work has extended OT to incorporate a fine-grained object versioning capability for isolating conflicting operations on the same object [23], and to support syntactic and semantic merging of multiple document versions in non-real-time collaboration [17], which is similar in concept but different in techniques to/from the work in [14]. No prior OT technique has the capability of creating new results from conflict operations on fine-grained objects. The CCR is compatible and can be integrated with OT: we have integrated the CCR capability into an OT-based generic collaboration engine [21].

CONCLUSIONS AND FUTURE WORK

In this paper, we have contributed a *Creative Conflict Resolution* (CCR) approach to explore positive aspects of conflict and support cooperative, competitive and explorative work in real-time collaborative editing. This approach is distinctive in creating new and alternative results based on collective effects of conflict operations on fine-grained objects in real-time, and allowing users to decide on suitable results if they wish to. Key technical contributions include: algorithms for consistent detection of effective conflict operations, methods for synthesizing conflict operations, creating new results, and maintaining alternative solutions, and interface techniques for supporting users in browsing and selecting conflict solutions. In this work, we have also contributed a taxonomy of conflict management approaches in real-time collaborative editing systems: from preventative, eliminative, arbitrative, preservative, to creative approaches, and a generic framework for supporting all these approaches and allowing users to tailor resolution strategies according to their needs.

The CCR approach uses synthesizers to create new effects from conflict operations, but it is independent of specific synthesizers, which necessarily vary from application to application. The CCR has a *creative* feature in the sense that it is able to *create* something new from conflict operations, but the creation methods may not necessarily demonstrate much *creativity* as judged by human intelligence. The simple and deterministic synthesization methods discussed in this paper mainly demonstrate the basic ideas of synthesization and show how synthesized effects can be achieved in the CCR framework. Inventing sophisticated and truly creative synthesization methods for real-world applications is one important direction of our future research.

The proof-of-concept implementation of the CCR approach in CoWord has mainly demonstrated the feasibility of the CCR, but no usability study of the CCR has been conducted using this prototype. We envisaged the CCR could be more useful and effective for collaborative digital media design, such as digital film making, animation, etc., due to the creative and explorative nature of such design processes. We are extending the CCR approach and mechanisms to real-time collaborative computer-aided design and digital media tools [1], and will evaluate the CCR usefulness and effectiveness in those novel collaborative applications in the future.

ACKNOWLEDGMENTS
We thank anonymous reviewers for their insightful and constructive comments and suggestions.

REFERENCES
1. Agustina, F. Liu, S. Xia, H. Shen, and C. Sun. CoMaya: incorporating advanced collaboration capabilities into 3D digital media design tools. In *Proc. of ACM Conf. on Computer-Supported Cooperative Work*, pages 5–8, November. 2008.
2. Agustina, C. Sun, and D. Xu. Operational transformation for dependency conflict resolution in real-time collaborative 3D design systems. In *Proc. of the ACM Conf. on Computer-Supported Cooperative Work*, Feb. 2012.
3. J. Begole, M. Rosson, and C. Shaffer. Flexible collaboration transparency: supporting worker independence in replicated application-sharing systems. *ACM Trans. on Computer-Human Interaction*, 6(2):95–132, 1999.
4. P. Dourish. Consistency guarantees: exploiting application semantics for consistency management in a collaboration toolkit. In *Proc. of the ACM Conf. on Computer-Supported Cooperative Work*, pages 268–277, November 1996.
5. S. Easterbrook, E. Beck, J. Goodlet, L. Plowman, M. Sharples, and C. Wood. A survey of empirical studies of conflict. In Steve Easterbrook, editor, *CSCW: Cooperation or Conflict?*, pages 1–68. Springer-Verlag, 1993.
6. W.K. Edwards. Flexible conflict detection and management in collaborative applications. In *ACM Symposium on User Interface Software and Technology*, pages 139–148, Oct. 1997.
7. C. A. Ellis, S. J. Gibbs, and G. L. Rein. Groupware: some issues and experiences. *Communication of ACM*, 34(1):39–58, Jan. 1991.
8. S. Greenberg and D. Marwood. Real time groupware as a distributed system: concurrency control and its effect on the interface. In *Proc. of the ACM Conf. on Computer-Supported Cooperative Work*, pages 207–217, Nov. 1994.
9. S. Greenberg, R. Roseman, and D. Webster. Issues and experiences designing and implementing two group drawing tools. In *Proceedings of the the 25th Annual Hawaii International Conference on the System Science*, pages 139–250, Jan. 1992.
10. R. Kanawati. LICRA: a replicated-data management algorithm for distributed synchronous groupware application. *Parallel Computing*, 22:1733–1746, Feb. 1997.
11. A. Karsenty, C. Tronche, and M. Beaudouin-Lafon. Groupdesign: shared editing in a heterogeneous environment. *Usenix Journal of Computing Systems*, 6(2):167–195, Spring 1993.
12. D. Li and R. Li. Transparent sharing and interoperation of heterogeneous single-user applications. In *Proc. of the ACM Conf. on Computer-Supported Cooperative Work*, pages 246–255, Nov. 2002.
13. T. Moran, K. McCall, B. van Melle, E. Pedersen, and F. Halasz. Some design principles for sharing in tivoli, a whiteboard meeting-support tool. In Saul Greenberg, editor, *Groupware for Real-time Drawings: A Designer's Guide*, pages 24–36. McGraw-Hill International(UK), 1995.
14. J. P. Munson and P. Dewan. A flexible object merging framework. In *Proc. of ACM Conf. on Computer-Supported Cooperative Work*, pages 231–242, 1994.
15. R.E. Newman-Wolfe, M.L. Webb, and M. Montes. Implicit locking in the ensemble concurrent object-oriented graphics editor. In *Proc. of the ACM Conf. on Computer-Supported Cooperative Work*, pages 265–272, November 1992.
16. M.O. Pendergast. Groupgraphics: prototype to product. In Saul Greenberg, editor, *Groupware for Real-time Drawings: A Designer's Guide*, pages 209–227. McGraw-Hill International(UK), 1995.
17. H.F. Shen and C. Sun. Flexible merging for asynchronous collaborative systems. In *Proceedings of Tenth International Conference on Cooperative Information Systems (CoopIS2002)*, pages 304–321, October 2002.
18. C. Sun and D. Chen. Consistency maintenance in real-time collaborative graphics editing systems. *ACM Trans. on Computer-Human Interaction*, 9(1):1–41, March 2002.
19. C. Sun, X. Jia, Y. Zhang, Y. Yang, and D. Chen. Achieving convergence, causality-preservation, and intention-preservation in real-time cooperative editing systems. *ACM Trans. on Computer-Human Interaction*, 5(1):63–108, March 1998.
20. C. Sun, H. Wen, and H. Fan. Operational transformation for orthogonal conflict resolution in real-time collaborative 2D editing systems. In *Proc. of the ACM Conf. on Computer-Supported Cooperative Work*, Feb. 2012.
21. C. Sun, Q. Xia, D. Sun, D. Chen, H.F. Shen, and W. Cai. Transparent adaptation of single-user applications for multi-user real-time collaboration. *ACM Trans. on Computer-Human Interaction*, pages 531–582, 2006.
22. D. Sun and C. Sun. Context-based operational transformation in distributed collaborative editing systems. 20(10):1454–1470, October 2009.
23. D. Sun, S. Xia, C. Sun, and D. Chen. Operational transformation for collaborative word processing. In *Proc. of the ACM Conf. on Computer-Supported Cooperative Work*, pages 437–446, Nov. 2004.
24. D. Terry, M. Theimer, K. Petersen, A. Demers, M. Spreitzer, and C. Hauser. Managing update conflicts in bayou, a weakly connected replicated storage system. In *Proc. of the Fifteenth ACM Symposium on Operating Systems Principles*, pages 172–182, New York, 1995. ACM.

Towards Self-Optimizing Collaborative Systems

Sasa Junuzovic
Microsoft Research
One Microsoft Way, Redmond, WA 98052
sasa.junuzovic@microsoft.com

Prasun Dewan
University of North Carolina at Chapel Hill
UNC, Chapel Hill, NC 27599
dewan@cs.unc.edu

ABSTRACT
Two important performance metrics in collaborative systems are local and remote response times. Previous analytical and simulation work has shown that these response times depend on three important factors: processing architecture, communication architecture, and scheduling of tasks dictated by these two architectures. We show that it is possible to create a system that improves response times by dynamically adjusting these three system parameters in response to changes to collaboration parameters such as new users joining and network delays changing. We present practical approaches for collecting collaboration parameters, computing multicast overlays, applying analytical models of previous work, preserving coupling semantics during optimizations, and keeping overheads low. Simulations and experiments show that the system improves performance in practical scenarios.

Author Keywords
Performance; response times; optimization; processing architecture; communication architecture; scheduling.

ACM Classification Keywords
C.2.4 [Computer-Communication Networks]: Distributed Systems – Distributed Applications, Client/Server; C.4 [Performance of Systems] Performance Attributes.

General Terms
Performance; Experimentation.

INTRODUCTION
As the landscape of available collaborative applications expands, it is critical for an application to differentiate itself from the rest of the field in a useful fashion. An important differentiation factor for these systems is performance. If an application does not respond to user actions in a timely fashion or quickly notify users of actions of others, users may get frustrated and switch to a different application.

In general, in computer science, the performance of a system is a function of available resources. If resources are abundant, then the system always performs well. On the other hand, if resources are insufficient, then the system never performs well. These two boundary cases bracket the case in which resources are sufficient but scarce, called the window of opportunity [9]. In the window of opportunity, a system can have good performance, but new algorithms and implementations may be necessary to achieve it.

In this paper we focus on the window of opportunity for improving the performance of collaborative systems. We present a new collaborative framework that can take advantage of this opportunity and meet performance criteria better than existing systems without requiring hardware, network, or user-interface changes. Several performance metrics have been identified, such as local [14] and remote [4] response time, throughput [5], bandwidth [7], jitter [6], task completion time [2], and frame rate [16]. While all of them are important, our focus is on response times.

Previous work has shown that response times depend on three important factors: processing architecture, communication architecture, and scheduling of tasks dictated by these two architectures [2,3,10,11]. This work has developed theoretical analytical models and used simulations to validate these models. In this paper, we present a system that keeps track of all three of these factors and dynamically adjusts them to improve response times.

A flavor of the kind of improvements the system can provide is shown in Figure 1. It shows the response times from an actual collaborative session and that they are better with than without the system. In fact, the performance with the system eventually approaches the x-axis, which is the theoretical best performance where response times are zero. More importantly, these improvements are noticeable to users. Human-perception studies by Youmans [17] and Jay

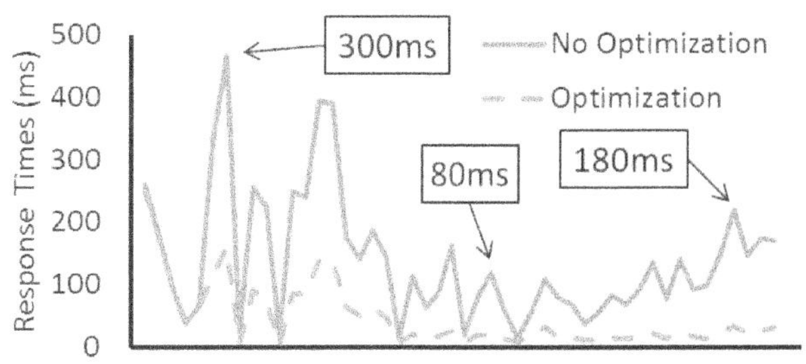

Figure 1. Response times during an actual collaboration session with and without the self-optimizing system

et al. [8] have shown that people can notice changes of 50ms in local and remote response times, respectively. As the response times in Figure 1 show, the system improves the response by as much as 300ms, which is noticeable.

The rest of this paper is organized as follows. First, we discuss background work that motivated the development of our system. We then present an issue based discussion of the implementation of the system. Following this, we present simulations and experiments that evaluate the benefits of the system in practical collaboration scenarios. Then, we discuss practical applications and broader impacts of the system. We end with conclusions and future work.

BACKGROUND WORK

Three important response time factors identified so far are processing architecture, communication architecture, and scheduling of tasks dictated by these two architectures.

Processing Architecture

Two main architectures have been used in the construction of collaborative systems [3]: centralized (client-server) replicated (peer-to-peer). In both cases, it is assumed that the shared application is logically divided into separate user-interface and processing components. The user-interface component transforms user input into input commands and sends these commands to the program component. Conversely, it processes output commands that it receives from the program component and transforms the result into updates to the display. The program component processes user input by converting input commands to output commands. The user-interface component is replicated on each user's computer and allows a user to manipulate application state not shared with the other users. The program component is logically shared by all users and may be physically centralized or replicated, depending on the processing architecture. Each user interface is mapped to exactly one program component.

In the centralized (client-server) architecture, all of the user-interface components are mapped to a single program component running on one of the user's computers. The computer running the program component is called the master and all of the other computers are called slaves. In the replicated (peer-to-peer) architecture, each user-interface component is mapped to the program component running on the local computer. Whenever a master receives a command from the local user, it sends the command to all of the other computers, thereby ensuring the program components on different masters are kept in sync.

The traditional rule of thumb has been that the replicated architecture provides the best response times. While there are scenarios in which this rule is accurate, Chung [2] was the first to show, both analytically and experimentally, that (a) low network latency actually favors a centralized architecture and (b) asymmetric processing powers actually favor a centralized architecture.

Communication Architecture

Regardless of whether a centralized or the replicated architecture is used, master computers transmit commands to all other computers. If commands are large or the number of users is high, then transmission costs can be high.

An important question when transmission costs are high is whether a master computer uses unicast or multicast to communicate with other computers. Junuzovic and Dewan [10] studied the use of multicast in realistic collaboration scenarios. They found that while multicast usually improves response times, it can harm them in some cases.

Scheduling Policy

Both the processing and the communication architecture mandate specific tasks that the users' devices must perform. The processing architecture determines which computers process input commands in addition to processing outputs, while the communication architecture dictates the destinations to which a computer transmits commands.

The order in which a computer carries out the processing and transmission tasks impacts response times. Four single-core policies for scheduling these tasks have been identified by Junuzovic and Dewan [11]. Three of these are straightforward: (a) process-first, which completes the processing task before starting the transmission task, (b) transmit-first, which does the reverse, and (c) concurrent, which creates a separate thread for each of these tasks and schedules these threads in a round-robin fashion. The fourth, called lazy, gives precedence to the processing task, but delays its execution and allows the transmission task to run during this delay if the resulting increase in local response times is not noticeable. As a result, a part of the transmission task can run earlier, thereby noticeably improving remote response times of some users.

On multi-core devices, intuitively the best response times will be obtained by executing the transmission and processing tasks in parallel on as many cores as possible. However, Junuzovic and Dewan [11] argue against this intuition. Specifically, they state that neither task should be scheduled on more than one core. Their reason for scheduling the processing task on one core is because in general the processing task is an application defined black box that cannot be parallelized by general frameworks. The reason for doing so with the transmission task is two-fold. First, using multiple cores for the transmission task makes it difficult to predict response times because the operating system can schedule the parallel send calls in an arbitrary order. Second, since the CPU is much faster than the network card, a single core saturates the network card. Thus there are no performance gains to using multiple cores to perform the transmission task.

They simulated performance with these policies in realistic scenarios. On single-core devices, they found that the (a) the lazy policy dominates the process-first policy and (b) none of the lazy, transmit-first, and process-first policies dominate each other. On multi-core devices, they found that (a) the parallel policy dominates all single-core policies and (b) using one core to perform both tasks can give performance that is equivalent to that of the parallel policy.

Summary

In summary, previous work has studied the impact of processing architecture, multicast, and scheduling policy on response times. Prior work shows that the combination of these three factors that provides the best response times depends on collaboration conditions. As these conditions can differ within and across collaborative sessions, it would be useful to develop a system that automatically optimizes the factors. In this paper, we present the first such system.

SYSTEM

In this first cut at the design and evaluation of a system that improves performance by automatically maintaining the processing architecture, communication architecture, and scheduling policy, we focused on three driving problems: a distributed PowerPoint presentation; a collaborative Checkers computer game; and instant messaging. They are important examples of real collaborative scenarios. Distributed presentations are becoming common, instant messaging is pervasive, and collaborative games, such as checkers, chess, and online poker, are extremely popular. In fact, by itself, distributed presentations are an important scenario as an entire industry has been created around them.

The self-optimizing framework both shares applications and improves their performance. These two responsibilities are carried out by the sharing and optimization sub-systems.

Sharing Sub-System

The sharing sub-system is a reimplementation of Chung's approach [2]. In Chung's work, a part of the system, which we refer to as the client component, is logically situated between the user-interface and program components on each computer. The application is not aware of the system component: to the user interface, it appears to be the program component, and to the program component, it appears to be the user interface. The client components communicate directly with each other. They can be setup to enforce replicated or centralized architectures. In our system, we modified these components to also support multicast. We also modified them to support scheduling policy enforcement. When they intercept a command, they create separate threads for processing and transmitting the command. By controlling when and on what core these threads execute, they can enforce any scheduling policy.

Optimization Sub-System

While modifying the sharing aspects of Chung's system is a contribution, our main contribution is the optimization sub-system and the implementation issues it raises.

Driving Optimization Decisions

The main question with any optimization system is how it derives optimization decisions. In our case, the question translates to how it predicts the combination of response time parameters that give the best response times.

One approach is to use learned rules of thumb. Wolfe et al. [16] developed a system called Fiia that uses rules of thumb along with developer hints to automatically centralize or replicate parts of the application at runtime in order to improve response times and frame rates. As mentioned earlier, however, an issue with using rules of thumb is that they do not always accurately predict performance. For instance, Chung showed that there exist collaboration conditions that favor a centralized architecture for good response times, which contrasts the rule of thumb that the replicated architecture provides the best response times.

An alternative approach that always accurately predicts performance is to use an analytical model. Ideally, an analytical model should predict the impact on performance of processing architecture, communication architecture, and scheduling policy since these have been shown to be response time factors. It should also support an arbitrary number of users and take advantage of the latest hardware and software trends such as multi-core CPUs and non-blocking communication. The only model of which we are aware that satisfies all of these requirements was presented by Junuzovic and Dewan [11], which predicts response times in centralized and replicated architectures with an arbitrary number of users. It supports think times, multicast, multi-core processors, and non-blocking communication.

An analytical model usually has a set of assumptions that define the scenarios in which the model applies. Junuzovic and Dewan [11] make only one assumption: an application implements only mandatory coupling functionality and no optional functionality, such as awareness and concurrency control. This assumption is satisfied by the applications that we target, namely, PowerPoint, Checkers, and IM. In general, however, applications implement optional functionality. We will return to the issue of optimizing these applications in more detail in the discussion section.

To apply the Junuzovic and Dewan [11] model, one must first collect values for all of its parameters. Moreover, while the model predicts performance with multicast, it does not actually build a multicast overlay. Therefore, one must also compute a multicast overlay before invoking the model.

Collecting Values of Collaboration Parameters

The parameters include for each computer the processing and transmission times of input and output commands, the think times, and network latencies to all other computers. While most of these parameters are self-explanatory, the transmission times warrant a second look. The transmission of a command is done in two steps: first, the CPU queues the command for transmission by the network card, and then the network card transmits the command. Thus, the time required for both steps needs to be collected.

Parameter values are measured by a client component of the optimization sub-system running on each computer. These components record the processing and transmission times of each command, as well as its think time if the local user entered it. They also measure network latencies to other computers, as well as, report the performance data.

Once parameters are collected during a session, it pays to save them as this can reduce the time the system takes to perform the first optimization in future sessions. For instance, processing and transmission costs measured for a computer in one session can be used as cost estimates for that computer in future sessions. Further reuse is possible by grouping and saving these costs based on processor type. Think times can also be reused by grouping them on a user or application basis. With the reuse of values of these parameters, the system can perform an optimization in a future session as soon as it collects network latencies. Such reuse is also useful when latecomers arrive. Specifically, if costs have been gathered for the latecomer's computer type, then the system can optimize response times as soon as it receives latencies among the latecomer and other users.

Computing Multicast Overlays
The idea of multicast requires the construction, for each source of messages, a multicast overlay that defines the paths a message takes to reach its destinations. We make two assumptions regarding multicast. First, because IP-multicast is not widely deployed, we assume an application-layer multicast in which end-hosts form the overlay. Second, as in peer-to-peer file sharing systems, we assume that only the users' computers can be used in the overlay. In this first-cut at a self-optimization system that uses multicast, we did not want to develop a new multicast scheme. Instead, we chose an existing application-layer scheme: the HMDM algorithm presented by Brosh and Shavitt [1]. It is the only algorithm of which we are aware that accounts for application-layer transmission costs.

Applying a multicast algorithm requires the collection of its parameters. The HMDM scheme parameters include network latencies and transmission costs. Since these parameters are also collected for the analytical model, no additional data needs to be collected by our system in order to build a multicast tree using the HMDM scheme.

An important issue is how many multicast trees are computed. One option is to compute a multicast tree rooted at every user, but HMDM's $O(number\ of\ users^3)$ runtime makes this approach impractical in large scenarios. A more practical alternative is to compute a single multicast tree that is shared by all users. An issue with this option is that a command from any user but the one who is at the root of the tree must first reach the tree, which increases the response times. Our system can be configured to create an arbitrary number of trees. The default is one.

Applying the Analytical Model
Once a multicast overlay is created, the system can use the analytical model to predict performance. Unfortunately, it may not be able to predict performance for all combinations of response time factors using only the reported values. The reason is that some parameter values may be missing because not all computers report values of all parameters at all times. For example, in a centralized architecture, a slave does not report input processing costs, so the collected values are not sufficient for predicting the performance of an architecture in which the slave is a master.

When parameter values are missing, it is possible to estimate them using the values of other parameters. One approach is to assume that the input and output processing cost ratio is the same for all computers. Since there is always a master computer, the ratio can be computed. Consider the missing input processing cost of a slave. A master's processing cost ratio and the slave's output processing cost can be used to estimate the missing value. Other parameters can be estimated similarly.

Estimated parameter values may not reflect the actual parameter values, however, so they may result in optimizations that degrade performance. Such degradations are temporary. As the optimization system gathers data, it will eventually discard estimated values. In addition, by reusing computer costs across sessions, eventually, it will know most if not all parameter values at session start time.

While the analytical model is able to predict performance for different configurations of a system, it does not predict which configuration gives the best performance. The simplest approach for picking a configuration is to pick the one with the best average response times. However, this approach does not account for the fact that response times are inherently partially ordered and external criteria must be used to create a total order. In general, infinitely many external criteria exist and their application depends on the response time requirements. To satisfy the requirements, we rely on the notion of a response time function introduced by Junuzovic and Dewan [11], which is an expression of the requirements. Their function distinguishes between primary and secondary users and between local and remote response times. It accepts response times of configurations, a list of inputting users, and identities of all users as parameters and returns a ranking of configurations from best to worst.

Preserving Coupling Semantics During Optimizations
Once the system begins to perform an optimization, it is important to ensure that the switch is performed atomically from the perspective of commands already in the system or those entered during the change. Otherwise, a command may not reach all of its intended destinations or it may reach a destination multiple times. For example, during processing architecture change, a computer that changed from a master to slave may receive an input command, which would be inconsistent with the notion of replicated and centralized architectures. Also, during a communication architecture change, a command may reach a destination multiple times since a computer may forward commands to different destinations in the old and the new architectures.

In some cases, an optimization may be performed when the shared application is in a quiescent state, in which case distribution semantics are not impacted by the change. For example, a switch may happen during think times if they are high. Alternatively, the system could ensure a quiescent state by delaying an optimization until users take a break.

In general, however, an optimization may be triggered when the shared application is in a non-quiescent state. One approach to performing the optimization atomically is to suspend user inputs during the switch and wait for the distribution of commands already in the system to complete before starting the optimization. An issue with this solution is that response times of commands can be high if the switch time is long. A more intelligent solution is to run the old and new configurations in parallel and switch to the new configuration when it is fully deployed, which is done by Chung for processing architecture changes [2]. As this approach has been implemented previously for processing architecture changes, we did not duplicate it in our system. However, as discussed below, our system demonstrates that the general idea of concurrently running two architectures can be applied to other reconfiguration steps. Specifically, a compromise taken by our system is to break the optimization into three sequential atomic sub-steps, one for each response time factor, and suspend user inputs only during the processing architecture change. Since the processing architecture defines which computers process inputs, it must be deployed before the communication architecture as the latter dictates how inputs are distributed. The scheduling policy can be changed last as it is independent of the two architectures.

Our system first changes the processing architecture by reconfiguring the client components of the sharing system. To bring program components up to date on computers changing from a slave to a master, it uses Chung's solution [2] of replaying input commands to these components. To support the replay, the system logs input commands on master computers. It picks one old master at random to replay commands to new masters. During the change, the system suspends user inputs.

One issue when deploying a new processing architecture is deciding what communication architecture and scheduling policy should be used until they are also changed. In particular, since the new processing architecture redefines which users process input commands, a previous multicast architecture may distribute input commands to new slave computers, which is inconsistent with the notion of collaboration architectures. Therefore, when changing the processing architecture, the system changes the communication architecture to unicast. The system must also choose a scheduling policy to use. It simply keeps the old scheduling policy since, as mentioned above, task scheduling is independent of the processing architecture.

Once the new processing architecture is deployed, the system resumes user inputs and begins the communication architecture change. During this step, the system changes the communication pattern among the client components. To handle user inputs, the system continues to distribute them using the old architecture while it deploys the new one. The new communication architecture is activated only once it has been deployed on all computers, and it is immediately used for all new commands.

An important aspect of the system is that it does not discard the old architecture immediately after activating the new one. The reason is that when the new architecture is activated, there may be commands that have been only partially distributed using the old architecture. Thus, the old architecture continues to distribute these commands. To help each other decide which architecture to use, source computers tag each command with the version number of the architecture that should be used to distribute it. The net effect of using the old architecture for commands entered before the new architecture is activated is that from the perspective of commands, the change is atomic because a command is distributed using only the old or only the new architecture. Eventually, the old architecture can be torn down. To ensure that it is not removed prematurely, the tear down should be delayed by the maximum response time. In our experience, a delay of several minutes is sufficient.

Finally, the system performs the scheduling policy change. A scheduling policy change is always atomic from the perspective of user commands because scheduling policies do not determine the distribution of commands. However, using a mix of old and new policies may lead to performance degradations because the performance was not predicted for any mix of policies. Fortunately, it is a temporary degradation; once the computers switch to the new policy, the performance will improve as predicted.

Minimizing Overhead Impact on Performance

The optimization steps described above require both CPU and network resources. Therefore, care must be taken so that they do not negatively impact performance.

Two of these steps have to be executed by the client components on the users' computers. Only these components can accurately measure the model parameters, and only they can reconfigure themselves when an optimization is performed. The data collection and reporting overheads can negatively impact the response times of the local user, although in our experiments they were insignificant. If these overheads are an issue, they can be reduced by increasing (a) the number of commands a client waits before reporting data, (b) reducing the network latency polling frequency of a client, and (c) reducing the number of destinations in each latency poll.

The remaining steps are particularly CPU intensive. One reason is that they involve the execution of the multicast algorithm, which requires heavy computation when there are many users. Fortunately, these steps do not need to be executed by the client components. We encapsulate them into a component called the server component. An important issue is the location of the server. We do not centralize it on a user machine for fear of degrading the user's response times. An alternative is to distribute the server among multiple machines. While this decentralized approach reduces the performance impact on any single user, such approaches in general suffer from a distributed consensus problem. To avoid the consensus issue, we centralize the server, but on an infrastructure (non-user) computer, such as the one running the session manager. Such a computer exists even in the most highly distributed systems, and is often called the bootstrapping node [15]. An issue with this approach is that computing an optimization may take a long time when there are many concurrent sessions. Fortunately, this issue is temporary, as the system eventually finishes the computation. More importantly, it does not degrade response times during this time.

EVALUATION

So far, we have presented the self-optimizing system. An important question is whether it has practical benefits.

Experiments vs. Simulations

In computer science, it is common that the performance of a system is evaluated through experiments and simulations. Experiments measure the performance of a system in use, while simulations estimate the performance of a system by using an analytical model of the system. Simulations are more than a pure theoretical evaluation, however. While theoretical evaluations can give trends and implications, simulations can also provide quantitative results.

The choice between experiments and simulations involves a tradeoff. Although experimental results are arguably more believable than simulated results, simulations generally require fewer resources than experiments making them easier to run. In fact, when large scale experiments are not possible because of a lack of resources, simulations may still be possible. In this case, one way of reducing the "believability gap" is to validate subparts of the simulation with small-scale experiments.

Whenever possible, we performed experiments instead of simulations. Unfortunately, in our lab, we do not have a sufficient number of machines to perform large experiments – we only have ten. Although public clusters, such as PlanetLab and Amazon's EC2, provide access to a large number of machines, they do not offer sufficient control needed for performance experiments. For instance, there is no way to ensure that the same set of machines is always used. In addition, in PlanetLab, machine loads can vary across experiments because users share machines. Thus, for our large scale scenarios, we had to use simulations.

When we performed large-scale simulations, we also carried out smaller-scale experiments that were possible on our equipment to validate subparts of the simulations. We used a virtualization approach in which we treat each user's computer as a virtual computer that is mapped to a physical computer. One physical computer may have multiple virtual computers mapped to it. We added the virtualization functionality to our framework. It supports mapping up to one hundred users onto a single computer before memory becomes an issue. The performance data for users who are not mapped to a dedicated physical computer must be discarded because when multiple users are mapped to a single physical computer, timing measurements for them and thus any users downstream from them are not reliable.

Processing Architecture Automation Experiments

We used experiments to study the impact on performance of processing architecture changes in practical scenarios. To obtain realistic user commands and think times, we logged a collaborative Checkers game in which users play together against the computer. We chose this program because it is a computer-intensive task and its transmission costs are low, allowing us to validate the effect of processing time differences. In the experiments we conducted to gather these logs, two users played together against the computer and both users made Checkers moves. We assumed that the data in the logs is independent of the number of collaborators, their devices, and network latencies.

We used three computers, a Core2 2.0GHz desktop, a P4 1.7GHz desktop, and a P3 500MHz desktop, which have processing power differences that can be expected when users collaborate. We use the P3 desktop to simulate next-generation mobile devices and current generation netbooks. The computers are connected on a local LAN. Thus, the latencies between them were low (i.e., ~0ms).

To replay the logs, we added functionality to our system that enables us to replay previously recorded logs. For fear of having our measurements affected by other applications, we removed as many active processes as possible on each computer, which is a common approach in experiments comparing alternatives. Nevertheless, as LAN delays and CPU loads vary during an experiment, we performed each one ten times and report the average performances.

We performed the following three-user experiment. Initially, two users are playing Checkers. $User_1$ is using the P4 and $user_2$ the P3 desktop. Suppose that the users are on the same LAN. Suppose also that after fifteen turns, $user_3$ joins using a Core2 desktop on the same LAN. We performed two sets of three experiments. In both sets, we used all three possible initial architectures: replicated, centralized on $user_1$'s P4 desktop, and centralized on $user_2$'s P3 desktop. In the first set of experiments, the optimization system was disabled so the architecture did not change during the session, while in the second set, it was enabled.

We did not provide any historical performance data to the optimization system; it collected all data from reports sent during the session. We configured (a) the client components to send reports after each command, (b) the clients to poll for network latencies every sixty seconds, and (c) the server component to perform optimizations every five commands. Finally, we used a total order function that ranks one system to be better than another if the former gives better response times to more users than the latter.

Architecture		$User_1$						$User_2$						$User_3$					
		1-5		6-20		21-48		1-5		6-20		21-48		1-5		6-20		21-48	
Initial	Opt?	Avg	Stdev	Avg	Stdev	Avg	Stdev	Avg	Stdev	Avg	Stdev	Avg	Stdev	Avg	Stdev	Avg	Stdev	Avg	Stdev
Cent on $User_1$	No	44.3	34.2	74.0	48.7	33.1	16.0	67.1	27.8	88.4	46.6	48.8	15.9			61.8	43.9	34.1	16.2
	Yes	44.8	33.8	75.4	48.9	19.2	6.25	64.0	30.8	87.4	47.7	29.6	7.16			63.0	46.6	16.9	6.42
Cent on $User_2$	No	128	91.3	217	139	98.9	49.3	131	89.0	221	139	104	49.3			174	121	98.1	49.1
	Yes	126	86.1	75.6	48.9	18.5	7.06	130	85.8	87.8	46.5	29.9	7.03			62.0	45.0	16.7	7.19
Rep	No	43.8	33.8	74.7	48.9	34.0	16.2	135	88.9	222	138	107	49.6			26.7	17.0	15.9	6.13
	Yes	43.9	33.6	75.3	48.4	19.4	6.45	133	86.3	88.9	46.2	29.1	6.64			62.6	44.3	17.1	6.73

Table 1. Response times (ms) measured during the Checkers architecture optimization experiment for commands before the first optimization (1-5), after the first but before the second optimization (6-20), and after the second optimization (21-48)

We expect two optimizations. We expect the first one to occur five moves into the game as the system gathers sufficient data by then. It should result in a switch to the centralized architecture in which the P4 is the master. The reason is that the P4 is more powerful than the P3. We expect the other optimization to happen after the twentieth move as this is five moves after $user_3$ joins, which means that sufficient data has been collected for $user_3$'s computer. It should result in a switch to the centralized architecture in which the Core2 is the master because it is the most powerful computer in the session. Specifically, we also expect that when the $user_3$ joins, the arrival does not trigger an optimization as there is no data for $user_3$'s computer. It should join as a slave of $user_1$. Since we expect optimizations after the fifth and twentieth commands, we present the average response times for commands one to five, six to twenty, and twenty-one to forty-eight (the end).

As Table 1 shows, in all cases except one, the performance is either better or no worse with than without optimization. As mentioned above, we consider a change of 50ms in response times significant. The highlighted cells in the table show noticeable improvements. Consider $user_2$'s response times. When the replicated architecture is used initially, the $user_2$'s average response times are improved by 133ms and 77.9ms after the first and second optimization, respectively.

The only case in which performance is worse with than without the self-optimizing system occurs for $user_3$ for commands six through twenty when the replicated architecture is used initially. This is actually expected. The reason is when the optimization system is running, by the time $user_3$ joins, the system had switched to the centralized architecture in which $user_1$'s computer is the master. Thus, when $user_3$ joins, $user_3$'s computer joins as a slave of $user_1$'s computer. On the other hand, when the system is not running, the architecture had not changed from replicated to centralized before $user_3$ joined. Thus, $user_3$'s computer would have joined as a master. Since $user_3$ has a more powerful computer than $user_1$, the architecture in which it is the master will offer better performance to $user_3$.

As described earlier, user inputs are paused during a processing architecture change. In our experiments, the pause did not negatively impact performance. The reason is that the maximum switch time, 360ms, was less than the minimum think time, 2134ms, so a switch could only happen either during think time or overlap with at most one command. The former was always true in our experiments.

System overheads also had no impact on response times. Such an impact would be betrayed in the response times for the first five commands. The reason is that in the case when our system is running, it does not change the architecture during the first five commands but it is still collecting data. As Table 1 shows, the response times for the first five commands with and without our system are the same.

Communication Architecture Automation Experiments

As mentioned above, the choice of unicast or multicast communication is important when the cost of transmitting commands is high. Thus, to study the effects of multicast on response times, we must consider large scale scenarios. Because large scale experiments were infeasible for us, we relied on simulations to evaluate the benefits of our system in large scale scenarios. Since simulations use an analytical model of a system to predict the performance of the system, the analytical model used in our simulations is the same as the model used by the self-optimizing system.

As was the case with experiments, we used realistic simulation data in the simulations. We considered a PowerPoint scenario in which the presentation is being given to 100, 200, 300, 400, and 500 audience members around the world. PowerPoint is a good choice of application for two reasons. It is perhaps a popular business collaborative application. Also, its transmission costs can be high, and thus multicast could help with its performance.

To obtain realistic PowerPoint commands and think times, we identified user-commands in logs of actual PowerPoint use. We analyzed recordings of two presentations. These recordings contain actual data and users' actions – PowerPoint commands and slides. We assumed that the data in the logs is independent of the number of collaborators, their devices, and network latencies.

To obtain the processing and transmission costs, we ran small scale distributed PowerPoint sessions with our system. We configured to system to just collect parameters without making optimization decisions. We then replayed the logs. To get costs for different machines, we repeated the procedure with four different computers: Core2 2.0GHz desktop; P4 1.7GHz desktop; P3 500MHz desktop; and 1.6GHz Atom netbook. As with the Checkers experiment, we removed all active processes that we could from the computers in order to reduce noise in the measurements.

Based on the published network latency data between 1740 computers [12], we set the network latencies between all users equal to those between a random subset of 100, 200, 300, 400, and 500 of the 1740 computers. Zhang et al. [18] showed that such subsets are representative of the entire set.

To create a multicast tree, we ran the HMDM algorithm with the latencies and measured transmission cost values.

Finally, we simulated the performance for a scenario in which (a) the centralized architecture is used, (b) the transmit-first policy is in effect, (b) the presenter is using a netbook, (c) the remaining users are using a random mix of netbooks and P3, P4, and Core2 desktops, and (d) a total order function that prioritizes maximum remote response times is used. We configured the system to use historical data and existing latencies instead of gathering them dynamically. We also configured it to begin performing the first optimization once the first command is replayed. We performed ten simulations and report the average results.

Table 2 shows the maximum remote response times as the number of users varied. The maximum remote response times increased much faster with unicast than with multicast as the number of users grew. As the number of users increased from 100 to 500, the maximum unicast remote response time grew by 5104ms, while the multicast remote response times grew only by 54.31ms. Also, the remote response times are noticeably better with multicast than with unicast for all sizes of collaborations: 1052ms better with 100 and 6102ms better with 500 users. The local response times are shown in Table 3. As Table 3 shows, with unicast, the local response time increased linearly with the number of users (427.6ms), while with multicast, it increased slightly (2.03ms). More importantly, local response times were significantly better with multicast than with unicast for all sizes of collaborations: 82.41ms better with 100 and 509.0ms better with 500 users. We did not find high maximum remote response time variability. The randomness in the simulations came mainly from randomly assigning realistic computer types to users and latencies among these computers, which mainly impact the multicast algorithm. The HMDM scheme was able to consistently navigate this randomness, which is a tribute to its design.

Num Users	100	200	300	400	500
Unicast	1651	2923	4227	5510	6756
Multicast	599.3	615.4	640.5	647.5	653.7

Table 2. Average maximum remote response times (ms)

Num Users	100	200	300	400	500
Unicast	164.2	271.2	378.1	485.0	591.9
Multicast	80.85	82.00	82.16	82.94	82.88

Table 3. Average local response times (ms)

The simulation results show that the system can noticeably improve performance through multicast. Whether the system would actually deploy multicast depends on the response time function. If the function favors configurations that minimize the maximum local or remote response times, then the system would deploy multicast. Also, although multicast appears to always be better than unicast, unicast is still useful. Unicast is easy to deploy and maintain while multicast requires computation for both. Thus, unicast can be the default option that is overridden by multicast only when it is noticeably worse than multicast.

Through limited experiments made possible by our virtualization approach described earlier, we compared the simulated and experimental values for a scenario with 2 and 100 users. We found that in all but one case, the simulated value was within 10ms of the measured value. The case it was not within 10ms was the maximum remote response time in the 100 user scenario, where it was 79.1ms lower. However, the measured value was 1415ms. Thus, the error, though higher than the noticeable threshold, was less than 6%. Even with the error, the response time trends predicted in the simulations were observed in the experiments.

Scheduling Policy Automation Experiments

We also measured the impact on response times of automating the scheduling policy maintenance. Because of space restrictions, we only give a summary of the results.

We wanted to verify that our system choses the same scheduling policies as those predicted by Junuzovic and Dewan simulations [11]. They found that on single-core devices, the lazy, transmit-first, and concurrent policies do not dominate each other. Hence, the one that optimizes response times depends on the users' response time requirements. They also show that on multi-core devices, the parallel policy dominates all single-core policies, although in some cases using a single-core policy on a single-core can give performance that is equivalent to that when using multiple cores with the parallel policy.

As for the communication architecture results, we used the simulation-and-validation approach. We showed that on single-core devices, our system chooses the scheduling policy that best meets response time requirements. In particular, if the response time function favors a system that (a) provides the best local response times, our system deploys the lazy policy, (b) provides the best remote response times to as many users as possible, our system switches to the transmit-first policy, and (c) improves as many remote response times as possible without noticeably degrading the local response times, the system deploys the lazy policy. In all simulations, the remote response time requirements would have been satisfied noticeably worse with other policies. Moreover, we show that on multi-core devices, the system uses the parallel policy only if it gives significantly better performance than all of the single-core policies. These results confirm simulations from prior work.

DISCUSSION

In this section, we discuss the broader impact and issues with the adoption of the self-optimization system.

Beyond the Scope

It is important to note that the limitations of the model used by our system are not limitations of the system. The implementation issues we presented are orthogonal to the choice of analytical model. Regardless of the model, it is necessary to gather its parameters, handle nuances in its application, and compute multicast overlays. The remaining issues, namely, the steps required to keep overheads low and preserve coupling semantics, are model independent.

On the other hand, the scope of applications whose performance can be improved by our system is dictated by the scope of applications supported by the analytical model it uses to predict performance. Since the applications in our driving problems had only coupling functionality, it was sufficient for our system to use a model that accounted only for coupling commands. As new performance models are created that relax this assumption, they can be used by our system to expand its application scope. For instance, new models that account for costs of consistency maintenance and conflict resolution could be used in our system to improve performance in scenarios where users generate a high rate of small actions, such as real-time editing systems.

Even with the current model, our system can still be useful for applications that have optional functionality. For instance, World of Warcraft has concurrency control. Thus, our system with the current model may not correctly predict performance when conflicts occur and may even degrade it. However, the model still applies to, and our system will still improve, the performance of, non-conflicting commands. Hence, if our system happens to degrade performance of conflicting commands, the degradation has to be weighed against the improved performance of non-conflicting commands. This is important given that the majority of commands do not conflict. In fact, sometimes conflicts do not occur at all. For instance, they did not happen in the collaborations we logged. Also, in some scenarios, social protocols prevent conflicts or users do not care about them.

In the scenarios we tested, users took turns to play a game and broadcasted a presentation. Ideally, we should also evaluate the system for scenarios with co-authoring actions, such as co-creating a presentation. Unfortunately, such logs are not publicly available, and we did not have an opportunity to observe and log any such sessions ourselves.

Immediate Applicability

An important question is whether performance of collaborative systems is an issue today. Consider Citrix GoToMeeting, Cisco Webex, and Microsoft Live Meeting, three of the most popular collaborative systems. Websites for all three products contain instructions on how to improve performance. Moreover, numerous unofficial websites offer help to users who are suffering from poor mouse and keyboard response times in these systems. Thus, performance of systems today does indeed matter.

We have shown that a window of opportunity for improving performance exists in some practical scenarios assuming that 50ms is a noticeable threshold. While 50ms is the only noticeable threshold reported by prior work, it was not studied using PowerPoint, Checkers, or Instant Messaging, so it is possible that it may not apply to these applications. More studies are needed to resolve this issue. Also, there is no guarantee that a noticeable improvement is always possible. We have shown that it is possible when resources are somewhat stressed. An important question is whether these conditions occur in practice.

Even if a noticeable performance improvement is possible, an important question is whether the complexity of the optimization system is worth it. As with any complex system, it has development and deployment costs, but it is not all or nothing. The components for optimizing each of the three factors are logically independent, and it is possible to implement some but not all of them to get some but not all of the benefits. The amount of implementation effort is proportional to the benefits it provides. For instance, applications typically support either centralized or replicated semantics. To get the full benefit of our system, they can be updated to support both architectures, or they stay unchanged but still get the benefit of our system's communication architecture and scheduling policy automation. This is consistent with the philosophy in successful commercial software, which provides features that are not used all the time. Also, in our case, the extra functionality does not have a performance overhead, as we see above, and unlike several commercial systems, no user overhead, as the user-interface is not changed. In general, implementation overhead is less important than performance or user overhead, as it does not deteriorate the end-user experience. Moreover, such a system has to be implemented and tested only once for all applications.

Additional complexity arises from the sharing sub-system, as the component situated between the user-interface and program components has to be implemented for each application. However, Chung [2] has already shown that its implementation is straightforward for applications with well-defined user-interface and program components and whose source code is available. In addition, we were also able to implement it for a black-box application, which, as a result, does not satisfy these requirements – PowerPoint. PowerPoint provides a COM interface. To bridge Java and COM, we used J-Integra, and then we were able to build the client component for PowerPoint. The process took two weeks. The majority of the time was spent on investigating COM-Java bridges. Thus, building the component for other COM applications will take less time. We anticipate similar investments for applications with other types of interfaces.

Future Applicability

An important question is whether our system will be useful in the future. For instance, as processor and network speeds improve, it may seem that processing and transmission costs will decrease. As a result, the choice of processing and communication architectures may not matter. However, historically, increasing processor and network speeds have resulted in more complex applications with increasing resource requirements. Also, on mobile devices, the hardware capabilities are developing less rapidly because of power conservation issues. Thus, architectures will continue to matter. Similarly, as devices become multi-core, it may seem that the choice of scheduling policy will not matter. Multi-core processors, however, are less power efficient, which is an issue for mobile devices. For this reason, many mobile devices still use a single-core processor. Thus, scheduling policies will continue to matter.

CONCLUSION

This paper makes two main contributions. First, it shows that it is possible to develop a self-optimizing system for collaborative applications that uses an analytical model to drive optimizations. It also presents new implementation issues relevant to all future self-optimizing frameworks. In addition, the presented system can be used as an instructional tool for teaching students about collaborative systems. In particular, students can use the system to experience the impact on response times of processing architecture, multicast, and scheduling policy. Currently, we are incorporating it into a graduate collaborative systems course and plan to make it available for download.

It will be useful to (a) extend the design space of applications that can benefit from our system; (b) improve the performance of massive online virtual worlds, such as Second Life; and (c) perform user studies to evaluate the perceived benefits of our system in actual collaborations. It is also important to study multi-pronged solutions to user experience issues caused by high response times. For instance, our work improves user experience by reducing response times. An orthogonal approach, taken by Savery and Graham in the TimeLines model [13], is to adjust processing of commands in a manner that masks them. Neither approach is perfect: ours does not reduce response times to zero and theirs does not perfectly mask them. It would be useful to first reduce responses times with our system and then use TimeLines to mask them as this may give a better user experience than with either system alone. It would also be interesting to add performance parameters that capture human factors as users can work around some performance issues. While functional, these workarounds may prevent optimal use of a system and may open other, potentially hidden, opportunities for improvement.

ACKNOWLEDGEMENTS

This research was funded in part by an NSERC scholarship, a Microsoft Research fellowship, and NSF grants IIS 0712794 and IIS-0810861.

REFERENCES

1. Brosh, E. and Yuval, S. Approximation and heuristic algorithms for minimum-delay application-layer multicast trees. *IEEE INFOCOM,* 2004.
2. Chung, G. Log-based collaboration infrastructure. *Ph.D. Dissertation, UNC Chapel Hill*, 2002.
3. Dewan, P. Architectures for Collaborative Applications. *CSCW: Trends in Software*, 7, 1999, edited by Beaudouin-Lafon, M.
4. Ellis, C.A, Gibbs, S.J., and Rein, G. Groupware: some issues and experiences. *ACM CACM,* 34, 1 (Jan 1991).
5. Graham, T.C.N., Phillips, W.G., and Wolfe, C. Quality analysis of distribution architectures for synchronous groupware. *CollaborateCom*, 2006.
6. Gutwin, C., Dyck, J., and Burkitt, J. Using cursor prediction to smooth telepointer actions. *ACM GROUP*, 2003.
7. Gutwin, C., Fedak, C., Watson, M., Dyck, J., and Bell, T. Improving network efficiency in real-time groupware with general message compression. *ACM CSCW*, 2006.
8. Jay, C., Glencross, M., and Hubbold, R. Modeling the effects of delayed haptic and visual feedback in a collaborative virtual environment. *ACM TOCHI,* 14, 2 (Aug 2007).
9. Jeffay, K. Issues in multimedia delivery over today's internet. *IEEE Multimedia Systems*. Tutorial. 1998.
10. Junuzovic, S. and Dewan, P. Multicasting in groupware? *IEEE CollaborateCom,* 2007.
11. Junuzovic, S. and Dewan, P. Scheduling in variable-core collaborative systems. *ACM CSCW*, 2011.
12. p2pSim: a simulator for peer-to-peer protocols. http://pdos.csail.mit.edu/p2psim/kingdata. Mar 4, 2009.
13. Savery, C. and Graham, T.C.N. It's about time: confronting latency in the development of groupware systems. *ACM CSCW*, 2011.
14. Shneiderman, B. Response time and display rate in human performance with computers. *ACM CSUR*, 16, 3 (Sep 1984).
15. Wikipedia. Bootstrapping Node, Dec 27, 2009.
16. Wolfe, C., Graham, T.C.N., Phillips, W.G., and Roy, B. Fiia: user-centered development of adaptive groupware systems. *ACM Symposium on Interactive Computing Systems,* 2009.
17. Youmans, D.M. User requirements for future office workstations with emphasis on preferred response times. *IBM United Kingdom Laboratories* (Sep 1981).
18. Zhang, B., Ng, T.S.E, Nandi, A., Riedi, R., Druschel, P., and Wang, G. Measurement-based analysis, modeling, and synthesis of the internet delay space. *ACM Conference on Internet Measurement*, 2006.

Author Index

www.ingramcontent.com/pod-product-compliance
Ingram Content Group UK Ltd.
Pitfield, Milton Keynes, MK11 3LW, UK
UKHW051420290926
15471UKWH00009B/1703

9 781450 319379